REEL
VIEWS

REEL

The Ultimate Guide to the Best 1,000 Modern Movies on DVD and Video

VIEWS

JAMES BERARDINELLI

creator of www.reelviews.net

Justin Charles & Co.
Boston

FIRST U.S. EDITION 2003

Every effort has been made to fulfill requirements with regard to reproducing copyright material. The author and publisher will be glad to rectify any omissions at the earliest opportunity.

ISBN 1-932112-06-5

Library of Congress Cataloging-in-Publication Data is available.

Published in the United States by Justin, Charles & Co., Publishers, 20 Park Plaza, Boston, MA 02116
www.justincharlesbooks.com

Distributed by National Book Network, Lanham, Maryland
www.nbnbooks.com

10 9 8 7 6 5 4 3 2 1

PRINTED IN THE UNITED STATES OF AMERICA

For Sheryl

Contents

FOREWORD

BY ROGER EBERT

Film critics are asked all the time: "Do you read the reviews of other critics?" The anticipated answer, I think, is "No, of course not! I exist in a pure and inviolate space occupied only by my own reviews." In this view, to read another critic would be cheating. My own answer is that I read other critics constantly. One of them, Stanley Kauffmann, I have been reading since 1960. I never took a film class—they were not offered when I was an undergraduate—but as a graduate student of English literature, I was expected to read the literature on an author or novel or poem before venturing to write my own essay. No serious scholar in any discipline would write about a subject without being familiar with the writing of those who had gone before.

That said, the experience of a film critic on deadline is a little different. James Berardinelli and I, and most of the other critics whose reviews appear on or before a movie's opening day, cannot read other critics most of the time, for the obvious reason that we are writing before any other reviews are available. If a film has already opened in England, say, or played for six months in San Francisco, there may be reviews online, but then there is another inhibiting factor: We don't want to come across an insight or a nice bit of phrasing that *we* might have thought of—and then feel that we can't use it, because we know that someone else already has.

Therefore, I prefer not to discuss movies with anyone before writing my review, and I rarely talk about them with other critics after a screenings. Case history. Some years ago there was a Chicago press screening of a film of truly awesome incompetence. As it happened, one of its reels was missing. In the dark, I smiled to myself, thinking, "If the missing reel contained the lost footage from *Greed,* it wouldn't help." The lights came up, a publicist appeared, and said "We have tracked down the missing reel and can show it to you after the second screening tomorrow." Gene Siskel said: "Even if it's the lost footage from *The Magnificent Ambersons,* it wouldn't help." Damn! Now how could I use my line?

So most of us write in a vacuum, sometimes by necessity, sometimes by choice. Once our reviews are written, however, of course I read others — especially if the movie is likely to divide critics, or is tricky or controversial in some interesting way. Most movies open on Fridays, and one of my Friday rituals is to visit a Web site like rottentomatoes.com, where the Tomatometer measures North American critical reaction and provides links to dozens of reviews. Other good sources are the Movie Review Query Engine (mrqe.com) and of course the invaluable Internet Movie Database (imdb.com).

For several years, one of my regular stops has been the ReelViews.net site of James Berardinelli, who was online even before the dawn of the Web. In an article about the best Web-based movie sites, for the first (June 1996) issue of *Yahoo! Internet Life* magazine, I wrote:

> . . . some of the Web-based critics are excellent, and there is one, James Berardinelli who stands above the crowd. Berardinelli describes himself as an electrical engineer from Morristown, N.J., who has written some 1,000 movie reviews over the last four years. That's more than many full-time critics manage. Berardinelli is literate, opinionated, well-informed and a good writer. He's also familiar with film history; unlike many Web critics, he knows the classics. A newspaper looking for a film critic would be well-advised to head for his URL and hire him immediately (assuming he could be wrenched away from electrical engineering).

Berardinelli and I struck up an e-mail friendship, and a year or so later I met him in person at the Philadelphia Film Festival. I found a man who was serious, focused, with a wry humor, fascinated by movies, and so thin that I never knew whether to talk movies with him, or take him out and try to get him to eat something.

I learned a little of his story. How his profession as a computer expert was matched with a passion for the cinema. How a sad loss in his life left him with a lot of free time, and he began posting reviews on the Web as a way of filling empty hours. How he had to drive to screenings in Philadelphia and New York. How nevertheless he found time to see a great many movies and to review them at full length, with insight and genuine feeling.

James and I have met several times since then, at the Toronto Film Festival and my own Overlooked Film Festival at the University of Illinois at Urbana-Champaign. I still believe a newspaper is missing a bet by not hiring him full-time, but I also understand that James is not looking for that: He likes the mix between his day job and his movies.

The Web is a remarkable democracy. Anyone can post a movie review there, and sometimes it seems like everyone does. Reviews appear on personal Web sites, on host sites, on newspaper and magazine sites, in webzines, at about.com and epinions.com, as "user comments" on the Internet Movie Database, as customer reviews on Amazon.com, and in places like the newsgroup rec.arts.movies.current-reviews. There are many sites dedicated to single directors or stars or genres. If you are a critic dealing with a genre you need to know more about, like Japanese anime, you can choose from dozens of sites via Google.

This vast and open democracy is like a testing-ground for the free marketplace of ideas. In theory, the best critics will rise to the top, and the lesser critics will find their sites visited only by their friends — maybe. Berardinelli's ReelViews now carries the top-page line, "The largest non-commercial movie site on the 'Net." Over a period of several years, many thousands of people looking for movie reviews have traveled the Web, and they have discovered Berardinelli, recognized the quality of his work, and kept coming back. As one who found him very early on, I agree with their discernment. I wanted to write this foreword because I admire the writing, and also because I admire the writer. Berardinelli is a valuable resource, and it is good to have his reviews — sane, accurate, passionate, generous in both praise and blame—between covers.

Many thanks to my parents & grandparents, for undying support;
to Martha Haigh and Roland LaVoie, for inspiring me to put pen to paper;
and to Roger Ebert and Harlan Jacobson for teaching me a few things
about expressing opinions about film.

INTRODUCTION

BY JAMES BERARDINELLI

The process of watching a movie isn't what it used to be. Not that long ago, seeing a film meant hiring a babysitter, driving to a theater, standing in line to buy a ticket, enduring the rudeness of fellow patrons, and being at the mercy of uncaring projectionists. Now, with the advent of home theater, the movie-going experience can be replicated to a degree in the comfort of one's house. All it takes is a trip to the video store or a few minutes browsing online. DVDs have elevated the audio and video quality far beyond what could be achieved with VHS tapes and laserdiscs. With a high-end speaker system and a big screen TV, home viewing can be nearly as immersive as theater going. And you don't have to deal with the kid behind you kicking the back of your seat or your shoes getting stuck to the floor.

One of the most daunting aspects of programming a home theater's screenings is choosing the movies. Walk into a video store, and you're faced with hundreds of titles, only a few of which (those that are relentlessly hyped in TV ads) sound familiar. It's worse online, where the selection is broader. The average video store around the corner may stock 1,000 titles; the most popular Internet rental sites stock ten times that. Granted, it's a lot cheaper to rent a movie than it is to see one in a theater, but the cost is not zero, and wasted time is still wasted time. Better to be prepared than to take a shot in the dark. Hopefully, that's where this book comes in.

The purpose of the book is twofold: to provide a list of recommended movies for viewing, and, hopefully, to offer a few hours of reading enjoyment. My view has always been that reviews, like any form of written criticism, should be seen as pieces of literature, to be read and enjoyed in their own right, regardless of whether you are familiar with the movie, or whether you agree with the review. Reviews are not solely designed as consumer guides for video renters/buyers, but as sources of information, inspiration, and entertainment. So, in compiling this book, I decided to reduce the number of titles in order to be able to present lengthier reviews. Call it quality over quantity.

You don't have to agree with a critic for him or her to be valuable. There's no such thing as an objective review. Reviews are informed opinions. They are useful to any reader who understands where the critic is coming from. After browsing through a number of the reviews in this book, you'll figure out a lot about me, and, using that information, you should be able to determine with reasonable accuracy from the text of any given review, whether the movie will interest you. You can't do that with one of those "every title under the moon" tomes, which assign zero to five stars and offer a 50-word synopsis.

The reviews are presented by category, much as the movies are to be found in most video stores. The placement of some titles presented difficulties. For example, more than a few movies straddle both the "Action/Adventure" category and the "Thriller" category. And should a romantic comedy be considered a "Romance" or a "Comedy?" In all cases, I have done my best to place each title where I believe it most appropriately to belong, but there may be cases where reasonable people will disagree.

There are roughly 1,000 reviews presented here. All have one thing in common: I recommend them. The assigned ratings – "Recommended," "Highly Recommended," or "Must See" — are indications of my enthusiasm. But there are no mediocre or bad movies to be found in this book. To one degree or another, I enjoyed every film that is reviewed in these pages.

The majority of the reviews are of movies released between 1990 and 2002. Since most video stores stock more new movies than older ones, this represents a good cross section of the most widely available titles. Blockbusters and obscure titles get equal treatment. There's also a small selection of older "classics" — pre-1990 movies that can be found in almost any video store and without which I would have felt this book to be incomplete. What kind of book would this be if there were no reviews of *Casablanca* and *Citizen Kane*? Admittedly, the choice of older reviews is somewhat arbitrary, but hopefully there are enough of those titles to satisfy anyone who is interested in earlier material.

Since all of these reviews are available online (at http://www.reelviews.net), it's a fair question to ask why it's worth investing in this book. I can think of a couple of reasons. The first is that the reviews here have been edited and condensed with a view toward enhanced readability. A great deal of extraneous information has been cut away, leaving behind a final article that is leaner and in many ways more literate than the Web site version. The second reason is one of convenience. Books are far more portable than computers. It's a lot easier to bring a book to a video store, or to curl up on a couch with a book, than it is a computer. As much as I value the Internet, I would be lost without my small library of printed material. Online material will never entirely replace books, just as home video will never completely supplant theatrical viewing.

It is my hope that everyone reading this book enjoys it for what it is — a collection of film-related essays written over a span of more than 10 years by someone whose love of movies has deepened during that period. No matter how closely your tastes match mine, you won't agree with everything I have written, but hopefully you will be entertained by every word.

I'll see you in line and online.

REEL
VIEWS

Action/Adventure

The 13th Warrior [1999]

Starring: Antonio Banderas, Diane Venora, Omar Sharif Director: John McTiernan Screenplay: William Wisher & Warner Lewis Running Time: 1:42 Rated: R (Violence, bloody carnage, headless bodies) Theatrical Aspect Ratio: 2.35:1

Admittedly, anyone expecting Shakespeare will be disappointed. Depth is not one of *The 13th Warrior*'s strengths. In fact, probably as the result of hasty editing, two subplots (one about internal politics and one featuring a romance) have been pruned to the point where their inclusions raise more questions than they answer. On the other hand, the main storyline is lean and tightly plotted, with the best sword-and-spear battle sequences since *Braveheart*. The movie is a lavish spectacle and does an excellent job of creating atmosphere and establishing an involving scenario.

Antonio Banderas plays Ahmed Ibn Fadlan, a 10th century Arab ambassador from Baghdad whose mission is to interact with and learn the ways of the Vikings. Although initially horrified by the Northmen's barbaric customs and lack of hygiene, Ahmed unexpectedly becomes one of their number when the Vikings' leader, Buliwyf (Vladimir Kulich), includes him in a small band of adventurers. Their goal: report to aging King Hrothgar (Sven Wollter) and offer their assistance in protecting his people from a scourge that is causing supernatural terror and decimating the population — half-men, half-beasts that attack during the night, decapitating their victims. Soon, Ahmed is on the front lines, fighting alongside Bulifwyf and his right-hand man, Herger (Dennis Storhøi), to defeat the creatures known as the "Eaters of the Dead."

What's interesting about *The 13th Warrior* is that it purports to be a deconstruction of the legend of Beowulf. According to the classic heroic poem (composed around 1000 A.D.), Beowulf is a great Scandinavian warrior who answers King Hrothgar's pleas for help to kill the man-eating monster Grendel. Later, after slaying the creature, Beowulf enters Grendel's lair to destroy his mother. *The 13th Warrior* argues that "Grendel" is not actually one creature, but a host of costumed men who assault under cover of darkness, pretending to be fearsome, demonic apparitions. Buifwyf/Beowulf earns his reputation by driving them back then leading a small party of warriors on a search-and-destroy mission for the female leader of the attacking tribe.

Admittedly, most of those venturing into a theater to see *The 13th Warrior* won't know anything about Beowulf or Grendel. But it's not necessary to make the connection. The movie can be enjoyed for what it is — an action/adventure picture filled with violent, bloody battles and larger-than-life heroic deeds. Think *Conan the Barbarian* crossed with *Braveheart*. There's more than a little of both to be found here — great deeds by great men in a forgotten era.

RECOMMENDED

Adrenaline Drive [Japan, 1999]

Starring: Masanobu Ando, Hikari Ishida, Kazue Matsugae, Yutaka Matsushige Director: Shinobu Yaguchi Screenplay: Shinobu Yaguchi Running Time: 1:51 Rated: Unrated (violence, profanity) Theatrical Aspect Ratio: 1.85:1 In Japanese with subtitles

To say that the "take the money and run" motion picture has been overdone is to understate the obvious.

Countless movies have used the basic premise of lovers on the run from gangsters whose money they have appropriated. The conceit probably worked the first few times, but, after having been twisted, regurgitated, and redone umpteen times, all promise and flair has been drained out of it. Improbably, however, Shinobu Yaguchi has rejuvenated the idea by coming at it from a different direction. Recognizing that the concept has become one big cliché, that's exactly how he treats it. *Adrenaline Drive* becomes a delightful exercise in spotting the many ways in which clichés and formulas are employed, and enjoying the times when the director gleefully sets us up for one particular outcome, then pulls the rug out from under us by giving us something unexpected.

The heroes are Suzuki (Masanobu Ando) and Shizuko (Hikari Ishida), two meek individuals who are thrown together by a whim of fate. When Suzuki is involved in an automobile accident with a gangster, the ominous Kuroiwa (Yutaka Matsushige), he is taken to the local yakuza headquarters to discuss reparations. While Suzuki is there, a gas explosion levels the building, killing everyone except Suzuki and Kuroiwa, who is badly injured. Shizuko, an off-duty nurse who is nearby, hears the explosion and rushes to help. Thinking there's no one to stop them, she and Suzuki take a case full of money from the gangsters' ruined headquarters. But Kuroiwa knows their identities and sends a gang of "junior" yakuza after them. Thus begins a bizarre and often-comic series of misadventures.

The reason *Adrenaline Drive* works on one level is because Yaguchi forms a bond between Suzuki & Shizuko and the audience. Their romantic relationship is nicely developed, but not to the point where it becomes cloying. The film is effective on a second level because the director enjoys crafting things with his tongue in his cheek, subtly winking and nodding at those who are paying attention. When big budget Hollywood directors adhere to formulas, they do so because they're afraid to try something different. When Yaguchi does the same thing, it is to gently mock the conventions. While Yaguchi's craft is evident, there's not a lot of depth, so *Adrenaline Drive* is best experienced as the cinematic equivalent of candy — something to be enjoyed for its transitory explosion of flavor and sweetness, but lacking the staying power to be savored for a long time afterwards. **RECOMMENDED**

Alive [1993]

Starring: Ethan Hawke, Vincent Spano, Josh Hamilton Director: Frank Marshall Screenplay: John Patrick Shanley Running Time: 2:06
Rated: R (Language, disturbing images, cannibalism) Theatrical Aspect Ratio: 1.85:1

In 1972, a chartered plane carrying 37 people — friends, family, and members of a Uruguayan rugby team — crash-landed in the Andes en route to Chile. For 72 days, the survivors struggled to prolong their existence, resorting to cannibalism to stay alive. *Alive*, based on Piers Paul Read's bestseller, is their story.

Alive will not be shown on any airplanes. The plane crash sequence, perfectly prefaced and executed, is hair-raising — perhaps the most terrifying crash ever shown in a movie. The tension of the moment is heightened, rather than diminished, by the knowledge of what is to come. The unpleasant subject of cannibalism is confronted in *Alive*. Because it was such an important factor to the survival of the 16, it could not be glossed over, but it is dealt with sensitively rather than sensationalistically. There are no gruesome close-ups of half-eaten bodies. The characters react with genuine horror at what they have to do. The most graphic scene occurs past the mid-point of the film, in a wide shot of the crash/camp site, where several stripped skeletons can be seen half-covered by snow.

One of the disadvantages of having so many characters is that few of them attain independence from the mass as far as the audience is concerned. As a result, most of the deaths are meaningless. There are only three characters who have enough screen time, dialogue, and interaction to achieve depth: Nando Parrado (Ethan Hawke), Antonio Balbi (Vincent Spano), and Roberto Cannessa (Josh Hamilton). It is primarily around these three that the story centers.

Alive is an adventure that grapples with issues more profound than most movies of the genre. The moral implications of eating the body of a dead friend or relative are not overlooked, nor is the spiritual cost of such a decision. The will to live demands sacrifices, none of which come cheaply. Religion and the existence of God are themes that *Alive* constantly returns to. Well-produced, acted, and scripted, this is a film that has to be seen to be experienced, even by those who know the entire tale. **RECOMMENDED**

Apollo 13 [1995]

Starring: Tom Hanks, Kevin Bacon, Bill Paxton Director: Ron Howard
Screenplay: William Boyles, Jr. & Al Reinert Running Time: 2:20
Rated: PG (Bodily functions) Theatrical Aspect Ratio: 2.35:1

The Apollo program was first announced in 1961. The climax came on July 20, 1969, when Neil Armstrong stepped out of Apollo 11's lunar module and issued his famous quote. Nine months later, with astronauts Jim Lovell (Tom Hanks), Fred Haise (Bill Paxton), and Jack Swigert (Kevin Bacon) aboard, Apollo 13 left the launch pad. Since moonshots were now regarded as commonplace, none of the three networks chose to air Lovell's first broadcast to Earth. However, when an explosion left the crew with a dwindling oxygen supply and failing power, television took notice, as did the entire world. This is the story told by Ron Howard in *Apollo 13*.

Perhaps the most impressive feat of this film is sustaining white-knuckle tension even though the chain of events is well known. The conclusion of the mission is a matter of recent historical record, yet recalling how it ends does nothing to lessen the excitement or dampen the emotional impact of several key moments. Such deft filmmaking is a prime reason why *Apollo 13* is an unqualified success.

It's not the only reason, however. During the 140-minute running time, we are essentially given three stories: the astronauts' struggle to stay alive, the controlled chaos at NASA as experts are forced to come up with unexpected solutions, and the trauma faced by the families of the men whose lives are in danger. With inserts of news footage from the time (much of which features Walter Cronkite), *Apollo 13* attains a level of verisimilitude few current features can match.

The effective, understated special effects never upstage any of the fine performances. All three actors playing the astronauts — Hanks, Paxton, and Bacon — have gotten under their characters' skins. Ed Harris exudes a palpable intensity in a supporting performance as Mission Controller Gene Kranz, the coordinator of the teamwork that goes into saving the space craft. Gary Sinise, reunited here with *Forrest Gump* co-star Tom Hanks, plays Ken Mattingly, the member of Lovell's team who, after being refused medical clearance to fly, plays a crucial role in the rescue.

The villain here is the vastness of space — an antagonist that refuses direct confrontation. There isn't a traditional bad guy to be found, but *Apollo 13* needs no such useless embellishment. Reality has a taste the likes of which fiction can rarely match. Those who recall that week in April 1970 will enjoy seeing the full story unfold; those who are too young to remember will get a feeling not only of what the individuals endured, but how the country as a whole reacted. **MUST SEE**

Bandit Queen [India, 1995]

Starring: **Seema Biswas, Nirmal Pandey, Manoj Bajpai**
Director: **Shekhar Kapur** Screenplay: **Mala Sen** Running Time: **1:59**
Rated: **R (Rape, violence, sexual situations)** In Hindi with subtitles

Two phrases encapsulate the backdrop against which *Bandit Queen* unfolds. The first is a quote shown on-screen at the film's start: "Animals, drums, illiterates, low castes and women are worthy of being beaten." The second is a statement by Phoolan Devi's father: "A daughter is always a burden . . ." It is into this male-centered culture that Devi is born in the late 1950s. Her entire life from the age of 11, when she is married to a much older man, is devoted to fighting for the rights of women and striking blows against a viciously prejudiced social structure.

After running away from her husband, Devi is captured and abused by bandits. Eventually, she joins a gang, and it isn't long before her reputation as a Robin Hood-like figure becomes known across India. She exacts revenge on those who betrayed her, becoming the chief instigator of 1980's Behmai Massacre, where 24 men are killed. The authorities prove unable to capture Devi, and she remains on the loose until 1983, when a deal with the Indian government brings about her surrender.

The picture of human indignity and suffering painted by *Bandit Queen* is on par with that of *Schindler's List*. As the Nazis treated the Jews like animals, so too do the upper caste Indians regard those born into poverty and squalor. Compared to some of the indignities experienced by Devi, death would have been quick and merciful. Multiple rapes and public humiliation are only a few of the torments she must endure, and each atrocity further hardens her heart. When it comes, Devi's revenge is indeed a dish best served cold.

Tightly-paced, powerfully-written, and well-acted, *Bandit Queen* is a first-rate adventure movie. Like *Schindler's List,* there is no political diatribe here. Actions and events are allowed to define the social climate. The film manages to grip the audience in a way that no preachy commentary ever will. Devi, as strikingly portrayed by actress Seema Biswas, becomes real, and it doesn't take long for us to feel her seething rage at the mountain of injustices rising above her. It is uncomfortable to sympathize with someone who becomes so ruthless and uncompromising, but that is the gut-wrenching path along which director Kapur drags us. *Bandit Queen* is not for the squeamish, or for those who prefer not to be challenged or unsettled by a motion picture. Because, whatever your feelings about the movie or its protagonist, *Bandit Queen* will not leave you apathetic. **HIGHLY RECOMMENDED**

Batman Forever [1995]

Starring: Val Kilmer, Tommy Lee Jones, Jim Carrey, Nicole Kidman, Chris O'Donnell Director: Joel Schumacher Screenplay: Lee Batchler, Janet Scott Batchler and Akiva Goldsman Running Time: 2:01 Rated: PG-13 (Violence, cartoonish garishness) Theatrical Aspect Ratio: 1.85:1

It's lighter, brighter, funnier, faster-paced, and a whole lot more colorful than before. There's a new actor underneath the cape, a new girlfriend on his arm, and a new partner by his side. The director is different and the composer has changed. The villains — Jim Carrey decked out in a neon question-mark jacket and Tommy Lee Jones with a face out of *The Elephant Man* — are making their debuts. Yet somehow, perhaps because of the costume, it still feels like the same *Batman* we've gotten to know in two previous films. The same, yet different — and much better.

This time around, the Caped Crusader (Val Kilmer) is faced with a new pair of dastardly bad guys: the Riddler (Carrey) and Harvey Two-Face (Jones). The Riddler, aka Edward Nigma, is a scientist working in Bruce Wayne's electronics factory. When he invents a device to beam television waves directly into the brain, then tries it on himself, he becomes unhinged ("wacko" is the "technical" term used). Now, he's out to control all of Gotham City and humiliate his former boss in the process. To that end, he joins up with Two-Face, who has a more modest goal: kill Batman, whom he blames for his disfigurement. Meanwhile, Bruce Wayne is falling for his third woman in three films. This time, it's a lady doctor with a name that sounds like two merged banks (Chase Meridian, played by Nicole Kidman). She's a psychiatrist who specializes in split personalities (something that afflicts just about everyone in this movie). And, in the person of Dick Grayson (Chris O'Donnell), who takes on the appellation Robin, Batman gets a sidekick to help use all his bat-gadgets and pilot his batmobiles, bat boats, bat planes, and bat subs.

Director Joel Schumacher's vision of Gotham is similar to, yet different from, Tim Burton's. The same bizarre, larger-than-life architecture is evident, but *Batman Forever*'s city is bigger and brighter. This is a jaunty, multi-hued place that reflects a lightening in the movie's tone. There's a lot going on in *Batman Forever* — probably much more than in either *Batman* or *Batman Returns* — yet Schumacher keeps things on an even keel, moving swiftly without creating such a strong undertow that the viewer loses his or her footing. The film is a blast and, ultimately, a very quick 2 hours. In a relatively short time, we get a solid action/adventure story, an odd romantic triangle, and the most detailed exploration of Batman's character to date. All-in-all, this is a very full motion picture. **RECOMMENDED**

Behind Enemy Lines [2001]

Starring: Owen Wilson, Gene Hackman, Joaquim de Almeida Director: John Moore Screenplay: David Veloz & Zak Penn Running Time: 1:43 Rated: PG-13 (Violence, profanity) Theatrical Aspect Ratio: 2.35:1

Behind Enemy Lines takes place at some unspecified, not-too-distant time in Bosnia, and does not attempt to dissect or explain the complicated social and political situation there. Instead, we are presented with a straightforward scenario. An American reconnaissance plane veers off course during a flyover and is shot down because its crew sees something they aren't intended to see. Once downed, Lt. Chris Burnett (Wilson) must flee for his life from a bunch of Bad Guys (identified only as being Serbs) who are out to get him. Meanwhile, back on his home aircraft carrier of the USS Carl Vinson, Admiral Reigart (Gene Hackman) is trying to organize a rescue effort. But he is being stymied by NATO Admiral Piquet (Joaquim de Almedia), who is concerned that a U.S. incursion into Bosnia at this critical time could cause a peace accord to disintegrate.

The film develops parallel storylines. The first involves Burnett's danger-laden trip to the town of Hac, where he is supposed to be lifted to safety. Along the way, he must avoid the well-armed troops of the local Serbian military leader, Lokar (Olek Krupa), and an assassin (Vladimir Maskov) whom Lokar has assigned to kill him. Meanwhile, on the ship, Reigart risks his career by trying to find a way to get Burnett out of harm's way without directly disobeying an order. Piquet becomes a villain of sorts simply because he comes across as a bureaucrat standing in the way of a righteous mission, but his form of villainy pales in comparison to that of the ruthless butchers seeking to eliminate Burnett.

Owen Wilson is a shrewd choice to play the film's

protagonist. Like Bruce Willis in *Die Hard*, Wilson brings an everyman quality to the role. We can easily identify with Burnett — he's not an Arnold Schwarzenegger, Sylvester Stallone, or Jean-Claude Van Damme. Gene Hackman, the consummate veteran, lends a hard-nosed dignity to the part of Admiral Reigart.

Even though this is only his debut, director John Moore has a clear sense of what works in this sort of motion picture. The premise is familiar and the storyline formulaic, yet the execution is effective enough that it keeps us involved for the running length. *Behind Enemy Lines* is a crowd-pleaser, and Moore rarely gives us enough down time to reflect on its weaknesses. In addition, the movie doesn't wear out its welcome. At just under 105 minutes, it's the right length. RECOMMENDED

Beyond Rangoon [1995]

Starring: Patricia Arquette, U Aung Ko, Frances McDormand, Spalding Gray Director: John Boorman Screenplay: Alex Lasker & Bill Rubenstein Running Time: 1:42 Rated: R (Violence) Theatrical Aspect Ratio: 2.35:1

One of the most difficult tasks a filmmaker faces when bringing to life a story with a particular political or social point-of-view is involving — not isolating — the viewer. It's far too easy for a "cause" motion picture to become dry and uninteresting. With *Beyond Rangoon*, director John Boorman (*Deliverance, The Emerald Forest*) has taken the situation in 1988 Burma and reduced it to a personal level.

Laura Bowman (Patricia Arquette) is a young American doctor visiting the Far East in hopes of finding escape from the recent tragedy which has ripped apart her life. One night while her tour group is staying in a Rangoon hotel, Laura wanders into the streets and becomes caught up in a pro-democracy rally led by charismatic activist Aung Sein Suu Kyi (who won the Nobel Peace Prize in 1991). The next day, Laura discovers that she lost her passport the previous night and, since the Burmese government will not let anyone leave the country without one, she is unable to depart as scheduled with her sister and the rest of her tour group.

After eventually acquiring a new passport from the U.S. Embassy, Laura decides to spend some time exploring. She soon locates an "unofficial" tour guide (U Aung Ko), and enlists his aid in bribing her way through checkpoints to meet people and go to places that no outsider normally sees. However, the tour guide turns out to be a pro-democracy activist and,

when the Burmese government declares martial law, Laura becomes caught up in a struggle she previously had no idea existed.

Besides being an intelligent and gripping thriller with a solid grounding in real, recent historical events, *Beyond Rangoon* also gives movie-goers a rare opportunity to watch a female hero. It's unusual to find a solid, well-rounded character the likes of Laura Bowman, and, while Patricia Arquette has a few awkward moments, she mostly does a credible job with a part that requires emotional and physical range.

Boorman has succeeded in an arena where Oliver Stone so often fails. By toning down the melodrama and manipulation, *Beyond Rangoon* calls attention to a situation without becoming overly didactic. Rarely does this film lose its edge — the characters are well-defined and the pacing is tight. And the message comes across — few who sit through this picture will react quite the same way when a story about Burma airs on the nightly news. RECOMMENDED

The Bourne Identity [2002]

Starring: Matt Damon, Franka Potente, Clive Owen, Chris Cooper Director: Doug Liman Screenplay: Tony Gilroy & William Blake Herron, based on the novel by Robert Ludlum Running Time: 1:58 Rated: R (Violence, profanity) Theatrical Aspect Ratio: 2.35:1

In all likelihood, Robert Ludlum fans will not be pleased by this adaptation of one of the spy master's best-received novels. That's because *The Bourne Identity* uses the premise, a few character names, and some isolated incidents from the novel, then runs off in its own direction. This version is nicely paced and fits the bill for those in search of 2 hours of spy-based action and martial arts. The movie has credibility issues, but none are insurmountable in the name of entertainment.

The Bourne Identity doesn't have much of a story to speak of — the plot is a jumping-off point and a means to keep things rolling from one action sequence to the next. Jason Bourne (Matt Damon) is a CIA assassin who loses his memory after a failed mission that results in him being shot twice and left floating in the ocean. However, while Jason doesn't know exactly who (or what) he is, he recognizes that someone is after him, and his training kicks in. That "someone" is his boss, Ted Conklin (Chris Cooper), who sees Bourne as a loose end that has to be eliminated. Jason meets Marie Kreutz (Franka Potente), a German wanderer who leaps at the chance to earn $20,000 by driving Jason to his Paris apartment. Once there, however, they encounter hit men and dead bodies, and Jason decides that the only way to save himself is to find out who he is and why someone wants him dead.

Action-oriented tension drives *The Bourne Identity*. While the movie pays lip service to solving the "mystery" of Jason's identity, this is pretty much a red herring. We figure things out early in the proceedings, so there are no surprises around the corner. The real question posed by the screenplay is how Jason will survive the hit men sent after him, especially the deadly Professor (Clive Owen), who seems to be his equal. In addition to a number of high-octane fight scenes and some cat-and-mouse games, the movie contains a lengthy car chase through the streets of Paris.

The Bourne Identity does not rely on special effects or science fiction-like plot elements to get by. It's a straightforward story of good guys against bad guys, with most of the moral ambiguities leached out. No matter who comes out on top, this is the kind of movie where the audience — at least an audience looking for 120 minutes of adrenaline-propelled escapism — wins. **RECOMMENDED**

Braveheart [1995]

Starring: Mel Gibson, Patrick McGoohan, Sophie Marceau
Director: Mel Gibson Screenplay: Randall Wallace Running Time: 2:50
Rated: R (Graphic violence, brief nudity) Theatrical Aspect Ratio: 2.35:1

Borrowing from masters like Sam Peckinpah and David Lean, actor/director Mel Gibson has crafted an exceptional cinematic tapestry in only his sophomore effort. Most of the time, 3-hour movies have a few flat spots, but *Braveheart* is constantly on the move — riveting from start to finish.

The title character is William Wallace (Gibson), a hero of Scottish history whose legend has surely outstripped fact (in its own unique way, the film acknowledges this). Wallace fought for Scotland's freedom in the late 13th century, wielding his broadsword and influence to defeat the forces of King Edward I (Patrick McGoohan), the British monarch who had declared himself king of Scotland upon the former ruler's demise.

Braveheart builds slowly to its first gritty climax. Much of the early film concentrates on Wallace's love for Murron (Catherine McCormack). Their courtship is unhurried, yet this is all preparation. The real meat of the story, which includes political machinations, betrayal, and dramatic battles, is yet to come. Patrick Henry once said, "Give me liberty, or give me death!" That might well be Wallace's motto. The nobles of

Scotland fight for land and riches, but Wallace stands for the individual, and earns respect with words and deeds.

Bulked up and wearing a long-haired wig, Gibson brings his usual wealth of charisma to the title role. Patrick McGoohan, best known from TV's *Secret Agent Man* and *The Prisoner,* is almost unrecognizable beneath a snowy beard. His Edward the Longshanks exudes an aura of cold menace. He's a worthy foe for Wallace because his intelligence matches his ruthlessness. Sophie Marceau, the French actress who plays Princess Isabelle, and Catherine McCormack are both immensely appealing.

Braveheart is a brutal, bloody motion picture, but the violence is not gratuitous. The maimings, decapitations, and other assorted gruesome details make Wallace's world seem real and immediate. In addition, few theatrical moments make a more eloquent statement against war than when Gibson shows women and children weeping over the dead on a body-littered battlefield. War is a two-headed beast, and both faces — the glorious and the tragic — are depicted. *Braveheart* offers an exhilarating, and occasionally touching, experience that has viewers leaving the theater caught up in an afterglow of wonder. These days, heroes like William Wallace are as rare as motion picture displays of this high, uncompromising quality. **MUST SEE**

Broken Arrow [1996]

Starring: John Travolta, Christian Slater, Samantha Mathis
Director: John Woo Screenplay: Graham Yost Running Time: 1:48
Rated: R (Violence, profanity) Theatrical Aspect Ratio: 2.35:1

According to the movie, a "broken arrow" is the military term for a lost nuclear weapon. Here, there are two, but they aren't really lost. Rather, they have been stolen by Air Force Major Vic Deakins (John Travolta at his most nasty). Vic thinks the military has done him a grave injustice by repeatedly passing him over for promotion, and he's out to get revenge. His demands are simple: $250 million or one major American city will be atomized.

The only things standing between Vic and a luxurious retirement are his ex-partner, Captain Riley Hale (Christian Slater), and a Utah park ranger, Terry Carmichael (Samantha Mathis). They hook up when Terry finds Riley after Vic ejects him from a stealth bomber. The rest of the film is a cat-and-mouse game, with Riley and Terry chasing Vic, or the other way around, depending on who has the missiles.

There are all the requisite close calls and narrow escapes, but nothing quite as nerve-wracking as watching a bus thunder towards a gap in a freeway-under-construction.

The writer of *Broken Arrow,* Graham Yost, also wrote *Speed,* which accounts for many of the similarities. Director John Woo seems very much at home in this high-tech arena. His characteristic trademarks, such as someone leaping through the air with guns blazing in both hands, are all in evidence. As always, Woo choreographs action like a ballet, creating some of the most artistic violence to be found anywhere.

After being typecast as a good guy, John Travolta finally gets a chance to try his hand at a despicable-to-the-core villain. And, boy, is he *cool.* Christian Slater's Riley doesn't have Vic's twisted charisma, but Slater musters enough screen presence to get us on his side. And, while it's nice to see him teamed up again with Samantha Mathis (the two previously joined forces in *Pump Up the Volume*), the two never really click.

The preposterous thrills in *Broken Arrow* take the characters from a fight aboard a stealth bomber to a car chase across the flats of Utah to the bowels of a disused copper mine to a speeding train. The pace is relentless; Woo never allows the excitement to flag. In the end, *Broken Arrow* is an exhilarating, if empty, experience. It's the kind of thing where you turn off your brain and dig your fingernails into the armrest.

RECOMMENDED

Brotherhood of the Wolf [France, 2001]

Starring: Samuel Le Bihan, Vincent Cassel, Emilie Dequenne, Monica Bellucci Director: Christophe Gans Screenplay: Stéphane Cabel & Christophe Gans Running Time: 2:26 Rated: R (Violence, gore, nudity, sex) Theatrical Aspect Ratio: 2.35:1 In French with subtitles

Brotherhood of the Wolf is a period-piece action/adventure movie with elements of the following genres thrown in for good measure: martial arts, horror, and mystery/intrigue. The events represented herein are based on an actual historical event, although, to paraphrase a popular saying, director Christophe Gans never lets the facts get in the way of a good story. Most of what transpires here is pure fantasy and has little to do with the real "Beast of Gevaudan," which roamed the remote countryside in 1764 France, killing several dozen women and children.

When the story opens, and Grégoire de Fronsac (Samuel Le Bihan) and his faithful Iroquois companion, Mani (Mark Dacascos), have arrived in Gevaudan to hunt down and kill the fearsome beast that has been terrorizing the district. Rumors about it abound, but the common belief is that it's a wolf-like demon. Fronsac, a man of science, disputes this. He believes that there is something more prosaic at work than the devil. Soon after arriving in Gevaudan, Fronsac meets the twisted Jean-François de Morangias (Vincent Cassel), a bitterly sardonic young man who has lost one arm, and his pretty sister, Marianne (Emilie Dequenne), who falls for Fronsac.

With the exception of a couple isolated fights, there's not much action during *Brotherhood of the Wolf*'s first hour — most of what transpires is exposition or used to establish characters and relationships. Indeed, we only catch half-glimpses of the Beast throughout the movie's first half. Once the action starts, however, it rarely lets up. We are treated to one martial arts showdown after another, leaving one to wonder whether an ancestor of Jackie Chan's roamed 18th century France dispensing fighting lessons.

Brotherhood of the Wolf isn't exactly a "guilty pleasure" — there is more artistry involved in the production than is immediately obvious — but its strongest appeal will be to those who don't mind movies that stray beyond the accepted boundaries of what we call "reality." The movie has something in it to appeal to just about everyone — religious politics, incestuous longing, a little gratuitous sex and nudity, savage fight scenes, a dollop of romance, and an impressive looking monster that is both more and less than it seems to be. In short, *Brotherhood of the Wolf* is daring in its approach and successful in its result — assuming the result is to provide pure entertainment to the viewer.

RECOMMENDED

Captain Corelli's Mandolin [United Kingdom/United States, 2001]

Starring: Nicolas Cage, Penelope Cruz, John Hurt, Christian Bale Director: John Madden Screenplay: Shawn Slovo Running Time: 2:07 Rated: R (Nudity, violence, sexual situations) Theatrical Aspect Ratio: 2.35:1

Captain Corelli's Mandolin, based on the "unfilmable" novel by Louis de Bernieres, represents the kind of old-fashioned romantic melodrama that hardly ever seems to reach multiplexes these days. Although there's nothing ground-breaking or otherwise extraordinary about the film, it is expertly directed, beautifully photographed, and (for the most part) nicely acted.

The movie opens on the eve of World War II in Greece. On the island of Cephalonia, life continues as usual. One of those "usual" events is the courtship of Pelagia (Penelope Cruz), the daughter of the resident doctor, Dr. Iannis (John Hurt), and Mandras (Christian Bale), a fisherman. The two announce their engagement on the day before Mandras goes off to war. He promises to write, but Pelagia hears nothing from him, her letters going unanswered. Meanwhile, Cephalonia comes under Italian occupation. The officer billeted in Dr. Iannis's house is the mandolin-playing, opera-loving Captain Antonio Corelli (Nicolas Cage). After initially resisting the attraction, he and Pelagia fall in love — just in time for Mandras to return. But the Italian officers face a moral crisis when Mussolini surrenders to the Allies and the Germans move in to take over the Italian occupation: do they give in and let the Germans take over, or do they fight against their former allies alongside the Greek rebels?

The most interesting aspect of *Captain Corelli's Mandolin* is the way the film explores the shifting relationship between the occupiers (Italians and Germans) and the occupied (Greeks). At first, there is a great deal of animosity, but, with the passage of time, as the two sides come to know one another, a wary camaraderie develops, especially between the Italians and the Greeks.

As Captain Corelli, Nicolas Cage is somewhat miscast. This isn't one of those incidents when the actor's presence in the role torpedoes the entire film, but there are instances when Cage doesn't seem comfortable living in Corelli's skin. He goes over-the-top and makes the title character more fatuous than he is meant to be. Penelope Cruz and Christian Bale are solid, but unspectacular.

For director John Madden (*Shakespeare in Love*), *Captain Corelli's Mandolin* represents an opportunity to indulge his preference for character-driven dramas. The movie also has a message to impart about the inhumanity of men to other men in war. But the glue that holds the movie together, and the element that will draw most viewers into the theater, is the romance between Pelagia and Corelli. Theirs isn't a love affair for the ages, but it's strong enough that *Captain Corelli's Mandolin* is likely to appeal to the *English Patient* audience. **RECOMMENDED**

Cast Away [2000]

Starring: **Tom Hanks, Helen Hunt** Director: **Robert Zemeckis**
Screenplay: **William Broyles, Jr.** Running Time: **2:24** Rated: **PG-13**
(Harrowing material, mild profanity) Theatrical Aspect Ratio: **1.85:1**

The year is 1995. Chuck Noland is an overworked Federal Express exec who zips from country to country troubleshooting problems and streamlining oper-

ations. Chuck is enjoying Christmas dinner with his girlfriend, Kelly (Helen Hunt), and his family, when a call comes in: he's needed in Malaysia. A short time later, he's airborne, flying through stormy skies over the South Pacific. Suddenly, there's an explosion, and Chuck finds himself underwater in the belly of a crashed plane. An inflatable life raft carries him to the surface and bears him to a deserted tropical island, where he learns that survival without the trappings of civilization is far more difficult than it's made out to be in books and in the movies. There may not be any humans on the island, but something is making noise in the jungle at night. And how is he to obtain food and fresh water? Without proper tools, simple tasks like opening a coconut or making a fire become herculean efforts.

Cast Away is divided into three clearly-defined acts: the setup, the main story, and the aftermath. Although the movie's centerpiece is the 75-minute portion detailing Chuck's experiences while marooned, it's the third act, which offers no easy solutions for difficult situations, that elevates the film from the level of a stirring, innovative adventure to a fully satisfying drama.

The scenes on the island are presented with uncommon intelligence. We follow Chuck on his step-by-step journey of survival, where even the smallest things become significant accomplishments. Zemeckis' approach to this segment of the film is flawless. He never cuts away from Chuck — there are no "back in Memphis" scenes that would have broken the mood, nor is there any incidental music. Also, the script doesn't cook up any hard-to-swallow, melodramatic situations or artificial conflicts.

For the level of his work in *Cast Away*, Hanks earned another Oscar nomination. The movie's success rests with him, since he is on screen by himself for more than half of the running time. It's one thing for an actor to triumph by playing off others; it's another thing altogether for him to excel with no one else around and virtually no dialogue to speak. In addition, the physical changes that Hanks had to go through to play the part are dramatic — he was forced to gain and lose weight quickly and in extraordinary amounts.

For as long as he works in Hollywood, Robert Zemeckis will be associated with *Forrest Gump*. As good a film as that was, it does not represent his finest work. In many ways, both *Contact* and *Cast Away* are stronger and more compelling features. *Cast Away* has all the hallmarks of a great motion picture: well-developed characters, solid drama, non-traditional adventure, and an intelligent script. It is one of the best of the year. MUST SEE

Charlie's Angels [2000]

Starring: Cameron Diaz, Drew Barrymore, Lucy Liu, Bill Murray
Director: McG Screenplay: Ryan Rawe, Ed Solomon & John August
Running Time: 1:38 Rated: PG-13 (Profanity, violence, sexual
innuendo) Theatrical Aspect Ratio: 2.35:1

Charlie's Angels approaches its subject matter in much the same way that *The Brady Bunch Movie* did. With tongue planted firmly in cheek for the entire 98-minute running length, the film simultaneously pays homage to and makes fun of the first television show to have gotten dads and daughters to bond in front of the set. *Charlie's Angels* is designed camp — a movie that openly acknowledges its dubious appeal and revels in it.

There is a plot — not that the specifics matter much. The current group of Angels — blond Natalie (Cameron Diaz), busty Dylan (Drew Barrymore), and leather-loving Alex (Lucy Liu) — are summoned to the Townsend Detective Agency building by Bosley (Billy Murray in the role originated by the late David Doyle). There, speaking from a remote location, the disembodied Charlie (voice of John Forsythe — the only returning participant from the TV series) informs his employees about their new assignment. Their client, Vivian Wood (Kelly Lynch), has suffered a catastrophic loss — her best friend and boss, the genius behind Knox Electronics, has been kidnapped, presumably by his chief rival, the dastardly Roger Corwin (Tim Curry). The Angels are to save Knox (Sam Rockwell) and recover the stolen technology Corwin has hidden deep in an ultra-secret vault.

It's hard to say whether *Charlie's Angels* contains more action scenes or flashes of flesh. Regardless, both are present in abundance. The film's director, making his feature debut, "McG" (short for Joseph McGinty Mitchell), pumps up the visual and audio volume, making *Charlie's Angels* a kinetic experience, even during the few "slow" sequences.

Fortunately, the actors are all in synch with the material. None of them tries to play things too seriously or too broadly. Barrymore, in addition to being one of the driving forces behind getting the movie made, is arguably the most luminous of the stars. Diaz borrows liberally from her *There's Something About Mary* character, although she appears (for lack of a better term) a little washed out. Lucy Liu is at her best when playing the part of a dominatrix disciplining a room full of sun-deprived engineers.

Feminists have always debated the merits of *Charlie's Angels* whether it deals in female exploitation or empowerment. This movie certainly isn't going to resolve the issue, since there's plenty of both going on. Ultimately, however, *Charlie's Angels* is far too light to promote any sort of serious or introspective discussion — and rightfully so. The movie is exactly what it needs to be to succeed: trashy, dumb, and flashy — in short, a guilty pleasure. RECOMMENDED

Courage Under Fire [1996]

Starring: Denzel Washington, Meg Ryan, Lou Diamond Phillips, Matt
Damon Director: Edward Zwick Screenplay: Patrick Sheane Duncan
Running Time: 1:57 Rated: R (Profanity, violence, mature themes)
Theatrical Aspect Ratio: 1.85:1

Courage Under Fire shows us another face of war's horrors, although this particular perspective is less bleak than that of a *Platoon* or an *Apocalypse Now*. Those movies were brutally effective because they reveled in bleakness, cynicism, and carnage; *Courage Under Fire* gains its power by affirming that the cost of war isn't the inevitable eradication of every trace of human dignity and heroism.

Lieutenant Colonel Nat Serling (Denzel Washington) was a tank commander during the Gulf War. On the night of February 25, 1991, his troops engaged the Iraqis, and, during the confusion, Serling mistook one of his own tanks for the enemy. He gave the order to fire, and ended up killing his best friend. Since then, Serling has been burdened by guilt.

Six months after the war's conclusion, Serling is working on the staff of General Hershberg (Michael Moriarty), investigating potential medal recipients. In that capacity, he is asked to rubber-stamp the approval of a posthumous Congressional Medal of Honor for Captain Karen Walden, a helicopter pilot who is credited for saving 5 lives at the cost of her own. As Serling begins his investigation, however, he discovers discrepancies in the stories of those involved. He digs deeper, and uncovers contrasting perspectives of the same events. Ilario (Matt Damon), one of the men in Walden's medi-vac unit, claims that "the heavier the pressure, the calmer she got." Monfriez (Lou Diamond Phillips), another of Walden's men, has a different story, stating emphatically, "She was afraid. . . . She was a coward. That's the bottom line. . . ."

Akira Kurosawa's *Rashomon* depicted a murder from several different viewpoints. *Courage Under Fire* uses a similar technique for events in the desert. Which Karen Walden is the real one: Ilario's, Monfriez's, or someone else's? Or is the truth unknowable? For Serling, whose honor demands that he get to the bottom of things, understanding what happened when Walden crash-landed becomes an obsession. His quest is like putting together a puzzle with pieces missing, and we work alongside him to unravel the mystery.

The campaigns of *Courage Under Fire* that leave the deepest impression aren't those involving ground troops and air cover. Rather, they're the deeper, more personal struggles of Nat Serling as he sifts through the war-ravaged elements of the human spirit for that "one little piece of shining something for people to believe in." *Courage Under Fire* is as profound and intelligent as it is moving. **MUST SEE**

Crouching Tiger, Hidden Dragon [China/Taiwan/United States, 2000]

Starring: Chow Yun-Fat, Michelle Yeoh, Zhang Ziyi Director: Ang Lee Screenplay: Wang Hui-Ling, James Schamus & Tsai Kuo Jung Running Time: 2:00 Rated: PG-13 (Violence, sex) Theatrical Aspect Ratio: 2.35:1 In Mandarin with subtitles

One of many things that can be said about director Ang Lee is that he's not afraid to take a chance. For his latest, most ambitious outing, Lee has turned his focus to a mythical China of several hundred years ago. The critically celebrated *Crouching Tiger, Hidden Dragon* is an epic martial arts film that combines incredible action sequences with elements of romantic melodrama and superhero derring-do. As visually stunning as it is inventive, *Crouching Tiger, Hidden Dragon* has gained an international following.

Taking place during the era of the Qing dynasty, *Crouching Tiger, Hidden Dragon* gives us a trio of larger-than-life characters: the great martial arts master, Li Mu Bai (Chow Yun-Fat), whose near-invincibility makes him the Superman of his day; the love of his life (for whom he has never openly acknowledged his feelings), female warrior Yu Shu Lien (Michelle Yeoh); and the powerful-but-innocent Jen (Zhang Ziyi), who is wandering down a path towards evil. The story hinges on Li Mu Bai and Yu Shu Lien's attempts to retrieve the legendary sword Green Destiny, which has been stolen from its rightful owner, and the manner in which that quest places Li Mu Bai into conflict with his old adversary Jade Fox (Cheng Pei-pei), the woman who killed his master.

Crouching Tiger, Hidden Dragon unfolds much like a comic book, with the characters and their circumstances being painted using wide brush stokes. Subtlety is not part of Lee's palette; he is going for something grand and melodramatic. His protagonists are bigger than life and their quest is the kind of epic endeavor that pits good against evil, with an innocent caught in between. The hallmark of *Crouching Tiger, Hidden Dragon* is its standout action sequences. All of them are eye-popping and spectacularly choreographed with special effects being used to enhance the natural athleticism of the participants.

Thematically, *Crouching Tiger, Hidden Dragon* has a rich underlying foundation. It ruminates on the true nature of freedom and how everyone, regardless of their circumstances, is a prisoner of one sort or another. Of equal importance is the way it balances the timeless equation of love, honor, and sacrifice. When viewed from any perspective, be it the lofty perch of a jaded critic or the less demanding vantage point of the average movie-goer, *Crouching Tiger, Hidden Dragon* stands out as one of the year's most complete, and exhilarating, motion picture experiences. **HIGHLY RECOMMENDED**

The Crow [1994]

Starring: Brandon Lee, Ernie Hudson, Michael Wincott Director: Alex Proyas Screenplay: David J. Schaw & John Shirley Running Time: 1:40 Rated: R (Graphic violence, profanity, sex, nudity) Theatrical Aspect Ratio: 1.85:1

The Crow is a gothic nightmare. With a view of Detroit that is every bit as bleak and dazzling as the urban panoramas presented in *Batman* and *Blade Runner*, this film makes it clear from the outset that wherever its flaws may lie, they will not be in the realm of visual presentation. Indeed, not only is *The Crow* a feast for the eyes, but it collides violently with another sense, utilizing a high decibel soundtrack to keep the energy level up.

There can be few in the audience upon whom the tragic irony of this picture will be lost. Lead actor Brandon Lee met his death in the final days of filming, killed as the result of a gun accident while acting the part of a man who returns from the dead to avenge his murder and that of his girlfriend (the film is dedicated to Lee and his fiancee, Eliza Hutton). It is a case of "art imitating death," and that specter will always hang over *The Crow*. Fortunately, however, the vision of director Alex Proyas lifts this film above its sad history.

Lee plays murdered rock star Eric Draven, who returns from the grave one year following his Devil's Night slaughter. His task is simple and bloody — avenge his death and that of his beloved Shelly by taking out each of the 4 killers. This he proceeds to do, with each murder becoming progressively more grizzly. Along the way, he teams up with a friendly cop (Ernie Hudson) who sympathizes with his goals.

The decision to tell the story, at least in part, from the perspective of young Sarah (Rochelle Davis) is an effective choice. By utilizing her point-of-view, *The Crow* attains an emotional level that it would not otherwise have reached. This is one of the few occasions when a voiceover works to advance, rather than hinder, the story.

Admittedly, the appeal of *The Crow* is entirely visceral. There's nothing intellectual about frying eyeballs and impaled bodies. No matter how stylish the direction and how captivating the action scenes, it's hard to see this film as much more than a highly-accomplished entry into the "revenge picture" genre. Nevertheless, as a project that the director and producer finished in memory of their young star, this film is a fitting epitaph. **RECOMMENDED**

Dangerous Lives of Altar Boys [2002]
Starring: Kieran Culkin, Jena Malone, Emile Hirsch, Vincent D'Onofrio, Jodie Foster Director: Peter Care Screenplay: Jeff Stockwell, Michael Petroni Running Time: 1:40 Rated: R (Profanity, violence, sexual situations, drug use) Theatrical Aspect Ratio: 1.85:1

Dangerous Lives of Altar Boys isn't your usual coming-of-age movie. Although elements of the film are reminiscent of *Stand By Me* (the group of male friends) and *Ghost World* (the dark, cynical undercurrent), *Dangerous Lives of Altar Boys* stands on its own legs. The serious issues are counterbalanced by a whimsical sense of humor. Among the most striking aspects of the movie are its occasional forays into animation.

Tim Sullivan (Kieran Culkin) and Francis Doyle (Emile Hirsch) are best friends and classmates at a Catholic high school. They spend their days and nights devising pranks and working on a comic book project that they call "The Atomic Trinity." Both Tim and Francis have graphic alter egos, and their nemesis is a caricature of the school's disciplinarian, Sister Assumpta (Jodie Foster). One day, Tim comes up with an idea for the ultimate prank — to drug a cougar at a local zoo, steal the dozing animal from its pen, and sneak it into Sister Assumpta's room. His plan is ambitious but seemingly without hope of success. Meanwhile, his constant co-conspirator, Francis, has

fallen for pretty Margie Flynn (Jena Malone), who is receptive to his advances.

Dangerous Lives of Altar Boys is told from the perspective of a couple of high-school outcasts. Thus, their parents play virtually no part in the movie, the adult figures at school come across as one-dimensional bad guys, and they live life with a sense of invulnerability. In a way, their superhero alter egos are more than drawings — they're an extension of how Tim and Francis feel about themselves.

There's a lot to like about *Dangerous Lives of Altar Boys*, even if, in the final analysis, there are some things that don't work. The animated sequences — lively, colorful, and energetic — are amongst the movie's high points, and director Care does a good job evoking the tribulations of adolescence. The romance is handled with the sensitivity demanded by the subject matter it encompasses, and the friendship between Francis and Tim is credible. *Dangerous Lives of Altar Boys* isn't the best coming-of-age story to hit the big screen, but it skirts new territory, and does so with a flair that earns it a recommendation. **RECOMMENDED**

Deep Blue Sea [1999]
Starring: Samuel L. Jackson, Saffron Burrows, Thomas Jane, Stellan Skarsgård, LL Cool J Director: Renny Harlin Screenplay: Duncan Kennedy, Wayne Powers & Donna Powers Running Time: 1:45 Rated: R (Violence, profanity) Theatrical Aspect Ratio: 2.35:1

At first glance, *Deep Blue Sea* might look like just another dumb, pointless monster movie crawling from the depths. However, while I won't argue that this creature feature is going to enrich the mind, the script is characterized by a certain flair and Renny Harlin's direction keeps things moving at a breakneck pace.

I like the way *Deep Blue Sea* is constructed. It takes a short time to introduce the characters and set up the situation, then gets right into the action. And, once the mayhem starts, the level of tension doesn't let up until the closing credits. The script borrows liberally from *Jaws*, *Jurassic Park*, *Alien(s)*, and *The Abyss*, but it doesn't try to hide its sources of inspiration. *Deep Blue Sea* knows it's not original, and it uses the audience's recognition of this as an asset rather than a detraction. The filmmakers play with our expectations by allowing events to happen in ways that they often don't in movies of this sort.

Nearly all of the action takes place on the Aquatica, an advanced deep sea research laboratory that looks like a "floating Alcatraz." It's there that a small group of marine biologists and other scientists are experimenting on three genetically altered Mako sharks that are bigger, smarter, faster, and deadlier than is typical for members of their species. The humans, led by Doctors Susan McAlester (Saffron Burrows) and Jim Whitlock (Stellan Skarsgård), believe that a protein found in the sharks' brains can cure Alzheimer's Disease. On the day that the project's funder, Russell Franklin (Samuel L. Jackson), is on the Aquatica, all hell breaks loose. The sharks turn violent, a tropical storm hits, and a helicopter crashes into the station. A group of 6 — McAlester, Franklin, shark handler Carter Blake (Thomas Jane), engineer Tom Scoggins (Michael Rapaport), preacher/cook Dudley (LL Cool J), and scientist Janet Winters (Jacqueline McKenzie) — are trapped below the surface, struggling against rising water levels while avoiding 3 pairs of dangerous jaws.

While *Deep Blue Sea* is mostly played straight, it's clear that Renny Harlin isn't beyond having a little fun with the material. But humor and drama are not the reason why audiences see a movie like *Deep Blue Sea,* and Harlin recognizes that. He gives viewers exactly what they want — a taut, exciting thriller that takes movie-goers and characters deep under water and leaves them gasping for breath. **RECOMMENDED**

Die Hard [1988]

Starring: **Bruce Willis, Alan Rickman, Bonnie Bedelia** Director: **John McTiernan** Screenplay: **Jeb Stuart & Steven E. de Souza** Running Time: **2:11** Rated: **R** (Extreme violence, profanity, brief nudity) Theatrical Aspect Ratio: **2.35:1**

Die Hard represents the class of modern action pictures and the standard by which they must be judged. Few films falling into the "mindless entertainment" genre have as much going for them as this movie. Not only is it a thrill-a-minute ride, but it has one of the best film villains in recent memory, a hero everyone can relate to, dialogue that crackles with wit, and a lot of very impressive pyrotechnics.

John McClane (Bruce Willis) had intended to spend a nice, quiet Christmas with his wife Holly (Bonnie Bedelia) and children, ironing out his marital problems caused by his working in New York City as a cop while her career keeps her in Los Angeles. Unfortunately for John, a group of terrorists, led by the suave Hans Gruber (Alan Rickman), has other ideas. After taking over the high rise Nakatomi Tower and holding the attendees of the Christmas party (including Holly) hostage, they begin the time-consum-

ing and complex procedure of breaking into the building's vault. However, one thing — perhaps the *only* thing — that Hans didn't plan on was John McClane, the self-professed "fly in the ointment," who is on the loose inside, and whose goals are in direct contradiction with those of the terrorists.

With *Die Hard,* director John McTiernan (*Predator*) has given us a modern action classic — a movie that doesn't slow down until the end credits are rolling to the tune of "Let It Snow." McTiernan is a master of pacing, and on those few occasions when the script lets him down, the camerawork of Jan De Bont comes to the rescue. This film is explosive in more ways than one — a lavish, noisy extravaganza that gets the adrenaline flowing.

Bruce Willis is perfect as the wisecracking John McClane, an "everyday" sort of guy who gets caught up in circumstances that force him to play the reluctant hero. Alan Rickman's Hans Gruber redefines the action genre villain. His charm lies in that volatile mixture of violence and cunning, all sheathed in a gentlemanly civility.

Whether Bruce Willis is climbing up an elevator shaft, throwing himself off an exploding building, or racing barefoot across a floor littered with glass shards, his John McClane holds our attention while we hold our breaths. *Die Hard* isn't motion picture poetry, but it shows the kind of raucous entertainment that the industry is capable of delivering. For what it is, this is the top model — flash, bang, and witty one-liners all included. **MUST SEE**

Die Hard 2 [1990]

Starring: **Bruce Willis, William Sadler, John Amos** Director: **Renny Harlin** Screenplay: **Steven E. de Souza & Doug Richardson** Running Time: **2:04** Rated: **R** (Extreme violence, profanity, brief nudity) Theatrical Aspect Ratio: **2.35:1**

It's rare that the sequel to a good movie lives up to expectations. Such is the case with *Die Hard 2,* the somewhat-muddled but still entertaining return of Bruce Willis' John McClane. Fortunately, the original *Die Hard* was good enough that there's room for the second installment to be enjoyable while still not matching the pace or possessing the flair of its predecessor.

It's Christmas Eve, and John McClane (Bruce Willis) is in trouble . . . again. This time, the scene is Dulles International Airport in Washington D.C., where a group of terrorists led by the renegade Colonel Stewart (William Sadler) has taken command of the runways and control tower. Unless their demands, which include the immediate release of the drug lord on his way to the United States for trial, are met, Stewart's band intends to start crashing planes. And Holly McClane (Bonnie Bedelia) is on one of those planes, endlessly circling above while a winter blizzard envelopes the already crippled airport. As before, it's up to John to save the day.

Die Hard 2 is not as tightly focused as the original, and this leaches away some of the excitement. The movie is still a thrill-a-minute ride, but much of the action is more pedestrian than stylish. Renny Harlin is a fair replacement for John McTiernan in the director's chair, but he lacks a measure of his predecessor's refinement.

Die Hard 2 is, in the final analysis, a worthwhile action film, but it doesn't deliver nearly as much as the first *Die Hard*. Nevertheless, those who enjoyed spending a couple hours with John McClane atop the Los Angeles skyline will find much to savor about this outing. It's not as crisply directed, and the plot holes are easier to find, but *Die Hard 2* is filled with the same sense of good-natured, wisecracking fun that infused the original. This is one sequel where déjà vu doesn't necessarily mean a rehash of what went before. **HIGHLY RECOMMENDED**

The Dirty Dozen [1967]

Starring: **Lee Marvin, Ernest Borgnine, Charles Bronson, Jim Brown**
Director: **Robert Aldrich** Screenplay: **Nunnally Johnson & Lukas Heller**
Running Time: **2:30** Rated: No MPAA Rating (Violence, mild profanity)
Theatrical Aspect Ratio: 2.35:1

More than 30 years after its initial release, *The Dirty Dozen* remains one of the most popular war films ever to grace the silver screen. A quintessential "guys' movie," *The Dirty Dozen* is best remembered for its tightly choreographed action sequences and testosterone-boosted storyline, but it was also one of the first movies to show the darker side of war — that the best soldiers are often society's outcasts, the sociopaths and misanthropes who kill and rape. War is not civilized, and there's no place for order or manners amidst the carnage of a battlefield.

The time period is 1944. D-Day is approaching. In addition to the overall invasion plan, the United States military has come up with an auxiliary mission designed to interrupt the German chain-of-command: raid a secluded mansion where high ranking German officers often come with their mistresses, and kill everyone there. To accomplish this suicide operation, the army has decided to use criminals who are either awaiting the execution of a death sen-

tence or who have been condemned to spend at least 20 years in prison.

The officer in charge of the operation, General Worden (Ernest Borgnine) has chosen Major John Reisman (Marvin) to train the men and lead them on the mission. Reisman is selected for a specific reason: he is a known discipline problem, and, if he fails, the army will be rid of him. Disgruntled but obedient, Reisman meets his group of 12 angry men — a sullen, antisocial lot, many of whom are convicted murderers and rapists. After convincing them that he is in charge, Reisman starts his version of boot camp in an atmosphere thick with tension. But, as the men learn to work together, a growing sense of camaraderie begins to develop, and, when Reisman stands up to a pompous colonel on behalf of his troop, they accept him as their leader.

Those who are sticklers for detail will find plenty to nit-pick about *The Dirty Dozen*. Its view of the military and of military procedures is slipshod, its handling of the wargames sequence is at times absurd, and its setup of the climax is contrived. Nevertheless, it's a testimonial to Aldrich's skill as a director that these problems don't interfere with the viewer's overall enjoyment of the film. *The Dirty Dozen* flows nicely, keeping things moving and drawing the audience along in its rapid current. The movie may not be a masterpiece but recent history has shown it to be an important motion picture, and the passage of 33 years has not dated it, nor has it diminished *The Dirty Dozen*'s enjoyability. **RECOMMENDED**

Dr. No [United Kingdom, 1962]

Starring: **Sean Connery, Joseph Wiseman, Jack Lord, John Kitzmiller, Ursula Andress** Director: **Terence Young** Screenplay: **Richard Maibaum, Johnanna Harwood & Berkely Mather** Running Time: 1:51
Rated: PG (Violence, sexual innuendo) Theatrical Aspect Ratio: 1.75:1

Barring a television adaptation of *Casino Royale* in the 1950s, 1962's *Dr. No* was the first opportunity fans of Ian Fleming's James Bond had to watch the intrepid superspy in action. However, producers Harry Saltzman and Albert Broccoli wanted their movie to appeal to a wider audience than just Fleming's readers. To that end, they altered the 007 of the novels to better fit the screen. Bond became more suave and witty, and less cold-blooded.

Story-wise, *Dr. No* isn't all that different from most of the other Bond plotlines, although it is a little more "bare bones." When a British agent assigned to Jamaica disappears, M (Bernard Lee) sends 007 (Sean Connery) to the Caribbean to look into the situation.

Upon arrival, Bond is immediately the target of a would-be assassin, and, as his investigation leads him closer to the truth, attempts on his life become more frequent. After joining forces with CIA operative Felix Leiter (Jack Lord), Bond enlists the aid of boat owner Quarrel (John Kitzmiller) to take him to Crab Key Island, which is ruled by the mysterious Dr. No (Joseph Wiseman). Once there, in addition to meeting a scantily-dressed young woman named Honey Ryder (Ursula Andress), 007 learns why no one ever returns from Crab Key.

With the exception of the big explosion during the film's finale, *Dr. No* is a low-key adventure. There are no gadgets, forcing Bond to rely on his ingenuity (in one scene, when he needs to breathe while submerged, he uses hollowed-out reeds as air tubes). The single car chase is reasonably straightforward. And, for the only time in the series, 007 is unmistakably brutalized, appearing bloody, beaten, and disheveled as a result. Regardless, he still defeats the villain and gets the girl. All-in-all, *Dr. No* is a successful, if not superlative, motion picture. While it may appear tame by the standards of the later productions, it's an entertaining look back in movie history at a project that developed into a worldwide phenomenon.
RECOMMENDED

El Mariachi [United States/Mexico, 1992]
Starring: Carlos Gallardo, Consuelo Gómez, Peter Marquardt, Reinol Martinez Director: Robert Rodriguez Screenplay: Robert Rodriguez Running Time: 1:24 Rated: R (Mature themes, violence) Theatrical Aspect Ratio: 1.66:1 In Spanish with subtitles

The title character of *El Mariachi* is the mariachi (Carlos Gallardo), an itinerant musician who goes from town to town in Mexico looking for a new place to play his music. Dressed in black and carrying his guitar in a case, he inquires for employment at various bars and restaurants. Unfortunately for the mariachi, Azul (Reinol Martinez) has just broken out of prison and is on his way to kill crime boss Roco (Peter Marquardt). No one except Roco has seen Azul, so the description of the escaped criminal is sparse: he dresses in black and carries a guitar case (which, instead of containing a musical instrument, has a selection of knives and guns). An obvious case of mistaken identity arises as Roco's thugs think the mariachi is Azul and try to gun him down. Fortunately, he finds a sympathetic ear in the person of Domino (Consuelo Gómez), but her introduction into his life only adds new and previously unforeseen complications.

El Mariachi is the $7,000 wonder. For less money than it costs to film a major television commercial, Robert Rodriguez took his crew to Mexico and filmed a gripping, tautly-paced action flick that outdoes most of Hollywood's similar output. This is clear evidence that film quality often has little to do with a production's budget.

El Mariachi is an old-fashioned thriller based on a case of mistaken identity. It's the kind of film that Humphrey Bogart would have been at home in. The only noticeable difference between this movie and something produced in the 1940s is the level of graphic violence. Rodriguez doesn't pull punches when it comes to showing people getting shot. There's enough blood and gore in this film to earn it the R rating.

On only a few occasions is it obvious that Rodriguez is a novice director working with almost no money. *El Mariachi* doesn't look like something out of Hollywood — the subtitles and the cleverness of the script make that much obvious — but neither does it look like the $7,000 project of a film student.
RECOMMENDED

Escape from L.A. [1996]
Starring: Kurt Russell, Stacey Keach Director: John Carpenter Screenplay: John Carpenter, Debra Hill & Kurt Russell Running Time: 1:40 Rated: R (Violence, profanity) Theatrical Aspect Ratio: 2.35:1

The prologue to *Escape from L.A.* takes place shortly after the conclusion of *Escape from New York*. On August 23, 2000, the "big one" hits the west coast, severing Los Angeles from the mainland. The new President of the Moral United States (Cliff Robertson, giving an eerily Reagan-esque performance) declares that L.A. is no longer part of the country. It becomes the deportation zone to which all those convicted of moral crimes are sent. Los Angeles is viewed as an island of depravity and violence, populated by psychos, criminals, and other assorted weirdoes — not that different, some would argue, from what it's like today.

Fast forward to 2013, where we once again meet the infamous criminal, Snake Plisskin (Kurt Russell). For a second time, the government needs him for a rescue-and-retrieval mission. This time, the object of his quest isn't a person, but a thing. The President's daughter, Utopia (A. J. Langer), has stolen the remote control unit for a doomsday weapon and given it to a guerrilla leader (George Corraface) on Los Angeles Island. So Snake, who has been injected with a virus that leaves him ten hours to live, has to go in, complete his mission, and escape to get the antidote.

If this premise sounds an awful lot like that of *Escape from New York,* it's no coincidence. John Carpenter isn't just making a sequel to the 1981 cult classic, but, armed with a considerable budget, he's also doing a partial remake. *Escape from L.A.* follows an almost-identical trajectory to its predecessor, only this time all the action takes place against the backdrop of the Hollywood Hills rather than under the shadow of the World Trade Center.

All things considered, *Escape from L.A.* is a significant improvement over the first Snake Plisskin adventure. The action sequences are better paced and directed. The erratic, tongue-in-cheek comedy of *New York* is back, but, in this picture, it is supplemented by a barbed satire of family values and political correctness. Best of all, however, the basic premise is satisfactorily explored rather than just existing as a jumping-off point.

The only returning actor is Kurt Russell, who slips effortlessly into his character as if a decade-and-a-half hadn't passed. Little has changed — Snake still talks with a Clint Eastwood-like rasp, sports a heavy five o'clock shadow, and openly despises authority. Though Snake may have aged, the self-deprecating, angry core that makes him more than a mere caricature hasn't changed one bit. Will Snake be back again? Probably not, but if he does return, at least there's no shortage of possibilities for the title. Anyone for *Escape from Chicago*? **RECOMMENDED**

Executive Decision [1996]

Starring: **Kurt Russell, Halle Berry, John Leguizamo, Oliver Platt, Joe Morton, David Suchet** Director: **Stuart Baird** Screenplay: **Jim Thomas & John Thomas** Running Time: **2:12** Rated: **R** (Violence, profanity) Theatrical Aspect Ratio: **2.35:1**

Kurt Russell as James Bond? Well, not quite, but in *Executive Decision*, it's not far off. As David Grant, PhD, Russell looks dashing and debonair in his tux as he sneaks on board a hijacked airplane to put pay to the bad guys. Using a mixture of brains and brawn, he performs some tricks that would make Sean Connery proud. The result is just the kind of tightly-scripted, well-paced white-knuckler that's needed to alleviate the late winter doldrums.

When it opens, *Executive Decision* looks suspiciously like a Steven Segal film. The stone-faced action hero portrays Lt. Col. Austin Travis, commander of an anti-terrorist operations unit. Fortunately, however, this isn't a Segal movie — in fact, those expecting a heavy dose of the martial arts master will be disappointed, since he's only on screen for about a quarter of the picture.

David Suchet plays the dastardly bad guy here, an Islamic fanatic named Nagi Hassan who hijacks a 747 bound from Athens to Washington D.C. On board are 406 passengers and a cache of nerve gas that, if it reaches the United States, could wipe out the Northeast. It's up to the anti-terrorist squad, led by Travis and Grant, to thwart the hijackers. To that end, they make use of the new, super-secret military plane that allows them to board the 747 undetected, while in flight. Then, the war of nerves begins . . .

Obviously, *Executive Decision* is a *Die Hard* wannabe, right down to the final shot. It's not a great clone, but it's still pretty good. *Executive Decision* isn't a start-to-finish string of shoot-outs and standoffs. In fact, barring a few fast-paced sequences, there's not that much action. Instead, this film relies on a growing sense of impending disaster to bring its audience to the edge of their seats.

It's refreshing to see a group of heroes who are as smart as their opponents, don't blunder around while attempting the rescue, and aren't bickering amongst themselves. Although Grant isn't a military man, he doesn't have to spend three-quarters of the film earning the others' respect; once they realize that he has a plan, they follow him without question.

Executive Decision certainly isn't quantum physics or advanced philosophy. It doesn't have a message, it's not overly-concerned with character development, and a fairly rigorous suspension of disbelief is mandatory. But, for uncomplicated excitement, the film offers a solid 130 minutes. **RECOMMENDED**

Face/Off [1997]

Starring: **John Travolta, Nicolas Cage** Director: **John Woo** Screenplay: **Mike Werb & Michael Colleary** Running Time: **2:20** Rated: **R** (Violence, profanity) Theatrical Aspect Ratio: **2.35:1**

Face/Off is in overdrive for about two-thirds of its running length. The rest of the movie is devoted to such mundane tasks as plot exposition, character and relationship development, and ruminations on philosophical issues like identity. While there's very little of the latter, there is enough to give *Face/Off* an interesting subtext. How much of who we are is determined by our physical appearance? And, if we're given the face of another, how like that person are we likely to become?

Such weighty questions are posed because the two

main characters swap faces and identities. Sean Archer (John Travolta) is a dedicated federal officer whose obsession with bringing down one particular master criminal, Castor Troy (Nicolas Cage), has blinded him to all other concerns. Six years ago, Troy's attempt to kill Archer went wrong, and Archer's young son was killed. Since then, a thirst for revenge has driven the FBI agent to pursue Troy with a single-minded relentlessness that has alienated both his wife (Joan Allen) and his teenage daughter (Dominique Swain). When the latest confrontation between the two leaves the criminal in a coma, Archer is forced to undergo a face transplant with Troy's features so that he can go undercover in a prison, interact with Troy's paranoid brother, Pollux (Alessandro Nivola), and learn the location of a bomb that is ticking away somewhere in downtown L.A. But, while Archer is masquerading as his arch-enemy, the real Troy regains consciousness and hijacks Archer's face.

The biggest hurdle to overcome while watching *Face/Off* is suspending disbelief. After all, the scenario that enables Troy and Archer to swap identities is preposterous. No matter how desperately Woo tries to make the procedure seem logically and medically feasible, it's all a little too much to swallow. Appreciating the movie as anything more than a series of flashes and bangs demands that the viewer accept, if not believe, that Troy and Archer can exchange features without showing any lingering signs of surgery or physical trauma.

There's almost too much action in *Face/Off*. After a while, no matter how much flair Woo invests in the project, the intensity starts to wear off and things become repetitive. *Face/Off* is primarily for hard-core action junkies and those who appreciate Woo's inimitable style. The movie is brash, loud, and far from the intellectual cutting-edge, but, on those occasions when *Face/Off* gets everything right, it's capable of moments of rare cinematic perfection. That alone makes it worth the price of admission. RECOMMENDED

For Your Eyes Only [United Kingdom, 1981]

Starring: Roger Moore, Carole Bouquet, Julian Glover, Topol
Director: **John Glen** Screenplay: Richard Maibaum & Michael G.
Wilson Running Time: **2:07** Rated: PG (Sexual innuendo, violence)
Theatrical Aspect Ratio: 2.2:1

With *For Your Eyes Only*, Roger Moore's fifth appearance as Bond and the twelfth entry in the long-running series, 007 enters the 1980s with a return to the "glory days" of the '60s. Realizing it would be tough to top the technical glitz of *Moonraker*, the film makers

wisely chose not to try, opting instead for a retro-Bond adventure that takes the intrepid superspy back into familiar territory: KGB involvement in a plan that centers on classified British secrets.

But that's not the only aspect of *For Your Eyes Only* that looks more to Bond's past than his future. Blofeld, the constant nemesis during the Connery years, makes a brief return appearance, and the film opens with 007 visiting the grave of his dead wife, Tracy. Bond's mission this time, "for [his] eyes only," is to locate and, if possible, recover Great Britain's ATAC equipment — a ship-based weapons system that allows the user to take control of the country's nuclear submarines, ordering them to attack any target. ATAC was on board a freighter that sank in the Ionian Sea, and Bond has at least one major rival, a sly villain named Kristatos (Julian Glover), who's after it as well. Joining 007 on his quest is Melina (French actress Carole Bouquet), the daughter of a scientist killed by Kristatos, who has vowed revenge against her father's murderers. Also along for the ride is the good-natured smuggler Columbo (Topol), who Kristatos set up as a fall guy.

Alas, Julian Glover's Kristatos won't be remembered as one of the great 007 bad guys. While the actor's ability is beyond question, it's usually not talent that makes for a memorable Bond villain, and Glover just isn't over-the-top or nasty enough. (One wonders if the film makers might have done better keeping Blofeld around for more than the pre-credits sequence.) Locque (Michael Gothard), Kristatos' henchman, is as dull as his master — he looks evil, but in the wake of Jaws, comes across as rather pathetic.

In the final analysis, *For Your Eyes Only* is a solid adventure, although it could have been better. There's enough action to hold those with even a short attention span, and Roger Moore's deft charm hasn't yet begun to wear thin. By the end of the '80s, Bond would be viewed as something of a relic, but at least the decade opened with an enjoyable outing. RECOMMENDED

From Russia with Love [United Kingdom, 1963]

Starring: Sean Connery, Daniela Bianchi, Pedro Armendariz, Lotte
Lenya, Robert Shaw Director: **Terence Young** Screenplay: Richard
Maibaum & Johanna Harwood Running Time: **1:50** Rated: PG
(Violence, sexual innuendo) Theatrical Aspect Ratio: 1.75:1

The elements of *From Russia with Love* move the movie closer to the recognizable "Bond formula" than was the case for its predecessor, *Dr. No*. Here, the action scenes are more numerous and generate added tension, the title sequence has a familiar flavor, John Barry's distinctive score replaces the workmanlike music of Monty Norman, Q makes his first appearance, and Connery tones up 007's sophistication while downplaying his cold-bloodedness.

Unlike the megalomaniacs in later Bond films, the villains in *From Russia with Love* aren't after world domination (at least not immediately). In fact, they want something significantly less ambitious: a Russian decoding device. Two of SPECTRE's top operatives are on the mission: #3, former KGB agent Rosa Klebb (Lotte Lenya), and #5, Kronsteen (Vladek Sheybal), a chess master who has meticulously plotted every move and weighed all alternatives. The pair reports directly to the mysterious #1, Blofeld.

Kronsteen's manipulative plan involves using Bond and Russian cipher clerk Tatiana Romanova (Daniela Bianchi) as pawns. Once the British agent has obtained the decoding device from Tatiana, SPECTRE thug Red Grant (Robert Shaw) is to take it from him, leaving behind a corpse. The plot is suitably complicated (but not so convoluted that the viewer will get lost), and, even though 007 suspects a trap, the lure of a beautiful woman and a valuable espionage coup is too enticing to resist. So he travels to Istanbul, where Tatiana has arranged to meet him.

From Russia with Love is among the most tightly-plotted of all the Bond films, and, as a result, is one of the shortest. It moves briskly, blending intrigue, romance, and action into an immensely satisfying whole. *Russia* exudes style, as typified by a fight in a gypsy camp where Bond offhandedly dispatches rogues to the strains of John Barry's "007 theme." This movie has several such memorable moments, including an inventively choreographed fight sequence with Bond and Grant going at it in the confined space of two train compartments. Shortly after that, there's a death-defying chase between Bond and a helicopter.

Standing at the pinnacle of the series, *From Russia with Love* shows how good a Bond film can be when all the ingredients mesh. This movie isn't just a fun popcorn-munching action adventure flick; it's a good motion picture by any standards. **HIGHLY RECOMMENDED**

The Fugitive [1993]

Starring: Harrison Ford, Tommy Lee Jones, Sela Ward, Jeroen Krabbe, Andreas Katsulas Director: Andrew Davis Screenplay: Jeb Stuart & David Twohy Running Time: 2:13 Rated: PG-13 (Violence, language, mature themes) Theatrical Aspect Ratio: 1.85:1

Despite his innocence, Dr. Richard Kimble (Harrison Ford) has been tried, convicted, and sentenced to die for the murder of his wife. On the bus ride that takes him to the prison where he will spend the rest of his days, Kimble is accompanied by 3 other prisoners. When they stage an attempted escape, the driver of the bus loses control and it plunges down an embankment. Kimble is free. Ninety minutes later, Federal Deputy Marshal Sam Gerard (Tommy Lee Jones) arrives on the scene to coordinate the search for the fugitive. So, while Kimble flees Gerard and his men, he begins his search for his wife's real killer — a mysterious one-armed man (Andreas Katsulas).

The Fugitive is loosely based on the 1960s television series that featured the late David Jansen in the title role. Even though *The Fugitive* is a chase movie, the scenes before the hunt begins are among the best of the movie. Everything surrounding the murder and trial, all told in a tremendously well-edited 15-minute prologue, is engrossing. The movie's pace flags somewhat during the second hour as the pursuit cools down and Kimble's own search for the one armed man takes up screen time. Most of *The Fugitive*'s problems center around this investigation. There are too many leaps of intuition and handily-placed clues. The murder mystery is not well-constructed; simplifying this aspect of the story might have resulted in a more tightly-constructed plot, and less confusion about the motivation of some of the characters.

With all apologies to Harrison Ford, the real standout is Tommy Lee Jones. He invests his character with charisma and energy and, as Gerard's grudging respect for Kimble grows, so does our appreciation of what Jones is doing with his seemingly-straightforward role.

While no one could accuse *The Fugitive* of having a masterful insight into human nature, that's not why this film was produced. There's an odd moment or two when an element of someone's behavior strikes a responsive chord, but basically the characters are developed only enough to keep us interested as the chase proceeds. They, like the sometimes overplotted story, are subordinate to the hunt. Fans of the old TV series will find echoes of the show here, but most of this version is new. "Innovative" is not a legitimate description of *The Fugitive*, but "entertaining" is. **RECOMMENDED**

Gladiator [2000]

Starring: Russell Crowe, Joaquin Phoenix, Richard Harris, Djimon Hounsou, Connie Nielsen Director: Ridley Scott Screenplay: David H. Franzoni, John Logan, William Nicholson Running Time: 2:35 Rated: R (Violence) Theatrical Aspect Ratio: 2.35:1

Gladiator is the kind of movie upon which Hollywood once built its reputation but rarely produces anymore: the spectacle. Filled with larger-than-life characters, gorgeous scenery, impressive set design, and epic storytelling, *Gladiator* is designed not just to entertain, but to enthrall. It draws audiences in and immerses them in a reality that is not their own. This is filmmaking on a grand scale.

Gladiator is set in 180 A.D., and uses actual historical personages and events for background. The latest Caesar, Marcus Aurelius (Richard Harris), is a scholar who has taken to the battlefield to repel a barbarian threat from Germania. To that end, he has invaded, relying upon the leadership and valor of his best general, Maximus (Russell Crowe), to win the day. Maximus does not disappoint, and the Emperor privately decides to name him as his successor — a decision that does not sit well with Commodus (Joaquin Phoenix), Marcus' son. In a fit of rage and grief, he kills his father, then has Maximus taken away to be executed. The general, however, escapes death, slaying his would-be killers, then races home to protect his wife and son. But he is too late — by the time he arrives, they are both dead, and he is soon taken prisoner by slave-traders. Along with his new friend Juba (Djimon Hounsou), he is bought by Proximo (Oliver Reed), an owner and trainer of Gladiators. Recognizing Maximus' potential, Proximo grooms him for a trip to Rome's Coliseum.

Gladiator weds the heroic scope of movies like *Ben-Hur, Spartacus, Braveheart,* and *Rob Roy* with the serpentine political treachery of *I, Claudius.* The film never fails to be involving and entertaining, and there are plenty of moments designed to stir the adrenaline. Additionally, the screenplay manages to avoid the trap of predictability. The villains are at least as smart as the heroes, and far more ruthless.

For New Zealand-born, Australian-bred actor Russell Crowe, *Gladiator* represents an opportunity to expand his reputation. This is Crowe's first opportunity to carry a big-budget motion picture, and he won a Best Actor Oscar for it.

One minor stumbling block is an occasional tendency towards moments of pretension. From time-to-time, a character will make a florid, preachy speech. There's nothing wrong with injecting social commentary about the bestial nature of human beings into a movie like *Gladiator* — my argument is that it should be more subtle. But that's a minor quibble. Like many of the great Hollywood historical epics, *Gladiator* is the story of the triumph of a heroic figure over seemingly-insurmountable odds. As spectacles go, *Gladiator* has a great deal to recommend it.

HIGHLY RECOMMENDED

Goldeneye [United Kingdom, 1995]

Starring: Pierce Brosnan, Sean Bean, Izabella Scorupco, Famke Janssen Director: Martin Campbell Screenplay: Jeffrey Caine & Bruce Feirstein Running Time: 2:10 Rated: PG-13 (Sexual innuendo, violence) Theatrical Aspect Ratio: 2.35:1

Like everything else, James Bond (Pierce Brosnan) has had to change for the nineties. The venerable 007 has taken on his sixth face, changed his mode of transport from an Aston-Martin to a BMW, and now answers to a female "M" (played dryly by Judi Dench). Bond's attitudes towards women have been modified — although not greatly. Also, there's more action in *Goldeneye* than in previous 007 entries — enough to keep a 90-minute film moving at a frantic pace. Unfortunately, this movie isn't 90 minutes long — it's 130, which means that fully ¼ of *Goldeneye* is momentum-killing padding.

As for the leading man, he's a decided improvement over his immediate predecessor. Brosnan has a flair for wit to go along with his natural charm; Dalton was stoic and sober. Of course, the newest Bond doesn't come close to Sean Connery's definitive portrayal, but he lacks the fatuousness that marred Roger Moore's tenure. Brosnan's approach has invigorated 007 enough to overcome a movie that seemingly never wants to end.

The story is standard fare, mixing and matching cliches of the genre. The Russian mafia obtains a space-based weapons system called *Goldeneye* that works by exploding a nuclear device in orbit, then crippling a ground location with the resulting electromagnetic pulse. It's up to Bond to save London from a vengeance-crazed megalomaniac. Along the way, he runs into such diverse characters as a beautiful computer programmer (Izabella Scorupco), a former partner (Sean Bean), a wisecracking CIA agent (Joe Don Baker), an ex-KGB officer with a score to settle (Robbie Coltrane), and a psychotic woman who likes squeezing men to death between her legs (Famke

Janssen). Brosnan is supported by an interesting troupe of actors, but the spotlight is always on him.

Goldeneye keeps Bond's comic book-like stunts at an appropriately absurd level. And, with its mixture of humor, interesting locales, high-speed chases, explosions, and action, *Goldeneye* represents solid entertainment. This updated Bond can stand toe-to-toe with today's crop of heroes. **RECOMMENDED**

Goldfinger [United Kingdom, 1964]

Starring: Sean Connery, Gert Frobe, Honor Blackman, Harold Sakata
Director: Guy Hamilton Screenplay: Richard Maibaum & Paul Dehr
Running Time: 1:52 Rated: PG (Violence, sexual innuendo) Theatrical
Aspect Ratio: 1.7:1

With 1964's *Goldfinger,* the third James Bond story to reach the screen, the "Bond formula" had reached maturity. One of the last Bond films to clock in at under two hours, *Goldfinger* is tightly-paced and economical in its usage of extraneous material. The character development of *From Russia with Love* is replaced by a greater attention to action. There are several memorable fight sequences (including a climactic struggle between 007 and Goldfinger's nasty henchman, Oddjob) and a lengthy car chase that has Bond's Aston Martin trailing smoke screens and oil slicks, firing built-in guns, and ejecting the passenger seat. The level of excitement in *Goldfinger* is up a notch from its predecessors.

When the British Secret Service decides that they want supposedly-legitimate bullion dealer Auric Goldfinger (Gert Frobe) under observation, agent 007 is chosen for the job. After Bond (Sean Connery) finds a naked, dead woman on his bed, covered head-to-toe with gold paint, the investigation takes on a new urgency. It seems that Goldfinger is planning something big — "Operation Grand Slam" — and anyone who interferes is targeted for elimination, including, of course, Bond. But, when Goldfinger captures the British agent in Switzerland, he decides to keep him as a hostage rather than kill him. So Bond accompanies the criminal and his entourage to Kentucky, where Goldfinger plans to engineer the greatest crime in history: knock over Fort Knox.

Sean Connery, back for the third time in the role that made him famous, plays the lead character with the same easy elegance and wit he displayed in *From Russia with Love.* The title character (played by Gert Frobe) isn't the most sinister or vicious villain to stand against 007, but he is intelligent, ingenious, and obsessed with gold. In addition to being one of the most

unforgettable of the "Bond Girls," Honor Blackman's Pussy Galore is one of the toughest and most self-sufficient women to cross 007's path. In her own words, she's immune to his charm, and, while this doesn't prevent her from sharing an intimate moment or two with him, she never yields her independence.

In the midst of Bond's "golden era" of the '60s, it's hard to single out one film as the best, but history has shown *Goldfinger* to be among the series' most enduring entries. Although more gimmicky than *From Russia with Love,* this film is equally as entertaining. And, of course, it takes the Bond films in a slightly different direction, blazing a trail that they have been following ever since. **HIGHLY RECOMMENDED**

The Horseman on the Roof [France, 1995]

Starring: Olivier Martinez, Juliette Binoche, Pierre Arditi, Carlo Cecchi
Director: Jean-Paul Rappeneau Screenplay: Jean-Paul Rappeneau,
Nina Companez & Jean-Claude Carriere Running Time: 1:57 Rated: R
(Violence, nudity, cholera) Theatrical Aspect Ratio: 2.2:1 In French with
subtitles

The year is 1832. Napoleon has fallen, leaving behind a vacuum of power. The Austrian empire is attempting a takeover of Italy, and many Italian patriots have fled to France to continue the fight from there. Meanwhile, a devastating cholera epidemic sweeps across France like wildfire, wiping out entire towns and generating a widespread fear of all strangers. Soldiers patrol the countryside, enforcing quarantines by lethal means. It's a grim era, and many superstitious folk think that God's judgment of the world has finally come.

This is the setting for Jean-Paul Rappeneau's *The Horseman on the Roof,* an old fashioned, historical, epic romance. These movies have certain common characteristics: a love affair involving two attractive protagonists; sweeping, beautifully-photographed backgrounds; and a tragic, tumultuous plot. Replete with heaving bosoms, thundering horses, energetic swordfights, and glorious widescreen cinematography, *The Horseman on the Roof* delivers what's expected.

The story opens with Angelo Pardi (Olivier Martinez), an Italian Carbonaro in exile, dodging a trio of Austrian assassins sent to Aix-en-Provence to murder him. With the killers hot on his trail, he flees to the city of Manosque. Before he can join up with a group of Italian refugees, he is accused of poisoning a water supply, and has to run from an angry mob. Angelo takes to the rooftops as riots break out in the streets below. When a thunderstorm strikes, he shelters in a house. The woman living there is Pauline (Juliette Binoche), a married French noblewoman, and, upon encountering Angelo, she reacts with unexpected calmness, inviting him to warm up and have some tea. Soon after, the two are paired in a flight across France to reunite Pauline with her husband and send Angelo back to Italy.

Although much of *The Horseman on the Roof* is more lighthearted than many sweeping melodramas, there are moments of stark, horrifying power. Most deal with the effects of cholera on France's unprepared populace. This is one of the most lavish, recent French exports, and the production values are top-notch. Rappeneau (*Cyrano de Bergerac*) directs with a sure hand, Martinez and Binoche do credible (if not spectacular) jobs, and cameos by Francois Cluzet and the ubiquitous Gerard Depardieu add a few brief moments of "star power." Despite all of this, however, *The Horseman on the Roof* is not a transcendent experience. But, while it doesn't have the power to get eyes misty and hearts aflutter, it's still entertaining nough to make the two hours pass quickly.
RECOMMENDED

In the Line of Fire [1993]

Starring: **Clint Eastwood, John Malkovich, Rene Russo** Director: **Wolfgang Petersen** Screenplay: **Jeff Maguire** Running Time: **2:03** Rated: **R (Language, mature themes, violence)** Theatrical Aspect Ratio: **2.35:1**

In 1963, Frank Horrigan was among the "best and brightest" of the Secret Service, the personal choice of President Kennedy. On November 22 in Dallas, an afternoon that Horrigan will never forget, he became one of the few living agents to lose a president. Now, decades later and only months before a presidential election, Mitch Leary (John Malkovich) is stalking the President. Believing there to be an intangible bond between himself and Horrigan (he says they were both betrayed by a government they had once loved), Leary makes contact with the Secret Service agent to discuss his intentions. Following his conversation with the potential killer, Horrigan acts quickly to get himself posted to protection duty. This time, he has no intention of failing and believes that, given the opportunity, he will take the bullet.

John Malkovich may be one of the screen's most overlooked actors. Or, at least he was until this performance. Hands down, Malkovich's assassin is the best thing about this solid thriller — a villain that rivals Hannibal Lecter for intelligence and cold, calculated viciousness.

Eastwood is Eastwood, albeit a more vulnerable version akin to what we saw in *Unforgiven*. He's still tough, and he isn't afraid to use his gun, but Frank Horrigan is haunted by his past. He's no longer sure whether it was simple indecision or an unwillingness to take a bullet that led to his not being there for Kennedy, and the possibility that the same situation might arise a second time troubles him day and night. Horrigan gives us the human side of Eastwood — the side we never see in a Dirty Harry film, the side that isn't afraid to shed a tear.

Plot-wise, *In the Line of Fire* is nothing extraordinary. It's basically a formula-type thriller with one or two twists thrown in to keep the viewer off-balance. However, strength of character, coupled with a consistently-high level of excitement, makes this film anything but ordinary. The most intriguing element of *In the Line of Fire* is the cat-and-mouse game between Horrigan and Leary. The relationship of these two is fascinating in a twisted way, as it explores psychological layers which many motion pictures find too difficult to convey realistically. For a couple of hours of entertainment, *In the Line of Fire* doesn't disappoint. **RECOMMENDED**

Iron Monkey [Hong Kong, 1993]

Starring: **Donnie Yen, Yu Rong-gwong, Jean Wang** Director: **Yuen Woo Ping** Screenplay: **Tsui Hark, Elsa Tang & Lau Tai Mok** Running Time: **1:25** Rated: **PG-13 (Violence)** Theatrical Aspect Ratio: **1.85:1** In Cantonese with subtitles

When it comes to action, *Iron Monkey* is every bit as astounding as either of Yeun Woo Ping's subsequent, more commercially successful features (he choreographed the fight scenes in both *Crouching Tiger, Hidden Dragon* and *The Matrix*). There are plenty of amazing fight scenes, each intent upon topping its predecessor. Many use wires, enabling the combatants to seemingly leap amazing distances and do all sorts of gravity-defying moves in mid-air. The climactic struggle, which features a duo of good guys against a mighty villain, has the participants balancing on poles over a raging inferno.

Iron Monkey is actually a prequel of sorts to the Tsui Hark/Jet Li 1991 collaboration, *Once Upon a Time in China*, about a 19th century Chinese folk hero named Wong Fei-hung. Here, Fei-hung is a 12-year old boy (played by a girl, Tsang Sze-man) who has come to the city of Chekiang with his father, kung fu master Wong Kei-ying (Donnie Yen). Shortly after their arrival, they are "recruited" by the corrupt governor (James Wong) to hunt down the notorious outlaw, Iron Monkey. Kei-ying is told that his son will be imprisoned until Iron Monkey is caught. But, as Kei-ying begins his task, he finds little help from the citizens of Chekiang. Iron Monkey is a popular figure, who, like Robin Hood, robs from the rich and gives to the poor. The only ones to show any sympathy to Kei-ying are the kindly Dr. Wang (Yu Ronggwong) and his lovely assistant, Miss Orchid (Jean Wang). The irony is that, by night, Dr. Wang is Iron Monkey.

Iron Monkey doesn't possess the epic feel of a *Crouching Tiger,* nor are the characters as well developed or effectively drawn. The storyline, despite having supposed historical underpinnings (like most legends), seems as simple and straightforward as something out of a comic book (with very few deaths). It also has a clear sense of good and evil.

Of course, the primary reason to see *Iron Monkey* isn't for a history lesson. Instead, *Iron Monkey* is all about action, a goal that Yuen pursues relentlessly, pausing only occasionally for short bursts of exposition before getting the adrenaline pumping again. His fights are innovative and intense, whether they're a whirlwind one-on-one duel or one of many struggles featuring multiple combatants. And he truly saves the best for last. **RECOMMENDED**

Kiss of the Dragon [France, 2001]

Starring: **Jet Li, Bridget Fonda, Tcheky Karyo** Director: **Chris Nahon** Screenplay: **Luc Besson & Robert Mark Kamen**, based on a story by Jet Li Running Time: **1:38** Rated: **R (Violence, sexual situations)** Theatrical Aspect Ratio: **2.35:1**

Whack! Thworp! Crack! Sometimes, it's fun to sit back and enjoy the spectacle of bad guys getting their heads beaten in. No political correctness. No toning down the violence to obtain the teen-friendly PG-13 classification from the MPAA. These things make a movie like *Kiss of the Dragon* a pure, if somewhat guilty pleasure. Of course, it helps that the lead actor is Jet Li, a man who oozes equal parts coolness and charisma.

Kiss of the Dragon doesn't have much of a plot. It's about a Beijing cop, Liu Jian (Jet Li), who's on assignment in France where he is framed by a local, high-ranking law enforcement officer, Inspector Richard (Tcheky Karyo). Jian's best hope to prove his innocence is Jessica (Bridget Fonda), a North Dakota girl who is hooking on the streets of Paris, but she won't speak out against Richard until Jian agrees to save her daughter from the dirty policeman's clutches. So the whole film is essentially one long chase, with Richard

trying to kill Jian before Jian can expose him as crooked.

As far as action icons go, Jet Li has more acting ability than most. Not only is he incredibly athletic and able to perform kicks, parries, and thrusts with blazing speed, but he has screen presence and is able to develop his character into a likable individual — at least to the degree allowed by the formula. Li has about a half-dozen standout action scenes, including one in which he goes up against an entire class of adult martial arts students, and one in which he faces off against two hulking Aryan brothers.

Kiss of the Dragon has been directed by newcomer Chris Nahoun, a protégè of French filmmaker Luc Besson (who co-wrote the script and co-produced the movie). Besson is one of a group of French directors who believe that for the French movie industry to be able to play on the international stage, it must make motion pictures that will succeed in the United States. As a result, even though events take place in Paris, everyone speaks English. *Kiss of the Dragon* stands out as a high-energy action movie that holds an audience's attention for its full running length, rather than losing viewers in a sea of plot contrivances and glitzy special effects. **RECOMMENDED**

The Last of the Dogmen [1995]

Starring: **Tom Berenger, Barbara Hershey, Kurtwood Smith, Steve Reevis** Director: **Tab Murphy** Screenplay: **Tab Murphy** Running Time: **2:00** Rated: **PG (Violence, mild profanity)** Theatrical Aspect Ratio: **2.35:1**

Take the mentality of an old-fashioned Hollywood Western, bleed in elements from Kevin Costner's *Dances with Wolves,* and start it out with a sequence culled from *The Fugitive,* and you get *The Last of the Dogmen* — a surprisingly entertaining, somewhat corny adventure film. And, while there's an obviously politically-correct slant to the story, that does nothing to dilute *The Last of the Dogmen*'s enjoyability.

Lewis Gates (Tom Berenger) is an old-time, macho cowboy who loves the rugged outdoors, carries a knife and a gun, and would rather not take a woman into "the roughest country God's ever put on a map." As the story opens, the local sheriff (Kurtwood Smith) has recruited Lewis, the best tracker in the area, to go into the Oxbow Quadrangle in search of three convicts. After some convincing, Lewis agrees, and it doesn't take him long to pick up his quarry's trail. But, by the time he catches up to them, all that's left are ripped clothes and a lot of blood. The bounty hunter returns to town empty-handed and full of questions.

For the answers, he goes to a leading Indian expert, Dr. Lillian Sloan (Barbara Hershey), telling her he believes there are lost warriors in the Oxbow. At first, she thinks he's deluded, but as he presents evidence accumulated from old newspaper clippings, her interest is piqued. Lewis wants one of her male associates to accompany him into the mountains — he needs someone who speaks Cheyenne. Much to his distress, however, she chooses to come herself, and together they go in search of the last of the Cheyenne dogmen — the possible descendants of survivors from 1864's Sand Creek Massacre.

Writer/director Tab Murphy pokes occasional fun at the macho cowboy image while simultaneously embracing it through Berenger's scruffy Lewis. But the main point of the movie is that when people finally find something they've spent their entire life searching for, they'll risk anything to protect it. The Cheyenne are Lewis' redemption, and his interaction with them saves a guilt-ravaged spirit. This simple theme lies at the core of an adventure that, while not original, is nevertheless satisfying. *The Last of the Dogmen* may recall *Dances with Wolves*, but it seems less a copy than a different story taking a similar path. **RECOMMENDED**

The Last of the Mohicans [1992]

Starring: Daniel Day-Lewis, Madeleine Stowe, Wes Studi, Russell Means, Jodhi May Director: Michael Mann Screenplay: Christopher Crowe, Michael Mann Running Time: 1:54 Rated: R (Violence, mature themes) Theatrical Aspect Ratio: 2.35:1

There is so little wrong with this film that I'll get the incidental negatives out of the way first. The introductory moments are somewhat confusing, and it takes about fifteen or twenty minutes to get the characters and situations straight. Madeleine Stowe's British accent is of the "now-you-hear-it, now-you-don't" variety, although her performance pretty much makes up for this inconsistency. Finally, the photography surrounding the waterfall is unconvincing. Other than that, *The Last of the Mohicans* is virtually flawless.

Cinematography and musical score combine in a breathtaking mosaic. Historical accuracy has been preserved (even if the movie takes liberties with James Fenimore Cooper's story). The battle scenes are easily the best choreographed since *Glory* — there's so much going on that one viewing isn't enough to pick up on everything.

From beginning to end, there isn't a weak performance. As the bare-chested central character, a native-raised white man named Hawkeye, Daniel Day-Lewis shines, bringing acting acumen to the role of romantic adventure hero. Madeleine Stowe, Richard Dreyfuss' girlfriend in *Stakeout,* is equally appealing as Hawkeye's upper-class British love interest. The major characters are fully fleshed-out, and there's more audience empathy for the minor characters here than the protagonists in many other films. As is common in a realistic depiction of a war, very little is absolutely good or evil.

Finally, there's the story, which, while not all that complex, is of epic nature — big, bold, and gloriously sweeping. It's about the love of Hawkeye, the adopted Mohican, and Cora, the daughter of a British commander stationed in America during the mid-1700s. War and tragedy swirl around them as they struggle to find their own kind of private solace. Bold and stirring with impeccable production values, *The Last of the Mohicans* is a memorable motion picture adventure. **MUST SEE**

Lethal Weapon 4 [1998]

Starring: Mel Gibson, Danny Glover, Joe Pesci, Renee Russo, Chris Rock, Jet Li Director: Richard Donner Screenplay: Channing Gibson, Alfred Gough, Miles Millar, Shane Black Running Time: 2:07 Rated: R (Violence, profanity, mayhem) Theatrical Aspect Ratio: 2.35:1

Given the expectations that constrain it, *Lethal Weapon 4* is probably the best motion picture that could possibly result from another teaming of Martin Riggs (Mel Gibson) and Roger Murtaugh (Danny Glover). The series has lost a lot of steam since the first two entries, and, although the fourth movie ratchets up the energy level from the moribund state of the disappointing *Lethal Weapon 3*, there's no sense of spontaneity. Too often, this film seems like a series of elaborate, skillfully-choreographed action sequences tied together by a flimsy plot. It's a calculated formula for success, and makes for entertaining viewing, but those expecting something with the spark of the first two pictures may be disappointed.

By returning director Richard Donner to the helm for the fourth time, the series assures a continuity in both plot and style. The same mixture of high-voltage action sequences and low-key comedy that succeeded in the original *Lethal Weapon* is in evidence here. And, in the tradition of the other films, one new character is added. In *Lethal Weapon 2*, it was Joe Pesci's Leo Getz. In *Lethal Weapon 3*, it was Renee Russo's Lorna Cole. And here, in *Lethal Weapon 4*, it's

Chris Rock's Lee Butters. Everyone else is back, creating a busy roster of supporting characters who sometimes appear to be struggling for screen time.

The plot, which is pretty thin, centers on Riggs and Murtaugh's first case after they have been promoted to captains (due to their propensity for destroying things, the police department couldn't purchase insurance until it got them off the street and behind a desk). After foiling a plot to bring illegal Chinese immigrants into the United States, the two cops become the targets of a top gangster (Hong Kong superstar Jet Li), who is more lethal than Riggs and Murtaugh put together. The battle becomes personal when the bad guys try to kill everyone, including Riggs' pregnant girlfriend, Lorna, by trapping them in a burning house.

Lethal Weapon 4 delivers just about what's expected from it — characters who we know and like, the camaraderie we demand, and Richard Donner's obsessive, must-top-anything-I've-ever-done attitude towards action sequences. When it comes to potential blockbusters, there are no guarantees, but, for a variety of reasons (most of which have to do with Gibson), it seems likely that this will be the final *Lethal Weapon*. If that's the case, there are worse ways to go out. **RECOMMENDED**

Licence to Kill [United Kingdom, 1989]

Starring: Timothy Dalton, Robert Davi, Carey Lowell, Talisa Soto, Anthony Zerbe Director: John Glen Screenplay: Richard Maibaum & Michael G. Wilson Running Time: 2:13 Rated: PG-13 (Sexual innuendo, violence) Theatrical Aspect Ratio: 2.2:1

Licence to Kill, Timothy Dalton's second and final outing as superspy James Bond is a most atypical adventure. Not since *Dr. No* has 007 been so cool and ruthless, and never has a plot been this close to realistic plausibility. The villain is not a megalomaniac, but a drug lord, and Bond's mission has nothing to do with Her Majesty's Secret Service. In fact, he's acting on a vendetta and the British government is trying to capture him and bring him back to London.

Paradoxically, while there are almost no gadgets in this film, the "gadget man" himself, Q (Desmond Llewelyn), has his biggest role to date. While taking a vacation, he seeks out Bond in South America and offers his help. Another returning character is Felix Leiter (David Hedison, the only man to play the part twice), who loses his leg to a shark. It's this brutal attack on Leiter and his wife (Priscilla Barnes) by drug kingpin Sanchez (Robert Davi) that leads to Bond's

abrupt resignation from MI6 so he can carry out a personal plan of revenge.

The dark, almost-ominous tone of *Licence to Kill* is unprecedented. This is an edgy movie, almost completely lacking in humor or flippancy. Dalton's 007 is angry and focused, and this portrayal is, at times, very like that of Connery at the beginning of *Diamonds Are Forever* (where Bond was hunting down Blofeld to avenge his wife's death).

For the most part, action is toned down in favor of plot development. This overemphasis on story may be a mistake, because there are times when *Licence to Kill*'s narrative bogs down. There are still two impressive action sequences, however. One involves an underwater struggle that develops into a mid-air fight. The other is a spectacular downhill chase featuring four loaded tanker trucks roaring along winding mountain roads. *Licence to Kill* may be taut and gripping, but it's not traditional Bond, and that, as much as any other reason, may explain the public's rejection of this reasonably well-constructed picture. **RECOMMENDED**

Light It Up [1999]

Starring: Usher Raymond, Rosario Dawson, Marcello Robinson, Vanessa L. Williams, Forest Whitaker Director: Craig Bolotin Screenplay: Craig Bolotin Running Time: 1:37 Rated: R (Violence, profanity) Theatrical Aspect Ratio: 1.85:1

Light It Up has all the trappings of an exploitation thriller about a group of high school students who hole up in a library with a hostage. There's a police negotiator, an overanxious SWAT team, and a media circus. Despite all of that, however, it's a relatively actionless film that's more concerned with developing characters and conveying a message than with carnage and pyrotechnics. As the story unfolds, *Light It Up* surprises by veering off into unexpected territory and defying the bloodthirstiness of some audience members in favor of attacking issues.

The film takes place in Queens' Lincoln High School on a seemingly normal day. When popular teacher Mr. Knowles (Judd Nelson) is suspended, a group of students organizes a sit-in. The arrival of police officer Dante Jackson (Forest Whitaker), in his first day on the job at the school, escalates an already tense situation. He becomes involved in a scuffle with two kids, Ziggy (Robert Ri'chard) and Lester (Usher Raymond), and soon his gun is in Ziggy's hands, he has been shot in the leg, and the school is being evacuated. Six students remain behind to hold

Jackson hostage. As a horde of cops gathers outside the building, the kids begin to realize the enormity of their situation, and the list of demands they present to the negotiator (Vanessa L. Williams) surprises nearly everyone.

Writer/director Craig Bolotin manages the difficult task of telling his story without exploiting current events — not an easy task considering how volatile the post-Columbine atmosphere is regarding kids and guns. Bolotin shines the spotlight on important social issues by developing a group of interesting characters and placing them in an untenable situation. He occasionally resorts to clichés (friction among the students, a cop who is anxious to drop the negotiations and storm the Bastille), but, for the most part, he keeps things fresh.

There are those who will see *Light It Up* as a left-wing sermon, but Bolotin de-politicizes the movie by highlighting the problem without offering specific solutions. In addition to being a cautionary tale, the movie also functions as a well-constructed, taut thriller. There's a great deal of tension in the situation, and Bolotin doesn't allow it to go to waste. Bolotin, his cast, and his crew have invested this motion picture with more than a flash of purpose and promise. **RECOMMENDED**

Limbo [1999]

Starring: Mary Elizabeth Mastrantonio, David Strathairn, Vanessa Martinez, Kris Kristofferson Director: John Sayles Screenplay: John Sayles Running Time: 2:07 Rated: PG-13 (Profanity) Theatrical Aspect Ratio: 1.85:1

There is little doubt that the most discussed aspect of writer/director/editor John Sayles' *Limbo* will be the ending. Unconventional and unexpected, the conclusion will inspire outrage in some movie-goers. Others, however, will recognize that Sayles chooses a resolution that is in keeping with the tone and artistic intent of the rest of the picture. Anything else would have been a capitulation to convention and traditional storytelling. With the exception of the atypical ending, *Limbo* ranks as one of Sayles' most accessible pictures. But mainstream audiences will *hate* what happens at the 2-hour mark.

If it's not obvious at first why this film is called *Limbo,* it will be by the time the proceedings have finished. The movie is about 3 characters trapped in an emotional paralysis from which only death will free them. In their own way, each of them is deeply troubled. Joe Gastineau (David Strathairn) is an introverted, lonely man who is haunted by a past that includes a tragic fishing accident in which two of his friends died. Donna De Angelo (Mary Elizabeth Mastrantonio) is a second-rate lounge singer whose life has consisted of a series of failed relationships. Her daughter, Noelle (Vanessa Martinez), is a disturbed teenager who entertains thoughts of suicide and self-mutilation. These three meet and interact in the town of Port Henry, Alaska, where Donna lands a gig at the local bar.

For a while, *Limbo* seems like it might be a slow-burning romance and tale of redemption, but, as is often the case, Sayles takes his audience in unexpected directions (unexpected because they defy comfortable, traditional narrative routes). Joe ends up in the middle of the mother/daughter struggle because he is involved with them both, albeit in different ways. Then his brother, Bobby (Casey Siemaszko), shows up in town looking for his help crewing a boat. Joe agrees, and invites Donna and Noelle to come along. Bobby is none-too-pleased by the inclusion of 2 passengers, and, after a while, it becomes apparent why: this isn't a routine trip; Bobby is being hunted by gangsters.

During the second half, when the 3 protagonists are stranded on a deserted island, Sayles enters seemingly familiar territory. It doesn't take long, however, for him to stake out his own patch of land. This is no lightweight romantic fantasy, nor is it an exploration of man's triumph over nature. As thrillers go, *Limbo* is a sedate film, but that's the point. It's not about vital characters striving to achieve great things; instead, it's about a trio of broken human beings who are trapped in stasis, heading for a dead-end. And, when you think about it, that's exactly what *Limbo*'s controversial conclusion depicts. **HIGHLY RECOMMENDED**

Mary Shelley's Frankenstein [United States/United Kingdom, 1994]

Starring: Kenneth Branagh, Robert De Niro, Helena Bonham Carter, Ian Holm, Tom Hulce Director: Kenneth Branagh Screenplay: Steph Lady & Frank Darabont Running Time: 2:04 Rated: R (Violence, gore) Theatrical Aspect Ratio: 1.85:1

With this cinematic depiction of Mary Shelley's classic monster movie, director (and uncredited co-writer) Kenneth Branagh has taken a less-traveled path. He has chosen to view *Frankenstein* as a tragedy of Greek (or, given his background, Shakespearean) proportions. What Branagh should recognize better than anyone, though, is that tragedy is at its most effective when allowed to cook slowly, basting in its own juices. This version of *Frankenstein* moves so frantically that far too many subtleties get lost along the way. The result is a rousing, occasionally-chaotic (especially during the choppily-edited first half-hour) piece of work that, while undeniably entertaining, lacks a depth that might otherwise have been attained.

As far as its faithfulness to the source material is concerned, *Mary Shelley's Frankenstein* frequently differs from the book on plot points, but the two are thematically in synch. The greatest strength of *Mary Shelley's Frankenstein* is that it illustrates both the good and evil qualities in each of its main characters. Of the two — Robert De Niro's creature and Kenneth Branagh's Frankenstein — the former is, perhaps surprisingly, the more sympathetic. In part because of the script and in part because of the acting (De Niro gives a far stronger performance than his director/co-star), the creature seems almost the more "human" of the two. In its own words, it is capable of great love and great rage. Frankenstein, on the other hand, often comes across as petty, self-serving, and ambitious. Only towards the end, when he finally grasps the full consequences of his actions, does the scientist capture a measure of our understanding.

Comparison's with 1992's *Bram Stoker's Dracula* are inevitable, especially since both came from Francis Ford Coppola's American Zoetrope production company. Considering the merits of both movies, however, there is little doubt which is more effective. Kenneth Branagh's film is stronger thematically and visually, possesses more solid characterization, and boasts Robert De Niro and Helena Bonham Carter rather than Keanu Reeves and Winona Ryder. *Mary Shelley's Frankenstein* may not be the definitive version of the 1817 novel, and the director likely attempted more than is practical for a 2-hour film, but overambition is preferable to the alternative, especially if it results — as in this case — in something more substantial than Hollywood's typical, fitfully entertaining fluff. **RECOMMENDED**

The Mask of Zorro [1998]

Starring: Antonio Banderas, Anthony Hopkins, Catherine Zeta-Jones, Stuart Wilson Director: Martin Campbell Screenplay: John Eskow, Ted Eliot & Terry Rossio Running Time: 2:15 Rated: PG-13 (Violence, sexual innuendo) Theatrical Aspect Ratio: 2.35:1

The Mask of Zorro treats us to the sight of not one, but two, Zorros. When the film opens in 1821, the mask is worn by Don Diego De La Vega (Anthony Hopkins). He is the original Zorro, the mysterious avenger who defends Mexico against its foes, including his arch-enemy, Don Rafael Montero (Stuart Wilson), the cruel governor of the region. But, on the night of Zorro's final public appearance, Montero learns his identity and takes a squadron of guards to De La Vega's abode. There, in a tragic accident, De La Vega's beloved wife is killed. Montero then imprisons his enemy and takes De La Vega's infant daughter as his own.

Twenty years later, that daughter, Elena (Catherine Zeta Jones), has grown into a beautiful woman. With her by his side, Montero triumphantly returns from exile with plans to turn California into an independent republic. Montero's reappearance awakens a long-dormant passion in De La Vega, who has spent two decades in dungeons, and he escapes. Soon after, he encounters a thief on the run from the law, Alejandro Murrieta (Antonio Banderas), who, as a child, once did Zorro a favor. After a brief period of deliberation, De La Vega decides that fate has brought them together ("When the pupil is ready, the teacher will find him"), and he agrees to take the man on as his protégé and groom him as the new Zorro. For his part, Murrieta is willing to endure De La Vega's tough training regimen, because he wants revenge on his brother's killer, Captain Harrison Love (Matt Letscher), who happens to be Montero's right-hand man.

Most recent superhero movies have been dark, bleak, and heavily reliant upon special effects. *The Mask of Zorro* is none of these. In many ways, it's a throwback to simpler times, before every new movie of this sort had to mimic *Batman*. There's something in the tone and style that recalls *Raiders of the Lost Ark,* and, while *The Mask of Zorro* isn't on the same level, it's not an altogether ridiculous comparison. Even though *Zorro* doesn't feature the non-stop cliffhanger adventure of *Raiders,* there's still plenty of action, tumult, and derring-do. And, like *Raiders,* this film never takes itself too seriously.

Like all great heroes, Zorro is bigger than life, and we wouldn't have it any other way. If the film makers can produce another one like this, here's hoping that Zorro rides again. **RECOMMENDED**

Maverick [1994]

Starring: Mel Gibson, Jodie Foster, James Garner Director: Richard Donner Screenplay: William Goldman Running Time: 2:09 Rated: PG (Mild profanity, implied sex) Theatrical Aspect Ratio: 2.35:1

Maverick may be as close as anything comes to perfect light entertainment (as opposed to a perfect movie). It has great action sequences, more than a splash of legitimately funny humor, solid performances from engaging actors, and a script that doesn't demand much mental exercise.

Lethal Weapon's Richard Donner and Mel Gibson have teamed up again in this comedy/adventure/ western that recalls, but does not imitate, the 1950s television series. Along for the ride is James Garner, who millions will remember as the original Bret Maverick, and Donner makes a wise decision in giving him more than a token speaking part. Garner's laid back persona is the perfect contrast to the high-voltage Gibson. Two-time Oscar winner Jodie Foster is effervescent in a role that requires little dramatic range but a flair for comedy. Foster's Annabelle Bransford is delightful, especially when paired with Gibson. There's a spark between them.

The story involves Maverick and Annabelle's attempts to get to a big Saint Louis riverboat poker game where the entry fee is $25,000. Each is short by a few grand, and they go from town-to-town trying to win, steal, or cheat others out of it. They meet in Crystal River, and soon find themselves on the same runaway coach out of town, in the company of itinerant lawman Zane Cooper (Garner).

Maverick features gun fights, fist fights, an attempted hanging, and a tête-à-tête with rattlesnakes — but none of these sequences are graphic or gory. The film is basically lighthearted, so there aren't too many deaths or maimings. Donner has a great deal of fun incorporating parodies of past movies into this one. The most inspired is a quick flash to his own *Lethal Weapon*. There's also an extended *Dances with Wolves* sequence, featuring *Wolves'* Graham Greene as a hip Indian who cheats the white man. *Maverick* also pays tribute to screenwriter William Goldman's *Butch Cassidy and the Sundance Kid*.

The strength of *Maverick* is the ease with which it switches from comedy to action, and back again. For the most part, the pacing is excellent, although at more than two hours, the film goes on for a little too long. No drama is needed, nor is it in evidence. The well-crafted *Maverick* does everything it sets out to do. To paraphrase the lead character, *Maverick* rarely bluffs and never, ever cheats its audience.

HIGHLY RECOMMENDED

Mission: Impossible II [2000]

Starring: **Tom Cruise, Thandie Newton, Dougray Scott, Ving Rhames**
Director: **John Woo** Screenplay: **Robert Towne** Running Time: 2:07
Rated: **PG-13** (Violence, profanity) Theatrical Aspect Ratio: 2.35:1

Chef Emeril Legasse is known for "kicking up" his food concoctions by adding a liberal dash of hot spices. Working from Robert Towne's pedestrian screenplay for *Mission: Impossible II,* that's what director John Woo has done with this cinematic entrée. The movie illustrates the kind of impact a stylish filmmaker can have on a project. In other hands, *Mission: Impossible II* might have been a run-of-the-mill action movie, but, emblazoned with Woo's trademark flourishes, the motion picture has been transformed into a high-energy, adrenaline-and-testosterone boosted ride. This is most definitely "a John Woo film."

The story concerns the quest of an ex-secret agent, Sean Ambrose (Dougray Scott), to obtain samples of both the killer virus Chimera and its antidote from the scientist who created them for Biocyte Pharmaceuticals in Sydney, Australia. Once he has the virus, Ambrose plans to unleash it in the streets of Sydney and get rich as his stock options in Biocyte skyrocket, since the drug company will be the only one producing the antidote. Of course, the Impossible Missions Force (IMF) cannot allow this to happen, so their leader, M . . . err, make that Swanbeck (Anthony Hopkins), calls on his top agent, Ethan Hunt (Cruise), interrupting his mountain climbing vacation.

Swanbeck sends Hunt to recruit Ambrose's old girlfriend, Nyah Nordoff-Hall (Thandie Newton), to spy for the IMF. On this mission, Hunt brings along an old buddy, Luther (Ving Rhames), and a new Aussie cohort (John Polson). Complications occur when Hunt unexpectedly falls — and falls hard — for Nyah, and his feelings are returned. Suddenly, saving her life becomes as important as saving the world, and, since we're deep in 007 territory for most of the movie, there's little question that both likelihoods will arise.

Woo is in fine form, employing every weapon in his considerable arsenal: slow motion shots, billowing clothing (scarves, loose jackets, the dresses on flamenco dancers), pigeons taking flight, lots of martial arts/WWF moves, and a fluid but constantly-moving camera. The soundtrack, which features a relentless Hans Zimmer score liberally sprinkled with a souped-up version of the "Mission: Impossible" theme, hammers the viewer's ears. As always, Woo choreographs his action scenes like ballet. The final chase/fight sequence, which features motorcycles zig-zagging through traffic and ends with a lengthy hand-to-hand duel in which both participants display superhuman stamina, is edge-of-the-seat material. It may sound clichéd and familiar, but Woo elevates it to another level. *Mission: Impossible II* is an exciting assault on the senses that doesn't tax the brain. RECOMMENDED

Moonraker [United Kingdom, 1979]

Starring: Roger Moore, Lois Chiles, Michael Lonsdale, Richard Kiel Director: Lewis Gilbert Screenplay: Christopher Wood Running Time: 2:06 Rated: PG (Sexual innuendo, violence) Theatrical Aspect Ratio: 2.2:1

Moonraker is a sort of James Bond meets *Star Wars*. While parts of *Moonraker* are rather silly (a trend during Roger Moore's tenure), solid special effects, well-executed action sequences, and a strict reliance upon the "Bond Formula" keep this film among Moore's better entries as the British superspy.

The film opens with the hijacking of a Moonraker space shuttle on loan from the United States to Great Britain. Anxious to get to the bottom of the situation, the British government sends agent 007 to investigate, beginning with Drax Industries in California, where the shuttle was produced. Bond arrives, starts poking around, and becomes the immediate target of several murder attempts. Along the way, he strikes up a relationship with Dr. Holly Goodhead (Lois Chiles), one of Drax's chief scientists, and encounters an old adversary — Jaws (again played by Richard Kiel).

While *Moonraker*'s centerpiece is the final half-hour, which takes place aboard an Earth-orbiting space station, this is actually the least entertaining portion of the film. It's essentially a special effects demonstration, with laser bolt shootouts and space shuttles firing at deadly satellites. Most of the tense action scenes occur before Bond blasts into outer space. If nothing else, this film proves that Bond is best on Earth.

Normally, characters in Bond films don't go through much development. Such is not the case with Jaws, however. One of 007's best adversaries returns for a second engagement (he was also in *The Spy Who Loved Me*). This time, however, the steel-toothed bad guy has mellowed as the direct result of falling in love. Although Jaws is still as indestructible as ever, we see a different side of him as *Moonraker* draws to a close. Just don't expect anything *too* dramatic — this is still a James Bond movie, after all.

As Roger Moore's fourth Bond outing, and the eleventh film in the series, *Moonraker* is a satisfying followup to *The Spy Who Loved Me*. Science fiction fans may be offended by some of the liberties taken here, but tolerance is necessary. The film is, after all,

geared towards a specific audience. Accent the "fiction" in science fiction, and recognize that with Bond, realism is the last thing anyone expects — or wants. RECOMMENDED

On Her Majesty's Secret Service [United Kingdom, 1969]

Starring: George Lazenby, Diana Rigg, Telly Savalas Director: Peter Hunt Screenplay: Richard Maibaum Running Time: 2:15 Rated: PG (Violence, sexual innuendo) Theatrical Aspect Ratio: 2.2:1

With the exception of one production aspect, *On Her Majesty's Secret Service* is by far the best entry of the long-running James Bond series. The film contains some of the most exhilarating action sequences ever to reach the screen, a touching love story, and a nice subplot that has agent 007 crossing (and even threatening to resign from) Her Majesty's Secret Service. The problem is with Bond himself. Following Sean Connery's departure, the film makers had to come up with a replacement. The man they chose, a model named George Lazenby, is *boring*, and his ineffectualness lowers the picture's quality.

Lazenby can handle the action sequences, but that's about all he masters. Even considering the leading man's limitations, however, *On Her Majesty's Secret Service* is still a fine motion picture. It's the only Bond film where 007 genuinely falls in love. The object of his affection, Tracy (Diana Rigg), is the troubled daughter of a European crime boss, Draco (Gabriele Ferzetti). After Bond saves Tracy's life and pays off a 20,000-franc debt, Draco becomes interested in acquiring the British agent as a son-in-law. Bond declines his offer of one million pounds to marry Tracy, then proceeds to fall in love with her anyway.

The movie isn't all love-and-kisses, however. The main storyline involves the return of Blofeld (Telly Savalas in this incarnation). This time, he plans a campaign of biological warfare to be waged from a "research clinic" high in the Alps. Posing as a genealogist, Bond visits the place. Despite their face-to-face meeting in *You Only Live Twice,* Blofeld doesn't recognize his adversary (maybe the change to Lazenby confused him), but a minor mistake blows 007's cover.

The climactic half-hour of *On Her Majesty's Secret Service* is almost non-stop action. There's a stunning night ski sequence, a car chase down icy streets and through the heart of a stock car race, an avalanche, a helicopter raid on Blofeld's clinic, and fisticuffs on a speeding bobsled. Director Peter Hunt has a flair for these kinds of scenes, and he keeps viewers on the edge of their seats. Even featuring an inferior 007, *On Her Majesty's Secret Service* is a landmark change-of-pace, and an exhilarating and affecting piece of entertainment. **HIGHLY RECOMMENDED**

The Perfect Storm [2000]

Starring: George Clooney, Mark Wahlberg, Diane Lane, William Fichtner, Mary Elizabeth Mastrantonio Director: Wolfgang Petersen Screenplay: Bill Witliff, based on the novel by Sebastian Junger Running Time: 2:08 Rated: PG-13 (Profanity, intense weather-related scenes) Theatrical Aspect Ratio: 2.35:1

In 1997, almost 6 years after the Great Halloween Nor'easter, journalist Sebastian Junger published *The Perfect Storm*, an account of some of the most dramatic and memorable events associated with the late-October 1991 weather system. The primary focus of the film (as well as the book) is the 6-man crew of the swordfishing vessel *Andrea Gail* — Bobby Shatford (Mark Wahlberg), Dale Murphy (John C. Reilly), David Sullivan (William Fichtner), Bugsy Moran (John Hawkes), Alfred Pierre (Allen Payne), and the captain, Billy Tyne (George Clooney). After returning to shore with a poor haul that earns him less than $6,000 (and members of his crew under $3,000), Tyne decides to take the *Andrea Gail* out one more time this season. The trip to the Flemish Cap is relatively eventless, but, as the *Andrea Gail* heads east, bad weather is brewing behind them, blocking their return home. Later, after they have filled their cargo holds and are on their way back, they lose radio contact and are unaware of the strength of the storm ahead of them.

The movie is at its best when it stays with the crew of the *Andrea Gail*, which it does most of the time. The opening half-hour, before the ship sails, does a good job introducing the characters and letting us know what makes them tick. The only piece of character interaction that isn't effective is the bickering between Murph and Sully (which leads to more than one passage of badly written dialogue). The sequences with these 6 men braving the rough seas and bad weather represent some of *The Perfect Storm*'s most suspenseful moments. For those who are unaware of the *Andrea Gail*'s fate, there will be more than one nail-biting moment.

Making use of impressive visuals (many of which were enhanced, if not generated altogether, by digital technology), *The Perfect Storm* gives a sense of the awe-inspiring power of a raging sea. With mountainous swells that dwarf even large boats and no place to

hide or take refuge, the ocean can easily become a very dangerous place. The movie is exciting, engaging, and, at times, majestic, but it does not change the historical facts to make for a more crowd-pleasing story. For the first time since *Das Boot*, Wofgang Petersen has taken his cast, crew, and cameras back into the water; the result is definitely *not* all wet. **RECOMMENDED**

Plunkett & Macleane [United Kingdom, 1999]

Starring: Robert Carlyle, Jonny Lee Miller Director: Jake Scott Screenplay: Robert Wade & Neal Purvis, Charles McKeawn Running Time: 1:35 Rated: R (Violence, sex, profanity) Theatrical Aspect Ratio: 2.35:1

Despite employing a modern techno score and MTV-style editing, there's something old fashioned and enjoyable about the pure spirit of adventure embraced by *Plunkett & Macleane*, an 18th century tale about a pair of bandits who become folk heroes. There's nothing deep or ambitious about this production — it's simply a rousing account of the exploits of two likable rogues and the bad-to-the-bone thief catcher who's on their trail. Those who are typically turned off by period pieces need not worry. The costumes and settings may date to England circa 1748, but the sensibilities, attitudes, and approach are turn-of-the-millennium. Jake Scott directs with flair and style.

The film opens with an unforgettable shot of a debtors' jail in Knightbridge. The gothic structure is surrounded by tombstones, and a thick fog is rolling in. Wolves can be seen in the background. The lone prisoner in this spare, squalid building is Captain James Macleane (Jonny Lee Miller), who lacked the financial wherewithal to pay back his creditors. Suddenly, Macleane's jail becomes the center of a pitched battle between a group of outlaws and the soldiers pursuing them. During the fray, Macleane is freed, joins up with one of the thieves — an unkempt man named Plunkett (Robert Carlyle) — then promptly ends up in another prison after the authorities catch him. But Plunkett has swallowed a large ruby, and, once he is able to pass it, he and Macleane buy their freedom. They then hatch a plan to strike it rich by stealing from others.

Parts of *Plunkett & Macleane* don't hold together upon close examination, but that doesn't prevent the movie from maintaining a sense of excitement. Even with the various contrivances demanded by the plot, it's still an involving picture. Visually, *Plunkett & Macleane* is a stylistic success, although Scott (making his feature debut) is overly fond of quick cuts. The film is also well paced; there aren't any dead spots to kill the momentum, and a fair amount of humor is stirred into the mix (sometimes of the laugh-aloud variety). The biggest challenge facing *Plunkett & Macleane* will be finding an audience. Entertaining as the picture is, it is being released in such a low-key fashion that many potential viewers may not find out about it until it's available on video. That's unfortunate, because *Plunkett & Macleane* is good enough to be appreciated during its theatrical run. RECOMMENDED

The Professional [France/United States, 1994]
Starring: Jean Reno, Natalie Portman, Gary Oldman Director: Luc Besson Screenplay: Luc Besson Running Time: 1:52 Rated: R (Violence, language, mature themes) Theatrical Aspect Ratio: 2.35:1

The career aspirations of Mathilda (Natalie Portman) aren't those of the average 12-year old girl. Instead of wanting to be a doctor, fashion model, teacher, lawyer, or nuclear physicist, Mathilda has decided to follow in the footsteps of her best friend, surrogate father, and protector, Leon (Jean Reno). The only problem is that Leon is a "cleaner" — a professional hit man. Mathilda comes from a *very* dysfunctional family. Her father is a drug dealer, his wife despises her, and her half-sister enjoys beating her up. Mathilda's chief pleasure is hanging out in her New York City tenement building's stairwell, smoking cigarettes.

One day, a crooked cop (played with typical over-the-top exuberance by Gary Oldman) decides to have Mathilda's whole family exterminated. When she arrives home to find them slaughtered, she goes to Leon, who lives down the hall, for help. Although he's at first reluctant to open his door to her, once he does, she worms her way into both his life and his heart. And she's not some wide-eyed innocent; her desire to learn about killing is fueled by the need to exact bloody revenge for her little brother's murder (she could care less about the other family members).

The real strength of *The Professional* is the central relationship between Mathilda and Leon. Although not well-founded in reality, these two characters mesh nicely. Despite an occasional low-key hint of sexual attraction, this is basically a father/daughter or mentor/apprentice relationship. There's nothing unique about a young girl melting the heart of a hardened loner except in the manner in which Luc Besson approaches the theme.

Because of the non-American flavor brought to this film by Besson, *The Professional* is anything but

typical fare. It is stylish, darkly humorous, and almost artsy in its approach to the genre. Nevertheless, it delivers what viewers want from any thriller: lots of action. With some surprisingly strong character interaction, there's a lot to like about this movie, at least for those willing to look beyond all the bloodshed.

At one point, Leon comments to an attentive Mathilda that "the closer you get to being a pro, the closer you can get to the client." Through the intimacy of the link forged by Besson with his audience, there's no doubt that he's as much the consummate professional as his implacable title character. RECOMMENDED

Queen Margot [France/Italy/Germany, 1994]
Starring: Isabelle Adjani, Daniel Auteuil, Jean-Hugues Anglade, Vincent Perez Director: Patrice Chereau Screenplay: Daniele Thmopson & Patrice Chereau Running Time: 2:23 Rated: R (Violence, gore, sex, nudity) Theatrical Aspect Ratio: 1.85:1 In French with subtitles

The ageless Isabelle Adjani, one of France's most beautiful faces, has an undeniable screen presence. And, with his lean, well-toned body and finely-sculpted features, Vincent Perez is equally pleasing to the eye. However, put them together with the expectation that they'll play off one another, and the love affair that's supposed to sizzle instead fizzles. Not only is there no chemistry between these two, but the cold-as-ice Adjani never thaws, and Perez shows that in France, like elsewhere, physical attractiveness does not equate to acting talent.

Fortunately, there's a lot more going on in *Queen Margot* than the relationship between Perez' gallant La Mole and Adjani's title character. The film's primary focus is the bloody 16th-century struggle between French Catholics and Protestants, and the resulting political intrigue in the court of King Charles XI. *Queen Margot* opens in 1572 at the ostentatious wedding of Margot — the Catholic daughter of Catherine de Medici (Virna Lisi) and the brother of Charles (Jean-Hugues Anglade) — to Henri of Navarre (Daniel Auteuil) — the leader of the Huguenots. While this arrangement is intended to secure peace between the rival religious factions, it is a marriage of convenience only. Margot makes it clear that Henri is not welcome in her bed.

Six days after the marriage comes the Saint Bartholomew's Day massacre, an event that sees the wanton slaughter of thousands of Protestants, including the king's confidante. Henri, like many of his subjects, is forced to convert to Catholicism to save his life. Meanwhile, Margot has taken a new lover — a brave and dashing Huguenot by the name of La Mole. Yet the *I Claudius*-like scheming and political machinations have just begun.

Most of *Queen Margot* is a top-notch historical epic featuring impeccable costumes and grand scenery. Unlike the "typical" French film, this is not at all talky. In fact, amidst the swordfights, carnage, and battle scenes, there are occasions when dialogue is at a premium. *Queen Margot* is a sumptuous movie — except when the focus switches to the poorly realized romance between Margot and La Mole.

Queen Margot has enough pomp and pageantry — not to mention melodrama — to alienate viewers who don't enjoy that sort of film. However, for those who appreciate bigger-than-life historical sagas, Chereau's entry is often impressive and almost always entertaining. RECOMMENDED

The River Wild [1994]

Starring: Meryl Streep, David Strathairn, Joseph Mazzello, Kevin Bacon, John C. Reilly Director: Curtis Hanson Screenplay: Dennis O'Neill Running Time: 1:52 Rated: PG-13 (Violence, language) Theatrical Aspect Ratio: 2.35:1

As thrillers go, *The River Wild* is a cut below a "white-knuckler," but it still has its share of spills and chills. Crafted by Curtis Hanson, *The River Wild* represents for its audience just about what you might expect from a film with that title.

It's the 10th birthday for Roarke (Joseph Mazzello), and his mother Gail (Meryl Streep) has agreed to take him white water rafting to celebrate the occasion. She knows the territory well, having spent years working as a guide. Workaholic dad Tom (David Strathairn) at first refuses to accompany them but, after a guilty conscience prods him to join the family outing, he seems determined not to enjoy himself. Brooding, not boating, is his specialty.

Also on the river are Wade (Kevin Bacon) and Terry (John C. Reilly), a pair of inept rafters who have supposedly lost their guide. Gail, not wanting to strand them 5 days from civilization, agrees to let them join her party. Along the trip downstream, as both parents' distrust of the strangers grows, Roarke becomes fascinated by his new friends, especially when Wade shows him a loaded gun. From that point, the story moves in a sinister direction, with hostages being taken and lives threatened.

The River Wild has its share of tense moments. The plot beneath the action is flimsy at best, but there's enough on-screen energy to overcome this defi-

ciency. Adding noticeable value is the fine quality of the cast. These aren't just personalities thrown into suitable roles. Meryl Streep and David Strathairn are well-respected actors who have done some incredible work in the past. Kevin Bacon, who typically plays a "nice guy," is effective cast against type as a ruthless killer.

Top-of-the-line production values are of equal importance. Expansive cinematography and an apt score transfer a portion of the rafting experience to the audience. No one is likely to get seasick from *The River Wild*, but the roller-coaster pace of the picture easily matches the ups and downs of the rapids.

With *The Hand that Rocks the Cradle*, director Hanson showed that he could manipulate characters and situations within the comfortable confines of a formula plot. With *The River Wild*, he does considerably more. The thriller framework is still familiar, but the results exhibit a welcome freshness. With a pace and level of excitement designed to submerge implausibilities and minor gaffes, *The River Wild* braves the rapids while keeping the viewer afloat amidst its churning waters. RECOMMENDED

Rob Roy [1995]

Starring: Liam Neeson, Jessica Lange, John Hurt, Tim Roth Director: Michael Caton-Jones Screenplay: Alan Sharp Running Time: 2:15 Rated: R (Violence, mature themes, sex, nudity, rape) Theatrical Aspect Ratio: 2.35:1

Ultimately, it's of minor import how much of *Rob Roy* is based upon historical fact and how much has been embellished by the pen of screenwriter Alan Sharp. As a hero of 18th century Scotland, Robert Roy Mac-Gregor is known to have walked through the mists of the Highlands, living by the code that made his name a legend. This film takes the skeletal myth and builds a real person around those bones. As embodied by Liam Neeson, Rob Roy is a tremendous protagonist — a naive man whose belief in honor and whose love for a woman, family, and clan make him a figure to cheer for.

Rob Roy has a great villain as well. Tim Roth, one of today's finest character actors, plays Cunningham, a fop with effete mannerisms and a deadly blade. He's a sociopath who kills and rapes without compunction or remorse, and whose primary goal in life is to make the best out of a tormented existence in Scotland. Hunting down Rob Roy gives him something to do — something he enjoys.

It's the forcefulness of the characters and the talents of the actors who play them that give *Rob Roy* its soul. After all, almost everyone loves a movie with admirable heroes and detestable villains. But there is more to this film than that. The story is well-developed, exciting, and visceral, and works equally well as an epic drama or an historical adventure.

The picture is well-crafted, with expert editing, impressive camerawork, and an atmospheric musical score. Composer Carter Burwell has combined traditional Scottish folk songs with original material to form an audio tapestry that complements the lens work of Karl Walter Lindenlaub. With all the elements coming together so flawlessly, director Michael Caton-Jones can be justifiably proud of *Rob Roy*, sure to be one of 1995's most absorbing and exhilarating epic adventures. **HIGHLY RECOMMENDED**

The Rock [1996]

Starring: **Sean Connery, Nicolas Cage, Ed Harris** Director: **Michael Bay** Screenplay: **David Weisberg, Donald S. Cook & Mark Rosner** Running Time: **2:15** Rated: **R (Violence, profanity, sex)** Theatrical Aspect Ratio: **2.35:1**

As is often the case with action films, a simple premise is the most effective. Here, it's that a group of ex-Marines have stolen 15 VX gas rockets and are threatening to launch a lethal strike on the San Francisco Bay area if their demands aren't met. Led by war hero and living legend Brigadier General Frank Hummel (Ed Harris), the crack platoon has holed up on Alcatraz, where they're holding 81 civilians hostage. The U.S. government responds by sending a troop of Navy SEALS on a secret raid, using the labyrinth of tunnels beneath the island as their entranceway. Their guide is the only man ever to escape from the legendary prison: ex-SAS operative, John Mason (Sean Connery). Also in the party is FBI agent Stanley Goodspeed (Nicolas Cage), an admitted "chemical superfreak" who has the knowledge and experience to defuse Hummel's rockets.

The cast is first rate. But the real standout is, of course, Connery. Having lost none of his charisma with age, the veteran actor puts to use his mastery of mixing humor and action. Just like Bond, Mason does all his shooting and battling with tongue in cheek. Along the way, he develops a nice rapport with Goodspeed, with the two actors clicking in the best "buddy movie" fashion.

The Rock's running time could have been trimmed. There's no reason for it to last a bloated 135 minutes. Much of the early, character-building material could have been shortened without damaging the complexity of the principal trio, and certain aspects of the

script might have benefiting from a little tightening up. Flaws aside, however, *The Rock* still represents a loud, fast-paced night's worth of entertainment. There are all the expected shoot-outs, explosions, and death-defying stunts. Director Michael Bay doesn't break new ground, but he displays his command of the genre by keeping the familiar from becoming boring. With Connery, Cage, Harris, and a host of harrowing action sequences, this is the kind of breath-stealing entertainment that audiences crave. Although not as expertly-crafted as *Die Hard* or *Speed*, *The Rock* is exhausting in its own right — and that's just one of several convincing reasons to see this film. **RECOMMENDED**

The Rocketeer [1991]

Starring: **Bill Campbell, Jennifer Connelly, Alan Arkin, Timothy Dalton** Director: **Joe Johnston** Screenplay: **Danny Bilson & Paul DeMeo** Running Time: **1:48** Rated: **PG (Mild violence)** Theatrical Aspect Ratio: **2.35:1**

The Rocketeer is a superhero movie, but it's a superhero movie of a different flavor. This isn't a *Batman* or a *Superman* clone. It isn't about a vigilante out to stomp out crime or a visitor from another world using his powers to advance truth, justice, and the American way. Instead, it's about an ordinary man who is briefly given the opportunity to do extraordinary things.

It's Hollywood, 1938. Although a war rages in Europe, the United States remains mostly isolated, and the West Coast mecca of motion pictures is deserving of the name of "Tinseltown." Cliff Secord (Bill Campbell) is a daredevil test pilot who enjoys his job but doesn't have much money. His girlfriend, Jenny (Jennifer Connelly), is an aspiring actress who loves Cliff, but thinks he takes her for granted. So it's no surprise that when the debonair Neville Sinclair (Timothy Dalton), the "third biggest box office draw," takes an interest in Jenny, she's smitten. Meanwhile, Cliff's career is in as much trouble as his love life. A plane he had hoped to fly in competition has crashed and burned, and he's left with too little money and too little time to set up something new. Then fate intervenes.

A gang of crooks has stolen a top-secret rocket backpack from Howard Hughes. Pursued by the FBI, they ditch it in Cliff's hanger, where he finds it. After a few experiments to see how it works, he straps it on and The Rocketeer (as the papers dub him) is born. But, while Cliff's intentions are to use the pack only for honorable purposes and return it to the legitimate owner upon request, others want it for darker reasons. Soon, Cliff finds himself pursued by gangsters, Nazis, and a big, ugly man with a rubber mask.

The film has something of the feel of the Indiana Jones movies, albeit without the self-referential humor. There's a lot of action and more than a few "How's he going to get out of this?" moments. As is often the case with movies of this sort, character development is not a focal point. As a result, we get thinly-sketched types: the likable hero, his irascible mentor, the gorgeous girlfriend, and the charming villain. They're comic book type individuals, which shouldn't be all that surprising, considering *The Rocketeer*'s pedigree. *The Rocketeer* may not be perfect, but it's an excellent example of how to adapt a comic book to the screen. RECOMMENDED

Set It Off [1996]

Starring: Jada Pinkett, Queen Latifah, Vivica Fox, Kimberly Elise
Director: F. Gary Gray Screenplay: Takashi Bufford & Kate Lanier
Running Time: 2:00 Rated: R (Violence, profanity, sex, mature themes)
Theatrical Aspect Ratio: 2.35:1

Set It Off, which chronicles the attempts of 4 young black women to take control of their lives, may sound like it's treading a similar path to the one blazed by the tepid *Waiting to Exhale*, but nothing could be farther from the truth. In the first place, although *Set It Off* contains some dramatic elements, it is, first and foremost, an action/caper film. Secondly, all things considered, this is a much better picture.

Jada Pinkett is one of the crop of fine young actresses working today, and she deservedly gets more screen time than her co-stars. As Stony, she's the most sympathetic of the quartet, and the only one who comes close to having a well-rounded personality. The film opens with her prostituting herself to get the money for her younger brother's college tuition. Shortly thereafter, he is dead, the victim of an accidental police shooting. Stony is devastated, and her anger at the system makes her vulnerable to the seductive lure of easy money through a bank robbery.

Her accomplices in crime are her best friends. The four women, who have always been there to support one another, share not only a common history but the dream of one day escaping from the projects where they have lived their entire lives. The plan's mastermind is Frankie (Vivica Fox), an ex-bank employee who was fired when she reacted improperly during a hold-up. Tisean (Kimberly Elise) needs the money to keep her young son from becoming a ward

of the State. And Cleo (Queen Latifah) wants in on the action so she can live the high life and buy nice clothes for her lesbian girlfriend. Together, after being kicked in the face once too often by society, these four don wigs, borrow some guns, walk into the South Los Angeles Bank, and take $12,000 in cash.

What sets this movie apart from the innumerable other entries into the action/caper genre is its social perspective. *Set It Off* doesn't preach, but you'd have to be blind not to recognize that there's a message here about the kind of desperation that can result from the familiar cycle of poverty, sexism, and racism. And, although the marketing for *Set It Off* is geared primarily towards African Americans, you don't have to be black to appreciate this effective, in-your-face style of film making. RECOMMENDED

Space Cowboys [2000]

Starring: Clint Eastwood, Tommy Lee Jones, James Garner, James Cromwell, Donald Sutherland Director: Clint Eastwood
Screenplay: Ken Kaufman & Howard Klausner Running Time: 2:10
Rated: PG-13 (Profanity, brief nudity) Theatrical Aspect Ratio: 1.85:1

In 1958, the 4 men of Team Daedalus were the most experienced and daring that the Air Force had to offer. Eventually, the team broke apart, each of them heading in separate directions — until 40 years later, when the orbit of the Russian communications satellite *Icon* begins to decay. The satellite has only five weeks before it burns up in the atmosphere, and the Russians are worried that its loss will cripple their telecommunications infrastructure and perhaps start a civil war. *Icon*'s antiquated guidance system will not respond to commands sent from Earth and no one currently at NASA knows how to fix it. So, grudgingly, NASA approaches Frank Corvin (Eastwood), the leader of Team Daedalus and the creator of *Icon*'s "dinosaur" guidance system. Frank agrees to help, but there's a condition: he and the other three members of his team — pilot Hawk Hawkins (Tommy Lee Jones), navigator Tank Sullivan (James Garner), and structural engineer Jerry O'Neill (Donald Sutherland) — must be on the space shuttle when it launches.

Those going to *Space Cowboys* expecting aliens and space warfare will have wandered into the wrong theater. The premise is not designed to test a viewer's willing suspension of disbelief. *Space Cowboys* uses technology that is currently available. As *Apollo 13* taught viewers, it's possible to have a low-key space adventure with a great deal of tension — all that must happen is for something to go wrong. And that's exactly what fuels this movie's climactic segments.

A significant portion of *Space Cowboys'* appeal results from the four leads, all of whom possess high viewer recognition and comfort levels. We like these guys and enjoy being in their company for two hours. Eastwood is careful to balance the ensemble, not giving himself all the prime material. This allows him to do what he does best — stay calm under pressure and perform some low-key heroics. The sense of camaraderie within the group is more tangible than in many of the conventional buddy movies that invade multiplexes on a regular basis.

In the movies, putting senior citizens in space is nothing new, but this is the first time it has been done semi-realistically. The screenplay incorporates a lot of material, including secret cold war politics, cover-ups, political infighting, melodrama, media manipulation, male bonding, and, of course, science fiction action/adventure. Some of these elements work better than others, but, taken as a whole, they make for an entertaining ride. *Space Cowboys* is a blast for those who don't mind geriatric heroes. RECOMMENDED

Speed [1994]

Starring: Keanu Reeves, Dennis Hopper, Sandra Bullock Director: Jan De Bont Screenplay: Graham Yost Running Time: 1:55 Rated: R (Violence, profanity) Theatrical Aspect Ratio: 1.85:1

It's an ingenious premise that first-time director Jan De Bont has turned into a tremendously well-executed motion picture. A mad bomber (Dennis Hopper) wants $3.7 million and to obtain a small measure of revenge on Jack Traven (Keanu Reeves), a cop who foiled one of his plots. So he rigs up a bomb on a bus that becomes armed when the vehicle goes over 50, and is primed to explode when it drops below that speed. And it's Jack's job to save all the people on board, including himself.

Good action movies are rare. Great action movies come along once every few years. *Speed* deserves a place in the latter category. This is a film that cries out for audience participation, whether it be the silent majority's digging of fingers into armrests or the vocal minority's cheers and catcalls.

With a single exception (that of the bus "flying" through the air), the stunts and special effects are flawlessly incorporated. And there are a lot of them. A *whole* lot. You could almost call this film *Planes, Trains, and Automobiles,* although for entirely different reasons than those behind the naming of the

Steve Martin/John Candy flick. *Speed* is clearly divided into three acts, each no less draining than the others. The first and last (which involve an elevator and a train, respectively) bookend the longer and better sequence on the bus. The film may clock in at nearly 2 hours, but the time, like the various vehicles, races. There is, quite literally, never a dull moment.

Of course, there are plot contrivances. How could there not be? But these are subtle and convincingly woven into the fabric of the story. While watching *Speed,* you may notice one or two (for an example, consider how a bus traveling at 52 mph can slam into a car and have its speed not drop below the red line), but you won't care much. The low-level but persistent humor is used to blot the tension. Most of the one-liners aren't as good as those in *Die Hard,* but a few are worth a chuckle, and they serve their purpose. This is not, after all, supposed to be a comedy.

This movie is a winner, and the closest you can get to an amusement park ride in a theater. Perhaps the same warning that's used for roller coasters should be applied here. You know, the one about high blood pressure and heart problems. HIGHLY RECOMMENDED

Spider-Man [2002]

Starring: Tobey Maguire, Willem Dafoe, Kirsten Dunst Director: Sam Raimi Screenplay: David Koepp Running Time: 2:01 Rated: PG-13 (Violence, sensuality) Theatrical Aspect Ratio: 1.85:1

Spider-Man is as critic-proof as movies come, so nothing that I say will make even a miniscule difference, but, for what it's worth, this represents the best kind of adventure movie — bold, colorful, and well-paced without numbing the mind or insulting the intelligence. On the scale of superhero movies, this one is about on par with *X-Men,* ahead of all of the *Batman* movies, but behind the grandly reverent *Superman.*

In comic book language, this is an "origin" story, meaning that it tells how Spider-Man came into being. The movie starts by introducing us to nerdy high school senior Peter Parker (Tobey Maguire), who is one of the least cool kids in school. He's shy and smart, and the girl of his dreams, Mary Jane Watson (Kirsten Dunst), doesn't know he exists. Peter's best friend is Harry Osborn (James Franco), the underachieving son of the rich and arrogant scientist Norman Osborn (Willem Dafoe). Peter lives with his uncle, Ben (Cliff Robertson), and aunt, May (Rosemary Harris), who are like a father and mother to him.

Things change rapidly for Peter when, while visiting a lab at Columbia University, he is bitten by a genetically altered spider. Overnight, Peter gains arachnid powers — unnatural strength and endurance, amazing agility, and glands on his wrist that allow him to spin webs. Eventually, Peter is forced to make a choice between hiding his abilities or coming into the open and helping humanity. Meanwhile, Spidey's first arch-rival is also in the making, as Norman Osborn's scientific experimentation gives him equal parts superhuman strength and madness, and his access to the latest technology allows him to don a horrific metal suit and ride a one-man jet-propelled glider. After his first public appearance, at which he wreaks mayhem, the press dubs him The Green Goblin.

Although it is first and foremost an action/adventure film, *Spider-Man* is many other things, as well. There's a fairly high romance quotient — after all, many of Peter's motivations are centered around his near-obsession with Mary Jane. These two make a cute couple, but the better part of their love story is still to come (although their kiss, with Spider-Man hanging upside down as they lock lips, is memorable). *Spider-Man* also offers occasional doses of morality, the biggest one coming from Uncle Ben's words of warning to Peter: "With great power comes great responsibility." In the comic book, that phrase became Spider-Man's credo.

This is a pure popcorn movie — the kind of film one can unabashedly enjoy for what it is. There's plenty of visual flash and dizzying action, but not at the expense of the other qualities that make for a complete motion picture experience. As a character in a comic book, Spider-Man is 4 decades old. His leap into this new medium has rejuvenated the legend, and offers movie-goers an opportunity to sit back and enjoy the birth of a new cinematic superhero. **RECOMMENDED**

Spy Game [2001]
Starring: **Robert Redford, Brad Pitt, Catherine McCormack**
Director: **Tony Scott** Screenplay: **Michael Frost Beckner & David Arata**
Running Time: **2:05** Rated: **R (Violence, profanity)** Theatrical Aspect
Ratio: **2.35:1**

Spy Game is an espionage thriller for viewers afflicted with Attention Deficit Syndrome. That's not to say it's a bad movie, but the frenzied approach doesn't allow much opportunity to absorb details. Despite the length, which exceeds 2 hours by a few minutes, *Spy Game* doesn't feel bloated or protracted. In fact,

given the amount of ground covered by the storyline, this could easily have been a much longer endeavor.

Spy Game centers on the mentor/protégé relationship between Nathan Muir (Robert Redford), a jaded CIA agent on the verge of retirement, and Tom Bishop (Brad Pitt), a young idealist. On his latest mission, in Beijing, Bishop has been captured by the Chinese government. With only 24 hours until his execution, the CIA is attempting to distance themselves from Bishop so that this international incident will not endanger trade talks. Muir, on the other hand, is appalled by the idea of hanging Bishop out to dry, and covertly develops a plan to affect a rescue. Meanwhile, Muir must relate his entire history with Bishop — how they met, why the older man recruited the younger one, and which missions they worked on together — in front of a room full of CIA bigwigs.

By using flashbacks, *Spy Game* covers four time periods. The film's present-day is 1991, when a new world order is developing from the ashes of the cold war. Michael Frost Beckner and David Arata's script also takes us back to the Vietnam war, where Muir and Bishop first meet; to '70s Berlin, where Bishop is assigned to bring an informant through Checkpoint Charlie; and to 1985 Beirut, where the CIA recruits terrorists to eliminate other terrorists. The manner in which the flashbacks are grafted into the main story is a little clumsy, but it succeeds in filling in the gaps and illuminating why Muir is determined to save Bishop.

Spy Game does not offer the attention to detail evident in the best spy thrillers. There's also no real build-up in tension, although this is principally a result of Scott's style and the screenplay's approach (it's difficult to develop suspense when flashbacks continually interrupt the main narrative thread). Overall, *Spy Game* is an engrossing, if flawed, endeavor — the kind of movie that represents an evening's solid diversion. **RECOMMENDED**

The Spy Who Loved Me [United Kingdom, 1977]
Starring: **Roger Moore, Barbara Bach, Curt Jurgens, Richard Kiel**
Director: **Lewis Gilbert** Screenplay: **Richard Maibaum & Christopher Wood** Running Time: **2:05** Rated: **PG (Sexual innuendo, violence)**
Theatrical Aspect Ratio: **2.35:1**

Of Roger Moore's 7 James Bond pictures, *The Spy Who Loved Me* stands out as the best. Stripped of the extreme silliness of *The Man with the Golden Gun* and packed with style, action, and wit, *The Spy Who Loved Me* ranks alongside the Connery Bonds as a memorable cinematic representation of Ian Fleming's superspy (although the screenplay is not based on Fleming's novel of the same title).

As usual, Bond's chief nemesis is a megalomaniac. This time, his name is Stromberg (Curt Jurgens), and he's out to destroy the world to fulfill his dream of creating and populating an underwater city. The first part of his plan involves destroying the over-water civilization by a nuclear holocaust. To that end, he steals British and Soviet submarines with the intention of using their nuclear capacity against the superpowers. 007, along with his Russian counterpart, Major Anya Amasova, aka agent Triple-X (Barbara Bach), is dispatched to stop this. There are complications, however, because, although the USSR and England are cooperating on the mission, Anya has a personal grudge against Bond, and she makes it perfectly clear that she intends to kill him at the first favorable opportunity.

The Spy Who Loved Me marks the first appearance of Jaws (Richard Kiel), who would prove to be 007's most dangerous and persistent adversary. So massive and powerful is Jaws that there's little Bond can do against him physically. He's the perfect supervillain, and it's great fun to see how 007 survives confrontations with the steel-toothed giant. Barbara Bach proves to be a pleasant addition to the cast as the latest "Bond girl." Major Amasova is attractive, smart, sexy, and (of course) dangerous. Her repartee with Bond is scripted with the usual attention to double entendres and witty retorts.

The Spy Who Loved Me has no shortage of gadgets. These include noxious cigarettes, ski pole projectiles, and, most impressive of all, a Lotus Esprit that swims rather than sinks. But such toys are only part of 007's appeal. Bond films attract audiences because they're solid fun — light, uncomplicated entertainment that requires no more from a viewer than that he or she sits back and enjoys. Despite the recycled plot, *The Spy Who Loved Me* deserves its popularity as one of Bond's most engaging outings. Even those who swore off the films with Sean Connery's departure might consider checking this one out. **RECOMMENDED**

Supercop [Hong Kong, 1993]

Starring: **Jackie Chan, Michelle Khan** Director: **Stanley Tong**
Screenplay: **Edward Tang, Fibe Ma & Lee Wai Yee** Running Time: **1:36**
Rated: **R (Violence)** Theatrical Aspect Ratio: **2.35:1** Dubbed into English

With its infectious mix of action and comedy, *Supercop* is vastly different from any big budget American picture. And the knowledge that Jackie Chan and his co-stars are doing their own stunts only sweetens the pot. Then there are the martial arts sequences (choreographed by director Stanley Tong), which are, quite simply, amazing, and remind the viewer that the fist is faster than the eye.

Supercop gives audiences an opportunity to appreciate the clown aspect of Chan's personality. Although he's best known as an action star, he's also a gifted comic. He has an expressive face — his features go through more contortions than his body. The dubbed English is actually an asset for this kind of film — the cheesy mis-synching of lips adds to the goofy fun.

Frankly, dialogue doesn't mean much in *Supercop,* nor does the plot. It's a framing device to get Chan into action. All we really need to know is which characters are the good guys and which ones are the bad guys, and, once that has been established, little else matters. For the record, *Supercop* pairs Chan's Hong Kong detective with a female Chinese security officer (Michelle Khan). Together, they go undercover to break a master criminal, Panther (Yuen Wah), out of prison, so he can lead them back to his drug lord brother (Ken Tsang). Their goal: infiltrate the organization and bring it down.

As is usual in a Chan film, the end credits (which show out-takes of failed stunts) are one of *Supercop*'s highlights. Ultimately, the closing montage points out one of the chief differences between Chan's stylized, fast-paced films and those of his American counterparts: this is action with a smile, not a grimace. **RECOMMENDED**

Swordfish [2001]

Starring: **John Travolta, Hugh Jackman, Halle Berry, Don Cheadle**
Director: **Dominic Sena** Screenplay: **Skip Woods** Running Time: **1:38**
Rated: **R (Violence, profanity, nudity, sex)** Theatrical Aspect
Ratio: **2.35:1**

Swordfish is escapist entertainment that requires a significant level of suspended disbelief. While this motion picture lacks the strong scripts and easy-to-identify-with central characters of its antecedents, its deficiencies in those areas don't detract significantly from its watchability. The screenplay, credited to Skip Woods, is silly and often preposterous, but it's not dumb. It pokes fun at itself on a fairly constant basis, although never straying so far over the line that it morphs into self-parody. Director Dominic Sena puts things into testosterone-and-adrenaline overdrive, delivering a healthy portion of chases leavened with high-tech gadgetry and a helping of raunchy under-the-table sex and high-profile nudity.

The story is presented in a convoluted manner, starting in the middle, flashing back for about an hour, then returning to the present. Gabriel Shear (John Travolta) is the film's charismatic villain, a man so wealthy and powerful that "he lives a life where nothing is beyond him." In this case, he's planning a $9.5 billion electronic bank robbery, the proceeds of which he can use to finance anti-terrorist terrorist activities. His surprisingly small crew includes the sexy Ginger (Halle Berry), who harbors a secret, and the stoic Marco (Vinnie Jones). Now, he wants to add ex-super hacker Stanley Jobson (Hugh Jackman) to his payroll. At first, Stanley isn't interested — he just got out of prison, and doesn't want to go back. Then Gabriel dangles an irresistible lure in front of him — the chance of regaining custody of his beloved daughter, Holly (Camryn Grimes), who is currently living with her porn-star mother. So Stanley agrees, and this places him once again into conflict with FBI agent Roberts (Don Cheadle), the man who previously busted him. Now, with his team assembled, Gabriel embarks upon the heist, using violent, amoral, pyrotechnic techniques and fooling his pursuers by pulling Houdini-like deceptions out of his bag of tricks.

By using computer hacking as a plot element, *Swordfish* attempts to be high-tech. There are some neat computer graphics and the dialogue occasionally sounds convincing (although those in the know will catch some laughable errors), but that's all window dressing for the caper action. The movie is loud, flashy, and violent, and certain viewers will probably be offended by the casual manner in which some of the deaths occur. But, for those on the lookout for this sort of motion picture, that's irrelevant. RECOMMENDED

Thunderball [United Kingdom, 1965]

Starring: Sean Connery, Claudine Auger, Adolfo Celi, Luciana Paluzzi Director: Terence Young Screenplay: Richard Maibaum & John Hopkins Running Time: 2:13 Rated: PG (Sexual innuendo, violence) Theatrical Aspect Ratio: 2.35:1

By the time *Thunderball*, the fourth in the "official" James Bond film canon, was released, the "Bond Formula" had already been perfected. It goes something like this: take the suave 007 (always impeccably dressed and ready with a witty one-liner) and add several beautiful, scantily-clad women, at least one exotic locale, a few neat gadgets, multiple polished

action sequences, a megalomaniac villain, and a musical score by the inimitable John Barry. These elements, taken together, made Bond a huge success in the 1960s and have kept him riding a crest of financial profitability for more than three decades.

As *Thunderball* opens, SPECTRE is again on the move. This time, the mission — to blackmail the United States and Great Britain — is headed by Number Two, Emilio Largo (Adolfo Celi). The plot he has masterminded involves stealing two nuclear weapons, then threatening to blow up a major city if the two countries don't pay the ransom. After the threat has been issued, M (Bernard Lee) calls in the "00" agents and assigns them to tasks around the world with the goal of finding and stopping Largo. 007 draws Nassau, where he encounters old friend Felix Leiter (played this time by Rik Van Nutter), Largo's lovely mistress, Domino (Claudine Auger), and a host of deadly adversaries.

At 2¼ hours, *Thunderball* runs too long. Certain squences could have been trimmed, especially the climactic underwater battle, which seems to take forever. The villain of the piece is a little weak, coming in the wake of such memorable adversaries as Dr. No and Goldfinger. While Adolfo Celi is suitably menacing, he plays Largo like a high-placed thug. There is some compensation for the deficiencies of the lead villain, however. It comes in the person of femme fatale Fiona (Luciana Paluzzi), whose sophisticated, black widow-like personality makes her more dangerous than any male SPECTRE agent.

The underwater sequences, which are choreographed and directed with great skill, are *Thunderball*'s standout feature. Connery is more often in a bathing suit than a tuxedo here. A fair amount of time is spent beneath the ocean's surface, and, down in Neptune's realm, the photography (by Lamar Boren) is clear and the action sequences are invigorating (when they don't seem to last forever, that is). *Thunderball* is classic 007 — not the best picture in the long-running series, to be sure, but a more-than-worthwhile diversion for the action-loving escapist in us all. RECOMMENDED

Titanic [1997]

Starring: Leonardo DiCaprio, Kate Winslet, Billy Zane Director: James Cameron Screenplay: James Cameron Running Time: 3:14 Rated: PG-13 (Mayhem, nudity, sex, profanity, mild violence) Theatrical Aspect Ratio: 2.35:1

Short of climbing aboard a time capsule and peeling back 8½ decades, James Cameron's magnificent *Titanic* is the closest any of us will get to walking the decks of the doomed ocean liner. Meticulous in detail, yet vast in scope and intent, *Titanic* is the kind of epic motion picture event that has become a rarity. You don't just watch *Titanic*, you experience it — from the launch to the sinking, then on a journey 2½ miles below the surface, into the cold, watery grave where Cameron has shot never-before seen documentary footage specifically for this movie.

Titanic is a romance, an adventure, and a thriller all rolled into one. It contains moments of exuberance, humor, pathos, and tragedy. In their own way, the characters are all larger-than-life, but they're human enough (with all of the attendant frailties) to capture our sympathy. Perhaps the most amazing thing about *Titanic* is that, even though Cameron carefully recreates the death of the ship in all of its terrible grandeur, the event never eclipses the protagonists. To the end, we never cease caring about Rose (Kate Winslet) and Jack (Leonardo DiCaprio).

Titanic sank during the early morning hours of April 15, 1912 in the North Atlantic, killing 1500 of the 2200 on board. The movie does not begin in 1912, however — instead, it opens in modern times, with a salvage expedition intent on recovering some of the ship's long-buried treasure. The bulk of the film — well over 80% of its running time — is spent in flashbacks. We pick up the story on the day that *Titanic* leaves Southampton, with jubilant crowds cheering as it glides away from land. On board are the movie's three main characters: Rose, a young American debutante trapped in a loveless engagement because her mother is facing financial ruin; Cal Hockley (Billy Zane), her rich-but-cold-hearted fiancé; and Jack Dawson, a penniless artist who won his third-class ticket in a poker game. When Jack first sees Rose, it's from afar, but circumstances offer him the opportunity to become much closer to her. As the voyage continues, Jack and Rose grow more intimate, but, when circumstances in the Rose/Cal/Jack triangle are coming to a head, *Titanic* strikes an iceberg and the "unsinkable" ship begins to go down.

A dazzling mix of style and substance, of the sublime and the spectacular, *Titanic* represents Cameron's most accomplished work to date. It's important not to let the running time hold you back — these 3+ hours pass very quickly. Although this telling of the *Titanic* story is far from the first, it is the most memorable. **MUST SEE**

Titus [1999]

Starring: Anthony Hopkins, Jessica Lange, Alan Cumming
Director: Julie Taymor Screenplay: Julie Taymore, based on the play by William Shakespeare Running Time: 2:42 Rated: R (Extreme violence, frontal nudity, sex) Theatrical Aspect Ratio: 2.35:1

Based on Shakespeare's play, *Titus* is a gory story of betrayal and revenge. It opens with Titus Adronicus (Anthony Hopkins), an aging and respected Roman commander, returning to Rome in the wake of a successful campaign against the Goths. He is greeted by his brother, Marcus (Colm Feore), who attempts to install him as Emperor. Titus refuses, instead throwing his support behind another candidate, Saturnius (Alan Cumming), who is quickly confirmed. One of Saturnius' first declarations as Emperor is that he will take Titus' daughter, Lavinia (Laura Fraser), as his bride. When Saturnius' brother, Bassianus (James Frain), objects on the grounds that he and Lavinia are already engaged, the Emperor is enraged, but he agrees to choose another. His alternate is Tamora (Jessica Lange), the queen of the Goths who was recently captured by Titus. Dripping honey from her forked tongue, she smoothes over quarrels and plays the peacemaker — all in preparation for a war of vengeance to be waged against Titus, who was responsible for the death of her eldest son. With the aid of her faithful Moor lover, Aaron (Harry J. Lennix), she causes the death of Bassianus, allows Lavinia to be raped and mutilated, and entraps two of Titus' sons. These actions drive the old commander into a state of towering rage and grief that sends him over the precipice of madness.

While the dialogue in *Titus* is taken verbatim from Shakespeare's text, the style is all Taymor's. In her feature debut, the acclaimed stage director categorically rejects a conventional interpretation of the play. Instead, she sets *Titus* in a nightmarish netherworld, where traditional Roman costumes and settings are married with trappings from other eras, particularly the 20th century.

Taymor's tone is not relentlessly bleak — there are bursts of kinetic action and certain scenes are suffused with wry, black humor. Also, she does not sensationalize the violence. Many of the bloodier acts are hidden from the camera's view. So, while we see the aftermath of the severing of hands and heads, we aren't afforded a direct shot of the actions occurring. Taymor finds the correct balance between indicating brutality and turning *Titus* into a bloodbath. One of the clearest indications that *Titus* succeeds is that, despite its nearly 3-hour running time, there are few dead spots. Taymor's visual flourishes prove to be an effective compliment for Shakespeare's text, rather than a distraction. HIGHLY RECOMMENDED

Tomb Raider [United States/United Kingdom, 2001]

Starring: Angelina Jolie, Daniel Craig, Iain Glen, Chris Barrie, Noah Taylor, Jon Voight Director: Simon West Screenplay: Patrick Massett & John Zinman Running Time: 1:38 Rated: PG-13 (Violence, profanity, brief nudity) Theatrical Aspect Ratio: 2.35:1

For what it is, *Tomb Raider* does a good job. It's like Indiana Jones meets James Bond with a female protagonist and most of the plot siphoned off. When you consider that Bond movies are not exactly known for their writing, this puts Lara Croft's first cinematic endeavor in perspective. Don't think too hard about the story — it simply won't stand up. Focus instead upon the action pieces, which are all expertly produced. (Although a slightly less hyperactive camera would have been appreciated — are all of those lightning-fast cuts really necessary?) *Tomb Raider* moves at a fast clip, and represents top notch eye candy.

It doesn't take a film critic to ascertain why *Tomb Raider* works. Her name is Angelina Jolie, and she imbues her character with a third dimension that didn't exist on the written page, where Lara Croft is all height and width with no depth. She's action and sex appeal blended and personified. We even feel for Lara at times — a sure sign that the character has managed to attain a semblance of life. Lara Croft may hail from a video game, but her first movie is all comic book in style and approach.

The story sounds like recycled *Dr. Who*. A fabled artifact called the Triangle of Light has been broken into two pieces. Now, as the 9 planets are about to align for the first time in 5,000 years, a secret society of Illuminati are trying to find these two hidden pieces and bring them together. If they succeed, they will have control over time. In their employ is Manfred Powell (Iain Glen), who oozes the kind of charm that only a villain can. In their way is Lara Croft, who is acting on written instructions from her dead, beloved father, Lord Croft (Jon Voight, Jolie's real-life dad), to stop them. This results in a showdown for the ages, with all sorts of special effects and *Matrix*-inspired action. It's involving, although not quite exhausting. *Tomb Raider* is a great way to cure the blahs, provided, as always with this kind of film, you short-circuit the thinking parts of your brain. RECOMMENDED

Tomorrow Never Dies [United Kingdom/United States, 1997]

Starring: Pierce Brosnan, Jonathan Pryce, Michelle Yeoh, Teri Hatcher Director: Roger Spottiswoode Screenplay: Bruce Feirstein Running Time: 2:00 Rated: PG-13 (Violence, mild profanity, sensuality) Theatrical Aspect Ratio: 2.35:1

Tomorrow Never Dies is a better film than *Goldeneye*. In fact, it's the best Bond film in many years. For the first time since the legendary Sean Connery left the part, this movie feels like a Connery Bond adventure. Pierce Brosnan, having left behind the jitters he occasionally exhibited during *Goldeneye,* now inhabits his character with a suave confidence that is very like Connery's. The villain of the piece, Elliot Carver (played with panache by Jonathan Pryce), is cut from the Blofeld/Goldfinger mold — sinister, cunning, and charismatic. Added to that are the usual Bond girls (Teri Hatcher and Michelle Yeoh), the gadgets, the chase scenes, the fights, the explosions, and a John Barry-esque score (by David Arnold) that makes repeated and effective use of the "James Bond Theme."

As is usually the case in a 007 flick, the bad guy is a megalomaniac. There's a twist, however — Carver doesn't want to rule the world, he wants to rule the world's media. Using the advanced technological capabilities of the Carver Media Group, he engineers a conflict in the South China Sea between two Chinese planes and the *HMS Devonshire.* War between China and Britain looms, with Carver having the inside story. And that's where Bond comes in.

Equipped with a brand new BMW that can almost drive itself, 007 goes undercover into Carver's empire, pretending to be a banker. At a posh party held by the tycoon, he meets Carver's wife, Paris (Teri Hatcher), an old flame. Also present is Wai Lin (Michelle Yeoh), a Chinese secret agent posing as a newswoman. It doesn't take long for Bond to rub someone the wrong way, and soon he's ducking behind a printing press to escape a hail of bullets, then racing through the streets of Hamburg in his souped-up car. With the clock ticking, Bond and Wai Lin have less than 48 hours to stop World War III.

The action sequences are suitably entertaining. It's impossible to count the number of bullets fired, and there are pyrotechnics aplenty, including exploding missiles, a fireworks show on the ground, and a fairly spectacular climactic conflagration. There are a couple of memorable chases, including one with a driverless car and another with a low-flying helicopter closing in on a motorcycle. For those who crave flashes, bangs, narrow escapes, and other action film staples, *Tomorrow Never Dies* delivers. RECOMMENDED

True Crime [1999]

Starring: Clint Eastwood, Isaiah Washington, Denis Leary, Lisa Gay Hamilton, James Woods Director: Clint Eastwood Screenplay: Larry Gross, Paul Brickman & Stephen Schiff Running Time: 2:07 Rated: R (profanity, violence, sexual situations) Theatrical Aspect Ratio: 1.85:1

True Crime has the potential to be a truly memorable film, and, for more than three-quarters of its running time, it is poised to live up to that potential. But then there are the final 20 minutes, which proffer the almost-painful experience of watching compelling drama devolve into mindless action. *True Crime*'s denouement is perplexing and exasperating, because, aside from generating some artificial tension, it contributes nothing to the story as a whole, and, consequently, serves only to cheapen it.

True Crime follows 24 hours in the lives of two men whose circumstances are vastly different, but whose destinies become intertwined. Frank Beachum (Isaiah Washington) is an innocent man on Death Row in San Quentin. A mere day away from his final meal, Frank is calm and resigned to his fate. Last minute reprieves are unlikely. Frank's wife, Bonnie (Lisa Gay Hamilton) and his young daughter are less stoic. Meanwhile, in the aftermath of the death of a colleague at the Oakland Tribune, veteran reporter Steve Everett (Clint Eastwood) is given the assignment of covering Frank's execution. Something isn't right, and, after only a few hours' digging, he thinks he knows why: Frank has been wrongfully convicted. Of course, the difficulty lies in proving it, and, the more of himself Steve invests in the story, the more apparent it becomes that his personal redemption is fused with Frank's salvation.

True Crime is not afraid to tackle difficult issues. While it does not attack the subject of capital punishment as directly as *Dead Man Walking*, it presents the frightening scenario of an innocent man awaiting execution. Eastwood, who is functioning with three hats (director, producer, star), depicts Frank's final day with the assurance and meticulous detail of a seasoned professional. From the guard who sits at a typewriter recording his every activity to Frank's agonizing final meeting with his family and the long walk to the Lethal Injection Chamber, Eastwood doesn't miss a beat.

I'll never understand why otherwise-intelligent motion pictures occasionally resort to the contrived tactics employed at the end of *True Crime*. We don't need the high-speed car chase and the race against the clock. Even with its flaws, *True Crime* is a fine motion picture, but I can't avoid asking the simple, clichéd question of "What if?" RECOMMENDED

True Lies [1994]

Starring: Arnold Schwarzenegger, Jamie Lee Curtis, Tom Arnold, Tia Carrere Director: James Cameron Screenplay: James Cameron Running Time: 2:20 Rated: R (Language, violence) Theatrical Aspect Ratio: 2.35:1

In the past, James Cameron has proven himself to be a master of action and suspense. Titles like *The Terminator* and *Aliens* speak volumes about his talent. His least original film, *T2*, was still a rollicking good time, if a little limited when it came to a plot. Now, with *True Lies*, the director has not only reaffirmed his ability to keep viewers on the edge of their seats, but he has shown himself capable of making an audience laugh. One of the best things about *True Lies* is that it's genuinely funny.

The storyline isn't really all that inventive, although it contains a few original moments. Arnold plays Harry Tasker, a man who leads a double life. At home, with his wife Helen (Jamie Lee Curtis) and daughter Dana (Eliza Dushku), he's a loving, if somewhat meek, husband and father. When he goes off to work, however, he doesn't travel to the sales office where Helen thinks he has a desk. Instead, he joins up with his partner Albert Gibson (Tom Arnold) to save the world. That includes romancing beautiful-but-deadly women like Juno Skinner (Tia Carrere) and squaring off against "wacko" terrorists like Salim Abu Aziz (Art Malik).

The point of *True Lies* is enjoyment. The plot is a little meatier than that of *Speed*, but until the last forty-five minutes, it doesn't thunder along at nearly the same breakneck pace. In fact, the main "terrorist-blackmailing-the-world" story stays in low gear until the film is 90 minutes along. Before then, a lot of time is spent examining the duplicitous relationship between Harry and Helen. When he suspects her of having an affair with a used car salesman (Bill Paxton), the results are hilarious.

There are the requisite spectacular explosions, coupled with an expectedly high body count. This is, after all, an Arnold Schwarzenegger motion picture, and certain things are expected. *True Lies* is an old-fashioned, high-tech, fun time at the movies. By not trying to "out-*Die Hard*" *Die Hard,* and relying instead on its own brand of mayhem and humor, this movie has injected some much-needed freshness into a genre that always threatens to turn stale. HIGHLY RECOMMENDED

Twister [1996]

Starring: Helen Hunt, Bill Paxton, Cary Elwes Director: Jan De Bont
Screenplay: Michael Crichton & Ann-Marie Martin Running Time: 1:52
Rated: PG-13 (Violent weather) Theatrical Aspect Ratio: 2.35:1

Twister, which follows a team of tornado chasers as they track down storms, is exciting, if a little shallow. This particular disaster movie, which pits man against an implacable, unstoppable enemy, owes as much to *Godzilla* and *Jurassic Park* as to *The Towering Inferno* and *The Poseidon Adventure.* It's a perfect motion picture roller coaster — fun, fast, and furious . . . as long as you don't think too hard.

Twister opens with a short prologue in June 1969. It's one of the film's most effective sequences, as a family of three flees into a shelter to escape an oncoming storm. The father is killed, sucked into the vortex while his wife and 5-year-old daughter, Jo, watch. More than 25 years later, that little girl has grown up to be a tornado chaser. Played by Helen Hunt, Jo is obsessed with increasing the pre-storm warning time. Accompanied by her old partner and soon-to-be-ex-husband, Bill Harding (Bill Paxton), her usual crew, and Bill's fiancee (Jami Gertz), Jo is about to try out "Dorothy," a specially-built instrument designed to spit out data from inside the vortex. So, in the midst of "the biggest series of storms in 12 years," Jo and Bill hit the road, vying with a rival scientist (Cary Elwes) to reach each new storm first.

Apparently, nature doesn't make a good enough villain, so the writers of *Twister* decided to add some nasty human rivals. Unfortunately, Cary Elwes' character is both unnecessary and irritating; the tornadoes are enough. Equally superfluous are the romantic complications in the relationship between Jo and Bill. It's a rather boring subplot, and, if these two had been together from the beginning, we would have been spared the presence of Jami Gertz' unappealing character.

Twister is peppered with bits of information about how to react if a tornado approaches, how dangerous the storms can be, etc. Despite these snippets of safety-conscious advice, the movie doesn't function as a public service announcement, nor should it. *Twister* doesn't have any pretensions. It is what it sets out to be: an effective piece of big money, early summer entertainment designed to blow viewers away. RECOMMENDED

U-571 [2000]

Starring: Matthew McConaughey, Bill Paxton, Harvey Keitel
Director: Jonathan Mostow Screenplay: Jonathan Mostow, Sam Montgomery, David Ayer Running Time: 1:55 Rated: PG-13 (Violence, mild profanity) Theatrical Aspect Ratio: 2.35:1

As submarine movies go, *U-571* gets the job done — that is to say, it tells an engaging (albeit predictable) story and features several scenes of nail-biting suspense. All of the usual plot staples are in evidence: tension between crew members, deep diving where the hull threatens to collapse, dodging depth charges, and sub-to-sub battles. Director Jonathan Mostow should be commended for taking a thin script and crafting a compelling film out of it. *U-571* doesn't hold together well upon reflection, but, while it's playing on screen, it works.

The storyline is simple enough. The crew of a U.S. submarine is sent on a top-secret mission to board a disabled German U-boat and steal a secret encoding device. The boarding crew is led by Lt. Andrew Tyler (Matthew McConaughey), whose relationship with his captain (Bill Paxton) is currently strained. Once Tyler's group has boarded the U-571, a German sneak attack destroys the U.S. sub, and the navy officers are forced to maneuver the crippled U-boat through enemy territory while being pursued by a German destroyer.

U-571 contains some great, sustained action sequences, the best of which is the climactic one, which features about ten minutes of nonstop tension as the submarine sinks to potentially fatal depths then ends up in a race against time. The battle scenes are well executed, with Mostow effectively conveying the confusion and chaos of what happens when a submarine is buffeted by depth charges that threaten to split it wide open. Bolts pop, water explodes through leaks, sparks fly, and fires start. The experience of watching these sequences is visceral.

On an intellectual level, the movie is less successful. The characters aren't just *under*developed — they are *un*developed. The only one with any backstory is Tyler, and all we know about him is that he was denied a promotion because his captain was unsure that he possessed the fortitude to send men to their deaths. We know nothing about the background or personality of any of the other men stuck on the U-571, except how they react to the crisis at hand. This complete lack of development makes it difficult to care about the characters. In terms of pure action/adventure, *U-571* is a strong contender, and its big name cast will give it a degree of visibility. Despite its weaknesses, this movie offers 2 hours of solid, kinetic entertainment. RECOMMENDED

Volcano [1997]

Starring: **Tommy Lee Jones, Anne Heche, Don Cheadle, John Corbett** Director: **Mick Jackson** Screenplay: Jerome Armstrong & Billy Ray Running Time: **1:53** Rated: **PG-13 (Death and mayhem)** Theatrical Aspect Ratio: **1.85:1**

For *Volcano*, character development fits into the "obligatory" category. Here, we have Mike Roark (Tommy Lee Jones), the head of Los Angeles' Office of Emergency Management (OEM), who smells a disaster around every corner. When a mild earthquake (4.9 on the Richter Scale) shakes the city, he abandons a vacation with his 13-year-old daughter (Gaby Hoffman) to come into work, uncertain how his second-in-command, Emmett Reese (Don Cheadle), will handle the situation on his own. Soon, however, strange things start happening. Several men working underground are scalded to death. The water temperature of a lake goes up by 6 degrees in 12 hours. And the La Brea tar pits begin to pop and bubble in earnest. Concerned that some geological cataclysm may be approaching, Roark requests the help of an expert. He gets Dr. Amy Barnes (Anne Heche), who believes that L.A. could be sitting atop a volcano that's about to become active.

In real life, I don't know anyone who believes that the residents of Los Angeles have anything to fear from volcanoes, but this film makes it very easy to suspend that particular disbelief. Not only is *Volcano* a hell of a ride, but the script has enough intelligence (relatively speaking, that is) that it's possible to become engrossed in the movie without constantly being jerked back to reality by stupid and obvious plot contrivances. Oh, there are missteps, such as an ill-conceived subplot about racial strife between a black youth and a white cop, but *Volcano* surprisingly manages to avoid many of the most common disaster movie pitfalls (probably because it keeps the number of major characters to a minimum).

All that most people want from a disaster movie is a jolt of adrenaline and a chance to "ooh" and "ahh," and *Volcano* fills both cravings. After all, there's a lot at stake — this isn't some sleepy Northwestern town, it's the second most populous city in the United States. The special effects are top-notch. When a lava river starts flowing down Wilshire Boulevard, we believe that it's actually happening. Although you see this film for the spectacle, the other stuff (characters, plot, etc.) doesn't get in the way, and that's the formula for success in this genre. *Volcano* triumphs with a resounding bang. RECOMMENDED

White Squall [1996]

Starring: **Jeff Bridges, Caroline Goodall, John Savage, Scott Wolf, Jeremy Sisto, Balthazar Getty** Director: **Ridley Scott** Screenplay: Todd Robinson Running Time: **2:08** Rated: **PG-13 (Profanity, mature themes, violence)** Theatrical Aspect Ratio: **2.35:1**

Based on the true-life memoirs of Chuck Gieg, *White Squall* introduces us to 13 high school students who have elected to spend the 1960-61 academic year on the American schoolship *Albatross* (a windjammer based out of Mystic, Connecticut). The Captain is Christopher Sheldon (Jeff Bridges), a man who preaches two lessons: the importance of unity among the crew and that "the ship beneath [them] is not a toy and sailing's not a game." His wife, Alice (Caroline Goodall), is the ship's doctor and the boys' science teacher. Other adults aboard are a Shakespeare-quoting English teacher (John Savage) and a Cuban cook (Julio Mechoso).

The young crew includes Chuck (Tom Cruise look-alike Scott Wolf), an all-American student who wants to break away from his parents' vision of what his future should be; Tod (Balthazar Getty), a tough-as-nails kid who hides a secret; Frank (Jeremy Sisto), who can't escape from under his rich father's thumbnail; and Gill (Ryan Phillipe), a young man with a desperate fear of heights. The trip on the *Albatross* is their rite of passage. By the end of *White Squall*, those who have survived are no longer boys, but men.

Given the title, it's no secret that the *Albatross* runs into real trouble. In nautical language, a "white squall" is a sudden, violent, wind-and-lightning storm that can take the sturdiest ship and snap it in two. However, this meteorological catastrophe doesn't make an appearance until the film's last 45 minutes. Until then, *White Squall* devotes itself to developing its young characters, their growing admiration for their skipper, and the relationships amongst them. While some of this drama relies on familiar formulas, a capable director like Scott can maintain the audience's attention through a long setup.

For nearly 2 hours, *White Squall* is a completely involving motion picture, keeping its comic, dramatic, and tragic elements in perfect balance. Unfortunately, the need to end with a *Dead Poets' Society*-like catharsis brings the conclusion down. Hopelessly corny and needlessly manipulative, the last scene is bad melodrama. Mercifully, it lasts only a few minutes, and the overriding image left with the viewer as the end credits roll is not of this silliness but of the *Albatross* riding the seas in the face of a hurricane-force wind. *White Squall* is a success because the good elements are so well orchestrated that they dwarf the few obvious flaws. This film offers just about everything, including a 20-minute white-knuckle sequence and a chance to shed a few tears. In short, it's first-rate entertainment. **RECOMMENDED**

The World Is Not Enough [United Kingdom/United States, 1999]

Starring: Pierce Brosnan, Sophie Marceau, Denise Richards, Robert Carlyle Director: Michael Apted Screenplay: Bruce Feirstein, Neal Purvis & Robert Wade Running Time: 2:08 Rated: PG-13 (Violence, sexual innuendo, brief nudity) Theatrical Aspect Ratio: 2.35:1

When it comes to Bond films, there's really only one question: Does it entertain for the entire running length? For *The World Is Not Enough*, as for the previous two endeavors with Brosnan, the answer is "yes." There's nothing special, shocking, or precedent-setting about the film, but it functions on a level that 007 fans will appreciate — as eye and ear candy for those who prefer action to exposition and character development. There are plenty of bangs, flashes, and chase sequences (on foot, on skis, and in the water), plus the usual array of beautiful women with skimpy outfits and funny names, science fiction-inspired gadgets (cars that drive themselves, x-ray glasses, a jacket that inflates into a survival bubble), and exotic locales (Azerbaijan, Kazakhstan, Istanbul).

With its emphasis on personal revenge, *The World Is Not Enough* hearkens back to *Licence To Kill*. Only this time it's "M" (Judi Dench) who's making things personal. When a good friend of hers is killed while inside MI6 headquarters, "M" is determined to have the murderer hunted down and brought to justice. She assigns her best agent, Bond (Brosnan), to protect her dead friend's daughter, Elektra King (Sophie Marceau). Bond soon discovers that the man who killed Elektra's father, and is now trying to eliminate

her, is a mysterious terrorist named Renard (Robert Carlyle), who is called "The Anarchist." Electra has previous ties to Renard. When she was younger, he kidnapped her, but she escaped before her father could pay the $5,000,000 ransom. But his purpose here seems more sinister than vengeance for a foiled plot. When Bond tracks him down, he finds Rendard about to steal a nuclear bomb from a group of scientists led by Dr. Christmas Jones (Denise Richards). And "M" arrives on the scene just in time to be captured.

The World Is Not Enough contains the usual array of eye-popping action sequences. In terms of genuine suspense, *The World Is Not Enough* is a cut below *Tomorrow Never Dies* — but only a tiny cut. For those who have enjoyed the other Bond movies or for anyone who appreciates fast-paced action films, *The World Is Not Enough* should prove to be a winner. Director Michael Apted may be best known for documentary efforts (the *Seven Up* series) and dramas (*Gorillas In the Mist, Nell*), but he proves to have a deft hand managing the taut pace and pyrotechnics of this kind of motion picture. When it comes to action and excitement, actors, directors, and screenwriters may change, but there's still only one James Bond. **RECOMMENDED**

X-Men [2000]

Starring: Patrick Stewart, Hugh Jackman, Ian McKellen, Halle Berry Director: Bryan Singer Screenplay: David Hayter Running Time: 1:40 Rated: PG-13 (Violence, mature themes, profanity) Theatrical Aspect Ratio: 2.35:1

X-Men's action takes place in the near future, when the United States Senate is debating a bill that will require all mutants (human beings who possess special powers as a result of DNA mutations) to register with the government. The leader of this movement, Senator Kelly (Bruce Davison), is a McCarthy-like personality who has whipped public opinion into a frenzy. One of the most powerful of the mutants, Magneto (Ian McKellen), believes that Kelly's words are the first volley of a battle that will turn into a war, and he intends to launch a preemptive strike for mutant-kind — something to head off the struggle before it begins. He is opposed by his old friend, the telepath Professor X (Patrick Stewart), and his band of "X-Men." The professor and those who study at his "School for Gifted Children" believe in the philosophy of peaceful co-existence. Meanwhile, a pair of newcomers have arrived at Professor X's school. They are Rogue (Anna Paquin), a frightened teenage girl who cannot touch another human being without draining that person's life energy, and Wolverine (Hugh Jackman), a fast healer with an adamantine skeleton and retractable claws that spring from the backs of his hands. These two, who have a big brother/little sister type of bond, are deciding whether to join Professor X when a move by Magneto takes matters out of the realm of free choice.

Compared to *Batman, X-Men* is an improvement. Style, not story, was that series' forte. The world created by Singer and his craftsmen is not as strange and gothic as Gotham City, but it is no less visually interesting. The climax, which involves the Statue of Liberty and Ellis Island, utilizes flawless, set-based duplications of reality (no significant footage was actually shot in or around New York). The giant spherical room within Professor X's school is impressive, as are chambers in Magneto's abode, and the glass-and-plastic apartment shown later in the film.

X-Men does not, however, top *Superman* as the most engaging superhero motion picture. The 1978 Richard Donner feature possessed an epic scope that *X-Men* doesn't approach. (Nor, in all fairness, does it aspire to.) This is a much simpler action/adventure effort, as the relatively short running length of 100 minutes betokens.

Most viewers will see *X-Men* as delivering what's expected of any summer movie. There are several in-jokes designed specifically for *X-Men* fans, none of which will confound someone who has never been exposed to this world before. *X-Men* brings to the screen the elements that any live comic book adaptation should offer, resulting in a lightly enjoyable cinematic experience. For escapism, *X* marks the spot. **RECOMMENDED**

Animated

Aladdin [1992]

Featuring the voices of: Robin Williams, Scott Weinger, Linda Larkin, Jonathan Freeman Directors: Ron Clements and John Musker Screenplay: Ron Clements & John Musker and Ted Elliot & Terry Rossio Running Time: 1:30 Rated: G Theatrical Aspect Ratio: 1.75:1

Like its immediate predecessors, *The Little Mermaid* and *Beauty and the Beast*, *Aladdin* features stunningly crisp visuals and wonderful song-and-dance numbers. Unlike those two films, however, the protagonist here is a boy. The other big change in *Aladdin* is the level of humor. *Beauty* and *Mermaid* had their comic moments, but they were essentially lightweight fantasy/dramas. Thanks to an incredibly lively vocal characterization by Robin Williams as the Genie, *Aladdin* is pretty much a straight comedy, with elements of romance, fantasy, and adventure thrown in almost as afterthoughts.

The story centers around the title character (voice of Scott Weinger), a homeless orphan living on the streets of the city of Agrabah. One day, while avoiding a contingent of the local law enforcement, Aladdin comes into contact with a young girl who is also hiding from the guards. She is actually the Princess Jasmine (Linda Larkin) in disguise, seeking shelter after having run away from home because of a disagreement with her father about his plans for her marriage. The gallant street urchin shows her his favorite place of concealment, then promptly falls in love with her. Soon, however, Aladdin has more to worry about than the guards or the sultan's daughter. The palace sorcerer, Jafar (voiced with relish by Jonathan Freeman), has divined that Aladdin represents the key to his plans. So, in the guise of an old man, Jafar tricks his unwitting victim into entering the mysterious Cave of Wonders, where undreamed-of treasures are hidden. There, Aladdin finds an ornate bottle, and, after accidentally rubbing it a few times, comes face-to-face with a blue genie (Williams), who is ready and willing to grant him 3 wishes. What follows is a basic formula tale as Aladdin, with the help of his sidekicks — a monkey named Abu and a flying carpet, seeks to win Jasmine's hand, defeat the evil Jafar and his vicious parrot, Iago (voiced with grating sarcasm by Gilbert Gottfried), and save Agrabah.

The mixture of Robin Williams' voice and the Disney animators' work makes the Genie a truly magical persona, stealing scene after scene from the rather bland title character. Even putting Williams' performance aside, there's still a lot to like about this film. The animation is almost as amazing as that in *Beauty and the Beast*. There are a number of wild action segments that are expertly executed. While the music isn't as important to *Aladdin* as it was to the previous two Disney animated films, there are still five new tunes, three of which are standouts. Perhaps best of all is that, as with *The Little Mermaid* and *Beauty and the Beast*, *Aladdin* can be enjoyed as much by adults as by children. This is a fun motion picture on all levels. **HIGHLY RECOMMENDED**

Anastasia [1997]

Featuring the voices of: Meg Ryan, John Cusack, Kelsey Grammer, Angela Lansbury, Christopher Lloyd, Hank Azaria Directors: Don Bluth, Gary Goldman Screenplay: Susan Ganthier & Bruce Graham, Bob Tzundiker & Noni White Running Time: 1:37 Rated: G Theatrical Aspect Ratio: 2.35:1

The first thing to note about this delightful animated adventure is that it should not be confused with an historical account of the Russian revolution. Aside from borrowing a few names, facts, and dates, this is pure, unadulterated fantasy. Someone expecting even a loose reliance upon history is going to be horrified, but then anyone who falls into that category probably doesn't belong at this movie in the first place.

The story opens in 1916 Russia, just before the revolution, and depicts the fall of Czar Nicholas II as the result of a curse placed upon him by the evil monk Rasputin (voice of Christopher Lloyd). Every member of the Romanov family is killed, except Nicholas' mother, Marie (Angela Lansbury), who escapes to Paris, and the Czar's youngest daughter, Anastasia (Kirsten Dunst), who is missing. Rasputin is also slain, but, because his curse was not fulfilled, he ends up languishing in limbo.

Fast-forward 10 years. Marie has offered a 10 million ruble reward for anyone who finds her granddaughter. Back in St. Petersburg, a pair of con artists, Dimitri (John Cusack) and Vladimir (Kelsey Grammer), are holding auditions for an "Anastasia" to take to Paris. When they discover Anya (Meg Ryan), little do they realize that the 18-year-old young woman is actually the real princess. Together, Dimitri and Vladimir teach Anya how to act like royalty, preparing her for an audience with Marie. Meanwhile, Rasputin finds a way out of his nether-domain and plots Anastasia's demise.

While the animation in *Anastasia* still doesn't quite match up to that of Disney's recent features, it's light years ahead of the likes of *The Land Before Time*, *Balto*, and even *An American Tail*. There are times when the characters' lips don't perfectly synch up with the vocals, and other occasions when the background detail is lacking, but, on the whole, *Anastasia*'s visual palette is quite rich.

Story-wise, *Anastasia* is every bit as strong as any new wave Disney film except *Beauty and the Beast*. There's a little adventure, a little romance, a little mysticism, and a little drama. The whole process of watching *Anastasia* is a thoroughly enjoyable one, and it proves that any studio willing to put forth the time, money, and effort can match Disney.

HIGHLY RECOMMENDED

Antz [1998]

Featuring the voices of: Woody Allen, Sharon Stone, Gene Hackman, Sylvester Stallone Directors: Eric Darnell, Tim Johnson
Screenplay: Tod Alcott, Chris & Paul Weitz Running Time: 1:17
Rated: PG (Mild profanity) Theatrical Aspect Ratio: 1.85:1

Antz is a very good movie, no matter how you look at it. Visually, it's more impressive than Disney's *Toy Story*, the pioneer in this burgeoning genre. On a script level, it was developed as much with a mature audience in mind as with the usual pre-pubescent crowd. A significant helping of *Antz*'s humor will go over the heads of the average under-12 viewer. Image-conscious adults should not feel embarrassed about sitting through this "kids' movie." The big-name vocal cast is expertly-selected. Where else can you find Woody Allen, Sylvester Stallone, Anne Bancroft, Christopher Walken, Sharon Stone, and Gene Hackman in the same film?

Antz follows the adventures of Z-4195 (Z for short), a neurotic worker ant whose voice is appropriately provided by Woody Allen. Z is in therapy because he's an individual in a colony where conformity is not only desirable, but mandatory. He's having trouble coming to grips with his insignificance and inadequacy. One night, while at a bar, he dances with Princess Bala (Sharon Stone), who's out incognito for a night of adventure. Z is immediately lovestruck and begins to plan a way to arrange another meeting with the princess. His scheme involves impersonating his friend, Weaver (Sylvester Stallone), a soldier ant. Things go wrong, however, when the evil General Mandible (Gene Hackman), arranges for the ant army to attack a nearby colony of termites, and Z finds himself in the midst of a battle. Surrounded by fierce fighters that look death in the face and laugh at it, this timid worker, whose preference is to "make belittling comments and snicker behind death's back," does the only thing he can: he hides.

Adults and children alike will be awestruck by *Antz*'s impressive production design. This animated effort has texture and depth. Story-wise, there's nothing here that is likely to confuse younger viewers. The basic plot is a cross between an adventure and a "Taming of the Shrew" romantic comedy. Or, as Z puts it, *Antz* is "your basic boy meets girl, boy likes girl, boy changes underlying social structure" tale. The dialogue is consistently smart, and has not been diluted to enable underage audience members to comprehend every line. Successful as an adventure, a surprisingly sophisticated comedy, a light romance, and a visual treat, there are few things that Eric Darnell and Tim Johnson's feature debut does not do. **HIGHLY RECOMMENDED**

Atlantis: The Lost Empire [2001]

Featuring the voices of: Michael J. Fox, James Garner, Cree Summer Directors: Gary Trousdale, Kirk Wise Screenplay: Tab Murphy Running Time: 1:33 Rated: PG (Cartoon violence) Theatrical Aspect Ratio: 2.35:1

Atlantis is from veteran Disney directors Gary Trousdale and Kirk Wise, whose previous credits include *Beauty and the Beast* and *The Hunchback of Notre Dame*. The vocal talents represent a large cross-section of Hollywood, including Michael J. Fox, James Garner, John Mahoney, Leonard Nimoy, and the late Jim Varney.

The story is simple enough. Nerdy Milo Thatch (voice of Michael J. Fox) is chosen to participate in an early 20th century expedition in search of the lost city of Atlantis. Milo, a linguist by trade (or, as some call him, an "expert in gibberish"), has earned that honor because his grandfather was the explorer who retrieved the journal that tells of the city's location. Milo is part of a party that includes a wisecracking cook, Cookie (Jim Varney); a bubbly teenage mechanic, Audrey (Jacqueline Obradors); an explosives authority, Vinny (Don Novello), a burly doctor, Sweet (Phil Morris); and The Mole (Corey Burton), an expert on digging. The group is led by the no-nonsense Commander Rourke (James Garner) and his equally humorless second-in-charge, Helga (Claudia Christian). After taking a submarine under water, battling a giant sea monster, and falling into the bowels of a dormant volcano, the group encounters the Atlantians, led by Princess Kida (Cree Summer) and her wary father, King Nedakh (Leonard Nimoy). Soon, Rourke's real objective in finding the city becomes apparent. He's not there for the "discovery, teamwork, and adventure" that drives Milo. His motive is purely mercenary — he sees dollar signs if he can bring back Atlantis' mysterious source of power. And the rest of the group is with him — at least to start with.

Atlantis contains less dialogue than some of the recent Disney animated features, replacing the songs and talking with some genuinely thrilling action sequences. There are submarine chase sequences, aerial dogfights, and a variety of daring escapes that feature all manner of pyrotechnics. Trousdale and Wise employ some bold camerawork, creating the animated equivalent of impressive tracking shots. There are also numerous panoramic sequences that involve a moving, rotating camera. The look of the characters is more angular than usual, giving the film a non-traditional appearance.

In terms of wit and character empathy, *Atlantis* is a notch below other recent Disney offerings, but, to a degree, the level of adventure spectacle compensates. On the whole, *Atlantis* offers 90 minutes of solid entertainment, once again proving that while Disney may be clueless when it comes to producing good live-action movies, they are exactly the opposite when it comes to their animated division. **RECOMMENDED**

Beauty and the Beast [1991]

Featuring the voices of: Paige O'Hara, Robby Benson, Jerry Orbach, David Ogden Stiers, Angela Lansbury Directors: Gary Trousdale, Kirk Wise Screenplay: Linda Woolverton Running Time: 1:30 Rated: G Theatrical Aspect Ratio: 1.66:1

"Irresistible" is an apt description of this film, because every frame is imbued with a magic that is rare for any motion picture, animated or otherwise. *Beauty and the Beast* is a triumph of artistry — a rare movie where all of the elements gel perfectly. It has set the standard for today's animated motion picture, establishing a level that no subsequent animated film has equalled.

Belle (voice of Paige O'Hara) is the most beautiful girl in a provincial town in France. Unfortunately for those who might want her as a wife, including the dim, narcissistic Gaston (Richard White), she's also one of the village's oddest denizens. She keeps to herself, helping her inventor father, Maurice (Rex Everhart), with his contraptions, and, in her spare time, devouring books. Then, one fateful day, her father disappears in the forest. Belle goes searching for him and stumbles upon a dark and scary castle. Venturing inside, she discovers a gallery of magical creatures — household objects that speak and move. Then there's the Beast (Robby Benson), the terrifying creature who rules over this domain and holds Maurice captive. Once a handsome prince, he has been cursed to remain a beast until he finds someone who truly loves him in spite of his appearance. Now, he is filled with equal parts hope and dread at Belle's arrival — hope that she might be "the one" to break the spell, and dread that she might be repulsed by his ugliness. Nevertheless, he agrees to release her father if she accedes to being his permanent guest. She makes the bargain, Maurice is set free, and she is trapped. In time, however, Belle discovers that life in the castle is not as dreadful as it initially seems.

As a romance, *Beauty and the Beast* is a delightful confection, creating a pair of memorable, three-dimensional characters and giving us reason to root for their union. Belle is strong-willed, independent, and smart. The real allure of the movie, however, is twofold: the amazingly-detailed animation and a half-dozen spectacular song-and-dance numbers. Visually, *Beauty and the Beast* is so carefully-constructed that repeated viewings reveal new details, like the wayward strands of hair that fall across Belle's forehead. The production numbers represent the best in Disney's considerable arsenal. They're the animated equivalent of Broadway show-stoppers, with all the energy and audacity of something choreographed by Busby Berkeley.

Combining all of these diverse elements, *Beauty and the Beast* attains a nearly-perfect mix of romance, music, invention, and animation. While many animated features claim to appeal equally to adults and children, *Beauty and the Beast* is one of the rare ones that actually achieves that lofty goal. It's a family feature that someone over the age of 18 can venture into without an accompanying child. **MUST SEE**

The Black Cauldron [1985]

Featuring the voices of: Grant Bardsley, Susan Sheridan, Nigel Hawthorne, John Byner, John Hurt Directors: Ted Berman and Richard Rich Screenplay: Ted Berman, Vance Gerry, Joe Hale, David Jones, Roy Monta, Richard Rich & Al Wilson Running Time: 1:20 Rated: PG (Potentially frightening moments) Theatrical Aspect Ratio: 2.35:1

The credits for *The Black Cauldron* claim that the film is based on Lloyd Alexander's "The Chronicles of Prydain." In actuality, it was inspired by *The Book of Three* and *The Black Cauldron,* 2 of the 5 books comprising the children's saga. While many of the characters and plot elements have survived the written page-to-screen transition, much of the depth and complexity is absent, turning *The Black Cauldron* into a fun-but-uninspired swords-and-sorcery story.

The film opens on a small farm in the mythical country of Prydain, where Taran the Assistant Pig Keeper (voice of Grant Bardsley) is caring for Hen Wen, a swine with clairvoyant capabilities. The farm is presided over by Dallben the Wizard (voice of Freddie Jones), who, upon viewing Hen Wen's latest prognostication sends Taran away from the farm to hide his pink charge. All does not go well, however, and Taran's journey turns into a rescue mission when Hen Wen is captured by the agents of the evil Horned King (voice of John Hurt), who intends to use the animal to discover the whereabouts of the Black Cauldron, a talisman of malevolent power that will enable him to take over the world. Along the way, Taran is joined by a petulant-but-pretty princess, Eilonwy (voice of Susan Sheridan); a cute, cuddly creature named Gurgi (voice of John Byner); and Fflewddur Fflam (voice of Nigel Hawthorne), a bard with a penchant for telling tall tales.

The Black Cauldron is not populated with a gallery of interesting characters. Taran is nobility personified, and, as such, is pretty boring. Eilonwy, despite showing signs of the backbone that later Disney heroines would display, isn't much more compelling than Taran. Fflewddur is used more for comic relief than anything else. As far as the villain goes, the only thing we learn about the Horned King is that he's evil and wants to take over the world. He looks and acts scary, but that's about it.

For those weaned on the slick animation of Disney's new wave features, some of the drawing in *The Black Cauldron* may seem a little rough or unfinished. Frankly, though, even judging by today's high standards, the artwork is impressive, especially during the late sequences when the Black Cauldron spews its magical contents skyward and an army of corpses begins its march.

To date, Hollywood has yet to make a truly rousing animated fantasy feature, making it perhaps the only genre to have eluded those who weave movie magic. Maybe because it is animated, *The Black Cauldron* is one of the more successful attempts. While the movie probably plays better to those who have not read Alexander's "Chronicles of Prydain," it's far from the failure it was once branded as. Now that it's available on video, it should find favor with a generation that never had the opportunity to see it during its brief theatrical tenure. **RECOMMENDED**

A Bug's Life [1998]

Featuring the voices of: Dave Foley, Kevin Spacey, Julia Louis-Dreyfus, Phyllis Diller Directors: John Lasseter, Andrew Stanton Screenplay: Andrew Stanton, Donald McEnery, Bob Shaw Running Time: 1:35 Rated: G Theatrical Aspect Ratio: 1.85:1

In *A Bug's Life*, the protagonist is Flik (voice of Dave Foley), an ant whose sole desire in life is "to make a difference." Flik is an inventor, and, when one of his experiments goes wrong, it brings the wrath of the grasshoppers, led by the dangerous Hopper (Kevin

Spacey), down upon the denizens of the ant hill. To protect the community, Flik, with the blessing of the ant queen (Phyllis Diller) and Princess Atta (Julia Louis-Dreyfus), ventures into the outside world and recruits "warrior insects" to defend the colony. The group of nine he collects is comprised of a praying mantis (Jonathan Harris, Mr. Smith from the TV version of "Lost in Space"), a butterfly (Madeline Kahn), a black widow spider (Bonnie Hunt), an unladylike ladybug (Denis Leary in a scene-stealing vocal performance), a walking stick (David Hyde Pierce), a caterpillar with a German accent (Joe Ranft), a rhino beetle (Brad Garrett), and a pair of unintelligible pillbugs (Michael McShane). There is a mistake in identity, however. Flik's "warrior bugs" are actually circus insects, and they accompany him under the false assumption that he is a talent scout. Things start to unravel once the ant and his elite corps discover the truth about each other.

The story presented in *A Bug's Life* works well on two levels. Children will appreciate the likable characters and fast-paced adventure; adults will marvel at the skillful animation and subtle humor. Visually, the film is both brilliantly detailed and wonderfully textured. *A Bug's Life* gives new dimensions to the diminutive world — a place where raindrops are dangerous projectiles, single berries provide full meals, and the most feared enemy is a bird.

Another thing *A Bug's Life* has is an ingenious series of end credits. Instead of just the latest lame Randy Newman song warbling over scrolling names, we are presented with a collection of mocked-up outtakes that parody the kinds of flubs and goofs which have come to decorate the credits of numerous comedies. It's brilliant in both conception and execution, and one could make a solid case that the last three minutes of *A Bug's Life* are its best.

Co-directors John Lasseter and Andrew Stanton understand that every story, even one with such an intense focus on visual elements, begins with a script and characters. *A Bug's Life,* like *Toy Story,* develops protagonists we can root for, and places them in the midst of a fast-moving, energetic adventure.

HIGHLY RECOMMENDED

Chicken Run [United Kingdom, 2000]

Featuring the voices of: Mel Gibson, Julia Sawalha, Miranda Richardson Directors: Nick Park, Peter Lord Screenplay: Kerey Kirkpatrick & Jack Rosenthal Running Time: 1:25 Rated: G Theatrical Aspect Ratio: 1.66:1

If the overall storyline of *Chicken Run* strikes a vague chord of familiarity, that's because it borrows loosely from the classic World War II adventure, *The Great Escape.* "Loosely," however, is the operative word. The movie is, appropriately enough, about a group of chickens, led by the hen Ginger (voice of Julia Sawalha), who are trapped on the farm of the stupid and greedy Mr. Tweedy (Tony Haygarth). Their lives are grinds: they produce eggs, which are collected by Tweedy and his wife (Miranda Richardson), then, when their egg-laying days are over, they become candidates for a chicken dinner. Unwilling to resign herself to such an existence, Ginger begins formulating escape plans. But, while getting one or two chickens off Tweedy's farm is feasible, freeing everyone seems to be an impossible task — until the unexpected arrival of Rocky the Flying Rooster (Mel Gibson), who crash-lands on the farm after escaping from a circus. In return for the hens hiding him, he agrees to teach them how to fly so they can sail over the fence penning them in. Unfortunately, Rocky isn't entirely trustworthy.

Although children will enjoy the film's likable animated protagonists and won't have any problem wrestling with the straightforward storyline, *Chicken Run*'s greatest appeal may be reserved for adults, who will appreciate the movie's singular wit. A fair amount of the dry, British humor is going to go over the heads of younger viewers. There are enough obvious jokes that kids won't be completely left out of the laughter loop, but my sense is that audience members over the age of 15 will find *Chicken Run* to be more amusing than those in the preteen and under-10 crowd.

Chicken Run is truly an unusual endeavor since, unlike every other animated motion picture reaching screens this year, its primary aim is not to astound viewers visually. In fact, with its old-fashioned approach to animation, it looks clunky in comparison to some of its competitors. Of course, that's part of *Chicken Run*'s charm.

At the dawn of the third millennium, animation has become the domain of the United States and Japan, so it's a rare pleasure to see another movie industry enter into the fray. With *Chicken Run*, Nick Park has taken all that was enjoyable about *Wallace & Gromit,* brought it into a barnyard, and extended it to feature length. Fans of the previous Aardman animated shorts (two of which have won Academy Awards) will undoubtedly shower Park with plaudits for what he has accomplished here. All that remains is for audiences at large to discover the simple-but-engaging entertainment of *Chicken Run*. RECOMMENDED

Dinosaur [2000]

Featuring the voices of: D.B. Sweeney, Julianna Margulies, Joan Plowright, Alfre Woodard Directors: Eric Leighton, Ralph Zondag Screenplay: John Harrison & Robert Nelson Jacobs Running Time: 1:24 Rated: PG (Dino violence) Theatrical Aspect Ratio: 1.85:1

While watching Disney's *Dinosaur*, with all of its incredibly rendered creatures and seamless blending of animated objects with real backgrounds, a question occurred to me: In movies like this, can the writing keep pace with the technology? As stunning as this movie is from a visual point-of-view, it boasts little else of great interest. Like so many big summer extravaganzas, this is a classic example of the triumph of style over substance.

Of course, since *Dinosaur* is a Disney animated effort and is geared primarily towards a younger audience, one has to make certain allowances. Kids will love the film. Although old and young alike will be awed by the spectacle of dinosaurs coming to life, the adventure, romance, and moralizing are all aimed squarely at the under-10 crowd. Children will enjoy *Dinosaur* as a fairly typical Disney-generated experience. Adults will appreciate it on another level, marveling at what cutting-edge special effects can accomplish while paying little or no attention to the rudimentary story and bland characterization.

There's not much to the plot. It's essentially a prehistoric road movie with a little *Tarzan* thrown in for good measure (once again, Disney recycles themes and ideas). Aladar (voiced by D.B. Sweeney) is a dinosaur who has been raised by a family of pre-monkey mammals. His mother (voice of Alfre Woodard), grandfather (Ossie Davis), and siblings are all cute, furry creatures that make the Ewoks look like grotesque monsters. Disney couldn't possibly have further ratcheted up the cuteness level. At any rate, after a good portion of the surrounding terrain is devastated by a meteor strike (not the Big One, apparently, since there's no lasting nuclear winter), Aladar and his mammal friends join a herd of dinosaurs who are on their way to The Nesting Ground (dinospeak for Eden). The journey is arduous, with danger coming from climate changes, roving predators, and in-fighting among the dinosaurs. In the end, it's up to Aladar to prove his mettle and be a hero.

Co-directors Eric Leighton and Ralph Zondag have crafted a film that will be an unqualified success with their primary target group. Children, more interested in fast-moving action than in a story with characters, will adore every moment of *Dinosaur*'s relatively short, 84-minute running time. Adults may be more restrained in their praise, but, even though the traditional aspects of cinema are lacking, it's hard not to be impressed by the package as a whole. *Dinosaur* is worth *seeing*. And seeing, as they say, is believing. RECOMMENDED

The Emperor's New Groove [2000]

Featuring the voices of: David Spade, John Goodman, Eartha Kitt, Patrick Warburton Director: Mark Dindal Screenplay: David Reynolds, Based on a story by Chris Williams & Mark Dindal Running Time: 1:15 Rated: G Theatrical Aspect Ratio: 1.85:1

The Emperor's New Groove represents Disney's first feature-length animated comedy. Although many of the Magic Kingdom's recent endeavors have included comedic characters (the genie in *Aladdin*, the dragon in *Mulan*, etc.), *The Emperor's New Groove* is the first motion picture to strive exclusively for comedy. Oh, there's a message buried in there (caring for others = good; selfishness = bad), but it isn't brought to the fore with sappy sentimentality. Instead, armed with what is arguably the most clever animated script in a long time, the movie makes its point through wit and gently barbed dialogue. The deeper one gets into *The Emperor's New Groove*, the less important the below average quality of the animation becomes.

Kuzco (voice of David Spade) is the emperor of all he can see — and has an ego to match his kingdom. With him, everything is "Me, Me, Me." Unbeknownst to Kuzco, his once-trusted advisor, the wizened witch Yzma (Eartha Kitt), is planning to depose him by poisoning a drink. Instead of causing the emperor's death as planned, however, Yzma's potion turns him into a llama. On all fours, he escapes from the clutches of Yzma's bumbling henchman, Kronk (Patrick Warburton), and joins forces with a kindly peasant, Pacha (John Goodman), who believes there is good in everyone — even the amazingly self-centered Kuzco. Together, these two work to restore Kuzco to his human body and his throne.

The screenplay offers plenty to laugh at for kids and adults. There's slapstick, self-mocking and self-referential humor, and amusing one-liners. The vocal casting is impeccable — perhaps the best Disney has done in 5 or 6 years. David Spade brings an edge to Kuzco, and he and John Goodman make an excellent team. Eartha Kitt finds the purr-fect tone for Yzma — bitchy, demanding, and over-the-top, but never frightening. The real scene-stealer, however, is Patrick Warburton, who sounds a great deal like Tim Allen as Buzz Lightyear. Warburton's good-natured mindlessness makes Kronk the film's constant comic highlight.

The Emperor's New Groove has gone through a major overhaul since it initially went into pre-production. Originally called *Kingdom of the Sun,* the movie was to have been a romantic comedy musical in the "traditional" Disney style. Director Mark Dindal indicated that the film's shift in course forced his team to employ "out of the box" thinking. The result, while not a groundbreaking effort for Disney, takes the animated division in a fresh direction by rejecting a number of expected conventions. *The Emperor's New Groove* is good, solid fun. RECOMMENDED

Fantasia 2000 [2000]

Hosted by: **Deems Taylor, Steve Martin, Quincy Jones, Bette Midler, Penn & Teller, James Levine, James Earl Jones, Angela Lansbury** Running Time: 1:15 Rated: G Theatrical Aspect Ratio: 1.85:1

Comparing *Fantasia 2000* to the original *Fantasia* is in some ways unfair, especially considering the way movie-going tastes have changed over the past 6 decades. Yet, even though the hand-drawn animation has been helped along by the latest in computer imaging and the running length is considerably shorter, the two movies have the kind of kinship one would expect from motion pictures under the same umbrella.

Of the 7 new segments, there are a couple of throw-aways. The opening sequence featuring a swarm of abstract triangles flying and dancing to Beethoven's Fifth Symphony, is dull and uninspired. Equally wasteful is a sequence featuring yo-yo-ing flamingos set to Camille Saint-Saen's "The Carnival of the Animals." And, while the animation for "Rhapsody in Blue," which tells a New York story, is interesting (and said to be based on the work of caricaturist Al Herschfeld), it seems to belong in another movie.

Balancing out the weaker entries are some new classics. The best of the three is "The Steadfast Tin Soldier," which mixes music (Shostakovich's "Piano Concerto No. 2"), top-notch animation, and an emotionally-rewarding story. More visually ingenious is the sequence based on Stravinsky's "The Firebird." Chosen to close the movie, this shows how a dryad-like spirit renews the earth after it has been blasted by a volcanic eruption. Finally, there's *Fantasia 2000*'s lightest episode, a charming tale of Donald Duck on Noah's Ark set to the familiar strains of "Pomp and

Circumstance." Children, who are not really *Fantasia 2000*'s primary audience (this is much more of an "adult" movie), will enjoy this one the best — either that, or "The Sorcerer's Apprentice," which is as delightful now as it was 20, 30, 60, or however many years ago you first saw it.

Although the overall quality of *Fantasia 2000* is considerably more variable than that of *Fantasia,* certain aspects of the experience are the same — namely, the ability to sit in a theater and listen to great music while being presented with a choreographed visual accompaniment. *Fantasia 2000* does not soar the way its predecessor did, but neither does it plummet to the earth. Instead, it occupies a middle territory, often hovering and drifting, but occasionally flying. RECOMMENDED

Final Fantasy: The Spirits Within [Japan/United States, 2001]

Featuring the voices of: **Ming-Na, Alec Baldwin, Steve Buscemi, Peri Gilpin, Ving Rhames, Donald Sutherland, James Woods** Director: **Hironobu Sakaguchi** Screenplay: **Hironobu Sakaguchi, Al Reinert, Jeff Vintar** Running Time: 1:45 Rated: PG-13 (Violence, mild profanity) Theatrical Aspect Ratio: 1.85:1

The aspect of *Final Fantasy* that has received the most attention is neither the storyline, nor the film's close kinship to anime, nor its roots in the gaming world. Rather, it's the movie's look, or, to be more precise, its attempts to realize computer-generated, synthetic actors as replacements for flesh-and-blood thespians. So, is it possible to tell that the individuals in *Final Fantasy* are animated, or do they look so real that they can be mistaken for actors? In medium and long shots, especially when the lighting is dim, the computer creations are extremely convincing. Up close, however, no one would confuse these creations with real people. There are all sorts of minor glitches that betray them.

The year is 2065. Earth is a battle zone, with pockets of humanity hiding behind barriers in megalithic cities from the "phantoms," alien invaders which have the capability of sucking the life force out of human beings. The war has raged since the arrival of the aliens in the Caspian Mountains, and all human settlements outside of the barriers have been laid waste. Dr. Aki Ross (voice of Ming-Na), an intrepid scientist and protégè of the revered Dr. Sid (Donald Sutherland), is "collecting" the 8 "spirits" that, when combined, will generate an energy wave to neutralize the aliens. She is aided by a small commando team comprised of Captain Gray Edwards (Alec Baldwin),

Neal Fleming (Steve Buscemi), Jane Proudfoot (Peri Gilpin), and Ryan Whittaker (Ving Rhames). While the council governing Earth backs Aki and Dr. Sid's plan, the ruthless and influential head of the military, General Hein (James Woods), advocates a more violent solution — using the Zeus cannon to obliterate the aliens, possibly damaging the Earth as well. It becomes a race against time, with Aki and her group trying to collect all the spirits before General Hein unleashes the power of the Zeus cannon.

Final Fantasy is a rousing science fiction adventure that contains enough action to keep the average viewer engaged. It pilfers shamelessly from other movies, but that's not necessarily a problem, since very little in the science fiction universe can claim to be original these days. Visually, the film is stunning, and it's not hard to understand the obvious advantages of doing this kind of project in the animated arena. *Final Fantasy* gives audiences a chance to glimpse the future of action/adventure/science fiction movies — its true achievement is to open a window onto the next frontier for computer animation. **RECOMMENDED**

Hercules [1997]

Featuring the voices of: Tate Donovan, Joshua Keaton, Roger Bart, Danny DeVito, James Woods, Susan Egan Directors: Ron Clements and John Musker Screenplay: John Musker, Ron Clements, Bob Shaw, Don McEnery, Irene Mecchi Running Time: 1:32 Rated: G Theatrical Aspect Ratio: 1.85:1

Students of mythology may be irritated by the changes made to the legend of Hercules. Many of these are understandable, given the studio's espousal of family values. After all, how much light-hearted fun can you have telling the tale of the bastard son of a god and mortal who grew up to kill his wife and children? So, instead, Disney has made Hercules the divine offspring of a couple that represents Olympian marital bliss: Zeus and Hera. Unfortunately, Hades, who is preparing a "hostile takeover bid" of the big mountain, has it on good authority that Hercules is the only one who can foul up his plans. So, using his inept assistants Panic and Pain, he has Hercules turned into a human. When Dad and Mom learn about this, they realize that their son, who is no longer immortal, cannot live on Olympus, and they allow him to be raised by Greek foster parents.

Hercules comes close to being a remake of the *The Little Mermaid* with a male hero. One could easily argue that all Disney animated films are similar, but *Hercules* is a little too blatant in its cannibalization of

past themes and plot points. Besides that, this film has a distractingly episodic feel. Instead of coming together as a cohesive story, it's like a bunch of thinly-related events strung one-by-one to reach a ninety-minute running time.

The most disappointing aspect of *Hercules* is the amateurish quality of the artwork. The "excuse" for this is that the animators at Disney were trying a new, angular style. In fact, this approach makes the film look rushed and, at times, incomplete. It is never a visual marvel — even the computer-generated scenes fail to impress. The sequences intended to offer the biggest spectacle — Olympus and the Underworld — provoke little more than a yawn.

So, although *Hercules* is undoubtedly a lightly enjoyable motion picture, I couldn't shake the feeling that it could have been and done more. Those on the lookout for another Disney masterpiece won't uncover it here. However, anyone with the modest goal of finding a screen solution to the problem of a family outing need not worry: Disney's 35th animated motion picture fills the prescription. **RECOMMENDED**

The Hunchback of Notre Dame [1996]

Featuring the voices of: Tom Hulce, Tony Jay, Demi Moore, Kevin Kline Directors: Gary Trousdale and Kirk Wise Screenplay: Tab Murphy Running Time: 1:30 Rated: G Theatrical Aspect Ratio: 1.66:1

Out of respect for the stunning visuals and family entertainment value of Disney's 34th animated feature, I can do no less than recommend *The Hunchback of Notre Dame*. All things considered, *The Hunchback of Notre Dame* isn't bad, it's just a little disappointing. Despite the over-hyped and overexaggerated "darkness" of the production, kids will love it.

It's curious that the Disney movie to use the most adult source material has yielded the least potent results. Obviously, Victor Hugo's vision of *The Hunchback of Notre Dame* couldn't be made into a Disney cartoon — it violates almost every aspect of the studio's traditional, feel-good/happy ending formula. So, predictably, the screenwriters diluted it. In doing so, they siphoned off the elements that give the story its unique power. With the darkest and most unpleasant aspects of Hugo's tragedy eradicated, there's not much left. The poorly-focused remains are likely to appeal most strongly to the under-12 crowd. Unlike past efforts, there aren't many in-jokes and double-entendres to catch the attention of the adults in the audience.

The film loosely follows Hugo's narrative. After

opening with a 6-minute prologue describing how Judge Claude Frollo (voice of Tony Jay) becomes the guardian of the deformed bell-ringer of Notre Dame, Quasimodo (voice of Tom Hulce), *Hunchback* launches into the meat of its story, which involves a curious love quadrangle. The center of attention is the gypsy Esmeralda (who looks and sounds like Demi Moore). Frollo, a powerful magistrate in 15th century Paris, whose self-proclaimed duty is to eradicate sin, wants all the gypsies dead, including Esmeralda. At the same time, however, he's having trouble fighting a lustful desire for her. The captain of his guards, Phoebus (voice of Kevin Kline), has fallen madly in love with the gypsy girl, as has Quasimodo, who becomes her friend and confidante. In Hugo's book, the interaction between these characters fuels a complex and multi-layered drama. Not so in this movie, where Quasimodo's 3 talking gargoyle companions exhibit more personality than the humans. For, although we come to feel for "Quasi," neither Esmeralda nor Phoebus makes a dent in our sympathy.

If you believe that the primary purpose for animated films is to enthrall children, *The Hunchback of Notre Dame* is an unquestionable success. If you're looking for entertainment for the whole family, this movie will fit the bill. But if you're anticipating something that's as diverting for adults as for younger viewers, *Hunchback* may disappoint. RECOMMENDED

Ice Age [2002]

Featuring the voices of: **Ray Romano, John Leguizamo, Denis Leary**
Director: **Chris Wedge** Screenplay: **Peter Ackerman, Michael Berg, Michael Wilson** Running Time: **1:22** Rated: **PG (Mild violence)**
Theatrical Aspect Ratio: **1.85:1**

Discounting *Final Fantasy*, which was aimed at a much different audience, *Ice Age* is the 8th Hollywood-financed computer animated film. It follows in the wake of, and borrows liberally from, both of 2001's blockbusters, *Shrek* and *Monsters Inc.* In fact, if *Ice Age* hadn't been in development before those movies arrived in multiplexes, one might be tempted to argue that the screenplay for this film took elements from its two immediate predecessors, jumbled them together, then dumped them out in the middle of a frozen tundra. Kids, of course, will love *Ice Age*. Adults will be entertained, but no more.

The time period is the Dawn of Man. The dinosaurs have long since vanished from the Earth, and an ice age is fast approaching. The animals, at least most of them, are headed south for the long, hard winter.

Among the exceptions are an industrious, frustrated squirrel, and 3 larger mammals: Manfred the Mammoth (voice of Ray Romano), Sid the Sloth (voice of John Leguizamo), and Diego the Sabertooth (voice of Denis Leary). These 3 have banded together on an unlikely quest: return a lost human baby to his tribe. However, while Manfred and Sid have the best intentions, Diego is pursuing his own agenda, which includes turning Manfred into dinner.

The contentious relationship turned to warm friendship between Manfred and Sid is virtually identical to that of Shrek and Donkey. The bonding that goes on between the animals and the baby recalls the way Boo worms her way into the big, bad monsters' affections. But, despite the many plot similarities, the humor and sophistication of *Ice Age* never quite reaches the level of the other computer animated endeavors — except on those occasions when the squirrel is on screen. Also, the quality of the animation is a notch lower. It's not *bad*, by any means, but it's a definite step backwards, often more resembling the look of a computer game than that of a big budget motion picture.

Ice Age's director is Chris Wedge, whose only previous experience behind the camera was making an animated short called "Bunny." His first foray into feature filmmaking is successful, although *Ice Age* is not a standout in the still-small subgenre of computer animated films. It's perfectly acceptable family entertainment — the kind of movie that parents can take their children to without worrying about inappropriate content (for either the youngsters or the adults). And, sometimes, that's about all you can ask for from a movie. RECOMMENDED

The Iron Giant [1999]

Featuring the voices of: **Eli Marienthal, Vin Diesel, Jennifer Aniston, Harry Connick Jr.** Director: **Brad Bird** Screenplay: **Brad Bird & Tim McCanlies, based on the book by Ted Hughes** Running Time: **1:20**
Rated: **PG (Mild profanity, cartoon violence)** Theatrical Aspect Ratio: **2.35:1**

The reason for *The Iron Giant*'s success isn't hard to discern — it has to do with the writing. The script is crisp, smartly-paced, intelligent, and emotionally satisfying. It recalls the strengths of *E.T.* without the weaknesses. It introduces real, likable characters worth caring about and rooting for. It's the kind of story with the power to engross 6-year olds and 60-year olds alike because it doesn't condescend. *The Iron Giant* is filled with small moments that only older viewers will get, but which pass so quickly that kids won't realize they have missed anything.

The place is Rockwell, Maine. The year is 1957. Grade schooler Hogarth Hughes (voice of Eli Marienthal) is forever looking for a pet that his mother, Annie (voice of Jennifer Aniston), will allow him to keep. One night while his mother is working late at the diner where she waitresses, Hogarth hears a noise outside. By the time he goes to check, nothing is there, but he can see a swath of destruction: broken fences, trampled ground, and downed trees. So he follows the trail into the forest to a nearby power station. It's there that he first glimpses the Iron Giant (voice of Vin Diesel) — a 100-foot tall robot from space that eats metal. When it runs afoul of some live wires, Hogarth finds the station's "Off" switch to cut the power, saving the Iron Giant from electrocution.

After another chance encounter the next day, Hogarth and the Giant become friends, but danger is lurking in the wings. A dastardly government agent, Kent Mansley (voice of Christopher McDonald), who tracks down unexplained phenomenon, is convinced that Hogarth knows something about the strange goings-on around Rockwell, and he is determined to use any means necessary to learn the truth.

The Iron Giant teaches lessons about friendship, tolerance, and sacrifice, without turning preachy. Although Hogarth is initially frightened by his huge friend (who wouldn't be?), he soon comes to realize that he's actually quite childlike and gentle. Hogarth becomes both his friend and his teacher, giving him speech lessons and occasionally discussing philosophical issues, like whether a robot can have a soul. The film also has a fairly strong anti-gun message. In addition to its effective dramatic elements, *The Iron Giant* contains a share of successful comedy. Some of the humor is fairly sophisticated, but most has a broad enough base to be enjoyed by everyone in the audience, regardless of age, gender, or race. And there's even a little flatulence, although it's considerably more tame than in most of today's films.

The Iron Giant's real strength lies in the story and character development. It's in this arena that this movie proves to be vastly superior, making this a top-notch family feature. **HIGHLY RECOMMENDED**

James and the Giant Peach [1996]

Cast: Paul Terry, Joanna Lumley, Miriam Margoyles, Pete Postlethwaite; and the voices of Richard Dreyfuss, Susan Sarandon, Simon Callow Director: Henry Selick Screenplay: Karey Kirkpatrick, Jonathan Roberts, and Steve Bloom based on the book by Roald Dahl Running Time: 1:20 Rated: PG (Scary situations) Theatrical Aspect Ratio: 1.85:1

Based (rather faithfully) on Roald Dahl's children's story, *James and the Giant Peach* uses a combination of live-action sequences and stop-motion animation to tell the tale of a lonely boy, James (Paul Terry), who finds love during a bizarre, transatlantic voyage in the innards of a gargantuan peach. His companions on the journey are a grasshopper, a centipede, a spider, an earthworm, a glow worm, and a ladybug. In the hands of Henry Selick, this weird story has been transformed into a playful, visually arresting experience with more than a few allusions to *The Wizard of Oz*.

In this case, the destination isn't Oz, but New York City, which, as envisioned by Selick, is a magical, ethereal place. The story takes place during an era when the Empire State Building is the world's tallest building, and *James and the Giant Peach* becomes the second movie to place an overgrown object at its pinnacle. Between England (where the story begins, with James suffering under the repressive thumbs of two ogre-like aunts) and New York, the peach, which is propelled by a flock of harnessed birds, has an ocean splashdown and takes a detour to frozen northern reaches.

Of course, all but the youngest children (who could be frightened by certain scenes) will be delighted by the film, and the script is written to succeed on more than one level. There are some deliciously wicked lines that few youngsters will get. This crisp dialogue is delivered by the likes of Susan Sarandon (the spider), Simon Callow (the grasshopper), David Thewlis (the earthworm), and Richard Dreyfuss (the centipede), actors with effective vocal presences.

Dorothy, accompanied by a dog, a Scarecrow, a Tin Man, and a Cowardly Lion, followed the yellow brick road. James, along with a pack of oversized bugs, follows his dreams. Both reach their destinations, and, once there, discover that it's what they learned on the trip that really matters. In the final analysis, *James and the Giant Peach* is undemanding entertainment with a subtle message. **RECOMMENDED**

The Lion King [1994]

Featuring the voices of: Jeremy Irons, James Earl Jones, Matthew Broderick, Whoopi Goldberg, Moira Kelly Directors: Rob Minkoff and Roger Allers Screenplay: Irene Mecchi & Jonathan Roberts Running Time: 1:27 Rated: G Theatrical Aspect Ratio: 1.66:1

Hamlet meets *The Jungle Book* — that's what *The Lion King* is — adding, of course, a few special touches all its own. *The Lion King* is primarily about guilt and redemption. Simba, a young lion cub and heir to his father's throne, is led to believe that he was the cause of the king's death. The trauma caused by this is so great that Simba goes into exile, attempting to find peace-of-mind through anonymity in the company of a warthog and a meerkat. But it's never that easy to escape the past . . .

The *Hamlet* parallels are all there for the discerning adult to note. Mufasa, king of the lions, is killed by a treacherous brother who subsequently takes over the rule of the kingdom. Simba, the beloved son, is wracked by guilt and impotence until the ghost of his father gives him instruction on what actions he should take. Death, something not really touched on in the last 3 animated Disney tales, is very much at the forefront of *The Lion King*. In a scene that could disturb younger viewers, Mufasa's demise is shown. It is a chilling moment that is reminiscent of a certain incident in *Bambi*. The film also contains a fair share of violence, including a rather graphic battle between two lions. Parents should carefully consider before automatically taking a child of, say, under 7 years of age, to this movie.

Scar, Simba's treacherous uncle, is the latest in a long line of Disney antagonists. Gone is the buffoonery that has marked the recent trio of Ursula, Gaston, and Jafar. Scar is a sinister figure, given to acid remarks and cunning villainy. The cold-hearted manner in which he causes Mufasa's death lets us know that this is not a lion to be trifled with.

The animation, as expected from any Disney film, is superior. As usual, as much attention is given to small background details as to foreground principals. Lighting and color are used to highlight the shifting tone of the picture (the sunny warmth of Mufasa's kingdom to the dreary barrenness of Scar's), and the animators have never lost sight that their subjects are not human.

With each new animated release, Disney seems to be expanding its already-broad horizons a little more. *The Lion King* is the most mature (in more than one sense) of these films, and there clearly has been a conscious effort to please adults as much as children. Happily, for those of us who generally stay far away from "cartoons," they have succeeded. **HIGHLY RECOMMENDED**

The Little Mermaid [1989]

Featuring the voices of: Jodi Benson, Samuel E. Wright, Pat Carroll, Christopher Daniel Barnes Directors: Ron Clements and John Musker Screenplay: Ron Clements & John Musker Running Time: 1:22 Rated: G Theatrical Aspect Ratio: 1.66:1

Despite revitalizing Disney's fortunes and introducing the present wave of big-screen cartoons, *The Little Mermaid* was not a groundbreaking motion picture, although it was the first animated movie to so thoroughly incorporate songs into the narrative. With big production numbers like "Under the Sea" and "Kiss the Girl," and several other hummable melodies, the film makers did their best to create the cartoon equivalent of a musical. Like all musicals, much of the enjoyment comes as a result of simply enjoying the singing, rather than being carried away by the relatively uncomplicated story.

The Little Mermaid is loosely based on the Hans Christian Andersen fable, albeit with a radically changed ending. Ariel (voice of Jodi Benson) is the rebellious teenage mer-daughter of Triton, King of the Sea (Kenneth Mars). She is obsessed with the culture of those who live on land, and keeps a secret treasure trove of objects recovered from shipwrecks. One day, while swimming around with her fish pal, Flounder (Jason Marin), and her chaperone, the crab Sebastian (Samuel E. Wright), Ariel comes upon a sinking ship and saves a handsome young human, who turns out to be a prince named Eric (Christopher Daniel Barnes), from drowning. Ariel is smitten, but when her father finds out about her excursions to the surface, he is furious. Hurt and desperate, the young mermaid falls into the trap of the sea-witch Ursula (Pat Carroll), who offers her a deal: in return for being transformed into a human, Ariel must cause Eric to fall in love with her in less than 3 days, otherwise her soul will belong to Ursula. To seal the bargain, Ariel gives her voice to the witch. What the mermaid doesn't know, however, is that Ursula has stacked the deck so that Ariel can't possibly emerge victorious.

The animation in *The Little Mermaid* isn't quite as accomplished or eye-popping as that of its successors, but it's still impressive, and hurried or unfinished cels are almost impossible to spot. What the film does expertly is to weave together music, likable protagonists, thoroughly nasty villains, and a fun plot into a cohesive whole, with a result that is nothing short of magical. And, although *The Little Mermaid* isn't among Disney's most "mature" animated movies, it offers enough entertainment, innocent romance, and low-key humor to keep adults involved. Children, of course, will love it. For 90 minutes of pure escapism, it's difficult to beat *The Little Mermaid*. **HIGHLY RECOMMENDED**

Monsters, Inc. [2001]

Featuring the voices of: Billy Crystal, John Goodman, James Coburn, Jennifer Tilly Directors: Peter Docter, David Silverman Screenplay: Dan Gerson, Andrew Stanton Running Time: 1:30 Rated: G Theatrical Aspect Ratio: 1.85:1

There's a world out there, somewhere under the rainbow, where monsters live. The sprawling city where they go about their daily lives is called Monstropolis — a vast, bustling place populated by all sorts of misshapen creatures who would cause the average human child to crawl under the covers. Energy in Monstropolis comes from an unusual source — the screams of children. Employees working for megacorporation Monsters, Inc. go through gateways into the bedroom of human kids on Earth, frighten them into screaming, capture the energy from the screams, and convert it to electricity in Monstropolis. But, since children are becoming harder to scare, Monstropolis is facing a "scream shortage."

The most successful scream team at Monsters, Inc. is comprised of Sulley Sullivan (voice of John Goodman) and Mike Wazowski (Billy Crystal). Sulley, really a gentle giant, is the scary one; Mike is his wisecracking partner. Together, they're approaching the all-time scream record. Their lone challenger is Randall Boggs (Steve Buscemi), who will stop at nothing to move past them. One night, after hours, Randall decides to cheat by making some unauthorized trips to the other side. Sulley accidentally discovers his plot. When he opens a door Randall has set up, a catastrophe occurs — a little girl, Boo (Mary Gibbs), crosses the threshold into the monsters' world. Suddenly, the greatest imaginable horror in monster society has occurred — a child from Earth has entered Monstropolis. Chaos reigns as Sulley and Mike try to hide the girl, protect themselves, and expose Randall's secret scheme.

Everything that was true of the two *Toy Story* movies and *A Bug's Life* can be said about *Monsters, Inc.* — this is the kind of movie that works on multiple levels — as fast-moving, lively fun for children and as slyly written, visually impressive entertainment for adults. *Monsters, Inc.* is one of those rare family films that parents can enjoy (rather than endure) along with their kids. And childless individuals venturing into a theater showing this picture need not worry that they'll be viewed as deviants — *Monsters, Inc.* is capable of drawing audience members from across the age spectrum.

The great strength of the previous Pixar films, as well as *Shrek*, is that they offer a genuine emotional component that runs deeper than that of the run-of-the-mill animated feature. Such is the case here, where the attachment between burly Sulley and tiny Boo touches the heart. The little girl brings out Sulley's soft side and smoothes some of Mike's rough edges.

Monsters, Inc. reaffirms the fact that a good animated film can be every bit as stimulating and emotionally satisfying a motion picture as a high quality live action endeavor. **HIGHLY RECOMMENDED**

Mulan [1998]

Featuring the voices of: Ming-Na Wen, Eddie Murphy, B.D. Wong, Miguel Ferrer Directors: Tony Bancroft, Barry Cook Screenplay: Eugenia Bostwick-Singer, Rita Hsiao, Philip LaZebnik, Chris Sanders, Raymond Singer Running Time: 1:25 Rated: G Theatrical Aspect Ratio: 1.85:1

The setting for this adventure is feudal China. An army of Huns under the command of the ruthless Shan-Yu (voice of Miguel Ferrer), has invaded the country, spreading death and disaster far and wide. The Chinese Emperor (Pat Morita) commands that one able-bodied male from every family must serve in an emergency army. Meanwhile, in a remote village, an independent-minded young woman named Mulan (Ming-Na Wen) has been rejected by a local matchmaker on the grounds that she is too willful. "You will never bring your family honor," decrees the matchmaker, causing Mulan to begin a period of soul-searching. When the Emperor's decree arrives, Mulan cuts her hair, dresses like a man, and enters the army in her father's place. With the help of her inept mythical guardian, the tiny dragon Mushu (Eddie Murphy), she seeks to win the confidence of her captain, Li Shang (B.D. Wong), and the acceptance of her fellow peasant-turned-warriors, while keeping her sex concealed from everyone.

Mulan is the first Disney animated film to deal with war and death on a large scale. The subject is not glossed over — the movie features several poignant sequences showing the devastation in the aftermath of a battle, including hundreds of lifeless bodies lying in the snow. Oddly, because there's nothing exploitative or gruesome about these images, they're more likely to affect older viewers, who will better understand the implications, than younger ones, for whom death is often a nebulous concept. In no way can it be said that *Mulan* is glorifying war.

The main character is cut from a familiar cloth. Although she looks different from Ariel, Belle, Jasmine, and Pocahontas, Mulan is very much the same type of individual: a woman with a strong, independent streak who is unwilling to bend to the customs of her culture, which decree that the role of the female is to be ornamental. The film isn't very subtle in reinforcing the idea of equality between the sexes, but the script contains a few amusing lines in this vein that will fly high over the heads of younger viewers.

As all Disney movies must, *Mulan* features a pair of new sidekicks. One, the second best-known cartoon cricket in the history of motion pictures, doesn't have a voice. The other, Mushu, never shuts up. It's clear that, in his vocal characterization of the dragon, Eddie Murphy is trying to top (or at least equal) Robin Williams' genie from *Aladdin*. Amazingly, he comes close. With his high-energy, often hilarious delivery, Murphy flies away with his scenes. Mushu is the primary reason kids will love *Mulan,* and he's not so fundamentally juvenile that adults won't get a few chuckles out of him, as well. **HIGHLY RECOMMENDED**

The Nightmare Before Christmas [1993]
Featuring the voices of: **Danny Elfman, Chris Sarandon, Catherine O'Hara, William Hickey, Ed Ivory** Director: **Henry Selick** Screenplay: **Caroline Thompson** Running Time: **1:15** Rated: **PG** (Cartoon monsters) Theatrical Aspect Ratio: **1.66:1**

The scene is Halloween Town where, not surprisingly, October 31 is the biggest night of the year. However, after arranging and carrying out his most devilish Halloween yet, Jack Skellington (voiced by Chris Sarandon when speaking, Danny Elfman when singing) is suffering the post-holiday blues. He craves something different in his life, something that can't be found in Halloween Town. Wandering out in a forest, he discovers gateways to different holidays, and finds his way to Christmas Town. There, he is captivated by the lights, the festivity, and the joy. He returns home to tell everyone that this year, Halloween Town is going to celebrate Christmas. To make things complete, he, Jack Skellington, will replace "Sandy Claws" on his yearly December 25 ride, delivering presents and spreading good cheer. Everyone is enthused by the idea except Sally (voiced by Catherine O'Hara), who has a premonition of doom if Jack goes through with his plans.

The Nightmare Before Christmas is a visual splendor. Done on the cheap, this could have been a gimmicky, unsatisfying experience, but, as the result of considerable time and effort, it is an unqualified success. All of the figures move smoothly and naturally, and the attention to detail is exquisite. We are given a group of cleverly-fashioned characters that look like refugees from Edward Gorey's sketchbook.

The film is designed for all but the youngest children, some of whom might be frightened by the bizarre inhabitants of Halloween Town. On its surface, the story is relatively straightforward, enabling younger viewers to enjoy the movie without becoming lost or bored. However, the film works on a second level, as well. The most deft humor is aimed at adults. Even those who aren't taken in by the charming tale or likable characters will be enthralled by the world Tim Burton and director Henry Selick have created. It is, quite frankly, an amazing achievement.

The Nightmare Before Christmas is *How the Grinch Stole Christmas* thrown into reverse (although clearly the Dr. Seuss tale had a part in formulating some of the images of Christmas Town). While the Grinch made Christmas better by trying to destroy it, Jack Skellington ruins the holiday by trying to improve it. But don't worry — everything turns out all right in the end. After all, this is a family film. **HIGHLY RECOMMENDED**

Pocahontas [1995]
Featuring the voices of: **Irene Bedard, Mel Gibson, Russell Means, David Ogden Stiers** Directors: **Mike Gabriel and Eric Goldberg** Screenplay: **Carl Binder, Susannah Grant, Philip LaZebrik** Running Time: **1:21** Rated: **G** Theatrical Aspect Ratio: **2.35:1**

Anyone who expects historical accuracy from a Disney animated feature should be ashamed of themselves. Those approaching *Pocahontas* in anticipation of a true-to-history account of the early days of Jamestown are in for a rude awakening.

Despite obvious similarities — Menken's music, a heroine who doesn't want her father to choose her husband, and a small legion of animals — *Pocahontas* is actually something of a departure from the recent batch of releases. This film isn't quite as cute; deals with some reasonably serious, "adult" issues; and contains an element of poignancy. The cartoonish animal sidekicks, which include a raccoon, a hummingbird, and a pug, are amusing as ever, but this time around, they don't have voices.

Pocahontas presents a fictionalized chronicle of the arrival of English settlers in Virginia. Led by a greedy, bombastic governor (David Ogden Stiers) and Captain John Smith (Mel Gibson), the explorers have come to the New World in search of gold. They promptly begin cutting down trees, digging holes, and preparing to kill the Indians. Meanwhile, a young native woman, Pocahontas (speaking voice of Irene Bedard, who was also the physical model for the character; singing voice of Judy Kuhn), observes the newcomers with a mixture of curiosity and trepidation.

Her father, Chief Powhatan (voice of Native American activist/actor Russell Means), is certain that the white mens' landing means war. And the only hope to avert a pitched battle arises as a result of the romance that develops between Smith and Pocahontas.

Several recognizable themes suffuse *Pocahontas*: the stupidity of wanton destruction, the need for tolerance between those of different races and cultures, and the forks in life's road offered by fate. While none is presented with any special subtlety (after all, children are supposed to get the message), there is surprisingly little preaching. It would have been easy to turn this into a "Native American good/White Man bad" film, but positive and negative traits are shown on both sides. **HIGHLY RECOMMENDED**

The Prince of Egypt [1998]

Featuring the voices of: Val Kilmer, Ralph Fiennes, Sandra Bullock, Jeff Goldblum, Michelle Pfeiffer Directors: Brenda Chapman, Steve Hickner, Simon Wells Screenplay: Philip LaZebnik Running Time: 1:39 Rated: PG (Slavery) Theatrical Aspect Ratio: 1.85:1

The subject matter of *The Prince of Egypt* is fairly sophisticated for animated fare (witness the PG rating). In keeping with Exodus, the mistreatment of the Hebrew slaves is depicted (albeit not graphically), as is the mass slaughter of Egyptian firstborns that leads to the Pharaoh's freeing of the slaves. And, as if the story wasn't grim enough to begin with, the screenwriters invented a friendship between Ramses and Moses to elevate certain aspects of *The Prince of Egypt* to the level of a Shakepearean tragedy. At times, Moses is depicted as a brooding, Hamlet-like hero.

The Prince of Egypt neither skims over nor dwells upon the least happy elements of the story. Overall, it's a story of triumph and adventure — of oppression ended and freedom begun. The comedy elements that have become an integral part of animated features are downplayed. The Pharaoh's two chief priests are sly and fatuous, and some of their antics are amusing, but they offer little more than occasional, momentary comic relief. For the most part, *The Prince of Egypt* plays it straight.

The animation in *The Prince of Egypt* is truly top-notch. The artists effectively mix hand-drawn and computer-generated images to good effect, the colors are rich and vibrant, and the characters' lip movements are in synch with the soundtrack. The final product is polished, with a number of standout sequences (the chariot race, the plagues, and the parting of the Red Sea).

As far as vocal talents are concerned, the film mak-ers have gathered an impressive cast, with even the minor characters being voiced by recognizable names. The plum roles of Moses and Ramses, the leader of the captive Hebrews and the King of Egypt, belong to Val Kilmer and Ralph Fiennes, respectively. Michelle Pfeiffer supplies the voice of Moses' wife, Zipporah; Sandra Bullock is his sister, the prophetess Miriam; Jeff Goldblum is his brother, Aaron; and Danny Glover is his father-in-law, Jethro. Other voices include Patrick Stewart and Helen Mirren as Ramses' parents, and the team of Martin Short and Steve Martin as the foolish Egyptian priests.

Jeffrey Katzenberg has gone out of his way to emphasize that *The Prince of Egypt* is not a religious movie, despite the nature of the source material. This is not intended to be a big budget Bible Story cartoon, but a rousing animated adventure. Consequently, this movie is worth a trip to the local multiplex by viewers of all ages, races, and religious persuasions. **HIGHLY RECOMMENDED**

Princess Mononoke [Japan/United States, 1999]

Featuring the voices of: Billy Crudup, Claire Danes, Gillian Anderson, Minnie Driver, Billy Bob Thornton Director: Hayao Miyazaki Screenplay: Hayao Miyazaki, Neil Gaiman (English version) Running Time: 2:13 Rated: PG-13 (Violence) Theatrical Aspect Ratio: 1.85:1

The director of *Princess Mononoke* is something of a living legend: Hayao Miyazaki, whom Roger Ebert called "a [Japanese] national treasure." Fans of anime uniformly praise his work, stating with enthusiasm that it puts even Disney's best to shame. There's such attention to detail that it's easy to lose oneself in the animation. Perhaps the best way to put it is that Miyazaki's films have a texture that is absent from even some of the most technically adept animated motion pictures.

Princess Mononoke has been "Americanized" by Miramax. No content has changed and no scenes have been cut, but familiar English-speaking actors (Billy Crudup, Gillian Anderson, Billy Bob Thornton, Claire Danes, Minnie Driver) have been brought in to record a new soundtrack. That means no subtitles, and, because dubbing isn't a major problem with animation, there's no obvious mismatch between lip movements and words.

The film, which takes place in ancient Japan at the dawn of the Age of Iron, is loosely based on Japanese mythology and is fundamentally about the eternal conflict between man and nature (as such, there's actually a conservationist message). When the story begins, a Curse God is approaching a small village in Northeast Japan, destroying everything in its path.

Ashitaka (Billy Crudup) rides out to stop it. However, while he succeeds in killing the creature, its touch afflicts him with a curse that will eventually kill him. The village wise woman tells Ashitaka that his only hope for survival is to travel West and find the Forest Spirit, who may deign to cure him. So, alone with his faithful mount, Ashitaka begins a long and perilous trek.

Eventually, Ashitaka comes to Irontown, a remote human settlement populated by society's outcasts and ruled by the Lady Eboshi (Minnie Driver). Irontown is under siege from samurai and is also waging a war with the Boar Gods and other Gods of the Mountains. During an attack by the Wolf God, Moro (Gillian Anderson), her two sons, and her human "daughter," San (aka "Princess Mononoke," voiced by Claire Danes), Ashitaka saves two men, and, as a result, is welcomed into Irontown by Eboshi. And, from that point, the story only grows more complex.

Is *Princess Mononoke* suitable for children? Probably not for the very young — the complexity of the story may confound them. (The violence isn't much of an issue, since it's not a great deal more intense than what kids see during some Saturday morning cartoons.) However, older boys and girls will be caught up in the film's adventure and impressed by its animation, although they will likely miss some of the plot's many subtleties. With a running length of nearly 2:15, this epic picture opens a vast world of romance, fantasy, and excitement that is unlike anything to emerge from a Western studio. **HIGHLY RECOMMENDED**

Shrek [2001]

Featuring the voices of: **Mike Myers, Eddie Murphy, Cameron Diaz, John Lithgow** Directors: **Andrew Adamson, Vicky Jenson** Screenplay: **Ted Eliot, Terry Rossio** Running Time: **1:27** Rated: **PG (Mild violence)** Theatrical Aspect Ratio: **1.85:1**

Dreamworks Pictures' wonderful, whimsical *Shrek* proves to be the latest family film to live up to its billing. With its blend of high adventure, light romance, and double-layered dialogue (which will take on a slightly different meaning for the under-and over-12 crowd), *Shrek* is capable of enthralling both children and their parents. In fact, this movie is so good that adults unaccompanied by offspring can venture into a theater without having to dress up in a disguise. *Shrek* is not a *guilty* pleasure for sophisticated movie-goers; it is, purely and simply, a *pleasure*.

Our protagonist is an ogre named Shrek (voice of Mike Myers, using a Scottish accent). Except for scaring off the odd knight who comes in search of his hide-out, Shrek leads a relatively peaceful life, until

the day that he stumbles into Donkey (voice of Eddie Murphy). Donkey is fleeing soldiers who are rounding up all the fairy tale creatures with the intent of resettling them. Unfortunately for Shrek, the local landholder, Lord Farquaad (John Lithgow), has decided to deport them to Shrek's swamp. This causes the irritated ogre, accompanied by his new best friend, Donkey, to head for the city of Duloc, where Farquaad holds court. There, he makes a deal with the noble — in return for getting back his swamp, Shrek will perform a quest and rescue Princess Fiona (Cameron Diaz) from the tower where she is held prisoner. The catch: she's guarded by a fire-breathing dragon. Farquaad wants Fiona for his wife (he chose her over Cinderella and Snow White), and figures that the ogre might be his best chance to rescue her. But what he doesn't count on, and what Shrek doesn't expect, is that the beauty and the beast will develop feelings for each other.

The interplay between Shrek and Princess Fiona is sweet and tender, while the exchanges between the ogre and the ass are often barbed and subversively funny. Like *The Princess Bride*, *Shrek* breaks with convention, but not so far that viewers will be put off by it. And, while there is a happy ending (as there must be in any fairy tale, no matter how unconventional), it's not necessarily the conclusion that many people will be expecting (at least up until the ⅔ point, when the movie reveals its hand). First-time co-directors Andrew Adamson and Vicky Jenson have crafted a movie to be proud of, and one that will hopefully receive a lot of attention, even during the crowded summer season. *Shrek* is easily one of the genre's most magical experiences. **HIGHLY RECOMMENDED**

South Park: Bigger, Longer and Uncut [1999]

Featuring the voices of: **Trey Parker and Matt Stone** Director: **Trey Parker** Screenplay: **Trey Parker & Matt Stone, Pam Brady** Running Time: **1:22** Rated: **R (Extreme profanity, cartoon nudity)** Theatrical Aspect Ratio: **1.85:1**

South Park is consistently rude, crude, and profane, with more than 200 obscenities being uttered in less than 90 minutes. The "R" rating is well deserved. But this production isn't all toilet humor, obscenities, and flatulence jokes. As is true of the TV series, there's a lot of subversive material to be found herein — satirical thrusts struck against a diverse array of opponents. Those include (but are not limited to) the MPAA and its ratings system, small town America, middle class "family values," traditional Judeo-Christian religious icons, Canada, wars, the Baldwin brothers, Bill Clinton, Bill Gates, and USO shows. In fact, it's hard to find a target that *South Park* doesn't savage in one way or another. And, while there aren't more than a handful of gut-busting, laugh-aloud moments, there is enough sly, slick humor to keep the average viewer chuckling throughout.

There is a plot, although the specifics of it don't much matter. Things get started when the 4 intrepid South Park heroes — Stan (Trey Parker), Cartman (Parker), Kyle (Matt Stone), and Kenny (Stone) — sneak into an R-rated movie to see a couple of Canadian stars singing profane songs and telling dirty jokes. The film makes such an impression on the youths that they can't stop swearing. Soon, everyone in school has seen the movie, and the classrooms have turned into hot beds of creative cursing. Canada gets the blame for this (after all, the movie was produced north of the border) and conservative organizations press President Clinton to declare war. Meanwhile, Kenny, who died after lighting fire to himself, is spending some time in Hell getting to know Satan and his gay companion, Saddam Hussein. When Kenny learns that the war between the U.S. and Canada could trigger the apocalypse, he decides to make a ghostly appearance to warn his former friends.

It will come as no surprise to fans of the show that *South Park* co-creators Trey Parker and Matt Stone are at the reins. Their trademark attacks on pop culture are much in evidence. *South Park* aficionados will doubtlessly be enthralled by the final product. Those who are new to the cartoon are advised to keep an open mind, and, since this is raw, ribald material, anyone who is easily offended should stay away. In the final analysis, *South Park* is an agreeable, albeit uneven, experience. RECOMMENDED

Spirit: Stallion of the Cimarron [2002]

Featuring the voices of: Matt Damon, James Cromwell, Daniel Studi
Directors: Kelly Asbury, Lorna Cook Screenplay: John Fusco Running
Time: 1:21 Rated: G Theatrical Aspect Ratio: 2.35:1

Spirit: Stallion of the Cimarron is a classic "kids' movie" — not a "family movie," as most recent animated movies have been described, but a "kids' movie." Frankly, aside from some gorgeous artwork, there's nothing in this movie to interest a viewer over the age of about 10. Dreamworks does try some interesting things with this movie. To begin with, it's a Western — a genre that has all but gone to Boot Hill. In the second place, the filmmakers have decided not to allow the animals to talk — a big plus as far as I'm

concerned, albeit a risky proposition. I don't think it would have worked if the horses had engaged in deep conversations with each other.

"They say that the history of the West was told from the saddle of the horse. But it's never been told from the heart of one before." With those words from the narrator (Matt Damon), *Spirit* opens with the birth of the title character, a mustang colt who grows into a mighty stallion. As an adult, Sprit finds his world threatened by the arrival of the White Man to the frontier. After a wild chase, a group of these interlopers capture the horse by throwing nooses around his neck. For a while, Spirit is penned inside a fort under the watchful eye of an army colonel who is determined to break him. But luck intervenes and Sprit escapes from the cavalry — only to be caught by Indians. But his treatment at their hands is more kind, and he learns that all human beings are not interested in subjugation. Also, during his time with the Indians, he meets the mare of his dreams.

The storyline for *Spirit* is infused with the kind of reverse approach to Westerns that has been in favor since *Dances with Wolves*. The Indians are the good guys; the cowboys and soldiers are the villains. *Spirit*'s twin morals of tolerance and harmony with nature are simplistic and unsubtle (as one would expect from a children's feature). An area in which *Spirit* excels is its animation. Easily the equal of anything to come out of Disney's studios in the past decade, *Spirit*'s artwork is virtually without flaw. Since the horses do not talk, the task falls to the animators to have the animals communicate and convey emotion through actions. As a result, there's a distinctly "human quality" to the horses' facial expressions.

Those for whom *Spirit* was made will find this to be a thoroughly enjoyable production. As a "kids' movie," *Spirit* is a resounding success. RECOMMENDED

Spirited Away [Japan/United States, 2002]

Featuring the voices of: Daveigh Chase, Jason Marsden, Suzanne
Pleshette, Michael Chiklis, Susan Egan Director: Hayao Miyazaki
Screenplay: Hayao Miyazaki Running Time: 2:04 Rated: PG (Scary
moments) Theatrical Aspect Ratio: 1.85:1

Spirited Away takes influences from *Alice in Wonderland* and *The Wizard of Oz* and uses them to fashion a highly original story about a 10-year-old girl, Chihiro (voiced by Daveigh Chase), who, along with her parents, ventures through a tunnel that leads to the world of spirits. After a witch, Yubaba (Suzanne Pleshette), turns Mom and Dad into pigs, Chihiro must find a niche in the spirit world, where humans are not well thought-of, and figure out a way to convince Yubaba to change her parents back into humans and send them all home. With help from Haku (Jason Marsden), Yubaba's boy apprentice, and Lin (Susan Egan), a "big sister" type, Chihiro gets a job at Yubaba's bathhouse for spirits, and there her quest to aid her family begins. But, as complications arise, she finds additional tasks to perform and other allies willing to help her.

The nature of the story is tailor-made for animation. Many of the characters engage in shape-shifting (boys become dragons, adults become pigs, a giant baby becomes a bloated mouse) and the bathhouse is frequented by a variety of strange and unusual creatures. While a few of the inhabitants of the sprit world look human, most appear to be anything but that. Take the boiler operator Kamaji (David Ogden Stiers), for example. At first glance, he's just a cranky old man with a frizzy beard. Then we notice that he has 8 legs and walks like a spider. We also find out that he's not as intimidating as he looks. His initially surly disposition melts away and he becomes of one Chihiro's numerous friends.

Miyazaki is an environmentalist, and his films often contain strong pro-environment messages. (This was a cornerstone to *Princess Mononoke*.) The film's animation is stunning, with richly-detailed backgrounds and flawless foregrounds. Unlike many animators, Miyazaki still relies almost exclusively upon hand-drawn artwork and his meticulous care shows.

Miyazaki does not dumb down *Spirited Away*, even though his stated target audience is children. This is a true family film, in that adults will be as enchanted by the characters and situations as children will. The pace is a little slower than the average animated film — there is not as much frantic action — but not so languid that younger viewers will become restless. The dubbing into English is very good, so there is no subtitle barrier. Miyazaki has provided another triumph, and, in the midst of the quality fall-off of Disney's in-house animated projects, a reason for animation-lovers to rejoice. **HIGHLY RECOMMENDED**

Tarzan [1999]
Featuring the voices of: Tony Goldwyn, Minnie Driver, Glenn Close, Lance Henriksen, Rosie O'Donnell, Brian Blessed Directors: Chris Buck, Kevin Lima Screenplay: Tab Murphy Running Time: 1:30 Rated: G Theatrical Aspect Ratio: 1.85:1

One thing viewers should never reasonably expect from an animated movie is faithfulness to the source material. Adult themes and unhappy endings rarely make it into a Disney movie. So those expecting *Tarzan*

to be a faithful recreation of the Edgar Rice Burroughs classic would do best to alter their expectations.

The movie opens on a high note, as Tarzan's mother and father, along with their baby boy, escape a burning shipwreck. They make it to shore, erect a treehouse, and start a life in Africa. Shortly thereafter, however, the two adults fall victim to a wild animal and the baby is adopted by a female gorilla. As he grows, Tarzan becomes an accepted member of the family, but he wonders why he looks different from everyone else. His questions — at least some of them — are answered with the arrival of Jane Porter, her father, and their guide, Clayton, to the jungle. Tarzan is surprised to find others like him, and, after he saves Jane from a band of angry baboons, he finds himself inexplicably drawn to her, and she to him.

From a purely visual standpoint, this may be the most impressive of all of Disney's traditionally animated features. The backdrops are lush, the characters are well realized, and the action sequences are dizzying, with frequent changes of perspectives and camera angles. No conventional animated film has been this ambitious before. Once again, Disney has made a series of wise decisions concerning vocal characterizations. Tarzan is voiced by Tony Goldwyn, who gives the hero a sort of ordinary voice. Minnie Driver's Jane is considerably more independent than the Rice Burroughs version, but she is allowed to keep her British accent. Nigel Hawthorne is Jane's father, Brian Blessed is the nefarious Clayton, Glenn Close is Tarzan's adopted mother, and Lance Henriksen is Kerchak, the fearsome leader of the gorillas.

One potential problem with *Tarzan* is the lack of a strong, central villain. Although Clayton eventually fulfills the bad guy role, he really doesn't assume the position until just before the anticlimactic final battle. Even then, he's not very frightening.

Through the years, Tarzan has proven to be an extraordinarily popular character with movie audiences. This new animated effort is sure to be a huge hit with children, and, while adults will find much to enjoy about the film, few will see this as the definitive screen version of the Edgar Rice Burroughs classic, and even fewer will herald this as one of Disney's greatest achievements. **RECOMMENDED**

Thumbelina [1994]
Featuring the voices of: Jodi Benson, Gary Imhoff, John Hurt, Carol Channing, Barbara Cooke, Gilbert Gottfried Directors: Don Bluth and Gary Goldman Screenplay: Don Bluth Running Time: 1:26 Rated: G Theatrical Aspect Ratio: 1.85:1

As her name indicates, Thumbelina (voice of Jodi Benson) is about the size of a finger. She lives a generally happy day-to-day life with her human mother and several animal friends, but something is missing — until she meets Cornelius (voice of Gary Imhoff), the Fairy Prince. One day, while out riding his bumblebee, Cornelius overhears Thumbelina singing. Circumstances bring the two together, and they are instantly smitten with each other. But, before Cornelius can propose marriage, Thumbelina is stolen away by a gruesome toad who also wants her for his wife.

The animation is crisp and visually striking, with careful attention paid to details. Thumbelina is perhaps not as completely-realized as Arielle, Belle, or Jasmine, but she's far better drawn than the women populating all the fringe big-screen cartoons. The same can be said of the other characters, most of whom are animals, and none of which embarrass their creators.

The storyline of *Thumbelina*, adapted from the popular Hans Christian Andersen fable, is relatively uncomplicated, and makes excellent material for an animated romance/adventure. There are several occasions when the plot seems rushed, especially towards the end. While children most likely won't notice this, adults will, although it shouldn't detract much from anyone's enjoyment of the film.

Entertainment comes in many forms, and *Thumbelina* is among the frothiest available. But the best thing is that not only is it fun — an eminently watchable — but it's a perfect "family film," capable of pleasing both children and their parents. With the exception of Disney fare, this has become an increasingly-rare commodity, and when an opportunity such as this occurs, it should be taken advantage of. RECOMMENDED

Titan A.E. [2000]

Featuring the voices of: Matt Damon, Drew Barrymore, Bill Pullman, Nathan Lane, Tone Loc Directors: Don Bluth, Gary Goldman Screenplay: Ben Edlund and John August and Joss Whedon Running Time: 1:34 Rated: PG (Violence, mild sensuality) Theatrical Aspect Ratio: 2.35:1

Titan A.E. represents an ambitious attempt by co-directors Don Bluth and Gary Goldman to fuse traditional animated techniques with the latest in computer graphics, and to present it all through a plot that owes more to Japanese anime than to classic Disney.

The year is 3028, and Earth has been destroyed by the merciless attack of an alien race known as the Drej. There are survivors, although the ragtag bunch of humans is scattered to the far corners of the quadrant, and the Drej, bent on genocide, pursue them doggedly

and seemingly without reason. For humanity, there is hope, however, in the form of a giant spaceship called *Titan*, which was successfully launched before the planet's destruction. But it is lost in deep space and only Cale, the young son of the *Titan*'s captain, possesses information about its location.

In 3042, Cale (voice of Matt Damon) is a young man living an aimless life on Salvage Station Tau 14. It is there that Captain Korso (Bill Pullman), an old friend of Cale's father, finds him. Korso has assembled a motley crew that includes a beautiful navigator, Akima (Drew Barrymore); an indolent first officer, Preed (Nathan Lane); a short-tempered weapons expert, Stith (Janeane Garafolo); and a brilliant-but-erratic scientist, Gune (John Leguizamo). Together, they have one goal: find the *Titan*, and they need Cale's help to do it. Although initially reluctant to join Korso's quest, Cale has a change of heart when he learns that the Drej are out to get him because they, like Korso, need the information he is in possession of.

Titan A.E. is action-oriented, with a number of high octane space chases and battles. The standout sequence occurs during the closing half-hour, when two ships are playing hide-and-seek in a field of giant, collapsing ice crystals. Not only are the visuals stunning, but there's a human element as well, because, by this point, we have come to care about the characters, so the sense of danger is genuine. Some of Bluth and Goldman's backgrounds are as impressive as the computer-generated foregrounds, featuring arrays of deep colors and brilliant detail. Despite technique mismatches, *Titan A.E.* is still a nice piece of visual candy.

Animation, especially of the non-Disney variety, is gradually moving in a more adult direction. *Titan A.E.* slides a little further down this slope, offering non-cute violence and blood. Such "innovations" may only be baby steps in the direction of *Heavy Metal* and countless Japanese features, but the payoff is evident: more challenging stories with interesting characters. RECOMMENDED

Toy Story [1995]

Featuring the voices of: Tom Hanks, Tim Allen Director: John Lasseter Screenplay: Joss Whedon, Andrew Stanton, Joel Cohen & Alec Sokolow Running Time: 1:21 Rated: G Theatrical Aspect Ratio: 1.85:1

Ever wonder how toys seem to get from one place to another with no human help? *Toy Story*, Disney's first feature-length foray into computer animation, postulates that they do it themselves. Toys have their own magical world which comes to life any time the lights are out or people aren't around. Any who doubt this should take a look at *Toy Story*. You'll never again feel quite the same way about Mr. Potato Head, Monkeys in a Barrel, or Slinkies.

Of course, the visual aspect is the centerpiece of *Toy Story*. The computer-generated effects are a marvel. Rich in unexpected detail (the grain of a wood floor, fingerprints and chipped paint on a door, reflections in polished surfaces, and so on . . .), this colorful and brilliantly-rendered aspect of the film would alone be worth the price of admission. It's something of a bonus that the characters, dialogue, and story provide entertainment value of their own.

Toy Story is a buddy movie/adventure tale with an understated lesson about the value of friendship. Parents might also be able to use some of what transpires to encourage their offspring to put away toys after playtime. While the screenplay isn't a marvel of originality, it is capable of holding the attention — light, undemanding fun that never gets too immature or syrupy. There's also quite a bit of intelligent wit that will go above the heads of younger viewers — that stuff's for Mom and Dad.

The two main characters are toys: cowboy Woody (voice of Tom Hanks), the old-time favorite, and space ranger Buzz Lightyear (voice of Tim Allen), the battery-operated newcomer. *Toy Story* opens with Buzz's arrival. Woody is upset that this high-tech neophyte has usurped his rightful place on the bedspread and in his 6-year-old owner's play time. The disgruntled cowboy comes up with a plan to eliminate Buzz, but it backfires, and soon the two rivals are out in the real world, forced to help each other in their struggle to escape the clutches of a toy-torturing juvenile delinquent.

How does *Toy Story* compare to Disney's more conventional animated features? They're really very different types of productions. This film is less artistic and more technologically impressive. Despite a few Randy Newman songs, it's not really a musical. Of course, the target audience is the same, and everything from Disney embraces "family values," but it's difficult — and unfair — to make an effective contrast of the two film making styles. **HIGHLY RECOMMENDED**

witty dialogue. The balance between what has been included for kids and what's there for adults is almost perfect. There are things that children will appreciate more than their parents, but other elements will go over the heads of shorter viewers. However, the majority of what *Toy Story 2* offers will delight everyone in the audience, regardless of their physical or mental age.

This film begins an unspecified time following the happily-ever-after conclusion to *Toy Story*. In the aftermath of their earlier adventures, Buzz (voice of Tim Allen) and Woody (voice of Tom Hanks) are now fast friends. One day, Andy's mother decides to have a yard sale, and she collects a few old toys from her son's room. Since one of these discards is a member of the moving toy gang, Woody goes to the rescue, leaving the safety of the house for the uncertainty of the front lawn in order to bring the toy back. Although his mission is successful, he is placed in a serious predicament when a toy collector named Al (voice of Wayne Knight) spies Woody while hunting through the wares available at the sale. The cowboy toy represents the final collectible needed to complete his collection of merchandise from the old TV series, "Woody's Roundup." If he can acquire Woody, Al can ship everything to a toy museum in Japan for a huge profit. So, after Andy's mother refuses to sell the wooden cowboy, Al steals him, and it's up to the other toys, led by Buzz, to go into the city to save their friend.

With all the elements working in perfect concert, *Toy Story 2* is a lot of fun. Viewers can expect a healthy dose of fast-moving action and broadly amusing comedy. And, although the primary thrust of the narrative is not drama, there is a moment of surprisingly affecting pathos where Jessie contemplates the pain of being outgrown by her child. It's a testimony to the skill of directors John Lasseter (who went solo on the original *Toy Story*), Lee Unkrich, and Ash Brannon that we develop such a strong bond with a group of computer generated toys. And, while *Toy Story 2* isn't quite the achievement that its predecessor represented, it is nevertheless a top example of family entertainment. **HIGHLY RECOMMENDED**

Toy Story 2 [1999]

Featuring the voices of: Tom Hanks, Tim Allen, Joan Cusack, Kelsey Grammer Directors: John Lasseter, Lee Unkrich, Ash Brannon Screenplay: Andrew Stanton, Rita Hsiao, Doug Chamberlin & Chris Webb Running Time: 1:30 Rated: G Theatrical Aspect Ratio: 1.85:1

One would have to be a hopeless curmudgeon not to be entertained by *Toy Story 2*'s remarkable visual style, quick-moving storyline, endearing characters, and

Treasure Planet [2002]

Featuring the voices of: Joseph Gordon-Levitt, Brian Murray, David Hyde Pierce, Emma Thompson Directors: Ron Clements, John Musker Screenplay: Kaan Kalyoun, Mark Kennedy, Sam Levine, Donnie Long, Frank Nissen Running Time: 1:35 Rated: PG (Mild violence, scary moments) Theatrical Aspect Ratio: 1.85:1

Treasure Planet is Disney's science fiction-style reimagining of Robert Louis Stevenson's *Treasure Island*.

The film uses a fair amount of computer-generated imagery to enhance the hand-drawn visuals and, to a layman like myself, the result is stunning. *Treasure Planet* is rich and colorful, with vivid foregrounds and richly detailed backgrounds. There are a number of standout action scenes and one bravura sequence in which the camera zooms in on a spaceport, starting from far away, then gradually moving closer, until we're in the midst of the bustling streets.

Needless to say, the story is a variation on *Treasure Island,* using many of the same characters and situations. When teenager Jim Hawkins (voice of Joseph Gordon-Levitt) comes into possession of a map that purports to show the location of the legendary "Treasure Planet," where the dreaded pirate Flint hid his stash, his mother's friend, Dr. Doppler (David Hyde Pierce), decides to fund an expedition. Doppler hires a stern captain, Amelia (Emma Thompson), to guide the ship, and a crew that seems comprised primarily of cutthroats — especially the Master of the Galley, John Silver (Brian Murray). Amelia is distrustful of the men on the ship, calling them "a ludicrous parcel of galloping galoots." Her concerns are not without merit, since Silver is planning a mutiny as soon as the ship reaches Treasure Planet.

With the exception of Jim and his mother, none of the characters in *Treasure Planet* are human. Silver is a cyborg, Dr. Doppler has canine features, Amelia appears to be descended from cats that walk upright, and the crew is comprised of all manner of beasts. There's even an arachnid. In the sidekick category, Jim ends up accompanied by a small creature called Morph that can change its shape at will and the robot B.E.N., whose missing memory chips have resulted in a bad case of cybernetic dementia.

Treasure Planet is perfectly pleasing animated action/adventure movie that seems better designed and better motivated than many of the Magic Kingdom's recent forays into hand-drawn motion pictures. As family films go, this one offers an engaging and exciting 90 minutes. RECOMMENDED

Waking Life [2001]

Cast: **Wiley Wiggins** Director: **Richard Linklater** Screenplay: **Richard Linklater** Running Time: **1:37** Rated: R (Profanity, mature themes) Theatrical Aspect Ratio: 1.85:1

After a short three-year hiatus, filmmaker Richard Linklater has returned to the world of cinema with the offbeat and ambitious *Waking Life*, an animated excursion through the dreams and philosophical musings of the main character. *Waking Life* is clearly an experiment, and, as such, looks and feels much different from anything else recently seen on a movie screen. When he introduced the film at its Sundance 2001 premiere, Linklater posed one question to the audience, and it goes a long way towards setting the stage for *Waking Life*. "How many of you out there are on drugs?" he asked. When a number of hands went up, he added, "Good. This is for you. The rest of you, just bear with me."

Waking Life is animated, but not in tradition of Disney features. Linklater filmed the entire movie in live action, then digitally transferred the images to computers, where his animators went to work. The final result is disjointed and dreamy, with images that are sometimes finely detailed and sometimes almost crude. The backgrounds frequently waver, making it look like all of the action is taking place on board a gently rocking ship. This is all intentional, since every moment of *Waking Life* is meant to be transpiring inside a dream.

The nameless protagonist is played by Wiley Wiggins, who is perhaps reprising his role from an earlier Linklater offering, *Dazed and Confused*. Also making a return appearance are Ethan Hawke and Julie Delpy, picking right up where they left off in *Before Sunrise*. They are present in an interlude, having an intriguing discussion about dream activity and reincarnation. Indeed, *Waking Life* is comprised of a series of philosophical discussions ranging from how language evolved to the role of the media in modern life to free will & quantum mechanics to the meaning of identity. For those who enjoy this kind of rambling, talky motion picture, *Waking Life* offers a full platter. Guest appearances by the likes of director Steven Soderbergh and Speed Levitch (the motor-mouthed protagonist of *The Cruise*) only up the ante. *Waking Life* certainly isn't for everyone, but, in large part because of its fresh approach and its endlessly fascinating discourses, it ends up staying with you long after the jittery animated images have faded from the screen. HIGHLY RECOMMENDED

Classics

2001: A Space Odyssey [United Kingdom/United States, 1968]

Starring: Keir Dullea, Gary Lockwood, William Sylvester
Director: **Stanley Kubrick** Screenplay: **Stanley Kubrick & Arthur C. Clarke** Running Time: **2:19** Rated: **PG (Mild violence, mild profanity)** Theatrical Aspect Ratio: **2.35:1**

In terms of its approach to the science fiction genre, *2001* stands alone. This is a space-based movie without zooming spaceships, laser shootouts, or explosions. The action, to the degree that there is action, is viewed from a detached perspective. Spacecraft move (relatively) slowly, they do not zip around at the speed of light. The result is a cold, majestic motion picture, a movie that seeks to remind us of the vastness of space and our relatively insignificant place in it. Kubrick's intention with *2001* was not to thrill us with battles and pyrotechnics, but to daunt us with the realization of how much there is that we do not understand. The movie's slowness (and it is slow) not only allows us to absorb the images, music, and atmosphere, but provides the opportunity to think about the implications of what Kubrick is saying. As enjoyable as *Star Wars* is, it does not encourage deep introspection. *2001* demands it.

Many viewers who understand *2001* through the first two hours leave the theater confused because the movie raises new questions during the last reel, when a conventional film would be providing solutions. However, for someone who enjoys the opportunity to ponder a filmmaker's intentions and delve deeply into a movie's subtext, the final act of *2001* is a godsend. As is true of every Kubrick film, the meticulous attention to detail is evident. Working in close concert with co-screenwriter Arthur C. Clarke and other scientific advisors, Kubrick made sure that every aspect of the film conformed to known scientific fact. His vision is eerily accurate, and, even though we have not attained Clarke's prophesied advancements, we are on the same track. Additionally, there isn't a moment in *2001* that seems dated.

2001 needs to be experienced to be appreciated. *2001* does not build bonds between the viewers and the characters or set up a straightforward, linear storyline. Instead, it challenges the audience and inspires wonder. Proponents argue that this is Kubrick's best film; regardless of whether or not that is true, there's no doubting that this movie represents the product of a great director at the height of his powers. Years after its release, *2001* has lost none of the qualities that make it an acknowledged masterwork.

MUST SEE

The Big Sleep [1946]

Starring: **Humphrey Bogart, Lauren Bacall, John Ridgely, Martha Vickers, Charles Waldron** Director: **Howard Hawks** Screenplay: **William Faulkner & Leigh Brackett & Jules Furthman,** based on the novel by **Raymond Chandler** Running Time: **1:54** Rated: **No MPAA Rating (Violence, sexual innuendo)** Theatrical Aspect Ratio: **1.33:1**

The Big Sleep is credited with having one of the most confusing storylines of any motion picture ever made. The reason that so many people get lost is probably because plot really isn't *The Big Sleep*'s focus. We get so caught up watching Bogart and Bacall — every nuance of their interaction is fascinating — and enjoying the sharp, smart dialogue with all of its double entendres, that it's almost impossible to keep track of what's going on and who's responsible for which murder. The ending is satisfying not because the killer (or, more appropriately, "one of the killers") has been caught, but because Bogart and Bacall are together. *The Big Sleep* is about atmosphere, tone, and, above all, star power.

The Big Sleep opens with private detective Philip Marlowe (Bogart) entering the house of General Sternwood (Charles Waldron), after having been invited for a discussion. Before Marlowe meets the general, he is introduced to his youngest daughter, the flirtatious Carmen (Martha Vickers). Sternwood has a job for Marlowe — he wants the detective to investigate the details of why someone is demanding money from him to cover up one of Carmen's indiscretions, and, once the facts are uncovered, make the blackmailer "go away." On the way out of the house, Marlowe meets the general's other daughter, Vivian (Bacall), who is as alluring as Carmen, but more mature.

From there, the mystery begins, and it doesn't take long to heat up. Shortly, there are two corpses, but those deaths are only the beginning. There are double-crosses, chases, shoot outs, and the undeniable and growing heat between Marlowe and Vivian. In essence, however, *The Big Sleep* is two capers in one. The first, which involves Marlowe's investigation into the blackmail, is concluded by the half-way point. The second, in which the detective looks into a related (but not directly connected) death and disappearance, comprises the movie's second half. Common characters, circumstances, and coincidences bridge the two, but they can (at least to an extent) be decoupled.

The Big Sleep remains one of Hollywood's most intriguing and enduring examples of film noir. It's a movie that every film student should study and every movie lover should watch at least once. Things may not always make sense, but the film's numerous delights completely eclipse its few, small weaknesses. **HIGHLY RECOMMENDED**

Butch Cassidy & the Sundance Kid [1969]

Starring: **Paul Newman, Robert Redford, Katharine Ross, Strother Martin** Director: **George Roy Hill** Screenplay: **William Goldman** Running Time: 1:50 Rated: PG (Violence, sexual situations) Theatrical Aspect Ratio: 2.35:1

Despite arriving during the era when this kind of movie was beginning a slow but inexorable fall from public favor, *Butch Cassidy and the Sundance Kid* remains one of the best crafted and most beloved of all the Westerns. In addition to launching Robert Redford's career into orbit and polishing Paul Newman's reputation as a leading man, *Butch Cassidy* also solidified screenwriter William Goldman's position in Hollywood.

The primary differentiator between *Butch Cassidy* and the hundreds of other films littering the genre is its lighthearted tone. The movie is jovial without being silly; it retains the sense of adventure that characterizes the Western, but replaces the often somber mood with one that is airy and, at times, almost comedic. To go along with its upbeat tone, it has a little of everything — comedy, action, adventure, drama, romance, and whimsy. It's hard to ask for much more than what this movie delivers.

The film can be loosely divided into three sections: the introduction, the posse chase, and the Bolivia adventures. Each has its own distinct mood. The introduction, when we meet Butch & Sundance and see them in action robbing a train, allows us a leisurely opportunity to get to know the characters. The posse chase, with the two protagonists being pursued by a relentless and seemingly unstoppable group of faceless bounty hunters, is the film's most tense sequence — 30 minutes of close calls culminating in Butch & Sundance's decision to leave the country. The Bolivia segment contains both the most overtly comical and the most dramatic sequences. At one point, the two men rob a bank where their inability to speak Spanish causes communication problems. Later, after Butch & Sundance have gone straight, they are forced into a gunfight with bandits. It is here that Butch, who avoided killing as a bank robber, takes his first life. Then, of course, there's the final shoot-out in San Vincente (the two go out more heroically on screen than they did in real life).

The success of *Butch Cassidy and the Sundance Kid* made it a template for countless later films. Although *Butch Cassidy* wasn't the first movie to pair up a couple of wisecracking best friends in an action/adventure setting, this film became the model of how well that approach could work when done right. It's easy to see a little of Butch and Sundance in nearly every action duo to reach the screens during the last 30 years. And that, more than anything, is a testimony to the lasting influence of one of the most atypical of all the Westerns. **HIGHLY RECOMMENDED**

Casablanca [1942]

Starring: Humphrey Bogart, Ingrid Bergman, Paul Henreid, Claude Rains Director: Michael Curtiz Screenplay: Julius J. Epstein, Philip G. Epstein, and Howard Koch Running Time: 1:42 Rated: No MPAA Rating (Mature themes) Theatrical Aspect Ratio: 1.33:1

It's probably no stretch to say that *Casablanca,* arguably America's best-loved movie, has had more words written about it than any other motion picture. Ultimately, however, while it's fascinating to examine and dissect all that went into the making of *Casablanca,* the greatest pleasure anyone can derive from this movie comes through simply watching it. Aside from some basic knowledge of recent world history, little background is needed to appreciate the strength and power of the film. *Casablanca* accomplishes that which only a truly great film can: enveloping the viewer in the story, forging an unbreakable link with the characters, and only letting go with the end credits.

Just about everyone knows the story, which takes place about a year after the Germans invaded France. Ilsa (Ingrid Bergman) and her husband, Czech freedom fighter Victor Laszlo (Paul Henreid), wander into Rick's Cafe in Casablanca. The two are on the run from the Nazis, and have come to the American-owned nightspot to lie low. But the German-controlled local government, headed by Captain Louis Renault (Claude Rains), is on the move, and Laszlo has to act quickly to get the letters of transit he came for, then escape. Little does Ilsa know that the cafe is run by Rick Blaine (Humphrey Bogart), the one true love of her life. When the two see each other, sparks fly, and memories of an enchanted time in Paris come flooding back.

Bogart and Bergman. When anyone mentions *Casablanca,* these are the two names that come to mind. The actors are both so perfectly cast, and create such a palpable level of romantic tension, that it's impossible to envision anyone else in their parts. Bogart is at his best here as the tough cynic who hides a broken heart beneath a fractured layer of sarcasm. Ilsa's arrival in Casablanca rips open the fissures in Rick's shield, revealing a complex personality that demands Bogart's full range of acting. As Ilsa, Bergman lights up the screen. What man in the audience wouldn't give up everything to run away with her?

Although just about everyone involved with this legendary motion picture has departed this life, the film itself has withstood the test of more than a half-century to rise, like cream, to the top. One can only imagine that, in another 50 years, its position in the hierarchy of all-time greats will be even higher. **MUST SEE**

Chinatown [1974]

Starring: Jack Nicholson, Faye Dunaway, John Huston Director: **Roman Polanski** Screenplay: **Robert Towne** Running Time: **2:11** Rated: **R** (Violence, profanity, sexual situations, brief nudity) Theatrical Aspect Ratio: **2.35:1**

Chinatown is unquestionably one of the best films to emerge from the 1970s, a period that has been called the "last great decade of American cinema" by more than one movie critic. The production, which went in front of the cameras without a final script, marks the high-water point in the careers of both lead actor Jack Nicholson and director Roman Polanski.

At first glance, Jake Gittes (Nicholson) seems like the kind of private investigator who would be at home in the pages of a Dashiel Hammett or Raymond Chandler novel. But that's an illusion. As we come to learn, Gittes isn't as thick-skinned as his numerous predecessors. He lives his life by a series of moral precepts that are not always governed by the principle of self-interest. Sure, Gittes can trade one-liners with the best of them, but his heart is bigger, and beats louder, than any of them.

Gittes' latest case starts innocently enough — those are the ones you have to watch out for — when a woman identifying herself as Mrs. Evelyn Mulwray (Diane Ladd) walks into his office and asks him to obtain evidence that her husband, Hollis (Darrell Zwerling), is having an affair. Jake does so, and soon finds that the photographs he has taken of Mr. Mulwray, the L.A. Water Commissioner, and a pretty blonde have been sold to a local paper. Into his office comes the *real* Mrs. Evelyn Mulwray (Faye Dunaway), and Jake knows he's been had. Someone has used him, and now he's determined to get to the bottom of it. Soon, however, his investigation leads to Mulwray's drowned body and Evelyn Mulwray's charming-but-sinister father, Noah Cross (John Huston), whose every word hints at past misdeeds too horrible to consider. Cross, who serves Jake a fish with the head still on for lunch, is clearly a man not to be trifled with. But Jake presses on.

Chinatown requires that the viewer pay attention, not because there are lots of twists, but because the plot is complex and doesn't stop every 10 minutes to bring slower audience members up to speed. Ever since film noir reached Hollywood, the detective has become a type, with film noir being his playground.

It takes a Herculean effort to transform this type into a character and to replace the formula with a story, and *Chinatown*'s success in both of these regards is one of the reasons it is universally viewed as a classic. The movie is a nearly flawless example of movie composition, with close examination revealing how carefully it was put together. For those who take a less studious and more visceral approach to movie viewing, it's also worth noting that *Chinatown* is a superior thriller — one that will keep viewers involved and "in the moment" until the final, mournful scene has come to a conclusion. **MUST SEE**

Citizen Kane [1941]

Starring: Orson Welles, Joseph Cotten, Dorothy Comingore, Agnes Moorehead Director: Orson Welles Screenplay: Herman J. Mankiewicz and Orson Welles Running Time: 1:59 Rated: No MPAA Rating (Mature themes) Theatrical Aspect Ratio: 1.33:1

Citizen Kane has been lauded as the greatest motion picture to come out of America during the black-and-white era (or any era, for that matter). It also represents the pinnacle of Orson Welles' film making career. For, although Welles lived for more than 40 years following the release of *Kane,* he never succeeded in recapturing the brilliance or fulfilling the promise of his first feature.

The movie opens with an unforgettable image of a distant, fog-shrouded castle on a hill. It's a classic gothic shot, and goes a long way towards establishing *Citizen Kane*'s mood. We quickly learn that this place, called Xanadu, is the dwelling of America's Kubla Khan, Charles Foster Kane (Welles), a one-time newspaper magnate who could have become President if not for an ill-advised extramarital affair. Xanadu, in the words of the faux newsreel that gives a brief history of Kane's life, is the "costliest monument of a man to himself." Any resemblance to The Ranch, William Randolph Hearst's real-life San Simeon abode, is *not* coincidental.

Within moments of the film's eerie, visually-stunning opening, Kane is dead, uttering the word "Rosebud" as he hunches over. When a reporter (William Alland) digs into Kane's past to learn the meaning of Rosebud, the mogul's history is unraveled through a series of extended flashbacks that represent the sometimes-overlapping, non-chronological accounts of five eyewitnesses. As the story unfolds, we see Kane, aided by his closest friend, Jedediah Leland (Joseph Cotton), build a nationwide newspaper empire out of one small paper with a circulation of less than 30,000. To do so, he displays equal parts ruth-lessness and generosity. By the time he marries Emily Norton (Ruth Warrick), the President's niece, Kane is one of the most powerful men in America.

Eventually, Kane moves into the political arena, but his bid for the governor's office crashes and burns when his rival, Boss Jim Gettys (Ray Collins), exposes Kane's affair with Susan Alexander (Dorothy Comingore). Following this failure, Kane divorces his first wife, marries Susan, then goes into seclusion in his unfinished palace of Xanadu. As the years pass, he becomes progressively more bitter and less approachable, until Susan, weary of Xanadu's isolation, leaves him. Alone and unloved, Kane awaits the inescapable hand of death.

As a film, *Citizen Kane* is a powerful dramatic tale about the uses and abuses of wealth and power. It's a classic American tragedy about a man of great passion, vision, and greed, who pushes himself until he brings ruins to himself and all around him. There's no denying the debt that the movie industry owes to Welles and his debut feature. Motion picture archives and collections across the world would be poorer without copies of this film, which will forever be recognized as a defining example of American cinema. **MUST SEE**

City Lights [1931]

Starring: Charlie Chaplin, Virginia Cherrill, Harry Myers Director: **Charles Chaplin** Screenplay: **Charles Chaplin** Running Time: **1:28** Rated: **No MPAA Rating (Nothing offensive)** Theatrical Aspect Ratio: **1.33:1**

Charlie Chaplin's the Tramp is front and center in *City Lights*. One night when he's out and about town, he prevents a drunk Millionaire (Harry Myers) from drowning himself. The Millionaire, realizing his folly, is grateful, and brings the Tramp home with him, much to the chagrin of the Millionaire's snobbish butler (Allan Garcia). In the morning, when the Millionaire has sobered up, he doesn't remember the Tramp. By nightfall, however, with the drink again in his veins, he greets his friend with warmth and good spirits, while the butler looks on with a pained expression.

Meanwhile, the Tramp has fallen in love with a gentle, blind Flower Girl (Virginia Cherrill). Using his last cent, he buys a flower from her and wears it in the lapel of his natty suit. The next day, flush with money provided by the Millionaire, he purchases her entire stock, then drives her home in his new friend's car. She mistakenly thinks he's a wealthy man, and that impression is re-enforced when he provides her with the money to pay her rent and travel abroad to have an operation to cure her blindness.

City Lights' ending is well known and has justly been described as one of the most perfect conclusions in the history of cinema. The Tramp, recently released from prison, encounters the Flower Girl, who can now see. At first, she doesn't recognize her benefactor, and takes pity on him because he looks poor and down-and-out. But, when she touches his hand, she understands who he is. Title cards are used to convey their sparse dialogue. Yet words would have ruined the moment, which features heartbreaking performances through body language and facial expression from both Chaplin and Cherrill. It is an indelible exchange that is often presented as a clip to illustrate the strength of silent films, but is inexpressibly powerful when shown in the context of the entire movie.

As compelling as *City Lights'* dramatic element is, the film is still primarily a comedy, and features several instances of Chaplin at his best. Indeed, the movie is pieced together like a series of shorts with several common characters. It's an episodic endeavor, with a host of classic comic vignettes. There is a paradoxical aspect to *City Lights*. When recalling its charm and humor, I don't think of it as a "silent film." Instead, it springs to mind as an example of a spry narrative brought to life by wonderful performances and talented direction. Yet the means of *City Lights'* presentation — without talking — is a necessary part of its charm and power. Dialogue can become a crutch. Here, the characters must emote their feelings without voice, and it results in some astounding moments. **MUST SEE**

Dr. Strangelove [United Kingdom, 1964]

Starring: Peter Sellers, George C. Scott, Slim Pickens, Sterling Hayden
Director: Stanley Kubrick Screenplay: Stanley Kubrick, Peter George, and Terry Southern Running Time: 1:33 Rated: No MPAA Rating (Mature themes, sexual innuendo) Theatrical Aspect Ratio: 1.33:1 & 1.66:1

Originally, director Stanley Kubrick envisioned Peter Sellers playing 4 unique roles. However, after filming 3 of them (President Merkin Muffley, RAF Group Captain Mandrake, and ex-Nazi scientist Dr. Strangelove), the actor broke his leg and was unable to complete the quartet. In his place, Slim Pickens was signed to portray Major "King" Kong. Other cast members include George C. Scott as General Buck Turgidson, Sterling Hayden as General Jack D. Ripper, and James Earl Jones (in his first film role) as Lieutenant Lothar Zogg.

The film opens with a deranged General Jack D. Ripper (Sterling Hayden) declaring a "Code Red," sealing off his airforce base, and ordering a nuclear attack on Russia. When his assistant, RAF Group Captain Mandrake (Peter Sellers), advises moderation, Ripper replies that he intends to launch a pre-emptive strike to stop a Communist infiltration which is "sapping and impurifying all of our precious bodily fluids."

In Washington D.C., an emergency meeting is called to determine how to react to the crisis. Present are President Merkin Muffley (Sellers), a man whose effete personality is adequately described by his name; General Buck Turgidson (George C. Scott), whose least favorite color is red; Dr. Strangelove, an ex-Nazi scientist who is now head of the United States' weapons development program; Soviet Ambassador de Sadesky (Peter Bull); and the rest of the higher-uppers at the Pentagon.

Meanwhile, aboard the bomber "Leper Colony," we are introduced to the crew that will play a vital role in the events about to transpire. Led by Major "King" Kong (Slim Pickens), an old-fashioned, gung-ho cowboy type (complete with hat and Texas accent), these men are as loyal and anti-Communist as they come.

As a story chronicling the potential countdown to humanity's end in a nuclear fireball, *Dr. Strangelove* is tightly-plotted and well-paced. As a black comedy, wielding a wit sharper than honed steel, the film is unparalleled. Kubrick's picture has so many targets that it's difficult to know where to begin. The genius of *Dr. Strangelove* is that it's possible to laugh — and laugh hard — while still recognizing the intelligence and insight behind the humor. The film is always saying something, and a viewer would have to be deaf and blind not to recognize the targets of the sarcasm. In fact, I'd worry about anyone who takes this movie *too* seriously. That, after all, isn't the kind of person *Dr. Strangelove* is aimed for; it's the kind this film takes aim at. **MUST SEE**

The Godfather [1972]

Starring: Marlon Brando, Al Pacino, James Caan, Robert Duvall
Director: Francis Ford Coppola Screenplay: Francis Ford Coppola and Mario Puzo based on the novel by Mario Puzo Running Time: 2:51 Rated: R (Violence, mature themes, language, brief nudity) Theatrical Aspect Ratio: 1.85:1

Rarely can it be said that a film has defined a genre, but never is that more true than in the case of *The Godfather*. Since the release of the 1972 epic, all "gangster movies" have been judged by the standards of this one. If *The Godfather* was only about gun-toting Mafia types, it would never have garnered as many accolades. The characteristic that sets this film apart from so many of its predecessors and successors is its ability to weave the often-disparate layers of story into a cohesive whole. The picture is a series of mini-climaxes, all building to the devastating, definitive conclusion.

The film opens in the study of Don Vito Corleone (Marlon Brando), the Godfather, who is holding court. It is the wedding of his daughter Connie (Talia Shire), and no Sicilian can refuse a request on that day. The family has gathered for the event. Michael (Al Pacino), Don Vito's youngest son and a second world war hero, is back home in the company of a new girlfriend, Kay Adams (Diane Keaton). The two older boys, Sonny (James Caan) and Fredo (John Cazale), are there as well, along with their "adopted" brother, Tom Hagen (Robert Duvall), the don's right-hand man.

With the end of the war, the times are changing, and as much as Don Vito seems in control at the wedding, his power is beginning to erode. His refusal to do business with drug supplier Sollozzo (Al Lettieri) strikes the first sparks of a war that will last for years and cost many lives. Each of the 5 major mob families in New York will be gouged by the bloodshed, and a new order will emerge. Betrayals will take place, and the Corleone family will be shaken to its roots by treachery from both within and without.

We come to *The Godfather* like Kay Adams — outsiders uncertain in our expectations — but it doesn't take long for us to be captivated by this intricate, violent world. The film can be viewed on many levels, with equal satisfaction awaiting those who just want a good story, and those who demand much more. *The Godfather* is long, yes — but it is 170 minutes well-spent. MUST SEE

The Godfather Part II [1974]

Starring: Al Pacino, Robert DeNiro, Robert Duvall, Diane Keaton
Director: Francis Ford Coppola Screenplay: Francis Ford Coppola and Mario Puzo based on the novel by Mario Puzo Running Time: 3:20
Rated: R (Violence, mature themes, language) Theatrical Aspect Ratio: 1.85:1

The Godfather Part II is a more ambitious production than the original since it attempts not only to tell a pair of completely disconnected stories, but to do so in parallel. The less time consuming of the two presents the early life of Vito Corleone (played by Robert DeNiro) in Sicily and New York, and shows how he came into power. The other tale picks up approximately a decade after the conclusion of *The Godfather*, and shows the means by which Michael Corleone (Al Pacino), now secure in his position, attempts to expand the family empire into Las Vegas and Cuba.

Michael lives his life and runs his business by two of his father's creeds: "A man who doesn't spend time with his family can never be a real man" and "Keep your friends close, but your enemies closer." There are times, however, when those precepts fail as guiding principles, such as when a betrayal occurs from within the family. Broken trust arising from so intimate a source can be devastating.

For a man constantly battling to keep his family together, a mournful irony of *The Godfather Part II* is that Michael's efforts succeed only in fragmenting it. If the end of the first film was numbing, this one is shattering. The flashback preceding the final scene presents a stark differentiation of how things once were from what they have become.

The traditional elements of the Tragedy introduced in *The Godfather* reach their maturity in *Part II*. Much of the humanity remaining to Michael at the outset is leached from him with each deception and setback. Late scenes with a resentful Fredo (John Cazale) and a bitter Kay (Diane Keaton) emphasize the price for Michael of continuing his father's dominion. His flaw is his imperceptiveness and, as is the case for any hero in a story of this nature, its effects are crippling.

Combined, *The Godfather* and *The Godfather Part II* represent the apex of American movie-making and the ultimate gangster story. Few sequels have expanded upon the original with the faithfulness and detail of this one. Beneath the surface veneer of an ethnic period piece, *The Godfather* is not so much about crime lords as it is about prices paid in the currency of the soul for decisions made and avoided. It is that quality which establishes this saga as timeless. MUST SEE

Gone with the Wind [1939]

Starring: Clark Gable, Vivien Leigh, Leslie Howard, Olivia De Havilland
Director: Victor Fleming Screenplay: Sidney Howard based on the novel by Margaret Mitchell Running Time: 3:42 Rated: G Theatrical Aspect Ratio: 1.33:1

Gone with the Wind is, simply put, a tale of two halves. The movie is divided by an intermission into a pair of roughly-equal segments. The first, which is brilliant and consistently captivating, covers the time period of the Civil War, beginning shortly after the election of Abraham Lincoln, and ending during Sherman's march through Atlanta. The post-intermission half, which dishes out the suds, picks up at the end of the Civil War and concludes about 8 years later. This portion of *Gone with the Wind,* while still retaining a degree of appeal and narrative interest, spins its wheels frequently.

Gone with the Wind has one of the best-known storylines of any film, due in large part to the popularity of the source material, Margaret Mitchell's best-selling 1936 book. The main character is Scarlett O'Hara (Vivien Leigh), the spoiled, manipulative daughter of an Irish immigrant plantation owner (Thomas Mitchell). Scarlett is secretly in love with Ashley Wilkes (Leslie Howard), who is about to marry the gentle, demure Melanie Hamilton (Olivia De Havilland). When Scarlett confesses her love to Ashley, he admits his feelings for her, but notes that Melanie will make a much better wife. Immediately after this meeting, Scarlett has her first encounter with the irrepressible Rhett Butler (Clark Gable), the cynical, smart hero who eventually falls in love with her. They are two headstrong likes who simultaneously repel and attract one another.

The bulk of the film follows a romantic quadrangle as it unfolds against the backdrop of war and reconstruction in and around Atlanta and the O'Hara plantation, Tara. Scarlett is in love with Ashley, or thinks she is, but he won't leave his wife. Melanie loves both her husband and Scarlett, who improbably becomes her best friend. Rhett is smitten with Scarlett, and she is clearly interested in him, but the real question is how long it will take for her to recognize the depth of her feelings.

To date, no film has sold more box-office tickets than *Gone with the Wind.* Of course, when the movie was first released, it wasn't just another motion picture — it was a spectacle, an event. Even though the habits of movie-goers have changed over the years, it's easy to see why this film provoked such an outpouring of praise and adulation during its initial release, and why its stature has grown with the passage of decades. *Gone with the Wind* has flaws, but it's still undeniably a classic and a legend. HIGHLY RECOMMENDED

It's a Wonderful Life [1946]

Starring: James Stewart, Donna Reed, Lionel Barrymore, Thomas Mitchell Director: Frank Capra Screenplay: Frank Capra, Frances Goodrich, Albert Hackett, and Jo Swerling Running Time: 2:09

Rated: No MPAA Rating (Nothing offensive) Theatrical Aspect Ratio: 1.33:1

What is it about this film, an uplifting, sentimental fable about the importance of the individual, that strikes a responsive chord with so many viewers? Some might argue that it has something to do with the season, but I don't buy that reasoning. *It's a Wonderful Life* is just as good in July as in December — the time of the year has little to do with motion picture quality. Rather, I think *It's a Wonderful Life* has earned its legion of followers because it effectively touches upon one basic truth of life that we all would like to believe — that each of us, no matter how apparently insignificant, has the power to make a difference, and that the measure of our humanity has nothing to do with fame or money, but with how we live our life on a day-to-day basis. *It's a Wonderful Life* asks and answers a question that all of us think of at one time or another: "What would this world be like if I had never been born?"

As almost every avid movie-lover knows, *It's a Wonderful Life* tells the story of George Bailey (James Stewart), the unsung, beloved hero of Bedford Falls. As a child, George was selfless, risking his own life (and losing his hearing in one ear) to save his brother from drowning. As an adult, he gave up his dreams of traveling the world and going to college to stay home and manage the Bailey Building and Loan Society after his father passed away. Throughout his life, George lived by a creed that always placed human need above riches, and, as a result, his only wealth was in his friends and family.

The film's villain is a miserly old man named Potter (played with consummate nastiness by movie great Lionel Barrymore), who uses his considerable wealth to bleed the citizens of Bedford Falls dry. The Bailey Building and Loan Society is the only institution in town that he doesn't own, and he's willing to do anything to get his hands on it — lie, cheat, bribe, steal . . . There's no end to the schemes that Potter devises to destroy George. Yet the Baileys always seem to end up on top.

Combine the characters, the story, the message, and the acting, and it's easy to see why *It's a Wonderful Life* isn't just a holiday favorite, but a great movie by almost any standards. There are a few cynics who will disparage this film, but, in a "feel good" genre clogged with imitators and inferior features, *It's a Wonderful Life* stands high above the rest. Whether you view this film in the middle of the summer or at Christmas, Capra's greatest film represents one of the most transcendent and joyful experiences any movie-lover can hope for. **MUST SEE**

King Kong [1933]

Starring: Robert Armstrong, Bruce Cabot, Fay Wray Directors: Merian C. Cooper and Ernest B. Schoedsack Screenplay: James Creelman and Ruth Rose Running Time: 1:45 Rated: No MPAA Rating (Violence) Theatrical Aspect Ratio: **1.33:1**

When released in 1933, *King Kong* was greeted with unprecedented amazement. State-of-the-art visual effects, an entertaining story, and a touching ending combined to bequeath upon this film the coveted label of a "classic." In its era — and, indeed, for decades after — no monster movie (whether made in the United States, Japan, or elsewhere) approached the lofty perch of this one. The title character, the creation of stop-motion effects wizard Willis O'Brien (mentor to Ray Harryhausen), captivated audiences and started a world-wide love affair with a giant ape.

The plot is reasonably straightforward — not a bad thing for a monster movie. A film crew headed by Carl Denham (Robert Armstrong) arrives at the mysterious Skull Island to do some location shooting for a new picture. However, the dark-skinned natives take a liking to Denham's leading lady, Ann Darrow (Fay Wray, in the role that immortalized her scream), and kidnap her as an offering to their god, Kong. Just as the cavalry, led by Denham and a hunky sailor named Jack Driscoll (Bruce Cabot), rushes in to save Ann, Kong — a 25-foot high ape (actually, his size varies throughout the film) — makes his appearance, snatching his prize from the altar and heading off into the jungle. Denham, Driscoll, and a search party set off in pursuit. Various encounters with Kong and a series of prehistoric relics decimate the group. In the meantime, we get to see battles between the giant ape and several dinosaurs. Eventually, Driscoll sneaks Ann away from Kong and, when the beast arrives at the natives' village to retrieve her, Denham uses sleeping gas to capture him.

Weeks later, a live show opens in New York City's Radio City Music Hall, with a chained Kong as the main attraction. He is, as the marquee proclaims, "The Eighth Wonder of the World." Despite Denham's best precautions, Kong breaks free on opening night, grabs Ann, wreaks havoc in the city, then climbs to the top of the Empire State Building. There, high atop New York, in one of cinema's most unforgettable moments, Kong fights a duel to the death with a group of biplanes.

Despite its various deficiencies and occasionally antiquated style, *King Kong* remains not only a milestone of movie-making, but a magical experience. Ultimately, the mystique of the film lies not so much in what it offers today, but what it has contributed during the course of the last 6 decades. Watching *King Kong* reminds us of what movies once were and what they have the potential to be, and that's something that *Jurassic Park* will never be able to do.
HIGHLY RECOMMENDED

Lawrence of Arabia [United Kingdom, 1962]

Starring: Peter O'Toole, Alec Guinness, Anthony Quinn, Jack Hawkins, Omar Sharif Director: David Lean Screenplay: Robert Bolt, based on "The Seven Pillars of Wisdom" by T.E. Lawrence Running Time: 3:37 Rated: PG (Violence, mature themes) Theatrical Aspect Ratio: 2.20:1

Lawrence of Arabia recounts the larger-than-life exploits of T.E. Lawrence (Peter O'Toole), an officer in the British army serving in the Middle East during World War I, who, according to one observer, "was a poet, a scholar, and a mighty warrior. He was also the most shameless exhibitionist since Barnum & Bailey." The film opens in 1935, with a prologue that shows Lawrence's death as a result of a motorcycle accident, followed by his funeral. The time frame then shifts back more than 20 years to Cairo, where Lawrence is about to begin the greatest adventure of his career. His commanding officer orders him to enter the desert and make contact with the Bedouin Prince Feisel (Alec Guiness), who is a British ally in the fight against the Turks. What follows is not only an account of how Lawrence became a pivotal figure in the Arab revolt against the Turks, but of the nearly-Shakespearean rise and fall of his character.

The most compelling aspect of *Lawrence of Arabia* is the way in which it dissects the fluid, often-contradictory personality of the title character. Like many of the best classic "war" movies, this one uses the battles as a backdrop for a character study. The combat sequences in *Lawrence of Arabia* are perfunctory, with few of the details shown. This allows us to focus on the individual at the epicenter of the storm.

As important as the actors are, however, they are often rendered insignificant by the scenery, and by the manner in which the perfectionist Lean and his cinematographer, Freddie Young, chose to shoot it. *Lawrence of Arabia* is littered with majestic, unforgettable shots. There's the famous "mirage scene," where

Ali first approaches Lawrence on horseback, emerging from a shimmering haze on the horizon. There's a transition in which, after Lawrence blows out a match flame, the camera cuts to a blazing sunset. There are images of majestic dunes with camel riders making their way along them, silhouetted against the sky. And there are shots of rock formations that one normally does not associate with the desert. Add to these moments the grandeur of Maurice Jarre's score, and *Lawrence of Arabia* has the power to overwhelm.

For David Lean, widely regarded as one of the masters of epic filmmaking, *Lawrence of Arabia* represented the most ambitious undertaking of a fruitful career. Restored to its full length in 1989, the version available today shows the story as Lean intended it to be seen. MUST SEE

My Fair Lady [1964]

Starring: Audrey Hepburn, Rex Harrison, Stanley Holloway Director: George Cukor Screenplay: Alan Jay Lerner, based on the play "Pygmalion" by George Bernard Shaw Running Time: 2:50 Rated: G Theatrical Aspect Ratio: 2.35:1

It could easily be argued that *My Fair Lady* is one of the richest and most intelligent romantic comedies ever produced. The dialogue, adapted by Lerner from Shaw's material, is brilliant: a perfect amalgamation of well-honed wit and barbed satire. The verbal jousting between Eliza Doolittle (Audrey Hepburn) and Professor Henry Higgins (Rex Harrison) is a delight, as is that between the various other characters.

The basic storyline concerns Eliza, a poor Cockney from Covent Garden who is transformed into a lady under the tutelage of Higgins. Although at first reluctant, Higgins, intrigued by the challenge of re-making a woman, agrees. He is ruthless in pushing Eliza. In addition to cleaning her up, teaching her how to behave in society, and instructing her about what to wear, he completely re-shapes her language skills. By depriving her of sleep and forcing her to repeat phrases like "The rain in Spain falls mainly in the plain," he hopes to rid her of her ghastly accent. "Think what you're trying to accomplish," he tells her. "Think what you're dealing with. The majesty and grandeur of the English language, it's the greatest possession we have. The noblest thoughts that ever flowed through the hearts of men are contained in its extraordinary, imaginative, and musical mixtures of sounds. And that's what you've set yourself out to conquer Eliza. And conquer it you will."

Few genres of films are as magical as musicals, and few musicals are as intelligent and lively as *My Fair Lady*. It's a classic not because a group of stuffy film experts have labeled it as such, but because it has been, and always will be, a pure joy to experience. It's also one of a very few 3-hour films that justifies the seemingly long running time. Rarely have so many minutes in a theater been passed this enjoyably. MUST SEE

Patton [1970]

Starring: George C. Scott, Karl Malden Director: Franklin J. Schaffner Screenplay: Edmund H. North and Francis Ford Coppola Running Time: 2:50 Rated: PG (Violence, language) Theatrical Aspect Ratio: 2.20:1

In early 1971, the Academy Awards saluted *Patton*. Capturing 8 Oscars — including best picture, best director, best actor, best screenplay, best editing, and best production design — the movie won every major battle of the evening. Such acclaim was richly deserved, for *Patton* remains to this day one of Hollywood's most compelling biographical war pictures.

With its larger-than-life, yet at the same time singularly human, portrayal of General George S. Patton, Jr., Franklin Schaffner's picture is an example of filmmaking at its finest. From production design and battle choreography to simple one-on-one dramatic acting, *Patton* has it all. There is no scene in all 170 minutes that doesn't work on some level.

The film opens in 1943 North Africa, with a brutal look at American casualties at the battle of Kasserine. Patton (George C. Scott) arrives from Morocco to take command of the U.S. army in Tunisia in preparation for fighting Rommel (Karl Michael Vogler) at el Gitar. From North Africa, Patton's forces move to Sicily, where they sweep north across the island, taking Palermo, then racing Montgomery (Michael Bates) to Messina. Along the way, Patton's verbal and physical abuse of a soldier suffering from "battle fatigue" — which the general brands as cowardice — becomes ammunition for his critics. He later offers a public apology, but this incident keeps him from the action for a while, and he must stand by as a decoy during the Normandy invasion. Later in the year, however, General Omar Bradley (Karl Malden) gives Patton command of the Allied Third Army, with which he pushes across Western Europe to stop the Germans at the Battle of the Bulge, the last major Nazi offensive of the war.

Those who have not seen *Patton*, or who have not watched the film carefully, might assume that this movie is about World War II and one of its most celebrated generals. In fact, they would be only partially correct. What *Patton* sets out to do is to demythicize its subject and show the forces that drove this man.

Brilliant tactician, merciless disciplinarian, tireless fighter, prima donna, and staunch patriot — Patton was all of these things and more. Life for him was the battlefield, and without war, his spirit was sapped. The German military recognized this when they noted that Berlin's fall would finish him. Patton was an anachronism — a man who belonged in another time. He was a warrior living in a time when victory in battle no longer meant the triumph it once had, a Roman conqueror who understood the meaning of the words that "all glory is fleeting." Above all, however, he was an icon whom millions cheered, millions hated, and few understood. **MUST SEE**

Psycho [1960]
Starring: Anthony Perkins, Vera Miles, John Gavin, Martin Balsam, Janet Leigh Director: Alfred Hitchcock Screenplay: Joseph Stefano based on the novel by Robert Bloch Running Time: 1:48 Rated: R (Violence) Theatrical Aspect Ratio: 1.85:1

With *Psycho*, Hitchcock dabbled in cinematic taboos, pushing the censorship envelope. For example, this was the first American motion picture to feature a toilet being flushed (most movies of the era didn't even acknowledge the existence of toilets). Also, Janet Leigh is shown in her underwear on more than one occasion, and, during the famous shower scene, it's possible to see hints of flesh (most of which belong to a body double). The script also features a man speaking the word "transvestite" — a line that survived in the film only after a Herculean struggle on Stefano's part.

The film starts out in traditional fashion for a Hitchcock thriller. A woman, Marion Crane (Janet Leigh), desperate to find a way to be with her lover, Sam Loomis (John Gavin), embezzles money from her boss, then goes on the lam. She's not an apt criminal, however, and she leaves a wide trail. A used car salesman assesses her nervous mood and uses it to bilk her out of some extra cash. A somewhat-ominous policeman shadows her, almost to the point of stalking. If anyone could ever be said to look and act guilty, it's Marion. Eventually, she ends up at the out-of-the-way Bates Motel, where the shy-but-kind manager, Norman Bates (Anthony Perkins), offers her a room, a meal, and a sympathetic ear. During her conversation with Norman, when he speaks

about the traps that life places everyone in, Marion resolves to return on the following morning and give back the money. Events of the night, which involve violence and the jealous rage of Norman's twisted mother, put an end to Marion's plans. Soon after, others arrive at the Bates Motel looking for her, including Loomis, a private investigator named Arbogast (Martin Balsam), and Marion's sister, Lila (Vera Miles). They all make horrifying discoveries.

Story-wise, *Psycho* is not extraordinary; its true ingeniousness lies in its construction. Hitchcock and Stafano have developed the movie in such a way that it consistently flouts expectations. There are 2 major surprises: the shower scene murder and the final revelation about Mother. A viewer who sees the film for the first time without knowing about either will experience the full impact of what Hitchcock intended.

Today, *Psycho* still holds up extraordinarily well. With the exception of *Halloween,* no latter-day horror/thriller has been capable of generating as many goosebumps. The painstaking care with which Hitchcock composed every scene is evident in the quality of the final product. *Psycho* may not represent the master director's pinnacle, but it is the motion picture for which he is best known, and its legacy is inarguably one of the most far reaching of any film to come out of a Hollywood studio. **HIGHLY RECOMMENDED**

Rear Window [1964]
Starring: James Stewart, Grace Kelley, Wendell Corey, Thelma Ritter, Raymond Burr Director: Alfred Hitchcock Screenplay: John Michael Hayes based on a short story by Cornell Woolrich Running Time: 1:53 Rated: PG (Mature themes, violence) Theatrical Aspect Ratio: 1.85:1

One of the most engrossing, and, in its own way, groundbreaking, studies of voyeurism is Alfred Hitchcock's *Rear Window*. The film is universally regarded as a classic, and a strong cadre of critics, scholars, and fans considers this to be the director's best feature. Not only does the movie generate an intensely suspenseful and fascinating situation, but it develops a compelling and memorable character: L.B. Jefferies (James Stewart), a top-flight photographer who, as the result of an accident that left him in a leg cast, is confined to his upper-story Manhattan apartment. He amuses himself by gazing out his window at the building opposite, and builds pictures of each of the inhabitants from the glimpses he catches of their lives. Some of them, like "Miss Torso," a lithe young ballerina who capers around in various stages of dress, and "Miss Lonelyhearts," a forlorn spinster, keep their curtains wide open. Others, like a newly-wed couple, pull down the blinds, leaving Jefferies to smile wryly as he guesses about their activities.

As Jefferies' days of confinement wear on, his fascination with his neighbors turns into an obsession. Their lives become more important than his. After all, they are vital and mobile; he is trapped and impotent. He has a charming and gorgeous young girlfriend, Lisa Fremont (Grace Kelly), but he is emotionally cool towards her, and their relationship is caught in the same stasis that paralyzes every other aspect of Jefferies' life. When he gropes for a reason why she wouldn't make a good wife, the only fault he can find is that she's "too perfect, too talented, too beautiful, and too sophisticated." Lisa may love him, but she is losing patience. Then, one day, Jefferies observes something that forces him to abandon his safe, cocooned role as a voyeur and become a participant. He sees — or *thinks* he sees — one of his neighbors, Lars Thorwald (Raymond Burr), commit a murder. When the police don't believe Jefferies, he is forced to take action without their help. Abetted by Lisa, he works to uncover evidence to prove that a crime was committed. However, with his mobility restricted, Jefferies can only watch through his rear window as Lisa puts herself in harm's way, and, when danger strikes, he is helpless to go to her rescue.

Simply put, *Rear Window* is a great film, perhaps one of the finest ever committed to celluloid. All of the elements are perfect (or nearly so), including the acting, script, camerawork, music (by Franz Waxman), and, of course, direction. The brilliance of the movie is that, in addition to keeping viewers on the edges of their seats, it involves us in the lives of all of the characters, from Jefferies and Lisa to Miss Torso. There isn't a moment of waste in 113 minutes of screen time. **MUST SEE**

Vertigo [1968]
Starring: James Stewart, Kim Novak, Barbara Bel Geddes Director: Alfred Hitchcock Screenplay: Samuel Taylor and Alec Coppel Running Time: 2:08 Rated: PG (Mature themes) Theatrical Aspect Ratio: 1.85:1

Vertigo opens with a short prologue that details the circumstances under which Detective John Ferguson (James Stewart) develops an acute case of acrophobia that leads to vertigo whenever he climbs a steep flight of stairs or gets more than a few feet above the ground. After leaving the police force because of this condition, John is approached by an old acquain-tance, ship yard magnate Gavin Elster (Tom Helmore), to tail his wife, Madeleine (Kim Novak). Gavin is concerned about Madeleine's health — she has frequent black-outs and he believes that the spirit of a dead woman is attempting to possess her.

As John follows Madeleine, watching her day after day, he falls for her. Eventually, the two meet and discover that the attraction is mutual. But even love is not enough to overcome John's vertigo, and he is unable to save her from a fall from the top of a church bell tower. Madeleine's death causes John to suffer a breakdown, and, during his recovery, a chance encounter on the street brings him face-to-face with a woman, Judy Barton (Novak), who is the spitting image of his dead love.

Hitchcock does a masterful job blending all of *Vertigo*'s diverse elements together. It's a love story, a mystery, and a thriller all rolled into one. It deals with issues of obsession, psychological and physical paralysis, and the tenuous nature of romantic love. *Vertigo* should really be seen more than once to be fully appreciated. Many of the darker, deeper aspects only begin to bubble to the surface on subsequent viewings.

Stylistically, perhaps the two most noteworthy elements of *Vertigo* are its distinctive color scheme, which features reds and greens, and the memorable, haunting score turned in by composer Bernard Herrmann. There are numerous, lengthy passages that pass without dialogue (most of these occur while John is trailing Madeleine), and Herrmann's music sustains Hitchcock's carefully-crafted tone. **HIGHLY RECOMMENDED**

The Wizard of Oz [1939]
Starring: Judy Garland, Frank Morgan, Ray Bolger, Bert Lahr, Jack Haley, Billie Burke Director: Victor Fleming Screenplay: Noel Langley and Florence Ryerson and Edgar Allan Woolf Running Time: 1:41 Rated: G Theatrical Aspect Ratio: 1.37:1

Throughout the years, there have been dozens of live-action films, stage plays, animated features, and TV programs based on L. Frank Baum's classic Oz stories. To one degree or another, almost all have been influenced by Fleming's telling of the tale. When anyone thinks of *The Wizard of Oz,* they see Judy Garland, Ray Bolger, Bert Lahr, and Jack Haley, and hear "Somewhere over the Rainbow" and "Follow the Yellow Brick Road."

Probably the most interesting aspect of *The Wizard of Oz* comes from interpreting what really happens during the bulk of the film. The story opens by introducing us to Dorothy Gale (Judy Garland), a young girl in Kansas who finds her wanderlust stirred by dreams of going "somewhere over the rainbow." When a tornado strikes the farm where she lives with her aunt and uncle, she is knocked unconscious. Upon waking up, she finds herself in the magical land of Oz, where she journeys in the company of a Scarecrow (Ray Bolger), a Tin Man (Jack Haley), and a Cowardly Lion (Bert Lahr) to defeat the Wicked Witch of the West (Margaret Hamilton) and find the all-powerful Wizard (Frank Morgan), who has the power to send her home. But is this a real trip, or is it all a dream? A strong case can be developed for either possibility, although it's ultimately up to each viewer to make up his or her own mind. Whichever way you lean, it doesn't detract from the movie's boundless capacity to entertain.

The Wizard of Oz has been subjected to the kind of scrutiny reserved for only the greatest of motion pictures. Volumes have been written about it, analyzing everything from its look to the urban legends that have sprung up around it. Ultimately, however, it doesn't take a lengthy study to understand why multiple generations find the movie so compelling. Not only is it wonderfully entertaining, but the issues it addresses, and the way it presents them, are both universal and deeply personal. And therein lies *The Wizard of Oz*'s true magic. **MUST SEE**

Comedy

8 Women [France, 2002]

Starring: Danielle Darrieux, Catherine Deneuve, Isabelle Huppert, Emmanuelle Béart, Fanny Ardant, Virginie Ledoyen Director: François Ozon Screenplay: François Ozon and Marina de Van, based on the play by Robert Thomas Running Time: 1:43 Rated: R (Sexual themes) Theatrical Aspect Ratio: 1.85:1

The product of French director François Ozon, *8 Women* offers as much delicious enjoyment to the viewer as it obviously did to the cast and crew when they were assembling it. Part satire, part comedy, part musical, and part murder mystery, this motion picture criss-crosses genre lines at will, offering just about every kind of pleasure imaginable, guilty or otherwise.

The 8 women of the title are Gaby (Catherine Deneuve); her daughters, Catherine (Ludivine Sagnier) and Suzon (Virginie Ledoyen); her mother (Danielle Darrieux); her sister, Augustine (Isabelle Huppert); her sister-in-law, Pierrette (Fanny Ardant); and her two maids, Louise (Emmanuelle Béart) and Chanel (Firmine Richard). These characters are trapped together in a house during a snowstorm with one dead body (Marcel, Gaby's husband) and cut phone lines. Tensions run high, with each woman suspecting the others of being the killer. Secrets, some silly and some shocking, are revealed. Suzon begins acting like Hercule Poirot, and everyone else takes an occasional break to lapse into song and dance. A more enjoyable confection cannot be found.

What a cast! No director could dream of a more talented and beautiful group of actresses to grace his film. The names read like a who's who of French film across 3 generations: the youngsters (Ledoyen, Sagnier, and Béart), the middle-aged stars (Deneuve, Huppert, Ardant), and the venerable grande dame (Danielle Darrieux). All of them are in top form and completely in step with what Ozon is attempting. In addition to paying homage to, as well as spoofing, Agatha Christie (via a '60s play written by Robert Thomas), he is re-creating the look and feel of a '50s or '60s Technicolor movie, complete with brightly-hued costumes, old-fashioned set design, and a lushly melodramatic score. Plus, for good measure, he throws in 6 musical numbers, allowing nearly all of the characters an opportunity to play the canary.

In many ways, *8 Women* is the ultimate feel-good movie, Ozon's valentine to those who have stuck with him through all of his previous, serious work. *8 Women* has the life and energy of a manic comedy, the spirit of a musical, and the heart of a mystery. And, believe it or not, despite all of the madcap zaniness going on, viewers come to care about the characters and are interested in knowing the answer to the crucial question of "Whodunnit?" In true Agatha Christie fashion, there's as much of a twist to that as there is to just about everything else in this wonderfully entertaining motion picture. **HIGHLY RECOMMENDED**

Adaptation [2002]

Starring: Nicolas Cage, Meryl Streep, Chris Cooper, Brian Cox, Tilda Swinton Director: Spike Jonze Screenplay: Charlie Kaufman and Donald Kaufman, based on *The Orchid Thief* by Susan Orlean Running Time: 1:50 Rated: R (Profanity, sexual situations, brief nudity, violence) Theatrical Aspect Ratio: 1.85:1

There is a concept in mathematics called "recursion." Charlie Kaufman and director Spike Jonze have apparently discovered the cinematic equivalent with *Adaptation,* an occasionally maddening and sometimes brilliant motion picture that varies between being insightfully sharp and insufferably self-indulgent. Regardless of whether you appreciate the movie or not, it's likely to stay with you.

Adaptation stars Nicolas Cage in a dual role as Kaufman and his fictitious brother, Donald. Meryl Streep is Susan Orlean, the writer of *The Orchid Thief;* Chris Cooper is Laroche; Brian Cox is Robert McKee, a real-life lecturer about the art of screenplay writing; and Tilda Swinton is Valerie, the one who commissions Kaufman to write the adaptation of the book. The film flips back and forth across time, alternating between the "present," in which Kaufman is trying to write the screenplay, and 3 years in the past, when the events recounted in *The Orchid Thief* are taking place. There are also various flashbacks and even an excursion to pre-historic times. Certain events take place on the set of Jonze and Kaufman's previous collaboration, *Being John Malkovich,* allowing actors like Malkovich and Catherine Keener to make cameos.

The title of *Adaptation* doesn't only refer to what Kaufman is doing to Orlean's book. It is also meant in the Darwinian sense — that humans adapt to circumstances. The movie is certainly as offbeat as *Being John Malkovich,* although it is neither as funny nor as accessible (if, indeed, *Malkovich* can be considered to be "accessible"). *Adaptation* has a serious point or two to divulge. In particular, it's about the importance of passion in every endeavor.

The movie comes across as chaotic, which I'm sure is intentional. With the multiple storylines, there's too much going on, and this damages *Adaptation*'s structure. Jonze does his best to bring a kind of order to the proceedings, but there are times when things get away from him. And there are instances when the movie comes across as being a little too clever. I can't imagine *Adaptation* having much mainstream appeal, but, for those who look for something genuinely off-the-wall in a motion picture, this will unquestionably strike a nerve. **HIGHLY RECOMMENDED**

The Adventures of Priscilla, Queen of the Desert
[Australia, 1993]
Starring: Terrence Stamp, Hugo Weaving, Guy Pearce
Director: Stephan Elliot Screenplay: Stephan Elliot Running Time: 1:32
Rated: R (Language, sexual themes, violence) Theatrical Aspect
Ratio: 1.85:1

The Adventures of Priscilla, Queen of the Desert is about the most fun you can have with 3 guys who like to dress up as women. The latest export from down under, *Priscilla* is the story of 3 drag queens — Bernadette/Ralph (Terrence Stamp), Mitzi/Tick (Hugo Weaving), and Felicia/Adam (Guy Pearce) — on their way across the Australian desert to play a gig. Along the way, their bus, Priscilla, breaks down, and they have to rely on help from strangers. And, while cross-dressing performers are accepted in the big city, their welcome in a less urban setting is not always warm and friendly.

The dance numbers are lavish and fun to watch, whether they're performed in the middle of the desert, atop a bar in some out-of-the-way town, or on a stage in Sydney. Mostly '70s disco hits (including once-popular tunes by Gloria Gaynor, the Village People, and ABBA), these songs are lip-synched and gyrated to with gusto by the transvestite trio as they don garish costumes and even worse makeup to wow their audiences.

There are moments of seriousness amidst all the zaniness as the twin specters of intolerance and homophobia (two sides of the same coin) cast a pall over the proceedings. Give director Stephan Elliot credit for not dwelling overmuch on these instances. He knows that their mere inclusion is sufficient to get the message across.

While each of the 3 leads is good, the standout performance belongs to normally-serious veteran actor Terrence Stamp, who has previously appeared in such diverse outings as *Billy Budd* and *Superman* (I and II). Here, he brings a quiet dignity to the role of Bernadette. That's not easy to do considering some of the outrageous costumes he's required to wear.

The Adventures of Priscilla, Queen of the Desert is a great deal more appealing than many might suppose it to be. It's a road movie that's anything but typical or traditional. So, whether or not you share the proclivities of Bernadette, Mitzi, and Felicia, the trio's cinematic cabaret is nevertheless something to smile and laugh your way through. **RECOMMENDED**

American Pie [1999]
Starring: Jason Biggs, Thomas Ian Nicholas, Chris Klein, Eddie Kaye Thomas, Eugene Levy Director: Paul Weitz Screenplay: Adam Herz
Running Time: 1:37 Rated: R (Graphic sexual activities of various sorts, nudity, profanity) Theatrical Aspect Ratio: 1.85:1

The point of every gross, eccentric, and vulgar moment in *American Pie* is to make the audience laugh.

First time director Paul Weitz and writer Adam Herz aren't going for anything remotely intellectual here — they're appealing to the least common denominator in us all. And it works. *American Pie* is consistently funny and sporadically hilarious. It should come as a surprise to no one that the most effective jokes involve some form of sex. There's also one instance of (literal) toilet humor that had the audience in stitches. *American Pie* descends into bad taste with its first scene and has the good sense never to rise above that level.

American Pie introduces us to a quartet of males with a serious problem: their high school senior year is coming to a close and they're all virgins. Jim (Jason Biggs), the film's ostensible hero, is an awkward guy who has trouble talking to females. Kevin (Thomas Ian Nicholas), the most average member of the group, is involved in a stable relationship with a beautiful girl, but he keeps stranding runners at third base. Oz (Chris Klein), a dumb jock, decides that the best way to meet members of the opposite sex is to join the glee club. And Finch (Eddie Kaye Thomas), the intellectual, is so tightly wound that he won't use the school restrooms. The egos of these 4 are badly bruised when evidence suggests that the biggest geek at East Great Falls High has had sex before them. So they make a pact to help each other lose their virginity before they graduate, and target one specific event: the Senior Prom.

Each of the guys is ultimately paired with a girl. For Jim, it's an oversexed exchange student named Nadia (Shannon Elizabeth), and, when that falls through, it's Michelle (Alyson Hannigan), a timid member of the school band. Oz falls for smart, pretty Heather (Mena Suvari), who generally has little time for jocks. Kevin's steady girlfriend is Vicky (Tara Reid), whose best friend, Jessica (Natasha Lyonne), encourages her to "do it." And Finch learns why *The Graduate* is such a popular movie.

The main difference between *American Pie* and most of the other teen-themed comedies flooding theaters these days is the take-no-prisoners edge. This film isn't going for "cute." It's not trying to earn a PG-13 for maximum exposure to the under-17 crowd. It takes risks; they don't always work, but, when they do, there's a payoff. There's nothing obtuse about the film's appeal. For those who think the moral level of Hollywood pictures is in a steep decline, *American Pie* provides evidence to support the theory. For just

about everyone else, it's a guilty (or, in some cases, a not-so-guilty) pleasure. RECOMMENDED

American Psycho [2000]

Starring: Christian Bale, Willem Dafoe, Jared Leto, Reese Witherspoon, Samantha Mathis Director: Mary Harron Screenplay: Mary Harron & Guinevere Turner, based on the novel by Bret Easton Ellis Running Time: 1:42 Rated: R (Violence, sex, nudity, profanity) Theatrical Aspect Ratio: 1.85:1

First and foremost, *American Psycho* takes a scathing look at the "me first" mentality of the mid-to-late-'80s. In fact, one of the reasons the film works so well is because of a take no prisoners attitude. We are given a gallery of despicable, amoral characters to observe. Anyone who identifies with them needs to consider seeking immediate psychiatric help. The most disturbing of them is Patrick Bateman (Christian Bale), a successful, wealthy commodities broker who believes himself to be untouchable and perhaps indestructible. Not content to destroy lives in the conventional manner embraced by his colleagues, Patrick has taken things one step further and become a serial killer. In fact, he has murdered so many times that he is losing track of the body count.

A crucial aspect of the movie's effective satire is the performance of Christian Bale, whose dead-on, straight man approach to the role gives *American Psycho* its punch. Bale's cold, charismatic, misogynist turn as the 27-year-old psycho is riveting. The supporting cast contains a number of familiar names — Reese Witherspoon as Patrick's superficial fiancée, Evelyn; Chloë Sevigny as his faithful secretary, Jean; and Willem Dafoe as a police detective.

In a voiceover, Patrick informs us that "There is no real me. I simply am not there." He sees himself as a façade — a perfectly sculpted body encompassing a black hole where his soul and conscience should be. "I have all the characteristics of a human being but not one discernible emotion except greed and disgust." He's a huge fan of pop music. Some of the film's creepiest and funniest scenes occur when he plays Huey Lewis and the News, Phil Collins, and Genesis as foreplay to violence. During sex, he spends as much time preening in front of a mirror as he does playing with the girl (or girls) he's with. When introducing himself at nightclubs, he claims to be in "murders and executions" not "mergers and acquisitions." And the people he uses that line with think it's funny.

In the recent tradition of movies like *Fight Club*, *American Psycho* employs a surprise ending. There is enough ambiguity about the last act revelations that one can interpret them in more than one way, but the most likely choice forces the entire movie to be re-interpreted through a different filter. In retrospect, the film holds together no matter which approach you accept, and the seams never show. **HIGHLY RECOMMENDED**

America's Sweethearts [2001]

Starring: Julia Roberts, Billy Crystal, Catherine Zeta-Jones, John Cusack, Hank Azaria Director: Joe Roth Screenplay: Billy Crystal & Peter Tolan Running Time: 1:40 Rated: PG-13 (Sexual situations, profanity) Theatrical Aspect Ratio: 2.35:1

Bruce Willis & Demi Moore. Meg Ryan & Dennis Quaid. Tom Cruise & Nicole Kidman. These are only three of the highest profile Hollywood "supercouples" to have blown apart in recent years, their splits enflaming the interest of gossip-mongers everywhere. It was only a matter of time before a group of filmmakers decided to make a movie about "Divorce — Hollywood Style." The talented trio to tackle the subject are veteran producer-turned-director Joe Roth and screenwriters Billy Crystal & Peter Tolan — all 3 of whom have their satirical razors sharpened to a keen edge for this endeavor. *America's Sweethearts* is first and foremost a lampoon of today's Hollywood, and its targets are as diverse as the cast. No one emerges unscathed from this comedy — not high-powered, egotistical producers; not self-absorbed actors; not film critics; and (especially) not publicists.

Eddie Thomas (John Cusack) and Gwen Harrison (Catherine Zeta-Jones) were America's most beloved husband-and-wife acting duo, with such titles on their combined resume as *Autumn with Greg & Peg, Requiem for an Outfielder,* and *Sasha and the Optometrist.* Of the 9 films they made together, 6 grossed more than $100 million. Then, 18 months ago, their fairy-tale story came to an end when Gwen began an affair with Spanish heartthrob Hector (Hank Azaria) and Eddie suffered a nervous breakdown. Now, after her solo film career has gone into a downward spiral steeper than the stairs in *Vertigo* and he has spent countless months in a "rest clinic," Eddie and Gwen are about to meet again to promote their final motion picture together: a science fiction spectacular called *Time Over Time.* Two publicists, studio flack, Lee (Billy Crystal), and Gwen's sister, Kiki (Julia Roberts), have the unenviable task of attempting to convince all the journalists on the press junket that Eddie and Gwen might be headed for a reunion. But there are complications — Kiki's long-harbored crush on Eddie threatens to turn everything on its head.

America's Sweethearts is characterized by sharp dialogue, comedy that varies from tame to ribald (Billy Crystal's encounter with a friendly Doberman is priceless), and a romance that adds a little sugar to the otherwise salty circumstances. The movie is more about the shenanigans that go on during the course of a press junket than about any particular character or relationship. It's the way all of the stories spin out of control and entwine with each other that makes the movie so enjoyable. Sure, the ending is predictable, but 95% of the fun is getting there, and, whenever things start getting too soft, there's always a vicious one-liner just around the corner. **RECOMMENDED**

Analyze This [1999]

Starring: Robert De Niro, Billy Crystal, Lisa Kudrow Director: Harold Ramis Screenplay: Peter Tolan, Harold Ramis & Ken Lonergan Running Time: 1:45 Rated: R (Profanity, violence, sex) Theatrical Aspect Ratio: 1.85:1

The greatest asset evidenced by Harold Ramis' gangster comedy, *Analyze This,* is that it doesn't try too hard for laughs. Instead of force-feeding audiences stale, predictable jokes about mobsters and mayhem, Ramis is content to let the humor evolve naturally out of the situations postulated by the script and the performances of lead actors Robert De Niro and Billy Crystal. The resulting movie, while not consistently uproarious, is frequently funny and occasionally hilarious.

De Niro is the straight man to Billy Crystal's Ben Sobel, a psychiatrist who has unwittingly become a name on Vitti's payroll. Crystal finds the right tone for Sobel early in the proceedings — he's a witty individual, but he doesn't go overboard. Crystal manages to be funny without destroying the integrity of his character — a crucial achievement for the movie to work on any level.

Vitti is not a "happy, well-adjusted gangster." Once, he was able to kill and brutalize without compunction, but now the day-to-day activities of a made guy are wearing him down. He's suffering from panic attacks and sentimental TV commercials cause him to break down and cry. If he's going to survive in a world where the appearance of machismo is everything, he has to banish his weakness through the most expedient manner possible — therapy. Because Sobel had the misfortune of giving his business card to Vitti's stooge, Jelly (Joe Viterelli), he becomes the mobster's first candidate. Soon, like it or not, Sobel is on call — even if it means interrupting his wedding to a pretty Florida news reporter (Lisa Kudrow).

Analyze This is not a great comedy, but it offers a fairly good time by poking fun at mobsters and psychiatrists. Both Freud and *The Godfather* take a pounding, but the best-conceived comic sequence comes near the end, when Crystal's Sobel is placed in a situation where he has to impersonate a Mafioso, and finds that he can't even pronounce "consigliere." The film contains several other memorable moments, such as Vitti's reaction to a Merrill Lynch TV spot and a fender bender that causes a couple of gangsters a few anxious moments.

Harold Ramis, the director of *Groundhog Day* and co-writer of *Ghostbusters,* knows a thing or two about comic timing, and his skill in this arena is in evidence here. The basic storyline is pretty much a throwaway; what makes *Analyze This* work is the interplay between the actors and the manner in which comic vignettes are incorporated into the plot. For those who have grown weary of lame gangster parodies, *Analyze This* offers a more intelligent, better conceived alternative. **RECOMMENDED**

Barcelona [1994]

Starring: Taylor Nichols, Chris Eigeman, Tushka Bergen, Mira Sorvino Director: Whit Stillman Screenplay: Whit Stillman Running Time: 1:41 Rated: PG-13 (Sexual situations, mature themes) Theatrical Aspect Ratio: 1.85:1

In *Barcelona,* nothing goes quite as you expect it to. In a broad sense, certain things are played out as anticipated, but there are always little quirks to be aware of. Filtered through a somewhat detached and ironic perspective, this film is the distillation of an intriguing blend of romantic comedy, satire, drama, and philosophy.

The first half of this movie races past at a frantic pace, its momentum gained more through its nearly-constant dialogue than because of any significant plot development. Things happen, to be sure, but everything is on a small scale. During the "last decade of the cold war," we're introduced to Ted Boynton (Taylor Nichols), an American salesman based in Barcelona, and his obnoxious cousin Fred (Chris Eigeman), a Navy officer. Fred drops in on Ted unexpectedly, announcing that he intends to stay for a while. Ted, too much the gentleman to say "no" to family, endures the unwanted intrusion. Despite a fair bit of friction, the two manage to coexist, going out on the town in search of love (in Ted's case) and sex (in Fred's). What they find is a group of attractive trade-fair girls and a match for each of them — or so it seems.

The best moments in *Barcelona* involve snippets of offbeat conversations about mundane facets of life. Some of these — like Fred's musings about the "correct" way to shave — are completely facetious, but others are designed to provoke a moment's genuine thought, such as Ted and Ramon's opposing views on the importance of physical beauty.

Barcelona is one of those movies that contains just about everything (and a lot of it) except action. The plot is a vehicle for the characters (and their intelligently-scripted dialogue) — a method, as Stillman says, of viewing different aspects of Ted and Fred's lives. However, while the film's initial charm may lie in its humorous perspective of this pair of mismatched cousins, its lasting impression (for men at least) may involve wondering exactly how to hold the razor. **HIGHLY RECOMMENDED**

Being John Malkovich [1999]

Starring: John Cusack, Cameron Diaz, Catherine Keener, John Malkovich Director: Spike Jonze Screenplay: Charlie Kaufman Running Time: 1:52 Rated: R (profanity, sexual situations) Theatrical Aspect Ratio: 2.35:1

These days, critics (and non-critics, for that matter) are fond of complaining about how multiplexes are populated by cookie-cutter motion pictures that follow safe, formula-derived patterns designed to please audiences who want a different version of a story they have already seen dozens of times. And, while there's some truth to the maxim that "there's nothing new under the sun," *Being John Malkovich* tries hard to be the exception. Admittedly, the themes addressed by the movie — those of identity, celebrity, and manipulation — are familiar, but the manner in which director Spike Jonze and writer Charlie Kaufman address them is fresh and inventive.

The premise is as intriguing and offbeat as it is difficult to adequately describe in a few sentences. Craig Schwartz (John Cusack) is a master puppeteer, but, after being out of work for a while, he is becoming restless, so his wife, Lotte (Cameron Diaz), suggests that he swallow his pride and get a job — any job. Since he has nimble fingers, he decides to apply for a position as a filing clerk. The job in question is on the 7½th story of a New York City office building — a floor that is 4 feet from carpet to ceiling ("low overhead") and can only be reached by stopping the elevator between the 7th and 8th stories and prying open the door with a crow bar. After a successful interview with the firm's sex-obsessed, carrot juice-drinking, 105-year-old boss, Dr. Lester (Orson Bean),

Craig gets the job and meets his co-workers, including Floris (Mary Kay Place), the hearing-impaired secretary, and Maxine (Catherine Keener), a sexy brunette.

One day, while searching for a lost file behind a cabinet in his office, Craig discovers a hidden door. Venturing through it, he is sucked into a portal that lands him inside the brain of John Malkovich, where Craig can look out the actor's eyes and experience what he feels. It's the ultimate in voyeurism, but it doesn't last for long. Fifteen minutes after Craig enters Malkovich, the portal spits him out, dropping him from the sky and landing him alongside the New Jersey Turnpike. He returns home and tells his wife, who wants to try the portal for herself. He also reveals the secret to Maxine, and, while he ponders "the metaphysical can of worms" the portal unleashes, she sees it as an opportunity to sell tickets: $200 a pop to be John Malkovich for 15 minutes.

The movie is surreal precisely because Jonze plays everything straight. The characters are not aware that they're in some kind of distorted reality, gazing through the looking glass darkly. This approach aids in the willing suspension of disbelief, drawing us into the story rather than distancing us and forcing us to gaze at the proceedings from the outside, looking for seams in the plot. *Being John Malkovich* is one of those rare cinematic experiences that works on one level or another for nearly everyone who sees it. It is a triumphant debut for Spike Jonze. **HIGHLY RECOMMENDED**

Best in Show [2000]
Starring: Christopher Guest, Eugene Levy, Michael McKean, Catherine O'Hara, Parker Posey, Fred Willard Director: Christopher Guest Screenplay: Christopher Guest & Eugene Levy Running Time: 1:30 Rated: PG-13 (Profanity, sexual themes) Theatrical Aspect Ratio: 1.85:1

Arguably the King of the Mockumentary, Christopher Guest goes that route again with his latest endeavor, using the familiar format of *This Is Spinal Tap* (which he co-wrote and in which he co-starred) and *Waiting for Guffman* (which he wrote, directed, and appeared in) and applying it to the unlikely subject of dog shows. As with *Guffman*, Guest's satire is pointed and occasionally hilarious, but it is not mean-spirited. The film is a parody, but it displays knowledge and understanding of the subject it is satirizing, and it never takes cheap shots.

The story is simple, as befits a movie of this sort. By using "interviews" and manufactured documentary-style footage, *Best In Show* follows the travels and travails of several groups as they converge upon Philadelphia for the Mayflower Kennel Club's annual dog show. We meet Hamilton and Meg Swan (Michael Hitchcock and Parker Posey), a yuppie couple who met at a Starbucks and share a love of J. Crew and L.L. Bean catalogues; Gerry and Cookie Fleck (*SCTV* vets Eugene Levy and Catherine O'Hara), a mild-mannered businessman and his wife, whose "loose" reputation precedes her; gay couple Scott Donlan (John Michael Higgins) and Stefan Vanderhoof (Michael McKean), who pamper their dog incessantly; North Carolina native Harlan Pepper (Guest), who runs a shop called The Fishin' Hole and hits the road in his RV with his bloodhound; and Sherri Ann Ward Cabot (Jennifer Coolidge), who shares a love of soup and snow peas with her rich, old husband, and is carrying on a lesbian affair with the handler of her dog.

The screenplay for *Best In Show* is funny in both subtle and overt ways. Some of the humor is sly; some is in-your-face. It's hard to imagine anyone sitting through this movie and not laughing on a fairly consistent basis. As in all of Guest's films, we come to care about the characters — perhaps not to the same degree that we might in a well-constructed melodrama or tearjerker, but, during the short span of 90 minutes, they become surprisingly real. And, while there's not a lot of tension surrounding the question of who eventually wins the "Best In Show" competition, Guest keeps us guessing, and rewards us with an unexpected twist or two. It's not great drama, but it prevents the story from dissolving into a series of loosely-connected comedy sketches. This is one rare occasion when we can be glad that the film industry is going to the dogs. **RECOMMENDED**

The Best Man [1999]
Starring: Taye Diggs, Nia Long, Morris Chestnut, Harold Perrineau Jr., Terrence Dashon Howard Director: Malcolm D. Lee Screenplay: Malcolm D. Lee Running Time: 1:58 Rated: R (profanity, sexual situations, violence, brief nudity) Theatrical Aspect Ratio: 1.85:1

The Best Man is not what it initially seems to be. Despite starting out with all the earmarks of a fairly ordinary romantic comedy, the project develops into a surprisingly effective look at a man's quest for rebirth after events topple him from a pedestal of arrogance. And, while there are plenty of laughs to be had, *The Best Man* functions better as a light drama than a straight comedy, with several scenes packing a punch because they're played straight. The film is the directorial debut of Malcolm D. Lee (Spike's cousin), who may have gotten this chance because of family connections but shows enough promise to earn further opportunities on his own.

The central character is, as one might anticipate from the title, scheduled to be the best man at a friend's wedding. Harper (Taye Diggs) is a Chicago-based writer who has just finished a novel called *Unfinished Business*. Although not yet published, it is described as a page turner, and Oprah has selected it for an upcoming book of the month. Like many good authors, Harper has filled his chapters with characters and events out of his past. And, just as a promising career is beginning to unfold before him, his girlfriend of 2 years, Robin (Sanaa Lathan), starts hinting that she wants a commitment that Harper is unwilling to give. He says he loves her, but he isn't ready for marriage.

Leaving Robin behind for a few days, Harper boards a New York-bound plane to participate in his best friend's wedding. There, he meets up with some old buddies. Much to Harper's dismay, just about everyone has read his book, even though it hasn't been published, and there are more than a few bruised feelings.

One cultural inequity that Lee dwells upon is the sexual double standard. Lance, the football gladiator, is essentially a throwback to the Stone Age. He believes that Mia should forgive him for his countless indiscretions; however, the thought that she might have slept with one other man fills him with a bubbling rage. Lee doesn't preach about this issue, but it's never far from the surface. Instead of applauding or condemning Lance's chauvinist perspective, he presents it neutrally and lets audience members draw their own conclusions. RECOMMENDED

The Big Lebowski [1998]

Starring: Jeff Bridges, John Goodman, Steve Buscemi, Julianne Moore Director: Joel Coen Screenplay: Joel & Ethan Coen Running Time: 1:55 Rated: R (Profanity, violence, nudity, drugs) Theatrical Aspect Ratio: 1.85:1

In a word, *The Big Lebowski* is a mess. But what a glorious, wonderfully-entertaining mess it is. Its single weakness, and what amounts to little more than a minor distraction, is that it doesn't have much of a plot, and what there is contains the kind of gaping holes that even the most obtuse viewer can identify.

The Coen Brothers begin by introducing us to their latest protagonist, The Dude (Jeff Bridges), a down-and-out, unemployed drifter who is still mentally mired in the '60s. Most of the time, The Dude is content to stay at home, which is why he's known as "the laziest man in Los Angeles County." That is, until a group of inept crooks confuse him with The Big Lebowski (David Huddleston), one of the city's richest businessmen.

It seems that Bunny Lebowski (Tara Reid), The Big Lebowski's ornamental wife, owes a great deal of money to porn producer Jackie Treehorn (Ben Gazzara). Treehorn's men mistake The Dude (whose real name is also Lebowski) for their quarry — and it takes them a while to realize their error (they're not Rhodes scholars). Irritated that his carpet has been ruined by the intruders, The Dude arranges a meeting with The Big Lebowski to extract compensation. But things don't go exactly as planned. Soon, The Dude finds himself on Lebowski's payroll as the bag man handling the ransom for his employer's kidnapped wife.

Much of the humor comes as a result of the sheer ineptitude of The Dude. This guy isn't a bad choice for handling the ransom drop in a kidnapping, he's the worst choice. He's a complete loser, and his friends (John Goodman, Steve Buscemi) aren't any better.

Problems with the plot notwithstanding, *The Big Lebowski* ranks as one of the most audacious comedies of recent years. The Coens keep the jokes coming, although some of them are so subtle they can easily be missed (for example, when The Dude writes a check for 69 cents). Profane, outrageous, and without inhibitions, *The Big Lebowski* further cements the Coens' reputation as *independent* film makers. RECOMMENDED

Big Trouble [2002]

Starring: Tim Allen, Rene Russo, Stanley Tucci, Omar Epps, Dennis Farina Director: Barry Sonnenfeld Screenplay: Robert Ramsey & Matthew Stone, based on the novel by Dave Barry Running Time: 1:22 Rated: PG-13 (Profanity, violence, brief nudity, sexual situations) Theatrical Aspect Ratio: 1.85:1

Big Trouble is a cinematic Rube Goldberg machine determined to prove the adage that the shortest distance between two points may be a straight line, but that is by no means the most interesting route. With a cast of characters so large that Robert Altman would feel at home, *Big Trouble* manages to do a lot of clever little things and generate quite a few big laughs without wearing out its welcome.

It's a mad, mad, mad world — a fact that Eliot Arnold (Tim Allen) is about to learn. A former Pulitzer Prize winning columnist for the Miami Herald, Eliot is currently stuck in a dead-end job running his own ad agency when destiny arrives in the form of a big metal suitcase containing a nuclear weapon that looks like a garbage disposal. With great rapidity, it changes hands. First, it's the property of a group of seedy Russian arms dealers. Then it's purchased by Arthur Herk (Stanley Tucci), a small-minded black-mailer with a foot fetish. Before Arthur has had a chance to become acquainted with his new property, it is stolen by the aptly named Snake (Tom Sizemore), who thinks it must be worth something. Eliot and Snake end up thrown together by circumstances, struggling with each other on a hijacked plane while the red digital display on the bomb counts down to zero. Thrown into the mix are Arthur's blond wife, Anna (Rene Russo); a hippie who's addicted to Fritos (Jason Lee); a couple of mismatched cops (Janeane Garofalo, Patrick Warburton); a frustrated hit man (Dennis Farina); and a young couple (Ben Foster, Zooey Descanel) whose idea of a good time is shoot-ing each other with water pistols. If all of this doesn't make any sense to you now, don't worry — it still might not after you have watched the movie.

Big Trouble's director is Barry Sonnenfeld, who is probably best known for *Men in Black*. Sonnenfeld's fondness for the warped and wacky is very much in evidence here. The high energy level and refusal to quit on the jokes reminded me of *Airplane*, and, al-though the movie primarily features stupid charac-ters, *Big Trouble* plays well to a smart audience.
RECOMMENDED

The Birdcage [1996]

Starring: Robin Williams, Nathan Lane, Gene Hackman, Dianne Wiest, Dan Futterman, Calista Flockhart Director: Mike Nichols Screenplay: Elaine May, based on *La Cage aux Folles* Running Time: 1:57 Rated: R (profanity, mature themes) Theatrical Aspect Ratio: 1.85:1

Mike Nichols, the director of such well-received films as *The Graduate* and *Working Girl*, has taken the out-rageous 1978 French farce, *La Cage aux Folles*, and, by tweaking, updating, and Americanizing it, come up with a huge winner. *The Birdcage*, as it's called, is one of those rare motion pictures with side-splitting laughs where the humor never stays dormant for long.

For some 20 years, Armand (Robin Williams) and Albert (Nathan Lane) have lived together as husband and wife (so to speak). Both are openly gay, and com-fortable with their sexuality. They are partners in business as well as out of it — Armand operates a drag nightclub where Albert is the star performer. They have a son, Val (Dan Futterman), the product of Armand's one-night tryst 21 years ago with big-time executive Katherine Archer (Christine Baranski). As far as his upbringing is concerned, Val is as much Albert's son as Armand's, and he's not ashamed of his unusual family situation — at least not in the normal course of things.

But things are no longer normal. Val is engaged to the 18-year-old daughter of Senator Keeley (Gene Hackman), the co-founder of the Coalition for Moral Order. Since there's no way that Keeley would sanc-tion a marriage between his daughter and the son of a gay couple, Val pleads with his father to pretend to be straight, if only for one night. The result of this, as might be expected, is a hilarious disaster.

Although most of the jokes come from Elaine May's screenplay, it's the performances that make them funny. Robin Williams, despite his reputation for unfettered mania, is surprisingly restrained throughout most of *The Birdcage*, doing a little seri-ous acting along the way. Nathan Lane, playing the effeminate Albert, is the real star, whether he's trying to swagger like John Wayne (to act manly) or cos-tumed like a housewife. Williams and Lane work well as a couple, feeding off one another in the fashion of all great comedy twosomes.

The structure of *The Birdcage* is designed to show us that there isn't much difference between conserv-atives and liberals or straight and gay people. Nichols' picture preaches tolerance and understand-ing, but neatly camouflages such themes beneath gaudy sets, colorful costumes, and unrestrained hu-mor. The script has a few lulls, and there are times when it doesn't make a lot of sense, but there are few better ways to spend an evening than peering through the bars of *The Birdcage*. **HIGHLY RECOMMENDED**

Black Cat, White Cat [Serbo-Croatia, 1998]

Starring: Severdzan Bajram, Florijan Ajdini, Salija Ibraimova, Branka Katic Director: Emir Kusturica Screenplay: Emir Kusturica & Gordan Mihic Running Time: 2:07 Rated: R (profanity, mature themes, drug use) Theatrical Aspect Ratio: 1.85:1 In Serbo-Croatian with subtitles

With all of the horrible things happening in the corner of the world once known as Yugoslavia, it's a pleasant change-of-pace to discover a comedy that transpires there. Set in the heart of a gypsy community, *Black Cat, White Cat* (so named for two animals that make frequent appearances) is a delightfully madcap romp featuring colorful characters, no holds barred humor, and a lively soundtrack. There's almost no political agenda, unless you count the occasional comment about the local discrimination against gypsies.

Matko Destanov (Severdzan Bajram) is a middle-aged con artist who makes his living by scamming people. He has a 17-year-old son, Zare (Florijan), who is in love with a blond waitress, Ida (Branka Katic). After letting Zare pursue her for a while, Ida finally gives in to his advances, just as Matko announces that he has arranged a marriage for his son as a way to pay off a debt to a lunatic business associate. Dadan (Srdjan Todorovic) wants to find a suitable husband for his sister, Afrodita (Salija Ibraimova), but her short stature has proven to be a stumbling block. Further complications arise when the son of a local gangster decides that Afrodita is his soul-mate. The ensuing wedding, complete with two deaths, multiple vows, and an outhouse incident, is an example of choreographed chaos that only an accomplished director could orchestrate. It is easily one of the most bizarre celebrations ever committed to celluloid.

Black Cat, White Cat has an earthy feel to it. Although expertly filmed, it lacks the polished glaze of most big budget features, but that's part of its charm. It's an entirely original comedy — some of the elements are familiar, but, taking things as a whole, I can't recall seeing anything exactly like *Black Cat, White Cat*. Although not a masterpiece, Emir Kusturica's latest film is a real treat for those in search of a healthy dose of laughter set in a culture whose intricacies are rarely captured on film. RECOMMENDED

Blast from the Past [1999]
Starring: Brendan Fraser, Alicia Silverstone, Christopher Walken, Sissy Spacek Director: Hugh Wilson Screenplay: Bill Kelly & Hugh Wilson Running Time: 1:46 Rated: PG-13 (Sexual themes, profanity) Theatrical Aspect Ratio: 2.35:1

Blast from the Past opens in 1962, when the Cold War is at its chilliest. Calvin and Helen Webber (Christopher Walken and Sissy Spacek) are regarded as eccentrics by their friends and neighbors. In a paranoid era when many affluent Americans are constructing their own personal fallout shelters, Calvin has taken things to an extreme. He has replicated his entire house underground. On the fateful night during the Cuban Missile Crisis, Calvin and Helen elect to play it safe and spend some time in their underground habitat. At the precise moment when they enter the shelter, a small plane falls out of the sky and crashes into their house. Convinced that a nuclear holocaust has begun, Calvin seals himself and his pregnant wife in. The locks on the shelter will not open for 35

years — the time Calvin has calculated that it will take for the surface to become habitable again.

Those 3½ decades pass quickly, and, by the late 1990s, Adam Webber, Calvin and Helen's grown son, is ready to venture forth into the world and find a wife. Considering his sheltered upbringing, he is ill-prepared for the pitfalls of making his way around present-day Los Angeles, but, when he hooks up with a young woman named Eve (Alicia Silverstone), he believes that not only has he found a guide and companion, but possibly a mate as well. Eve, who is being paid to help Adam, views things differently.

While it's possible to see *Blast from the Past* as a fairly traditional romantic comedy, the film is really more than that. It's a slick, clever satire of American culture, both as it exists today and as it was more than 3 decades ago. Director Hugh Wilson invested a great deal of thought and consideration into designing the look of the fallout shelter and the portion of 1998 Los Angeles into which Adam first emerges. For those who care to notice, there are numerous background sight gags. And the relationship between Adam and Eve is a little more substantial than just boy-meets-girl; it's about finding the middle ground between two radically different cultures.

Blast from the Past is arguably a little too ambitious. A subplot involving a religious cult isn't well-realized and a segment featuring a social worker is poorly integrated. Those are relatively minor hiccups in an otherwise frothy and enchanting motion picture. RECOMMENDED

Blues Brothers 2000 [1998]
Starring: Dan Aykroyd, John Goodman, Joe Morton, J. Evan Bonifant Director: John Landis Screenplay: Dan Aykroyd & John Landis Running Time: 2:05 Rated: PG-13 (Profanity, violence, sensuality) Theatrical Aspect Ratio: 1.85:1

They're back, and this time they're not on a mission from God. Strictly speaking, however, only one of the original Blues Brothers has returned — Dan Aykroyd's Elwood. His partner, Jake (played by the late John Belushi), died in prison, so now it's up to the survivor to find a new lead singer, re-form the group, hit the road, run from the police, and end up in a band competition to end all band competitions. Any similarities between the sequel and its classic inspiration are entirely intentional. In fact, in many ways, *Blues Brothers 2000* is as much a remake as it is a follow-up. The familiar elements are certainly all there. The difference between the two Blues Brothers movies can be summed up simply: the original 1980 release worked as a musical and a comedy; the 1998 installment functions as a musical masquerading as a comedy.

This time around, there are 4 men in black. Aykroyd plays Elwood much the same as he did 18 years ago. In fact, with the hat, suit, and sunglasses covering up the most obvious signs of aging, it's hard to believe that so much time has passed. Taking over for John Belushi is John Goodman as the surprisingly timid Mighty Mack. Initially, this role was earmarked for Jim Belushi, but scheduling conflicts prevented him from appearing. Joe Morton joins the group as a cop who undergoes a conversion to the blues. Then there's 10-year-old Buster (played by J. Evan Bonifant), who specializes in stealing scenes.

Blues Brothers 2000 is the kind of movie that needs to be seen with an audience to be fully appreciated. Almost like a live concert, the energy of the viewers adds to the atmosphere. The film also has the good sense to build to something, leaving the dullest, least-invigorating elements for the first two reels. By the time the end credits arrive, the production is on a roll. **RECOMMENDED**

Bowfinger [1999]

Starring: Steve Martin, Eddie Murphy, Heather Graham, Christine Baranski, Terence Stamp Director: Frank Oz Screenplay: Steve Martin Running Time: 1:37 Rated: PG-13 (Profanity, sexual situations) Theatrical Aspect Ratio: 1.85:1

Over the years, there have been a number of good films about the process of making a bad movie. *Bowfinger* is the latest entry into this semi-elite group. Powered by a hilarious, high-octane performance by Eddie Murphy and a witty, boisterous script by his co-star, Steve Martin, *Bowfinger* offers 90-plus minutes of solid entertainment. It's a comic oasis in the midst of the mid-August desert of motion picture mediocrity, and contains some of the biggest laughs of the year.

When Bobby Bowfinger (Martin) reads the script for *Chubby Rain* and decides that this is *the* movie he has been waiting for, Bowfinger is already in dire financial straits, but he manages to round up a group of performers, "borrow" the necessary equipment, and acquire the green light from high-power producer Jerry Renfro (Robert Downey Jr.). There's only one catch — for Renfro to back the movie's distribution, Bowfinger has to land action mega-star Kit Ramsey (Eddie Murphy) as his lead. And, when Kit sees the script, his immediate reaction is an emphatic "NO!" But that's only a minor bump in the road for Bowfinger. He forges ahead, using a hidden camera

to photograph Kit as his actors come up to the star on the sidewalk and in restaurants saying their lines. Soon Kit, paranoid at the best of times, is convinced that aliens are out to get him. And, when he disappears, Bowfinger must hire a lookalike replacement.

Bowfinger does what all good comedies do — it builds comic momentum as the film unfolds. This isn't just a series of gags strung together; it's a carefully orchestrated composition that delivers bigger and bigger laughs the longer it runs.

Bowfinger saves the best for last. The concluding series of scenes (excerpts from another Bowfinger masterpiece) are worth the price of admission in their own right. They're funny not just because they're madcap and silly (which they are), but because they display a knowledge of the subtleties of movie-making and utilize this know-how to create an unforgettable send-up of chop-socky action sequences. Not since Keenan Ivory Wayans' *I'm Gonna Git You Sucka* has a fight scene been done with this many winks at the audience. (None of the hero's punches or karate chops comes anywhere close to the bad guys). With all of the ingredients blended effectively together, director Franak Oz, Martin, and Murphy can be credited for supplying a deliciously amusing confection. **HIGHLY RECOMMENDED**

Bridget Jones' Diary [United Kingdom/United States, 2001]

Starring: Renee Zellweger, Colin Firth, Hugh Grant Director: Sharon Maguire Screenplay: Richard Curtis, Andrew Davies, based on the novel by Helen Fielding Running Time: 1:35 Rated: R (Sex, profanity, violence) Theatrical Aspect Ratio: 2.35:1

The film tells the story of a year in the life of an average, single, 30-something British woman, who, armed with only her wits and charm (and a diary), goes in search of the ever-elusive Mr. Right. Unlucky-in-love Bridget (Renee Zellweger) has two candidates: the fun and sexy Daniel Cleaver (Hugh Grant) and the dour Mark Darcy (Colin Firth), whom she overhears calling her a "verbally incontinent spinster" when they first meet at a party. Not surprisingly, she goes for Daniel, but he turns out to be a less-than-perfect catch. Then, just when her interest in Mark begins to emerge, he hooks up with man-eating lawyer Natasha (Embeth Davidtz), who is determined to marry him. Meanwhile, her parents' marriage is on the rocks and she embarks upon a career in television news.

In England, the casting of American Renee Zellweger was initially greeted with much resistance by the press and the public. It was argued that not only was Zellweger an American, but she was too skinny to play the chubby Bridget. Well, some time between casting and shooting, Zellweger put on a few pounds and worked hard to perfect a British accent. These qualities, coupled with her natural charm and screen presence, make her a flawless choice for the lead. Zellweger embodies Bridget, and is a huge reason why the movie works.

Those who have read Jane Austen's *Pride and Prejudice* will find some familiar characters and elements in *Bridget Jones's Diary*. It doesn't take much deduction to determine that Helen Fielding is an Austen admirer, and that all of the nods to *Pride and Prejudice* are intentional. While it would be unfair to call *Bridget Jones's Diary* a 20th-century re-interpretation of *Pride and Prejudice,* there are some parallels — at least one of which the filmmakers have decided to emphasize.

The casting of Colin Firth as Mark Darcy is inspired. Firth, who essayed Mr. Darcy in the hugely popular 1995 BBC/A&E television production of *Pride and Prejudice,* plays this part exactly as he played the earlier role, making it evident that the two Darcys are essentially the same.

Bridget Jones's Diary is filled with moments of truth and flashes of humor (sometimes the two are the same). The direction, by newcomer Sharon Maguire, shows the deftness of a veteran. The energy level is consistently high and the characters (especially Bridget) don't take long to endear themselves to the audience. Congratulations to all involved. *Bridget Jones's Diary* is a triumph. **HIGHLY RECOMMENDED**

The Brothers McMullen [1995]
Starring: Mike McGlone, Edward Burns, Jack Mulcahy, Connie Britton, Shari Albert, Maxine Bahns Director: Edward Burns Screenplay: Edward Burns Running Time: 1:37 Rated: R (Profanity, sex) Theatrical Aspect Ratio: 1.85:1

Love, passion, and Irish Catholicism collide in *The Brothers McMullen,* writer/director Edward Burns' feature debut. Although it generally stays true to the clichés and plot turns of the genre, *The Brothers McMullen* is smart and honest rather than manipulative. Instead of resorting to hard-to-swallow story complications, this film stays on-target from its opening moments. Along the way, the empty dialogue too often incipient in this sort of picture is replaced by intelligent, insightful conversations.

One of *The Brothers McMullen*'s top assets is the brothers themselves. Despite their flaws (and each

has a reasonably obvious one), Patrick (Mike McGlone), Jack (Jack Mulcahy), and Barry (Edward Burns) are likeable guys. They drink beer together, reminisce none-too-fondly about their dead father, and discuss topics ranging from true love to whether there's a hell.

Patrick, the youngest, has just graduated from college and is getting cold feet about the prospect of spending the rest of his life with his Jewish girlfriend, Susan (Shari Albert). Jack, the oldest, is happily married to Molly (Connie Britton), the love of his life. But, as her maternal instincts assert themselves, Jack's eye begins to roam. Barry, the middle brother, is the most cynical of the three. ("Being a pessimist," he says, "makes it easier to deal with my inevitable failure.") A screenwriter on the verge of a big breakthrough, Barry goes from relationship to relationship without ever finding love. Then he meets Audrey (Maxine Bahns), and suddenly nothing is quite so clear-cut.

If this film was only about the 3 men and their relationships, it would be enjoyable, but not particularly noteworthy. However, Burns has given his characters a slew of interesting things to say, and he hasn't reduced the women to pawns in male-centered romantic fantasies. In fact, in *The Brothers McMullen,* the female halves of the relationships are often smarter and hipper than their male counterparts. When one of the brothers thinks he's putting something over on his wife/girlfriend/lover, he's more likely just fooling himself.

Despite its occasional forays into weighty matters, *The Brothers McMullen* largely stays on the light side, where all good romantic comedies reside. The tone is upbeat and the script is laced with wit and, upon occasion, there are moments guaranteed to cause deeper, louder laughter. You don't have to be Catholic, or Irish, or even American, to "get it." Burns' language, despite originating on Long Island, is universal in appeal and meaning. **HIGHLY RECOMMENDED**

Bullets Over Broadway [1994]
Starring: John Cusack, Dianne Wiest, Chazz Palminteri, Jennifer Tilly, Mary-Louise Parker Director: Woody Allen Screenplay: Woody Allen & Douglas McGrath Running Time: 1:38 Rated: R (Violence, mature themes, language) Theatrical Aspect Ratio: 1.85:1

Bullets Over Broadway is the most insightful and deliciously droll look at show business since Robert Altman skewered Hollywood in 1992's *The Player.* The film questions what real art is. Just because a play is compromised, does that make it a less valid expression of ideas? And is it possible to get anything made without giving in on some element of artistic integrity? Woody Allen toys with those issues, taking playful jabs at his audience, himself, and the entertainment industry as a whole.

David Shayne (John Cusack as Allen's alter-ego) is a playwright with a brilliant script that no one wants to produce. Since it's "art," the belief is that it's destined for obscurity. ("If the common people don't understand your work, you're a genius.") Then, along comes a gangster (Joe Viterelli) looking for a role for his manifestly untalented actress girlfriend Olive (Jennifer Tilly). For the price of including her in the play, David can have all the money he needs. Despite a pricking conscience and the warnings of his girlfriend (Mary-Louise Parker), he agrees.

To round out the cast, David chooses as his leading lady Helen "Don't Speak" Sinclair (a wonderfully over-the-top Dianne Wiest), a star with an ego to match her mammoth reputation, and as his leading man, British thespian Warner Purcell (the always-reliable Jim Broadbent), a food addict who falls off the dieting wagon whenever he gets nervous.

With its legitimate issues couched in laughter, *Bullets Over Broadway* is a delight to experience. Solid performances, a clever script (which contains at least one truly outrageous twist), and a jaunty soundtrack of '20s songs keep this movie a notch above many of Allen's recent films. And good Woody Allen is always a sure bet for entertainment. **HIGHLY RECOMMENDED**

Bulworth [United States, 1998]

Starring: Warren Beatty, Halle Berry, Oliver Platt, Don Cheadle
Director: Warren Beatty Screenplay: Warren Beatty & Jeremy Pikser
Running Time: 1:48 Rated: R (Profanity) Theatrical Aspect Ratio: 1.85:1

In one sense, the film, put out by Warner Beatty with little concern for whose toes might get stepped on, can be summed up as an attack on the growing conservatism of the Democratic party, which is becoming increasingly more difficult to distinguish from its Republican rival. *Bulworth* is unrepentantly cynical in its view that all politicians are in the back pockets of big business and that every elected official, whether Democrat or Republican, is a member of an exclusive club. Hypocrisy, self-interest, and greed are the 3 forces that drive every campaign, and Senator Jay Billington Bulworth (Beatty) has had enough.

It's mid-March 1996, and Bulworth, an incumbent Senator from California, is running for re-election. However, he has reached the breaking point. After taking out a $10 million life insurance policy with his 17-year-old daughter as the sole beneficiary, he puts out a contract on his own life, then goes on the warpath against special interest groups. Suddenly, Bulworth's "tell it like it is" philosophy is a national sensation, attracting the attention of millions, including a young black woman named Nina (Halle Berry), who is determined to show the Senator what life is like for those who live in South Central L.A. Right in the middle of everything, Bulworth suddenly decides that he wants to live, but learns that calling off a hit isn't as easy as setting one up.

Bulworth's only real weakness (and it's more in the nature of a minor inconvenience than a significant flaw) is the backstory, which, with its disguised hit men, car chases, and bungled assassination attempts, takes up a little too much time. The political satire, on the other hand, is brilliant. Not only is it honed to a viciously sharp edge, but it's frequently hilarious. Beatty manages to lampoon controversial issues, like kids selling drugs for dealers because they're too young to go to prison, while simultaneously making serious points. In addition to the political material, there are other targets, including the easy marks of tabloid reporters and TV news programs.

Bulworth is an angry movie, but Beatty is savvy enough to recognize that people respond better to comedies than serious "issue films," so he has camouflaged his message beneath the surface of this original, incisive satire. The movie has a take-no-prisoners attitude, and in today's climate of suffocating political correctness, that's a welcome trait.
HIGHLY RECOMMENDED

The Castle [Australia, 1997]

Starring: Michael Caton, Anne Tenney, Stephen Curry, Anthony Simcoe, Sophie Lee Director: Rob Sitch Screenplay: Santo Cilauro, Tom Gleisner, Jane Kennedy, Rob Sitch Running Time: 1:27 Rated: R (Profanity) Theatrical Aspect Ratio: 1.85:1

Fans of quirky Australian fare will appreciate *The Castle*'s offbeat sense of humor. The movie will probably not generate many belly laughs (although there are at least two hilarious sequences), but it will have all but the most die-hard curmudgeons smiling frequently. The feature debut of director Rob Sitch, *The Castle* represents a pleasant blend of gentle satire and feel-good comedy.

Michael Caton plays Darryl Kerrigan, the happiest homeowner in Australia. His abode at 3 Highview Crescent is his pride and joy, even though it's next door to an airport on one side and a high voltage tower on the other. Darryl lives in the ramshackle little house with his beloved wife, Sal (Anne Tenney), who makes the best meals of any woman on the face of the planet, and his two sons, narrator Dale (Stephen Curry) and "idea man" Steve (Anthony Simcoe). A third son, Wayne (Wayne Hope) is in jail, and a daughter, Tracy (Sophie Lee), has recently entered a life of wedded bliss. For the eternally optimistic Darryl, life couldn't be better. But storm clouds are on the horizon.

The airport wants to expand, and, under an agreement with the government, they demand the compulsory acquisition of Darryl's home. Instead of accepting their generous offer and moving, he and a few neighbors decide to fight back. They hire a lawyer, Dennis Denuto (Tiriel Mora), to challenge the constitutionality of the airport's case. Unfortunately, Dennis isn't a very good attorney — he can't even get his copier to work — and he botches things up. All is not lost, however. The venerable Lawrence Hammill (Charles 'Bud' Tingwell) takes an interest in Darryl's seemingly lost cause, and intends to pursue the matter to the highest court in the land.

Although *The Castle* is a comedy, it's not entirely without themes and serious ideas. The central conflict is a classic David vs. Goliath (big business infringing on personal liberties) — something that almost everyone (except Fortune 500 CEOs) can relate to. Also, the concept of a "home" is presented as a deeply personal thing. One individual's shanty might be another's dream house. It's not just a case of bricks and mortar, but the whole package: memories, feelings, and other associations (both good and bad). Buildings do not have identities, but homes do. We don't just exist in them, we live there. *The Castle* is not an overly ambitious motion picture, but it has a point to make, and does so in an undeniably entertaining manner. **RECOMMENDED**

Children of the Revolution [Australia, 1996]

Starring: Richard Roxburgh, Judy Davis, Sam Neill, Geoffrey Rush, Rachel Griffiths, F. Murray Abraham Director: Peter Duncan
Screenplay: Peter Duncan Running Time: 1:40 Rated: R (Profanity, sex) Theatrical Aspect Ratio: 1.85:1

Children of the Revolution opens in 1951 Sydney, where die-hard communist Joan Fraser (Judy Davis) is drumming up support to defeat a ballot referendum that would outlaw the party. Joan's mantra, which she utters at every possible opportunity, is taken directly from Marx: "From each according to his capacity to each according to his means." One of her fellow communists, a conventional fellow named Zachary Welch (Geoffrey Rush), proposes marriage,

but Joan refuses, claiming that she's not in love with him.

Every week, she writes a new letter to her hero, Joseph Stalin (F. Murray Abraham). When the dictator finally gets around to reading her missives, he is so touched by her enthusiasm that he arranges for her to visit Moscow for the 1952 Communist Party Conference. There, on the night that Stalin dies, she sleeps with both him and an Australian/Russian double agent (or perhaps triple agent) named David Hoyle. Nine months later, when Joan is back in Sydney and married to Zachary, she gives birth to a baby boy. But is the child, Joe Welch (played by Ben McIver as a youngster; Richard Roxburgh as an adult), the offspring of Stalin or Hoyle?

Smartly written and adroitly developed, *Children of the Revolution* fires verbal and visual volleys at multiple bullseyes, from communism and Stalin to the news media and McDonalds. Not all of the satirical jabs hit their mark, but there are so many of them that most of the misses go unnoticed. And several that do work are just short of brilliant. One of the more absurd scenes, which calls to mind Mel Brooks' "Springtime for Hitler" (from *The Producers*), has Stalin singing and dancing to "I Get a Kick Out of You." There's also a sequence that details a "macabre and barbaric" means of breaking a hunger strike: blow the scent of sizzling bacon into the cell of the striking prisoner. *Children of the Revolution* uses a fresh approach to take aim at a broad range of targets, and the result is both decisive and incisive. **RECOMMENDED**

Citizen Ruth [1996]

Starring: Laura Dern, Swoosie Kurtz, Kurtwood Smith, Mary Kay Place
Director: Alexander Payne Screenplay: Alexander Payne & Jim Taylor
Running Time: 1:46 Rated: R (Profanity, mature themes) Theatrical Aspect Ratio: 1.85:1

The average movie about the abortion debate tends to be preachy, melodramatic, and unbearably solemn. So, it comes as something of a shock that the latest venture to the front line of the pro-life/pro-choice battle is actually a *comedy*. Director/co-writer Alexander Payne has taken the slogans, name-calling, and behind-the-scenes tactics, and created a vicious satire that skewers (and probably offends) those on both sides of the issue. There's a serious message here, as well — that in a war between ideologies, it's too easy to lose sight of the individual.

Laura Dern (*Rambling Rose*) is Ruth Stoops, a glue-sniffing, alcoholic drifter who has been arrested 16 times for "hazardous vapor inhalation." She has given birth to 4 children, all of whom have been taken away from her by the government. Her family and friends have disowned or abandoned her. Now, after being jailed for getting high on patio sealant, she learns that she's pregnant again. The judge decides to allow charges of felony criminal endangerment of the fetus, but tells Ruth that if she gets an abortion, he'll reconsider. Suddenly, Ruth's case becomes a lightning rod for local activists. The struggle for Ruth's conscience pits the Baby Savers, run by an evangelical husband-and-wife team (played by Kurtwood Smith and Mary Kay Place), against a pro-choice organization headed by a lesbian feminist (Swoosie Kurtz). The situation rapidly develops into a war where the weapons are coercion and bribery, and the last thing anyone seems to care about is Ruth.

Laura Dern gives an excellent performance, allowing herself to be photographed in an extremely unattractive fashion, with no makeup, dark circles under her eyes, and lank, unwashed hair hanging below her shoulders. She plays Ruth as a selfish, but very human, character who only cares about the pro-life and pro-choice movements in relation to how she can benefit from them (preferably financially).

Citizen Ruth has its share of bitingly funny moments, and some of the comedy is quite inventive. By structuring the film as a satire, Payne is able to make statements about the abortion issue that no straight film would likely attempt, and, as is often the case, there's a great deal of truth buried in the humor. In fact, *Citizen Ruth*'s weakest moments occur not when it's savaging social causes and political concerns, but when it attempts to inject conventional drama into its exaggerated, outrageous milieu. **RECOMMENDED**

Clerks [1994]

Starring: Brian O'Halloran, Jeff Anderson Director: Kevin Smith
Screenplay: Kevin Smith Running Time: 1:37 Rated: R (Graphic language, mature themes) Theatrical Aspect Ratio: 1.85:1

The comedy found in *Clerks* is raw and ribald, varying from somewhat off-color to truly tasteless. Nothing, no matter how outrageous, is beyond director Kevin Smith, and his willingness to flaunt cinematic taboos is one of the reasons why *Clerks* is such a unqualified success. The dialogue accurately captures the street language common in the part of the country where the movie was filmed. There are a few lines that come across as scripted, but this is often the result of the manner in which they're delivered (the ac-

tors are good, but not seasoned). As far as the level of profanity is concerned, anyone spending time on a Monmouth County (New Jersey) street won't be shocked, but those who are offended by such language should beware.

By Smith's own admission, there isn't much of a plot — just a loose framework to hold together a series of scenes featuring odd personalities in bizarre situations. The main characters are Dante (Brian O'Halloran), a Quik Stop clerk who does his best to cater to his customers, and Randal (Jeff Anderson), the man behind the counter at a local video store who spends his time insulting and offending every potential renter. Also wandering in and out of the story are a local drug-dealer, Jay (Jason Mewes), and his sidekick, Silent Bob (Kevin Smith), as well as Dante's current girlfriend, Veronica (Marilyn Ghigliotti), and his ex, Caitlin (Lisa Spoonhauer).

It's rare for a motion picture to maintain the level of irreverence and humor of *Clerks* for its full running length. In his first outing behind the camera, Kevin Smith has given his audience the kind of film at which veteran film makers often fail. As the final credits roll with the promise that "Jay and Silent Bob will return in *Dogma*," we can be thankful that this isn't the last we'll see of Smith or his cast of offbeat characters. **HIGHLY RECOMMENDED**

Clockwatchers [1997]

Starring: Toni Collette, Parker Posey, Lisa Kudrow, Alanna Ubach
Director: Jill Sprecher Screenplay: Jill Sprecher, Karen Sprecher
Running Time: 1:36 Rated: PG-13 (Profanity) Theatrical Aspect Ratio: 1.85:1

Clockwatchers opens with a brilliant scene that is repeated daily, all across the country, in hundreds of work places. A secretarial temp, Iris (Toni Collette), arrives to start a new assignment with Global Credit. She gets there a few minutes early and is ignored by the receptionist, who doesn't go on duty until the clock strikes 9. Then, she is shown into the office complex, where she is told to wait until someone comes to tell her what to do. Two hours later, she's still waiting. During all that time, no one has shown the slightest interest in her; she's a temp, and, therefore, beneath notice. In terms of the office food chain, she's plankton.

Four temps work for Global Credit, filing papers, making copies, and stuffing envelopes. In addition to the meek, mousy Iris, there's Margaret (Parker Posey), a rebel who doesn't mind raising eyebrows by speaking her mind; Paula (Lisa Kudrow), an airheaded blond with acting aspirations; and Jane (Alanna Ubach), a woman with low self-esteem who is willing to marry an insensitive fiancé just to get out of the corporate rat race. For its first 50 minutes, *Clockwatchers* explores the developing friendship among these 4 as their common employment status forms a natural bond. Then, during the film's second half, Sprecher investigates how the existence of an office kleptomaniac fosters distrust and paranoia, elevating the level of tension and fragmenting friendships.

The thing I liked best about *Clockwatchers* is its understanding and subtly satirical presentation of life in a rigidly conservative office, where anything other than strict conformance is regarded with a frown. Many employees have so little work that, in Margaret's words, "The . . . real challenge is trying to look busy when there's nothing to do." One man guards his stash of pencils, pens, and rubber bands like they are precious jewels. Meanwhile, everyone counts down the minutes remaining until quitting time.

Clockwatchers is billed as a comedy, and, in many ways, it is one. But there's also a lot of drama here, and, as the film moves along, there are fewer and fewer laughs. Essentially, this is an autopsy of a lifestyle, and, while a lot about it seems funny at first, the more we get to know the characters and understand the futility of their lives, the more disheartening it becomes. With *Clockwatchers,* director Jill Sprecher has created a setting that may be bizarre to those unfamiliar with the world of office temping, but will seem on-target for anyone who has endured a foray into this lifestyle. *Clockwatchers* offers a perspective of the American corporate office that is both viciously satirical and depressingly accurate. RECOMMENDED

Cold Comfort Farm [United Kingdom, 1996]
Starring: Kate Beckinsale, Eileen Atkins, Rufus Sewell, Ivan Kaye, Ian McKellan Director: John Schlesinger Screenplay: Malcolm Bradbury, based on the novel by Stella Gibbons Running Time: 1:44 Rated: PG-13 (Sexual situations) Theatrical Aspect Ratio: 1.66:1

Using an almost-apologetically gentle satire, *Cold Comfort Farm* parodies Merchant-Ivory films and their ilk. Transpiring in the 1920s, the movie takes us to the dilapidated rural estate of Cold Comfort Farm, where recently-orphaned Flora Poste (Kate Beckinsale) has come to stay with distant relatives. In some way, the Starkadders, who inhabit Cold Comfort, owe a debt to her father, but, while no one will say what it is, they agree to give her free room and board. For her part, Flora intends to organize the untidy farm, as well as the lives of everyone who call it home.

The residents of Cold Comfort Farm are a strange lot. There's Judith Starkadder (Eileen Atkins), a middle-aged widow who continually prophesies disaster for her family. There are her sons, Seth (Rufus Sewell), who loves movies, and Reuben (Ivan Kaye), who loves farming. Judith's brother, Amos (Ian McKellan), is a fire-and-brimstone preacher. Her mother, Ada Doom (Sheila Burrell), the Cold Comfort matriarch, remains locked in her room. Also living in the house are Elfine (Maria Miles), a beautiful-but-flighty young woman who wants to marry a member of the gentry, and Adamsbreath (Freddie Jones), the family's faithful retainer.

With comic efficiency, Flora sets to work giving each member of the Starkadder clan what they want. There are no real characters here — each member of the cast plays a certain period piece type to good effect. We sympathize with the men and women of Cold Comfort Farm largely because of strong performances, not because they're written with any depth or breadth. As is often true of satire, the people don't matter as much as the situations they're placed in.

Cold Comfort Farm is not a vicious lampoon. The script cares about its characters and doesn't want to distance the audience. Some of the best satire comes near the end, while the various subplots are reaching happy conclusions. Schlesinger uses "Tara's Theme" from *Gone with the Wind* to put the hilarious punctuation on a very funny scene. This sequence, the movie's comic highlight, had me nearly doubled over with laughter. There may not be intellectual enrichment forthcoming, but there's undeniable pleasure to be gained from watching Flora bring warmth to *Cold Comfort Farm*. RECOMMENDED

Commandments [1997]
Starring: Aidan Quinn, Courteney Cox, Anthony LaPaglia Director: Daniel Taplitz Screenplay: Daniel Taplitz Running Time: 1:26 Rated: R (Profanity, sex, mature themes) Theatrical Aspect Ratio: 1.85:1

Commandments, the first major feature from writer/director Daniel Taplitz, is a satire of faith, religion, and hypocrisy. Strangely enough, it's also the most offbeat disaster movie to come along in years (note: that's "disaster movie" *not* "movie disaster"). In fact, for the price of admission, we're treated to 3 different manifestations of Mother Nature's wrath: a tornado, a violent thunderstorm (with associated lightning strike), and a hurricane.

Taplitz obviously intended this to be a black comedy, and, viewed as such, it's reasonably successful. It is also potentially offensive to anyone who considers himself (or herself) a deeply religious person. *Commandments* dares to call God "a raging psychotic" (and mean it) and postulates that the reason he allows suffering is that he's either a fraud or malevolent. A few of the theological questions posed here are ones that fundamentalists tend to sidestep or talk around because they raise disturbing possibilities. And some of the satire is as vicious as it is risky, which may alienate mainstream viewers.

The main character, Seth Warner (Aidan Quinn), was a nice, well-adjusted True Believer — until God chose him to live a '90s remake of the Book of Job. Within a short time, he lost his wife and unborn child, his home, and his job. When he demands an answer from the Almighty, he gets struck by lightning and ends up in the hospital. While convalescing there, he comes up with an audacious scheme to show his contempt for God. He's going to break every one of the Ten Commandments. When he confesses the plan to his brother-in-law, Harry (Anthony LaPaglia), it doesn't provoke much of a reaction. It seems that Harry routinely breaks 5 or 6 commandments a day without much thought. "Get back to me when you start breaking some really serious ones," he says. Meanwhile, Harry's wife, Rachel (Courteney Cox), is far more sympathetic to Seth's circumstances, and it doesn't take long before she becomes his primary target for Commandment #7 ("Thou shalt not commit adultery").

Although the script isn't a masterpiece of twists and surprises, not everything goes as expected, and the audience isn't quite as far ahead of the characters as it initially thinks. For anyone who isn't easily offended and doesn't mind forthright irreverence, *Commandments* is worth checking out — at least you haven't already seen 5 movies like it already this year. **RECOMMENDED**

The Cook, the Thief, His Wife and Her Lover
[United Kingdom/France, 1989]

Starring: Richard Bohringer, Michael Gambon, Helen Mirren, Alan Howard, Tim Roth Director: Peter Greenaway Screenplay: Peter Greenaway Running Time: 2:05 Rated: NC-17 (Sex, nudity, violence, profanity, rotting fish and meat) Theatrical Aspect Ratio: 2.35:1

If there's anything disgusting or grotesque that *The Cook, the Thief, His Wife, and Her Lover* doesn't dabble in, I'm at a loss to figure out what it is. This film, a wildly exuberant, bitingly satirical examination of excess, bad taste, and great acting, is the kind of over-the-top experience that will have timid movie-goers running (not just walking) for the exits. Taboos? If director Peter Greenaway has any, you can't tell by this film.

Roughly ⅔ of the film takes place inside the fine French restaurant, Le Hollandais. With a dungeon-like kitchen that looks like it was snatched out of Terry Gilliam's *Brazil,* this is a fantastically bizarre place to eat dinner. The chef, Richard (French actor Richard Bohringer), is a gastronomical genius who cares as much for the artistry of a meal as for its taste. Le Hollandais' owner, an uncouth rogue by the name of Albert (Michael Gambon), visits the restaurant nightly in the company of his wife, Georgina (Helen Mirren), and a flock of toadies. There, sitting in the center of Le Hollandais' dining room, at the biggest table, Albert holds court, spouting often-absurd discourses about any subject he can think of. But, while he's talking, his neglected wife catches the eye of a nearby diner (Alan Howard), and soon those two sneak away for a tryst in the Ladies' Room.

The Cook, the Thief, His Wife, and Her Lover is well-written, with dark humor and irony peppering nearly every conversation and monologue. Set design is top notch. Le Hollandais is a surreal place. This is also a movie of vivid colors: reds for the dining room, pinks for the rest rooms, and greens for the kitchen. *The Cook* is always visually interesting, even on those rare occasions when other aspects of the production aren't as arresting.

One message that Greenaway clearly conveys is the association between two of life's most obvious sensual pleasures: eating and sex. He litters this picture with the brutal and the grotesque — including murder, covering someone with excrement, and cannibalism. *The Cook* is always as visceral as it is visual, with Gambon on hand to provide acid commentary for everything (he never seems to stop talking). Then there's the ending, which contradicts the saying that revenge is a dish best served cold. In this case, it's warm, and very, very appropriate. **HIGHLY RECOMMENDED**

Cookie's Fortune [1999]

Starring: Glenn Close, Julianne Moore, Liv Tyler, Chris O'Donnell, Charles Dutton, Patricia Neal Director: Robert Altman Screenplay: Anne Rapp Running Time: 1:58 Rated: PG-13 (Sensuality, suicide) Theatrical Aspect Ratio: 1.85:1

Cookie's Fortune deserves to be appreciated on its own terms. A less-ambitious outing from veteran director Robert Altman, this movie delivers agreeable performances and a charming, amusing story that offers little in the way of substance. The movie is set in the deep South. Actually, let me amend that — it's set is a world that is a gentle caricature of the deep South, a place which is manufactured from a combination of reality and the outsider's preconceptions. As is often Altman's method, *Cookie's Fortune* was developed as an ensemble piece. The title character, played by Patricia Neal, is a Southern matriarch in her waning years. She's an odd but likable old lady who has an easy rapport with her close friend, confidante, and odd-jobs man, Willis (Charles S. Dutton). In addition to being fond of Willis, Cookie has a soft spot in her heart for Emma (Liv Tyler), the young daughter of her dim, gullible niece, Cora (Julianne Moore). Cookie also has another niece, the intolerant, image-conscious Camille (Glenn Close), who thinks of herself as the most important person in Holly Spring.

After spending some time introducing the characters and defining their relationships, *Cookie's Fortune* shifts into high gear with a change in tone. While the early portions of the film set us up for a lighthearted melodrama, Altman eventually guides his picture into the realm of farce and dark comedy. Despondent about her failing health, Cookie resolves to take her own life. When Camille finds the body, she decides to fake a burglary and murder, because "suicide is undignified." After eating Cookie's suicide note, she enlists Cora's aid in concocting a complicated cover-up that fools the local police.

The result of all this is a madcap plot that involves jailhouse trysts, paternity revelations, and all sorts of other intrigue. With a sly, clever script (by Anne Rapp) that consistently ratchets up the comic momentum and even throws in a little genuine suspense, *Cookie's Fortune* builds to a delightfully funny climax. Some of the best moments are provided by small, aside jokes, such as when one character literally gets caught with her hand in the cookie jar. And, while *Cookie's Fortune* never devolves to the level of mindless comedy offered by the many lowbrow films populating multiplex screens, this isn't intellectual humor, either. It's entirely accessible to anyone willing to invest 2 hours.
RECOMMENDED

Cradle Will Rock [1999]

Starring: Emily Watson, John Turturro, John Cusack, Joan Cusack, Hank Azaria, Angus MacFadyen, Susan Sarandon Director: Tim Robbins Screenplay: Tim Robbins Running Time: 2:15 Rated: R (Nudity, profanity, mature themes) Theatrical Aspect Ratio: 2.35:1

Cradle Will Rock is Tim Robbins' most challenging feature to date. A combination screwball comedy and period piece drama, the film makes us laugh while presenting themes that are as relevant today as they were 6 decades ago. Intertwining the stories of more than a dozen characters and using a style that variously recalls the work of Preston Sturges, Orson Welles, and Robert Altman, Robbins generates a pace that is often frantic.

Cradle Will Rock is, according to the film, (mostly) based on a true tale. Actually, it's more like 5 episodes that are thematically and, at times, narratively, linked. The primary story tells of the efforts of director Orson Welles (Angus MacFadyen), producer John Houseman (Cary Elwes), writer Marc Blitzstein (Hank Azaria), and their cast to put on the pro-Union play "The Cradle Will Rock" despite attempts by the U.S. government to close it down. Folded into this tale are the struggles of Hallie Flanagan (Cherry Jones) to keep the Dies Committee from cutting financial support to the WPA (which funded the Federal Theater program) because of alleged pro-Communist propaganda in the plays. Meanwhile, Nelson Rockerfeller (John Cusack) hires artist Diego Rivera (Ruben Blades) to paint a mural in the lobby of Rockerfeller Center, then balks when he sees the final product. Steel magnate Gray Mathers (Philip Baker Hall) flirts with Mussolini's mistress, Margherita Sarfatti (Susan Sarandon), while his flighty wife, the Countess (Vanessa Redgrave), pursues social causes. And an alcoholic ventriloquist (Bill Murray) believes that communists are infiltrating vaudeville, but his attempts to do something about them alienate him from everyone he knows.

Cradle Will Rock treads into fascinating territory with some of its meatier issues. How far does freedom of expression go? Does the government have the right to arbitrarily determine what "art" it will fund, or is that censorship? And, when a person owns a piece of art, does he or she have the right to determine when or how it is displayed, or whether it can be changed, defaced, or destroyed? None of these questions have easy answers, and *Cradle Will Rock* doesn't pretend they do, but it addresses all of them during its 135-minute running time. **RECOMMENDED**

Crocodile Dundee [Australia, 1986]

Starring: Paul Hogan, Linda Kozlowski, John Meillon, David Gulpilil, Mark Blum Director: Peter Faiman Screenplay: John Cornell, Ken Shadie, Paul Hogan Running Time: 1:33 Rated: PG-13 (Profanity, mild violence, sexual innuendo) Theatrical Aspect Ratio: 2.35:1

Crocodile Dundee is a breezy, fun affair — a trifle that is extremely pleasant to sample and leaves no bitter aftertaste. It's a fantasy that's part romantic comedy and part fish-out-of-water, and, while most of the elements are familiar in a different context, *Crocodile Dundee's* method of merging them is unconventional enough that the film seems as fresh and unsullied as the Australian bush in which the first half of the movie transpires.

The film opens with New York journalist Sue Charlton (Linda Kozlowski) hunting down the legendary Michael J. 'Crocodile' Dundee (Hogan) in the small rural Australian town of Walkabout Creek. She makes contact with Walter Reilly (the late John Meillon), the co-proprietor of "Never Never Safari Tours," who promises to send her on a 3-day, 2-night trip with Mick. Local myth states that Mick survived a one-on-one encounter with a crocodile, then, after having half his leg bitten off, he crawled back home. Sue wants to see where it happened so she can prepare a feature on Mick and his ordeal. After spending about 48 hours together in the bush, Mick and Sue have bonded, and she invites him to come back to New York with her. So, for the first time in his life, Mick leaves Australia for the wilds of Manhattan, where he encounters a stranger breed than anything found in the bush.

Crocodile Dundee is peppered with memorable moments, most of which occur during the second half, while Mick is navigating the ins-and-outs of New York City. In addition to his encounter with a mugger with a knife, he also plays the gallant gentlemen to a pair of hookers, and comes up with an infallible (if untactful) way of determining whether a woman is really a woman, or just a man dressed in drag. All the while, he and Sue have time to fall in love, which leads to the grand fairy tale ending in the subway station.

The movie works entirely because of Hogan. It's not hard to understand why American movie-goers reacted so positively to him; his Mick Dundee has a natural, unforced charm that is hard for even the best actor to artificially generate. Mick is the kind of guy all men would like to have for a buddy and all women would like to have for something a little more.

Many years after its initial release, *Crocodile Dundee* is still as fresh and enjoyable as ever. Little in the film seems dated, and Hogan's affability shines through. What the storyline lacks in ambition, it makes up for in sheer, unfettered likability.
RECOMMENDED

The Daytrippers [1996]

Starring: Hope Davis, Pat McNamara, Anne Meara, Parker Posey, Liev Schreiber, Stanley Tucci Director: Greg Mattola Screenplay: Greg Mattola Running Time: 1:28 Rated: R (Mature themes, profanity) Theatrical Aspect Ratio: 1.85:1

Pity poor Eliza (Hope Davis). On the surface, her family seems normal. She lives with her husband, Luis (Stanley Tucci), in a nice, Long Island home only a short distance from her parents' house. Under that roof are her mom, Rita (Anne Meara), dad, Jim (Pat McNamara), sister, Jo (Parker Posey), and her sister's SO, Carl (Liev Schreiber). When Eliza discovers incriminating evidence indicating that Luis could be cheating on her, she is bundled into the car by the rest of her family for a sleuthing day trip to New York City. By the time night falls, Eliza will probably wish she had stayed in bed.

The Daytrippers, from first time director Greg Mattola, starts out as a droll comedy about a group of oddball characters forced by circumstances to spend a day together, but finishes as a slightly overbearing drama about relationships in crisis. The change in tone from playful to somber, which takes place about ¾ of the way through, is jarring. The melodrama that follows, while adequate to wrap up the story, isn't nearly as effective as the offbeat comedy that persists for most of the running length.

Leaving out the final act, which includes a lot of bickering, anger, and one "shocking" revelation, *The Daytrippers* satirizes a suburban family's trip into a big city. Of course, they're there on a mission — to spy on Eliza's husband. They hang around outside the possible address of his mistress, waiting. When he finally appears and jumps in a cab, the chase is on. Unfortunately, a red light immediately intervenes, resulting in "the world's shortest car chase." Undaunted, however, Rita leaps out of the car to follow her son-in-law on foot, or, as Jo puts it, "My mom suddenly turns into Wesley Snipes."

The Daytrippers is at its best using parody to paint an incisively humorous picture of a modern American family. We see here just how dysfunctional the typical nuclear family can be, and that "family values" aren't always the solution. Even though *The Daytrippers* is played primarily for laughs, there's a lot of truth lurking beneath the comic exterior. The message comes across to anyone who wants to listen:

preserving the family is about fostering communication, not mouthing platitudes. Unfortunately, that's something that the film makers understand far better than most politicians. RECOMMENDED

Deconstructing Harry [1997]
Starring: Woody Allen, Judy Davis, Elizabeth Shue, Kirstie Alley, Bob Balaban Director: Woody Allen Screenplay: Woody Allen Running Time: 1:38 Rated: R (Profanity, mature themes, sexual situations, nudity) Theatrical Aspect Ratio: 1.85:1

How much of Woody Allen is there in Harry Block? This is undoubtedly one of the questions likely to be foremost in any viewer's mind after watching Allen's 1997 feature, *Deconstructing Harry*. It's also the question most often asked of the director in interviews about the film. Allen has been understandably evasive, stating repeatedly that, while there may be some similarities between Harry and himself, the movie is a work of fiction and Harry is nothing more than a character.

So who is Harry Block? He is, by some accounts, one of the most unpleasant men alive. Since he's played by Woody Allen, he's also an insecure and self-absorbed individual, as well. Professionally, he's a world-famous, bestselling author who writes thinly-veiled autobiographical tales about his relationships with his 3 ex-wives. Personally, he's a wretch — a pill-popping, alcoholic lout who has few friends and can't stay faithful to one woman. Ostensibly, the film is about Harry's trip to upstate New York, where a college that expelled him as an undergraduate now wants to honor him as a distinguished alumnist. At the same time, he's looking to overcome a severe case of writer's block. Along with Cookie (Hazelle Goodman), a hooker he hired for the day; Richard (Bob Balaban), a friend with a bad heart; and Hilly (Eric Lloyd), his son, Harry heads north.

Allen's script isn't linear, but it isn't difficult to piece together. The intent is to amuse, not to confuse. However, aside from piquing the viewer's curiosity about how much of Allen is in Harry, there's not a whole lot of depth to *Deconstructing Harry*. It's a movie of moments, some of which are side-splittingly funny. Arguably, this is the most uproarious comedy that Allen has ever done. The dialogue is almost always as brilliant and witty as it is profane. Then there's Robin Williams, who, in a cameo, has never been so delightfully out of focus.

Deconstructing Harry is an uneven piece of work, but the high level of comedy covers up many of the rough spots. We may never know how much of this film is pure fiction and how much is self-analysis, but one thing is for sure — once the laughter has subsided and the end credits have rolled, audience members will begin deconstructing Woody. RECOMMENDED

Double Happiness [Canada, 1994]
Starring: Sandra Oh, Alannah Ong, Stephen Chang Director: Mina Shum Screenplay: Mina Shum Running Time: 1:40 Rated: No MPAA Rating (Mature themes, sexual situations, profanity) Theatrical Aspect Ratio: 1.85:1

Mina Shum's debut feature, *Double Happiness*, chronicles the tribulations of one Chinese-Canadian young woman as she struggles to develop her own identity in a family where her parents are bound by traditions she views as outdated and short-sighted.

The comic tone of *Double Happiness* has a unique flavor. Shum is clearly interested in making her points through laughter rather than tears. The film opens by introducing us to the protagonist, an unmarried 20-ish woman named Jade, as she delivers a short monologue about what it was like being raised in her family. "I grew up wondering why we couldn't be the Brady Bunch," she confides, later adding that the Bradys never needed subtitles. During the course of the film, Jade isn't the only one who speaks directly to the camera. Among others, her grandmother, father, and a *fen shwei* master (a sort of soothsayer) are all given similar opportunities.

Jade, as played by actress Sandra Oh, is a wonderful character: likable, bubbly, optimistic, funny, and — most important of all — believable. She's the kind of person worth building a movie around, and that's exactly what has happened here. There are several subplots going on, but this is ultimately Jade's story

Like many of the best comedies, this one is funny because it deals with the realities of life and the human condition — circumstances and situations that everyone can relate to, regardless of ethnic heritage. *Double Happiness* is often as insightful as the most serious motion pictures, only it chooses a lighter tone to impart its message. There are moments of silliness here, as well, but they're not so extreme or out-of-place that they confuse the movie's primary itent.

What Mina Shum has achieved here is impressive for a first-time film maker. *Double Happiness* has the look and feel of a seasoned director's work. It uses techniques rarely embraced by novices (such as unusual camera angles to advance the narrative), and the script is filmed with a delicacy of touch that makes the humor all the more effective. This is truly a wonderful motion picture and an unexpected find. **HIGHLY RECOMMENDED**

Election [1999]

Starring: Matthew Broderick, Reese Witherspoon, Chris Klein, Jessica Campbell Director: Alexander Payne Screenplay: Alexander Payne & Jim Taylor Running Time: 1:44 Rated: R (Sexual themes & situations, profanity) Theatrical Aspect Ratio: 2.35:1

Reese Witherspoon plays Tracy Flick, a model student who is running unopposed for the highest student office. She's an overachiever's overachiever. Witherspoon, who has shown her range in a variety of roles, presents Tracy as all seemingly-perfect students should be presented: superficially good-natured and perky, but a real bitch underneath. Teacher Jim McAllister (Matthew Broderick) doesn't like Tracy (she was the "victim" in a sex scandal that led to the firing of his best friend), so he decides to encourage another student to run against her in the election. His choice is Paul Metzler (Chris Klein), one of the best-loved and most sincere students at Carver. He's also a football star with a broken leg, and his intelligence is on the level expected from a jock. Paul is popular, but he runs an inept campaign. His idea of addressing the student body is reading a speech as a single run-on sentence, delivered in a monotone. There's also a surprise entrant into the election: Paul's sister, Tammy (Jessica Campbell), an angry lesbian whose view of student elections is that they're "pathetic charades." The race turns into a tight tug-of-war with Paul remaining completely honest, Tammy seeming not to care, and Tracy resorting to unethical stunts. Meanwhile, McAlliester, unable to remain a spectator, begins to harbor sexual fantasies about Tracy even as he works to orchestrate her downfall.

Election is the sharpest satire of any teen movie made in years. Like the best lampoons, it attacks by exaggerating reality ever-so-slightly and targeting a broad range of subjects. There are no cheap shots and no grotesquely distorted performances. Those who have been involved in school elections will recognize the accuracy of director Alexander Payne's portrayal. Actually, it's not just school elections that Payne is taking a swipe at, but elections in general.

Election doesn't pull any punches. Its frank view of sexuality is in stark contrast with the cute or crude versions presented in most teen stories. The film is frequently funny, but, as with all dark comedies, our laughter isn't always comfortable. The use of multiple narrators allows the viewer to understand the different perspectives. The ending is laced with the perfect touch of irony. *Election* may not present the most flattering portrait of today's teenager, but there's a lot of truth in the picture it paints. **HIGHLY RECOMMENDED**

Faithful [1996]

Starring: Cher, Chazz Palminteri, Ryan O'Neal Director: Paul Mazursky Screenplay: Chazz Palminteri Running Time: 1:31 Rated: R (Profanity, sexual situations, violence) Theatrical Aspect Ratio: 1.85:1

Faithful is less of a black comedy than a disquieting drama laced with wit. Adapted by Chazz Palminteri from his off-Broadway play, the film, as directed by Paul Mazursky (*Down and Out in Beverly Hills*), unfolds like a 3-act theatrical piece: lots of dialogue and not much action. Only 3 actors have significant roles, and there are a limited number of sets.

Cher plays Maggie, an unhappy housewife who, on the 20th anniversary of her marriage to an unfaithful husband, Jack (Ryan O'Neal), decides to kill herself. But, before she can down the bottle of pills, she receives a visitor. Tony (Chazz Palminteri), a trash-talking, borderline-manic mafia hit man ostensibly hired by Jack, breaks into her palatial home, ties her up, then tells her he's going to murder her. Unfortunately, he has to wait for Jack's go-ahead signal, and, to pass the time, he and Maggie converse about everything from the question of what really constitutes sex to why couples stay together when a marriage is dead.

At one point, Tony confesses that he has "problems like everyone else." In fact, however, his trauma runs much deeper than the average person's. Both he and Maggie are in therapy (in fact, Tony calls his shrink from the scene of the hit), and Jack should probably join them. These are 3 very disturbed individuals, none of whom is satisfied with the status quo. Maggie sees her marriage, and, by extension, her life, as a failure. Tony is saddled by guilt at the part he played in his beloved sister's death. And Jack is looking for a way to pacify his young, impatient girlfriend. For over an hour, *Faithful* allows this trio of characters to work through their problems. They argue, shout, plead, cajole, and, at long last, understand and accept.

At times, *Faithful* is amusing, although most of the humor is of the gallows variety (such as Tony's objection to Maggie's having a last cigarette because of the danger to him from secondary smoke). More importantly, the unique perspectives created by the unusual situation allow the film to offer insight into the issues of fidelity, love, and marriage. Although Palminteri doesn't write with the verve of David

Mamet, he employs enough crisp dialogue in the service of an interesting premise to keep the audience involved for most of the 90-minute running length. **RECOMMENDED**

Fierce Creatures [1997]
Starring: John Cleese, Jamie Lee Curtis, Kevin Kline, Michael Palin
Directors: Robert M. Young and Fred Schepisi Screenplay: John Cleese
& Iain Johnstone Running Time: 1:33 Rated: PG-13 (Profanity, sexual
situations) Theatrical Aspect Ratio: 2.35:1

After the unexpected success of 1988's *A Fish Called Wanda*, John Cleese began planning a movie that would reunite the entire cast. After flirting with the concept of a direct sequel, he decided instead to invent new characters for the actors to play. Now, 8 years later, Cleese's idea has finally reached screens, and, while it's not quite as bold, funny, or endearing as *Wanda*, it's still good for numerous hearty laughs, which is more than can be said for most comedies these days.

Cleese's script (co-written with Iain Johnstone) reads like a series of skits loosely connected by a flimsy storyline. The chief pleasure here is that several of the individual sketches are gut-bustingly funny. One of Cleese's fortes has always been humor based on mistaken assumptions, and *Fierce Creatures* features quite a lot of these. There's also enough crude (but still effective) sexual innuendo that an "R" rating wouldn't have been out of the question (although the MPAA granted a "PG-13"). Only the flatulence bits don't really work.

The rather convoluted storyline starts in Atlanta, where Willa Weston (Jamie Lee Curtis) arrives for work in her new post with Octopus Inc. to find out that multi-billionaire Rod McCain (Kevin Kline) has changed her job description. Now, along with his bumbling son, Vince (Kline again), she's supposed to go to England to take over management of the Marwood Zoo, which has to boost its profits by 20% or face closure. Meanwhile, the current zoo manager, Rollo Lee (John Cleese), has decided that the best way to increase revenue is to promote violence ("Sylvester Stallone did not get where he is today by playing in Jane Austen," he says). As a result, only fierce creatures are to be retained in captivity. Much to the consternation of the various animal keepers (Michael Palin, Cynthia Cleese, Ronnie Corbett, ex-Bond girl Carey Lowell), Lee decides that all the tame, cuddly animals must be eliminated — one way or the other.

Even when *Fierce Creatures* doesn't have you doubled over with laughter, it's still amusing. There are plenty of moments that, while not worth laughing aloud at, are capable of bringing a smile to the face. This isn't a great movie — the comedy is uneven and the connecting storyline is weak — but it's still a lot of fun, and I welcome any film that keeps me entertained for nearly the entire running length. **RECOMMENDED**

A Fish Called Wanda [1988]
Starring: John Cleese, Jamie Lee Curtis, Kevin Kline, Michael Palin
Director: Charles Crichton Screenplay: John Cleese Running Time: 1:48
Rated: R (Profanity, sexual situations, brief nudity, violence) Theatrical
Aspect Ratio: 1.85:1

A Fish Called Wanda represents the high point of John Cleese's motion picture career. The film, which sprang from his pen and was directed by Charles Crichton, not only highlights Cleese's comic aptitude, but also that of co-stars Michael Palin, Jamie Lee Curtis, and Kevin Kline (who won a Best Supporting Actor Oscar for the part). The script contains enough hilarious moments to allow each member of the cast to have a chance to shine while the audience is kept in stitches.

The story centers around a quartet of jewelry store robbers. George (Tom Georgeson) is the ringleader, the man who has masterminded the theft. He is assisted by his stuttering, animal-loving friend, Ken (Michael Palin), and his girlfriend, Wanda (Jamie Lee Curtis). But Wanda wants the loot all to herself, and, to aid her in getting it away from George, she brings her psychotic, Nietzche-reading lover, Otto (Kevin Kline), into the gang. After the heist is successfully completed, Wanda and Otto place an anonymous call to the cops, and George is arrested. But, before he's hauled off to prison, he hides the jewels where Wanda and Otto can't find them.

In order to reduce his sentence if he's found guilty, George hints that he might be willing to turn over the location of the jewels to his barrister, Archie Leach (Cleese). As a result, the next step in Wanda's plan is to seduce Archie, a mild-mannered lawyer looking for a little romance and excitement. Soon, he's embroiled in the hilarious caper, and, as the situation grows progressively more convoluted, he learns that stolen jewels can make for very strange bedfellows.

Nothing is sacred to Cleese, who flouts every possible definition of political correctness by satirizing homosexuals, the British, the Americans, and stutterers. And, just to prove that he's got nothing to hide, Cleese does one of the most side-splitting stripteases ever to appear on screen. It's not erotic, but what happens immediately afterwards will have you doubled over with laughter. Despite the non-stop zaniness, Cleese manages to fashion his screen personae into a likable hero. We quickly come to sympathize with Archie, an appealing loser who's finally getting a chance to break out of the constrictive shell that has held him back all his life.

A Fish Called Wanda is one of the best-constructed, funniest, and most clever comedies to grace motion picture screens in recent years. It's outrageous, offensive, and even a little sick — and all the more enjoyable because of it. John Cleese has spent his entire career rejecting conventional comedy, and, on this occasion, there's no denying that he has hit paydirt. **MUST SEE**

Flirting with Disaster [1996]

Starring: Ben Stiller, Patricia Arquette, Tea Leoni, Mary Tyler Moore, George Segal, Alan Alda, Lily Tomlin Director: David O. Russell Screenplay: David O. Russell Running Time: 1:32 Rated: R (Sex, profanity, mature themes) Theatrical Aspect Ratio: 1.85:1

Ben Stiller's neurotic Mel Copland is going through a mid-life crisis long before mid-life. A control freak no longer in control, Mel, who was adopted as a baby, is on a quest for his biological parents. In fact, he's so hung up on the issue of his "true identity" that he hasn't been able to name his 4-month old son. Mel's long-suffering wife, Nancy (Patricia Arquette), is trying to be supportive, but, as Mel's obsession deepens, it becomes more difficult. Finally, one day, the adoption agency locates Mel's mother: a middle-aged woman living in San Diego. With Tina Kalb (Tia Leoni), a leggy counselor-in-training from the agency, in tow, Mel and Nancy head west. And that's where the disasters, which start with a mistaken identity and end with a flight across the border into Mexico, begin. Before it's all over, Mel will have become acquainted with 4 parents, 2 gay federal officers, and a brother who tries to send him on a bad acid trip. All the while, he'll be trying to figure out who he is, whether he wants Tina or Nancy, and why he bothered searching for his roots in the first place.

Director David O. Russell takes the traditional road picture and does some really strange things with it. With a view of middle America that David Lynch would applaud, Russell peels back the layers of normalcy to reveal the twisted and absurd things that go on underneath. However, where Lynch makes his case through violence and mysticism, Russell uses outrageous humor and parody. The results are no less telling, however.

Each new port of call offers a surprise. If it's not a false lead, it likely involves some time in handcuffs. Russell delights in stringing us along with Mel as his search becomes increasingly more surreal — he is trapped by circumstances beyond his control. But if there's one lesson he learns, it's that sometimes it's better to appreciate what you have instead of yearning for what you don't. To be sure, Mel grows from his experience, but if he had it to do over again, he'd probably stay home.

Russell has paced his film perfectly, gradually building from the relatively normal to the extremely strange, and heightening the humor with each new twist. *Flirting with Disaster* has its tongue firmly planted in its cheek the entire way; there's no opportunity for serious introspection. By the time the ninety-minute film has expired, you'll be glad you joined Mel and company on this hilariously eccentric journey. **HIGHLY RECOMMENDED**

Four Weddings and a Funeral [United Kingdom, 1994]

Starring: Hugh Grant, Andie MacDowell, Kristin Scott Thomas, Simon Callow, John Hannah Director: Mike Newell Screenplay: Richard Curtis Running Time: 1:57 Rated: R (Language, sexual situations, mature themes) Theatrical Aspect Ratio: 1.66:1

The simplest and most honest expression of praise that I can offer Mike Newell's movie is that it represents 2 hours of solid movie magic. *Four Weddings and a Funeral* possesses the rare ability to make an audience laugh (and laugh hard) and cry, without ever seeming manipulative or going hopelessly over-the-top.

Charles (Hugh Grant), now in his 4th decade of life, is a "serial monogamist" — someone who moves from girlfriend to girlfriend without ever falling in love. His friends have started down the matrimonial road, but not Charles. Thoughts of spending the rest of his life with someone never enter his head, until one day at a wedding when he encounters Carrie (Andie MacDowell), an American fashion editor. And, although the two enjoy a brief tryst at an inn, Charles' typical British reticence kicks in, and Carrie is on her way back to America before he realizes he should have said something.

Four Weddings and a Funeral is about, well, 4 weddings and a funeral (actually, if you want to be picky, it's about 3 weddings, a funeral, and another wedding). While the central story of this charming motion picture is fairly common romantic comedy fare, it is framed by a plot filled with little twists and turns, lots of laughs, and a frothy, intoxicating atmosphere.

Four Weddings and a Funeral is a modern comedy with a very traditional theme. It blends good breeding and bad language; laughter and tears; and marriage and friendship into a thoroughly enjoyable whole. Mike Newell knows what his viewers want, but appreciates them enough not to give it in a predictable or obvious manner — and that is the greatest pleasure of all in watching this movie. HIGHLY RECOMMENDED

Free Enterprise [1998]

Starring: Rafer Weigel, Eric McCormack, Audie England, William Shatner Director: Robert Meyer Burnett Screenplay: Mark A. Altman & Robert Meyer Burnett Running Time: 1:56 Rated: R (Profanity, sex, nudity) Theatrical Aspect Ratio: 1.85:1

The *Free Enterprise* version of William Shatner is probably very little like the real man. But it plays nicely off the image that the public has developed of the actor whose name will forever be linked with that of his most famous TV character, James T. Kirk. *Free Enterprise*'s Shatner seems like a real man who has lost touch with reality. His dream is to put on a musical version of Shakespeare's *Julius Caesar* with himself in all of the male roles.

Free Enterprise isn't really about Shatner, which is a shame in some ways, because he's the most interesting character to cross the screen. Instead, the focus is on would-be filmmakers Robert (Rafer Weigel) and Mark (Eric McCormack), two *Star Trek*, comic book, and science fiction fans who haven't outgrown what most people would consider to be a teenage addiction. Emotionally, they're in a state of severe arrested development. Mark is anal and Robert is a womanizer. It's not surprising that these two are the best of pals — both of them believe that the answers to all of life's questions can be found in one of the original *Star Trek* series' episodes. And, as children, they both had Captain Kirk/William Shatner as an imaginary friend.

Two events occur to change Robert and Mark's lives. The first is that, while browsing through a bookstore, they encounter their idol, Shatner, leafing through a porn magazine. The second, and perhaps more remarkable, occurrence is that Robert falls in love. He meets the object of his affection, Claire (Audie England), in a comic book store. For him, she's the perfect mate — she has the face and body of a model and a passion for comics and science fiction to match his own.

When compared to other entries from the recent crop of new filmmakers crafting movies about their lives, *Free Enterprise* stands out as one of the most entertaining and least pretentious efforts. And, because of the deluge of often-obscure references, the movie is a must-see for anyone who loves, or has ever loved, *Star Trek*. The rest of the movie-going world will see this as a genial, amusing comedy with surprisingly broad-based appeal. *Free Enterprise* never received a significant theatrical distribution. Now, on video, it has a chance to find its audience. RECOMMENDED

The Great White Hype [1996]

Starring: Samuel L. Jackson, Jeff Goldblum, Damon Wayans, Peter Berg, Jon Lovitz, Corbin Bernsen Director: Reginald Hudlin Screenplay: Tony Hendra & Ron Shelton Running Time: 1:30 Rated: R (Profanity, violence) Theatrical Aspect Ratio: 1.85:1

The Great White Hype takes the boxing industry and rips it open, displaying the rotting, putrid innards for all to see. There are times when this movie is so vicious that it ceases to be funny. While *The Great White Hype* has its share of comical, occasionally-hilarious moments, don't expect a non-stop laughfest on par with *This Is Spinal Tap*.

James "the Grim Reaper" Roper (Damon Wayans) is the most devastating heavyweight champion since Mike Tyson. With his 38-0 record, he's a force to be reckoned with. Or is he? Is Roper undefeated because he's so good, or because his flamboyant, publicity-loving manager, Reverend Fred Sultan (Samuel L. Jackson), only lets him fight stiffs?

The pay-per-view revenue for Roper's last fight is down — way down. The money isn't rolling in the way it used to, and Sultan knows the reason. People need a white hero — someone with a "clean-cut," "all-American" image. And, Sultan adds, if he doesn't exist, "I'll create him." When one of Sultan's assistants uncovers the name of Terry Conklin (Peter Berg), the only man ever to knock out Roper (albeit in an amateur bout more than 10 years ago), Sultan has his man. With his entourage in tow, the promoter pays a visit to Cleveland, where Conklin is acting as lead singer for a bad heavy metal band. After making one $10 million offer to the ex-Golden Glove Champ, Sultan has his "great white hope" — Irish Terry Conklin (who's not Irish), defender of the homeless (he gives large donations to that cause) and challenger for the heavyweight championship.

Ably directed by Reginald Hudlin (*Boomerang*), *The Great White Hype* never lets up with its pummeling of the boxing industry and its image-obsessed attitudes. The film also presents a timely message about how racial divisiveness can be exploited in sports (especially boxing) to bring in big bucks. Shelton and Tony Hendra's script sparkles with nasty, incisive wit — their pens were sharpened to finely-honed points before they began this skewering.

The Great White Hype is still the kind of first-rate satire that would make Jonathan Swift proud. By the time this hyper-energetic, unapologetically politically incorrect motion picture draws to a close, boxing has been dealt a knock-out punch. **RECOMMENDED**

Gridlock'd [1997]

Starring: Tim Roth, Tupac Shakur, Thandie Newton, Vondie Curtis Hall, Bokeem Woodbine Director: Vondie Curtis Hall Screenplay: Vondie Curtis Hall Running Time: 1:31 Rated: R (Profanity, violence, drug use, nudity) Theatrical Aspect Ratio: 1.85:1

Gridlock'd is about people caught in one of life's most absurd traffic jams, and the lengths that they'll go to in order to get moving again. It's a darkly humorous, vicious satire, and, like all the best satires, it works because so much of what transpires on screen not only could happen, but does happen — every day in every major urban area across the country. First time writer/director Vondie Curtis Hall sees the comedy in the situation and uses it to deliver a blistering attack on the social system and its attendant bureaucracy.

Spoon (Tupac Shakur) and Stretch (Tim Roth) are a '90s odd couple. Spoon is a mature, even-tempered black man; Stretch is a childish, borderline-manic white guy. Yet, even though their personalities are 180 degrees apart, they're as close as brothers. They work together, live together, get high together, and, when they decide to free themselves from drugs, they try to kick the habit together.

The occasion for this momentous decision is an overdose by Cookie (Thandie Newton), Spoon's lover and the third member of their performance art group. While she lies in a coma at a nearby hospital, Spoon and Stretch come to grips with the precariousness of their lives. "I don't want to go out like that," laments Spoon (his words eerie in retrospect, considering the fate of the actor speaking them), "Lately, I've been feeling like my luck's running out." Getting into a detox program, however, proves to be next-to-impossible. Spoon and Stretch spend one long day racing from social service locale to locale, taking blood tests, filling out forms, waiting on lines, and being chased by both cops and drug dealers — all in a hopeless attempt to get a little help to "kick it."

Gridlock'd is refreshing because it's different. The subject matter isn't new, but the approach and tone are. For Vondie Curtis Hall, this is the promising beginning of what will hopefully be a long and fulfilling career. For Tim Roth, it's another fine performance to add to his ever-growing resume. And for Tupac Shakur, who displays genuine talent here, it's a fitting epitaph. Hopefully, *Gridlock'd* won't get lost in the traffic jam of low-quality, mid-winter releases that surround it. **RECOMMENDED**

Grosse Fatigue (Dead Tired) [France, 1994]

Starring: Michel Blanc, Carole Bouquet, Philippe Noiret Director: Michel Blanc Screenplay: Michel Blanc Running Time: 1:24 Rated: R (Double entendres, profanity) Theatrical Aspect Ratio: 1.85:1 In French with subtitles

There are two types of satire: high concept and low concept. Both lampoon specific targets, but while the latter does so with more concern for belly-laughs than subtle, thought-provoking amusement, the former is often characterized by wit and intelligence. *Grosse Fatigue*, a quirky, unique product of French writer/director/actor Michel Blanc, is a high concept farce. During most showings of this film, smiles and chuckles — not uncontrollable laughter — will be in abundance.

One common disclaimer reads: "The names have been changed to protect the innocent." In *Grosse Fatigue*, names are precisely what have *not* been altered. The personalities portrayed by Blanc, Carole Bouquet, and Philippe Noiret retain the actors' real names. In *Grosse Fatigue* as in life, Blanc is a famous French movie maker/actor. Bouquet is a glamorous actress and Noiret is the suave, cultured man who graced international screens in *Cinema Paradiso* and *The Postman*. Only a special sort of director would dare take such obvious jabs at his own celebrity status, and part of *Grosse Fatigue*'s appeal is that this film plays off egos rather than pandering to them.

The premise, which demands a fair (but not unreasonable) level of suspended disbelief, postulates what might happen if a famous person had a double, and that double chose to masquerade as the star. In this case, the celebrity victim is Blanc, and the man cashing in on the resemblance is a nobody named Patrick Olivier (also played by Blanc). The impostor is so good that Blanc's relatives and friends (like Carole Bouquet) doubt the identity of the true man. By the time Blanc figures out what's going on and decides to take action, it may already be too late.

In the way it toys with reality and fantasy, *Grosse Fatigue* is a fascinating exploration of life as seen through the eyes of a perceptive and humorous director. Blanc never allows his film to degenerate into

a series of pointless jokes, but the serious side is also kept at bay. *Grosse Fatigue* is smart in both script and approach, and this makes for a lighthearted 90 minutes where turning off the thinking portions of the brain is not a prerequisite to enjoyment.
HIGHLY RECOMMENDED

Groundhog Day [1993]

Starring: Bill Murray, Andie MacDowell, Chris Elliot Director: Harold Ramis Screenplay: Danny Rubin & Harold Ramis Running Time: 1:41 Rated: PG (Little offensive) Theatrical Aspect Ratio: 1.85:1

The date is February 2 and the place is Punxsutawney, Pennsylvania. Pittsburgh weatherman Phil Connors (Bill Murray), on hand to cover the Groundhog Day ceremony, is having one of the most unpleasant experiences of his life. It's one of those days when Murphy's Law seems to be in full effect. But Phil soon discovers that things are worse than they first seemed, because for him, and him alone, time has stopped. Now, he's trapped in a bizarre time loop that forces him to re-live Groundhog Day over and over, with no hope of reprieve or release, and no way of explaining the situation to anyone else since he's the only one who realizes what's happening.

It's déjà vu gone mad. *Groundhog Day* is one of the most original comedies to grace the screen in months. With as much repetition as there is, it would be easy for the film to get bogged down. Solid directing, combined with judicious editing, eliminate the problem. The only time we see a scene repeated is when there's something new added, and even then we are re-shown little more than what's necessary for the effect.

The humor is of a higher caliber than that found in most so-called comedies. *Groundhog Day* finds its humor in situations and characters. Making use of Bill Murray's talent as a comedian, the film encourages him to play off of the more serious Andie MacDowell. While the chemistry between them isn't smouldering, they work well together. Their characters' romance is credible because it's low-key.

Groundhog Day isn't a science fiction or fantasy film, so it's not interested in answering the technical questions of how the time loop came about, or what might happen if Phil stayed up all night. Instead, it presents the situation to the audience on a take-it-or-leave-it basis. I'll wager that there are few who will choose the latter option.

With all of the formula-driven, painfully unfunny comedies available today, it's a pleasure to uncover something as unique as *Groundhog Day*, especially in the month of February, which isn't known for strong releases. This movie has all the qualities necessary to be a crowd-pleaser: likable characters, charismatic performers, a strong, capably-executed premise, and lots of laughs. **HIGHLY RECOMMENDED**

Grumpy Old Men [1993]

Starring: Jack Lemmon, Walter Matthau, Ann-Margret, Burgess Meredith, Ossie Davis Director: Donald Petrie Screenplay: Mark Steven Johnson Running Time: 1:43 Rated: PG-13 (Language, mature themes) Theatrical Aspect Ratio: 1.85:1

John Gustafson (Jack Lemmon) and Max Goldman (Walter Matthau) have been neighbors since they were kids, and the feud between them has lasted almost as long. A state of uneasy coexistence is in place, with namecalling and practical jokes being the most heated their exchanges get. Their rivalry turns more serious, however, when both of them become interested in the new neighbor across the street. Ariel (Ann-Margret) is vivacious, beautiful, and alluring, and both John and Max are smitten.

While not without its problems (some of which are readily apparent), *Grumpy Old Men* works more often than not. It's an example of a frothy, good-natured holiday picture that adults can relax and enjoy. As a comedy, the movie contains enough fresh humor to keep the laughs coming. Dramatically, however, it's rather feeble. There are formulas at work here, and anyone admitting to be surprised by the "plot twists" should hang his or her head in shame.

Lemmon and Matthau are perfect for their roles as lifelong sparring partners. Of course, these two are no strangers to this sort of interplay, having done it several times before, most memorably in *The Odd Couple*. This is an example of perfect casting, as is the choice of Burgess Meredith as the tough-talking, dirty-minded patriarch of the Gustafson family.

Fortunately, drama always plays second fiddle to comedy, and this is a consistently funny motion picture. There's everything from slapstick to puns, with a lot of clever references and gags. Witness Jack Lemmon and Walter Matthau's "performances" to the song "I'm too Sexy," Lemmon's send-up of Macaulay Culkin's aftershave scream from *Home Alone*, and the little dance number Lemmon does in his underwear. The end credit outtakes are perhaps the comic highlight of the movie. Most attending a showing of *Grumpy Old Men* will leave the theater with a smile,

and that's basically what the movie is aiming for.
RECOMMENDED

Happy, Texas [1999]

Starring: Jeremy Northam, Steve Zahn, William H. Macy, Ally Walker, Illeana Douglas Director: Mark Illsley Screenplay: Ed Stone, Mark Illsley & Phil Reeves Running Time: 1:44 Rated: PG-13 (Profanity, sexual content, violence, mature themes) Theatrical Aspect Ratio: 1.85:1

Happy, Texas doesn't exactly shatter expectations by breaking new cinematic ground, but that's part of its charm. We're on a road that has to conclude with a happy ending; the fun is in the trip, not at the destination. A pair of escaped cons, the laconic Harry Sawyer (Jeremy Northam) and the dimmest bulb in the pack, Wayne Wayne Wayne Jr. (Steve Zahn), are looking for a place to lie low while the police are scouring the countryside for them. When they arrive in the small hamlet of Happy, Texas ("the town without a frown") in a stolen Winnebago, they are mistaken for the pair of gay beauty pageant consultants who have been hired to help the little girls of Happy win the 18th annual "Little Miss Fresh Squeezed" talent contest. Since this kind of impersonation seems like a great way to steer clear of the cops, the pair decides to play along with the town's enthusiastic residents. So, while Wayne, under the watchful eye of the local school teacher, Ms. Schaefer (Illeana Douglas), ineptly tries to instruct his charges on the finer points of winning a pageant, Harry plans a robbery of the local bank. But there are two complications — he is falling for the bank president, Josephine McLintock (Ally Walker), while being courted by the sheriff, Chappy Dent (William H. Macy), who thinks he finally has found a soul mate.

Jeremy Northam, as suave as always even out of period costume, gives a low-key rendering of Harry — he's the prototypical "likable crook" because, deep inside, he has a heart of gold, no matter how much he likes to pretend otherwise. With Northam playing the straight man, that leaves it up to Steve Zahn to generate most of the laughs — a task for which he is eminently suited. The only actor who stands a chance of upstaging Zahn is William H. Macy. For most of the film, Macy's reserved sheriff is content to remain in the background, but, as events shift into high gear, he emerges from the closet to add a dash of pathos to the proceedings.

If there's a down side to *Happy, Texas,* it's that the ending doesn't deliver the expected comic punch line — instead, it gets stuck incorporating a little too much action. That's really a minor quibble, however. The real pleasure of this film isn't that many of the jokes work, but that Illsley's affection for the characters carries over to the audience. **RECOMMENDED**

High Fidelity [2000]

Starring: John Cusack, Jack Black, Lisa Bonet, Joan Cusack, Iben Hjejle Director: Stephen Frears Screenplay: D.V. DeVincentis, Steve Pink, John Cusack & Scott Michael Rosenberg, based on the novel by Nich Hornby Running Time: 1:50 Rated: R (Profanity, sex) Theatrical Aspect Ratio: 1.85:1

Based on the novel by Nick Hornby, *High Fidelity* is a quirky comedy that explores the romantic misfortunes of the main character. Rob is the owner of "Championship Vinyl," a music store that specializes in LP's. Along with his assistants, belligerent Barry (Jack Black) and meek Dick (Todd Louiso), Rob does his best to keep his shop afloat, even though it's barely making enough for him to keep him off welfare. Rob is a neurotic, and he obsesses over his lackluster romantic history. Fond of making Top 5 lists, Rob has recently composed his "Top 5 all-time breakups," and he re-lives each of them in his head, from a high-school sweetheart he kissed under the bleachers to the beautiful Charlie (Catherine Zeta-Jones), who is even more self-absorbed than Rob. His latest loss, however, has hit Rob the hardest, because he belatedly realized she may have been "the one." Her name is Laura (Iben Hjejle), and, after growing weary of Rob's general listlessness and unwillingness to commit, she decided to leave him and move in with a former neighbor, new wave guru Ian (Tim Robbins).

As far as the plot goes, there really isn't one — *High Fidelity* is a movie driven by characters (Rob's in particular) and situational comedy. A significant portion of the film takes place in the record store, and it's there that *High Fidelity* shines, with Barry verbally abusing ignorant customers and Dick shyly making advances towards a girl (Sara Gilbert) he finds attractive. For the most part, Rob stays in the background during these scenes, watching bemusedly as his two cohorts conduct business. He comments that he can't fire them because he "hired [them] for 3 days a week, then they started showing up every morning — that was 4 years ago."

There's no deep meaning to *High Fidelity,* although it occasionally toys with the importance of pop music to a person's psychological development. At one point early in the film, Rob muses, "Did I listen to pop music because I was miserable, or was I miserable because I listened to pop music?" There's more than a hint of Woody Allen in the project, from the neuroses of the main character to the *Annie Hall*-type dissection of a failed romance, but without the stigma that some movie-goers attach to anything Allen does. Because of its quirky characters, smart dialogue, and occasional bursts of penetrating humor, *High Fidelity* stands out as a "small" motion picture that deserves wide exposure. **RECOMMENDED**

House of Angels [Sweden/Norway/Denmark, 1992]

Starring: Helena Bergstrom, Rikard Wolff, Sven Wollter, Viveka Seldahl Director: Colin Nutley Screenplay: Susan Falck Running Time: 1:59 Rated: R (Language, nudity) Theatrical Aspect Ratio: 1.85:1 In Swedish with subtitles

House of Angels begins in a small farming community somewhere in Sweden, where a local citizen is about to meet his death in an automobile accident. At his funeral, his sole surviving relative arrives — a long-lost granddaughter named Fanny (Helena Bergstrom). She is accompanied by a gay companion, Zac (Rikard Wolff), who's the perfect picture of a biker: leather jacket, sunglasses, and five o'clock shadow. The pair are from Berlin, and have big city customs that don't fit in the small town setting, so when they move into the dead man's house, the residents of the village become uneasy. The women are afraid that Fanny will steal away their menfolk, and the men are uncertain what to make of their new neighbor. Only one person has a clear goal. Axel (Sven Wollter), the local bigshot, wants Fanny out so he can buy up her land.

Things aren't always what they seem — a point that *House of Angels* is adept at illustrating. Fanny and Zac look like the wild, drug-addicted deviants that the townspeople believe them to be, but few are willing to get to know the pair well enough to test their preconceived convictions. Once the label is affixed, nothing Fanny can do will remove it. Eventually, she decides to give people what they expect, but this leads to her own disillusionment.

The small town/big city conflict is played out with conformity as the principal weapon. Too many of the villagers don't want something new or different in their midst, and so are threatened by what Fanny and Zac represent. Rather than concede the potential value in diversity, they attempt to squash it.

House of Angels is an excellent example of how lighthearted film can be used to probe deeper, more intense issues without becoming preachy or overbearing. There's a priest in this film, but the movie isn't given to sermonizing. The picture's sense of fun rarely flags, nor does the inner core of drama that underlies each scene. *House of Angels* has a lot to say, and the best thing is that the audience enjoys every word that's spoken. **HIGHLY RECOMMENDED**

The House of Yes [1997]

Starring: Parker Posey, Josh Hamilton, Tori Spelling, Freddie Prinze Jr., Genevieve Bujold Director: Mark Waters Screenplay: Mark Waters, based on the play by Wendy MacLeod Running Time: 1:25 Rated: R (Sex, profanity, mature themes) Theatrical Aspect Ratio: 1.85:1

Going home to meet your fiance's family seems like the normal thing to do. Intimidating, perhaps, but normal. And Lesly (Tori Spelling) is a *very* normal girl, albeit not a particularly bright one. In fact, that's why Marty Pascal (Josh Hamilton) is attracted to her — he has a craving for normalcy, something that he never got from his family. His twin sister, Jackie-O (Parker Posey), is obsessed with the former First Lady, even going so far as to dress up as her and stage re-creations of JFK's final moments. And the relationship between Marty and Jackie-O isn't a typical sibling connection; it's more like a brother/sister affair. Mom (Genevieve Bujold) and little brother Anthony (Freddie Prinze Jr.) are aware of the situation, but, in the best interests of all involved, they turn a blind eye.

Then, on Thanksgiving Day in 1983, Marty shows up at his Washington D.C. home in the midst of a hurricane. He's not alone — Lesly, the proud bearer of a new engagement ring, is with him. Jackie-O's reaction upon learning that her beloved brother is no longer all hers is to let out a piercing scream. Mom is a little more reserved. On her way back into the kitchen, she calmly notes, "I'm going to go baste the turkey and hide the kitchen knives." Over the next 24 hours, Lesly will learn all there is to know about Marty and Jackie-O while capturing Anthony's affection and earning Mom's enmity.

Although *The House of Yes* is dark, bleak, and occasionally disturbing, it is subversively funny — and I mean laugh-aloud funny. Admittedly, most of the humor is warped (how else could you describe a comedy with central themes of incest and an obsession with JFK's assassination), but it would take an exceedingly bland viewer not to find at least a few amusing elements in the film. Consider, for example, the delightfully matter-of-fact manner in which Genevieve Bujold delivers her biting dialogue. Or the wonderfully off-the-wall way in which Parker Posey brings Jackie-O to demented life.

The House of Yes is what happens when a film takes the dysfunctional family melodrama to its farthest reaches. It's a bold, gutsy movie that's definitely not for everyone. But, for those who are always looking for the next daring motion picture and who aren't offended by off-color humor, *The House of Yes* offers 90 minutes of solid entertainment. Not every chance taken by Mark Waters works, but enough are successful to produce some memorable motion picture moments. **RECOMMENDED**

The Hudsucker Proxy [1994]

Starring: Tim Robbins, Jennifer Jason Leigh, Paul Newman, Charles Durning Director: Joel Coen Screenplay: Joel & Ethan Coen and Sam Raimi Running Time: 1:52 Rated: PG (Mature themes) Theatrical Aspect Ratio: 1.85:1

When he wanders into Hudsucker Industries for a job in the mail room, Norville Barnes (Tim Robbins) is an imbecile from Muncie with a single idea for a children's toy. Coincidentally, as Barnes is going in, the president of the company, Waring Hudsucker, is on his way out — through the window of the board room on the 44th floor (not counting the Mezzanine). Hudsucker's death sets off a panic; company rules state that since he died without having a will or living relatives, his majority share must be sold on the open market. Determined to devalue the stock so that the current board members can afford to buy it, Chief exec Sidney J. Mussberger (Paul Newman) devises a scheme to destroy the Hudsucker reputation by choosing a complete incompetent for the top seat. At that moment, he meets Norville Barnes . . .

From the opening sequence, soaring through the snow over the benighted building tops of New York, it's apparent that *The Hudsucker Proxy* is going to be a awe-inspiring visual experience. Given that the producer/director pairing is brothers Joel and Ethan Coen, who headed such projects as *Blood Simple, Miller's Crossing,* and *Barton Fink,* the emphasis on set design, artwork, and innovative cinematography (by Roger Deakins), shouldn't come as a surprise.

The Hudsucker Proxy skewers big business on the same shaft that Robert Altman ran Hollywood through with *The Player.* From the *Brazil*-like scenes in the cavernous mail room to the convoluted machinations in the board room, this film is pure satire of the nastiest and most enjoyable sort. In this surreal world of 1958 can be found many of the issues confronting large corporations in the 1990s, all twisted to match the filmmakers' vision.

The dialogue crackles, with one-liners and double entendres peppering the character exchanges. A Hula Hoop is referred to as an "Extruded Plastic Din-

gus," and a very un-Wim Wenders-like angel makes an appearance singing "She'll Be Comin' Round the Mountain." With its refined wit and glorious vision, *The Hudsucker Proxy* is certainly deserving of a wide audience. **HIGHLY RECOMMENDED**

An Ideal Husband [United Kingdom/United States, 1999]

Starring: Rupert Everett, Julianne Moore, Jeremy Northam, Cate Blanchett, Minnie Driver Director: Oliver Parker Screenplay: Oliver Parker, based on a play by Oscar Wilde Running Time: 1:36 Rated: PG-13 (Sensuality, brief nudity) Theatrical Aspect Ratio: 1.85:1

An Ideal Husband is a delightful parfait — an irresistible concoction of brilliant dialogue, sumptuous set design, top-notch acting, and a plot littered with Machiavellian twists. Possessing a light tone tinged with an acerbic accent, *An Ideal Husband* represents about the best that the motion picture industry can offer. It's an exquisitely crafted movie that can be appreciated from start to finish. Writer/director Oliver Parker has taken Oscar Wilde's play and tweaked it in such a way that the playwright's best lines remain intact while the setting has been opened up to offer a fresh perspective.

The film begins by taking us to England at the end of the 19th century. There, we are introduced to Lord Arthur Goring, played with panache by the underrated Rupert Everett. Goring is described by friends as "the idlest man in London"; his favorite pastimes are engaging in slothful activities, flirting with Mabel Chiltern (Minnie Driver), and avoiding being pushed into marriage by his stodgy father, the Earl of Caversham (John Wood).

Lord Goring's closest friends are Sir Robert Chiltern (Jeremy Northam) and his wife, Lady Gertrude (Cate Blanchett). Robert is an upright man of impeccable reputation and his wife, an independent-minded woman, is devoted to him. Several days before Robert is to speak before Parliament to denounce potential British support for an act to cut a canal through Argentina, he is approached by the devious Mrs. Laura Cheveley (Julianne Moore), who has just returned to London from Vienna. She offers him money to support the canal, and when he refuses, she comments that every man has his price. Her next action is to blackmail him — unless he capitulates, she will ruin his career and wreck his marriage by revealing the secret of how he acquired his wealth.

The plot has all the twists and turns of a David Mamet effort, yet remains surprisingly easy to follow. And it's a good thing, because unnecessary concentration on the mechanics of the story would take away from our ability to savor Wilde's dialogue, which never flags. Although the film's tone is primarily playful, there are serious moments, and it's during these that we gain genuine insight into the characters. Actually, some of the best interaction has less to do with words than with actions.

These days, with flashy action/adventure films and big budget science fiction flicks claiming the lion's share of the box office, it's easy to forget the simple, undeniable pleasure of watching a movie like *An Ideal Husband*, where dialogue, performances, and story construction combine to perfect the experience. **HIGHLY RECOMMENDED**

Igby Goes Down [2002]

Starring: Kieran Culkin, Susan Sarandon, Jeff Goldblum, Claire Danes, Ryan Phillippe Director: Burr Steers Screenplay: Burr Steers Running Time: 1:37 Rated: R (Profanity, sex, nudity, drugs, violence) Theatrical Aspect Ratio: 2.35:1

Igby (Culkin) hasn't had the greatest childhood. His father, Jason (Bill Pullman), is in a mental institution after suffering a breakdown while Igby was in grade school. His pill-popping mother, Mimi (Susan Sarandon) is cold, unfeeling, and more concerned about how Igby's frequent failures will reflect upon her reputation. His Young Republican brother, Oliver (Ryan Phillippe), appears embarrassed to be related to his undisciplined sibling. The only one Igby can rely upon is his open-minded, wealthy godfather, D.H. Baines (Jeff Goldblum), who views Igby's upbringing as his personal charity.

Igby fails at school because of his indifference. He has been expelled from one private institution after another until he finally ends up in military school. He doesn't last there, and ends up in rehab. Soon, he's hanging out in New York, acting like a bohemian. He lives in the same flat as D.H.'s artist mistress, Rachel (Amanda Peet), with whom his relationship quickly evolves from a platonic liaison to a sexual one. He gains an older girlfriend, the improbably-named Sookie Sapperstein (Claire Danes), who stays with Igby until someone better comes along — namely his brother, Oliver. Meanwhile, Igby is hiding out from his detested mother and trying to figure out what to do with his existence. Despite his glib tongue and bravado, he is deeply insecure about the future. His major in life may be attitude, but on more than one occasion, he admits to being scared.

Igby Goes Down is one of those films where the whole is more than a sum of the pieces. There isn't much of a plot — this is basically just a series of episodes that, when strung together, present a patchwork tapestry of whom the main character is and how he got to be that person. With a less deft script, this could have been a thuddingly dull motion picture, but Steers finds the right balance between irony and pathos. Despite some heavy drama, things never become overly somber. As a first-time director, Steers is adequate — where he really shines is as a writer.

Igby Goes Down ends pretty much where it begins, with the majority of the story being told in flashback. For the most part, *Igby Goes Down* is lightweight, although it exhibits enough heft for us to develop an emotional connection with the main character. I have always appreciated a smartly written motion picture, and, whatever flaws *Igby Goes Down* may possess, it is undeniably that. **RECOMMENDED**

The Impostors [1998]

Starring: Oliver Platt, Stanley Tucci, Alfred Molina, Lili Taylor, Tony Shalhoub Director: Stanley Tucci Screenplay: Stanley Tucci Running Time: 1:41 Rated: R (Profanity, sexual comedy) Theatrical Aspect Ratio: 1.85:1

The Impostors is retro in almost every sense of the word. The only thing '90s about the movie are the actors, and the fact that the film stock is in color. The script and style hearken back to the early days of the motion picture industry. Savvy film-goers will recognize more than a little of the Marx Brothers, Charlie Chaplin, and Buster Keaton in the director's sophomore effort. This is the first screwball comedy in years that actually works, and that's mainly because Tucci hasn't tried to update the genre for a "modern" audience. Instead, he has crafted this film exactly as it might have been made 50 years ago. And, for those who want to look even further back into motion picture history, the opening sequence, which is done entirely without sound, is the director's homage to the great silent farces of the '20s.

The Impostors doesn't have much in the way of a plot. It's about the exploits of two Depression-era, unemployed actors, Arthur (Tucci) and Maurice (Oliver Platt), a likable Laurel and Hardy duo who would rather con people out of money and food than work for a living. After getting involved in a scrape with a famous Shakespearean actor, the absolutely awful Jeremy Burtrom (Alfred Molina), they end up as stowaways on a cruise ship bound from New York to Paris. They spend the rest of the film trying to avoid Burtrom, who's also on board, while unearthing a plot to blow up the ship.

Tucci pursues laughter with relish. An uncredited

cameo by Woody Allen is only the tip of the iceberg. In the best tradition of the screwball comedy, there are role reversals and gender benders (look for Oliver Platt in drag). And, as the title implies, almost no one is who they seem to be, and much of the fun results from the various impostors being unmasked. No, there aren't any surprises for the audience, but it's entertaining to observe how the characters react to these revelations.

The goal of *The Impostors* is to tickle the funny bone, and it achieves that aim. Although I recognize that the appreciation of comedy is extremely subjective, it's hard to imagine anyone sitting through this film and not being captured by its infectious energy.
RECOMMENDED

In and Out [United Kingdom/United States, 1997]
Starring: Kevin Kline, Tom Selleck, Joan Cusack, Matt Dillon, Debbie Reynolds Director: Frank Oz Screenplay: Paul Rudnick Running Time: 1:30 Rated: R (Profanity, mature themes) Theatrical Aspect Ratio: 1.85:1

From the very first scene, you know that *In and Out* has struck a rich satirical vein. The movie opens in Greenleaf, Indiana, a conservative, family values-oriented town in middle America that seems to be stuck in the '50s. Director Frank Oz has photographed Greenleaf as a place with a gauzy, fairy tale-like quality that, along with some very pointed dialogue, gently pokes fun at cherished, *Leave it to Beaver* impressions of the "ideal" community. Unlike David Lynch, who has repeatedly attacked this image in his films, Oz and Rudnick are content to have a little affectionate fun with it.

We are introduced to Howard Brackett (Kevin Kline), one of the local high school's most popular teachers. Day-in and day-out, Howard attempts to stir the minds of his young charges to embrace Shakespeare and other forms of English literature. And, while the kids appreciate Howard's teaching methods, they're more interested in his recollections of Cameron Drake (Matt Dillon), a pupil from several years ago who has gone on to become a teen heartthrob and the odds-on favorite to win this year's Best Actor Oscar. Howard is less interested in whether Cameron wins, however, than he is in planning his upcoming wedding to a fellow teacher, Emily Montgomery (Joan Cusack), with whom he has been engaged for 3 years. No one is more excited about the wedding than Howard's mother (Debbie Reynolds), who sees the ceremony as the culmination of a lifelong dream.

Then comes the bombshell. During his internationally-televised acceptance speech for the Academy Award, Cameron goes out of his way to thank "Howard Brackett," adding, rather unexpectedly, that "He's a gay teacher." Everyone, including Howard, is shocked by the statement. The next day, reporters converge on Greenleaf, looking for a story. One of them, Peter Malloy (Tom Selleck), manages to confront Howard alone, and what he reveals causes the confused teacher to question his own sexuality.

In and Out has a thinking person's script, and, as such, works on several levels. It can be seen as a light comedy, a biting satire, and/or a morality play that uses humor to examine society's approach to sexual identities. *In and Out* definitely isn't a pointless comedy of the *Dumb and Dumber* variety — it deals with issues in a shrewd manner, using a creative and well-written script to camouflage with wit any preaching. Regardless of your opinion of the gay community, *In and Out* is more than worth an evening's admission — provided, of course, that you like to laugh.
HIGHLY RECOMMENDED

Irma Vep [France, 1996]
Starring: Maggie Cheung, Jean-Pierre Leaud, Nathalie Richard, Antoine Basler Director: Olivier Assayas Screenplay: Olivier Assayas Running Time: 1:37 Rated: No Rated (Sexual situations, profanity, nudity) Theatrical Aspect Ratio: 1.66:1 In French and English with subtitles

Irma Vep, Olivier Assayas' incisive and entertaining 1996 feature, takes an offbeat look at the current state of French cinema. Assayas turns the camera on the behind-the-scenes process, and the results are both comic and revealing. In a picture that has a lot to say about the film making process and the people who engage in it, Assayas has not restricted his commentary to the French movie industry — he has words for the American and Hong Kong brands, as well.

Irma Vep isn't lacking when it comes to a drawing card. The sight of actress Maggie Cheung garbed in a skintight, black latex outfit should be enough to create lines at the box office. Cheung is playing herself here — a successful Hong Kong actress who has been pegged by an aging French director, Rene Vidal (Jean-Pierre Leaud), to play the part of Irma Vep in his remake of Louis Feuillade's 1915 silent serial, *Les Vampires*. Vidal's vision is to have Cheung dressed like Michelle Pfeiffer in *Batman Returns*, slinking around the Paris underworld. And, out of some misplaced artistic sentiment, he has decided to honor the original by filming the new version as a silent, black-and-white offering that's more strange than it is compelling.

Irma Vep works extraordinarily well on two levels. It explores the movie-making process, and, in doing so, exposes the fakery and hypocrisy that often emerges in the self-serving, so-called "intellectual cinema." One character states that many French movies have become boring because they're intended only for the elite, and that the tendency of French directors to embrace such limited projects is contributing to the death of the movie industry. Assayas has fun with this idea, and gets quite a bit of mileage playing off the commonly-held perception that French cinema is dull and talky. There's also a more serious point to this aspect of the movie, as it will prod viewers into considering what they look for and appreciate in a film, and whether the true strength of the medium lies in its variety and versatility.

Are French films stuffy? At times, yes, and that's one of many reasons why even the most "accessible" French movies are relegated to art cinemas in this country. *Irma Vep* gleefully defies such facile labeling, however. This is a sly, sexy endeavor that presents its audacious viewpoint with style and intelligence. **HIGHLY RECOMMENDED**

Jeffrey [1995]

Starring: Steven Weber, Michael T. Weiss, Patrick Stewart, Bryan Batt, Sigourney Weaver Director: Christopher Ashley Screenplay: Paul Rudnick Running Time: 1:32 Rated: R (Profanity, sexual candor) Theatrical Aspect Ratio: 1.85:1

Jeffrey is a gay romantic comedy with a very impressive laugh-to-running time ratio. Written by *Addams Family* scribe Paul Rudnick (based on his play of the same name), this film is about as eccentric and quirky as they get. Rudnick throws everything at the viewer except the kitchen sink, and if he'd been able to find a way to get that in, he probably would have included it. And, despite all the mirth and mayhem, deep within *Jeffrey*'s core is a message everyone can relate to, regardless of their sexual orientation.

Jeffrey (Steven Weber) is a sexually compulsive, young, gay man. After a number of bizarre in-bed experiences, he decides to give up sex cold turkey. It's not an easy decision to begin with, but it becomes almost impossible when he meets Steve (Michael T. Weiss) at a gym. Jeffrey is immediately attracted to Steve, but his current celibate state makes a relationship difficult. However, Steve is patient, and it doesn't take long before Jeffrey starts to weaken. Then the bombshell is dropped — Steve is HIV+. At first, Jef-

frey says it doesn't matter, but he's lying, and the moment he cancels a dinner date, Steve knows too.

Jeffrey never attempts to simulate real life. It's filled with asides to the audience, strange interludes (including a faux game show and a ghostly hospital encounter), and parodies of parodies. One hilarious segment has Sigourney Weaver playing "the nation's hottest post-modern evangelist." Another has Jeffrey talking frankly about sex to his mother and father. Then there's Nathan Lane as a randy priest who tries to seduce Jeffrey before breaking into a chorus of "Everything's Coming Up Roses." If nothing else, Rudnick and director Christopher Ashley know how to keep the audience off balance and in stitches.

You don't have to dig too deeply to find *Jeffrey*'s simple message, which is essentially the same as the one put forth by 1992's *Strictly Ballroom*: "A life lived in fear is a life half-lived." The AIDS epidemic has scared Jeffrey, and now he's not only hiding from his own sexuality, but from life in general. Darius, despite being mortally ill, describes Jeffrey as the saddest person he's ever known and offers this advice: "Hate AIDS, Jeffrey, not life." Ultimately, this is the point of *Jeffrey*, and it's what makes this film more than just a laugh-a-minute riot. **RECOMMENDED**

Joe Versus the Volcano [1990]

Starring: Tom Hanks, Meg Ryan, Lloyd Bridges Director: John Patrick Shanley Screenplay: John Patrick Shanley Running Time: 1:37 Rated: PG (Profanity) Theatrical Aspect Ratio: 2.35:1

The great god Big Woo, lord of the orange-soda swilling natives of Waponi Woo, demands a sacrifice. Big Woo is a volcano, and, unless someone jumps into its maw, the unappeased god will sink the island under the Pacific, drowning the Waponis. So along comes Joe (Tom Hanks), a man worn down by a drab life and a dead-end job. Joe has lost his self-respect — he lacks the courage even to ask out the boss' mousy secretary (Meg Ryan). Then, one day, Joe learns that he is afflicted with a terminal condition called a "brain cloud." Suddenly free from the constraint of worrying about his mortality, he accepts the offer of a wealthy tycoon (Lloyd Bridges) to live out his last days "like a man," then die like a hero. In his case, being heroic means offering himself to Big Woo.

John Patrick Shanley's script can best be described as "quirky." Stretches of *Joe Versus the Volcano* are nearly perfect. On the other hand, the ending really doesn't work. In fact, the whole last act has problems. Once Joe and his love interest, Patricia (Ryan), reach

Waponi Woo, things start to unravel. Shanley's attempts to have fun with the Waponi culture don't succeed. The satire isn't well-focused and the humor is flat. It's a shame, because this segment seems ripe with promise, all of which is wasted. Shanley never finds the right tone.

In fact, the second half of the film suffers from a mild case of split personality. On one hand, Shanley wants to continue the offbeat, delicious rhythm initiated with the opening credits, but, on the other hand, he wants to explore the romance between soul-sick Patricia and life-weary Joe. While the two motives aren't necessarily in conflict, each leeches time away from the other. Ultimately, the real reason we care about the pairing of Patricia and Joe has less to do with the script than with the appeal and charisma of the two leads, Tom Hanks and Meg Ryan.

Joe Versus the Volcano is difficult to review because some parts are fresh, inventive, and entertaining, while others are near-misses or even complete failures. On balance, however, I readily admit liking this movie, although the second half pales in comparison to the first. But, if only for the pleasure of its best moments, or the enjoyment of savoring Hanks and Ryan's chemistry (pre-*Sleepless in Seattle*), *Joe Versus the Volcano* is worth the price of a rental. **RECOMMENDED**

Life [1999]

Starring: Eddie Murphy, Martin Lawrence Director: Ted Demme
Screenplay: Robert Ramsey & Matthew Stone Running Time: 1:40
Rated: R (Profanity, crude humor) Theatrical Aspect Ratio: 1.85:1

Most of *Life* takes place in a Mississippi State prison that could only exist in the movies. Of course, this is a comedy, so it wouldn't do to set up a grim, ugly locale where every day is worse (or at least no better) than the last. Consequently, director Ted Demme fashions a cozy prison that bears little resemblance to reality, and, for the most part (as long as you're not looking for realism), it works.

One of *Life*'s weaknesses is the lengthy and cumbersome setup necessary to get New Yorkers Ray (Murphy) and Claude (Lawrence) arrested for murder in Mississippi and sentenced to life. The film follows the turbulent relationship of Ray and Claude across the span of 65 years. Demme uses an episodic approach, first checking in with the pair in the 1930s, then returning in the 1940s, the 1970s, and the 1990s. Thanks to a reasonably convincing job by Hollywood makeup specialist Rick Baker, Murphy and Lawrence (as well as Obba Babatundé, who plays a fellow pris-

oner, and functions as the narrator) look like old men rather than younger men wearing multiple layers of latex. Through the years, Ray and Claude maintain a lively verbal repartee that hides a deep friendship.

Life moves along at a breezy clip, but there's a little more going on here than the sophomoric hijinks that characterize most Murphy films. Demme utilizes humor to tackle a serious issue as Ray and Claude are refused service in a whites-only diner. The point is made without preaching, because we're too busy laughing. *Life* also has its sentimental moments, especially as the years move by and many of Ray and Claude's longtime companions pass into the prison cemetery. Demme doesn't give us any death scenes — he merely has the characters fade away.

For those in search of a "true" Eddie Murphy picture, *Life* fills the bill. It has its share of flatulence jokes, homophobic double entendres, and gross-out moments, but there's enough going on here beyond that base level of comedy to allow acceptance and enjoyment by a more mainstream audience. Those who are turned off by Murphy's humor probably won't find a whole lot to like about *Life*, but, for everyone else, the movie represents a charming diversion that re-affirms the likability and comic aptitude of both co-stars. **RECOMMENDED**

Living in Oblivion [1994]

Starring: Steve Buscemi, Catherine Keener, Dermot Mulroney, James LeGros Director: Tom DiCillo Screenplay: Tom DiCillo Running Time: 1:31 Rated: R (Profanity, sexual situations, brief nudity) Theatrical Aspect Ratio: 1.85:1

Living in Oblivion details one day in the life of director Nick Reve (Steve Buscemi), who is trying to put together an independent film on a shoestring budget. This particular morning, he's due to shoot scene 6. Little does he know that Murphy's Law is in full force. Nightmares — real, figurative, and cinematic — will plague the production, and what eventually emerges will be nothing like what anyone envisioned.

Reve's leading lady, Nicole (played by a shining Catherine Keener), is fraught with angst about her career choice. Does she belong in front of the camera or behind the counter at some greasy dive? The male lead, a stuck-up star by the name of Chad Palomino (James LeGros), has no worries about his ability. With an ego too big for the tiny set, Chad spends most of his time complaining to Reve and flashing smiles at the assistant director (Danielle Von Zerneck) and script girl (Hilary Gilford). The cinematographer

(Dermot Mulroney), an eye-patched character who looks like Rambo but has the emotional sensitivity of Alan Alda, rarely lets a take go by without arguing the choice of shot.

The mishaps of scene 6 provide 90 minutes of unbridled fun. There are missed shots, booms in frame, exploding smoke machines, actors with bad breath, a vomiting camera operator, a senile mother on the set, and an irate dwarf in a red room (an obvious poke at David Lynch and *Twin Peaks*). Life imitates art, art imitates life imitating art, and all this happens in switches from black-and-white to color.

Living in Oblivion is packed with laughs and twists, and comes to an end far too soon. It's rare that a movie rolls the credits too early, but when this film fades to black, we're still longing for at least one more scene with Reve, his cast, and crew. While it's true that we don't get much sense of these people off the set, they're so wonderful in and around the camera that it doesn't matter. Best of all, *Living in Oblivion* doesn't demand that the viewer be a film buff — just that he or she enjoys laughing. **HIGHLY RECOMMENDED**

Love and Death on Long Island
[Canada/United Kingdom, 1997]
Starring: John Hurt, Jason Priestley Director: Richard Kwietniowski
Screenplay: Richard Kwietniowski, based on the novel by Gilbert
Adam Running Time: 1:33 Rated: PG-13 (Infrequent but extreme
profanity, non-explicit sexual content) Theatrical Aspect Ratio: 1.85:1

Everyone knows someone like Giles De'Ath: stuffy, arrogant, set in his ways, and at war with anything that could in any way be associated with "progress." This is the kind of role that could easily be turned into a flat stereotype, but John Hurt, in what is certainly his best performance in a decade and possibly the most impressive of his long and distinguished career, turns "erstwhile fogy" Giles into a three-dimensional human being. Giles, who is a widower and a recluse, does not frequent the cinema, but when he learns that an E. M. Forster film is playing at the local theater, he screws up his courage and decides to go. What he doesn't realize is that the movie house is showing 2 films: the Forster adaptation and a teen exploitation flick called *Hotpants College II*. A nonplused Giles ends up sitting in a darkened room watching buff male and female bodies in various states of undress. Just as Giles is about to leave, however, he notices Ronnie Bostock (Jason Priestley) and, suddenly, it's love at first sight. Giles is enraptured, and the moment *Hotpants College II* is over, he begins to scour

stores for Bostock memorabilia, including teen magazines and video tapes. (In order to watch those tapes, Giles must buy a VCR, but he initially doesn't realize that he needs a TV to use the VCR.)

Eventually, not satisfied with being the world's foremost authority on Bostock, Giles boards a plane and travels to Long Island, where his idol's home is located. Bostock is away when Giles arrives, but the wily Englishman manages to befriend Ronnie's supermodel girlfriend, Audrey (Fiona Loewi). Eventually, the actor arrives home and, impressed with Giles' demeanor and intelligence, he begins to rely on the older man's advice. But, while Giles' affection runs deep, Ronnie's feelings are less constant.

Love and Death on Long Island is many things wrapped into one: a social commentary (it tackles the thorny issue of film as pure art versus film as mindless entertainment), a buddy picture/love story (Ronnie and Giles have one of the most interesting relationships found anywhere on a movie screen these days), and a "fish out of water" tale (Victorian relic Giles forced into the modern world). Yet, despite the many laughs *Love and Death* offers, it never takes cheap shots. It has a vibrant, beating heart — and that makes the comedy all the more worthwhile. **RECOMMMENDED**

Lovely and Amazing [2001]
Starring: Catherine Keener, Brenda Blethyn, Emily Mortimer, Raven
Goodwin Director: Nicole Holofcener Screenplay: Nicole Holofcener
Running Time: 1:30 Rated: R (Profanity, nudity) Theatrical Aspect
Ratio: 1.85:1

Somewhere between the whimsy of a fluffy romance and the grit of an uncompromising character study lies the realm of *Lovely & Amazing*, a dramatic comedy from Nicole Holofcener that tells the tale of a mother and her 3 children. *Lovely & Amazing* is the kind of motion picture that can make you laugh one moment and cry the next. It is at times serious and at times very funny. But it is always perceptive, and that quality, more than any other, is what makes it worth a recommendation.

At first glance, there couldn't be 4 more different people than Jane (Brenda Blethyn) and her daughters, Michelle (Catherine Keener), Elizabeth (Emily Mortimer), and Annie (Raven Goodwin). Jane is a good-natured, caring, middle-aged women. Michelle is trapped in an unhappy marriage while working an unfulfilling job at a photograph development shop. Elizabeth is a mostly unsuccessful actress who is questioning her career and her choice in men. And Annie, an adolescent African-American girl adopted by Jane, is struggling with the rigors of puberty. Yet there is a common thread that connects these women: insecurity about their personalities and bodies. Jane is undergoing liposuction to lose inches around her waist. Michelle, aware that her husband is unfaithful, contemplates dallying with an underage boy who finds her attractive. Elizabeth worries that she's not sexy enough to get the right roles. And Annie's answer to problems is to pig out on McDonald's food, even though everyone comments that she's getting fat.

It's Holofcener's insight into the female psyche that makes *Lovely & Amazing* such an engrossing motion picture. The director has recruited a talented cast to bring these characters to life. Brenda Blethyn, Emily Mortimer, and Catherine Keener are all good. On the male side, we are treated to appearances by James LeGros (as Elizabeth's emotionally detached lover), Jake Gyllenhaal (as the teenage object of Michelle's fantasies), and Dermot Mulroney (as a big-time Hollywood actor).

Holofcener crafts each of her characters carefully, showing their creativity and neuroses. And, while there's plenty of humor to be found in this 90-minute feature, there's never an occasion when we're laughing at the characters. We come to like these people, warts and all. RECOMMMENDED

The Man Who Knew Too Little [1997]

Starring: Bill Murray, Joanne Whalley, Alfred Molina, Peter Gallagher Director: Jon Amiel Screenplay: Robert Farrar & Howard Franklin, based on the novel "Watch That Man" by Robert Farrar Running Time: 1:33 Rated: PG (Sexual innuendo, cartoon violence, mild profanity) Theatrical Aspect Ratio: 1.85:1

With a title like *The Man Who Knew Too Little*, one might reasonably assume that actor Bill Murray's latest endeavor is a parody of Hitchcock's twice-made film, *The Man Who Knew Too Much*. In fact, although the movie takes a few stabs at mocking Hitchcockian plot twists, it's mainly a satire of the James Bond pictures. Unlike many similar productions, this one has a smart, knowing script that understands just how to play up all the tricks and contrivances of the secret agent genre to their best comic effect. It's a breezy, fun film that offers more than a few solid laughs.

Murray plays Wallace Richie, an American from Des Moines who decides to celebrate his birthday by purchasing a plane ticket and flying to see his brother, James (Peter Gallagher), and sister-in-law,

Barbara (Anna Chancellor), in London. And, while James is delighted to see Wallace, the visit comes at an inopportune time — he is on the verge of closing a big deal with some German businessmen and he needs an quiet, conservative dinner party without a wild card like Wallace around to disturb things. So, for a birthday present, James gives Wallace an evening's participation in the "Theater of Life," an experimental form of entertainment that allows normal people to act out their fantasies. Only, instead of becoming involved in this "Theater of Life," Wallace accidentally intercepts a phone call intended for a real hit man, and, as a result, he becomes embroiled in a web of espionage, attempted assassinations, and a would-be terrorist attack at the signing of a peace treaty between Russia and England.

It's virtually impossible for the premise of a mistaken identity to sustain an entire motion picture, but *The Man Who Knew Too Little* employs enough variations that, until the very end, proceedings remain surprisingly lively. Of course, it could be argued that the situation in this film is so outrageous that it's as much a "fish out of water" scenario as a "mistaken identity" one. Wallace is, after all an "innocent" American thrown into the midst of a European game of murder, mayhem, and blackmail.

Despite a floundering ending, *The Man Who Knew Too Little* leaves a favorable impression. Although *The Man Who Knew Too Little* is less audacious than *Austin Powers* and lacks all of the '70s references, it's frequently as enjoyable, if not more so, and that makes it a worthy choice for a frothy, funny evening. RECOMMMENDED

Manhattan Murder Mystery [1993]

Starring: Woody Allen, Diane Keaton, Alan Alda, Anjelica Houston, Jerry Adler Director: Woody Allen Screenplay: Woody Allen & Marshall Brickman Running Time: 1:48 Rated: PG (Mature themes) Theatrical Aspect Ratio: 1.85:1

Carol Lipton (Diane Keaton) and her husband Larry (Woody Allen) are caught in a routine, commonplace marriage — until Carol turns into Nancy Drew following the death of a neighbor. It all seems like a open-and-shut case of a heart attack, and the police aren't thinking foul play, but Carol becomes suspicious when the widower of the dead woman (Jerry Adler) doesn't mourn "enough" ("What should he do," asks Larry, "walk down the street sobbing?"). With the help of Ted (Alan Alda), a close friend who encourages her sleuthing, she begins to assemble "clues" to fit her pet theory of a murder. But the evidence is weak, and Larry becomes concerned that his wife is obsessed with a macabre fantasy. He tries to be the voice of reason, but when no one listens to him, he ends up playing along.

Part of the fun of *Manhattan Murder Mystery* is guessing whether or not Lillian House was murdered, as Carol believes, or simply died of a heart attack. In a sense, that's the mystery of the film, and Woody Allen brings across the solution with his characteristic mix of madcap comedy and on-target realism.

Film buffs will find the usual number of references to look for, although these are perhaps more explicit than in many Allen movies, and include *Double Indemnity, Rear Window,* and *The Lady from Shanghi.* There certainly may be others, as Allen has a habit of putting more into his films than anyone can hope to get in one sitting.

Woody Allen is rarely a big commercial draw, and whether his off-screen antics will boost his box-office take remains to be seen, but *Manhattan Murder Mystery* may be his most accessible film since *Hannah and Her Sisters.* This movie is still pure Allen, but the humor is broad-based, and the "quirkiness" often associated with the director is kept to a minimum. Frankly, it's been years since I've enjoyed the director's work this much. **HIGHLY RECOMMENDED**

Me, Myself & Irene [2000]

Starring: Jim Carrey, Renee Zellweger, Chris Cooper, Robert Forster
Directors: Bobby Farrelly, Peter Farrelly Screenplay: Peter Farrelly, Mike Cerrone & Bobby Farrelly Running Time: 1:55 Rated: R (Profanity, vulgarity, sexual situations, brief nudity, violence)
Theatrical Aspect Ratio: 1.85:1

Me, Myself & Irene highlights the continuing evolution of Jim Carrey as an actor (as opposed to a comic phenomenon). This is Carrey's second outing for the Farrellys, and his work here is by far the better of the two. Unlike in the previous film (*Dumb and Dumber*), which was essentially a group of thinly-connected dumb jokes, Carrey's comic energy is effectively focused. He's not trying so hard to be funny that he becomes irritating.

Carrey is Charlie and Hank, two faces of the same man. Charlie is meek, kind, and ineffectual. Hank, on the other hand, is aggressive and dumb, with an attitude and voice to match Dirty Harry. Charlie is one of the best liked members of the Rhode Island State Police Force, but, when he loses control of his mind and body and Hank emerges to go on a rampage, his career is in jeopardy. His captain (Robert Forster) sends him to deliver a female prisoner, Irene (Renee Zell-

weger), to an upstate New York police station. After that, he is supposed to take a little R&R. However, it turns out that Irene, the head groundskeeper at a golf course that was a front for criminal activity, may have seen something she shouldn't have, and, as a result, she has been marked for death by some crooked cops (Chris Cooper and Richard Jenkins). So, accompanied by an albino serial killer named Whitey (Michael Bowman), Charlie and Irene go on the lam.

As with the Farrellys' previous directorial outings, the plot is the least important aspect of the proceedings. It's there to move things along and provide a clothesline upon which the various comic situations can be hung. Thinking about it or pondering its coherence is not a good approach, because it doesn't make a lot of sense. In fact, things are so convoluted that a voiceover narrator is needed to keep audiences from becoming lost. And, for such a weak plot, there's too much of it. The movie runs nearly 2 hours, which is easily 20 to 30 minutes too long. The laugh quotient is down significantly during the final half-hour as the Farrellys make the mistake of concentrating a little too much on the story.

Ultimately, *Me, Myself & Irene* is a comedy, and it works because it does its job of making viewers laugh. It is perhaps a slight notch below *There's Something About Mary* on the Farrelly entertainment scale, but it's a significant improvement over either *Dumb and Dumber.* The film is less successful as a romance, primarily because of the weakness in Irene's character. Those who are offended by vulgar material certainly won't embrace this movie, but fans of the Farrellys, Carrey, and humor in the worst possible taste will find plenty to enjoy. **RECOMMENDED**

A Midwinter's Tale [United Kingdom, 1995]

Starring: Michael Maloney, Richard Briers, Julia Sawalha, John Sessions Director: Kenneth Branagh Screenplay: Kenneth Branagh
Running Time: 1:38 Rated: R (Profanity, mature themes) Theatrical Aspect Ratio: 1.66:1

A Midwinter's Tale is loaded with allusions, both cinematic and literary. The most obvious are those from Shakespeare, which understandably permeate the film. Not only are the characters attempting to perform *Hamlet,* but certain scenes from the play hit a little too close to home for several of them. Director Kenneth Branagh also simultaneously pays homage to and pokes fun at one of the most respected British filmmakers of all time: Sir Laurence Olivier. Elements of *A Midwinter's Tale*'s presentation recall the work of Woody Allen, and the ensemble cast is the kind that

Allen usually gathers — although Branagh uses British names while Allen typically assembles Americans.

With all of Branagh's energy focused on directing (he never appears on screen), *A Midwinter's Tale* is almost always on-target. Most of the so-called dramatic aspects of this film are subtle parodies of traditional Hollywood cliches: the struggling actor choosing love over fame, a reconciliation between a long-separated father and son, and a man finally earning his mother's approval after a lifetime of failure. Branagh handles these themes deftly, treating each with enough respect to create emotional arcs for the characters, but making sure the audience knows he's fully aware of how overused the material is.

The main character is actor/director Joe Harper (Michael Maloney, whose acting style echoes Branagh's), who, during a slow time in his career, risks bankruptcy to stage an experimental Christmas-time production of *Hamlet* in his home town of Hope. Unfortunately, auditions don't go well — all the respected theatrical talent is involved in one production or another of *A Christmas Carol* — and Joe finds only 6 willing participants. Since the text necessitates 24 roles, everyone is forced to play multiple parts. Thus, Hamlet's Ghost, Claudius, and the Player King all bear a strong resemblance to one another, Laertes is moonlighting as about 5 other people, and Rosencrantz and Guildenstern are one. Gertrude is played by a drag queen (John Sessions), Ophelia is essayed by an amazingly nearsighted actress (Julia Sawahla), and Horatio is a drunk (Gerard Horan).

Branagh has fun with his material, weaving a tale likely to generate guffaws even for those with little knowledge of the play upon which it is based. No current film maker appears to love and understand Shakespeare as well as Branagh, and never has his affection for the Bard been more apparent than here. This picture succeeds as a comedy, a satire, and even, to a certain extent, as a mild melodrama about choosing between a paycheck and the nourishment of the soul. HIGHLY RECOMMENDED

Mighty Aphrodite [1995]

Starring: Woody Allen, Mira Sorvino, Helena Bonham Carter, Peter Weller, Michael Rapaport Director: Woody Allen Screenplay: Woody Allen Running Time: 1:38 Rated: R (Sexual situations, mature themes, profanity) Theatrical Aspect Ratio: 1.85:1

The film opens in an amphitheater in Greece, with an appropriately-garbed Greek chorus chanting of the deeds of Achilles and Oedipus. Suddenly, unexpect-

edly, the masked men and women decide to switch to the tale of Lenny Weinrib (Woody Allen) — definitely *not* a name known from mythology. And, as things go from slightly absurd to completely ridiculous, the Chorus, led by F. Murray Abraham, say things like "Oh cursed fate! Some thoughts are better left unthunk!" and breaking into verses of "When You're Smiling." And all this is accomplished with an appropriate level of pomposity.

The story starts out with Lenny and his wife, Amanda (Helena Bonham Carter), discussing adoption. Lenny doesn't want a child, but Amanda does, although she isn't willing to sacrifice a year of her life to have one the normal, biological way. Eventually, Lenny gives in and the couple gets a healthy male infant, whom they name Max. As the child grows and Amanda becomes more wrapped up in her attempts to procure her own art studio, Lenny fights a growing curiosity to learn more about his son's natural mother. Eventually, he sneaks a peek at the adoption agency's records. This leads to a meeting with Linda Ash (Mira Sorvino), the woman who gave birth to Max. Much to Lenny's dismay, she turns out to be a statuesque blond with a helium voice and little in the way of intelligence. Worse still is how she makes her living — her dual career involves starring in porn films and turning $200 tricks for a bald-headed, homicidal pimp.

The most original element of *Mighty Aphrodite* is the use of the Greek Chorus. However, what starts out as a clever, innovative device quickly becomes tedious through overuse. The Chorus seems always to be on hand to make pithy remarks, and their presence becomes intrusive. At times, it's as if Woody Allen is attempting to take a page out of the *Monty Python* book, and those two very different styles of humor do not mix well.

While not up to the level of many of Allen's recent films, *Mighty Aphrodite* is nevertheless an entertaining diversion. The comedy, most of which is light and easily accessible, is worthy of some laughs, and the movie has a good sense of irony. *Mighty Aphrodite* is far from a tour de force, and some Woody Allen die-hards may be disappointed, but there's enough in this picture to recommend it. RECOMMENDED

Mother [1996]

Starring: Albert Brooks, Debbie Reynolds, Rob Morrow Director: Albert Brooks Screenplay: Albert Brooks & Monica Johnson Running Time: 1:45 Rated: PG-13 (Mature themes, mild profanity) Theatrical Aspect Ratio: 1.85:1

In the formula-laden playground of modern comedies, *Mother* comes as a breath of fresh air. The film relies on smart humor rather than slapstick, puns, and dumb jokes with quick payoffs. Albert Brooks doesn't use the *Airplane* approach to comedy. His films aren't loaded with hit-and-miss gags. The director/writer strives for quality over quantity, and when he wants the audience to laugh, they generally do so.

Brooks plays John Henderson, a 40-year-old B-grade science fiction writer (his published books include *Planet Seven* and *Planet Eight*) who is going through his second divorce. For John, this is only the latest in a long line of failed relationships. In the words of a friend he meets at a bar (John C. McGinley), "You've gotta know what you're looking for [in a woman], and you don't have a clue." After a great deal of soul-searching, John decides that to better understand women, he needs to investigate his strained relationship with his mother, Beatrice (Debbie Reynolds). So, much to the surprise of his friends and his younger brother, Jeff (Rob Morrow), he decides to move back into his childhood home in Sausalito and live with her. Thus begins an odyssey of mother/son bonding that not even John is prepared for.

It would have been easy for Brooks' script (co-written by Monica Johnson) to treat Mrs. Henderson as a caricature. Most comedies would have opted for that route, I think. The result might have been funny, but it wouldn't have been as meaningful. As the film progresses, Beatrice is allowed to fill out into a full-fledged character, complete with her own desires, dashed hopes, and simmering dreams. We, like John, gradually recognize why she reacts to him the way she does.

Although *Mother* boasts a host of hilarious one-liners, the best moments are the extended episodes that delve into everyday life. One features John's attempt to start an intelligent conversation with a vacuous date (*Friends*' Lisa Kudrow). There are also the scenes with Mom: a trip to the grocery store, an excursion through the mall, and an afternoon at the zoo. All of these sequences could have been short, but Brooks allows them to develop and play out naturally, letting the comedy bubble to the surface rather than escape in one sudden, contrived explosion. RECOMMENDED

Muriel's Wedding [Australia, 1994]

Starring: Toni Collette, Rachel Griffiths Director: P.J. Hogan
Screenplay: P.J. Hogan Running Time: 1:46 Rated: R (Language, sexual candor, mature themes) Theatrical Aspect Ratio: 1.66:1

Muriel Heslop (the vibrant, energetic Toni Collette) is a hopeless romantic. She spends her days locked in her bedroom, listening to ABBA songs and dreaming of the day she'll be able to put on a wedding dress. Her walls are covered with momentos of her two favorite things in life: posters of the singing group and pictures of brides-to-be. Part of her reason for living in a fantasy world is that her family life is so depressing. Her brothers and sisters spend all day lounging in front of the television. Her mother (Jeane Drynan) is oblivious to the goings-on around her, and her father (Bill Hunter) doesn't miss any opportunity to brand Muriel as "useless." In fact, he derides her as the *most* useless of his children. On top of that, her bitchy friends call her an embarrassment and announce that they don't want her accompanying them on a vacation.

Muriel takes all this to heart and decides that the only way to change her life is to leave the town of Porpoise Spit and find a man. To this end, she follows her friends to the resort of Hibiscus Island. Once there, she encounters Rhonda (Rachel Griffiths), an old school chum. In this wild party girl, Muriel discovers something she has never before had — a *real* friend, someone who actually cares about her.

One of the most pleasant aspects of *Muriel's Wedding* is the distinctly unconventional third act. No one seeing this movie will confuse it with a Hollywood picture, as it continually flouts the "feel good" formulas that typically characterize this sort of romantic comedy. The ending is far-from-perfect, but it's a great deal better than several obvious alternatives.

Nevertheless, parts of *Muriel's Wedding* are heavy-handed and, as a result, needlessly uncomfortable to view. There are times when Hogan almost seems to enjoy belittling and degrading Muriel. While it's necessary to understand her low self-image, the director goes to excessive, almost-sadistic, lengths to get his point across. Balancing these moments are some high-energy scenes, including a wonderful lip-synch of ABBA's "Waterloo" by Muriel and Rachel, Muriel trying on wedding dresses to the tune of "Dancing Queen," and an almost-sex scene featuring sofa cushions being unzipped instead of skirts.

Muriel's Wedding isn't a perfect comedy, tragedy, or drama, but it contains enough original elements of each to make it worth a look. Ultimately, however, individual enjoyment of this picture may be in direct proportion to a viewer's ability to tolerate ABBA's omnipresent music. RECOMMENDED

My Big Fat Greek Wedding [2002]

Starring: Nia Vardalos, John Corbett, Michael Constantine, Lainie Kazan Director: Joel Zwick Screenplay: Nia Vardalos Running Time: 1:34 Rated: PG (Mild profanity, sexual situations) Theatrical Aspect Ratio: 1.85:1

My Big Fat Greek Wedding starts out as a modern day Cinderella story and culminates with the traditional end to most fairy tale romances — the wedding, with all of its associated complexities and mishaps. There's a significant element of cultures clashing here, as well. The 3 primary rules of life for a young Greek woman are to (1) marry a Greek boy, (2) make Greek babies, and (3) feed everyone for the rest of your life. So, when Toula Portokalos (Nia Vardalos) becomes involved with the not-at-all-Greek Ian Miller (John Corbett), she's set to create a family uproar.

When the film opens, Toula is a seating hostess at her father's downtown Chicago Greek restaurant, "Dancing Zorba's." At age 30, Toula has pretty much given up hopes of romance and marriage, as indicated by her frumpy appearance. Then Toula decides to embark upon a course of self-improvement, the first step of which is taking computer classes as a local college. Then she meets Ian.

Actually, the two had previously met, albeit briefly, when Ian stopped in for a bite to eat at "Dancing Zorba's." On that occasion, Toula was struck dumb by Ian's handsome visage. This time, the attraction is mutual. Soon, they are dating, then sleeping together, then are engaged. And that's when things get tricky. Toula's father, who was unhappy to learn that she was dating a non-Greek, nearly has an apoplexy when his daughter breaks the news to him that she intends to marry someone whose parents are as "white bread" as they come.

My Big Fat Greek Wedding is more in the nature of an embrace and celebration of Greek culture than it is a lampoon. Sure, there are times when it pokes fun, but, on those occasions, it is gentle and kind-hearted, not nasty or sarcastic. The movie is consistently funny without ever going over the top — a rarity in movies. While some of the comedy is more witty than sidesplitting, there are plenty of opportunities for belly laughs. And, in the process of boosting the laugh quotient, *My Big Fat Greek Wedding* does not lose sight of the characters. That's an important quality for any movie that wants to keep its audience invested in the eventual outcome. The result is an appealing blend of laughter, romance, and ethnic flavoring — an independent production to be appreciated for its likability and humor. RECOMMENDED

Mystery Men [1999]

Starring: Ben Stiller, William H. Macy, Hank Azaria, Geoffrey Rush, Janeane Garofalo, Greg Kinnear Director: Kinka Usher Screenplay: Neil Cuthbert, based on the comic book created by Bob Burden Running Time: 1:57 Rated: PG-13 (Violence, profanity, innuendo) Theatrical Aspect Ratio: 1.85:1

Mystery Men isn't just clever — it's genuinely funny, as well. Comic book and superhero fans will be pleased that *Mystery Men* isn't just a parody, but an homage. The film introduces us to a bunch of blue-collar superheroes. In Champion City, a stylized metropolis that looks like a cross between the futuristic world of *The Fifth Element* and *Batman*'s Gotham City, Captain Amazing (Greg Kinnear) is every little boy's idol. Children revere this Superman clone, and why not? He has singlehandedly cleaned up the city. But there's more to being a superhero than simply restoring law and order. During his period of fighting evil-doers, Captain Amazing has hired a publicist and earned sponsors. Now times are getting a little difficult. Without any supervillains to defeat, Captain Amazing's shining star is dimming, so he decides to help engineer the parole of his arch nemesis, Cassanova Frankenstein (Geoffrey Rush), so that he'll have someone to save the city from. Unfortunately, Cassanova proves to be smarter than Captain Amazing, and soon Champion City's #1 champion is nowhere to be found.

Enter the Mystery Men — 3 ordinary guys who want to be superheroes. Their powers are less than astonishing. Mr. Furious (Ben Stiller) supposedly shows amazing strength when he gets mad, but the depth of his abilities is exaggerated. The Blue Raja (Hank Azaria) is an "effete British superhero" who can do some impressive things with forks and spoons. And the Shoveler (William H. Macy) calls a spade a spade, then clanks people over the head with it. Unfortunately, these three aren't too successful in battle, and, when it comes to rescuing Captain Amazing, they're in over their heads — and they know it. So they do a little recruiting. Soon, their group has expanded, and, armed with some really cool weapons, they decide to storm Cassanova's castle and save Captain Amazing and the city.

Mystery Men offers a broad base of humor with something for everyone. There are puns, sight gags, fairly sophisticated satire, lowbrow humor, and fart jokes. The best scene in the film is arguably the one in which Mr. Furious, the Blue Raja, and the Shoveler interview new candidates. Some of the rejected wannabe superheroes have names like Ballerina

Man, Pencil Man, and PMS Avenger. Another candidate for the most memorable moment is when the Mystery Men attempt to rescue Captain Amazing — with unexpected results. RECOMMENDED

Nurse Betty [2000]
Starring: Renée Zellweger, Morgan Freeman, Chris Rock, Greg Kinnear, Aaron Eckhart Director: Neil LaBute Screenplay: John Richards and James Flamberg Running Time: 1:48 Rated: R (Profanity, violence, sex) Theatrical Aspect Ratio: 1.85:1

Nurse Betty's two hallmarks are originality and star quality, both of which combine to draw the viewer through the film's occasional rough spots. Neil LaBute has put together an offbeat production that combines elements of fantasy, drama, satire, and black humor. It has an unusual tone that successfully encourages the willing suspension of disbelief and allows one to become involved in a story that, at least from the outside, is patently absurd.

Betty is a part-time housewife/part-time waitress living in a small, dead-end Kansas town. She's sweet, oblivious, and innocent, and allows herself to be taken advantage of by everyone around her, especially her philandering husband, Del (Aaron Eckhart). Because her own life is so empty, Betty is a fervent fan of the soap opera *A Reason To Love*, where her favorite character is Dr. David Ravell (Greg Kinnear). However, aside from getting her daily soap fix, making dinner for her husband, and serving coffee to regulars like the local sheriff (Pruitt Taylor Vince) and the town's only reporter (Crispin Glover), Betty doesn't have much to do.

Then, one day, a couple of strangers named Charlie (Morgan Freeman) and Wesley (Chris Rock) arrive at Del's Used Car lot, looking to do business with him. The end up back at his house for drinks, but things get ugly and Del doesn't survive. Unbeknownst to Charlie and Wesley, Betty sees the entire incident. Post traumatic stress from witnessing the murder pushes her into a half-fantasy world where she suddenly believes that characters from *A Reason To Love* are real people, and that she was once engaged to David Ravell. Armed only with her shaky sanity, she heads for Los Angeles, where her lost love "lives." Meanwhile, Charlie and Wesley, convinced that Betty could be a threat to them, start to search for her.

The best part of *Nurse Betty* is the climax, which gains a comic momentum of its own. Without revealing any details, I can say that a few unexpected things happen during this sequence, which also offers the most overtly humorous moments of the film. LaBute

ends on a high note, which is a credit to him, his cast, and screenwriters John Richards & James Flamberg. Once again, the director has distinguished him as that rare Hollywood commodity: someone who is willing to take a chance on an unconventional project and turn it into something enjoyable. RECOMMENDED

The Object of My Affection [1998]
Starring: Jennifer Aniston, Paul Rudd, John Pankow, Timothy Daly Director: Nicholas Hytner Screenplay: Wendy Wasserstein, based on the novel by Stephen McCauley Running Time: 1:50 Rated: R (Sexual themes, profanity) Theatrical Aspect Ratio: 1.85:1

The Object of My Affection, based on the novel of the same name by Stephen McCauley, is a pleasant romantic comedy that asks (and tries to answer) questions about the nature of love, sex, family, and friendship. And, while some of the solutions are a little facile, the film nevertheless succeeds, due in large part to a luminous performance by Jennifer Aniston and the effectively-developed central relationship between Aniston's Nina Borowski, a pregnant twentysomething heterosexual, and George Hanson (Paul Rudd), a gay man in the same age range.

In most movies, friendships are the equivalent of cinematic side orders. Especially in contemporary productions, almost every main character has to have a best friend. This facilitates character development and allows secondary interaction. Rarely, however, is friendship the *point* of a movie. That's not the case in *The Object of My Affection*, which, although it is a little about sex and love, is much more about the undemanding, casual affection that builds between real friends. The chemistry between Aniston and Rudd is perfect in establishing this relationship. They have a real camaraderie which is only occasionally spiced up by a hint of sexual tension.

George and Nina meet at a dinner party that neither of them is enjoying. They soon discover that they have a great deal in common, and the fact that she's straight and he's gay makes them ideal candidates for roommates. Once George's current relationship with a egotistical doctor (Timothy Daly) comes to an end, George moves into a bedroom in Nina's Brooklyn apartment. The two quickly become best friends, with a closeness that is so extreme that, when Nina becomes pregnant by her boyfriend, Vince (*Mad About You*'s Ira, John Pankow), she tells George first. Problems arise, however, when Nina begins to fall for George while he simultaneously becomes interested in a young actor (Amo Gulinello).

This is apparently director Nicholas Hytner's push

to make a mainstream Hollywood movie. Although many of the secondary relationships are sketchily-developed and occasionally hard-to-swallow, the connection between George and Nina is so strong and believable that it draws us into their world and allows us to root for the seemingly-improbable happy ending. RECOMMENDED

The Opposite of Sex [1998]
Starring: Christina Ricci, Martin Donovan, Lisa Kudrow Director: Don Roos Screenplay: Don Roos Running Time: 1:45 Rated: R (Sexual themes, profanity, violence) Theatrical Aspect Ratio: 1.85:1

Christina Ricci's performance is only one reason why Don Roos' *The Opposite of Sex* is a success. This is the kind of daring feature that doesn't open every Friday at the local multiplex; its frank, sometimes politically incorrect approach towards the act and politics of sex is refreshing. And, in addition to dealing with intrinsically provocative material, first-time director Roos uses the unique approach of satirizing the conventions of road pictures and dysfunctional family dramas to tell his story. In particular, he has a lot of fun with the voice-over. The glib narrator, Deedee Truitt (Ricci), is aware that she's speaking to a movie audience, and, as a result, can't resist the opportunity to have some fun at the viewer's expense.

Although Deedee is the narrator, she's not the film's central character. That role belongs to her half-brother, Bill (Martin Donovan), "the definition of a softy." Bill, a gay high school teacher, has been leading a peaceful existence until his pregnant sister runs away from home and comes to him for shelter. He lets Deedee stay, and she repays his kindness by seducing his live-in lover, Matt (Ivan Sergei), who, after his fling with Deedee, decides that he's not really a homosexual — he's a bisexual. Another constant presence in Bill's life is the always-miserable Lucia (Lisa Kudrow), the sister of his dead true love. Then there are Jason (Johnny Galecki), who falsely tells the police that Bill molested him, and Sheriff Carl Tippett (Lyle Lovett), the genial cop who investigates the boy's claims.

As comedies go, *The Opposite of Sex* is consistently funny. Of course, humor is subjective, and I'm known for being a little warped in that area, so Roos' flamboyant, out-on-a-limb approach is perfect for someone like me. The dialogue is crisp and distinctive, occasionally invoking the spirit of something written by Kevin Smith. However, it's obvious to Roos (and to us) that this kind of slick, unconventional style can have trouble sustaining a feature-length movie. So the

writer/director changes gears during the second half. Although *The Opposite of Sex* never completely loses its satirical, self-mocking edge, the final 50 minutes are more serious than what precedes them, and the humor is leavened by a couple of earnest, surprisingly-effective messages.

The tag line for *The Opposite of Sex* is: "You'll laugh, you'll cry, you'll be offended." While that's perhaps overstating the movie's impact, it's not completely off-base. The film manages to mix a portion of successful drama into its primarily-comic foundation, and conservative movie-goers will likely be turned off by the no-punches pulled, occasionally raunchy look at sex. However, with its memorable dialogue, solid performances, and idiosyncratic style, *The Opposite of Sex* is sure to be appreciated by those who aren't frightened away by the cinematic equivalent of hot chili. HIGHLY RECOMMENDED

The Original Kings of Comedy [2000]
Starring: Steve Harvey, D.L. Hughley, Cedric the Entertainer, Bernie Mac Director: Spike Lee Running Time: 1:53 Rated: R (Profanity, Sex related humor) Theatrical Aspect Ratio: 1.85:1

Concert films, regardless of whether they're music shows or comedy acts, run the gamut from excellent to unwatchable. The key to such a movie's success is its ability to capture the "you are there" feeling — a task that *The Original Kings of Comedy* is largely effective at. Admittedly, there's no way that sitting in a motion picture auditorium can duplicate the experience of being live, but, by using digital sound, uncomplicated shots that don't call attention to the camerawork, and simple editing techniques, Lee draws the viewer in.

The Kings of Comedy road tour showcased the talents of 4 of black America's hottest male comedians: Steve Harvey (the host of *It's Showtime at the Apollo* and the star of TV's *The Steve Harvey Show*), D.L. Hughley (of TV's *The Hughleys*), Cedric the Entertainer (also of *The Steve Harvey Show*), and Bernie Mac (of TV's *Moesha*). During the course of the movie/show, each has approximately 30 minutes of stage time, and, while their styles are different, there's enough synergy between them to make the program seem like a cohesive whole rather than a series of unrelated segments (a frequent drawback to many comedy club shows). The 4 men complement each other, and each seems to have just about the right amount of time to forward his comic cause.

The material is frequently ribald, often racy, and always laced with profanity. Those who are offended by the use of four-letter words in comedy will be openly horrified by what transpires here. No apologies are offered or needed, however, because the movie is consistently funny — often side-splittingly so. *The Original Kings of Comedy* only features a few dead patches, none of which last very long. And, while I found certain of the entertainers to be more enjoyable than others (Hughley being the most consistently humorous and Harvey getting the biggest laugh with his rap sketch), none of them are duds.

The stage personalities of Harvey, Hughley, Cedric, and Mac come across unfettered and bigger-than-life. Lee's 3 or 4 attempts to take us backstage slow things down for a few minutes, but they aren't long enough to kill the momentum. Overall, Lee takes a step back, allowing *The Original Kings of Comedy* to be about the Kings, not the filmmaker — and that's the way it should be, because these men are more than capable of holding anyone's attention for the nearly 2-hour running length. RECOMMENDED

Planes, Trains and Automobiles [1987]
Starring: Steve Martin, John Candy, Laila Robins Director: John Hughes Screenplay: John Hughes Running Time: 1:33 Rated: R (Profanity, mature themes) Theatrical Aspect Ratio: 1.85:1

Planes, Trains, and Automobiles is a Murphy's Law story. For salesman Neal Page (Steve Martin), everything that can possibly go wrong is about to do so. This is like Martin Scorsese's *After Hours* on a grander, less psychotic scale. It all starts in New York City, 2 days before Thanksgiving. Neal is eager to get home into the bosom of his family so he can enjoy the holiday. But bad weather intervenes. His flight from LaGuardia to O'Hare is diverted to Wichita, Kansas after a snowstorm hits Chicago. What makes the trip even longer is that Neal is stuck next to one of those good-natured, annoying talkers who won't shut up. The man's name is Del Griffith (John Candy), and he's a shower curtain ring salesman armed with an endless supply of dumb jokes and pointless anecdotes. This isn't the first time Neal has run into him, either. Earlier in the day, when Neal was trying to get to the airport, Del stole his cab, getting their relationship off to a rocky start.

In the time-honored tradition of the buddy comedy, *Planes, Trains, and Automobiles* throws these two mismatched individuals together and allows them to suffer all sorts of bizarre misfortunes as they try to get home before the turkey is served. They spend a night in a cramped hotel room sleeping in the same bed, endure the blatant incompetence of uncaring rental

car clerks, suffer through transportation breakdowns, and watch one of their last hopes literally go up in smoke. We know they're eventually going to reach the Windy City, so the fun is watching their slow, reluctant bonding as they take planes, trains, automobiles, and tractor trailers to get there.

Planes, Trains, and Automobiles is one of those rare movies that manages to mingle outrageous comedy and light drama in such a way that we aren't repulsed or offended by its simplicity and occasional mawkishness. It's a fine cinematic treat that doesn't demand much from a viewer, but gives back a lot, both in terms of laughter and good feeling. RECOMMENDED

Private Parts [1997]
Starring: Howard Stern, Mary McCormack, Robin Quivers Director: Betty Thomas Screenplay: Michael Kalesniko & Len Blum, based on the book by Howard Stern Running Time: 1:49 Rated: R (Profanity, vulgarity, nudity) Theatrical Aspect Ratio: 1.85:1

Will the real Howard Stern please stand up? For, in truth, the man who haunts the airwaves of nearly three-dozen radio stations each morning seems vastly different from the kinder, milder version who graces the screen in Betty Thomas' sweet, often-hilarious biopic. Based on the bestselling book of the same name, *Private Parts* relates some of the details of Stern's life — his romance with his wife, Alison (Mary McCormack), his early radio failures, his development into America's foremost "shock jock," and his vitriolic war with NBC's top brass. Along the way, we get to know Howard as a tender, intelligent, affable guy who just happens to do an "offensive . . . obnoxious . . . disgusting" radio show.

The film begins when Howard is a child and traces his life to the present. His sidekicks are accounted for — Fred Norris, whom he met while working in Hartford during the late '70s; Robin Quivers, who started as a newswoman in Washington D.C. before becoming his friend; joke writer Jackie Martling; producer Gary Dell'Abate; and even Stuttering John Melendez, who pops up for an unforgettable cameo. Much of *Private Parts* details Howard's always-loving, occasionally-rocky marriage to Alison, who's played with warmth and charm by *Murder One*'s Mary McCormack. The battles with the FCC have been relegated to a minor annoyance, although the ongoing feud with a WNBC program director takes center stage during the film's final ⅓.

It will probably come as no surprise to Stern fans to learn that their hero has an undeniable screen presence. Unlike many personalities-turned-actors, he never seems awkward or out-of-place. Stern's surprisingly subdued portrayal of himself may open a few eyes, however. He's never out-of-control, and the only time he plays a "sexist, racist pig" is when he's on the air.

Private Parts is aimed primarily at a mainstream audience. The humor here is racy, but also universal, and many of the jokes will cause viewers to double over with laughter. And, as bizarre as it may sound, Stern is the kind of guy you can't help pulling for. Most who take a chance, regardless of what prejudices they harbor against WXRK's top personality, will find themselves rewarded by a surprisingly pleasant two hours. **RECOMMENDED**

Pumpkin [2002]

Starring: **Christina Ricci, Hank Harris, Brenda Blethyn, Dominique Swain** Directors: **Anthony Abrams, Adam Larson Broder** Screenplay: **Adam Larson Broder** Running Time: **1:55** Rated: **R** (Profanity, sexual situations, mature themes, brief nudity) Theatrical Aspect Ratio: **1.85:1**

For approximately ¾ of its nearly 2-hour running time, *Pumpkin* finds the right balance between satire, black comedy, and offbeat drama. However, the quirky independent film loses its focus on its way to the finish line, stumbling through several "false endings" and ultimately concluding with a whimper. The film's last act problems do not obscure *Pumpkin's* two greatest strengths: the majority of the film is original and engaging, and Christina Ricci turns in another fine performance. This pair of assets alone is worth the price of admission.

Carolyn McDuffy (Ricci) is the ideal sorority sister. The right-hand woman of Alpha Omega Pi's leader, Julie (Marisa Coughlan), Carolyn is as vacuous and peppy as any of the members of the rival house, Tri-Omega. As in the past, this year, Alpha Omega Pi and Tri-Omega are locked in a heated battle for the coveted title of "Southern California State University Sorority of the Year," and Julie is determined to win. To aid the cause, she decides that the sisters are going to perform mentorship duties for a group of physically and mentally handicapped individuals preparing for the "Challenge Games" (think Special Olympics). Carolyn's charge is a young man named Pumpkin (Hank Harris), who doesn't talk much and can only get out of his wheelchair for a few moments at a time. He is immediately smitten by Carolyn, and, after only a session with her, begins to show enough determination to improve his physical condition that his mother (Brenda Blethyn) notices. Meanwhile,

Carolyn is freaked out by working with Pumpkin, and considers quitting. But she can't, and, despite having the "perfect" boyfriend, tennis star Kent Woodlands (Sam Ball), she finds herself increasingly attracted to Pumpkin.

There's a little of the satirical tone of *Bring It On* and *Legally Blonde* in *Pumpkin's* approach, but, in this movie, it is better integrated into the overall story. *Pumpkin* is straightforward in choosing its targets — the "Stepford wife" mentality of sorority sisters, the lack of tolerance amongst supposedly-liberal college students, and society's views of the handicapped as second-rate citizens. The primary target of the screenplay's scorn, at least early in the film, is Carolyn, who represents all of these things. As her personality changes, and she becomes more "real," the movie develops a dramatic arc. Ultimately, while the relationship between Carolyn and Pumpkin is never played entirely straight, it makes for an effective motion picture romance. This particular *Pumpkin* deserves to be picked, not left out on the vine to wither away. **RECOMMENDED**

The Real Blonde [1998]

Starring: **Matthew Modine, Catherine Keener, Maxwell Caulfield, Bridgette Wilson** Director: **Tom DiCillo** Screenplay: **Tom DiCillo** Running Time: **1:30** Rated: **R** (profanity, sexual situations) Theatrical Aspect Ratio: **1.85:1**

The Real Blonde examines the difference between illusion and reality, and satirizes the acting industry. Although the seams in the plot are visible (the movie plays best as a series of loosely-connected comic vignettes), there's enough light substance and lighter humor to warrant a recommendation.

The principals are Joe (Matthew Modine) and Bob (Maxwell Caulfield), a pair of out-of-work actors who are making a living waiting tables for the ever-stern Ernst (Christopher Lloyd). Joe believes in the purity of his craft — the only kinds of acting jobs he's interested in are "serious" ones. His resolve is tested, however, when Bob gets a plum role on the soap opera *Passion Crest*. There's nothing remotely respectable about the part, but it offers Bob a regular income of $3,600 per week and turns him into an overnight heartthrob. Suddenly, a jealous Joe, with some prodding from his live-in girlfriend, Mary (Catherine Keener), decides that if he's going to be an actor, he's going to have to compromise his values. So he goes to his agent (Kathleen Turner) and tells her he's willing to do anything — even a TV commercial or a music video.

The title comes from an obsession of Bob's — for

him, Ms. Right has to be a "real blonde." His on-again, off-again girlfriend, insecure supermodel Sahara (Bridgette Wilson), is a sweet, gorgeous girl, but she's got a dye job. Bob finds what he thinks he wants in Kelly (Daryl Hannah), his leading lady on the soap. He soon learns, however, that just because a woman really has blond hair doesn't mean that there's nothing artificial about her personality.

One aspect of American culture that *The Real Blonde* successful captures (and skewers) is the hollowness of what we're exposed to through the media. Image and fantasy are everything; reality is valueless. Bob is obsessed with a "real blonde" because he's tired of fake women — the irony is that he's just as artificial as any of the girls he goes out with. What's authentic in an industry of make-believe?

The Real Blonde would have been even more satisfying if it had seemed like a coherent whole rather than a batch of skits loosely connected by DiCillo's story arc of a struggling actor trying to remain true to both his calling and the woman he loves. Nevertheless, in part because of Catherine Keener's appeal and in part because DiCillo gets his point across with a successful portion of humor, *The Real Blonde* is enjoyable and inviting. RECOMMENDED

Romy and Michele's High School Reunion [1997]

Starring: Mira Sorvino, Lisa Kudrow, Janeane Garofalo, Alan Cumming Director: David Mirkin Screenplay: Robin Schiff Running Time: 1:31 Rated: R (Profanity, mature themes) Theatrical Aspect Ratio: 1.85:1

The title characters (played by Mira Sorvino and Lisa Kudrow) are blond Southern California babes who have been rooming together since they moved to the L.A. area after graduating from high school. They have been friends for a lot longer — two inseparable peas in a pod who have never fit in with the hip crowd and have never cared that they're outsiders. Now, a decade after brushing the dust of Tucson, Arizona from their heels, the receive word that the Sagebrush High School Class of '87 is holding a 10-year reunion. So, armed with lies about how they have become successful business women, they head east to impress the classmates who used to taunt and ridicule them.

Although I smiled frequently during the film, I didn't laugh too often. Perhaps surprisingly, a lot of the humor is low-key, and there are very few truly hilarious moments. Another problem is that the script unsuccessfully attempts to inject a little lame drama with a moral ("be true to yourself") into the mix. I have no problem with ambitious comedies introduc-

ing dramatic elements into the storyline, but those aspects should be less banal than the ones pulled off the "stock plot device" shelf for this movie. *Romy and Michele* is at its best when it's being lighthearted and at its weakest when it takes a halfhearted stab at semi-seriousness.

Romy and Michele's High School Reunion is one of those pleasant movie-going experiences that doesn't offend, excite, or challenge anyone. There are all sorts of likable things about it — Sorvino and Kudrow, accessible humor, and an '80s soundtrack that's the most definitive survey of the decade in pop music since *Peter's Friends*. First-time director David Mirkin brings a lot of energy to the production, always keeping things moving. And, perhaps most intriguingly, anyone who has ever gone to a reunion will recognize a kernel of truth lurking under all of *Romy and Michele*'s blond and brainless icing. RECOMMENDED

The Royal Tenenbaums [2001]

Starring: Gene Hackman, Anjelica Huston, Ben Stiller, Gwyneth Paltrow, Luke Wilson Director: Wes Anderson Screenplay: Wes Anderson & Owen Wilson Running Time: 1:46 Rated: R (Profanity, brief nudity, sexual situations, mature themes) Theatrical Aspect Ratio: 2.35:1

For those who enjoy skewed, deadpan humor, *The Royal Tenenbaums* has enough to sate the appetite. The movie is a twisted satire on the feel-good genre in which an estranged family member returns to the fold and redeems himself. It's Frank Capra crossed with David Lynch, with a little Monty Python thrown in on the side. The movie is rarely (if ever) side-splittingly funny, but there are so many clever moments that nasty chuckles and devilish smiles come at frequent intervals. The movie doesn't have more heart than Anderson's vastly overrated *Rushmore,* but it's a smarter, more sophisticated endeavor — a clear indication that the filmmaker has grown.

The Tenenbaums are dysfunctional in only a way a movie family can be dysfunctional. Royal Tenenbaum (Gene Hackman), the patriarch, is not a good father. Although he and his wife, Etheline (Anjelica Huston), have raised 3 gifted children, all of them have grown up to be burnt-out neurotics with "issues." Chas (Ben Stiller), a real estate wheeler-dealer in high school, is afraid of his own shadow. Margot, a promising playwright (and the adopted daughter), is trapped in a loveless marriage with a much older man (Bill Murray). And Richie, a former U.S. Open tennis champion who had the biggest meltdown in the history of the sport, pines for his true love — his sister.

Royal, meanwhile, has left the family home to live in a hotel. Although he has never officially divorced Etheline, he has not seen her or his children for 3 years. Then comes the news that Etheline is considering the marriage proposal of Henry Sherman (Danny Glover), and Royal decides he wants to win her back. So, faking a terminal illness, he returns to the Tenenbaum home — at about the same time that Chas, Margot, and Richie all show up. Suddenly, all the members of this none-too-happy clan are back together under the same roof. The Waltons, they aren't.

Anderson doesn't seem to mind breaking movie taboos. Not only does he have a lot of fun with the incestuous relationship of Richie and Margot, but he does something no director seems willing to do these days: kill a pet dog. Much of the humor is sly and dry, not outrageously flamboyant. Dramatically, *The Royal Tenenbaums* is on uncertain ground. Anderson wants the characters to grow on us, and seems to believe that Royal's Scrooge-like transformation should have some meaning, but it doesn't really work. Lovers of *Rushmore* will probably be delighted, but *The Royal Tenenbaums* contains enough that even those who were put off by the earlier movie may find something here worth savoring. **RECOMMENDED**

The Rules of Attraction [2002]

Starring: James Van Der Beek, Shannyn Sossamon, Ian Somerhalder Director: Roger Avary Screenplay: Roger Avary, based on the novel by Bret Easton Ellis Running Time: 1:52 Rated: R (Sexual situations, profanity, nudity, drug use, violence) Theatrical Aspect Ratio: 1.85:1

Once you get past all of the wild camera tricks and visual gimmickry, you arrive at the core of *The Rules of Attraction* and find out that it's really *about* something other than replicating the party life at a New England college. Working from his own screenplay, which has its roots in the Bret Easton Ellis novel, writer/director Roger Avary spins a yarn about the pain of unrequited love that is at times darkly funny and at other times depressingly tragic. It's safe to say there aren't any movies out there quite like this one.

It is possible to consider *The Rules of Attraction* to be an anti-romantic comedy. The Hollywood convention is that, whenever a boy meets a girl, love will follow as quickly as the clichés allow. In real life, sex and romance are less perfect, and, in not giving in to the "love conquers all" mentality, Avary's film uncovers an important truth about male/female relationships — that attraction isn't always mutual, and, even when it is, happily-ever-after is frequently not the result. Each of the 3 protagonists in this movie is in love

(or lust, or whatever), but none of them finds their feelings reciprocated to the same degree.

James Van Der Beek plays Sean Bateman, a student at Camden College who spends most of his time dealing drugs and sleeping with women. Sean is attracted to Lauren (Shannyn Sossamon), and is convinced that she has been leaving anonymous love letters in his mailbox. Meanwhile, although Lauren isn't indifferent to Sean, she has given her heart to her bum of a boyfriend, Victor (Kip Pardue), who has taken off to spend some time wandering around Europe. It is her intention to lose her virginity to him. (She spends her spare time studying pictures of the effects of STDs in an effort to keep her hormones under control.) Then there's Paul (Ian Somerhalder), who used to date Lauren but is currently exploring his bisexual side and has developed a huge crush on Sean. Sean, being self-centered and strictly hetero, is oblivious to Paul's feelings.

As with *Killing Zoe*, Avary has decided to focus upon a group of nihilistic, self-absorbed, drugged out individuals. Avary's view of his characters is cynical and unsympathetic, sometimes to the point of cruelty. *The Rules of Attraction* is not mainstream fare, but it is quirky and interesting, and worth a look for those who don't mind movies where you end up despising just about everyone who has a speaking part. **RECOMMENDED**

Saving Silverman [2001]

Starring: Jason Biggs, Steve Zahn, Jack Black, Amanda Peet, R. Lee Ermey, Amanda Detmer Director: Dennis Dugan Screenplay: Hank Nelken & Greg De Paul Running Time: 1:40 Rated: PG-13 (Profanity, crude humor, violence) Theatrical Aspect Ratio: 2.35:1

Jason Biggs, hopelessly typecast, is back in the same kind of role he played in both *American Pie* and *Loser*: a healthy, young American male who has limited social skills and no success with women. This time, however, he gets lucky. His character, Darren Silverman, is in the right place at the right time, and thus is able to hook up with the "queen of all hotties," Judith (Amanda Peet), who turns out to be a maneater. In no time, she has Darren following her around like an obedient puppy, much to the dismay of his two longtime best friends, Wayne (Steve Zahn) and J.D. (Jack Black). They are aghast when Darren announces his engagement to Judith, and they resolve to stop the relationship before their buddy gets to the altar. To that end, they concoct an amazingly idiotic plan that involves kidnapping Judith; persuading Darren to go out with Sandy (Amanda Detmer), the girl he pined for in high school (and who is in training to become a nun); and getting some help from Darren's idol, Neil Diamond.

Not surprisingly, most of the comedy in *Saving Silverman* has something to do with sex. There are plenty of jokes about masturbation, homosexuality, and various permutations of male/female physical interaction. There's also a welcome absence of toilet humor. *Saving Silverman* has its share of pratfalls and slapstick moments, but there's almost no flatulence. This, more than anything, is an indication that the comedy is being pitched at an older audience than grade-schoolers (or those with a grade school mentality).

Saving Silverman offers the kind of unpretentious entertainment that only this sort of dumb comedy can aim for. And, because the humor works more often than not, the protagonists are affable (if not terribly bright), and R. Lee Ermy's performance is superlative, *Saving Silverman* represents one of those pleasantly unexpected diversions that occasionally crop up during the bleakness of the winter movie season. **RECOMMENDED**

Scary Movie [2000]

Starring: Anna Faris, Shawn Wayans, Marlon Wayans, Cheri Oteri, Shannon Elizabeth Director: Keenen Ivory Wayans Screenplay: Keenen Ivory Wayans, Marlon Wayans, Shawn Wayans, Phil Beauman, Jason Friedberg, Buddy Johnson, Aaron Seltzer Running Time: 1:22 Rated: R (Profanity, explicit sexual language & images, nudity, violence) Theatrical Aspect Ratio: 2.35:1

Offended by gay and anti-gay humor? Avoid *Scary Movie*. Shocked by the sight of an erect (albeit prosthetic) penis? Avoid *Scary Movie*. Horrified by the thought of seeing grandma take a header down the stairs then get run over by a piano? Avoid *Scary Movie*. Put off by the concept of a character so stoned that when he gets shot in the lung, smoke puffs out of the hole? Avoid *Scary Movie*. Embarrassed to laugh at some admittedly juvenile humor? Avoid *Scary Movie*. But if all those things are your cup of tea, you might think this is among the funniest movies around.

Only about 30-40% of the jokes in *Scary Movie* work. There are a lot of clunkers, and some that are simply too dumb to generate a response. However, considering the sheer quantity of material that is thrown at us, even a failure rate of more than 50% represents a lot of laughs.

The central target of the Wayans' wit is *Scream*. It's certainly not the only movie to be skewered by *Scary Movie*, but it's the most obvious. The film opens with

bodacious high school student Drew Becker (Carmen Electra, who cheerfully toys with her image) making popcorn when the phone rings. A voice on the other end inquires what her favorite scary movie is and she immediately replies, "*Kazaam!*" Soon, she's running through sprinklers in her underwear with a masked man in pusuit. The next day, her murder is big news at the local high school, and pushy reporter Gale Hailstorm (Cheri Oteri) is on hand to get the story. Meanwhile, cute and innocent Cindy (Anna Faris) begins to worry that the murder might have something to do with a man she and her friends accidentally killed last Halloween. Her closest pals, Buffy the bimbo (Shannon Elizabeth) and Brenda (Regina Hall), and her boyfriend, Bobby (Jon Abrahams), try to convince her otherwise. But the killer is soon stalking her, and not even the efforts of Deputy Dufy (Dave Sheridan) can save the day.

One inherent problem with this type of motion picture is a tendency to lose comic momentum, and *Scary Movie* suffers from the malaise. The film has a significantly higher laugh quotient at the beginning than near the end, and there are several noticeable dead spots during the final half-hour. A shorter, tighter version of *Scary Movie* probably would have been better, but the film's lean running length of 82 minutes is already on the low side of what will play in a multiplex. Nevertheless, the material generates so much laughter that the overriding post-viewing impression is of an uneven film that's definitely worth the time investment. **RECOMMENDED**

Scotland, PA [2001]

Starring: James LeGros, Maura Tierney, Christopher Walken, Kevin Corrigan Director: Billy Morrissette Screenplay: Billy Morrissette, based on a story by William Shakespeare Running Time: 1:35 Rated: R (Profanity, violence) Theatrical Aspect Ratio: 1.85:1

Billy Morrissette has taken the premise behind *Macbeth* and shifted it several centuries, to the 1970s. Morrissette does not rely on Shakespeare's dialogue (although some of the play's most famous lines can be heard in the background, often coming out of a radio), but anyone remotely familiar with the play will recognize the similarities. Morrissette hasn't even bothered to change the names (well, at least not much). What he has done is played with tone and intent, resulting in a motion picture that is undeniably *Macbeth* and unquestionably a comedy.

The themes and ideas underlying the play — revenge, manipulation, guilt, and fate — remain in place, but the changes result in additional layers.

Morrissette's approach allows him to broadly satirize fast-food, suburbia, and, most obviously, the 70s. Joe and Pat McBeth (James LeGros and Maura Tierney) are workers at Duncan's hamburger joint in the tiny town of Scotland, PA. Tired of taking orders and getting no recognition for their valuable contributions, Joe and Pat decide to take action. Prodded by the musings of three hippies (Andy Dick, Speed Levitch, and Amy Smart), they plot the death of their boss, Duncan (James Rebhorn). The crime is committed, and it looks like the McBeths have gotten away with it, until police lieutenant Ernie McDuff (Christopher Walken) starts investigating. That puts him and Joe on a collision course.

Scotland, PA is peppered with witty dialogue and inventive moments. Early in the film, there is a scene in which Joe throws two troublemakers out of the restaurant. Morrissette films this like high drama, in slow motion with a soaring melodramatic score. The result is very funny. We learn that Duncan made his fortune by selling a chain of donut stores. And we're treated to lines like (from Pat McBeth), "We're not bad people — we're just underachievers that have to make up for lost time."

This movie won't help kids looking for essay answers for their English class, but, for those who don't take their Shakespeare too seriously, *Scotland, PA* is a lot of fun. Who would have imagined that such a funny motion picture would have its roots in one of the Bard's bloodiest plays? **RECOMMENDED**

Secretary [2002]

Starring: James Spader, Maggie Gyllenhaal Director: Steven Shainberg Screenplay: Erin Cressida Wilson, based on the short story by Mary Gaitskill Running Time: 1:45 Rated: R (Sexual situations, S&M, nudity, profanity) Theatrical Aspect Ratio: 1.85:1

Secretary is just your regular, garden-variety romantic comedy with heavy doses of S&M/B&D. The movie enters a realm where few non-porn films venture, and comes across as darkly funny, energetic, and surprisingly gentle. Part of the reason that *Secretary* succeeds is that it doesn't treat S&M relationships only as the butt of jokes or purely for their shock value — when we laugh, it's because the director intended us to laugh, not because we're uncomfortable or being exposed to a dirty little secret. While being aware of the absurdity of an S&M relationship, filmmaker Steven Shainberg recognizes that there are legitimate psychological reasons why people engage in this behavior. He is also careful not to make the actions of the characters too extreme.

The film opens by introducing the protagonist, Lee Holloway (Maggie Gyllenhaal). Lee has just been released from a mental institution where she was treated for her self-mutilation tendencies. Whenever the stress in her life becomes unbearable, she removes a sharp object from a small bag she carries and opens a wound on her thigh. No sooner has Lee emerged from treatment than her father's drinking binge veers her back towards the edge. In an attempt to fend off her condition, she decides to look for a job, and finds employment for a stern, emotionally closed-off lawyer, E. Edward Grey (James Spader).

At first, Lee's job entails little more than the daily rigors expected of a secretary — answering the phones, typing letters, and so forth. Gradually, however, Edward becomes more domineering in reprimanding Lee for typos, and, on one occasion, when his anger at her errors results in a spanking session, both Lee and Edward realize they have stumbled upon a taboo desire that fulfills them both. However, while Lee relishes her part as the submissive, Edward is tormented by his inability to give up his addiction to domination. Only when Lee begins to express genuine feelings for Edward does he become frightened enough to put an end to the non-business aspects of their relationship. Lee is crushed — and realizes that she loves Edward.

Secretary is less about sex than it is about human interaction outside of what society deems normal. Tone is critical, and that's where Shainberg hits pay dirt. *Secretary* has enough genuine laughs to eliminate the potential twitters and snickers, and it treats Edward and Lee as people. Some of the credit must go to Spader, who is his usual solid self, and Gyllenhaal, who is amazing, but the director knows exactly where he wants his characters to go, and successfully takes them there. *Secretary* is a romantic comedy for those who go into sugar shock from the usual entries into the genre. **HIGHLY RECOMMENDED**

Sliding Doors [United Kingdom, 1998]

Starring: Gwyneth Paltrow, John Lynch, John Hannah, Jeanne Tripplehorn Director: Peter Howitt Screenplay: Peter Howitt Running Time: 1:45 Rated: R (Sex, profanity) Theatrical Aspect Ratio: 1.85:1

Film makers are no less fascinated by issues of destiny than anyone else, and that's why there's no shortage of movies about this subject. While this approach has been the fodder for several notable dramatic films, *Sliding Doors* is the first romantic comedy to plumb its depths. The "road not taken" approach isn't just a plot device, either. Writer/director Peter Howitt expands upon both possible fates of a character after she just misses/catches a train. The audience watches, with ever-growing fascination, how this one event impacts upon every aspect of her life: her future career, where she lives, whom she loves, and whether she has a family. As her separate destinies diverge and then re-converge, she becomes two completely different individuals.

That woman is Helen, played by Gwyneth Paltrow as a long, dark-haired Brit. One day, after losing her job as an advertising executive, she decides to return home in the middle of the day. The scene of the pivotal moment is a train platform. In scenario #1, she just slips through the sliding doors before the train pulls out of the station. On board, she meets the cheerful, talkative James (John Hannah), a *Monty Python* fan who is taken with her beauty. Minutes later, in her flat, she walks in on her lover, Gerry (John Lynch), in bed with another woman (Jeanne Tripplehorn). In scenario #2, she misses the train and, shortly thereafter, is the victim of an attempted mugging. She doesn't meet James and fails to make it home in time to discover Gerry's infidelity. Juxtaposed one against the other, while sharing many places, cues, and characters, the two stories proceed in parallel from there.

On one level, for viewers who enjoy pondering the workings of fate, *Sliding Doors* can be viewed as a deep and wonderful experience. But, for those who just appreciate a romantic comedy characterized by solid acting, a script with a few twists, and a great deal of genuinely funny material, *Sliding Doors* still fits the bill. One of its most obvious strengths is that it can satisfy many different types of audiences — those who demand something substantial from their motion pictures, and those who couldn't care less. HIGHLY RECOMMENDED

Slums of Beverly Hills [1998]

Starring: **Natasha Lyonne, Alan Arkin, Marisa Tomei, Kevin Corrigan** Director: **Tamara Jenkins** Screenplay: **Tamara Jenkins** Running Time: **1:31** Rated: **R** (Sex, nudity, profanity, drugs) Theatrical Aspect Ratio: **1.85:1**

Our guide through the *Slums of Beverly Hills* is Vivian Abramowitz, who is played by Natasha Lyonne in a star-making performance. Lyonne makes Vivian instantly likable. She's a tough-talking girl whose uncertainty about her own sexuality and her developing body reveals an inner innocence and vulnerability. Her uncertain lifestyle doesn't make it easy to deal with the effects of hormones racing out of control.

Her father and mother are divorced, and she lives with her dad, Murray (Alan Arkin), and her two male siblings. Consequently, there is no woman around to shepherd her through experiences like her first period. So, when her perpetually-stoned cousin, Rita (the always energetic Marisa Tomei), comes to stay, Vivian is suddenly on the fast track to learning about sex.

The Abramowitzes are nomads. They don't have much money, so they move from cheap apartment to cheap apartment, often skipping out in the middle of the night to avoid paying the rent. They stay just within the limits of Beverly Hills because of the schools. As Murray states, "Furniture is temporary, education is forever." When Rita comes to live with them, however, her rich father (Carl Reiner) pays Murray enough money that he and his family can afford to move into a ritzy place. While there, Vivian meets and falls for a gentle-but-strange neighbor, Eliot (Kevin Corrigan), who is fixated with Charles Manson.

Slums of Beverly Hills is by turns funny and poignant, and it effectively expresses the various traumas of young womanhood. However, although Vivian is at the center of Jenkins' movie, the other characters are not ignored. Murray in particular is fleshed out, due in no small part to the contribution of veteran actor Arkin, who injects the right amount of wit into an otherwise straight performance. Murray is not the perfect father, but he loves his children and is trying to provide the best life he can for them.

First-time writer/director Jenkins has admitted in interviews that *Slums of Beverly Hills* contains a high quotient of autobiographical material. The truth of this shows in the insight she brings to Vivian's experiences. The character's struggles with the pitfalls of adolescent development may be particular to women, but many of the emotional ramifications will strike a chord of familiarity for men, as well. It's the differences in addition to the similarities that make all coming-of-age stories compelling to members of both sexes, and *Slums of Beverly Hills* is an example of how engaging one such tale can be. RECOMMENDED

The Snapper [United Kingdom/Ireland, 1993]

Starring: **Colm Meaney, Tina Kellegher, Ruth McCabe** Director: **Stephen Frears** Screenplay: **Roddy Doyle** Running Time: **1:34** Rated: **R** (Language, mature themes) Theatrical Aspect Ratio: **1.85:1**

In the Curley household, unwed motherhood isn't the disaster it might be elsewhere. When 20-year-old Sharon (Tina Kellegher) informs her father, Desi (Colm Meaney), and mother, Kay (Ruth McCabe), that she's "up the pole," they aren't thrilled, but there's no display of histrionics. After asking who the father is (and not being told), Desi invites his daughter out to the local pub for a drink. Sharon's friends are as interested as her family in the father's identity, but she resolutely keeps mum about the truth until an event in the neighborhood brings it into the open.

The Snapper is a very funny production, and it gets funnier as the movie progresses. Some of the humor has a distinctly Irish flavor, and it takes a while to get used to the ebb and flow of certain jokes. The biggest obstacle to laughter in *The Snapper* may be getting past the heavy accents. Wisely, however, Miramax has decided against subtitles, which would have ruined the subtlety of many of the wittier moments.

Those who think this is just another "unmarried girl gets pregnant" motion picture are in for a surprise. Rarely has a movie honestly, yet humorously, shown how the pressures of pregnancy can tear at the fabric of a close-knit, working-class family. The relationship between Sharon and her dad is more intimate than that of most daughter/father pairings, and the things these two have to admit to one another are often heartrendingly difficult to say.

In fact, the dramatic elements of *The Snapper* hold the humor in check. It's hard to let loose with unrestrained laughter when you recognize the pain underlying a scene. There are several sequences that move from laughter to tears back to laughter, bringing the audience along on the roller coaster ride. This structure doesn't always work, and that occasionally leads to an unsettled feeling.

It's refreshing to see an old subject dealt with in the open and original manner that *The Snapper* handles pregnancy. The marriage of humor and drama is admittedly imperfect, but it works well enough to occasionally spawn laughter and touch the heart, and there's a crucial scene between Colm Meaney and Tina Kellegher that is beautifully written, acted, and directed. Even those who have trouble understanding the accents will find that once the language barrier is broken and the slang deciphered, *The Snapper* has a surprising amount of depth. **RECOMMENDED**

State and Main [2000]

Starring: Alec Baldwin, Charles Durning, Philip Seymour Hoffman, William H. Macy Director: David Mamet Screenplay: David Mamet Running Time: 1:45 Rated: R (Profanity) Theatrical Aspect Ratio: 1.85:1

State and Main chronicles the trials and tribulations of a production crew trying to make a movie on-loca-

tion in the small town of Waterford, Vermont. Although this is a farce, one has to wonder how many of the incidents related in the film represent episodes from director David Mamet's experience. The characters are a mix of Hollywood big shots and small town types. Arriving in Waterford are Walt Price (William H. Macy), the director; Marty Rossen (David Paymer), the producer; Bob Barrenger (Alec Baldwin), the male lead with a penchant for underage girls; Claire Wellesley (Sarah Jessica Parker), the female lead; and Joseph Turner White (Philip Seymour Hoffman), the sensitive writer. Greeting the movie-makers are the likes of Waterford's mayor, George Bailey (Charles Durning); the mayor's domineering wife, Sherry (Patti LuPone); the local bookseller, Ann Black (Rebecca Pidgeon); and the young and flirtatious Carla (Julia Stiles).

Problems crop up almost immediately. The town's historical old mill, where much of the film's action was to have taken place, burned down more than 30 years ago. Barrenger's notorious appetites get him in trouble the minute he meets Carla. Claire wants an additional $800,000 to appear topless (despite the fact that the American public can "draw her [breasts] from memory"). Rossen is pushing the product placement of bazoomer.com, even though the movie is a period piece set in 1895. And White falls for local girl Ann, enraging her lawyer/fiancé.

State and Main is not consistently funny, but it contains a number of winning scenes and barbed one-liners. Mamet's talent for writing shines through with comments like: "It's not a lie, it's a gift for fiction," "An associate producer credit is what you give your secretary instead of a raise," and "The better part of valor is to step away, or you, your kids, and your grandkids will die in poverty." There's a brief-but-timely exchange on how absurd the American electoral process is (ironically, the film was made long before the current Presidential situation). And, while Mamet's view of Hollywood types is sharp and cynical, it isn't nearly as nasty as what was portrayed in Robert Altman's *The Player*.

Mamet has a reputation for creating daring and powerful motion pictures. *State and Main* is neither daring nor powerful, but its lightness and lack of complexity should not necessarily be viewed as a negative. It's highly watchable, and, at times, humorously compelling. The film probably doesn't deserve the large crowds and long lines it generated at film festivals, but, in the more comfortable venue of a local theater, it offers 2 hours' diverting entertainment. **RECOMMENDED**

Strictly Ballroom [Australia, 1992]

Starring: **Paul Mercurio, Tara Morice, Gia Carides** Director: **Baz Luhrmann** Screenplay: **Baz Luhrmann & Andrew Bovell** Running Time: **1:34** Rated: **PG (mature themes)** Theatrical Aspect Ratio: **1.85:1**

Scott Hastings (Paul Mercurio), one of Australia's best ballroom dancers, is targetted for a number of championships until he abandons the Dance Federation's rigid steps in favor of his own moves. Horrified by his unorthodox behavior, his partner, Liz (Gia Carides), leaves him, and Scott is forced to take up with an amateur. Fran (Tara Morice) matches Scott's zest for life, but one question hangs over them as they teach each other about life, love, and dancing: can they win by rejecting tradition?

Strictly Ballroom, based on an Australian play of the same name, was one of that country's biggest 1992 screen hits. It's easy to see why. The movie is funny, energetic, and enjoyable — the perfect film for a night or an afternoon out, regardless of what mood you're in. While the plot and characters don't boast any special depth, there's enough freshness to hold just about anyone's interest.

The movie possesses an inventive sense of humor that becomes apparent in the riotously funny opening scenes. Although *Strictly Ballroom* never recaptures the brilliantly offbeat quality of its beginning, there are still numerous laughs peppered throughout, and its upbeat sense of fun is infectious. *Strictly Ballroom* is filled with energy and color. The dance numbers are splendidly choreographed and the soundtrack is vibrant and varied. The romantic elements, while skillfully downplayed, are relegated to the background.

Like *Dead Poets' Society, Strictly Ballroom*'s motto might be "Seize the day!" When Scott is dancing to satisfy everyone else's expectations, he isn't happy, but when he takes a chance and does his own thing, he finds fulfillment, and, with Fran, love. In a world where winning means everything, Scott learns how hollow victory can be if the price is stifling creativity. His own father, as it turns out, is a living example of this.

Strictly Ballroom represents the best in light entertainment, and, apart from a slight fall-off during the second half, there aren't many flaws. The movie has

wit, style, and a special brand of irreverence that allows it to work as a love story, a comedy of manners, and a satire. **HIGHLY RECOMMENDED**

The Stupids [1996]

Starring: **Tom Arnold, Jessica Lundy, Bug Hall, Alex McKenna** Director: **John Landis** Screenplay: **Brent Forrester** Running Time: **1:30** Rated: **PG (Nothing offensive)** Theatrical Aspect Ratio: **1.85:1**

The Stupids is a pleasant surprise: a comedy about dumb characters that doesn't insult the audience's intelligence. John Landis' brand of humor doesn't rely on flatulence jokes, double entendres, or sexual innuendo. *The Stupids* is relatively clean, entirely suitable for family viewing, and much funnier than countless films with harsher Rateds.

Brent Forrester's script is a Machiavellian masterpiece of misdirection, misrepresentation, and mayhem. And be forewarned — appearances can be deceiving. Despite the title, this film is going to appeal more to the thinking viewer than someone who prefers to sit back and laugh at mindless gags. The best aspect of *The Stupids* is seeing events from two perspectives — that of a "normal" person and that of our intrepid heroes, a family so dense that, put together, their combined IQs would have trouble reaching the triple-digit level.

With a vacuous affability, Tom Arnold plays Stanley Stupid, the good-natured head of the Stupid clan. Decked out in an outdated plaid sportscoat and straw hat, Stanley and his wardrobe both appear stranded in an earlier decade. His wife, Joan (Jessica Lundy), and children, Buster (Bug Hall) and Petunia (Alex McKenna), are just as intellectually dim and fashion impaired. Joan looks like she just stepped out of an episode of *Leave It to Beaver*.

The story begins innocently enough. Stanley goes out one morning to find his curbside trash cans empty. Someone has stolen the garbage again! Unlike in the past, however, he's no longer going to sit back and allow this sort of thing to continue. So, several nights later, after setting the bait, he hides in the bushes and waits. When a huge truck comes along and the men inside take not only his garbage, but that of his neighbors, Stanley reaches a stunning conclusion: this is a conspiracy of global proportions. Someone is draining the world of one of its most valuable resources: garbage. A typically illogical leap leads Stanley to connect this latest caper to a scheme he uncovered years ago while working for the Postal

Service, where thousands of letters never reached their destinations because they were being diverted to a mysterious Mr. Sender. The only evidence of this tampering was a message stamped on the envelope: "Return to Sender." Soon, the Stupids are hunting down this dangerous enemy, overcoming obstacles by relying on "techniques that defy description."

The Stupids is loaded (if not overloaded) with all sorts of humor — everything from satire and word-play to slapstick. Not a moment goes by when something amusing isn't happening, even if it's taking place in the background. *The Stupids* will be seen in different ways by different people, but one thing is abundantly clear: the film makers deserve congratulations for coming up with something this diabolically clever. **RECOMMENDED**

Sweet and Lowdown [1999]

Starring: Sean Penn, Samantha Morton, Uma Thurman Director: Woody Allen Screenplay: Woody Allen Running Time: 1:35 Rated: PG-13 (Sexual situations, drug use) Theatrical Aspect Ratio: 1.85:1

Presented as if it's the bio-pic of a real person, *Sweet and Lowdown* mixes reminiscences with legends and "facts" to present a fragmented portrait of the lead character. As essayed by Sean Penn, Ray is a brilliant but egotistical and erratic artist whose personality traits included an inferiority complex to a French gypsy guitarist named Django Reinhardt, a mild case of kleptomania, and a tendency to show up "late, drunk, or not at all" for shows. Ray comes alive through a series of episodic vignettes, many of which are more in the nature of tall tales than historically believable recreations. (In one instance, we're even offered a multiple choice resolution for one of Ray's "legendary" escapades.) Along with various jazz authorities who appear in "talking head" segments, Allen provides some of the linking narration between episodes; other than that, the director is absent from the screen.

Sweet and Lowdown is arguably the least ambitious and most atypical entry into Allen's '90s canon. Perhaps ironically, it is all the more pleasant for those qualities. The shift back in time and the lack of an obvious Allen-like central figure help things immeasurably — we don't spend the movie on the lookout for self-referential insights about the man behind the camera. The movie looks great, and, as one might expect from this sort of production, there's a top-notch jazz score. Ultimately, *Sweet and Lowdown* isn't a monumental event, but it represents an enjoyable diversion. **RECOMMENDED**

Tadpole [2002]

Starring: Sigourney Weaver, Aaron Stanford, John Ritter, Bebe Neuwirth Director: Gary Winick Screenplay: Heather McGowan and Niels Mueller Running Time: 1:15 Rated: R (Sexual situations, profanity) Theatrical Aspect Ratio: 1.85:1

Oscar Grubman (Aaron Stanford) is not an average 15-year-old high school sophomore. Aside from the fact that he attends an exclusive prep school, he reads (and quotes) Voltaire, is more interested in a woman's hands than any other physical assets, and makes shocking statements to the effect that life "isn't all about getting laid." According to his best friend, Charlie (Robert Iler, Tony Jr. from "The Sopranos"), he's like a 40-year old trapped in a 15-year-old's body. And, indeed, Oscar's taste in women runs to those who are decades his senior. He is hopelessly infatuated with his step-mother, Eve (Sigourney Weaver), and endlessly plots how to reveal his feelings. He is convinced that her marriage to his father, Stanley (John Ritter), has left her unfulfilled and has a vague notion that he might be able to fill the vacuum. Then, when he's home in Manhattan for Thanksgiving, he makes the mistake of getting drunk, then compounds that error by sleeping with Eve's best friend, Diane (Bebe Neuwirth). He then spends the rest of the vacation trying to hide his indiscretion from his parents while subtly wooing Eve.

The script, credited to Heather McGowan and Niels Mueller, is smart, witty, and occasionally very funny. The top-notch cast brings the story to life with aplomb. As the man-eating (or should that be "boy-eating") Diane, Bebe Neuwirth displays impeccable comic timing. She's the main reason why one of *Tadpole*'s standout scenes, a quiet little restaurant dinner, delivers as many laughs as it does. Newcomer Aaron Stanford makes a solid feature debut, although no one is going to mistake the 25-year old for someone 10 years his junior. Maybe one of the reasons this movie doesn't make us squirm as it flirts with pedophilia is that Stanford's Oscar looks like he's legally an adult.

Tadpole captures not the ebb and flow of average teenage relationship angst, but the currents that direct Oscar's atypical life. Of course, it's far off the beaten path for a high school student to lust after his step-mother and consummate a relationship with her best friend, but I find that to be a little more stimulating than watching Freddie Prinze Jr. and Sarah Michelle Gellar figuring out who's going to the prom with whom. As is astutely observed by Charlie, Oscar's life has the potential to become a Greek tragedy, but Winick keeps things light enough that it resolutely stays a comedy. RECOMMENDED

There's Something About Mary [1998]

Starring: Ben Stiller, Cameron Diaz, Matt Dillon Directors: Peter Farrelly & Bobby Farrelly Screenplay: Ed Decter & John J. Strauss and Peter Farrelly & Bobby Farrelly Running Time: 1:57 Rated: R (Profanity, gross-out jokes, fake nudity, cruelty to animals and human beings) Theatrical Aspect Ratio: 1.85:1

When we first meet the narrator of the story, Ted (Ben Stiller), it's 1985 in the small town of Cumberland, Rhode Island. The occasion is Ted's Senior Prom, and he is about to attend it with Mary (Cameron Diaz), the girl of his dreams. Ted can't believe this is really happening, but Mary, after breaking up with a longtime boyfriend, took a liking to Ted when he stood up for her mentally handicapped brother, Warren (W. Earl Brown). Things are going along perfectly for Ted until he makes a pit stop in Mary's bathroom while she's upstairs changing. Failure to tuck himself in properly before zipping up leads to one of the film's most painful comedy sequences and ruins Ted's chance for a date with Mary.

Cut to 1998. Ted, now a moderately successful writer, still carries the torch for Mary. On the advice of his best friend, Dom (Chris Elliott), he hires Pat Healy (Matt Dillon), a sleazy private investigator, to track down Mary, who now lives in Florida. Pat finds and falls for his quarry, then lies to Ted about her whereabouts so he can pursue her on his own. But Ted, unconvinced by Pat's information, decides to check things out on his own, and soon finds himself in the middle of a bizarre romantic pentagon that also involves a British architect (Lee Evans) and a famous NFL quarterback.

Perhaps the most surprising thing about *There's Something about Mary* is that, while the film relies heavily on crude humor, it's also unexpectedly effective as a sweet, albeit offbeat, romantic comedy. Granted, if you're not at least open to laughing at the kinds of gags that the Farrellys bombard their audience with, it's doubtful that this aspect of the film will save it. But, for those who embrace the humor in all of its perversity, the effectiveness of the romance is a distinct plus.

To be fair to the Farrellys, not every joke in this film centers on genitals, breasts, bodily fluids, or an assortment of other, tasteless subjects. Granted, this isn't subtle or intellectual humor (two words that don't apply to any Farrelly Brothers production), but it is less earthy than their usual material. The Far-

rellys couldn't care less whether viewers are affronted by their material. In fact, they probably set out with the intention of offending at least 99% of the audience. RECOMMENDED

To Die For [1995]

Starring: Nicole Kidman, Matt Dillon, Joaquin Phoenix, Casey Affleck Director: Gus Van Sant Jr. Screenplay: Buck Henry, based on the novel by Joyce Maynard Running Time: 1:43 Rated: R (Profanity, sex, violence) Theatrical Aspect Ratio: 1.85:1

Told in an effectively disorganized fashion that jumps back and forth in time and includes pseudo-interviews and pieces of "actual" story, *To Die For* gradually unravels the tale of TV weatherperson Suzanne Stone (Nicole Kidman), who gains national notoriety as the result of a murder conspiracy rap that she beats. Her face and story are everywhere — *Donahue*, *USA Today*, and smaller talk shows across the country. For someone with Suzanne's vapid philosophy that "You're not anyone in America unless you're on TV," this is paradise.

More than a year before the end of the film (which is also the beginning), Suzanne is a single young woman in the town of Little Hope, New Hampshire. She has the looks, but not much intelligence to go with them. Despite that (or perhaps because of it), she catches the eye of local hunk Larry Maretto (Matt Dillon), an all-around nice guy and the son of a reputed mobster. Larry falls head-over-heels, and there are soon nuptials, with Suzanne wearing an exact replica of Maria Shriver's wedding veil. Not long after that, Larry has been transformed from "Van Halen to Jerry Vale" and is beginning to bore Suzanne with his desire to become a father, especially now that her career is taking off with a daily job as the weathergirl at a local cable station.

Van Sant, whose previous efforts include *Drug Store Cowboy* and *My Private Idaho*, is not an accomplished satirist, but his screenwriter, Buck Henry (adapting from a book by Joyce Maynard), is. The humor in this film is more often intellectually tantalizing than laugh-aloud funny. Suzanne is the embodiment of the extreme celebrity worship that has made the O.J. Simpson circus into the biggest TV event of all time. In the main, Van Sant and Henry know just how to exploit that element of their film.

To Die For has its share of truly delicious sequences, and some biting dialogue worth killing for. The best moments occur during a taped interview with Suzanne where she discusses her frighteningly shallow theories about life, death, television, and keeping her maiden name for on-air work. In the end, however, *To Die For* doesn't go quite far enough — there are times when Van Sant stays a little too conventional, and this causes the picture to have only teeth when it could have had fangs. **RECOMMENDED**

Twelfth Night [United Kingdom/United States, 1996]

Starring: Helena Bonham Carter, Imogen Stubbs, Nigel Hawthorne, Richard E. Grant, Ben Kingsley Director: Trevor Nunn Screenplay: Trevor Nunn, based on the play by William Shakespeare Running Time: 2:14 Rated: PG (Mature themes) Theatrical Aspect Ratio: 1.85:1

Twelfth Night opens with a scene alluded to, but never presented in Shakespeare's original text. Twin siblings, Viola (Imogen Stubbs) and Sebastian (Steven Mackintosh), are aboard a ship that is wrecked off the coast of the imaginary country of Illyria. Although both characters escape the disaster, they are separated, and each believes the other to be dead. In order to survive more easily in a "man's world," Viola cuts her hair, glues on a fake mustache, and dresses in men's clothing. Going by the name of Cesario, she enters the service of a local Duke, Orsino (Toby Stephens). Orsino is madly in love with a young countess, Olivia (Helena Bonham Carter), who steadfastly refuses his advances. Orsino sends Viola to woo Olivia in his name. Olivia immediately falls for Viola/Cesario, while, at the same time, Viola realizes that she is in love with Orsino. And so the triangle is established.

A secondary story concerns the goings-on in Olivia's household, where the countess' frequently drunk uncle, Sir Toby Belch (Mel Smith); her maid, Maria (Imelda Staunton); a foppish noble, Sir Andrew Aguecheek (Richard E. Grant); and an itinerant entertainer, Feste (Ben Kingsley), plot the downfall of Olivia's bad-tempered steward, Malvolio (Nigel Hawthorne).

Twelfth Night is chiefly about the similarities and differences between the sexes. By dressing Viola as a man, Shakespeare establishes an opportunity to explore through one character the different manners in which men and women approach the same situation, especially if it involves love. The play also addresses the deceptiveness of judging by appearance. After all, appearance, especially as it relates to identity, is an important aspect of *Twelfth Night*.

With *Twelfth Night*, as with any of the Bard's comedies, there's always a question of how well the humor will translate to a modern audience. Fortunately, in large part due to a wonderful comic turn by Nigel Hawthorne, the film offers plenty to laugh at. The finale, where all the mistaken identities are unraveled, is an example of how perfect timing can accentuate comedy.

Shakespeare aficionados will probably be pleased that so much of the written word has made it to the screen, but the 2+ hour running length is a bit burdensome. Nevertheless, the slow spots are worth sitting through, because, as a whole, this is solid entertainment. **RECOMMENDED**

Undercover Brother [2002]

Starring: Eddie Griffin, Chris Kattan, Denise Richards, David Chappelle Director: Malcolm D. Lee Screenplay: John Ridley & Michael McClullers Running Time: 1:23 Rated: PG-13 (Profanity, sexual situations, cartoon violence) Theatrical Aspect Ratio: 1.85:1

The filmmakers atop *Undercover Brother* understand that parody, no matter how inherently witty, cannot last for 90 minutes. Repetition will give birth to boredom. Thus, to keep the audience's interest, the film changes tone and focus on a fairly regular basis. By re-inventing itself every 20 minutes or so, *Undercover Brother* plays more like a series of thinly-connected skits than a coherent motion picture; however, for this kind of production, that's not a detriment. Also, director Malcolm D. Lee (cousin of Spike Lee) and his cast understand the meaning of the term "comedic timing." Because of that, jokes work here that might not have worked in other, similar endeavors.

Anton Jackson (Eddie Griffin) is Undercover Brother, a very conspicuous guy whose wardrobe and appearance are stuck in the '70s, and who is devoted to the cause of the Black Man. One day, Undercover Brother's path inadvertently crosses that of B.R.O.T.H.E.R.H.O.O.D., an organization dedicated to opposing the schemes of The (White) Man and his assistant, Mr. Feather (Chris Kattan), whose goal is to promote racial divisiveness. When the Chief of B.R.O.T.H.E.R.H.O.O.D. (Chi McBride) is impressed by Undercover Brother's moves, he offers the ultra-cool guy with the mega-afro a position in B.R.O.T.H.E.R.H.O.O.D.'s inner circle, joining the likes of Sista Girl (Aunjanue Ellis), Conspiracy Brother (David Chappelle), Smart Brother (Gary Anthony Williams), and Lance (Neil Patrick Harris), the white, affirmative action intern. Undercover Brother's first assignment: go undercover playing the black sellout in a white corporation and discover how Mr. Feather has managed to force a Colin Powell-type Presidential candidate (Billy Dee Williams) to abandon politics in favor of opening a fried chicken fast food chain.

The most consistently funny parts of *Undercover Brother* — and there are surprisingly quite a few to choose from — involve Undercover Brother losing himself in white corporate America. The movie uses humor to make its points, but it does so gently, not stridently, and with a smile, rather than an angry grimace. Of course, *Undercover Brother* is more interested in getting laughs and appealing to a wide audience than in making a social statement. Consequently, it takes equal jabs at black and white culture.

Undercover Brother needn't be a guilty pleasure — it's made with enough savvy to be appreciated on its own terms. There are laughs aplenty, and, as a bonus, viewers don't have to worry about being subjected to farts, urine, feces, semen, or any of the other foul substances that have overrun modern-day comedies.
RECOMMENDED

Wag the Dog [1997]
Starring: Robert De Niro, Dustin Hoffman, Anne Heche, Woody Harrelson Director: Barry Levinson Screenplay: David Mamet & Hilary Henkin, based on the book by Larry Beinhart Running Time: 1:35 Rated: R (Profanity, mature themes) Theatrical Aspect Ratio: 1.85:1

Hollywood and Presidential politics — perfect together. Anyone who doubts this simple maxim will face a challenge to their opinion when they see *Wag the Dog*, the hilarious satire from director Barry Levinson. For, although this film is one of the funniest comedies out there, it also carries a serious, thought-provoking message about the relationship between politics and mass-market entertainment. This is one of Levinson's best films, and the screenplay, co-penned by noted writer David Mamet (along with Hilary Henkin), is brilliantly on-target.

The premise is relatively simple. Only 2 weeks before election day, a sitting president is hit by a sex scandal. A brief dalliance with a Firefly Girl becomes public knowledge, and now his 17% lead is about to plummet. Winifred Ames (Anne Heche), one of the President's top aides, calls in spin doctor extraordinary, Conrad Bream (Robert De Niro). Conrad goes to work immediately, deciding that the best way to get the public's mind off the Firefly Girl is to give them something bigger to think about. "Change the story, change the lead" is his motto, so he decides to manufacture a war against Albania. Why Albania? Because the name sounds sinister and no one in the United States knows anything about the country.

Conrad decides that he and Winifred can't do it alone. They need help, so they go to big-time Hollywood producer Stanley Motss (Dustin Hoffman). He has never won an Academy Award, but he's more than willing to help stage the war. They'll need slo-gans, a theme song, merchandising links, and sympathetic characters. Soon, carefully-controlled leaks to the press make it to the evening news, and everyone is reporting about the outbreak of hostilities between the United States and Albania, even though no troops have been moved and no shots have been fired. Actual battles don't matter, however, because, if it's on television, it must be real.

To avoid making *Wag the Dog* sound too much like an intellectual challenge, let me make this clarification: the movie is intelligent, but it's also a lot of fun. This is the kind of film that you can laugh and think your way through. I look forward to seeing *Wag the Dog* another time, and I think I'll enjoy it as much, if not more. No matter what your political persuasion is, or how cynically you regard the goings-on in Washington, you will be entertained. Let's just hope *Wag the Dog* isn't *too* close to the mark in its depiction of specific events. **HIGHLY RECOMMENDED**

Waiting for Guffman [1996]
Starring: Christopher Guest, Eugene Levy, Catherine O'Hara, Fred Willard, Parker Posey Director: Christopher Guest Screenplay: Christopher Guest & Eugene Levy Running Time: 1:24 Rated: R (Profanity, mature themes) Theatrical Aspect Ratio: 1.85:1

Because the title sounds like *Waiting for Godot*, some viewers may be fooled into expecting highbrow entertainment from *Waiting for Guffman*. They are in for a huge surprise, for, although Christopher Guest's film is exceptionally perceptive, there's nothing remotely artsy or pretentious about it. This "documentary," which chronicles the production of an amateur play to celebrate the sesquicentennial of the fictitious town of Blaine, Missouri, offers one laugh after another.

Blaine has two claims to fame — it's the "stool capital of the United States" and it was visited by a UFO before Roswell was ever heard of. In fact, when the aliens landed in Blaine, they invited the residents on board their ship for a pot luck dinner, and when they took off, they left behind a circular landing site within which the weather never changes (67 degrees with a 40% chance of rain). Now, Blaine is 150 years old, and, to celebrate the occasion, the town council has decided on a number of special events, all to culminate with the play "Red, White, and Blaine," which is to be produced at the local high school.

Directing this play is off-off-off-off-Broadway exile Corky St. Claire (Christopher Guest), the man who attempted to turn *Backdraft* into a stage production. Corky is ably assisted by his music director, Lloyd

Miller (Bob Balaban), and has a fine cast of 6. They are the husband-and-wife team of Ron and Sheila Albertson (Fred Willard and Catherine O'Hara), Blaine's travel agents (who have never been outside of Blaine), local dentist Allan Pearl (Eugene Levy), Dairy Queen waitress Libby Mae Brown (Parker Posey), auto mechanic Johnny Savage (Matt Keeslar), and an old coot by the name of Clifford Wooley (Lewis Arquette). Abandoning their day jobs, they come together to breathe life into a musical version of Blaine's history.

There are numerous reasons why *Waiting for Guffman* works. In the first place, it has intimate knowledge of the objects of its satire. Anyone who has ever participated in a high school play will be struck with an eerie sense of familiarity. And those who have lived in communities like Blaine will immediately recognize the acuteness of Guest's perception. Secondly, *Waiting for Guffman* doesn't go for cheap laughs. The play comes off much as it might in real life. And, perhaps unsurprisingly, there's the same kind of charm about "Red, White, and Blaine" that there is about any amateur production where the players substitute enthusiasm for talent.

There is such a thing as comic momentum, and Guest has a good sense of what that means. Comic momentum doesn't refer to nonstop jokes, but to an atmosphere that is always ripe for humor. By utilizing accomplished performers and crisp editing, the director achieves this. HIGHLY RECOMMENDED

Waking Ned Devine [Ireland, 1998]

Starring: Ian Bannen, David Kelly, Fionnula Flanagan, Susan Lynch, James Nesbitt Director: Kirk Jones Screenplay: Kirk Jones Running Time: 1:35 Rated: PG (Nudity, mature themes) Theatrical Aspect Ratio: 2.35:1

Ned Devine is dead. The news that he was holding a lottery ticket worth over 6.8 million pounds was too much for old Ned's heart. Now, the tiny Irish village of Tullymore has a decision to make: do they bury Ned's ticket along with him or do they choose one of their own to impersonate Ned and collect the money, then split it 52 ways? Although the answer to this question may not be surprising, the smoothly entertaining manner of the storytelling is.

Waking Ned Devine is an unabashed excursion into feel good territory. Director Kirk Jones, making his feature debut, revels in the film's lightheartedness. And, although his movie is not entirely without substance (themes about religion, morality, and spirit-

uality abound, as one can guess from the title character's name), it's basically designed to allow the audience to have fun. The two main characters, Jackie O'Shea (played by veteran Irish actor Ian Bannen) and Michael O'Sullivan (David Kelly, best known as O'Reilly in John Cleese's *Fawlty Towers*), are as likable as any screen pair, and, even though they're committing a crime, we're with them all the way.

The crime in question is fraud — defrauding the lottery, to be specific. After Jackie and Michael learn that someone from Tullymore is holding the lucky ticket, they set out to discover who it is. Their intention is to "find the winner and make sure we're their best friends when they cash the check." Ultimately, the search leads to the very dead Ned Devine. Rather than let the money go unclaimed, they decide that Michael will pose as Ned, and, when the lottery officials arrive, the rest of the townspeople confirm his identity. Everyone is in agreement, except one disgruntled woman, who claims she can get more money by turning in the population of Tullymore than by participating in the scam.

Waking Ned Devine is filled with wonderful, magical moments and excursions into humor guaranteed to provoke laughter. Who can miss the comedy inherent in the sight of a buck-naked old man zipping along the roads around Tullymore on a motor scooter? Then there's the scene where Jackie and Michael are replacing dead Ned's dentures. For the most part, the humor in *Waking Ned Devine* is innocent, although there are a few biting gems in the dialogue.

Jones has fashioned a visually lush motion picture that captivates with its images of the rolling hills and steep cliffs of a coastal Irish village. Combined, these elements make *Waking Ned Devine* a delightful 95-minute excursion in the company of people who are worth spending the time with. RECOMMENDED

The Wedding Banquet [Taiwan/United States, 1993]

Starring: Winston Chao, May Chin, Mitchell Lichtenstein, Sihung Lung Director: Ang Lee Screenplay: Ang Lee, Neil Peng, James Schamus Running Time: 1:49 Rated: Unrated (Mature themes, sexual situations, brief nudity) Theatrical Aspect Ratio: 1.85:1 In Mandarin and English with subtitles

Wai-Tung (Winston Chao) has a problem. Living in New York with a well-paying job, a nice home, and a stable relationship (with Simon, played by Mitchell Lichtenstein), everything appears to be going his way. But his parents, unaware of his homosexual proclivities, are expecting a marriage and grandchildren, and Wai hasn't been able to get up the courage to tell them that he's gay. Meanwhile, Wei Wei (May Chin), a tenant in a building owned by Wai, has to find a way to obtain a green card or be deported. A solution to both problems is proposed: a marriage of convenience. Once agreed to by both parties, the arrangements are made, and everything seems to be working out well until Wai's parents arrive from China to plan the wedding banquet.

What at first seems like a simple romantic comedy is actually a deceptively perceptive look at cultural, sexual, and generational differences. And, despite *The Wedding Banquet*'s often-light, occasionally-playful tone, a forceful dramatic structure underlies the film. Of course, this is what usually makes for the best kind of comedy — a movie that cares more about its story and characters than making people laugh. Chinese-American writer/director/producer Ang Lee displays a remarkable aptitude for presenting a balanced view of issues while avoiding the dangerous trap of clichés and stereotypes. All the characters have their own unique identities.

While there isn't anything revolutionary in the story, and some of the "twists" are easy to predict, it's never clear until the end how everything is going to be resolved. And, although it deals with potentially-weighty issues and some very powerful emotional impulses, *The Wedding Banquet* never becomes bogged down by its own seriousness. Lee manages to keep the production buoyant by including scenes that are often riotously funny. There is enough depth in this picture to fill up several movies, yet *The Wedding Banquet* shortchanges none of its interwoven storylines. While I won't go so far as to say that this is a magical motion picture, it certainly serves as excellent entertainment on more than one level. **RECOMMENDED**

When the Cat's Away [France, 1996]

Starring: Garance Clavel, Zinedine Soualem, Olivier Py, Renee Le Calm
Director: **Cedric Klapisch** Screenplay: **Cedric Klapisch** Running Time: **1:35** Rated: **R (Sexual situations, profanity)** Theatrical Aspect Ratio: **1.66:1** In French with subtitles

Part documentary, part narrative fiction, *When the Cat's Away* represents one of the year's most offbeat approaches to a character study. Set in Paris' Bastille quarter, Cedric Klapisch's film offers an involving, oc-

casionally poignant portrait of an insecure twentysomething woman named Chloe (Garance Clavel). At the same time, the movie examines the changing face of the city, as trendy shops replace older, family-run businesses, supermarkets supplant Mom and Pop stores, and apartment buildings are renovated to cater to a younger crowd.

When the Cat's Away begins with the search for a lost animal, but develops into something more sublime and revealing. At the film's opening, we meet Chloe as she is making final preparations for her first vacation in 3 years. Up to this point, however, she has been unable to find anyone to care for her beloved cat, Gris-Gris. Her gay roommate, Michel (Oliver Py), is unwilling to put himself out, so she is forced to ask around the neighborhood. Her inquiries lead her to Madame Renee (Renee Le Calm), a known cat-sitter. Chloe leaves Gris-Gris with the elderly woman, then leaves for 2 weeks at the seaside. She returns to learn that Gris-Gris has run away, leaving Madame Renee in a state of near-panic.

The film progresses with Chloe searching the neighborhood for Gris-Gris. In the process, she meets many of the people who live nearby, but with whom she has never come into contact. There's a shy, insecure young Arab named Djamel (Zinedine Soualem) who is more than willing to help Chloe as she scours the streets, a grungy musician (Romain Duris) who catches her eye, and, most memorably, a group of Madame Renee's friends, all of whom seize upon this minor emergency as a means of adding spice to routine existences.

As she interacts with neighbors for the first time and later sits alone at home, listening to her roommate entertaining a lover, Chloe becomes aware of her own isolation and loneliness. Suddenly, *When the Cat's Away* is no longer about finding Gris-Gris, it's about Chloe discovering meaning in her life. Her plaintive question of "Why am I all alone?" is one that many individuals across the world can relate to.

When the Cat's Away claims a premise so simple that it's easy to wonder how a full length feature could be developed from it, but the results are profound and moving. There's a little bit of Chloe in all of us, I think, and that's why it's so easy to relate to this searching young woman. **HIGHLY RECOMMENDED**

Documentary

4 Little Girls [1997]

Director: **Spike Lee** Running Time: **1:42** Rated: **No MPAA Rating** (Violence, mature themes) Theatrical Aspect Ratio: **1.66:1**

Basically, there are two types of documentaries: those set in the present or the near-past that feature numerous video images to support their thesis, and those based in a time that's decades or centuries ago, for which only paintings or still photos remain. *4 Little Girls*, feature director Spike Lee's first foray into the documentary realm, is in the time period of the former, but uses the techniques of the latter. Although the central event of the film — the bombing of the Sixteenth Street Baptist Church in Birmingham, Alabama where 4 little girls were killed — took place on September 15, 1963, the only surviving records of the victims exist as a series of black-and-white photographs.

4 Little Girls begins on the morning of September 15, 1963, with the atrocity that brutally killed 11-year-old Denise McNair, 14-year-old Carole Robertson, 14-year-old Cynthia Wesley, and 14-year-old Addie Mae Collins. In the absence of live footage to display the event, Lee must rely upon photographs taken in the aftermath. Intercut with them are pictures of the girls superimposed upon images of their tombstones. Through it all, we can hear the voice of Joan Baez singing "Birmingham Sunday," a song that recounts the tragedy.

During the 90 minutes that follow the stirring opening, Lee takes pains not only to detail the political climate in which this occurred, but, more importantly, to give us a sense of who the girls were and what their loss meant to the community. The words of Rev. Jesse Jackson, Coretta Scott King, Rev. Reggie White, and Walter Cronkite establish the girls' place in history; the words of Maxine McNair, Chris McNair, and Alpha Robertson express the crushing impact of the event in personal terms. It is a pain that, even after 3 decades, has not fully healed. As the sister of one of the victims explains, "You may not remember the details, but know how you felt [at the time]."

4 Little Girls therefore works on several levels, and that's the true nature of its mastery. Not only is it an excellent piece of historical research, but it's also a solid piece of drama. It's one thing to hear a talking head drone on about the importance of this event to the future of civil rights, but another thing altogether to hear the tearful, heartwrenching account of a mother as she tries to describe the depth of her loss. **HIGHLY RECOMMENDED**

42 Up [United Kingdom, 2000]

Director: **Michael Apted** Running Time: **2:15** Rated: **PG** (Mature themes) Theatrical Aspect Ratio: **1.66:1**

42 Up is the latest, and perhaps final, installment in Michael Apted's long-running *Up* series. When the filmmaker began this project in 1964, he came armed with a simple concept: interview 14 British children, all age 7, representing a wide range of classes and backgrounds. Then, every 7 years for the remainder of the century, he would seek out those same 14 people and spend a day catching up with them. Those who have seen the other *Up* movies will recognize that the series really starts to get interesting with

21 Up, the 1978 entry. Each succeeding segment has grown progressively more engrossing as we see Apted's subjects mature before our eyes. *42 Up* represents the best of the movies to date.

Of the 14 original interviewees, 11 continue to co-operate, with 3 having elected to drop off. Between *35 Up* and *42 Up,* there has been one defection — Peter, who is curiously not mentioned during the movie, even though Charles and John, who haven't participated in a long time, are accorded screen time. Of the other 11, some seem more reluctant than others to dredge up older memories and recap recent occurrences. Watching *42 Up,* you get the sense that if Apted makes a *49 Up,* he might lose another participant or two. Then again, several of his subjects would probably stay with the project to their dying day.

The men and women of *42 Up* represent a reasonably comprehensive cross-section of British society, although not all of them still live in the United Kingdom. Nick, an engineering professor, has moved to the United States, and Paul resides in Australia. Most of the interviewees have been married, several are divorced, and only two don't have children. Nearly everyone in *42 Up* has been forced to cope with the loss of their parents. A good sampling of the class system and economic spectrum is presented — from the homeless Neil (who is getting his life together after bottoming out around the time of *35 Up*) to the comfortably situated Andrew.

There's something incredibly simple yet profound about what Apted has done with this series. It's an amazing achievement — not only is it a sociological masterpiece, but it's a fine example of how real-life drama can often be more compelling than fiction. We feel a kinship with these men and women because, in a very real sense, we have watched them grow up. These days, web cams allow us to enter the homes and lives of a wide variety of individuals, but such short-term, voyeuristic views are only appetizers to the kind of multi-course meal that the *Up* series offers. **HIGHLY RECOMMENDED**

American Movie [1999]

Director: **Chris Smith** Running Time: **1:47** Rated: **R (Profanity, fake gore)** Theatrical Aspect Ratio: **1.66:1**

To succeed in the independent film industry, a director must possess 3 critical attributes: luck, drive, and talent. The absence of any one of those characteristics can be fatal. *American Movie* is the story of Wis-

consin filmmaker Mark Borchardt, a man with plenty of drive, but not much talent, and even less luck. He is one of those directors who invests his heart, soul, and sweat into a product that few will see and even fewer will appreciate.

In addition to being an examination of the genesis and development of a low-budget, independent film, *American Movie* is also a study of one average guy and his dream. Making movies is Borchardt's passion; it's the thing that keeps him going. Sure, he wants the expensive car and the big house, but one senses that these things are secondary. For Borchardt, obtaining the dream is not as important as pursuing it. In one way or another, this is something we can all relate to, even if our dream is vastly different. Crafting movies imparts meaning to Borchardt's life and gives him something to strive for. His enthusiasm is the one thing that differentiates him from everyone else in the film. They're reactive; he is proactive.

Directed by Chris Smith, who almost never intrudes himself or his camera into the action but allows it to play out in front of him, *American Movie* chronicles nearly 2 years in Borchardt's life. Ultimately, this film runs a little too long. Judicious trimming of about 15 to 20 minutes would have eliminated some of the slow spots and evened out the pacing. Nevertheless, even on those occasions when it drags, *American Movie* never fails to fascinate. Not only does it offer a worthwhile portrait of an individual who embodies aspirations and desires that we can all identify with, but it shows him doing something about them. *American Movie* may seem to be about filmmaking (and, to a degree, it is), but it's actually much more about the man behind the camera, and all that he represents. **RECOMMENDED**

Anne Frank Remembered [United Kingdom, 1995]

Director: **Jon Blair** Running Time: **2:02** Rated: **PG (Mature themes)** Theatrical Aspect Ratio: **1.66:1**

Those who have read the diary are aware of Anne's indomitable spirit, but, in terms of an historical perspective, her writings cover only 2 years. Blair's film fills in factual gaps, providing previously-unrevealed tidbits about the Frank family. More importantly, however, the movie extends the tale beyond August 1944, when the last journal entry was made. During the second half of this film, we follow the ultimately-fatal journey that took Anne from her family's hiding place in Amsterdam to Gestapo headquarters to Auschwitz and, finally, Bergen-Belsen, where she died in February 1945 of typhus (one month before the camp was liberated by advancing allied troops). Of the 7 who went into hiding with Anne, only one survived the war — her father, Otto Frank, who devoted the rest of his life to keeping his young daughter's memory alive.

Anne Frank Remembered interviews a number of people who knew Anne, either before or after she was sent to the concentration camps. Miep Gies, one of the quartet who concealed the Frank family from the Nazis in Amsterdam for over a year, offers extensive recollections of Anne, her father, and the war. Anne's lone surviving relative, Bernd Elias, expresses his feelings about his cousin. Excerpts from 1976 and 1979 interviews with Otto Frank (who died in 1980) are included. Together with many other testimonials, these form a compelling picture of events not covered by Anne's diary.

Perhaps the most remarkable piece of archival footage presented in this film is a small, one-second film clip of Anne on a balcony — the only known moving picture ever taken of her. It represents a tenuous link to a girl who is known to so many people through her diary. Even Otto Frank admitted that he never really knew his daughter until he read what she had written.

Anne Frank Remembered is as important for what it will preserve for posterity as for the story it tells today. The message emerging from the Holocaust has always been "Never Forget," and films of this quality make it impossible not to remember. If the story of each of Hitler's victims was told with the sensitivity and power of *Anne Frank Remembered,* there would not be enough buckets in the world to hold all the tears. **HIGHLY RECOMMENDED**

Bowling for Columbine [2002]

Director: **Michael Moore** Running Time: **2:00** Rated: **R** (Violence, profanity) Theatrical Aspect Ratio: **1.85:1**

While there will always be a debate about the authenticity of Michael Moore's documentary techniques, there's no arguing that *Bowling for Columbine* succeeds equally well as a provocative essay on gun violence in America and an opportunity for the writer/director to engage in some heavy self-promotion. Whether you like him or hate him, it's impossible to deny Moore's charisma and persuasiveness as a showman. He takes a thesis and runs with it, and, while some of his conclusions may be a little farfetched, his probing often pays unexpected dividends.

Regardless of how dubious its documentary tactics may be, *Bowling for Columbine* is powerful, thought-provoking, and, upon occasion, bitingly funny. Moore's easygoing tone never makes the viewer feel threatened — just as his rumpled personal appearance puts his victims and adversaries at ease. He's a predator in disguise. The movie offers something for everyone. Even those who disagree with Moore's politics will find themselves *thinking* during and after the movie. Whether you agree with the director's conclusions isn't the issue — it's that you recognize the problem.

The point of the film is to determine why gun violence, especially that of children on children, is rampant in this country. At first, Moore is guided by the precept that easy access to guns is the cause. And, despite being a card-carrying NRA member, he is more than willing to point the finger at Heston and his cronies. But, along the way, Moore makes a discovery — there are more guns per household in Canada than in the United States, yet the death toll, even when adjusted to consider the unequal populations, is much lower. This forces Moore to conclude that, while the ready availability of firearms in the United States may be a contributing factor to the high number of gun-related homicides, it's not the primary reason. Eventually, after conducting various interviews and hopping around the country (and out of it), Moore suggests that fear, enhanced by the media's obsession with death and violent crime, may be the root cause of America's death-by-gun problem.

I can predict with a large degree of certainty that *Bowling for Columbine* will outrage viewers whose political leanings are conservative. The film is at times laugh-aloud, viciously funny (provided you aren't among Moore's targets). But, above all, no matter how much you love or despise the messenger and his means, there's no denying that the message bears consideration and rumination. Imperfect as it may be, *Bowling for Columbine* is riveting stuff. **HIGHLY RECOMMENDED**

The Celluloid Closet [1996]

Directors: **Rob Epstein and Jeffrey Friedman** Running Time: **1:40** Rated: **R** (Mature themes, sexual situations, nudity, profanity) Theatrical Aspect Ratio: **1.85:1**

The thesis of Rob Epstein and Jeffrey Friedman's film, *The Celluloid Closet,* can be summarized by a line from the production: "Hollywood, that great maker of myths, taught straight people what to think about gay people, and gay people what to think about themselves." Unfortunately, most of those lessons have been negative. *The Celluloid Closet* presents a fairly comprehensive overview of how the gay/lesbian community has been portrayed in American films. Clips from dozens of motion pictures are included — everything from 1912's *Algie, the Miner* to 1993's *Philadelphia*. Well-known gay and straight personalities are on hand to offer opinions and observations. These include Tom Hanks, Whoopi Goldberg, Susan Sarandon, Tony Curtis, and Harvey Fierstein.

In the silent era, gay characters were used for comic relief. With exaggeratedly effeminate gestures, these thinly-drawn caricatures were foils for numerous silent stars, including Charlie Chaplin, who kissed a cross-dresser in *Behind the Screen*. With the arrival of the talkies, "the sissy," Hollywood's first stock gay character, arrived. This clichéd image of the gay man could be found in such films as *The Gay Divorcée* and *Call Her Savage*. In the 1930s, Hollywood decided to begin censoring its own films. The result was the infamous, and largely ineffective, Hays Code. While the Code didn't eliminate the presence of gay characters in films, they became less obvious. It wasn't until the late '60s when a few films appeared that dealt intelligently and sympathetically with homosexuality. With the 1968 British film, *The Detective*, and 1970's *The Boys in the Band*, a slow change was initiated. The attitude shift took a long time to grow roots, however, as the '70s and '80s saw many more films with gays as victimizers than as genuine characters.

The Celluloid Closet is one of the most fascinating documentaries to put Hollywood under the microscope. In about 100 minutes, this film convincingly defends its thesis. *The Celluloid Closet* is top-notch entertainment, not only because it's enjoyable, but because it argues its case with an effectiveness that would impress even a first class, homophobic attorney. **HIGHLY RECOMMENDED**

The Cruise [1998]

Director: **Bennett Miller** Running Time: **1:16** Rated: **No MPAA Rating** (Mature themes) Theatrical Aspect Ratio: **1.85:1**

There are two characters in *The Cruise*, director Bennett Miller's documentary debut — tour guide Timothy Levitch and New York, the city that barely contains his seemingly-boundless energy. This is not, however, a New York that can be found anywhere but on the screen for the 76-minute running length of this black-and-white motion picture. It is a stylized, surreal window onto the city as Levitch sees it — a place where the past and the present collide, where lore is more important than historical accuracy, and where sexual gratification can be obtained by gazing at the ornate side of a building.

Who is this Timothy Levitch? You may not know the answer to that question before entering a theater showing *The Cruise*, but you certainly will know it once the end credits have rolled. Levitch is New York's latest offbeat celebrity — a fast-talker, philosopher, and actor who is never without something strange and compelling to say. Many of his observations are witty, a few are insightful, and some are pretentious. His knowledge of New York minutia astounds, even when you realize that half of it is made up. For him, giving a tour of the city is meant to be a transformative experience, an awakening to a world that most people pass through without noticing.

Levitch has been a New York tour guide since graduating from NYU in 1992. During that time, he has also been voluntarily homeless, preferring to "couch surf" from the house of one friend to that of another instead of tying himself down to one place. You don't have to be a New Yorker to be captivated by Levitch — in fact, one could argue that he has more appeal to out-of-towners than to residents. Regardless, because of the dominance of the central figure and the way in which *The Cruise* has been assembled, it functions more as a character study than a travelogue, and that makes for an engaging time in a darkened theater. **RECOMMENDED**

Crumb [1994]

Director: **Terry Zwigoff** Running Time: **1:59** Rated: **R** (Profanity, sexual candor, mature themes) Theatrical Aspect Ratio: **1.85:1**

Upon viewing the completed version of this film, cartoonist Robert Crumb, whose story it tells, informed director Terry Zwigoff, "After I saw it I had to go for a walk in the woods, just to clear my head. I took my favorite hat off, this hat that I've had for 25 years, and I threw it off a cliff. I don't want to be R. Crumb anymore." Considering the material, the reaction is understandable. This is the sort of movie capable of prompting a viewer to question and evaluate a great deal more than the inner workings of a single man. In addition to presenting one of the most compelling filmed documentary character studies of all time, *Crumb* asks a lot of pointed questions about life and art that no one can possibly answer, least of all the misanthropic genius at the center of the portrait.

Crumb's claim to fame is founding the underground comics movement in 1967, when issue #1 of his "Zap Comix" was released. Crumb is also the creator of the "Keep on Truckin'" logo, the artist for the LP cover of Big Brother and the Holding Company's *Cheap Thrills,* and the originator of Fritz the Cat, which Ralph Bakshi turned into the first X-rated animated feature (a film that Crumb hates).

Is Crumb a misogynist? Probably, since, in his own words, he harbors inner hostility towards women. But there's more than that to his work. Is Crumb obsessed with sex? No doubt. Apparently, there was a time when he masturbated 4 to 5 times each day, and everyone seems to agree that he finds his own work sexually stimulating. Is Crumb disgusted with popular culture and fame? In his own words, "As a teenager . . . I realized I was an outcast, I became a critic, and I've been disgusted with American culture from the time I was a kid. I started out by rejecting all the things that the people who rejected me liked, then over the years I developed a deeper analysis of these things."

Whatever opinion a viewer has of Crumb at the end of this film, an apathetic reaction is unthinkable. Empathy, fascination, disgust, or anger are all likely, but not disinterest. R. Crumb is the sort of person it's impossible to ignore, and Zwigoff's film creates such an honest portrayal of him that some sort of response is demanded. **MUST SEE**

Dadetown [1996]

Director: Russ Hexter Running Time: 1:33 Rated: No MPAA Rating (Profanity, slaughtered deer) Theatrical Aspect Ratio: 1.85:1

Dadetown is a "meta-documentary" about small-town America in the 1990s. Is a rural, close-knit community still the "American dream," or, with the closing of factories, has it become a kind of American nightmare? A stunning only feature from director Russ Hexter, who died at the age of 26, *Dadetown* leads to an unforgettable revelation during the closing credits.

"The small town is the backbone of America," asserts one of Dadetown's residents in the interview that begins the film. Indeed, Dadetown, NY is one of many nameless, faceless American towns where family and religious values define the community. All is not right in Dadetown, however. Gorman Metal, the industry which has employed most of Dadetown's men for decades, is downsizing. The result is unemployment. Even as Gorman's fortunes decline, a new

corporation, American Peripheral Imaging (API), relocates to the upstate New York community, bringing more than 100 employees from places like Buffalo and Philadelphia. These newcomers, with fancy houses and yuppie lifestyles, don't mesh well with the "hick" longtime residents of Dadetown, and a cultural schism develops.

Dadetown is the most thought-provoking examination of the collapse of a community since *Roger and Me.* Absent here is Michael Moore's sarcasm — *Dadetown* opts instead for a more serious account of events. The result, partially achieved through effective editing, is a compelling and emotionally-stirring account of cultural friction and how mass unemployment damages the psyche of a town.

Yet there is another issue addressed with unexpected force by *Dadetown* — the intrusiveness of documentary film makers when producing their features. Do they merely record events or do they become part of what they're filming? *Dadetown* takes matters to the next level, however, with a unique punchline that calls into question the role and responsibility of documentary film makers. Whatever you do, don't leave before the final credits have rolled. *Dadetown*'s most startling surprise is reserved for them. **HIGHLY RECOMMENDED**

The Endurance [United States/United Kingdom, 2001]

Director: George Butler Running Time: 1:33 Rated: No MPAA Rating (Mature themes) Theatrical Aspect Ratio: 1.85:1

Sir Ernest Shackleton, a veteran explorer who visited Antarctica on several occasions (once almost becoming the first man to reach the South Pole), began planning a cross-continent expedition in late 1913. To obtain a crew, he used the following advertisement: "Notice: Men wanted for hazardous journey. Bitter cold. Small wages. Long months of complete darkness. Constant danger. Safe return doubtful. Honour and recognition in case of success." From the thousands of respondents, Shackleton hand-picked a crew of 28 (including himself and several men he had previously worked with). The endeavor that followed, which is chronicled in George Butler's documentary, *The Endurance,* was equal parts disaster and tragedy, and illustrated why Shackleton has since come to be regarded as one of the greatest leaders ever to tread the paths of humanity.

For those who go into the movie knowing the fate of *The Endurance* and the 28 men aboard, this motion picture represents a fascinating inspection of what happened every step of the way. For those who see *The Endurance* without previous knowledge of anything about Shackleton or his trips to Antarctica, the movie represents a rousing adventure film filled with high suspense. Butler is careful not to give away the ending too early; the words spoken by Liam Neeson in the running voiceover narration reveal things only when appropriate to the movie's internal chronology.

Unlike "talking head" documentaries, which stay on a airy, philosophical plane, *The Endurance* draws you into the story. The characters, especially Shackleton, are rich and the setting is vivid. The means by which Butler brings all of this together is perfect for the story. We do not have to sit through scene after scene of Polar Exploration scholars discussing Shackleton's importance to history (there is one of these individuals, but his comments are limited). Instead, Butler's new footage shows us the terrible beauty of Antarctica, the relatives' contributions further humanize the participants, and the stock images crystallize everything. *The Endurance* is many things, including a compelling adventure saga. However, above all, it is a testimony to the triumph of the human spirit, and a reminder that, under the right leadership, humankind is capable of virtually anything. In Shackleton's own words: "We have seen God and his splendors, heard the text that nature renders. We have reached the naked soul of man." You will leave the theater uplifted, exhilarated, and perhaps a little chilly. HIGHLY RECOMMENDED

Fast, Cheap & Out of Control [1997]

Director: Errol Morris Running Time: 1:22 Rated: PG (Nothing offensive) Theatrical Aspect Ratio: 1.85:1

Fast, Cheap & Out of Control isn't much like any of Errol Morris' other well-known films — *Gates of Heaven* (about a pet cemetery), *The Thin Blue Line* (about a murder), and *A Brief History of Time* (about science, space, and infinity). In fact, at first glance, this movie appears startlingly unambitious by comparison. But there's more to *Fast, Cheap & Out of Control* than initially meets the eye. Not only is there a great deal of craft involved in the film's production, but its underlying themes are compelling and universal.

The basic framework for *Fast, Cheap & Out of Control* has Morris interviewing 4 men with unique, but not terribly interesting, professions. Dave Hoover is a wild animal trainer who works with lions and tigers in the circus ring. George Mendonca is the topiary

gardener (the person who sculpts hedges into lifelike shapes) for Green Animals' Gardens. Ray Mendez is a mole-rat specialist (mole-rats are hairless mammals that live in insect-like colonies). And Rodney Brooks is a robot scientist who works in an artificial intelligence lab at M.I.T. All 4 of these individuals are among the best in their respective fields, and it's their passion for their jobs, rather than anything especially startling or hypnotic about the work itself, that piques our interest.

As we watch, however, we become aware that, by structuring *Fast, Cheap & Out of Control* as he does, Morris is doing far more than merely presenting a series of talking-head interviews. By piecing the film together with fast cuts and sequences where the soundtrack of one interview overlaps images depicting the activities of another of the subjects, Morris explores at least two intriguing, interrelated themes: the evolution of humankind and our never-ending attempt to control our environment.

One thing that never changes, however, is man's desire to regulate everything around him. Brooks speaks of his robots being the forerunners of a new breed of silicon-based life form that may eventually render our species extinct. Despite his assertion that he is only an observer, Mendez takes an important role in shaping the existence of his mole-rats, hoping to learn more about himself through their actions. Hoover's entire livelihood is based on mastering creatures that are more powerful and dangerous than himself. And even the mild-mannered Mendonca alters the course of nature by twisting and shaping bushes into works of art. In one way or another, all 4 are playing god. HIGHLY RECOMMENDED

The Girl Next Door [1999]

Director: Christine Fugate Running Time: 1:24 Rated: No MPAA Rating (Sex, frequent frontal nudity, profanity, graphic plastic surgical procedures) Theatrical Aspect Ratio: 1.85:1

Her stage name is "Stacy Valentine," and her list of credits list more than 65 adult movies, including a number of popular titles. She has been working in the porn industry since 1995, when she escaped from an abusive marriage in Oklahoma and surfaced in Hollywood. It was there that documentary filmmaker Fulgate made contact with her, and the result is a fascinating chronicle of 2 years in Stacy's life, including highs and lows. Stacy gives Fulgate surprisingly candid access, allowing the director to film her during some of the darkest moments of this period.

Although *The Girl Next Door*'s primary goal is to offer a well-rounded cinematic representation of Stacy The Person (not just Stacy The Porn Star), the cameras also reveal something about the world around her. Without being judgmental, Fulgate gives us an unvarnished look into the heart of the porn industry. *The Girl Next Door* isn't an expose, nor is it intended to be — the movie doesn't dwell on drugs, violence, and sleaze. Instead, it depicts the hollowness of this lifestyle. All that glitters is not gold, and, in this case, the glamour is all artificial and the adoration is skin deep.

Just as nothing about the industry is real, nothing about "Stacy Valentine" is either — not her name or her body. Fulgate's job is to peel away the porn star personality worn like a gaudy garment by Stacy Baker and reveal the naked character of the girl underneath. Stacy Valentine is a product of her environment — her breasts have been augmented more than once, her thighs and legs have been liposuctioned, and her lips have been injected with fat removed from her hips. On one occasion, she mentions that she hardly recognizes herself when she looks in the mirror.

Fans who have bought into the fantasy image of Stacy Valentine may find *The Girl Next Door* to be a disillusioning experience. After seeing this film, it is impossible to objectify her; she has become a real person. For Fulgate, *The Girl Next Door* represents nearly 4 years worth of effort — 2 years to find her subject and another 2 years to film her. For Stacy Baker/Valentine, it's an opportunity to open up before the camera and bare her soul in a more explicit manner than she has ever displayed her body. For the viewer, this is a rare chance to voyeuristically experience the life of a woman who occupies the fascinating position of being one of the adult entertainment industry's top draws. **RECOMMENDED**

God Said "Ha!" [1998]

Director: **Julia Sweeney** Running Time: **1:25** Rated: **PG-13** (Mature themes, mild profanity) Theatrical Aspect Ratio: **1.85:1**

Julia Sweeney's *God Said "Ha!"* is a no-frills adaptation of her one-woman stage show. A comedienne who is best known for a stint on *Saturday Night Live,* a starring role in the disastrously bad *It's Pat,* and as a good buddy of Quentin Tarantino's, Sweeney shows a different side of herself here. She tells a deeply personal story that intersperses comic vignettes with moments of genuine, almost heart-wrenching pathos. Her descriptions are vivid — characters

come alive through her vocal inflections. By the end of the film, we feel that we have met her mother, father, and brother, Mike, even though they never once appear on screen.

God Said "Ha!" is a comedy about tragic events. It takes a gently humorous look at the absurdities of life without losing the human aspect of the story or turning the events into a farce. Sweeney never forces any of her jokes — that approach would have felt wrong and painfully awkward. When she's funny (and she frequently is *very* funny), we laugh, but there are times when we're just a hair's breadth away from crying. It's easy to empathize with Sweeney because, to one degree or another, her experiences are universal. It doesn't require a big stretch to understand what she's talking about. All we have to do is examine our own lives.

Throughout this film, Sweeney speaks conversationally, as if we're intimate friends that she's confiding in. She paints amazing pictures with words, creating three-dimensional characters that come to life in our minds. How much of our own mothers and fathers do we recognize in Sweeney's impersonations? Her affection for her family is real, even though she ruthlessly satirizes them for nearly 90 minutes. Her tone speaks of her love, even as her words provide a parody. This is the kind of genuine tale that each member of the audience can relate to on his or her own terms. Everyone's life story may contain the content to develop a film like *God Said "Ha!",* but there aren't many who possess Sweeney's style — and, in this case, it's the style that gives power to the substance. **RECOMMENDED**

Home Page [1998]

Director: **Doug Block** Running Time: **1:42** Rated: **No MPAA Rating** (profanity, nudity, sexual themes) Theatrical Aspect Ratio: **1.33:1**

The function of *Home Page,* a documentary by Doug Block is not to present some sort of all-encompassing overview of the Internet, but to offer a sampling of viewpoints and personalities, with a heavy dosage of high-level pop psychology and sociology. In the end, we get as much from inferring how Block's topics relate to our own lives as from observing what's on the screen.

Watching *Home Page* is like surfing the Web. There is a trajectory of sorts, but it's a strange, rambling one, filled with stops, starts, dead-ends, odd tangents, and abrupt leaps. By the end, we feel like we have gone on a journey, although it's not entirely clear what sort.

Block introduces us to a number of colorful Web eccentrics and celebrities (Justin Hall, Harold Rheingold, Jaime Levy, Julie Petersen, Carl Steadman), offering glimpses into their often dysfunctional real lives. And, in a way, *Home Page* represents a tour of self-discovery for Block. He starts out like any other indie documentary maker, then ends up creating his own home page, exploring a new world, and re-connecting with his wife.

One of the issues addressed by *Home Page* is what underlies the growing trend of on-line exhibitionism — men and women who place the most intimate details of their life on the Web (either via tell-all journals or the ever-popular cams, which often leave nothing to the imagination). Different theories are espoused, but the most convincing is that people do this because they crave the attention that making shocking revelations will earn them. They want their 15 minutes of fame, and outrageous content on a home page offers that opportunity. Another theme Block explores is how the growing sense of alienation in society has given birth to a generation that is becoming more comfortable with the anonymous, faceless communication of the Internet than with the face-to-face rigors of interpersonal interaction. Real-life communities are being replaced by virtual ones.

Home Page is probably more intriguing and interesting than it is compelling. Block doesn't offer any astounding revelations and his techniques are a little rough around the edges — this is not slick, accomplished filmmaking, but, considering the low budget, it works. **RECOMMENDED**

Hoop Dreams [1994]

Director: **Steve James** Running Time: **2:51** Rated: **PG-13 (Mature themes, language)** Theatrical Aspect Ratio: **1.33:1**

Hoop Dreams, the tale of two high school basketball players, is less a story about the sport than it is a chronicle of life in the inner city and of following Aldous Huxley's advice that "a man's reach should exceed his grasp." *Hoop Dreams* follows two Chicago youths, William Gates and Arthur Agee, from their Freshman year of high school to their first year of college. In addition to documenting the inevitable on-court maturation process, the movie illustrates the difficulties of balancing sports with scholastic and family pressures. Neither William nor Arthur are advanced academically, and both suffer through a variety of away-from-school crises.

At the start of *Hoop Dreams,* when William and Arthur are 14, each appears to be a solid prospect for recruiting by "white" suburban basketball powerhouse St. Joseph High School and its legendary coach, Gene Pingatore. Arthur has the quickest step one talent scout has seen in 5 years, and William looks like the "next Isiah Thomas." One point explored by this film is that no matter how "can't miss" a prospect is, and regardless of their level of talent and enthusiasm, most of them, in fact, fail. Being the star of a high school team does not guarantee a trip to the NBA, and realizing this represents a rude awakening for William and Arthur.

While William quickly becomes Coach Pingatore's "go-to-guy" on the varsity squad, Arthur's slow development as a player allows him to be dropped from the Freshman team. When his parents can no longer afford St. Joseph's tuition, Arthur is cut loose and sent back to public school. His home life is further disrupted by financial struggles and the departure of his father. William, on the other hand, suffers a series of knee injuries that erode his confidence, and the unexpected arrival of a baby daughter throws his personal life into further turmoil.

The rich texture of *Hoop Dreams'* drama is its greatest asset. This is a film that goes beyond the verisimilitude of something to come from the pen of Spike Lee or John Singleton, into the realm of real life. The shattered illusions of William and Arthur are all the more poignant because these are not the dividends of a screenwriter's fertile imagination. And the drug deals depicted are chilling for exactly the same reason. If any single line sums up the lessons learned by the two protagonists, it comes late in the movie, and is spoken by William in his Marquette University dorm room: "People always say to me, 'When you get to the NBA, don't forget me.' Well, if I don't get to the NBA, *you* don't forget about *me.*" **HIGHLY RECOMMENDED**

The Last Days [1998]

Director: **James Moll** Running Time: **1:28** Rated: **No MPAA Rating (Holocaust images)** Theatrical Aspect Ratio: **1.85:1**

When it comes to 20th-century events, few have generated more unforgettable documentary footage than the Holocaust. For those who normally avoid this sort of production, *The Last Days* offers a compelling reason to make an exception. Like all filmed Holocaust essays, it is disturbing and wrenching, but there is also an undercurrent of inspiration and optimism in the portraits painted by film maker James

Moll. At its core, *The Last Days* is more about lives rebuilt than lives destroyed. It is a testimony to the resiliency of the human spirit.

For *The Last Days*, Moll has interviewed 5 survivors of Hitler's "Final Solution," all of whom currently live in the United States. He accompanies these Hungarian Jews as they return to the land of their birth, searching for closure and catharsis. Seeking solutions to unanswerable questions, they also visit the locations of their most nightmarish recollections — the remains of Auschwitz and Berkenow. And they bring their children and grandchildren with them, entrusting memories of their experiences to future generations.

The most prominent of the 5 subjects interviewed in Moll's film is U.S. Congressman Tom Lantos, who was part of the Jewish underground in Hungary. He, along with many others, worked to provide fake Swedish passports for Jews seeking to escape from a homeland that had turned rank and deadly. Bill Basch was also a member of the Resistance. His most telling memory is of the day the Americans liberated the camp — how the former prisoners literally tore some of their captors to pieces. Alice Lok Cahana, an artist who paints as a way to memorialize the dead, returns to Europe to make peace with her ghosts. Renee Firestone goes back to Auschwitz to uncover details about her sister's death, even going so far as to question Dr. Hans Munch, the doctor in charge of the section of the camp where her sister was held. Finally, Irene Zisblatt tells a moving tale about the diamonds she now wears on a tear-shaped pendant. They are the only tangible momento she has of a mother who did not survive the ordeal.

While much of the archival footage presented in *The Last Days* is new, the substance is familiar. These are the kinds of images that no Holocaust film can ignore, because they drive home the horror of what transpired 5 decades ago, half a world away. For added impact, Moll interviews a handful of American servicemen who participated in the liberation of Dachow. What they saw and experienced there, they will never forget. The same will be true of those who view this film. **HIGHLY RECOMMENDED**

Looking for Richard [1996]

Director: **Al Pacino** Running Time: **1:52** Rated: **R** (Violence, profanity)
Theatrical Aspect Ratio: **1.85:1**

Any traditional version of Shakespeare's *Richard III* will open with "Now's the winter of our discontent made summer by this son of York," the first line of one of the Bard's best-known soliloquies. It's a telling point, therefore, that *Looking for Richard* starts with a stentorian voice declaring: "Our revels now are ended." This movie, a labor of love for Al Pacino, who makes his directorial debut, does not intend to present a complete, unabridged version of the text. Like all film makers who take on Shakespeare, Pacino's goal is to give life to his own passion for the plays. His methods are decidedly unconventional. *Looking for Richard* is a condensed version of *Richard III* wrapped in a stream-of-consciousness documentary.

Pacino begins the film as a documentary investigating what modern day audiences think of Shakespeare's works. The answers he gets during person-on-the-street interviews are predictable: "it sucks," "it's boring," "huh?" The director's motivation for making the movie is stated up front: "It has always been a dream of mine to communicate how I feel about Shakespeare to others." After this lengthy introduction, Pacino moves on to the play. We glimpse the casting process and are given an impromptu history lesson about the War of the Roses. The second half of *Looking for Richard* concentrates on performing select scenes from the play.

A number of familiar faces fill roles here. Pacino, of course, is Richard, complete with faux hunchback and limp. Alec Baldwin plays Clarence, and Harris Yulin is King Edward. Penelope Allen is Queen Elizabeth, Kevin Spacey is Buckingham, Aidan Quinn is Richmond, and Winona Ryder is Lady Anne.

Looking for Richard is a fascinating piece of film making, but I don't think it does anything so revolutionary that non-believers will be suddenly converted. Pacino's passion is obvious, but it's not universally contagious. However, those who enjoy Shakespeare, or are at least open-minded, will find much to appreciate here. **RECOMMENDED**

Microcosmos [France, 1996]

Directors: **Claude Nuridsany & Marie Perennou** Running Time: **1:17**
Rated: **G** Theatrical Aspect Ratio: **1.85:1**

Microcosmos is a delightful little documentary — emphasis on *little*. This film offers a view into a world more bizarre than anything depicted in the most special effects-intensive science fiction. Intrigued? Well, if not, you will be once you start watching *Microcosmos*, Claude Nuridsany and Marie Perennou's fascinating portrait of life "beyond anything we could imagine, and yet almost beneath our notice."

Microcosmos literally has a cast of thousands — insects, that is. Beetles, ants, bees, wasps, dragonflies, butterflies, snails, mosquitoes, darning needles, and dozens of other assorted bugs fill the screen, going about their everyday chores. They build nests, find food, pollinate flowers, battle over territory, and procreate. For viewers with spiritual inclinations, there's a fair amount of quasi-religious imagery: mantises that pray and bugs that walk on water.

The microscopic drama of *Microcosmos* is surprisingly engrossing, primarily because of the exquisite detail of the photography. Nuridsany and Perennou's cameras take us from normal-scale overviews of their locale deep into the world of the insects, where blades of grass are as tall as houses, trees are unimaginably large, and lakes become oceans. Everything is shown up close and personal, with a level of clarity and intimacy never previously obtained in nature films.

Transpiring in a specially created "field studio" in Aveyron, France, *Microcosmos* took 3 years to film and 6 months to edit, but the results more than justify the necessary time, effort, and patience. After watching *Microcosmos,* it will be impossible to take a walk in the woods without being aware of the amazing tapestry of activity going on all around, yet out of sight. **HIGHLY RECOMMENDED**

Mr. Death: The Rise and Fall of Fred A. Leuchter Jr. [1999]

Director: **Errol Morris** Running Time: 1:36 Rated: PG-13 (Mature themes) Theatrical Aspect Ratio: 1.85:1

To begin with, who is Fred Leuchter, and why has a filmmaker of Morris' caliber used him as the subject of a major documentary? By his own admission, Leuchter is an "execution technologist," who, from an early age, has harbored a fascination with death. As he grew older and became an engineer, Leuchter used his knowledge to design new, "more humane" (his words, not mine) electric chairs intended to eliminate the kind of horror stories that are often told and occasionally shown about electrocutions. This goal of this new approach was to make electrocution a safer, cheaper, and less horrific means of state-mandated killing. And, after achieving success with the electric chair, Leuchter was asked to stretch his scientific know-how to design a lethal injection machine for the state of New Jersey. At one point, he comments, "I sleep well at night — people executed by my machines have dignified, painless deaths."

Eventually, Leuchter's reputation as an "execution technologist" was eclipsed by another aspect of his life. This happened a decade ago when he became a key witness in the trial of Ernst Zundel. Zundel, a neo-Nazi, selected Leuchter as an expert witness to corroborate his assertion that the Holocaust was a hoax. On his 1988 honeymoon, Leuchter could be found poking around the ruins of Auschwitz, taking samples and evaluating the evidence. His conclusion: the so-called "showers" could not have been used as gas chambers without killing everyone in the camp (including the Nazis). Further studies led Leuchter to believe that Zundel was correct: 6 million Jews were not killed in death camps. In his opinion, it was not scientifically feasible. And, at least on the surface, his arguments *sound* persuasive.

It would be easy to label Leuchter as a hate-monger and an anti-Semite, but, as the film illustrates, he is neither. The man does not hate Jews, nor is he a neo-Nazi supporter. Leuchter, who lacks an imposing physical presence, is motivated by scientific principles. The problem is, his methods are flawed. He developed a hypothesis, but, in gathering the evidence to support it, he ignored facts that pointed to another conclusion. He cannot see another possibility because he isn't looking for one. He disproved the existence of the Holocaust based on a faulty premise and through an investigation that was riddled with inaccuracies. By presenting Leuchter sympathetically, Morris disallows us the comfort of simply labeling the man as "evil" and moving on to another target. *Mr. Death* is a compelling film because it paints Leuchter in three dimensions. **HIGHLY RECOMMENDED**

Paradise Lost: The Child Murders at Robin Hood Hills [1996]

Directors: **Joe Berlinger** and **Bruce Sinofsky** Running Time: 2:25 Rated: No MPAA Rating (Gruesome murder scene photographs) Theatrical Aspect Ratio: 1.33:1

On the night of May 5, 1993, three 8-year-old boys, Steven Branch, Christopher Byers, and Michael Moore, were tortured and murdered in Robin Hood Hills, West Memphis, Arkansas. The community, understandably outraged, cried out for blood. It took the police a month to make arrests. The eventual suspects were Jessie Misskelly, age 17; Damien Echols, age 18; and Jason Baldwin, age 16. Jessie, who has a 72 IQ and was subjected to a grueling 10-hour interrogation, confessed to his involvement in the killings, but later recanted the confession, claiming to have been coerced. He was tried, convicted, and sentenced to life plus 40 years. Likewise, Damien and Jason were found guilty. Damien was sentenced to die by lethal injection; Jason was to spend the rest of his life in jail without the possibility of parole.

Paradise Lost follows events surrounding the crime, from the discovery of the bodies to the verdicts. Berlinger and Sinofsky painstakingly chronicle 10 months worth of developments, illustrating how easily justice can be swayed. There's no way that this movie can answer the question of the defendants' guilt or innocence, but one piece of information is clear from *Paradise Lost*: Jessie Misskelly, Damien Echols, and Jason Baldwin did not receive fair trials.

There was almost no physical evidence connecting the three to the crime. Jessie's confession was, at best, obtained under dubious circumstances. But the town of West Memphis needed scapegoats, people they could demonize. Because Damien was "different" by his own admission — he wore black, listened to Metallica, and had shown interest in the Wicca religion — he made an excellent target. Suddenly, news reports were full of allegations of Satanic rituals and occult ceremonies, with intimations of human sacrifice and sexual perversity. Damien, Jessie, and Jason were tried and convicted by the media. They didn't have a chance in court.

Berlinger and Sinofsky have obtained an amazingly in-depth and intimate picture of the situation. Their cameras were allowed in the courtrooms, behind closed-door strategy sessions, and in the prisons where the accused were being held. The friends and families of the victims and the defendants cooperated with the film makers, enabling them to get close to both sides. As a result, there are no faceless entities here — all of the participants have personalities.

Watching Berlinger and Sinofsky's movie is like witnessing an execution: it's horrifying, gut-wrenching, and impossible to turn away from. Anyone with an interest in law and order, the American justice system, or the role of the media, should seek it out. **MUST SEE**

Unzipped [1995]

Director: **Douglas Keeve** Running Time: **1:13** Rated: **R (Profanity)**
Theatrical Aspect Ratio: **1.66:1**

Unzipped is a cinematic portrait of Isaac Mizrahi, an artist whose palette is fabric. Ostensibly, the film is a documentary, but use of that term requires stretching its meaning. Many scenes appear staged, and a great deal of cutting-and-pasting has been done in the editing room. The cinema verité effect is a conceit — genuine spontaneity is at a premium, and everyone is aware of and playing to the camera (especially would-be actresses like Cindy Crawford). Director Douglas Keeve (who was Mizrahi's lover at the time) freely admits that he "couldn't care less about the truth" but was more interested in capturing "the spirit and love in Isaac and in fashion."

Despite violating nearly every rule of "legitimate" documentary film making, however, *Unzipped* is a remarkably enjoyable piece of entertainment. While it sheds only a little light on the behind-the-scenes world of the fashion industry, it presents a fascinating, if incomplete, picture of designer Mizrahi. This man is the perfect subject for this kind of study — he's funny, energetic, and eminently quotable. He has unusual views on just about everything, from fashion ("It's about women not wanting to look like cows.") to Mary Tyler Moore ("Between her and Jackie Kennedy, they shaped this country.") to style ("It's almost impossible to have style nowadays without the right dogs.").

Unzipped also gives a glimpse into the creative process by which Mizrahi turns an idea into a dress. It's almost certainly different that anyone would imagine. The designer draws on a variety of sources for his look, including *Nanook of the North* and old Bette Davis movies, then enlists the aid of a Ouija board to help form the collection. In particular, *Unzipped* traces Mizrahi's development of his Fall 1994 line from its inception in the Spring to the final fashion show, which highlights a number of prominent models, including Cindy Crawford, Naomi Campbell, Kate Bush, and Linda Evangelista.

While *Unzipped* isn't an expose on the fashion industry per se, Keeve has enough clips of petulant models to make the viewer realize how tame Robert Altman was with *Ready to Wear*. Overall, however, this movie is far more about Mizrahi than anything else, and only when viewed from that perspective does *Unzipped* succeed. When the designer declares that "everything is frustrating except designing clothes — that's beautiful and liberating," it fits perfectly with the image of him that *Unzipped* has constructed. **RECOMMENDED**

Visions of Light: The Art of Cinematography [1992]

Directors: **Arnold Glassman, Todd McCarthy, and Stuart Samuels**
Running Time: **1:31** Rated: **No MPAA Rating (Nothing offensive)**
Theatrical Aspect Ratio: **1:33:1**

Often, one of the most overlooked elements of a film is its cinematography. Paradoxically, it is also the most important, whether specifically noticed or not. Movies are a visual medium where the pictures shoulder the lion's share of the burden. A movie can have a good director, accomplished actors, and a riveting script, but if the photography is poor, the production is doomed.

Visions of Light states that cinematography is the art of light — blending it so it enhances the director's vision. Much time is spent discussing this subject as well as various other technical aspects of the craft (the role of close-ups, the importance of showing a performer from a particular angle, and the advantages and disadvantages of certain shots). If all this sounds dry, be assured that it isn't. There are clips from over a hundred movies to revel in — everything from *The Cabinet of Doctor Caligari* to *Goodfellas*.

The film is divided into 3 sections. The first, and shortest, traces the early days of Hollywood and the importance of camerawork in silent films. Several of the interview subjects lament the introduction of sound into the movies so early, feeling that another decade of silence could have advanced their craft by leaps and bounds.

The second section deals with the black-and-white era after the introduction of sound. Covering roughly the years between 1930 and 1960, much attention is paid to the role of contrast and shadow (gray versus black, for example) in these movies. *Citizen Kane* is given a lengthy treatment with its many photographic innovations discussed at some length.

Finally, color movies are presented. From *Gone with the Wind* to films of the '80s, the various techniques used by color photographers to achieve moods and portray emotions are detailed. During this part, time is spent on movies such as *Annie Hall, Jaws, Blue Velvet,* and the aforementioned *Goodfellas* (including a discourse on the genesis of one of that film's most unusual shots).

Visions of Light is somewhat didactic and doesn't attempt any ground breaking documentary techniques. But its mixture of information and film clips maintains an effective pace. This film will add a dimension to the knowledge of those familiar with the work of cinematographers, and give an appreciation of a different facet of filmmaking to those who are not. RECOMMENDED

The War Room [1993]

Directors: D. A. Pennebaker and Chris Hegedus Running Time: **1:36**
Rated: No MPAA Rating (Language) Theatrical Aspect Ratio: **1:66:1**

The War Room is the story of James Carville and George Stephanopoulos, and their efforts on behalf of Bill Clinton throughout the 1992 Presidential campaign. From the New Hampshire primary to election night, *The War Room* depicts Carville and Stephanopoulos' backroom strategy sessions and public moves as they catapulted their man from a virtual unknown to President Elect.

This is not Bill Clinton's story, nor is it an account of how he beat the odds to become the first Democratic President in 12 years. Rather, *The War Room* is an examination of two of the men instrumental in the victory: James Carville, the "Ragin' Cajun," and, to a lesser extent, the yuppiesque George Stephanopoulos.

Carville, with his buoyant personality and glib one-liners, naturally steals every scene from the soft-spoken Stephanopoulos. Without Carville, this could have been yet another dry documentary on the behind-the-scenes political process. Stephanopoulos is intelligent, but he's not particularly interesting. Carville, on the other hand, is magnetic, not only because of his keen intellect, but because everything he does is suffused with a sense of sincerity.

While most of the movie focuses on Carville's professional activities as he heads the efforts to defuse the Gennifer Flowers situation, prepares a television commercial, and leads the attack on the Republicans, we are given a glimpse into his personal life. His girlfriend, Mary Matalin, appears several times — albeit doing her job as President Bush's campaign strategist.

Clinton, Bush, and Perot have peripheral roles in this film that concentrates its attention on the people behind the Democratic campaign strategies. While elements of the tactics used by the members of the so-called "War Room" are revealed (including a fascinating discussion of the relative importance of the colors of Clinton/Gore signs at the Democratic Convention), the movie is less concerned with political maneuvering than with the maneuverers. RECOMMENDED

When We Were Kings [1996]

Director: Leon Gast Running Time: **1:28** Rated: **No MPAA Rating**
(Boxing action) Theatrical Aspect Ratio: **1:85:1**

When We Were Kings, a documentary about the Muhammad Ali/George Forman heavyweight "Rumble in the Jungle" boxing match, is a wonderfully nostalgic, and occasionally insightful, window into the recent past. While *When We Were Kings* is not a biography of Ali, it offers a great deal of insight into why the boxer was equally beloved and despised during his heyday. It's easy to forget how controversial a figure Ali was in the '60s and '70s, when he constantly proclaimed himself "the greatest," refused to register for the draft, and said things like "Damn America. I live in America, but Africa's my home." Age and Parkinson's Disease have softened the man's image, and, as Spike Lee comments, it's shocking to realize how few young people understand who Muhammed Ali was.

From the early press conferences to the aftermath, *When We Were Kings* chronicles the meeting of these two titans. At times, the structure is uneven, especially when the film goes on a tangent detailing the start of Don King's career, but the bulk of the material is engrossing. Since most of the footage was shot in 1974 (with the exception of "talking head" interviews with Spike Lee, Norman Mailer, and George Plimpton), watching this film is like taking a little time trip. Ali and Forman appear on-screen, but only as they did around the time of the fight. No retrospective interviews with either are presented.

When We Were Kings has several high points, including footage of Ali's press conference and coverage of the "Black Woodstock" event that was supposed to precede the fight (the music festival went off as scheduled, but the fight was postponed for more than a month). Unsurprisingly, however, the most involving portion of the film is the coverage of the match, which details exactly how Ali was able to use the now-famous "Rope-a-Dope" tactic to pull off what is probably boxing's greatest upset. This match, which took place at 4 a.m. local time on October 30, 1974 in Kinshasa, Zaire, marked the point at which Ali's image began to change from that of anti-hero to that of hero. For sheer dramatic impact, "The Rumble in the Jungle" exceeds even the best fictional boxing stories, including *Rocky*.

To use the old cliché, you don't have to be a sports fan to enjoy this motion picture. All you need is an appreciation of recent history and a desire to learn more about an event that had far more importance in the world's eyes than any other heavyweight bout in the history of boxing. **RECOMMENDED**

Drama

8 Mile [2002]

Starring: Eminem, Kim Basinger, Brittany Murphy Director: Curtis Hanson Screenplay: Scott Silver Running Time: 1:50 Rated: R (Profanity, violence, sex, brief nudity) Theatrical Aspect Ratio: 2.35:1

At its heart, *8 Mile* is a very conventional motion picture. By applying the traditional sports formula to hip-hop music, it manages to extend a familiar plot structure into a new arena. So, instead of the climactic struggle taking place in a boxing ring or on a baseball field, it takes place in a club where two rappers battle it out to see who takes home the crown. And, as is usually the case with a well-made sports movie, you don't have to appreciate the particular sport in order to enjoy the movie. *8 Mile* has not been made solely with fans of hip-hop music in mind.

8 Mile has a grim, gritty feel. The camera captures the seedier quarters of Detroit in a way that will do nothing for the city's tourist industry. There aren't many smiles, either, or, for that matter, many reasons to smile. The people in this film are impoverished and struggling to make ends meet. In order to pay the rent, they have to hope that they win at bingo. Sex isn't about love; it's about surcease and forgetting, if only for a moment.

The controversial and high-profile rap artist Eminem plays Jimmy "B-Rabbit" Smith Jr., a worker at an automobile factory whose real passion is hip-hop. He's a master rhymer, but, upon entering a competition, he is overcome by stage fright. One day, he hopes to earn enough money to make a demo tape, but that day seems far off. In the meantime, he struggles through his daily life, living in a trailer with

his mother (Kim Basinger) and stealing the occasional moment with his trampy girlfriend, Alex (Brittany Murphy). Then, one day, B-Rabbit gets a chance at redemption by taking on the current champion in a rap contest. It is an opportunity he cannot pass up.

Formulaic movies can work if they are well-made, and *8 Mile* qualifies. The movie's generally downbeat tone is relieved by the failsafe of a triumphant ending, but, along the way, the filmmakers aren't afraid of showing blue-collar life as it really is. Also, in an intriguing switch, the black/white racial division works in reverse. *8 Mile* is about a white guy trying to make it in a world dominated by African Americans. B-Rabbit's audience is black, making skin color the first obstacle he has to overcome. We have seen this theme explored before, but not from this angle. RECOMMENDED

25th Hour [2002]

Starring: Edward Norton, Philip Seymour Hoffman, Barry Pepper, Rosario Dawson, Anna Paquin, Brian Cox Director: Spike Lee Screenplay: David Benioff, based on his novel Running Time: 2:14 Rated: R (Profanity, sexual situations) Theatrical Aspect Ratio: 2.35:1

Spike Lee's *25th Hour* puts a new spin on an old question: what would you do if you knew you had less than 24 hours to live? In this case, the protagonist, Monty Brogan (Edward Norton), isn't headed for the embrace of the Grim Reaper, but he's getting the next best thing. Convicted on a major drugs charge (possession of more than one kilo with intent to distribute), he is headed for an overcrowded, maximum security prison where he will serve a 7-year sentence. He has less than a full day of freedom before he must present himself at the penitentiary (*why* he is free is never explained). In that time, he tries to tie up as many loose ends in his life as he can, spending time with his two close friends — insecure Jakob (Philip Seymour Hoffman), a high school teacher, and fiery Frank (Barry Pepper), a Wall Street broker; his girlfriend, Naturelle (Rosario Dawson); one of Jakob's students, Mary (Anna Paquin); and his father (Brian Cox).

Going to prison isn't Monty's only choice. A three-pronged fork in the road looms ahead. One branch takes him behind bars. Another branch takes him on the run, fleeing to some nameless town to spend the rest of his life in obscurity. The final branch involves putting a bullet through his brain. Don't expect to get a definitive answer to which path Monty chooses. *25th Hour* is deliberately (and, some might argue, maddeningly) open-ended, although it offers a tantalizing glimpse of one possibility.

25th Hour moves slowly — it's an unhurried, talky affair that consists primarily of members of the small group of characters interacting, while flashbacks reveal how and why Monty is in his current predicament. The movie seems largely detached from reality, although the tableau is more of a nightmarescape than a dreamscape. There's a sense of time (with the relentless clock ticking away) and place (a cold, inhospitable, post-9/11 New York City). Lee's decision to use digital video and desaturate the color enhance the gloomy atmosphere. *25th Hour* is not a happy experience, and there are times when it seems to drag, but there's no denying that it lingers in the mind long after the impressions left by other movies have evaporated. RECOMMENDED

About a Boy [United Kingdom/United States, 2002]
Starring: Hugh Grant, Toni Collette, Rachel Weisz, Nicholas Hoult Directors: Chris Weitz, Paul Weitz Screenplay: Peter Hedges and Chris Weitz & Paul Weitz, based on the novel by Nick Hornby Running Time: 1:40 Rated: PG-13 (Profanity, sexual situations) Theatrical Aspect Ratio: 2.35:1

Will Freeman (Hugh Grant) is the ultimate slacker. Living off the royalties of his one-hit-wonder father's Christmastime jingle "Santa's Supersleigh," Will is proud of never having had a job or, indeed, having done much of anything. He's not interested in a serious relationship — casual sex and one-night stands are his forté. Then he makes a mistake. On the prowl for easy female prey, he ventures into a single parents' group meeting, creating a fictitious son for himself. Soon, he is dating a woman who is babysitting for her friend's son, Marcus (Nicholas Hoult). This wouldn't mean much to Will, except that Marcus

takes a liking to him and decides that Will might be the perfect match for his emotionally disturbed mother, Fiona (Toni Collette). Then the strangest thing happens — Will and Marcus strike up an unusual friendship. But complications ensue when Will falls for another single mother (Rachel Weisz) and wants Marcus to pretend to be his son.

Even though they use a stock plot, *About a Boy* injects enough fresh attitude to provide an enjoyable 100 minutes. There's nothing terribly challenging or original about the production, but it boasts nicely rounded, amiable characters, a fairly consistent sense of self-deprecating wit, and the occasional belly laugh. We grow to care about the protagonists, and the Weitzes manage the difficult task of making the big climax satisfying while, at the same time, they avoid pushing it over the top to the point where it becomes overly sentimental claptrap. We get to see Will move from his state of perpetual adolescence. His interaction with Marcus gives him a perspective on life that he never had. Suddenly, his insular lifestyle seems shallow and superficial, and, even though it's "hard work to be wonderful all the time," it's worth the sacrifice.

The key to the movie's success is the slightly irreverent tone adopted by the directors. The Weitzes know when to wink at the audience, and they employ internal monologues (for Will and Marcus) to provide biting commentary on what's going on. It is smart enough to avoid sit-com and movie-of-the-week situations. Hugh Grant is in rare form, toeing the line between his "aw shucks" good guy and the cad from *Bridget Jones's Diary*. In Will, Grant gives us a character whose obvious flaws are a primary reason for his appeal. Meanwhile, Nicholas Hoult shows legitimate screen presence, and he and Grant generate some chemistry.

About a Boy is not a daring film, but it is immensely likable. Every once in a while, a movie comes along that, despite traversing familiar terrain, is made with enough all-around skill that it overcomes its clichéd origins. *About a Boy* is such a movie. RECOMMENDED

About Schmidt [2002]
Starring: Jack Nicholson, Hope Davis, Kathy Bates Director: Alexander Payne Screenplay: Alexander Payne & Jim Taylor, based on the novel by Louis Begley Running Time: 2:04 Rated: R (Profanity, nudity) Theatrical Aspect Ratio: 1.85:1

Until recently, Warren Schmidt (Jack Nicholson) was like so many millions of American workers, leading a life bounded by conformity and routine. Now, at age

66, he has been forced to leave behind his assistant vice president job at a Nebraska-based insurance company, and amble into the great unknown of retirement. Suddenly, life seems to be closing in on Warren. Helen (June Squibb), his wife of 42 years, is getting on his nerves, he despises the man (Dermot Mulroney) about to marry his beloved daughter, Jeannie (Hope Davis), and, most importantly, when he looks back at his 6+ decades of life, he can't see any way that he has made a difference. So, after watching a television infomercial, he writes out a check to a "Save the Children" organization and "adopts" a 6-year-old Tanzanian boy named Ndugu. Then, unexpectedly, Helen dies and Warren finds himself alone. So he packs his bags, climbs into the spacious RV sitting in his driveway, and heads off to visit his daughter — after making a few stops along the way.

About Schmidt is an unsentimental yet effective portrait of a character struggling with the essential questions of life. Although it has moments of cynicism, this is not a cynical film. Although it contains instances of humor, it is not a comedy. And, although it contains elements of the road trip genre, it is not a road trip movie. Instead, this is an opportunity to spend 2 hours in the company of a fairly ordinary man who no longer understands the point of anything.

One thing that is rock-solid throughout is the performance of Jack Nicholson. Nicholson carries the movie, and does so by not just being Jack, but by using an understated approach to playing Warren. This isn't a flamboyant, over-the-top individual, but a sad, quiet man who looks at the world though lenses tinted with despair. This is one of Nicholson's best acting assignments in years.

About Schmidt is on the long side. Some of the road trip detours drag a little and there are perhaps a few too many "colorful" characters. The catharsis at the end hits the right note, giving the viewer a sense of closure without betraying the character or cheapening what has gone before. On balance, I recommend the movie both for Nicholson's performance and for the opportunity to spend some time with the kind of man that we often meet in real life, but rarely see on screen. **RECOMMENDED**

The Accompanist [France, 1993]

Starring: **Romane Bohringer, Richard Bohringer, Elena Safonova**
Director: **Claude Miller** Screenplay: **Claude Miller and Luc Beraud**
Running Time: **1:50** Rated: **PG (Mature themes)** In French with subtitles

It is 1942-43 in German-occupied France. Charles Brice (Richard Bohringer), a French businessman, is regarded as a collaborator because he's making money with the Germans in charge. His wife, singer Irene Brice (Elena Safonova), is beloved by both French nationals and the occupying power. Into this world of wealth and privilege comes a talented young pianist by the name of Sophie Vasseur (Romane Bohringer), who auditions to be Irene's accompanist. Irene, amazed by the young woman's remarkable ability, hires her, but Sophie soon learns that working with the singer demands more sacrifices than she could have dreamed possible.

The Accompanist is told in 3 parts. The first, which takes place in France, focuses on Sophie, exploring her life, feelings, and the love/hate relationship that develops between her and Irene. The second part, the journey from France to England, is more the singer's story, while the third segment, in England, concentrates on Charles and the demons of insecurity and jealousy that haunt him.

Despite the varying emphases of the different portions of *The Accompanist,* the central character is always Sophie, although she is rarely more of an observer. She has given up her own life to follow Irene, and off-stage as well as on, she is always in the background. Even as Sophie is obsessed with a woman whom she both despises and is jealous of, so Irene comes to depend on the young woman who plays the piano for her.

The third member of the trio is Charles, who at first appears to be a supremely confident, smug man whose business acumen has made him a force to be reckoned with. It isn't until Sophie has begun living under the Brices' roof that she learns how thin that veneer is. Charles is far more dependent upon his wife than Irene is on him, and this forms the backdrop for *The Accompanist's* final scenes.

All three principal actors, as well as the members of the supporting cast, give fine performances. Romane Bohringer, who won the 1992 Cesar Award as Most Promising New Actress, is exceptional, bringing a silent expressiveness to the role of Sophie that would be beyond many veterans of the screen. Ms. Bohringer's rapport with her father Richard is evident in their many scenes together.

Ultimately, *The Accompanist* holds the viewer's attention through the power of its depiction of the bonds that develop between the singer, her husband, and her pianist. The story that conveys this relationship is neither original nor exceptional, but writer/director Claude Miller's presentation of the intricate and conflicting emotions makes this an experience that is always absorbing, and occasionally wrenching. **HIGHLY RECOMMENDED**

The Adventures of Sebastian Cole [1999]
Starring: Adrian Grenier, Clark Gregg, Aleksa Palladino, Margaret Colin, John Shea, Marni Lustig, Gabriel Macht   Director: Tod Williams   Screenplay: **Tod Williams**   Running Time: **1:39**   Rated: R (Profanity, sexual situations, drug use)   Theatrical Aspect Ratio: 1.85:1

It's June 1983 in Dutchess County, New York. The Cole family, which consists of 16-year-old Sebastian, his older sister, Jessica (Marni Lustig); his mother, Joan (Margaret Colin); and his stepfather, Hank (Clark Gregg), is a relatively normal, stable unit until Hank makes a startling pronouncement — he's going to undergo a sex-change operation. Shortly thereafter, Sebastian is on his way to London with his mother, who has decided that life in a lesbian relationship isn't for her. But Sebastian doesn't fare well in England, and, in time for the next school year, he is back in New York, living with Hank (who now goes by the name of Henrietta). Sebastian's confused relationship with Hank/Henrietta impacts every aspect of his life, including his ability to function in school and the way he treats his girlfriend, Mary (Aleska Palladino).

For the most part, this is a serious motion picture about the common traumas encountered during the teenage years — alienation from the family, the need to rebel, the difficulties of love and sex, and the confusion of planning for the future — as well as at least one unusual one — relating to a parent undergoing a gender identity crisis.

The relationship between Hank/Henrietta and Sebastian is well realized and poignantly real. Although we never learn much about the factors that drive Hank/Henrietta to need the operation, his interaction with his step-son is effectively presented. The same is true of many of the other individuals — they are carefully developed when they enter Sebastian's orbit, but sketchy and incomplete outside of it. This approach serves to make Sebastian the most rounded character in the film. It's not difficult to understand what motivates his disruptive and occasionally self-destructive actions.

The Adventures of Sebastian Cole, which premiered in competition during the 1999 Sundance Festival, is a little more on the fringe than the bulk of its cinematic kin. Instead of offering the common delin-quency/redemption cycle encompassed by most coming-of-age movies, it offers a fragmented slice of life with minimal closure. The protagonist does not sink to the depths reached by many central figures in films like this nor does he ever set his feet on the path to leading a productive life. *The Adventures of Sebastian Cole* isn't about telling a complete story; it's about giving the audience an opportunity to spend 90 minutes observing an interesting character during a critical period of his life. **RECOMMENDED**

The Advocate [United Kingdom, 1993]
Starring: Colin Firth, Ian Holm, Nicol Williamson, Amina Annabi, Donald Pleasance, Jim Carter, Lysette Anthony   Director: Leslie Magahey   Screenplay: Leslie Magahey   Running Time: 1:50   Rated: R (Sex, violence, nudity, mature themes, language)

In the Middle Ages in France, the laws of the time applied not only to humans, but to some very unlikely subjects. Since it was the common belief that everything was created by God, all things — including animals, inanimate objects, and natural phenomena — could be held accountable for crimes.

The main character in this tale is Richard Courtois (Colin Firth), a young advocate who has abandoned Paris for the 1452 French countryside. There, he expects to find relative peace marred by only occasional land disputes and petty quarrels. Instead, he enters a hotbed of murder, rape, beastiality, and sorcery. People — and animals — are being tried and hanged for the most heinous crimes.

Joining Firth is a supporting cast of stellar quality. Donald Pleasance (attempting to shine up an image tarnished by four *Halloween* films) plays Pincheon, the local prosecutor, who has little difficulty attempting to convict a pig for the murder of two young Jewish boys. Ian Holm is Albertus, a Catholic priest whose personal beliefs fail to match those he publicly espouses. Nicol Williamson is a merchant-come-seigneur who freely and willfully abuses his considerable power. Together, they make a jab or two at the legal profession, raise serious questions about the nature of justice, and present a case against bigotry ant intolerance.

Leslie Magahey has penned an insightful and witty script whose underlying themes and currents are as valid today as they were 500 years ago in another part of the world. The deepest indictment in *The Advocate* is not of the practitioners of law, but of the system itself, and how easy it is to pervert the course of justice. Legal trickery is as old as the courts, and those who make the laws are easily motivated by self-interest. Few have the moral fiber to pass a law that hurts themselves, regardless of how many others it benefits.

Then there's *The Advocate*'s non-sermonizing approach to racial prejudice. Amina Annabi plays a dark-skinned gypsy who fascinates Courtois. Hers is the pig in danger, but the men and women of Abbeville view the woman as little better than the jailed animal. By sleeping with her, the advocate opens himself to a charge of bestiality — engaging in sexual activity with someone viewed as less-than-human.

Despite the rather dreary mystery subplot, the case for *The Advocate* is a strong one. Leslie Megahey's picture contains enough successful elements that it's possible to push aside those that don't work while concentrating on the ones that do. Taken at face value, this movie presents a view of a Medieval village caught in the grip of fear. Below that surface, however, can be found the themes and convictions which give this film its true victory. **RECOMMENDED**

An Affair of Love [France/Belgium, 1999]
Starring: **Nathalie Baye, Sergi Lopez** Director: **Frederic Fonteyne** Screenplay: **Philippe Blasband** Running Time: 1:20 Rated: R (Sex, nudity) Theatrical Aspect Ratio: 2.35:1 In French with subtitles

Meticulously crafted by director Frederic Fonteyne (in his second feature outing) and flawlessly acted by leads Nathalie Baye and Sergi Lopez, *An Affair of Love* offers the kind of deeply reasoned and rewarding romance that is almost never presented in traditional motion pictures (such as the slicker, high-profile American productions that dominate the world market).

The underlying premise represents a fairly typical foundation for a motion picture romance — two individuals, initially drawn to each other for purely sexual reasons, fall in love. The mechanism of their first encounter is a personal ad that the woman (Baye) places in a magazine. The man (Lopez) answers, the two arrange a meeting, then, after a short introduction, they retire to a room in a hotel. We never learn exactly what they do behind the closed door of that room, but both acknowledge that it's out-of-the-ordinary. After their first encounter, they meet weekly for trysts, until, eventually, they decide they want to try making love "normally." Following this, they begin to realize that they have come to regard each other as more than sexual objects. Even though they don't

know each other's names, ages, or professions, there is a deep connection. They feel comfortable and relaxed with each other. While sex is still an important part of their relationship, it is no longer the *only* part: they have fallen in love. Yet neither knows how to handle the unexpected turn of events.

Fonteyne is methodical in his approach to the subject matter; he chronicles the affair from start to finish — from the nervous uncertainty of the first meeting to the sad, final encounter. Intercut with scenes featuring the two unnamed characters conversing with each other in Paris cafes and discussing life and love in a hotel room are clips from faux interviews conducted with them an unspecified time after the end of their affair. In addition to providing some important background information, the interview segments offer a sense of closure — from the earliest moments in the film, we know that these characters will not end up together in some fairytale, happily ever after state, but that they will move on with their lives.

Ultimately, miscommunication and a fear of intimacy doom the relationship, but Fonteyne builds slowly to the inevitable break-up, allowing us to explore every stage in the couple's interaction. Baye and Lopez are on equal footing, each matching the other's performances scene-for-scene, fully inhabiting the skins of their characters. We learn almost nothing about these two as far as their lives apart from each other are concerned, but we come to know them through this relationship. We discover them as they discover each other. **HIGHLY RECOMMENDED**

Affliction [1998]
Starring: **Nick Nolte, Sissy Spacek, James Coburn, Jim True, Holmes Osborne, Willem Dafoe, Mary Beth Hurt, Brigid Tierney** Director: **Paul Schrader** Screenplay: **Paul Schrader** based on the novel by Russell Banks Running Time: 1:54 Rated: R (Profanity, violence) Theatrical Aspect Ratio: 1.85:1

Wade Whitehouse (Nick Nolte) sees the world a little differently from everyone else. Alienated from his pre-teen daughter, Jill (Brigid Tierney) and unhappily divorced from his wife Lilllian (Mary Beth Hurt), he thinks he can get a lawyer and restructure his custody agreement. Likewise, when his best friend, Jack Hewitt (Jim True), accompanies a man on a hunting expedition, and the man accidentally shoots and kills himself, Wade begins to suspect a conspiracy, despite a lack of evidence. Unwilling to accept Jack's story of a simple, tragic mishap, Wade wonders about mob involvement, cover-ups, and hit men.

As a child, Wade was brutalized by an unloving father (James Coburn). The experience left profound scars, and old wounds are re-opened every time he visits his parents, who still live in the area. Fortunately for Wade, there is one stabilizing influence in his life — Maggie Fogg (Sissy Spacek), a local waitress who genuinely cares for him and is willing to sacrifice her personal comfort to ensure that he has a chance at happiness.

All of these elements are woven together in a tapestry that is part drama, part mystery, and part psychological exploration of a compelling character. The glue that holds everything together, and the driving reason to see *Affliction*, is Nick Nolte. Nolte has always been regarded as a good actor, but, during his long and successful career, rarely has he poured himself into a part the way he does here. His portrayal of Wade is riveting. With his eyes, his voice, and his every body movement, he forces us to understand what it means to live in Wade's tortured skin. On an intellectual level, we realize that Wade is headed for a meltdown, but that doesn't lessen the connection between the character and the audience — a connection that Nolte is instrumental in forming. By the time the end credits roll, we know Wade inside out. We understand the forces that drive him, and recognize the inevitability of what transpires. In fact, the way Schrader chooses to present it, Wade's "criminal behavior" is almost an epilogue. *Affliction* is not about the crimes; it's about what leads up to them.

Affliction successfully and effectively navigates treacherous and complex psychological territory without ever missing a beat. Although many of the plot details can be found in any dysfunctional family drama, the vividness of Wade's character is what makes this film especially compelling. Presentation is everything, and this is far more powerful than any TV movie of the week about the effects of child abuse. *Affliction* is for anyone willing to take the journey into the heart and soul of a troubled man on the edge.
HIGHLY RECOMMENDED

After Life [Japan, 1998]
Starring: Arata. Erika Oda, Taketoshi Naito, Susumu Terajima, Takashi Naito Director: Hirokazo Kore-eda Screenplay: Hirokazo Kore-eda Running Time: 1:58 Rated: No MPAA Rating (Mature themes) Theatrical Aspect Ratio: 1.85:1 In Japanese with subtitles

What happens after death? Director Hirokazo Kore-eda's vision, as shown in *After Life,* is that when someone dies, they go to a spiritual halfway house that looks like a country lodge. There is no heaven or hell, no god or religion. The dead stay at this place for exactly one week. During that time, they must choose the one memory from their life that they want to keep; the rest will all be erased. That memory is then re-created and filmed, and it becomes their constant and sole companion as they pass into the afterlife.

Kore-eda uses this premise as a springboard for numerous interwoven tales, telling us stories both of those who are passing through the way station on their way to the sweet hereafter and those who "live" and work there. There's one simple requirement for becoming a counselor at the halfway house: refuse to choose a memory. No one can pass on until they do.

After Life is intellectually satisfying, but emotionally cool. There are too many characters, and little time is accorded to any of them. The only three given more than token screen time are Ichiro Watanabe (Taketoshi Naito), a 70-year old businessman who died in the wake of an unhappy life of drudgery, and his afterlife case workers, Takashi Mochizuki (Arata) and Shiori Satonaka (Erika Oda). As Watanabe views videotapes of his life in order to select a memory, Takashi and Shiori are drawn into his drama, breaking the cardinal rule of not becoming involved. When it becomes apparent to Takashi that he and the old man share a past, he removes himself from the case. His subsequent decision causes a crisis of confidence for Shiori.

It's interesting to consider some of the memories most cherished by the characters. One man, who speaks ceaselessly about his sexual conquests, eventually chooses his daughter's wedding day. A teenage girl rhapsodizes about a trip to Disneyland, then, after learning that it's a common choice for children her age, decides on something more personal. There are as many memories as there are people — memories for everyone except the few who intentionally shun them.

Kore-eda's film also expends time exploring the world where the counselors reside, and the kind of existences they lead. The way station is virtually identical to a segment of modern-day Japan, complete with a city where people hustle to their destinations, traffic jams during rush hour, and stores decorate for the Christmas season. In many ways, it's the ordinariness of Kore-eda's limbo and of those who inhabit it that make this vision of the afterlife so fascinating. With Kore-eda's skillful hand behind both the camera and the pen, the result is a rewarding cinematic experience. **RECOMMENDED**

Afterglow [1997]

Starring: Nick Nolte, Julie Christie, Lara Flynn Boyle, Jonny Lee Miller
Director: Alan Rudolph Screenplay: Alan Rudolph Running Time: 1:54
Rated: R (Profanity, sex, brief nudity) Theatrical Aspect Ratio: 1.85:1

Afterglow introduces you to two unhappily married couples. Jeffrey Byron (Jonny Lee Miller) is a cold, seemingly-heartless businessman who is sexually indifferent to his young wife, Marianne (Lara Flynn Boyle). For her part, Marianne is so obsessed with having a baby that she never attempts to interact with her husband on a human level. All she's interested in is seducing him during those few days when she's ovulating. After he refuses to make love, she decides to find someone else to play the role of sperm donor.

The other couple, Lucky (Nick Nolte) and Phyllis Mann (Julie Christie), are an older pair, but they're no more content than Jeffrey and Marianne. A mysterious fracture in their past relationship has driven them apart. They remain married as a matter of convenience, but they have an unspoken agreement whereby Lucky can fool around as much as he wants. The landscape of emotional pain between them is palpable.

The four characters begin interacting when Marianne hires Lucky as a handyman to fix up the inside of the apartment she shares with Jeffrey. The two of them are immediately attracted to one another, and it doesn't take long before they're lounging together, naked, in her pool. Meanwhile, Jeffrey, who is captivated by older women, runs into Phyllis in a hotel bar, is smitten, and invites her to accompany him on a weekend retreat to the mountains.

The romantic couplings of the characters are interesting in that they illustrate the multiple faces of love. Sex means something different to everyone — to Jeffrey, it's an unpleasant chore, a loss of control; to Marianne, it's a means to a maternal end. Ultimately, none of these characters appears to love anyone else as much as they love themselves.

The greatest strength of the film lies not in the script, but in the performances. The clear standout, however, is Julie Christie, who is nothing short of delicious as the world-weary Phyllis. Her often wry, occasionally cutting asides are the source of much of the film's humor, and there's hardly ever a moment when she doesn't steal the spotlight from her co-stars.

I don't know if *Afterglow* is the film to convert Rudolph-detractors, but it seems that this movie is a little more accessible than some of the director's earlier productions. Enough of his trademark style remains, however, to reassure his supporters. *Afterglow* is basically a four-pronged character study. The plot is not especially compelling, but the character interaction is, and that's the real reason to see this motion picture. Rudolph has painted an able picture of the non-romantic side of love — the one that has more to do with tolerance and familiarity than with affection and attraction. **RECOMMENDED**

The Age of Innocence [1993]

Starring: Daniel Day-Lewis, Winona Ryder, Michelle Pfeiffer, Miriam Margoyles, Richard E. Grant, Geraldine Chaplin Director: Martin Scorsese Screenplay: Martin Scorsese and Jay Cocks, based on the novel by Edith Wharton Running Time: 2:13 Rated: PG (Mature themes) Theatrical Aspect Ratio: 2.35:1

It's New York City in the 1870s, a society ruled by expectations and propriety, where a hint of immorality can bring scandal and ruin. Into this world arrives Countess Ellen Olenska (Michelle Pfeiffer), a woman who has spent much of her life in Europe and is now escaping from a disastrous marriage. Her initial adult meeting with Newland Archer (Daniel Day-Lewis) is sedate — he is engaged to her cousin May (Winona Ryder) — but there is a subtle fire smouldering from the first glance. From that point on, Archer's dilemma becomes painfully clear — marry the rather vapid May, or allow his heart and passions to carry him far from the realm of what is conventionally acceptable.

Martin Scorsese has made a reputation from making movies that show a profound perceptiveness of human nature through their images of toughness and violence. Scorsese has placed his indelible stamp on this picture, not only through the camerawork, but in the potent tension that builds between the main characters. For while blood has often been Scorsese's method, the characters, and what exists between and within them, have always been his ends.

Adapting from the 1921 Pulitzer Prize-winning novel by Edith Wharton, Scorsese and Jay Cocks have successfully incorporated the conflict of emotion against societal pressures that lie at the heart of *The Age of Innocence*. It is a sumptuous motion picture, a feast for the senses. The colors are vivid, from the red and yellow of roses to the flashes of crimson and white that transition scenes. The powerful score moves along with the story, in perfect counterpoint to the visuals — never intrusive, but always effective.

Daniel Day-Lewis never fails to impress, even when he appears in a poor film. Here, Day-Lewis immerses himself in the character of Newland Archer, and it's no great stretch for the audience to accept him. I have never subscribed to the widely held belief that Michelle Pfeiffer is a ravishing beauty. In fact, in *The Age of Innocence*, she looks rather plain (an impression that, in my opinion, heightened the impact of the story). Ellen is exotic, certainly, but beautiful? Nevertheless, there is no denying the stirring, heartfelt passion of Pfeiffer's performance. Outstripping anything she has done in the past, the role of Ellen can be considered a pinnacle.

There are few films this year that I recommend as heartily as *The Age of Innocence*, which has the rare distinction of being more of a cinematic experience than a simple movie. Something that transcends the medium like this shouldn't be set aside for viewing on the small screen. For those who expect more from their films than a lot of bangs and flashes, *The Age of Innocence* is not to be missed. MUST SEE

Ali [2001]

Starring: **Will Smith, Jamie Foxx, Jon Voight, Mario Van Peebles**
Director: **Michael Mann** Screenplay: **Stephen J. Rivele & Christopher Wilkinson and Eric Roth & Michael Mann** Running Time: **2:35** Rated: **PG-13** (Profanity, violence, sexual situations) Theatrical Aspect Ratio: **2.35:1**

Ali, Michael Mann's attempt to chronicle 10 pivotal years in the life of former heavyweight boxing champion Muhammed Ali, suffers from the most common ailment of motion picture biographies — trying to do too much in a limited time. During the height of his career, Ali was reviled by much of white America — he was seen as a rebellious and divisive figure. Two decades later, the majority view of Ali has softened considerably. Age and Parkinson's have leached away much of the perceived arrogance that irritated many of Ali's critics. Consequently, the aging pugilist is now a revered figure. Ali's faults tend to be glossed over (we don't learn about his frequent philandering until the movie is almost over), while his praiseworthy tendencies are overemphasized. Even considering those flaws, *Ali* still manages to deliver. Every time the movie threatens to bog down, Mann takes us into the ring and re-invigorates the film with his fantastic boxing sequences.

Little blame for *Ali*'s weaknesses can be laid at the feet of actor Will Smith, who put his whole heart and mind into the performance. The actor bears only a passing physical resemblance to Ali, but Smith proves that great acting can overcome the need to look like a twin. This portrayal is at times passionate and fiery, and at others, quiet and thoughtful. Smith's Ali is a portrait of a man who was a fighter both inside and out of the ring. His work here will force those who doubted his selection to eat their words.

Smith casts such a long shadow that no one else appearing in the film can be considered as anything more significant than a supporting player. Jamie Foxx, who, like Smith, is better known for comedy than drama, offers an effective representation of Bundini, Ali's cornerman (he created, "Float like a butterfly, sting like a bee"). Then there's Jon Voight's interpretation of legendary sportscaster Howard Cosell, whose on-screen verbal sparring and off-screen friendship with "the champ" would mark a cornerstone of Ali's public life. Unrecognizable under layers of garish makeup, Voight at times looks like a moving, talking waxwork. But the voice and inflection are perfect, and, every time Voight opens his mouth, he becomes Cosell.

There's no debating that *Ali* could have been a far more impressive motion picture than what Mann has brought to the screen. It fails to deliver the hoped-for knockout, but also avoids the pitfalls of an early round collapse. *Ali* tells an involving story of individual heroism, and does so in a manner that keeps the audience engaged. In the genre of boxing movies, *Ali* falls short of the likes of *Raging Bull* and *The Hurricane*, but, just because this movie doesn't connect with every punch should not disqualify it from consideration as a way to spend a Saturday night. RECOMMENDED

Alice and Martin [France, 1998]

Starring: **Juliette Binoche, Alexis Loret, Mathieu Amalric**
Director: **André Téchiné** Screenplay: **Olivier Assayas, Gilles Taurand, André Téchiné** Running Time: **2:04** Rated: **R** (Sexual situations, nudity, profanity, violence) Theatrical Aspect Ratio: **1.66:1** In French with subtitles

When it comes to movies about dysfunctional family relationships and emotionally damaged individuals, few active filmmakers do a better job than veteran French director André Techiné. He uses the canvas of *Alice and Martin* to explore the delicate and uncertain balance of the relationships between lovers, siblings, parents, and children in an unstable family environment. The film delves into the price of obsessive love and the way in which secrets and their associated guilt have the capacity to poison everything they touch.

Martin (Jeremy Kreikenmayer) is the bastard child

of a successful business man, Victor Sauvagnac (Pierre Maguelon), and a young beautician. Martin is sent as a child to live in his father's mansion. Ten years later, Martin (Alexis Loret) is shown fleeing through the gates of that mansion, pursued by unidentified demons. After a brief sojourn in the mountains, he ends up in Paris at the apartment of his half-brother, Benjamin (Mathieu Amalric). Benjamin shares his flat with Alice (Juliette Binoche), a violinist with whom he has a close, platonic friendship. Martin's entrance into their lives upsets the quiet stability of their relationship, especially when it becomes clear that he is deeply fascinated by Alice. She does not immediately reciprocate Martin's feelings, but once he has had some success in his new modeling career, he challenges her to acknowledge what is between them or stop seeing him.

As is his trademark, Techiné leaches the melodrama out of the situation, leaving the viewer with starkly detailed but not always comfortable pictures of the protagonists. There is no emotional manipulation here, just honest characterization. Martin is a deeply disturbed, brooding individual whose increasingly erratic behavior is explained once his secret is revealed. And Alice learns what it means to surrender her heart to someone like Martin. Their relationship begins with the kind of giddy euphoria that marks the early days of nearly every romantic liaison, but the baying of Martin's demons eventually grows too strident to be ignored. Meanwhile, Benjamin looks on with ill-concealed jealousy at what they have.

Two of the most powerful human emotions are love and guilt. In uplifting romantic fantasies, love can provide a wellspring of redemption, but *Alice and Martin* doesn't offer such a facile resolution. For Martin, love is a distraction, not a panacea; he needs to atone for that which defines his present existence. The need to be judged is too strong to be denied. Like a zealot who demands a public flagellation to expiate his sin, Martin's thirst for punishment grows until his mental health is in doubt. Alice, unable to stand by helplessly, chooses to work with him rather than at cross-purposes, and, by disturbing a few skeletons, she learns the reasons behind the haunted look in her lover's eyes. RECOMMENDED

All About My Mother (Todo Sobre mi Madre)
[Spain, 1999]
Starring: Cecilia Roth, Eloy Azorín, Marisa Paredes, Penelope Cruz
Director: Pedro Almodovar Screenplay: Pedro Almodovar Running

Time: **1:45** Rated: **R (Sex, nudity, profanity, drug use)** Theatrical Aspect Ratio: **2.35:1** In Spanish with subtitles

On the cusp of his 17th birthday in Madrid, Esteban (Eloy Azorín) is blossoming into an accomplished writer. He jots down in his journal that he wishes his mother, Manuela (Cecilia Roth), would tell him the story of his father, whom he has never met. After Esteban makes his feelings known to her, Manuela promises to tell him, but tragedy strikes before she has an opportunity. While running after a taxi to get the autograph of a star he admires, Esteban is struck and killed by a car. A grieving Manuela then decides to travel from Madrid to Barcelona, where Esteban was conceived, to find her ex-husband and inform him that the son he never knew about is dead.

Arriving in Barcelona, Manuela runs into her old friend, Agrado (Antonia San Juan), a transvestite prostitute, who informs her that her former husband, who goes by the name of Lola, has vanished. Together, Manuela and Agrado visit Rosa (Penelope Cruz), the young nun who last saw Lola. Although Rosa does not know Lola's current location, she is anxious to find him. While she was shepherding him through a drug detox program, Rosa became sexually involved with Lola, and she now carries his child. Meanwhile, Manuela takes time out of her schedule to see the Tennessee Williams play *A Streetcar Named Desire*. While there, she meets Huma Rojo (Marisa Paredes), the actress whose autograph Esteban was pursuing when he was killed.

As the title implies, *All About My Mother* is about mothers and their relationships with their natural or surrogate children. It's also about the other roles that women occupy when they're not caring for their sons and daughters. There are no significant male characters in the film. Esteban dies early and Agardo, while born a male (and still possessing male genitalia), thinks and behaves like a woman. The absence of men allows Almodovar to explore interpersonal interaction without being concerned about testosterone interference. This results in a thoughtful and emotionally rich tapestry.

For his principals, the director has mined the best of Spain's talent. Penelope Cruz and Marisa Paredes, both veterans of Almodovar's past work, breathe life into their characters. Cruz, as usual, is extremely likable, and Paredes brings a mixture of toughness and world weariness to the part of Huma. There's a particularly poignant scene in which she recognizes that though she may be successful, after you've had success for a while, you no longer notice it. The center-piece of *All About My Mother* is Cecilia Roth. Almodovar has used her several times before, but never has she been as vibrant as she is here. For Almodovar, this picture represents the latest high point in a lively career. **HIGHLY RECOMMENDED**

All Over Me [1997]

Starring: Alison Folland, Tara Subkoff, Cole Hauser Director: Alex Sichel Screenplay: Sylvia Sichel Running Time: 1:30 Rated: R (Sex, drugs, violence, profanity) Theatrical Aspect Ratio: 1.85:1

Welcome to Hell's Kitchen: a part of New York City that's not on many visitors' tour maps. It's the quintessential inner city: no one has any money, crime is rampant, and everyone dreams of getting out. It makes a great backdrop for a motion picture, provided that you want your story to be set against a world of poverty, violence, and drug abuse.

At the center is Claude (Alison Folland), a slightly overweight, somewhat insecure 15-year-old whose whole life revolves around her best friend, Ellen (Tara Subkoff). As Claude is beginning to recognize that her feelings for Ellen may run deeper than friendship, Ellen becomes involved with a local drug dealer/bad boy, Mark (Cole Hauser), and Claude's importance in Ellen's life plummets. To fill the void, Claude begins exploring new relationships — a casual acquaintanceship with Luke (Pat Briggs), a gay musician who moves in downstairs, and a tentative friendship with a lesbian guitar player (Leisha Hailey). Through it all, Claude realizes that what she wants more than anything is to recapture her closeness with Ellen, but a series of events may make that goal impossible to achieve.

Part of the reason *All Over Me* possesses such a stark sense of realism is because of the keenly-observed, unaffected performances of the lead actors. Alison Folland, who attracted attention for her role as a troubled teen in *To Die For,* is exceptionally strong, realizing all of the angst and conflict churning within Claude. As Ellen, Tara Subkoff has a less demanding part, but is no less effective in it. Subkoff is called upon to present a character trapped in a cycle of drug and alcohol abuse. The supporting cast includes Cole Hauser as the irredeemably nasty Mark, singer Leisha Hailey (of the group The Murmurs) as Claude's would-be girlfriend, and Psychotica band member Pat Briggs as the sensitive Luke.

The setting and music of *All Over Me* play an im-portant part in developing the story. These elements don't just function as background, but are integral to Claude's life choices. As uncertain as she is about her sexual identity, there is one thing she's sure of — that she loves playing the guitar. Her dream has been to start a band with Ellen. When that is no longer possible, she is forced to consider the likelihood that their futures will diverge and that their irreplaceable friendship will become a memory.

All Over Me falls loosely into the same genre as *Girls Town* — entirely-believable stories of the troubles faced by girls growing up in a '90s inner city environment. With all the truth inherent in the story, it could easily be depicting the life of someone we might pass on the street. And that makes it very easy to care about Claude, Ellen, and their lives during a few short summer weeks in Hell's Kitchen. **HIGHLY RECOMMENDED**

Almost Famous [2000]

Starring: Patrick Fugit, Kate Hudson, Billy Crudup, Frances McDormand, Jason Lee, Phillip Seymour Hoffman, Anna Paquin, Fairuza Balk, Noah Taylor Director: Cameron Crowe Screenplay: Cameron Crowe Running Time: 2:05 Rated: R (Profanity, sexual situations, drug use, brief nudity) Theatrical Aspect Ratio: 1.85:1

Almost Famous looks back at the world of rock 'n roll as it existed in the early 1970s. Fifteen-year-old William Miller (Patrick Fugit), a San Diego high school senior who skipped 2 grades in elementary school, gets to spend a few weeks on the road with his favorite band, Stillwater, and write an article about them for *Rolling Stone* magazine. His mentor, *Creem* rock critic Lester Bangs (Phillip Seymour Hoffman), gives him one key piece of advice: "You cannot make friends with the rock stars." William, however, allows himself to be seduced into the lifestyle by the group's guitarist, Russell Hammond (Billy Crudup). He also falls in love with one of Stillwater's groupies, Penny Lane (Kate Hudson), who has a "thing" going on with Russell. Back home, William's mother (Frances McDormand), does her best to keep tabs on her son's whereabouts by calling the hotels where he's staying, leaving one clear message: "Don't use drugs!"

Almost Famous isn't really about the '70s or the music scene. These are little more than background elements to William's coming-of-age story. The movie's central element is its depiction of how the socially immature William comes to grips with who he is, what he wants to do, and who he will become. For him, the trip with the band is about exploring his sexuality and learning how to live outside of his mother's protective umbrella. In the process, he loses his virginity, rejects the drug scene, forms a few lasting friendships, and saves a life.

Almost Famous contains a number of memorable characters: William, the ordinary young man who provides our portal into the movie, is effectively underplayed by actor Patrick Fugit. Kate Hudson (*Desert Blue*) gives a luminous star turn as Penny Lane, the girl who is at the center of the movie's romantic triangle. As William's mother, Oscar-winner Frances McDormand not only has some of the best scenes, but represents the movie's only truly unique character — a mother who is struggling to find the right balance between smothering her children and giving them their freedom. Phillip Seymour Hoffman has a wonderful turn as Lester Bangs (he gives a great speech about the benefits of being "uncool"), and Billy Crudup and Jason Lee are solid in their rolls as rock stars.

Almost Famous will be hard to top for its sheer exuberance and high feel-good quotient. The film's ecstatic atmosphere is only briefly interrupted by the sense of longing that is associated with first love and the pain that accompanies the inevitable separation between a child and a parent. Crowe's fourth feature represents another master stroke for the director, who has yet to have a bad outing. *Almost Famous* is an unqualified success. **HIGHLY RECOMMENDED**

Amelie [France, 2001]

Starring: Audrey Tautou, Mathieu Kassovitz, Rufus, Dominique Pinon, Isabelle Nanty, Serge Merlin Director: Jean-Pierre Jeunet Screenplay: Jean-Pierre Jeunet, Guillaume Laurant Running Time: 2:00 Rated: R (Sexual content, brief nudity) Theatrical Aspect Ratio: 2.35:1 In French with subtitles

Amelie is Amelie Poulain (brought to life with a delightful mix of shyness, energy, and mischievousness by Audrey Tatou), a young woman who has spent most of her life existing in the background. As a child, she was discouraged from having friends by her neurotic mother and emotionally distant father. As an adult, she has no boyfriend, no confidantes, and no real sense of purpose in life. That all changes with one small event — the discovery of a box of old snapshots and toys in a hidden compartment in her apartment. She sets out to find the owner of the box, and her quest eventually leads him to reconcile with his son. Emboldened by her success, Amelie decides to become a force for good in her small corner of the world, helping others around her. In the process, she

encounters Nino Quincampoix (Mathieu Kassovitz), who may be her soulmate — if she can ever find the courage to talk to him face-to-face and admit her feelings for him.

Mathieu Kassovitz (the director of *Hate*) makes Nino an effective match for Amelie. Kassovitz underplays the part perfectly, showing that Nino, like Amelie, is shy about their relationship, but he is determined to pursue it. Since she never approaches him directly, but is content to leave him clues and anonymous messages, he is forced into the role of detective and pursuer. Other supporting performers include Jeunet regular Dominique Pinon as a disgruntled customer at the café where Amelie works, and Serge Merlin as Amelie's painter neighbor, who gives her advice on life and love.

One of the most intriguing aspects of the film, aside from its visual vivaciousness, is the manner in which Amelie chooses to help others. Rather than going about things in a straightforward manner, she devises stratagems, the complexities of which are analogous to the workings of a Rube Goldberg project. Her father has a hidden desire to travel, so, in order to bring his interest to the surface, Amelie kidnaps his garden gnome and has it photographed in front of various geographical landmarks around the world. For a neighbor who cherishes old love letters from her dead husband, Amelie fakes one that was "recently found." Throughout this movie, Jeunet keeps us guessing whom Amelie will help next, and how she will choose to do so.

By shooting all around Paris, Jeunet uses the city as more of a character than a mere backdrop, although the director's surreal and timeless vision should not be confused with the place seen by tourists (or even ordinary citizens). This is Jeunet's city, where magic abounds in the strangest places, where fate and predestination lurk around every corner, where photographs talk, and where one sprightly young woman can orchestrate small miracles. **HIGHLY RECOMMENDED**

American Beauty [1999]

Starring: Kevin Spacey, Annette Bening, Thora Birch, Wes Bentley, Mena Suvari Director: Sam Mendes Screenplay: Alan Ball Running Time: 2:00 Rated: R (Profanity, nudity, sexual situations, drugs, violence) Theatrical Aspect Ratio: 2.35:1

Most teenagers think their parents are strange, but, in the case of Jane Burnham (Thora Birch), this is as much a state of reality as it is a state of mind. Her father, Lester (Kevin Spacey), is suffering through a mid-life crisis. At the age of 42, he has become apathetic to everything. Jane's mother, Carolyn (Annette Bening), places such value on status that she has turned into a "bloodless, money-grubbing freak" who has no time for any form of intimacy. She and Lester continue in their dead marriage for their daughter's sake and so they'll look normal to the outside world. In a moment of clarity, Lester admits, "Our marriage is just for show — a commercial for how normal we are, when we're anything but."

We see how these characters grow, and the catalysts that break them out of their near-catatonic existences. Happiness, the goal of youth, is replaced by the desire for the artificial comfort that comes through the numbing sameness of repetition. Loveless marriages like Lester and Carolyn's exist because neither partner possesses the willingness to break the cycle. And the children they think they're protecting by staying together are often the biggest victims of their sham.

Lester's awakening is prompted by two events, the first being that he might lose his job. Lester faces this possibility with dread. But as he dissects the situation in his mind, he sees how liberating it can be. Then there's Jane's best friend, Angela (Mena Suvari), an attractive teenager who captures his attention and arouses his sexual interest. Lester's desire to have this girl reawakens his long-dead libido. While Lester goes through a complete reconstruction of his outlook on life, Carolyn's perspective is also changing. Frustrated by her relationship with her husband, she begins an affair with a fellow real estate agent who calls himself "The King" (Peter Gallagher).

Then there's sullen Jane, who's caught between the two of them. Displeased with her physical appearance, she is saving up for breast augmentation surgery (something she *clearly* does not need). She also develops an unusual relationship with Ricky Fitts (Wes Bentley), the boy next door. Ricky has his own problems — his mother (Allison Janney) is virtually withdrawn from life and his father (Chris Cooper) is an ex-Marine neo-Nazi who submits his son's urine for drug testing every 6 months. Meanwhile, Jane also has to deal with Angela's growing fascination with the possibility of sleeping with Lester.

American Beauty is emotionally satisfying. While it's not a groundbreaking movie, its presentation of vivid characters in interesting situations makes the story seem fresh. There's a sense of poignancy at the end, but also the feeling that we have been on an incredible trip through the lives and souls of three perfectly-realized characters. **HIGHLY RECOMMENDED**

American Buffalo [1996]

Starring: Dustin Hoffman, Dennis Franz, Sean Nelson Director: Michael Corrente Screenplay: David Mamet Based on a David Mamet play Running Time: 1:28 Rated: R (Profanity, mature themes) Theatrical Aspect Ratio: 1.85:1

American Buffalo starts out torturously slowly, with lots of cryptic dialogue about not confusing business with pleasure, a "broken toaster," and some kind of "job" that a couple of down-on-their-luck guys are preparing to pull. Those men are Don (Dennis Franz), the owner of a New York junk shop, and Teach (Dustin Hoffman), a '90s version of *Midnight Cowboy*'s Ratso Rizzo. The third character in the story is a teenage boy named Bobby (Sean Nelson) who wants to help in the upcoming job, but the two adults are reluctant to get him involved.

The film improves considerably after the unpromising opening. Don and Teach are planning to rob some rich guy's coin collection (the title, *American Buffalo*, refers to the pre-Jefferson nickel), but they don't have a plan or a clear sense of what they're doing. Teach, a take-things-as-they-come person, wants to get down to the action. Don, a more careful man, wants everything planned out in advance. This conflict leads to a fascinating scene where the two men sitting in the back of Teach's car, discussing the psychology of home safes.

Like a well-written musical composition, *American Buffalo* builds to a crescendo. The climax features a three-way confrontation between Teach, Don, and Bobby, and raises the specter that one or more might be double-dealing and committing a betrayal. The sense of paranoid claustrophobia makes the tension almost unbearable.

Dustin Hoffman plays Teach with caged energy. He's all mannerisms and nervous tics — the waiting is unbearable; he wants to *act*. He's the consummate failure who never gives up hoping for that one big score. But, by harkening back to *Midnight Cowboy* and resurrecting aspects of the long-dormant Ratso Rizzo, Hoffman makes this role his own.

Dennis Franz, an Emmy winner for *NYPD Blue*, holds his own opposite Hoffman. His Don is the picture of a man wracked by uncertainty. Should he do the job or not? Does he need the money badly enough to put up with all this aggravation? Meanwhile, Sean Nelson brings an enigmatic mixture of hardness and innocence to his portrayal of Bobby, keeping us unsure of his character's motives. Unfortunately, he doesn't quite have the screen presence to stand toe-to-toe with his experienced co-stars.

American Buffalo is an intense, but flawed, piece of drama. The ending winds the tension so tautly that everything feels ready to snap. To reach that point, it's necessary to plod through a murky beginning. Mamet's play may be 20 years old, but the themes of loyalty, betrayal, and ruthlessness are as applicable to the current social and economic environment as they were in the '70s. And that's a compelling reason why, if you don't mind the initial discomfort, it's worth staying for the entire film. RECOMMENDED

American Heart [1993]
Starring: Jeff Bridges, Edward Furlong, Lucinda Jenny Director: Martin Bell Screenplay: Peter Silverman Running Time: 1:53 Rated: R (Language, violence, nudity, mature themes)

Jack Kelson (Jeff Bridges) is an ex-con just out of jail, trying to get his new chance at life off to a good start. Unfortunately, circumstances are conspiring against him. His 14-year-old son, Nick (Edward Furlong), has run away from Jack's sister's farm, where he was staying, to seek him out. At first, Jack intends to send the boy back, but when Nick won't budge, he has no choice but to let him stay. With each passing day, problems mount, and the easy money offered by Jack's old way of life becomes increasingly more difficult to resist.

Set against a backdrop of poverty and violence in the underprivileged sections of Seattle, *American Heart* dramatizes a dysfunctional father/son relationship. Jack and Nick don't have a great rapport, but as the movie progresses, they struggle to find some sort of connection. Jack doesn't know how to be a good parent, and really doesn't want to start trying, but it's obvious that he loves his kid and wants Nick to have better opportunities than he had.

Jack has a relationship with Charlotte (Lucinda Jenny), a female pen-pal he started corresponding with while in prison. Nick resents Charlotte's presence, feeling that she takes away time that Jack should be spending with him. As the film progresses, Nick gets a girlfriend of his own — Molly (Tracey Kapisky), a 15-year-old streetwalker whose mother dances topless. Molly introduces Nick to drugs and crime and despite Jack's warnings that she'll break his heart, Nick can't stay away. She's as addictive as the marijuana that he smokes with her.

Then there's the constant re-appearance of Jack's old partner, Rainey (Don Harvey), who wants either Jack or Nick to accompany him on his next job — a jewelry store robbery. Considering the poor state of Jack's finances, it's a tempting offer, but he realizes that to attain his modest dream of traveling north to live in Alaska, he has to keep his hands clean. Whether Nick can resist the lure is another matter altogether.

Jeff Bridges, who has shown a capacity for playing grungy, downtrodden men throughout his career, turns in a heartfelt, entirely-believable performance. Would that the same could be said of Edward Furlong, who displays a distressing lack of range. He seems to have two modes: a blank face and a peeved expression. Anything else is a bonus. Fortunately, few scenes demand that Furlong carry them, and he is supported by a fine cast.

American Heart is the kind of hard-hitting, issue-confronting drama that throws formulas out the window. The atmosphere is stark, but not so relentlessly bleak that there isn't room for a little comic relief. Nevertheless, by not adhering to traditional Hollywood staples, this film sets itself up as an intellectually and emotionally challenging alternative. HIGHLY RECOMMENDED

American History X [1998]
Starring: Edward Norton, Edward Furlong, Beverly D'Angelo, Avery Brooks, Stacy Keach, Fairuza Balk Director: Tony Kaye Screenplay: David McKenna Running Time: 1:57 Rated: R (Profanity, violence, sex) Theatrical Aspect Ratio: 1.85:1

In the world of the skinhead neo-Nazi, slogans replace thought, fueling a mindless hatred that is startling in its intensity. Derek Vinyard (Edward Norton) is one of the most fervent members of the Venice Beach White Supremacist movement. An avowed hater of everyone who is not a white Protestant, he has risen to the top of a ragged group of hate-mongers. Derek is the disciple of Cameron (Stacy Keach), who stays behind the scenes to keep his record clean. Derek's followers include his younger brother, Danny (Edward Furlong), who worships him; and his girlfriend, Stacey (Fairuza Balk), who thoughtlessly parrots his words. Derek's mother, Doris (Beverly D'Angelo), and sister, Davin (Jennifer Lien), are frightened of and for him. On one fateful night, Derek uses deadly force to stop a pair of black youths from stealing his car. He ends up in prison for 3 years. While on the inside, he learns some hard truths about life from a fellow inmate (Guy Torry) and from the principal of his old high school (Avery Brooks). When Derek emerges with a desire to change attitudes, he finds that words are not enough.

American History X is in no way a comprehensive look at racism, hatred, or inner city violence. Instead, it examines the various ways these elements tear at the fabric of a family. The film emphasizes that actions have consequences, and that attaining redemption isn't as easy as saying "I'm sorry." The price for a change of heart can be, and often is, brutal. The final sequence in the film is shocking not because it's unexpected, but because it illustrates this truth.

The chief weakness in *American History X* is that we're presented with only one truly three-dimensional character. As portrayed by Edward Norton (who gained 30 pounds for the role), Derek is a fully-developed individual. We see the subtle elements that prime Derek for racist attitudes, follow the events that push him over the edge, then watch the trajectory of his life as his hatred spirals out of control before being reined in. Unfortunately, no one else in the movie comes close to being as real as Derek. Actors like Edward Furlong, Beverly D'Angelo, Fairuza Balk, and Avery Brooks do the best they can with lean material, but it falls on Norton's shoulders to carry the film.

The director, Tony Kaye, imbues *American History X* with a relentlessly ominous tone, especially during the final half hour, when we're expecting something grim to occur. Not all of Kaye's moves work — it seems unnecessarily showy for all of the "past" sequences to be in black-and-white, while the "current" ones are in color — but, on balance, Kaye displays ability in the motion picture arena. *American History X* may be flawed, but it's not easily forgotten. RECOMMENDED

American Me [1992]

Starring: Edward James Olmos, William Forsythe, Pepe Serna, Evelina Fernandez Director: Edward James Olmos Screenplay: Floyd Mutrux and Desmond Nakano Running Time: 2:04 Rated: R (Violence, profanity, nudity, mature themes)

Gut-wrenching, brutal, and powerful, *American Me* is not enjoyable in the conventional sense, but stands out as one of the most impressive purely dramatic offerings of 1992. It's a story of violence and its dehumanizing consequences that is reminiscent of *The Godfather*, with characters that echo those from the Puzo/Ford-Coppella epic. Director Edward James Olmos fearlessly takes aim at the culture of machismo which has enveloped so many inner city youths. This is an unrelenting, unallayed condemnation of that lifestyle, a portrait of the sort of brutality that violence begets.

The story centers around Santana (Olmos), a small

time hood on the outside who becomes a big time prison gang leader on the inside. Santana supposedly organizes his fellow prisoners in an attempt to improve their conditions, but what he's really after is power. Once he has tasted it, he can't get enough. Those who stand against him are ruthlessly trodden underfoot, often ending up in the morgue.

As powerful as this film is, it has a few drawbacks, the most notable of which is the acting. Many of the players don't have much range. Olmos, the most-accomplished of them, tries to portray his character over a span of nearly 20 years without ever seeming to age. As a 40-year-old, he's believable, but no amount of makeup can make him look 25. There are times when Olmos' appearance detracts from his fine performance, and suspension of disbelief is difficult in a picture so well grounded in a cruel reality.

Olmos isn't especially interested in giving the audience characters they can sympathize with, and this may be a mistake, since it limits the force of the climactic scenes and eventual resolution. That's not to say that the characters aren't three-dimensional, because they generally are. There simply isn't any emotional empathy created between them and the audience. Difficult as this may be to accomplish, it can be done — numerous other films have succeeded (Quentin Tarantino's *Reservoir Dogs*). Here, however, Olmos doesn't try.

American Me is definitely not for everyone. This isn't escapist entertainment. It carries out its agenda with little concern for eliminating the "comfort barrier" that exists between the screen and the audience. Those daring to see the movie should be prepared to be disturbed. HIGHLY RECOMMENDED

An American Rhapsody [United States/Hungary, 2001]

Starring: Nastassja Kinski, Scarlett Johansson, Tony Goldwyn Director: Eva Gardos Screenplay: Eva Gardos Running Time: 1:44 Rated: PG-13 (Mature themes, profanity) Theatrical Aspect Ratio: 1.85:1 In English and Hungarian with subtitles

An American Rhapsody opens in 1965, with American-raised teenager Suzanne (Johansson) standing on the Chain Bridge in Budapest and saying in a voiceover, "I was 15 and my life was already falling apart, so I came back to Hungary, where it all began." With those words, the film transports us through time to the beginning, via an extended flashback. Suzanne is a baby and her mother, Margit (Kinski), and father, Peter (Goldwyn), facing persecution and arrest, decide to flee the country. But circumstances conspire to keep Suzanne in Hungary, where she grows up as the daughter of foster parents. Meanwhile, in Los Angeles, Margit and Peter begin to make a life for themselves, all the while planning ways to get Suzanne to join them.

The opportunity arrives when Suzanne is 6 years old (and played by Kelly Endresz-Banlaki). She is whisked away from her foster parents, placed on a plane, and flown to the United States. There, the confused little girl is re-united with the family she does not remember. Her adjustment to her new life is not easy — she misses her mama and papa, and can't think of what to call Margit other than "lady." Events skip forward 10 years, to an older Suzanne who can't figure out where she belongs. In an attempt to answer her questions, she returns to Hungary.

Gardos looks back on her life through an unfogged lens — she views all of the characters sympathetically. The only villain is the faceless totalitarian system of government which forces the separation of Suzanne from her birth family. The movie is exceptional in the way it presents the various characters' mindsets. Margit and Peter miss their daughter desperately and try everything possible to get her back — a process that takes 6 years. And Suzanne is bewildered and frightened by the sudden shift in her life, as her home is replaced by something altogether different.

The film stars Scarlett Johansson, one of today's finest young actresses. She presents Suzanne as a child-woman struggling with all the usual problems of girls her age (boys, curfews, overly restrictive parents) while suffering through an identity crisis. Her sense of frustration, and, later, of loss, is palpable. Nastassja Kinski and Tony Goldwyn offer Johansson effective support and hold the movie together during the early scenes when she is not on screen.

If there's a problem with the movie, it occurs at the very end, when Gardos rushes an emotional catharsis that feels forced and artificial. Perhaps it's difficult to conclude a film like this, but the ease with which everything is neatly wrapped via a short conversation feels too much like a cheat. That's only a few minutes, however. Everything that comes before it is as perceptive as it is involving and touching. RECOMMENDED

Amistad [1997]

Starring: Djimon Hounsou, Matthew McConaughey, Morgan Freeman, Anthony Hopkins, Nigel Hawthorne Director: Steven Spielberg
Screenplay: David Franzoni Running Time: 2:37 Rated: R (Violence, mature themes, nudity) Theatrical Aspect Ratio: 1.85:1

One stormy night during the summer of 1839, the 53 men imprisoned on the Spanish slave ship *La Amis-*

tad escape. Led by the lion-hearted Cinque (Djimon Hounsou), they take control of the vessel, killing most of the crew. Adrift somewhere off the coast of Cuba and uncertain how to make their way back to Africa, they rely on the two surviving Spaniards to navigate the eastward journey. They are tricked, however, and the *La Amistad* is eventually captured by an American naval ship near Connecticut. The kidnapped Africans are shackled and thrown into prison, charged with murder and piracy.

The first men to come to the Africans' defense are abolitionists Theodore Joadson (Morgan Freeman) and Lewis Tappan (Stellan Skarsgård). They are soon joined by Roger Baldwin (Matthew McConaughey), a property attorney of little repute. Baldwin proves a more persuasive orator than anyone gave him credit for, and his central argument — that the prisoners were illegally kidnapped free men, not property — convinces the judge. But powerful forces have aligned against Baldwin's cause. Current President Martin Van Buren (Nigel Hawthorne), eager to please Southern voters and 11-year-old Queen Isabella of Spain (Anna Paquin), begins pulling strings behind-the-scenes to ensure that none of the Africans goes free.

At its heart, *Amistad* is a tale of human courage. Cinque is a heroic figure whose spirit remains unbreakable regardless of the pain and indignity he is subjected to. Effectively portrayed by Djimon Hounsou, Cinque is the key to viewers seeing the *Amistad* Africans as more than symbols in a battle of ideologies. They are individuals, and our ability to make that distinction is crucial to the movie's success. To amplify this point, Spielberg presents many scenes from the Africans' point-of-view, detailing their occasionally-humorous observations about some of the white man's seemingly-strange "rituals."

Matthew McConaughey successfully overcomes his "pretty boy" image to become Baldwin, but the lawyer is never particularly well-defined outside of his role in the *La Amistad* case. Likewise, while Morgan Freeman and Stellan Skarsgård are effective as Joadson and Tappan, they are never anything more than "abolitionists." Nigel Hawthorne, who played the title character in *The Madness of King George*, presents Martin Van Buren as a spineless sycophant to whom justice means far less than winning an election. Finally, there's Anthony Hopkins, whose towering portrayal of John Quincy Adams is as compelling as anything the great actor has done.

Amistad is thematically rich, impeccably crafted,

and intellectually stimulating. *La Amistad* is a part of American social and legal fabric. It is an important American film. **HIGHLY RECOMMENDED**

. . . *And Justice for All* [1979]

Starring: Al Pacino, John Forsythe, Jack Warden Director: Norman Jewison Screenplay: Barry Levinson and Valerie Curtin Running Time: **2:00** Rated: R (Profanity, mature themes) Theatrical Aspect Ratio: **1.85:1**

Al Pacino plays Arthur Kirkland, a defense attorney who has been in practice for 12 years. His caseload is heavy; however, Kirkland isn't in the game for money, prestige, or power. He's one of those rare lawyers who believes in the judicial system and wants to help people. He'll spend a night in jail for contempt of court rather than let a judge ignore a crucial piece of evidence. Yet all of Kirkland's principles are about to be called into question when he is asked to defend a hard-line justice, Judge Fleming (John Forsythe), who is accused of rape. Kirkland's dislike of Fleming runs deep, but circumstances force the lawyer to take this case.

The more you consider . . . *And Justice for All*'s message, and the means by which it is delivered, the more aware you become of how uncompromising director Norman Jewison's attack is on the legal system. Insane and corrupt judges dole out life-and-death sentences with as much thought as a butcher would give to carving a side of beef. Attorneys view the courtroom as an arena where they can grapple with an opponent without concern for the cost in human pain and tears. And those who genuinely care about their clients are foiled at every turn by the deeply-rooted hypocrisy and cynicism that defines American law.

Pacino earned an Academy Award nomination for his work in . . . *And Justice for All*. However, of all his Oscar nominations, this is probably the least-deserved. Of the supporting performers, John Forsythe and Jack Warden leave the strongest impressions. Forsythe, known best at the time for being the faceless Charlie of *Charlie's Angels,* is the perfect picture of cold, controlled arrogance. There's nothing vaguely human about him except his capacity for vice. Whether guilty or innocent of rape, he's still a villain. Warden plays a suicidal, borderline-lunatic judge whose continued presence on the bench makes a mockery of every trial he presides over. Jeffrey Tambor is a lawyer who undergoes a crisis of conscience when a man whose acquittal he facilitated commits a double murder.

. . . *And Justice for All* ends with the kind of bravura outburst by Pacino that one might easily assume is designed to entice cheers and applause from the audience. Here, the actor's words radiate real outrage, and what he says caps the film's central ethical dilemma about a lawyer defending a man he knows to be guilty. This is a powerful, cathartic moment that's neither exhilarating nor uplifting. Like most of what precedes it, the climax of . . . *And Justice for All* underscores Jewison's message about how hollow and diseased the process of law has become. We need look no further than the fiasco of the O.J. Simpson trial to understand everything that this film is trying to say. **HIGHLY RECOMMENDED**

Angel Baby [Australia, 1995]

Starring: John Lynch, Jacqueline McKenzie, Colin Friels, Deborra-Lee Furness, Daniel Daperis Director: Michael Rymer Screenplay: Michael Rymer Running Time: **1:45** Rated: No MPAA Rating (Sex, nudity, mature themes) Theatrical Aspect Ratio: **1.85:1**

Angel Baby, a tale of love, loss, and mental illness from Michael Rymer, swept through the 1995 Australian Film Awards, winning seven, including best picture, best director, best actor (John Lynch), and best actress (Jacqueline McKenzie). However, unlike *Shine,* which was similarly lauded at the 1996 AFIs, no overseas distributor rushed to pick up *Angel Baby.* The reason? Despite certain thematic similarities, *Shine* is an upper; *Angel Baby* is a downer.

Depressing or not (I suppose it depends on your point-of-view), there's no denying *Angel Baby*'s emotional power. This is the sort of film that lays it all on the line, and requires the kind of intense commitment from its lead actors that few motion pictures demand. John Lynch (*Some Mother's Son*) and Jacqueline McKenzie (*Romper Stomper*) deliver intense, passionate portrayals that obliterate the barrier of the screen. In large part, *Angel Baby* succeeds because of their work.

Lynch plays Harry, a schizophrenic who, thanks to medication, is able to move through society in a relatively normal fashion. Harry is an outpatient at a psychiatric clinic called "the Club House." One day, while there, he catches sight of Kate (Jacqueline McKenzie), a new client. She ignores him, but, shy and smitten, Harry decides to follow her as she makes her way from the clinic to the halfway house where she lives. Realizing that she's being shadowed, Kate confronts Harry, and, after a few tender getting-to-know-each-other scenes, they are frantically in love. The sheer intensity of their emotion has disastrous consequences, for, although Harry and Kate believe their love is strong enough to overcome anything — even insanity — the reality is far less romantic or forgiving.

Writer/director Michael Rymer's imperfect narrative contains a few contrived missteps, but the characters and their relationships are so effectively conceived and expertly realized that it's difficult to fault the film much for this. *Angel Baby* is well-focused on an emotional level, and I found myself unexpectedly touched by this unconventional love story. The tenderness, eroticism, and ecstasy of their interaction leaves the most forceful impression. We can't help becoming involved as they walk an uncertain mental tightrope, clutching at each other all the way.

Having seen *Angel Baby,* it's easy for me to understand why major distributors like Fine Line and Miramax stayed away. Much like *Breaking the Waves,* it's a raw, intense, carnal film that will appeal most strongly to adventurous movie-goers. Actually, it's ironic that the very qualities which scared off everyone except Cinepix Film Properties are those that give *Angel Baby* its unique identity and make it such a compelling viewing experience. **HIGHLY RECOMMENDED**

Angela's Ashes [United Kingdom/United States, 1999]
Starring: Emily Watson, Robert Carlyle, Joe Breen, Ciaran Owens, Michael Legge Director: Alan Parker Screenplay: Laura Jones and Alan Parker, based on the novel by Frank McCourt Running Time: 2:25 Rated: R (Profanity, nudity, sex, violence, mature themes) Theatrical Aspect Ratio: 1.85:1

Angela's Ashes is based on the memoirs of Frank McCourt. The film follows roughly 10 years in Frank's life, beginning when he's 5 years old (going on 6), and ending some time shortly after his 16th birthday. During the course of the movie, he is played by 3 different actors: Joe Breen (the young Frank), Ciaran Owens (the middle Frank), and Michael Legge (the older Frank). Breen, Owens, and Legge are all capable performers, and their physical appearances are similar enough that the changes are not jarring.

The film opens in 1935 Brooklyn, where Frank's family is struggling to ward off poverty and disease. Frank's father, Malachy McCourt (Robert Carlyle), is unemployed and his mother, Angela (Emily Watson), has just given birth to a baby girl — the 5th child in the family. But the new addition doesn't live long, and, after her death, the family decides to return to Ireland. Things, unfortunately, are even worse across the Atlantic. The house into which Frank's family moves is damp. Due to its proximity to the community privy, there's a permanent stench. When it rains,

which is almost all the time, the first floor floods. In quick succession, Frank's two youngest brothers fall ill and die. Meanwhile, every scrap of money that Malachy earns goes to buying a pint or two at the pub. He comes home drunk at night and spends his days in a fruitless search for a new job. Through all of this, Frank faces the usual traumas of youth: peer pressure, learning about sexuality, and enduring the necessary Catholic rites of passage — especially the First Confession and First Communion.

Despite having first billing, Emily Watson plays a supporting character. This is Frank's story. His mother occupies a critical role, but she is rarely the focal point of the tale. Her performance is quiet, subdued, and powerful. Like Watson, Robert Carlyle does not seek the spotlight. His part is that of the flawed-but-loving father who cares for his family, but also carries a great burden of guilt. Carlyle shows that he, like Watson, is capable of underplaying a part.

Angela's Ashes is a deftly realized and beautifully filmed story of a boy coming of age during the 1930s and 1940s in the Catholic portion of Ireland. There have been movies of this sort before, and most of them end in an ideological clash between the Irish Catholics and their Protestant counterparts. Here, the primary foe is not religious intolerance. It is one of the oldest enemies of humanity: poverty and hunger. Yet, while the film contains lengthy stretches in which the characters are subjected to ever more demeaning spates of pain and abject misery, the movie as a whole turns out to be a quietly triumphant experience — a testimony to the fortitude of the human spirit under even the worst circumstances. **HIGHLY RECOMMENDED**

Angels and Insects [United Kingdom/United States, 1995]
Starring: Mark Rylance, Patsy Kensit, Kristin Scott Thomas Director: Philip Haas Screenplay: Philip Haas and Belinda Haas based on the novella *Morpho Eugenia* by A.S. Byatt Running Time: 1:57 Rated: R (Sex, nudity, mature themes) Theatrical Aspect Ratio: 1.85:1

Angels and Insects, based on A.S. Byatt's novella *Morpho Eugenia,* opens in Victorian England with the arrival of naturalist William Adamson (Mark Rylance) at the demesne of the Alabaster family. William was recently shipwrecked on his return journey from South America. Reverend Alabaster (Jerermy Kemp), keen to have an educated scientist help with a book he is writing, invites William to live in his house. Once there, he becomes infatuated with the serenely beautiful-but-cold Eugenia (Patsy Kensit), the eldest daughter of the Alabasters. Although not hopeful that a match is likely, William nevertheless courts Eugenia, and is greatly surprised when she accepts his marriage proposal. But a dark secret in her past cannot stay buried forever.

In many ways, this film is a study in contrasts: the passionate abandon of the South American natives to the structured restraint of England's Victorian aristocrats, butterflies to ants, and beauty to intelligence. Philip Haas wants us not only to understand the rigidity of life on the Alabaster estate, but to see the decadence that bubbles just beneath the surface. Eugenia's apparent physical perfection — which enthralls William — hides a dead, ravaged soul.

Haas has elected not to reveal the horror of Eugenia's situation in one melodramatic moment of discovery. Instead, he gradually unfolds the truth, feeding it to the audience bit-by-bit, clue-by-clue, so that when the generally oblivious William finally learns his wife's secret, we are already cognizant of it. The entire narrative of *Angels and Insects* is fashioned like this, with slow, steady revelations.

If Eugenia is the butterfly — beautiful, fragile, and as vapid as "colored air" — then Matty Crompton (Kristin Scott Thomas), an educated woman living with the Alabasters, is the ant: plain, resourceful, and intelligent. It doesn't take William long to learn that he has married the wrong woman. Matty is his perfect companion, but he recognizes too late how little value should be placed on physical appearance.

The drawback of *Angels and Insects* is a combination of lackluster characterization and mediocre acting. None of the men or women populating this film grab our sympathy. In the case of someone as shallow as Eugenia, this is entirely appropriate, but William remains strangely distant, in part because of a bland performance by Mark Rylance. This leads us to watch him with interest, but never become emotionally engaged in his travails.

The reason to see *Angels and Insects* is for its keen and intricate explorations of human sexual and social interaction. In the world of insects, there is only one layer, but men and women hide truth beneath many facades. Yet perhaps the most striking similarity is how members of both species are capable of stinging without remorse, unconcerned about the consequences. That's an uncomfortable message that everyone can relate to. **RECOMMENDED**

Angie [1993]

Starring: Geena Davis, Aida Turturro, James Gandolfini, Philip Bosco, Stephen Rea, Jenny O'Hara Director: Martha Coolidge

Screenplay: **Todd Graff** Running Time: **1:47** Rated: **R** (Language, brief nudity, mature themes)

Martha Coolidge's *Angie* begins as a delightful, if somewhat familiar, romp through romantic comedy territory. Then, somewhere in the middle, it becomes something completely different. Depending on the individual, this shift may be seen as a welcome surprise or an unpleasant diversion. There are those who will find it to be both. One thing *Angie* is not, however, is typical.

Born in Bensonhurst in 1961, Angie (Geena Davis) grew up without her mother, who ran away when she was three. She spent her formative years living with her father (Philip Bosco) and stepmother (Jenny O'Hara), a woman whom she never liked. Now in her early thirties, Angie finds herself pregnant by her boyfriend, Vinnie (James Gandolfini), who, upon learning of the happy event, promptly decides that they should get married. Angie reluctantly agrees, but it isn't until she meets a blarney-spewing Irishman named Noel (Stephen Rea) that she has the courage to face Vinnie with her doubts.

No one is going to find themselves in unfamiliar territory at the outset of *Angie*. For the first half, the storyline is pure romantic comedy, complete with the two boyfriends and the various subplots and complications. Then, following a hilarious birth scene that features profane renditions of Marvin Hamlisch songs, the tone and intent of *Angie* shifts to melodrama, and there aren't many additional laughs forthcoming. This frothy motion picture turns serious in a hurry.

Some might find the abrupt shift in mood disconcerting or annoying, and, to a degree, it is both. But it's also a welcome change that the film is willing to break away from the expected norms and spring a series of surprises on the audience. There's nothing more bland than a predictable romantic comedy that runs on too long. *Angie* may be flawed in a number of ways, but this isn't one of them.

The movie survives the second-half melodrama because the acting keeps things at a high level, even when the dialogue becomes stilted. Geena Davis is consistently strong, and Stephen Rea is a whirlwind of energy and charm. Together, the two work perfectly. The rest of the cast is adequate at worst, including Aida Turturro in a part that could have been written for Rosie O'Donnell.

The key to enjoying *Angie* is not to anticipate the expected. What the film starts as is not what it is by the time that the final credits roll. Those who go in with an open mind and a willingness to overlook a number of minor faults are more likely to enjoy the picture than those who approach it with preconceived notions. The transition is not elegant or seamless, but it gives this movie a mark of originality, a trait which has become increasingly scant in Hollywood productions. RECOMMENDED

The Anniversary Party [2001]

Starring: Alan Cumming, Jennifer Jason Leigh, Kevin Kline, Phoebe Cates, Jane Adams, John C. Reilly, Jennifer Beals, Denis O'Hare, Mina Badie, Gwyneth Paltrow, Michael Panes, Parker Posey Directors: Alan Cumming, Jennifer Jason Leigh Screenplay: Alan Cumming, Jennifer Jason Leigh Running Time: 1:55 Rated: R (Profanity, drug use, nudity, sexual situations) Theatrical Aspect Ratio: 1.85:1

Jennifer Jason Leigh and Alan Cumming first decided that they wanted to do a movie together when they shared the stage for a recent revival of *Cabaret* (she playing Sally Bowles and he playing the Master of Ceremonies). At the time, neither was aware that their intended collaboration would force them to wear so many hats: co-writer, co-producer, co-director, and co-star. And, even though there was very little money and a short shooting schedule (4 weeks), they were able to use their clout in the business to line up an impressive cast, including the likes of the husband-and-wife pair of Kevin Kline and Phoebe Cates, indie icons John C. Reilly and Parker Posey, and Gwyneth Paltrow, who seems willing to try just about anything at least once.

There isn't much of a plot. This is an actors-and-their-characters piece, and, to that extent, it's almost like a filmed play. Joe (Cumming) and Sally (Leigh) are celebrating the 6th anniversary of their stormy marriage by inviting a few friends over for a party. Joe is an author who is about to try his hand at directing and Sally is a once-hot actress on the downside of her career. Among the guests are Cal and Sophie Gold (Kline and Cates), a fading screen icon and his ex-actress spouse, who gave up the business to raise their children; a well-regarded director (Reilly) and his neurotic wife (Jane Adams); a sexy photographer (Jennifer Beals); a likable guy (Michael Panes); two sourpuss neighbors (Denis O'Hare and Mina Badie); and high-salaried actress Skye Davidson (Paltrow), who is set to make $4 million for starring in Joe's upcoming film.

The most riveting scene is a vicious shouting match between Joe and Sally during which each exposes the other to a few cold, cruel facts. Filmed starkly, with no camera tricks, this represents an intense 5 minutes of acting by Cumming and Leigh. After it's finished, things kind of fizzle out. By then, the story has essentially been told and the end credits are not far away. Along the way to this sequence, there are some other nice moments, and almost every member of the large ensemble cast gets an opportunity to shine. Yet, while Cumming and Leigh don't hog the spotlight, in the end, their work is what we remember.

There's an almost voyeuristic appeal to this sort of film, and that aspect of *The Anniversary Party* is emphasized by the setting — a house that seems to be made entirely of glass. There's hardly any privacy. Because so many of the actors are playing variations of their public images, it adds a layer of verisimilitude. And the acting is what makes this picture worth framing. RECOMMENDED

Antonia's Line [Netherlands/Belgium/United Kingdom, 1995]

Starring: Willeke Van Ammelrooy, Jan Decleir, Els Dottermans, Thyrza Ravesteijn, Dora Van Der Groen, Marina De Graaf Director: Marleen Gorris Screenplay: Marleen Gorris Running Time: 1:42 Rated: No MPAA Rating (Nudity, sex, profanity, mature themes, violence) Theatrical Aspect Ratio: 1.85:1 In Dutch with subtitles

Opening shortly after the end of World War II and continuing for over 40 years, *Antonia's Line* introduces us to 4 generations of women — Antonia (Willeke Van Ammelrooy), her daughter Danielle (Els Dottermans), her granddaughter Therese, and her great-granddaughter Sarah. The film begins in the post-war Netherlands with Antonia returning to the village of her birth. In her company is her young daughter, whose initial impression of the town is that it's an unpromising place. Antonia, who left 20 years ago, has come back to bury her mother and take over running her inherited farm.

The movie progresses by highlighting various episodes in the lives of the characters. Aside from Antonia's family, we're introduced to many of the town's other residents: Farmer Bas, who carries a torch for Antonia; Crooked Finger, a student of Schopenhauer and Nietzsche; retarded Deedee, who is raped by her own brother; Mad Madonna, who bays at the full moon; and many others. Together, these misfits and outcasts form Antonia's tight-knit community — those friends and neighbors who are always ready to support one of their own, regardless of the circumstances.

Gorris imbues each of her characters with a sense of uniqueness, and we come to care about them, whether they're around for the entire film or just a small portion of it. The story flows smoothly from event to event, balancing such disparate elements as madcap humor (Danielle's vision of her grandmother rising from a coffin and breaking into a chorus of "My Blue Heaven") and shocking violence (two rapes). The only obvious flaw in the structure of *Antonia's Line* is its over-reliance upon a voiceover narrative; there are times when the plot is too easily advanced by telling instead of showing.

Antonia's Line is a thematically rich motion picture, with a visual style similar to that of Dennis Potter's work (*Pennies from Heaven, The Singing Detective*). In addition to the evident message about the importance of community, the film challenges different philosophies about death, from those of Schopenhauer to those of the Catholic church. It condemns the hypocrisies of organized religion while endorsing the concept of "church" as a gathering place. And it gently advances the director's feminist agenda, illustrating that women can thrive (not just survive) without men. Antonia doesn't want a husband and Danielle's lover is a lesbian.

The final lines of *Antonia's Line* are: "And, as this long chronicle draws to a conclusion, nothing has ended." Such is often the case for life stories brought to the screen with heartfelt realism. Aided by a fine cast giving unaffected performances, Gorris has fashioned a rare and wonderful world capable of provoking both laughter and tears — sometimes at the same time. **HIGHLY RECOMMENDED**

Antwone Fisher [2002]

Starring: Derek Luke. Joy Bryant, Denzel Washington Director: Denzel Washington Screenplay: Antwone Fisher Running Time: 1:57
Rated: PG-13 (Mature themes, mild profanity, violence) Theatrical Aspect Ratio: 2.35:1

For his directorial debut, Denzel Washington has used basic filmmaking techniques to tell a story that, although conventional, is at times deeply moving. The autobiography of Antwone Fisher (Derek Luke), who wrote the screenplay, is an inspirational tale that uses themes of family, courage, and the will to overcome as its building blocks. One could easily argue that Washington's relatively simple approach (he uses traditional camera placement, uncomplicated shots, and, from a storytelling perspective, doesn't do anything more radical than employ frequent flashbacks) is perfect for the material. The result speaks for itself.

When we first meet Antwone, he is an enlisted man in the U.S. Navy who is prone to uncontrollable outbursts of anger. One such incident earns him a reduction in rank and a visit to psychiatrist Jerome Davenport (Denzel Washington), who must determine whether Antwone is fit to continue serving his country. At first, Antwone and Jerome have a frosty relationship. Eventually, however, the doctor's nonconfrontational attitude breaks through Antwone's silence, and he begins relating details about his past. Born in prison to a convict mother who abandoned him, Antwone spent the first 2 years of his life in an orphanage. He then moved in with a foster family and was physically, emotionally, and sexually abused until a bout of willfulness got him thrown out of the house. After a stint in reform school and a short period of life on the streets, he joined the Navy.

In short order, Jerome becomes a surrogate father to Antwone, whose biological male parent died before he was born. The young man also begins to cultivate a tentative relationship with Cheryl (Joy Bryant), a girl he has been attracted to for some time. Eventually, Jerome advises that Antwone search for his blood relatives. He reasons that only by locating them can Antwone free himself so he can go on with his life.

There are a few occasions when *Antwone Fisher* crosses the line to become too syrupy. (One such instance occurs during the speech used to conclude the movie.) For the most part, however, the production radiates emotional honesty. Some of the events of Fisher's real-life story may have been fictionalized in the name of producing a better narrative, but there's little doubt that this tale of genuine human courage will find favor with nearly everyone who sees it. **RECOMMENDED**

Anywhere But Here [1999]

Starring: Susan Sarandon, Natalie Portman, Eileen Ryan, Ray Baker, John Diehl, Shawn Hatosy, Bonnie Bedelia Director: Wayne Wang Screenplay: Alvin Sargent, based on the novel by Mona Simpson Running Time: 1:54 Rated: PG-13 (Profanity, sexual content) Theatrical Aspect Ratio: 2.35:1

When we first meet Adele August (Susan Sarandon) and Ann (Natalie Portman) they are loading up the car to leave Bay City, Wisconsin. Adele is anxious to get on the road, but Ann is heartbroken about leaving behind her friends and stepfather. The mother/daughter cross-country sojourn to Beverly Hills does not get off on the right foot. At first, it appears that Adele's motives are selfish. She's restless and being stifled by life in a small town. Her main motivation — which we don't recognize until later in the proceedings — is every parent's goal: to offer her child a better life. Adele thinks she knows what's best for Ann when she may not, and the thought of consulting her daughter on the matter never occurs to her. So, she heads to California with the intention of getting a job as a teacher and starting up Ann's acting career. But there's a problem — Ann wants to go to college and has no interest in entering show business.

The mother/daughter interaction is a tempestuous tug of war. In emotional terms, something of a role reversal is in play, with Ann being the sensible, responsible one and Adele needing grounding. Ann wants stability and normalcy, but Adele is incapable of providing either. She views her mother as irresponsible, impractical, and tyrannical, but Ann also catches enough glimpses beneath Adele's façade to recognize the loneliness and uncertainty hidden there. Adele does not live for herself — she lives for her daughter, and the thought of losing Ann is her greatest fear.

One of the best sequences in the film comes when Ann and Adele return to Bay City for a visit. For Ann, what should be a homecoming of sorts turns out to be a strange experience. Her relationships with her friends have cooled and she begins to recognize what Adele saw when she decided to hit the road. In her voiceover, Ann remarks, "The streets didn't seem as wide, the trees seemed lower and the houses smaller." And someone else remarks to her, "I think if you would have stayed, you'd be just like your mom — always wanting to go away."

There are times when *Anywhere But Here* becomes uncomfortable because of the rawness of emotions it churns up. On one occasion, Adele butts her way into an audition she has forced Ann to take, and sees her daughter performing a cruel mimicry of her. At another time, Adele misconstrues a night of casual sex for something more meaningful, with painful and embarrassing results. For the most part, Wang keeps the movie's tone light and playful, but, in moments such as these, he allows the audience to feel the characters' discomfort. Although men cannot have first-hand experience with the mother/daughter bond, they should not dismiss the movie — well-made pictures like this cross the boundaries between sexes.

RECOMMENDED

The Apostle [1997]

Starring: Robert Duvall, Miranda Richardson, Farrah Fawcett, John Beasley, Walter Goggins, Rick Dial, Billy Joe Shaver, Billy Bob Thornton Director: Robert Duvall Screenplay: Robert Duvall Running Time: 2:12 Rated: PG-13 (Mature themes, mild profanity, brief violence) Theatrical Aspect Ratio: 1.85:1

A relatively simple tale about a far-from-simple character, *The Apostle* never falters in its portrayal of Euliss "Sonny" Dewey (Robert Duvall) as a real, flesh-and-blood human being. *The Apostle* is a character study, and, like all motion pictures of this sort, its ultimate success depends upon how compelling the protagonist is. As essayed by Duvall, arguably one of America's ten-best living actors, Sonny is the kind of complex individual we could watch for hours on end without ever losing interest.

The film opens with a brief prologue in 1939 Texas that shows Sonny, as a boy, at a Pentecostal church service. *The Apostle* then fast-forwards nearly 6 decades. Now, Sonny is an aging preacher who spends most of his time on the road, leading revivals all across the deep South. His long-suffering wife, Jessie (Farrah Fawcett), grows tired of his never being home, and wants a divorce. The already-uncomfortable situation is further exacerbated when Jessie and her lover, a young minister named Horace (Todd Allen), use church by-laws to steal Sonny's congregation away from him. In a moment of jealous rage, Sonny attacks Horace, and the result of that confrontation forces him to flee his home state and change his identity. Bearing the name and title of "The Apostle E.F.," he soon re-surfaces in a small bayou community in Louisiana with the intention of starting a Pentecostal ministry. His enthusiasm is so great that a respected, local black pastor (John Beasley) agrees to help him.

Like many flawed heroes, Sonny is a good man who is haunted by one tragic mistake. His entire life becomes devoted to redemption and atonement. He cannot take back what he did, but he is determined to act in a manner that will bring good into the lives of everyone he meets. Sonny has moments of weakness, but his sincerity never wavers, even when his ministry flourishes and the temptation for self-aggrandizement grows. He is a powerful, charismatic figure with a real gift for preaching. Watching Sonny lead revivals, it's easy to understand the appeal of an energetic preacher, and how some of the most popular achieve a status not unlike that of a rock star.

To enhance *The Apostle*'s verisimilitude, Duvall relied primarily on non-professional church-goers and evangelists (rather than experienced actors) in supporting roles. For the picture's style, he admits to being inspired by the near-documentary quality of Ken Loach's films. As a result, *The Apostle* possesses a truer and more intimate feel than it would have with slick camerawork. Sonny's character shines through clearly as he struggles to find a path that has meaning. *The Apostle* is not the kind of movie that provokes a profound change in the viewer, but it offers a balanced portrait of a unique personality. **RECOMMENDED**

Artemisia [France, 1997]

Starring: Valentina Cervi, Michel Serrault, Miki Manojlovic
Director: Agnes Merlet Screenplay: Agnes Merlet, Christine Mille
Running Time: 1:42 Rated: R (Graphic sexuality, frontal nudity, violence) Theatrical Aspect Ratio: 1.85:1 In French with subtitles

Born on July 8, 1593 in Rome, during an era when many professions were forbidden to women, Artemisia Gentileschi was one of the first female painters to make a living as an artist. In the immediate centuries following her death, her work was largely forgotten, only to be re-discovered in the last forty years. Her best-known painting, *Judith Beheading Holophernes,* was completed in 1612, and has often been cited as one of the most passionate and proficient works of art crafted by a woman during the 17th century. Today, Artemisia's surviving canvasses are recognized throughout the West, and several of them reside in the Louvre.

Agnes Merlet's speculative treatment of a chapter in Artemisia's life (many of the actual details from the period are unknown, so the film maker is able to fashion her own interpretation of the historical record) begins in 1610, the year when her artistic urges become too powerful to suppress, and ends in 1612, after a rape trial separates her from her mentor and lover, Agostino Tassi. Tassi, an artist working with Artemisia's father, Orazio, agreed to teach Artemisia after the girl's request for admission to the males-only Academy of Fine Arts was rejected. Their relationship eventually turned sexual, and led to Tassi's arrest on rape charges.

Italian-born Valentina Cervi plays the lead character with the right mix of innocence and sensuality. As essayed in this film, Artemisia is a brilliant, headstrong, passionate woman whose tribulations made her a better artist. Cervi's portrayal is stunning, giving us another young international actress who is as talented as she is beautiful. Appearing opposite Cervi is Miki Manojlovic, whose interpretation of Tassi is that of an older man hopelessly enraptured by a woman who should remain forbidden to him. Rounding out the main cast is veteran French actor Michel Serrault, who brings an air of quiet dignity to his performance as Orazio.

It's debatable how accurate Merlet's treatment of Artemisia's affair with Tassi is (the surviving court records of the rape trial indicate that it was a somewhat less romantic liaison than is presented here), but it makes for a compelling story. Especially noteworthy are the scenes in which Tassi instructs Artemisia about the techniques of art, reigning in her natural passion and allowing her to harness a burgeoning talent. Tassi is presented as a volatile man who loves his student as much as his craft. Artemisia's fascination with sex and the naked male body leads to an ever-present subtext about the relationship between eroticism and art — a subject that has fascinated scholars and laymen alike throughout history. In the context of this film, it not only impels the narrative, but captures and holds the viewer's attention. With *Artemisia*, Merlet paints a beautiful and intriguing, if somewhat incomplete, picture. **RECOMENDED**

Auto Focus [2002]

Starring: Greg Kinnear, Willem Dafoe, Maria Bello, Rita Wilson
Director: Paul Schrader Screenplay: Michael Gerbosi, based on the book *The Murder of Bob Crane* by Robert Graysmith Running Time: 1:47 Rated: R (Sex, nudity, violence, profanity) Theatrical Aspect Ratio: 1.85:1

Auto Focus is the story of the rise and fall of actor Bob Crane. Just about everyone in America is familiar with Crane, or, more precisely, with his television alter-ego, Col. Hogan of *Hogan's Heroes*. If every actor has a defining role, Crane's was unquestionably that of Hogan. The series opened on CBS during the 1965-66 TV season and was an immediate success. *Hogan's Heroes* lasted for 6 years before taking its 180-plus episodes into syndication, where it continues to play on cable stations to this day — 24 years after the tragic, unsolved murder of its lead actor.

When the film begins, Crane (Greg Kinnear) is a disc jockey for KNX radio. He seems happy — he has been married for 15 years to his childhood sweetheart, has a delightful family, and attends church regularly. Then his agent brings him the script for *Hogan's Heroes* and Crane's life changes almost overnight. Fame is a heady tonic, but Crane is able to keep on an even keel until he meets audio/video salesman John Carpenter (Willem Dafoe), a seedy individual who befriends Crane and introduces him to late-night sex parties, the swinging circuit, and provides him with the equipment to videotape his sexual exploits. For a while, Crane is able to lead a double life — nice guy in public, sex addict in private. Eventually, however, things spiral out of control. His wife, Annie (Rita Wilson), leaves him. And, once *Hogan's Heroes* is cancelled, he can't get another job because his reputation is badly soiled. His sole friend remains Carpenter, who has leeched onto Crane like a parasite — in large part because of an unconsummated homosexual longing on Carpenter's part.

Auto Focus is loaded with sex and nudity, as might be expected from a film with this subject matter, but Schrader manages to keep things at a level where we never sense a whiff of exploitation. There's as much here (no more, no less) as is necessary for the story to be properly told. The result is a compelling motion picture that illustrates an American tragedy and shows the transformation of a decent family man into someone whose struggles with addiction and association with the wrong man bring him to an untimely end, with no hope of retribution. **RECOMMENDED**

Autumn Tale (Conte d'automne) [France, 1998]
Starring: Marie Rivière, Béatrice Romand, Alain Libolt, Didier Sandre, Alexia Portal Director: Eric Rohmer Screenplay: Eric Rohmer Running Time: 1:50 Rated: none (Mature themes, sexuality) Theatrical Aspect Ratio: 1.66:1 In French with subtitles

Eric Rohmer has been taking his time turning out his Tales of Four Seasons cycle. The final chapter is *Autumn Tale* (*Conte d'automne*), which, in many ways, is the sunniest of the quartet. The picture is both penetrating and effervescent — a joyous romantic comedy filled with subtle humor and stunning performances. Unlike many directors, Rohmer allows his actors to take center stage as they chew on the lines he has given them; he never upstages them with scenery or visual gimmicks, and he never cuts away from scenes too quickly.

Autumn Tale centers on a middle-aged woman's quest for love. Magali (Béatrice Romand), the widowed owner of a vineyard and the mother of 2 grown children, is lonely for a romance. But, in her words, "At my age, it's easier to find buried treasure" than a man. Her best friend, Isabelle (Marie Rivière), who suggests that she place a Lonely Hearts ad. When Magali rejects the idea, Isabelle does it for her, then carefully interviews Gerald (Alain Libolt), who answers the ad. Soon, Isabelle has contrived a meeting between Magali and Gerald. However, she isn't the only one playing matchmaker. Rosine (Alexia Portal), Magali's son's girlfriend, decides to introduce Magali to a former flame of hers, Etienne (Didier Sandre). Complications arise when the men selected by Isabelle and Rosine both arrive to meet Magali in the same place at the same time. The result is a farcical scene of great warmth and intelligence, and one of the most overtly humorous sequences ever to appear

in a Rohmer movie. With *Autumn Tale,* the director uses common romantic comedy plot elements, such as the mistaken identity, in new and thoroughly enjoyable ways.

It goes without saying that the acting is superlative across the board. Béatrice Romand and Marie Rivière don't just play their characters; they inhabit them. By the end of the film, we are convinced we have spent 2 hours with a group of likable, familiar friends. Romand is vivacious and attractive, but we can feel her loneliness and despair that late middle age may have robbed her of a last chance at romance. Also impressive is the supporting cast, which features Alain Libolt as the solid, reliable Gerald and Didier Sandre as Etienne, a stuffy professor still pining for lovely Alexia Portal's Rosine.

Autumn Tale isn't Rohmer's most impressive work; in fact, it's not even the best of the Tales of Four Seasons group (that honor belongs to *A Winter's Tale*), but it's a solidly entertaining effort — the kind of movie that can be enjoyed by anyone who appreciates discerning comedy. There are a few minor missteps, but those don't significantly detract from the viewing experience. The characters, their relationships, and the things they say to one another are the highlights of *Autumn Tale.* **HIGHLY RECOMMENDED**

Baby Boy [2001]
Starring: Tyrese Gibson, Adrienne-Joi Johnson, Ving Rhames, Taraji P. Henson, Snoop Doggy Dogg Director: John Singleton Screenplay: John Singleton Running Time: 2:08 Rated: R (Profanity, sex, violence, nudity) Theatrical Aspect Ratio: 1.85:1

For director John Singleton, *Baby Boy* represents a return to his old cinematic stomping ground. The film, described as a "companion piece" to his debut feature, *Boyz 'N the Hood,* is set in the same rough-and-tumble Southern California neighborhood as the 1991 motion picture, although the tone and intent are radically different. *Baby Boy* doesn't deal with gangs or gangland violence (although there is one drive-by shooting). Instead, it concentrates on the relationships between parents, children, and lovers in a segment of modern-day society where the concept of the so-called "nuclear family" has long since imploded.

In terms of dramatic impact, *Baby Boy* falls somewhere in between Singleton's most powerful efforts (the aforementioned *Boyz 'N the Hood, Rosewood*) and his failures (*Poetic Justice, Higher Learning*), and is certainly an improvement over the testosterone-propelled *Shaft. Baby Boy* uses well-developed characters to address real issues, then cheats a little with resolutions that are too facile. The film's ending is disappointing in that it belongs in a different, more standard feature than in a movie attempting to make a statement about the ills of society.

Singleton's thesis is that many adult black men are trapped in a state of perpetual emotional infancy. They call their women "mama," their friends "my boys," and their place "the crib." Jody (Tyrese Gibson) is a classic example of this. Despite being 20 years old and having fathered two children by different women, Jody has been unable to cut the apron strings. At one point, his 36-year-old mother, Juanita (Adrienne-Joi Johnson), notes, "Why are you so afraid to grow up and leave the nest?" Indeed, he still lives at home when he could easily stay with Yvette (Taraji P. Henson), the mother of his son. Things come to a head when Juanita's new boyfriend, Melvin (Ving Rhames), a reformed gangster, moves in and rubs Jody the wrong way.

The movie is neither hard-hitting nor gritty (both qualities which could be ascribed to *Boyz 'N the Hood*). In fact, the quotient of melodrama occasionally approaches soap opera levels. But there is a twofold key to *Baby Boy*'s success: it almost always seems real (at least until the end) and it addresses meaningful issues. In a consumer environment when it's often unpopular to take any kind of social stance, Singleton is bucking a trend. The movie asks us to think, observe, and consider — characteristics that are not popular among the many movie-goers who like to disengage their brains and watch all the pretty explosions. *Baby Boy* is not original, but, in its presentation of familiar issues, it is provocative and involving, and capable of holding an audience's attention for the full 128-minute running time. **RECOMMENDED**

The Basketball Diaries [1995]

Starring: Leonardo DiCaprio, Mark Wahlberg, James Madio, Patrick McGaw, Lorraine Bracco Director: Scott Kalvert Screenplay: Bryan Goluboff based on the novel by Jim Carroll Running Time: 1:42 Rated: R (Drug use, profanity, sexual themes, violence)

The best anti-drug movies are the ones that eschew sermons. Nothing turns off an audience faster than a film that becomes pedantic. However, when a production gets the message across through a story that lacks even a trace of artifice, its effectiveness is indisputable. Such is the case with *The Basketball Diaries*, film maker Scott Kalvert's updating of Jim Caroll's autobiographical novel. The tale related here isn't all that original, but the honest presentation lends impact to a wrenching scenario.

Jimmy Carroll (Leonardo DiCaprio) is a star basketball player on his New York City Catholic school team. Fellow roundballers Mickey (Mark Wahlberg) and Neutron (Patrick McGaw) and unofficial cheerleader Pedro (James Madio) are Jimmy's closest friends, and whenever trouble stalks one, it invariably affects them all. So, when the drug cycle starts, it quickly spreads to each of the 4 corners of the friendship. What begins as casual use first becomes a weekend habit, then an everyday obsession. Grades plummet, on-court performance becomes unreliable, and crime looms as the only means to pay for a seemingly-endless supply of uppers, downers, cocaine, and heroin.

There have been quite a few addiction movies, but most are surface melodramas, concerned with busting the bad guys or facilitating a Hollywood-style transformation from user to productive member of society. Films like with *The Basketball Diaries*, which paint a stark, ugly portrait of drug abuse, are rare. This is not the type of picture likely to draw big at the box office. Much of what's shown is simply too raw for audiences out for a couple hours' entertainment.

In Collard's *This Boy's Life*, Leonardo DiCaprio played a young man coming of age in the Pacific Northwest. Here, though his character undergoes a far different change, the actor's performance is equally on-target. Because it demands so much range, the role of Jimmy Carroll requires more effort, but DiCaprio doesn't miss a beat.

The decay of the individual always makes for powerful drama. Such was the case with Cyril Collard's *Savage Nights,* and it is no less true here. The teen years — an age of rebellion and uncertainty in the best of circumstances — can be devastating when an individual loses control. *The Basketball Diaries* captures this with brutal effectiveness. Facile escapes are rejected, and the resolution is acceptable because we can believe it. In fact, that's the reason this film works as well as it does: credibility. You won't need many fingers to count the times when scenes ring false. By another name, call this *Hoop Nightmares*.
HIGHLY RECOMMENDED

Beau Père [France, 1981]

Starring: Patrick Dewaere, Ariel Besse, Maurice Ronet Director: Bertrand Blier Screenplay: Bertrand Blier Running Time: 2:03 Rated: No MPAA Rating (Sex, nudity, profanity, mature themes) Theatrical Aspect Ratio: 2.35:1 In French with subtitles

Beau Père begins by introducing us to Remy (Patrick Dewaere), a sadsack restaurant piano player whose marriage is falling apart. For the last 8 years, Remy has been married to Martine (Nicole Garcia) and has cared for her daughter, Marion (Ariel Besse), as if she was his own. But Martine is fed up with his lack of earning power and ambition and is ready to leave him. As she's going to work following an argument, she is killed in an automobile accident. Remy is left to care for Marion alone. His initial reaction is that the girl should live with her alcoholic father, Charly (Maurice Ronet), but she resists the idea.

It soon becomes apparent that Marion's reasons for wanting to stay with Remy have little to do with the affection of a daughter for her father. He has become the object of her sexual fantasies, and she makes it apparent that her feelings go far beyond what is proper. Equally attracted to her but unwilling to admit it, Remy puts up token resistance, but his attempts to ward off Marion are halfhearted at best. Eventually, he gives in and a sexual relationship is consummated.

In the end, Blier does not give us an overwrought conclusion featuring histrionics, threats, recriminations, and police action. It's clear that both Remy and Marion have been damaged by their sexual encounters, although neither seems willing or able to recognize that any aspect of their personality has been distorted. Marion's social development has been retarded; it is clear that she holds boys her own age in the lowest regard. Meanwhile, by crossing a dangerous line, Remy has taken the first steps down a slope that may lead him to become the stereotypical predator of young girls.

One often-neglected aspect of this kind of relationship that Blier focuses on is how the introduction of sex destroys the natural boundaries between father and daughter. Remy loses his place as an authority figure, and, when he tries to assert himself, he is shown to be impotent. Indeed, as the film progresses, it becomes increasingly apparent that Marion has all the power in the relationship. Both emotionally and practically, she pulls the strings.

Beau Père's success results from a combination of a provocative script featuring well defined characters and a pair of powerful performances. In particular, Ariel Besse is stunning. Her portrayal of Marion is unfeigned; she effectively mixes the innocent girl and the tempting, seductive woman. In fact, she's so good that at times it can be unsettling to watch her aggressive sexual behavior. Working opposite her, Patrick Dewaere has the difficult task of not being upstaged by his young co-star. His Remy is a sad, psychologi-

cally tortured individual with virtually no confidence. While *Beau Père* is not an easy film to watch, it is undeniably rewarding. **HIGHLY RECOMMENDED**

A Beautiful Mind [2001]

Starring: Russell Crowe, Ed Harris, Jennifer Connelly, Christopher Plummer Director: Ron Howard Screenplay: Akiva Goldsman, based on the book by Sylvia Nasar Running Time: 2:12 Rated: PG-13 (Profanity, sexual situations, violence) Theatrical Aspect Ratio: 1.85:1

Affecting without being overtly manipulative, *A Beautiful Mind* tells the life story of John Nash, a Nobel prize winner who struggled through most of his adult life with schizophrenia. As directed by Ron Howard, this becomes a tale not only of one man's battle to overcome his own disability, but of the overreaching power of love.

While the gross facts may be accurate, one must expect embellishment of the details. Narrative features are not constrained by the same rules that limit documentaries. We first meet Nash as a student at Princeton in 1947. He is brilliant but erratic — a mathematical genius who lacks social skills. Years later, following an astounding breakthrough that revolutionizes economics, John is teaching at M.I.T. and doing code-breaking work for a shady government agent, William Parcher (Ed Harris). It's at this time that John meets, falls in love with, and marries Alicia (Jennifer Connelly). But his happy world soon starts to crumble. John is afflicted with paranoid hallucinations; by the time he is taken to a mental hospital under the care of the mysterious Dr. Rosen (Christopher Plummer), he is diagnosed as having an advanced case of schizophrenia.

For Russell Crowe, this is another opportunity to broaden his range. Crowe successfully buries his personality beneath Nash's, allowing the character to come to the fore. And, when it comes to the sequences depicting Nash battling his demons, Crowe's performance is utterly convincing. Meanwhile, Jennifer Connelly is luminous as Alicia. Although the showier performance belongs to Crowe, it is Connelly's complex work, depicting a woman torn by love for and fear of the same man, that elevates the film to a higher level.

A viewer certainly doesn't have to be a mathematical expert to appreciate what *A Beautiful Mind* offers, although those with a strong left-brain component may relate better to John Nash than right-brainers. The movie tosses mathematical theories and theorems in the audience's direction, but explains them simply and lucidly; no one is going to become lost or bored. *A Beautiful Mind* isn't about mathematics except as a symbol. It's about human frailty and the ability to triumph over it. Nash could just as easily be a doctor, a lawyer, or a construction worker and the essence of the story would not change.

The strength of the writing and production values elevate it far above "disease of the week movie" quality. At the core of the picture lies the relationship between John and Alicia, and the tribulations that the strength of their bond allows them to overcome. *A Beautiful Mind* defies the conventional Hollywood wisdom that love is passion and romance. For John and Alicia, it is painful, heartbreaking work. And, while hearts and flowers are great for a fantasy, this is the kind of expression of emotion that touches a deeper chord. **HIGHLY RECOMMENDED**

Beautiful People [United Kingdom, 1999]

Starring: Charlotte Coleman, Charles Kay, Rosalind Ayres
Director: Jasmin Dizdar Screenplay: Jasmin Dizdar Running Time: 1:47
Rated: R (Violence, drug use) Theatrical Aspect Ratio: 1.85:1

In what can only be viewed as a change-of-pace for movies about Bosnia and Bosnians, *Beautiful People* has a generally upbeat perspective. While recognizing the tragedy inherent in the current conflict, Jasmin Dizdar chooses not to dwell upon it. Instead, he focuses on the absurdities and ironies that the civil war has created, and how the situation has allowed some people to find the strength and courage to live a better life. *Beautiful People* is about men and women of different cultures coming together.

The film has an ambitious agenda. It tells 6 stories that are often separate, but occasionally intersect, merge, or break apart. Each of these tales has at least one connection to the people or events currently transpiring in war-torn Bosnia. Some are richer and more substantive than others, but Dizdar works hard to ensure that they all hold our interest. The only problem with his approach is that it necessitates the passing of roughly ⅓ of the film before the viewer has become immersed in Dizdar's world.

Beautiful People opens by introducing us to a Serb (Dado Jehan) and a Croat (Faruk Prutti) who encounter each other on a London bus. Fisticuffs break out, and the two end up brawling their way through the city's streets, eventually ending up in the same hospital room, recovering from their wounds. Meanwhile, another former Yugoslavian, ex-basketball player Pero (Edin Dzandzanovic), is brought to the hospital after being struck by a car. A nurse, Portia (Charlotte Coleman), falls in love with him, and, after

his release, brings him home to meet her upper crusty family. A doctor (Nicholas Farrell) is distressed over the break-up of his marriage and the likelihood that his wife will take away his 2 children. Despite that, he does his best to help a pregnant woman and her husband come to grips with the harsh reality that the child she is about to give birth to is the product of a rape that happened before they left Bosnia.

It's worth noting that the perspective embraced by *Beautiful People* offers North American viewers an opportunity to see events from a closer vantage point. In this part of the world, Bosnia is a remote place, separated from us not only by differences in culture but by half a globe's distance. However, in London, the travel time is not as great and the circumstances are far less remote. Although, as Dizdar points out on more than one occasion, there are members of British society who would prefer to ignore the existence of any problems associated with the former Yugoslavia.

The most impressive thing about this film is the accessibility of the humor. While *Beautiful People* is best described as a black comedy, it is funny, not merely grimly amusing. This makes *Beautiful People* a very intriguing and thought-provoking comedy. **RECOMMENDED**

Beautiful Thing [United Kingdom, 1996]

Starring: Glen Berry, Scott Neal, Linda Henry, Tameka Empson, Ben Daniels Director: Hettie Macdonald Screenplay: Jonathan Harvey
Running Time: 1:30 Rated: R (Profanity, mature themes) Theatrical Aspect Ratio: 1.66:1

Beautiful Thing tells of two teenage boys, Jamie (Glen Berry) and Ste (Scott Neal), who live next door to each other in southeast London's Thamesmead Estate. When Ste's chronically abusive father and older brother apply a fresh beating to him, he goes to Jamie's mother, Sandra (Linda Henry), for sanctuary. Ste ends up spending several nights in Jamie's room, and, as the days pass, the boys recognize a burgeoning attraction. However, each of them is apprehensive not only about acting upon it, but about even admitting it. Nevertheless, as others begin to notice the changing dynamic in their relationship, Jamie, the less popular of the two, becomes the target of his schoolmates' derision.

The central story is handled with warmth and intelligence by Hettie Macdonald, who is directing from a script adapted by Jonathan Harvey from his play. The relationship between Jamie and Ste comes across as surprisingly heartfelt yet unsentimental. There's all the angst and uncertainty one would expect from boys struggling with a foreign sexual identity, recognizing that if they choose what comes naturally, they will face society's contempt. But this is also a case of first love for both of the principals, each of whom, in addition to facing their homosexuality, must struggle with the distress and rapture of a passionate adolescent infatuation. Macdonald manages to capture the nuances of the situation, exploring the emotional complexity of the circumstances without resorting to melodrama.

Unfortunately, *Beautiful Thing* has a plethora of subplots, none of which comes close to the main story in terms of richness or sensitivity. Jamie's stormy relationship with his mother represents the kind of dysfunctional family situation that has become a motion picture cliche. The same is true for Ste's interaction with his father and brother. A neighborhood girl, Leah (Tameka Empson), initially looks like she might play an important part in the film, but she ends up in a supporting role, offering occasional comic relief and providing much of the soundtrack as a result of her obsession with Mama Cass (of the Mamas and Papas). Despite having the potential to be *Beautiful Thing*'s most interesting character, she remains severely underdeveloped and underused.

Beautiful Thing uses numerous conventions of urban dramas and forbidden love stories in its framework, but, because Macdonald keeps the focus intimately on Jamie and Ste, the result is still satisfying. Only the ending, which gives a false sense of closure to an otherwise well-balanced narrative, feels wrong. Otherwise, *Beautiful Thing* represents a keen, personal look at the difficulties of growing up gay in a heterosexual world. RECOMMENDED

Before and After [1996]

Starring: Meryl Streep, Liam Neeson, Edward Furlong, Julia Weldon, Alfred Molina Director: Barbet Schroeder Screenplay: Ted Tally based on the novel by Rosellen Brown Running Time: 1:48 Rated: PG-13 (Violence, profanity) Theatrical Aspect Ratio: 1.85:1

As an indictment of American Law, director Barbet Schroeder's *Before and After* has little new to offer. Numerous films over the years, from *Twelve Angry Men* to *Eye for an Eye*, have voiced various views about what's right and wrong with the U.S. criminal justice system. This particular film has the perspective that "truth" is relative and has little to do with whether someone is convicted or not. Trials are all about credibility, and doubt is the defendant's greatest ally.

However, as an examination of family dynamics,

Before and After presents an incisive and stirring picture. And, ultimately, this movie is less about culpability than how a family copes with the realization that one of them may be a murderer. To what lengths should they go to protect him? And which is more important — faith in his innocence or practical action in case he's guilty?

Schroeder forges this tale about a family bound by love, yet torn apart by uncertainty. Jacob (Edward Furlong), the 16-year-old son of Carolyn (Meryl Streep) and Ben Ryan (Liam Neeson), is suspected of murdering his girlfriend, Martha (Alison Folland). Her body was found in the snow near where she and Jacob had been seen together in his car. Now, Jacob has disappeared and the police want to question him. When Ben conducts a cursory examination of Jacob's car, he finds gloves and a car jack, both covered with blood. He burns the gloves and washes the jack, deciding that protecting his son is more important than destroying evidence.

For those who want a little mystery, the truth about Martha's death isn't revealed until past the film's midpoint. The majority of the film is structured around Jacob's attempts to cope with the situation, his mother's faith, his father's steadfast refusal to abandon him, and the town's need for retribution. The central relationship is between Jacob and his father. Ben goes to great lengths to prove his love and, consequently, Jacob's actions and reactions are designed not to let this man down.

A degree of *Before and After*'s success must be ascribed to the performers. Meryl Streep and Liam Neeson are in fine form, as is the much younger Edward Furlong. Julia Weldon is Jacob's younger sister, Judith, and Alfred Molina has an energetic turn as a defense attorney who cares more about what's on his sandwich than whether his client is innocent. John Heard and Ann Magnuson both make cameo appearances.

Despite an overly-melodramatic climax, *Before and After* is, in large part, an affecting study of a family under pressure. It's easy to love when things are going well, but far more difficult in a crisis, especially when the difference between right and wrong isn't clear-cut. RECOMMENDED

Before Night Falls [2000]

Starring: Javier Bardem, Olivier Martinez, Andrea Di Stefano, Sean Penn, Johnny Depp, Michael Wincott Director: Julian Schnabel Screenplay: Cunningham O'Keefe, Lazaro Gomez Carriles, Julian Schnabel Running Time: 2:13 Rated: R (Sexual situations, violence, nudity) Theatrical Aspect Ratio: 1.85:1

For the director, who is world-renowned for his painting, the appeal of a man like Reinaldo Arenas (the central character of *Before Night Falls*) is not difficult to understand. The outstanding question is not whether Schnabel is fascinated by his subjects, but whether he can make them as compelling on film to an audience as they are in real life to him.

The somewhat disjointed narrative manages to cover episodes throughout Arenas' life, although they are often disconnected. While Schnabel clarifies the time periods by employing captions, some of the fast-forwards are jarring. The first incident we see is Arenas' birth in 1943 rural Cuba. Following glimpses of his poverty-stricken childhood, the scene switches to Holguin in 1958, where Arenas becomes a revolutionary; by 1964, his status as a homosexual, an intellectual, and a writer has made him anathema to Castro's regime. For the next 15 years, he shuttles back and forth between jail and freedom, finally going into exile in New York City in 1981. Ten years later, at the age of 47, Arenas dies of AIDS.

In many ways, it's hard to fault Schnabel's storytelling choices. Since it's impossible to represent a man's complete life in 133 minutes, the filmmaker is content to hit as many highlights as he can. Although the result may leave us wondering a little about what happened during the interim between some scenes, *Before Night Falls* successfully paints a picture depicting the influences behind Arenas' writing: his difficult childhood, his conflicted feelings for his mother, coming to terms with his sexuality, the revolution in Cuba, and the pain of being an outcast in his own country. Arenas' writing is poignant, lucid, and intelligent — three characteristics that can easily be ascribed to the man who penned it.

At the center of *Before Night Falls* is actor Javier Bardem. With the film moving rapidly through the years and from location to location, Arenas becomes the only constant character, so it is up to Bardem to hold the film together. He gets some help from an effective supporting cast, including the likes of Sean Penn and Johnny Depp, but this is Bardem's show, and Schnabel's ability to recreate Arenas' life rests squarely on his shoulders. The Spanish-born actor is up to the challenge. This is a startlingly real and believable performance, with Bardem being credible as Arenas from his early twenties through his late forties.

Before Night Falls received its world premiere at the 2000 Venice Film Festival and its North American premiere at the 2000 Toronto Film Festival. It was lauded with critical praise at both venues, taking a number of top prizes in Venice. It is an intriguing and sporadically powerful motion picture with a stellar central performance. **RECOMMENDED**

Beyond Silence (Jenseits der Stille) [Germany, 1996]

Starring: Sylvie Testud, Tatjana Trieb, Howie Seago, Emmanuelle Laborit Director: Caroline Link Screenplay: Caroline Link, Beth Serlin Running Time: 1:50 Rated: R (Nudity, sex) Theatrical Aspect Ratio: 1.85:1 In German and DGS (German Sign Language) with subtitles

Beyond Silence has the capacity to appeal to a broad range of audiences, because the subject material is so rich and multi-layered. The protagonist is Lara, the sprightly and gifted daughter of a deaf man, Martin (Howie Seago), and a deaf woman, Kai (Emmanuelle Laborit). When we first meet her, Lara is a precocious 8-year-old child (played by Tatjana Trieb) who is wise beyond her years. She is devoted to her parents, and uses her ability to sign (their language) and speak (society's) to translate for them in business meetings. She is the bridge between their realm of silence and the noisy world outside. Lara idolizes her musician-aunt, Clarissa (Sybille Canonica), a red-headed clarinet player who is engaged in a long-standing sibling feud with Martin. When Clarissa presents Lara with a clarinet, the little girl is enthralled, and immediately sets about learning how to play. Martin is angry, in part because of Lara's infatuation with something he cannot understand or participate in, and in part because he is jealous that the childless Clarissa is attempting to steal his daughter. Kai advises patience, however, warning that if Martin does not treat Lara gently, he risks losing her.

Flash-forward 10 years. Lara (Sylvie Testud) is now a young woman and an accomplished clarinet player. She is so good that both Clarissa and her music teacher encourage her to study professionally at a renowned German conservatory. Martin opposes the idea, but, with a little prompting from Kai, he allows Lara to spend the summer with Clarissa and her husband, Gregory (Matthias Habich), in Berlin, where she can prepare for the entrance exam. While there, she meets Tom (Hansa Czpionka), a teacher of deaf children, and falls in love. But tragedy is about to strike.

The most impressive portrayal is split between Sylvie Testud and Tatjana Trieb, both of whom play Lara. Not only are the actresses singularly effective, but they fit together so well that the viewer never loses sight of the character, not even for a moment, when the changeover occurs. Mannerisms, facial expressions, and even vocal inflections transfer from one actress to the other. Testud and Trieb immerse themselves in this role with astonishing results. Apparently, several hundred girls auditioned before Link settled on Trieb, who is making her feature debut. Testud, a theatrically-trained French actress, is appearing in her second film.

Beyond Silence has the capacity to appeal to a broad range of audiences, because the subject material is so rich and multi-layered. It truly involves the viewer; the characters and situations become so immediate and real that you feel like dancing or weeping with Lara as she grows into being her own person. **MUST SEE**

The Big Kahuna [1999]

Starring: Kevin Spacey, Danny DeVito, Peter Facinelli Director: John Swanbeck Screenplay: Roger Rueff, based on his play, "The Hospitality Suite" Running Time: 1:30 Rated: R (Profanity) Theatrical Aspect Ratio: 1.66:1

The Big Kahuna is driven entirely by character development and dialogue. There's a setup, but no story to speak of. Three salesmen for Lodestar Laboratories are operating a hospitality suite on the top floor of a hotel in Wichita, Kansas. Their goal is to attract the attention of "The Big Kahuna" — a corporation president who may have interest in buying Lodestar's industrial lubricants. But, as the evening wears on, it becomes clear that these 3 men may have different agendas.

Performances dominate this intimate piece. Bob, the youngest member of the Lodestar trio, is played by Peter Facinelli. Facinelli does an effective job conveying Bob's sense of arrogant superiority. He's a deeply religious man who never questions his beliefs and has a tendency to view others with a hint of condescension. Kevin Spacey (who also helped produce this film) plays Larry, the most driven of the 3 — someone who sees his entire future with the company married to this potential sale. Finally, there's Danny DeVito's Phil, a man on the far side of middle age who is beginning to view life from an existential perspective. Although Spacey's performance is the most dynamic and showy, DeVito's introspective turn as Phil represents *The Big Kahuna*'s best work.

From early in the evening until well past midnight, we see these characters trading jabs, exchanging stories, and reflecting on what is meaningful to them.

Each represents a distinct stage in life. Bob is the callow youth — brimming with self-confidence and certain that his path is the right one. Larry is more mature in his outlook, but he is no less driven than Bob. However, while the younger man's motivator is religious zeal, Larry's impetus is a need to land the client. Because they are so alike in many ways, a clash is inevitable. Finally, there's Phil, who was once much like Larry, but now is growing older and weary. By default, he becomes the referee in the philosophical struggle between Bob and Larry. When it comes to an outlook on life, the men span the spectrum: Bob is an idealist, Larry is a cynic, and Phil is a pragmatist.

The Big Kahuna starts brilliantly and ends brilliantly, but there is a bit of a sag in the middle. With a few minor exceptions, the entire movie unfolds in one room, and the production's theatrical origins are evident. Director John Swanbeck, making his big-screen debut, and cinematographer Anastas Michos do their best to make the experience visually interesting, but there are limits to what can be accomplished in such a confined locale. *The Big Kahuna* is not the most visually dynamic motion picture. Then again, odd camera angles and other such trickery would have detracted from the performances, which are the movie's foundation. **RECOMMENDED**

Big Night [1996]

Starring: Stanley Tucci, Tony Shalhoub, Isabella Rossellini, Ian Holm, Minnie Driver Directors: Campbell Scott and Stanley Tucci Screenplay: Joseph Tropiano and Stanley Tucci Running Time: 1:55 Rated: R (Profanity, mature themes) Theatrical Aspect Ratio: 1.85:1

During the 1950s in the seaside resort of Keyport, New Jersey, two brothers — master chef, Primo Pilaggi (Tony Shalhoub) and his maitre d' brother, Secondo (Stanley Tucci) — open an authentic Italian restaurant called the Paradise. Not many customers frequent this small establishment, however — there aren't free side orders of pasta, the lovingly-prepared food takes too long to reach the tables, and there's no live performer. Across the street is Pascal's Italian Grotto, which nightly draws full houses for its cheap, plentiful, familiar Italian fare. In fact, many evenings after closing the Paradise, Secondo stops by to have a drink with his friend, the exuberant Pascal (Ian Holm, in a deliciously over-the-top role).

Not surprisingly, the Paradise is in financial trouble. Foreclosure is imminent. Secondo wants to make a few changes to broaden the restaurant's popularity, but Primo is against capitulating to

"Philistines" who can't recognize good food from "the rape of cuisine" that is available at the Italian Grotto. For Primo, an uncompromising purist, "to eat good food is to be close to God."

Pascal, who respects both Primo and Secondo, offers his help. He assures the brothers that when famous singer Louis Prima is in town next week, he will invite him and his band to dine at the Paradise. To celebrate the event, Primo and Secondo prepare the feast of a lifetime, aware that if everything doesn't go right, this one expensive evening could turn out the be their Last Supper.

The centerpiece of *Big Night* is, obviously, the big night — everything from the preparation to the serving of the dishes comprising the multi-course dinner. For everyone, it's an evening to remember as Primo finds himself, Secondo wonders what he really wants from life, and the two brothers rediscover something they've known all along: that food, like love, is an unspoken, universal means of communication. This realization is cemented the next morning, when, in an unbroken 5-minute take, Secondo prepares an omelet that he and his brother wordlessly share.

While Primo and Secondo anchor the film, the guests at the party add flavor and color to the night's festivities. They include Pascal's mistress, the sensuous Gabriella (Isabella Rossellini); Secondo's earthy, charming girlfriend, Phyllis (Minnie Driver); and Primo's would-be flame, Ann (Allison Janney).

The cast is wonderful, as is the direction by Scott and Tucci. The bond between brothers is developed in a believable way, with the usual mix of friction and wordless affection. In addition to their deft skill with light drama, the directors understand well-placed humor, and throw just the right amount of comedy into the mix to make *Big Night* fun without turning it into an outright farce. When it comes to seeing *Big Night,* two words say it all: *Bon appetit!*

HIGHLY RECOMMENDED

Billy Elliot [United Kingdom, 2000]

Starring: Jamie Bell, Gary Lewis, Julie Walters, Jamie Draven
Director: Stephen Daldry Screenplay: Lee Hall Running Time: 1:50
Rated: R (Profanity) Theatrical Aspect Ratio: 1.85:1

In Margaret Thatcher's United Kingdom, the coal miners are on strike and the police are mobilized daily to put down potential riots. Scabs who cross picket lines are in bodily danger, and only the presence of numerous armed officers keeps the conflagration from exploding. Billy Elliot (Jamie Bell) is an 11-year old boy whose life has been turned upside down by the strike, since both his father, Jackie (Gary Lewis), and his brother, Tony (Jamie Draven), are among those currently not bringing home a paycheck. While they're out manning the picket lines, Billy is left home to care for his senile grandmother. His own mother is recently deceased and Billy, who visits her grave regularly, misses her more deeply than he is willing to admit.

Billy Elliot begins in much the same manner as many movies about amateur boxing providing a valuable outlet for youthful aggressions. But Billy is inept in the ring, and he soon finds his attention wandering to a ballet class that is being taught within the walls of the same gym. At first, Billy simply watches as the teacher, Mrs. Wilkinson (Julie Walters), puts her students through the moves, but it isn't long before he's paying 50 pence per lesson and learning that he may have the raw ability to succeed in an audition for the Royal Ballet School. Unfortunately, while dancing may be Billy's dream for himself, it's not his father's. When Jackie finds out what his son has been up to, he explodes with the expected testosterone-induced reaction: "Lads do football, boxing, or wrestling — not friggin' ballet!" He questions Billy's sexuality and demands that he immediately cease having anything to do with Mrs. Wilkinson and her classes.

The acting is of consistently high quality, and is one of the reasons why the movie is as effective as it is. *Billy Elliot* wins over viewers because of its characters, not its plot, and these individuals are imbued with life by the actors inhabiting their skins. Newcomer Jamie Bell infuses Billy with boundless enthusiasm. He's a raw talent, but it's impossible not to be impressed by the way he throws himself into the role. Gary Lewis brings a quiet dignity to his passionate portrayal of Jackie, the man who would be the film's villain if he wasn't so human. And screen veteran Julie Walters lends her support as solid, determined Mrs. Wilkinson, who will not allow Billy's talent to go wasted and unrecognized.

With an audition that recalls Jennifer Beals' in *Flashdance, Billy Elliot* moves out of the tricky, murky waters of family dynamics and into the realm of formula plot development. Then there's a brief epilogue which, while not adding anything new to the story, provides a satisfactory sense of closure. *Billy Elliot* ends on a high note that will have many movie-goers smiling as they leave the theater. **RECOMMENDED**

Three Colors: Blue [France/Poland/Switzerland, 1993]

Starring: Juliette Binoche, Benoit Regent, Florence Pernel, Charlotte Very Director: Krzysztof Kieslowski Screenplay: Krzysztof Kieslowski and Krzysztof Piesiewicz Running Time: 1:38 Rated: No MPAA Rating (Sexual situations, mature themes, nudity) Theatrical Aspect Ratio: 1.85:1 In French with subtitles

One moment, Julie (Juliette Binoche) had everything; the next, her husband and daughter have been killed in a car accident and her own face is a patchwork of lacerations. The physical recovery proves less difficult than the emotional one, and Julie ends up selling her house, burning her late composer-husband's compositions, putting her mother in a home, and running off to live in relative anonymity, with "no memories, no love, no children." Life, however, is intent on forcing Julie to confront certain elements of her past that she might rather not face.

Juliette Binoche, in what amounts to a one-woman show, manages to bring an element of humanity and sympathy to a potentially unsympathetic character. There is little in Julie, as written, for the audience to latch onto, but Binoche provides the emotional link to the story. In *Blue,* we delve deeply into the psyche of Julie and perhaps examine our own perspectives on life, loneliness, and liberty as we watch her cope with her new, and dramatically different, existence. We are also reminded that control is often an illusion.

Along with director of photography Slawomir Idziak, Krzysztof Kieslowski has created one of the most technically impressive productions in recent years, rivaling Martin Scorsese's *The Age of Innocence* for sheer visual impact. Kieslowski uses light and shadow like a painter uses his palette, and even some of the most simple images — such as a sugar cube absorbing coffee — are memorable. Then there's the use of color — and one color in particular. In addition to blue filters and blue lighting, any number of objects are blue — a foil balloon, a tinted window, awnings, a folder, the walls of a room, coats, skirts, scarves, blouses, jeans, shirts, trash bags, crystals, a lollypop and its wrapper, binders, graffiti, a pool, a van, and a pen. Each use of the title color underlines the central messages.

Coping with loss and trying to build life anew is certainly not a unique theme, but the manner in which *Blue* portrays one woman's journey along this path is fresh and eye-opening. As rich in emotional impact as in style, this motion picture sets a high standard that we as viewers can only hope the other two chapters of the trilogy will match.

HIGHLY RECOMMENDED

Blue Chips [1994]

Starring: Nick Nolte, Mary McDowell, J.T. Walsh, Alfre Woodard, Shaquille O'Neal, Anfernee Hardaway Director: William Friedkin Screenplay: Ron Shelton Running Time: 1:47 Rated: PG-13 (Language) Theatrical Aspect Ratio: 1.85:1

Coach Pete Bell of Western University (Nick Nolte) is going through a nightmare season. After a decade of winning, his team is about to finish with a sub-.500 record for the first time in his tenure. The Western University Dolphins are thin on talent, so getting several blue chip prospects becomes the driving motivation for the off-season. Coach Bell singles out 3 (Shaquille O'Neal, Anfernee Hardaway, and Matt Nover). They all like Western U, but two are demanding a little something "under the table," which goes against Coach Bell's principles. Nevertheless, he is forced to consider that cars and cash might not be the worst price to pay.

Perhaps the best decision made by writer Ron Shelton and director William Friedkin was to focus on the off-court politics of recruiting rather than on the team's wins and losses. In the end, that's what makes *Blue Chips* different from so many other, similarly-marketed movies. There is a big showdown at the end, but the basketball game becomes peripheral to a more important crisis. It is a catalyst, not a conclusion.

Those who expect Shaquille O'Neal to dominate the film will be disappointed. While the NBA star has his share of scenes, the acting required is limited. From start to finish, this is Nick Nolte's picture, with his energetic performance approaching the point of frenzy. It doesn't take long to discern that Coach Bell is modeled after Indiana's Bobby Knight (who, along with numerous other basketball luminaries, makes an appearance).

The central moral dilemma facing Coach Bell is whether or not to pay off players with alumni money. While this goes against everything he believes in, it becomes apparent that it may not be possible to field a winning team without breaking the rules. There's a good dose of reality in this story, even if the script occasionally becomes too preachy. The end sequences especially could have been toned down.

Blue Chips is peppered with subtle humor and in

jokes. One prime example is former UNLV coach Jerry Tarkanian (who was constantly accused of recruiting violations by the NCAA) expressing genuine concern about whether a prospective college player has the grades to stay academically eligible. The film's conclusion also features a droll parody of the "what happened to our characters after this movie ends . . ." messages that reality-based dramas often scroll across the screen.

Blue Chips will obviously appeal more to basketball aficionados than to those who are indifferent to the sport. Despite an advertising blitz of slam-dunks and crisp passes, this film has a story to tell that doesn't require much on-court savvy. The theme, which involves facing the consequences of one's actions, is universal, even if the attraction of "the Shaq" isn't. RECOMMENDED

The Blue Kite [China, 1993]

Starring: Chen Xiaoman, Zhang Wenyao, Yi Tian, Lu Liping, Pu Quanxin, Li Xeujian, Guo Baochang Director: Tian Zhuangzhuang Screenplay: Xiao Mao Running Time: 2:18 Rated: No MPAA Rating (violence) Theatrical Aspect Ratio: 1.85:1 In Mandarin with subtitles

The narrator of *The Blue Kite* is Tietou (played by Yi Tian as an infant, Zhang Wenyao as a young boy, and Chen Xiaoman as an adolescent), whose 1953 birth occurs early in the film. His parents, librarian Shalong (Pu Quanxin) and teacher Shujuan (Lu Liping), are supporters of the Maoist revolution, but that doesn't prevent Shalong from being accused of counterrevolutionary activities and sent off a labor camp, where a tree falls on him and kills him. Shujuan and Tietou's struggles through this and subsequent trials form the background of Tian Zhuangzhuang's motion picture.

The Blue Kite recounts how a child and his mother survive through the turbulence of China during the 1950s and '60s, when political beliefs that were proper one year might be deemed counterrevolutionary the next. It is a troubling climate, where nothing is certain, and the greatest difficulty of growing up lies in determining what is proper behavior and what is likely to get you taken away for "reform."

Tian's criticism of the Chinese revolution is effective because of its subtlety. As was true in Chen Kaige's *Farewell My Concubine,* the characters' stories are used to represent the injustices of the system. If anything, the methods employed in this film are less direct than those in *Concubine,* but no less disturbing. Tietou's courage, Shujuan's spirit, and the love between mother and child are the immutable ele-

ments of *The Blue Kite*. No matter what year it is or how dire the characters' circumstances are, these 3 things are constant.

Tian's method of storytelling, while reasonably straightforward, will be unfamiliar to many American movie-goers. Careful attention is demanded, especially for those who don't know the historical background. Because numerous scenes end abruptly and are often followed by sudden time changes, it's easy to lose track of what's going on in *The Blue Kite*.

Many of the movies coming from so-called "Fifth Generation" Chinese filmmakers (such as Chen Kaige and Zhang Yimou) are either banned in their native country, or heavily censored. The government has shown an unwillingness to allow any criticism of their policies, either past or present. However, one proverbial "silver lining" in this cloud of controversy has been the greater worldwide recognition and distribution of productions such as *The Blue Kite*. We in the West should feel fortunate to be exposed to such well-crafted, provocative motion pictures. RECOMMENDED

Body Shots [1999]

Starring: Sean Patrick Flanery, Jerry O'Connell, Amanda Peet, Tara Reid Director: Michael Cristofer Screenplay: David McKenna Running Time: 1:42 Rated: R (profanity, graphic sex-related dialogue, sex, nudity, drug use, violence) Theatrical Aspect Ratio: 2.35:1

Body Shots is a graphic and sporadically compelling motion picture that uses equal parts comedy, introspection, and tragedy to offer a measure of social commentary about the confusion and frustration faced by superficial 20-somethings as they navigate a treacherous sexual road map. It's an edgy movie that doesn't pull any punches, and, despite some of the most frank discussions about oral sex in any multiplex-bound film, *Body Shots* managed to avoid the NC-17 kiss of death.

Filmmaker Michael Cristofer refuses to adhere to traditional narrative methods. His characters frequently address the camera directly, as if they are answering questions for a documentary interview. Add to that a lively camera that prefers odd angles, unusual visual effects such as filming at 6 frames per second to make objects appear to move fast, and a pulsing soundtrack, and *Body Shots* never lets the energy level dip.

The characters in *Body Shots* are all looking for human contact. They'll take sex, but they want love. In addition to exploring the difference between lust and love, *Body Shots* takes time out to give tips on oral sex and explain why nice guys are boring. Much of the film's second half deals with the controversial issue of what constitutes date rape. As has been illustrated repeatedly in the courts, a line that should be clear often becomes blurred, especially when alcohol and low self-esteem are involved.

There are 4 girls and 4 guys — all physically attractive, all immature and self-obsessed, and all with a lot of money to burn. The women are Jane (Amanda Peet), Sara (Tara Reid), Whitney (Emily Procter), and Emma (Sybil Temchen). The men are Rick (Sean Patrick Flanery), Michael (Jerry O'Connell), Trent (Ron Livingston), and Shawn (Brad Rowe). These two quartets meet at a club, where most of them get drunk, then pair off for the night. Jane goes with Rick, and Sara leaves with football player Michael, even though she has been dating nice guy Shawn. Distressed at seeing his girlfriend depart with another man, Shawn proves he's not all that nice when he corners Emma in an alley for a hot encounter. Meanwhile, Trent learns that Whitney has some kinky sexual preferences.

Late at night, a bleeding and disheveled Sara arrives at Jane's door, claiming to have been raped by Michael. Two versions of events — his and hers — are depicted, and it's clear that more than just a misinterpretation of words and gestures has taken place. Someone is lying. And the question isn't just "Who?" but "Why?" The resolution isn't likely to satisfy anyone, and is a case of filmmakers taking the easy way out. This movie is designed to stir up controversy and fuel discussions outside of the theater, and it certainly has the content and capacity to fulfill that goal. **RECOMMENDED**

Bogus [1996]

Starring: Whoopi Goldberg, Gerard Depardieu, Haley Joel Osment
Director: **Norman Jewison** Screenplay: **Alvin Sargent** Running
Time: **1:51** Rated: **PG (Mild profanity)** Theatrical Aspect Ratio: **1.85:1**

Bogus is a lightly-dramatic fantasy and is sentimental without being mawkish. Only at the very end is there a brief, and largely inoffensive, slip into melodrama. As the film opens, we're introduced to Lorraine Franklin (Nancy Travis), a bubbly single mom with a delightful, 7-year-old son, Albert (Haley Joel Osment). Lorraine is part of the Circus Phantastique, a traveling band of performers currently based in Las Vegas. Albert has formed an attachment with the group's magician, Antoine (Denis Mercier), who acts as a substitute father. When Lorraine is killed in a traffic accident, Albert finds himself alone in the world. Antoine helps him with his grief, but he cannot be a full-

time caretaker, and the young boy faces becoming a ward of the state.

To avoid that eventuality, Lorraine had drafted a will of sorts that names her one-time foster-sister, Harriet (Whoopi Goldberg), as Albert's guardian. Reluctantly, Harriet agrees to take the boy in, even though, by her own admission, she doesn't have a "motherly bone" in her body. Indeed, Harriet is not a good parent, and, to compensate for her inadequacies and fill a void in his life, Albert invents a good-natured, invisible friend named Bogus (Gerard Depardieu). Harriet, of course, doesn't believe in Bogus' existence, but a series of events makes her question her views of reality.

It's said that many intelligent, creative children invent imaginary friends. Considering that Albert has just lost his mother and surrogate family, and has been forced to move to Newark, New Jersey (ugh!), he has plenty of reasons to dream up Bogus. As the movie unfolds, we learn that, despite the weighty subject matter, *Bogus* isn't a downer. It's a magical excursion into the worlds of imagination and potential. Lorraine's death is just the starting point — the real story is about how Albert and Harriet grow close and learn that neither of them is so different from the other after all.

Whoopi Goldberg, who seems determined to act here rather than just rely on her goofy personality, turns in a sympathetic and multi-layered performance. Gerard Depardieu has finally found a solid English-language role to place aside his numerous critically-acclaimed French parts. His ability to mix light comedy with pathos makes Bogus more than just a cardboard character. Then there's Haley Joel Osment, who has as much charisma and screen presence as any under-10 performer.

Bogus is a well-crafted and moving motion picture. The film asks, but doesn't answer, the question of whether the process of growing up is worth the sacrifice of innocence and trust. The director doesn't attempt too much, and his weaving of several themes into one is masterfully handled. Children and adults of all ages will be enchanted by this movie, which is the exact opposite of its title. **RECOMMENDED**

Boogie Nights [1997]

Starring: **Mark Wahlberg, Burt Reynolds, Julianne Moore, Don Cheadle, Heather Graham, John C. Reilly** Director: **Paul Thomas Anderson** Screenplay: **Paul Thomas Anderson** Running Time: **2:28** Rated: **R (Sex, nudity, profanity, violence)** Theatrical Aspect Ratio: **2.35:1**

Boogie Nights isn't an exposé of the porn industry — it's a provocative and involving character study. One of the movie's greatest, and most immediately obvious assets is its ability to capture the feel and mood of the late '70s and early '80s. At different times throughout the film, Anderson uses long, single takes where the camera pans from one character to another, putting the viewer in the midst of a swirl of activity. The director also has a talent for picking just the right songs for each scene, making the soundtrack an integral part of the movie rather than just a jumbled collection of old disco hits. Add to that the hairdos, clothing, decor, and attitudes of the era, and you have an effective re-creation of recent history.

At *Boogie Nights*' center is Eddie Adams (Mark Wahlberg), a waiter at a San Fernando Valley night club who is "discovered" by idealistic porn movie producer/director Jack Horner (Burt Reynolds). Jack's dream is to make a movie that is "true, and right, and dramatic," and his vision excites Eddie, who changes his name to Dirk Diggler and quickly becomes the hottest young stud in the industry. Together, the director and his star seek to elevate the Adult Film to the next level.

Dirk isn't the only one under Jack's wing. There's Amber Waves (Julianne Moore), a top female star who has lost custody of her son because of her involvement with Jack. Rollergirl (Heather Graham) is an airheaded young starlet who drops out of high school to be in the movies. Buck Swope (Don Cheadle) is one of Jack's veterans, but his dream is to have a wife, a family, and his own hi-fi equipment store. Reed Rothchild (John C. Reilly) is a hanger-on who becomes close friends with Dirk. And Little Bill (William H. Macy) is a behind-the-scenes worker who never feels comfortable with the kind of movies that he's involved in. His resolution to this dilemma leads to *Boogie Nights*' change of direction.

Although Mark Wahlberg has the starring role, he is easily overshadowed by two more impressive portrayals. Burt Reynolds, doing his best motion picture work in recent memory, develops Jack into a three-dimensional individual who really believes in his job until disillusionment hits. Matching Reynolds' performance step-by-step is Julianne Moore, who can add her role in *Boogie Nights* to an ever-increasing list of interesting and challenging characters. Meanwhile, Heather Graham, Don Cheadle, and William H. Macy are impressive in smaller parts. And porn

icon Nina Hartley gets some mainstream exposure, and even a few lines, as Little Bill's wife.

Boogie Nights is a dramatically rich and visually arresting motion picture that has earned (and is deserving of) comparisons to the films of Robert Altman. Anderson takes risks with this movie, few of which fall short. The result is a memorably penetrating motion picture. **HIGHLY RECOMMENDED**

The Borrowers [United Kingdom/United States, 1998]
Starring: John Goodman, Jim Broadbent, Mark Williams, Hugh Laurie Director: Peter Hewitt Screenplay: Gavin Scott and John Kamps based on the books by Mary Norton Running Time: 1:23 Rated: PG (Cartoon violence) Theatrical Aspect Ratio: 1.85:1

A missing cufflink. A misplaced watch. A lost set of keys. In general, we attribute these absences to a faulty memory, but could there be another explanation? They live under the floorboards of our houses, and only emerge when the coast is clear to do their "borrowing," then are gone before any human can see them. That's the premise of *The Borrowers,* a new family film from director Peter Hewitt based on the series of children's books by Mary Norton.

In *The Borrowers,* the viewer isn't forced to identify with an animatronic rodent or an irritating child actor. Instead, we have Pod Clock (Jim Broadbent); his wife, Homily (Celia Imire); and their children, teenager Arrietty (Flora Newbigin), and 9-year-old Peagreen (Tom Felton). Then there's Pete Lender (Bradley Pierce), the human boy who befriends the borrower family. The villain is the nefarious Ocious P. Potter (John Goodman).

Pete's family is being forced to move out of their house because the unscrupulous Potter has stolen the will that leaves the property to them. The house is to be torn down to make way for apartment buildings. Pete informs his new friends that they have to depart. However, in transit to the new house, the borrower children become separated from their parents. Arrietty and Peagreen return to the old dwelling in time to learn that Potter has cheated Pete's family out of their rightful property. So the two young borrowers set out to rectify matters.

Much of the violence found in *The Borrowers* is of the live-action cartoon variety — that is to say, it's wildly exaggerated and no one really gets hurt. Overall, it's not as mean-spirited as we've come to expect from this sort of movie. Aside from a massive electrical shock, nothing horrible happens to anyone. No irons fall on people's heads, no one tumbles out of a third-story window, and no one gets tarred and feathered.

One of the nicest surprises about *The Borrowers* is that it's not only charming, but genuinely funny. Granted, there aren't many belly laughs, but the screenplay offers plenty of opportunities for smiles and chuckles, and there's nothing here that kids need to be shielded from. Likewise, *The Borrowers* stays at a high enough level to involve adults. From time-to-time, some offbeat bit of humor coupled with the creative set design generates a distant echo of Terry Gilliam's brilliant *Brazil*. Best of all, however, is that *The Borrowers* doesn't limit its capacity for pleasure to any particular age group. It's a most delightful family film. **RECOMMENDED**

The Boxer [Ireland, 1997]
Starring: Daniel Day-Lewis, Emily Watson, Brian Cox, Ken Stott, Gerard McSorley, Ciaran Fitzgerald Director: Jim Sheridan
Screenplay: Jim Sheridan & Terry George Running Time: 1:48 Rated: R (Violence, profanity) Theatrical Aspect Ratio: 1.85:1

Although it takes place in Belfast, *The Boxer*'s themes are universal. This is a meditation on hatred and intolerance, and upon the "kill or be killed" mentality that fuels many conflicts. Director Jim Sheridan (*In the Name of the Father*) refuses to demonize or lionize the IRA, exposing the deep fissures within the organization that crack open in the wake of a cease-fire. To one group, peace means an end to the brutal cycle of violence. To others, inured to bloodshed and all-too-willing to continue it, peace means selling out to the English and betraying the memories of hundreds of dead IRA "soldiers."

At the center of all the turmoil is Danny Flynn (Daniel Day-Lewis), a boxer by trade and a Catholic native of Belfast by birth. After serving 14 years in prison for terrorist activities, Danny has just been released because of good behavior. At age 18, he was a staunch soldier in the IRA, and, when he was captured, he refused to name his co-conspirators. Now, free again at age 32, he wants nothing more to do with his former associates. In his view, they have stolen the best years of his life. He wants to rebuild the community, and, with the help of his old trainer, Ike Weir (Ken Stott), he intends to re-open the Holy Family Boxing Club — a non-sectarian training center where Catholics and Protestants can practice together.

The IRA in Belfast is split. The main branch, headed by Joe Hamill (Brian Cox), is negotiating with the British government to establish a peace treaty. A group of mavericks, led by an embittered man (Gerard McSorley) whose only child perished as a result of a British military action, threaten to break the cease-fire. Danny, a high profile figure, is caught in the middle. And he's not the only one. His one-time girlfriend, Maggie (Emily Watson), whose husband is in prison, becomes another central figure in the power struggle. It's only a matter of time before the bubbling tension and hatred boil over.

The Boxer's story is presented with a sense of overwhelming pathos and sadness, and it's not hard to empathize with the characters' despair. When members of the younger generation are drawn into the struggle, Danny realizes that something — anything — must be done to change the situation.

The film is not without weaknesses, chief of which is an erratic pace. The beginning is slow and murky, and the end seems rushed and incomplete. *The Boxer* doesn't offer more than a token sense of closure, but that's in keeping with the current situation in Ireland, which is anything but stable. The symbolism — especially the relationship between boxing and politics — is at times a little too obvious. The same is true of the parallels between the physical and emotional barriers within Belfast. **RECOMMENDED**

Boys Don't Cry [1999]
Starring: Hilary Swank, Chloë Sevigny, Peter Sarsgaard, Brendan Sexton III Director: Kimberly Peirce Screenplay: Kimberly Peirce, Andy Bienen Running Time: 1:56 Rated: R (Violence, rape, nudity, sex, profanity, mature themes) Theatrical Aspect Ratio: 1.85:1

On December 30, 1993 in Falls City, Nebraska, two men, John Lotter and Tom Nissen, shot and killed 21-year-old Brandon Teena. Brandon, a young woman who was actually born as Teena Brandon, had been living as a man in preparation for an eventual sex change operation, and had presented himself as such to Lotter and Nissen, with whom he became friendly. When they learned the truth, they reacted violently, humiliating Brandon in front of his girlfriend, Lana, then kidnapping and raping him. After Brandon reported the incident to the police, Lotter and Nissen resorted to murder. Because of the lurid details surrounding the case (sex, lesbianism, a woman masquerading as a man), the "Brandon Teena murder" fed national news headlines.

Most of the action takes place in the small town of Falls City. For a while, Brandon has both acceptance and friendship, but that all changes very quickly. The violence of his so-called friends' reactions makes a horrific statement about the deep-seated vein of homophobia that characterizes many rural, Midwestern communities. Lotter and Nissen are the only convicted killers, but they are aided and abetted by Lana's mother, the local sheriff (who treats Brandon, the victim, like some kind of sick, twisted criminal), and most of the other "good" citizens of Falls City.

The cast, which is comprised primarily of actors who have made their marks in small, low-budget features, is nearly perfect. The lion's share of the praise goes to Hilary Swank, who, with her hair cut short and her chest wrapped, bears a remarkable resemblance to the real Brandon Teena. This is raw, courageous work that draws the audience in. We feel Brandon's confusion, uncertainty, and alienation.

Chloë Sevigny (*The Last Days of Disco*) plays Lana, an affection-starved young woman with such a low sense of self-esteem that she deludes herself into believing that Brandon is actually a man, even after a sexual encounter. She provides the counterbalance to the tide of hatred that drowns the last act of the film. Even after Lana is forced to confront the truth, she will not abandon her lover. Peter Sarsgaard and Brendan Sexton III play Lotter and Nissen as typical redneck, "good ole boys." The most chilling thing about these two characters is that some people in this country regard them as heroes.

Sitting in a theater watching *Boys Don't Cry* is like observing a speeding train rushing headlong towards a certain crash. The ending, a matter of recent historical record, assures that there will be no room for an upbeat twist. We view events with a growing sense of discomfort as the inevitable catastrophe looms nearer. Ultimately, Pierce tells a story of great human tragedy — one that has happened before and is almost certain to be repeated more than once in the years to come. What human beings do not understand, they destroy. **HIGHLY RECOMMENDED**

Brassed Off! [United Kingdom, 1996]
Starring: Pete Postlethwaite, Tara Fitzgerald, Ewan McGregor, Jim Carter   Director: Mark Herman   Screenplay: Mark Herman   Running Time: 1:47   Rated: R (Mature themes, profanity)   Theatrical Aspect Ratio: 1.85:1

Unemployment is a bane almost everyone can appreciate. While the loss of each individual job is traumatic, that's nothing compared to what happens when the livelihood and identity of an entire community are jeopardized by a round of mass layoffs. *Brassed Off!*, written and directed by Mark Herman,

takes a look at the plight of the British coal miner. Once, mining was a thriving industry in rural England, with whole towns built around each mine. During the early 1980s, the Tory government began converting the country to nuclear power. The resulting drop in demand devastated the coal industry, with hundreds of pits being closed and a quarter of a million miners made "redundant."

Grimley Colliery is a mine on the verge of shutting down. To sweeten the bitter taste for the workers, a healthy severance package has been offered. Still, there are those who are willing to fight to the end, believing that no amount of money can make up for the damage that Grimley's closure will bring. Among the most vocal of the anti-closing brigade are Andy (Ewan McGregor), a brash, young miner whose lungs are still relatively clean, and Phil (Stephen Tompkinson), a family man who's deep in debt and needs his job to make ends meet. Meanwhile, Phil's father, Danny (Pete Postlethwaite), wants the mine to stay open for a different reason. He's the conductor of the Grimley Colliery Brass Band. If the mine closes, the band will come to an end. Several members are considering tendering their resignations to Danny until a pretty young trumpet player, Gloria (Tara Fitzgerald), arrives in town and asks to sit in on the practice sessions.

The best acting turn belongs to Pete Postlethwaite (*In the Name of the Father*), whose Danny is poignant and proud, followed closely by such British stalwarts as Jim Carter, Philip Jackson, Peter Martin, and Stephen Tompkinson. If Danny represents *Brassed Off!*'s heart, then the miners represent its body and soul.

McGregor and Fitzgerald appear to be on hand largely to inject some youthful appeal into the film. Neither of their characters is particularly necessary or effective. Without their rather unconvincing romantic subplot, the movie probably wouldn't reach as wide an audience. They may not do much, but they're there, and their characters fall in love. That will be enough for certain viewers who would otherwise ignore a dramatic comedy about a bunch of old geezers who play in a colliery brass band.

The plot itself is littered with familiar feel-good elements: the big competition, the critical illness of a key character, and the redemption of someone who's viewed as a betrayer. Despite this, or perhaps partially because of it, *Brassed Off!* successfully presents its theme without ever becoming overbearing. Certainly, this isn't a hard-hitting motion picture, but its heart is in the right place, it has a great soundtrack, and it keeps the viewer entertained. RECOMMENDED

Bread and Roses [United Kingdom, 2000]
Starring: Pilar Padilla, Adrien Brody, Elpidia Carrillo, Jack McGee, George Lopez Director: Ken Loach Screenplay: Paul Laverty Running Time: 1:50 Rated: R (Profanity, mature themes) Theatrical Aspect Ratio: 1.85:1 In English and Spanish with subtitles

British filmmaker Ken Loach has devoted his career to a code of honor that acknowledges the basic dignity of a human being, regardless of income or social status. Loach is an activist, and every film he has made illustrates one aspect or another of his world view. *Bread and Roses,* his follow-up to *My Name Is Joe,* brings him for the first time to the United States. Set in Los Angeles in the immigrant community, Loach examines the inequities faced by minorities who are forced to subsist on poverty-level wages because they lack the skills and organization to unionize. He personalizes the struggle by focusing on a small group of characters who work as non-union janitors in a downtown high rise.

The film opens with the arrival of Maya (Pilar Padilla) in Los Angeles. Her sister, Rosa (Elpidia Carrillo), has paid for her to be brought across the border from Mexico. When Rosa is unable to come up with the agreed-upon price, Maya is required to make up for the difference with her body. She escapes and flees to Rosa's house, where the sisters have a joyous reunion. Money is a problem for Rosa, whose husband's doctor's bills eat up much of the income she makes from working long hours as a janitor. Maya also needs work, and Rosa helps her to get a job with her company. Meanwhile, a local activist, Sam (Adrien Brody), is seeking to unionize the workers in the building where Maya and Rosa work — an intention that creates friction between the sisters. Maya believes that it is a cause worth fighting for. Rosa, who cannot afford to lose her job, is unwilling to take any risks.

Loach's pro-union stance emerges loud and clear. In fact, there are times when the film edges close to sermonizing. However, as is always true of the director's films, we become so engrossed in the lives and relationships of the characters that the presentation of the message seems like a natural extension of the story, not something grafted heavy-handedly onto the plot.

Several name actors have lent Loach their support for this film by making cameo appearances. They include Lara Belmont and Tim Roth, as well as William Atherton and Ron Perlman. Their presence adds to the film's credibility, but the work of the leads is what gives *Bread and Roses* its strength. The film is not without faults — it tends to lionize the pro-union movement without acknowledging certain terroristic tactics — but that doesn't diminish its overall impact, nor does it in any way invalidate the important message that Loach is championing. RECOMMENDED

The Breakfast Club [1985]
Starring: Emilio Estevez, Anthony Michael Hall, Judd Nelson, Molly Ringwald, Ally Sheedy Director: John Hughes Screenplay: John Hughes Running Time: 1:37 Rated: R (Profanity, mature themes) Theatrical Aspect Ratio: 1.85:1

The Breakfast Club is a small group of high school students, who, during the course of a 9-hour Saturday detention, are transformed from complete strangers to confidantes. For each of them, it is an unforgettable day, and, while the friendships they form between 7 a.m. and 4 p.m. may disintegrate once they get back into the real world, feelings are explored and emotions unearthed that give them insights into their own lives and the forces that drive the others. These are the kinds of realizations which, if more high school students understood them, might make grades 9 through 12 a little less traumatic.

The characters trapped in detention are all very different individuals. Hughes sets them up as traditional stereotypes, then delights in slowly peeling back the layers, showing how each suffers from surprisingly similar problems. There's the jock, wrestling star Andrew Clark (Emilio Estevez); the most popular girl in school, Claire Standish (Molly Ringwald); the all-brains, no-brawn geek, Brian Johnson (Anthony Michael Hall); the rebel without a cause, John Bender (Judd Nelson); and the outcast, Allison Reynolds (Ally Sheedy). It turns out that none of them communicates well with their parents, all are under tremendous pressure from their peers, and each is beset by angst about the future.

John Hughes has assembled a unique and singularly effective cast. Emilio Estevez, although a little too old to play a high school teenager (he was 22 at the time of filming), does a good job presenting the human side of the athlete on a pedestal. Judd Nelson is believable as the James Dean-type who is looking for some kind of acceptance and uses his pugnaciousness as a defense mechanism. Molly Ringwald, the star of 3 Hughes films (the other 2 being

Sixteen Candles and *Pretty in Pink*), gives the strongest performance by showing the ugly, shallow side of being Ms. Popularity. Ally Sheedy is suitably weird as a compulsive liar and thief who takes a long time to open up. Anthony Michael Hall looks the part of the geek, but, of the 5 lead actors, his is the least impressive portrayal; Brian has trouble escaping from the stereotypical sinkhole in which he begins the movie.

Few will argue that *The Breakfast Club* is a great film, but it has a candor that is unexpected and refreshing in a sea of too-often generic teen-themed films. The material is a little talky, but it's hard not to be drawn into the world of these characters. The depiction of high school is evocative because it's so accurate (an actual suburban Illinois high school was used as the filming location). Unlike many teen films, which seem to transpire in some kid's dirty imagination, this picture, despite its occasional flights of fancy, is grounded in reality. In *The Breakfast Club*, Hughes has created a surprisingly enduring motion picture. RECOMMENDED

Breaking the Waves [Denmark/France, 1996]
Starring: Emily Watson, Stellan Skarsgård, Katrin Cartlidge, Jean-Marc Barr, Adrian Rawlins, Udo Kier Director: Lars von Trier
Screenplay: Lars von Trier Running Time: 2:39 Rated: R (Violence, sex, nudity, profanity) Theatrical Aspect Ratio: 2.35:1

According to writer/director Lars von Trier, *Breaking the Waves* is "a simple love story," but "simple" hardly begins to describe this deeply disturbing, multi-layered drama. In fact, nowhere is the picture's complexity more evident than in its study of contrasts — it is highly spiritual yet anti-religious, triumphant yet tragic, and personal yet universal.

This epic-length film is divided into 9 sections: a prologue, 7 "chapters," and an epilogue. Most of the action occurs in a closed village with deeply-rooted fundamentalist Christian beliefs. According to the elders who rule with an iron fist, life isn't for enjoyment; it's for serving God. Outsiders aren't welcome; they're consigned to hell. So when meek, kind-hearted Bess (Emily Watson) announces that she intends to marry oil-rig worker Jan (Stellan Skarsgard), an unbeliever, the entire community is stunned.

Despite the stern disapproval of all the elders, the marriage goes ahead, and Bess finds herself happier than she ever could have imagined. But heartbreak looms ahead. Jan returns to his rig, leaving a lonely Bess behind. Even her best friend and sister-in-law, Dorothy (Katrin Cartlidge), can't lift her out of her profound depression, but when a local doctor (Adrian Rawlins) is called in to evaluate her mental state, he proclaims her sane. Then tragedy strikes as a freak work accident renders Jan paralyzed from the neck down.

Central to the narrative is Bess' relationship with God. For most of the movie, von Trier keeps it ambiguous whether she is psychotic or truly involved in some kind of special communion with the Almighty. Does she really hear God's voice, or is she exhibiting signs of a split personality? Is she His instrument of salvation, or is she merely experiencing potentially self-destructive delusions? Unfortunately, in a late scene, von Trier tips the balance in favor of one interpretation, and this dilutes the film's overall impact.

As the deeply disturbed Bess, British stage actress Emily Watson turns in an award-worthy performance. Since Bess must endure a number of physically and mentally degrading events while her volatile personality veers from emotional calm to complete hysteria, Watson's task of creating a believable character becomes more difficult as the movie progresses. To her credit, she never falters. The supporting players, including Stellan Skarsgård and Katrin Cartlidge, do fine jobs, but none captures the lens the way Watson does.

There's no denying that *Breaking the Waves* is a difficult motion picture to endure. Excepting the chapter breaks, there isn't a wasted moment. And, if not for a somewhat forced catharsis during the epilogue (the weakest segment of the movie), *Breaking the Waves* would have been more wrenching than it is. This achievement announces that von Trier's aptitude for fashioning characters equals, if not exceeds, that which he has previously displayed for images. HIGHLY RECOMMENDED

The Bridges of Madison County [1995]
Starring: Clint Eastwood, Meryl Streep Director: Clint Eastwood
Screenplay: Richard LaGravenese based on the novel by Robert James Waller Running Time: 2:15 Rated: PG-13 (Mature themes, brief nudity) Theatrical Aspect Ratio: 1.85:1

Clint Eastwood plays Robert Kincaid, the male protagonist in the motion picture adaptation of Robert James Waller's *The Bridges of Madison County*. Kincaid is a sensitive loner, and while the actor is certainly known for his portrayal of independently-minded individuals, one would be hard pressed to describe Dirty Harry as a model of sensitivity. Nevertheless, this is not the first time Eastwood has successfully stretched his range.

As good as Eastwood is, however, it's his co-star, Meryl Streep, who really shines. After taking a break from drama, she returns to the kind of role that made her famous, and gives perhaps her best performance since *Sophie's Choice*. Streep is Francesca Johnson, a lonely housewife whose eyes and heart are opened to true love when Robert arrives in Iowa to take pictures of Madison County's covered bridges.

Francesca's husband and 2 children are away for 4 days at the Illinois State Fair, leaving her home alone when Robert stops for directions to the Roseman Bridge. Since the roads are unmarked, she guides him there in person, and the pair end up spending the rest of the day — into the evening — together. They start as friends with an endless capacity for conversation, but less than 24 hours later, they are in love.

The Bridges of Madison County is a beautiful film, not only in the way it was photographed, but for the manner through which the characters are revealed to us. Eastwood will not be hurried, choosing a relaxed pace for the unfolding of this romance. There's a lot of dialogue — some mundane and some touching on the quintessential aspects of the human experience. The Bridges of Madison County presents a richly-textured emotional tapestry.

In the book, Francesca is not an especially strong character — things happen around her and she's swept up in the current. Richard LaGravenese's screenplay rectifies this, creating a dynamic personality for Streep to work with. In fact, the actress commented that she was "blind to the book's power" but thought the script was "beautifully crafted."

There aren't many intelligent motion picture romances. But here, there is a profound sense of inevitability permeating the atmosphere, a realization that this magical time must come to an end — and soon. *In The Bridges of Madison County,* we know the conclusion before we learn the beginning and this lends an air of poignancy to the proceedings.

It's easy to believe that Francesca and Robert's love is deep and special, but perhaps the real test of the film's power is whether the statements, situations, and characters transcend the screen to leave a lasting impression. Not many pictures are created with the necessary skill to challenge our perceptions and beliefs, but *The Bridges of Madison County* is a rare exception. **HIGHLY RECOMMENDED**

Bringing Out the Dead [1999]

Starring: Nicolas Cage, Patricia Arquette, John Goodman, Ving Rhames, Tom Sizemore Director: Martin Scorsese Screenplay: Paul Schrader, based on the novel by Joe Connelly Running Time: 2:00
Rated: R (profanity, violence, drug use) Theatrical Aspect Ratio: 2.35:1

Nicolas Cage is Frank Pierce, a NYC Emergency Medical Technician ambulance driver. He and one of his partners, Larry (John Goodman), Marcus (Ving Rhames), or Tom (Tom Sizemore), respond to 911 emergencies barked across the ambulance's two way radio. Lately, Frank has been in a rut. His patients are all dying on him; he hasn't saved anyone in months. The frantic lifestyle is taking its toll on him. He rarely eats, surviving instead on an unhealthy mixture of booze and caffeine. His eyes are hollow and red-rimmed, but nightmares deprive him of sleep. And he has begun to see the ghosts of the many men and women he has lost.

Frank needs redemption, and he spends the entire film trying to find it. We first meet him on a Thursday, when he and Larry are called to help a man who has collapsed from a heart attack and is apparently dead. The man's daughter, Mary (Patricia Arquette), is in hysterics by his side as Frank goes to work with CPR. He revives the patient, then transports him to the hospital, where he remains in a coma. For the next 2 days, nearly every time Frank brings someone in, Mary is there, waiting and wondering if her father will ever get better. Soon, she and Frank realize that they have much in common.

Frank remains something of an enigma. We're aware of who he is here and now, and, in part because of Cage's voiceovers, we know what he's thinking, but his past and his relationships with his co-workers are shrouded in mystery. We get clues, but nothing more — he was married, his parents are still alive, his close working relationship with Tom fell apart, and he was once one of the best ambulance drivers in New York. But we never see where he lives, nor do we meet anyone that could be considered close to him. Perhaps there is no one. Even his developing relationship with Mary is uncertain and tentative.

Patricia Arquette plays the only other genuine character in *Bringing Out the Dead*. Everyone besides Frank and Mary functions as little more than a catalyst or a mouthpiece for bits of philosophy. Arquette draws on a wellspring of pain and darkness for this portrayal; the sultry vixen she often essays is completely sublimated. Mary is just another wretch in need of some sort of solace, and she doesn't care how that relief comes. Like Frank, we learn little about Mary's past, except that she was heavily into the sex-and-drug scene, has been clean for 2 years, and is estranged from her dying father.

This is not one of Martin Scorsese's best films. Despite the lack of energy and the lethargic pace, there's something darkly compelling about *Bringing Out the Dead*. It's an uncomfortable excursion, sort of like a ride in a hearse to a funeral. See this film if you appreciate bleak character portraits that do not feel the need to let a little sunshine in. RECOMMENDED

A Bronx Tale [1993]

Cast: Robert De Niro, Chazz Palminteri, Lillo Brancato, Francis Capra, Taral Hicks Director: Robert De Niro Screenplay: Chazz Palminteri based on his play Running Time: 2:01 Rated: R (Violence, language) Theatrical Aspect Ratio: 2.35:1

It's New York City in 1960 — the Fordham neighborhood. Living at East 187th Street is the family of Calogero (played at age 9 by Francis Capra and at age 17 by Lillo Brancato). Calogero's father Lorenzo (Robert De Niro) believes that a man should work hard for a living, and thus refuses to be involved in anything that has illegal overtones, such as working for Sonny (Chazz Palminteri), the local "boss." Calogero has different views, however. He idolizes Sonny and, given a chance to help the "boss" beat a murder rap, Calogero takes it. A grateful Sonny brings the 9-year old under his wing and, despite the protestations of Lorenzo, a bond develops. Soon, Calogero has two fathers — each giving different advice and neither respecting what the other has to say.

Robert De Niro has appeared in some of the greatest gangster films of the past 2 decades, working for directors such as Francis Ford Coppola (*The Godfather 2*), Brian DePalma (*The Untouchables*), and, of course, Martin Scorsese (*Goodfellas*). As a result, it shouldn't come as a surprise to anyone that De Niro has chosen this genre for his first behind-the-camera motion picture.

A Bronx Tale covers little new ground, but the material's presentation is anything but ordinary. On the surface, it's another gangster movie, but the story, like the deeply-realized characters, is multi-layered. It could be accused of tackling too much, and perhaps its few failures are because of an overly-ambitious scope, but the film has impressive vision and packs a legitimate emotional punch.

While there is violence in *A Bronx Tale*, it isn't a focal point. Most of the violent scenes are fairly "clean" — graphic beatings, but little blood). Instead, as they should be, the characters are kept at the center. The three principles — Calogero, Sonny, and Lorenzo — are all well-realized. This is as much a credit to the writing of Chazz Palminteri and the direction of Robert De Niro as to the quartet of fine actors essaying the characters.

If the movie takes a wrong turn, it's in trying to incorporate an anti-racist theme by having Calogero fall for Jane, a black girl. Today, mixed race relationships are subject to various tensions and pressures, but that's nothing compared to how it was in 1968. This isn't as successful putting these issues in perspective as when it deals with the complex relationship of Calogero and his "two fathers."

De Niro successfully varies the tone, keeping it light and playful at times, dark and somber at others. *A Bronx Tale* is his triumph, and a testimony that all those years of watching the best in the business have borne fruit. If what is yet to come has any of the promise shown by this debut, we may be witnessing the birth of yet another directing talent.

HIGHLY RECOMMENDED

Bully [2001]

Starring: Brad Renfro, Rachel Miner, Nick Stahl, Bijou Phillips, Leo Fitzpatrick Director: Larry Clark Screenplay: Zachary Long, Roger Pullis, based on the book by Jim Schutze Running Time: 1:52 Rated: No MPAA Rating (Nudity, sex, violence, profanity, drug use) Theatrical Aspect Ratio: 1.85:1

Nearly every neighborhood has a bully, and some are worse than others. In the Hollywood, Florida suburb where Marty Puccio (Brad Rendfro) and his family live, that bully is Marty's "best friend," Bobby Kent (Nick Stahl). Bobby is a smart boy with a bright future — he gets good grades and is college-bound. But he has a dark side. He constantly abuses and humiliates Marty, and often displays an unchecked penchant for sexual violence. He likes rough sex, and has acquired a taste for rape. He's the kind of person who used to be known as a "bad seed."

Individually, none of the characters arrayed against Bobby would be capable of a homicidal act. Marty has spent so much time enduring Bobby's taunts and torments that it has become second nature to him. Lisa (Rachel Miner), Marty's girlfriend, has self-esteem problems. Lisa's pal, Ali (Bijou Phillips), is into kinky sex, and her friends, Donny (Michael Pitt) and Heather (Kelli Garner), are in constant pursuit of a drug-related high. Finally, there's Derek (Daniel Franzese), Lisa's neighbor and "protector," who spends most of his free time playing video games. All 6 are harmless on their own, but, when put together with a common goal — to kill Bobby — they become lethal.

These are teenagers who, instead of acting to better themselves, are content to be carried by the inertia of their wasted lives. When the idea of killing Bobby is broached, Lisa, Marty, and the others are galvanized. The murder, as viewed from afar, gives them the opportunity to break the monotony of their existences. They mark the approaching event much as they would a holiday — with excitement and anticipation.

Clark's brutal style is mostly successful, although there are some minor miscues along the way. In one scene, he puts the camera in the midst of a group of characters and rotates it for a needlessly long period of time, creating a dizzying effect. This is as close as I have ever come to being motion sick in a movie theater. *Bully* does not shy from shocking scenes — there is a lot of graphic simulated sex, full frontal nudity, and unvarnished violence. Had the movie been submitted to the MPAA for classification (which it was not), there's no doubt it would have received an NC-17.

Bully is one of those films that stays with you long after you have left the theater. It isn't a perfect motion picture, but it is a powerful one, and leaves a lasting impression. Adapted from Jim Schutze's "true crime" novel, *Bully* takes a seemingly straightforward tale of revenge and turns it into a cautionary narrative offering a few dark psychological insights. For those who can stomach its bleak vantage point, it is not to be missed. **HIGHLY RECOMMENDED**

Burnt By the Sun [Russia/France, 1994]

Starring: **Nikita Mikhalkov, Ingeborga Dapkounaite, Oleg Menchikov, Nadia Mikhalkov** Director: **Nikita Mikhalkov** Screenplay: **Nikita Mikhalkov and Roustam Ibraguimbekov** Running Time: **2:14** Rated: **R** (Violence, sex, mature themes) Theatrical Aspect Ratio: **2.35:1** In Russian with subtitles

Burnt by the Sun attempts, with only limited success, to combine two segments of radically different pacing and temperament. The film takes place in 1936 Russia, 19 years after the Communist Revolution and well into Stalin's reign of terror. We are introduced to Colonel Serguei Kotov (Nikita Mikhalkov), hero of the Revolution, and his family: young wife Maroussia (Ingeborga Dapkounaite) and 6-year-old daughter

Nadia (Nadia Mikhalkov). They are spending a happy, peaceful summer at a rural retreat. Into this idyllic setting comes Dimitri (Oleg Menchikov), an old lover of Maroussia's who was once in exile. His appearance irrevocably alters the loving relationship between Kotov and his wife as secrets come to light, and buried jealousy bubbles to the surface.

Director Nikita Mikhalkov is up front about the ultimate meaning of his film, dedicating it to "everyone who was burnt by the sun of the Revolution." This movie is very much an attack on the policies and paranoia of Stalin. The chilling final scenes emphasize the theme as we come to realize just how far-reaching the dictator's grasp was, and how insecure even the most loyal patriots were.

Burnt by the Sun's most apparent flaw is the stagnancy of its first two-thirds, which are scripted like Checkov in slow-motion, but without depth. Other than establishing relationships and hinting at past misdeeds, this portion of the film serves little purpose beyond presenting impressive views of Russian country vistas and highlighting several fine performances. Only in the final 1/3 does the plot begin to explore issues of substance and power.

Symbolism plays a key part in *Burnt by the Sun*. Some of it, like a huge, billowing portrait of Stalin, is obvious, but much is obscure. It's left up to the individual viewer to determine how literally to take several instances of magic realism — not that a particular interpretation will more than subtly change anyone's appreciation of the film. Mikhalkov makes sure that his principal thesis is conveyed in such a manner that it's impossible to overlook or misunderstand.

This is the first anti-Stalin film to come out of post-Communist Russia, and the new freedom shows in the full scope of what Mikhalkov is able to criticize. This story is the latest to illustrate the age-old injustices inherent in absolute power and how easily past loyalties are betrayed. After the protracted and sluggish setup, the meat of *Burnt by the Sun* is as gripping as that of any "serious" motion picture — it's getting to that point that's the main difficulty. **RECOMMENDED**

The Butcher Boy [Ireland/United States, 1998]

Starring: **Eamonn Owens, Stephen Rea, Fiona Shaw, Alan Boyle** Director: **Neil Jordan** Screenplay: **Patrick McCabe and Neil Jordan** based on the novel by Patrick McCabe Running Time: **1:48** Rated: **R** (Violence, profanity) Theatrical Aspect Ratio: **1.85:1**

The Butcher Boy takes place during the early 1960s, when the fear of atomic obliteration was on everyone's mind, even the denizens of out-of-the-way villages like the one pictured here. Twelve-year-old Francie Brady (Eamonn Owens) is the local bully. He and his best friend, Joe (Alan Boyle), delight in tormenting other kids, especially the shy Philip (Andrew Fullerton), whose mother, Mrs. Nugent (Fiona Shaw), is Francie's personal nemesis. According to him, everything that's bad in the world can be traced back to her. Meanwhile, Francie's home life is less-than-ideal. His mother (Aisling O'Sullivan) is on the verge of a breakdown, and his father (Stephen Rea), "the best drinker in the town," is frequently drunk and abusive.

At first, we view Francie as a fairly typical product of a dysfunctional home, but it soon becomes apparent that his problems run much deeper. This isn't the story of a prankster who finds redemption in a Dickensian fashion — it's a darker, more ominous tale about a boy whose hostile surroundings feed his inner anger and paranoia and turn him into an amoral monster. Most coming-of-age films are about kids triumphing by overcoming adversity. *The Butcher Boy* shows what happens when a child fights back not by bettering himself, but by lashing out at others.

Neil Jordan presents *The Butcher Boy* as more of a black comedy than a tragedy. Francie's internal monologues (the film is infected with the dreaded voiceover narrative) are sometimes corrosively funny, especially his descriptions of certain characters. He shows contempt for just about everyone except his best friend, Joe, and, at times, his mother and father. By playing up the most absurd aspect of almost every situation, Jordan manages to find the humor in even the most horrific sequences.

Without a doubt, Jordan has a good sense of time and place, and uses it to the film's advantage. This is a world where people go about their daily work under the constant threat of nuclear annihilation (the Cuban missile crisis occurs during the course of the film). The accepted treatment for psychiatric patients is shock therapy. And the influence of Catholicism is all-pervasive.

Jordan's occasional use of preposterous images and magic realism are designed to draw us into Francie's world. In reality, however, they accomplish the opposite by erecting an artificial barrier between the audience and the character. There's no debating that Francie is a fascinating individual, or that newcomer Eamonn Owens gives an amazing performance, but this boy doesn't burrow under our skin in the same way that the two girls from *Heavenly Creatures* (a not entirely dissimilar film) do. We see Francie's explosive rage clinically, from a distance. We do not experience or participate in it, and that keeps *The Butcher Boy* from being a truly memorable motion picture.
RECOMMENDED

Butterfly (La Lengua de las mariposas) [Spain, 1999]

Starring: Fernando Fernan Gomez, Manuel Lozano, Uxia Blanco
Director: Jose Luis Cuerda Screenplay: Rafael Azcona, Jose Luis Cuerda, Manuel Rivas Running Time: 1:35 Rated: R (Sex, nudity, mature themes) Theatrical Aspect Ratio: 2.35:1 In Spanish with subtitles

Set in the winter of 1936, *Butterfly* tells of the unique relationship between 8-year-old Mocho (Manuel Lozano) and his kindly teacher, Don Gregorio (Fernando Fernan Gomez). From the first day the sensitive boy enters his classroom, Don Gregorio recognizes the child's limitless potential. With patience and affection, the elderly man imparts life lessons to his young charge, instructing him on the finer points of literature, nature, and how to woo a girl. But storm clouds are gathering over Spain as the political situation becomes a powder keg, and Mocho learns his most unpleasant lesson. Despite being well-respected in the village, Don Gregorio is an atheist and a Republican, and, under the rising tide of fascism, those qualities mark him as a potential enemy of the State.

Politics do not become a significant factor until the end of the movie, although they linger in the background throughout. There's always a hint of darkening gloom during the otherwise sunny days, especially when the chill of winter gives way to the glories of a new spring. *Butterfly*'s first three-quarters are designed as a series of vignettes that develop Mocho's character and illustrate facets of his relationships with Don Gregorio, his companions, and family. We observe Mocho and a school friend as they curiously follow a young man of the village when he sneaks out to meet his sweetheart. Mocho "courts" Aurora, a girl his age who has caught his eye. And, while on a road trip with a group of musicians, Mocho's older brother is smitten by the young Chinese wife of the man who provides him with a bed for the night.

Mocho's home life is simple. His parents love him, as well as each other. Mocho and his brother get along uncommonly well for siblings who share a bedroom. Meanwhile, viewers who have seen their share of foreign imports in recent years may find a degree of familiarity in the relationship between Mocho and Don Gregorio. It's a give-and-take friendship that benefits both participants, often in unexpected ways. Don Gregorio finds someone thirsty for his company and eager to learn the knowledge he can convey, and Mocho discovers things about life he could never learn from anyone else.

Butterfly has the virtue of mixing a pleasant tale about growing up with a harder-edged conclusion. However, this is not a case of an ending redeeming an otherwise mediocre motion picture, because Cuerda's feature is worthwhile throughout. *Butterfly* makes a powerful statement about the dark side of human nature and the traits that characterize it: cowardliness, betrayal, and mean-spiritedness. The brutal manner in which these are depicted elevates *Butterfly* to a level it would not have attained had it remained in the arena of placid sentimentality.
RECOMMENDED

Camera Buff (Amator) [Poland, 1979]
Starring: Jerzy Stuhr, Malgorzata Zabkowska, Ewa Pokas, Stefan Czyzewski Director: Krzysztof Kieslowski Screenplay: Krzysztof Kieslowski and Jerzy Stuhr Running Time: 1:52 Rated: No MPAA Rating (Mature themes, sex) Theatrical Aspect Ratio: 1.33:1 In Polish with subtitles

Call *Camera Buff* a case of art imitating life. Although director Krzysztof Kieslowski admitted that this film doesn't tell his own story it will undoubtedly strike a responsive chord with many amateur and professional film makers. Although the film deals with serious themes: obsession, censorship, and the battle between artistic integrity and personal sacrifice, Kieslowski never allows the proceedings to grow maudlin or overly-introspective. The script is peppered with serio-comic incidents that leaven what could have been a staid, sober story.

The main character, Filip Mosz, is played by Jerzy Stuhr. In anticipation of his new baby's birth, Filip spends 2 months' pay on an 8mm camera to record of his child's first few years. But, from the moment he looks through the lens, Filip is hooked. He begins filming almost anything that moves. His boss at the factory (Stefan Czyzewski) appoints Filip as the establishment's official chronicler. At first, the manager is pleased with the films, and he allows Filip to proceed as he sees best. But, when the films begin to attract attention, winning amateur prizes and appearing on TV shows, the manager attempts to restrict Filip's work. Heedless of the personal cost (his wife leaves him) and risking his job, Filip pushes forward, only to stumble into a trap set for him by the factory's management. In the end, he faces a painful choice:

destroy his own work or allow it to be used for a purpose he cannot condone.

All the dilemmas in *Camera Buff* center on Filip. He becomes so obsessed with film making that he neglects his family, eventually losing not only his wife, but his young daughter and unborn child. He also confronts censorship when his manager demands that scenes be edited out to make a film more complimentary to the factory. Eventually, when his employers attempt to suppress an entire movie and determine the content of another, Filip faces a crisis of conscience. Why does he make films? And do they mean anything if they are reduced to propaganda pieces instead of genuine depictions of the world as he sees it? When his immediate boss is fired because of a film's content, Filip finally sees how serious his "harmless" hobby has become.

This all sounds rather grim, but, perhaps surprisingly, *Camera Buff* may be the funniest of Kieslowski's features. None of the humor is excessive or intrusive, but there are moments of the absurd that maintain a relaxed tone, and Filip's enthusiasm is infectious. Kieslowski isn't attempting to bludgeon us with preachy morality lessons; his intent is to explore certain issues in an entertaining manner. And, while *Camera Buff* lacks some of the artistry evident in the director's later projects, it's worth seeing not only as an example of Kieslowski's early work, but as an important film in its own right. **HIGHLY RECOMMENDED**

Career Girls [United Kingdom, 1997]
Starring: Katrin Cartlidge, Lynda Steadman, Kate Byers, Mark Benton, Joe Tucker Director: Mike Leigh Screenplay: Mike Leigh Running Time: 1:28 Rated: R (Profanity, sexual situations, brief nudity) Theatrical Aspect Ratio: 1.66:1

Simplicity is *Career Girls*' greatest asset. Because the plot is so threadbare, it allows us to delve more deeply into the personalities of the two protagonists. They are Hannah (Katrin Cartlidge) and Annie (Lynda Steadman), a pair of 30-ish former university roommates-turned-business women who are spending a weekend together in London. Once, Hannah and Annie were inseparable, but, since completing their terms at college 6 years ago, they have become victims of the gulf that time and distance often build.

Mike Leigh uses the "fly on the wall" perspective to give us insights into the most mundane aspects of the women's weekend. We see them eating, drinking, and getting ready for bed. Their topics of conversation are often banal, but the intelligence of the writing keeps us involved even when the subject matter is stale.

And, to give us a sense of perspective about Hannah and Annie's past, Leigh employs numerous flashbacks to allow us to share their memories.

The reunion is presented believably, with the initial awkwardness and tension giving way to the gradual recapturing of an easy familiarity. Reunions give us a chance to take a step back and examine how the years have altered our lives and those of others. This is the feeling that Leigh has captured here, by introducing not only Hannah and Annie, but 3 other important individuals from their past: the "idiot savant" Ricky (Mark Benton), the callous Adrian (Joe Tucker), and another former roommate, Claire (Kate Byers). Coincidence also plays a role in *Career Girls*, although Leigh seems a little self-conscious using this device, since he keeps mentioning it.

Career Girls is peppered with humor, although some of the comedy is underpinned by a bittersweet aura. The most memorable of this film's episodes has Hannah and Annie, who are looking at expensive condos without any intention of buying, encountering a sleazy owner who seems as interested in getting them into bed as in showing off his high-rise domicile.

Career Girls is a wonderful diversion — expert film making that's all the more effective because it seems so natural and effortless. The movie effectively transforms two strangers into people worth caring about. *Career Girls* can be regarded as nothing less than a success. **RECOMMENDED**

Carried Away [1996]

Starring: Dennis Hopper, Amy Locane, Amy Irving, Gary Busey, Hal Holbrook, Julie Harris Director: Bruno Barreto Screenplay: Ed Jones and Dale Herd based on the novel *Farmer* by Jim Harrison Running Time: **1:44** Rated: R (Nudity, sex, profanity) Theatrical Aspect Ratio: **1.85:1**

It's difficult to say what *Carried Away* is primarily about, because it deals with so many issues: how we view sexuality, how love compares to lust, and how everyone — men and women — have a tendency to become stale and complacent with the approach of late middle age. Joseph Svenden (Dennis Hopper) knows about this latter issue first-hand. At age 47, he's dissatisfied with his life, but doesn't know what to do about it. He's engaged to a woman, Rosealee Henson (Amy Irving), whom he has loved since high school, but something lifeless in their relationship keeps him from actually tying the knot. He hasn't found anything that he's truly good at — he's a mediocre teacher and a worse farmer. He lives with his dying mother (Julie Harris) in the house where he

has spent his entire life. Joseph is trapped, both in an infirm body, and in his village.

Relief — or at least a modicum of excitement — arrives in the person of Catherine Wheeler (Amy Locane), a sexually precocious 17-year old with a killer body. Her parents move into one of Joseph's neighboring houses, and she becomes his student at the small two-classroom school where he teaches. In her own way, Catherine feels as trapped as Joseph. Her mother is a drunk and her father is more interested in shooting pheasants than caring for her. So, looking for an escape, she discovers her teacher, whom she clumsily seduces. Joseph is quite willing, and, though he feels guilty at first, he gradually comes to view his relationship with Catherine as a liberating experience . . . until she begins to fantasize about marrying him.

In addition to Hopper's fine job, the principal supporting players are solid. Amy Irving bears all (literally and figuratively) in a performance of surprising emotional depth. Rosealee is a sad figure who, like Joseph, wants something that she doesn't understand and can't put into words. As Catherine, Amy Locane (*Blue Sky*) exudes not only sexuality, but vulnerability. Locane offers us glimpses of the hurt, confused child carefully concealed beneath the brazen exterior. Gary Busey, as Catherine's father, is uncharacteristically restrained, and Hal Holbrook provides most of the comic relief as a small town doctor.

Although Catherine is developed as a real character with real problems, *Carried Away* isn't as much about her as it is about Joseph's reaction to her. This is, after all, his story. Although these two profess to love one another, they are both lying, perhaps as much to themselves as to each other. Their reasons for having sex are far more complex than simple "love," and Barreto's film has the courage to examine those reasons. *Carried Away* is erotic, but it's also thoughtful and intelligent, and, coupled with Hopper's extraordinary performance, that's reason enough to be carried away by this motion picture. **HIGHLY RECOMMENDED**

Carrington [United Kingdom, 1995]

Starring: Emma Thompson, Jonathan Pryce, Steven Waddington, Samuel West, Rufus Sewell Director: Christopher Hampton Screenplay: Christopher Hampton based on the book *Lytton Strachey* by Michael Holroyd Running Time: **2:02** Rated: R (Mature themes, sex, violence, discreet nudity) Theatrical Aspect Ratio: **1.85:1**

Screenwriter Christopher Hampton makes a successful directorial debut with this picture, an artistic and emotional examination of the 17-year liaison between

Dora Carrington (Emma Thompson) and Lytton Strachey (Jonathan Pryce). *Carrington* is a special love story that challenges the intellect with as much vigor as it touches the heart. Hampton shows that it's possible to have souls in synch even when their sexuality is incompatible. Though Dora, a heterosexual woman who didn't lose her virginity until she was in her 20s, and Strachey, an avowed homosexual, each had an assortment of male bed partners, they were intensely devoted to each other with a passion that was "all absorbing" and "self-abasing." Even without a sexual element, their love was transcendent, majestic, and ultimately tragic, for one could not live without the other.

Lytton Strachey was born in 1880, 15 years before Dora Carrington. The two met shortly after the onset of World War I. At that point, he was a confirmed pacifist; she wanted nothing more than to be a man so that she could fight. The 1918 publication of *Eminent Victorians* cemented Strachey's literary reputation. Dora, on the other hand, remained a little-known talent during her lifetime, since she painted just for herself and Strachey, not to exhibit or sell.

Carrington is divided into 6 chapters, most named after the men who float in and out of the title character's life. Of course, Strachey is there all the time, a constant supportive and loving presence. In one segment, Dora loses her virginity to ardent suitor Mark Gertler (Rufus Sewell). In another, she marries Ralph Partridge (Steven Waddington), primarily because Strachey is attracted to him. This leads to a bizarre triangle where only one relationship is consummated.

The film is beautifully photographed, with each scene carefully composed. One of *Carrington*'s most poignant images is of Dora sitting outside of Ham Spray House at night. As she gazes in through lighted windows at the various couplings taking place, it's possible to feel her loneliness. The stunning sequence is made all the more impressive by the slow, deliberate manner in which it was filmed.

Thompson, as always, is a joy to behold. Here, with a Buster Brown haircut, the actress gives a carefully restrained, subtly nuanced performance. The versatile Jonathan Pryce is every bit Thompson's equal. It's a rare pleasure to watch two top-notch equals play off one another. There is tangible chemistry between them, although not of the conventional sort.

Carrington's tone is not one of restraint. Strachey and Dora don't have sex, but their love is definitely neither unrequited nor unacknowledged. This is a passionate, although never gratuitous, motion picture, with a clear view of how it wants to portray its characters and their complex relationship. The result is a memorable portrait of two of history's most unique lovers. **HIGHLY RECOMMENDED**

Casino [1995]

Starring: Robert De Niro, Joe Pesci, Sharon Stone, Don Rickles, James Woods Director: Martin Scorsese Screenplay: Nicholas Pileggi & Martin Scorsese based on the book by Nicholas Pileggi Running Time: 2:58 Rated: R (Violence, profanity, drug use, sexual situations) Theatrical Aspect Ratio: 2.35:1

Casino opens with short sequence in 1983 before moving on to the meat of the story, which is related through flashbacks. Director Martin Scorsese makes heavy use of voiceovers, employing disembodied monologues by both lead actors — Robert De Niro and Joe Pesci — to fill in gaps. The sheer volume of words sporadically detracts from character development, but it is integrated successfully enough not to seem overly intrusive. While the intelligence and wit of the voiceovers makes them palatable, such nonstop talking isn't always the best way to convey a story — the temptation to *tell* something, rather than *show* it, is too great.

During its 3-hour running time, *Casino* tells the story of two men's intermingled lives. Sam "Ace" Rothstein (Robert De Niro) was a gambler who never lost. He researched all his bets carefully, and rarely made a bad pick. His winning tendencies gained him popularity and favor with the local mob, who used Nicky Santoro (Joe Pesci) to shadow and protect him. Now that Ace has moved to Vegas to manage the Tangiers Casino, Nicky isn't far behind. And, while the two gravitate to opposite sides of the law, with Ace keeping his fingers clean and Nicky taking over the local crime scene, their paths continue to cross, and their encounters become increasingly less friendly. Stirred into the mix is Ace's girlfriend, Ginger (Sharon Stone), an expert hustler who attracts men like flies. Although she agrees to marry Ace, she continues a liaison with her former pimp (James Woods) while encouraging Nicky's affections.

Supporting players include a restrained James Woods, comedian Don Rickles in a serious role, Alan King (also playing it straight), and Kevin Pollak. Scorsese's mother has a brief (and very funny) appearance as the no-nonsense parent of a bumbling, small-time gangster. And faces associated with Vegas, like Steve Allen, Frankie Avalon, Jayne Meadows, and Jerry Vale, have cameos.

Casino was filmed in Las Vegas, and this shows in the splashiness and energy of nearly every scene. By using gaudy costumes and a '70s soundtrack, Scorsese takes us back some two decades. Starting with the vivid opening credits *Casino* sparkles like its fake diamond of a host city. The cinematography, which uses surprisingly few tricks other than freeze-framing to emphasize key moments, is crisp and clean.

By now, audiences have come to expect forceful films from Martin Scorsese. With *Casino,* he doesn't disappoint. The movie is long, but, with a fast-moving storyline, escalating tension, and surprisingly robust humor, the 3 hours move quickly. Several flaws, mostly minor, keep *Casino* on a plateau slightly below that of the director's best (*Mean Streets, Raging Bull, Taxi Driver, Goodfellas*), but this is worth making an effort to see. **HIGHLY RECOMMENDED**

The Cat's Meow [Canada/Germany/United Kingdom, 2001]

Starring: Kirsten Dunst, Cary Elwes, Edward Herrmann, Eddie Izzard, Joanna Lumley, Victor Slezak, Jennifer Tilly Director: Peter Bogdanovich Screenplay: Steven Peros, based on his play Running Time: 1:50 Rated: PG-13 (Sexual situations, violence) Theatrical Aspect Ratio: 1.85:1

Hollywood is built on the myths and legends of the past — its reputation rests upon the closeted skeletons of the movers and shakers of its early days. One of many such half-whispered stories occurred during a weekend in November 1924 on a boat owned by publishing magnate William Randolph Hearst. The "official" account, backed up by the coroner's report, stated one thing, while the gossip columns and underground murmurs related another. For *The Cat's Meow,* director Peter Bogdanovich, working from Steven Peros' screenplay (which is an adaptation of his stage play), has chosen to present the most lurid version of what may have transpired during those few days nearly 80 years ago. And, while this movie may not represent historical fact, it's a fun sort of conjecture.

The people are real; the circumstances are highly speculative. There's Eddie Izzard as Charlie Chaplin, the movie star/director who is readying his next effort, something called *The Gold Rush.* Edward Herrmann is William Randolph Hearst, one of the wealthiest and most powerful men in the world. Hearst had a famous feud with Orson Welles, but he didn't like Chaplin much, either. The reason was starlet Marion Davies (Kirsten Dunst), Hearst's mistress,

whom he suspected of engaging in an affair with Chaplin. Helium-voiced Jennifer Tilly is gossip columnist Louella Parsons, and Joanna Lumley is author Elinor Glyn. The occasion that has brought these notable personages (and a few lesser-known ones) together on Hearst's ship is the birthday of movie producer Thomas Ince (Cary Elwes). By the time the weekend was over, Ince was at death's door. *The Cat's Meow* observes that the reason was not "acute indigestion" or "heart failure" (as the official reports stated) but a gunshot wound accidentally inflicted by a jealous lover.

There are three standout roles: Izzard's Chaplin commands the screen; Herrmann, who shows both sides of Hearst — the dark and the playful; and Joanna Lumley, who imbues Elinor Glyn with a ferocity to match her dry wit. Since she's playing a fatuous character, Jennifer Tilly manages not to seem too out-of-place. Good character actor that he is, Cary Elwes essays his part without stealing scenes. And, for Kirsten Dunst, this represents an opportunity to move away from playing teenagers. Her Marion is bubbly, but she does not captivate the camera the way some of her co-stars do.

Director Peter Bogdanovich made this film because this is a story he wanted to tell, and, from an artistic and entertainment perspective, it is the best movie he has made in the better part of a decade. *The Cat's Meow* isn't quite good enough to elicit a purr, but it represents better-than-average movie making that doesn't demand a dumb, distracted audience. **RECOMMENDED**

Caught [1996]

Starring: Edward James Olmos, Maria Conchita Alonso, Arie Verveen, Bitty Schram, Steven Schub Director: Robert M. Young Screenplay: Edward Pomerantz based on his novel, *Into It* Running Time: 1:59 Rated: R (Sex, nudity, violence, profanity) Theatrical Aspect Ratio: 1.85:1

Because it lacks a precise ideological agenda, *Caught* is something of a departure for veteran director Robert M. Young, a film maker known for socially and politically-motivated dramas. In fact, this is little more than an erotic, contemporary tale that plays like a Greek tragedy (*Oedipus,* to be exact). *Caught* cross sections a dysfunctional family whose uncomfortable stability is disturbed by the introduction of an outsider.

That outsider is Nick (Arie Verveen), a homeless Irish drifter trying to survive on the streets of Jersey City. When he ducks into a fish store to escape the police, the owners, Joe (Edward James Olmos) and his wife, Betty (Maria Conchita Alonso), take pity on him. They offer him a room, board, and $80 a week to work as Joe's assistant. Nick accepts, not intending to stay for long. But days turn into weeks, then months, and, soon, the young Irishman is more dear to Joe and Betty than their real son, Danny (Steven Schub).

Nick treats Joe like the father he never knew, but his feelings for Betty are more complex. Although he regards her as a mother at the outset, he is powerless to stop a growing attraction. Eventually, after one-too-many moments of hightened sexual awareness, their relationship is consummated. From that point on, Nick and Betty are all over each other at every opportunity. A further complication arises when Danny returns home with a wife and son to find that his place has been usurped.

Caught examines psychological and emotional family bonds as they apply to the "real" son and the "adopted" one. The film also explores the most intense kind of sibling rivalry, a jealousy that is rooted in Oedipal impulses. Danny has many reasons to hate Nick, but he doesn't go over the edge until he recognizes the sexual nature of Nick and Betty's relationship.

The final scenes close the story in an unforgettably stark manner. Although a relentless premonition of doom hangs over this picture, we're still not quite prepared for the brutal twist of events that marks *Caught*'s climax. Even though the movie's overall arc is somewhat predictable, and occasionally melodramatic, it's impossible to deny the cumulative impact.

Caught opens and closes with an image of fish caught in a net, struggling to escape. It's an apt metaphor, since all the characters in this film are trapped by fate in one way or another. A thought-provoking tragedy like this deserves a place in American cinema. **RECOMMENDED**

The Celebration (Festen) [Denmark, 1998]

Starring: Ulrich Thomsen, Thomas Bo Larsen, Paprika Steen, Henning Moritzen Director: Thomas Vinterberg Screenplay: Thomas Vinterberg, Mogens Rukov Running Time: 1:45 Rated: R (Strong sexual content, profanity, nudity, mature themes) Theatrical Aspect Ratio: 1.37:1 In Danish and English with subtitles

It is the 60th birthday of the family patriarch, Helge (Henning Mortizen). Everyone is coming home for the party, including Helge's sons, Christian (Ulrich Thomsen) and Michael (Thomas Bo Larsen), and his daughter, Helene (Paprika Steen). Missing from the roster of invitees is Christian's twin sister, Linda, who

recently committed suicide. The reason for her action, and the repercussions from it, form the basis of the shocking and painful events that transpire during a 24-hour period. In the midst of dinner, Christian makes a startling accusation, and, even as the disbelieving guests are choosing sides, the film slowly unwraps the truth.

Filmed using a shaky, hand-held camera with natural lighting and little or no post-production, Verterberg's approach mimics the look of a home movie. If the style looks familiar, that's because it resembles the approach used by director Lars Von Trier in *Breaking the Waves*. Von Trier, Vinterberg, and two other Danish directors signed a pact called "Dogme 95." A rejection of Hollywood's fascination with special effects, Dogme 95 touts the value of cinematic simplicity: hand-held cameras, natural sound and lighting, location filming only (no sets), and no computer manipulation of images.

Vinterberg and Mogens Rutov have penned a tight, taut screenplay that addresses twisted family dynamics in an immediate way, by combining effective drama with an undercurrent of dark humor. The film touches on issues like child and spousal abuse, racism, and revenge, and, in the process, it shows how difficult it can be to differentiate between love and hate when the line between them becomes blurred.

Christian is played with coiled intensity by Ulrich Thomsen. By nature, he is not the kind of man who seeks a confrontation, but this is one struggle he cannot run from, and Thomsen does an excellent job of conveying his unease. Christian's polar opposite is his brother Michael, who is essayed by Thomas Bo Larsen. Larsen's portrayal presents Michael as a thoughtless, vicious brute who terrorizes his wife and anyone else who doesn't agree with him. The third child, Helene, is a portrait of camouflaged sadness. Like Thomsen and Larsen, Paprika Steen uses her skills as an actress to bring her alter-ego to life. The other major character, Henning Mortizen's Helge, is something of an enigma. Mortizen gives human dimensions to a man who, in another movie, might have been a banal villain.

The Celebration has been accorded the kind of international recognition that is often given to challenging motion pictures. It was an official selection at numerous film festivals, including Cannes (where it was the co-recipient of the Jury Prize), Toronto, and New York. *The Celebration* rips apart the placid facade of a familiar subject, leaving its audience stunned. As difficult as the film can at times be, the patient viewer will be rewarded. **HIGHLY RECOMMENDED**

The Cement Garden [France/Germany/United Kingdom, 1993]

Starring: Andrew Robertson, Charlotte Gainsbourg, Alice Coultard, Ned Birkin, Sinead Cusack Director: Andrew Birkin
Screenplay: Andrew Birkin based on the novel by Ian McEwan
Running Time: 1:45 Rated: No MPAA Rating (Mature themes, nudity, sex, language) Theatrical Aspect Ratio: 1.66:1

Considering the rancid, nightmarish quality of his books, it's somewhat amazing that a writer like British author Ian McEwan could have 3 of his works filmed by now. In addition to *The Cement Garden*, *The Comfort of Strangers* has been made into a movie (by Paul Schrader in 1991), and *The Innocent* (directed by John Schlesinger) is due to be released. The most controversial of these, however, is *The Cement Garden*, principally because of its subject matter: teenage incest.

An entire family is together at the outset of the film, but not for long. After the father collapses and dies of a heart attack, the mother (Sinead Cusack) becomes confined to bed, stricken by a mysterious and debilitating illness. This leaves the eldest sister and brother, Julie (Charlotte Gainsbourg) and Jack (Andrew Robertson), to care for their younger siblings, Sue (Alice Coultard) and Tom (Ned Birkin). These 4 are not what most people would define as "normal." Julie and Jack are drawn to each other by a forbidden sexual attraction that neither can deny, despite the obvious taboo.

The incest issue is dealt with in a straightforward and non-prurient fashion. Director Andrew Birkin is not attempting to shock his audience, but rather to candidly represent the factors that lead to this relationship. His style is sensitive, not exploitative, which makes all the difference to the success of *The Cement Garden*. The film works because the characters are alive, and morality is shown to be relative.

As dark as the subject matter is, Birkin still culls laughter from the audience. This isn't the nervous tittering of uncomfortable viewers, but a genuine reaction. Much of the humor is relatively harmless, although a few of the jokes are off-color.

The relationship between Jack and Julie holds the film together. This is a mutual seduction, and both play their parts. Julie has all the responsibility in the household, while Jack, on the other hand, gets away with doing as little as he can, preferring to spend his time masturbating in secret places or admiring himself in a mirror. Julie is a more likable character than her brother, but only because it's difficult to love a narcissist.

The Cement Garden makes no apologies. The quality of fascination is as much a credit to those producing the film as to the unorthodox — and grim — central theme. *The Cement Garden* is occasionally grotesque, frequently disturbing, and, at times, surprisingly humorous. No matter what else it may be, however, this movie is always thought-provoking, and it's hard to imagine anyone leaving without the strongest of opinions. **HIGHLY RECOMMENDED**

Central Station [Brazil, 1998]

Starring: Fernanda Montenegro, Vinicius de Oliveira, Marilia Pera, Soia Lira Director: Walter Salles Screenplay: Joao Emanuel Carneiro, Marcos Bernstein Running Time: 1:46 Rated: PG-13 (Profanity, mature themes) Theatrical Aspect Ratio: 2.35:1 In Portuguese with subtitles

Walter Salles' *Central Station* opens inside a large train station in Rio de Janeiro, where Dora (Fernanda Montenegro) is going about her daily job. At a dollar's price, she will write a letter for one of the many illiterate passers-by in the station, then seal it in an addressed envelope. When it comes to mailing the letters, however, Dora is not trustworthy. Based on an arbitrary criteria, she posts some letters, tears up others, and stashes a few in a drawer. Dora doesn't care when she betrays a trust; she has made the determination of what's best, and decides whether or not to send a letter based on that judgment. She stands aloof and uninvolved, making her assessments dispassionately. Until she meets Josue (Vinicius de Oliveira).

Josue is the 9-year-old son of a woman who dictates a letter to Dora. In it, she asks the boy's father if they can be reunited. When leaving the station afterwards, the woman is struck by a bus and killed. Josue, with nowhere to go, begins to loiter around the station, acting pugnacious and withdrawn. His plight stirs something in Dora, who brings him home, then sells him to an adoption agency. However, when her best friend notes that the organization may be a front for organ thieves, Dora kidnaps the boy from the agency, then goes on a journey with him, searching for his father.

Regardless of the political issues the film touches upon or its travelogue aspect, the real heart of *Central Station* is the relationship between Dora and Josue. As in the best of this sub-genre of movies, the two change each other in profound ways. Dora fills the maternal role left vacant in the boy's life by the unexpected demise of his mother. In turn, her cynicism melts away and she discovers that she still retains the capacity to love, to sacrifice. Salles develops the relationship perfectly. It is certainly a familiar story, but in this context, it seems fresh.

The two leads both do superlative work. Fernanda Montenegro believably conveys the changes in Dora as her relationship with Josue transforms her inner self. It's a finely-tuned portrayal that doesn't ask the audience to accept any sudden or hard-to-swallow shifts in behavior. Dora's rebirth is gradual. Newcomer Vinicius de Oliveira doesn't have as complex as role, but his performance as a young, lost boy touches the heart. Together, the two actors create a palpable, and very special, bond.

Central Station is both literate and emotionally-powerful — an increasingly rare combination. It does not rely upon camera tricks or overwrought performances to touch the viewer. There's manipulation going on here, but it's subtle and skillful, and, as a result, we don't feel like our heartstrings are being twisted and pulled by an unseen puppeteer. For that reason, *Central Station* is well worth seeing, especially if you're in the mood for an affecting drama.

RECOMMENDED

The Chambermaid on the Titanic [France/Spain/Italy, 1997]

Starring: Olivier Martinez, Romane Bohringer, Aitana Sanchez Gijon, Didier Bezace Director: Bigas Luna Screenplay: Bigas Luna, Cuca Canals, Jean-Louis Benoit adapted from the novel by Didier Decoin Running Time: 1:36 Rated: No MPAA Rating (Sensuality) Theatrical Aspect Ratio: 2.35:1 In French with English subtitles

Despite the title, *The Chambermaid on the Titanic* is not actually about the sinking of the famous ship. It functions as an exploration of the creative process and a subversive and subtly funny satire of the genre of overblown melodramas of which James Cameron's *Titanic* is a distinguished member. The script turns out to be a lot more clever than it initially seems, and it's up to the viewer to what's real and what's imaginary.

The lie is the foundation of almost every good story. Most creative people are, by nature, good liars. *The Chambermaid on the Titanic* examines the evolution of one lie from a simple embellishment to the basis of a man's fame and fortune. In the process, it spotlights certain aspects of human nature, particularly our endless craving for the kind of entertainment that can vicariously take us to a place where we can't go on our own.

The film opens in the grim, gray confines of the Simeon Foundry in Northern France during the Spring of 1912. Horty (Olivier Martinez), one of the workers, wins the factory's version of the triathlon. The prize is an all-expenses paid trip for one to Southampton to watch the departure of the *Titanic* on its maiden voyage. Leaving behind his devoted wife, Zoe (Romane Bohringer), Horty heads for England. While there, he meets Marie (Aitana Sanchez Gijon). She's a chambermaid on the *Titanic*, but, on the night before the ship leaves, there are no hotel rooms in Southampton, and Marie needs a place to stay. Horty, who is smitten by the brunette beauty, offers his bed — he'll sleep in a chair. What happens (and doesn't happen) that night becomes crucial to Horty's future once he returns to Simeon and his wife. After his friends see Horty's photograph of Marie, they press him for details, and, when the truth doesn't satisfy them, he begins embellishing. His simple story of one night's indiscretion turns into an incredibly over-the-top romantic melodrama guaranteed to bring tears to the eyes of every listener. Soon, Horty has become a local attraction, but his fame has its down side. Zoe, as convinced by his stories as everyone else in the region, believes that Horty is madly in love with the memory of a woman who probably perished when the ship went down.

Oliver Martinez's looks are more impressive than his performance. Romane Bohringer (*Savage Nights*) is fine as the mousy Zoe and Aitana Sanchez Gijon (*A Walk in the Clouds*) radiates a healthy sexuality as Marie. This is not, however, an actors' film; *The Chambermaid on the Titanic*'s strength is in the script, which attempts a number of things, and succeeds at most of them. The presence of the name "Titanic" in the title might be what gets some moviegoers into theaters showing this film, but *The Chambermaid*'s unique narrative strengths will be what keeps them there. **RECOMMENDED**

Character (Karakter) [Netherlands, 1997]

Starring: Fedja Van Huet, Jan Decleir, Betty Schuurman, Victor Low, Tamar van den Dop, Hans Kesting Director: Mike van Diem Screenplay: Mike van Diem, Laurens Geels, Ruud van Megen based on the novel by Ferdinand Bordewijk Running Time: 2:00 Rated: R (Violence, sexuality) Theatrical Aspect Ratio: 1.85:1 In Dutch with subtitles

Character is a fine motion picture about the relationships within a dysfunctional family in the Netherlands during the 1930s. The film tells the story of Katadreuffe (Fedja Van Huet), a young man who has made his mark in the world despite the conspiracy of numerous, diverse forces to keep him suppressed. As a child, he wasn't an orphan, but he might as well have been. His unmarried mother, Joba (Betty Schuurman), is a harsh, unloving woman who rarely speaks to her son. His father, Dreverhaven (Jan Decleir), is the city's most detested bailiff. After being rejected by Joba, Dreverhaven wants nothing to do with his son, and works actively to place obstacles in his path. The struggle between Katadreuffe and Dreverhaven turns into a personal war of attrition. This fuels Katadreuffe's single-minded goal to rise through the legal system, but costs him a chance at true happiness.

Through his entire life, Katadreuffe is impelled by a need to escape from the shame of his birth and upbringing. He uses Dreverhaven's contempt as a catalyst to push himself harder. Dr. De Gankelaar (Victor Low), a lawyer who represents Katadreuffe in a bankruptcy hearing, sees great potential in the young man, and takes him on as an assistant. From there, using money borrowed from Dreverhaven's bank, Katadreuffe applies himself exclusively to his studies in law.

Although Katadreuffe is *Character*'s protagonist, the most fascinating individual in the film is Dreverhaven, who is played with a combination of malice and world-weariness by veteran actor Jan Decleir (*Antonia's Line*). Dreverhaven's motives are far more complex than those of a typical villain. Underneath his cold, harsh exterior, he is tortured by inner demons. His feelings towards his son are unclear — a mixture of shame, anger, bitterness, and, curiously, perhaps even pride. He claims that his financial assault is designed to strengthen Katadreuffe's character, but it's really an attempt to assert control and prove his superiority. Despite all of his money and his respected position in society, Dreverhaven is filled with self-loathing and disgust with the odious process of living. He risks his life frequently, causing many to wonder whether he's brave or seeking his own death.

Dickensian elements abound, from the travails of the poverty-stricken masses to the struggles of an (almost) orphan. Director Mike van Diem has crafted the look of Rotterdam in the 1930s to resemble London of a century earlier. Politics play a small-but-important role in the film as Katadreuffe enjoys a brief flirtation with the communist movement, which stands in direct opposition to Dreverhaven and all that he stands for. Ultimately, everything comes down to the relationship between Katadreuffe and Dreverhaven, and the manner in which their constant power struggle shapes their futures. RECOMMENDED

Chariots of Fire [United Kingdom, 1981]

Starring: Ben Cross, Ian Charleson, Nigel Havers, Nicholas Farrell, Ian Holm, John Gielgud Director: Hugh Hudson Screenplay: Colin Welland Running Time: 2:04 Rated: PG (Nothing offensive) Theatrical Aspect Ratio: 1.85:1

Chariots of Fire, the Oscar-winning 1981 film, transports us to the 1924 Olympics, and, in the process, highlights such commendable qualities as commitment, perseverance, and fraternity. That's not to say that winning isn't important to the competitors in Hugh Hudson's film. On the contrary, for British track stars Harold Abrahams (Ben Cross) and Eric Lidell (Ian Charleson), it's a paramount concern, but neither is so obsessed by their goal that they lose sight of the larger picture. Eric is a devout Christian who runs because he believes it glorifies God. Harold is a Jew who competes as a way of proving his worth. Both are driven by an inner fire, and have nothing but respect for their rivals.

Chariots of Fire tells the story of the British triumphs at the 1924 Olympics, where the UK representatives took a number of medals over the heavily-favored Americans. With Abrahams and Lidell leading the way, the British track team had one of their best-ever showings. This film traces the two principal athletes' paths to the Paris games, where their on-field successes form a surprisingly low-key climax. *Chariots of Fire* doesn't rely on worn-out sports film clichés; it's more interested in motivation and character development. Yes, it's important to know that Abrahams and Lidell win, but the real meat of the story is contained in what leads up to the races. Like in Sylvester Stallone's first *Rocky*, it's possible to claim victory before the competition begins — Lidell because he has holds fast to his beliefs and Abrahams because gives all he has to give.

There's barely a whiff of melodrama in *Chariots of Fire*, which makes the film-watching experience all the more effective — director Hugh Hudson shows respect for the integrity of his material and the intelligence of his audience. The absence of mawkish moments provides the narrative with a genuine quality that supports its factual background. Not only do we care about the characters, but we accept that they really existed. In fact, the entire production claims that same sense of verisimilitude. Most sports movies rely on nostalgia and adrenaline — *Chariots of Fire* stands on strong writing, direction, and acting. Appreciation of this picture doesn't demand a love of sports, merely an understanding of human nature. **HIGHLY RECOMMENDED**

Children of Heaven (Bacheha-Ye aseman)
[Iran, 1997]
Starring: Mohammad Amir Naji, Amir Farrokh Hashemian, Bahare Seddiqi Director: Majid Majidi Screenplay: Majid Majidi Running Time: 1:28 Rated: PG (Mild profanity) Theatrical Aspect Ratio: 1.85:1
In Farsi with subtitles

Children of Heaven opens in the poor quarter of an Iranian city. There we meet Ali (Mir Farrokh Hashemian), a 9-year-old boy going home with his sister's worn, pink shoes, which he has just taken to a cobbler for repairs. On the way, he stops at a fruit and vegetable stand to buy some potatoes. He puts the shoes down, and, while he's sorting through a bin, a rag picker mistakenly takes the shoes, thinking they're part of the stand owner's refuse. When Ali arrives home empty-handed, his 7-year-old sister, Zahra (Bahare Seddigi), is in tears. What will she wear to school?

Ali has a solution. She goes to school in the morning; he attends in the afternoon. They can share a pair of sneakers. Once her day is done, she can rush home and give the sneakers to him. Unfortunately, there's not enough time for the swap, and Ali arrives late to his first class. Meanwhile, on a day off, he accompanies his father (Amir Naji) to the city's wealthy section in search of work as a gardener — work that will pay enough to give the family a little extra money. And, at school, Ali discovers a possible solution to the shoe dilemma. Third place in a foot race is a pair of new sneakers (first and second prize are more lucrative, but Ali has no interest in them). All Ali has to do is beat out several hundred children and lose to only two, and his sister will be happy.

There are a number of reasons to like *Children of Heaven*, not the least of which is its inherent sweetness. Unlike many American movie kids, Ali and Zahara truly care for one another. Ali is deeply upset about losing the shoes, and the two siblings work together to find a solution without placing an additional financial burden upon their beleaguered parents. Seeing the film in North America also offers the fascination of looking through a window at a different culture and recognizing that it's not fundamentally different from our own.

The film's single weakness is the central conceit, which seems contrived. There's a sense of falseness in the way Ali loses his sister's shoes — a few too many coincidences occur for the viewer to miss the screenwriter's hand at work. Ironically, the awkwardness with which Majidi starts out his tale stands out only because the majority of the movie is so carefully constructed. In a big, flashy, Hollywood-style production, this kind of mistake wouldn't be noticed, but, in such a low-key picture, it calls attention to itself.

Children of Heaven isn't about Zahra's lost shoes, Dad's difficulty finding work, or Ali's placement in the race. It's about how those things define one family, and why the characters make worthwhile companions for 90 minutes of our time. There's certainly nothing epic about Majidi's narrative, but sometimes, as in *Children of Heaven*, an inconsequential and intimate story can provide a satisfying emotional payoff. **RECOMMENDED**

Chuck & Buck [2000]
Starring: Mike White, Chris Weitz, Lupe Ontiveros, Beth Colt, Paul Weitz Director: Miguel Areta Screenplay: Mike White Running Time: 1:36 Rated: R (Sex, language, homosexual themes) Theatrical Aspect Ratio: 1.85:1

In childhood, Buck (Mike White) and Chuck (Chris Weitz) were best friends. They did everything together, from climbing trees to the kind of innocent sexual exploration that occasionally happens between 11-year-old boys. For Chuck, this was a stepping-stone to a healthy, well-adjusted adulthood. Now living in Los Angeles, he is a high-powered executive in the recording industry with a gorgeous house, plastic friends, and a beautiful fiancée (Beth Colt). Buck, on the other hand, became stuck in adolescence. At age 27, he is socially unformed, mentally immature, and fixated on his limited sexual experience with Chuck. When his sick mother dies, it galvanizes him into action.

Buck invites Chuck to the funeral, and the two meet for the first time in 15 years. Chuck is a different person, but Buck is not, and it doesn't take Chuck long to realize that his former friend is afflicted with a bizarre personality, and is no longer the kind of individual he wants to have contact with. However, an obsessed Buck follows Chuck to the West Coast, where the haunting and stalking begins. When Chuck tries to explain that the past — as well as their friendship — has been buried, Buck doesn't want to hear it. He blames Chuck's fiancée, Carlyn, for ruining their relationship, and sinks all of his savings into producing a play, *Hank and Frank*. Written by Buck, this is a thinly-veiled account of his friendship with Chuck transplanted into an Oz-like setting. The play's director, the quick-witted Beverly (Lupe Ontiveros), calls it "a homoerotic, misogynistic love story" — a label that confuses Buck, who sees it as an innocent fairy tale about how he lost Chuck to Carlyn.

Hollywood delights in turning mental instability into a "cute" condition, and making individuals afflicted with it quirky and likable. *Chuck & Buck* does no such thing. Buck, ably portrayed by writer Mike White, is a disturbing person. We're never entirely comfortable when he is on screen. He's an innocent in an unkind world that he is unequipped to deal with, and the potential for harm (either to him or to someone else) is incipient in every scene. The goal of *Chuck & Buck* is to offer a realistic depiction of how the naiveté of a childhood friendship cannot survive intact into adulthood, not to present a feel-good account of two old friends reconnecting. *Chuck & Buck* is *not* a buddy movie.

Chuck & Buck is being referred to as a comedy in some quarters, but that's a misleading label. It is too unsettling to be genuinely funny. It's also not a love story. Buck is obsessed, not in love, and the object of his obsession is not the idealized image he envisions. By the end of the film, we understand Buck, even if we don't connect with him on an intimate, emotional level. And it's nice to note that *Chuck & Buck* closes on a hopeful note that allows us to leave the theater satisfied but not depressed. RECOMMENDED

Chungking Express [Hong Kong, 1994]

Starring: Brigitte Lin, Takeshi Kaneshiro, Tony Leung, Faye Wang
Director: Wong Kar-wai Screenplay: Wong Kar-wai Running Time: 1:30
Rated: R (Mature themes, sexual situations, profanity) Theatrical
Aspect Ratio: 1.85:1 In Chinese with subtitles

In any given day, each person comes into contact with dozens, if not hundreds, of others. Many are simply men and women we pass on the street. There's no interaction other than the occasional meeting of eyes. Consider, however, that each face conceals a life's tale. How many of those stories are similar, and how many are truly unique? This is the focus of *Chungking Express*. Wong Kar-wai believes that, while every person's narrative has a percentage of singular elements, there's always a certain commonality that falls under the broad umbrella of the "human experience."

To illustrate his point, Wong brings us two disparate tales. The only connection between them is a Hong Kong snack bar. The parallel course of love and loss charted by each underlines the primary theme. The first centers on a young policeman, He Qiwu (Takeshi Kaneshiro), who desperately misses his ex-girlfriend. After they were together for 5 years, she walked out on him, and he is keenly aware of the hole in his life. So, to ease the pain, he decides to fall in love again — this time with a blonde beauty (Brigitte Lin) who crosses his path. Of course, Qiwu isn't so much attracted to her as he is to the basic idea of being in love.

The second story introduces another man (Tony Leung) who has been dumped by his girlfriend. Faye (Faye Wang), one of the girls who works at the snack bar he frequents, becomes attracted to him. After obtaining a key to his apartment, she starts sneaking in while he's at work. His remarkably poor powers of observation allow Faye to clean the place and even do some minor redecorating without his noticing.

The loneliness of both male protagonists is palpable, and the females are each seduced by the lure of American culture. The object of Qiwu's desire dresses like a femme fatale out of a '40s movie and spends much of her time in a bar where everyone speaks English. Faye talks about moving to the United States and is forever playing her favorite song, "California Dreamin'." While the two stories are separate, the crisscrossing of themes and common elements can confuse inattentive movie-goers. *Chungking Express* requires unflagging vigilance.

Like John Woo, Tsui Hark, and other directors who learned their craft in Hong Kong, Wong infuses his films with style and energy. His hand-held camera is restless, always moving and shifting. The action sequences are punctuated with unusual shots and stop-motion jumps. By filming *Chungking Express* in such rich, vibrant manner, the director uses visual images to underscore his themes. Once the viewer gets past bouts of confusion (the film demands more than one viewing), the result is a uniquely memorable look at the ties that bind all people, as presented through two deceptively simple stories. HIGHLY RECOMMENDED

Ciao, Professore! [Italy, 1994]

Starring: Paolo Villaggio, Isa Danieli, Esterina Carloni Director: Lina Wertmuller Screenplay: Lina Wertmuller, Leo Benvenuti, and Piero De Bernardi based on *Me, Let's Hope I Make It* by Marcello D'Orta Running Time: 1:40 Rated: No MPAA Rating (Language) Theatrical Aspect Ratio: 1.85:1 In Italian with subtitles

Ciao Professore! is the story of Marco Sperelli (Paolo Villaggio), a northern Italian teacher who gets dumped in the southern Italian town of Corzano because of a bureaucratic screw-up. At the De Amicis school, he has been assigned to teach 3rd grade, but when he arrives, he finds the place run by the janitor. Only 3 of his 15 students are in class — the rest are out working on the streets, helping their families make ends meet. So, taking matters into his own hands, Sperelli makes a trip through the village to collect his delinquent pupils personally.

Wertmuller, who learned some of her craft from Fellini (she was his assistant director on *8 1/2*), has primarily been known for controversial films. Those used to her normal fare (such as *Swept Away* and *Seven Beauties*) will find *Ciao Professore!* a distinct departure. Instead of focusing on issues like sexuality, revenge, and madness, this movie makes do with a simple message of hope.

The bonding of Sperelli with his students is achieved with care and consideration. There is no single incident that galvanizes the process. Trust comes slowly, especially after the teacher slaps a belligerent young boy. Yet, as they spend more time together, each side discovers a little more about the other, and, through that learning, gains understanding. By the end, it's difficult to decide who has changed more: the professor, his pupils, or their families.

Given the time constraints of keeping this film to a reasonable length, Wertmuller does a marvellous job fleshing out a unique personality for each of the students. This is not a motion picture where the children blend together into a faceless mass, with only one or two standouts. Through a series of short vignettes, the director tells something about the conditions that have shaped their individual lives.

Ciao Professore! is rich in humor, much of which is grounded in the raw language used by the children. Even in the most serious circumstances, Wertmuller never allows this motion picture to become maudlin or melodramatic. A relentlessly upbeat, occasionally-playful atmosphere pervades the film, as typified by the repeated use of the song "What a Wonderful World."

Ciao Professore! premiered to high acclaim on the international film festival circuit (where it was called by its original title, *Me, Let's Hope I Make It*). The accolades are well-deserved. This is a rare movie-going experience — an artistic film that's both unpretentious and optimistic. **HIGHLY RECOMMENDED**

The Cider House Rules [1999]

Starring: Tobey Maguire, Charlize Theron, Delroy Lindo, Paul Rudd, Michael Caine Director: Lasse Hallström Screenplay: John Irving, based on his novel Running Time: 2:11 Rated: PG-13 (Sexual situations, violence) Theatrical Aspect Ratio: 2.35:1

Most of Lasse Hallström's *The Cider House Rules* transpires during the mid-1940s in an America that has added its strength to the Allied forces. Homer Wells (Tobey Maguire) is ineligible to join the military because of a bad heart. He has spent his entire life at an orphanage in St. Clouds, Maine as the special project of Dr. Wilbur Larch (Michael Caine), who sees great promise in the boy and imparts valuable medical knowledge to him. By the time he has reached adulthood, Homer is as good a doctor as Larch, albeit without a degree. There is also a moral divide between them: Larch will perform abortions (even though they're illegal), but Homer will not. Life changes for Homer with the arrival of Air Force officer Wally Worthington (Paul Rudd) and his girlfriend, Candy Kendall (Charlize Theron). She's at the orphanage for an abortion, and, after a brief stay, she is ready to go home. Homer chooses this moment to hitch a ride with them out of St. Clouds so he can see the world and establish a life for himself.

The script was written by John Irving and based on his novel of the same name. The impetus behind *The Cider House Rules* is Homer's search to find himself. During his time at St. Clouds, the course of his life has been mapped by the expectations of others. He is a big brother to the other orphans and a helper to Dr. Larch, but, trapped within such an insular community, he has never had the opportunity to unlock the real Homer Wells. The arrival of Wally and Candy opens a door to the outside, and Homer rushes through it. Only after he has discovered himself can he chart his future.

The film addresses two serious issues: abortion and incest. There really aren't two sides to the latter subject, and *The Cider House Rules* doesn't pretend that there are. It shows the kind of emotional wreckage that can result from a twisted family relationship. Meanwhile, by having main characters on both sides of the abortion issue, *The Cider House Rules* manages to give the debate a reasonably balanced perspective, and the 1943 setting makes the proceedings seem more fresh than is often the case for films that tackle this subject. At first glance, it appears that Irving and Hallström may be short-changing the anti-abortion side, but, upon closer inspection, it becomes apparent that there's real sense of fairness to the film's approach. Impressively, the movie manages to make its points without resorting to sermonizing.

In a little over 2 hours, with a strong cast, an accomplished cinematographer, and a well-tuned script, Hallström has fashioned a motion picture of visual splendor and emotional depth. *The Cider House Rules* defies conventions as it successfully turns back the clock to the wartime years and tells a story that is unique, despite a number of familiar elements. Few films offer a more fulfilling experience than the one promised, and delivered, by *The Cider House Rules*. **MUST SEE**

Cinema Paradiso [Italy, 1988]

Starring: Philippe Noiret, Salvatore Cascio, Marco Leonardi, Jacques Perrin Director: Giuseppe Tornatore Screenplay: Giuseppe Tornatore Running Time (original): 2:03 Running Time (director's): 2:54 Rated: PG (Mature themes) Theatrical Aspect Ratio: 1.66:1 In Italian with subtitles

As a fatherless child, Salvatore (Salvatore Cascio) loved the movies. He would abscond with the milk money to buy admission to a matinee showing at the local theater, a small place called the Cinema Paradiso. The Paradiso became his home, and the movies, his parents. Eventually, he developed a friendship with the projectionist, Alfredo (Philippe Noiret), a lively middle-aged man who offered advice on life, romance, and how to run a movie theater. Salvatore worked as Alfredo's unpaid apprentice until the day the Paradiso burned down. When a new cinema was erected on the same site, an adolescent Salvatore (Marco Leonardi) became the projectionist. But Alfredo, now blind because of injuries sustained in the fire, remained in the background, filling the role of confidante and mentor to the boy he loved like a son.

Once Salvatore has grown into his teens, *Cinema Paradiso* shifts from being a nostalgic celebration of movies to a traditional coming-of-age drama, complete with romantic disappointment and elation. Salvatore falls for a girl named Elena (Agnese Nano), but his deeply-felt passion isn't reciprocated. So he agonizes over the situation, seeks out Alfredo's advice, then makes a bold decision: he will stand outside of Elena's window every night until she relents. In the end, love wins out, but Salvatore's joy is eventually replaced by sadness as Elena vanishes forever from his life.

The Screen Kiss is important to *Cinema Paradiso*. Early in the film, the local priest previews each movie, using the power of his office to demand that all scenes of kissing be edited out. By the time the new Paradiso opens, however, things have changed. The priest no longer goes to the movies and kisses aren't censored. Much later, following the funeral near the end of *Cinema Paradiso*, Salvatore receives his bequest from Alfredo: a film reel containing all of the kisses removed from the movies shown at the Paradiso over the years. The deluge of concentrated ardor acts as a forceful reminder of the simple-yet-profound passion that has been absent from his life since he lost his one true love, Elena.

Thoughts about the "Director's Cut": When *Cinema Paradiso* was released in the late 1980s, the version seen by Italian movie-goers was much different than the cut shown to North American viewers. The truncated edition is still a stunning, masterful production, but it leaves the audience with a nagging question: What really happened to Elena? The answer is provided in a 35-minute sequence that never made it into the 1988 American release, but which has now been restored.

For lovers of *Cinema Paradiso*, this restored version is unquestionably a "must see." The magic and poetry of the original remain, but the added scenes fashion a different, more complete cinematic experience. For those who have never seen Tornatore's masterpiece, this is an excellent opportunity to view it for the first time. **MUST SEE**

Cobb [1994]

Starring: Tommy Lee Jones, Robert Wuhl, Lolita Davidovich Director: Ron Shelton Screenplay: Ron Shelton based on *Cobb: A Biography* by Al Stump Running Time: 2:08 Rated: R (Violence, language, nudity) Theatrical Aspect Ratio: 2.35:1

A notorious drunkard, bigot, and womanizer, the "Georgia Peach" had few qualities to praise other than his ability to hit a baseball. He claimed to be misunderstood, but the sad truth is that he was understood too well. Described at various times as "difficult at best, psychotic at worst" and someone whose "brooding soul . . . bubbled with violence," Ty Cobb represented the kind of man who could be admired only from a distance — the farther the better.

In 1960, with death stalking him, Cobb (Tommy Lee Jones) decides that he wants his story told. To write this tale of a "prince among men," he recruits sportswriter Al Stump (Robert Wuhl) to do the typing. At first, Stump is ecstatic at the opportunity to spend days on end with the greatest baseball player of all time — until he meets him, that is. Cobb's poisonous personality quickly convinces him that little pleasure will be derived from the task. Yet, despite continual verbal and physical abuse, Stump stays with Cobb, and even drives him across country from his Nevada home to Cooperstown. Friendship is never the lure, however; Stump is seduced by the need to understand greatness. And, in the end, he compromises his principles to capture his own small measure of it.

With a lead character as abrasive as they come, *Cobb* is not always a pleasant movie. At times, it is downright uncomfortable. The film is perhaps too long; much of the last half-hour feels excessive and redundant. Nevertheless, given such a forceful anti-hero, the viewer's horrified fascination lasts all 128 minutes, even to the end of the credits when Cobb declares, "Baseball is 100% of my life."

Jones' on-target portrayal of the dying athlete is mesmerizing. Robert Wuhl has considerably less screen presence, but this serves only to highlight Jones. Wuhl gives his co-star someone to play off of. There is a share of male bonding here, but not enough to turn *Cobb* into a cloying buddy picture. And, thankfully, the title character is never redeemed. Cobb remains detestable to the day of his death.

Image has little to do with reality. Tremendous statistics do not make for a tremendous person. When our heroes turn out to be less like Dale Murphy and more like Ty Cobb, we feel betrayed and slighted. On those occasions, we have only ourselves to blame because in our society, it's the .367 lifetime batting average that earns the reverence, regardless of how despicable the man holding the bat is. **RECOMMENDED**

Colonel Chabert [France, 1994]

Starring: Gerard Depardieu, Fanny Ardant, Fabrice Luchini, Andre Dussolier Director: Yves Angelo Screenplay: Yves Angelo and Jean Cosmos based on the novel by Honore de Balzac Running Time: 1:50 Rated: No MPAA Rating (Violence, mature themes) Theatrical Aspect Ratio: 2.35:1 In French with subtitles

A snow-covered battlefield littered with the dead. Bodies stripped of armor and clothing, then tossed naked into mass graves. Seemingly uninjured young men whose throats are uncovered to reveal mortal wounds. Unmoving horses dragged through the snow to join their fellows on an ever-growing pyre. And one man, still breathing, mistakenly thrown into a pit along with countless numbers of his dead compatriots.

This still-living man is Colonel Chabert (Gerard Depardieu), the hero of 1807's battle of Eylau between Napoleon and the Russians. However, due to injuries, Chabert is unable to declare himself, and is presumed dead. His wife (Fanny Ardant) re-marries, and takes Chabert's considerable fortune with her. Ten years later, however, in a *Return of Martin Guerre*-like turn of events, the Colonel comes back to Paris with the intention of re-claiming his lost life. After finding a sympathetic lawyer (Fabrice Luchini), Chabert confronts his former wife, now the Countess Ferraud.

One of the underlying questions in *Colonel Chabert* is whether it's possible to resurrect a life that no longer exists. Just because Chabert presents himself in the flesh doesn't mean that the hero of Eylau has come home. After 10 years spent in poverty and near-madness, the Colonel has become aware of how little intrinsic value there is in money and material possessions. It's unclear whether his primary motive in revealing himself is to regain what he lost or to exact revenge upon those he views to have taken it from him.

Colonel Chabert is not a romance about two former lovers finding each other after a tragic 10-year separation. Any real affection between the title character and his former wife has long since burned out. Instead, this film is about how those two manipulate one another in vying for control of a fortune that each has a legitimate claim upon. Cupidity and backstabbing lie at the center of *Chabert*, and there's enough legal and political maneuvering to satisfy any who enjoy those sorts of murky machinations.

Wonderfully photographed and deliberately directed, *Colonel Chabert* progresses slowly (sometimes painfully so), often lingering on images rather than proceeding to the next scene. There are times when this method of storytelling works exceptionally well, but others when the attention to detail causes the plot to grind to a halt. Fortunately, however, novice director Yves Angelo is savvy enough never to lose his characters amidst all the cinemtographic splendor.

Depardieu says he was attracted to this film version of Honore de Balzac's novel because he was fascinated by the opportunity to play in this sort of tragedy. The question that looms large throughout the movie is not whether Chabert will regain his honor and fortune, but whether there's enough of him left to appreciate it. Death, after all, has many faces, and just because the body goes on doesn't mean the personality still exists. This is why *Chabert* possesses a level of subtlety beyond that of most historical dramas. **RECOMMENDED**

Courage (Amor Propio) [Spain, 1994]

Starring: Veronica Forque, Fernando Valverde, Antonio Valero, Antonio Resines   Director: **Mario Camus**   Screenplay: **Mario Camus**   Running Time: **1:50**   Rated: No MPAA Rating (Mature themes, profanity)   In Spanish with subtitles

Like Hal Hartley's *Amateur, Courage* develops as a noir thriller while simultaneously spoofing the genre. This film has all the right elements: a dark, evocative atmosphere, double and triple-crosses, multi-million dollar scams, and an appealing heroine. It's a difficult task to pay homage to a film style while simultaneously parodying it. However, director Mario Camus establishes the perfect tone, leading to an entertaining romp through familiar-seeming territory that is subtly transformed by his lighthearted methods.

Played with unbridled energy and enthusiasm by helium-voiced Veronica Forque (from *Kika*), Juana is placed in a desperate position when her husband Simon, a frequenter of Spain's high finance inner circles, disappears — apparently with a lot of money. Everyone — police, gangsters, and bankers — wants something from Juana, but she knows nothing and refuses to lose faith in her beloved husband. Things change, however, when Juana discovers that Simon has a mistress. Suddenly, it's pay back time.

Courage displays a lot of offbeat humor as it toys with typical noir plot elements. The ending is such a masterpiece of timing and trickery that it may surprise even thriller veterans. Don't expect the traditional here — Camus shuns anything remotely somber and his heroine is far from the usual femme fatale. The result is a film that never takes itself too seriously, and, consequently, is a whole lot of fun to watch. **HIGHLY RECOMMENDED**

Crooklyn [1994]

Starring: Alfre Woodard, Delroy Lindo, Zelda Harris, Carlton Williams, David Patrick Kelly   Director: **Spike Lee**   Screenplay: Joie Susannah Lee, Cinque Lee, and Spike Lee   Running Time: **1:55**   Rated: **PG-13** (Language, mature themes)

From *Malcolm X* to *Crooklyn*, Spike Lee has moved from heavy, epic drama to something significantly more lighthearted. Instead of drifting back to the first half of this century, we're only going to 1973, a year when afros and bellbottoms were in fashion; when the Knicks won the basketball championship; and

when there were enough pop tunes to fill a soundtrack.

Told from the point-of-view of 10-year-old Troy Carmichael (Zelda Harris), *Crooklyn* is the story of how one family struggles to survive and stay together. With Troy's musician dad Woody (Delroy Lindo) busy in the basement composing, the full burden of running the family and bringing home the money falls on Troy's mom, Carolyn (Alfre Woodard). This inevitably leads to tension between the two adults, and, when one particularly nasty fight explodes, Woody is out the door.

Producer/director Spike Lee has woven an evocative drama that has one major stumbling block. Two-thirds of the way through the movie, Troy goes south to visit a hyper-religious aunt. To emphasize how distorted the little girl's perception of this vacation is, Lee shoots this portion of the movie with an anamorphic lens, causing everything to seem elongated. While that's fine for short sequences, in this case it goes on for too long, becoming an annoying trick that nearly undermines the entire production.

Aside from this 20-minute detour, there aren't many overt flaws in *Crooklyn*. All but the most comic of urban violence has been removed, and we're left with a somewhat-idealized view of an early-'70s Brooklyn. Lee is as talented as any director is capturing an era, and some of the early scenes perfectly recall the mood of the time. The pop soundtrack may be a little too obvious, but it gets the job done.

Crooklyn comes to the screen with an upbeat tone and a lot of heart. The world of a child — especially one pushed all-too-soon into adulthood — is never easy, and this film captures the facets of Troy's odyssey. If Lee errs with his "Southern vacation" scenes, he recovers to fashion an ending that is both touching and hopeful. Beneath the surface of this deceptively simple motion picture lurks a keen insight. **RECOMMENDED**

The Crucible [1996]

Starring: Daniel Day-Lewis, Winona Ryder, Joan Allen, Paul Scofield   Director: **Nicholas Hytner**   Screenplay: Arthur Miller based on his play   Running Time: **2:04**   Rated: **PG-13** (Mature themes, brief nudity)   Theatrical Aspect Ratio: **1.85:1**

Arthur Miller's 1953 play, *The Crucible*, was written during Senator Joseph McCarthy's House Un-American Activities Committee hearings (for which Miller was called to testify in 1956). And, although the play is an historical allegory for the McCarthy period, its true power lies in its ability to be re-interpreted to fit any time period. Indeed, its fertile themes — the lure of power, the gullibility of those who believe they have a moral imperative, and the nature of truth — are universal in scope. Events such as those depicted in *The Crucible* have recurred with alarming predictability throughout human history.

The film opens with a seemingly-harmless event — Abigail Williams (Winona Ryder), Mary Warren (Karron Graves), Mercy Lewis (Kali Rocha), and several other Salem village girls attend a secret voodoo ritual in the woods. Tituba (Charlayne Woodard), a native of Barbados, presides over the ceremony, which involves drinking chicken blood, dancing naked, and casting charms to ensnare boys. However, when the local preacher, Reverend Parris (Bruce Davison), stumbles upon the proceedings, witchcraft is suspected, and an expert in the field, Reverend Hale (Rob Campbell), is brought in to investigate.

To save themselves from the noose, which is the penalty for a witch who does not admit to consorting with the Devil, Abigail and her cohorts plead for their lives. However, they not only confess to performing witchcraft, but name other townspeople as servants of Satan. Soon, with the arrival of Judge John Danforth (Paul Scofield), the girls, now turned back to "the ways of God," are regarded as unimpeachable witnesses. Those whom they condemn are arrested, and the innocent who refuse to confess are hanged. Abigail's real reason for starting the charade is to eliminate Elizabeth Proctor (Joan Allen), the wife of John Proctor (Daniel Day Lewis), the man she loves. Although Abigail and John once had an affair, he will not abandon his wife for his former mistress, and his staunch defense of Elizabeth places him in jeopardy, especially when he accuses Danforth's court of "pulling down heaven and raising up a whore!"

In *The Crucible,* there are heroes and villains, but nothing is black and white. Shades of gray permeate every action. Abigail is the spark that ignites the inferno of mistrust; however, she is guided not by malice, but by a misplaced, obsessive love. John Proctor, the most upright man in the film, is an adulterer whose own actions indirectly lead to the tragedy. He is noble only to a point, and his character faults make him easy to identify with as a human being.

Whether on stage or on film, *The Crucible* is a powerful, thought-provoking production. This version illuminates the story's numerous strengths, resulting in a motion picture of surprising emotional and intellectual impact. **HIGHLY RECOMMENDED**

Cry, the Beloved Country [1995]

Starring: James Earl Jones, Richard Harris, Vusi Kunene, Charles Dutton Director: Darrell James Roodt Screenplay: Ronald Harwood based on the novel by Alan Paton Running Time: 1:48 Rated: PG-13 (Mature themes) Theatrical Aspect Ratio: 1.85:1

In the aftermath of World War II, South Africa is a divided country — a land of growing injustice where the white man prospers through the efforts of the black man, and where the majority of the wealth is in the hands of the racial minority. Whites live in beautifully-constructed mansions with immaculately-groomed gardens. Blacks are often forced to eke out an existence by turning to crime and living as squatters in a shantytown. The specter of fear looms large over everything. All men, black and white alike, feel its oppressive, pervasive influence.

In this climate, two very different men come to the city of Johannesburg. The first is a black pastor, Reverend Stephen Kumalo (James Earl Jones), who has left behind his poor community to make the journey in search of his son. The second is a white landowner, James Jarvis (Richard Harris), who has come to Johannesburg to bury his only child, Arthur, the victim of a shooting by 3 black youths, one of whom was Absalom Kumalo (Eric Miyeni), Stephen's son.

Arthur Jarvis was a well-known activist for native rights who devoted his life to improving circumstances for the blacks of Johannesburg. Whites did not understand him; blacks embraced him. Those at the Claremont African Boys Club, where he was president, loved him not only for the money he spent on the facility, but for the time he freely gave. In his writings, he spoke of South African whites as "tyrants, oppressors, and criminals."

The meat of *Cry, the Beloved Country* concerns how events in the wake of the shooting transform the lives of Stephen Kumalo and James Jarvis. Each is forced to abandon their naïveté and confront the grim truths of reality. For Stephen, this means a crisis of faith and a re-assessment of his role in the world. For James, it means coming to terms with the core of his son's beliefs and seeing his own bigotry for what it is. In the end, each gains more than he loses, yet the price of that new knowledge cuts deeply.

Rarely does a motion picture touch the heart so deeply, with no hint of artifice or manipulation. Producer Anant Singh has said he wanted to wait to film this version of *Cry, the Beloved Country* until after apartheid's death so that the new climate in South Africa could provide a more hopeful backdrop. *Cry, the Beloved Country* shows the path of tolerance and compassion that the leaders of South Africa have finally found. **MUST SEE**

Dance With Me [1998]

Starring: Vanessa L. Williams, Chayanne, Kris Kristofferson, Jane Krabowski, Beth Grant Director: Randa Haines Screenplay: Daryl Matthews Running Time: 2:06 Rated: PG (Mild profanity, mild sensuality) Theatrical Aspect Ratio: 1.85:1

Dance with Me isn't intended to be a deeply introspective look at the struggles of a man and woman to overcome their individual emotional troubles and find each other. Instead, it uses these familiar, lightweight plot elements as a foundation for the series of colorful, energetic dance sequences that represent the real reason to see this movie. Vanessa Williams, the former Miss America-turned singer-turned actress, plays Ruby, a by-the-book professional dancer who's looking to win a World Latin Dancing Championship before she hangs up her shoes and costumes. Chayanne (the Latino sensation who isn't as well-known north of the Border as he is south of it) is Rafael, a free-spirited Cuban who has come to Texas in search of the father he never knew. Like Ruby, he's an accomplished dancer, but he's strictly an amateur. For him, what he does on the dance floor isn't a matter of pre-arranged moves; it's what the music tells him to do.

Ruby and Rafael fall in love. While the two stars strike a few sparks (as in the bathroom scene where Rafael is dressed only in a towel), theirs isn't a smoldering, hard-to-forget coupling. Both Williams and Chayanne are hot enough on their own, however, that the lack of palpable chemistry doesn't do irreparable harm. Anyone expecting to be swept away on the currents of a soaring love story may be a little disappointed.

Rafael is also struggling to communicate with the man he came to Texas to meet. John Burnett (Kris Kristofferson) is the father he never knew, but, while Rafael knows his sire's identity, John isn't even aware that he has a son. Meanwhile, Ruby is trying to get over the heartbreak caused by her breakup with her longtime partner, Julian (Rick Valenzuela, doing his best to outsneer Billy Zane's *Titanic* character), who also happens to be the father of her son.

The pedestrian narrative of *Dance with Me* is a necessary nuisance. One could argue that all it really succeeds in doing is taking away time from the dance sequences. The characters aren't well-developed and the drama, such as it is, is merely adequate. Fortunately, when it comes to choreography, Haines is aware of what the audience wants, and obliges with some breathtaking moments. The energy level is consistently high, and, even when we're forced to endure a painfully trite moment with John and Rafael bonding at the end of a fishing pier, we know that something delightful is just around the corner.

When I left *Dance with Me*, I was smiling. As far as feel-good movies go, this one works in spite of a bloated running length (over 2 hours) and a plot that could use an injection of originality. The dance sequences, which comprise roughly half of the screen time, have it all — great music, wonderful choreography, and attractive participants — and this makes up for many of the film's deficiencies.
RECOMMENDED

Dancer In the Dark [Denmark/France/Sweden, 2000]

Starring: **Björk, Catherine Deneuve, David Morse, Peter Stormare** Director: **Lars von Trier** Screenplay: **Lars von Trier** Running Time: 2:20 Rated: **R** (Violence, profanity) Theatrical Aspect Ratio: 2.35:1

Dancer In the Dark takes place in Washington State during 1964. The characters all live in the same small town and many of them work at the local J. Anderson Tool Company. Selma (Björk) is a Czechoslovakian immigrant who came to the United States with her son, Gene (Vladica Kostic), to find a better life. She lives in a trailer on the property of a local policeman, Bill (David Morse), and his wife, Linda (Cara Seymour). Selma's best friend is Kathy (Catherine Deneuve), and she is courted by the shy, undemanding Jeff (Peter Stormare). When she's not working, Selma spends her time at the movies watching Hollywood musicals and practicing for a local production of *The Sound of Music*, in which she plays Maria.

Selma and Bill are close, and, late one night, they trade secrets. He is broke, and, unless he can find a way to make his mortgage payment, the bank will foreclose on his house. Not only will he lose his property, but he is sure that his materialistic wife will dump him as well. Selma, on the other hand, is going blind. She suffers from a hereditary, degenerative condition that she has passed on to Gene. There is an operation to cure it, but the procedure is expensive. Selma has been scraping together every dollar she can save so that Gene can have the surgery. When Bill hears this, he wonders if Selma's nest egg might prove to be the solution to his problem, but his plan to get the money has catastrophic consequences for everyone involved.

Lars von Trier fused in elements of an homage to old Hollywood musicals (including an overture). As a result, there are about 6 instances in which all the action stops so the characters can sing and dance their way through elaborate production numbers. Unfortunately, it doesn't always work, but it is consistently interesting. And it certainly takes a hell of a lot of guts to incorporate traditional musical elements into a dark, thought-provoking drama.

The acting standout is Björk. She is capably supported by fine performances from, in particular, David Morse as the decent-but-flawed Bill and an underused Catherine Deneuve as Kathy. For an actress of Deneuve's stature and ability, it's surprising that von Trier didn't offer her a meatier role. Cameo roles are filled by Stellan Skarsgård (whose career has gone into high gear since he appeared in *Breaking the Waves*), Udo Kier, and stage and screen veteran Joel Grey, who gets to participate in one of the song-and-dance numbers.

Lars von Trier's movies speak for themselves — loudly. The filmmaker is a talented risk-taker, and instances of failure in his features are often more invigorating than instances of success in the work of less ambitious directors. *Dancer In the Dark* does something almost inconceivable in the way it merges two disparate genres. The result represents a thought-provoking, emotionally resonant, and innovative cinematic experience. **HIGHLY RECOMMENDED**

Dangerous Beauty [1998]

Starring: Catherine McCormack, Rufus Sewell, Oliver Platt, Moira Kelly
Director: Marshall Herskovitz Screenplay: Jeannine Dominy based on *The Honest Courtesan* by Margaret Rosenthal Running Time: 1:51
Rated: R (Nudity, sex, profanity, violence) Theatrical Aspect Ratio: 2.35:1

In 1583 Venice, women were regarded as little more than possessions. Education and willfulness were negative traits, reserved only for those who plied their bodies for money. Marriage had nothing to do with love — it was a contract made based exclusively on considerations of wealth and position. If a girl's family didn't have money, she had no hope of marrying an "important" man, no matter how deeply the two loved each other. In a situation like that, if she

wanted him, her only hope was to become his mistress. And, if she was truly ambitious and skilled, she could become a courtesan, a mistress to dozens of men, all willing to pay for her services.

Such are the circumstances of Veronica Franco (Catherine McCormack), who is desperately smitten with Marco Vernier (Rufus Sewell) — and he with her. But the difference in their social position makes a legal relationship impossible. When Marco, not wanting to lead Veronica on, informs her of this harsh truth, she is devastated, and chooses to follow the advice of her mother (Jacqueline Bisset) and become a courtesan. Soon, she is the most prized prostitute in Venice, desired by everyone from the local bishop to the King of France. But, during the age of the Spanish Inquisition, power gained through "sinful" means can be a tenuous thing.

Against the backdrop of Veronica and Marco's tumultuous relationship, director Marshall Herskovitz explores the injustices visited upon women at a time when they were universally viewed as inferior to men. The obedient wives are presented as timid, uncertain creatures who dream of a better lot for their daughters while secretly envying Veronica's freedom. For her part, although Veronica uses every weapon at her disposal to hold her own in power struggles with men, she would give all that she has away for a life with Marco.

As is the case with too many melodramas designed to give the audience a triumphant rush, *Dangerous Beauty* goes over the top in its closing moments, offering speech-making and grandstanding that undercuts some of the film's drama. A "commercial" finale isn't the worst thing that could happen in a picture like this — it may be emotionally manipulative, but, on a certain level, it works. *Dangerous Beauty* isn't great art, but it is good entertainment. **RECOMMENDED**

Dead Man Walking [1995]

Starring: Susan Sarandon, Sean Penn, Raymond J. Barry, R. Lee Ermey Director: Tim Robbins Screenplay: Tim Robbins based on the nonfiction book by Sister Helen Prejean Running Time: 2:02 Rated: R (Profanity, violence, mature themes) Theatrical Aspect Ratio: 2.35:1

As a film about capital punishment, *Dead Man Walking* is effective, but the true brilliance of this picture is that it deals with so much more. Touching such universal themes as revenge and redemption, crime and punishment, and fear and salvation, the movie explores the relationship between Matthew Poncelet

(Sean Penn), a convicted rapist/murderer on death row, and his spiritual advisor, Sister Helen Prejean (Susan Sarandon). The bond that develops between them is, paradoxically, both exceedingly complex and deceptively simple, and Robbins, with considerable help from his actors, captures it perfectly. *Dead Man Walking* could easily be manipulative or exploitative, but it's neither.

Sean Penn, in a remarkable performance, brings Matthew to life. There's never any doubt that Matthew was involved in the crime for which he is going to die, although he denies pulling the trigger. And *Dead Man Walking* doesn't attempt to portray him as a wrongly accused innocent man or someone misunderstood by society. He's a nasty piece of work — an arrogant, trash-talking racist. But, beneath all the bluster, he's lonely and frightened, as Helen discovers when she starts to probe.

Sarandon's Catholic nun is at the focal point of *Dead Man Walking* — and it's a performance to match her co-star's for aptness and intensity. Helen is the one we identify with, and the person around which all the moral and spiritual crises revolve. She is exposed to everyone's pain: Matthew's, his family's, and that of the victims' relatives. It's almost more than one woman can bear, but Helen is strong — strong enough to offer love to one of the most detestable human beings she has ever met.

Ultimately, the questions come back to capital punishment. They're all familiar. Is Matthew going to be executed because he was too poor to hire a fat-cat lawyer? Is there a moral difference when the State kills as opposed to an individual? Should justice be based on the "eye for an eye" edict or the one that says to "turn the other cheek"? Only in subtle details does it becomes clear that the director cannot condone the government taking a life.

I defy anyone to sit unaffected through *Dead Man Walking*. This is as powerful as motion pictures get, yet it doesn't descend into a valley of spiritual gloom. There are moments of comic relief, and, even if some of the humor is of the gallows variety, it keeps this 2-hour odyssey from becoming unbearably intense. Although this is only his second directorial outing, actor-turned-film maker Robbins has clearly mastered his craft. There's no sophomore jinx here.

Dead Man Walking refers to what the people on death row are called as they take that final walk towards their execution. It's ironic that a film with this title should be among the most vital, alive, and challenging cinema experiences of the year. **MUST SEE**

Decalogue [Poland, 1988]

Starring: (Part 1): Henryk Baranowski, Wojciech Klata, Maja Komorowska; (Part 2): Krystyna Janda, Aleksander Bardini; (Part 3): Daniel Olbrychski, Maria Pakulnis; (Part 4): Adrianna Biedrzynska, Janusz Gajos; (Part 5): Miroslaw Baka, Krzysztof Globisz; (Part 6): Grazyna Szapolowska, Olaf Lubaszenko; (Part 7): Anna Polony, Maja Barelkowska, Wladslaw Kowalski; (Part 8): Maria Koscialkowska, Teresa Marczewska; (Part 9): Ewa Blaszczyk, Piotr Machalica, Jan Jankowski; (Part 10): Jerzy Stuhr, Zbigniew Zamachowski Director: Krzysztof Kieslowski Screenplay: Krzysztof Kieslowski and Krzysztof Piesiewicz Running Time: 9:31 (in 10 parts) Rated: No MPAA Rating (Mature themes, violence) Theatrical Aspect Ratio: 1.33:1 In Polish with subtitles

Decalogue was initially produced as a series of 10 1-hour films for Polish television. Two of the episodes, parts 5 and 6, were expanded to full-length features released internationally under the titles of *A Short Film About Killing* and *A Short Film About Love*. Each segment of *Decalogue* ostensibly concentrates on one of the Ten Commandments.

Kieslowski first envisioned *Decalogue* as a project to give young Polish directors their first shots at film making. He and his writing partner, Krzysztof Piesiewicz (who also co-authored *No End*, *Veronique*, and *Three Colors*) scripted the episodes, intending for a different director to helm each one. However, when the screenplays were complete, Kieslowski realized they were too good to hand over to someone else. In the end, he directed all 10 — completing the entire series in under a year.

Anyone can make a movie about the Ten Commandments, but few such productions would share the subtlety and depth which characterize Kieslowski's vision. It isn't the subject matter per se that gives *Decalogue* its greatness — it's the manner in which the director handles his material. For part 5, those expecting to see a morality play about the evils of killing are in for a surprise. To be sure, this episode is about murder and its ramifications, but the issues examined are far more complex, and Kieslowski shuns absolutes of good and evil.

Each episode of *Decalogue* has a different tone. Part 1 starts out playful as we're introduced to a loving father and son. Part 2 is somber. And so on. Certainly, one of the many elements that makes *Decalogue* so powerful is that, among the dozens of primary actors, there are no inadequate performances. Every character is portrayed naturally, and each story unfolds without uneven acting creating a question of authenticity. For those familiar with other Kieslowski films, there are several recognizable faces. Zbigniew Zamachowski, who starred in *White*, plays a lead in part 10. Jerzy Stuhr, from *Camera Buff* and *White*, is also in the same segment. And Grazyna Szapolowska, Magda in part 6, also appeared in *No End*.

Throughout the history of film, there has been a select group of standout pictures — movies that, for technical or artistic reasons, have made an indelible imprint on viewers. Taken as one 10-hour exploration of the human experience, this is the product of a expert storyteller/filmmaker at the height of his craft, creating a masterwork the likes of which comes along only once in a great while. There is no other motion picture out there like *Decalogue*, which makes it more the pity how difficult it is to hunt down in North America. But, for those who take the trouble, the payoff is more than worth the effort. **MUST SEE**

The Dish [Australia, 2000]

Starring: Sam Neill, Kevin Harrington, Tom Long, Patrick Warburton, Genevieve Mooy Director: Rob Sitch Screenplay: Santo Cilauro, Tom Gleisner, Jane Kennedy, Rob Sitch Running Time: 1:37 Rated: PG-13 (Occasional profanity) Theatrical Aspect Ratio: 1.85:1

The Dish takes us back to the third week in July 1969, when all eyes were cast in the direction of our nearest celestial neighbor, where Neil Armstrong was about to take the most famous documented step in modern human history. July 20, 1969 was one of those rare days when most of humanity was focused on an event that had more to do with the triumph of the human spirit than with war, religion, or death. *The Dish* successfully transports us back in time to that slightly different era without resorting to the clichés that are often used to indicate a time shift to late '60s or early '70s.

Most movies made about the moon landing have a decidedly American viewpoint. *The Dish* is an exception, and its different vantage is one of its strongest assets. The film transpires in the rural Australian town of Parkes, where the largest radio telescope in the southern hemisphere is being "borrowed" by NASA to track Apollo 11 on its famous trip. This is a source of tremendous civic pride, despite the fact that the Parkes radio telescope is located in the middle of a sheep paddock.

The telescope is operated by Cliff Buxton (Sam Neill), the "dishmaster," a hard-working, knowledgeable man who lost some of the joy of life when his wife died the year before. He is joined by his two assistants, Mitch (Kevin Harrington) and Glenn (Tom Long), and a NASA representative, Al Burnett (Patrick Warburton). Together, these four are responsible for handling the operations that will allow Houston to keep in constant contact with the spacecraft and to allow the world to see Armstrong's historic space walk. Of course, there are difficulties — such as a power failure and an inconvenient wind storm — but nothing the intrepid team cannot handle.

With his quiet, unforced performance, Sam Neill towers over the production. His Cliff Buxton is a fully realized character — a man of great inner strength and integrity who occasionally shows a hint of sadness. The reason for this is explained, but not dwelt upon, and it never becomes the fuel for a silly or melodramatic moment. American actor Patrick Warburton is also a standout, managing to both embody and defy worldwide preconceptions about American arrogance. Finally, mention should be made of the job done by Tayler Kane, who, as the dish's security officer, provides a lion's share of the film's funniest moments.

The Dish is a comedy with a heart — a rare thing in the movies these days. And for those old enough to recall the moon landing, it will inevitably merge with personal memories. For those who think motion pictures have become a largely joyless affair, *The Dish* provides a pleasant counter-example. **RECOMMENDED**

Dolores Claiborne [2000]

Starring: Kathy Bates, Jennifer Jason Leigh, Christopher Plummer, David Strathairn Director: Taylor Hackford Screenplay: Tony Gilroy based on the book by Stephen King Running Time: 2:11 Rated: R (Mature themes, language) Theatrical Aspect Ratio: 2.35:1

Dolores Claiborne begins as a dark and dreary murder mystery set in the small town of Little Tall, Maine. The skies above this village are continually congested with clouds, the streets are slick with rain, and the sea is gray and angry. Yet this story, which starts out as an investigation of a suspicious death, soon takes on a more grim and disturbing tone. Memories crowd out the present as the narrative takes us back 18 years to expose the ugly roots of one family's dysfunction.

Two deaths lie at the center of *Dolores Claiborne* — Vera Donovan's (Judy Parfitt) in the present and Joe St. George's (David Strathairn) in the past. After Joe fell into a partially-concealed well during the total solar eclipse of 1975, his wife Dolores (Kathy Bates) was suspected, but never convicted, of murder. The death was eventually ruled as accidental, splotching the previously-perfect record of Detective John Mackey (Christopher Plummer). Now, Dolores stands accused of killing her invalid employer, and Mackey is determined to get a conviction.

Dolores' daughter Selena (Ellen Muth at age 13; Jennifer Jason Leigh at age 31), a reporter living in New York city, receives a fax of an article in a Bangor newspaper detailing her mother's suspected involvement in Vera's death. Haunted by her muddled recollections of her father's death, and driven by an unshakable conviction that her mother is guilty, she takes a brief leave-of-absence to go home. Once there, she is confronted not only by the unpleasantness of the present, but by the ghosts of the past.

The main characters, mother and daughter, are well-written and effectively portrayed. Dolores is a sad, lonely survivor who has, perhaps unjustly, endured a lifetime of misery. Secrets can be an oppressive burden, and Dolores has been worn down by them. Selena, on the other hand, has become an alcoholic and drug-abuser as the result of what she has repressed. Bates and Leigh are in peak form as they settle into the lonely isolation of their characters.

There's a lot to digest in *Dolores Claiborne*. The subtle visual effects, which mix digital animation and live-action, form an effective backdrop for a story teeming with emotional turmoil. With their unique method of delineating shifts in time, the flashbacks are invested with a degree of eerie immediacy. Although the forced ending weakens the climactic catharsis, it doesn't diminish the naked honesty, which forms the foundation of *Dolores Claiborne*.
RECOMMENDED

Donnie Brasco [1997]

Starring: Al Pacino, Johnny Depp, Michael Madsen, Bruno Kirby, James Russo, Anne Heche Director: Mike Newell Screenplay: Paul Attanasio based on the book *Donnie Brasco: My Undercover Life in the Mafia* by Joseph Pistone with Richard Woodley Running Time: 2:06 Rated: R (Profanity, violence, mature themes) Theatrical Aspect Ratio: 2.35:1

Donnie Brasco is based on the true story of FBI agent Joe Pistone (Johnny Depp), who went undercover and infiltrated the New York City mob during the late 1970s. Joe, who went by the name of "Donnie Brasco," played his role so effectively that he rose to extraordinary heights within the organization, holding a place alongside his mentor, Lefty (Al Pacino), in the inner circle of boss Sonny Black (Michael Mad-

sen). But, the more time he spent with members of the Mafia, the more like them he became. And, after a while, Joe could no longer tell where his true loyalties lay: to his wife (Anne Heche), family, and government, or to the wiseguys who had adopted him into their lifestyle.

Perhaps the most impressive thing that Newell has done with *Donnie Brasco* is to cull an atypically low-key and introspective performance from Al Pacino, an actor known for manic, scenery-chewing efforts. Lefty is a world-weary hit man with 26 kills under his belt and little to show for it. His dream is to buy a boat and sail far away from civilization, but he doesn't have the money or the gumption to chase that golden fantasy. Pacino presents Lefty as a tragic, and at times pathetic, character who earns our pity and understanding, if not our sympathy.

While not on Pacino's level, Johnny Depp is competent as the title character, a man who loses his perspective as he becomes seduced by the mobster's lifestyle. Depp lets us see the conflict within Joe as his friendship with Lefty grows into something real and as his wife and children become little more than distant images. Near the beginning of *Donnie Brasco*, Joe attempts to prevent a hit; by the end, he comes perilously close to taking part. If there are times when Joe's character doesn't seem whole, the blame lies more with the script's failure to provide the needed background or motivation than with Depp's performance.

Although *Donnie Brasco* is set against a backdrop of crime and violence, it, like many better gangster films, is really about family and relationships. Lefty and Joe have a surrogate father/son bond that gradually supersedes all other attachments in either of their lives. It's because *Donnie Brasco* focuses on characters and relationships that it makes for compelling viewing.

Although the film contains many of the usual mob clichés and stock secondary characters, these don't detract much from the viewer's enjoyment. The film has all the right little touches to be believable, such as Lefty's fascinating lesson to his protégé about how to dress, act, and speak to be respected in wiseguy circles. *Donnie Brasco* takes us into a world that the movies frequently open to us, but somehow this trip seems more real and less glamorized than most. The result is a satisfying film-going experience.
RECOMMENDED

Down In the Delta [1998]

Starring: **Alfre Woodard, Al Freeman Jr., Mary Alice, Esther Rolle, Loretta Devine, Wesley Snipes** Director: **Maya Angelou**
Screenplay: **Myron Goble** Running Time: **1:51** Rated: **PG-13 (Profanity, drug-related material)** Theatrical Aspect Ratio: **1.85:1**

Down in the Delta opens in Chicago, where one three-generation family is falling apart, despite the best efforts of the matriarch, Rosa Lynn (Mary Alice), to hold it together. Her daughter, Loretta (Alfre Woodard), is hooked on drugs and booze. Her grandson, Thomas (Mpho Koaho), makes money on the streets by selling polaroids to tourists for $5, and her granddaughter, Tracy (Kulani Hassan), is autistic. As a mother, Loretta is unfit. Her idea of keeping little Tracy happy is to fill her bottle with cola, and she's more interested in getting her next drink than in caring what her children are doing. Recognizing that her family's current path leads inevitably to disaster, Rosa Lynn calls her brother-in-law, Earl (Al Freeman Jr.), and arranges for Loretta and her children to spend a summer at his place on the Mississippi Delta. Loretta agrees to go, albeit reluctantly, and, with Thomas and Tracy in tow, she heads south. And, while the initial transition is difficult, she eventually finds herself, and connects with her family.

Down in the Delta suffers from some narrative hiccups. The most obvious of these is the quickness of Loretta's transformation from down-and-out loser to responsible mother and entrepreneur. The resolution is also a little too facile to be entirely believable. Fortunately, however, while Myron Goble's script may not be airtight, Angelou's cast is consistently reliable. Alfre Woodard becomes Loretta — there's not a moment when we doubt this performance. As the stubborn-but-wise uncle we all wish we had, Al Freeman Jr. is a commanding presence.

Down in the Delta doesn't just deal with healing through a change in locale, but regeneration through coming to grips with the past. As Loretta learns the history of "Nathan" (the name of a family heirloom — a candlestick holder passed down through the family from the time of slavery), she begins to understand that, by wasting her life, she is demeaning the sacrifices of those who came before her.

Maya Angelou is one of the most influential and powerful author/poets of the second half of the 20th century and this is her first stint as a director. While there's nothing groundbreaking in her approach, she does a highly credible job, and shows particular promise in handling actors.

Down in the Delta does not purport to offer an answer to the problem of inner city social decay. But, while the specifics of the film's solution are confined to this story, Angelou makes it clear that all healing must begin with self-respect, close-knit family connections, and an appreciation of personal history. Those are the life lessons Loretta must learn before she can move on, and, through her growth and development, Angelou teaches us without ever seeming preachy or didactic. With its rich characters and flawless performances, *Down in the Delta* is a fully-satisfying emotional experience that offers all we might expect from an individual of Angelou's accomplishments. **HIGHLY RECOMMENDED**

The Dreamlife of Angels (La Vie Rêvée des Anges) [France, 1998]

Starring: **Élodie Bouchez, Natacha Régnier, Grégoire Colin, Jo Prestia, Patrick Mercado** Director: **Erick Zonca** Screenplay: **Erick Zonca & Roger Bohbot** Running Time: **1:53** Rated: **NC-17 (Sex, nudity, drugs)** Theatrical Aspect Ratio: **1.66:1** In French with subtitles

Those who see *The Dreamlife of Angels*, the powerful 1998 feature from director Erick Zonca, will immediately notice the irony of the title. Not only is the film about reality of the grittiest sort, but the two main characters, Isa (Élodie Bouchez) and Marie (Natacha Régnier), are as earthy and non-angelic as they come. It isn't difficult to describe the picture's narrative thrust. *The Dreamlife of Angels* focuses on the intense friendship between two 20-something girls in Lille, France. Both are poor and have trouble holding a steady job, but that's where the similarities end. Personality-wise, they're polar opposites. Dark-haired Isa is a tempestuous free-spirit — an outgoing girl with a big heart and bigger smile. Marie, on the other hand, is withdrawn and emotionally cloistered. The flames of their friendship quickly die out, leaving behind smoldering embers and growing bitterness. *The Dreamlife of Angels* can be considered an autopsy of a friendship — a chronicle of its development from beginning to end.

The two live together in a flat that Marie is watching for a mother and daughter who are in the hospital following a car accident. Isa finds the girl's diary, and, in one of the movie's more interesting subplots, pays a visit to the hospital. She learns that the girl, Sandrine, is in a coma and that her mother has died. Thereafter, Isa becomes a regular visitor, spending hours reading to the unconscious girl and holding her hand. It's a uniquely touching relationship that fundamentally alters Isa's perception of life. But, as her one-way emotional bond with Sandrine strengthens, her relationship with Marie starts to disintegrate.

Zonca keeps the situations genuine and the characters authentic. He never takes more than a minimal dramatic license, allowing events to transpire in much the same way they might in the real world. Isa and Marie's friendship is developed with great care and attention to detail. As is almost always true of French films, the performances are superlative. Both Élodie Bouchez and Natacha Régnier are in fine form, giving life and personality to Isa and Marie. Their chemistry is perfect for the material. International star Grégoire Colin is the perfect choice for the hard-hearted Lothario who captures, then breaks, Marie's heart. Jo Prestia and Patrick Mercado have supporting roles as a pair of leather-jacketed bouncers who are attracted to the girls.

This is a basic yet sublime motion picture. The greatness of this movie lies in its essential simplicity. Zonca has crafted a pair of individuals so well rounded and effectively defined that we can relate to them on a personal basis. We aren't just watching Isa and Marie endure the tiny triumphs and hardships of their lives; we're experiencing those ups and downs alongside them. HIGHLY RECOMMENDED

Drumline [2002]
Starring: Nick Cannon, Zoe Saldana, Orlando Jones, Leonard Roberts Director: Charles Stone III Screenplay: Tina Gordon Chism and Shawn Schepps Running Time: 1:58 Rated: PG-13 (Profanity, sexual innuendo) Theatrical Aspect Ratio: 2.35:1

Drumline introduces viewers to the competitive world of collegiate marching bands, for whom "halftime is game time." Devon (Nick Cannon) is a highly sought-after drummer who is attending Atlanta A&T on a full band scholarship. Devon is more cocky than the average freshman, wooing Laila (Zoe Saldana), an upperclass philosophy major with a passion for dance, and openly feuding with his section leader, Sean (Leonard Roberts). He also believes that the numbers chosen by the band leader, Dr. Lee (Orlando Jones), are outmoded and boring. His tendency towards flamboyancy makes him a controversial individual, but, when he is unable to repress his need for individual glory and live by Dr. Lee's motto of "one band, one sound," he finds himself on the sidelines heading into the BET Big Southern Classic band championship against A&T's arch-rival, Morris Brown University.

Drumline is a star vehicle for Nickelodeon staple Nick Cannon, who is making his first significant foray onto the big screen. Cannon carries himself well, coming across as self-confident and charismatic, without taking things to the level that would make him abrasive. He's more Will Smith than Martin Lawrence. If he chooses his roles wisely, there's no reason he can't find the same kind of mainstream success achieved by Smith. During the course of *Drumline*, he shows an affinity for both light drama and restrained comedy, having no difficulty with scenes that require pathos or intensity.

The soundtrack for *Drumline* — undoubtedly one of the film's selling points — is cross-generational, with the band playing more than just traditional marching tunes. But those performances are just color. At *Drumline*'s heart are the characters and the behind-the-scenes politicking that goes on whenever money is involved. (The leader of Morris Brown's band is eager to pull Devon away from Atlanta A&T — not only because he's a good drummer, but because of the insider information he can provide about what Dr. Lee is planning for the BET.) Director Charles Stone never strays too far from the familiar, but there are nice little twists that keep the production fresh. (Yes, Devon and Sean's relationship softens, but Dr. Lee never turns into Mr. Chips, and, in fact, he is forced to compromise his high values in order to keep his job.) Coming in the midst of so many high-profile, end-of-the-year motion picture, *Drumline* is a pleasant, and very welcome, surprise.
RECOMMENDED

East Is East [United Kingdom, 1999]
Starring: Om Puri, Linda Bassett, Jimi Mistry, Raji James, Archie Panjab Director: Damien O'Donnell Screenplay: Ayub Khan-Din, based on his play Running Time: 1:36 Rated: R (Profanity, violence, artistic depictions of male & female genitalia) Theatrical Aspect Ratio: 1.85:1

East Is East stars the great Om Puri in another riveting performance. Here, he plays George Khan, a Pakistani immigrant to Salford, Manchester. The year is 1971 and, back in his native country, a war is raging with India. Thousands of miles away, George is trying to instill Pakistani traditions in his 6 sons and 1 daughter — a task made difficult by their immersion in English culture and by the fact that their mother (George's second wife), Ella (Linda Bassett), is British. In fact, even though he won't admit it (or perhaps he doesn't realize it), George is a hypocrite. Twenty-five years ago, he left Pakistan to come to England to make his fortune. Instead of bringing his first wife with him, he left her behind and married Ella. Now, the couple operates "George's English Chippy" together. Despite his own poor example, George is determined to make his children into good Pakistanis, even if it's physically painful. The problem is that they see themselves as English and are angered by their father's restrictions.

When George isn't looking, his kids dabble in Catholicism, eat bacon and sausages, and (in the cases of the older boys) fool around with white girls. His daughter, Meena (Archie Panjabi) is a tomboy who likes playing soccer. College student Saleem (Chris Bisson) pretends to be studying engineering when he's actually an art major. Only one of the middle children, Maneer (Emil Marwa), holds Islam in high regard. When Nazir (Ian Aspinall), the eldest son, rejects an arranged marriage at the altar, his father disowns him. But, despite that disaster, George moves forward with plans to marry off Tariq (Jimi Mistry) and Abdul (Raji James) to docile, homely Pakistani girls. Those plans provoke a conflict that threatens the family's already shaky stability.

East Is East is about cultural differences and the difficulties of assimilation. It's about the dangers of losing one's unique identity when leaving behind one country for another. Above all, however, it's about family dynamics, and how children inevitably rebel against their parents' beliefs and traditions.

The most powerful performance belongs to Om Puri, although his character, George, is little more than a one-dimensional monster. As impressive is Linda Bassett, the only actor from the stage play to appear in the film. Bassett captures her character's essential humanity — at times playful, at times shaken, and at times resolute. She loves her husband and children and is torn by the potential of having to side with one against the other.

East Is East ponders a lot of questions, and, as with all well made motion pictures, doesn't offer simple, cut-and-dried answers for any of them. When the movie draws to a close, there is a conclusion, but it's relatively open-ended. In cinematic terms, *East Is East* offers a more satisfying meal than one might expect to get at George's English Chippy. **RECOMMENDED**

Eat Drink Man Woman [Taiwan, 1994]

Starring: Sihung Lung, Kuei-Mei-Yang, Chien-Lien Wu, Yu-Wen Wang, Winston Chao Director: Ang Lee Screenplay: Ang Lee, James Schamus, and Hui-Ling Wang Running Time: 2:04 Rated: No MPAA Rating (Mature themes) In Mandarin with subtitles

Who said foreign films can't be fun? Ang Lee's followup to *The Wedding Banquet* is a delicious examination of the relationship between aging Chinese master chef Tao Chu (Sihung Lung) and his 3 daughters. The oldest, Jia-Jen (Kuei-Mei-Yang), is an unmarried school teacher in her late 20s. The middle daughter, Jia-Chen (Chien-Lien Wu), is a thriving corporate airline executive whose career comes before all else. The youngest, Jia-Ning (Yu-Wen Wang), is a 20-year-old romantic who works at a Wendy's fast food joint.

Eat Drink Man Woman is an accomplished motion picture. The comedy is spontaneous and relaxed, the drama is finely-tuned, and the plot is seasoned with unexpected little twists. The script delights in occasional forays just beyond the typical bounds of a screenplay.

Though filmed entirely in Taiwan, the themes of *Eat Drink Man Woman* are universal. The problems faced by the Chu family happen all around the world, and the difficulty of communicating across the generation gap is something almost everyone has experienced at one time or another. Love, especially that of Chu for his daughters, often goes unspoken, for to express emotion is to admit vulnerability.

With an ease that marks the true craftsman, Ang Lee develops a rapport between his characters and the audience. These people have a richness, texture, and depth that no stereotype could hope to match. The perfectly-proportioned measures of comedy and drama emerge through character interaction, not as a result of contrived situations and silly one-liners.

Food is as much a backdrop as a recurring symbol. Chu's failing taste buds parallel his loss for the zest for life. Jia-Chen's love of cooking harkens back to a frustrated childhood desire, and Jia-Ning's work at a Wendy's makes a statement about the infusion of Western culture into modern-day China. Nevertheless, *Eat Drink Man Woman* could perhaps be frustrating to any who view it on an empty stomach.

Eat Drink Man Woman is basted in its own wonderfully seasoned juices. Chu may have lost his taste, but writer/director Ang Lee has definitely not. A treat for those not scared off by subtitles, this movie provides one of the year's most sincere views of family dynamics. Dealing with subjects that could easily have emerged half-baked, Lee instead applies his talent and comes up with a dish cooked to perfection. **HIGHLY RECOMMENDED**

Elizabeth [United Kingdom, 1998]
Starring: Cate Blanchett, Geoffrey Rush, Christopher Eccleston, Joseph Fiennes, Richard Attenborough, Fanny Ardant Director: Shekhar Kapur Screenplay: Michael Hirst Running Time: 2:01 Rated: R (Violence, sex, nudity) Theatrical Aspect Ratio: 1.85:1

In 1554, the Catholic Queen Mary (Kathy Burke), the daughter of Henry VIII, sat on the throne. Frightened that her younger half-sister, Elizabeth (Cate Blanchett), is involved in a plot to usurp her crown, Mary has her heir thrown into the Tower of London. Elizabeth survives the ordeal and, upon Mary's death, assumes the throne. Immediately, she is confronted by a legion of problems: a dry treasury, a weak army, the need to marry to secure the blood line, and a growing threat from Mary of Guise (Fanny Ardant), who is massing troops to move against England. There are also dangers within Elizabeth's court, the most notable of which comes from the dangerous Duke of Norfolk (Christopher Eccleston), who wants her dead. And, because Elizabeth is a Protestant, Pope Pius V (John Gielgud) declares her a heretic and issues a proclamation releasing all English Catholics from following her. To help her in her struggles, Elizabeth has 3 strong allies: the ever-faithful William Cecil (Richard Attenborough), the wily and dangerous Francis Walsingham (Geoffrey Rush), and the love of her life, Lord Robert Dudley (Joseph Fiennes).

From a general perspective, *Elizabeth* offers a reasonably accurate overview of the 16th century monarch's character and life. When it comes to specifics, however, the film is sorely lacking. Much of what happens in *Elizabeth* did not happen that way, and, if the plot occasionally seems unnecessarily convoluted and confusing, it's understandable, since writer Michael Hirst has chosen to compress many of the key events of Elizabeth's lengthy reign into a 5-year period. There are also several outright distortions of the historical record. In reality, for example, Mary of Guise's fate was significantly different than what the film depicts. Ultimately, however, all of this is, if not irrelevant, then inconsequential. Those who want a factual account of Elizabeth's reign can read a history book; *Elizabeth* does what it sets out to do: provide a solidly entertaining 2 hours.

One of the primary reasons *Elizabeth* works is because of the superlative performance of Cate Blanchett. Not only does Blanchett look like Elizabeth, but she acts the part of a fiery, determined young woman riddled by the uncertainty of a precarious position. She breathes life into the revered historical figure, transforming her from an old picture on an encyclopedia page to a flesh-and-blood individual whom an audience can root for and care about.

In addition to its factual inaccuracies, *Elizabeth* possesses a few weaknesses. The movie's editing is uneven, a situation that can result in occasional bouts of confusion when trying to unravel the Byzantine plotting going on at court, and the ending seems a little too pat. RECOMMENDED

The Emperor's Club [2002]
Starring: Kevin Kline, Emile Hirsch, Embeth Davidtz Director: Michael Hoffman Screenplay: Neil Tolkin, based on the short story "The Palace Thief" by Ethan Canin Running Time: 1:49 Rated: PG-13 (Profanity, sexual situations) Theatrical Aspect Ratio: 1.85:1

The Emperor's Club starts out predictably, taking us back in time 25 years and introducing us to the reliable, enthusiastic, ethically unimpeachable Mr. William Hundert (Kevin Kline, in fine form), who educates the students at St. Benedict's School for Boys about the Greeks and the Romans while providing life lessons on the side. Enter the Troublemaker, Sedgewick Bell (Emile Hirsch), a stereotypical smart kid with a bad attitude. Mr. Hundert makes it his business to mold Sedgewick into the kind of person who realizes his potential and thereby makes a difference.

So far, so good. All of this is standard material culled from Screenwriting 101. But then comes the twist. Mr. Hundert fails with his pet project, and in a pretty big way. At first, it looks like Sedgewick has turned a corner, but then he shows his true colors. He falls from grace, backsliding all the way to the starting line. To exacerbate matters, Mr. Hundert has compromised his own ethics in his zeal to reform Sedgewick. And things get worse when we catch up with the characters in the modern time period. Mr. Hundert still believes in Sedgewick, even after so many disappointments, but the up-and-coming politician is as much a cheater and a manipulator as ever.

Ultimately, *The Emperor's Club* doesn't quite have the guts to follow this story to its natural, cynical conclusion. There are some feel-good elements thrown in that allow the movie to end on an upbeat note. The results of one scene convince Mr. Hundert that his career as an educator should be judged not by one failure, but by numerous successes. Nevertheless, the cheerful sheen can't obscure the fact that *The Emperor's Club* isn't business as usual for this sort of picture. It dares to be a little different, and that shading is what makes it worthwhile.

The Emperor's Club doesn't have a lot of heft. It's a relatively light-weight story that is carried more by the well-defined characters than by plot developments. In the end, we get a sense that it has all been worthwhile, not only for Mr. Hundert, but for those of us sitting in the audience. It helps, of course, that the movie confounds our expectations yet still delivers a positive message. There's still quite a bit of the essence of *Dead Poets Society* in *The Emperor's Club*. Thankfully, however, the level of schmaltz and manipulation has been greatly reduced. **RECOMMENDED**

The Emperor's New Clothes [Germany/Italy/United Kingdom, 2001]

Starring: Ian Holm, Iben Hjejle, Tim McInnerny, Tom Watson, Nigel Terry Director: Alan Taylor Screenplay: Kevin Molony, Alan Taylor, Herbie Wave, based on "The Death of Napoleon" by Simon Leys Running Time: 1:45 Rated: PG Theatrical Aspect Ratio: 1.85:1

According to the history books, Napoleon Bonaparte died in May 1821 on the island of St. Helena. According to Alan Taylor's *The Emperor's New Clothes*, it wasn't Napoleon who ended his days on St. Helena, but an imposter. Napoleon had previously escaped his captors and returned to France, where the news of his death made it difficult for him to be accepted as anything other than a melon seller with delusions of grandeur. Thus, Napoleon, once the most powerful man in the world, was forced to live as a commoner, and, in the process, understand that some things in life are more satisfying the power.

The movie begins on St. Helena, the island to which Napoleon (Ian Holm) was exiled following his defeat at Waterloo. He has a plan to escape — his aides have smuggled a lookalike, Eugene Lenormand, to the island. Eugene and Napoleon will switch places and he will make his way to Paris, pretending to be a deck hand. Once he is there, Eugene will announce himself to be a fraud, Napoleon will declare himself, and the people will rise up for their emperor. But, once Napoleon has returned home, he discovers that fate has conspired against him. Eugene likes playing the part of the emperor too much, and is unwilling to relinquish the fruits of the role. So Napoleon must live the life of a commoner, and, in the process, he has the good fortune to fall in love with a peasant woman, Pumpkin (Iben Hjejle), who does not believe that Eugene is *the* Napoleon, but will accept him as *her* Napoleon.

The Emperor's New Clothes is a lighthearted, feel-good film that embraces the time-honored truth that the most powerful thing in life is love. Granted, the real Napoleon never would have settled down to live with a common woman, but *this* Napoleon does, and, in the doing so gives us the moral of this story — acceptance of the changing world and our place in it is the only way to keep time from passing us by. The film also toys with issues of identity.

Playing the dual role of Napoleon as Eugene and Eugene as Napoleon, Ian Holm turns in another fine performance. Quirks in mannerisms and body language easily differentiate the two individuals. This is actually the third time Holm has played Napoleon. He previously essayed the part in a mid-1970s mini-series called "Napoleon and Love," then again in *Time Bandits*. Iben Hjejle is affable as the unaffected Pumpkin, the woman who teaches Napoleon things he never knew about life when he was a world leader.

The film's director is Alan Taylor, whose primary experience is in television. Taylor's approach to this material — mixing occasional humor with undemanding drama — works well enough that we don't care about the logical inconsistencies and plot holes. To that end, *The Emperor's New Clothes* ends up as a pleasant diversion. **RECOMMENDED**

The End of the Affair [United States/United Kingdom, 1999]

Starring: Ralph Fiennes, Julianne Moore, Stephen Rea, Ian Hart, Sam Bould, Jason Isaacs Director: Neil Jordan Screenplay: Neil Jordan, based on the novel by Graham Greene Running Time: 1:44 Rated: R (Sex, nudity) Theatrical Aspect Ratio: 1.85:1

The End of the Affair takes place during the days and months following World War II. We meet the not-so-happily married couple of Sarah (Julienne Moore) and Henry Miles (Stephen Rea). Henry, a workaholic, admits to not having been much of a husband and never having been a true lover to his wife. During the summer of 1939, novelist Maurice Bendrix (Ralph Fiennes) and Sarah met and began a torrid affair. They professed undying love for one another, and, while Henry worked long hours on the war effort, Maurice and Sarah spent the time in Maurice's flat. But, on a night when Maurice was seriously wounded in a German air raid, the relationship abruptly ended. When Sarah left him, he was bitter and angry, and all of his love turned to rage and hatred. Sarah, on the other hand, believed in a pure love — a kind that would endure to her dying day, even if circumstances prevented her from ever seeing Maurice again.

Several years after the end of the affair, Maurice has a chance meeting with Henry, who confesses to his old friend that he believes Sarah is being unfaithful. The ugly specter of jealousy rears its head for Maurice — even though he has not seen Sarah in years, he cannot bear the thought of her being with someone else. Pretending to act on Henry's behalf, he hires a private investigator (Ian Hart) to follow Sarah and learn the identity of her new lover.

The End of the Affair is more satisfying on an intellectual level than it is on an emotional one. In addition to probing into the depth of the spiritual and physical components of love, Jordan explores the ways in which the vagaries of fate and/or the Hand of God shape people's destinies. In an attempt to maintain a balance between Sarah and Maurice's often contradictory perspectives, Jordan allows certain key scenes to be repeated twice — once from Sarah's point-of-view (using her words in a voiceover) and once from Maurice's (employing his words).

The End of the Affair is based on a semi-autobiographical novel by Graham Greene. Even with its flaws, it still possesses the quiet power to involve the viewer in a simple tale that is likely to invoke his or her own feelings about love, fate, and God.
RECOMMENDED

The English Patient [1996]
Starring: Ralph Fiennes, Kristin Scott Thomas, Juliette Binoche, Willem Dafoe, Colin Firth, Naveen Andrews Director: Anthony Minghella Screenplay: Anthony Minghella based on the novel by Michael Ondaatje Running Time: 2:40 Rated: R (Sex, nudity, violence, profanity) Theatrical Aspect Ratio: 1.85:1

For those who have forgotten the depth of romance and passion that the movies are capable of conveying, Anthony Minghella's *The English Patient* can remedy the situation. This well-crafted story, brought to the screen with great care by British playwright and director Anthony Minghella (*Truly, Madly, Deeply*) and based on the prize-winning novel by Michael Ondaatje, serves up the love of Almasy (Ralph Fiennes) and Katharine (Kristin Scott Thomas) in a way that is simultaneously epic and intimate.

The opening sequence, which takes place during World War II, shows a British plane being shot down over the North African desert. The pilot, a Hungarian count named Laszlo Almasy, is badly burned in the ensuing crash. Years later, in 1944 Italy, we meet him again. Although his outward injuries have healed, leaving his features scarred beyond recognition, he is dying. He has also supposedly lost his memory. Hana (Juliette Binoche), the Canadian nurse who cares for

him, takes him to an isolated, abandoned church to allow him to die in peace. There, injecting him with morphine and reading to him from his beloved volume of Herodotus, Hana seeks to stimulate his memories. Meanwhile, others arrive at the church — a mysterious, crippled war veteran named Caravaggio (Willem Dafoe), and a pair of bomb experts, the British Sgt. Hardy (Kevin Whately) and his Sikh superior, Kip (Naveen Andrews), who becomes Hana's lover.

Eventually, through dreams and waking flashbacks, Almasy's memories come flooding back, although Caravaggio asserts that he hasn't really forgotten anything — he just *wants* to forget. The story then flip-flops between the present and a period during the late-'30s and early-'40s, when Almasy is part of a British map-making effort surveying the Sahara. It's then that he meets Katharine Clifton, the wife of a good-natured pilot (Colin Firth) who is helping with the project. Almasy and Katharine fall for each other, and the stage is set for a classic exploration of love and betrayal set against the dangerous background of Nazi aggression.

Ralph Fiennes gives us an Almasy who seems loosely based on *Casablanca*'s Rick — strong and silent until the right woman releases all of his pent-up passion. Kristen Scott Thomas is luminous as Katharine, effortlessly conveying to the audience the energy and zest for life that Almasy finds irresistible. Together, these two are hotter than the desert heat that simmers around them.

The English Patient is the sort of intelligent, epic love story that seems so rare these days. There's something about this film that lingers long after the end credits have rolled — a desire to re-experience all the feelings generated by the movie, perhaps. One of the reasons for *The English Patient*'s power is that it strikes universal chords. **HIGHLY RECOMMENDED**

Ethan Frome [1993]
Starring: Liam Neeson, Patricia Arquette, Joan Allen Director: John Madden Screenplay: Richard Nelson (based on the novel by Edith Wharton) Running Time: 1:43 Rated: PG (Mature themes)

When we first meet Ethan Frome (Liam Neeson), he is a broken man hobbling around town. The new preacher takes an interest in him and soon learns the tragic tale of Frome's life. Years ago, as a younger and healthier man, Ethan married Zeena (Joan Allen), perhaps mistakenly, as "compensation" for her giving up part of her life to nurse Ethan's mother. Zeena, however, is a sickly woman who becomes susceptible to almost every kind of illness. When she proves unable to adequately keep house, she calls on a poor cousin, Mattie (Patricia Arquette), to come to help. What Zeena cannot foresee is the attraction that develops during the course of a year between her husband and Mattie.

Based on Edith Wharton's novel, the plot contains elements of many genres — mystery, drama, tragedy, and romance, none of which are overplayed. One strength of *Ethan Frome* comes from its essential simplicity. There are no convoluted subplots to muddy the waters. Given the opportunity to focus on 3 people living one story, the viewer quickly learns who these characters are and what's going on.

The greatest asset of *Ethan Frome,* however, and the most crucial to successfully transferring the story from the written page to the screen, is the acting. Liam Neeson is entirely convincing in this role. Everything about him, from his mimicking of the injured man's walk to the pained facial expressions in close-ups, shows how in touch he is with the role. Neeson took a serious reduction in pay in order to play the title character.

Although free from profanity, nudity, and overt sex, this is not a movie for children. *Ethan Frome* tells a powerful, ultimately affecting tale of passion, loss, and consequences — themes that form the core of the so-called "human experience." The material is adult in nature because maturity is needed for the viewer to become immersed in the slow, deliberate magic woven by director John Madden and his superlative cast. **RECOMMENDED**

Evelyn [Ireland, 2001]

Starring: Pierce Brosnan, Aidan Quinn, Julianna Margulies, Stephen Rea Director: Bruce Beresford Screenplay: Paul Pender Running Time: 1:34 Rated: PG-13 (Mature themes, profanity) Theatrical Aspect Ratio: 2.35:1

Evelyn is a shamelessly uplifting motion picture that attains its feel-good status by forging a deep emotional connection between the undertrodden protagonist and the audience. The bulk of the film transpires during 1954 in Dublin, and concerns a court case that resulted in sweeping changes being made to Irish custody laws. *Evelyn* bears the "based on a true story" label, but, considering the flow of the narrative, my guess is that only the bare-bones facts remain. I don't mind when a screenwriter takes a fair amount of artistic license with the historical record,

and the strength of Paul Pender's script argues that he and Beresford made the right choices.

Desmond Doyle (Pierce Brosnan) is an average working-class Irishman, who happens to be out of work at the moment because of an employment shortage. His wife chooses this moment to run off with her wealthy lover, leaving Desmond alone to support his two young sons and his only daughter, Evelyn (Sophie Vavasseur). However, because Desmond has no job, the courts take his children away from him, placing his sons in a Catholic Boys' Home and Evelyn in a convent. Eventually, Desmond rights his financial situation, but discovers that he cannot regain custody of his children without his wife's consent — and she is nowhere to be found. So he rounds up a legal team comprised of 3 local lawyers (Aidan Quinn, Stephen Rea, and Alan Bates) with the intention of fighting the church and the government. With the support of those 3 men and a local woman, Bernadette (Julianna Margulies), he goes to battle to retrieve Evelyn and her brothers. (There is a romantic rivalry between Quinn's character and Desmond for Bernadette. Fortunately, the contest is friendly and free of the usual bickering and squabbling that often accompanies this kind of subplot.)

The film's root theme — a father's love for his children — is a proven cinematic favorite, and Beresford develops it perfectly. *Evelyn* offers plenty of light-hearted humor and gently manipulative melodrama, but the climactic moment seems to come from the heart. The performances of Brosnan and Vavasseur are on the mark, and the tactic of using a sports commentator to provide a running "play-by-play" of the courtroom action is a nice twist. It's easy to view this kind of movie with cynicism, but, as long as you're not too jaded, the film's ample good will should draw you in. I believe that virtually everyone who sees this motion picture will enjoy it. **RECOMMENDED**

Eve's Bayou [1997]

Starring: Samuel L. Jackson, Lynn Whitfield, Jurnee Smollett, Meagan Good Director: Kasi Lemmons Screenplay: Kasi Lemmons Running Time: 1:49 Rated: R (Profanity, sex, mature themes) Theatrical Aspect Ratio: 1.85:1

Eve's Bayou takes us to the Tennessee Williams country of the deep south and introduces us to the rarest of motion picture institutions: an affluent black family. Ultimately, however, this film is not about skin color, but about the deeply-rooted bonds that join women together, which not even the most tragic of mistakes can obliterate. The setting — a small town in Louisiana during the 1950s — serves its purpose, but the themes broached by the writer/director are anything but parochial in nature.

The focus of the film is on the 5-member Batiste family. There's Louis (Samuel L. Jackson), a prominent and respected doctor; Roz (Lynn Whitfield), the beautiful, elegant mother of a son and two daughters; and their children — 14-year-old Cisely (Meagan Good), 10-year-old Eve (Jurnee Smollett), and 9-year-old Poe (Jake Smollett). Members of the extended family, particularly Louis' mother (Ethel Ayler) and sister, Mozelle (Debbi Morgan), are never far away. On the surface, Louis is the perfect husband and father, but he doesn't pay much attention to his marriage vows. When his daughter Eve catches him in the act, the issue becomes a festering sore in the family's stability. The situation is further exacerbated when Cisely's near-worshipful affection for her father threatens to cross a forbidden barrier.

Louis pays both an emotional and a tangible price for his many affairs. Cisely's clouding of the truth has its own unfortunate result. And an ill-considered yet passionate decision on Eve's part has devastating ramifications. The film also makes a point of showing that everything is not as it seems, especially in the tangled web of family relationships.

The strongest element of *Eve's Bayou* is the character interaction. Every member of the family (except young Poe) is developed into a unique individual, and all of the relationships are well-defined. What family doesn't go through an upheaval when secrets come into the open? The low-key plot, with its elements of voodoo and spiritual sight, allows us to the opportunity to get to know the Batistes. Lemmons' fine writing is complimented by a series of strong performances. Samuel L. Jackson is as solid as ever in a role that requires a less flamboyant portrayal than we have become accustomed to. Lynn Whitfield radiates cool beauty while Debbi Morgan emanates sensual heat. Jurnee Smollett and Meagan Good, the young actors playing Eve and Cisely, are both believable as sisters with close ties and hidden jealousies.

A subtle picture that treads a delicate line between drama and psychological thriller, *Eve's Bayou* is refreshing. Rather than perpetuating racial stereotypes, *Eve's Bayou* defies them, creating several well-rounded characters and placing them in a deceptively complex story that builds to a forceful conclu-sion. It's a movie like no other on the market today, and deserves to find its audience. **RECOMMENDED**

Exotica [Canada, 1994]

Starring: Bruce Greenwood, Mia Kirshner, Elias Koteas, Don McKellar, Arsinee Khanijian, Sarah Polley Director: Atom Egoyan Screenplay: Atom Egoyan Running Time: 1:43 Rated: R (Sex, nudity, language, mature themes) Theatrical Aspect Ratio: 1.85:1

The Exotica is a strip club in Toronto, where men go to watch, but not touch, a variety of unclothed women who strut their stuff to the pulsing sounds of a rich and varied soundtrack. Christina (Mia Kirshner) is a sultry brunette who comes on stage in a school girl costume and is introduced by the deejay Eric (Elias Koteas) as a "sassy bit of jailbait." Her gyrations as she unbuttons her white blouse give the illusion of corrupted innocence — a fantasy with its basis in reality. Mia Kirshner, with her combination of sensuality and thinly-veiled pain, arrests the viewer's attention.

One of the club's regulars is Francis (Bruce Greenwood), a lonely government auditor who spends hours paying out money for Christina to dance privately for him. The bond between these two is more profound than that of a normal dancer and client. When Francis utters his refrain of "How could anyone hurt you?" to Christina, we're not aware of all the layers inherent in his words.

Paralleling Francis' story is that of Thomas (Don McKellar), a gay pet shop owner who runs a lucrative smuggling operation. Currently, his business is being investigated by Francis, and this forms the narrative link by which everything is eventually tied together. Thomas is the shy, nerdy sort who doesn't know how to go about picking up men, until fate deals him a pair of opera tickets and a means by which to find a seemingly-limitless supply of partners. But for Thomas, filling that aching void of the soul involves paying a hefty material price.

On the surface, *Exotica* might seem to be about sex and lust. Nothing could be further from the truth. Those elements are a slick sheen of polish over the real core. While it's true that strip joints normally reek of excess, Egoyan's story seeks a more fundamental emotional level. This film is driven by the grief and isolation of the characters. The interpersonal connections made in *Exotica* are often obscure, and the reasons underlying otherwise-inexplicable actions are complex.

Everyone deals differently with loss, but Francis' problem is that he can't accept the tragedy which has defined his life. The effects are too devastating, so he huddles behind a curtain of illusion spun by Christina, trying to reduce his crushing despair to something more bearable. It's easy to mistake Francis for a dirty-minded middle-aged voyeur until you begin to understand what *Exotica* is saying. And it's not until the final credits roll that the last word of that litany is spoken. Very little about this picture is either predictable or conventional.

As movies go, this one is painful — painful because it exposes so much truth. *Exotica* becomes a journey of self-discovery. As the mysteries underlying the actions of Francis, Christina, Eric, and Thomas are slowly unwrapped, we learn as much about ourselves as we do about Egoyan's characters. When any motion picture succeeds at that, it deserves recognition as nothing less than a profound cinematic experience. MUST SEE

The Family Man [2000]

Starring: Nicolas Cage, Tea Leoni, Jeremy Piven, Don Cheadle, Harve Presnell Director: Brett Ratner Screenplay: David Diamond & David Weissman Running Time: 2:02 Rated: PG-13 (Nudity, sexual situations, profanity) Theatrical Aspect Ratio: 1.85:1

The Family Man proves to be an effective, if not truly impressive, look at the road not taken. Nicolas Cage plays Jack Campbell, a wheeler-dealer who's the toast of Manhattan and "a credit to capitalism." He is willing to do anything to close a deal, including forcing his entire team to work late on Christmas Eve then come in for a "strategy session" on Christmas Day. Family has no meaning for Jack. Then, on his way home after work late on Christmas Eve, he encounters a street hustler (Don Cheadle) who turns out to be an angel of sorts. When Jack claims that he has everything in life that he needs, the angel decides to prove that's not the case, and transports Jack into an alternate universe where he has been married for 13 years to Kate (Téa Leoni), his college girlfriend. He is no longer rich, he works at a tire dealership, he has 2 kids, and he lives in a small house in Teaneck, New Jersey. Jack is initially horrified, but, in true *It's a Wonderful Life* fashion, he begins to connect with this lifestyle, which focuses on people and relationships rather than money and possessions.

Boiled down to its essence, *The Family Man* is a romantic comedy dressed up with a lot of intriguing philosophical side issues. At the core of the film is the relationship between Jack and Kate, and how her love (and the affection of his children) redeems him and proves the old-fashioned ideal that true wealth comes from having a family, not a 10-figure bank account. For the most part, this relationship works. Neither Cage nor Leoni does groundbreaking work here, but they're both effective and likable, and, when together, they click. And, although Cage is not recognized as an actor with great range, he capably handles Jack's transition from self-centered bachelor to giving husband and father.

The Family Man is not a flawless exploration of this scenario. At a little over 2 hours in length, the movie wears out its welcome. Director Brett Ratner has a tendency to include redundant scenes, especially late in the film as Jack is coming to the realization that he likes his "new" life. Ratner seems unsure how much the audience needs to buy Jack's conversion, and he ends up belaboring the point. The conclusion is lame, as if the filmmakers couldn't decide how to wrap things up and went with a "you can have your cake and eat it" option. For a story that is in large part about sacrifice, this doesn't work.

Overall, however, *The Family Man* is a pleasant motion picture. Despite its flaws, the screenplay is effective enough to get us thinking about a few philosophical issues while it tells a worthwhile story. RECOMMENDED

A Family Thing [1996]

Starring: Robert Duvall, James Earl Jones, Michael Beach, Irma P. Hall, David Keith Director: Richard Pearce Screenplay: Billy Bob Thornton and Tom Epperson Running Time: 1:49 Rated: PG-13 (Violence, profanity, mature themes) Theatrical Aspect Ratio: 2.35:1

Richard Pearce's *A Family Thing* is a pleasant, if not especially groundbreaking, motion picture that takes the "buddy movie" concept a step forward by introducing themes of race relations and kinship. All the topics presented on an intimate level are equally applicable to society as a whole, which has become more sensitive to issues of skin color than those of basic humanity.

A Family Thing's premise is that Duvall's character, Earl Pilcher, has been raised as the son of white parents, even though his real mother was black. After the death of the woman he called "Mom," Earl learns about his true heritage, and heads north to Chicago to meet his half-brother, Raymond (Jones). However, Ray is less than pleased to see Earl, because he associates his white sibling with tragedy. His mother died giving birth to Earl, and Ray has nursed this bitterness for more than 60 years.

For Earl, the challenge is putting aside the bigotry bred into him by his rural Arkansas environment. Learning the truth about his mother forces him to abandon his black-and-white perceptions. As *A Family Thing* chronicles one man's gradual acceptance of himself, it reminds us that skin color is an artificial, not a natural, barrier. After meeting Ray, Earl realizes that intolerance is the product of ignorance, and, when it comes down to it, he and his black brother aren't fundamentally very different.

One character central to bringing Earl and Ray together is their blind aunt, played brilliantly by scene-stealing Irma P. Hall. In Aunt T's words, she doesn't "have the blessing of being able to separate people by looking at them." So what if Earl's skin is lighter than Ray's — that doesn't change their shared parentage. She recognizes that the rift between the brothers is carved out of pride and stubbornness, and decides that it's her job to bridge it. To that end, she forces Ray to stop blaming Earl for his mother's death while encouraging Earl to embrace his heritage. Gradually for both men, stereotyping gives way to understanding, and understanding to brotherhood.

Most of *A Family Thing* is devoted to Earl and Ray's struggles to reach common ground. The usual "mismatched buddy" film conventions are present: initial resentment and dislike that leads to a physical confrontation, followed by bonding and grudging admiration that grows into genuine affection. With actors of Duvall and Jones' caliber, however, such formulas attain a higher-than-ordinary level.

Overall, this film is an agreeable exploration of what it means to be part of a family. *A Family Thing* isn't just about accepting one's circumstances, but embracing them. The actors, playing characters it's easy to sympathize with, bring the story alive. Because Duvall and Jones establish a successful rapport, it has an unexpectedly strong emotional resonance, and that's a key reason why viewers are likely to leave this movie satisfied. RECOMMENDED

Far from Heaven [2002]

Starring: Julianne Moore, Dennis Quaid, Dennis Haysbert
Director: Todd Haynes Screenplay: Todd Haynes Running Time: 1:47
Rated: PG-13 (Mature themes, brief profanity & violence) Theatrical
Aspect Ratio: 1.85:1

Welcome to the world of "Father Knows Best," white picket fences, and brilliant fall colors. Todd Haynes' *Far From Heaven* takes us to Hartford, Connecticut, circa 1957. However, unlike most traditional period piece dramas, the intention here isn't just to replicate an American community as it was a half-century ago, but to emulate that community as it would have been

portrayed in a movie of the era. One of Haynes' goals in crafting *Far From Heaven* is to emulate the so-called "women's films" of Douglas Sirk. In terms of style, visual approach, and general thematic content, Haynes has come as close as it's possible to in re-creating a '50s domestic melodrama for '00s consumption.

Cathy Whitaker (Julianne Moore) has a seemingly perfect life. Her husband, Frank (Dennis), is a recognized TV salesman. As per the American dream, she has two children and a comfortable home. She is content with the way things are, until Frank inadvertently provides a shock to her system. One night, when he is supposedly working late, Cathy hand-delivers him dinner, only to find him in a torrid embrace with another man. Afterwards, Frank confesses that he has always had homosexual feelings and promises to seek out a doctor to help him "beat this thing." While Frank is struggling with his sexuality, Cathy finds herself drawn to the quiet, kind gardener, Raymond (Dennis Haysbert). Raymond is black, and, on an occasion when he and Cathy are seen in public, a firestorm of nasty rumors begins. Raymond's idealistic belief that color should not be a social barrier is soon put to the test, and Cathy finds that her platonic relationship with Raymond is as much of a danger to her family as is Frank's homosexuality.

Haynes' style and approach draw the viewer in gently, but firmly. Once we are established in the seemingly-perfect world of Cathy and Frank, he allows their marriage and their lives to unravel before our eyes. *Far From Heaven* is not "realistic" in the traditional sense of the word (Haynes calls it "hyper-realistic"), but the emotions of the characters are genuine, and we feel for them and with them. In the end, *Far From Heaven* tells a simple story, but there's nothing remotely simple about the impact it has upon the viewer. HIGHLY RECOMMENDED

Farewell My Concubine [China, 1993]

Starring: Leslie Cheung, Zhang Fengyi, Gong Li Director: Chen Kaige
Screenplay: Lilian Lee and Lu Wei based on the novel by Lilian Lee
Running Time: 2:38 Rated: NR (Violence, mature themes, sexual situations) In Mandarin with English subtitles

In 1924 Beijing, the youthful Douzi and Shitou are brought together under the thumb of the strict master of a small acting troupe. It quickly becomes apparent that these are the most talented of the master's pupils, and he pushes them harder than his other students. Thirteen years later, their suffering has paid off. Douzi, now going by the name of Chen Dieyi (Leslie Cheung), and Shitou, called Duan Xiaolou (Zhang Fengyi), are major opera stars, and their production, *Farewell My Concubine* is nationally known. The two are inseparable, until the woman Juxian (Gong Li) comes between them.

The first portion of the film is devoted to the early lives of Dieyi and Xiaolou as they form an unshakable bond under the often-cruel punishments of their master. Years later, when we meet them again, the bond has only strengthened. These two are as close as men can be — yet Dieyi wishes for even greater intimacy. The subject of homosexuality is only once overtly referred to in *Farewell My Concubine,* but its presence is never far from the surface. While Xiaolou remains blissfully unaware of the nature of his friend's love, Dieyi is tortured by it. The introduction of Juxian, a prostitute who becomes Xiaolou's companion, creates a moral dilemma for Dieyi. Chen Kaige has done a fabulous job portraying these various relationships with depth, sensitivity, and realism.

Dieyi is the most fascinating character. From the beginning, his sense of identity is confused. Not only is he attracted to men, but his role as a woman in *Farewell My Concubine* creates a certain ambivalence about his own gender. In childhood, the refrain of "I am a girl" is drilled into him so that he can effectively assume the role of the concubine in the opera but, as another character observes, the line between reality and acting has become blurred.

Xiaolou has a more straightforward personality, at least on the surface. Nevertheless, through his ever-changing relationships with Dieyi and Juxian, he proves that this apparent simplicity often hides strong undercurrents. One of his actions ultimately propels the movie to its literal and emotional climax.

Juxian appears to be little more than a scheming whore frantic to capture a wealthy husband but, like everyone else, she is capable of a few surprises, including an entirely-unexpected streak of kindness towards Dieyi, who shows her nothing but contempt. Starting out as a wedge between the two friends, Juxian ends up a crucial element in their relationship.

It's no wonder that this film was initially banned in China. The Communist movement is not shown in a positive light. No film can ever hope to convey the complex mosaic of cultural upheaval caused by everything that happened between 1924 and 1977, but *Farewell My Concubine* does an excellent job pre-senting samples of the flavor while telling a story that is both epic and intimate. **MUST SEE**

Felicia's Journey [Canada/United Kingdom/United States, 1999]

Starring: Bob Hoskins, Elaine Cassidy, Arsinée Khanjian, Peter McDonald Director: Atom Egoyan Running Time: 1:56
Screenplay: Atom Egoyan, based on the novel by William Trevor
Rated: PG-13 (Mature themes) Theatrical Aspect Ratio: 2.35:1

Felicia's Journey concentrates on two characters, switching between them, choosing transition points that italicize their similarities and differences while never causing the narrative to lose momentum. The first person we meet is Joe Hilditch (Bob Hoskins), who is introduced at the end of the opening credits. Hilditch is an old-fashioned man. His house is filled with things of the past: rotary phones, antique appliances, and a small, black-and-white TV.

Meanwhile, the title character (Eileen Cassidy), a teenager from Ireland, has arrived in England searching for her boyfriend. She comes from a Catholic, Republican family and has been disowned for literally sleeping with the enemy. But she's a stranger with nothing more than a vague sense of geography to go on until she meets Hilditch, who offers her aid and advice. Soon, he has agreed to help her find her beloved Johnny, but we begin to suspect his motives, especially when we realize he has been videotaping his interaction with Felicia, and this isn't the first time he has offered a kind, sympathetic ear to a lonely, young girl.

Felicia's Journey grows more fascinating with every frame, as each of the characters comes into clearer focus and the narrative intensity builds. We begin to understand what motivates Hilditch and Felicia, and why they are the way they are. Yet, the deeper we get into the story, the more disquieting it becomes. Emotionally and spiritually, these people are not whole. The grim reality is that any kind of relationship between them, whether platonic or not, will lead inevitably to disaster.

A simplistic label like "villain" does not apply to Hilditch. Even as we despise his actions, we feel pity for him. Bob Hoskins' gestures, vocal mannerisms, and body language make Hilditch into a real person rather than a mere writer's construct inhabited by an adept performer. Hoskins is a recognizable face, but he submerges himself so effectively beneath the character's skin that we lose sight of the actor. And, on those occasions when the camera looks into

Hilditch's haunted features and catches a glimpse of hell, one can only marvel at the intensity of Hoskins' work.

Elaine Cassidy exhibits expert poise and ability in a role that requires great range and subtlety. She displays the necessary mix of naiveté, vulnerability, and emotional toughness that one would expect from someone like Felicia, who has defied her family in a moment of passion and now finds herself alone in a strange country.

Admittedly, *Felicia's Journey* can be a troubling and difficult film to sit through, and there is a contrivance near the end that fails to convince 100%, but the production's overall ability to leave a lasting impression is undeniable. This is not the kind of facile motion picture that is easy to shake off after leaving the theater; it lingers and ripens in the mind for days afterwards. Once again, Atom Egoyan has boldly stepped forward, deepening and broadening his reputation as one of the world's best living filmmakers.

HIGHLY RECOMMENDED

Fearless [1993]

Starring: Jeff Bridges, Isabella Rossellini, Rosie Perez, Tom Hulce, John Turturro Director: Peter Weir Screenplay: Rafael Yglesias based on his novel Running Time: 2:04 Rated: R (Mature themes, language, charred bodies) Theatrical Aspect Ratio: 1.85:1

Fearless opens with Max Klein (Jeff Bridges) striding purposefully through a head-high field of corn, a baby in his arms and a young boy by his side. These three are among the survivors of a brutal plane wreck which has strewn death and debris all over a southern California corn field. After delivering the boy to the authorities and the baby to its tearful mother, Max walks away from the scene of the accident and heads to Los Angeles, where he holes up in a motel, not even calling his wife Laura (Isabella Rossellini) to let her know that he's alive. Eventually, he is forcibly brought back to his San Francisco home, where his family finds him a changed man. Eventually, Max is introduced to another survivor, Carla Rodrigo (Rosie Perez), a young woman who lost her son in the crash. Perhaps not unexpectedly, the two embark upon an unusual, deeply emotional friendship.

Jeff Bridges, who tends to play his roles with more stoicism than emotion, finds the right balance. He gives us a Max that we aren't likely to identify with, but who doesn't promote audience apathy, either. Isabella Rossellini is not as effective as Laura, but her part doesn't demand the same level of intensity. Best of the 3 principles is Rosie Perez, whose portrayal of a grief-stricken mother unable to deal with the death of her son, comes across with stark believability. For the most part, Perez's acting is understated, which makes sudden bursts of emotion all the more forceful.

The theatrical trailers for this movie would lead you to believe that it's an uplifting experience. Nothing could be further from the truth. While there are a few moments of emotional exultation, most of the movie explores darker elements of human nature. The tangible presence of the Grim Reaper hangs above *Fearless* from start to finish.

While the relationship between Max and Carla is developed to perfection, there are a few offshoots of the main story that are never plumbed satisfactorily. Great care is taken to show the hero worship exhibited by the boy who followed Max out of the plane, but beyond the setup, little is done. There are indications of the stress that this places on Max's relationship with his own son, but the situation is given perfunctory treatment. Director Peter Weir fails to draw upon the possibilities of one of *Fearless*'s most emotionally-wrenching scenes: a group therapy session where survivors relate their memories of the crash.

Fearless is still an impressive film, even considering the untapped potential. The interactions of the 3 main characters are potent without being shocking or sensationalistic and the import of the questions raised isn't diminished because of the lack of firm answers. **HIGHLY RECOMMENDED**

Feast of July [United Kingdom, 1995]

Starring: Embeth Davidtz, Tom Bell, Gemma Jones, Ben Chaplin Director: Christopher Menaul Screenplay: Christopher Neame based on the novel by H. E. Bates Running Time: 1:58 Rated: R (Sexual situations, violence) Theatrical Aspect Ratio: 2.35:1

By turns tragic and beautiful, but always atmospheric, *Feast of July*, an adaptation of H.E. Bates' novel, focuses on the dark side of love and the grotesque capacity for violence hidden deep within the meekest human being.

The film opens with a pregnant young woman, Bella Ford (Embeth Davidtz), struggling across the windswept countryside of late Victorian England. Unmarried and alone, she is undergoing a 30-mile journey to find the father of her unborn child. By the time she reaches the town where he claims to live (but in fact doesn't), she has miscarried. Exhausted and weak, she is taken in by a kindly local family, and soon becomes a member of the household. The sons — Con (Ben Chaplin), Jedd (James Purefoy), and Matty (Kenneth Anderson) — vie with each other for her attention. For her part, Bella is attracted to all 3, although one eventually rises above the others in her estimation. But he must compete with Bella's memories of her lost love, a scoundrel who suddenly re-appears.

There's no doubt that *Feast of July* is, at heart, a tragic melodrama. But, at least in its appraisal of human nature, it aspires to something greater. Despite the trappings of civilization, man is still an animal, and even the gentlest of people can be driven by uncontrollable passions to do terrible things. Reason has never been able to master love, and *Feast of July* illustrates the devastating results of one moment's irrational blindness. For, in this sort of fiction, if not always in real life, crime has consequences.

As is almost always the case in British productions, the sense of atmosphere is masterful. Director Christopher Menaul (*Prime Suspect*) has used all the tools at his disposal, including rich cinematography by Peter Sova and a haunting score by longtime Kieslowski collaborator Zbigniew Preisner, to craft a realistic portrait of a private tragedy. Even though the circumstances are outdated, the emotional core of *Feast of July* is timeless.

Joy is a scarce commodity in this film, and there's little opportunity for comic relief to lighten the tension. *Feast of July* is not for those seeking an uplifting motion picture experience. As accomplished as Menaul's technique is, the film is a real downer — tissues are a recommended accessory. The main dish served up at this particular *Feast* is raw emotion.

RECOMMENDED

Finding Forrester [2000]
Starring: Sean Connery, Rob Brown, F. Murray Abraham, Anna Paquin
Director: Gus Van Sant Screenplay: Mike Rich Running Time: 2:18
Rated: PG-13 (Profanity, mature themes) Theatrical Aspect Ratio: 2.35:1

In Gus Van Sant's *Finding Forrester*, newcomer Rob Brown plays Jamal Wallace, a Bronx high schooler whose stunning achievement test scores and standout performance on the basketball court earn him the notice of officials at the exclusive Mailor-Callow Prep School, where he is offered a full scholarship as a junior. Jamal's mother (April Grace) and brother (Busta Rhymes) are thrilled by the offer, and, realizing that going to Mailor will allow him to advance his prospects, Jamal agrees to attend. Although his streetwise background makes him a social outsider amidst a sea of rich, pampered kids, Jamal's performance on the court and in the classroom earns him the

respect of many of his teachers and peers, including Claire (Anna Paquin), the pretty daughter of the head of Mailor's board of directors.

Jamal inadvertently discovers the whereabouts of the reclusive author William Forrester (Sean Connery), a former Pulitzer Prize winner who disappeared from the public eye after writing "the Great 20th Century Novel," *Avalon Landing*. Forrester owns an apartment overlooking the blacktop where Jamal and his friends play pickup games, and, one day, after making a brazen statement, Jamal is forced to back up his words by sneaking into Forrester's apartment to steal something. He is caught in the act and accidentally leaves behind his backpack, which contains his journals. Forrester writes comments in the notebooks and returns the backpack. Thus begins a peculiar mentor/student relationship, with Jamal agreeing not to reveal Forrester's whereabouts in return for Forrester's instruction in the craft of writing.

At the core of *Finding Forrester* is a familiar "buddy story" — about how a brilliant, outcast youngster simultaneously learns from and teaches life lessons to a weary old-timer. Forrester tutors Jamal about how to be an author; Jamal encourages Forrester to shake off his fear of the outside world.

As Jamal, Rob Brown displays a natural, unforced charisma. There isn't a hint of artifice in his performance, and it's easy to understand why the filmmakers chose him instead of a better established actor. For his part, the eternally watchable Connery doesn't test the limits of his acting ability to play the curmudgeonly Forrester. This is a case when an actor's reputation works in the character's favor. As written, Forrester is an irascible, unpleasant fellow, but audiences are so used to liking Connery that it's impossible to accept that there isn't a heart of gold hidden beneath the aging author's thick skin.

With *Finding Forrester*, Van Sant appears to have put an exclamation mark on his intention to move into mainstream filmmaking. Viewers unaware of Van Sant's history will not be clued into it by anything found on-screen in this movie. *Finding Forrester* is well made but conventional, and, depending on your mood, that represents either its greatest strength or its most telling weakness. **RECOMMENDED**

The Five Senses [Canada, 1999]
Starring: Mary-Louise Parker, Nadia Litz, Daniel MacIvor, Molly Parker, Gabrielle Rose Director: Jeremy Podeswa Screenplay: Jeremy Podeswa Running Time: 1:45 Rated: R (Profanity, nudity, sex)
Theatrical Aspect Ratio: 1.85:1

The central conceit embraced by *The Five Senses* is that each of the primary characters represents a sense. Cake baker Rona (Mary-Louise Parker) is taste; sulky, voyeuristic teenager Rachel (Nadia Litz) is sight; Richard (Philippe Volter), an eye doctor losing the use of his ears, is hearing; cleaning man Robert (Daniel MacIvor), who has an odd habit of sniffing people's odors, is smell; and masseuse Ruth (Gabrielle Rose) is touch. The central connecting event is the disappearance of a 3-year-old child while in Rachel's care. The mother, Anna (Molly Parker), makes a public plea for help and the case becomes the central focus of the Toronto news scene.

Rona is involved with an Italian boyfriend with whom she can't communicate (he speaks Italian; she speaks English). Her bisexual best friend, Robert, is looking up old boyfriends and girlfriends to see whether any of those relationships can be resurrected. Richard silently broods about his loss of hearing and makes up a list of sounds he wants to experience one last time before the chance is gone forever. He desperately misses his estranged wife and daughter, and seeks solace from a prostitute who has a deaf child. Ruth feels intense guilt for the young girl's disappearance because Rachel is her daughter. And Rachel dissociates herself from the entire incident, seeking comfort in the company of a boy her age who is also one of society's outcasts.

The characters in *The Five Senses* radiate a strong, almost overpowering sense of loneliness. It is their constant companion, and the lesson that each must learn (and not everyone does) is that genuine intimacy requires the use of all 5 senses, not just 1 or 2. Admittedly, the idea underlying the movie sounds pretentious, but the execution is not.

Each character is looking for something. Those who can define it, like Robert, are no closer to attaining it than those who are groping in the dark. A mother and daughter, both sharing a loss, have become strangers. To one degree or another, these are problems we are all familiar with. Rona's relationship with her Italian boyfriend is symbolic of this malaise of the soul — they have sex and eat, but, because of the language gap, they cannot engage in a meaningful conversation.

Underlying *The Five Senses* is a sharp understanding of the natures of grief, loneliness, and communication. As the film progresses, the importance of the individual senses is downplayed. The movie is not so much about the five senses as it is about how we process the information they provide. RECOMMENDED

Focus [2001]

Starring: William H. Macy, Laura Dern, David Paymer, Meat Loaf Aday Director: Neal Slavin Screenplay: Kendrew Lascelles, based on the novel by Arthur Miller Running Time: 1:47 Rated: PG-13 (Mature themes, violence) Theatrical Aspect Ratio: 1.85:1

It's a little disconcerting to watch something as timely and eerily prescient as Neal Slavin's *Focus*, which touches on many current "hot button" issues. The film is based on a 1945 novel by playwright Arthur Miller — a fact that illustrates the sad truth that, no matter how hatred and bigotry metamorphose, they remain constants of the human experience — dark, shadowy companions during our sojourn in this life.

Lawrence Newman (William H. Macy) lives in a quiet, middle-class neighborhood with his mother (Kay Hawtrey). Lawrence is a bit of a recluse. He'll politely greet his neighbors if he sees them on the street, but he rarely goes out of his way to start a conversation. His next-door neighbor, Fred (Meat Loaf Aday), is wary of Lawrence, failing to understand why an upstanding Protestant man avoids coming to a series of "neighborhood meetings" designed to discuss what to do about the unwanted presence of a local Jewish shopkeeper, Finkelstein (David Paymer). Then, Lawrence gets spectacles, and suddenly people begin to notice that he looks Jewish. When he meets, then marries, Gertrude (Laura Dern), suspicions deepen because, like Lawrence, Gertrude "looks" Jewish. Suddenly, these two Protestants have been blacklisted as Jews and are subject to the same persecution being visited upon Finkelstein.

Focus is an examination of the pervasive and uncompromising nature of hatred. The central irony is, of course, that neither of the main characters is a member of the race being singled out for vilification. Because of this, Slavin is able to show how truly irrational any form of group-specific hatred is. *Focus* also makes a statement about the fear of involvement. Lawrence believes the creed "see no evil, hear no evil, speak no evil." Little does he realize that it's only a matter of time before he becomes an outsider and everyone in the neighborhood turns a blind eye to his plight.

A secondary theme in *Focus*, and perhaps one of more immediate interest, is that of the resolve to stand firm in the face of terrorist threats. Both Lawrence and Finkelstein grow increasingly isolated and threatened. One option that is repeatedly suggested to them is that they move away, but they refuse to budge. This is their home and fear will not drive them from it. They stand resolute, regardless of how ugly circumstances become.

Few things, when taken to extremes, have positive results. *Focus* shows what can happen when patriotism and religious zeal turn sour. Hatred has no justification, but it always seeks an excuse, and, in the reactionary politics and misguided advocacy of a close-minded preacher, it finds one. *Focus* explores how acts of hatred begin small, then snowball out of control. Slavin's film is not without its faults, but, especially in today's climate, it's a fascinating motion picture, and its diverse-yet-interrelated subject matter can provide fodder for lengthy post-movie discussions. **RECOMMENDED**

For Love of the Game [1999]

Starring: Kevin Costner, Kelly Preston, John C. Reilly, Jena Malone Director: Sam Raimi Screenplay: Dana Stevens, based on the novel by Michael Shaara Running Time: 2:17 Rated: PG-13 (Profanity, sexual situations) Theatrical Aspect Ratio: 2.35:1

For Love of the Game is appropriately named. Crafted with respect for the game and an eye towards accuracy, the best scenes are some of the most true-to-life baseball moments ever presented in a non-documentary form on celluloid. The rest of the film tells a rather corny love story that is occasionally hamstrung by ripe dialogue. The romantic angle is necessary to the overall plot because it provides a sense of balance in the main character's life, but it is not written or developed as well as the baseball aspect.

Kevin Costner plays Billy Chapel, a pitcher who has thrown every major league pitch in his 19-year career for the Detroit Tigers. When the team won the World Series in 1984, Chapel was a big part of the victory. This has not been a good year, and the baseball gods haven't been kind to him — his record is a lackluster 8-11. Now, the team's owner has informed him that if he doesn't retire after today's game, the season finale against the Yankees in New York, he will be traded.

Weary in body, Billy takes the mound and gives it everything he has. As the innings go by, his mind drifts back through the last 5 years, recalling the only love of his life besides baseball. She is Jane Aubrey (Kelly Preston), and she has just broken things off with him so she can go to England to advance her career. Billy remembers key moments in their relationship — the first time they met, the time

she surprised him at Spring Training when he was with another woman, and the night he rescued her teenage daughter (Jena Malone). Then, as the number of outs remaining drops into the single digits, everyone in the stadium, from the beer-guzzling fans in the stands to the announcers in the booth (Vin Scully and Steve Lyons), recognizes that Billy has a chance to pitch a perfect game. For 7 innings, no one has gotten on base. But, as anyone who watches baseball knows, the last 6 outs are always the hardest.

The film's structure — cutting back and forth between the final game of the season and the flashback highlights of Billy and Jane's romance — works. The problem is that the script isn't as smart or insightful when it deals with a man's love for a woman as it is when it concentrates on that same man's love for baseball.

In many ways, *For Love of the Game* is an old fashioned motion picture. Although it acknowledges the state of the game today, it views the sport with the respect it once had when it was America's Pastime. Today, winning has become everything. No one seems to care about the simple rhythm of 9 innings. As baseball movies go, this one isn't a home run — it's more of a single or a double. But, as any fan knows, that's still a hit, and it can generate some excitement. **RECOMMENDED**

Forrest Gump [1994]

Starring: Tom Hanks, Robin Wright Penn, Gary Sinise, Mykelti Williamson, Sally Field Director: Robert Zemeckis Screenplay: Eric Roth based on the novel by Winston Groom Running Time: 2:22 Rated: PG-13 (Mature themes, implied sex, discreet nudity, language, violence) Theatrical Aspect Ratio: 2.35:1

Passionate and magical, *Forrest Gump* is a tonic for the weary of spirit. For those who feel that being set adrift in a season of action movies is like wandering into a desert, the oasis lies ahead. In *Forrest Gump*, the main character remains a child in heart and spirit, even as his body grows to maturity.

Forrest Gump (Hanks), named after a civil war hero, grows up in Greenbow, Alabama, where his mother (Sally Field) runs a boarding house. Although Forrest is a little "slow" (his IQ is 75, 5 below the state's definition of "normal"), his mental impairment doesn't seem to bother him, his mother, or his best (and only) friend, Jenny Curran (played as an adult by Robin Wright Penn). In fact, the naïveté that comes through a limited understanding of the world around him gives Forrest a uniquely positive perspective of life.

During the next 30 years, Forrest becomes a star football player, a war hero, a successful businessman, and something of a pop icon. Through it all, however, there is one defining element in his life: his love for Jenny. She is never far from his thoughts, no matter what he's doing or where he is.

A trio of assets lift *Forrest Gump* above the average "lifestory" drama: its optimism, freshness, and emotional honesty. Though the movie does not seek to reduce every member of the audience to tears, it has moments whose power comes from their simplicity. Equally as important is laughter, and *Forrest Gump* has moments of humor strewn throughout.

Through the miracle of visual effects, Forrest meets his fair share of famous people — George Wallace, Presidents Kennedy, Johnson, and Nixon, and John Lennon. While mixing the real footage of these notables with new images featuring Hanks is not a seamless process, the result is nevertheless effective.

Tom Hanks won an Academy Award for *Philadelphia*, but his performance here is more impressive. The Alabama accent may seem a little awkward at first, but it doesn't take long for the acting to dwarf the twang. Hanks has no difficulty creating a totally human character who is free of guile and deceit, and barely able to comprehend a concept like evil. Looking and seeming like a younger Jessica Lange, Robin Wright Penn is believable as the object of Forrest's undying affection. The real scene-stealer, however, is Gary Sinise. In this movie, his Lieutenant Dan Taylor is riveting. The passion and pain he brings to the middle portions of *Forrest Gump* hold together some of the film's weaker moments.

This is a marvelous motion picture — a mint julep on a hot summer's afternoon. MUST SEE

Frankie Starlight [Ireland, 1995]

Starring: Anne Parillaud, Gabriel Byrne, Matt Dillon, Alan Pentony, Corban Walker, Georgina Cates, Rudi Davis Director: Michael Lindsay-Hogg Screenplay: Ronan O'Leary and Chet Raymo based on the novel *The Dork of Cork* by Chet Raymo Running Time: 1:40 Rated: R (Profanity, sexual situations) Theatrical Aspect Ratio: 1.85:1
In English and French with subtitles

Frankie Starlight is ambitious, and, as is often true of movies that attempt too much, it's only partially successful. The story tells the tale of a modern-day Irish author, Frank Bois (Corban Walker), who is submitting his manuscript, *Nightstalk* (as in *Nights Talk*, not *Night Stalk*), to an editor. The book is immediately snapped up by Penguin Press for publication. An overnight success, Frank can't help but wonder whether his good fortune is due to the quality of his work or to his physical stature — he's a dwarf.

According to Frank, *Nightstalk* is an intermingling of astronomy with the stories of his and his mother's lives. *Frankie Starlight*'s ambitious agenda is to transform the events of *Nightstalk* from text to screen images by means of lengthy flashbacks. These forays into the past start out with promise, as we first meet Bernadette (Anne Parillaud), Frank's mother, in Normandy, days before the Allied invasion. The setting soon changes to Ireland. Unfortunately, once the shores of France are behind Bernadette, the story starts glossing over key plot elements. *Frankie Starlight* is saved from incoherent oblivion by the birth of Bernadette's son. Soon, our attention — not to mention our sympathy — is vested exclusively in him. Bernadette becomes an almost unwanted distraction.

The last ⅓ of the movie is by far the best. Taking place in the present, it brings together several loose threads from the past and weaves them into a touching love story. There's more emotional depth to Frank's relationship with his soul mate than is initially obvious, with director Michael Lindsay-Hogg handling this aspect of his film adeptly.

Throughout the entire picture, stars are a key symbol. Frank eventually becomes an amateur astronomer, and many of the film's best sequences take place on a rooftop with thousands of points of light twinkling in the darkened canopy above. It is there that father figure Jack Kelly (Gabriel Byrne) first teaches young Frank stories about the constellations, and that draws the film to a close.

Connections, both made and missed, and the vagaries of life that lead us to react differently to the same people in diverse circumstances, form *Frankie Starlight*'s thematic backbone. Parillaud's acting is too flat, and the sketchiness of the screenplay, which follows her life in broad strokes with few details, doesn't help. We're sure how and why Frank connects with others; the same can rarely be said about his mother.

Frankie Starlight is more satisfying taken as a whole than when its individual parts are examined. The film is flawed, but there's still enough magic and genuine emotion to make for a pleasant movie-going experience. Affability is perhaps *Frankie Starlight*'s strongest quality. No matter how many problems you

uncover along the way, when the final credits roll, you're more likely to be smiling than frowning.
RECOMMENDED

Fresh [United States, 1994]

Starring: Sean Nelson, Giancarlo Esposito, Samuel L. Jackson, Cheryl Freeman, N'Bushe Wright Director: Boaz Yakin Screenplay: Boaz Yakin Running Time: 1:54 Rated: R (Violence, language, drugs) Theatrical Aspect Ratio: 1.85:1

Never has chess been a more apt metaphor for life than in Boaz Yakin's feature debut, *Fresh*. Samuel L. Jackson sits in New York's Washington Square playing speed chess and dispensing valuable lessons about life. (As a trivia note, the chess advisor for this film was Bruce Pandolfini, whose real-life character was portrayed by Ben Kingsley in *Searching for Bobby Fischer*.) His son Michael (played with astonishing ability by Sean Nelson) eats up those lessons and promptly applies them to a far more dangerous game than the one in the park.

Michael, nicknamed Fresh by the drug lords who use him as a runner, has had the grisly misfortune of watching 2 children gunned down in cold blood. He knows the killer, and decides that if he orchestrates his revenge cleverly, he may be able to get both himself and his sister Nichole (N'Bushe Wright) out of the cycle of poverty and drugs they're trapped in. To succeed, however, he must play the perfect match. A false move means death at the hands of his mentor, Esteban (Giancarlo Esposito), the local smack distributor.

Fresh takes the setting and tone of *Boyz 'N the Hood* and *Menace II Society* and applies it to a thriller. Gone is the documentary-like quality of filmmaking as well as the gritty sense of immediacy. *Fresh* uses higher-quality film stock and a more traditional cinematographic style to distance the audience ever-so-slightly from the characters. This way, it's easier to appreciate the complexity of Michael's plan and the manner in which he arranges his masterful scheme of manipulation.

With a script as smart as the title character, *Fresh* keeps its viewers guessing. Having a 6th grader as the protagonist is a stroke of genius that adds a further layer of tension to an already taut storyline. Thirteen-year-old Sean Nelson's performance would make many older actors envious. Without a hint of awkwardness, he conveys the sharp intelligence behind Michael's wide-eyed, seemingly innocent looks.

Samuel L. Jackson is a scene-stealer as Michael's near-vagrant speed chess playing father. The role isn't large, but this is an example of an actor at his most focused. Michael's father advises him that any piece on the chess board can be sacrificed to get the king. It is a lesson he takes to heart. Everyone becomes an expendable pawn in the high-stakes game, and there are casualties. The price of winning at all costs is depicted in the film's final shot. That's just one of the images that marks *Fresh* as an atypical thriller — a film that succeeds because it defies many conventions of its genre. **HIGHLY RECOMMENDED**

Fried Green Tomatoes [1991]

Starring: Mary Stuart Masterson, Mary-Louise Parker, Kathy Bates, Jessica Tandy Director: Jon Avnet Screenplay: Fannie Flag and Carol Sobieski based on the book *Fried Green Tomatoes at the Whistlestop Café* by Fannie Flag Running Time: 2:19 Rated: PG-13 (language, mature themes)

Fried Green Tomatoes is a thoroughly enjoyable movie-going experience, replete with laughter, tears, triumph, and tragedy. Unfortunately, it has been sanitized and "Hollywoodized," with the relationship between the two 1930 female leads left ambiguous, and a few too many scenes going over-the-top to manipulate an emotional reaction. So, while providing 2+ hours worth of solid entertainment, director Jon Avnet's picture lacks the crucial ingredient which would have lifted it above the level of a tearjerker to that of the extraordinary.

The acting can easily be counted among *Fried Green Tomatoes*' strengths. Especially noteworthy are the performances by Mary Stuart Masterson (as Idgie) and Mary-Louise Parker (as Ruth), who make their characters' improbable friendship come alive. Oscar-winners Kathy Bates and Jessica Tandy are fine, although their characters aren't as compelling, nor does their relationship have the same dynamics.

Some viewers have labeled this film a "woman's movie," which it is in the sense that the 4 protagonists are female. The themes and plot are universal, as male audience members who aren't afraid of sentiment will discover. *Fried Green Tomatoes* is 2 stories in one, both of which ultimately work as well as they can, given what the film is trying to do. It should be noted that the present-day scenes aren't as involving as those that take place in the 1930s. The structure is unusual, with the modern day scenes "framing" the flashbacks. Because the differences in the time periods are so marked, this may have not been the best way to handle the dual storylines. There are some awkward moments when the 1930s/1990s parallelism seems forced.

The greatest flaw of this movie is that Avnet tries relentlessly to get his viewers to reach for the box of tissues. A little manipulation is expected in any melodrama, but *Fried Green Tomatoes* goes overboard. That's not to say that the audience is likely to be weeping through the entire film, but Avnet isn't particularly subtle about what he's trying to do.

Because of its strong sense of character development, *Fried Green Tomatoes* touches a plethora of emotional chords. At times, it is gritty and inspirational, while still maintaining enough comedy to offset the less-comfortable instances of emotional upheaval. For mystery-lovers, there's even a murder thrown in. The film isn't perfect, but it has enough going for it to make it worthy entertainment.

HIGHLY RECOMMENDED

From the Journals of Jean Seberg [1996]

Starring: Mary Beth Hurt Director: Mark Rappaport Screenplay: Mark Rappaport Running Time: 1:37 Rated: No MPAA Rating (Profanity, violence, nudity) Theatrical Aspect Ratio: 1.33:1

Part biography, part social autopsy, and part movie criticism, *From the Journals of Jean Seberg* is a fascinating perspective of the life and films of the former film star. From director Mark Rappaport, he gives a posthumous (Seberg committed suicide in 1979), speculative interpretation of what the actress might have said about her career. Played by Mary Beth Hurt, Rappaport's vision of Seberg speaks with a barbed tongue that spares no one.

Seberg burst on the movie scene in 1957, when, at the age of 17, she beat out 3,000 contenders for the title role in Otto Preminger's epic biopic, *Joan of Arc*. The movie was a disappointment, due in large part to Seberg's horrible miscasting, but Preminger used her in his next film, *Bonjour Tristesse,* an examination of a daughter's obsessive love for her father (David Niven). Few people saw the movie, but among those who did was Jean Luc Godard, who instantly wanted Seberg for 1959's *Breathless*. Suddenly, she was a celebrated actress.

Breathless and 1964's *Lillith* represented the heights of Seberg's uneven career. After those films, she appeared in a number of awful-to-middling pictures, often as a nymphomaniac. Several years later, in 1969, Seberg appeared opposite Clint Eastwood in the failed musical *Paint Your Wagon*. Her swansong screen appearance in 1976 was in a nondescript role in a virtually forgotten picture called *The Wild Duck*. Three years later, with her personal and professional life in shambles, she took an overdose of sleeping pills.

From the Journals of Jean Seberg draws parallels between Seberg, Jane Fonda, and Vanessa Redgrave. All were political activists — Fonda against Vietnam, Redgrave for the PLO, and Seberg for the Black Panthers (an affiliation for which she was hounded by J. Edgar Hoover and the FBI). All were connected, in one way or another, by their husbands, lovers, or previous directors.

Jean Seberg's social viewpoint is indisputably cynical. With a deceptively bland expression, Mary Beth Hurt delivers scathing line after line, contemptuous of everything from the roles of women in film (either mad, oversexed, objectified, or some combination of all 3) to the influence that Clint Eastwood's screen personae had on Presidents Reagan and Bush. It's a vivid, feminist perspective that strikes more than a few raw nerves because of its acuteness.

Jean Seberg's career began with her being burned at the stake (literally and figuratively) in *Joan of Arc*. It ended when the FBI's relentless persecution, coupled with various personal problems, pushed her to suicide. *From the Journals of Jean Seberg* examines the public life bookended by those events. There are some aspects of Seberg's career that perhaps deserved more screen time, and certain tangents that could have been reduced or eliminated. On the whole this is certainly one of the most innovative pseudo-biographies ever to reach the screen. **HIGHLY RECOMMENDED**

The Full Monty [United Kingdom, 1997]

Starring: Robert Carlyle, Tom Wilkinson, Mark Addy, Steve Huison, Paul Barber, Hugo Speer Director: Peter Cattaneo Screenplay: Simon Beaufoy Running Time: 1:30 Rated: R (Profanity, nudity) Theatrical Aspect Ratio: 1.85:1

The Full Monty combines humor with light drama to explore the manner in which a group of men cope with the emotional and financial toll of being "force adjusted." The movie opens in Sheffield, England, a major steel working city whose central industry has been modernized and mechanized. Productivity is up, but the victims of the automation are the workers, many of whom have been laid off. *The Full Monty* focuses on one such man, Gaz (Robert Carlyle), who is hundreds of pounds behind on child support payments to his ex-wife, Mandy (Emily Woof). Gaz's best friend, Dave (Mark Addy), and his former boss, Gerald (Tom Wilkinson), are also unemployed. Their collective inability to find work is eating into their self-esteem. Gaz's son doesn't want to spend time at his dad's house because it's always cold, Gerald is frightened to tell his credit card-obsessed wife that he doesn't have a job, and Dave loses his ability to perform sexually.

Things change when the Chippendales arrive in Sheffield to perform a show. The tremendous crowds that turn out for the event give Gaz an idea. If male strippers who don't take it all off can rake in the money, what about those who are willing to show "the full monty"? In short order, Gaz has recruited an unlikely group of dancers: a sad loner (Steve Huison), an aging black man with rhythm and a bad hip (Paul Barber), and a cheerful, well-endowed young man (Hugo Speer) who has the body but not the moves. Drawing upon Gaz's enthusiasm and Gerald's experience as a ballroom dancer, the band of 6 develop a routine, dancing with and without clothes to the songs of Donna Summer, Gary Glitter, and Tom Jones.

The Full Monty throws pretended eroticism out the window. There isn't a sexually provocative moment in the film. The nudity is discretely handled, although the actors did in fact perform a live strip show in front of 400 extras in a sequence that was, according to the director, "a one-take deal." This lends a degree of spontaneity to *The Full Monty* that makes the movie's climactic scenes more believable and enjoyable.

The 6 members of the group relate well to each other and engage our sympathy. Robert Carlyle plays Gaz with the right mix of pathos and energy. Tom Wilkinson (*Sense and Sensibility*) has the "stuck up bastard with a good heart" role down pat. And, as the overweight Dave, Mark Addy brings to the fore feelings of insecurity that almost anyone can relate to.

The Full Monty is basically about overcoming adversity and succeeding is spite of certain perceived shortcomings. What *The Full Monty* lacks in depth, it makes up for in good will and likeability. This isn't a great movie, but it's breezy, enjoyable, and easy to sit through. And sometimes, even when dealing with a serious issue like unemployment, that can be the perfect tone to drive home a message. **RECOMMENDED**

Gas Food Lodging [1992]

Starring: Brooke Adams, Ione Sky, Fairuza Balk, James Brolin Director: Allison Anders Screenplay: Allison Anders based on the novel *Don't Look and It Won't Hurt* by Richard Peck Running Time: 1:42 Rated: R (Language, nudity, mature themes) Theatrical Aspect Ratio: 1.85:1

Generally, people go to the movies to escape from reality. *Gas Food Lodging* provides this escape by mirroring life so perfectly that the audience feels like they're watching real people in real situations rather than actors in a film. The dialogue, actions, and movements are as genuine as can be found in any motion picture.

This is director Allison Anders' first feature, and she readily admits that much of the story is culled from her own experiences (even though the screenplay is based on a novel by Richard Peck). In *Gas Food Lodging*, she wanted to present the difficulties of being a single mother in a setting where the economic climate is bleak. It's a scenario that many will be able to relate to on a personal level.

The plot is effective in its simplicity, and there is enough quiet intensity to keep it from becoming stagnant. *Gas Food Lodging* follows about a year in the life of a 3-female household (mother and 2 teenage daughters). There are numerous subtle touches which underscore Anders' aptitude with the material and her cast. The messages in *Gas Food Lodging*, all of which deal with consequences, are presented obliquely.

This film is highlighted by several noteworthy performances. Ione Skye (of *Say Anything*) takes on the less-than-glamorous role of Trudi, an affection-starved girl who believes that using her body is the only way to get men to like her. As believable as Skye's performance is, she's upstaged by the younger Fairuza Balk (as Shade), with her wonderfully expressive wide eyes. Brooke Adams and James Brolin round out the cast as Nora and John, the divorced parents of the two girls.

Gas Food Lodging deals with issues, but its strength lies in the characters that struggle at the heart of the story. Anders has made this film far from the glitz of Hollywood and the money that comes with the limelight. Hopefully, for her next project, she'll be able to maintain the gritty quality which makes her debut such a memorable effort. **HIGHLY RECOMMENDED**

Georgia [1995]

Starring: Jennifer Jason Leigh, Mare Winningham, Ted Levine Director: Ulu Grosbard Screenplay: Barbara Turner based on a story by Barbara Turner and Jennifer Jason Leigh Running Time: 1:58 Rated: R (Profanity, mature themes, sex, nudity) Theatrical Aspect Ratio: 1.85:1

Georgia is a slice-of-life motion picture that lacks a definite beginning and end. It's a dual character study of 2 sisters and an examination of the complex dynamic which fuels their atypical relationship. While the movie could easily be called *Sadie*, because it's more about Jennifer Jason Leigh's character than her older sister, Georgia (Mare Winningham), the film makers have chosen their title carefully, because everything in this movie comes back to Georgia — even Sadie, who often defines herself in terms of her relationship to her sister.

The sisters are classic opposites. Sadie is passionate, generous, giving, and emotionally open. She loves singing with her whole heart — it's her reason for being alive — yet she is painfully bereft of talent. Conversely, while Georgia is reserved and emotionally shackled, her glorious voice has made her a hugely successful Country/Western singer. So, as Georgia performs in packed arenas, Sadie must make do in front of a few drunks at a local night club.

Yet Sadie never resents Georgia's success. She attends her sister's concerts, applauding unreservedly after each song, and repeatedly identifies Georgia as the "only one who matters" to her. But Sadie's untempered, desperate passion and ambition terrify Georgia. In her view, Sadie has latched onto her and won't let her go, and someone as balanced as Georgia cannot cope with the all-consuming suffering and triumph that defines Sadie's existence. Like magnets of shifting polarity, these 2 are both drawn to and repelled by each other.

Leigh infuses Sadie with an inextinguishable inner fire. There are times when it's uncomfortable to watch this performance because it's so powerful — Sadie is raw passion coupled with a total lack of talent. Never is this more apparent than when she sings from the heart. The emotion is there, but not the ability. The one thing Sadie wants more than anything else, she cannot have, and this realization incites her spiral into drugs and alcohol.

Georgia was a personal project for Leigh (her mother wrote the screenplay), and it shows in her presentation of Sadie. Director Ulu Grosbard opts for a stark, simple style that underlines the tremendous swings of emotion that characterize the film. *Georgia* doesn't possess an amazingly original narrative, but what distinguishes this picture is the depth of the characters and the amazing power with which the two leads breathe life into them. **HIGHLY RECOMMENDED**

Get On the Bus [1996]

Starring: Charles Dutton, Ossie Davis, Thomas Jefferson Byrd, Andre Braugher Director: Spike Lee Screenplay: Reggie Rock Bythewood Running Time: **2:00** Rated: R (Profanity, mature themes) Theatrical Aspect Ratio: 1.85:1

The Million Man March, which took place on October 16, 1995, was arguably the most important display of male black solidarity since the '60s. As depicted in *Get on the Bus,* it was about unity, self-discovery, and taking responsibility. *Get on the Bus* investigates the spirit and meaning of the March as seen through the eyes of a group of diverse men taking the long bus trip from Los Angeles to Washington D.C. for the event. Unfortunately, many of the bus riders are just variations of stock characters. Neither Lee nor screenwriter Reggie Rock Bythewood crafts more than one or two well-realized personalities.

The men who board the "Spotted Owl" bus in South Central L.A. are certainly not all cut from the same mold. There's Gary (Roger Guenveur Smith), a half-white cop who's insecure about his "blackness." Evan (Thomas Jefferson Byrd) and his son, Junior (De'aundre Bonds), are shackled together by court order. "Dog," as Junior calls him, is trying to make up for years of absent parenting by taking his reluctant, delinquent offspring to this historic event. Two homosexual lovers, Kyle (Isaiah Washington) and Randall (Harry J. Lennix), are in the midst of a breakup. An up-and-coming actor, Flip (Andre Braugher), is waiting to hear whether he'll get the co-starring role in a new Denzel Washington movie. Also along for the ride are Xavier (Hill Harper), an aspiring film student; and Jeremiah (Ossie Davis, in a standout performance), the aging voice of wisdom and experience.

There isn't enough screen time to develop these stories more than fitfully. Some get better exposure than others. The struggle of the homosexuals to attain acceptance is handled in a superficial manner. The battle lines between gay rights supporters and homophobes are clearly established on the bus, with each side mouthing the requisite slogans. Lee doesn't really offer anything new as far as the plight of the gay black man is concerned, and appears to have included this pair primarily as a means of illustrating diversity within the community.

The melodramatic ending, which includes a sermon on unity, is excessively manipulative. And there are several instances throughout when Lee uses contrived events to advance the plot. Still, all things considered, *Get on the Bus* presents an involving, intimate portrait of a group of men gathered for a common purpose. Artificial plot devices don't divert our attention from the strong, heartfelt performances.

Some moments in *Get on the Bus* cut to the heart of what the Million Man March symbolized. One such occasion has the characters singing an improvised "Roll Call," introducing themselves to each other in song. Another is an intense confrontation between Gary and Jamal about street violence, a topic that has a deep, personal meaning for each of them. Scenes like these, ripe with genuine emotion, are the most compelling reason to take this trip with director Spike Lee and his talented cast. RECOMMENDED

Ghost World [2001]

Starring: Thora Birch, Scarlett Johansson, Steve Buscemi, Brad Renfro
Director: Terry Zwigoff Screenplay: Daniel Clowes & Terry Zwigoff,
based on the comic book by Daniel Clowes Running Time: 1:51
Rated: R (Profanity, sexual situations) Theatrical Aspect Ratio: 1.85:1

Ghost World could easily be considered an "anti-Hollywood coming of age story." It is based on the comic book of the same name, which was devised by Daniel Clowes. In addition to co-writing the screenplay, he was available to help director Terry Zwigoff in a consultant capacity. *Ghost World* is being marketed as a comedy, and while that's technically correct, it should be noted that this is a bleak comedy.

The movie opens at a high school graduation. Best friends Enid (Thora Birch) and Rebecca (Scarlett Johansson) are preparing to venture into the "real world" together. They intend to get jobs, then rent an apartment together. College isn't in the cards for either of them. However, despite being inseparable during high school, Enid and Rebecca begin to drift apart as their maturing life goals take them in different directions. Rebecca is embracing conventionality — a steady job (at a coffee shop), a "regular" apartment, and plans for the future. Enid, on the other hand, is wandering aimlessly, entering into a semi-romantic relationship with a much older, timid jazz-lover, Seymour (Steve Buscemi), failing to hold down a job for more than a day, taking a remedial art class, and continuing to live in her father's house. The more the rift between Enid and Rebecca widens, the less likely it is that they will be able to bridge it.

The real strength of *Ghost World* are the characters. Enid in particular, who has the most screen time, develops into a well-rounded individual. She has her rough edges (she's not the easiest person to get along with), but it doesn't take long for us to be rooting for her. In portraying Enid, Birch weds quirkiness with an underlying sense of melancholy and ennui.

Scarlett Johansson, provides an appealing Rebecca, although her role is a little underwritten (especially in comparison with Birch's). Meanwhile, indie favorite Steve Buscemi has the opportunity to play a kind of part he is rarely accorded — a romantic lead. Of course, Seymour doesn't represent the typical male half of a romantic pairing — he's emotionally withdrawn, painfully shy, and inexperienced with women — in short, a traditional dork. Seymour's relationship with Enid represents a non-traditional May/December pairing, although the manner in which their interaction is handled rings true.

Ghost World offers interesting characters, smart dialogue, biting satire (the concept of "high art" gets shredded), and dark comedy. Zwigoff, who brought us the brilliant portrait of cartoonist R. Crumb in the documentary *Crumb,* clearly feels at home in this territory. RECOMMENDED

Ghosts of Mississippi [1996]

Starring: Alec Baldwin, Whoopi Goldberg, James Woods, Craig T. Nelson, Diane Ladd, Bonnie Bartlet, Bill Cobbs, William H. Macy
Director: Rob Reiner Screenplay: Lewis Collick Running Time: 2:10
Rated: R (Mature themes, profanity, violence) Theatrical Aspect Ratio: 1.85:1

Shortly after midnight on a steamy June evening in 1963, civil rights activist Medgar Evers was shot to death outside his home in Jackson, Mississippi. One shot, fired from a high-powered rifle, exploded through his chest, ripped through the nearby wall of his house, ricocheted off a refrigerator, and broke a coffee pot. The assassin was white supremacist Byron De La Beckwith, a man with such an intimidating personality that even the KKK feared him. De La Beckwith was captured, but, after two trials ended in hung juries, he went free. When, 30 years later, at the behest of Evers' widow, Myrlie, Assistant DA Bobby DeLaughter re-opened the case, he had no idea of the difficulties he would face in obtaining a new indictment. Evidence was missing, witnesses had died, and even the official court transcripts of the original trials could not be located. On top of that, the new trial re-opened old wounds in the community. DeLaughter's life was threatened, and many people — including his own wife — turned against him. Undaunted, he pursued the case, determined to see it through to the end.

As a courtroom drama, *Ghosts of Mississippi* is reasonably successful. The trial, which carefully follows the actual transcript from 1994, avoids the contrived, theatrical twists that mar many similar films. There are no surprise witnesses or unexpected moves by either the prosecution or the defense. Each side presents its case, then leaves the final decision in the hands of the jury. As a result of this verisimilitude, the courtroom aspects of *Ghosts of Mississippi* are intelligent rather than over-the-top. We care about the characters and what happens to them.

As an examination of how the Civil Rights movement has changed lifestyles and attitudes in Mississippi (and, by extension, across the entire country) during the last 30 years, *Ghosts of Mississippi* is less effective. Reiner investigates two prevalent, albeit contradictory, views of how the Civil Rights movement has changed the nation. Either we are making slow progress, step by step, to a better future, or, "emotionally, we will always be segregated." DeLaughter's conscience becomes the battleground for these viewpoints. But, although the script is tightly-written for the most part, there are times when it lapses into sermonizing (such as when DeLaughter tries to explain to his young children why Evers was a great man).

At times, *Ghosts of Mississippi* resembles nothing more lofty than a toned-down, historically-grounded version of *A Time to Kill*. (A white man in the "new" South faces racism and personal danger for defending the "black" perspective.) So, although I recommend *Ghosts of Mississippi* and believe that it deserves to find a wide audience, I am cognizant that this is not a perfect motion picture. It is occasionally thought-provoking, but rarely haunting. RECOMMENDED

Girl, Interrupted [1999]

Starring: Winona Ryder, Angelina Jolie, Clea DuVall, Brittany Murphy Director: James Mangold Screenplay: James Mangold and Lisa Loomer and Anna Hamilton Phelan, based on the book by Susanna Kaysen Running Time: 2:07 Rated: R (Profanity, sexual situations, violence) Theatrical Aspect Ratio: 1.85:1

When it comes to sexual promiscuity in America, is there a double-standard? Of course, and it was even more evident during the mid-to-late-1960s, the era in which *Girl, Interrupted* is set. As Susanna (played by Winona Ryder), the lead character, puts it, "How many girls would a 17-year-old boy have to [sleep with] to earn the label 'compulsively promiscuous'? And how many boys for 17-year-old girls?" The answer is telling. A teenage boy with multiple partners would be considered "virile" or would be viewed good-naturedly as "sowing his wild oats." At best, a girl who approached sex with a similar vigor would be called a "slut." At worst, as was Susanna's case, she would be classified as having a "borderline personality disorder."

Of course, enjoying sex isn't Susanna's only problem — she also occasionally hallucinates, and, after attempting suicide, she is encouraged to check into Claymoore, a suburban Boston mental hospital that's more like a country club than an asylum. Only after signing the admission papers does she learn that she can't just walk out — the hospital has to release her. So Susanna is stuck for the long haul, which turns out to be nearly 2 years.

Susanna's time in Claymoore is a period of self-discovery. At first, she is angry and antisocial, and gravitates naturally towards Lisa, (Angelina Jolie) the ward's most consistent troublemaker. Eventually, however, she learns that Lisa's cruel streak has a vicious edge that she doesn't want to be associated with. So she concentrates on writing in her journal and making a conscious effort to rehabilitate.

For the most part, the film manages to avoid seeming like a rip-off of *One Flew Over the Cuckoo's Nest* with women. Director Mangold ably mines the talent of his cast. Winona Ryder brings Susanna to life in a low-key, subtly powerful performance that allows Susanna to seem strangely normal compared to her fellow inmates. Give the film credit for having the courage to run with a protagonist who isn't entirely likeable: in addition to suffering delusions, Susanna is presented as spoiled, selfish, and occasionally unkind. Compared to Lisa, however, she's an angel. In *Girl, Interrupted*'s most visible role, Angelia Jolie shines like a supernova, radiating flamboyance. It's an electric performance that energizes every scene in which she appears, recalling but not imitating Jack Nicolson's turn as Randle P. McMurphy in *Cuckoo's Nest*.

Marred (not fatally) by a somewhat pat ending, *Girl, Interrupted* is a fine film about relationships and self-discovery. While the movie may not entirely capture the tone and spirit of the book, it stands solidly on its own, separate yet never entirely divorced from its source material. RECOMMENDED

Girlfight [2000]

Starring: Michelle Rodriguez, Jaime Tirelli, Paul Calderon, Santiago Douglas, Ray Santiago Director: Karyn Kusama Screenplay: Karyn Kusama Running Time: 1:50 Rated: R (Profanity, sex, violence) Theatrical Aspect Ratio: 1.66:1

The focal point of one of the 2000 Sundance Film Festival's more serious bidding wars, first-time director Karyn Kusama's *Girlfight* is a well crafted and emotionally satisfying debut — a fine drama about self-discovery and female empowerment. It's about taking charge of one's own life when it appears to be hurtling out of control towards disaster.

Girlfight tells the story of a would-be girl boxer. Diana Guzman (Michelle Rodriguez in a coming-out performance that is equal parts fire and luminosity) is a frequent troublemaker at school, where she's just a few months shy of graduation. However, her propensity for getting into fights has her one demerit away from expulsion. She has no boyfriend, and her few girlfriends are wary of her volatile nature. Her home life isn't much better. Her mother has been dead for years and there's a slow-burning, mutual antagonism between Diana and her father (Paul Calderon). The only one she seems to care for is her geeky brother, Tiny (Ray Santiago). One day, after dropping something off at the Brooklyn Athletic Club, Diana decides that she wants to take boxing lessons. She coaxes one of the trainers, Hector (Jaime Tirelli), into teaching her for $10 a session. Soon, she is channeling her hostility and energy into the sport and is becoming less disruptive at school. At home, however, her relationship with her father edges closer to an explosion of physical violence.

These days, boxing mostly gets a bad rap; thugs dominate the ring and crooks manage them. Though once a Hollywood staple, boxing movies that show a positive aspect to the sport — getting fighters off the street and giving them a focal point for pent-up adolescent angst and anger — are now rare. Rarer still is *Girlfight*'s finely modulated sense of drama, in a genre prone to sensationalism and fervent sermonizing. And, unlike in most sports movies where the underdog must inevitably triumph at the end, the victor's identity in *Girlfight* is very much in doubt, partly because the outcome of the "big bout" isn't all that important. This picture is much more about Diana's succeeding in life than it is about her winning in the ring.

Girlfight has a hard side, because it's about characters who have been dealt a bad hand by life, but it is ultimately emotionally satisfying because it explores the way they fight and struggle to right themselves. **HIGHLY RECOMMENDED**

Gods and Monsters [1998]

Starring: Ian McKellen, Brendan Fraser, Lynn Redgrave, Lolita Davidovich Director: Bill Condon Screenplay: Bill Condon based on the novel *Father of Frankenstein* by Christopher Bram Running Time: 1:45 Rated: R (Homosexual themes, nudity, mild profanity) Theatrical Aspect Ratio: 1.85:1

Frankenstein. The Old Dark House. The Invisible Man. The Bride of Frankenstein. Show Boat. Although this may sound like a "which one of these things doesn't

belong" game, there is a common element to all 5 of these '30s motion pictures — they are the enduring legacy of director James Whale. Whale, an Englishman who started on the British stage, came to Hollywood in 1930, and, with the release of *Frankenstein* in 1931, established himself as a premiere horror film maker. Whale's career spanned the '30s, but, after the spectacular failure of 1937's *The Road Back* (a picture on which he claims to have lost creative control), his star dimmed. By the mid-'40s, he was out of the motion picture industry and had turned his attention to painting. In 1957, following a stroke that left him in a state of constant mental deterioration, he drowned himself in a swimming pool. *Gods and Monsters* presents a fictionalized account of the last month of Whale's life, and is replete with flashbacks to his boyhood, his time in the trenches during World War I, and his movie-making heyday.

The film explores the relationship between Whale (Ian McKellen) and his lawn cutter, Clay Boone (Brendan Fraser). Although Whale is homosexual, Clay is not, so their connection is strictly platonic. In Clay, Whale finds a willing audience for his stories, and a means to work through a painful event from his past. In Whale, Clay finds a sympathetic figure to replace the cold, harsh father who never understood him. While the primary focus of *Gods and Monsters* is their relationship, the movie also has a great deal to say about the process of filmmaking. We see a flashback to the creation of a classic scene from *The Bride of Frankenstein* (actress Rosalind Ayres bears a striking resemblance to Elsa Lanchaster), experience a lavish Hollywood party given by George Cukor (the director of *The Philadelphia Story* and *A Star Is Born*), and listen with rapt attention as Whale tells stories of his triumphs and tragedies behind the camera. The "gods and monsters" of the title have many meanings in this story, but the most apparent is the one relating to the film maker and his creations. Throughout this movie, we wonder whether Whale is shaping Clay into his final monster.

Most of us know James Whale's monsters — the stiff Karloff creature (whose appearance was suggested by Whale), the bizarrely beautiful Bride of Frankenstein, and Claude Rains' Invisible Man — but we know little of the individual who gave them life, and faced his own private demons on a daily basis. *Gods and Monsters* is a rich, multi-layered portrait of a director from Hollywood's Golden Age whose own life was as interesting as any of his movies.

RECOMMENDED

Going All the Way [1997]

Starring: Jeremy Davies, Ben Affleck, Amy Locane, Rachel Weisz, Rose McGowan, Jill Clayburgh, Lesley Ann Warren Director: Mark Pellington Screenplay: Dan Wakefield based on his novel Running Time: **1:43** Rated: R (Sexual situations, nudity, profanity, violence) Theatrical Aspect Ratio: 1.85:1

Going All the Way, based on Dan Wakefield's 1970 bestselling novel of the same name, is a coming of age story with characters who are a little older than usual in this genre. While most stories about the rituals of entering adulthood are set in high schools, *Going All the Way* looks at two 20-something men who, having served during the Korean War, are fresh out of the army and trying to find their place in the world. And, since the movie is set in 1954, it addresses the roles of religion and sex in the rites of passage — this is, after all, an era when the latter was taboo and the former was de rigueur.

Sonny (Jeremy Davies) and Gunner (Ben Affleck) are an unusual pair of close friends. Although both attended the same high school and each joined the army after graduation, that's where the similarity ends. Sonny is a shy, alienated young man who comes from a deeply conservative family and who gets tongue-tied around pretty girls. His war experience was limited to guarding the home front from Kansas City. Gunner, on the other hand, is an ex-jock who spent time in Korea and Japan. He's popular, well-liked, and can get any girl he wants. His mother (Lesley Ann Warren), a swinging bachelorette, treats him more like a boyfriend than a son. Yet, despite the differences in their personalities and backgrounds, Sonny and Gunner have very similar concerns and questions about the mysteries of life, love, and the future.

Women are, of course, the great unsolved (and perhaps unsolvable) mystery. Gunner falls for a sexy art student named Marty (Rachel Weisz, sporting an unbelievably irritating faux American accent), while Sonny is looking for a way out of a dead-end relationship with his high school sweetheart, the loyal-but-uninteresting Buddy (Amy Locane). He finds his escape in Gale (Rose McGowan), but learns the hard way that dream girls are sometimes better left in dreams.

The movie, adapted by Wakefield and directed by MTV alum and first time feature filmmaker Mark Pellington, is at times uneven. *Going All the Way* con-

tains elements of comedy ranging from subtle humor to blatant satire (most of the latter involve a scathing view of religion and conservatism in the '50s). Not all of these blend seamlessly with the movie's more dramatic elements, and several of the comic-to-serious transitions are jarring (such as the tragedy that follows closely upon Sonny's surreal trip into a fundamentalist church where he asks directions to a whore house).

Going All the Way is a pleasant way to spend an evening, and the characters are fashioned with enough detail for us to care about them, but this is in no way a seminal or transforming movie. The only thing that sets it apart from so many forgettable period piece coming-of-age stories is that it has been put together with a degree of care and skill.

RECOMMENDED

The Good Girl [2002]

Starring: Jennifer Aniston, Jake Gyllenhaal, John C. Reilly Director: Miguel Arteta Screenplay: Mike White Running Time: **1:33** Rated: R (Sexual situations, profanity, violence) Theatrical Aspect Ratio: 1.85:1

For Justine Last (Jennifer Aniston), the comfort of routine has crippled her. By her own admission, she feels like she's in a prison on death row. She has a job, a husband, and a home, but none of those things mean anything, except to offer the bland assurance that they were there yesterday, are there today, and will be there tomorrow. She's a retail clerk at a place called Retail Rodeo, an establishment that makes Wal-Mart look upscale. Her husband, Phil (John C. Reilly) is a house painter who spends his days working and his evenings sitting in front of the TV and smoking pot with his best friend, Bubba (Tim Blake Nelson). Then along comes Holden Worther (Jake Gyllenhaal), a 22-year old who joins the Retail Rodeo staff. He keeps to himself and reads *Catcher in the Rye* during his lunch breaks. Holden is a lost soul. Like Justine, he is dissatisfied with the routine of his life. She is drawn to him, and he becomes obsessed by her. Soon, they have embarked upon the kind of explosive affair that can only result when two people are drowning in desperation.

For Jennifer Aniston, this is clearly an attempt to escape the *Friends* typecasting. Her performance is forceful and effective — she effortlessly submerges herself into the role, and, after only a moment's hesitation, Aniston has vanished and all that's left is lonely, trapped Justine. Many actors, especially those who are identified with one particular role, bring a great deal of baggage with them to any part. That's not the case here. Meanwhile, John C. Reilly plays Phil as a dullard without ambition, and Jake Gyllenhaal is creepy as the too-intense Holden.

Some Aniston fans may be disappointed — this isn't the kind of lighthearted, throw-away film she has done in the past. It's a work of some substance that requires an investment of attention and effort on the part of the viewer. *The Good Girl* is not mainstream fare. It does not have happy ending (instead, it has a *fitting* one) and ignores the traditional formulas. Instead, *The Good Girl* offers nothing more spectacular than a character study. And, although *The Good Girl*'s protagonist may be trapped by routine, that's one claim that can never be made about the movie.
RECOMMENDED

Good Will Hunting [1997]

Starring: Matt Damon, Robin Williams, Ben Affleck, Stellan Skarsgård, Minnie Driver, Casey Affleck, Cole Hauser Director: Gus Van Sant Screenplay: Matt Damon and Ben Affleck Running Time: 2:06 Rated: R (Profanity, mature themes, violence) Theatrical Aspect Ratio: 1.85:1

Will Hunting is a troubled young man. As a child, he was the frequent victim of abuse. An orphan, he was in and out of foster homes on a regular basis. Now, not yet 21 years old, he has accumulated an impressive rap sheet. He has a short temper and any little incident can set him off like a spark in a tinder box. But he's a mathematical genius with a photographic memory and the ability to conceive simple solutions to complex problems. While working as a janitor at MIT, he delights in anonymously proving theorems on the math building's hall blackboards. Then, one evening, his anonymity is shattered when Professor Lambeau (Stellan Skarsgård) catches him at work. Will flees, but Lambeau tracks him down. Unfortunately, by the time the professor finds him, Will is in jail for assaulting a police offer.

The judge agrees to release Will under two conditions: that he spend one day a week meeting with Lambeau and that he spend one day a week meeting with a therapist. Eventually, once several psychologists have rejected the belligerent young man, Sean McGuire, a teacher at Bunker Hill Community College, agrees to take the case. After a rocky start, the two develop a rapport and Will begins to explore issues and emotions he had walled up behind impregnable armor. And, as Will advances his self-awareness in sessions with Sean, he also learns about friendship from his buddy, Chuckie (Ben Affleck), and love from a Harvard co-ed named Skylar (Minnie Driver).

Director Gus Van Sant (*Drugstore Cowboy, To Die For, Finding Forrester*) culls genuine emotion from his actors, and this results in several affecting and powerful scenes. There's an edginess to some of the Sean/Will therapy sessions, and the offscreen chemistry between Matt Damon and Minnie Driver (who became romantically linked while making this film) translates effectively to the movie — the Will/Skylar relationship is electric. Likewise, the companionability of Damon and Affleck is apparent in the easygoing nature of Will and Chuckie's friendship. The outstanding performance of the film, however, belongs to Robin Williams, whose Sean is sad and wise, funny and somber. This is arguably the best dramatic work in the actor's career, alongside *The Fisher King*.

Good Will Hunting is an ordinary story told well. Taken as a whole, there's little that's special about this tale — it follows a traditional narrative path, leaves the audience with a warm, fuzzy feeling, and never really challenges or surprises us. But it's intelligently written (with dialogue that is occasionally brilliant), strongly directed, and nicely acted. **RECOMMENDED**

Goodfellas [1990]

Starring: Robert De Niro, Ray Liotta, Joe Pesci, Lorraine Bracco, Paul Sorvino Director: Martin Scorsese Screenplay: Nicholas Pileggi & Martin Scorsese, based on "Wiseguy" by Pileggi Running Time: 2:26 Rated: R (Graphic violence, profanity, drug use) Theatrical Aspect Ratio: 1.85:1

There are two kinds of Mafia movies: those that romanticize the life, and those that show its brutality and squalor. The best known and most accomplished of these films, *The Godfather*, towers above the first camp. *Goodfellas* stands atop the other. Both pictures are epic in scope, but Coppola's *Godfather* embraces the mythos of the gangster, while Scorsese's exploration is more pragmatic. Violence is a key component of each, but it is a more brutal companion in *Goodfellas* than in *The Godfather*.

Written by Scorsese and Nicholas Pileggi, *Goodfellas* is based on a true story originally recounted in Pileggi's book *Wiseguy,* a rich and multi-layered study of three characters and the culture that shaped their lives. It's a fascinating exploration of a lifestyle that has beguiled Americans for most of this century, whether in movies, in novels, or on television.

The story opens by introducing us to 13-year-old Henry Hill (played by Christopher Serrone as a youngster and by Ray Liotta as an adult), our narrator. It's the '50s in New York City, and becoming a member of the mob looks like one of the coolest employment opportunities around. "As far back as I can remember," Henry recollects, "I wanted to be a gangster." And no wonder — to a kid just entering his second decade of life, these men have everything: friends, girls, cars, cash, and, most importantly, respect. Henry pursues his goal and soon has become a gofer for the brother of Paul Cicero (Paul Sorvino), the neighborhood boss. His first taste of the life is a heady experience. "At 13, I was making more money than most of the adults in the neighborhood."

The story, which spans a quarter of a century, has an epic feel despite its intimate perspective. The first 40 minutes, which detail Henry's childhood and his acceptance into mob life, is presented almost as a fairy tale, using the same kind of romanticized approach embraced by *The Godfather*. The purpose of this segment is to forge a bond between the audience and the main character while he is still relatively innocent. Henry does not grow up to be a nice man, but, because of the way Scorsese has structured the early portions of the film, we remain sympathetic to him throughout.

Goodfellas begins calmly, but, by the time the final credits roll, there has been a great deal of blood shed. Some of the violence is sudden, shocking, and visceral. One death in particular comes as a total surprise, and leaves the viewer momentarily stunned and disoriented. Even after I have seen the film numerous times, this scene remains unsettling. *Goodfellas* does not rely on plot twists to hold the viewer's attention, but one of the film's strongest traits is the sense of uncertainty that hangs over every frame. Scorsese's tactic of using two narrators even leaves open the possibility that Henry might not survive the film.

Film critics will argue over which represents Scorsese at his best — *Taxi Driver, Raging Bull,* or *Goodfellas.* Taken together, these 3 films offer insight into the themes and ideas that are closest to Scorsese's heart. Taken individually, each represents an amazing motion picture accomplishment, with *Goodfellas* standing alongside *The Godfather* as the two greatest mob stories told on film. MUST SEE

Gosford Park [2001]

Starring: Emily Watson, Derek Jacobi, Maggie Smith, Kristin Scott Thomas, Kelly Macdonald, Clive Owen, Stephen Fry, Ryan Phillippe, Jeremy Northam, Helen Mirren, Michael Gambon Director: Robert Altman Screenplay: Julian Fellowes Running Time: 2:18 Rated: R (Violence, profanity, mature themes) Theatrical Aspect Ratio: 2.35:1

Gosford Park is an ensemble movie, with perhaps the largest and most distinguished group of actors direc-

tor Robert Altman has ever worked with. The cast list reads like a who's who of British cinema, including Derek Jacobi, Emily Watson, Michael Gambon, Maggie Smith, Kristin Scott Thomas, Stephen Fry, Helen Mirren, Jeremy Northam, and Clive Owen. Thrown in for good measure are a Scottish lass (Kelly Macdonald) and two Americans (Ryan Phillippe, who doesn't seem out of his depth, and Bob Balaban). With such a roster, two things are never in doubt: (1) the film features some of the best acting in any 2001 feature, and (2) nearly everyone is underused.

Gosford Park takes place in November 1932 during a shooting party at the rural estate of Gosford Park, the home of Sir William and Lady Sylvia McCordle (Michael Gambon and Kristin Scott-Thomas). Their guests include other members of the local nobility, such as Lord Stockbridge (Charles Dance), the Honorable Freddie Nesbitt (James Wilby), and the Countess of Trentham (Maggie Smith), and some members of the movie-making community: actors Ivor Novello (Jeremy Northam) and Henry Denton (Ryan Phillippe), and producer Morris Weissman (Bob Balaban). As the story progresses, we become privy to the friction generated by old romances and new rivalries. Even more is going on below the stairs, where the servants live and work. The head of the household, Mrs. Wilson (Helen Mirren), is harboring a long-buried secret that is clawing its way from the grave. Housemaid Elsie (Emily Watson) is secretly carrying on an affair with Sir William. Probert (Derek Jacobi), Sir William's valet, is constantly jumping to fill his master's unusual requests. Into this mix are thrown Mary (Kelly Macdonald), the Countess' maid, and Robert Parks (Clive Owen), Lord Stockbridge's valet, both of whom are new at service. Things are proceeding as smoothly as possible until the unthinkable occurs — a murder. And, with no shortage of suspects both upstairs and downstairs, a top-notch detective is needed to solve the crime. Unfortunately, Inspector Thompson (Stephen Fry) is assigned to the case, and he's more concerned about people mispronouncing his name than about gathering physical evidence.

Altman is widely regarded as a master of the ensemble film, but in *Gosford Park* he seems unable to wrap his arms completely around the large and talented cast. This is a hugely ambitious undertaking, and it's a pleasure to see so many accomplished actors on screen in one film. But perhaps Altman tries to cram a little too much into his 138-minute running length. Things go by too fast and there's little opportunity to identify with anyone in a more than perfunctory manner. Nevertheless, overshooting the mark is infinitely preferable to undershooting it, which is the failing of far too many films. *Gosford Park* is not an uncontested triumph, but it is thoroughly enjoyable. **RECOMMENDED**

The Governess [United Kingdom, 1998]

Starring: Minnie Driver, Tom Wilkinson, Florence Hoath, Jonathan Rhys-Meyers Director: Sandra Goldbacher Screenplay: Sandra Goldbacher Running Time: 1:54 Rated: R (Sex, nudity) Theatrical Aspect Ratio: 2.35:1

Before seeing *The Governess,* I never thought of Minnie Driver as a sex symbol. A good actress with charismatic screen presence, yes . . . but a sex symbol? In her previous films her characters have been more cute and bubbly than sexy. That has changed with *The Governess,* a period drama set in 19th century Great Britain.

Driver plays Rosina, a 20-something Jewish girl living in London who has eschewed marriage so that she can pursue a career as an actress. When her father is murdered, her family is left in heavy debt and she must either marry a rich man or seek employment. Unwilling to sell herself into a loveless union, she applies for a position as the governess of a girl living on the Isle of Skye in Scotland. And, because a woman of solid Christian values is sought, she assumes the pseudonym of Mary Blackchurch, and uses her acting skills to disguise herself as a "Gentile and a gentlewoman." Her application is readily accepted.

Rosina soon finds herself in a strange land, surrounded by people with bizarre customs. Not only do the Gentiles make her uneasy, but she finds the green, wide-open spaces of Scotland disconcerting. "I long for cities and chimneys," she remarks in a voiceover narration. Her employers are the Cavendishes. Mrs. Cavendish (Harriet Walter) is a relentlessly proper woman whose chief characteristics are prudishness and humorlessness. In Rosina's words, she's seems like "she has a lemon up her posterior." Mr. Cavendish (Tom Wilkinson) is a mysterious man who spends nearly all of his waking hours working on a project in his laboratory. Rosina's charge, 13-year-old Clementina (Florence Hoath), is a "rodent in lace" who is quickly subdued by a few pointed threats. Then there's Clementina's older brother, Henry (Jonathan Rhys-Meyers), who is almost immediately infatuated by the governess.

Rosina's natural curiosity leads her to explore Cavendish's laboratory. There she finds that he is experimenting with a new process called photography. Soon, the two are working as a team to find the critical agent that will allow the images captured by the camera to remain permanent. Initially, he resists taking a picture of Rosina, but eventually she wears him down, and, the more she bares herself to the camera, the more deeply Cavendish falls under her spell, even though he resists his own feelings every step of the way.

The Governess is solidly entertaining material with enough substance to lift it above the traditional period drama. Goldbacher's script takes the time to develop each of the major characters, which allows the climax and denouement to have greater impact. In addition to flawless acting by Driver and Wilkinson, the film is highlighted by Ashley Rowe's sumptuous photography. *The Governess* is far more absorbing than one might guess from the accurate, if plain, title. **RECOMMENDED**

Great Expectations [1998]

Starring: Ethan Hawke, Gwyneth Paltrow, Anne Bancroft, Robert DeNiro Director: Alfonso Cuaron Screenplay: Mitch Glazer based on the novel by Charles Dickens Running Time: 1:51 Rated: R (Sex, nudity, profanity) Theatrical Aspect Ratio: 2.35:1

You have to give a film maker credit for having the chutzpah to take one of the most beloved classics in the English language and transform it into a modern-day morality play/romance. *Great Expectations* is considered by many to be Dickens' finest novel; it is certainly among his darkest. With the setting changed from 19th century England to contemporary Florida and New York, the social minefield of Dickensian England has lost some of its menace. Surprisingly, however, the story survived the transition relatively unscathed.

Even as the setting has changed, so have the names and occupations of many of the characters. The lead is no longer Pip; he's now called Finn, and is played by Ethan Hawke (with an assist from Jeremy Kissner as a 10-year-old). Estella, the love of Finn's life, is still Estella, and she is portrayed by a radiant-yet-restrained Gwyneth Paltrow (and Raquel Beaudene at a younger age). Mad Miss Havisham has become the equally deranged Miss Dinsmore, who spends her days in a ruined house mourning a wedding that never took place. With Anne Bancroft in this part, it's easy to imagine that Nora Dinsmore could be Mrs. Robinson gone bonkers, 30 years later. The criminal Magwich has become Lustig, an escaped death row inmate, and is played by Robert DeNiro. Finally, Chris Cooper (*Lone Star*) plays Finn's "uncle," Joe Gargery (no name change), and Hank Azaria is Walter Plane, Finn's rival for Estella.

Finn first meets Estella in the late 1970s, when both are 10 years old. Neither has any parents. Finn lives with his sister and her boyfriend; Estella has been adopted by Miss Dinsmore, who (though crazy) is one of the richest women in Florida. Despite a warning from the old lady that Estella will break his heart, Finn falls for the golden-haired girl, but their relationship never progresses beyond wet kisses at a water fountain. Finn is in earnest, but Estella likes to tease. More than a decade later, they meet in New York City. He's there to break into the Manhattan art scene (and earn enough money to impress her), while she's contemplating marriage to a man named Walter Plane, who has commitment problems. And, hidden beneath the love story, there's a mystery. Someone is bankrolling Finn's success. He assumes it's Miss Dinsmore, but is the truth perhaps less obvious?

The actors do admirable jobs, and all of the performances feed into the essence of *Great Expectations,* with its elements of unrequited love, broken class barriers, and unexpected revelations. Any missteps here are not so much the result of shifting the novel in time and place, but of condensing it to feature-length. Nevertheless, while *Great Expectations* falls short of being the definitive interpretation of the novel (for that, see David Lean's 1946 version) it still offers an entertaining 2 hours. RECOMMENDED

The Green Mile [1999]

Starring: Tom Hanks, David Morse, Bonnie Hunt, Michael Clarke Duncan, James Cromwell, Michael Jeter, Graham Greene, Doug Hutchison, Sam Rockwell, Barry Pepper, Jeffrey DeMunn, Patricia Clarkson Director: Frank Darabont Screenplay: Frank Darabont, based on the novel by Stephen King Running Time: 3:08 Rated: R (Violence, profanity, sex-related material) Theatrical Aspect Ratio: 2.35:1

Stephen King stories generally come in two flavors — the kind that top level directors fashion into powerful motion pictures (*Stand By Me, The Shining, The Shawshank Redemption, Dolores Claiborne,* etc.) and more schlocky, exploitative fare. Generally speaking, *The Green Mile* falls into the first category.

"The Green Mile" is the nickname given to the Coal Mountain Louisiana State Penitentiary's death row. The year is 1935, and narrator and main character Paul Edgecomb (Hanks), is head guard of The Green

Mile. Four others work with him — his best friend, Brutus Howell (David Morse); the handsome and somewhat impetuous Dean Stanton (Barry Pepper); the veteran Harry Terwilleger (Jeffrey DeMunn); and the newcomer, a sadist and coward named Percy Wetmore (Doug Hutchison). Percy has a promotion to a desk job at a mental institution waiting for him — he's only on the Mile so he can see an execution. Paul would dearly like to get rid of him, but Percy has highly placed connections and cannot be transferred until he submits a request.

A new inmate, John Coffey (Michael Clarke Duncan), has come to The Green Mile, joining the two who are already awaiting signed death warrants. They are a Cajun named Eduard Delacroix (Michael Jeter) and a Native American, Arlen Bitterbuck (Graham Greene). John is a giant of a man, but he is quiet, simpleminded, and surprisingly docile: surprising considering the shocking crime he was arrested for — the brutal murder of two little girls. While Percy delights in tormenting the prisoners, both new and old, Paul and the other guards form tentative bonds with them. And, because of that, Paul makes a remarkable discovery about John, and realizes that something extremely unusual may be at work on The Green Mile.

With 3 hours to work with, it's no surprise that Darabont does an excellent job of character development. Realistically, however, the film probably would have been as effective at about two-thirds that length. The film also includes a strong Judeo-Christian message, and at times the symbolism is laid on a little thickly. Problems aside, *The Green Mile* is at times a powerful motion picture. The characters are well-drawn and ably portrayed, with Tom Hanks filling the shoes of the likable protagonist as only he can, and Doug Hutchison doing a good job making us hate him. Sam Rockwell gets an opportunity to chew on the scenery as an out-of-control, bad-to-the-bone nutcase who is shut up in a cell. Bonnie Hunt, who gets better with every movie, is Paul's wife. But the real standout is Michael Clarke Duncan, who easily acts circles around Hanks — his portrayal of John is often touching and occasionally wrenching. RECOMMENDED

The Grey Zone [2001]

Starring: David Arquette, Daniel Benzali, David Chandler, Steve Buscemi, Harvey Keitel Director: Tim Blake Nelson Screenplay: Tim Blake Nelson Running Time: 1:33 Rated: R (Holocaust images, nudity, violence) Theatrical Aspect Ratio: 1.85:1

Auschwitz, 1944. One of the darkest times in one of the darkest places in recent human history. It is into this nightmarish world that director Tim Blake Nelson plunges us with *The Grey Zone*, a harrowing film about compromise, betrayal, and moral ambiguity that tells the tale of the 12th Sonderkommando at Auschwitz — the only group ever to lead an armed uprising at the death camp. (The term "Sonderkommando" was coined by the Germans to describe those Jews who agreed to collaborate with the Nazis.)

In the darkness of the death camp, an armed uprising is being planned by the Sonderkommandos, who have been stockpiling illicitly gained explosives and guns. While some of the organizers, such as the self-serving Abramowics (Steve Buscemi), plan to use this as an opportunity to escape, others, such as Hoffman (David Arquette), Rosenthal (David Chandler), and Schlermer (Daniel Benzali) are more pragmatic. Their intention is to blow up the crematoriums, then die fighting. They do not believe they will ever again see anything outside of the walls of Auschwitz. Thirsty for some form of redemption, these men leap to the aid of a 14-year-old girl (Kamelia Grigorova) who miraculously survives a gassing. They hide her, and, with the aid of Dr. Nyiszli (Allan Corduner), Mengele's Jewish assistant, bring her back to consciousness. Even when Muhsfeldt (Harvey Keitel), the Nazi camp commander, learns of her presence, they stubbornly refuse to let her die, even when their actions endanger the uprising.

The Grey Zone is as powerful as it is grim. The film illustrates the darker side of the human instinct for survival — how men can be capable of things they never would have thought possible in the face of death. In order to spare their consciences, the members of the Sonderkommando display an amazing ability to lie to themselves, but, the more aware they become of their culpability in what is transpiring around them, the greater their need is for a taste of redemption.

With its numerous complex issues, the Holocaust has formed the backdrop for countless powerful, emotionally wrenching dramas. And, with so many stories to tell, redundancy does not seem to be a problem — each new motion picture puts a face on another previously anonymous body. *The Grey Zone* gives life and meaning to an event that is little more than a footnote in history books (if that). Like so many of its fellow Holocaust dramas, *The Grey Zone*

seeks not to comfort audiences, but to remind them.
RECOMMENDED

Guinevere [1999]
Starring: Stephen Rea, Sarah Polley, Jean Smart, Gina Gershon
Director: Audrey Wells Screenplay: Audrey Wells Running Time: 1:47
Rated: R (Profanity, sex, nudity) Theatrical Aspect Ratio: 1.85:1

Every year has a set of breakout performances. In 1999, one of those belonged to Sarah Polley in *Guinevere*, a smartly written, insightful coming of age movie. Considering that 90% of the entries in this genre deal with the trials and tribulations of young men, the protagonist's gender alone makes *Guinevere* noteworthy.

Portraying 21-year-old Harper Sloane, Polley is a standout from the moment she appears in the first scene. The event is her older sister's wedding, and it's immediately clear that the only thing the family considers Harper good for is acting as a gofer. She's told to locate the photographer, but, after unsuccessfully searching the grounds, she finds an isolated spot to wrestle with the cork on a champagne bottle. Enter the photographer, Connie Fitzpatrick (Stephen Rea), a genial, middle-aged man whose bohemian charisma immediately captures Harper's affection-starved attention.

It doesn't take long for Harper to become Connie's apprentice (both in the study of life and photography). He wants to release the talent he senses bubbling just beneath her surface. Following his advice, she decides not to go to law school — an action that enrages her parents, who are both attorneys — but she isn't certain that Connie is right about her artistic ability. "I've got no talent," she remarks. "You're mistaking me for someone with potential." It doesn't take long for Harper and Connie to become lovers, too, and for her to leave her parents' sterile mansion and move in with him. However, an encounter with one of Connie's former "pupils" (Gina Gershon) provokes Harper to wonder whether she's really special, or just another one of Connie's conquests.

Although Polley steals the spotlight, she is given strong support by Stephen Rea, Jean Smart, and (though in a small role) Gina Gershon. Of the three, Rea has the most difficult task — playing a middle-aged loser with no future who is, as seen through Harper's eyes, also a figure of kindness, wisdom, and charm. Rea finds the right balance, allowing the audience to observe both aspects of his character. As Harper's mother, Smart leaps off the screen during her few scenes and proves the old adage that the tongue can cut more deeply than the knife. Gershon brings a cocky cynicism to the role of Billie, illustrating the kind of life that a relationship with Connie can lead to.

Guinevere has a clear-headed view of its characters and their situations. Unfortunately, for the epilogue, Welles switches the focus away from Harper and towards Connie, and uses an unwelcome fantasy sequence to offer closure. Other than that, *Guinevere* is a successful feature debut for Audrey Welles, and an opportunity for Sarah Polley to display the full range of her considerable acting ability. RECOMMENDED

Hamlet [United Kingdom/United States, 1996]

Starring: Kenneth Branagh, Derek Jacobi, Julie Christie, Richard Briers, Nicholas Farrell, Kate Winslet Director: Kenneth Branagh Screenplay: Kenneth Branagh based on the play by William Shakespeare Running Time: 4:02 Rated: PG-13 (Mature themes, brief nudity, sex, violence) Theatrical Aspect Ratio: 2.35:1

This is not only the best filmed version of *Hamlet,* but the best film of *any* of Shakespeare's plays I have ever seen. *Hamlet* has long been something of a private obsession for actor/director Kenneth Branagh; now that vision has been realized, and with every line from the original play intact, it takes approximately 4 hours to run. It is a well-spent 4 hours.

Part of the enduring appeal of *Hamlet* lies in its complex characterization and twisty, tragic plot. *Hamlet* deals with, among other things, madness and revenge, sex and love, and ghosts, both real and figurative. There is also a great deal of humor, and good old-fashioned adventure. *Hamlet* can literally make you laugh and cry, hiss and cheer. It contains a slew of the most famous lines in English lit, including "To thine own self be true," "Something is rotten in the state of Denmark," "Brevity is the soul of wit," "The play's the thing," "The lady doeth protest too much," and, of course, "To be, or not to be, that is the question."

The story takes place in 12th-century Denmark. Prince Hamlet (Branagh), is mourning the death of his beloved father (Brian Blessed) and the untimely (and according to custom, unseemly) wedding of his mother, Gertrude (Julie Christie), to his uncle, Claudius (Derek Jacobi). Hamlet sees his mother's hasty remarriage as a betrayal of her union with his father, but worse news is yet to come. An apparition of the dead King haunts Elsinore Castle, and when Hamlet confronts it the ghost claims Claudius poisoned him to claim both queen and crown for himself. Hamlet vows revenge, and thus begins either his

slow spiral into madness or his carefully orchestrated act to appear insane.

Meanwhile, Fortinbras (Rufus Sewell), the nephew of the King of Norway, is massing armies to attack Denmark. Ophelia (Kate Winslet), Hamlet's lover, has been forbidden to have any further contact with the prince. A group of traveling actors has come to Elsinore. And two old school mates of Hamlet's have been employed by Claudius to betray their old friend.

Branagh has assembled a top-notch international cast. Well-known actors like Charlton Heston (as the Player King), John Gielgud (Priam), Judi Dench (Hecuba), and Robin Williams (Osric) fill small roles. The leads are all in peak form. Richard Briers adds layers of guile and intelligence to his interpretation of the fatuous Polonius. Brian Blessed makes us feel the power and malevolence of the ghost. Julie Christie's wonderful Gertrude allows us to understand why Claudius would resort to murder to win her. And Derek Jacobi's cultured, politically savvy, yet privately tortured Claudius is richly portrayed.

Then there's Kenneth Branagh, the film's undisputed star. For Hamlet's calmer, quieter scenes (such as the soliloquies), Branagh brings a contemplative and introspective quality to his performance. But for the emotionally rousing sequences, his interpretation is brash and forceful, drawing us into the pure drama of the situation. It's a marvelous portrayal that complements those of the many other cast members.

From the moment it was first announced that Branagh would attempt an unabridged *Hamlet,* I never doubted that it would be a worthy effort. I have seen dozens of versions of this play (either on screen or on stage), and none has ever held me in such a grip of awe. This may be Kenneth Branagh's dream, but it is our pleasure. MUST SEE

Hamsun [Denmark/Sweden, 1996]

Starring: Max von Sydow, Ghita Nør Director: Jan Troell Screenplay: Per Olov Enquist based on *Processen mod Hamsun* by Thorkild Hansen and *Regnbuen* by Marie Hamsun Running Time: 2:40 Rated: No MPAA Rating (Mature themes) Theatrical Aspect Ratio: 1.85:1 In Danish, German, Norwegian, and Swedish with subtitles

Nobel prize winning writer. Nazi sympathizer. Deep thinker. Naïve fool. To some, Knut Hamsun was a hero, but to most, he was a villain and a coward who sold out to Hitler for the price of safety and respect. In *Hamsun,* a powerful 1996 feature from renowned Swedish director Jan Troell (*The Emigrants*), the tragedy of Hamsun's life is laid bare before the camera over a 17-year period (from 1935 until his death in

1952). This is a singularly striking and unforgettable portrayal of a great man whose hubris led to his fall. Shakespearean in its approach and structure, *Hamsun* represents the first time I have ever felt real pity and sorrow for a figure linked by history to the rise of the Third Reich.

In his heyday, Hamsun was one of the most revered men in Norway. Awarded the 1920 Nobel Prize for literature, he became a national hero. But, during Hitler's rise in the '30s and '40s, Hamsun sided with Quisling's puppet government, and, in the years after World War II, his very name was anathema. The reasons for Hamsun's political stance are a key aspect of this riveting drama. Was it because, as he publicly declared, he harbored an intense hatred of British imperialism and believed the best path for a free Norway was to side with Germany? Or was there a more personal influence, such as the singleminded drive of his wife? *Hamsun* offers a wealth of possibilities, but no real answers. The film also makes it clear that, although the title character supported Hitler, he failed to comprehend the depth of the German leader's anti-Semitism, and the lengths to which he would go to carry out his genocidal goals.

As the elderly Hamsun, Max von Sydow gives the crowning performance of an impeccable career. Cantankerous, aloof, thoughtful, intellectually astute, and, in the end, frail and emotionally ruined, von Sydow's Hamsun is a fully realized individual. Nearly his match is co-star Ghita Nørby, who portrays Hamsun's controlling, bitter wife, Marie. Knut and Marie's union is as dysfunctional as a marriage can get, and the actors effectively present complex interpretations of characters whose vicious psychological struggles have bound them together while scarring their children.

At 160 minutes, *Hamsun* probably runs a little too long, and there are a few slow parts, but the cumulative effect is devastating. *Hamsun* goes to extraordinary lengths to present one of history's villains as nothing more demonic than a deeply flawed human being. **HIGHLY RECOMMENDED**

Happenstance [France, 2000]

Starring: **Audrey Tautou, Faudel, Eric Savin, Eric Feldman, Lysaine Meis** Director: **Laurent Firode** Screenplay: **Laurent Firode** Running Time: **1:37** Rated: **R (Nudity, sexual situations, profanity)** In French with subtitles

Chaos theory, that arcane branch of mathematics with the cool name, has been showing up in some surprising motion pictures (see *Jurassic Park*). And

why not? It all has to do with cause-and-effect — a perfect film vehicle — and is the subject of French filmmaker Laurent Firode's debut, *Happenstance*.

The central character, Irene, is played by the luminous Audrey Tautou, star of *Amelie*. "Central" is perhaps a misleading term. Although Irene has more exposure than anyone else, and the story keeps returning to her, she's just one of many faces to populate the screen.

We first meet Irene on a subway train during her daily commute to work. When a woman reads Irene's horoscope out loud, Younes (Algerian singer Faudel) realizes it is his as well because he and Irene share the same birthday. The horoscope speaks of discovering one's true love on the day of the full moon, which happens to be that day. So, Younes spends the rest of his waking hours searching for Ms. Right. Irene, meanwhile, undergoes one mishap after another, until she finally decides to pack up her things, leave Paris, and go home to her mother. We meet others whose paths cross those of Irene and Younes: Richard (Eric Savin), a married man carrying on an affair with Elsa (Lysaine Meis); Luc (Eric Feldman), a charming liar who seems incapable of being truthful around women; Stephanie (Irene Ismailoff), whose reunion with an old lover turns into a nightmare; an old woman (Francoise Bertin), who tries to return a coffee maker to the store where she bought it; a pickpocket (Said Serrari), who chooses an unfortunate victim; and many others.

The film is openly interested in the vagaries of chance and fate. It's a delight to watch the plot unfold, and to become aware of how a small, random action by one person can impact the life of another. Does the film overplay its hand and rely too much on coincidence? Only to those who aren't fascinated by the idea. In some ways, Firode's effort works better on a second viewing, when the characters and their relationships to one another have been established; but whether seen once or multiple times, *Happenstance* is an intriguing meditation on the unseen forces that no one can escape. **RECOMMENDED**

Happiness [1998]

Starring: **Jane Adams, Dylan Baker, Lara Flynn Boyle, Philip Seymour Hoffman, Cynthia Stevenson, Jared Harris, Ben Gazzara, Louise Lasser, Camryn Manheim** Director: **Todd Solondz** Screenplay: **Todd Solondz** Running Time: **2:12** Rated: **No MPAA Rating (Graphic sexual situations, profanity, nudity)** Theatrical Aspect Ratio: **1.85:1**

Happiness, director Todd Solondz's second feature, is an ensemble piece of several different stories, all of which revolve around the Jordan sisters. Trish (Cynthia Stevenson), the oldest, is apparently living the American dream: she has a beautiful house, a loving husband, and 3 children. Helen (Lara Flynn Boyle), a successful author, leads a life of wealth and glamour. Joy (Jane Adams) is alone and lonely, and the only men she attracts turn out to be losers, cheats, and degenerates. Trish and Helen both pay lip service to their concern for Joy, but, in reality, they're so wrapped up in their own lives that they could care less. Self-centeredness is the chief characteristic of nearly everyone in this film.

Helen feels that she's a fraud, and, tired of empty nights of sex with good-looking men, she's in search of something adventurous. She finds it through Allen (Philip Seymour Hoffman), a repressed computer geek who derives sexual fulfillment from making obscene phone calls.

Meanwhile, Trish's marriage hides a dark secret. Her proper and caring psychiatrist husband, Bill (Dylan Baker), is a pedophile, and, while he presents the facade of the perfect family man, his obsession is always lurking just beneath the surface. For a while, he is content with masturbating to pictures of good-looking teen idols, but, when the opportunity presents itself, he drugs and rapes the best friend of his adolescent son. With the genie out of the bottle, there is no stopping him.

Finally, there's Lenny and Mona (Ben Gazzara and Louise Lasser), the retired parents of Joy, Trish, and Helen. After 40 years of marriage, Lenny decides that he needs to be alone. He doesn't want a divorce, but he craves "more space."

Solondz's overriding message is that true happiness is a myth. There is no such thing. Some are pragmatic enough to accept that fact and live with it. Others delude themselves into believing that it might be possible, only to be slapped down when faced with the truth. In *Happiness*, the disconsolate Joy is no less cheerful than the perfectly-married Trish or the financially-assured Helen.

It took me more than one viewing of *Happiness* and a lot of thought to clarify my feelings about this movie. One thing is for certain: *Happiness* is not for everyone. John Waters (director of *Pink Flamingos* and *Pecker*) has lavished praise upon Solondz and *Happiness*. The Farrelly Brothers (*There's Something about Mary*), on the other hand, were quoted in the New York Times Magazine as calling the picture "sick." Audience reaction for this audacious experiment is no less divided. Love it or hate it, however, *Happiness* is not easily forgotten. **HIGHLY RECOMMENDED**

Hate (La Haine) [France, 1995]

Starring: Vincent Cassel, Hubert Kounde, Said Taghmaoui, Francois Levantal, Marc Duret Director: Mathieu Kassovitz Screenplay: Mathieu Kassovitz Running Time: 1:35 Rated: R (Profanity, violence) Theatrical Aspect Ratio: 1.66:1 In French with subtitles

If there's one thing that Mathieu Kassovitz's black-and-white feature proves, it's that hate knows no boundaries — international, racial, or generational. With a perspective that's part *Kids*, part *Boyz 'N the Hood*, part Scorsese, and part all its own, *Hate* offers a raw, powerful look at urban class struggles in and around Paris. If not for the subtitled French dialogue, this story could just as easily have taken place in New York, Los Angeles, London, or dozens of other cities.

Hate, which captured three Cesar awards in 1994, is an angry film from a passionate young film maker. The narrative is sparse, bordering on nonexistent, and the trio of main characters aren't the sort of people you'd want to meet in real life. But *Hate* never asks its audience to sympathize with the protagonists, only to understand some of the factors that make them act as they do. For 90 minutes, they rail against "the system" which has warped their existence, until the consequences of violence overtake them. You can only run so far, so fast.

The first of the 3 principals is Said (Said Taghmaoui), a French youth of Arab decent who often represents the voice of reason (such as it is). Next, there's Vinz (Vincent Cassel), a Jew who sees himself as a thug in the Robert De Niro mold (he does a pretty good imitation of *Taxi Driver*'s "You talking to me?" line). The other member of the small group is Hubert (Hubert Kounde), an African French teen. *Hate* follows these characters for 24 hours as they meander through Paris' seedier districts. They have many enemies — the police, skinheads, and the privileged, to name a few, and, when Vincent confesses that he has a gun, each of the 3 feels a thrill of power. Suddenly, they have the means to strike back, if only briefly, against the forces that have penned them into their unpromising life.

In *Hate*'s culture, going to jail is a badge of honor and guns are viewed with awe (in France, they aren't as readily available as in the United States). Death doesn't mean much — it is taken as inevitable, either sooner or later. The film uses a repeated, and somewhat chilling, metaphor comparing life in urban France to someone jumping off a skyscraper. All the way down, with each passing floor, the jumper thinks "So good, so far." Then he hits bottom. In the end, it's not how far you fall that matters, but how you land. *Hate* may portray young men who explode on impact, but the film itself has a solid touchdown. **HIGHLY RECOMMENDED**

He Got Game [1998]

Starring: Denzel Washington, Ray Allen, Rosario Dawson, Milla Jovovich Director: **Spike Lee** Screenplay: **Spike Lee** Running Time: 2:11 Rated: R (Profanity, nudity, sex, violence) Theatrical Aspect Ratio: **1.85:1**

Writer/director Spike Lee is a huge basketball fan (specifically, a New York Knicks fan), and *He Got Game* has been called "Lee's basketball film." Such a label is misleading. *Hoosiers* is a basketball movie; *He Got Game* is a story about life, relationships, and the pressures of fame.

The story opens with Jake Shuttleworth (Denzel Washington) serving a lengthy sentence in Attica for killing his wife. Meanwhile, on the outside, his son, Jesus (Ray Allen), has become the top-rated high school basketball player in the country, and is being recruited by every major college. In the words of one expert, he's "the best thing to happen to the game since the tennis shoe was invented." The warden of Attica (Ned Beatty) comes to Jake with a deal: convince Jesus to go to the governor's alma mater, Big State, and Jake's sentence will be reduced or commuted. To allow Jake to make contact with his son, he is given one week of freedom. There's a problem, though — Jesus doesn't want to have anything to do with his father, and Jake's increasingly desperate attempts at a reconciliation run into a brick wall.

The other aspect of *He Got Game* is the high-pressure salesmanship designed to encourage Jesus to sign a letter of intent with a college or to hire an agent and go pro. While there's something vaguely comical about many of these scenes, Lee conveys the strain that highly-touted, young athletes are under. With surreptitious cash payments and all sorts of perks so readily available, it's understandable why some high-schoolers make the choices and mistakes that they do. In its depiction of this side of the sports business, *He Got Game* makes an effective companion piece to *Hoop Dreams* and *Blue Chips* (which explored college recruiting from the coach's perspective).

Beyond Washington and Allen, Lee has populated the film with a number of credible supporting performers. Zelda Harris (the lead in *Crooklyn*) is delightful as Jesus' little sister. Rosario Dawson is con-

vincing as Lala, Jesus' sexy girlfriend. Bill Nunn and Hill Harper provide comic relief as Jesus' uncle and cousin, respectively. And Milla Jovovich, best known for her work in *The Fifth Element*, is surprisingly sympathetic as a down-on-her-luck prostitute who connects with Jake during his week out of prison. There are cameos from the likes of Charles Barkley, Larry Bird, Michael Jordan, Shaquille O'Neal, John Thompson, and Reggie Miller.

While the father/son reunion gives the film its emotional core, the basketball recruiting sequences provide a cynical edge. Stylistically, *He Got Game* is uneven. Narratively, the film is hurt by a contrived setup and a hokey, overly-sentimental final scene. It's the stuff in between that makes this a worthwhile experience, however, which it surely is. **RECOMMENDED**

Heavy [1995]

Starring: Pruitt Taylor Vince, Liv Tyler, Deborah Harry, Shelley Winters Director: **James Mangold** Screenplay: **James Mangold** Running Time: 1:45 Rated: No MPAA Rating (Profanity, mature themes) Theatrical Aspect Ratio: **1.85:1**

The characters in James Mangold's debut feature, *Heavy*, are the flotsam and jetsam of life. They all wash up at Pete and Dolly's Restaurant, a Hudson Valley roadhouse where a smile is just about the last thing anyone expects to see.

The roadhouse is owned and run by Dolly Modino (Shelley Winters), an aging woman in failing health. Dolly spends much of her time reminiscing about the past when her husband was still alive. Delores (Deborah Harry) is a frumpy waitress who has engaged in a 15-year war of words with Dolly. Life-weary and looking for a little affection, Delores drifts from day-to-day, not seeming to care what comes next. Leo (Joe Grifasi) is Pete and Dolly's most loyal customer, a perpetually drunk loser who hangs around the roadhouse hoping that Delores will agree to take him home. Callie (Liv Tyler) is the new employee, a college dropout in need of money who is saddled with a loutish boyfriend and may or may not be pregnant.

Then there's Victor (Pruitt Taylor Vince), the film's protagonist. Painfully shy and convinced that his overweight condition makes him unattractive, Victor lives in the shadow of his mother, Dolly. He's the restaurant's cook and the object of Delores' affection. With the arrival of Callie, Victor finds something to brighten up his days. He is instantly smitten with her, and, when she has a few kind words for him and seems interested in a friendship, Victor is eager to oblige. Nevertheless, his feelings for Callie are clearly not reciprocated on the same level, and lead to inevitable heartbreak.

Dialogue is sparse in *Heavy*, so it's left up to the actors to form and develop their characters with mannerisms and facial expressions instead of scripted lines. Considering that the cast is not made up of "great" names, this is a daring move by Mangold. Fortunately, it pays off, largely due to a gargantuan performance by Pruitt Taylor Vince (*Nobody's Fool*), who creates a heartwrenchingly sympathetic man we can't help caring about. Deborah Harry is also good, giving us the kind of waitress who would have made *Frankie and Johnny* a memorable movie. Liv Tyler (*Stealing Beauty*) gets by more on looks than ability, but she has her moments. And Shelley Winters is refreshingly low-key.

Heavy is not the kind of film to view when you're looking for something upbeat. It's too real, and, as a result, potentially too painful. Mangold captures the nuances of life perfectly, and, by never cheapening his vision through facile resolutions, he fashions a memorable cinematic portrait. **HIGHLY RECOMMENDED**

Henry Fool [1997]

Starring: Thomas Jay Ryan, James Urbaniak, Parker Posey, Maria Porter, James Saito, Kevin Corrigan, Chuck Montgomery Director: Hal Hartley Screenplay: Hal Hartley Running Time: 2:18 Rated: R (Profanity, sex, violence) Theatrical Aspect Ratio: 1.66:1

Henry Fool, maverick director Hal Hartley's most accomplished movie to date, explores the age-old debate between art and morality. If a work of art presents certain ethically reprehensible ideas, does that somehow reduce its artistic merit? Should a controversy of this sort make any property, regardless of its intrinsic value, a hot commodity? *Henry Fool* isn't the first movie to tackle these questions, but the story it tells is fresh and surprising.

The film's title is obviously intended to be ironic, because Henry (newcomer Thomas Jay Ryan) is anything but a fool. He's cultured, educated, and erudite, not to mention somewhat taken with his own supposed brilliance. The other central figure, Simon Grim (James Urbaniak), is an introverted garbage man, who becomes Henry's best friend. Henry sees something in the quiet, unsure man that others have missed (as a child, everyone thought he was "retarded"), and encourages Simon to put down his thoughts in writing: the result is a poem that fills up several composition books. Simon's poem becomes a lightning rod for controversy, and publishers are suddenly clamoring to make a deal. Meanwhile, the mysterious Henry stands slightly in the background, carrying on an affair with both Simon's mother, Mary (Maria Porter), and his sister, Fay (ubiquitous indie star Parker Posey), while hoping that Simon's newfound popularity will somehow enable his own opus, *The Confession,* to be published.

Simon's untitled poem is the film's Maguffin — it is critical to all that transpires, and it is mentioned frequently, but we never hear a line of it. Hartley has a little fun with the way the poem affects different people: its power causes a mute woman to sing, it brings on Fay's period a week and a half early, and it drives one individual to commit suicide. People on both sides of the art vs. pornography debate react passionately, with free-thinkers like Camille Paglia gushing over the poem while right-wing politicians denounce it from their position of moral superiority. Hartley never gets too serious about this debate, preferring to keep the tone light and slightly satirical.

Hartley (*Simple Men, Flirt*) has designed *Henry Fool* to play like an offbeat, modern fable. Much of what happens in the film isn't believable in real-world terms. It's unlikely that Simon's poem, no matter how cutting-edge, would become so popular so quickly (Hartley's view of the Internet is particularly naïve), but that doesn't matter in the movie's context. All of the characters have arcs, there are a couple of diverting subplots, and the secondary theme — about the value and importance of friendship — provides for a satisfying, if over-the-top, conclusion.

As is always true of a Hartley film, one thing to savor about *Henry Fool* is the dialogue, which is often clever and frequently brilliant. It's great to hear characters say things like "You need to do something to be ashamed of every once in a while" and "I've been bad. Repeatedly." In the case of *Henry Fool*, the dialogue isn't the only thing — it's the icing on the cake. **HIGHLY RECOMMENDED**

Hideous Kinky [United Kingdom, 1998]

Starring: Kate Winslet, Said Taghmaoui, Bella Riza, Carrie Mullan Director: Gillies MacKinnon Screenplay: Billy MacKinnon from the novel by Esther Freud Running Time: 1:39 Rated: R (Sex, profanity, brief nudity) Theatrical Aspect Ratio: 2.35:1

Gillies MacKinnon's *Hideous Kinky* is a road movie, but one of a very different sort. Set in 1972 Morocco, it follows the quest of a young British woman to discover herself and give her two daughters a taste of the world.

When her longtime lover and the father of her two children moves on to another woman, Julia (Kate Winslet) quits the gray sadness of London for the warm brightness of Marrakech. However, although Morocco offers the promise of spiritual enlightenment to the 25-year-old mother, a lack of financial resources limits her prospects. She wants to travel to Algeria, where one of the great mystics resides, but, with barely enough money to live off of, the possibility of moving on seems remote. And, while 6-year-old Lucy (Carrie Mulligan) is happy in this new, strange country, 8-year-old Bea (Bella Riza) wants nothing more than to return to a "normal" life. One day, Julia's goals and priorities are re-arranged when she meets Bilal (Said Taghmaoui), a charming acrobat who quickly insinuates himself into the vagabond family as Julia's lover and Lucy and Bea's father figure. Soon, the quartet is off on a short vacation to Bilal's home village, but that trip turns into a more revealing sojourn than anyone expected.

MacKinnon (*Regeneration*), directing from a script written by his brother and based on the novel by Esther Freud, captures time and place perfectly. The camera captures the stark beauty of the desert (complete with at least one memorable sunset) and a riot of colors marking the bustling city streets.

Kate Winslet, whose performance is top-notch, shows here that she's more interested in advancing her craft than in basking in publicity and trying to get a big paycheck.

Opposite Winslet is Said Taghmaoui (*Hate*), whose infectious charisma makes him a perfect choice for the part of the likable, roguish Bilal. As Julia's children, both Bella Riza and Carrie Mullan are making their feature debuts. Each displays natural talent; rarely is there even the barest hint of artifice in either performance. Also in the cast is veteran French actor Pierre Clementi, who plays a European who opens his villa to Julia and her daughters.

For all that *Hideous Kinky* introduces us to an unusual culture and takes us on a whirlwind trip of Morocco, the central feature of the film is the human element. It's the sacrifices Julia must ultimately make for her children that makes *Hideous Kinky* more than just a lush travelogue. MacKinnon has not allowed the glorious setting to overwhelm the characters. Through everything, Winslet's Julia remains the rock upon which the story is founded and developed.

RECOMMENDED

Hilary and Jackie [United Kingdom, 1998]

Starring: Emily Watson, Rachel Griffiths, James Frain, David Morrissey, Charles Dance, Celia Imrie, Auriol Evans, Keeley Flanders Director: Anand Tucker Screenplay: Frank Cottrell Boyce, based on "A Genius in the Family" by Hilary and Piers du Pré Running Time: 2:00 Rated: R (Sex, profanity, debilitating disease) Theatrical Aspect Ratio: 2.35:1

The story of celebrated cellist Jacqueline du Pré is too good not to have been made into a movie. Add the best female performance of 1998, a glorious soundtrack, and vibrant cinematography, and *Hilary and Jackie* stands as a towering achievement for Director Anand Tucker.

Jaqueline du Pré (Emily Watson) was one of classical music's brightest stars during the 1960s and early '70s. After making her professional debut as a teenager, she became one of the most in-demand cellists of her time, and was known not only for her peerless technique, but for the passion she exhibited by swaying to the music as she played. In 1973, while at the height of her popularity, Jacqueline was diagnosed with Multiple Sclerosis. The disease put an end to her career, and, following a 15-year battle, her life.

As the title makes clear, this film isn't just about the life of Jacqueline du Pré, but about her tempestuous relationship with her sister, Hilary (Rachel Griffiths). When they were both children they were inseparable soul-mates. Hilary, a flutist, was considered the greater talent. She was invited to play with orchestras and make special appearances. Through practice and hard work, however, Jackie elevated herself to her sister's level, then beyond. Hilary came to resent Jackie's success as her own musical aspirations floundered, and as an adult, Hilary all but gave up the flute in favor of marriage and a family, while Jacqueline chose fame. The price Jackie paid was a desperate yearning to have the stability and happiness that Hilary possessed. Then, when MS ended her career and left her alone and dependent, she had to cope with the loss of the music that defined her, unaccustomed powerlessness, and death.

As Jackie, Emily Watson gives a stunning performance. Watson, who earned an Oscar nomination for her courageous work in *Breaking the Waves*, is even better here, capturing every nuance of a character trapped between genius and madness, whose playing defines her existence. ("When you play, everyone loves you. When you stop, you're alone.")

Despite being in Watson's shadow, Rachel Griffiths acquits herself nicely. In fact, the relationship between the two sisters works because Griffiths is able to rise to Watson's level, and, on those occasions when the film focuses on Hilary, Griffiths' performance holds our attention.

Stylistically, the film is a success. The music is used extraordinarily effectively, especially when the Elgar Concerto (in a recording by Jackie) is played over the closing sequence. It's a poignant piece that plays as if composed just for that scene. *Hilary and Jackie* tells a heartbreaking tale of vividly-developed characters. It is a triumph. MUST SEE

Hollow Reed [United Kingdom, 1997]

Starring: Martin Donovan, Joely Richardson, Sam Bould, Jason Flemyng, Ian Hart Director: Angela Pope Screenplay: Paula Milne Running Time: 1:46 Rated: No MPAA Rating (Violence, sex, mature themes) Theatrical Aspect Ratio: 1.66:1

Angela Pope's *Hollow Reed* can be extremely difficult to watch. In examining how the physical abuse of a child affects an already broken family, the film doesn't pull any punches, literally or figuratively. Yet, *Hollow Reed*'s real subject matter is the hypocrisy of a legal system that would rather let a child live in danger than grant custody to his gay father. Lawyers and judges can mouth PC platitudes, but when it comes to handing over a child into the custody of a gay household, the deep-rooted ugliness of homophobia rears its head.

Part of the reason that *Hollow Reed* is so punishing is that it's told from a child's point-of-view. That child is Oliver (Sam Bould), a quiet, introverted boy who seems to be the perfect son and student. He's a *Star Wars* fan, and spends hours in his room playing with Luke Skywalker action figures and remote-controlled cars. His parents are divorced, and their relationship is far from amicable. Oliver lives with his mother, Hannah (Joely Richardson), and her boyfriend, Frank (Jason Flemyng). Meanwhile, Oliver's father, Martyn (Martin Donovan), an out-of-the-closet homosexual who shares a home with his lover, Tom (Ian Hart), has only the right of "reasonable access" to his son.

The film opens with Oliver arriving at his father's door late one evening with a bleeding, bruised face. Although Oliver claims that he was beaten up by a group of local thugs, Martyn has his doubts. Days later, when the boy shows up at school with a crushed hand, Martyn goes to the police, requesting that they investigate whether Frank has been abusing his son. He then instigates a custody lawsuit, with the intention of taking Oliver away from Hannah if she doesn't

kick Frank out. And, as the case goes before a judge, all sorts of ugly truths about society's perception of homosexuals are unveiled.

Both Martin Donovan and Joely Richardson do fine jobs as Oliver's parents. Richardson (Disney's live-action *101 Dalmatians*) arguably has the more difficult role playing the torn woman who doesn't want to believe a horrible truth. Oliver's silence allows her to remain in blissful denial. Donovan portrays a man who, despite having the moral high ground, is powerless to save his son. The key to Donovan's performance is that it starts out low-key, so as the situation becomes increasingly desperate, he never seems over-the-top. However, all of the adults, including Richardson, Donovan, and the fine supporting cast, are outacted by young Sam Bould, who captures the essence of Oliver without a hint of the confusion and awkwardness that sometimes marks child performances.

This is not the sort of motion picture that's likely to find favor with the "feel good" crowd, but, if you aren't afraid of a movie that is capable of challenging convictions and wrenching emotions, *Hollow Reed* makes for an unforgettable 2 hours.

HIGHLY RECOMMENDED

Homage [1996]

Starring: Frank Whaley, Blythe Danner, Sheryl Lee, Danny Nucci, Bruce Davison Director: Ross Kagan Marks Screenplay: Mark Medoff Running Time: 1:37 Rated: R (Violence, sex, profanity) Theatrical Aspect Ratio: 1.85:1

An edgy, unsettling look at obsession and its potentially catastrophic results, *Homage* is a dramatic character study; and though it features a number of questionable creative choices, a trio of powerful performances makes this film worthwhile.

The most dubious decision regarding *Homage* was forcing it into a non-linear chronological structure. The film begins at the end, with TV star Lucy Samuel (Sheryl Lee, in the best performance of her career) being gunned down by psychotic fan Archie Landrum (Frank Whaley), while her mother, Katherine (Blythe Danner), looks on in horror. So much for any suspense about how things are going to be resolved. From that point, the narrative alternates between the present and the past, using flashbacks and a contrived pseudo-documentary style to chronicle events leading up to the shooting, while giving us glimpses of an imprisoned Archie in the aftermath, and detailing the tactics employed by his public defender

(Bruce Davison) to beat the charges. Along the way, director Marks also takes an occasional detour to shish-kabob celebrity worship and paparazzi.

Frank Whaley's portrayal of Archie is chillingly effective. Archie has a Ph.D. in math, but, in his own words, is "an inept human being." Katherine sees him as lonely and harmless, not recognizing that his personality is dangerous. He's extremely intelligent, but lost, and the more Lucy rejects him, the more determined he becomes to win her — at all costs. This is the obsession of someone with no sense of self-worth. The only way to validate his own existence is to become part of Lucy's life, and she thinks he's a creep. It's disturbing to watch the seemingly-normal Archie come completely unglued.

Meanwhile, Sheryl Lee returns to familiar territory with Lucy — a character who is idolized in her home town while secretly battling addictions to drugs and booze. She keeps a private diary, and, in the end (or should I say, the beginning), is murdered. Lee's career started as Laura Palmer in David Lynch's *Twin Peaks,* and there are numerous similarities here. The marked difference is in the performance, however. When she appeared in *Peaks* (and reprised the role in the big-screen's *Fire, Walk with Me*), Lee was new at her craft. Here, she displays a depth and maturity that Lynch never captured.

The third member of the trio, Blythe Danner, is no less impressive than her co-stars, although her performance is more low-key. Nevertheless, it is only through Katherine's agonized reaction to her daughter's death that *Homage*'s most compelling tragedy becomes apparent.

There's something haunting and forceful about *Homage,* but I attribute that power more to what Whaley, Lee, and Danner do with the material than with the material itself. **RECOMMENDED**

Hoodlum [1997]

Starring: **Laurence Fishburne, Tim Roth, Andy Garcia, Vanessa L. Williams, Chi McBride, Clarence Williams III** Director: **Bill Duke** Screenplay: **Chris Brancato** Running Time: 2:10 Rated: R (Violence, profanity, brief nudity) Theatrical Aspect Ratio: 1.85:1

Hoodlum is a period-piece gangster film, harkening back to Depression-era Harlem. While Al Capone was king in Chicago, Lucky Luciano (Andy Garcia) ruled New York, parceling out the city to members of his "Sicilian Syndicate." The 1930s were the mob's heyday, when no cop, special prosecutor, or judge was too expensive to buy, and when the only real law was

the one laid down by Luciano or one of his many "associates." Of course, in a place as big as New York, there were bound to be wild cards. One was Dutch Schultz (Tim Roth), a former partner of Luciano's whose forays into the uptown numbers racket put him on a collision course with the Queen of Harlem, Stephanie St. Clair (Cicely Tyson), and her trustworthy friend and protector, Bumpy Johnson (Laurence Fishburne). The resulting turf war between Schultz and the St. Clair/Johnson camp littered the streets of Harlem with bodies, and threatened the mob's security in New York when the violence spread to downtown targets.

Hoodlum's storyline is similar to the one told in Francis Ford Coppola's 1984 feature, *The Cotton Club.* The setting is the same, many of the characters are the same, and certain aspects of the storylines intersect. The perspective, however, is different. Unlike *The Cotton Club,* which focused on the lives of many of the "normal" people who frequented and played in the nightclub, *Hoodlum,* as Bumpy's story, is a relatively straightforward gangster yarn that melds fact with fiction to create a dramatically compelling 2 hours.

The acting is top notch. As Bumpy, Fishburne is mesmerizing, displaying his range as an actor by subtly and effectively presenting the variety of emotions that lurk just beneath Bumpy's seemingly-placid exterior. Tim Roth, the versatile British actor who has portrayed almost every kind of character imaginable during his career, brings a flamboyant mix of impatience and casual viciousness to Dutch Schultz. Andy Garcia, on the other hand, is low-key in his approach to Lucky Luciano, presenting the famed mobster as charismatic, urbane, and intelligent, with only a hint of the danger he represents. Of the supporting players, only Vanessa L. Williams seems off-key. Chi McBride (as Bumpy's cousin and right-hand man, Illinois) and Clarence Williams III (as one of Schultz's most dangerous henchmen) are memorable.

Overall, *Hoodlum* may be the best depression-era gangster film since Brian DePalma's *The Untouchables.* The movie's decision to take the point-of-view of several black characters lends a fresh angle to a fairly well-known historical account. *Hoodlum* may not be the definitive chronicle of New York mob activity during the 1930s, but it's a welcome contribution. **RECOMMENDED**

The Horse Whisperer [1998]

Starring: Robert Redford, Kristin Scott Thomas, Sam Neill, Scarlett Johansson Director: Robert Redford Screenplay: Richard LaGravenese, Eric Roth based on the novel by Nicholas Evans Running Time: 2:50 Rated: PG-13 (Accident scene) Theatrical Aspect Ratio: 1.85:1

The Horse Whisperer is a powerful and moving tale of love and loss that eschews melodramatic manipulation in its pursuit of a simple, honest tale.

The film opens peacefully enough, with two teenage girls leaving their houses in the early morning hours for a horseback ride. The sunrise is brilliant, and, as snow begins to fall later in the day, the fields and forest are turned into a winter wonderland of blues and silvers. Everything is picture perfect until tragedy strikes, brutally and without warning. One of the girls' mounts loses his footing on an icy hill and, suddenly, the two friends are in the path of a skidding 18-wheeler. One girl and her horse die. The other pair, Grace MacLean (Scarlett Johansson), and her beloved steed, Pilgrim, are badly injured. Grace loses the lower half of one leg. Pilgrim is driven mad, and everyone advises that he be put to sleep.

Grace's parents, Annie and Robert MacLean (Kristin Scott Thomas and Sam Neill), are ill-prepared to help their daughter cope with her physical disability and the mental scars of having seen her best friend run down by an out-of-control truck. Annie decides that Grace's recovery will be aided if she can find a way to heal Pilgrim (the film's only dubious contrivance). So, with her daughter and the horse in tow, Annie heads out to Montana, where a legendary "horse whisperer," Tom Booker (Robert Redford), lives and works on a ranch. After seeing Pilgrim, Tom agrees to try to help the horse, and so begins a long period of restoration for 4 souls: Pilgrim, Grace, Annie, and Tom.

Everyone in this film has their own demons to wrestle with. Grace, who retreats into a sullen cocoon after the accident, is raw on the inside, but won't let it out. She resents her mother's emotional distance and is frightened that the loss of her leg makes her useless and will doom her to a life alone. ("Nobody will want me like this!") Annie, who is used to being in charge, doesn't know how to cope with the situation, and, when she takes the time to examine her life, she recognizes how the pressures of her career have leached away her humanity. Meanwhile, Tom, who is basically at peace with himself, begins to re-discover what it means to love, something he had lost when his wife left him.

Emotionally, *The Horse Whisperer* finds the perfect pitch, and as a director, Redford has never shown greater mastery of his material. His presentation of Montana, with all of its glorious open spaces, is enough to make anyone in the theater think about heading west. He also manages to make the day-to-day activities of running a ranch and working with horses seem interesting. All in all, *The Horse Whisperer* is as rich in its emotional resonance as it is in its visual presentation. **HIGHLY RECOMMENDED**

The Hours [2002]

Starring: Meryl Streep, Nicole Kidman, Julianne Moore, Ed Harris Director: Stephen Daldry Screenplay: David Hare, based on the novel by Michael Cunningham Running Time: 1:54 Rated: PG-13 (Mature themes, brief profanity) Theatrical Aspect Ratio: 1.85:1

With superb acting and a complexly structured narrative, *The Hours* tells the story of three women living in different times and places. Thematically, as well as concretely, there are connections, but the fabric that binds them the most strongly is Virginia Woolf's fourth novel, *Mrs. Dalloway*. Nearly everything of importance that occurs in this film pertains to that book. The first segment transpires in 1923 (with brief flash-forwards to 1941) on the day that Woolf (Nicole Kidman) begins committing *Mrs. Dalloway* to paper. The second episode occurs in 1951 Los Angeles, where a lonely, depressed housewife, Laura Brown (Julianne Moore), begins to discover some things about herself and her life by reading *Mrs. Dalloway*. The third piece takes place in 2001 New York City, where a modern day Mrs. Dalloway, Clarissa Vaughn (Meryl Streep), arranges a party for her terminally ill ex-husband, Richard (Ed Harris).

The Hours contains some rather dense and weighty material, and will have the strongest appeal for those who are familiar with *Mrs. Dalloway*. The movie does not immediately exclude anyone unfamiliar with Woolf's first great novel, but their appreciation will be limited. My sense is that those who consider themselves to be fans of Woolf and her book will regard *The Hours* as a brilliant, literate motion picture. Those who don't know Woolf from Brontë will find Stephen Daldry's film to be pretentious and glacially paced.

The Hours is a triumph of acting. The portrayal most likely to garner notice is Nicole Kidman's — in large part because she undergoes a physical transformation that renders her nearly unrecognizable. Wearing a prosthetic nose and buried under layers of makeup that hide her beauty, she comes across as sickly, homely, and somewhat demented. However, although Kidman's acting is strong, she overshadows neither Julianne Moore nor Meryl Streep, both of whom give taut, tightly controlled performances. The most notable supporting work is provided by Ed Harris, whose character represents a thread connecting two of the episodes.

The Hours isn't the kind of film that's going to stir a lot of widespread enthusiasm. The film's emotional frigidity is offset by its literate and artistic qualities. I'm sure mainstream audiences will be baffled, but, for those with at least a minimal appreciation of Woolf and Clarissa Dalloway, *The Hours* represents two of those well spent. RECOMMENDED

How Stella Got Her Groove Back [1998]

Starring: Angela Bassett, Taye Diggs, Whoopi Goldberg, Regina King, Suzzanne Douglas, Michael J. Pagan Director: Kevin Rodney Sullivan Screenplay: Ron Bass and Terry McMillan based on the novel by Terry McMillan Running Time: 2:05 Rated: R (Sex, profanity, nudity) Theatrical Aspect Ratio: 1.85:1

How Stella Got Her Groove Back is a surprisingly low-key romantic melodrama dealing with the issues that arise when a woman "of a certain age" defies convention and falls for a younger man.

The film (and the novel that inspired it) is loosely based on writer Terry McMillan's own experience of falling in love and setting up house with a Jamaican man young enough to be her son. Perhaps this semi-autobiographical background is the reason why the characters resonate with warmth and believability. They're easy to like, and even easier to root for, and *How Stella Got Her Groove Back* is a fresh, sassy source of entertainment.

Stella Payne, the main character and McMillan's alter ego, is brought to life through a superior performance by Angela Bassett. Not only is Bassett gorgeous at the age of 40, but she has a body to die for and the acting skills to make us believe that she is Stella. The film begins by introducing the title character as an independent woman who is raising a son by herself and doesn't crave the constant company of a man. However, when her high-pressure job as a San Francisco-based stock broker gets to be too much for her, Stella decides to take a vacation. Along with her best friend, Delilah (Whoopi Goldberg), she books a trip to Jamaica. While there, she begins flirting with a 20-year-old hunk improbably named Winston Shakespeare (Taye Diggs). Soon Stella, who embarked upon the vacation in an uptight and unsettled mood, is beginning to unwind and rediscover the part of her that had gotten lost under the business suits. Within a

matter of days, she finds that her fling with Winston is becoming serious, and her feelings for him don't dissipate once she's back in the Bay Area.

While Bassett is clearly the film's star, she is surrounded by a fine cast. Fresh face Taye Diggs does exactly what's demanded of him for this part: he portrays the too-good-to-be-true Winston with perfect sincerity while showing off a very impressive physique. The supporting cast includes a pair of wonderfully amusing performances from Whoopi Goldberg as the obligatory Best Friend, and Regina King (Cuba Gooding Jr.'s wife in *Jerry Maguire*) as Stella's chatty sister, Vanessa. We expect Goldberg to be funny, but King's comic aptitude is a revelation.

How Stella Got Her Groove Back is aimed at the black female audience, but this movie can be enjoyed by members of both genders of any race. It isn't the kind of "chick flick" that will have men looking at their watches every 5 minutes. And the film has a thing or two to say about older women and younger men. As *Stella* shows, there are times when the vapid cuteness of a young nymph can't hold a candle to the practiced sensuality of a mature woman. RECOMMENDED

How To Make an American Quilt [1995]

Starring: Winona Ryder, Ann Bancroft, Ellen Burstyn, Maya Angelou Director: Jocelyn Moorhouse Screenplay: Jane Anderson based on the novel by Whitney Otto Running Time: 1:56 Rated: PG-13 (Mature themes, brief nudity, mild profanity) Theatrical Aspect Ratio: 1.85:1

American movies are filled with male bonding rituals; *How to Make an American Quilt* offers a feminine alternative. Here, 7 quilters imbue their creation with passion and vitality. The "quilting bee" consists of 7 members: sisters Gladys (Ann Bancroft) and Hy (Ellen Burstyn); Sophia (Lois Smith), a woman known for frightening children; Emma (Jean Simmons), the timid wife of a perpetually unfaithful man; Constance (Kate Nelligan), who has been having an affair with Emma's husband; Anna (Maya Angelou), the leader of the group; and Marianna (Alfre Woodard), Anna's daughter. The project they're busy with is the wedding quilt for Hy's granddaughter, Finn (Winona Ryder), who has just become engaged. She's spending the summer with Hy and Gladys, and away from her fiancé, to decide whether a lifelong commitment is really what she wants, and whether it's better to marry a friend or a lover.

There are probably too many characters. So, instead of really getting to know a few of them, we are presented with quick glimpses into a single defining event in each of their lives. We learn about the root of the smoldering resentment between Gladys and Hy, and are told the reasons why Emma stays with her husband and Sophia is so irascible. There are other episodes as well: the love of Anna's life, Marianna's soul mate, and a look at the reasons why Constance entered into an affair with her friend's husband. The sum total of these tales is meant to provide the framework for Finn's story: whether to go forward with her marriage or dally with a hunky stranger.

On the whole, *How to Make an American Quilt* is a nicely-understated drama that has a lot to say about love, passion, and monogamy in relationships. There is no emotional epiphany in the movie. The stories are all well-told, but it's difficult to really connect with the characters — their moments pass so quickly. Finn's segment is by far the most compelling, because she's the focal point: her actions are shaped by everyone else's experiences. The other patches of this American Quilt are successful only to varying degrees, but the privilege of seeing such a fine cast in top form allows a viewer to enjoy this picture even if the story is somewhat conventional. **RECOMMENDED**

Hugo Pool [1996]

Starring: Alyssa Milano, Patrick Dempsey, Malcolm McDowell, Cathy Moriarty, Robert Downey Jr., Richard Lewis, Sean Penn Director: **Robert Downey Sr.** Screenplay: **Robert Downey Sr. and Laura Downey** Running Time: 1:32 Rated: No MPAA Rating (Brief nudity, mature themes, profanity) Theatrical Aspect Ratio: 1.85:1

Robert Downey Sr. is an American original. He has been at his craft as an independent filmmaker for more than 30 years now — his debut, *Chafed Elbows,* came out in 1965. His best known work, the trilogy of *Putney Swope, Pound,* and *Greaser's Palace,* was released between 1969 and 1972. Downey has always taken his own road, never worrying about or giving into commercial pressure. When asked by the producer of one of his films whether it would make money, he replied "Not a dime."

Hugo Pool — an upbeat, quirky romantic comedy that reminds us how stale most entries in this genre are — is essentially a day in the life of Hugo (Alyssa Milano), a Southern California pool cleaner. As she goes from house-to-house, we meet members of her strange gallery of clients: Franz Mazur (Robert Downey Jr.), a deranged film director who murdered one of his extras; Chic Chicalini (Richard Lewis), a gangster with a killer stare; and Floyd Galen (Patrick Dempsey), a victim of ALS (commonly known as Lou Gehrig's Disease), who ends up joining Hugo on her

rounds. Also lending a hand are Hugo's burnt-out father, Henry (Malcolm McDowell), and her gambling-obsessed mother, Minerva (Cathy Moriarty).

The romance of *Hugo Pool* is between Hugo and Floyd, and it's touching, sweet, and funny. Despite Floyd's considerable disability, the attraction between the two grows as the film progresses. Patrick Dempsey, whose character can't move or talk, does all of his acting with his face and eyes. Alyssa Milano, whose resume includes several B-grade exploitation flicks, is a real revelation. As Hugo, she's great — tough, energetic, and charming. If she wants to impress directors in the future, she should show them her work in *Hugo Pool.*

Like David Mamet and Quentin Tarantino, Downey writes some of the best dialogue around, and his script sparkles with it. His words aren't the kind of things real people would say, but they have a rhythm and charm all their own. Characters make comments like "Chances are taken, not given," "I'm too superficial to be hurt," and "If words could speak, I still would have nothing to say." Out of context, these phrases are clever; when seen as part of the film, they're uproarious.

As Hollywood churns out $100 million blockbusters and the Miramaxes and Fine Lines of the world go after the next *The English Patient* or *Shine,* idiosyncratic, thoroughly delightful features like *Hugo Pool* are becoming more and more of an endangered species. Thankfully, there are still directors out there like Robert Downey Sr. who don't care what the market will bear and are willing to do whatever's necessary to get their own singular vision to the screen. **HIGHLY RECOMMENDED**

Hurlyburly [1998]

Starring: Sean Penn, Kevin Spacey, Robin Wright Penn, Chazz Palminteri, Garry Shandling, Anna Paquin, Meg Ryan Director: Anthony Drazan Screenplay: David Rabe based on his play Running Time: 2:02 Rated: R (Profanity, drug use, sex, violence) Theatrical Aspect Ratio: 1.85:1

Hurlyburly is a talky film — the entire movie is constructed around lengthy sequences of dialogue where the characters talk and talk and talk, often saying nothing. But in Anthony Drazen's adaptation of the David Rabe play, that's the point. Because the vocal rhythms are so perfect, the words so well-chosen, and the performances so powerful, listening to this much talk is a pleasure, not a chore.

Eddie (Sean Penn), is a fast-talking, coke-sniffing

Hollywood casting agent whose contempt for others is exceeded only by his contempt for himself. Eddie has surrounded himself with 3 equally degenerate friends: his housemate and business partner, Mickey (Kevin Spacey), a mindless thug named Phil (Chazz Palminteri), and a sycophantic writer, Artie (Gary Shandling). Women have no real place in this mens' world, except as sexual objects and punching bags. Three female characters drift through the movie: Darlene (Robin Wright Penn), the love of Eddie's life; Donna (Anna Paquin), a hitchhiker who trades sex for lodging; and Bonnie (Meg Ryan), a perpetually stoned stripper with an oral talent.

If this sounds misogynistic, it is, but it's the characters that display that trait, not the movie. These 4 men are among the least likable individuals you'd ever run across, and Drazan makes no attempt to hide their shortcomings. As one character notes, Eddie surrounds himself with losers so that no matter how far he falls, there will always be someone in his immediate circle who is lower.

Sean Penn gives a towering, intense performance as Eddie, getting into the character's skin and inhabiting him completely. It's an amazing turn and a frighteningly believable portrayal of an opportunist on the edge. Penn's 3 male co-stars — Chazz Palminteri as the talentless actor whose chief ability is to whack people (women in particular), Kevin Spacey as the amoral but amusing Mickey, who's never without a dry comeback, and Gary Shandling as the oily Artie — are capable of holding their own in scenes with him, which is a testament to the strength of their performances. Those who think of Meg Ryan as all sugar and spice will be surprised to see her in this role, where she radiates a slutty sexuality. And Anna Paquin is effective as a vapid, oversexed girl who trades her body for a bed. Actually, it's almost a shame that Ryan and Paquin are so good — they make us want to see more of their characters.

It's hard to say whether *Hurlyburly* is a black comedy or a tragedy. For, while the film contains its share of absurd and darkly comical moments, the overall portrait is a grim one. The characters are bottom-feeders — scum that prey off the weaknesses of others and revel in the bleakest aspects of the Hollywood culture. *Hurlyburly* would be easier to take if its portrayals weren't so dead-on. But the sheer pleasure of watching such virtuoso performances makes it worthwhile. **RECOMMENDED**

The Hurricane [1999]

Starring: Denzel Washington, Vicellous Reon Shannon, Liev Schreiber, Deborah Unger, John Hannah, Dan Hedaya Director: Norman Jewison Screenplay: Armyan Bernstein and Dan Gordon, based on *Lazarus and The Hurricane* by Sam Chaiton and Terry Swinton, and *The 16th Round* by Rubin 'Hurricane' Carter Running Time: 2:05 Rated: R (Violence, profanity) Theatrical Aspect Ratio: 1.85:1

"Hate put me in prison. Love's gonna bust me out." Those words, spoken by Rubin "Hurricane" Carter (Denzel Washington), form the thematic foundation of Norman Jewsion's film, *The Hurricane*. Alternatively tragic and triumphant, it is an exhilarating trip through the life and times of the title character, a championship boxer from Paterson, New Jersey, who spent 19 years behind bars for murders he did not commit. *The Hurricane* not only details the crime and the miscarriage of justice that followed, but shows how Carter survived the long, lonely years in prison, and how the devotion of a small group of Canadians led to his redemption.

It's difficult to state exactly where and when the movie begins, since, especially during its first half, it jumps around freely and frequently in time. There are numerous flashbacks, but the editing is clean and sharp, which keeps the potential for confusion to a minimum.

There are two primary time periods. The first begins in 1963, when The Hurricane defeats Emile Griffith for the World Welter Weight title, and continues through 1966, when he is arrested and tried for murder, then into the 1970s, when he is incarcerated at Trenton State Prison on a life sentence. The second time period occurs during the 1980s, when Lesra Martin (Vicellous Shannon), a Brooklyn teenager living in Canada, buys a copy of Carter's autobiography, *The 16th Round*, and develops a passion to meet Carter. Encouraged by the 3 older people he is living with — Sam (Liev Schreiber), Terry (John Hannah), and Lisa (Deborah Unger) — he opens a correspondence with Carter, then travels to New Jersey to visit him. Following the face-to-face meeting, Lesra becomes determined to free Carter, and enlists the aid of Sam, Terry, and Lisa in his struggle.

Many people became aware of Carter's plight as a result of Bob Dylan's mid-70s ballad, "The Hurricane" (which is featured on two separate occasions during the course of the film). Over the years, a number of celebrities have leant their support to Carter's cause, but none of the marches or protests had any effect. What made the difference was the commitment of the group from Toronto, who gave up their jobs, moved to New Jersey, and literally risked their lives to find the evidence to prove Carter's innocence and to bring to light the corruption of the Paterson police lieutenant (Dan Hedaya) who hunted The Hurricane like a dog. Their efforts turn *The Hurricane* into a story of victory rather than defeat. **HIGHLY RECOMMENDED**

I Shot Andy Warhol [1996]

Starring: Lili Taylor, Jared Harris, Stephen Dorff, Martha Plimpton, Lothaire Bluteau, Donovan Leitch, Tahnee Welch Director: Mary Harron Screenplay: Mary Harron and Daniel Minahan Running Time: 1:40 Rated: R (Profanity, sex, violence) Theatrical Aspect Ratio: 1.85:1

The script for *I Shot Andy Warhol* began life as a documentary before the producers convinced writer/director Mary Harron to transform it into a dramatic interpretation. The result is an impressive feature debut — a provocative look at Valerie Solanas, the intellectual, possibly psychotic prefeminist who shot Warhol in 1968.

Most of *I Shot Andy Warhol* takes place in New York City from 1966 to 1968, chronicling the period in Valerie Solanas' (Lili Taylor) life when she wrote her definitive work, *SCUM Manifesto*, was introduced to Andy Warhol (Jared Harris), became a fringe member of his circle, and eventually shot him. Valerie, who had a "pitiful childhood" characterized by abuse and molestation, is subversive and disturbed, but many of her theories, as outlandish as they initially seem, are consistent, logical, and thought-provoking.

SCUM, or the Society for Cutting Up Men, was the prefeminist organization formed by Valerie (she was also the only member). It was founded on a number of basic principles — the male is a biological accident, women are the naturally superior gender, the female function is to create a "magical world," and men are sex-obsessed machines. *The SCUM Manifesto* represents Valerie's legacy (it's still in print today).

Those offended by the "male bashing" aspect of *Thelma and Louise* may become apoplectic during *I Shot Andy Warhol*. Since the film is essentially a character study of Valerie, it gives an uncompromising presentation of her views and experiences. She despises "men, married women, and other degenerates," and makes no secret of her feelings. She's a "butch dyke," and proud of it, and the only time she has any sexual interaction with men is when she gets paid.

Lili Taylor, who, like Eric Stoltz, has gravitated towards independent features, gives a powerful, passionate portrayal, bringing out Valerie's anger and disgust with the world.

Jared Harris (the son of Richard Harris), manages to capture not only Warhol's strange magnetism, but his aloof, almost-shy nature. Stephen Dorff (*Backbeat*) plays Candy Darling, Valerie and Warhol's transvestite companion. Supporting roles are filled by Martha Plimpton (as Valerie's best friend), Lothaire Bluteau (as Maurice Girodius, the publisher who buys the rights to Valerie's writing), and Tahnee Welch (as a member of Warhol's circle).

I Shot Andy Warhol is a toned-down, nostalgic look at New York in the late 1960s as well as the subculture that took root around Warhol — the wild, bohemian lifestyle, the drugs and sex. Primarily, however, this is Valerie's story — an invitation to explore her theories and understand her motivation, even if you can't relate to such a disagreeable personality. **RECOMMENDED**

The Ice Storm [1997]

Starring: Kevin Kline, Sigourney Weaver, Joan Allen, Tobey Maguire, Christina Ricci, Jamey Sheridan, Elijah Wood Director: Ang Lee Screenplay: James Schamus based on the novel by Rick Moody Running Time: 1:52 Rated: R (Sexual situations, profanity) Theatrical Aspect Ratio: 1.85:1

It is Thanksgiving week of 1973 in New Canaan, Connecticut. On the political front, the nation is bathed in the aftermath of Vietnam, and President Nixon's regime is beginning to crumble as the Watergate scandal escalates. With trust in the government giving way to cynicism and disillusionment, it is the end of an era — politically, socially, and culturally.

The Hood family is the poster household of the times: poised and perfect on the outside, riven by doubt and guilt within. Paul (Tobey Maguire) is an average 16-year old off at prep school learning about Dostoevsky in the classroom and the difficulties of romance outside of it. His younger sister, Wendy (Christina Ricci) is a restless 14-year old, intensely curious about sexual matters, and willing to explore them beyond the bounds of prudence. Paul and Wendy's parents, Ben and Elena (Kevin Kline and Joan Allen) appear at first glance to be the perfect mother and father. But their perfection is a sham, and while Ben dallies with a willing neighbor (Sigourney Weaver), Elena stews in her own loneliness. Sexually and socially, everyone in this film is groping for answers, whether their age is 14 or 40. More often than not, the children in *The Ice Storm* are open about what they want. The adults, on the other hand, feel the need to resort to deception and wife-swapping games to achieve the same ends.

Lee accurately captures the "feel" of the early '70s,

which is ironic since, during the year when *The Ice Storm* transpires, he didn't speak English and hadn't yet set foot in America. However, for those of us who lived through that era, there are plenty of familiar images and items. Some, like the bellbottoms, wide-collared shirts, and gas-guzzling cars, are expected. Others, like the bubble umbrella and the anti-pollution TV spot featuring a crying Native American, show that Lee was willing to take things to another level of detail. While it's true that *The Ice Storm* may not represent the reality of the '70s, it effectively fits our memories of the time.

The ice storm of the title is a presence throughout the film. It is crucial to the narrative resolution, but its vivid presentation makes it almost a character in its own right as it coats trees, power lines, and streets with ice and turns the world into a beautiful-but-deadly place.

The Ice Storm is at times funny, poignant, moving, and sensitive; it is perceptive about people, relationships, and human nature, and there's not a single moment in the entire 112 minute running length that rings false. **MUST SEE**

I'm Not Rappaport [1996]

Starring: Walter Matthau, Ossie Davis, Amy Irving, Boyd Gaines, Martha Plimpton, Craig T. Nelson Director: Herb Gardner
Screenplay: Herb Gardner based on his play Running Time: 2:15
Rated: PG-13 (Profanity, mature themes) Theatrical Aspect Ratio: 1.85:1

I'm Not Rappaport, Herb Gardner's production of his own 1986 Tony award winning play, revolves around the unlikely friendship of two 80-year-old men who, despite infirm bodies and failing eyesight, aren't ready to give up on life. Together, Nat (Matthau) and Midge (Davis) sit around on benches in New York's Central Park, argue with each other, discuss life and philosophy, reminisce about better days, argue some more, share a joint, and try to do their small part in righting the world's wrongs. And, while most of their efforts are ultimately ineffective, it isn't until the very end that we, like them, recognize that even apparent failures can be successes.

Several minor characters occasionally cross Nat and Midge's paths. Nat's daughter, Clara (Amy Irving), doesn't trust her father on his own and wants to put him in an old age home. Laurie (Martha Plimpton), an attractive artist, watches the pair from afar, sketching them. The Cowboy (Craig T. Nelson), a high-testosterone drug dealer, roams the park on business. Danforth (Boyd Gaines), the yuppy spokesman of the group that wants to fire Midge from his

maintenance job, breaks the bad news only to have the situation unexpectedly blow up in his face. And a mugger (Guillermo Diaz) tries to extort protection money from Nat.

For the most part, the plot is incidental. What matters in *I'm Not Rappaport* are the characters and their dialogue. Over the 2+- hour running time, Nat and Midge touch on an amazing variety of subjects: unions and bosses ("their tactics haven't changed in one century"), age ("an old man like me, I could wander through the world like a ghost"), memories ("nostalgia kills more of us than heart disease"), and the war between idealism and realism ("I got smarter — I fought in battles I thought I could win"). They talk and talk and talk, and they're always a delight to listen to, whether we're hearing Nat's tall stories or Midge's less fanciful reflections.

I'm Not Rappaport is the kind of movie that grows on you. It's obviously a play that has been adapted for the cinema, but that doesn't take anything away from the delicate magic that Gardner has conjured by his use of sly comedy and keen social insight. While it's true that this is essentially a buddy movie, it's a very special one. Nat and Midge's friendship reminds us of what bonding really is — and it doesn't have anything to do with dodging bullets or running away from exploding buildings. In the final analysis, this motion picture is far more about a rapport than a Rappaport. **HIGHLY RECOMMENDED**

In the Bedroom [2001]

Starring: Tom Wilkinson, Sissy Spacek, Nick Stahl, Marisa Tomei, Deborah Derecktor, Veronica Cartwright Director: Todd Field
Screenplay: Robert Festinger, Todd Field, based on the short story by Andre Dubus Running Time: 2:16 Rated: R (Profanity, violence, mature themes) Theatrical Aspect Ratio: 2.35:1

The stunning feature debut of Todd Field, *In the Bedroom* deals with issues that are rarely approached with this degree of sensitivity on film. The movie, set in Maine, stars Tom Wilkinson and Sissy Spacek as Matt and Ruth Fowler, a seemingly perfect middle-aged couple. Their only son, Frank (Nick Stahl), is spending the summer working on a lobster boat before going off to an Ivy League school in the fall. His latest girlfriend, Natalie Strout (Marisa Tomei), is an older woman with two young children. These characters are bound together when a criminal act results in a tragedy.

The movie is close to flawless. The set-up is sympathetic and involving; the crime is shocking; and the aftermath has the inevitability of tragedy. *In the Bed-*

room shows how the pressure of a tragedy can put strain on even the most solid marriage. For Matt and Ruth, their quiet camaraderie gradually dissolves into anger and recrimination. One explosive confrontation between them leads directly to an action that brings catharsis and closure to one while causing the other to engage in deeper soul-searching.

The movie also presents some of the most poignant reminders of the little things that often cause the greatest pain in the wake of a tragedy. The narrative gathers an unwavering momentum as it moves towards the climax. *In the Bedroom* also addresses the frustration and anguish of crime victims, especially in cases when the perpetrators of a crime appear beyond the reach of legal punishment. The tendency in motion pictures these days is to develop sympathy for the criminal; it is rare that a film addresses the other side of the equation with this degree of intelligence and sensitivity.

The performances are all astonishing. Wilkinson, perhaps best known for his work in *The Full Monty,* imbues Matt with a quiet dignity, a deep wellspring of grief, and a simmering fury. Sissy Spacek's Ruth is a volcano that lies dormant for a while before erupting. Nick Stahl brings depth and strength to a character that could have turned into a one-dimensional type. Marisa Tomei impresses in yet another supporting role far away from the Hollywood spotlight (although her inconsistent New England accent is a little distracting).

In the Bedroom is the kind of motion picture that it's almost impossible to forget. It epitomizes what an American independent film can be when the director is willing to abandon the safety net. **MUST SEE**

In the Mood For Love [Hong Kong, 2000]
Starring: Tony Leung, Maggie Cheung, Lai Chen, Rebecca Pan
Director: Wong Kar-wai Screenplay: Wong Kar-wai Running Time: 1:38
Rated: PG (Mature themes) Theatrical Aspect Ratio: 1.85:1
In Cantonese and French with subtitles

Longing — it is one of the great motivators of the human experience. It has driven poets to write sonnets, painters to create artwork, and composers to fashion music to wrench the soul. Hong Kong filmmaker Wong Kar-wai understands longing and, the sublime *In the Mood for Love* brings it to life on the screen.

The plot is simple, and is really just a vehicle for the characters and their delicate ballet of hidden feelings and concealed emotions. The film takes place in 1962 Hong Kong, where Chow (Tony Leung) meets Li-zhen (Maggie Cheung) when they become next-door neighbors in an apartment building. He's a journalist

with dreams of publishing pulp martial arts books; she's a secretary. After learning that Chow's wife is having an affair with Li-zhen's husband, the two become close friends, and the attachment between them grows into something deeper and more lasting than a casual liaison. But, because of cultural issues and feelings of guilt (the guilt of things considered in the mind but never committed in the body), they never act upon those impulses. They remain true to their marriage vows even though their respective spouses do not.

The tone is languorous, allowing the shadings of the characters to deepen as the storyline advances. The camera makes us more of a voyeur than usual, as Wong employs unusual shots to imprint upon the film a unique look. There are times during conversations between Chow and Li-zhen when the camera frames one in the shot without the other, or peeks at them from between objects. In addition, Wong limits the number of people and locales. Chow's and Li-zhen's spouses remain faceless entities — they never appear on-screen — and the majority of *In the Mood for Love*'s scenes take place indoors.

For his lead characters, Wong couldn't have selected two better-suited actors. Both Tony Leung (*Chungking Express*) and Maggie Cheung (*Irma Vep*) have international followings, and neither has been better than they are here.

The Hollywood version of this motion picture would have a radically different ending — one that would satisfy the standard romantic formula even as it betrays the material and the characters. Wong's film is as anti-Hollywood as a motion picture can be. It is slow, it does not pander, it allows the characters room to breathe, and, in the end, it has an impact. *In the Mood for Love* is a powerful study of longing that uses innovative camera techniques, evocative music (mournful violins), and strong performances to bathe the audience in the mood of the characters — one of poignant yearning for something that both desire but which neither can find the courage to express. **HIGHLY RECOMMENDED**

Indochine [France, 1992]
Starring: Catherine Deneuve, Linh Dan Pham, Vincent Perez
Director: Regis Wargnier Screenplay: Louis Gardel, Erik Orsenna, Regis Wargnier, Catherine Cohen Running Time: 2:35 Rated: PG-13 (Mature themes, violence, brief nudity) Theatrical Aspect Ratio: 1.66:1
In French and Vietnamese with English subtitles

Indochine is, at its heart, a love story. Despite all the political turmoil that functions as the film's backdrop, the central element of the movie is the tale of how Camille (Linh Dan Pham) and Jean-Baptiste (Vincent Perez) meet, fall in love, and confront an uncertain future. The scenes focusing on the relationship between these two are electric. Unfortunately, the movie isn't nearly as engaging when the legions of other performers fill the screen. Catherine Deneuve's Eliane, while well-acted, is not as intriguing a character, so many of her scenes lack thrust.

The pace of *Indochine* as a whole is leisurely, although there are three instances when the slow progression of events is suddenly shattered by a barrage of violent action. *Indochine* is of epic scope and, at times, it appears that scenes have been cut for the sake of brevity. Regardless of what was sacrificed, however, the final product remains a well-plotted and superbly-acted piece.

Linh Dan Pham is excellent. Much of the depth attained by Camille is a product of a strong screen portrayal, since the character is not strongly written. Vincent Perez's Jean-Baptiste is better rounded on the written page than his lover, and the actor's passionate performance amplifies what the screenplay envisioned.

Set in French Indochina on the brink of revolution in the 1930s, *Indochine* tackles numerous social and political issues, many of which are still relevant today. This is both the picture's strength — because its range is so broad — and its weakness — because it occasionally loses its focus. Nevertheless, *Indochine* is successful far more often than not, and, when it works, it works beautifully. **HIGHLY RECOMMENDED**

Infinity [1996]

Starring: **Matthew Broderick, Patricia Arquette, Peter Riegert, Dori Brenner, Peter Michael Goetz, Zelijko Ivanek, James LeGros** Director: **Matthew Broderick** Screenplay: **Patricia Broderick** based on the books of Richard Feynman Running Time: **1:56** Rated: **PG (Mature themes)** Theatrical Aspect Ratio: **1.85:1**

Infinity is a biographical look at the early life of Richard Feynman (Matthew Broderick), the noted speaker, writer, and Nobel Prize-winning physicist who died in 1988.

Infinity tells two stories: Feynman's relationship with his beloved first wife, Arline (Patricia Arquette), and his involvement in the Manhattan Project's development of the first atomic bomb. While the tales cannot be split, it's clear that the film has a much better feel for Feynman's personal life than for his ethical struggles about unleashing a force of mass destruction. As background, the Los Alamos material is effec-

tive, but, on those occasions when it is thrust into the foreground, it pales in comparison to the love story.

The bulk of the film has nothing to do with Los Alamos or the bomb. Rather, it's about Richard and his intense, unwavering love for Arline. He meets her one day in 1934, when both are still in high school. He wanders into a room where she's singing and playing the piano, and is immediately smitten. The attraction is mutual, and, from that day forward, they are a couple.

In 1941, however, Arline falls ill, and the initial diagnosis is Hodgkin's Disease, a fatal ailment. Eventually, however, it turns out to be tuberculosis, the AIDS of the time. Over the protests of his family, who are afraid that he might contract the disease, Richard decides to marry Arline, then accept a government job so he can support her. Shortly after they elope, he moves to Los Alamos to join the Manhattan Project as a theoretical physicist, and the head of the project, J. Robert Oppenheimer, makes sure that Arline has a place in an Albuquerque sanitarium, where Richard can visit her each weekend. For two years, things continue like this, until Arline's illness reaches its crisis point just as victory is declared in Europe.

As told here, Arline and Richard's touching love story is devoid of sensationalism. Only in the end, when Richard fails to display any significant emotion following Arline's death, does *Infinity* strike a wrong chord. Feynman may have really given this rather clinical, dispassionate assessment: "Everybody dies. It doesn't stop the world." But it's tough to get an audience to accept that a loving husband could turn into such a cold fish.

Knowledge of physics and mathematics isn't necessary to enjoy the film. Arline is, after all, an artist, so Feynman has to explain his work in a manner that she, and the audience, will understand. *Infinity* represents a journey of emotional and scientific discovery. It's just unfortunate that the ending isn't more fundamentally satisfying. That single flaw keeps this from being a remarkable feature. **RECOMMENDED**

The Insider [1999]

Starring: **Al Pacino, Russell Crowe, Christopher Plummer, Diane Venora, Philip Baker Hall** Director: **Michael Mann** Screenplay: **Eric Roth & Michael Mann**, based on the *Vanity Fair* article "The Man Who Knew Too Much" by Marie Brenner Running Time: **2:37** Rated: **PG-13 (Profanity)** Theatrical Aspect Ratio: **2.35:1**

The Insider tells the story of CBS News's blackest hour — a time when greed and bad judgment overcame journalistic integrity. A story for *60 Minutes* compiled by correspondent Mike Wallace (played in the film by Christopher Plummer) and producer Lowell Bergman (Al Pacino) was killed when a potential lawsuit by tobacco giant Brown & Williamson threatened a buyout of CBS that would make a number of high-placed corporate executives very rich. The story: an interview with Jeffrey Wigand (Russell Crowe), a fired B&W corporate V.P. who had decided to blow the whistle on his former boss' lies to congress.

As a scientist, Wigand was deeply disturbed by the results of a study he ran, which showed that the tobacco companies deliberately manipulate the levels of the drug in their product to promote addiction. He first met Bergman when the *60 Minutes* producer was looking for an expert to translate industry-specific technical jargon. As the two spent time together, Bergman realized that Wigand knew an explosive secret, but was constrained from talking by a confidentiality agreement he had signed upon leaving B&W (the terms of which guaranteed his severance pay and continued medical coverage). Bergman, believing he knew a way around a breach of contract, offered Wigand the opportunity to be subpoenaed to testify in a Mississippi wrongful death class action lawsuit against the tobacco companies. Once his testimony was a part of the public record, he could go on *60 Minutes* to state his case. Even before Wigand agreed, he and his family became the targets of terrorist threats from anonymous sources. After risking everything (including his marriage and the possibility of going to jail), Wigand learned that *60 Minutes* had decided to cut the interview, rendering his sacrifices moot. Wigand had been betrayed, Bergman had been hung out to dry, and the Court of Public Opinion would not hear the truth about the tobacco giants.

The Insider is arguably a little too long with a few too many minor subplots thrown in (such as one about the Unibomber). However, when the movie is on-target, which is most of the time, it is riveting. Mann generates tension without resorting to the boring stand-bys of shootouts and chase scenes. The actors play their roles as if there's something tangible on the line, and those performances heighten the level of suspense.

The result is a compelling and engaging motion picture that weds the tautness of a thriller with the depth and impact of a drama. HIGHLY RECOMMENDED

Inventing the Abbotts [1997]

Starring: Joaquin Phoenix, Billy Crudup, Liv Tyler, Joanna Going, Jennifer Connelly, Will Patton, Kathy Baker, Barbara Williams
Director: Pat O'Connor Screenplay: Ken Hixon Running Time: 1:50
Rated: R (Sex, profanity, brief nudity) Theatrical Aspect Ratio: 1.85:1

Inventing the Abbotts begins with a voiceover, "The end of my innocence and childhood began in 1957." Openings like this are not promising, usually heralding overwrought coming-of-age melodramas of the most unremarkable sort. But while no one is going to mistake this for groundbreaking cinema, for what it is, *Inventing the Abbotts* does a more-than-acceptable job.

The film centers around two brothers: The older is Jacey Holt (Billy Crudup, from *Sleepers*) and the younger is Billy (Joaquin Phoenix, from *To Die For*), our narrator. Through the superfluous voiceover, we're given a quick rundown on the boys. Jacey is hard-working, obstinate, and gets all the girls; Billy is less sure of himself or where his life is going. The Holt boys are devoted to their mother, Helen (Kathy Baker), who brought them up on her own — their father died before Billy was born.

Next door to the Holts live the upper-class Abbotts. There are three daughters: Alice (Joanna Going), the "good girl" eldest child; Eleanor (Jennifer Connelly), the "bad girl" middle child; and Pamela (Liv Tyler), the youngest, who describes herself as "the one who sort of gets off the hook." Jacey is madly in lust with Eleanor, but it's a match that the Abbott patriarch (Will Patton) regards with ill-disguised contempt. Billy is friends with Pam, but, although theirs is a platonic relationship, it's clear that Pam would like it to go further. Billy, however, is wary, telling us that "I witnessed enough of my brother's social agony early on to know that I would never let the Abbotts matter to me." We in the audience, having seen this all before, know better.

Inventing the Abbotts is a routine Hollywood drama, which is to say that it doesn't take any chances and adheres rigorously to certain time-honored romantic conventions. The boy and girl appear fated to get together, but not until the last reel, and only after all sorts of social and emotional roadblocks have been cleared. The main story — Billy's relationship with Pam — is arguably the least interesting aspect of the film. In fact, the most compelling characters aren't necessarily the central figures. Jennifer Connelly's confident portrayal of Eleanor crackles with open sexuality; it's a shame that the film discards her so quickly. Likewise, Billy Crudup's Jacey is far more complex than his rather bland brother.

Watching *Inventing the Abbotts* is a comfortable experience. It would have been a better movie without the voiceover, but that particular narrative contrivance aside, the film comes across a genial, undemanding tale of love and life in the late '50s. And, while it's hard to get worked up about such a low-key motion picture, that doesn't diminish the simple enjoyment that the movie is capable of offering. **RECOMMENDED**

Iris [United Kingdom/United States, 2001]

Starring: Judi Dench. Jim Broadbent, Kate Winslet, Hugh Bonneville, Penelope Wilton, Juliet Aubrey Director: Richard Eyre
Screenplay: Charles Wood, Richard Eyre, based on *Iris: A Memoir and Elegy for Iris* by John Bayley Running Time: 1:30 Rated: R (Nudity, sex, profanity) Theatrical Aspect Ratio: 1.85:1

Those who have had a loved one fall prey to the ravages of Alzheimer's will see in *Iris* a depiction so lucid and accurate that it may be painful to watch. Based on the memoir of John Bayley, *Iris* tells of the first and last days of his relationship with his wife, philosopher and novelist Iris Murdoch. It's a powerful, affecting tale that uses scenes of the young couple's new love as a counterpoint to Iris' final days — memories of a brightest spring echoing in the darkest depths of winter.

Iris' main storyline unfolds in the early 1990s, when Iris (Judi Dench), regarded by some as the "foremost novelist of her generation" begins to experience the first stirrings of the disease that would eventually reduce her to a state of childlike helplessness. At first, she forgets things, and, for someone with a deep and abiding passion for words, her inability to recall the best one becomes a frustrating experience. Eventually, she loses more than just words. She can no longer write or even think coherently. The unknown frightens her. She sits in front of the television, watching shows designed for children. Her husband, John (Jim Broadbent), comfortable for 40 years being the "weaker" half of the union, is now thrust into the role of caregiver. There are times when he is found lacking, but his love for his wife ensures that he will not give up on her until the end.

Intercut with the '90s scenes are sequences from the '50s, when John (Hugh Bonneville) first meets and falls in love with the young, vivacious Iris (Kate Winslet), who loves nude swimming, fast biking, and no-strings-attached sex. Unaccountably, Iris is as drawn to John as he is to her, and it's not long before some of her free-spiritedness rubs off on him. They are a classic case of opposites attracting. She introduces him to sex and he shows her the rewards of simple, honest tenderness. It is in these flashback moments that *Iris* derives a measure of its power.

Through them, we see Iris at her strongest, and understand the foundation of her relationship with John.

Lest *Iris* seem like too much of a downer, there are moments of light humor to go along with the poignancy. Iris and John's courtship is presented playfully, and Eyre's decision to sprinkle the flashbacks throughout the film (rather than present them in one long block) gives us moments of needed respite from the sadness that accompanies Iris' downward spiral. And, while this is a story about the effects and ramifications of a disease, it is also a tale of the unbreakable power of love. While Alzheimer's defeats Iris' intellect, it never sunders the bond that she and John have formed. **HIGHLY RECOMMENDED**

It Could Happen to You [1994]

Starring: Nicolas Cage, Bridget Fonda, Rosie Perez, Wendell Pierce, Isaac Hayes, Stanley Tucci Director: Andrew Bergman Screenplay: Jane Anderson Running Time: 1:51 Rated: PG (Language, mature themes) Theatrical Aspect Ratio: 1.85:1

Those with a cynical bent will not enjoy *It Could Happen to You*. If you don't like happy endings, think Christmas is just for kids, and feel vaguely ill while watching *It's a Wonderful Life*, you would do well to stay away from this movie. On the other hand, if you're looking for a "feel good" romantic comedy, there aren't too many around more affable than this one.

Charlie Lang (Nicolas Cage) is a New York cop, and a genuinely nice guy — so nice, in fact, that when he doesn't have the change to tip his coffee shop waitress Yvonne (Bridget Fonda), he promises to split his winnings from a lottery ticket with her — if he wins, that is. Yvonne, who is having a bad day (she declared bankruptcy before coming to work), doesn't give the offer a second thought — until Charlie returns the next day with the news that he's $4 million richer. Despite the pleadings of his wife Muriel (Rosie Perez) to "stiff" the waitress, Charlie lets his conscience guide him, and sticks to his promise.

Love is in the air, as the old John Paul Young tune goes. You know from the beginning that Charlie and Yvonne are going to get together. If you can't figure that out, you've probably rented the wrong movie. The chemistry between Fonda and Cage is tangible — not the sultry, sexy kind that often characterizes boy-meets-girl stories, but something cuter and more fanciful.

Often, relationships in romantic comedies are contentious. Not so in *It Could Happen to You*. Charlie and Yvonne are two kind-hearted people who don't yell at each other. Instead, all scenes of conflict are reserved for vain, gold-digging Muriel, who begrudges Charlie every penny he gives away. She's the obvious villain of the piece, *It Could Happen to You*'s version of Mr. Potter.

I'm not sure if Rosie Perez does a great job of acting or not, but her character is really, really annoying. The word "shrill" doesn't begin to do her justice. Watching most of her scenes is like sitting in a classroom while someone scrapes their fingernails across the blackboard. Screeeeeeeeech!

It Could Happen to You is the most inoffensive of motion pictures, and that's precisely where the core of its charm lies. Other than a little suspension of disbelief, it doesn't demand a heavy investment from its audience. Of course, you have to enjoy this sort of movie to appreciate its appeal. If you do, *It Could Happen to You* will convince you that the magic of Frank Capra isn't dead in Hollywood after all. RECOMMENDED

Jack [1996]

Starring: Robin Williams, Diane Lane, Brian Kerwin, Jennifer Lopez, Adam Zolotin, Bill Cosby, Fran Drescher Director: Francis Ford Coppola Screenplay: James DeMonaco & Gary Nadeau Running Time: 1:53 Rated: PG-13 (Mature themes) Theatrical Aspect Ratio: 1.85:1

This feel-good motion picture is intelligently written and expertly directed: cross *Big* with *Forrest Gump*, and you get an idea of where *Jack*'s appeal lies.

The premise for *Jack*, although seemingly simple, is riddled with potential problems — nearly all of which the script not only addresses, but answers without a whiff of condescension. Jack is born when his mother is only 10 weeks pregnant. The doctors are immediately aware that something strange is going on. Eventually, they arrive at an explanation. The child has an internal clock that's ticking 4 times faster than usual. So, by the time Jack turns 10, he appears like a 40-year old man (Robin Williams).

Until the fall of his 11th year, Jack has been taught by a tutor (Bill Cosby). But, after careful consideration, his mother (Diane Lane) and father (Brian Kerwin) agree that he should give public school a try, despite children's' propensity for name-calling and finger-pointing. So, one morning, Jack ventures into Nathaniel Hawthorne Elementary School to meet his 5th grade teacher, Miss Marquez (Jennifer Lopez), and his classmates.

The film has an excellent grasp of what it's like to be in 5th grade. Jack endures all the painful isolation

of a "different" child, but, gradually, as he makes friends (by dominating schoolground basketball games and offering to buy *Penthouse* magazines), he begins to fit in. It's perhaps an idealized vision of elementary school, but there are enough aspects of reality not to jolt our suspension of disbelief. *Jack* is rarely maudlin, and manages to be affecting without heavy-handed manipulation.

One of the most difficult issues *Jack* has to deal with is the title character's rapid aging. If he looks like he's 40 at 10, that means he'll be lucky to live past 20. When his teacher asks him what he wants to be when he grows up, Jack's answer is succinct and poignant: "Alive." Mr. Woodruff, Jack's tutor, describes him this way: "You're a shooting star amongst ordinary stars . . . A shooting star passes quickly, but, while it's here, it's the most beautiful thing you'll ever want to see." The movie never shies away from confronting Jack's mortality.

Robin Williams is entirely believable as a 10-year-old. He has all the mannerisms and vocal inflections perfected — whining when he doesn't get his way, pulling at his shirts, adjusting his pants, and so forth. It's almost as if he regressed back into childhood for the duration of filming. (Then again, has Williams ever really grown up?)

Jack has something to offer just about everyone. It's good-natured, funny, heartwarming, and capable of being viewed on more than one level. Children will relate to *Jack* differently than their parents, although, with its "soft" PG-13, the film isn't for the very young. RECOMMENDED

Jane Eyre [France/Italy/United Kingdom, 1995]

Starring: Charlotte Gainsbourg, William Hurt, Joan Plowright, Josephine Serre, Anna Paquin, Geraldine Chaplin, Elle Macpherson, Amanda Root Director: Franco Zeffirelli Screenplay: Hugh Whitemore and Franco Zeffirelli based on the novel by Charlotte Bronte Running Time: 1:57 Rated: PG (Mature themes) Theatrical Aspect Ratio: 1.85:1

One of the best-loved of all the Victorian novels, *Jane Eyre* combines social commentary with gothic romance. This film, directed by Franco Zeffirelli (best known for his 1968 Oscar-nominated *Romeo and Juliet*), remains faithful to the original narrative in general, if not in all the particulars.

We are introduced to 10-year-old Jane (Anna Paquin) in the early 1830s at Gateshead Hall, where she lives with her aunt and cousins. Orphaned at an early age, Jane has grown up unloved and unloving, and now her aunt has decided to send her to the Lowood Charity School, citing her as willful, obstinate, deceitful, and in need of a stern upbringing. At Lowood, Jane finds life difficult under the tutelage of the cold-hearted Mr. Brocklehurst (John Wood) and Miss Scatcherd (Geraldine Chaplin), but she forms a pair of solid friendships that help her through the hardest times.

After 10 years at Lowood, an older, wiser, but still-spirited Jane (now played by Charlotte Gainsbourg) accepts a position as governess for the young French ward of Edward Rochester (William Hurt), master of Thornfield Hall. Jane settles in quickly, forming solid relationships with her charge, Adele Varens (Josephine Serre), and Thornfield's housekeeper, Mrs. Fairfax (Joan Plowright). However, the master of the house makes the strongest impression on the young woman. From her first meeting with Edward, when she offers aid after he is thrown from a horse, she is infatuated, but his natural reticence keeps her from confessing her feelings. But there is something other than Edward for Jane to consider as she beomes established in her new situation, because Thornfield Hall hides a secret. Who, or what, lives in the attic, under the stern and watchful eye of the semi-vigilant Grace Poole (Billie Whitelaw)?

Jane Eyre is a love story, but, instead of the lighter romance and humor of Jane Austen's novels, this tale is marked by stark realism and a pervasive sense of misery. The meticulously accurate settings and beautiful-but-gloomy cinematography establish the atmosphere. Even the daytime scenes are drab and colorless, and many of the interior shots are so dark that it's difficult to see the characters' expressions.

Charlotte Gainsbourg (*The Cement Garden*) brings Jane to life, and, on those occasions when the script fumbles because it's painting the narrative in too-broad strokes, she holds our attention and captures our sympathy. Unfortunately, Gainsbourg's opposite, William Hurt, lacks presence. His is a passionless portrayal of a tragic figure.

For Bronte aficionados, lovers of Victorian romance, or those who simply appreciate literate love stories, *Jane Eyre* offers 2 hours of quality entertainment. **RECOMMENDED**

Jason's Lyric [1994]

Starring: Allen Payne, Jada Pinkett, Forest Whitaker, Anthony "Treach" Criss, Suzanne Douglas, Bokeem Woodbine Director: Doug McHenry Screenplay: Bobby Smith Jr. Running Time: 1:59 Rated: R (Language, violence, nudity, sex, mature themes) Theatrical Aspect Ratio: 1.85:1

Doug McHenry's tale of life for an urban black family is an extraordinary achievement, filled with passion, romance, and complex tragedy. *Jason's Lyric* is not so much a poem as a saga, and there is no part of this motion picture that ever feels contrived or forced.

This film is about many kinds of love, and the rage and jealousy that often go hand-in-hand with them. Only the strongest of emotions can provoke a violent reaction, and this is a truth that *Jason's Lyric* illustrates. A common adage states that there's a fine line between love and hate. If that's true, the characters in this film cross over and back several times.

The setting is Houston. We are introduced to the two young sons of Gloria Alexander (Suzanne Douglas): Jason (played as an adult by Allen Payne), the elder, and Joshua (played as an adult by Bokeem Woodbine), the younger. As children, the two are forced to defend their mother when their drunken father Maddog (Forest Whitaker) storms into the house in a rage.

A decade and a half later, Joshua has become a criminal and Jason is living life on the "straight-and-narrow." The two could not be more dissimilar, but the ties binding them are stronger than their differences. Until Jason falls in love, that is. The object of his affection is Lyric Greer (Jada Pinkett), the sister of a local drug kingpin (Anthony "Treach" Criss). As soon as Joshua recognizes that this woman could come between his brother and him, he develops a powerful dislike of her.

As rich a story as this is, it would never have attained such an impact without a spate of strong performances. From Bokeem Woodbine, who plays the haunted, angry Joshua, to Forest Whitaker, as a man whose soul was lost in Vietnam, to Suzanne Douglas, the torn mother, there isn't an instance of weak or sub-par acting. Allen Payne and Jada Pinkett, playing the title characters, possess that rare chemistry that so many screen couples lack. Their interaction drives *Jason's Lyric* to its inevitable climax.

Whether love is healing or destructive, any giving of this emotion demands opening one's heart, and an open heart can easily be broken. *Jason's Lyric* is about consequences — those that come about as a result of trusting, loving, and even living. The result showcases the talent of all involved, and weaves a rare and unforgettable story. **HIGHLY RECOMMENDED**

Jefferson in Paris [United States/United Kingdom, 1995]

Starring: Nick Nolte, Greta Scacchi, Thandie Newton, Gwyneth Paltrow, Lambert Wilson, Simon Callow Director: James Ivory Screenplay: Ruth Prawer Jhabvala Running Time: 2:22 Rated: PG-13 (Mature themes)

The Bostonians. A Room With A View. Mr. and Mrs. Bridge. Howards End. The Remains of the Day. These represent the best of Merchant-Ivory — a category to which *Jefferson in Paris* does not belong.

Nick Nolte looks like Thomas Jefferson, and his reputation as a fine actor is wholly deserved. But Nolte is inexplicably flat in a part that seems to smother him. He's adequate, but no emoting is involved, and there are many sequences where Jefferson comes across as stiff and lifeless. Nolte never successfully forges a bond between his character and the audience.

Four principal storylines are developed throughout the movie. The first relates to Jefferson's burgeoning friendship/romance with painter Maria Cosway (Greta Scacchi). The second follows the changes in his relationship with one of his slaves, 15-year-old Sally Hemings (Thandie Newton). Another examines the jealous reactions of his daughter Patsy (Gwyneth Paltrow) to his mistresses. The final, and potentially most interesting, is an observation of the political events leading up to the French Revolution, and how Jefferson (who was the U.S. minister to France between 1784 and 1789) reacts to these.

In general, it's the secondary performers who are most impressive. Thandie Newton brings life and vibrancy to Sally (although there is one horribly over-the-top scene where she dances for Jefferson in the privacy of his bed chamber). Gwyneth Paltrow gives a multi-dimensionality to a character conflicted by love, commitment, and jealousy. Simon Callow (*Four Weddings and a Funeral*) has a delightful turn as the gay husband of Scacchi's Maria.

When it comes to issues, *Jefferson in Paris* is feeble and fumbling. After introducing the ironic hypocrisy of Jefferson's having written a document claiming that "all men are created equal" while nevertheless maintaining a significant contingent of slaves, little more of substance is presented on the subject. The conflicts and ideologies underlying the French Revolution are given equally short shrift. Aside from a few brief discussions filled with facile arguments, this particular element of the plot seems designed more as an historical backdrop than anything else.

Impressions of *Jefferson in Paris* are likely to be based largely upon expectations. Those anticipating something with the depth and breadth of a *Howards End* will be disappointed. Regardless, though it may be occasionally slow-moving and perhaps a half-hour too long, this film is put together with care and a mindfulness of quality. Little here is exceptional, but, fortunately, less is below par. In the end, *Jefferson in Paris* is just another *Masterpiece Theater*-style costume drama. **RECOMMENDED**

Jesus' Son [Canada/United States, 1999]

Starring: Billy Crudup, Samantha Morton, Denis Leary, Jack Black, Will Patton, Holly Hunter, Dennis Hopper Director: Alison Maclean Screenplay: Elizabeth Cuthrell, David Urrutia, and Oren Moverman, based on the novel by Denis Johnson Running Time: 1:48 Rated: R (Drug use, nudity, sex, profanity, violence) Theatrical Aspect Ratio: 2.35:1

It's neither new nor revolutionary for a motion picture to be presented from the point-of-view of someone who is perpetually stoned. However, unlike most movie spirals into the drug culture, Alison Maclean's *Jesus' Son* offers a perspective that embraces, not alienates, the audience. The film's protagonist, the appropriately named "Fuckhead" (played with wide-eyed innocence by Billy Crudup), is impossible not to like, even though, like an inverted King Midas, everything he touches turns to dross.

In its own peculiar way, *Jesus' Son* is a road movie. Fuckhead and his girlfriend, Michelle (Samantha Morton), are constantly on the move, usually in his VW Bug, crashing in cheap motels and rarely spending more than a few weeks in any one place. Along the way, they meet a number of odd characters — the ill-fated Wayne (Denis Leary), who offers Fuckhead a job even though the work messes with his high; Georgie (Jack Black), a hospital orderly who steals uppers and downers from medical cabinets; John Smith (Will Patton), who offers Michelle a better life; and Mira (Holly Hunter), whose husbands and boyfriends have a history of dying.

Jesus' Son is hard to classify. The film is surprisingly funny, and could almost be described as a dark comedy. The movie's structure is unusual — the story is presented as a series of narrated flashbacks that are often disconnected. For the most part, they're offered in chronological order, but not always. And, on one occasion, Fuckhead stops one flashback in the middle because he forgot to tell another story. So he goes back to the other incident before returning to where he left off.

The acting is superlative. Billy Crudup, who is not a big name despite a fairly lengthy resume, has the ability to disappear into his character — a trait that serves him well here. Matching Crudup beat-for-beat is Samantha Morton, who has the rare gift of being able to meld sweetness, vulnerability, and earthy sexuality into her portrayal. Other performers, such as

Denis Leary, Dennis Hopper, Holly Hunter, and *High Fidelity*'s Jack Black, have small (but colorful) parts.

Addiction is one of the key themes explored by *Jesus' Son*, but it's not only the inescapable lure of heroin. Fuckhead is as addicted to Michelle as he is to drugs, and she proves to be a more difficult habit to shake than anything he can inject into his veins. The result is a film that is odd, engaging, often comedic, and sometimes even a little haunting. RECOMMENDED

The Journey of August King [1995]

Starring: Jason Patric, Thandie Newton, Larry Drake, Sam Waterston, Sarah Jayne Wylde Director: John Duigan Screenplay: John Ehle based on his novel Running Time: 1:32 Rated: R (Mature themes, execution) Theatrical Aspect Ratio: 1.85:1

The Journey of August King is as close to a flawless motion picture as is likely to be produced by the film industry (independent or mainstream). In a performance that is remarkable because of its reserve and restraint, Jason Patric plays the title character, a widowed frontiersman making his way home from town in 1815 North Carolina. He has just used the year's gains to buy a milk cow, a boar, and 2 geese. Along the road, he meets up with a runaway slave girl (Thandie Newton), heading for the freedom of the North. Her owner, Olaf Singletary (Larry Drake), desperately wants her back and is offering a handsome reward for her return — 5 acres of land and a good horse. August thinks this is too cheap a price for a human life, but is still reluctant to help the girl because it's against the law. Eventually, however, her bleak circumstances prick his conscience, and he allows her to hide in his wagon. Thus begins his complicity in an act that could lead to his ruin.

Australian director John Duigan, whose previous efforts include *The Year My Voice Broke, Flirting,* and *Sirens,* is in complete control of the material. Working with his best script yet, Duigan displays his mastery of tone and pacing. *The Journey of August King* advances slowly and deliberately, allowing the characters necessary time to breathe and expand. Nothing is hurried or forced; Duigan understands how to move action and transform personalities without cheating or manipulating his audience.

Thandie Newton, who starred in Duigan's *Flirting,* and later appeared in *Jefferson in Paris,* brings a mix of quiet dignity and desperation to Annalees, as well as a subtle eroticism of which the character is ignorant. Newton and Patric work well together, with Annalees' spirit counterbalancing August's reticence. Larry Drake (*Darkman*) creates a complex antagonist

in Olaf Singletary, a man who is not so much evil as he is torn by the conflict between his own needs and society's expectations.

Although it is most obviously a tale of redemption, *The Journey of August King* is also a love story (in the most basic sense of the word "love"). There's no doubt that an intimate bond develops between August and Annalees, although it's *not* the one most movies would choose. Each learns from the other and, by the end, it's unclear who has gained more from the exchange. The toll of the journey seems a small price to pay for what they achieve, separately and together. *The Journey of August King* offers a look through the window of a rare and special story. MUST SEE

The Joy Luck Club [1993]

Starring: Ming-Na Wen, Tamlyn Tomita, Lauren Tom, Rosalind Chao, Kieu Chinh, Tsai Chin, France Nuyen, Lisa Lu Director: Wayne Wang Screenplay: Amy Tan and Ronald Bass based on the novel by Amy Tan Running Time: 2:19 Rated: R (Language, mature themes, violence) Theatrical Aspect Ratio: 1.85:1

The Joy Luck Club is a collection of Chinese women bound together more by hope than joy or luck. The 4 women — Suyuan (Kieu Chinh), Lindo (Tsai Chin), Ying Ying (France Nuyen), and An Mei (Lisa Lu) — came to America many years ago to escape China's feudal society for promise of a better life. Now, however, Suyuan has died and the 3 surviving members of the club invite her daughter June (Ming-Na Wen) to take her place. June belongs to the "new" generation, those of Chinese heritage who grew up speaking English and learning American customs. Also of roughly the same age are Waverly (Tamlyn Tomita), Lindo's daughter; Lena (Lauren Tom), Ying Ying's daughter; and Rose (Rosalind Chao), An Mei's daughter. *The Joy Luck Club* tells of the varied difficulties and tragedies involved in these mother/daughter relationships.

Co-writer Ronald Bass (who, along with Amy Tan, adapted from Tan's novel) says that there are 16 separate stories in *The Joy Luck Club*. These vignettes explore common themes that give solid grounding and greater resonance to the overall film. As Bass comments, "I saw all the mothers' and daughters' stories as facets of the same experience. Put together, they formed a mosaic."

The Joy Luck Club is clearly — perhaps too clearly — an adaptation of a book. The dialogue is often too poetic to be real, and the story too clearly plotted to be acceptable as anything more than an imperfect reflection of the world we live in. The line between drama and melodrama is a fine one, and, while *The Joy Luck Club* most often successfully navigates the tightrope, there are times when it slips and comes across as heavy-handed.

The characters are the movie's real strength. Many are played by more than one actor (as children then adults, for example), but all transitions are smooth and seamless. It's as easy to accept both a little girl and the beautiful, sophisticated-looking Tamlyn Tomita as Waverly, and that's because the characters transcend the performers portraying them.

It's fascinating and satisfying the way the diverse threads are knitted together into a single tapestry. *The Joy Luck Club*'s message is one of hope — that catharsis and emotional fulfillment often come through tragedy. Sure, a lot of bad things happen during the course of this film, but at the end, the tears are of happiness and new beginnings, not loss. **RECOMMENDED**

Jude [United Kingdom/United States, 1996]

Starring: Christopher Eccleston, Kate Winslet, Liam Cunningham, Rachel Griffiths, June Whitfield Director: Michael Winterbottom Screenplay: Hossein Amini based on *Jude the Obscure* by Thomas Hardy Running Time: 2:02 Rated: R (Nudity, sex, animal slaughter, mature themes) Theatrical Aspect Ratio: 2.35:1

Jude is an ambitious, big-screen adaptation of Thomas Hardy's heartbreaking classic, *Jude the Obscure*. This is a film of tremendous scope and emotional depth that uncovers the soul of a novel and brings it to life on the screen.

In every way that matters, *Jude* is faithful to its print inspiration. The rhythm of some of the dialogue has been changed to make it sound more natural to contemporary viewers, and a number of minor characters have been deleted, but the story arc is rigorously true to Hardy's vision.

As the film opens, young Jude (James Daley) has accompanied his beloved school teacher, Phillotson (Liam Cunningham), to the top of a hill outside his town of Marygreen. Phillotson is traveling to Christminster to become a scholar, and, with Jude by his side to bid him farewell, he points out the distant place, shimmering and gleaming on the horizon like Camelot. This vision becomes a driving force in Jude's life. Though he grows up to be a stone mason by trade, his dream is of scholarship, so he spends long hours studying, hoping eventually to follow Phillotson.

Years later, in the wake of a failed marriage to a pig farmer's daughter (Rachel Griffiths), Jude (now played by Christopher Eccleston) finally journeys to

Christminster. And, although he fails in his quest for admission to a university, he meets his beautiful, young cousin, Sue Bridehead (Kate Winslet), a modern woman who refuses to be governed by religious superstitions. As she and Jude spend time together, they fall hopelessly in love. But, because they can never marry, the pressures of society doom their relationship. (In fact, it was Hardy's harsh condemnation of society's intransigence, in addition to his sexual frankness, that caused such a stir when *Jude the Obscure* first reached the public.)

Jude couldn't have been more perfectly cast. Christopher Eccleston (*Shallow Grave*) develops Jude as a somewhat naive dreamer who is forever chasing an elusive image of happiness. For a while, that's the existence of a scholar, then, for the bulk of the film, it's a life with Sue. Eccleston gets us to care about Jude, a development that is critical to the film's success. His chemistry with his leading lady, Kate Winslet, is electric. When Phillotson says of Jude and Sue, "Sometimes I think [those] two are one person split in two," we believe him. Their initial sexual encounter is both funny and touching.

The emotional intensity of *Jude* rivals that of films like *Carrington* and *The Remains of the Day*. Top notch production values and strong performances help, but more important is the universality of the sad, unforgettable love story that Thomas Hardy first told, and Michael Winterbottom has so effectively reinterpreted. **HIGHLY RECOMMENDED**

Judy Berlin [1999]

Starring: Barbara Barrie, Bob Dishy, Edie Falco, Aaron Harnick, Bette Henritze, Madeline Kahn, Julie Kavner, Anne Meara Director: Eric Mendelsohn Screenplay: Eric Mendelsohn Running Time: 1:33 Rated: No MPAA Rating ("R"-level profanity) Theatrical Aspect Ratio: 1.85:1

Judy Berlin is filmed in glorious black-and-white — a perfect choice for the subject matter — an unforced meditation on the pressure of monotony in suburbia. The film opens with scenes of late-'90s suburbia — a local elementary school, houses lined up neatly in rows with cars in driveways, electric meters, and street lights winking out as the day begins. Events, to the extent that anything happens, take place during a September day in the community of Babylon, Long Island. It's the second day of the new school year, but, more importantly, it's the day of a total solar eclipse. However, once the sun disappears behind the moon, it never re-emerges, so more than half of *Judy Berlin* takes place in the *Twilight Zone* of a pitch black summer afternoon.

Against this backdrop, we meet and spend time with a small group of characters. Thirty-year-old David Gold (Aaron Harnick) is a failed Hollywood director who has returned to Babylon in despair. As the film opens, he is crying in the bathroom. Later, he wanders outside and encounters an old high school classmate, the irrepressible Judy Berlin (Edie Falco), who is about to embark on the journey David just came back from — a trip to California, which seems to her like a land of milk and honey. She's a wannabe actress (and, by all accounts, not a very good one) and has dreams of "making it big." Meanwhile, Judy's mother, Sue (Barbara Barrie), a grade-school teacher, is not coping well with her daughter's impending departure. She turns for comfort to the school's principal, Arthur Gold (Bob Dishy), David's father. Like Sue, Arthur is going through a bad time. He is sick of the tediousness of his life, of his son's listlessness, and of the whining of his wife, Alice (Madeline Kahn). So, as David and Judy spend the day walking around Babylon, revisiting the past and wondering about the future, Sue and Arthur try to define their feelings for one another. And Alice seems to be the only one taking notice that the eclipse is lasting far longer than it should be.

To be appreciated, *Judy Berlin* has to be savored — accept that nothing will happen and simply enjoy the experience exploring the interaction of characters who seem as three-dimensional as anyone you might meet in everyday circumstances. As one critic put it, "You can believe these characters existed before the film started and that they'll continue existing after it ends."

Although best known for light roles in Mel Brooks comedies, Madeline Kahn (whose last role this was, before her death in 1999) here adds weight to this depiction of the so-called American Dream slipping a few gears into the American Nightmare. **RECOMMENDED**

K-PAX [2001]

Starring: Kevin Spacey, Jeff Bridges, Mary McCormack, Alfre Woodard, Brian Howe   Director: Iain Softley   Screenplay: Charles Leavitt, based on the novel by Gene Brewer   Running Time: 2:04
Rated: PG-13 (Profanity, mature themes)   Theatrical Aspect Ratio: 2.35:1

All movies require of their audience a "willing suspension of disbelief." Watching a movie like *K-PAX* demands an abandonment of cynicism, as well. Because the movie tends towards melodrama, more hardened viewers may tune out without bothering to look beneath *K-PAX*'s surface to discover that there are some interesting themes and issues lurking there. The premise, although not original, is intriguing, and the overall impact is helped immeasurably by the competent performances of lead actors Kevin Spacey and Jeff Bridges.

Prot (Spacey) is the newest patient to be admitted to the Psychiatric Institute of Manhattan. He's a gentle, intelligent man who seems abnormally sane and lucid until he starts talking about his origins. According to Prot, he's not a resident of Earth, but merely a visitor. He hails from the planet of K-PAX, located 1,000 light years away in the constellation of Lyra. He traveled here on a beam of light with the intention of investigating the population of a "BA-3 planet" — a world in the early stages of evolution with an uncertain future. His doctor is Mark Powell (Bridges), the Chief of Clinical Psychiatry. Of course, Mark doesn't believe that Prot is from K-PAX, but he acknowledges that the man's delusions are more detailed than usual, and he is at a loss to explain how the patient knows things about star systems that only a few eminent astronomers are aware of and how he can make calculations on paper that those same scientists require a computer for. Instead, he believes that Prot has fashioned a fantasy cocoon as a result of a traumatic event in his life, and it's up to Mark to ferret out the truth of what happened.

Thematically, the movie is concerned with the importance of families and human contact in everyday existence. Mark is a workaholic who often neglects his wife (Mary McCormack) and children in favor of his latest patient. Working on Prot's case, however, Mark begins to realize how desolate it can be for a person to be alone in the universe, with no family or friends to turn to. When Mark makes an offhand comment about accompanying Prot back to K-PAX, Prot responds that he should explore more of his own planet first.

Of course, the mystery at the core of *K-PAX* is whether Prot is really an alien sojourning for a time in our corner of the galaxy or whether he's a man with a deeply troubled past. In the end, the truth about Prot is only pointed at; there is some wiggle room for varying interpretations. What is clear is that Prot represents something a little different to everyone who knows him: patient, friend, savior, simpleton, genius. With versatile character actor Kevin Spacey playing the part, there's never any difficulty accepting Prot as any of these things. RECOMMENDED

Kandahar [Iran, 2001]

Starring: Nelofer Pazira, Hassan Tantaï, Sadou Teymouri
Director: Mohsen Makhmalbaf Screenplay: Mohsen Makhmalbaf
Running Time: 1:25 Rated: Unrated (Mature themes) Theatrical Aspect
Ratio: 1.85:1 In Farsi with subtitles

When *Kandahar* had the first of its two screenings at the 2001 Toronto International Film Festival on September 8, most of the Western world knew very little about the Taliban. One week later, at the time of *Kandahar's* second Toronto screening, everything had changed.

Nafas (Nelofer Pazira) is a female journalist returning to her birthplace in Afghanistan for the first time in over a decade. When she fled the country for Canada, she was forced to leave behind a sister who had been maimed by a landmine. Now, that sister, despondent as a result of the Taliban's oppression, has decided to kill herself during the final solar eclipse of the second millennium. When Nafas learns of this, she decides to travel to Kandahar to prevent the suicide. But getting to the city, especially with time working against her, is not an easy task. Disguised under an all-concealing burka (the head-to-toe garment worn by fundamentalist Muslim women), she is accompanied by various others on this trek, including an American living in Afghanistan (Hassan Tantaï), a child seeking to make money, and a one-armed man trying to sell an artificial leg. She is Dorothy traveling a demented yellow brick road, but her destination is not Oz.

Kandahar's narrative is just a skeleton that Makhmalbaf can use to expose the social system of Afghanistan under the Taliban. It would be easy to mistake *Kandahar* for a grim fantasy or something set in a long-forgotten land. It's difficult to believe that any modern country could be this backward and unenlightened, but during the course of the movie, one character remarks, "weapons are the only modern thing in Afghanistan."

Many of the episodes in *Kandahar*, including the exchanges at the Red Cross tent where artificial legs are handed out, the way in which doctors examine female patients (through a sheet with a hole in it, so faces cannot be seen), and the wedding procession, are drawn from things Makhmalbaf encountered during a clandestine trip into Afghanistan while preparing for the film. No professional actors are used, and filming was done near the Iran/Afghanistan border, less than a mile outside of Taliban-controlled territory.

Kandahar's story — that of Nafas' episodic journey — will likely be quickly forgotten. As a character, she is not well-developed and her situation, while tragic, pales in comparison with what will linger: the portrait of Afghanistan that Makhmalbaf paints on this cinematic canvas. For better or for worse, the reign of the Taliban appears to be over. But, as *Kandahar* shows, the end of that government does not mean an end to Afghanistan's problems. RECOMMENDED

The Keeper [1996]

Starring: Giancarlo Esposito, Regina Taylor, Isaach De Bankole
Director: Joe Brewster Screenplay: Joe Brewster Running Time: 1:30
Rated: No MPAA Rating (Violence, profanity) Theatrical Aspect
Ratio: 1.85:1

Joe Brewster's *The Keeper* is a compelling look at what can happen when a man loses his faith in humanity. This multi-layered psychological drama uses fine performances by Giancarlo Esposito (*Do the Right Thing*), Regina Taylor (*A Family Thing*), and French actor Isaach De Bankole (*Night on Earth*), as well as an intelligent script by writer/director Brewster, to tell a suspenseful tale.

The Keeper introduces us to Paul Lamont (Esposito), a New York City cop with dreams of becoming a lawyer. Paul takes his job seriously and has a tendency to bring his problems home with him. But Paul is also a firm believer in justice, and when he sees a man, Jean Baptiste (De Bankole), thrown into jail for a rape he probably didn't commit, Paul advances the Haitian-born immigrant the $1,500 bail money. Later, when Jean comes to Paul for a place to stay, the cop reluctantly offers him a place on the couch. Paul's wife, Angela (Taylor), is initially horrified at the thought of a possible rapist sleeping in her home, but, with the passage of time, she and Jean form a special bond. As they grow closer, however, Paul begins to feel alienated, and his growing disillusionment with the system, coupled with questions about his wife's fidelity, fuel a churning, unpredictable anger.

Brewster is a psychiatrist, so it's no surprise that the psychological elements of *The Keeper* are the most engrossing. As the story progresses, not only does Paul question his own system of beliefs, but he becomes conflicted about his identity. Paul's father was Haitian, but he has long denied that part of his heritage, shrinking away from the customs of the

Caribbean and trying to fit in as a generic New Yorker. On the other hand, Jean still embraces Haitian traditions, and his flaunting of those customs drives Paul to a crisis point. Is Paul jealous of Jean, or of Jean's clear sense of identity?

The Keeper isn't just powerful drama, it's an effective thriller. A subplot about how cops abuse their power dovetails nicely with the resolution of the main story, and the film's closing images are some of its most memorable. Brewster doesn't follow conventional formulas, and, although there are surprises, all are perfectly logical considering the nature of the people involved. Taken as a whole, *The Keeper* is a disturbing portrait of a modern America where homogeneity and conformity threaten not only our cultural identities, but our individuality. HIGHLY RECOMMENDED

Kids [1995]

Starring: Leo Fitzpatrick, Justin Pierce, Chloë Sevigny, Rosario Dawson, Yakira Peguero Director: Larry Clark Screenplay: Harmony Korine Running Time: 1:35 Rated: No MPAA Rating (Profanity, sex, violence, drugs) Theatrical Aspect Ratio: 1.85:1

The vision presented in Larry Clark's *Kids* is as bleak as things get — an ugly portrait of amoral youths who resort to drugs and sex not as a form of rebellion, but to fill the void of otherwise empty and meaningless lives.

On the outside, Telly (Leo Fitzpatrick) is the kind of clean-cut teenage boy any mother might let her daughter go out with. He looks "normal" — perhaps even a little nerdy — and can be polite and sincere when it suits him. But Telly is an inveterate liar. He will say or do anything to satisfy his addiction for deflowering virgins. Sexually uninitiated girls present the greatest challenge and, as a bonus, are guaranteed disease-free. Not that he believes in AIDS anyway — condoms, in his opinion, are a waste of time.

Telly's best friend is Casper (Justin Pierce). While Casper also enjoys sex, his partners don't have to come with their hymens intact. And Casper's as much into drugs and drink as sleeping with girls. Like Telly, he's not concerned about the future or the consequences of his actions. He takes life as it comes, whether that means inhaling dope, raping a stoned girl, or beating someone half to death with a skateboard.

Then there's Jennie (Chloë Sevigny), who's only had sex once, but, without protection, that was enough to do irreparable damage. When her HIV test comes back positive, her life collapses around her. Nothing

makes sense. Her best friend, Ruby (Rosario Dawson), has had sex with at least 8 guys, yet she's clean. And when Jennie rushes to stop another girl from sharing her fate, she arrives too late.

Kids is shot like a documentary and, in its uncompromising depiction of every aspect of the characters' social and sexual interactions, it seems almost too raw for fiction. Clark has meticulously designed this movie to blur the lines between reality and scripted story, hiring 20-year old Harmony Korine to write a screenplay that reflects what's really going on in the streets. The actors are all newcomers, and their unfamiliar faces and unpolished-yet-effective performances add to the documentary-like effect.

Kids shows what happens when children are set adrift in a heartless world, and warns us what happens — and is already happening — in the absence of love and guidance. If people lose their souls as children, what happens when they grow up? This is a tragedy without a last act — a wrenching experience that offers no catharsis. HIGHLY RECOMMENDED

The King of Masks (Bian Lian) [China, 1996]

Starring: Zhu Xu, Zhou Ren-ying, Zhao Zhigang Director: Wu Tianming Screenplay: Wei Minglung Running Time: 1:41 Rated: PG-13 (Mature themes, mild profanity) Theatrical Aspect Ratio: 1.85:1 In Mandarin with subtitles

The King of Masks is melodrama of the highest order: manipulative and occasionally overacted yet deeply affecting. The film draws from a rich tradition of stories about children melting the hearts of lonely older men or women, but its cultural backdrop — China in the 1930s — lends depth and freshness to familiar themes.

Bian Lian Wang (Zhu Xu), the so-called King of Masks, is a locally renowned street performer whose magical ability to instantaneously switch between various facial coverings makes him a crowd favorite. A famous opera singer, Liang Sao Lang (Zhao Zhigang), is so impressed with the King's show that he asks to learn the old man's tricks. The King gently, but firmly, refuses, stating that "While my talents may be meager, only a son may inherit them." His family has a long tradition of passing their secrets from fathers to sons (no daughters). However, the King has no child — his only boy died at the age of 10, 21 years ago. So, to ensure that he has an heir, the King goes to a slave market where he buys Doggie (Zhou Ren-ying), an affable 8-year old. At first, the King is delighted by this new presence in his life — someone who readily calls him "grandpa." Then he learns he has been duped. The "boy" he purchased is actually a girl.

The emotional fulcrum of *The King of Masks* is the relationship between the caring Doggie and the crusty King. After learning that his charge isn't a boy, the King is initially cold and insensitive, but the dire nature of Doggie's circumstances convinces him that turning his back on her would be wrong (she has already been sold 7 times). So he allows her to remain with him, provided that, instead of calling him "grandpa," she refers to him as "boss." Predictably, the longer the two remain together, the closer their bond becomes. Doggie is openly devoted to the King, and, although he will not admit it, he comes to love her. She eventually becomes part of the King's act, although, because she is not a male, he will not reveal his secrets to her.

While a host of movies to have emerged from China during the '90s have been political in nature (often overtly so, resulting in bans), *The King of Masks* is an exception. Despite being uniquely Chinese in many ways, the basic narrative has a universal appeal. The touching, human aspect of this story has the capacity to warm the hearts of all but the most cynical moviegoer. RECOMMENDED

King of the Hill [1993]

Starring: Jesse Bradford, Jeroen Krabbe, Lisa Eichhorn, Adrien Brody, Spalding Gray, Elizabeth McGovern, Karen Allen Director: Steven Soderbergh Screenplay: Steven Soderbergh based on the memoirs of A. E. Hotchner Running Time: 1:49 Rated: PG (Mature themes) Theatrical Aspect Ratio: 2.35:1

In St. Louis during the Great Depression, Aaron Kurlander's (Jesse Bradford) family is falling apart. His little brother has been shipped off to live with an uncle, his sick mother (Lisa Eichhorn) has been admitted to a sanitarium, and his father (Jeroen Krabbe) must go on the road to make money. So Aaron is left on his own in a fleabag hotel, with no money and few friends. Life becomes a struggle for the 12-year-old — the hotel wants to evict him and his meager supply of food is running dangerously low — and it's only through his remarkable resourcefulness that he manages to survive.

Writer-Director Steven Soderbergh brings 1933 St. Louis to life with uncompromising accuracy. Many period pieces give only token acknowledgment to the era in which they take place, but *King of the Hill* has the Great Depression woven inextricably throughout.

Jesse Bradford does an excellent job as Aaron. His performance is unforced, regardless of the complexity of emotions he is expected to show. Take, for example, the touching, bittersweet relationship that develops between Aaron and a lonely, epileptic girl living down the hall. These scenes have a remarkable resonance.

Soderbergh's style is frank, not quirky, and yields up a number of powerful images: a starving boy cutting out pictures of food and serving them on a plate, a homeless man waving hello, and a puddle of blood-tainted water seeping from underneath a closed door. With an accomplished director at the helm, *King of the Hill* becomes a remarkable odyssey about a resilient young hero who uses both his imagination and his sense of reality to survive. HIGHLY RECOMMENDED

Kolya [Czech Republic, 1996]

Starring: Zdenek Sverak, Andrej Chalimon, Libuse Safrankova, Ondrej Vetchy, Stella Zazvorkova, Ladislav Smolijak Director: Jan Sverak Screenplay: Zdenek Sverak Running Time: 1:45 Rated: R (Mature themes, sexual situations, brief nudity) Theatrical Aspect Ratio: 1.66:1 In Czech with subtitles

Prague, 1988: the twilight of communism in the Czech Republic. As the Iron Curtain begins to collapse all across Eastern Europe, the collective voice of the Czech people is finally heard in what became known as the "Velvet Revolution." Even with such world-shaping events happening in the background, *Kolya* is still a deeply personal motion picture that has far more to do with the human soul than with the political restructuring of a country.

The film opens by introducing us to Louka (Zdenek Sverak, the director's father, who also wrote the script), a 55-year-old professional cellist who has three great passions in life: music, women, and disdain for the Russians occupying his country. Because of a past blunder, Louka is forbidden to perform in the Czech Philharmonic Orchestra, where he once held a revered post. Instead, he must work menial jobs, such as refurbishing grave headstones and playing his instrument at cremations. Louka is fighting a losing battle against poverty — he's in debt and sinking fast. However, financial stability becomes a tantalizing possibility when his friend, Broz (Ondrej Vetchy), offers him a proposition.

If Louka, a confirmed bachelor, agrees to a marriage of convenience with a young Russian woman (she needs Czech citizenship), he'll be rewarded handsomely. Against his better judgment, he agrees, but the results are disastrous. His new bride runs off to West Germany to be with her lover, and Louka is left behind minding her 5-year-old son, Kolya (Andrej Chalimon). Then a strange thing begins to happen — the harder Louka tries to get rid of the boy, the more he becomes attached to Kolya.

One of the reasons why *Kolya* satisfies is that it effectively synchronizes the changing political landscape with the changes in Louka's personal circumstances. Essentially, this is a tale of new beginnings. Louka, who has wandered through life living only for his music and never wondering what it might be like to have a family, experiences not just a rejuvenation of his soul, but a rebirth, even as a different country is rising out of the ashes of the former socialist dictatorship. Kolya opens Louka to experiences and emotions he never believed possible, and at age 55, he discovers new meaning in an isolated existence that had grown repetitious.

Kolya is beautifully photographed, with an almost poetic quality to many of the scenes. The film also boasts a strong cast. Zdenek Sverak bears a resemblance to Sean Connery not only in appearance but in screen presence. Complimenting him is young Andrej Chalimon, whose unaffected performance allows us to forget that we're watching an inexperienced actor. Finally, Libuse Safrankova brings a great deal of appeal to the role of Louka's would-be girlfriend, Klara. *Kolya* is charming and warm-hearted. **HIGHLY RECOMMENDED**

La Promesse [Belgium/France, 1996]

Starring: Jeremie Renier, Olivier Gourmet, Assita Ouedraogo, Rasmane Ouedraogo Directors: Jean-Pierre and Luc Dardenne Screenplay: Jean-Pierre and Luc Dardenne Running Time: 1:35 Rated: No MPAA Rating (Mature themes, violence) Theatrical Aspect Ratio: 1.66:1 In French with English subtitles

La Promesse, a rare import from Belgium, tells the story of 15-year-old Igor (Jeremie Renier), who is trapped into choosing between his father, Roger (Olivier Gourmet), and the demands of his conscience.

When the film opens, Igor is already wise beyond his years. He's an active participant in his father's shady, "immigration service" business. For exorbitant fees, they smuggle illegal immigrants into Belgium, forge false work permits for them, and set them up in slum-like apartments (with unreasonably high rents). Many of the immigrants also work at Roger's construction site, where they are paid a pittance for hard, dangerous work. Igor serves as his father's assistant, and has learned to lie, cheat, and steal just as well as his old man.

Roger has trained himself (and is training Igor) to objectify the men and women he smuggles into the country, adopting the same basic philosophy as the Belgian police: "Illegals don't exist." To Roger, the immigrants are a less-than-human source of income, and that is a philosophy he attempts to pass on. Dad's lessons are leaving an impression upon Igor until an event occurs that forces him to reevaluate what he has learned.

One of Roger's workers, Amidou (Rasmane Ouedraogo), falls from a scaffold and is critically injured. As he lies dying, he extracts a promise from Igor to care for his wife, Assita (Assita Ouedraogo), and infant boy. Rather than taking Amidou to a hospital (where all sorts of difficult questions would arise), Roger elects to let the man bleed to death, then buries him under a thick layer of cement. He encourages Igor to forget the incident, but the boy cannot, and his attempts to honor his promise to the dying Amidou generate friction between himself and his father. Worse still, Assita is often a grudging, if not openly unwilling, recipient of Igor's aid.

Essentially, *La Promesse* is a variation of that motion picture staple, the "coming of age" story. The difference here, however, is that the choices faced by Igor are more complex than usual. Becoming an adult does not mean, as his father asserts, learning how to drive and "getting laid" — it means assessing the value of his word and heeding the call of his conscience, regardless of the price. No matter what Igor does, he will betray someone — and he must decide which betrayal he can live with. *La Promesse* speaks volumes about how we treat other human beings and what it means to truly grow up. **HIGHLY RECOMMENDED**

Ladybird, Ladybird [United Kingdom, 1994]

Starring: Crissy Rock, Vladimir Vega, Sandie Lavelle, Mauricic Venegas Director: Ken Loach Screenplay: Rita Munro Running Time: 1:42 Rated: No MPAA Rating (Language, violence, mature themes) Theatrical Aspect Ratio: 1.66:1

Theoretically, the function of the social worker is to help families through difficulties. In Ken Loach's latest, *Ladybird, Ladybird,* good intentions don't always have the best results. Loach's films (such as *Riff-Raff* and *Raining Stones*) are always doped with social commentary, and this one is no different. Here, the villain is a process that places regulations over human interests, where a child becomes a pawn in a struggle between the State and the Mother.

In this case, the Mother is Maggie (Crissy Rock), a passionate and lively woman with 4 children —

each from a different liaison. The latest's father, with whom Maggie is now living, is violently abusive. To get away from him, Maggie checks into a woman's shelter, but an accident there nearly causes her oldest child to die in a fire, and the social agencies take all four children into custody. Court appearances turn into bitter shouting matches, and Maggie's offspring are placed into foster care.

Meanwhile, Maggie has met Jorge (Vladimir Vega), a rare "good" man. He's a political refugee from Paraguay whose English visa has expired. But he remains as an illegal alien and takes a low-paying job in order to stay with Maggie. Together, the two have a child (her fifth; his first), but social workers have long memories and all it takes is one nasty word from a nosy neighbor to put Maggie's maternal fitness in question once more.

As powerful and stinging a story as *Ladybird, Ladybird* is (and it's based on real events), it's the performance of Crissy Rock that makes the film work. Rock, a standup comic with no previous acting experience, is incredible. Her high-voltage rendering of Maggie is so emotionally volatile that the movie becomes a draining experience to view. You don't just watch Maggie; you experience along with her — and what she's going through isn't the sort of thing that anyone wants to be a part of.

The questions raised by *Ladybird, Ladybird* are compelling, if not unique. Loach frequently uses film to examine the inadequacies of the British social system, and here we're forced to consider the issue of when a woman is truly incapable of raising a child. While there seems to be reasonable justification for taking Maggie's first 4 offspring, what happens thereafter illustrates the kind of capricious horror that can occur when those in power don't really understand a situation.

Ladybird, Ladybird is an unforgettable portrait of human anguish and the price that any society must pay when its best intentions go awry.

HIGHLY RECOMMENDED

Lamerica [Italy, 1994]

Starring: **Enrico Lo Verso, Carmelo Di Mazzarelli, Michele Placido**
Director: **Gianni Amelio** Screenplay: **Gianni Amelio, Andrea Porporati, and Alessandro Sermoneta** Rated: **No MPAA Rating (Mature themes)**
Theatrical Aspect Ratio: **2.35:1** In Italian with English subtitles

To understand *Lamerica*, which takes place in 1991 Albania, a little history is necessary. In 1939, as documented by black-and-white news reel footage shown during the opening credits, Mussolini invaded and occupied Albania. Following World War II, a Soviet-supported Socialist dictatorship came into power, and nearly all communications with the tiny Balkan nation were cut off. No one was aware of the staggering level of poverty that persisted until 1991, when the government was overthrown, the borders were opened, and 40,000 Albanians fled to Italy. The immigrant crush was like the European influx into the United States earlier in the century, with Italy being viewed by the Albanians as "their America" (hence the title, with the absent apostrophe in "L'America" intended to represent the semi-literacy of the Albanians).

Once Albania converted to democracy, some of the first foreign investors came from Italy, and many of their proposals were thinly-veiled con games. *Lamerica* opens by introducing two such swindlers, Fiore (Michele Placido) and his assistant Gino (Enrico Lo Verso, last seen in *Farinelli*), who claim to be in the shoe-making industry. They choose a random homeless man who has suffered in a Socialist jail for 50 years as their company's chairman (corporations fronted by anti-Communist heroes are guaranteed government support). All they need is a "straw man" without relatives, so that once the deals are set and the financial aid comes in, they can take the money and run. But problems arise when their chosen chairman turns out not to be an Albanian native, but an Italian World War II deserter who was captured after the end of the war and thrown into prison.

The "chairman," Michele Talarico (Carmello Di Mazzarelli) by name, was born in Sicily some 70 years ago, but his identity is now obscured by the passage of time. His papers say he's Albanian, but he calls Italy his home. He has blocked out the 50 years spent in jail, so he believes that he's only 20, and holds to this fiction no matter what evidence is presented to the contrary. As the film progresses, Gino — a young, brash, ignorant Italian at the outset — gradually loses his own sense of national identity until he's as much an Albanian as the hundreds around him, including Talarico. Italian, Albanian, or something else — in the trenches of life, at the most basic level of humanity, nationality has no meaning. When it comes to survival, who cares about politics?

Lamerica certainly isn't for everyone. In fact, the average moviegoer may find this to be a dull 2 hours. For those in search of a deeper film experience, however, *Lamerica* is a welcome arrival. **HIGHLY RECOMMENDED**

Land and Freedom [United Kingdom, 1995]
Starring: Ian Hart, Rosana Pastor, Iciar Bollain, Tom Gilroy, Frederic Pierrot, Marc Martinez, Suzanne Maddock, Mandy Walsh
Director: **Ken Loach** Screenplay: **Jim Allen** Running Time: **1:49**
Rated: No MPAA Rating (Violence, profanity, mature themes)
Theatrical Aspect Ratio: 1.66:1

The Spanish Civil War was like no other uprising in history. It was a messy, disorganized affair with pro-communist and pro-democracy forces fighting each other instead of uniting against their common enemy. This lack of organization among the country's landless workers led to victory by Franco, who was backed by both Mussolini and Hitler. Some, including Loach, believe that the pernicious influence of the Stalin-backed Communist party fostered the divisiveness among the revolutionaries that resulted in the fascist victory.

Land and Freedom opens in present-day England, with a young woman (Mandy Walsh) reading the diaries and letters of her late grandfather, who was part of the multinational Republican Militia fighting against Franco. David (Ian Hart), a card-carrying member of the Communist Party, was unemployed in Liverpool when the call went out from Spain for support in the war against fascism. Driven by idealism, David left his wife behind to join a ragtag division of one of many local militias struggling to defeat Franco.

There are several gritty battle scenes in *Land and Freedom*, but, as with all of Loach's movies, this one is impelled by ideas. It's unlikely that you've seen a war movie quite like *Land and Freedom*. After the militia liberates a small town, they join the local workers in a lengthy argument about the pros and cons of collectivization. It's a rich, spirited discussion, and both sides make excellent points. *Land and Freedom* is filled with such scenes as characters talk about things that mean something, like why they should reject the organized Communist army and why they shouldn't moderate their slogans just to gain the support of other nations.

The story unfolds as seen through David's eyes. This is his tale, and, like all epic journeys of the heart and spirit, it involves triumph, tragedy, love, passion, and pain. Torn between supporting the organized resistance and continuing to be a part of an isolated but autonomous militia, David makes the "safe" decision, then, to his dismay, learns the reason why

Franco is winning the war — the Stalinists are more interested in suppressing the *real* freedom fighters than opposing the fascists.

While in Spain, David falls in love with a Blanca (Rosana Pastor), a fiery Spaniard who has already paid a terrible price in the war. This relationship forms the film's emotional center, but, like everything else that David holds dear, it is endangered by his ambivalence about which revolutionary arm to support.

Land and Freedom reminds us of the price of fighting for beliefs, and the greater price of being abandoned by supposed allies during that fight, a lesson just as valuable today as it was for David, Blanca, and all the other members of the Republican Militia who fought facism. **MUST SEE**

The Last Castle [2001]
Starring: Robert Redford, James Gandolfini, Mark Ruffalo, Delroy Lindo, Steve Burton Director: Rod Lurie Screenplay: David Scarpa and Graham Yost Running Time: **2:10** Rated: R (Violence, profanity)
Theatrical Aspect Ratio: 2.35:1

The Last Castle, from director Rod Lurie (*The Contender*), is a rousing adventure film that entertains despite a raft of plot implausibilities. With its themes of courage, honor, and redemption, it lands squarely in the ranks of old-style, flag-waving American cinema.

Robert Redford, taking a break from behind the camera to do some acting-only work, plays decorated 3-star general Eugene Irwin, who has been court martialed as a result of disobeying an Executive Order. For his crime, Irwin has been sent to the military prison "The Castle," where he will serve out his ten-year sentence. The warden, Colonel Winter (James Gandolfini), is a huge supporter of Irwin's; however, when Irwin voices his disapproval of Winter's methods of discipline, a power struggle ensues. Winter's attempts to break Irwin will backfire — the general's weathering of the warden's punishment earns him respect amongst his fellow prisoners. Soon, Irwin mounts a challenge to Winter's authority with the intent of removing the warden — even if it means taking over The Castle.

The struggle between Irwin and Winter plays out like a chess game between a Grand Master missing a few pieces and a lesser-skilled opponent with all of his intact. While Winter scores a few minor victories because of his initial superior position, Irwin sacrifices the occasional pawn in going after bigger prizes. The chess metaphor is apt (especially since the script mentions it on more than one occasion), but it is not meant to over-intellectualize the story. Lurie's film works because it generates suspense without going overboard. There are pyrotechnics, but they are not the sole point. The characters are developed with enough dimensions that they become more than cardboard figures moving through a plane of action. Even Winter, who is the clear villain, is given an understandable motive and a few redeeming qualities. And Irwin *is* guilty of the crime that landed him in prison; he's not someone wrongly condemned.

In the world of "chick flicks" and "guy flicks," *The Last Castle* falls in the latter camp. That's not to say that women won't enjoy the film — the emotions it generates are universal — but there will be a greater appeal to men. At 130 minutes, this is fairly lengthy, but Lurie keeps things moving so that the proceedings never bog down. *The Last Castle* is winning entertainment, a bold cinematic tapestry. **RECOMMENDED**

The Last Days of Disco [1998]

Starring: Chloë Sevigny, Kate Beckinsale, Christopher Eigeman, MacKenzie Astin, Matthew Keeslar, Robert Sean Leonard, Tara Subkoff, David Thornton, Jennifer Beals Director: Whit Stillman Screenplay: Whit Stillman Running Time: 1:55 Rated: R (Sexual themes and discussion, brief nudity, drug use) Theatrical Aspect Ratio: 1.85:1

Popular culture has an imponderable fascination with things 20 years past. With *The Last Days of Disco*, independent writer/director Whit Stillman chooses to view the early '80s through a lens coated with satire. There's the requisite disco soundtrack loaded with tunes from Sister Sledge, Donna Summer, and others, and there are plenty of scenes featuring oddly-attired young people dancing under the flashing light of a strobe, but this film is packed with Stillman characters, and, more importantly, Stillman dialogue. There are discourses about whether yuppies really exist, why VDs aren't all bad, how virginity is defined, and whether it's a good idea to follow Shakespeare's maxim, "To thine own self be true." Plus, there's a hilarious deconstruction of Disney's *Lady and the Tramp*, where one character claims the movie's function is to "program women to adore jerks."

The Last Days of Disco opens during "the very early 1980s" in Manhattan at a packed disco obviously inspired by Studio 54. There we meet the two main characters, a pair of recent college graduates named Alice (Chloë Sevigny) and Charlotte (Kate Beckinsale), who are out for a night of dancing. Since they're young and attractive, they're able to get into the club without having to stand in the ever-growing line. Inside, they meet some of the other regulars, including

Jimmy (MacKenzie Astin), an advertising executive; Josh (Matthew Keeslar), an assistant D.A.; and Tom (Robert Sean Leonard), an environmental activist. The club's womanizing manager, Des (Christopher Eigeman), is also on hand. Having just dumped his latest girlfriend by telling her he's gay, he is on the prowl for a new catch.

Kate Beckinsale is impeccable as the bitchy Charlotte. With a perfect American accent and a demeanor that recalls Parker Posey, Beckinsale fashions her character as the picture of the shallow, vain party girl. Chloë Sevigny makes Alice a warm, sympathetic character in the midst of a soulless world. By forging an emotional connection with the audience; Sevigny becomes our way into the story. Stillman regular Christopher Eigeman is delightfully self-centered as the callous Des, and Robert Sean Leonard plays a seemingly-charming guy who turns out to be a cad.

There's nothing inherently brilliant about the movie or its theme of shallow hedonism in the early Reagan era, but the combination of sharply-realized dialogue and infectiously energetic dance sequences keeps *The Last Days of Disco* from losing steam. And when the "Love Train" rolls through the New York subway at the end of the movie, it's almost impossible to keep from smiling. **RECOMMENDED**

The Last Good Time [1995]

Starring: Armin Mueller-Stahl, Olivia D'Abo, Maureen Stapleton, Lionel Stander, Adrian Pasdar Director: Bob Balaban Screenplay: Bob Balaban and John McLauglin based on the novel by Richard Bausch Running Time: 1:29 Rated: R (Language, nudity, mature themes) Theatrical Aspect Ratio: 1.85:1

On any given day, you can walk down a street in New York City (or any other city, for that matter) and pass hundreds of people, most of whom will be gazing straight ahead, wrapped in their own thoughts. Take a moment to consider the untold story behind each face. Most of the time, it won't be anything flashy or exotic — just a normal tale of the minor ups and downs of day-to-day life. *The Last Good Time* chronicles one of those simple-yet-affecting stories.

Approached with less sensitivity and intelligence, this movie could have been exploitative. The subject — the relationship between an older gentleman and a much younger woman — is, by nature, delicate. However, there is nothing salacious about *The Last Good Time*; instead, it's an examination not so much of sexuality, but of friendship, need, and platonic love. The story opens where most of the scenes take place: in a small apartment rented by Joseph

Kopple (Armin Mueller-Stahl), an over-70 widower living a lonely life governed by a regimented daily routine. Every morning, he wakes up at 7:10, takes the bus to visit his friend Howard (the late Lionel Stander) in a nursing home, eats a TV dinner, then goes to sleep. There's no variety, but the unceasing blandness gives him a measure of comfort.

Then, as is often the case, things change suddenly and dramatically. Charlotte Zwicki (Olivia D'Abo), one of Joseph's upstairs neighbors, has a violent fight with her boyfriend (Adrian Pasdar). When she needs a place to stay, circumstances bring her to Joseph's door. After a few days, the pair form an unusual and fragile bond. There is a certain degree of sexual tension in their relationship, but it's neither provocative nor gratuitous.

Veteran actor Mueller-Stahl shows tremendous range in a role that demands the expression — and repression — of a variety of emotions. Much of Joseph's inner self is conveyed to the audience through body language and facial expressions. Dialogue is used exclusively as a supplement.

Olivia D'Abo, while not given the opportunity to show the same breadth of character as her more experienced co-star, displays impressive depth. In what is by far her best screen performance to-date, D'Abo uses Charlotte's raw energy to ignite her scenes. This memorable performance is all the more surprising coming from an actress who hasn't previously shown such ability.

Supporting the fine performances and well-crafted script is the evocative and atmospheric cinematography of Claudia Raschke. Working with a palette of shadow and light, she uses contrast and camera angles to amplify the relationship between the two leads. The filmmakers' willingness to proceed with patience, allowing the drama to unfold naturally, affords the audience an opportunity to experience a marvelously complex, character-based study of two apparently dissimilar people who recover lost fragments of their selves through each other.

HIGHLY RECOMMENDED

Last Night [Canada, 1998]

Starring: Don McKellar, Sandra Oh, Callum Keith Rennie, David Cronenberg, Tracy Wright, Geneviève Bujold, Roberta Maxwell, Robin Gammell, Sarah Polley Director: Don McKellar Screenplay: Don McKellar Running Time: 1:33 Rated: R (Sex, nudity, profanity, mature themes) Theatrical Aspect Ratio: 1.85:1

Of all the movies about the end of the world, it is significant and ironic that the best is the one with both the lowest profile and the smallest budget. That's because Don McKellar's *Last Night* isn't concerned about the how and why of Armageddon. Instead, it focuses on far more interesting and existential questions. Rather than showing space shuttles blasting off to blow apart an asteroid, *Last Night* stays grounded on Earth, and depicts the final hours of a small group of characters as they struggle to come to grips with their mortality and what life meant, and means, to them. Sometimes movie characters don't have pasts; these men and women lack futures.

The story opens at 6 p.m. on December 31, 1999 — 6 hours before the earth's existence will wink out. (The film never explains the cause of the world's end. The only clues we have are that there wasn't much time for preparation, and that the sun now shines 24 hours a day.) Of the men and women introduced here, everyone has their own idea of what a perfect last night entails. For Patrick (McKellar), it's abandoning friends and family, going back to his apartment, and listening to music by himself. For Patrick's best friend, Craig (Callum Keith Rennie), the end is an opportunity for nonstop sex. Patrick's parents (Roberta Maxwell, Robin Gammell) spend their last hours at home together, while his sister, Jennifer (Sarah Polley), goes out partying. Meanwhile, one distraught woman, Sandra (Sandra Oh), is having trouble getting home to her husband (David Cronenberg). A series of misfortunes befalls her, and, with public transportation down and taxis ignoring fares, her chances of making her way across Toronto look bleak until she hooks up with Patrick.

The Canadian filmmaking community is a small and close one, so many of the participants in *Last Night* will be familiar to those who have seen a Canadian film or two in recent years. The writer/director/actor, behind the camera for the first time, is Don McKellar, who was involved in scripting both *Thirty-two Short Films About Glenn Gould* and *The Red Violin*, and appeared in Atom Egoyan's *Exotica*.

Last Night succeeds where so many other films have failed because it concentrates on the element that its predecessors have ignored: the human factor. It's only mildly diverting to watch end-of-the-world pyrotechnics, but it's endlessly fascinating to observe how seemingly normal people react to a catastrophe of unimaginable proportions. While limiting its canvas to the lives of a few characters, *Last Night* manages to capture aspects of every possible reaction, from nihilism and anarchy to stoic acceptance.

McKellar doesn't cheat his characters, and more importantly, doesn't cheat his audience. RECOMMENDED

The Last September [United Kingdom/Ireland, 1999]
Starring: Keeley Hawes, Maggie Smith, Michael Gambon, Jane Birkin, Fiona Shaw Director: Deborah Warner Screenplay: Deborah Warner, based on the novel by Elizabeth Bowen Running Time: 1:43 Rated: R (Nudity, sex, violence) Theatrical Aspect Ratio: 1.85:1

The time is the early 1920s, and the location is County Cork, Ireland. The hostilities between the Irish Republicans and the British are heating up. Caught in the middle are the so-called Anglo-Irish, those British citizens who moved to Ireland decades before to "oversee" the country, and who now consider themselves to be Irish. Many of the locals, however, still view them as foreigners. As a result, the Anglo-Irish find themselves in a difficult situation, not belonging fully to either side, and thus earning a measure of distrust from both. Halcyon days are past; darker seasons are coming.

Sir Richard and Lady Myra Naylor (Michael Gambon and Maggie Smith) are an affluent Anglo-Irish couple who live in County Cork during these troubled times. Also dwelling in their spacious house is the young and vivacious Lois Farquar (Keeley Hawes), Sir Richard's motherless niece, whose father is a world traveler. Lois is being courted by Captain Gerald Colthurst (David Tennant), a British officer stationed in the area. But, although she is friendly with the upright young man, her passion is stirred instead by a young Irish hothead, Peter Connolly (Gary Lydon), who is part of a terrorist gang roaming the countryside, killing English soldiers. Eventually, the violence will reach into their lives and their home. Yet Sir Richard and Lady Myra wear blinders, continuing to host tennis and dinner parties while a "war" rages outside the borders of their property. One of their guests puts it best when he states, "When this house burns, we will all be so careful not to notice."

The Last September is really Lois' story — she is the fulcrum and the emotional centerpiece. She is so involved in her own drama of being torn between a Republican lover and a proper Englishman that she has little time to reflect on the nature of the larger conflict. For her, it's all very personal, and, like the overall struggle, it is destined to end tragically.

The Last September features several noteworthy performances. Maggie Smith and Michael Gambon are in top form, she blending tart humor with an upper-crusty seriousness, and he radiating a gentle, paternal wisdom. Fiona Shaw is a delight as a woman who speaks her mind regardless of the consequences. Keeley Hawes is an excellent find; she shines in a role that demands a complex spectrum of feelings and reactions. Lois is the romantic whose illusions are brutally shattered.

Despite occasional bursts of humor, the prevalent tone throughout the movie is somber. This is a film about the impending end of an era, and an autumnal sense of loss hangs over everything. RECOMMENDED

Leaving Las Vegas [1995]
Starring: Nicolas Cage, Elisabeth Shue, Julian Sands Director: Mike Figgis Screenplay: Mike Figgis based on the novel by John O'Brien Running Time: 1:52 Rated: R (Profanity, violence, sex, nudity) Theatrical Aspect Ratio: 1.85:1

Around the time that Mike Figgis began production of *Leaving Las Vegas*, John O'Brien, the author of the book upon which the film is based, shot himself in the head. This story, according to O'Brien's father, is his son's suicide note. And what an epitaph it is.

Leaving Las Vegas tells the story of Ben (Nicolas Cage), an unapologetic drunk, and Sera (Elisabeth Shue), a prostitute. After Ben loses his L.A. job, he takes his termination pay and heads to Vegas, that American mecca of glitz and greed where souls go to die. His intent is not to gamble, however, but to do something more certain: take a room in a flea-bag motel, buy as much booze as he can afford, and drink himself to death. By his estimation, that should take only a few weeks. But Ben is a lonely man and, even as his body craves alcohol, his heart yearns for companionship. So, when he sees Sera walking the streets, he offers her $500 for an hour. As it turns out, though, what he needs more than sex is a friendly ear. Thus begins the relationship that forms the film's core.

One of the reasons *Leaving Las Vegas* is so heartbreakingly haunting is that the unconditional love between Ben and Sera blossoms against a backdrop of desperation, loneliness, and self-destruction. Ben's only plea to Sera is that she never try to stop him from drinking. This is not a lesson movie like *When a Man Loves a Woman,* where the triumph over alcoholism forms the central dynamic. Instead, *Leaving Las Vegas* is about passion that flares brightly for a moment before being extinguished. The audience understands when Sera says, "We both realized that we didn't have that much time. I accepted him as he was and didn't expect him to change. He needed me. I loved him — I really loved him."

Leaving Las Vegas wouldn't be as difficult to sit

through — equal parts transcendent beauty and unbearable pain — if it weren't for a pair of magnificent performances. Nicolas Cage, who has a track record of immersing himself in parts, gives one of his most powerful acting turns, a complex, multi-layered portrayal. Meanwhile, Elisabeth Shue, whose filmography is far less impressive, matches Cage scene-for-scene, emotion-for-emotion. There's no glamour in this role, but we still see the beauty that attracts Ben — tarnished and dulled, perhaps, but still obviously there.

Leaving Las Vegas has no taboos. It doesn't moralize about its characters. Like great poetry where each verse strives for new highs and lows, *Leaving Las Vegas* draws its audience along a rarely-traveled path whose scope can only be fully appreciated in the silence of the aftermath. HIGHLY RECOMMENDED

The Legend of 1900 [Italy, 1998]

Starring: Tim Roth, Pruitt Taylor Vince, Mélanie Thierry, Bill Nunn, Peter Vaughan, Clarence Williams III Director: Giuseppe Tornatore Screenplay: Giuseppe Tornatore, based on the book by Alessandro Baricco Running Time: 2:04 Rated: R (Profanity) Theatrical Aspect Ratio: 2.35:1

The entire tale of *The Legend of 1900* takes place aboard a cruise ship during the early decades of the 20th century, but this is no *Titanic*. Told in flashback by a down-on-his luck trumpet player named Max (Pruitt Taylor Vince), the movie is presented as half-fable, half-melodrama. The main character, Danny Boodman T.D. Lemon 1900, or 1900 for short (played by Tim Roth), is found abandoned as a child on board the ocean liner *The Virginian* by an engine room worker (Bill Nunn), who keeps him and gives him his name (based on the year of his birth). 1900 grows up to be an agoraphobe who never knows life outside the ship. He is a genius at the piano, and his reputation spreads far and wide across the globe, but he never leaves *The Virginian* to claim the slice of fame that could be his. Even love cannot lure him from the open sea. On one occasion, he falls for a pretty passenger (Melanie Thierry), but lacks the courage to follow her into the city when the ship docks. *The Virginian* was where he was born and where he intends to die

As characters go, 1900 is a little underdeveloped, and no one else gets enough screen exposure to function as more than a secondary player. Tim Roth, as engaging as ever, brings 1900 to life, imbuing him with energy and charisma. Pruitt Taylor Vince plays an adequate second fiddle as 1900's best friend. Even

though the movie is told from his point-of-view, however, Max is not fleshed out as anything more substantive than a narrator. Melanie Thierry offers viewers (and 1900) a pretty face to look at, but nothing more. The film's standout supporting role belongs to Clarence Williams III, who plays real-life jazz pianist Jelly Roll Morton. In *The Legend of 1900*'s standout sequence, Jelly Roll boards the ship to challenge 1900 to a piano duel. The smokin' results are pure magic.

Director Giuseppe Tornatore (who also made the great *Cinema Paradiso*) has a talent for developing stories that are pleasantly sentimental without turning mawkish. The director has blended one part fantasy, one part whimsy, one part comedy, and one part drama into a whole that stirs the spirit. *The Legend of 1900* is an uplifting experience — the kind of movie that can make a hardened moviegoer laugh and cry at the same time. RECOMMENDED

Les Miserables [France, 1995]

Starring: Jean-Paul Belmondo, Michel Boujenah, Alessandra Martines, Salome Lelouch Director: Claude Lelouch Screenplay: Claude Lelouch, inspired by the novel by Victor Hugo Running Time: 2:54 Rated: R (Violence, mature themes) Theatrical Aspect Ratio: 2.35:1 In French with English subtitles

Les Miserables, Victor Hugo's sprawling epic of love, honor, fortitude and social injustice has been brought to the screen many times. In this version, Director Claude Lelouch has retained the heart, guts and muscle of the story, but shed its 19th century skin by setting it in WW II-era France.

It is impossible to overstate what Lelouch has accomplished here. No film that I'm familiar with has so ably intersected a classical novel with a modern tale. It's been tried, most frequently with Shakespeare, but never has the result been such an unqualified success. This version of *Les Miserables* is a masterpiece precisely because it doesn't merely regurgitate Hugo's tale. It's something simultaneously new and timeless.

The film centers around 4 people whose lives are inextricably entwined. They come together, offer redemption and salvation to each other, then are ripped apart. The outsider is Henri Fortin (Jean-Paul Belmondo), a former middleweight boxing champion-turned-truck driver who has agreed to aid a Jewish family in their flight from Nazi occupied France to Switzerland. The refugees are Andre Ziman (Michel Boujenah), a renowned defense attorney; Elise Ziman (Alessandra Martines), a prima ballerina; and their young daughter, Salome (Salome Lelouch).

As Henri and his charges trundle across the French

countryside, the illiterate driver requests that Andre read aloud to him from Victor Hugo's *Les Miserables*. As the story-within-the-story unfolds, Henri is enraptured, seeing parallels in his own life to both *Les Miserables*' Jean Valjean and Cosette. Like Valjean after meeting the little chimney sweep, Henri is determined to devote the rest of his life to the selfless aid of others.

The rest of the film follows Henri, Andre, Elise, and Salome as their paths diverge and converge. Like a master composer, Lelouch overlays elements of Hugo's novel on each of their stories. One recurring theme throughout *Les Miserables* is that there are really only two or three stories that continuously repeat themselves throughout history. What makes a story great, whatever the medium chosen for its telling, is that in it we see ourselves and people we know. Themes echo and resonate and events inevitably recur as Lelouch masterfully mixes tales from two different centuries.

Les Miserables is a story of the indomitable nature of the human spirit. Despite the title and its attendant images of misery, poverty, injustice, and oppression (all of which are present in one form or another), the movie is a decidedly uplifting experience, because its concentration is on the power to overcome. To be sure, there's much evil in this world, but there's good as well. For every Gestapo officer, there's a Henri Fortin or Jean Valjean willing to risk everything to save a small child. **MUST SEE**

Les Miserables [1998]

Starring: Liam Neeson, Geoffrey Rush, Uma Thurman, Claire Danes, Hans Matheson Director: Bille August Screenplay: Rafael Yglesias, based on the novel by Victor Hugo Running Time: 2:15 Rated: PG-13 (Mild violence, sexual situations) Theatrical Aspect Ratio: 2.35:1

If Claude Lelouch's 1995 *Les Miserables* is a brilliant re-imagining of Hugo's classic, this edition, by director Billie August, is a faithful and heartfelt rendering, true in its period setting and detail, and true, most importantly, to the characters of Jean Valjean, Javert, and Cosette.

Towering over the film is Liam Neeson, the Irish actor who seems at home in any kind of picture, whether set in contemporary America (*Nell*), World War II Germany (*Schindler's List*), or centuries-ago Scotland (*Rob Roy*). Here, the setting is France during the 1820s and 1830s. Using all of his considerable powers as an actor, Neeson buries himself in the role of Jean Valjean, a convicted thief, who, after serving 19 years in prison, is released on parole. Valjean is a bitter, dejected man who is headed back to a life of crime until a monsignor takes pity on him, and, through a simple act of kindness, causes Valjean to re-evaluate his life and dedicate himself to the betterment of others. As brought to the screen by Neeson, Valjean is not only a grand, heroic figure, but a distinctly human individual as well, with frailties aplenty.

Valjean's opposite is Inspector Javert, an inflexible man who pursues the former criminal in part because he sees much of himself in his quarry. The one thing that separates the two is that, while Valjean lives a life of love and kindness, Javert is consumed by a fear of transgressing the law that he clings to like a lifeline. Geoffrey Rush, as dislikable here as he was likable as David Helfgott in *Shine*, makes Javert a memorable villain, but he avoids the obvious temptation of turning the inspector into a cartoonish bad guy. As Valjean has his failings, so Javert has his virtues, and there are many times when we pity him more than hate him.

For the most part, *Les Miserables* is the story of Javert's attempts to track down and punish Valjean. It's an obsession that blinds Javert to all else, and consumes his entire life. Other characters enter and leave as the tale progresses. There is Fantine (Uma Thurman), a poor, sick prostitute who Valjean takes under his protection, and with whom he forms a powerful bond. Cosette (Mimi Newman and, later, Claire Danes) is Fantine's bastard daughter, who Valjean raises after her mother's death. And Marius (Hans Matheson) is a fiery revolutionary who captures Cosette's heart even as he plans to restore the Republic to France.

While this version of *Les Miserables* lacks the cleverness and contemporary spin of Lelouch's, it ably demonstrates the great and satisfying virtues of the well-made period film. **RECOMMENDED**

Liam [Germany/United Kingdom/France, 2000]

Starring: Ian Hart, Claire Hackett, Anthony Borrows, David Hart, Megan Burns Director: Stephen Frears Screenplay: Jimmy McGovern Running Time: 1:30 Rated: R (Nudity, profanity) Theatrical Aspect Ratio: 1.85:1

Throughout a long and varied career, Stephen Frears has proven to be one of those few, rare filmmakers who feels comfortable and has success working on both sides of the Atlantic. He has achieved artistic — if not always commercial — success with such films as *My Beautiful Laundrette, Prick Up Your Ears,* and *Dangerous Liaisons.*

Liam is set in depression era Liverpool, where jobs are hard to come by and the seemingly-omnipotent Catholic Church controls charity. Liam Sullivan (David Hart) is the school-age son of a proud father (Ian Hart) and a loving, determined mother (Claire Hackett). He also has an older brother and a sister, Theresa (Megan Burns), with whom he shares a close relationship. The story is told mostly through the naïve eyes of young Liam, who becomes our gateway into the streets of Liverpool. We see his father lose his job then struggle with his inability to find meaningful work. His mother pawns off clothing and jewelry to keep food on the table. And Theresa, who works as a maid in a Jewish household, becomes her family's sole provider, bringing home table scraps to go along with the coins she is paid. Meanwhile, unrest on the streets grows as anti-Semitic fascists clash with Communists. And Liam discovers the pervasive power of religion, as his pre-First Communion lessons convince him that, after seeing his mother naked, he is headed for hell.

If an impoverished, 1930s Liverpool is *Liam*'s setting, the teachings of Catholicism function as its foundation. Frears does a better job than most directors of presenting the guilt and fear used by the Church to influence its members without demonizing the men and women who deliver the message. The film offers an honest representation of the teachings that are drummed into the hearts and minds of children: the stain of sin can only be wiped away by confession, failing to make a true confession is a sacrilege, and those who die without having their souls washed clean will burn forever in hellfire. The language of the priests and schoolteachers is persuasive; watching *Liam*, it's not difficult to understand the Church's power in a neighborhood where Catholicism is a way of life and where not attending Sunday mass will set tongues to wagging.

Liam is the kind of movie that leaves an impression. Its masterful depiction of time, place, and characters, and its willingness to tell a story unfettered by formulaic cliches set up an ending with a powerfully ironic, poignant turn of fate that illustrates how deeply the sword of hatred can cut. **HIGHLY RECOMMENDED**

Liberty Heights [1999]
Starring: Adrien Brody, Ben Foster, Orlando Jones, Bebe Neuwirth, Joe Mantegna, Rebekah Johnson Director: **Barry Levinson**
Screenplay: **Barry Levinson** Running Time: **2:07** Rated: **R** (Sexual situations, profanity) Theatrical Aspect Ratio: **1.85:1**

Liberty Heights is the fourth installment (so far) in Barry Levinson's overstuffed "Baltimore Trilogy," joining *Diner*, *Tin Men*, and *Avalon*.

The movie begins in the Fall of 1954, and follows the lives of the Kurtzman family: our narrator, Ben (Ben Foster), his older brother, Van (Adrien Brody), and their father, Nate (Joe Mantegna). According to Ben, who relates the story as a reminiscence (with sparingly used voiceovers), his family lived in an all-Jewish neighborhood in northwest Baltimore. When he was young, he thought everyone was Jewish. It wasn't until he started attending public school that he recognized that there was "the other kind." By the time *Liberty Heights* takes place, Ben is a senior in high school, and his brother, Van, has already graduated. Nate is a wealthy man as a result of an illegal numbers racket he runs, and he uses his profits to take care of his wife, Ada (Bebe Neuwirth), and children. For the most part, the film is a series of tiny vignettes strung together to form a cohesive and likable whole, but three narrative strains eventually emerge — one for each of the male characters. Ben becomes attracted to Sylvia (Rebekah Johnson), the lone black girl in his home room, and, despite racial boundaries and parental objections on both sides, he attempts to build a relationship with her. Van is also involved in a romantic dilemma — he meets his "dream girl" (Carolyn Murphy) at a Halloween party and is so flummoxed that he forgets to ask her name. And, when he finally discovers who she is, it turns out that she's dating the son of one of Baltimore's wealthiest men. Meanwhile, Nate finds himself in trouble when a small-time drug dealer, Little Melvin (Orlando Jones), strikes it big on the numbers. Nate ends up owing Little Melvin more cash than he has in reserve, and the impatient winner wants his money.

The film doesn't shy away from difficult issues, like racial and religious prejudice, but it plays up the absurdities of such bigotry without becoming heavy-handed. For example, there's a scene in which a black and a Jew are discussing how their races are viewed by White America, and the conversation devolves into an argument about which group has been more oppressed. The moment could have been tense and angry, but Levinson keeps things light, resulting in a sequence that is genuinely funny, but, at the same time, makes a point.

Liberty Heights is smart in the way it views the adolescent years. Levinson may not have constructed this story specifically out of events from his own life, but the quality of the remembrances depicted here have an authentic feel. RECOMMENDED

Life as a House [2001]

Starring: Kevin Kline, Kristin Scott Thomas, Hayden Christensen, Jena Malone, Mary Steenburgen Director: Irwin Winkler Screenplay: Mark Andrus Running Time: 2:03 Rated: R (Profanity, sex, nudity) Theatrical Aspect Ratio: 2.35:1

Things are not going well for George (Kevin Kline). Divorced from his ex-wife, Robin (Kristin Scott Thomas), and estranged from his rebellious son, Sam (Hayden Christensen), he lives in a run-down shack overlooking the ocean. Things go from bad to worse when he loses his job, then learns that he has terminal cancer. Knowing that the best he can hope for is another 4 months to live, he decides to spend his last summer with his son, tearing down the shack and building his dream home. Sixteen-year-old Sam, needless to say, is unhappy about exchanging a wild summer of drinking and drugs for several months of working alongside the father he doesn't really like. Once living with George, Sam considers running away, but the pretty girl next-door, Alyssa (Jena Malone), gives him something to stick around for. As the summer wears on and the old house comes down, Robin begins stopping by, and, during the course of these visits, she and George re-connect.

Life as a House derives its strength from its performances. As George, Kevin Kline is in the limelight for most of the film, and his portrayal is effective. He presents George as a man in search of a catharsis and personal redemption. Knowing that his days are numbered, George wants to make a difference to someone before he leaves this planet. It is important to him that Sam thinks of him as a father, not as a stranger. (It is also worth noting that, unlike many individuals in movies who look better as their terminal diseases progress, George actually looks like he's dying.) Yet, as good as Kline is, he is arguably out-acted by Kristen Scott-Thomas, who brings passion and humanity to her conflicted character. Scott-Thomas makes this role her own, elevating Robin beyond the constraints of the stereotyped "still-loved ex-wife." Hayden Christensen, soon-to-be Anakin Skywalker, does solid work, and up-and-coming Jena Malone (most recently seen in *Donnie Darko*) is delightful as the surprisingly mature Alyssa.

The script gets some of the relationships just right, and I was fascinated by some of the details surrounding the demolition of the old house and the erection of the new one. Unfortunately, a few scenes, including the last one, try too hard to wring emotion from the material, and end up being laughably absurd. This is a case of filmmakers not recognizing when they're taking things too far.

Overall, however, the movie gets us to feel about the characters, their relationships, and their circumstances, and that goes a long way towards allowing us to forgive the screenplays' occasional missteps and wrong turns. Like most houses, this one is far from perfect, but it's a pleasant place to visit for a couple of hours. RECOMMENDED

Life Is Beautiful (La Vita e Bella) [Italy, 1997]

Starring: Roberto Benigni, Nicoletta Braschi, Giustino Durano, Sergio Bini Bustric, Marisa Paredes, Horst Buchholz, Giorgio Cantarini Director: Roberto Benigni Screenplay: Roberto Benigni, Vincenzo Cerami Running Time: 1:54 Rated: PG-13 (Mature themes, off-screen violence) Theatrical Aspect Ratio: 1.85:1 In Italian with subtitles

For the first 45 minutes of *Life is Beautiful*, the Italian comedy star Roberto Begnini tricks us into believing that it's nothing more than a pleasant-but-uninspired romantic comedy set in Fascist Italy, with Guido (Benigni) seeking to woo a pretty girl, Dora (Nicoletta Braschi, Benigni's real-life spouse), away from her stuffy fiancé.

But 50 minutes into *Life is Beautiful*, there is a transition. The year is 1945, and Guido and Dora have a 5-year-old son, Giosue (Giorgio Cantarini). The second World War is in its final days, and Jewish Italian families like Guido's are the recipients of nonstop persecution. One day, the police break into Guido's home and take his family into custody. Soon after, they are herded like cattle into a train bound for a nameless concentration camp. It is a place of horror and death, where healthy men and women work all day long melting down metal for weapons while those who are too old, too infirm, or too young to endure hard labor are sent to the showers.

Guido is well aware of what is happening, and is determined to shield his son from the terrifying reality of the situation. So he carefully concocts a story-teller's web of fantasy around Giosue, informing the boy that this is all part of an elaborate game. The object is to get 1,000 points; the winner gets a real tank, not one of the toys Giosue is used to playing with. The rules constantly change, but they usually involve a lot of hide-and-seek, plenty of make-believe, and something called "silence." The police aren't really bad guys; they're just acting that way because that's how they win. Anyone complaining about not having enough food is disqualified and has to go home. By deflecting or laughing off his son's most serious concerns (such as a rumor that the camp prisoners are all going to be "cooked in the oven" to become "buttons and soap"), Guido manages to transform Giosue's ordeal into what seems like a vacation.

While I have no reservations about *Life is Beautiful*'s second hour, I'm less enthused about the breezy material that precedes it. Even though this portion of the movie accomplishes its aim of introducing the characters and setting up the background, it consumes too much screen time for its weaknesses to be ignored. And, as forceful as the rest of the movie is, the awkwardness of the first 50 minutes mutes its overall impact.

Nevertheless, by the time the end credits begin rolling, this is all a dim memory. The best part of *Life is Beautiful* redeems the rest with its utter assurance that people will do whatever is necessary to protect what is most dear to them. In its perspective on the Holocaust, Benigni's film is unique. But it's the depiction of the love and sacrifice of a father for a son that makes *Life is Beautiful* worthwhile. RECOMMENDED

Little Odessa [1994]

Starring: Tim Roth, Edward Furlong, Moira Kelly, Vanessa Redgrave, Maximilian Schell Director: James Gray Screenplay: James Gray Running Time: 1:38 Rated: R (Sex, violence, brief nudity) Theatrical Aspect Ratio: 2.35:1

Because of the richness of the subject matter and the complexity of the characters, gangster movies, especially those with strong ethnic overtones, make excellent vehicles for social commentary. *Little Odessa* is a case in point.

Joshua Shapiro (Tim Roth), is a deeply-troubled, emotionally detached hit man who has come home to Brooklyn to commit an assassination. Although difficulties in his past make it dangerous for him to be seen near Brighton Beach, the real impediment to his return is his father, Arkady (Maximilian Schell). For, while Josh loves his dying mother, Irina (Vanessa Redgrave), and his younger brother, Reuben (Edward Furlong), there is nothing but antipathy between father and eldest son. Nevertheless, left without a choice, Josh ventures back to the Russian/Jewish community, and eventually encounters all the members of his family. While there, he also hooks up with an old girlfriend, Alla Shustervich (Moira Kelly), a young woman who is reluctantly attracted to the lonely killer.

At the opening of *Little Odessa*, Josh is in a hell of his own making. During the course of the film, there are opportunities for redemption and love, all of which are rejected. Josh has no emotional capacity; when he makes love to Alla, the act is passionless and mechanical. He is unable to respond to his brother's simple offer of devotion. He cannot cry when he faces his dying mother. Only his father provokes a reaction, and that is a decidedly negative one. By this performance, Tim Roth adds yet another impressive credit to his resume.

Equally complex is Josh's tormented, self-pitying father — a man who has lost all authority over his household and his existence. Assimilation to the American way of life is a continuing struggle for someone like him, born and raised on traditions and values that his children don't share. Arkady loathes Josh as much as he hates himself. He has a mistress, but feels guilty about not being with his dying wife. He is educated, yet is forced by economic circumstances to run a newsstand. He loves Reuben, yet his actions seem always to hurt his younger son. Maximilian Schell, an accomplished actor who hasn't had much screen exposure in the past few years, encourages in viewers a mixture of resentment and sympathy.

The violence of *Little Odessa* is brutal, quick, and always shocking. Scenes of bloodshed are presented graphically, but never gratuitously. Director James Gray was only 24 when he made this film, yet with an emotional impact as strong as its intellectual appeal, *Little Odessa* can sit alongside some of the best gangster films of the last 20 years. HIGHLY RECOMMENDED

Little Voice [United Kingdom, 1998]

Starring: Brenda Blethyn, Jane Horrocks, Michael Caine, Jim Broadbent, Ewan McGregor, Annette Badland, Philip Jackson Director: Mark Herman Screenplay: Mark Herman based on the play "The Rise and Fall of Little Voice" by Jim Cartwright Running Time: 1:39 Rated: R (Profanity, brief nudity) Theatrical Aspect Ratio: 1.85:1

Mari Hoff (Brenda Blethyn) is a late middle-aged widow with two passions: drinking and sex. She lives with her daughter, Laura (Jane Horrocks), above the disused record store that her late husband ran. Laura, whose nickname is "Little Voice," is a shy, quiet young woman. She rarely speaks or leaves her tiny attic room where she spends her days and nights listening to her father's extensive collection of record albums and conversing with his ghost. She has become an expert at mimicking the vocal styles of Billie Holiday,

Shirley Bassey, Judy Garland, Marilyn Monroe, Marlena Dietrich, and others. When she sings "Somewhere Over the Rainbow," a local nightclub owner (Jim Broadbent) who hears her from the street below her window swears that it's Garland.

Mari's latest boyfriend, failed talent agent Ray Say (Michael Caine), sees $$$$ when he hears Little Voice sing. He immediately begins planning her show biz debut, even though she is petrified of performing in public. Meanwhile, Laura meets and forms a fragile relationship with an introverted telephone repairman, Bill (Ewan McGregor), who raises homing pigeons.

The most flamboyant performance in *Little Voice* is given by Brenda Blethyn, who earned an Oscar nomination in 1997 for her work in *Secrets and Lies*. Here, she relishes the opportunity to create a larger-than-life character. However, while there's nothing subtle about Blethyn's work, it is not a thoughtless or cartoonish performance. Mari is the kind of woman who lives life to its fullest, and Blethyn invests this portrayal with enough humanity to keep her from coming across as a pure caricature. She is not a nice woman. She's vain, vapid, and motivated purely by self-interest, but it's hard not to feel pity for her in the film's later stages. Underneath all of her bluster, Mari is a sad, pathetic soul.

If Blethyn's Mari is all sound and fury, Jane Horrocks' Laura is the exact opposite. She's the typical shy wallflower who blossoms under the spotlight. The highlight of the movie is a sequence in which Laura performs a tribute to her father's favorite artists. The actress sings all of her own songs, and her ability to mimic great female singers is astounding. Hearing her belt out "That's Entertainment" or "Big Spender" will give you chills.

Little Voice is incontrovertible evidence of how superior acting can turn a good movie into a great movie. By offering opportunities to laugh, cry, and cheer, *Little Voice* satisfies in a big way.

HIGHLY RECOMMENDED

Little Women [1994]

Starring: Winona Ryder, Trini Alvarado, Claire Danes, Kirsten Dunst, Samantha Mathis, Susan Sarandon, Christian Bale, Gabriel Byrne, Eric Stoltz Director: Gillian Armstrong Screenplay: Robin Swicord based on the novel by Louisa May Alcott Running Time: 1:50 Rated: PG (Nothing offensive) Theatrical Aspect Ratio: 1.85:1

This third, and most recent, film adaptation of Louisa May Alcott's classic 1868 novel about family and crossing the barrier between girlhood and womanhood, is a treatment for today's audiences. As faithful to the original story as a 2-hour production is likely to be, *Little Women* is in ways similar and dissimilar to its two cinematic predecessors (released in 1933 and 1949).

This tale of 4 independent sisters of differing temperaments is undeniably melodramatic, but it's very good melodrama, with an accumulation of vitality and charm that elevates the movie to an unexpectedly high level. The basic plot of *Little Women* isn't terribly original or invigorating; it's the effective realization of several memorable characters that gives this film its strength.

For those not familiar with the novel, it centers around the March demesne of Orchard House in Concord, Mass. With her husband away fighting in the Civil War, Marmee (Susan Sarandon) is left alone to care for her 4 daughters: the volatile and imaginative Jo (Winona Ryder), the sophisticated Meg (Trini Alvarado), the compassionate Beth (Claire Danes), and the romantic Amy (Kirsten Dunst as a child and Samantha Mathis as an adult). The girls share a bond that no outsider can penetrate, although there are some willing to make the attempt — most of whom are men. There's Laurie (Christian Bale), a neighbor with a passion for the piano who becomes a friend to all the Marches; John Brooke (Eric Stoltz), a poor tutor who is smitten with Meg; and Professor Bhaer (Gabriel Byrne), a German immigrant who develops a friendship with Jo.

With rich, colorful cinematography and a fine score by Thomas Newman, *Little Women* is technically accomplished. It's the performances, however, that make this movie special. Winona Ryder fashions a near-perfect Jo, Alcott's headstrong alter-ego in the fictional autobiography. Had it been demanded of her, the actress undoubtedly could have carried the entire film. However, this version allows the other sisters some development independent of Jo, and all the actresses hold their own. The only hiccup comes as a result of the change in the aging Amy from the energetic and charismatic Kirsten Dunst to the more sedate Samantha Mathis.

Christian Bale, after a couple of extremely weak performances (in *Newsies* and *Swing Kids*), finally displays some recognizable talent. In fact, Bale is so solid as Laurie that it's hard to credit this actor as the same one who joined Robert Sean Leonard in the streets of Nazi Germany.

Perhaps the greatest fault — and some may not

see it as such — is that even the best-developed characters in *Little Women* display an alarming lack of character flaws. Rare are the moments when someone says something nasty or does something unsavory. So much niceness occasionally makes *Little Women* seem too sugary and scripted. Nevertheless, the tale is engrossing enough, and the film put together with such obvious affection, that it's not hard to dismiss those things as necessary elements of a beloved period piece. RECOMMENDED

Live Flesh (Carne trémula) [Spain, 1997]

Starring: Liberto Rabal, Francesca Neri, Javier Bardem, Angela Molina, Jose Sancho, Penelope Cruz Director: Pedro Almodovar
Screenplay: Pedro Almodovar, Jorge Guerricaechevarria, Ray Loriga based on the novel by Ruth Rendell Running Time: 1:40 Rated: R (Sex, profanity, nudity, drugs) Theatrical Aspect Ratio: 1.85:1

Almodovar. To those familiar with his body of work, that name is more than just a way to identify one of today's premiere directors — it offers valuable insight into the scope and intent of a movie. Since his debut in 1980 with *Pepi, Luci, Bom,* Almodovar has been the "bad boy" of Spanish cinema. Now, however, there are indications that Almodovar is maturing. With *Live Flesh,* based loosely on a novel by Ruth Rendell, Almodovar is back in fine form, yet signs of restraint are evident in nearly every frame of this movie. By toning down his visual flourishes and curbing his tendencies towards excess, Almodovar has created what might be the finest work of his career to date.

The 5 principals come together on one fateful night in 1992 Madrid. Victor (Liberto Rabal) has fallen for a woman, Elena (Francesca Neri), whom he had sex with a week ago. Elena, however, wants nothing more to do with Victor, and, when he shows up at her apartment, she uses a gun to scare him away. A shot is fired and the cops are called. Arriving at Elena's apartment are two partners, David (Javier Bardem) and Sancho (Jose Sancho), who are in the midst of a crisis in their friendship. Sancho believes that his wife, Clara (Angela Molina), is having an affair, and he suspects David of being Clara's lover. What happens when the police break down the door to Elena's apartment sets off a chain of events that reverberate through time to a period 4 years later, when circumstances bring the characters together once again.

Live Flesh is really a mystery, which is why I won't give a more detailed plot description. This isn't a crime thriller, however — it's an exploration of characters' motives, secrets, and true emotions. They are all wrapped in a web of consequences, with each one hurting the others multiple times, and the strands around them growing ever thicker. The ending is surprising, not because it doesn't fit, but because, knowing all that we do about the involved parties, it's the perfect way to offer closure to the tale.

With *Live Flesh,* Almodovar offers a controversial viewpoint that seemingly contradicts the romantic's first rule of true love being the glue in long-term relationships. Time and time again, *Live Flesh* shows that "true love" is overrated. The married couples in this film love each other, but they're hopelessly, helplessly trapped. Almodovar isn't denying the value of romance, but he's emphasizing the complexities of any love-based relationship and affirming that sex is far from irrelevant.

One of the most delicious aspects of *Live Flesh* is its keen sense of irony. There's also a fair amount of humor, some of which borders on the absurd. Yet there is never a time when Almodovar's appreciation of offbeat comedy endangers the integrity of the characters or the story. Like the gorgeous cinematography, this is all part of Almodovar's stylistic package. Never has it been more impressive than here, where everything (not just the flesh) is vibrant with life. HIGHLY RECOMMENDED

Live Nude Girls [1995]

Starring: Dana Delaney, Kim Cattrall, Cynthia Stevenson, Lora Zane, Laila Robins, Olivia D'Abo Director: Julianna Lavin Screenplay: Julianna Lavin Running Time: 1:32 Rated: R (Frank sexual dialogue, nudity)
Theatrical Aspect Ratio: 1.85:1

It would be impossible to write a review of this film without discussing the title. How many viewers will see Julianna Lavin's feature debut because it's called *Live Nude Girls*? And how many will avoid it for the same reason? There's little doubt that the title was chosen for its provocative value, because, although the movie deals with live girls, they're mostly clothed. The nakedness in this picture is of the emotional, not the physical, variety.

In essence, *Live Nude Girls* features 5 women in their early-30s hanging out and talking. It's 90 minutes of simple, pleasant conversation. Nothing earth-shattering occurs, and no one attempts to answer, or even raise, any meaningful, philosophical questions. One-by-one, these characters open up to one another about relationships, love, and sex, while those of us in the audience are transformed into flies on the wall.

In movies, slumber parties have been used as settings for everything from teen sex comedies to soft porn. Here, writer/director Julianna Lavin resorts to this overused plot device one more time. The occasion for the slumber party is the approaching wedding of one of the women, Jamie (Kim Cattrall). Four of her friends — Georgiana (Lora Zane), Rachel (Laila Robins), Jill (Dana Delaney), and Marcy (Cynthia Stevenson) — have decided to hold a girls-only get-together on the night of the groom-to-be's bachelor party. Hanging around on the periphery of this group is Chris (Olivia D'Abo), Georgiana's lesbian lover.

The reason *Live Nude Girls* works is that all 6 major actresses give unaffected performances. Each of them (even Kim Cattrall, who isn't known for her acting ability) slides effortlessly into her role, and their interpersonal interaction is relaxed. Perhaps because it was written and directed by a woman, *Live Nude Girls* has a genuine "feel." Everything from the petty bickering of two sisters (Jill and Rachel) to the frank, raunchy discussions about sex has a ring of truth.

Live Nude Girls mixes humor with the drama. On one occasion, Jamie is obsessing about the reprehensible acts her fiance might be engaged in at his bachelor party. The scene then cuts to 4 guys sitting around a table at a bar, drinking beer and guessing how much money a nearby jukebox brings in on a weekly basis. It's not exactly the sex-crazed nightmare of Jamie's vision. Although it isn't hilarious, this sequence is cleverly-constructed, and there are several more like it throughout the film. Beneath the familiar plot contrivances, there's a core of honesty that delivers a satisfying motion picture experience. **RECOMMENDED**

Living Out Loud [1998]

Starring: Holly Hunter, Danny DeVito, Queen Latifah, Martin Donovan, Richard Schiff, Elias Koteas Director: Richard LaGravenese
Screenplay: Richard LaGravenese Running Time: 1:42 Rated: R
(Profanity, drug content, sex) Theatrical Aspect Ratio: 2.35:1

The best thing about Richard LaGravenese's directorial debut, *Living Out Loud*, are the characters; the minimal plot is almost inconsequential. LaGravenese's strength is developing multidimensional, wholly believable protagonists. In this film, which draws its inspiration from the Anton Chekhov short stories "The Kiss" and "Misery," they are Judith (Holly Hunter) and Pat (Danny DeVito), two lonely, middle-aged New Yorkers who find a measure of comfort in each other's company.

As the movie opens, Judith and Pat are both picking through the wreckage of collapsed existences. Judith, a nurse who has been dumped by her wealthy doctor/husband of 16 years, doesn't seem to know what to do with her life, because, at least in part, her identity was defined by her husband. No matter what went wrong, she could always rely on saying, "At least I'm married. At least I'm safe." But no longer. Pat, the doorman at the apartment building where she lives, is at a similar dead-end junction. His marriage is over, his daughter has recently died, and he's up to his ears in gambling debts. Somehow, he and Judith connect, and what begins as a form of casual interplay blossoms into a friendship that offers comfort to both of them.

Pat gradually becomes infatuated with Judith, but her feelings towards him remain platonic. To her, he's a reliable companion but not a good partner — she's looking for something more spontaneous and romantic in a relationship. Then, one night at a jazz club, she encounters the unexpected when a mysterious stranger kisses her. The friendship at the core of *Living Out Loud* is never allowed to go too far too fast, and both of the characters are intensely sympathetic. Judith can unburden her soul to Pat, telling him her secrets, and, although his feelings for her run deeper, he is content to fulfill that role.

LaGravenese manages to give *Living Out Loud* a light (and occasionally quirky) touch by mixing in frequent doses of comedy and fantasy. Both characters are capable of laughing at their own failings, and they sometimes find themselves in absurd situations. From time-to-time, we see events from two different perspectives — as they really are and as Judith dreams they might be. *Living Out Loud* is not a monumental motion picture. In fact, in many ways, it's quite the opposite — a quiet, unassuming story of friendship and love that uses richly-developed characters to charm its audience. **RECOMMENDED**

Local Hero [United Kingdom, 1983]

Starring: Burt Lancaster, Peter Riegert, Fulton Mackay, Denis Lawson, Norman Chancer, Peter Capaldi, Rikki Fulton, Jenny Seagrove
Director: Bill Forsyth Screenplay: Bill Forsyth Running Time: 1:51
Rated: PG (Mature themes) Theatrical Aspect Ratio: 1.66:1

Local Hero is a fragment of cinematic whimsy — a genial dramatic comedy that defies both our expectations and those of the characters. Director Bill Forsyth (*Gregory's Girl*) finds the perfect tone for this not-quite-a-fairy-tale set in a quaint seaside Scottish village named Ferness. By injecting a little (but not too much) magical realism into the mix, Forsyth leavens his pro-environmental message to the point that those not looking for it might not be conscious of its presence.

The film stars Peter Reigert as Mac MacIntyre, a deal-closer for Knox Oil who is picked by the corporate head, Felix Happer (Burt Lancaster), to travel to Scotland and buy up an entire fishing village where the company can build a refinery. MacIntyre is chosen because of his name, even though he does not, in fact, have any Scottish ancestry. And, before he leaves, his boss gives him a secondary duty, which, in some ways, seems more important to Mr. Happer than the primary job: MacIntyre is to keep his eyes on the night sky, watching for new, previously-undiscovered comets. Huppert has decided that the best way to immortalize his name is to get it attached to a celestial body.

Once in Scotland, MacIntyre meets his local liaison, Danny Oldsen (Peter Capaldi), who turns out to be a likable twit. Together, the two make the trip to their destination, where they encounter the colorful locals: their landlord (who also happens to be the town's only accountant), Gordon Urquhart (Denis Lawson); the hermit who owns the beach, Ben Knox (Fulton Mackay); the local priest, Reverend Macpherson (Christopher Asante), who came to Scotland on a mission from Africa and stayed; the appropriately named Marina, a marine biologist with certain mermaid-like characteristics (Jenny Seagrove); and others. It is MacIntyre's job to get everyone to agree to give up their homes in exchange for a cash payment.

Local Hero is suffused with the kind of almost magical color that typically characterizes comedies set in Scotland, Ireland (*Waking Ned Devine*), and Wales (*The Englishman Who Went Up a Hill But Came Down a Mountain*). For films like *Local Hero*, the setting is often as important a character as any being played by a human being. Indeed, in this film, it isn't the veteran Lancaster or the bewitching Seagrove who steals the most scenes, but the village and its surroundings. This is the best kind of light fare: a motion picture that offers a helping of substance to go along with an otherwise frothy and undemanding main course. **HIGHLY RECOMMENDED**

The Locusts [1997]

Starring: Vince Vaughn, Jeremy Davies, Kate Capshaw, Ashley Judd, Paul Rudd, Daniel Meyer, Cynthia Capshaw Director: John Patrick Kelley Screenplay: John Patrick Kelley Running Time: 2:05 Rated: R (Sexual situations, mature themes, violence, profanity) Theatrical Aspect Ratio: 2.35:1

In the dusty, dry world of *The Locusts* — a Midwestern American cattle ranch during the late 1950s — everyone has a secret. But, unlike films that live or die on the basis of unexpected plot disclosures, secrets are only important to *The Locusts* in the way they define the characters, explain their motivations, and drive their actions.

The Locusts opens with a rugged stranger, Clay Hewitt (Vince Vaughn), entering the town of Sealy, Kansas. He claims to be looking for temporary work to finance his cross-country trip to California, where his brother, a marine, is stationed. Clay finds a job and a place to live at a local cattle ranch run by Delilah Ashford Potts (Kate Capshaw), who has a reputation for giving her ranch hands "a room, a job, and a whole lot more than [they] bargained for." While there, Clay strikes up a fragile friendship with Flyboy (Jeremy Davies), Mrs. Potts' emotionally-damaged son. Flyboy is known for his isolation and passivity — he speaks only to a "pet" bull — until Clay's easy manner and persistence encourage Flyboy to open up. Meanwhile, Clay also becomes friendly with a local girl named Kitty (Ashley Judd), who is willing to help with his project to rebuild Flyboy's confidence and psyche. But change is one thing Mrs. Potts will not tolerate, and, on the ranch, she wields all the power. *The Locusts* is rich in themes of atonement, redemption, revenge, and a particularly brutal examination of the shifting balance of power between men and women, and parents and children.

The narrative for *The Locusts* does justice to each of these motifs as it gradually peels back the onion-like layers of the characters to reveal the complexity that lies beneath. The film doesn't offer any simpleminded solutions to difficult issues, and there are two very different ways to interpret the ending (depending on whether you're an optimist or a pessimist). If there's one misstep in *The Locusts*, it's that the meaning of the title (which is a metaphor) is explained a little too obviously. But that's an extremely minor quibble and it does little to detract from the strength of this film. **HIGHLY RECOMMENDED**

Lolita [United States/France, 1997]

Starring: Jeremy Irons, Dominique Swain, Melanie Griffith, Frank Langella Director: Adrian Lyne Screenplay: Stephen Schiff based on the novel by Vladimir Nabokov Running Time: 2:17 Rated: R (Sex with a minor, nudity, profanity, violence, mature themes) Theatrical Aspect Ratio: 1.85:1

Adrian Lyne's *Lolita* is a stately, non-gratuitous adaptation of Nabokov's controversial novel. It does not titillate or exploit; the only scenes of a nude girl are shadowy and indistinct. Despite that, the subject matter alone — pedophilia — was enough to scare off nearly every major American distributor. Interestingly, in many ways, the concept underlying *Lolita* is more provocative than the actual material, which tends to be a bit long-winded.

The pedophile is Humbert Humbert, brought to life by Jeremy Irons, an actor who enjoys playing deranged characters (he won an Oscar for his portrayal of Claus von Bülow in 1990's *Reversal of Fortune*). Humbert is not presented as a soulless monster or an evil predator, as most motion picture pedophiles are. Instead, *Lolita* attempts to understand Humbert, and allows us to sympathize with him without condoning his actions. He may be a deviant, but he is still a man. He recognizes that his obsession is unhealthy, but he cannot stop himself. Heedless of the fact that he is destroying three lives, he plunges on recklessly, letting an infatuation develop into a taboo physical relationship.

Dolores "Lolita" Haze (Dominique Swain) is the "nymphet" who becomes the object of Humbert's desire. At the tender age of 14, she's a character of contradictions — vixen and virgin at the same time. It's clear from the beginning that she knows the effect she's having on Humbert, and revels in the way a flash of her legs or the touch of a bare foot on his skin arouses him. Yet, despite her apparent sexual maturity, she's still a child in many ways, and, by responding to her teasing, Humbert turns her into a schemer and a whore.

Humbert first meets Lolita in 1947, after he travels across the Atlantic to New England, where he's to become a college professor. While lodging in the house of Charlotte Haze (Melanie Griffith), he falls for her daughter, whom he sees as a substitute for a lost love of his youth. Eventually, Humbert marries Charlotte to avoid losing Lolita, but his new wife finds out about his illicit desires. Before she can confront her daughter, however, she is killed in a car accident, and Humbert finds himself as Lolita's guardian. Together, the two begin a road trip that takes them to random destinations across America. As they travel, their relationship develops from playful to sexual to strained. Then another man, a sinister pedophile named Clare Quilty (Frank Langella), enters the picture, and draws Lolita away from Humbert. It is a rejection he cannot endure.

Lolita is not a sex film; it's about characters, relationships, and the consequences of imprudent actions. And those who seek to brand the picture as immoral have missed the point. Both Humbert and Lolita are eventually destroyed — what could be more moral? The only real controversy I can see surrounding this film is why there was ever a controversy in the first place. RECOMMENDED

Lone Star [1996]

Starring: Chris Cooper, Elizabeth Pena, Joe Morton, Ron Canada, Miriam Colon, Clifton James, Kris Kristofferson, Matthew McConaughey   Director: John Sayles   Screenplay: John Sayles   Running Time: 2:15   Rated: R (Mature themes, profanity, violence, sexual situations)   Theatrical Aspect Ratio: 2.35:1

In *Lone Star*, writer/director John Sayles (*City of Hope*, *Passion Fish*) cannily blends drama, romance, mystery, and social observation into a satisfying, if slightly overlong, whole. In the hands of a lesser film maker, this material could easily have degenerated into routine melodrama, but Sayles keeps it on a consistently high level.

Lone Star opens in the present time frame, and most of the narrative takes place there, with the exception of several, seamlessly-interwoven flashbacks to 1957 and 1973. These are necessary to breathe life into the film's mystery and love stories, and Sayles gives us just enough to satisfy the script's dramatic needs.

In 1996, the sheriff of Rio County is Sam Deeds (Chris Cooper). He's been on the job for 2 years, and he's filling huge footsteps. His late lawman father, Buddy (Matthew McConaughey), is a local legend, and Sam won election more because of his last name than because voters respected his talents. For a variety of reasons, Sam's image of Buddy is far more tarnished than the one endorsed by the community, and, when the corpse of a bigoted ex-sheriff (Kris Kristofferson) is found on an abandoned rifle range, Sam tries his best to pin the 40-year-old murder on his father.

Several other stories occur in parallel with Sam's investigation. One involves the sheriff's old flame, Pilar (Elizabeth Pena), trying to explain to concerned parents why she's teaching high school history with a nontraditional slant. Instead of relying on the accepted anglo-approved text, she's attempting to show how "cultures come together in both negative and positive ways." In the meantime, she's wrestling with her feelings for Sam and coping with an unruly teenage son.

We also get to know Colonel Del Payne (Joe Morton), the new commanding officer of Fort McKenzie, which is due to close. Del's father, Otis (Ron Canada), lives in the area. He and his son haven't spoken for decades, but, while Del is bitter about the estrangement, it's impossible for the two men to avoid each other.

Lone Star contains a number of "escape hatches" — points when the story could have moved in a safe, predictable direction, but Sayles uses few of these. The weakest aspect of the movie is the mystery, but it's also the least important. *Lone Star* is most intimately concerned with how different cultures and generations mix, match, and interact. Sayles explores the bipolar issues of racial divisiveness and tolerance, both as they exist today and as they were nearly 40 years ago, and does so without ever losing sight of the characters. With its numerous strengths and few weaknesses, *Lone Star* is an example of why Sayles' films are so engrossing despite lengths which consistently exceed 2 hours. **HIGHLY RECOMMENDED**

Lorenzo's Oil [1992]

Starring: Nick Nolte, Susan Sarandon, Peter Ustinov, Zack O'Malley Greenburg Director: George Miller Screenplay: George Miller and Nick Enright Running Time: 2:15 Rated: PG-13 (Mature themes) Theatrical Aspect Ratio: 1.85:1

Lorenzo's Oil is based on the true story of Augusto Odone (Nick Nolte) and his wife, Michaela (Susan Sarandon), as they fight to save the life and sanity of their son, Lorenzo (Zack O'Malley Greenburg). Lorenzo, diagnosed in early 1984 as a victim of ALD, an incurable degeneration of the brain, is beyond the help of conventional medicine. His parents, unwilling to give up the struggle even after participating in several failed therapies, begin their own investigation of the disease. *Lorenzo's Oil* follows the triumphs and tragedies of this search.

The film is unique in that it avoids the obvious trap of becoming a melodramatic, tear-jerking soap opera. Instead of focusing primarily on a family being torn apart by guilt and pain, *Lorenzo's Oil* follows Augusto and Michaela's attempts to understand their son's disease and discover a method of treatment. This search is fascinating — a unique odyssey of discovery. Even though it delves into medical terminology that few laymen will grasp, simple metaphors, such as those of a kitchen sink and a chain of paper clips, are used to clearly and concisely explain the causes and effects of ALD. Comprehension is necessary to the success of the film, and *Lorenzo's Oil* easily overcomes what might seem a troublesome barrier.

Lorenzo's Oil is at its weakest when it steers away from the investigation to present "character moments." Most of these scenes are of the hit-and-miss

variety. The only example of overacting in the film comes in one of these instances, when Nolte's Augusto slides down a flight of stairs, howling in agony. His pain is telegraphed with all the subtlety of a jackhammer.

Much of *Lorenzo's Oil* is based on true events, but there are at least a few moments when Hollywood intrudes, creating occasional leaps of exultation that are contrived (such as what happens when the results of Lorenzo's Oil are revealed to a group of ALD parents). Fortunately, the director/writer team of George Miller and Nick Enright have curbed excesses in this area. In the final analysis, when *Lorenzo's Oil* is stripped to the bare story, it's about the war for knowledge and the victory of hope through perseverance. And, for more than 2 hours, audience members are brought along to witness each battle. **RECOMMENDED**

Losing Isaiah [1995]

Starring: Jessica Lange, Halle Berry, David Strathairn, Samuel L. Jackson, Cuba Gooding Jr. Director: Stephen Gyllenhaal Screenplay: Naomi Foner based on the novel by Seth Margolis Running Time: 1:46 Rated: R (Mature themes, drug use, language) Theatrical Aspect Ratio: Not Given

Losing Isaiah tries very hard to make its viewers cry — and succeeds. But the chance to shed a few tears is not all this thought-provoking and dramatically-solid motion picture offers. An emotionally-charged issue is handled with balance and care. Excepting circumstances, there are no villains here, and the case for each side is presented in a compelling manner.

The issue in question is whether a black crack child, abandoned by a drug-addicted mother shortly after birth, is better off with that now-reformed woman or with the white adopted family with whom he has spent the first 4 years of his life. Everyone loves little Isaiah (Marc John Jefferies): his birthmother, Khaila (Halle Berry); his white parents, Margaret and Charlie (Jessica Lange and David Strathairn); and his adopted sister, Hannah (Daisy Eagan). But love often leads to pain, as becomes evident when Khaila goes to an activist lawyer (Samuel L. Jackson) to seek custody of her son.

Much of *Losing Isaiah* is wrenching, and all of it is well-acted. Here, Jessica Lange gives the kind of performance for which an Oscar nomination is deserving (unlike her over-the-top caricature in *Blue Sky*). Halle Berry is equally moving in a role that requires more range. Lange needs only to play the devastated mother; Berry must do double-duty as an addict and a woman trying to regain her son. David Strathairn and Samuel L. Jackson, two actors who almost always impress, are solid in less-visible parts. Marc John Jefferies is amazingly believable and shows none of the awkwardness that often accompanies the debut of a child actor.

The end of *Losing Isaiah* is something of a cheat, but the eventual resolution is neither badly handled nor overly-melodramatic. Numerous scenes stand out, but there is one image — Jackson and Lange standing side-by-side under an overhang during a rainstorm — that summarizes everything about this film. Brief in duration but undeniable in impact, that moment has everything: pain, uncertainty, and the unbridgeable gulf existing between the issue — "black babies belong with black mothers" — and the real people involved. There is virtually no dialogue; it isn't needed. It's instances like this, which are scattered throughout, that give depth and poignancy to a story that daringly probes a volatile question for which there are no straightforward answers. **RECOMMENDED**

The Loss of Sexual Innocence [1998]
Starring: Julian Sands, Saffron Burrows, Stefano Dionisi, Kelly MacDonald, Gina McKee Director: Mike Figgis Screenplay: Mike Figgis Running Time: 1:46 Rated: R (nudity, sexual situations, profanity, violence) Theatrical Aspect Ratio: 1.85:1

The Loss of Sexual Innocence is from the director of *Leaving Las Vegas*, Mike Figgis, and as the title implies, the film deals with the issue of sexual identity. *The Loss of Sexual Innocence* follows the life of Nic, a film ethnographer (played as a teenager by Jonathan Rhys-Meyers and as an adult by Julian Sands), through different periods in his life — as a young boy growing up in Kenya, as an adolescent coping with his first sexual encounters, and as a grown man involved in a stale marriage. Other tales are interwoven with Nic's, most notably those of twins (both played by Saffron Burrows) who were separated at birth but fleetingly encounter each other in an airport. There's also a stylized re-telling of Adam and Eve's expulsion from Paradise that takes a vicious jab at organized religion.

While there's nothing prurient to be found in *The Loss of Sexual Innocence* (in fact, considering the title, it's a relatively chaste film, although the "R" rating is deserved), a key theme relates to the importance of sex to the human experience. The characters are defined, at least in part, by their sexual activities. The central event of the film (which happens in the closing few minutes) occurs because of a sexual indiscretion on Nic's part — an impropriety that is built up to by his entire sexual history. Likewise, Figgis' version of the forbidden fruit is sex, and that's what causes Adam and Eve's fall.

More interesting than the film's thematic content, however, is the manner in which it is presented. Linear storytelling is out the window. *The Loss of Sexual Innocence* refuses to stay anchored in one time period, presenting disjointed pieces of a story without offering many clues about how they should be put together (although Figgis' use of amber filters helps a little). The production rejects the traditional narrative form, preferring instead to try something experimental. The result is curiously satisfying, because, while it leaves countless unanswered questions and loose ends, it demands thought and intellectual participation.

When asked his reasons for presenting the film in this manner, Figgis denounced the way the 3-act structure has become the filmmaker's Bible, then went on to attack the manner in which commercialism has destroyed the artistic elements of film. *The Loss of Sexual Innocence* is his attempt to restore art to the medium, and to prove that an involving, compelling experience can result from a fragmented narrative that relies more on music and images than dialogue. For the most part, *The Loss of Sexual Innocence* proves Figgis' point. **RECOMMENDED**

Love & Basketball [2000]
Starring: Sanaa Lathan, Omar Epps, Alfre Woodard, Dennis Haysbert, Debbi Morgan Director: Gina Prince-Bythewood Screenplay: Gina Prince-Bythewood Running Time: 2:04 Rated: PG-13 (Profanity, sex) Theatrical Aspect Ratio: 1.85:1

Love & Basketball is, as one can infer from the title, about love and basketball. The film follows the lives of two next-door neighbors, one male and one female, from their first meeting on the court at the age of 11 until a fateful night a dozen years in the future. Through all this time, their passion for basketball is equaled only by their passion for each other, but it's never clear for either of them which takes precedence — the game or the relationship. In the final analysis, the feature debut of writer/director Gina Prince-Bythewood (backed by producer Spike Lee) succeeds better as a sports movie than as a romance. While the sports clichés are kept to a minimum in favor of a *Hoop Dreams*-type view of basketball, the love story follows a familiar trajectory.

The two protagonists are Monica Wright (Sanaa Lathan) and Quincy McCall (Omar Epps). She is determined to become the first woman ever to enter the NBA; he is driven by the need to better the accomplishments of his father, Zeke (Dennis Haysbert), a star for the Los Angeles Clippers. *Love & Basketball* is divided into "quarters" like a basketball game, with each segment chronicling a different period in Monica and Quincy's lives. The first quarter, set in 1981, details their meeting and their brief relationship as an 11-year-old "couple." The second quarter skips ahead seven years to high school, where both Monica and Quincy are stars. However, since he's a male and she's a female, his future in the sport appears to be set while hers is uncertain. When it comes to choosing a college, she has to wait anxiously to hear from a recruiter while he plans a press conference to announce his choice. Quarter number 3 transpires during the pair's freshman year at college, when she faces pressure from a demanding coach and he struggles with salacious revelations about his father. Finally, in the fourth quarter, the film shows the degree to which Monica and Quincy's dreams are realized both on and off the court.

Even though every major cast member of *Love & Basketball* is black, the film is essentially color-blind. However, while race is a non-issue, gender is not. The film illustrates, among other things, the vast gulf of inequality that exists between male and female athletes. By dramatizing Monica and Quincy's lives in parallel, Pince-Bythewood is able to explore the inequities. Despite having the same drive, ambition, and passion, they cannot reach the same peak, nor are the plateaus along the way on the same level. Although not a slam-dunk, it's a satisfying lay-up. RECOMMENDED

Love! Valour! Compassion! [1997]

Starring: John Glover, Stephen Bogardus, Jason Alexander, Randy Becker, John Benjamin Hickey Director: Joe Mantello Screenplay: Terrence McNally Running Time: 1:54 Rated: R (Graphic nudity, profanity, sex, mature themes) Theatrical Aspect Ratio: 1.85:1

While *Love! Valour! Compassion!* will obviously appeal to gay audiences (considering that *all* 8 characters are homosexual), the film has plenty to offer straight viewers as well. Much of the humor and drama presented here is universal — love is, after all, love, regardless of whether it's between a man and a woman, a woman and a woman, or a man and a man. *Love! Valour! Compassion!* doesn't use homosexual shock tactics to enliven the proceedings. Instead, it carefully and realistically examines a series of relationships, both sexual and platonic, between men.

Over the course of 3 holiday weekends during one summer, a group of 8 friends gathers together at a secluded Victorian house for swimming, picnicking, volleyball, and talking. The house is owned by

an aging dance choreographer, Gregory (Stephen Bogardus), who lives with his younger, blind companion, Bobby (Justin Kirk). Their guests include John Jeckyll (John Glover), a surly British composer, and his current lover, Ramon (Randy Becker); John's twin, James (also Glover), who is as nice as his brother is nasty; Buzz Hauser (Jason Alexander), a flamboyant showtune aficionado whose HIV+ status casts a grim shadow over his life; and Arthur (John Benjamin Hickey) and Perry (Stephen Spinella), a couple who have been together for 14 years. As the season progresses from Memorial Day to Independence Day to Labor Day, relationships begin and end, revelations occur, and betrayals are committed.

As is often true of stage productions adapted for film, *Love! Valour! Compassion!* turns out to be a talky affair, and, even though the dialogue is rich, there are times when the characters seem to be speaking just to hear the poetry of their words. The film also takes a while to get going. This is not an unusual trait for an ensemble piece — until you get to know the characters a little, it's difficult to become involved in the story. After about the first half-hour, however, *Love! Valour! Compassion!* hits its stride, and, from that point on, it becomes consistently more engrossing.

As play-to-movie transitions go, *Love! Valour! Compassion!* is about average. Mantello, who helmed the stage version but has never before directed a film, doesn't do anything especially interesting or radical. He opens things up a little bit, and occasionally uses the closeup effectively, but this is by no means a stunning motion picture debut. Nevertheless, the material he's working with is so strong that even a mundane approach like this fashions a funny, poignant motion picture that's worth seeing regardless of your sexual orientation. RECOMMENDED

Lucas [1986]

Starring: Corey Haim, Kerri Green, Charlie Sheen, Courtney Thorne-Smith, Winona Ryder Director: David Seltzer Screenplay: David Seltzer Running Time: 1:40 Rated: PG-13 (mature themes) Theatrical Aspect Ratio: 1.85:1

In the decade of the 1980s, when the teen movie was redefined as either a juvenile sex comedy or a bloody slasher movie, *Lucas* became one of the few exceptions to try a different approach. Even today, *Lucas* remains one of the best films to tackle the themes of first crushes and the adolescent angst of not fitting in. It's a poignant and effective character study that manages not only to explore important teenage issues without condescending to the audience, but to offer an upbeat ending without descending into mawkishness.

Lucas (Corey Haim) is a misfit, but he's not a misanthrope. A 14-year-old accelerated high school student with far more intelligence than common sense, he is the prototypical nerd. Like most children who are all brains and little brawn, Lucas is an outcast at school — he is relegated to a clique of others like him, whose scholastic aptitude overshadows their social maturity. Although Lucas has friends, he is pretty much a loner. His home life is not a happy one, and, rather than spend time in the trailer where he lives with his alcoholic father, he prefers to be outside, catching insects in a net or earning a few dollars cutting lawns. Being with other people is not Lucas' style — until he meets Maggie (Kerri Green).

Maggie's new in town and doesn't yet have any friends. The fact that she's 2 years older than him doesn't mean much to Lucas, and he cheerfully takes on the task of being Maggie's constant companion. It's the middle of the summer, and they spend a few idyllic weeks together sharing a variety of experiences. For a short period, they are in a magical world all their own until reality, in the form of school, intrudes. As Maggie meets other people and becomes increasingly popular, the green-eyed monster of jealousy begins to grip Lucas. His emotional crisis reaches a pinnacle when Maggie starts dating Cappie (Charlie Sheen), a football player. Cappie is the only jock at school to treat Lucas with respect, but that doesn't mean much to the younger boy when he sees his special relationship with Maggie slipping away. And it also doesn't matter to Lucas that Maggie never saw him as more than a friend, or that there's another girl at school who is desperate to be his girlfriend.

Lucas is fiction, but it touches the heart like real life, and the title character is so strongly drawn that it's hard to identify with him as nothing more than an artifact of a writer's imagination. In the end, *Lucas* manages to be touching, sad, thoughtful, funny, and joyous — it's a nearly-perfect portrait of the incredible highs and lows that accompany the high school journey of a square peg who doesn't fit into a round hole. **HIGHLY RECOMMENDED**

The Luzhin Defence [United Kingdom/France, 2000]

Starring: John Turturro, Emily Watson, Geraldine James, Stuart Wilson Director: Marleen Gorris Screenplay: Peter Berry, based on the novel by Vladimir Nabokov Running Time: 1:48 Rated: PG-13 (Sensuality, mature themes) Theatrical Aspect Ratio: **1.66:1**

The Luzhin Defence is a motion picture from feminist director Marleen Gorris, whose past cinematic efforts have included *Antonia's Line* and *Mrs. Dalloway*. Based loosely on the novel by Vladimir Nobokov (who is perhaps best known for penning the controversial *Lolita*), this movie tells the unlikely story of a socially inept Chess Grand Master who finds love just as he is about to face the most pressure-packed challenge of his life.

Luzhin (John Turturro) is recognized as one of the greatest chess players of his era (which happens to be the late 1920s). Since the age of 10, his entire life has been devoted to chess. It has been an obsession and an addiction. It's the only thing he is good at and the only thing that has meaning for him. Until, while in Italy to play a match against his chief rival, he meets Natalia (Emily Watson), an elegant beauty who instantly captures his heart. He, in turn, despite his awkward manner and social ineptitude, touches her deeply — so much so that she describes him as the most "fascinating, enigmatic, and attractive man" she has ever met — much to the horror of her mother (Geraldine James), who wants her to marry someone better. But, even as Luzhin is finding a life outside of chess with Natalia, forces are conspiring against him. His old teacher (Stuart Wilson) wants to see him lose the match, and has taken steps to increase the pressure on Luzhin to the point where he will crack.

While one might initially suspect that a movie about chess would inherently be dull (the game itself not necessarily being the best spectator sport), *The Luzhin Defence* is actually an involving and compelling tale. The story is presented in two pieces: events unfolding in the film's present and flashbacks that illuminate how Luzhin became the person he is today. Both timelines converge at the end, when the movie reaches its powerful climax. Gorris frequently toys with symbolism concerning how Luzhin's life replicates the game he plays, but the film never becomes overbearing or bogged down in making such parallels.

With its sumptuous photography and deeply realized characters, *The Luzhin Defence* offers everything one could ask from a period piece, including an emotional release at the end that lacks the artifice associated with manipulative melodramas. This is a fine, thoughtful motion picture that effectively combines the maneuvers of the chessboard with the unfathomable intricacies of the human heart. **RECOMMENDED**

Ma Vie en Rose (My Life in Pink) [France/Belgium/United Kingdom, 1997]

Starring: Georges Du Fresne, Michele Laroque, Jean-Philippe Ecoffey, Helene Vincent Director: Alain Berliner Screenplay: Chris Vander Stappen, Alain Berliner Running Time: 1:30 Rated: R (Profanity, mature themes) Theatrical Aspect Ratio: 1.85:1 In French with subtitles

Equal parts fantasy, satire, and pathos, *Ma Vie en Rose* investigates the role of sexual stereotypes in today's culture, and shows how the more conservative elements of society encourage conformity and stifle diversity. In terms of both its style and story, this is one of 1997's few unique motion pictures.

Pierre (Jean-Philippe Ecoffey) and Hanna (Michele Laroque), along with their 4 children, have just moved into a nice house in a suburban Paris neighborhood. Three of the kids are normal and well-adjusted, but the fourth, Ludovic (Georges Du Fresne), a 7-year-old boy, is showing "alarming" tendencies. His favorite toys are Barbie-like dolls, he expresses a desire to marry a male classmate when he "grows up and becomes a girl," and he shows up at a party dressed like a pink princess. His mother, convinced that this is a harmless phase, tries to be as supportive as possible, but, when pressure from unsympathetic and close-minded neighbors mounts, she begins to turn on Ludovic. Meanwhile, Pierre doesn't know how best to cope with his son's tendencies, and Ludovic's sometimes-embarrassing displays of femininity threaten to derail his career.

Ludovic can't understand what the fuss is about. After all, everything seems clear to him. When God was giving out chromosomes, his second "X" (of the "XX" pair that signifies a female) was lost in the trash and he somehow got stuck with a "Y" instead (for the male "XY" pair). As a result, he's a "girlboy," but, when he grows up, he's convinced that he'll be a woman. So why shouldn't he wear makeup and dresses, and play with dolls? And why is it wrong if he arranges a mock marriage with a boy in his class? When his parents and his schoolmates react angrily, he doesn't understand their surprise, discomfort, and rage. He just wants to do what feels right, yet everyone hates him for it. Those who assume that he's gay have missed the point entirely — sexuality isn't even an issue, at least not at this young age. *Ma Vie en Rose* isn't concerned with Ludovic's eventual sexual orientation.

Although the most memorable element of *Ma Vie en Rose* is the forceful visual style, the director proves himself to be an apt student of human nature. The film works because we understand the central characters and their tribulations. When Ludovic is teased and tormented, it's easy to remember how much unthinking cruelty there is in this world, whether the setting is Paris or next door. But, when all is said and done, *Ma Vie en Rose* is more of a fantasy than a straight drama, and Berliner's lighthearted touch keeps the film buoyant when it could easily turn grim. **RECOMMENDED**

Ma Saison Préferée (My Favorite Season) [France, 1993]

Starring: Catherine Deneuve, Daniel Auteuil, Marthe Villalonga, Jean-Pierre Bouvier, Chiara Mastroianni, Anthony Prada Director: André Téchiné Screenplay: Andre Téchiné Running Time: 2:04 Rated: No MPAA Rating (Nudity, mature themes, profanity) Theatrical Aspect Ratio: 2.35:1 In French with subtitles

Ma Saison Préferée is about relationships and communication. It's about sacrifice and misunderstandings. And, above all, it's about the ties of family and how the passage of time constantly distorts and reinvents our relationships with those we are closest to. André Téchiné's masterful story probes these issues, constantly digging deeper to uncover hidden motivations. In the process, a pair of multi-dimensional, completely believable personalities are created. These characters get under our skin and stay there.

Ma Saison Préferée features international film icon Catherine Deneuve as Emilie and French star Daniel Auteuil (*Jean de Florette, Un Coeur en Hiver*) as her estranged brother, Antoine. The rift between these two has existed for 3 years, a time during which they haven't spoken. When their mother, Berthe (Marthe Villalonga), suffers a stroke, Emilie brings the older woman to her house to live. Bruno (Jean-Pierre Bouvier), Emilie's husband, resents Berthe's presence, and is even less pleased when Emilie breaks the silence with Antoine and invites him to Christmas dinner. On that night, with the snow falling outside, the tangled skein of Emilie and Antoine's relationship begins to untangle, causing Emilie to leave her husband and reach a new understanding with her brother.

When *Ma Saison Préferée* begins, none of the characters are happy with themselves, their lives, their relationships, or each other. As time passes, however, and Emilie and Antoine re-discover the closeness they once shared, they uncover their lost humanity. But how deep is this new understanding, and what level of sacrifice can it survive? Téchiné goes to great pains to illustrate that there are no easy answers to life's most difficult questions, and that no aspect of human interaction can avoid change.

A varied and intriguing group of supporting characters populate this film. The most important is Berthe, whose circumstances and actions impel change in Emilie and Antoine's relationship. We also meet Emilie's troublesome adopted son, Lucien (Anthony Prada), and her daughter, Anne (Chiara Mastroianni, the real-life offspring of Deneuve and actor Marcello Mastroianni), who feels unloved and neglected. These two members of the younger generation have their own stories, pieces of which we see when they intersect aspects of Techine's main narrative.

Ma Saison Préferée is the sort of intelligent, sensitive drama that we need more of. It engages the intellect without ignoring the emotions. **HIGHLY RECOMMENDED**

Maborosi [Japan, 1995]

Starring: Makiko Esumi, Takashi Naitoh, Tadanobu Asano
Director: Hirokazu Kore-eda Screenplay: Yoshihisa Ogita based on the short story by Teru Miyamoto Running Time: 1:50 Rated: No MPAA Rating (Mature themes, brief nudity) Theatrical Aspect Ratio: 1.66:1
In Japanese with subtitles

In an era when MTV-inspired film making techniques have begun to dominate motion pictures, its refreshing to see something with the simple, unhurried style of Japanese director Hirokazu Kore-eda's feature debut, *Maborosi*. This film, which is really little more than a series of images connected by a bare-bones plot, explores the evolution of one woman's emotion as she ponders the unexplained (and seemingly inexplicable) death of her first husband.

The film opens with a brief prologue during which a young Japanese girl watches her beloved grandmother leave home, never to return. On that same day, she meets the boy who will eventually become her husband. When we next encounter her, Yumiko (Makiko Esumi) is 20 years older. She's married to Ikuo (Tadanobu Asano) and has a 3-month old son. She is content, and her happiness is shown through a playfulness that permeates every action. Then, one night, everything changes. Ikuo commits suicide by walking in front of a train. Yumiko is plunged into an extended period of mourning from which she only begins to emerge when she re-marries, this time to a widower named Tamio (Takashi Naitoh). To be with Tamio, Yumiko leaves the city of Osaka to live in a tiny fishing village. But she is a haunted woman, and her fear of intimacy keeps her emotionally isolated from her new husband.

Kore-eda has chosen not to illustrate Yumiko's emotions through traditionally melodramatic meth-

ods. In fact, it's rare that she sheds a tear, although the face of model-turned-actress Makiko Esumi is certainly capable of expressing a surprising range of feeling. Instead of relying on the character, however, Kore-eda uses Yumiko's surroundings. When she's on the way to the police station to identify her husband's body, the weather weeps for her, streaking the car windows with rain. After Ikuo's death, the director, much like Ingmar Bergman, uses spatial relationships to highlight her emotional isolation. She is often distanced from others, frequently appearing alone and shrouded by shadow. Towards the end of *Maborosi*, there is a memorable sequence when Yumiko, depicted in silhouette, is set far apart from everyone else. Kore-eda also uses certain sounds to contribute to the sense of solitude — the crashing of the waves and the roar of the wind, in particular.

Maborosi is a worthwhile movie experience not because it ventures into virgin territory, but because its presentation is so precise and unique. This is a haunting cinematic portrait, where the almost-poetic visual images and their associated emotional meaning hold the viewer enraptured. **HIGHLY RECOMMENDED**

The Madness of King George [United Kingdom, 1994]

Starring: Nigel Hawthorne, Helen Mirren, Ian Holm, Amanda Donohoe, Rupert Graves, Rupert Everett Director: Nicholas Hytner Screenplay: Alan Bennett based on his stage play "The Madness of George III" Running Time: 1:50 Rated: No MPAA Rating (Mature themes) Theatrical Aspect Ratio: 1.85:1

Opening in 1788, more than 5 years after England lost her North American colonies, *The Madness of King George* relates a dark episode in the king's reign. Bothered by increasingly painful abdominal pains, George (Nigel Hawthorne) begins to act irrationally and belligerently. The doctors — mostly a bunch of jumped-up quacks — do nothing for him. His eldest son and heir, the Prince of Wales (Rupert Everett) is eager to see his father declared mad so he can take over as regent. Ministers, retainers, and others at court begin to scheme how to get the most out of the king's indisposition. At last, when all appears lost, Prime Minister Pitt (Julian Wadham), aided by Queen Charlotte (Helen Mirren); her Mistress of the Robes, Lady Pembroke (Amanda Donohoe); and Greville (Rupert Graves), one of the king's aides; sends for Dr. Willis (Ian Holm), a doctor of the mind with a reputation for curing dementia.

The Madness of King George is much more than a simple study of one man's descent into insanity. With a style that's more tongue-in-cheek than melodramatic, the film is always witty and occasionally satirical. The characterizations are flawless (as well as historically accurate), and the political wrangling of the Tories and Whigs (led by PM Pitt and Charles Fox, respectively) provide a deliciously complex backdrop.

Medical historians are generally agreed that the cause of George's madness was something called porphyria, an acute, intermittent, hereditary disease that is physical (rather than mental) in nature. The king's symptoms, including blue urine and gastric crises, match those of porphyria, although some have postulated that there may have been a secondary affliction, such as manic-depression, involved. Whatever the case, as this film illustrates, it's clear that there were times when George was unfit to rule.

Despite allusions to *King Lear,* this movie's strength is in its story breadth, not its depth. A lot happens here, but few of the themes take root beyond their surface meaning. Adapted from Alan Bennett's play *The Madness of George III,* the film trims copious portions of dialogue, leaving behind a tightly-paced picture that has the feel of something created for the screen rather than for the stage. Certain subplots are watered down or eliminated, but what survives is more than enough to keep *King George* a source of solid entertainment. **HIGHLY RECOMMENDED**

Magnolia [1999]

Starring: Jason Robards, Philip Baker Hall, Tom Cruise, John C. Reilly, Melora Walters, Julianne Moore, William H. Macy, Philip Seymour Hoffman Director: Paul Thomas Anderson Screenplay: Paul Thomas Anderson Running Time: 3:05 Rated: R (Profanity, violence, sex) Theatrical Aspect Ratio: 2.35:1

With *Magnolia,* director Paul Thomas Anderson has created a fascinating and worthwhile motion picture that manages to keep viewers interested in the plights of 10 different characters for nearly its full 3-hour length — right up to and through the improbable climax.

In order to get a sense of where *Magnolia* is going, it is necessary to introduce the various characters. At the center of events is Earl Partridge (Jason Robards), a television producer who, stricken by cancer, lies on his deathbed. His young wife, Linda (Julianne Moore), is desolate with grief and guilt, and has trouble coping with her impending loss. His estranged son, Frank Mackey (Tom Cruise), the charismatic guru of the "Seduce and Destroy" lifestyle, has worked hard to sever all connections with Earl. His nurse, Phil Parma (Philip Seymour Hoffman), seeks to fulfill his employer's dying wish and reunite him

with Frank. Meanwhile, Jimmy Gator (Philip Baker Hall), who is the host of Earl's most popular TV show, the long-running "What Do Kids Know?," also has terminal cancer. Like Earl and Frank, a rift exists between him and his child. When he attempts a reconciliation with Claudia (Melora Walters), she rebuffs him. Later, she embarks on a strange relationship with a gentle but ineffectual police officer, Jim Kurring (John C. Reilly). And Jimmy must explain to his wife, Rose (Melinda Dillon), why Claudia hates him so intensely. At the same time, Stanley Spector (Jeremy Blackman), a child genius on Jimmy's show, finds that the only way to get his father's attention is to win money. And, as Stanley continues to answer questions right, a former quiz show star, Donnie Smith (William H. Macy), watches the remains of his life go up in smoke. Together, these characters make up the leaves and branches of this tree.

Like Robert Altman's *Short Cuts, Magnolia* is a finely-tuned ensemble piece. Yet a direct comparison between the two films would be somewhat misleading. Thematically, at least when considering the role played by chance, there are similarities, but Altman used a different, more languid style than Anderson does. *Magnolia* is a kinetic picture that doesn't stop moving and rarely stays with one story for more than a couple of minutes before moving to the next. This approach allows us to get to know the principals quickly, and keeps us engaged by all of the storylines. *Magnolia* is admittedly not for everyone, but those who "get" the film are in for something that ranks as more of a cinematic experience than a mere movie. **HIGHLY RECOMMENDED**

The Majestic [2001]

Starring: Jim Carrey, Martin Landau, Laurie Holden, Bob Balaban Director: Frank Darabont Screenplay: Michael Sloane Running Time: 2:32 Rated: PG (Mature themes, profanity) Theatrical Aspect Ratio: 1.85:1

Once in a while, a movie arrives on the scene that immediately causes critics far and wide to compare it to the work of a legendary director, such as Hitchcock, Wilder, or Welles. In this case, it's Frank Capra. Typically, an effort associated with Capra will fall into the feel-good category, may engage in shameless manipulation, and will bring to mind words like "wholesome" and "sentimental." *The Majestic* has all the elements to be a crowd-pleaser. The only potential negatives are its languorous pace and long running time, which may cause some MTV-bred viewers to squirm in their seats.

The Majestic takes place in the early 1950s. The Cold War is well underway and Sen. Joseph McCarthy's anti-Communist fervor is at its peak. No one is safe from government bullying — especially in Hollywood, long viewed as a hotbed of seditious activity. Screenwriter Peter Appleton (Jim Carrey), whose movie, *Sand Pirates of the Sahara,* has just reached screens, is no exception. Years ago in college, he attended a pro-Communist meeting to impress a girl. Now, that simple action has come back to haunt him, as he finds himself blacklisted and called to testify in front of Congress. The night when Peter learns that his life will never be the same, he drinks himself into a stupor, then crashes his car into a river. He wakes up on a beach with no memory of who he is. But the citizens of the small, nearby town have no such uncertainty — he is Luke Trimble, a war hero who was reported missing in action 9½ years earlier. Luke is welcomed home by everyone, including his aging father, Harry (Martin Landau), the mayor (Jeffrey DeMunn), and the love of his life, Adele Stanton (Laurie Holden). With the help of the townsfolk, Luke and Harry set to work restoring the local movie theater, The Majestic, to its former glory. But not everyone believes in the miracle of Luke's return, and the government is looking for Peter Appleton.

Most people will leave *The Majestic* with a smile reflecting the warm glow within. The film is unashamed of its feel-good intentions and, in that, is a throwback. There's no sex or violence, and very little in the way of profanity. Had *The Majestic* been made in black-and-white with a less high-profile cast, one might have assumed it to be the product of Hollywood during a kinder, gentler era. For those craving a large helping of nostalgia with a topping of crowd-pleasing patriotism, there are few choices better than *The Majestic.* **RECOMMENDED**

Malena [Italy/United States, 2000]

Starring: Monica Bellucci, Giuseppe Sulfaro, Luciano Federico, Matilde Piana Director: Giuseppe Tornatore Screenplay: Giuseppe Tornatore, based on a story by Luciano Vincenzoni Running Time: 1:32 Rated: R (Nudity, sexual situations, violence) Theatrical Aspect Ratio: 2.35:1
In Italian with subtitles

Malena is a curious mix of whimsy and tragedy. Director Giuseppe Tornatore's blending of the divergent tones is not entirely successful — there are several jarring moments — but, on the whole, *Malena* works as an affecting coming-of-age story set against the backdrop of Fascist Italy and filtered through the memories of the narrator. Along the way, Tornatore

sticks to the same basic style that served him well in his 1989 international hit, *Cinema Paradiso,* by employing equal parts nostalgia, comedy, and drama.

The year is 1940 and the place is the picturesque (and fictional) town of Castelcuta, Sicily. 13-year-old Renato Amoroso (Giuseppe Sulfaro) is about to experience his first major adolescent crush when he catches a glimpse of Malena Scordia (Monica Bellucci). Malena, the daughter of Latin teacher Professor Bonsignore (Pietro Notarianni), has come to Castelcuta to care for her father while her husband is away at war. As Malena walks by, every man's head turns and women's tongues wag with scathing gossip. Then Malena's husband is killed in the war and she becomes free to pursue and be pursued by Castelcuta's male population. Meanwhile, Renato, whose infatuation develops into an obsession, begins spying on Malena and, in the process, learns that the "real" Malena is much different than his idealized portrait of her.

Malena begins as a lighthearted drama that recalls one of Federico Fellini's best-known works, *Amarcord.* Tornatore does not have Fellini's deft hand, however, and the story eventually takes a dark turn, with some of its themes and ideas recalling the late Krzysztof Kieslowski's *A Short Film About Love,* in which a young voyeur has his fantasy picture of a woman brutally shattered by an encounter with her.

One of the most powerful elements of *Malena* is the music, by frequent Tornatore collaborator and legendary composer, Ennio Morricone. Combined with cinematographer Lajos Koltai's sweeping camera work and beautifully photographed vistas, the music gives *Malena* a glorious backdrop against which the story can unfold. This is not the writer/director's most accomplished feature, but it offers a strong central character, an interesting historical subtext, and a coming-of-age narrative that most people will be able to relate to on one level or another. **RECOMMENDED**

A Man of No Importance
[Ireland/United Kingdom, 1994]

Starring: Albert Finney, Brenda Fricker, Rufus Sewell, Tara Fitzgerald, Michael Gambon Director: Suri Krishnamma Screenplay: Barry Devlin Running Time: 1:38 Rated: R (Mature themes, sex, nudity, violence)

As it turns out, the only thing of real importance in *A Man of No Importance* is Albert Finney's performance. His turn as bus conductor Alfie Byrne is yet another extraordinary credit to add to an already-impressive resume. The man who played Tom Jones in the 1960s matured into of the best character actors of the 1990s, with memorable appearances in such films as *The Playboys, Rich in Love,* and *The Browning Version.* Even when these movies had little to offer, Finney's presence was a saving grace.

When he's not entertaining his regular passengers with readings of Oscar Wilde, Alfie is a would-be director who delights in putting on not-so-successful amateur productions. In the past, he has been known for doing *The Importance of Being Earnest,* but this time around, Alfie has chosen to attempt *Salome.* This decision is crystalized when he finds the perfect choice for the title role — an enchanting young woman named Adele (Tara Fitzgerald) who wanders on his bus one day.

But Alfie's personal life isn't nearly as joyful as his public personae might lead others to believe. Despite attempts by his sister (Brenda Fricker) to find him a wife, Alfie steadfastly resists the idea, primarily because women don't interest him. However, the only one to whom he has openly admitted his homosexuality (or "the love that dare not speak its name," as Wilde called it) is himself. In Alfie's world of 1963 Dublin, tolerance for gays is in short supply.

If *A Man of No Importance* is anything other than a nicely-detailed portrait of one unfulfilled middle-aged Dubliner, it's about the value of friendship. Although Alfie never finds the love for which he so desperately searches, he discovers a far more valuable commodity. In Adele, he uncovers someone else who hides a secret. The two are kindred spirits and there are times when their interaction has a closeness that lovers often strive for. Then there's the driver of Alfie's bus, a young man named Robbie (Rufus Sewell), to whom Alfie is attracted. Because Robbie is straight, Alfie never reveals his feelings, choosing instead to pursue a platonic friendship.

"The only way to get rid of temptation is to yield to it," wrote Oscar Wilde, but when Alfie tries to apply this lesson, the results are — to put it mildly — unfortunate. That life cannot be lived without risk and failure is certainly one of *A Man of No Importance*'s more emphatic messages. **RECOMMENDED**

Man on the Moon [1999]

Starring: Jim Carrey, Danny DeVito, Paul Giamatti, Courtney Love, Jerry Lawler Director: Milos Forman Screenplay: Scott Alexander & Larry Karaszewski Running Time: 1:59 Rated: R (Profanity, sexual situations, nudity) Theatrical Aspect Ratio: 2.35:1

During his lifetime, Andy Kaufman was regarded by fans as a comic genius and by detractors as an out-of-control lunatic. Most of the American public simply didn't understand him, and the numerous outrageous antics of his later life alienated many of those who had initially enjoyed him in the role of Latka Gravas in the TV series *Taxi.*

In telling its story of Kaufman's rise to fame and fall out of favor, *Man on the Moon* briefly visits him as a young boy, then zooms ahead to the mid-'70s, when he is starting his career as a stand-up comedian in improv clubs. One night, agent George Shapiro (Danny DeVito) sees him perform and decides that he wants to represent him. When the two later meet, Kaufman confides to Shapiro that he considers himself to be a song & dance man, not a comedian. "I don't do jokes. I don't even know what's funny." Following his signing with Shapiro, Kaufman makes an appearance as a "musical guest" on the first episode of *Saturday Night Live,* then goes on to star in *Taxi.* Along with his writing partner, Bob Zmuda (Paul Giamatti), he pens a prime time special that ABC executives nix, calling it bizarre and unfunny. Meanwhile, Kaufman is living a double life — his alter ego is an offensive and thoroughly untalented lounge singer named Tony Clifton.

Once he has the spotlight, Kaufman is unwilling to become creatively apathetic. He enjoys playing with his mercurial image and toying with the lines between fantasy and reality. So he sets himself up as a sexist wrestler who will only wrestle women. His first public "bout" occurs on the Merv Griffin show, where he defeats a woman named Lynn Marguiles (Courtney Love), with whom he later falls in love. Other matches follow, until Kaufman is challenged to go one-on-one with the King of Wrestling, Jerry Lawler.

Kaufman becomes so adept at the art of deception and illusion that, when he discovers he has terminal cancer, no one believes him. His family views it as the latest in a series of cruel practical jokes and believes that his doctor is a paid actor. Like the boy who has cried wolf once too often, Kaufman must struggle to convince those around him that, for once, he is serious.

Man on the Moon does not whitewash its lead character, but he is presented as a likable, albeit strange, protagonist. And, as a side benefit, we are given the opportunity to peer behind the scenes at some of the goings-on in Kaufman's projects. There are many reasons to see *Man on the Moon,* but the two most compelling are to appreciate the way the movie works on many levels and to experience what has the potential to be the crowning performance of Jim Carrey's career. **HIGHLY RECOMMENDED**

Manny & Lo [1996]

Starring: Scarlett Johansson, Aleksa Palladino, Mary Kay Place
Director: Lisa Krueger Screenplay: Lisa Krueger Running Time: 1:25
Rated: R (Profanity, sex, mature themes) Theatrical Aspect Ratio: 1.85:1

Manny & Lo, the debut feature from writer/director Lisa Krueger, is a wonderfully-textured comic fantasy about family life. With only a few missteps along the way, this film takes us on a deceptively complex journey of discovery into a world that is similar, yet different, from the one we travel through every day. For, although Krueger presents her characters as the human flotsam of modern-day life, there is a timeless, placeless quality to this story. Ultimately, it doesn't matter *when* or *where Manny & Lo* takes place, but *how* the characters' trajectories bring them together at their final destination.

Eleven-year old Amanda (or Manny, played by Scarlett Johansson) and 16-year-old Laurel (or Lo, played by Aleksa Palladino) are sisters on-the-run. After the death of their mother, they were placed in separate foster homes, only to be reunited after Lo ran away and "so-called kidnapped" Manny from her substitute family. Together, the pair live life on the road, watching out for state troopers who may have their description, stealing food from small convenience stores, sleeping in model homes, and checking the milk cartons to make sure that their pictures aren't on the "missing" panels.

Their unorthodox lifestyle is seriously disrupted, however, when Lo becomes pregnant. By the time she acknowledges that it's not just a few extra pounds, she's too far advanced for an abortion. Unwilling to turn herself in for medical care, but recognizing that she needs help, Lo decides to kidnap Elaine (Mary Kay Place), a "baby expert." With Manny's help, Lo uses a shotgun to encourage Elaine to accompany her to a deserted mountain cabin retreat. There, the 3 of them, captors and captive, await the baby's arrival while growing into a strange pseudo-family.

The best parts of *Manny & Lo* are the quiet, character-driven scenes, when it's just the 3 women alone, exploring their new relationship and contemplating the future. A subplot involving the cabin's owner (Paul Guilfoyle) shows us something about how desperately Elaine wants to be part of Manny and Lo's life, but there are aspects of this sequence that strain the film's delicately-struck balance between reality and fantasy.

There's something magical about the way Lisa Krueger's film transports us to its unique reality. There have been many films about family and belonging, but none with quite the same perspective as this one. *Manny & Lo* is always pleasant, never confrontational, and comes to a conclusion that is emotionally true. With its carefully-modulated combination of light comedy and drama, the film casts a gentle spell. **HIGHLY RECOMMENDED**

Mansfield Park [United Kingdom/United States, 1999]

Starring: Frances O'Connor, Jonny Lee Miller, Embeth Davidtz, Alessandro Nivola, Harold Pinter Director: Patricia Rozema
Screenplay: Patricia Rozema, based on Jane Austen's novel *Mansfield Park*, her letters and early journals Running Time: 1:50 Rated: PG-13 (Sex, nudity, mature themes) Theatrical Aspect Ratio: 1.78:1

There are 3 primary problems associated with filming Jane Austen's most confounding novel, *Mansfield Park*. In the first place, the text is long (this is Austen's second most verbose novel). Secondly, it's a deeply introspective work, with much of the "action" taking place inside the heroine's head. Finally, that heroine, Fanny Price, is passive and difficult to like. To put her on screen the way she is on the written page would risk driving viewers away. Canadian director Patricia Rozema's innovative (and possibly controversial) solution has been to change the text. In streamlining the plot, scenes and characters have been eliminated. Rozema also allows Fanny Price to address the camera, reducing the use of the voiceover narrative. And, most importantly, the director has altered Fanny's personality by injecting a great deal of Austen into her. The result is a hybrid of author and creation.

The film begins just after the turn of the 18th century. Young Fanny Price (played by Hannah Taylor Gordon as a child and Frances O'Connor as an adult) is shipped off from her squalid home in Portsmouth to live with wealthy relatives in the country estate of Mansfield Park. Because of her inferior social class, she is treated as an outcast by most of the family: Sir Thomas Bertram (Harold Pinter), Lady Bertram (Lindsay Duncan), and cousins Tom, Maria, and Julia. Only Edmund (Philip Sarson as a child, Jonny Lee Miller as an adult), the Bertrams' second son, is kind and open. He takes an interest in Fanny's writings, and, over the years, they become friends — and perhaps a little more. Although Edmund is seemingly oblivious to it, Fanny has fallen in love with him, and her affection is more than that of one cousin for another.

The scene shifts ahead several years, and life at Mansfield Park is considerably shaken by the appearance of Henry and Mary Crawford (Alessandro Nivola and Embeth Davidtz), a cosmopolitan brother and sister who arrive from London in search of marriageable prey. Much to Fanny's dismay, Mary sets her sights on Edmund, and he appears receptive to her overtures. Meanwhile, although Henry initially flirts with all the eligible young women at Mansfield Park, his attention eventually focuses on Fanny. He likes a challenge, and she provides it. Her reluctance only fuels his desire, but she does not trust him and she is distracted and dismayed by the growing bond between Edmund and Mary.

Of all the Austen novels to reach the big or small screen during the '90s, this one makes the most departures from its source material. From a technical standpoint, *Mansfield Park* is gorgeously composed, with standout production design and stunning cinematography. The screenplay achieves the difficult goal of making *Mansfield Park* both accessible to and engaging for a modern audience. Overall, this is a fine addition to the filmed Austen canon. Rozema's *Mansfield Park* should slake nearly every movie-goer's thirst for the most beloved female author of the pre-Victorian 1800s. **RECOMMENDED**

Marvin's Room [1996]

Starring: Meryl Streep, Leonardo DiCaprio, Diane Keaton, Robert DeNiro Director: Jerry Zaks Screenplay: Scott McPherson based on his play Running Time: 1:38 Rated: PG-13 (Mature themes, profanity) Theatrical Aspect Ratio: 1.85:1

Scott McPherson's play, *Marvin's Room,* debuted on stage in New York 6 years ago. McPherson went on to write the film's screenplay before succumbing to AIDS-related complications. And, while the narrative is not intended to be biographical, McPherson nevertheless drew heavily on his own experiences while writing it. Director Jerry Zaks widens the canvas here, expanding the film's locales to a Florida beach and Disneyworld while continuing to maintain the level of emotional intensity that makes this a memorable story.

Bessie (Diane Keaton) and Lee (Meryl Streep) are sisters who have gone their separate ways. Twenty years ago, a bitter quarrel over family responsibilities split them, and they haven't spoken since. Bessie gave up her life to return to the family home in Florida and play the role of caregiver for her father, Marvin (Hume Cronyn), who had a stroke, and her bedridden aunt (Gwen Verdon). Lee, unwilling to accept such a personal sacrifice, went her own way. She had 2 children, Hank (Leonardo DiCaprio) and Charlie (Hal Scardino), that she has struggled to raise on her own.

Now, Bessie has been diagnosed with leukemia, and her survival may depend on a bone marrow transplant from a family member. This leads to an awkward and inevitable reunion between the sisters. Lee and her two sons travel to Florida — Lee to revisit the past; Charlie and Hank to meet the aunt they never knew. But all is not well between these characters. Hank's rebelliousness, which landed him in a mental institution, threatens to explode into the open, and the tension between Lee and Bessie is palpable.

Marvin's Room deals with a number of potentially-depressing subjects: mental illness, child abuse, repressed memories, buried guilt, and terminal cancer. In many ways, however, this film is not a downer, because it encourages us to look at the good things in a day-to-day existence. *Marvin's Room* is about three people in damaged relationships coming together. Nothing is really resolved by the time we reach the somewhat abrupt ending, but the seeds of hope have been planted.

It takes a lot of thought and reflection to untangle all the complex relationships revealed throughout *Marvin's Room.* In the end, however, the image that lingers is one of promise. Sure, there's a tragedy here, but, ultimately, I think the tone of *Marvin's Room* is far more positive than the subject matter might lead anyone to believe. **HIGHLY RECOMMENDED**

Me Without You [United Kingdom, 2001]

Starring: Michelle Williams, Anna Friel, Kyle MacLachlan Director: Sandra Goldbacher Screenplay: Sandra Goldbacher, Laurence Coriat Running Time: 1:47 Rated: R (Profanity, sexual situations, drug use, nudity) Theatrical Aspect Ratio: 2.35:1

The movie opens in 1973 London, where best friends Holly (Ella Jones) and Marina (Anna Popplewell) are finding ways to spend the long summer days. Despite their differences, Holly and Marina are inseparable. Holly is the "clever" one, whose looks and self-confidence don't match the strength of her mind. Marina, on the other hand, is pretty, uninhibited, and not Holly's intellectual equal. Despite her wildness, however, she's actually vulnerable, with her outward boldness hiding a deep insecurity. Marina is clearly the dominant one in the relationship; Holly follows along, at times almost in awe.

The scene shifts to 1978. Both girls are now in their late teens and into the punk rock scene. Holly (now played by Michelle Williams) is as much of a wallflower as ever, and Marina (Anna Friel) is even more brash and outgoing. One night at a party, while Marina is doing heroin, Holly loses her virginity to Marina's older brother, Nat (Oliver Milburn). This creates a rift between the friends. Four years later, while at college, they both have affairs with the same professor (Kyle MacLachlan). Each is hurt to learn of the other's "betrayal" of sleeping with "her" man. Meanwhile, Nat makes an appearance, and it's clear that he's as besotted with Holly as she is with him. But a jealous Marina pushes them away from each other, and Nat goes to France to patch things up with his actress girlfriend.

The relationship between Holly and Marina starts as a typical teenage friendship before developing into something dark and unhealthy. In the early years, the two share everything and are as necessary to one another as oxygen. As they grow older and Marina's dominance strengthens, the downward spiral begins. Jealousy gradually poisons what exists between them. By the time the movie has reached its third act in the late '80s, these two women are together simply because they have been close for so long that the idea of splitting up seems unthinkable. Yet their friendship is dysfunctional. The bonds between them are rotten, and the situation has become suffocating.

Too few dramas these days have an arc such as the one traversed by *Me Without You*. The story works because it's about ordinary people — women you wouldn't look at twice if you passed them on the sidewalk. *Me Without You* offers more insight into the experience of female bonding that dozens of Hollywood features about the same subject. Touching and sincere, this film deserves to be seen by anyone who is searching for a movie about compelling characters in real circumstances. **RECOMMENDED**

Men with Guns [1998]

Starring: **Federico Luppi, Dan Rivera Gonzalez, Damian Delgado, Tania Cruz** Director: **John Sayles** Screenplay: **John Sayles** Running Time: **2:08** Rated: **R** (Profanity, violence) Theatrical Aspect Ratio: **1.85:1** In Spanish with subtitles

Men with Guns is a very good film. It stars Argentinean actor Federico Luppi (*Cronos*) as Dr. Fuentes, an aging medical practitioner in an unnamed Central American country. With retirement upon him, Fuentes is determined that some part of his teaching will outlast him. He believes that his legacy lies in the contribution he made to a project that trained young men and women to be doctors before sending them out as "ambassadors of health" to remote Indian villages. It has been years since Fuentes has heard from any of his former students, and he decides to take a trip out of the city to look for a few of them. The deeper he gets into the wilderness, the more horrified he becomes by what he finds in different Indian villages. Poverty and lawlessness are the chief characteristics of life. To the common farmer eking out a living, there's no difference between guerrillas and soldiers — they're all men with guns who steal and kill.

Along the way, Fuentes assembles an unusual group of traveling companions. The first to join him is an orphaned young boy (Dan Rivera Gonzalez), who knows the way of the back roads that the doctor must traverse. The next member of the group is a solider who has deserted (Damian Delgado) and whose prized possession, a revolver, has no bullets. Later, the band is enlarged by a priest who has lost his faith (Damian Alcazar) and a mute woman (Tania Cruz) who is in search of solace.

One of the most vociferous arguments to develop against *Men with Guns* focuses on the setting. Sayles has placed all of the action in a fictitious Latin American country, declining to indict any particular government for the travesties that are shown (guerrillas killing men for helping soldiers; soldiers killing men for helping guerrillas). And, while there is a legitimate argument for "naming names," Sayles' point is that the themes and issues he addresses are universal in nature, and that there's no reason to pin down a specific country. These kinds of human rights abuses have happened throughout history and are still taking place all across the world wherever oppressors with superior technology use their position of strength to dispossess and suppress the indigenous population.

Reduced to broad generalizations, *Men with Guns* is an adventure story — a sort of *Don Quixote* meets *Heart of Darkness*. What marks this film as special isn't just that the surface details are believable, but that there is great richness and breadth to the issues addressed within. Where does innocence end and ignorance begin? How much responsibility do we bear for circumstances when we hide from them? And, if we learn the truth, how do we respond when all roads lead to desperation, futility, and failure? While *Men with Guns* ends on an artificially uplifting note, the prevailing tone is one of bleak hopelessness. This is a thought-provoking motion picture that, like many of Sayles' other efforts, demands that we ponder complex questions. **HIGHLY RECOMMENDED**

Menace II Society [1993]

Starring: Tyrin Turner, Larenz Tate, Jada Pickett, Charles S. Dutton Director: Allen and Albert Hughes Screenplay: Tyger Williams Running Time: 1:37 Rated: R (Language, violence, sexual situations, mature themes) Theatrical Aspect Ratio: 1.85:1

As a child, Caine (Tyrin Turner) was raised in a "den of thieves," with a heroin-addicted mother and a gun-toting, drug-pushing father. At the age of 5, Caine learns how to shoot a gun and witnesses his father kill someone in cold blood. By the time of his high school graduation, he's already a seasoned drug pusher. One night, he and his friend O-Dog (Larenz Tate) go into a store to get a beer. O-Dog takes exception to a remark made by the owner, and, with Caine standing by his side, guns the man down. Starting at this moment, the pair start down a road of crime that nothing can rescue them from — not even the fear of death. In fact, when Caine's grandfather asks him if he wants to stay alive, his response is, "I don't know."

The setting for *Menace II Society* and John Singleton's remarkable *Boyz 'N the Hood* is the same, and the overwhelming specter of explosive violence hangs over both. Each, in its own way, is a powerful indictment of what life has become for a black man in the inner city, and how the only escape through violence is into the grave. While *Boyz 'N the Hood* has as its main characters a couple of "good" kids, *Menace II Society* focuses on the other side. Caine and O-Dog are criminals, given to using their guns to solve problems. Nevertheless, they are portrayed sympathetically and the audience comes to understand and even care about Caine, even though it's impossible to endorse his actions.

The story and characters are well-developed, and we are given a graphic, firsthand depiction of the wages of Caine and O-Dog's lifestyle. The lure of money, prestige, and power are realistically presented, but no more so than the brutal payment that is exacted to obtain them. *Menace II Society* also explores the necessity for a person to accept the consequences of his actions, and how an apparently inconsequential event can trigger a disastrous chain-reaction.

This film is too stark and powerful to function as simple entertainment. Those that chose to view *Menace II Society* should prepare for a gut-wrenching, emotionally turbulent experience. It won't be a fun time — at least not in the conventional sense — but you'll sit through a 97-minute odyssey that won't be quickly forgotten. **HIGHLY RECOMMENDED**

Message in a Bottle [1999]

Starring: Kevin Costner, Robin Wright Penn, Paul Newman, Illeana Douglas, Robby Coltrane Director: Luis Mandoki Screenplay: Gerald DiPego, based on the novel by Nicholas Sparks Running Time: 2:10 Rated: PG-13 (Sexual themes, mild profanity) Theatrical Aspect Ratio: 2.35:1

In addition to being a beautifully-photographed motion picture with a solid (albeit melodramatic) storyline and good acting, *Message in a Bottle* was also Kevin Costner's bid to once again be taken seriously in the wake of several unfortunate career choices (capped off by the disastrous *The Postman*).

Message in a Bottle starts out with single mom Theresa Osborne (Robin Wright Penn), leaving her young son, Jason (Jesse James), in the care of his father, with whom he's visiting for a few weeks. After that, she takes a stroll along a New England beach, where she finds a bottle with a message in it. The note is addressed to someone named Catherine, and appears to be a heartfelt letter of love and loss. The writer calls the woman his "true North," expresses how much she means to him, and laments her loss. Theresa is deeply touched, and, when she returns home to Chicago, she shows the missive to her friends and co-workers at the Tribune. The next day, the letter is printed in the paper, and the resulting reader response is overwhelming. Contained in the stacks of mail delivered to the Tribune are two other messages, both found in bottles, that appear to be from the same source. Using her investigative instincts, Theresa tracks down the writer, a North Carolina ship repairman named Garret Blake (Kevin Coster), and, without revealing her profession, she strikes up a friendship with him. It turns out that Garret is still grieving for his dead wife, Catherine, and his life has been an empty shell for the past 2 years. But, through his interaction with Theresa, he begins to shake off some of the cobwebs of loneliness and pain.

The movie's premise promises more than the rather standard grief-assuaged-by-new-love story that's ultimately delivered. The first half-hour of *Message in a Bottle* is engrossing because it appears to be going in a completely new direction. After that, things fall into familiar patterns. Once the initial 30 minutes are over, the best part of *Message in a Bottle* is the character interaction.

Working from a script by Gerald DiPego (based on Nicholas Sparks' novel), director Luis Mandoki has fashioned one of his most complete films to date. Credit both the actors and the material for making *Message in a Bottle* a worthwhile 2 hours. It's not a great film, but it succeeds in being both tender and cathartic, and, unlike *Patch Adams* and *Stepmom*, it isn't unbearably cloying in the process. **RECOMMENDED**

Michael Collins [United Kingdom/United States, 1996]
Starring: Liam Neeson, Aidan Quinn, Julia Roberts, Alan Rickman, Stephen Rea, Ian Hart, Brendan Gleeson Director: Neil Jordan
Screenplay: Neil Jordan Running Time: 2:12 Rated: R (Violence, profanity) Theatrical Aspect Ratio: 1.85:1

Neil Jordan's *Michael Collins* is a biopic of the man who co-founded the IRA and signed the 1921 treaty that partitioned Ireland and provoked the 1922 civil war. Even before its release, the film fanned passions in the United Kingdom, where is was tagged with such diverse labels as "ammunition for IRA recruiting sergeants and fund-raisers" (Ruth Dudley Edwards) and "as important a film as ever to be made in Ireland about Ireland" (Art Cosgrove).

While its clear that *Michael Collins* does distort elements of history, most of the changes and compressions are dramatically effective. Certain characters are combined, a few deaths happen differently from what history records, and events have been streamlined. This aside, however, viewers are left with an expertly-directed and well-acted historical epic that disappoints only in its shallow perspective of the Irish/British and Irish/Irish conflicts.

Michael Collins opens in 1916 Dublin, with the infamous Easter Rising, where the better-organized British troops rout the Irish Volunteers. From there, the movie progresses rapidly through the next 2 turbulent years, tracking Collins' rise in power and popularity and De Valera's ascension to the head of Sinn Fein. Then, while De Valera is in America drumming up support for an independent Ireland, Collins' campaign of urban guerrilla warfare against the British proves to be a spectacular success. Rejecting conventional tactics, he uses an "invisible army" that strikes unexpectedly with whatever means are available. Informers are shot and England's Irish intelligence operation is brought to its knees. By late 1921, Churchill and Lloyd George are willing to talk peace, and De Valera sends Collins as the Irish representa-

tive. The resulting controversial treaty, the best Collins felt he could get at the time, fuels the drama of *Michael Collins'* final act. Because the agreement still requires that the Irish pay fealty to England's king and because it divides the country in two, De Valera rejects it, labeling it as a betrayal. Civil war ensues, and, on August 22, 1922, Collins is assassinated while in his home district of Cork.

In tone and spirit, if not in time and place, this film shares a great deal with Oscar-winning *Braveheart*. Michael Collins, like William Wallace, fought for independence, and, in the end, was its victim. Neil Jordan felt that this story was so important that he nurtured the script for 13 years until he had the clout to command the actors and budget he wanted. The ultimate result may not quite match his ambitions, but it was one of 1996's most talked-about motion pictures. **HIGHLY RECOMMENDED**

Midnight in the Garden of Good and Evil [1997]
Starring: John Cusack, Kevin Spacey, Jack Thompson, Lady Chablis, Alison Eastwood, Irma P. Hall Director: Clint Eastwood
Screenplay: John Lee Hancock based on the novel by John Berendt Running Time: 2:35 Rated: R (Mature themes, profanity, violence) Theatrical Aspect Ratio: 1.85:1

Clint Eastwood's *Midnight in the Garden of Good and Evil* is a compelling but meandering tale of lust, murder, sex, voodoo, and betrayal. Despite the presence of so many titillating elements, the film's nearly somnambulant pace makes it easy for a viewer to lose his or her concentration.

Midnight in the Garden is the story of New York journalist John Kelso (John Cusack), who travels to Savannah when *Town and Country* magazine hires him to write a story about the much-ballyhooed annual Christmas bash held by millionaire Jim Williams (Kevin Spacey). After a brief discussion with Jim's football-loving lawyer, Sonny Seiler (Jack Thompson), John meets Jim, who turns out to be a suave, appealing gentleman with extravagant tastes. The writer is given a brief tour of Jim's opulent house, which was built by the grandfather of songwriter Johnny Mercer. Over the course of the next twenty-four hours, as he waits for the party to begin, John meets some of the locals: a man who walks an imaginary dog, a sexy young woman named Mandy (Alison Eastwood), an attorney-turned-housesitter (Joe Odom), and the brash, cocky Billy Hanson (Jude Law), who is Jim's lover. Then, suddenly, after the party, when John is getting ready to go home, *Midnight in the Garden* turns into a murder story. Jim shoots and kills Billy under mysterious circumstances, and the question of his innocence is put before a jury. John, seeing the potential to expand his short article into a full-length book, begins his own investigation of the incident, and his detective work leads him to two more unusual citizens of Savannah: transvestite Lady Chablis (playing herself) and Minerva (Irma P. Hall), a voodoo priestess.

Midnight in the Garden demands a certain temperament to enjoy a long, unhurried experience like this. And, while the movie doesn't succeed in effectively developing all of the subplots and secondary themes in its complex tapestry, its main point — that morality is a relative, not an absolute, quantity — is presented in a striking fashion. With *Midnight in the Garden of Good and Evil,* Eastwood has captured a peculiar yet involving slice of life. **RECOMMENDED**

Mifune [Denmark/Sweden, 1999]

Starring: Iben Hjejle, Anders W. Berthelsen, Jesper Asholt, Emil Tarding, Anders Hove, Sofie Gråbøl Director: Søren Kragh-Jacobsen Screenplay: Søren Kragh-Jacobsen, Anders Thomas Jensen Running Time: 1:38 Rated: R (Profanity, sexual situations, violence) Theatrical Aspect Ratio: 1.66:1 In Danish with subtitles

It's refreshing to see a movie in which there are no special effects, no camera tricks, and no incidental music to strum on a viewer's emotional strings. These are some (but certainly not all) of the tenets of Dogma 95, the much-ballyhooed "cinematic vow of chastity" taken by four Danish directors, one of whom, Søren Kragh-Jacobsen, is responsible for this film.

Mifune takes its title from the name of the legendary Japanese actor Toshiro Mifune, who starred in many of Akira Kurosawa's films, including the classic *The Seven Samurai.* Mifune died around the time that this movie, then simply called *Dogma 3,* was going into production. Director Kragh-Jacobsen decided that he wanted to find a way to honor Mifune's memory, and so was born a storyline in which one character dresses up as a Samurai named "Mifune" in order to please his mentally retarded brother. That's how a Danish film came to be named after a Japanese icon.

Mifune opens with a wedding. Kresten (Anders W. Berthelsen) is marrying Claire (Sofie Gråbøl), a domineering woman who happens to be the daughter of Kresten's boss. The two haven't been united in marital bliss for long when Kresten receives a phone call: his father has died and he has to return home to care for his brother, Rud (Jesper Asholt), and to prepare the funeral. All of this comes as a great surprise to Claire, who didn't realize that her husband had any

surviving family. She offers to accompany him, but Kresten doesn't want her meeting Rud (whom he views as an embarrassment) or seeing the seedy, run-down farm where he grew up and from which he fled. When he arrives, the place is in a mess, as is his brother. Looking for someone to help clean up as well as to babysit Rud, Kresten places a newspaper ad for a housekeeper. The only one who responds is Liva (Iben Hjejle), a young, attractive blond who is running from demons of her own. She is a prostitute who is fed up with selling her body just to keep her ungrateful brother, Bjarke (Emil Tarding), in boarding school.

Some have argued that the tenets embraced by Dogma 95 amount to little more than a marketing tool — an attempt by a group of underappreciated Danish directors to obtain wider distribution for low-budget motion pictures. And, while there may be some truth to those charges, there's no denying the artistic and entertainment value of a movie like *Mifune.* **RECOMMENDED**

Moll Flanders [Ireland/United States, 1996]

Starring: Robin Wright, Morgan Freeman, Stockard Channing, Brenda Fricker, John Lynch Director: Pen Densham Screenplay: Pen Densham based on the character devised by Daniel Defoe Running Time: 2:02 Rated: PG-13 (Violence, nudity, mature themes) Theatrical Aspect Ratio: 2.35:1

Literature purists are likely to have an apoplexy when faced with Pen Densham's *Moll Flanders.* Very little of Daniel Defoe's novel has survived in Densham's screenplay, with the notable exceptions of the time period, the lead character's name, and a few plot points. However this free adaptation is not an embarrassment to either the original author or the production team.

The narrative structure is unnecessarily clumsy. The film opens with the ever-faithful Hibble (Morgan Freeman), a onetime acquaintance of Moll's, rescuing her 9-year-old daughter, Flora (Aisling Corcoran), from an orphanage. While taking Flora on the long trek across the Atlantic Ocean from Europe to America, Hibble relates the mother's story to the daughter. Thus, through flashbacks, we are introduced to the life and times of Moll Flanders.

As a young woman on the streets of London, Moll (Robin Wright) is in desperate need of food and shelter. The red lantern of a whorehouse beckons, and soon Moll is working for the establishment's proprietress, Mrs. Allworthy (Stockard Channing). By respecting a secret that she learns about Hibble, Moll earns the man's friendship and trust. Later, after falling in love with one of her clients, a painter (John Lynch), Moll finds a way out of the bordello.

Though this may sound like the stuff of an historical romance novel, *Moll Flanders* is actually more substantial than that. Eighteenth-century England is a place of violence and disease, both of which are shown in gruesome, and somewhat graphic, detail. As was true of *The Horseman on the Roof,* we aren't left with pretty illusions about the delights of living during this era. It was a hard time, when women of no means had to resort to prostitution to survive, and epidemics of fatal diseases stalked city streets. *Moll Flanders* is a thoughtful and subdued attempt to document this. **RECOMMENDED**

Mona Lisa [United Kingdom, 1986]

Starring: Bob Hoskins, Cathy Tyson, Michael Caine, Robbie Coltrane, Sammi Davis Director: Neil Jordan Screenplay: Neil Jordan, David Leland Running Time: 1:44 Rated: R (Sexual themes, violence, profanity, nudity) Theatrical Aspect Ratio: 1.85:1

Although Cathy Tyson's character, the prostitute Simone, is the representation of the Mona Lisa in Neil Jordan's *Mona Lisa,* the central character is an everyman named George, played by Bob Hoskins. It is George's obsession for Simone that validates the title. For him, she is the Mona Lisa — beautiful, mysterious, and unattainable. From his limited contact with her, and based on the stories she tells him (some true, some not), he concocts an image of the woman he wants her to be. In the end, when he discovers that the reality is nothing like his fantasy, he is stunned and hurt.

Jordan has skillfully developed this story not only to examine George's fascination for Simone, but to dissect their relationship. Although Simone does not return George's feelings, she is attuned to them, and uses them to her own ends. But she does not think harshly of George. He is kind towards her, and she appreciates that. Both of them need each other, albeit in different ways, so, in a sense, the relationship is mutually beneficial. But, in the end, once Simone has gotten what she wants, George realizes that he can never have what he hoped for.

The story takes place in the seedier parts of London. George has just been released from a lengthy term in prison. His first stop is to visit his old home. Initially, his daughter doesn't seem to recognize him, but his ex-wife does, and she throws him out. At that point, an old friend of George's, Tommy (Robbie Coltrane), shows up and offers his mate a place to

sleep. On the way back to Tommy's, George stops in at a bar to find Mortwell (Michael Caine). It seems that his prison term was in some way connected to this man, and he feels that he is owed something. Mortwell's henchman gives George work as the driver for Simone (Cathy Tyson), a local prostitute.

The initial meeting between George and Simone is not promising. By virtue of her profession, George sees her as somewhere below him on the social scale, and is contemptuous of being ordered around by her. His coarse manner irritates Simone, and his careless approach to dressing offends her sensibilities (for her, a high priced call girl, clothes are everything). But Simone immediately recognizes something in George that can satisfy a need she has, and she sets about trying to win his confidence, first by buying him expensive suits, and then by telling him her life's story. George responds as she knows he will — by offering to help her. He soon learns that Simone is in trouble. An ex-pimp is anxious to cut her face, and Mortwell is somehow involved.

In an era when movies about love almost always invariably devolve into formulaic affairs, Neil Jordan's *Mona Lisa* stands out as an often-surprising, multi-layered achievement. By offering a rumination on a wide variety of love — real, imagined, romantic, sexual, and platonic — *Mona Lisa* defies easy categorization and offers a complex and superior 100 minutes for all who view it. **MUST SEE**

Monsoon Wedding [India/United States/Italy/France, 2001]

Starring: Naseeruddin Shah, Lillete Dubey, Shefali Shetty, Vijay Raaz, Tilotama Shom Director: Mira Nair Screenplay: Sabrina Dhawan Running Time: 1:54 Rated: R (Mature themes, profanity) Theatrical Aspect Ratio: 1.85:1

Monsoon Wedding, an infectious celebration of life and love, is an effort from Indian director Mira Nair (*Salaam Bombay!, Mississippi Masala, Kama Sutra*). Throwing caution to the wind with an invitation to the hedonist in us all, Nair has constructed this motion picture in such a way that even the most cynical curmudgeon with find himself or herself smiling at one time or another.

The primary story concerns the impending nuptials of Aditi (Vasundhara Das) and Hemant (Parvin Dabas), a couple who are getting to know one another after agreeing to participate in an arranged marriage. Aditi is a lively young woman who is trying to conclude a dead-end relationship with her boss. Hemant is an engineer who lives in Houston, Texas and is interested in finding a bride who shares his roots and heritage. As Aditi and Hemant are forging a fragile bond, Aditi's boss predatorily moves back into the picture and threatens both the marriage and Aditi's future happiness.

Complementing Aditi's story are a pair of other tales — one dark and one light. The wedding coordinator, Dubey (Vijay Raaz), suddenly and unexpectedly falls for the shy and insecure Alice (Tilotama Shome), Aditi's maid. Their gentle, tentative courtship is presented with a mixture of humor and tenderness. Meanwhile, Aditi's cousin, Ria (Shefali Shetty), reveals a malignant secret she has kept for nearly 2 decades about how she was sexually abused as a child by a family member who may be attempting to repeat the offense with another young girl.

Most of *Monsoon Wedding* is frothy and enjoyable, with the lush, varied music of Mychael Danna heightening the delicious sense of celebration. (Nair's film borrows from the Bollywood tradition of incorporating vivid musical numbers into the main story.) Visually, the film also tantalizes the senses, with nearly every scene offering a riot of color. Ria's story provides the dramatic glue that keeps the film grounded — the theme of sexual abuse is treated sensitively, but nothing can hold this irrepressible motion picture down for long.

The actors all do fine jobs, especially lovely Vasundhara Das as Aditi. But the real star of this movie is its director, who, in cooperation with screenwriter Sabrina Dhawan, has crafted the kind of motion picture that represents 2 hours of pure, unfettered joy. Typically, movies that offer this much fun do so because they are mindless and inconsequential. Nothing could be further from the truth where *Monsoon Wedding* is concerned. This film manages to be delightful without insulting the characters or the audience. **RECOMMENDED**

Monster's Ball [2001]

Starring: Billy Bob Thornton, Halle Berry, Peter Boyle, Heath Ledger, Sean Combs, Coronji Calhoun Director: Marc Forster Screenplay: Milo Addica & Will Rokos Running Time: 1:51 Rated: R (Sex, nudity, profanity) Theatrical Aspect Ratio: 2.35:1

Monster's Ball is a powerful and poignant motion picture not about racism and redemption, as one might initially suppose, but about one of the most urgent and universal of human needs — that of finding solace for pain and loneliness. Though it has some of the trappings of an interracial romance, *Monster's Ball* is not that, either. The sex in this movie is not a precursor to love; it is a means by which two people can find

temporary refuge from their otherwise bleak existences. An orgasm is an effective way to wipe away everything else, if only for a few moments.

Coincidence forms the fulcrum of *Monster's Ball's* storyline. The principle male character is Hank Grotowski (Billy Bob Thornton), a corrections officer who is greatly respected at work, but whose home life is a disaster. It's hard to say whether he has a worse relationship with his surly, racist father (Peter Boyle) or his soft-hearted son (Heath Ledger). Hank is charged with supervising the execution of death-row inmate Lawrence Musgrove (Sean Combs), a cop killer who has exhausted 11 years' worth of appeals. Lawrence has a son, Tyrell (Coronji Calhoun), who idolizes him, and a wife, Leticia (Halle Berry), who can't stand him. Following the execution, both Hank and Leticia suffer shocking, unexpected tragedies, and, in the wake of one of these, they are thrown together. And, because they happen to be there, they turn to each other.

This is a brave movie requiring courageous performances. With this role, Halle Berry sheds years of lightweight baggage and a deserved Oscar win. Billy Bob Thornton matches her intensity pace-for-pace. These two radiate neediness and anguish. We can see their inner torment mirrored in their eyes and faces. The hand of Job is upon them both.

Hank is, in many ways, an ugly individual. He is a racist who has inherited his feelings from his father. As the film wears on, his tolerance for blacks grows. This is not the result of some sudden enlightenment, but because the passion necessary to sustain prejudice has drained out of him. Leticia, too, is no angel, either. She abuses her son, both verbally and physically, because he eats too much. She has trouble keeping her job and is on the verge of being evicted from her home.

This is the second feature from director Marc Forster, whose debut, *Everything Put Together*, was never widely seen outside of the film festival circuit. Thus, *Monster's Ball* has become Forster's calling card, and it makes a bold statement. **HIGHLY RECOMMENDED**

Monument Ave. [1998]

Starring: Denis Leary, Ian Hart, Jason Barry, John Diehl, Famke Janssen, Colm Meaney, Billy Crudup Director: Ted Demme Screenplay: Mike Armstrong Running Time: 1:30 Rated: R (Violence, profanity) Theatrical Aspect Ratio: 1.66:1

Monument Ave. is set in Boston's Charlestown neighborhood, where the influx of yuppies and "new money" is threatening to stifle the old, established

Irish community which has been in place for decades. The film is a study of the ways that the men and women of Charlestown respond to internal and external pressures — how they close ranks, shut their mouths, and mete out their own brand of justice. Outside help is not wanted; in fact, it is met with anger and resistance. *Monument Ave.* examines how a series of volatile incidents bring the current social situation to a boil.

The boss in the blue collar community is Jackie O'Hara (Colm Meaney), a tough guy who doesn't challenge many Irish gangster clichés. In his view, there's just one unpardonable sin: disloyalty. When a local boy, Teddy (Billy Crudup) gets out of prison early because he is suspected of having ratted on Jackie, the older man has him gunned down in a pub, then appears at the funeral with words of comfort for the family and a few dollars to cover the expenses. Feelings for Jackie in the neighborhood are complex — he is feared and respected, but nearly everyone resents his all-encompassing control.

Bobby O'Grady (Denis Leary) and Mouse Murphy (Ian Hart) are a couple of working stiffs trapped by the daily grind that is life in Charlestown. With their dull-witted cab driver friend, Digger (John Diehl), and Bobby's cousin from Dublin, Seamus (Jason Barry), they form a quartet that steals new cars from the cross-town yuppies and turns them over to Jackie's chop shop. These nightly forays provide them with enough cash to fuel a substantial cocaine habit. However, when Teddy is killed while enjoying a drink in their company, Bobby's anger towards Jackie begins to simmer, and the arrival of a cop from the outside (Martin Sheen) adds another wild card to an increasingly-unstable situation.

Stories about closed communities ruled by shady types represent fairly standard motion picture fare, especially on the independent circuit. Several such features are released each year, and, after a while, they all tend to blur together. With fresh dialogue and a willingness to show his protagonists in a less-than-favorable light, Demme has found a way to make this entry memorable. **RECOMMENDED**

Mr. Holland's Opus [1995]

Starring: Richard Dreyfuss, Glenne Headly, Olympia Dukakis, W.H. Macy, Jay Thomas, Alicia Witt, Jean Louisa Kelly Director: Stephen Herek Screenplay: Patrick Duncan Running Time: 2:22 Rated: PG (Mild language) Theatrical Aspect Ratio: 2.35:1

Mr. Holland's Opus, a Capra-esque motion picture in its sentimentality, persuades its audience that no life

spent in a worthy pursuit is ever wasted. However it doesn't stoop to heavy-handed proselytizing.

Mr. Holland's Opus spans 31 years in the life of a high school music teacher. When Glenn Holland (Richard Dreyfuss) first comes to the newly-dedicated JFK High School in 1964, he has a dream of spending a few years teaching to accumulate a nest egg, then returning to his true passion: composing. His loving wife, Iris (Glenne Headly) is completely supportive — until she becomes pregnant. After that unexpected event, teaching is no longer just Glenn's "fall back position." It has become his means to provide for his family.

Yet Glenn finds that instructing students in music appreciation has its rewards. When lectures and text assignments don't fire his pupils' passion for the subject, Glenn tries unique ways of encouraging an understanding that "playing music is supposed to be fun — it's about heart . . . not notes on a page." Repeatedly during his 3 decades of teaching, Glenn chooses boys and girls with special skills to nurture and encourage. In the process, he creates a deep loyalty among JFK's student body while straining the harmony of his home life. His wife and son wonder if Glenn cares more about his pupils than about them.

The musical metaphors in *Mr. Holland's Opus* are rather obvious, and the soundtrack is an effective mix of pop tunes, classical compositions, and Michael Kamen's score.

In recent years, it has become common practice for movie studios to release at least one emotionally stirring drama around the holiday season. Flaws aside, one common element in these films is that each focuses on the triumph of the human spirit, using a story that seeks to touch the heart. *Mr. Holland's Opus* deserves a place in their ranks. It's a symphony of solid storytelling and good feeling that pays tribute to Hollywood's rarely-seen, gentler side.
HIGHLY RECOMMENDED

Mrs. Brown [United Kingdom, 1997]

Starring: Judi Dench, Billy Connolly, Geoffrey Palmer, Richard Pasco, Anthony Sher Director: John Madden Screenplay: Jeremy Brock Running Time: 1:43 Rated: PG (Mature themes, violence) Theatrical Aspect Ratio: 1.85:1

Mrs. Brown is a love story much in the same vein as *Carrington* in that it deals with platonic affection that runs deeper and truer than that of the motion picture staple romantic variety. These days, it seems that whenever we see a male/female friendship on screen, it's just a setup for the inevitable moment when the two realize that they're fated to be lovers. Not so with *Mrs. Brown*. It shows, amongst other things, that it's possible to love completely and with unflagging devotion without sex ever becoming an issue.

Queen Victoria was born on May 24, 1819 and died nearly 82 years later, in the first month of 1901. Her reign as England's monarch, which began in 1837, lasted more than 6 decades and left such an indelible impression upon the country that, upon hearing of her death, author Henry James wrote, "We all feel a bit motherless today." *Mrs. Brown*, which is based on actual events and uses historical figures, transpires during one of the darkest periods of Victoria's reign — a 4-year segment from 1864 to 1868 (with a brief epilogue in 1883). Still mourning the death of her beloved husband, Prince Albert, who died over 2 years earlier, the Queen (Judi Dench) is in virtual seclusion at Windsor. She sees no one outside of her servants and her immediate family, rarely goes out, and has no taste for politics. In the words of her loyal secretary, Henry Posonby (Geoffrey Palmer), they are all "prisoners of the queen's grief." So, in an attempt to revive Victoria, Posonby summons John Brown (Billy Connolly), the highlander who runs the queen's Scottish retreat of Balmoral, to Windsor. It's Posonby's hope that Brown will "appeal to the queen's sentimental belief that all highlanders are good for the health."

Brown arrives and proves to be a breath of fresh air. Before he enters Windsor, the castle is a place of icy silence and solitude. Director John Madden so effectively conveys this atmosphere that we become keenly aware of such things as a ticking clock and a cleared throat. Brown's attitude of speaking what he thinks, regardless of the consequences, horrifies the servants and family. But, after initially being annoyed, Victoria warms to his methods, and it isn't long before the two develop a unshakable friendship. They become so close, in fact, that wags begin calling the Queen "Mrs. Brown." The Prince of Wales, wary of Brown's growing influence over his mother, seeks to have the highlander sent back to Scotland. And the Prime Minister, Disraeli, wonders whether Brown is more likely to be a valuable ally or a dangerous enemy.

Perhaps the best thing of all about *Mrs. Brown* is that it doesn't offer any hokey, Hollywood-type moments. *Mrs. Brown* is a fascinating character study, a wonderful love story, and a brilliant period piece that will delight and touch any viewer who seeks it out.
HIGHLY RECOMMENDED

Mrs. Dalloway [United Kingdom, 1997]
Starring: Vanessa Redgrave, Natascha McElhone, Rupert Graves, Michael Kitchen, John Standing Director: Marleen Gorris
Screenplay: Eileen Atkins based on the novel by Virginia Woolf
Running Time: 1:37 Rated: PG-13 (Mature themes, brief nudity)
Theatrical Aspect Ratio: 1.85:1

In 1996, director Marleen Gorris, who hails from the Netherlands, entered the international spotlight when her 1995 feature, *Antonia's Line*, won the Best Foreign Film Oscar. Two years later, Gorris' follow-up to that much-lauded effort arrived in the form of *Mrs. Dalloway*, an adaptation of Virginia Woolf's classic novel. Because of its strong leading character and female-oriented themes, it's easy to understand why the film held such appeal for an avowed feminist like Gorris. In conjunction with Vanessa Redgrave, the director paints a probing-but-flawed portrait of a thoughtful woman.

Mrs. Dalloway is a "day in the life" motion picture that uses flashbacks to broaden the time span from a single day in June 1923 to a lifetime. The film begins by introducing viewers to Clarissa Dalloway, the upper class wife of Richard Dalloway (John Standing), a wealthy Member of Parliament. Clarissa, who lives a life that is safe, isolated, and dull, is planning a gala party for the evening. Clarissa is well-known for her parties, and they have become social events in London society. Then something happens to shatter the stillness of Mrs. Dalloway's life — a man named Peter Walsh (Michael Kitchen), an old flame from 30 years ago, shows up on her doorstep. This leads Clarissa to think back to the choices she made during the summer of 1890, and how they shaped the rest of her life.

Juxtaposed with Mrs. Dalloway's story is that of a young, shell-shocked soldier, Septimus Warren-Smith (Rupert Graves), who has never recovered from his experiences in World War I. This material, although thematically relevant to the main plot, causes unwanted interruptions in the narrative that threaten to derail the picture. Graves plays the part effectively, and the story of the young man's loss of identity is tragic, but I found the Warren-Smith scenes to be more of a distraction than a crucial subplot.

Not surprisingly, the acting is top-notch. Redgrave shines, whether she's gazing back through the mists of the past or, in the film's best sequence, making pithy asides to expose the true nature of the guests at her party. Michael Kitchen and John Standing are solid as the two men who were once rivals for Clarissa's affections, and who have changed very little over time. In flashbacks, Natascha McElhone (*Surviving Picasso*) brings a sparkle to the young Clarissa, and Alan Cox cuts a dashing figure as Peter. The 1890 scenes also feature Lena Headley as Clarissa's best friend, and there are hints of a subtle lesbian attraction.

Mrs. Dalloway will probably appeal most strongly to those who appreciate Merchant-Ivory's unhurried pace. The story, which is more of a character study than a plot-oriented narrative, moves slowly and deliberately, giving us a crystal-clear picture of the many faces of Clarissa Dalloway — who she was, who she might have been, and who she has become. **RECOMMENDED**

Mrs. Parker and the Vicious Circle [1994]

Starring: Jennifer Jason Leigh, Campbell Scott, Matthew Broderick, Gwyneth Paltrow Director: Alan Rudolph Screenplay: Alan Rudolph and Randy Sue Coburn Running Time: 2:04 Rated: R (Sex, nudity, language, mature themes) Theatrical Aspect Ratio: 2.35:1

Mrs. Parker and the Vicious Circle is set primarily against the backdrop of the roaring '20s, with critic/poet/writer Dorothy Parker (Jennifer Jason Leigh) as the centerpiece. Parker was by far the best known female member of the famed Algonquin Round Table — a collection of journalists, actors, writers, and other artists who gathered daily for lunch at a 44th Street Manhattan hotel. Also included in the membership of this exclusive circle were Robert Benchley (Campbell Scott), Harold Ross (Sam Robards), and Charles MacArthur (Matthew Broderick). Among their successes, the Algonquin clique could claim Pulitzer Prizes, Oscars, successful stage shows, and bestselling books. To the outside world, they were celebrities; to some on the inside, they were "just a bunch of loudmouths showing off."

Dorothy Parker is perhaps best remembered for her tart sayings and pithy turns of phrase, and that's the tone that this movie initially adopts — playful and clipped. However, as the screenplay delves beneath the surface of its lead character's personality, a grim, more serious mood becomes pervasive, turning Dorothy's witticisms into self-contemptuous jabs or cries for help.

Arguments can be made about the historical accuracy of the film. Many of the events related herein are based on Parker's own statements, and she was notorious for exaggerating — if not outright lying —

about her past. Regardless of how faithfully it records its title character's life, however, *Mrs. Parker and the Vicious Circle* is a top-notch movie. Everything is in place — a striking lead performance from Jennifer Jason Leigh, solid supporting players, a well-written script, and, above all, expert direction to merge the ingredients. In a case like this, "truth" may not be the most important factor to consider in the overall evaluation. **HIGHLY RECOMMENDED**

Murder in the First [1995]

Starring: Christian Slater, Kevin Bacon, Gary Oldman, R. Lee Ermey, Embeth Davidtz Director: Marc Rocco Screenplay: Dan Gordon Running Time: 2:01 Rated: R (Violence, torture, mature themes, language) Theatrical Aspect Ratio: Not Given

Murder in the First is another example of a movie that strays from historical reality to create a more dramatically-appealing product. And, regardless of how this version raises the hackles of Alcatraz aficionados, Marc Rocco's movie is a solid and affecting example of film making.

It's March 25, 1938, and an escape attempt from the maximum security federal penitentiary at Alcatraz has failed. Two of the 4 escapees are dead, a third — the informant — is returned to his cell, and the fourth — a 25-year-old named Henri Young (Kevin Bacon) — is placed into a dark, grimy cubicle deep beneath the ground. There, for 3 interminable years, his only respite from loneliness are the frequent visits of guards and Associate Warden Glenn (Gary Oldman), and the beatings they administer.

When his long stint in solitary confinement ends and Young is re-integrated into normal prison society, revenge consumes him — a need to lash out against the man who blew the whistle on the escape. This he does, driving a spoon through the victim's throat, tearing away his life. With no regard for the barbaric treatment which turned a petty thief into a killer, the government tries Young for first-degree murder — a crime that carries a death sentence. Assigned to defend him is an up-and-coming member of the public defender's office named James Stamphill (Christian Slater), perhaps the only man to believe in his client's innocence.

Murder in the First is as much an indictment of the penal system as an account of one man's fight against a first degree murder rap, and that's where the picture's strength lies. The events leading to Young's actions are graphically rendered, and little doubt remains about where the responsibility lies. The questions that arise are whether Stamphill can prove it and, in the process, how much of his personal security he's willing to sacrifice.

Unlike *The Shawshank Redemption*, this movie isn't about triumph behind prison bars. Instead, *Murder in the First* is an unrelenting look at the dehumanizing effects of prison life, and what can happen when power is abused. Some scenes may be too graphic for audience members to view comfortably, but "comfort" isn't on director Rocco's agenda. Little that occurs towards the end to affect a false sense of dramatic closure reduces the power of bearing witness to the exposure of Henri Young's soul — or what's left after Glenn and Alcatraz have finished with it. **RECOMMENDED**

My Family [1995]

Starring: Jimmy Smits, Eduardo Lopez Rojas, Jenny Gago, Edward James Olmos, Esai Morales Director: Gregory Nava Screenplay: Gregory Nava and Anna Thomas Running Time: 2:07 Rated: R (Violence, profanity, sex, nudity) Theatrical Aspect Ratio: 1.85:1 In English with Spanish subtitles

My Family, a portrait of a Mexican-American family living in East Los Angeles, boasts a series of distinguished thematic antecedents, including Francis Ford Coppola's *The Godfather* and Zhang Yimou's *To Live*. Here, as in the 1972 gangster saga, the significance of family is a central issue, although each movie chooses to explore this differently.

My Family opens in 1926 Mexico, as Jose Sanchez heads north to California to find a long-lost relative. Once there, he meets and marries Maria, who bears him a son and daughter. She is pregnant with their third child when immigration officials illegally deport her. The rest of this segment concentrates on her attempts to return to her husband and family.

The 1958 and 1980s episodes present the fortunes of two of the Sanchez children: Chucho (Esai Morales) and Jimmy (Jimmy Smits). Chucho is a brash youth who leads a gang, incurs the wrath of his father when he sells marijuana, and is constantly skirting trouble with the police. Jimmy idolizes his older brother and eventually follows in his footsteps, but the underlying pain of one shared, tragic moment haunts Jimmy's future. It is only during a watershed scene, when the anger and grief are released, that Jimmy is able to agree that "tomorrow matters."

My Family is amazingly rich, with themes that are topical-yet-timeless, a solidly constructed story to give them vitality, and superlative production values. Cinematographer Edward Lachman has photographed all three eras differently, and his visual flair adds another layer to this production. *My Family* gives us culture shock and class distinctions, metaphors involving owls and bridges, and the struggle between traditional values and modern ethics. It never dwells on gang violence, crime, or racism; but ignores none of these three. Above all, however, it is faithful to its title, presenting the newest portrait of an ancient truth — of all the ties that bind humans to each other, none is more lasting than that of birth and blood. **HIGHLY RECOMMENDED**

My Life So Far [United Kingdom, 1999]

Starring: Robbie Norman, Colin Firth, Rosemary Harris, Irène Jacob, Tchéky Karyo, Mary Elizabeth Mastrantonio, Malcolm McDowell Director: Hugh Hudson Screenplay: Simon Donald, based on *Son of Adam* by Sir Denis Forman Running Time: 1:33 Rated: PG-13 (Mature themes, brief nudity, animal sex) Theatrical Aspect Ratio: 1.85:1

My Life So Far is a pleasantly nostalgic look at a few transformative months in the life of a 10-year-old Scottish boy. *My Life So Far* provides 90 minutes of solid entertainment that runs the gamut from outright hilarity to melodrama. The film doesn't offer many surprises or deep insights into human nature, but it possesses an easygoing charm and likability that overcomes such potential deficiencies.

The place is Argyll, Scotland. The time is the late-1920s, a "safe" era in Europe when the horrors of the Great War are receding into the past and Hitler's proclamations are not yet shaking the firmament. Fraser Pettigrew (Robbie Norman) is an average child growing up in a somewhat abnormal household. He lives with his family on the estate of Kiloran, a vast, sprawling piece of the countryside that houses The Pettigrew Sphagnum Moss Factory. Fraser's father, Edward (Colin Firth), is an unsuccessful inventor with two passions: Beethoven and the Bible. He has a deep and abiding love for his children, and shares a special bond with Fraser. Also living in Kiloran Castle are Edward's wife, Moira (Mary Elizabeth Mastrantonio), and his mother-in-law, Gamma Macintosh (Rosemary Harris), who owns the land. Moira's brother, Morris (Malcolm McDowell), is a frequent visitor. His relationship with Edward is stormy but he gets along well with his nephews. The catalyst for change is the arrival of Morris' finacée, a French cellist named Heloise (Irène Jacob), who is half her intended husband's age. Fraser develops a childlike crush on the beautiful, soft-spoken woman, but Edward's infatuation is of a more adult, and potentially damaging, nature.

During the course of *My Life So Far,* Fraser learns truths about hypocrisy, death, and sex. He spends quite a bit of time in an attic, looking at pictures of naked women and reading through an "Encyclopedia of Ethics" that elaborates subjects he doesn't always understand. His incomplete comprehension of the activities performed by a prostitute leads to an uproarious scene that is as funny as anything this side of *American Pie.* Fraser also enjoys bath time, because it gives him an opportunity to peek down the dress of the maid who bathes him, an experience he describes as being "better than looking at the pictures."

My Life So Far features many beautiful shots of the Scottish countryside as it tells the story of a group of generally well-detailed characters traipsing through a series of anecdotes. The film doesn't so much unravel a traditional narrative as it allows us to roam around for a short while in a different time and place. The difference between success and failure for a picture of this sort is whether the filmmakers engage the audience's attention and sympathy, and provoke an emotional response. With *My Life So Far,* Hudson's ability to meet those criteria makes this a rewarding movie-going experience. RECOMMENDED

My Name Is Joe [United Kingdom, 1998]
Starring: Peter Mullan, Louise Goodall, David McKay, Anne-Marie Kennedy, David Hayman, Gary Lewis Director: Ken Loach Screenplay: Paul Laverty Running Time: 1:45 Rated: R (Extreme profanity, drug use, brief nudity) Theatrical Aspect Ratio: 1.85:1

Movie-goers attend Ken Loach movies for a variety of reasons, but one of them is not to have a "feel good" experience. The reason? Loach consistently looks at believable characters in realistic situations. His pictures are not escapist; they're frequently grim and sometimes downright depressing. They're about the trials and tribulations of those who engage in back-breaking labor on a daily basis trying to scrape enough together to put bread on the table. They're about men and women trapped by poverty and a social system that doesn't care whether they live or die. And they're about the sometimes-tragic consequences of the actions some people take in a vain attempt to liberate themselves from their circumstances. (A few titles: *Riff-Raff, Raining Stones, Ladybird Ladybird,* and *Land and Freedom.*)

My Name Is Joe is perhaps in some way Ken Loach's most accessible film. As the title suggests, the name of the main character is Joe — Joe Kavanagh, to be precise. Joe is a recovering alcoholic who has been on the wagon for 10 months. A believer in the 12-step program, he attends AA meetings regularly where he speaks his mantra: "My name is Joe and I'm an alcoholic." Actor Peter Mullan, who plays Joe, gives a tremendously natural, Oscar-caliber performance. His Joe is a boisterous, likable fellow — the kind of guy we all wish could be our neighbor.

Joe is the coach of a perennially inept soccer team, and, although he acts as a father-figure to all of the young men, he has taken a special interest in Liam (David McKay), a former drug dealer who is trying to walk the straight-and-narrow. Liam has a heroin-addicted wife, Sabine (Anne-Marie Kennedy), and a 4-year-old son, and his financial situation is hopeless. Sabine's habit has put him deep in debt to a local mobster, McGowan (David Hayman), and, if he can't pay, he has two choices: let McGowan pimp Sabine or get both of his legs broken. Meanwhile, Joe has become involved with Liam and Sabine's health visitor, Sarah (Louise Goodall). Although she resists his initial advances, Joe's reckless charm eventually wins her over, but dark times loom ahead.

Although addiction is a key element of *My Name Is Joe,* the movie is not as much about substance abuse as it is about accepting the consequences of one's actions. The greatest strength of *My Name Is Joe* is the sense of stark reality. The humor and tragedy are presented without a whiff of melodrama, and the movie will leave almost any viewer with a sense of disquiet. If the definition of a great film is a picture with two memorable scenes and no bad ones, then *My Name Is Joe* unquestionably makes the cut. HIGHLY RECOMMENDED

The Myth of Fingerprints [1996]
Starring: Noah Wyle, Julianne Moore, Roy Scheider, Blythe Danner, Michael Vartan, Laurel Holloman, Hope Davis Director: Bart Freundlich Screenplay: Bart Freundlich Running Time: 1:33 Rated: R (Sex, profanity, mature themes) Theatrical Aspect Ratio: 1.85:1

With *The Myth of Fingerprints,* writer/director Bart Freundlich has scored a coup: he has created a low-key holiday drama that's refreshing not only because it lacks the big discovery melodrama of most similar movies but because it's entirely believable.

The Myth of Fingerprints begins with the familiar process of the family re-assembling at Mom and Dad's New England house during Thanksgiving week. The only one who still lives with her parents (who are ably portrayed by Roy Scheider and Blythe Danner) is Leigh (Laurel Holloman), the sprightly youngest child who has a boundless well of enthusiasm and good cheer. The same cannot be said of most of the returning children. There's Warren (Noah Wyle) who hasn't been home in 3 years since breaking up with his high-school sweetheart (Arija Bareikis). The perpetually-cranky Mia (Julianne Moore) arrives with her latest significant other, therapist Elliot (Brian Kerwin), in tow. Their relationship is clearly on the rocks, and Mia's fascination with an old grade school pal (James LeGros) doesn't help matters. Jake (Michael Vartan) shows up with his flighty girlfriend, Margaret (Hope Davis), who amuses Jake's Mom by insisting that she and her boyfriend share the same bed.

At its best, *The Myth of Fingerprints* is a sensitive, intelligent examination of the dynamics of a dysfunctional family (note: families in movies like this must always be dysfunctional, otherwise there wouldn't be much of a story). At its worst, which isn't often, Freundlich's feature debut runs into difficulties with cliches: the overbearing father who has left his "fingerprints" on the lives of each of his offspring, the search by various couples to rekindle the old flame, etc.

The Myth of Fingerprints contains a number of noteworthy scenes, including some strangely quiet dinners and awkward moments between estranged siblings. But the best sequence occurs early in the film, on the night when everyone has finally assembled under one roof. One-by-one, the various couples begin to make love, and the concert of moans, thumps, and squeaks creates an atmosphere that is both poignant and funny, especially as we observe Warren's reaction to all the noise around him.

Nothing much happens during *The Myth of Fingerprints,* but that's the point. For 90 minutes, Freundlich opens a window into the lives of a few characters, and our perspective is so clear that we feel we get to know them. So, although the material is not especially challenging, the results are among the best for an American film of this genre. For those who appreciate this sort of simple drama, *The Myth of Fingerprints* is worth a trip to the theater. **RECOMMENDED**

Naked [United Kingdom, 1993]

Starring: **David Thewlis, Lesley Sharp, Katrin Cartlidge, Greg Cruttwell, Claire Skinner, Peter Wight** Director: **Mike Leigh** Screenplay: **Mike Leigh** Running Time: **2:12** Rated: **No MPAA Rating (Violence, sexual violence, language, sex, nudity)** Theatrical Aspect Ratio: **1.66:1**

Mike Leigh has always been known as a creator of exceptional, insightful character studies. Often, his films do little more than trace activities in the life of a person or persons over a several-day period. However, whereas comedies such as *Life is Sweet* and *High Hopes* showed Leigh's whimsical side, *Naked* is anything but charming. This movie is brutal and raw, and its sense of humor comes with a serrated edge.

We meet Johnny (David Thewlis) on the benighted streets of Manchester, pinning a woman against a building as he rapes her. Then, threatened with bodily harm, Johnny heads for London to find his old girlfriend, Louise (Lesley Sharp). Their reunion is less-than-affectionate, and propels Johnny into a violent and self-destructive sexual relationship with Louise's flatmate, Sophie (Katrin Cartlidge). Not long after, Johnny starts to feel trapped by his new lover's unexpected dependence, and he takes to the streets, wandering through the backways and alleys of the city's underprivileged districts (where a rat is always less than 30 feet away), meeting an assortment of people even more bizarre than himself.

There are so many thought-provoking themes and issues addressed by *Naked* that it's impossible to mention them all, let alone do them justice, in the space of a movie review. Johnny, despite having the appearance of a tramp, has the heart and mind of a philosopher, and isn't afraid to express his views. In line after line of energetic, dazzling dialogue delivered at a rapid-fire pace, we are exposed to the lead character's views on why everyone is bored, the importance of cliches, the interrelationship between the past, present, and future, the Apocalypse, evolution, God's relationship to man, and life in general. He's not particularly choosey about his listeners, entering into conversations with the vacuous Sophie, a middle-class guard named Brian (Peter Wight), a lonely woman who he initially observes from afar through a window, and a man putting up posters.

David Thewlis didn't get his deserved Oscar nomination, but his work here is extraordinary, and possibly better than that of any of the 5 nominees (including Anthony Hopkins). Thewlis creates an amazing character — someone with a keen intellect and ugly appetites, who can be reviled, understood, and respected.

Naked is one of those rare motion pictures that refuses to slip easily from memory. Its images and themes linger long after the viewer has left the theater. Those in search of escapism should not look to this motion picture, but anyone willing to assume the risk of facing the ugliness of Johnny's world will find a startling, gut-wrenching, eye-opening experience. **HIGHLY RECOMMENDED**

Nell [1994]

Starring: Jodie Foster, Liam Neeson, Natasha Richardson, Richard Libertini, Nick Searcy Director: Michael Apted Screenplay: William Nicholson and Mark Handley based on the play "Idioglossia" by Mark Handley Running Time: 1:52 Rated: PG-13 (Nudity, language) Theatrical Aspect Ratio: 2.35:1

In *Nell*, a lush, green world of rolling hills and crystal pools, technology is an unwelcome intruder; civilization, a threatening monster. Both are slaves to the avaricious. *Nell* is about the importance of communication and interaction, about how the events of childhood shape a life, and about the difficulty — and rewards — of reaching out to others.

Nell (Foster) has lived her entire life alone in the woods with an aging mother. She is eventually discovered by a local doctor, Jerome Lovell (Liam Neeson), who comes to her secluded, ramshackle hut after her mother's death. Nell's panicked and hostile response to strangers forces Jerome to travel to nearby Charlotte to recruit the expert assistance of Dr. Paula Olsen (Natasha Richardson). After meeting the young woman, Paula's impression is that Nell should be committed. Jerome, horrified by this possibility, obtains a court order to stop it. The two opposing sides eventually argue the case before a judge. Deferring his verdict for 3 months, the judge gives the two doctors that time to observe their subject, learn her language, and present him with enough evidence to make an informed decision.

Jodie Foster's Oscars are no fluke, as her simple-yet-profound performance in *Nell* illustrates. She is one of only a few actors capable of so fully immersing herself in a character that it's possible to forget the star behind the performance. With Jack Nicholson or Al Pacino, you watch a variation of the same personality; with Jodie Foster, you see a new individual.

Nell is an almost-childlike woman who speaks her own fractured form of English, hides inside her house by day, and takes moonlight swims in a nearby lake. In Jerome and Paula, she finds a substitute father and mother, and together, these three attempt to breach the non-physical walls between them. This, the real meat of *Nell,* is where the film attains its depth and richness.

It is difficult to deny *Nell*'s intelligence and sensitivity. We approach this story with the same fascination that Nell faces each day, seeing, if only for a short time, how different the world — and people — *can*

be. It is this impression more than any other that stays with the viewer after the drama has been played out and the final credits roll. **RECOMMENDED**

Nicholas Nickleby [United States/United Kingdom, 2002]

Starring: Charlie Hunnam, Jamie Bell, Christopher Plummer, Jim Broadbent, Anne Hathaway, Romola Garai Director: Douglas McGrath Screenplay: Douglas McGrath, based on the novel by Charles Dickens Running Time: 2:12 Rated: PG (Mature themes) Theatrical Aspect Ratio: 1.85:1

Writer/director Douglas McGrath has successfully condensed Charles Dickens' *Nicholas Nickleby* to the point where it can fit into a time span of less than $2\frac{1}{4}$ hours without doing irreparable damage to the story's essence. The narrative shows occasional hiccups, but, considering how it has been shoehorned, it is reasonably clear. This still *feels* like Dickens, perhaps because the best things about *Nicholas Nickleby* remain, including the uniquely Dickensian setting (19th century England) and characters.

The title character is played by British TV actor Charlie Hunnam, whose good looks prove not to be a detriment to his ability to play the 19-year old only son of a recently deceased country gentleman. When Nicholas' father dies, leaving behind a legacy of debt, the young man is forced to travel with his mother and sister, Kate (Romola Garai), to London to seek the assistance of Nicholas' uncle, Ralph (Christopher Plummer). A notorious miser with little concern for his poorer relations, Ralph nevertheless appears to show signs of humanity by securing a position for Nicholas as the assistant headmaster at a rural boys' school, working for Wackford Squeers (Jim Broadbent). Soon, however, Nicholas learns that his uncle has given him an unbearably odious job — Squeers is a sadist who delights in punishing the children in his charge. One day, when Squeers is beating the crippled boy Smike (Jamie Bell), Nicholas loses patience with the headmaster and turns the cane on him. He then departs, taking Smike with him. This action enrages Ralph, exacerbating his already prickly relationship with Nicholas and encouraging Ralph to take revenge upon Kate, who is under his "protection."

McGrath's *Nicholas Nickleby* is set up as a struggle of good, as personified by Nicholas, against evil, as represented by Ralph. Each of these characters has various allies, but the final struggle is between the two of them. The progression of the story is somewhat episodic, as is characteristic of many of Dickens' tales. Purists and die-hard aficionados of the novel may be dismayed by the manner in which it has been adapted, with all of the fat trimmed off (and, as I'm sure some will comment, some of the meat and bone with it), but, for a general movie-going audience, *Nicholas Nickleby* works. This is the engaging story of an upright man's quest to protect his family, find love, and see justice done. As a means to bring a classic novel to the attention of a modern audience, McGrath's *Nicholas Nickleby* is a success. **RECOMMENDED**

Night Falls on Manhattan [1997]

Starring: Andy Garcia, Ian Holm, Richard Dreyfuss, Lena Olin, James Gandolfini Director: Sidney Lumet Screenplay: Sydney Lumet based on the novel *Tainted Evidence* by Robert Daley Running Time: 1:55 Rated: R (Profanity, violence, mature themes) Theatrical Aspect Ratio: 1.85:1

With *Night Falls on Manhattan*, which is based on a fact-inspired novel by New York writer Robert Daley, director Sidney Lumet is in top form. The basic framework is familiar: corrupt cops, tainted evidence, and a big trial that will make or break the hotshot lawyer protagonist. But, if you think you've seen this story already, be prepared for more than one surprise.

Sean Casey (Andy Garcia) is an earnest young lawyer fresh out of school. A former cop, he's one of the few in his profession who still cares about the importance of justice. He goes to work as an assistant district attorney not because he views it as a stepping stone to the next plateau of his career, but because he cares about the cases. The situation becomes personal when his police detective father, Liam (Ian Holm), is shot in a drug bust gone bad. Liam is the lucky one — 3 of his fellow officers are dead. The suspect, a drug kingpin (Shiek Mahmud-Bey), turns himself in via a media circus that's carefully orchestrated by his attorney, Sam Vigoda (Richard Dreyfuss).

For the D.A., Morgenstern (Ron Leibman), it's an election year, and he decides on a risky strategy that, if it works, could give him a publicity edge. He chooses Sean to prosecute the case, with Liam as the star witness. The media goes wild with the story, Sean sees this as his big chance, and Liam is bursting with pride. But there's an obstacle — Vigoda is a brilliant lawyer, and he has an ax to grind. From the moment the defense attorney presents his opening argument, it's clear that his tactic will involve putting the entire N.Y.P.D. on trial.

Night Falls on Manhattan is savvy about a number of things. Not only does it have a good feel for both sides of the police corruption issue, but it's aware of the political rivalries and behind-the-scenes deal-making that keeps a city running. The script is smart, and the characters are better realized than their counterparts in countless similar-yet-inferior motion pictures. Sean may be the knight in shining armor trying to stay afloat in a sea of corruption, but it doesn't take long for him to recognize that survival demands compromise.

Sidney Lumet has done something that I wasn't sure was possible in this age of instant, formulaic gratification: make a riveting cop movie without a car chase and a courtroom thriller without cheap theatrics. *Night Falls on Manhattan* isn't about the trappings of these situations; it's about their inner workings, their underlying issues, and the men and women who keep things moving. **HIGHLY RECOMMENDED**

Nil By Mouth [United Kingdom, 1997]

Starring: Ray Winstone, Kathy Burke, Charlie Creed-Miles, Laila Morse, Edna Dore, Jamie Forman Director: Gary Oldman Screenplay: Gary Oldman Running Time: 2:08 Rated: R (Frequent, extreme profanity, violence, nudity, drug use) Theatrical Aspect Ratio: 1.66:1

There is a scene in *Nil by Mouth*, actor Gary Oldman's directorial debut, that is excruciatingly difficult to watch. It's not especially graphic, since the gruesome details take place out of frame, but anyone with an imagination can conjure up an image to chill the blood. The sequence depicts a particularly brutal instance of spousal abuse, and is perhaps only recently rivaled in intensity by a similar occurrence in *Once Were Warriors*.

From the beginning, it's clear that three elements are going to be critical to the events that transpire during *Nil by Mouth*: alcohol, drugs, and poverty. They are facts of life in contemporary South London, where the movie is set. Our first glimpse of the main character, Raymond (Ray Winstone, in a stunningly forceful performance), is in a pub where he and some friends are sitting around drinking lager and trading profane stories. Oldman allows the film to develop slowly, giving us a feel for Ray and his buddies. They are all victims of society, but do the best they can to get by, and use alcohol to dull the pain of not having any real purpose in life.

Ray is a family man. He has a wife, Valerie (a heartwrenching Kathy Burke, who won the Best Actress prize at the 1997 Cannes Film Festival), and a young daughter. But all is not well under his roof. When he has had a few pints, Ray is prone to explosive exhibits of violence. With little or no provocation, he will lash out at anyone in range. His favorite target is his wife's drug-addicted brother, Billy (Charlie

Creed-Miles), who lives with Ray's family. When Billy isn't around, there are other possibilities, including his wife. And, although Ray never harms his daughter physically, there is little doubt that his behavior leaves deep psychological scars.

Nil by Mouth does not sympathize with Ray, but it forces us to understand him. He is the product of a dysfunctional family and the son of a man who was incapable of expressing affection (the film's title refers to this). He loves his wife and daughter, but, like too many men under the influence of alcohol, he cannot control himself, and the most base impulses of his nature emerge with devastating consequences.

Nil by Mouth is as powerful as it is uncomfortable, and those in search of a pleasant movie-going experience would be best served looking elsewhere. It approaches a serious social issue in the best, most dramatically true manner. Instead of resorting to lugubrious sermons or prettying things up Hollywood-style, it tells a simple, psychologically-exact tale that illustrates the depth and breadth of pain caused by domestic abuse. *Nil by Mouth* leaves an impression that is hard to shake off, and that's the mark of an top-notch film. **HIGHLY RECOMMENDED**

Nixon [1995]

Starring: Anthony Hopkins, James Woods, Paul Sorvino, Joan Allen, Powers Boothe, Ed Harris Director: Oliver Stone Screenplay: Oliver Stone, Stephen J. Rivele, and Christopher Wilkinson Running Time: 3:10 Rated: R (Language, mature themes) Theatrical Aspect Ratio: 2.35:1

It's always a tricky proposition to make a motion picture based on recent history — and the more public the episode, the more difficult it is for the film maker to balance drama with accuracy. This is especially true when that film maker is Oliver Stone, a director known more for self-aggrandizement than for the thoughtful handling of difficult issues. Under Stone, *JFK,* for instance, turned into a 3-hour paranoid ordeal with a conspiracy theory 10 times less plausible than the Warren Commission's "one bullet" hypothesis.

It's entirely because of Stone's reputation that the even-handedness of *Nixon* is such a surprise. While not an unassailable portrait of the late president, this movie at least attempts to present Nixon as a human being, with all the failings and greatness inherent in a man of his stature. Nixon is portrayed as neither demonic nor angelic.

Nixon is not a simple regurgitation of historical events. In fact, history is used primarily as the backdrop against which this character study takes place. Less a biography than an impressionist's vision, the film may disappoint those expecting a vitriolic attack on someone who is surely not among Stone's heroes. But the lead persona, as realized by Anthony Hopkins, isn't reduced to an unthinking, unfeeling caricature. While Nixon is depicted as a paranoid, borderline-megalomaniac, he's also shown to have deep moral convictions, a strong sense of loyalty, and a love of his country. The drama plays out in a Shakespearean fashion, with Nixon's tragic flaw of hubris clearly in evidence. Hopkins is not heavily made up — and therefore doesn't really look like his character — but his mannerisms are perfect and he is allowed a full range of facial expressions (unlike Robert Duvall in *Stalin*). Hopkins does far more with acting than fake jowls could ever accomplish.

The film's structure is disjointed, especially during the first hour, as the narrative skips back and forth through time from Watergate to 1960 to the 1920s and 30s. Stone is giving us a snapshot of Nixon's life, but it comes in such a random and haphazard fashion that it dims the dramatic impact and dilutes early character development. It's not until the film's second hour, as Nixon faces the dilemma of how to end the Vietnam War, that Hopkins' character starts to click.

Nixon really doesn't offer any surprising insights, nor does it break new ground for the director. This is a dynamic — if flawed — look at the man who, for better and for worse, changed America's place in the world and its perception of itself. There are few who do not have an opinion of Nixon. In this motion picture, Oliver Stone presents his vision of the forces that drove and motivated the late President. And, factual or not, there's no denying that *Nixon* has moments when it is nothing short of compelling. **RECOMMENDED**

No End [Poland, 1984]

Starring: Grazyna Szapolowska, Maria Pakulnis, Aleksander Bardini, Jerzy Radziwillowicz, Artur Barcis Director: Krzysztof Kieslowski Screenplay: Krzysztof Kieslowski and Krzysztof Piesiewicz Running Time: 1:47 Rated: No MPAA Rating (Mature themes, sex, nudity) Theatrical Aspect Ratio: 1.66:1 In Polish with subtitles

No End, the first collaboration between writer-director Krzysztof Kieslowski and lawyer-turned-screenwriter Krzysztof Piesiewicz, takes place in a Poland that is under the cloud of martial law. More than any of the director's other internationally-screened features, this one requires some (however rudimentary) knowledge of the political situation in Poland during the early-to-mid-'80s. Martial law was declared in late 1981, and, in the resulting climate of uncertainty and tension, the courts began to pass 2–3 year sentences on anyone caught painting graffiti, found in possession of an underground newspaper, breaking curfew, or participating in strikes or other resistance activities. One of Kieslowski's objectives in *No End* was to explore potential ramifications of this situation from a noncritical perspective.

No End is really three stories in one, all of which revolve around people connected to a lawyer, Antoni Zyro (Jerzy Radziwillowicz), who dies just before the film begins. There's Ulla (Grazyna Szapolowska, who later appeared in *Decalogue 6, A Short Film About Love*), the lawyer's widow. Only after his death does she realize how much she loved her husband and how little meaning her life has without him. Then there's Dariusz (Artur Barcis), Antoni's client, who has been jailed for leading a labor strike. After Antoni's death, Dariusz is forced to employ an older, more cautious lawyer (Aleksander Bardini), who believes in compromising with the state to obtain a lenient sentence. Finally, there's the ghost of Antoni, who silently haunts his friends and family, watching as they continue their lives.

The three motifs of *No End* frequently cross and occasionally entwine. Kieslowski doesn't always handle these interconnections well; in fact, there are times when the different stories mesh clumsily. Nevertheless, the film is so packed with ideas that there's never any shortage of material worth pondering, and Ulla's emotional torment touches the heart. Looking back on the full body of Kieslowski's films, *No End* can be viewed as an important entry, because, despite its flaws, we can observe embryonic forms of several themes that the director explored more fully in *Decalogue* and *Three Colors*. Thus, *No End* functions both as a compliment and a precursor to the director's most lasting works. **HIGHLY RECOMMENDED**

Nobody's Fool [1995]

Starring: Paul Newman, Dylan Walsh, Jessica Tandy, Melanie Griffith, Bruce Willis Director: Robert Benton Screenplay: Robert Benton based on the novel by Richard Russo Running Time: 1:52 Rated: R (Profanity, brief nudity) Theatrical Aspect Ratio: 1:85:1

Nobody's Fool is about as sublime a motion picture as is likely to come out of Hollywood. With a structure that contravenes the norm, this film concentrates on character first, letting the plot fall naturally into place. Situations are forced on neither the film's inhabitants nor the audience. It's rare to sit through a drama and not feel manipulated, but the feelings generated by Robert Benton's movie are entirely natural, and likely to bring a smile to the heart.

Paul Newman gives an unforgettable performance as Donald Sullivan (or Sully), a cantankerous, aging man living in the small, snowbound town of North Bath, New York. With the spirit of a mischievous teenager but the body of a 60-year-old, Sully has the kind of infectious presence that, in his own words, "grows on you." He delights in flirting with women half his age, and engages in a game of theft where he and his sometimes-boss, Carl Roebuck (Bruce Willis), take turns devising creative means by which to steal a snow blower from one another.

Nobody's Fool is as much about regrets as about choices made; as much about the road not taken as the one travelled. It's about families broken apart, and parent/child relationships mended. Sully's father was a ruthless, violent drunk whom he never forgave, and that is perhaps why he was such a poor father to his own son, Peter (Dylan Walsh). Now, decades later, the abandoning father is trying to make amends — not only to his son, but to his grandchildren as well.

Offering the best in easygoing, unconfrontational drama, the story is told with wry, intelligent humor. For Melanie Griffith, this is the best acting she has done in a long time. After a string of lackluster comedies (the last one of which was *Milk Money*) and ineffective thrillers (*Shining Through, A Stranger Among Us*), *Nobody's Fool* offers a role for which she is suited. Playing the dowdy wife of a perpetual womanizer, she finds the right mixture of strength and pathos.

Also holding his own is Bruce Willis, here in his second consecutive solid performance (on the heels of *Pulp Fiction*). Jessica Tandy, to whom the film is dedicated, is as effective as ever. Of course, no one can quite match Newman, who shows a chameleon-like ability to shed his star image and don a most atypical personality. This is the sort of part normally associated with a character actor of Albert Finney's status.

Quiet and enchanting in its simplicity, *Nobody's Fool* is a joy. Admittedly, it meanders a bit, but that's part of its charm. The intelligent sensitivity of the script, coupled with Newman's powerfully understated performance, make this motion picture special. There aren't many of them like this out there. **HIGHLY RECOMMENDED**

Normal Life [1996]

Starring: Ashley Judd, Luke Perry Director: John McNaughton Screenplay: Peg Haller and Bob Schneider Running Time: 1:42 Rated: R (Profanity, nudity, sex, violence) Theatrical Aspect Ratio: 1:85:1

Fine Line Features, *Normal Life*'s distributor, elected not to release the film in theaters, opting instead for a run on HBO. This infuriated director John Mc-Naughton (*Henry: Portrait of a Serial Killer*), who claimed that he never would have directed the movie had he been aware of Fine Line's intentions. Now, *Normal Life* is out on video cassette, and its availability should generate a wider audience.

Normal Life is a character study loosely based on a true-life crime spree that occurred in Chicago's western suburbs. It is compelling because of the characters' twisted, co-dependent relationship, and not because it falls into the often-sordid category of having its narrative built around a real criminal case.

Those characters are the husband-and-wife team of Chris and Pam Anderson (Luke Perry and Ashley Judd), and *Normal Life* tells their story over a 2-year period. The two meet in a bar one night when Pam has a fight with her boyfriend and cuts her hand on a broken glass. Chris comes to the rescue, bandages the wound, then asks her to dance. Soon thereafter, they are married, and that's when the trouble begins.

Despite her cheerleader looks, Pam is not the perfect wife. Sexually, she's frigid; emotionally, she's unstable, and has self-destructive tendencies. Yet, through all of this, her husband sticks by her. There's something about Pam that holds him in thrall.

When Chris loses his job, Pam's profligate spending traps the couple in an ever-widening vortex of debt. To save them, Chris robs a bank. Then another. Then another. It appears he's good at it. Soon, he and Pam have moved into an upscale townhouse. Then, by chance, Pam finds out about her husband's new source of income. The idea excites her. She joins him in a robbery and, afterwards, experiences her first-ever orgasm during sex. But the pattern of self-destruction returns, and the resolution is inevitable.

Normal Life isn't really about whether Pam and Chris get away with their crimes — they don't, and that point is never in doubt. Rather, it's about how they relate to each other, and how Pam's manic-depressive behavior destroys not only her own life, but Chris's as well. Why would someone stay with a woman like this? Watching Ashley Judd's wrenching, uninhibited portrayal of Pam, it's easy to understand the reasons. Buried beneath the madness, there's a sweetness and vulnerability that cries out for protection and nurturing. Luke Perry, giving the most convincing performance of his career to date, makes it clear how desperately, hopelessly smitten Chris is by his wild, troubled wife.

I have watched *Normal Life* twice now, and I don't understand Fine Line's decision regarding the movie's distribution. By depicting the sham of "normality," *Normal Life* reminds us how fictitious and unattainable the "American dream" can be. **RECOMMENDED**

O [2001]

Starring: Mekhi Phifer, Josh Hartnett, Julia Stiles, Elden Henson, Andrew Keegan, Rain Phoenix, John Heard, Anthony Johnson, Martin Sheen Director: Tim Blake Nelson Screenplay: Brad Kaaya, based on "Othello" by William Shakespeare Running Time: 1:35 Rated: R (Violence, profanity, sexual situations, drug use) Theatrical Aspect Ratio: 1:85:1

There are two ways to adapt Shakespeare into a contemporary setting. The first is to take the story and dialogue and dump them wholesale into modern times. The second is to extract the essence of the material and re-work it for our era. Tim Blake Nelson's *O*, based on *Othello*, takes the latter route, and the result is a stirring and affecting piece of drama.

O re-locates the story into a United States high school circa 2000, and in keeping with the violent nature of Shakespeare, doesn't shy away from bloodshed. A simple emotion (in this case, it's jealousy), unchecked and stoked, forms the foundation of this violence. Mixed with the rampant hormones of the teen years, *O* demonstrates this combination to be as explosive and unstable as nitroglycerine.

The Othello of *O* is Odin James (Mekhi Phifer), the god of the Palmetto Grove basketball team. He's the lone black student in an all-white prep school, but he has a good heart, is smart, and is unstoppable on the court. He has won the love of the dean's daughter, Desi (Julia Stiles in the Desdemona role), and the respect of his teammates — all except one. Hugo (Josh Hartnett as Iago) is keenly jealous of Odin because Hugo's own father (Martin Sheen), the coach of the basketball team, considers Odin to be more of a true son than Hugo. This breeds resentment and hatred, and Hugo puts a plan in place to destroy Odin by sowing seeds of doubt about the legitimacy of Desi's love and fidelity. Odin, who is on some level insecure, reluctantly takes the bait.

The single most memorable aspect of any Shakespeare play is the dialogue. Yet, in *O*, where all of those lines have been stripped away, the strength and universality of the play's themes come to the fore. The intent of director Tim Blake Nelson (*Eye of God*) is to fashion a dramatic milieu that approximates high school in the '00s. He is not looking for a hard-core, gritty reality.

In the wake of the Columbine tragedy, Miramax Films, the company that owned the rights to *O* at the time, shelved it because they feared controversy. Obviously they ignored the fact that this picture has a message that is thought-provoking rather than exploitative. Eventually, Lions Gate picked up the rights and the movie was able to see the light of day. And that's a good thing for everyone who appreciates Shakespeare or a serious examination of the volatile issue of school violence. **RECOMMENDED**

October Sky [1999]

Starring: Jake Gyllenhaal, Chris Cooper, Chris Owen, William Lee Scott, Chad Lindberg, Laura Dern, Natalie Canerday Director: Joe Johnston Screenplay: Lewis Colick, based on the book "Rocket Boys" by Homer H. Hickam Jr. Running Time: 1:43 Rated: PG (Mature themes, mild profanity) Theatrical Aspect Ratio: 1.85:1

There has always been a distinction between high school nerds and jocks. Those in the former category are on the chess club, play Dungeons & Dragons, and participate in academic contests, while those in the latter are guided by testosterone, muscles, and not much else. Jocks look forward to winning the big championship game and being scouted by college coaches. Nerds hope to score a 1600 on their SATs or take first prize at a national science fair, thereby attracting a university's attention. There's always been a social dividing line between the grunts and the geeks, and it's very much in evidence here.

October Sky is based on the book by Homer Hickam, and relates the true story of 4 boys who experimented with home made rockets during the autumn of 1957, the year that the Soviet satellite Sputnik blasted into orbit. Set in the coal mining town of Coalwood, West Virginia, this movie is about one boy's struggles to escape from a lifestyle that he views as an unsafe and unhealthy prison.

Homer (Jake Gyllenhaal), along with his 3 friends, Quentin (Chris Owen), Roy Lee (William Lee Scott), and O'Dell (Chad Lindberg), is determined to make a rocket that will soar. His primary adult ally in this endeavor is his teacher, Miss Riley (Laura Dern), who supports and encourages his dream. But his father, John (Chris Cooper), who runs the local coalmine, dismisses his son's avocation as foolish. Football and mining are acceptable; hoping to get into college by

winning a national science fair is a waste of time and effort. Indeed, for a while, it looks like all of Homer's efforts are doomed to failure as rocket after rocket explodes on the launch pad, but, when the 4 boys discover the secret to success, they become local celebrities — until one of their rockets is suspected of starting a forest fire. And, when an accident at the mine threatens to ruin Homer's family, the idealist must choose between preserving his dream and working to allow his parents to keep their home.

There are a lot of reasons to like *October Sky*, but the most compelling is the multi-faceted, complex relationship between Homer and John. This isn't the kind of one-dimensional interaction we have come to expect from movie fathers and sons; it's characterized on both sides by anger, jealousy, resentment, bitterness, respect, pride, and love. While at first it appears that the rocket building lies at the movie's heart, we gradually realize that the connection between Homer and his father is more important.

October Sky gets a lot of the details right. With its use of period costumes and accessories, the film has the proper look for the late-1950s, and the soundtrack contains numerous pop hits from the time. Believable, subtle, and consistently intelligent. **HIGHLY RECOMMENDED**

Oleanna [1994]

Starring: William H. Macy, Debra Eisenstadt Director: David Mamet Screenplay: David Mamet based on his play Running Time: 1:30 Rated: R (Mature themes, violence, language) Theatrical Aspect Ratio: 1.66:1

Two people approach an intersection from different vantage points. When an accident occurs, they both observe the same facts, yet afterwards their versions of events differ considerably. Neither is lying; rather, the subjective element of their experience accounts for this gap in perception. This sort of difference of perspectives (albeit in other circumstances) is one theme explored by writer/director David Mamet in *Oleanna*.

Sexual harassment is certainly an issue of some importance in today's society. Ultimately, perhaps the question in *Oleanna* is not whether sexual harassment has been committed, but exactly who is persecuting whom. *Oleanna* also examines the significance of today's college education. Is it more important to go through the expected routines — taking notes, reading texts, and passing exams — than it is to have one's intellect stimulated and one's interests awakened? To use Mamet's words, "Is higher education useful?"

Faithfully adapted by the director from his own play, *Oleanna* is a two-character piece. For the most part, the dynamics are played out in a series of rooms on an unnamed northeastern college campus. The only two speaking parts belong to William H. Macy as a middle-aged professor and Debra Eisenstadt as Carol, a student who comes to him to discuss why she's failing his course. Needless to say, these characters are central to Mamet's presentation of certain themes. Their relationship is developed through 3 acts, each showing a new phase of their interaction. In some ways, the progression of *Oleanna* is more like that of a psychological thriller than a drama. The film spirals in on itself, twisting from sanity and reason to primal emotion.

As is always the case, Mamet's dialogue has a rhythm and cadence all its own. Early in the film, this, combined with a sluggish tone, causes *Oleanna* to seem staged and unnatural. Later, however, as the pace builds, the strengths of what the actors are saying — and how they're saying it — outstrip the weaknesses. By photographing *Oleanna* using dim lighting frequently designed to hood the eyes, motives, and feelings of the characters, cinematographer Andrezej Sekula (*Reservoir Dogs, Pulp Fiction*) enhances the sense of claustrophobia created by Mamet's restrictive setting. By the end of the movie, we in the audience feel as trapped as the characters on screen.

Oleanna probes deeply into some of the darker facets of human interaction, and anything with this keen an edge will cause discomfort. This film has been made for those willing to look beneath the surface to see a taut, intellectual sparring match where there is no absolute truth. For such an audience, this picture will leave an indelible imprint.

HIGHLY RECOMMENDED

Olivier Olivier [France, 1992]

Starring: Gregoire Colin, Marina Golovine, Francois Cluzet, Brigitte Rouan Director: Agnieszka Holland Screenplay: Agnieszka Holland Running Time: 1:48 Rated: R (Nudity, sexual situations, mature themes) In French and English with subtitles

Nine-year-old Olivier is what his mother describes as a "delicate child." His relationship with his older sister Nadine is somewhat tempestuous. The two enjoy playing together, and there is genuine affection between them, but Nadine is jealous of all the attention that Olivier gets from their mother. It's obvious to both children who the favorite is. Then, one day while running an errand for his father, Olivier disappears. Police and civilian investigations turn up nothing. Nadine (Marina Golovine) is devastated and the already-strained marriage of Olivier's parents, Serge (Francois Cluzet) and Elizabeth (Brigitte Rouan) can't weather the strain. The scene then switches to 6 years later in Paris, where a boy claiming to be Olivier (Gregoire Colin), and knowing a lot about his life and family, appears.

In many ways, the central story of *Olivier Olivier* is a cross between the French film *The Return of Martin Guerre* and the Josephine Tey novel *Brat Ferrar*. Both are about the re-appearance of someone believed dead. However, where *Brat Ferrar* and *Martin Guerre* focus primarily on questions of identity, *Olivier Olivier* is more concerned with family dynamics. Olivier's relationship with Nadine, which involves both passionate jealousy and sexual tension, forms the fulcrum around which the best aspects of the movie are developed.

Olivier Olivier takes approximately a half-hour to strike into the meat of the story, but the 30 minutes of background are crucial to appreciating what comes afterwards. We are given an opportunity to get to know the characters in all their complexity. Great care is also taken in making the setting real, developing an understanding of where this story unfolds and how a child can disappear with so little trace.

As is almost always the case with French-made films that obtain United States theatrical release, the acting is superb. All 4 leads play their roles flawlessly. Perhaps the most difficult and convincing task is given to Marina Golovine as Nadine, and she carries it off with aplomb. Brigitte Rouan's Elizabeth is in some ways reminiscent of Susan Sarandon's character in *Lorenzo's Oil*. Gregoire Colin retains an air of mystery around Olivier that keeps us guessing about his identity and motives.

Olivier Olivier is not without problems. There are some unanswered questions that nag at the viewer's mind and the eerie, mystical powers attributed to Nadine serve little purpose. The story could have been as strong — if not stronger — without them. Overall, however, director/writer Agnieszka Holland has crafted a powerful, effective film that surpasses *Europa Europa*, her well-received previous effort. Where that movie occasionally sputtered, this one sails through to a memorable conclusion.

HIGHLY RECOMMENDED

Once Upon a Time . . . When We Were Colored
[1996]

Starring: Charles Earl Taylor Jr., Willis Norwood Jr., Damon Hines, Al Freeman Jr. Director: Tim Reid Screenplay: Paul W. Cooper based on the novel by Clifton Taulbert Rated: PG (Violence, mature themes) Theatrical Aspect Ratio: 1.85:1

In a time when intelligent family pictures are at a premium, intelligent African American family pictures are virtually nonexistent. Filling this void is *Once Upon a Time . . . When We Were Colored,* Tim Reid's feature adaptation of Clifton Taulbert's memoirs. Blending sepia-toned nostalgia with harder-hitting, passionate themes, Reid has crafted a portrait of growing up in the middle-of-the-century South the likes of which is rarely found in any medium.

In *Once Upon a Time,* a sense of quiet dignity has replaced the rage that often typifies films targeted for black audiences. Yet this movie is no less emotive or potent because of it. Issues of equality, fairness, and self-respect form the cornerstones of the subtext for this coming-of-age story. Although *Once Upon a Time* is rooted in a setting that will have greater resonance for black Americans, much of what this film says has universal scope and intent.

Once Upon a Time . . . When We Were Colored opens in 1946, in Colored Town, the black companion community to Glen Allen, Mississippi — the year and place of Clifton Taulbert's birth. The film traces his first 16 years, ending in 1962 when Cliff decides to leave his home and family, and go to work in the cotton fields for the promise of the North. Although *Once Upon a Time* is occasionally disjointed, and some of the transitions are abrupt, it nevertheless offers a compelling chronicle of one man's growth into adulthood during volatile times, when courageous men and women began challenging an unjust system.

Once Upon a Time . . . When We Were Colored is about growing up and breaking free, both as an individual and as a community. It's about standing up for denied rights and not backing down in the face of pressure. Moreover, it's an intimate odyssey through the kind of childhood that is forever lost in the not-so-distant-past, when, despite the plague of legal racism throughout the South, the closeness of a community still offered support, comfort, and love. In Cliff's words, "All that I am or ever will be comes from growing up with my extended family in . . . Colored Town." That simple statement embodies the core of the film's message to viewers of all races and generations. **HIGHLY RECOMMENDED**

Once Were Warriors [New Zealand, 1994]

Starring: Rena Owen, Temuera Morrison, Mamaengaroa Kerr-Bell, Julian Arahanga, Taungaroa Emile, Cliff Curtis Director: Lee Tamahori Screenplay: Riwia Brown based on the novel by Alan Duff Running Time: 1:39 Rated: R (Violence, rape, language) Theatrical Aspect Ratio: 1.85:1

Once Were Warriors is centered upon the touchy yet timely topic of domestic violence. It is not, however, merely another "domestic violence motion picture." With its complex cultural backdrop and its stark view of this societal cancer, *Once Were Warriors* attains a level where it is equally painful and potent.

The critical themes of this movie are universal, even though there is a great deal of background that only a New Zealander can appreciate. Nevertheless, though many elements of the subtext may be lost to outside viewers, the key issue — the brutal cycle of violence and denial within a family — is brought to the fore in a manner that necessitates no special awareness.

Equality is not a basic tenant of the Maori lifestyle (Maoris are the Polynesian warrior-race who settled New Zealand some 1,000 years ago), at least as depicted in this film. However, alcoholism and unemployment are. It's the lot of the woman to work, while the man — the "protector" — spends all day at the local pub getting drunk. Wife-beating, while distasteful, is acceptable behavior, especially if the woman has the audacity to talk back to her husband.

Once Were Warriors takes place in an urbanized area of south Auckland, where Beth and Jake Heke (Rena Owen and New Zealand soap stud Temuera Morrison) live in a small house with 4 of their 5 children. The fifth, Nig (Julian Arahanga), has moved out to join a local gang. At first glance, Beth and Jake seem to have a solid marriage. But when Jake is drunk (which is frequently), his temper is easily ignited, and when one of Beth's barbs pushes him too far, the bloody and violent results are terrible to behold. Many films have depicted wife-beatings. Few have been as graphic and difficult to watch.

The acting throughout *Once Were Warriors* is uniformly strong, with leading and supporting actors turning in performances that range from credible to electric. The musical score, by Murray McNabb, is evocative, and a perfect match for the drab, dreary colors suffusing Stuart Dryburgh's camerawork. Great pains have been taken to emphasize that everyone in this film is trapped by one thing or another — if not their circumstances, then their personality. The only moment of serenity — the opening scene depicting a pastoral setting — turns out to be an illusion: a billboard in the midst of a gray city.

By anchoring *Once Were Warriors* in the turmoil of a Maori family, director Lee Tamahori takes full advantage of an opportunity not only to dissect the forces that lead to domestic violence, but also to focus on the clash between Maori traditions and modern values. The snares laid for men and women are not the only concepts put forth to ponder. *Once Were Warriors* works, to some degree, on 3 levels: the visceral, the emotional, and the intellectual, and it is the amalgamation of these that makes this a memorable film. HIGHLY RECOMMENDED

One True Thing [1998]

Starring: Meryl Streep, Renée Zellweger, William Hurt, Tom Everett Scott Director: Carl Franklin Screenplay: Karen Croner based on the novel by Anna Quindlen Running Time: 2:07 Rated: R (Language, sexual situations, mature themes) Theatrical Aspect Ratio: 1.85:1

Sometimes, the performance of one actor can elevate a mediocre script to the level of solid entertainment. This is a phenomenon we see again and again, and *One True Thing* is a good example of this. Perhaps surprisingly, however, that performance does *not* come from veteran screen presence Meryl Streep, who plays a woman dying of cancer. Streep is good in the role, but, frankly, this is the kind of part she could play in her sleep. Likewise, Oscar winner William Hurt is solid, but not spectacular. The one who rivets our attention with her pouty expression and subtle demonstrations of pain is Renée Zellweger.

Zellweger is Ellen Gulden, an ambitious young writer working for a New York-based magazine. When the film opens, it's 1988, and Ellen is being questioned in connection with the death of her mother. Kate Gulden (Streep), beloved member of a small upper New York state community, died in her sleep at the age of 48. At the time, she was suffering from advanced, terminal cancer, but the cause of death was a morphine overdose. Also under suspicion is Kate's husband, George (Hurt), a local college professor.

The story gradually evolves in flashback, showing Ellen's sometimes-contentious relationship with her mother and her unswerving devotion to her father. When Kate's condition is diagnosed, George pleads with Ellen to quit her job and come home to help around the house. Somewhat resentfully, Ellen agrees to return to the nest. Soon, she finds herself losing her own identity as her mother's lifestyle swallows her up.

Director Carl Franklin (*Devil in a Blue Dress*) has chosen to model the movie as a tearjerker, albeit a superior one. There are plenty of moments of sentimental melodrama, but there are also instances of surprisingly keen character insight. Although George, Kate, and Ellen start out as stereotypes, they quickly evolve beyond that baseline level. The relationships between these individuals are suitably complex; there are no clear-cut boundaries separating love, admiration, and resentment. And the issue of euthanasia is handled sensitively and intelligently, without the filmmakers getting on a pulpit to preach down to us.

One True Thing will undoubtedly be pigeonholed as a "chick flick," and it's not an unreasonable classification. Like *Terms of Endearment,* the movie deals with the two issues most likely to draw raves from the average female viewer: a well-defined mother/ daughter relationship and a slow death. However, I would argue that *One True Thing* is a little less overt than *Terms* in its approach to these issues, and that makes it a less cloying experience. There's no denying that *One True Thing* is affecting, and, although the plot rarely excels, the actors bring enough to their roles to transform this motion picture into a satisfying weeper. RECOMMENDED

Oscar and Lucinda [Australia/United States, 1997]

Starring: Ralph Fiennes, Cate Blanchett, Ciaran Hinds, Tom Wilkinson, Richard Roxburgh Director: Gillian Armstrong Screenplay: Laura Jones based on the novel by Peter Carey Running Time: 2:10 Rated: R (Violence, sex, mature themes) Theatrical Aspect Ratio: 2.35:1

Oscar and Lucinda opens in the mid-1800s, with parallel story lines in New South Wales, Australia, and Devon, England. As the narrative voice of Geoffrey Rush informs us, Lucinda Leplastrier (Cate Blanchett) is a headstrong young woman being raised in the Australian outback. Meanwhile, half the world away, Oscar Hopkins (Fiennes) has broken with his puritanical father over religious issues, and has gone away to school to study to be an Anglican priest. Lucinda is fascinated with glass; Oscar is obsessed with theology. Lucinda is rich; Oscar is poor. Lucinda is forward and self-assured; Oscar is timid and uncertain of himself. Yet one characteristic unites these two diverse individuals — the compulsion to gamble, whether it's on horses, dogs, cards, or the flip of a coin. And fate has decreed that they will one day meet.

That day doesn't occur until 45 minutes into the film, when Oscar boards a ship bound for Sydney, Australia, where he hopes to change his life and minister to anyone in need of his help. Another of the passengers is Lucinda, who is returning from England where she has been shopping for machinery to equip her newly-acquired glassworks factory. At first, their relationship is that of a reverend and a confessor, but it doesn't take long for both of them to recognize a kindred spirit in the other. A friendship is born, and, once they reach Australia, it develops into something more potent. But Oscar is uncertain of Lucinda's affection, and feels he must do something to prove himself worthy of her.

Oscar and Lucinda isn't beyond a little manipulation to get the desired emotional response, and there are times when the story line curves in preposterous directions. On more than one occasion, it's apparent that events are occurring specifically to funnel the characters into a position where there is only one possible route. Coincidence is a crucial plot device; without it, this movie can't go anywhere. The voiceover narration is also too verbose and breaks into the story at undesirable moments.

There's a real magic in the way director Gillian Armstrong develops the story, keeping things moving in unexpected directions without lingering too long on any one moment or sequence. With the skill of a consummate storyteller, she weaves romance, friendship, passion, humor, and tragedy together into a complete package. The characters, with all of their human foibles and neuroses, are wonderfully developed by Fiennes and Blanchett. So who cares if the storyline is a little ripe and unwieldy? *Oscar and Lucinda* still offers abundant pleasures to reward the viewer. RECOMMENDED

Othello [United Kingdom/United States, 1995]
Starring: Laurence Fishburne, Irene Jacob, Kenneth Branagh, Nathaniel Parker, Michael Maloney Director: Oliver Parker Screenplay: Oliver Parker based on the play by William Shakespeare Running Time: 2:04 Rated: R (Nudity, sex, violence) Theatrical Aspect Ratio: 1.85:1

To condense *Othello* into a reasonable, 2-hour running time, writer/director Oliver Parker has lopped approximately 50% of Shakespeare's original text from the screenplay. Yet, even with so much gone, the movie remains faithful to the play's central themes and conflicts, and the streamlined narrative is surprisingly easy to follow. For sheer impact, this *Othello* can stand side-by-side with the versions brought to the screen by Orson Welles (as restored in 1992) and Lawrence Olivier.

Laurence Fishburne plays the Moor Othello, a gifted general who is commissioned to confront a Turkish army at Cyprus. Always by Othello's side are his two

right-hand men: Cassio (Nathaniel Parker) and Iago (Kenneth Branagh). However, for reasons that are never fully explained, Iago is not the faithful retainer Othello believes him to be. In fact, hatred bubbles just beneath Iago's cool, rational exterior, and he has put a plan into action by which he intends to cause Othello's downfall and shatter the relationship between the Moor and his devoted wife, Desdemona (Irene Jacob).

Laurence Fishburne, a black actor playing the black title role (in some of his various other film incarnations, Othello has been essayed by the likes of Orson Welles, Lawrence Olivier, and Anthony Hopkins — none of whom are black), gives a stirring and powerful interpretation of a man haunted by uncertainty about his wife's faithfulness. Irene Jacob (*The Double Life of Veronique, Red*) imbues Desdemona with far more vitality than she has had in any other movie version. Kenneth Branagh, perhaps better focused since he's only acting in this piece, makes Iago a chillingly rational character whose acerbic asides to the camera draw the audience into his plot almost as an accomplice.

Certain Shakespeare purists will probably dismiss Parker's *Othello* because of the sex scenes and liberal cuts. Such a reaction might be a mistake, however, since this director's view of Othello's tragedy has an unusual slant. Parker is careful to play up the love affair between the title character and his wife so that when the inevitable occurs, it has a more profound impact. When Othello declares, "My life upon [Desdemona's] faith," you believe him.

With this version of *Othello*, Parker wanted to create a Shakespearean film that anyone could see, relate to, and enjoy. In large part, he has accomplished this. *Othello* has never been one of my favorites of the Bard's plays, but, at times, I found myself engrossed by this adaptation. Using the visual aspects of film to enhance certain story elements, Parker has crafted a fine motion picture. RECOMMENDED

Outside Providence [1999]
Starring: Shawn Hatosy, Alec Baldwin, Amy Smart, Jon Abrahams, George Wendt Director: Michael Corrente Screenplay: Peter Farrelly & Michael Corrente & Bobby Farrelly Running Time: 1:30 Rated: R (Profanity, drug use, sexual situations) Theatrical Aspect Ratio: 1.85:1

Outside Providence is a simple coming of age story, a nostalgia-soaked trip back to the mid-'70s when the social fabric of the American youth was stitched together by sex, drugs, and rock music. The film, despite never venturing into uncharted territory, is funny, warm, and endearing, and features a protagonist who grows on the audience. Because the themes are universal (first love, rebellion against restrictive authority, generational friction), nearly everyone, regardless of their age or gender, should be able to relate to the experiences of Timothy "Dildo" Dunphy.

The film opens in Pawtucket, Rhode Island during the summer of 1974. Timothy Dunphy (Shawn Hatosy), or Dunph, as his friends call him, has nothing better to do than to while away the days smoking dope and hanging out with friends with names like Drugs Delaney (Jon Abrahams). One evening, however, while stoned, Dunph gets into an accident with a parked cop car. His father (Alec Baldwin) is furious, and promptly pulls a few strings to get Dunph sent off to the Cornwall Academy, an exclusive prep school that has a reputation for academic excellence and discipline.

Cornwall has a seemingly endless list of rules, but the three most important are no drugs, no alcohol, and no sex. Dunph, of course, manages to break all three on numerous occasions. The game is to avoid being caught. During his time at Cornwall, Dunph falls in love with an "unattainable" girl, wins her affections in return, becomes serious about studying, and turns his life around. The material is standard fare for this kind of motion picture, but the script handles the familiar situations well and presents us with several likable characters. The voiceover narration is kept to a minimum, although Corrente relies on a few too many montages to convey advances in relationships.

Outside Providence effectively treads the line between comedy and drama, providing us with an enjoyable confection that's neither too leaden nor too airy. As a coming of age story, it's comfortable and effective; it hits all the high points and follows the expected general structure. There are serious moments, such as when Joey makes a surprising confession, or when Dunph learns a lesson about mortality. But, as one would expect from a Farrelly Brothers screenplay, there are quite a few laughs to be had, as well — and some of them are pretty big. But none of the jokes are as over-the-top or outrageous as we have come to expect. Instead of bodily fluid hair gel, we have verbal ripostes and modern-day proverbs ("Sex is like a Chinese dinner — it ain't over till you both get your cookies"). Overall, while *Outside Providence* isn't the kind of movie that challenges an audience, it is likely to cause most viewers to leave the theater with a warm, pleasant feeling inside. RECOMMENDED

Palookaville [1996]

Starring: William Forsythe, Vincent Gallo, Adam Trese, Gareth Williams, Frances McDormand Director: Alan Taylor Screenplay: - David Epstein Running Time: 1:33 Rated: R (Profanity, brief nudity) Theatrical Aspect Ratio: 1.85:1

Palookaville (the title is from the classic Marlon Brando line in *On the Waterfront* about losers) is the debut feature for director Alan Taylor, who has used the stories of post-WWII Italian author Italo Calvino and the 1956 comic heist movie, *Big Deal on Madonna Street,* as inspirations. This film, which takes place in Jersey City, New Jersey, chronicles the failed robbery attempts of three inept protagonists: Sid (William Forsythe), Russell (Vincent Gallo), and Jerry (Adam Trese). The problem is, while these "self-unemployed" men need money to pay the rent, none has the kind of personality necessary for a life of crime. As Jerry says, "We're not really cut out for this. Some people are. For instance, criminals."

Palookaville opens with a jewelry store robbery gone bad — but not in *Reservoir Dogs* fashion. Here, it's a bloodless, customerless night operation, with Russ and Jerry knocking a hole in the back brick wall while Sid stands guard out front. The problem is, they've got the wrong store — it's a bakery adjacent to the jewelers, and the booty ends up being jelly donuts and pastries instead of diamonds and gold.

Following this first failed caper, the gang tries to go straight, but their good intentions don't last long. Eventually, they hatch a plot to rob an armored car. It's not a very good plan — parts are culled from the old RKO movie, *Armored Car Robbery* — but they seem to think it's foolproof. Inevitably, however, when it comes to pulling the heist, Murphy's Law is in full force, and nothing goes the way anyone expected.

Although this film is sprinkled with comic moments and its tone is basically lighthearted, it treats its protagonists seriously. Sid, Russ, and Jerry seem like real people — losers with good hearts who want to commit crimes but lack the requisite toughness and cynicism. Through their relationships with women and their illegal activities, each of *Palookaville*'s main characters learns something about himself and the world.

With an evocative score by Rachel Portman and cinematography by John Thomas, *Palookaville* has a feel that belies its $1 million budget. At times, the movie is funny, touching, and quirky. There are a few isolated scenes that don't work, but, in general, *Palookaville* represents insouciant entertainment bolstered by an unforced message about not taking the "American dream" too seriously. And, although it may appear Tarantino-inspired at a glance, once you get into *Palookaville*, you'll understand that it has a much kinder, gentler story to tell. **RECOMMENDED**

The Paper [1994]

Starring: Michael Keaton, Glenn Close, Robert Duvall, Marisa Tomei, Randy Quaid Director: Ron Howard Screenplay: Stephen and David Koepp Running Time: 1:51 Rated: R (Profanity, mature themes) Theatrical Aspect Ratio: 1.85:1

Ron Howard has a history of making entertaining films with weak conclusions. For something that starts out as a boisterous, amusing, potentially-incisive look at the newspaper business and the people who run it, *The Paper* finishes with a relative whimper.

Henry Hackett (Michael Keaton) is at a watershed, and the next 24 hours are going to determine a lot — perhaps more than he could imagine. Caught in a dilemma between two jobs — his current one at the tabloid-like *New York Sun* and an offer from the prestigious *New York Sentinel* — Henry must make a decision. On one hand, there are factors that argue for the career change: his pregnant wife Martha (Marisa Tomei) wants security, and his bitter feud with his boss Alicia Clark (Glenn Close) is getting nastier by the moment. On the other hand, Henry doesn't want to leave the friendly chaos of *The Sun* and the friends he has made while there.

No viewer is likely to be bored by *The Paper*. The film moves along quickly, using mobile cameras and rapid cuts to keep the energy level high and the pacing crisp. This is especially true in the newsroom scenes, as director Ron Howard attempts to convey the spirit and atmosphere of the disorganized-but-productive work environment. His eye for detail is evident.

Away from the paper's offices, the movie is less successful. The personal lives of Henry and his co-workers aren't all that interesting, and seem scripted rather than real. This is especially true during the drawn-out melodrama that characterizes the last 15 minutes. There are also several out-of-place scenes with Robert Duvall and Jason Alexander commiserating at a bar. The contrivance used to incorporate these into the overall plot is a little too obvious.

But there's a lot in *The Paper* that works. Although most of the characters are types, the actors portray them with sympathy and understanding. Three-dimensionality may not be achieved, but attempts are made to give the men and women in this film some depth, and the freshness of the performances helps a great deal.

The Paper is a crowd pleaser, and, regardless of any viewer's experience (or lack thereof) with the behind-the-scenes wrangling that goes on in newspaper offices, the story is affable and entertaining. While there are no startling revelations, the film's atmosphere contains enough strength of realism that more than one viewer may momentarily think of the goings-on at *The Sun* as they sit down with their morning cup of coffee and look at the day's headlines. **RECOMMENDED**

Pay It Forward [2000]

Starring: Haley Joel Osment, Kevin Spacey, Helen Hunt, James Caviezel, Jay Mohr Director: Mimi Leder Screenplay: Leslie Dixon, based on the novel by Catherine Ryan Hyde Running Time: 2:05 Rated: PG-13 (Profanity, mature themes, sexual situations) Theatrical Aspect Ratio: 1.85:1

Things start out simply enough in *Pay It Forward*: it's the first day of school for 7th grader Trevor McKinney (Haley Joel Osment), who finds himself face-to-face with the realities of middle school in Las Vegas — including metal detectors and bullies who find ways to sneak knives past the security checkpoints. Trevor's social studies teacher, Eugene Simonet (Kevin Spacey), is a challenging and unconventional sort of educator — he doesn't just want his pupils to learn places and dates, he wants to prepare them to face life. "What does the world mean to you?" he asks. "What does the world expect of you?" In Trevor's case, the answers aren't positive ones — his mother, Arlene (Helen Hunt), is an alcoholic who works two jobs to pay the bills then drinks like a fish when she thinks no one is looking, and his father (Jon Bon Jovi) has long since split. Yet when Mr. Simonet offers his students an extra-credit project, "Think of an idea to change our world — and put it into action," Trevor attacks it with all the vigor he can muster. The result is something he calls "Pay It Forward."

The idea is more profound than one might normally expect from a child. Trevor will perform 3 acts of unsolicited kindness with the only requirement being that each recipient of his goodwill must "pay it forward" to 3 other people. It's a practical application of karma, and Mr. Simonet is impressed, even as he wonders whether it's an "overly utopian idea."

Nevertheless, Trevor gets to work, setting his sights first on a homeless man (James Caviezel), whom he invites inside for a meal and a place to sleep. His second target is Mr. Simonet, a lonely man Trevor thinks would make a perfect companion for his mother. But, as Trevor learns, kindness and the best intentions are not always enough.

Not everyone is going to appreciate *Pay It Forward*. People react differently to sentiment, and there's no doubt that this film operates in the arena of skillful manipulation. The key here is the word "skillful." *Pay It Forward* is not mawkish, crass, or clumsy. It does not attempt to turn our emotions into a cat's cradle like the latest dying-of-a-mysterious-disease movie. Instead, it offers an intelligent screenplay that tells an intriguing story about interesting characters, and, in the process, allows us to believe in an improbable dream. It's about lonely people reaching out and coming together, not disconnecting.

Pay It Forward reserves its greatest rewards for those who give in to the experience. There's a textual richness to the screenplay that likely owes a debt to Catharine Ryan Hyde's source novel. Issues such as child/spousal abuse and addiction are used more meaningfully than as a convenient plot device. Cynics may scoff at the film's apparently old-fashioned values, but there's a quiet power at work here that is hard to deny. RECOMMENDED

The People vs. Larry Flynt [1996]

Starring: Woody Harrelson, Courtney Love, Edward Norton, James Cromwell Director: Milos Forman Screenplay: Scott Alexander and Larry Karaszewski Running Time: 2:09 Rated: R (Nudity, sex, profanity, mature themes) Theatrical Aspect Ratio: 2.35:1

Larry Flynt, the self-proclaimed king of smut, as an American hero? Unlikely as it may seem, that's the scenario set up and successfully pursued by Milos Forman's (*One Flew Over the Cuckoos Nest, Amadeus*) *The People vs. Larry Flynt*. While this movie doesn't say anything that we haven't learned in high school civics classes, it gives names and faces to the subjects. Instead of "righteous" men stepped upon by the system, we're presented with a person who has been demonized not only by the religious right, but by the mainstream press. Nevertheless, when Larry Flynt won his case before the Supreme Court in 1987, we all emerged victorious. His wasn't just a fight for his own rights, but a battle for everyone who cherishes the freedoms afforded by the First Amendment.

The People vs. Larry Flynt picks up Flynt's story in 1972, when he's trying to drum up business for his "Hustler" go-go clubs. His solution: start a "newsletter" with lots of pictures of naked women. Soon, *Hustler* is a nationwide publication, but poor sales threaten to financially ruin its publisher. Then Flynt manages an amazing coup. The *Hustler* issue featuring pictures of a naked Jacqueline Kennedy Onassis sells in excess of 2,000,000 copies and puts the magazine in the big leagues. Suddenly, Flynt becomes the target of obscenity and pandering law suits, with big guns like Charles Keating (James Cromwell) and Jerry Falwell (Richard Paul) lined up against him.

Perhaps the most obvious flaw in *The People vs. Larry Flynt* is making the central figure too likable. He's played by Woody Harrelson, an actor who has been synonymous with good-naturedness since his days on *Cheers*. And, with the real Flynt taking a bit part (an unsympathetic judge who presides over the first trial), and his lawyer, Alan Isaacman, acting as consultant, it's reasonable to wonder how much the publishing magnate's image has been smoothed over to make him more palatable to an unbiased viewing audience. It's no great stretch to assume that Flynt wasn't the civil rights advocate he comes across as being, since, by his own admission, he was "just trying to make an honest buck."

Why is *The People vs. Larry Flynt* entertaining? Probably because the lead character is so much bigger than life, and perhaps because, by making him into a sympathetic man, we're spared the darkest portions of his personality. There's no doubt that Flynt is a compelling figure, but his crusade for personal freedom is only part of the reason. Sex undoubtedly sells, and Forman doesn't skimp on it here. Ultimately, it doesn't matter much how true-to-life everything on screen is. What's important is that *The People vs. Larry Flynt* tells a good, intelligent story that keeps us interested and involved. Since that's what happens, the verdict is clear: see the movie. You don't have to like the man to support his struggles and enjoy this dramatization of them. HIGHLY RECOMMENDED

A Perfect World [1993]

Starring: Kevin Costner, T. J. Lowther, Clint Eastwood, Laura Dern Director: Clint Eastwood Screenplay: John Lee Hancock Running Time: 2:18 Rated: PG-13 (Language, violence, sexual situations, mature themes) Theatrical Aspect Ratio: 2.35:1

Upon cursory examination, *A Perfect World* may seem like a buddy movie crossed with a road picture, but the film's surprising emotional depth transcends that which is normally found in either genre.

Halloween, 1963 is just another day for 8-year-old

Phillip Perry (T. J. Lowther), since his mother, a devout Jehovah's Witness, refuses to let him go trick-or-treating. In fact, that's not the only thing on the boy's "forbidden" list. He can't celebrate Christmas, has never eaten cotton candy, and hasn't ridden a roller coaster. For Phillip, life is dull until Butch Haynes (Kevin Costner) bursts into his kitchen. Recently escaped from prison, Butch is in need of a hostage, and Phillip happens to be in the wrong place at the wrong time. Strangely, the boy instinctively trusts Butch, and accompanies him meekly. The ride starts out a little bumpy, with Butch's sadistic fellow escapee attempting to molest the hostage — a situation that Butch corrects. Then, when it's only the two of them, Butch and Philip head across Texas with Police chief Red Garnett (Clint Eastwood) and his band of Rangers in pursuit.

Those who understand the psychology of hostage situations are aware of the bond that develops between captive and captor. The case presented in *A Perfect World,* however, is far from normal, even for these circumstances. The connection between Kevin Costner's Butch and T. J. Lowther's Phillip isn't something nebulous, but a father-and-son-like relationship that profoundly affects them both. Once they're together, neither of them can be the same — not spiritually, physically, or morally.

Like his star, Kevin Costner, Clint Eastwood is a better director than actor. In *A Perfect World,* he again wears both hats, although his on-screen appearances are limited. Eastwood the actor has two modes — the cynical tough guy and the sensitive tough guy, both of which are present here (the former more often than the latter). He's in fine form, but it's his behind-the-scenes work that really deserves the credit. There are moments when *A Perfect World* manipulates, but they are masterfully subtle.

A Perfect World is evidence that Hollywood is still capable of producing the kinds of moving, intelligent movies that have increasingly become the province of independent filmmakers. The characters here have depth and breadth, and the themes and relationships are complex. Clint Eastwood won an Oscar for directing *Unforgiven,* and *A Perfect World* shows that the wellspring of talent is still bubbling energetically. May it never run dry. **HIGHLY RECOMMENDED**

Permanent Midnight [1998]

Starring: Ben Stiller, Elizabeth Hurley, Maria Bello, Janeane Garofalo, Owen Wilson Director: David Veloz Screenplay: David Veloz based on the book by Jerry Stahl Running Time: 1:25 Rated: R (Drug use, profanity, sex) Theatrical Aspect Ratio: 1.85:1

If the progress of one man's descent into drug abuse in *Permanent Midnight* looks familiar, that's because the patterns of addiction are universal. It doesn't matter what an individual's demon is — alcohol, speed, cocaine, gambling, sex, or one of a hundred other vices. In this case, David Veloz's adaptation of Jerry Stahl's autobiography, the substance is heroin. The resulting spiral into dependence, debauchery, degradation, and disaster is as predictable as it is sad. And, for every lucky man like Stahl who manages to recover after hitting bottom, there are numerous nameless, faceless statistics who never again rise from the depths to which they have sunk.

Back in the 1980s, Jerry Stahl was a highly-successful TV sitcom writer (his best-known credit was *Alf*). Every week, he pulled in $5,000. The problem was, he had a smack habit that was costing him $1,000 more than that. What began as a minor recreational activity developed into an all-consuming obsession. Stahl couldn't function without heroin, but, after sticking a needle in a vein, he was "a real stud." Eventually, after being caught high while driving a car with his own baby in the passenger seat, Stahl straightened out his life.

As gritty as most of *Permanent Midnight* is, it doesn't wallow in unrelieved depression. The script injects a fair amount of black humor into the situation. The dialogue is smart and the narrative voiceover is riddled with cynical, self-deprecating observations. Because the film is structured as an extended series of flashbacks after Stahl has successfully made it through rehab, we know that he's going to be all right in the end, so that allows us to laugh at the jokes while still recognizing the seriousness of the situation.

Ben Stiller portrays a man on the edge, driven by forces he loses control of. There's one scene in particular that stands out in my memory. Unable to find a vein in his arm for the heroin injection, Stahl plunges the needle into his neck. On another occasion, we see him rooting through a trash bin in search of the residue of someone else's fix. Through all of this difficult material, Stiller is entirely convincing.

Permanent Midnight doesn't offer much in the way of surprises or revelations. It is largely what you expect it to be — the story of a man ruining his life because of his endless, desperate quest to inject a dangerous fluid into his bloodstream. Nevertheless, as familiar as the material may be, Veloz and Stiller invigorate it, making *Permanent Midnight* a more compelling and effective motion picture than one might normally anticipate from an entry into what has become a crowded field. RECOMMENDED

Philadelphia [1993]

Starring: Tom Hanks, Denzel Washington, Jason Robards, Mary Steenburgen, Antonio Banderas Director: Jonathan Demme
Screenplay: Edward Saxon and Jonathan Demme Running Time: 2:05
Rated: PG-13 (Mature themes, language, brief nudity) Theatrical
Aspect Ratio: 1.85:1

Some will argue that a film, being essentially a means of entertainment, can do little to change a national consciousness. Others, citing the power of the medium, will claim that motion pictures possess this rare and extraordinary ability. In Jonathan Demme's *Philadelphia*, the question is not whether we sympathize with Tom Hanks' AIDS-afflicted, gay character, but whether that sympathy opens up a different perspective on the victims of the disease in the real world.

Andrew Beckett (Tom Hanks), a hotshot law graduate from Penn, has a promising career ahead of him when he discovers that he has AIDS. Choosing not to tell his mentor at the firm, Charles Wheeler (Jason Robards), of either his disease or his sexual orientation, Andrew moves forward with his caseload as a senior associate. But the partners learn of his affliction, and while their dismissal is couched in terms of incompetence, Andrew knows that his AIDS and homosexuality are the root cause. He takes his case to a number of lawyers, including ambulance-chaser Joe Miller (Denzel Washington), none of whom is willing to represent him — until Miller has a change of heart, recognizing a hint of familiar discrimination in the way Andrew is being treated.

Tom Hanks gives what has rightly been called "the performance of his career," lending humanity and vibrancy to the victim. We feel for Andrew Beckett because he seems to be a genuine human being, not because the script and production have twisted circumstances to manipulate our emotions.

The work of Denzel Washington, while less obvious, is as impressive. Washington plays the "everyman," the on-screen representation of those in the audience who harbor homophobic tendencies. He, like many viewers, is forced to examine his bigotry and reassess his feelings about the gay community as he comes to know them as people rather than symbols and caricatures.

Symbolism is crucial to the story; the most obvious example is the role of physical space between Beckett and Miller. Before the AIDS revelation, they are shoulder-to-shoulder, two lawyers on opposite sides. Then Beckett drops his bombshell, and Miller moves to the other side of the room. As the film progresses, they grow gradually closer, sitting across a table at a library, then side-by-side in court. Finally, past the moment of Miller's crisis of conscience, he drops all barriers by lifting an oxygen mask to Andrew's face, momentarily touching flesh to flesh.

Even as it stands, with its faults, *Philadelphia* is still a remarkable expression of honesty and openness. Miller's court statements about this country's fear of homosexuals are frank and to-the-point. The story is timely and powerful, and the performances of Hanks and Washington assure that the characters will not immediately vanish into obscurity. And as long as people remember, there's a chance they can change. HIGHLY RECOMMENDED

The Pianist [United Kingdom/France/Germany/Poland/Netherlands, 2002]

Starring: Adrien Brody, Thomas Kretschmann Director: Roman Polanski Screenplay: Ronald Harwood, based on the book by Wladyslaw Szpilman Running Time: 2:28 Rated: R (Violence, profanity) Theatrical Aspect Ratio: 1.85:1

To lump *The Pianist* in with all of the other Holocaust stories brought to the screen does a great disservice to this powerful, compelling motion picture. Crafted without a whiff of melodrama, this motion picture takes a steady, unflinching look at the plight of Jews in Warsaw during the years when Poland was occupied by the Nazis. For director Roman Polanski, this represents his most effective film in nearly 3 decades. Not since 1974's *Chinatown* has Polanski reached such dramatic heights.

How is *The Pianist* different from an "average" Holocaust drama (if there can be said to be such a thing)? To begin with, there are no concentration camp scenes. In addition, Polanski does not flinch from showing the naked horrors perpetrated by Nazis on Jews. There is no attempt to sugar-coat this bitter pill — we see frequent gunshots to the head, torture, and the effects of starvation. The tone and style of the film are documentary-like — Polanski observes from a detached perspective, detailing atrocities without manipulating his audience. The result is bleak and powerful, and may overcome more sensitive viewers.

The Pianist opens in 1939 Warsaw, shortly after Poland's defeat to Germany. The film's protagonist is celebrated Jewish pianist Wladyslaw Szpilman

(Adrien Brody), who, along with his family, is forced to watch as the restrictions against Jews become increasingly more odious. Initially, Jews are forbidden from eating in certain establishments, walking in public parks, or sitting on public benches. Soon, they must wear distinguishing armbands, bow to Nazis passed in the streets, and walk in the gutters. Eventually, all Jews in Warsaw — approximately 500,000 — are moved into a ghetto, where whole families are crammed into single small rooms. After the Nazis begin implementing their "Final Solution," most of the Jews in Warsaw are shipped to the concentration camps to be exterminated. Only those capable of labor are allowed to remain behind. Wladyslaw is separated from his family at this point. He remains behind as part of a work force, while his family is herded into a cattle car. Eventually, with the help of the underground, Wladyslaw escapes into hiding, where he battles starvation, disease, and cold until the arrival of the Soviets.

With *The Pianist,* Roman Polanski has not only given us the most recent motion picture to remind future generations of what happened under Hitler's regime, but he has also provided us with hope that his own career, after numerous dead-ends, may finally be back on track. **HIGHLY RECOMMENDED**

The Piano [Australia/New Zealand/France, 1993]
Starring: Holly Hunter, Harvey Keitel, Sam Neill, Anna Paquin
Director: **Jane Campion** Screenplay: **Jane Campion** Running Time: **2:01**
Rated: **R** (Nudity, sex, violence, mature themes) Theatrical Aspect
Ratio: **1.85:1**

The Piano is about passion, the most basic and primal element of human nature. No matter how thick the veneer of civilization is, or how deeply-buried beneath layers of social repression those latent emotions are, passion ultimately cannot be denied. This is something that the 3 principals of this movie learn in various, often unpleasant, ways.

In the mid-1800s, Ada (Holly Hunter) arrives on the stormy shores of New Zealand, a mute bride sold by her father to a British emigrant named Stewart (Sam Neill). In addition to a normal assortment of baggage, Ada brings with her 8-year-old Flora (Anna Paquin), her illegitimate daughter, and a piano. Initially, Stewart declares that the piano is too bulky to move from the beach, and resists bringing it to his house despite Ada's wordless pleadings. Next, he sells it to fellow Englishman Baines (Harvey Keitel), a man who has embraced the local Maori ways. In addition to the piano, Baines wants a reluctant Ada as his teacher.

When he offers her a deal to get the instrument back, she is unprepared for the price she must ultimately pay.

Jane Campion's story is often stirring and occasionally gut-wrenching; the latter perhaps to a fault. There is a single visceral scene in this movie which becomes the most stark and enduring image taken from the theater. While definitely an expression of passion, this is perhaps not intended as the single defining moment of *The Piano,* although it may be remembered as such.

As affecting as Campion's basic story is, both characterization and technical presentation are lacking. Taken in tandem, these flaws prevent *The Piano* from attaining its full potential. The editing is choppy, at times causing the narrative to become disjointed or confusing. More than one transition is jarringly abrupt.

While Ada is as fully-rounded as she can be, the others all have elements missing from their personalities. Stewart never attains three-dimensionality, despite Sam Neill's best attempts, and Baines is occasionally little more than a sounding board for Ada's emotions to reverberate off of. Flora's personality undergoes a radical shift that, at best, is only partially-motivated by what we see on screen.

The Piano is a solid motion picture with a universal message and occasional splashes of genius, but it is remarkable only as Holly Hunter's performance is concerned. **RECOMMENDED**

Picture Bride [United States/Japan, 1995]
Starring: Youki Kudoh, Akira Takayama, Tamlyn Tomita, Cary-Hiroyuki Tagawa, Toshiro Mifune Director: **Kayo Hatta** Screenplay: **Kayo Hatta** and Mari Hatta based on a story by Kayo Hatta, Mari Hatta, and Diana Mei Lin Mark Running Time: **1:30** Rated: **PG-13** (Mature themes, brief nudity) Theatrical Aspect Ratio: **1.85:1** In English and Japanese with subtitles

At the beginning of the 20th century, Hawaii's economy was dominated by the output of its sugar cane plantations. To boost production, plantation owners imported workers from China, Japan, Korea, the Philippines, and other countries. Men arrived in droves, with illusions of getting rich. Reality, of course, was far from the dream, and the immigrant workers had little choice but to accept their lot and limit their expectations. So, instead of wealth, they sought the comfort and stability of a family. Attaining even this modest goal proved difficult, however, as Hawaii lacked an abundance of available women. The eventual solution was the concept of the "photo marriage" — arranged matches established through photographs and letters sent between the plantation workers and their prospective partners across the sea.

Writer/director Kayo Hatta spent 5 years researching stories of the picture brides, and at one point considered producing a documentary rather than a feature. In the end, however, she blended real-life anecdotes with historical facts to form what is, in essence, a simple love story. Hatta tells her tale with a heartfelt sincerity that comes across on the screen, and the Hawaii of the early 1900s is realistically portrayed. *Picture Bride* has its faults, but artifice and melodrama are not among them.

The title character is Riyo (Youki Kudoh), a 16-year-old girl from Yokohama who has come to Hawaii to escape her past and begin a new future with Matsuji (Akira Takayama). When she first meets her husband-to-be, she is shocked: the aging plantation worker barely resembles the young man in her photograph. Somewhat shamefacedly, Matsuji admits that he didn't have a good recent likeness, so he sent one taken a long time ago.

The marriage starts on shaky ground. Riyo will not sleep with Matsuji, and thinks of nothing but earning the money to return to Japan. With wages of about $11 a month, however, raising the necessary $300 seems an impossible task. And, as Matsuji informs her, "After a while you think of the homeland less and less. Going back to Japan becomes an old dream." Kana (Tamlyn Tomita), a veteran worker of the cane fields who also came to Hawaii as a picture bride, befriends Riyo and attempts to bring a little harmony to her unsettled marriage.

Picture Bride depicts the struggle of a strong-willed, female Asian American protagonist. As an attempt to re-create a segment of Hawaii's colorful history, this film is extremely effective. As a love story, it is only marginally less so. Through much of *Picture Bride,* we feel like we're viewing the story rather than experiencing it. We understand the motives of Riyo, Matsuji, and Kana, but moments of intimate identification are rare. For Kayo Hatta, *Picture Bride* represents a satisfying culmination to a labor of love.

RECOMMENDED

Playing by Heart [1998]

Starring: Sean Connery, Gena Rowlands, Gillian Anderson, Madeleine Stowe, Angelina Jolie, Dennis Quaid Director: Willard Carroll Screenplay: Willard Carroll Running Time: 2:01 Rated: R (Profanity, sexual situations, mature themes) Theatrical Aspect Ratio: 2.35:1

Playing by Heart is an ensemble dramatic comedy about the many faces of love: romance, longing, loss, sex, and lust. Set in modern-day L.A., the film tells 6 seemingly-unrelated tales about men and women finding each other, losing each other, unearthing long-buried secrets, and discovering things about themselves and others. Nothing in *Playing by Heart* is groundbreaking. In fact, one could argue that every one of the stories is unremarkable to the point of being trite. But the movie is consistently well-acted and features a gallery of characters so affable that it's difficult to actively dislike any of them, or, for that matter, the film as a whole.

The biggest name in the cast is undoubtedly Sean Connery, who plays Paul, a robust man afflicted with a brain tumor. Paul is dying, but you'd never know it to look at him. Connery is in fine form, with a mischievous twinkle in his eye and not a hint of James Bond in his performance. It's a pleasure to see the actor in a low-profile role like this. Paul is married to Hannah (the always-reliable Gena Rowlands), the host of a successful TV cooking show. After 40 years of marriage, the two think they know everything about each other — until Hannah's discovery of a 25-year-old photograph forces Paul to reveal several long-buried secrets.

Shaking her popular TV image, Gillian Anderson plays Meredith, a lonely young woman whose disastrous romantic history has caused her to give up on love. Madeleine Stowe is Gracie, a woman who engages in frequent affairs to plug the void in her sexually-unfulfilling marriage. Dennis Quaid is Hugh, an individual whose personality and life story changes from night to night. Ellen Burstyn and Jay Mohr are Mildred and Mark, a mother and son coming to grips with the latter's impending death from AIDS complications. And Angelina Jolie, who gives the film's standout performance, is luminous as the sassy, self-confident Joan, a Generation X-er in search of Mr. Right. Also in the cast are Jon Stewart, Anthony Edwards, Nastassja Kinski, and Ryan Phillippe as partners for the various main characters.

Love is an emotion that everyone experiences at one time or another. For that reason, at least one of the stories in *Playing by Heart* is likely to touch each viewer to some degree. Cynics may balk at the audience-friendly disposition of the film, but that's usually only a bad thing when melodrama suffocates intelligence, which only happens here on rare occasions. On the surface, the title doesn't mean much but, after seeing the film, it seems to fit the mood. *Playing by Heart* will not make many Top 10 lists, but, as a way to spend a January afternoon or evening, it's an enjoyable diversion. **RECOMMENDED**

Ponette [France, 1996]

Starring: Victoire Thivisol, Matiaz Bureau, Delphine Schiltz, Xavier Beauvois, Claire Nebout Director: Jacques Doillon
Screenplay: Jacques Doillon Running Time: 1:37 Rated: No MPAA Rating (Mature themes) Theatrical Aspect Ratio: 1.66:1 In French with English subtitles

Few of us who call ourselves "adults" truly remember the experience of childhood, except as a dim and distant illusion. Oh, we can recall what we did as a child, and often our memories of that period are among our most precious, but, looking back, we view things through the haze of maturity. Every once in a while, however, something comes along that breaks through that filter — a movie, a scene on television, a page in a book, or a moment in real life. Jacques Doillon's *Ponette* is one such catalyst. By presenting the world through the eyes of a grieving 4-year-old, *Ponette* manages to do what few motion pictures can — regress an audience into childhood.

Ponette works in large part because of its simplicity and realism. The plot is minimal — just enough to give us a reason to stay with the tiny protagonist for ninety minutes. Ponette has recently lost her mother in a car accident. Her father, a somber, emotionally-detached man, informs her that "Mommy was broken," then disappears for a while, leaving his daughter in the care of her aunt. So, with the aid of two cousins and, later, a group of other school children, Ponette must grapple with confusing religious issues while trying to understand the meaning of life and death.

The film effortlessly takes us into the magical world of a 4-year-old, where stuffed animals have extraordinary powers, dolls are more than inanimate objects, and God is someone you can talk to and expect an answer from. Some of the most memorable moments in *Ponette* center around the innocent conversations of children — how Catholics are different from Jews, what it means to be "single," and how eating a certain candy can make you fall in love forever.

For more than 80 minutes, *Ponette* continues strongly, but, in the end, writer/director Jacques Doillon seems at a loss how to end the movie. His choice, while admittedly cathartic, feels like a cheat. The pseudo-realistic, almost-documentary quality of the film evaporates; *Ponette*'s final scenes jar us out of the fragile reverie generated by what preceded them. Fortunately, the contrived ending does little to dampen my enthusiasm for the picture as a whole. When I recall *Ponette*, the first thing I think of is the heartbreakingly pure performance of young Victoire Thivisol.

From start to finish, Thivisol is nothing short of amazing. This is the kind of portrayal that would be labeled as a standout from an actor of any age, but, from someone who's only four, it's astonishing. A share of the credit must be lavished upon Doillon — it takes a masterful filmmaker to elicit this kind of unforced performance from a child. Had Thivisol shown a hint of artifice, *Ponette* would not have worked. The strength and consistency of her acting keeps this film on a high level. **RECOMMENDED**

The Portrait of a Lady [United Kingdom/United States, 1996]

Starring: Nicole Kidman, John Malkovich, Barbara Hershey, Martin Donovan, Mary-Louise Parker Director: Jane Campion
Screenplay: Laura Jones based on the novel by Henry James Running Time: 2:25 Rated: PG-13 (Mature themes, brief nudity) Theatrical Aspect Ratio: 2.35:1

The Portrait of a Lady, the first motion picture adaptation of Henry James' beloved classic, presents a stark contrast to the light-and-sunny Jane Austen movies. Although it examines some of the same issues as *Pride and Prejudice, Sense and Sensibility,* and *Emma,* the perspective is much darker. Those expecting a light romance from *The Portrait of a Lady* are in for a rude awakening.

Kidman plays Isabel Archer, a headstrong-but-naive young woman who, as the story opens in 1872, has recently arrived in England from America. While there, she's staying at the estate of her aunt (Shelly Winters) and uncle (John Gielgud). Her closest companion and confidante is her cousin, Ralph Touchett (Martin Donovan), a consumptive who encourages his father to will a large sum of money to Isabel. She is also pursued by two suitors: the rich and unexciting Lord Warburton (Richard E. Grant) and the dashing Caspar Goodwood (Viggo Mortensen). She rejects both, saying "I don't want to be a mere sheep in the flock. I shall probably never marry." Her desire is to explore the world and forge her own way in it.

When her uncle dies, leaving her a fortune of 70,000 pounds, she has the financial means to do so. She begins to travel, spending a great deal of time in Italy. But her naïveté enables her to be led astray by the sinister

Madame Serena Merle (Barbara Hershey), whom she falsely believes to be her friend. Madame Merle contrives a meeting between Isabel and the dangerous Gilbert Osmond (John Malkovich). Soon, Isabel, seduced by Osmond's promises of love, agrees to marry him. Too late, she recognizes Osmond's true nature.

Those familiar with Jane Campion's previous effort, *The Piano,* will not be surprised by the dismal tone of *The Portrait of a Lady,* which, if anything, is even grimmer than that of the novel. Campion films over half of the scenes in dim light, making effective use of contrast to highlight character attributes. Isabel is frequently shown standing in patches of light while Madame Merle and Osmond keep to the shadows. Occasionally, Campion gets a little too artsy, as in a surreal, black-and-white dream sequence where Isabel's subconscious wrestles with Osmond's declaration of love.

The Portrait of a Lady is a difficult story to film, and Jane Campion and screenwriter Laura Jones have done an admirable job with this adaptation. The motifs of love, betrayal, and accepting the consequences of one's actions are well-established. The movie does not attain the emotional depth of Michael Winterbottom's *Jude,* but there are definite thematic and tonal similarities. The result is a fascinating portrait not only of a lady, but of the society and marriage that entrap, then attempt to destroy, her. RECOMMENDED

The Postman (Il Postino) [Italy, 1995]

Starring: Massimo Troisi, Philippe Noiret, Maria Grazia Cucinotta, Linda Moretti Director: Michael Radford Screenplay: Anna Pavignano, Michael Radford, Furio Scarpelli, and Massimo Troisi based on the novel *Burning Patience* by Antonio Skarmeta Running Time: 1:55 Rated: PG (Mature themes) Theatrical Aspect Ratio: 1.85:1 In Italian with subtitles

The Postman, an Italian film from British director Michael Radford, is a charming piece of cinema that takes several comfortable formulas and expands upon them in ingenious and emotionally-satisfying ways. There's a little of everything here: poetry, politics, humor, love, and heartbreak. Best of all, these elements flow together seamlessly in a production characterized by solid acting, balanced pacing, and eye-catching cinematography.

Mario (played by the late Italian writer/director/ actor Massimo Troisi) is a postman in a fishing village on a small island off the coast of Italy. Arriving there in 1953 is famed Chilean poet Pablo Neruda (Philippe Noiret), exiled from his native country for espousing communist doctrine. Mario is curious about this new resident who, despite his advancing age, has a seemingly magical power over women. Eventually, after delivering Neruda's mail for a while, he gets up the courage to engage the poet in a conversation about writing. This begins an unusual collaboration, with Mario providing a sounding board for Neruda's ideas and Neruda teaching Mario about poetry and its relationship to life.

In the final performance of a great career, Massimo Troisi (who died at the age of 41, shortly after completing this picture) gives us a memorable character. Hesitant, shy, and uncultured, Mario has the heart of a poet, but little talent with words. In this post-*Forrest Gump* era, it would be easy to compare him to the Tom Hanks character, but Mario is really a more complex individual. He occasionally makes some startlingly insightful observations, such as "the whole world is a metaphor for something," often without realizing how thought-provoking his comments are. *The Postman* is about Mario, and Troisi imbues him with a captivating humanity.

Philipe Noiret's Pablo Neruda is the perfect foil for Mario — a kindred spirit with all the experience and talent that the postman lacks. Noiret plays Neruda as part father-figure, part dreamer, and part realist. When Mario asks him how to become a poet, the older man responds by advising his "pupil" to take a walk along the island's shoreline and see what images come to mind. After Mario has fallen for the stunning Beatrice (Maria Grazia Cucinotta), Neruda tells him about the many women of that name to have inspired poets.

For 2 hours, it's possible to fall under *The Postman*'s spell and be completely enchanted. There is more vitality and genuine passion here than in any ten big-budget extravaganzas. This movie about words and images will delight not just because it entertains, but because it takes the motion picture experience one step further, and fulfills. MUST SEE

Priest [United Kingdom, 1994]

Starring: Linus Roache, Tom Wilkinson, Cathy Tyson, Robert Carlyle Director: Antonia Bird Screenplay: Jimmy McGovern Running Time: 1:40 Rated: R (Mature themes, sex) Theatrical Aspect Ratio: 1.66:1

The Catholic community struggled with *Priest* when it was first released, and, in light of more recent events, it will doubtlessly seem more timely viewing than ever.

The main character is Father Greg Pilkington (Linus Roache), a by-the-book, straightlaced Roman Catholic priest who is new to a rural parish in Great Britain. Father Greg is the sort who believes his job is to give moral advice, not act as a social activist — a charge he levels against fellow priest Father Matthew Thomas (Tom Wilkinson).

While trying to serve his flock, however, Father Greg has his own personal demons to wrestle. Not only is he unable to keep his vow of celibacy, he breaks it with another man — something many of his less-tolerant parishioners would surely view as an "abomination" if they learned of it. Even as he struggles with his sexual identity and its implications, Father Greg is forced to endure an additional crisis of faith when a 14-year-old girl (Christine Tremarco) comes to him under the seal of confession and admits to being sexually molested by her father.

Jimmy McGovern's script does an excellent job of dovetailing the two main elements of the film — Greg's homosexuality and Lisa's sexual abuse — into a compelling whole, often using unexpected bursts of humor to keep the level of tension from becoming too intense. Arguably, the more stirring story centers on the priest's battles with his conscience over how to help Lisa, but this film wouldn't have the same emotional resonance without the other pieces. In fact, the final scene incorporates several threads into a moment that, while perhaps a little overdone, is nonetheless powerful.

Priest addresses both social and religious themes. At its core, however, is the question of absolute certainty versus faith. There is, of course, no answer to most of the questions that Greg agonizes over, but these — such as how Christ could expect him to keep silent when that silence condemns a girl to continued suffering — are presented for the audience's consideration. It is by his reaction to the issues that Greg's true character is slowly revealed. It doesn't take long for us to realize that our first impression of the man is as false as his facade.

Provocative films like *Priest* rarely arrive without creating some sort of controversy. By not compromising her vision (which is similar to that of fellow British film maker Ken Loach), director Antonia Bird has fashioned a picture that not only stirs up a hornet's nest of timely and volatile spiritual issues, but faces up to homosexuality and incest with a frankness which few films dare. *Priest* is effective not only because of all the ground it traverses, but because the final turn brings closure without excess.

HIGHLY RECOMMENDED

The Princess and the Warrior [Germany, 2000]

Starring: Franka Potente, Benno Furmann, Joachim Król, Marita Breuer
Director: **Tom Tykwer** Screenplay: **Tom Tykwer** Running Time: **2:09**
Rated: **R** (Violence, profanity, sexual situations) Theatrical Aspect
Ratio: **2.35:1** In German with subtitles

German filmmaker Tom Tykwer first gained a measure of international recognition in 1997, when his second feature, *Winter Sleepers* received attention outside of his native Germany. Then came the 1998 Toronto Film Festival and the debut of *Run Lola Run*, which became one of the hottest and most talked about properties in Toronto that year.

Although Tykwer uses many of the same flourishes that made *Lola*'s style unique, the tone and pacing of *The Princess and the Warrior* are much different. *Lola* was an explosion of riotous color and kinetic energy; this movie is more restrained and thoughtful. It also has greater thematic depth and resonance.

Franka Potente, who has traded in her bright red hair from *Lola* for blond tresses, plays Sissi, a meek nurse at a psychiatric hospital whose daily life represents a sea of monotony. One day, her path crosses that of Bodo (Beno Furmann), an ex-army officer who can't hold down a stable job. Because of something Bodo does, Sissi is struck by a truck while crossing a street. Unaware that he was the cause of the accident, Bodo slips underneath the stopped truck to escape the policemen who are pursuing him. There he finds Sissi, immobilized and struggling to breathe. Acting quickly, Bodo saves her life, then vanishes. Two months later, once her recovery is complete, Sissi seeks out her savior, only to find a bitter individual who wants nothing to do with her. But his rejection is not enough for Sissi, who believes that destiny brought them together, so she continues to pursue Bodo — only to have fate throw another curve ball in her direction.

Thematically, *The Princess and the Warrior* has a lot going on. One of Tykwer's pet issues — that of fate and coincidence guiding our lives — is in play here, as it was in both *Winter Sleepers* and *Run Lola Run*. The film also explores ideas about life, death, guilt, salvation, and male anger towards women. Tykwer finds a way to blend everything together into a production that challenges as much as it entertains.

Often, a director's follow-up to an acclaimed work

results in a letdown. Thankfully, *The Princess and the Warrior* represents a step forward for Tykwer, not a step backward. Those who like stories with clean, unambiguous resolutions will probably not appreciate (or understand) the freedom and latitude offered by *The Princess and the Warrior*'s conclusion. But for anyone who esteems the experience of participating in a movie rather than being a passive observer, this film comes with a "Do Not Miss" label. It is the reason I review movies. **MUST SEE**

Prisoner of the Mountains [Russia, 1996]

Starring: **Sergei Bodrov Jr., Oleg Menshikov, Jemal Sikharulidze, Susanna Mekhralieva** Director: **Sergei Bodrov** Screenplay: **Arif Aliev, Sergei Bodrov, Boris Giller** based on the short story "Prisoner in the Caucasus" by Leo Tolstoy Running Time: **1:39** Rated: **R** (Profanity, violence, nudity) Theatrical Aspect Ratio: **1.85:1** In Russian with subtitles

Lyrical and evocative, *Prisoner of the Mountains* represents a balanced and telling examination of the absurdity of war. Director Sergei Bodrov uses an intimate tapestry depicting two Russian captives and their small band of captors to illustrate the similarities of human beings on either side of the battle lines. There's nothing fundamentally new about this observation, of course, but the manner in which *Prisoner of the Mountains* presents it is unique.

After a brief opening sequence showing the physical examinations of would-be recruits to the Russian army, the scene shifts to the Caucasus mountains, where Chechnyan rebels ambush a group of Russian soldiers. Two — Vanya (the director's son, Sergei Bodrov Jr.) and Sacha (Oleg Menshikov, *Burnt by the Sun*) — are taken prisoners. The patriarch of the village, Abdul-Mourant (Jemal Sikharulidze), wants to trade the Russians for his son, who is a captive of the army. But mistrust on both sides scuttles a deal. Unwilling to give up his son so easily, Abdul-Mourant demands that Vanya and Sacha write to their families so that their mothers can attempt to broker a settlement. Meanwhile, the captor's young daughter, Dina (the delightful Susanna Mekhralieva), takes an almost-proprietary interest in the prisoners.

There's an old saying that goes something like: "We have met the enemy and they are us." Words to that effect could easily describe the growth process undergone by the characters in *Prisoner of the Mountains* as they come to understand how little there is that separates them. Often, it's the little things that emphasize the connection. Vanya repairs Abdul-Mourant's watch. When she comes to bargain for her son's life, Vanya's mother tells the patriarch that she, like his son, is a teacher. Dina offers the Russians bread and water. Vanya, in turn, makes a toy for her. The participants on both sides of the struggle have to consider what the word "enemy" means and whether the phrase "It's war" is a good enough justification for a killing.

Prisoner of the Mountains makes us think about the absurdity of war. It brings the toll of battle down to a personal level, but without the bitterness and rancor evident in American productions like *Platoon* and *Apocalypse Now*. There's quite a bit of low-key humor to be found here, which may account for the tone being lighter than the subject matter might suggest. However, the final, darkly ironic sequence of the film drives home Bodrov's point with brutal clarity. The machines of war don't take into account the human pain that they inflict. **HIGHLY RECOMMENDED**

Proof [Australia, 1991]

Starring: **Hugo Weaving, Geneviève Picot, Russell Crowe** Director: **Jocelyn Moorhouse** Screenplay: **Jocelyn Moorhouse** Running Time: **1:30** Rated: **R** (Sex, nudity, profanity) Theatrical Aspect Ratio: **1.85:1**

Proof is a delightful and dark dramatic comedy that can be hilarious one moment and poignant the next. The script is intelligent, the acting is brilliant, and the overall result is fabulously entertaining.

For Martin (Hugo Weaving), trusting has never been easy. He has been blind his entire life, and, as a boy, he believed his mother lied to him when she described the sights around him. Why? Because she could. Martin was sure that his mother never loved him, but merely put up with him out of a sense of responsibility. When she died at a young age, he thought it was all a ruse so she could get away from him. Those beliefs followed him into adulthood, where he became a recluse, unwilling to let anyone into his life or his heart beyond what was absolutely necessary. Martin has an interesting pastime for a blind man — he's a photographer. He takes pictures, then has someone describe them to him. In his words, the photographs are proof that what he senses is what others see.

Martin has a housekeeper, a 30-year-old woman named Celia (Geneviève Picot). She's in love with him to the point of obsession. Like Martin, Celia dabbles in photography, but she only has one subject — him. The walls and tables of her home are covered with pictures of Martin. But theirs is not a cordial relationship. Celia torments Martin and, in response, he humiliates her. Celia wants Martin's trust and respect, but those are things he is unwilling to part with, especially to her. So they continue in a state of unhealthy co-dependency, where each needs something from the other, and both are unhappy.

Enter Andy (Russell Crowe in an early role), the outsider who impels the relationship between Martin and Celia out of its stasis. Andy is a waiter at a local restaurant who befriends Martin, and, after a short while, becomes his regular describer of photographs. When Andy meets Celia, he is immediately smitten, but all she sees in Andy is a rival for Martin. So Celia concocts a plan designed to discredit Andy and finally give her what she wants — Martin, all to herself.

The soundtrack of *Proof* is remarkable in the way it amplifies the blind man's perspective. We hear bracelets jingling, rain pattering on ceilings, cats purring, dogs panting, truck breaks squeaking, distant phones ringing, the hum of fluorescent lights, footsteps, wine being poured into glasses, and a china teacup rattling on a saucer. Moorhouse makes us aware of sounds in a way that most directors don't. It isn't necessary to the plot, but it's one of those touches that elevates the movie's impact. *Proof* would have been a fine feature without such details and subtleties. With them, it's a tour de force for a first-time director, and the kind of motion picture that deserves to be playing in VCRs, not sitting untouched on video store shelves. **HIGHLY RECOMMENDED**

Quills [2000]

Starring: Geoffrey Rush, Kate Winslet, Joaquin Phoenix, Michael Caine, Amelia Warner Director: Philip Kaufman Screenplay: Doug Wright, based on his play Running Time: 2:03 Rated: R (Sexual situations, sex-related dialogue, nudity, profanity, violence) Theatrical Aspect Ratio: 1.85:1

Two assumptions can readily be made about any motion picture centered around the Marquis de Sade. The first is that the material will be of a sexual nature. The second is that the movie will not be a lighthearted romp. Both of these presumptions are true in the case of Philip Kaufman's *Quills*, arguably the most provocative and best historical melodrama of 2000.

Count Donatien-Alphonse-François de Sade, better known as the Marquis de Sade, lived from 1740 until 1814, although his infamous reputation has survived for nearly 2 centuries since his remains were scattered. For most of his adult life, the Marquis was in and out of prison, as his penchant for deviant sex-

ual behavior (which typically included torture) continually put him at odds with the law. Following the French Revolution and the storming of the Bastille, he was incarcerated in the Charenton Asylum for the Insane, where he resided for a year. After his release, he spent approximately a decade writing scandalous manuscripts and putting on plays before his activities once again landed him at Charenton, where he spent the rest of his life.

Quills, although a fictionalized account of the Marquis' last years, is moderately faithful to the historical record. The characterization of the title character, despite being softened to make the man bearable to a mainstream audience, captures some of Sade's essence. As portrayed by the energetic Geoffrey Rush in a brilliant turn that avoids the easy path of caricaturization, Sade is a shrewd, dangerous man with an intelligence that is matched in magnitude by his perverse sexual desires.

Kate Winslet plays Madeleine, a chambermaid at the asylum who is engaged in a clandestine (albeit platonic) relationship with the Marquis. His writing fascinates her, and she smuggles his manuscripts out of Charenton so that they can be published. Winslet's performance, while generally low key, is so strong that she is able to stand toe-to-toe with the more flamboyant Rush. Joaquin Phoenix turns in solid work as a priest who conceals romantic feelings for Madeleine. Finally, Michael Caine's portrayal of Dr. Royer-Collard, the "man of science" sent by Napoleon to oversee Charenton, results in a memorably detestable villain.

For those who aren't offended by the idea of a movie that presents the Marquis de Sade as a multi-dimensional character rather than a cartoon-like pervert, *Quills* has much to offer. It is based on a play by Doug Wright, and, while the dialogue has the intelligence and crispness of something originally designed for the stage, Wright and Kaufman have done an excellent job of opening up the setting. Employing the talents of a top-flight cast and working from a screenplay that uses the historical backdrop as a means to deal with issues of contemporary import, *Quills* offers a thoroughly compelling 2 hours. **HIGHLY RECOMMENDED**

Quiz Show [1994]

Starring: Ralph Fiennes, Rob Morrow, John Turturro, Paul Scofield, David Paymer Director: Robert Redford Screenplay: Paul Attanasio based on *Remembering America: A Voice from the Sixties* by Richard N. Goodwin Running Time: 2:13 Rated: PG-13 (Profanity, mature themes) Theatrical Aspect Ratio: 1.85:1

1958. Television quiz shows like "Twenty-One" are ratings hits. Americans tune in every week to root for the charming, erudite Charles Van Doren (Ralph Fiennes) in his quest to vanquish new challengers. Following his defeat of the previous champion, Herbie Stempel (John Turturro), Van Doren, the son of the well-known poet Mark Van Doren (Paul Schofield), has become a national celebrity, sending sales of Geritol, the sponsor of "Twenty-One," through the roof. But all is not well behind the scenes. Van Doren's victories are cheats, the results of pre-supplied answers guaranteed to keep him on the air. When a bitter Stempel decides to go public, and Congressional investigator Dick Goodwin (Rob Morrow) listens to him, a national scandal erupts.

The clearest message of *Quiz Show* is a cynical truth: the entertainment industry is a business where ethics are meaningless when it comes to winning a ratings war. This is hardly a revelation, of course. No American in 1994 is naïve enough to blindly accept anything they see on television. "Twenty-One," however, is where that disillusionment started.

One of the reasons that *Quiz Show* is so extraordinary is because it spins a story as compelling on the personal level as on the national one. Ralph Fiennes' Charles Van Doren is a fascinating individual, equally seduced and repelled by greed. Desperate to escape his father's shadow, he wallows in public adulation until it begins to stink from his own hypocrisy. On the other side of the father/son conflict is Paul Scofield's character. Masterfully rendered, Mark Van Doren is far more than the usual stern, disapproving patriarch. He is a man with keen insight and sensitivity who looks sadly upon the track of his son's ambitions.

John Turturro is exceptional as the uncharismatic Herbie Stempel, a man so petty and dislikable that it's impossible to sympathize with him even when he's presented as a victim. Rob Morrow is good enough not to be completely overshadowed by his co-stars, although his forced accent could have been toned down. Mira Sorvino provides a spark as Goodwin's wife.

Towards the end of the movie, David Paymer's Dan Enright comments that the sham of "Twenty-One" created a situation in which nobody lost — not the sponsor, NBC, the public, or the contestants. Viewers of *Quiz Show,* however, are likely to form the opposite impression — that, in the end, there were no winners. **HIGHLY RECOMMENDED**

Raining Stones [United Kingdom, 1993]

Starring: **Bruce Jones, Julie Brown, Ricky Tomlinson, Gemma Phoenix, Tom Hickey** Director: **Ken Loach** Screenplay: **Jim Allen** Running Time: **1:31** Rated: **No MPAA Rating (Profanity, violence)** Theatrical Aspect Ratio: **1.66:1**

Simplicity, sincerity, and realism are the hallmarks of Ken Loach's *Raining Stones.* With an uncompromising look at England's lowest class, this film explores the facets of living hand-to-mouth in a society where work is scarce and a pint at the pub offers life's sole release.

Bob (Bruce Jones) and his family are barely making ends meet before two events upset the careful balance. First, Bob's van is stolen, then he learns that the outfit for the First Communion of his daughter, Coleen (Gemma Phoenix), is going to cost more than 100 pounds. His wife, Anne (Julie Brown), and pastor (Tom Hickey) advise him to take a less expensive route, such as renting a dress, but Bob will have none of that. Nothing but the best for his daughter on this special occasion. The problem is, since he's on the dole, money is hard to come by, and odd jobs don't pay much.

Although possessing the grittiness and rare honesty of Loach's previous project, *Riff Raff,* this is not a re-telling of the same story. Anyone familiar with the director's work, however, will recognize the characteristic style. Dark locales, underexposed interiors, and actors with accents so thick that some might find subtitles helpful — all these elements are synthesized to deliver an amazingly real portrait of life as a member of Middleton's unemployed and underprivileged.

There's no preaching in *Raining Stones,* and the narrative never condescends to the characters, no matter what their circumstances are. This movie presents life as it is — no regrets or complaints. Without ever mentioning politics, Loach makes the most powerful and effective of political statements — one that relies on subtlety and the intelligence of the audience.

Raining Stones is a mirror that reflects our times, with universal themes. You don't have to be a resident of Middleton to understand what director Ken Loach is saying. That there is humor and warmth in the midst of such poverty speaks volumes for the indomitable human spirit, not to mention the strength of this movie's ability to capture that.

HIGHLY RECOMMENDED

Raise the Red Lantern [China, 1991]

Starring: Gong Li, Cao Cuifen, He Caifei, Jin Shuyuan, Kong Lin, Ma Jingwu, Zhao Qi Director: Zhang Yimou Screenplay: Ni Zhen based on the novel *Wives and Concubines* by Su Tong Running Time: 2:05 Rated: No MPAA Rating (Mature themes) Theatrical Aspect Ratio: 1.85:1 In Mandarin with subtitles

Raise the Red Lantern is one of those all-too-rare motion pictures capable of enthralling an audience while they're watching it, then haunting them for hours (or days) thereafter. With its simple story and complex themes and emotions, *Raise the Red Lantern* hints at the kind of film a great director like Ingmar Bergman might have made had he attempted a story set in mainland China.

The difference between Songlian (Gong Li), the fourth wife of a rich landowner, and the other three spouses, is that she is educated, and has been married (by her mother) against her will. Now, her whole world is reduced to one small compound, and the only people she sees are her husband, his family, and their servants. She is given a maid (Kong Lin) that she doesn't get along with, and finds her new home to be a cheerless place, despite all the bright colors that adorn the inside walls.

It's the master's tradition to light lanterns outside the house of the wife he intends to join for the night. Since Songlian is new to the compound, it is expected that he will spend much of his time with her. However, on their first night together, the master is called away to soothe his pampered third wife (He Caifei), who complains of an ailment. From then on, Songlian realizes that she'll have to resort to deceit and manipulation to retain her husband's interest. And, while she doesn't necessarily appreciate his attentions, she realizes that her status in the household is directly proportional to how highly she is favored.

Within days of her arrival, Songlian's relationships with her "sisters" are established. The first wife (Jin Shuyuan), an aging woman with a grown son, does her best to ignore Songlian's presence. She is tolerant — no more, no less. The third concubine, a beautiful ex-opera singer, is fiercely jealous of Songlian, worried that the master will find his new, educated bride more enticing. However, the second concubine (Cao Cuifen) offers friendship and kindness to the newest member of the family — or so it initially seems.

The film is beautifully photographed using a process that captures the vividness of the many colors employed by the director. *Raise the Red Lantern* is visually stunning, and the appeal to the eye only heightens the movie's emotional power. The fullness of reds, oranges, and yellows is unlike anything that has been seen in an American film for years. Zhang clearly understands at least one of the fundamental rules of film making: that a great-looking picture will enhance a superior story.

Songlian's ultimate fate is wrenching, and the closing scene represents a sad epilogue to a unique motion picture experience. I don't think I've ever seen a movie quite like *Raise the Red Lantern,* and, since I consider it to be a defining example of Chinese movie-making and one of the best films of the '90s, I doubt that I ever will again. **MUST SEE**

Real Women Have Curves [2002]

Starring: America Ferrera, Lupe Ontiveros, Ingrid Oliu, George Lopez Director: Patricia Cardoso Screenplay: George LaVoo and Josephina Lopez Running Time: 1:30 Rated: PG-13 (Profanity, sexual situations) Theatrical Aspect Ratio: 1.85:1

Ana (America Ferrera) is an 18-year-old second generation Mexican American living in Los Angeles. She's an excellent student — good enough, in fact, that her English teacher, Mr. Guzman (George Lopez), believes that she has a chance for a scholarship to a good college. But Ana's mother, Carmen (Lupe Ontiveros), is against Ana continuing her education — she wants her youngest daughter to work at a dress-making shop run by her eldest daughter, Estela (Ingrid Oliu). Ana agrees, albeit reluctantly and petulantly. She still dreams of college and freedom from her mother — dreams that grow stronger when she begins a fling with an Anglo classmate, Jimmy (Brian Sites).

Real Women Have Curves does little to hide its primary, female-empowerment theme: that a woman should be judged by the quality of her mind and thoughts, not by how closely her body matches the so-called "ideal." Certainly, it's a laudable stance for a movie to take, but director Patricia Cardoso and writer Josephina Lopez become too strident in their advocacy of it.

At the core of the movie is Ana's tempestuous relationship with her mother. Carmen, who sees any form of "progress" as evil, wants her daughter to follow in her footsteps: find a man, get married, and have children. She criticizes Ana's weight because she believes that a fat girl won't be able to catch a husband. She is adamantly opposed to further education for Ana because that would take the girl away from home. There's also probably some sublimated jealousy here, with Carmen being envious of all of Ana's opportunities — opportunities she never had.

For Ana's part, living with her mother is stifling her. She recognizes that Carmen manipulates her life, and is resentful of it. She sees a college education as the way to broaden her horizons — a sentiment that is shared by her father, grandfather, and teachers. Once it becomes clear that Carmen will not change, Ana comes to the sad conclusion that she may be forced to chose between her mother and her future. One of the reasons the film resonates is that the final break of independence is something every individual must face, regardless of the family relationship. RECOMMENDED

Three Colors: Red [France/Switzerland/Poland, 1994]

Starring: Irene Jacob, Jean-Louis Trintignant, Frederique Feder, Jean-Pierre Lorit Director: Krzysztof Kieslowski Screenplay: Krzysztof Kieslowski and Krzysztof Piesiewicz Running Time: 1:40 Rated: R (Mature themes, sexual situations, nudity) Theatrical Aspect Ratio: 1.85:1 In French with subtitles

Red, the final chapter of Krzysztof Kieslowski's *Three Colors* trilogy, is a subtle masterpiece. With its satisfying exploration of such complex and diverse themes as destiny and platonic love, *Red* is not only a self-contained motion picture, but also a fitting conclusion to the series. Through one brief-but-important scene, this movie adds closure to both *Blue* and *White*, tying both to each other and to *Red*, and thereby reinforcing the commonality of ideas threaded through all three.

This time around, the protagonists are a young woman named Valentine (Irene Jacob, who starred in Kieslowski's *The Double Life of Veronique*) and a crotchety retired judge, Joseph Kern (Jean-Louis Trintignant). Valentine, a fashion model, meets the judge after running down his dog in the street and taking the injured animal to the address listed on the collar. Kern is initially indifferent to his pet's predicament, telling Valentine to keep the dog if that's what she wants. She does; however, the animal eventually runs away and finds its way back to the judge. When Valentine goes searching, she inadvertently learns Kern's secret — he enjoys spying on people by illegally tapping into their phone conversations.

Told in parallel with the chronicle of the unusual friendship between Valentine and the judge is the story of two lovers that Kern spies upon. Auguste (Jean-Pierre Lorit) and Karin (Frederique Feder), seem devoted to each other, but fate has already cast its die against them. For Auguste's life is eerily similar to that of Kern 30 years ago and, like the older man, he is drawn by forces beyond his control towards Valentine.

Thematically, *Red* is the strongest of the three films. Its construction allows hardly a moment to pass when the viewer isn't considering how fate manipulates the lives of Valentine, Auguste, Kern, and Karin. Then there's the meaning of platonic love (or "fraternity") — friendship completely divorced from sexual overtones. Kieslowski shows exactly how multi-faceted any relationship can be, and what occasionally must be sacrificed to the basic human need of finding a kindred spirit.

Red virtually demands more than one viewing for an appreciation of the picture's ambitious scope. It's a tragedy that this movie was not eligible for the Best Foreign Film Oscar (Switzerland, the country of origin, decided to reject *Red* because of its strong French and Polish production elements), but the lack of official recognition does not alter the fact that this is one of 1994's exceptional motion pictures. MUST SEE

The Red Violin (Le Violon Rouge) [Canada, 1998]

Starring: Samuel L. Jackson, Don McKellar, Carlo Cecchi, Irene Grazioli, Jean-Luc Bideau Director: François Girard Screenplay: François Girard, Don McKellar Running Time: 2:11 Rated: R (Nudity, sex, mature themes) Theatrical Aspect Ratio: 1.85:1 In English, French, German, Mandarin, and Italian with subtitles

What do the following people have in common: a 17th century fiddle-maker in Cremona, Italy; a young orphan with a prodigious musical talent in 18th century Vienna; a famous British Lord performing during the reign of King George III; a lover of Western music struggling through the Chinese Cultural Revolution; and a musicologist in modern-day Montreal? The answer: the Red Violin. Not only is that the name of the instrument that lies at the center of François Girard's new film, it's the movie's title, as well. Appropriately, the picture relates the story of the violin from its genesis in 1681 to its sale at auction in 1997.

Girard has assembled a huge international cast to present 5 key episodes in the violin's history. In the first, the creator, Nicolo Bussotti (Carlo Cecchi) labors on the instrument as a present for his unborn child. Meanwhile, his wife, Anna (Irene Grazioli), uncertain about the stability of her pregnancy, seeks advice on the future from a fortune-teller. A century later, the violin has become the property of an orphanage outside of Vienna. It is there that Georges Poussin (Jean-Luc Bideau) discovers it in the possession of an amazing prodigy, young Kaspar Weiss (Christoph Koncz), whom he intends to instruct himself. Soon afterwards, Lord Frederick Pope (Jason Flemyng), a popular concert violinist, takes possession of the fiddle and makes it his instrument of choice. But, as his career flourishes, his personal life is thrown into turmoil when his beloved mistress, Victoria (Greta Scacchi), leaves him behind to take a trip to Russia. By the early 20th century, the violin has come into the possession of Xiang Pei (Sylvia Chang) in Shanghai, but she must hide it or face punishment from an establishment that deems all Western instruments to be a corrupting influence. When the violin re-surfaces in 1997 Montreal, Charles Morritz (Samuel L. Jackson) and Evan Williams (Don McKellar) work to restore the instrument so it can bring a huge price at auction.

Movies that follow objects rather than characters are always difficult to craft, and the central item often ends up being little more than a gimmick used to tie together unrelated narratives. Girard and McKellar avoid that trap, which is one reason why *The Red Violin* works. Another is that the film offers a wonderful trip through three centuries and across several countries. *The Red Violin* may not succeed on every level, but it's still a pleasing and fascinating excursion.

RECOMMENDED

The Remains of the Day [United States/United Kingdom, 1993]

Starring: Anthony Hopkins, Emma Thompson, James Fox, Christopher Reeve Director: James Ivory Screenplay: Ruth Prawer Jhabvala based on the novel by Kazuo Ishiguro Running Time: 2:14 Rated: PG (Mature themes) Theatrical Aspect Ratio: 2.35:1

Most of *The Remains of the Day* is presented as a series of flashbacks, with a 1950s James Stevens (Anthony Hopkins) recalling his days of service under the late Lord Darlington (James Fox), especially during the years leading up to the second world war. However, at the center of the tale is Stevens' never-defined relationship with the head housekeeper, Sally Kenton (Emma Thompson). They love each other, but that love remains unvoiced, for no matter how hard Miss Kenton tries to draw him out, Mr. Stevens can not admit his feelings, not even to himself.

This relationship is explored under the shadow of the Nazis' rise to power in Germany. Lord Darlington, a German sympathizer who believes that the Treaty of Versailles was cruel, is determined to fight for peace, no matter what the cost. Some of those that he

invites to stay under his roof are not as enthusiastic, including U. S. Congressman Lewis (Christopher Reeve), who warns Darlington that he is an amateur playing a game best left to professionals. The warning is prophetic, but its consequences are not explored as fully as they might have been.

Anthony Hopkins has the central role, and he portrays Stevens to perfection. Hopkins is forced to employ a great deal of subtlety to exhibit the turmoil beneath the surface. Stevens is tortured by his love, but the need to express his feelings cannot overcome his deep reserve. Emma Thompson does her usual solid job with her part, but the role of Ms. Kenton lacks the substance of the actress' character in *Howards End*.

Christopher Reeve is a perfect choice to play the "typical American." No one would confuse Congressman Lewis with a real character, but it doesn't seem that James Ivory was interested in presenting more than a stereotype. Lewis is involved for two reasons, and once both aims are accomplished, there's no real reason for him to be in the story at all. He serves his purpose, and that's good enough.

The Remains of the Day is an engaging and powerful motion picture, every bit the equal of Merchant-Ivory's best work, and certainly the most emotionally-wrenching tale they have brought to the screen. Tragic love stories often hit with the hardest impact, and few are better-crafted and more intelligently presented than that of Mr. Stevens and Miss Kenton.

HIGHLY RECOMMENDED

Remember the Titans [2000]

Starring: Denzel Washington, Will Patton, Wood Harris, Ryan Hurst, Ethan Suplee, Hayden Panettiere Director: Boaz Yakin Screenplay: Gregory Allen Howard Running Time: 1:53 Rated: PG (Mature themes, mild violence) Theatrical Aspect Ratio: 2.35:1

If viewed as a crowd-pleasing, feel-good sports movie, *Remember the Titans* is an unqualified success. However, if seen as a socially conscious retrospective on race relations in the South during the early 1970s, it can best be described as timid and unexceptional. In soft-peddling the theme of intolerance, the picture refuses to take even the smallest chance. From the beginning, we are meant to know that the events portrayed in *Remember the Titans* have their roots in historical fact, as if the "based on a true story" caption lends added credibility to the story.

With the exception of a pair of bookend scenes transpiring in 1981, the film takes place a decade earlier in the town of Alexandria, Virginia, where the T.C.

Williams High School has just been integrated. This means that not only will whites and blacks be mingling in the halls, but on the football field as well. And, in a place like Alexandria, the composition of the T.C. Williams Titans is a serious matter, as is the identity of the coach. So, when the eminently qualified local choice, Bill Yoast (Will Patton), is passed over in favor of an out-of-towner named Herman Boone (Washington), the citizens are in an uproar, especially since they believe Boone has been selected based not on his qualifications but because of his race. The commonly held opinion is that school board hopes the presence of a black coach might be able to calm the tensions that are threatening to turn Alexandria into another Watts.

Boone is initially uncomfortable with his reasons for getting the job, but he vows to be color-blind in his treatment of his players. He invites Yoast to be his defensive coordinator — an offer that is reluctantly accepted. Then, over the course of a grueling, late-summer boot camp for would-be football players, he concentrates on destroying the preconceptions of all of his charges, both black and white. In the process, some of the players become fast friends, and Boone and Yoast develop a bond. But the team's new-found internal harmony does not necessarily reflect that of the outside world, which regards the racially integrated team with mistrust and, at times, disdain.

As sports films go, *Remember the Titans* is a notch above the average entry in part because its social message creates a richer fabric than the usual cloth from which this kind of movie is cut. The film's racial slant gives the football games a little more meaning and energy, and the characters come across as more sincere and less self-centered. Still, when compared to a high school sports classic like *Hoosiers,* which contained many of the same elements, *Remember the Titans* shows a few flaws. Fortunately, they aren't serious enough to lower the film's broad-based appeal or to diminish its quotient of feel-good moments. **RECOMMENDED**

Requiem for Dream [2000]

Starring: Ellen Burstyn, Jared Leto, Jennifer Connelly, Marlon Wayans Director: **Darren Aronofsky** Screenplay: **Darren Aronofsky**, based on the novel by Hubert Selby Jr. Running Time: **1:42** Rated: Unrated (Drug use, sex, nudity, violence, profanity) Theatrical Aspect Ratio: **1.85:1**

Requiem for a Dream presents the darkest take imaginable on a story of hopes and dreams shattered by drug addiction. There's no preaching or sermonizing here, just an almost-clinical depiction of lives laid to waste. This is not a film for the weak of mind or soul. It is a force to be reckoned with.

The movie starts slowly, introducing each of the characters and establishing their relationships. Visually, Aronofsky tries for something a little different here, employing a split-screen approach that neither enhances nor detracts from the narrative. (It isn't around long enough to become distracting.) The central figure is Harry (Jared Leto), a young man who lives hand-to-mouth because nearly every cent he saves, earns, or steals goes towards buying something he can inject into his veins. His best friend and business partner is Tyrone (Marlon Wayans, playing it straight and doing so effectively), who shares many of Harry's aspirations. His girlfriend is Marion (Connelly), who, like Harry and Tyrone, is an addict. The fourth significant player is Harry's widowed mother, Sara (Ellen Burstyn), who is as addicted to television as Harry is to drugs. When she learns that a marketing company may be able to offer her a spot in the studio audience of a live TV broadcast, she decides to lose weight. Following a visit to the doctor's, she is on her way to dropping 30 pounds and becoming hooked on the uppers and downers that comprise her diet.

For these characters, drugs gradually take the place of everything else — food, sex, aspirations, and even the day-to-day impulse to live. They become the sole sources of pain and pleasure. They form the core of relationships. Would these people have anything to do with one another if they weren't bound by the ceremony of the injection? Perhaps it's not that way in the beginning, but the life-destroying power of drugs is insidious and undeniable, and the spiral of all-consuming addiction is what Aronofsky has captured with unnerving effectiveness.

Requiem for a Dream certainly isn't the first recent motion picture to offer an unpleasant picture of what happens when an individual becomes hooked on drugs, but its quadruple character study is unsparing. This is in large part because of the brilliant final fifteen minutes, which is a tour de force of direction and editing. Employing hundreds of cuts, Aronofsky careens back and forth between his 4 main players, showing their increasingly dire circumstances and allowing those to escalate to a brutal climax. Don't be fooled by the passively poetic title; there's nothing serene or restful about this motion picture. *Requiem for a Dream* gets under your skin and stays there. **MUST SEE**

Restoration [United Kingdom/United States, 1995]

Starring: Robert Downey Jr., Sam Neill, Meg Ryan, Ian McKellan, Hugh Grant Director: Michael Hoffman Screenplay: Rupert Walters based on the novel by Rose Tremain Running Time: 1:57 Rated: R (Sex, nudity, plague) Theatrical Aspect Ratio: 1.85:1

The setting for *Restoration* — England in the 1660s — represents one of the most interesting eras in European history. Following the death of Oliver Cromwell, Charles II returned from exile to reclaim the throne for the Stuart family. His coronation heralded the Restoration — a time of great enlightenment and debauchery. Then, in 1665, the Great Plague struck, and in 1666, London burned. The film *Restoration* attempts to incorporate all of these events into its 2-hour story. Those hoping for historical accuracy will be sorely disappointed, however. The 1660s serve as little more than a backdrop for the action. The costumes and sets are authentic-looking, but little else has more than a flavor of the period. Even the dialogue is frequently anachronistic.

Historical authenticity aside, *Restoration* is still a worthy source of entertainment. The narrative has numerous dramatic hiccups — most caused by trying to cram too much into too little time — but, overall, it tells an engrossing tale. The film, which opens in 1663 London, follows the rise and fall of Robert Merivel (Robert Downey Jr.), a reluctant physician. Despite his undeniable medical gifts, he would rather spend time drinking and whoring. When King Charles II (Sam Neill) needs someone unconventional to heal his ailing dog, he sends for Merivel. The animal's recovery assures the doctor a place at court, where he is gradually transformed from physician to fool.

One of the most unusual services demanded of Merivel by the King is that he marry the royal Mistress, Celia Clemence (Polly Walker). The doctor is told in no uncertain terms that the marriage is never to be consummated — it is in name only ("I need a man far too enamored of women in general to love one in particular," Charles tells Merivel). Unfortunately for his status at court, Merivel falls for Celia, and when the King learns of this, he dispatches Merivel from his service. The now-penniless physician ends up in a Quaker community with an old friend (David Thewlis). It is there that he discovers the true nature of his talents.

Restoration is developed as a series of episodes which combine to form a story arc taking Merivel's character from debauchery to poverty to redemption. Flaws aside, the film is a sumptuous, affecting tale about the most roguish of men making good. And, despite assorted tragedies along the way, the tone and intent are decidedly upbeat.

As a well-developed, fast-paced movie that tells a "feel good" story, *Restoration* is a welcome entry. As a history lesson, it's a failure. The British are famous for their period pieces, and, while *Restoration* isn't among the best (all of Jane Austen's adapted novels are superior), it's still solid entertainment. **RECOMMENDED**

Rich in Love [1993]

Starring: Kathryn Erbe, Albert Finney, Kyle MacLachlan, Piper Laurie, Suzy Amis Director: Bruce Beresford Screenplay: Alfred Uhry based on the novel by Josephine Humphreys Running Time: 1:45 Rated: PG-13 (Mature themes) Theatrical Aspect Ratio: 1.85:1

One day, Lucille Odom (Katherine Erbe) comes home from school to find that her mother (Jill Clayburgh) has left. According to the short farewell note, it's not a sudden decision, but something that has been building for a long time. Predictably, Lucille's father, Warren (Albert Finney), is devastated by what has happened. When he seems unable to put his life back together, Lucille calls on her big sister, Rae (Suzy Amis), for help. Rae arrives with her husband, Billy (Kyle MacLachlan), in tow, and a surprise: she's pregnant.

Rich in Love is rich in character but lean in plot. The movie boasts a group of believable, three-dimensional personalities. We can understand and empathize with each of them — their flaws, their fears, their dreams, and their hopes. Due in large part to a screenplay that shies away from stereotyping, these people come across more as human beings than scripted characters, with the strengths and foibles common to real people.

For the most part, the story is told through the eyes of Lucille, the youngest of 2 daughters. As she watches her family fall apart, she tries to be brave, but the front she puts on is a sham that, in Billy's words, hides a lot of love. Kathryn Erbe, the young actress who plays Lucille, gives a genuine, heartfelt performance.

Albert Finney, who seems at home in almost any role, conquers this one with aplomb. He masters Warren with as much ease as he does the Southern accent. As written, Finney's character might not be the most interesting of men, but the actor infuses him with life and keeps him from becoming the maudlin cliché that is the unfortunate destiny of many abandoned motion picture spouses.

Rich in Love is mostly about emotions and relationships. The plot itself is unremarkable. Not a lot happens — the movie depends upon the characters to enrapture the audience. There are several story lines with dramatic potential that are accorded only cursory attention. One of these (relating to Lucille's birth) had me thinking and wondering long after the people on screen had put it aside.

Rich in Love is a slice-of-life film in the truest sense of the word. As such, although it has a clearly-defined beginning, the end is less obvious. An attempt at closure is made, but the final scene rings false. The ending aside, *Rich in Love* has a lot going for it, including a certain warmth and character insight that many movies lack. The story may be out-of-focus, but that's generally the way life is. RECOMMENDED

Richard III [United Kingdom/United States, 1995]

Starring: Ian McKellan, Jim Broadbent, Annette Bening, Kristin Scott-Thomas Director: Richard Loncraine Screenplay: Ian McKellan and Richard Loncraine based on the play by William Shakespeare as adapted for the stage production by Richard Eyre Running Time: **1:45** Rated: R (Violence, sexual candor, brief nudity) Theatrical Aspect Ratio: **2.35:1**

Opening in a 1930's England war room with a tank crashing through a wall, one is immediately struck by the realization that, whatever else *Richard III* is doing, it certainly isn't preserving the story's original time frame. However, while the sets and costumes have been moved to a mythical, Nazi-like pre-WWII England, the dialogue, characters, actions, and themes remain unchanged from the original text by Shakespeare. While this curious clash between a near-modern setting and the much older source material might seem confounding, it actually serves to energize the play, as well as making it more palatable to present-day audiences.

Richard III is the last in the series of Shakespeare histories to chronicle England's tribulations during the period before the Tudors took the throne (an event which occurs at the end of *Richard III*, when Henry VII, the first of the Tudors and grandfather to Shakespeare's Queen Elizabeth, becomes King). This play tells of the machinations of Richard (Ian McKellan), a royal prince with a twisted spine and grotesque physical appearance, to place himself in power. Richard is a spiteful person who kills without compunction and, in the process, earns nothing but

enmity from all around him. There are 4 bodies that impede his march to the crown: two of his brothers — Clarence and King Edward — and the king's two young sons. One-by-one, Richard has them removed, caring only that he should one-day rule England.

Does Richard have a conscience? Can evil such as his triumph completely, with no recompense expected on this side of the grave? Can the British monarchy exist without venom and corruption filtering up to the highest levels? These are a few of the more cogent questions addressed by *Richard III*, and McKellan and director Richard Loncraine make sure that they remain intact in the final version of the film.

In its own bloody way, *Richard III* is as enjoyable to watch as any recent screen production of Shakespeare, and the shift to the 1930's with its attendant Nazi imagery (parallels between Richard III and Hitler abound) gives the film a twist that conventional productions do not have. If there's a flaw to the movie, it's that this is one of Shakespeare's least ambitious and less thematically rich plays. Nevertheless, since the only memorable motion picture version is Lawrence Olivier's 1956 version, *Richard III* doesn't suffer from overexposure, and this interpretation offers an unconventional — and easily accessible — perspective. RECOMMENDED

Ridicule [France, 1996]

Starring: Charles Berling, Jean Rochefort, Fanny Ardant, Judith Godreche Director: Patrice Leconte Screenplay: Remi Waterhouse Running Time: **1:42** Rated: R (Nudity, mature themes) Theatrical Aspect Ratio: **1.85:1** In French with subtitles

In Patrice Leconte's *Ridicule*, the pen — or rather the word — is truly mightier than the sword. In late 18th century France, before the advent of the guillotine, wit was used as often for pain and humiliation as it was for pleasure. Those who had mastered the art of ridicule could, with one turn of phrase, strip a less adept opponent of pride and position, hurling him from the pampered confines of Louis XVI's court into the hostile world beyond, where indignities and possibly death awaited.

Ridicule is not meant to be taken as a rigorous historical account, but, as with all French movies, the period detail is impeccable. The general atmosphere, if not the specifics, reflects 1783 Versailles, where a witty conversationalist was greatly prized as a source of entertainment, and where those with a gift for bon mots could attain a position of importance at the king's court.

Gregoire Ponceludon de Malavoy (Charles Berling), a baron from the rural province of Dombes, comes to Versailles to obtain money for an ambitious engineering scheme that would drain southwest France's swamps to reduce disease and pestilence. Ponceludon entertains a hope that the king, known to be intrigued by science, might take an interest in the project and offer to fund it. However, what he discovers at Versailles disheartens him. Gaining an audience with the king has more to do with one's ancestors, bedpartners, and verbal agility than with the merits of one's proposal.

Undeterred, Ponceludon finds a local sponsor, Bellegarde (Jean Rochefort), who sees promise in the idealistic newcomer and offers lessons of how to survive in Versailles ("Don't laugh with your mouth open," "We call puns the death of wit," "The soul of wit is to know one's place"). While the young nobleman is learning the rules of acceptable court behavior, he falls for Bellegarde's beautiful, young daughter, Mathilde (Judith Godreche). But, when Ponceludon's would-be romance with Mathilde flounders because of her impending marriage, he seeks the sexual (and political) favors of Madame de Blayac (Fanny Ardant), a fixture at court who consorts with all the finest wits. Ponceludon then becomes involved in a series of contests with the appropriately-named Vilecourt (Bernard Giraudeau) to see whose wit is the most corrosive.

Leconte's film is tightly-plotted and well-paced, with few wasted or unnecessary scenes. The script does have lapses, such as a sequence that uses a conventional duel to generate unnecessary tension and uncertainty, but, on the whole, the writing is *Ridicule*'s greatest asset. The carefully-rendered French-to-English subtitles do justice to the sparkling dialogue, making the verbal matches between Ponceludon, Madame de Blayac, and Vilecourt one of *Ridicule*'s highlights. For those who appreciate movies with a bite, *Ridicule* shows its teeth early and keeps them razor-sharp throughout. **RECOMMENDED**

Riff-Raff [United Kingdom, 1993]

Starring: Robert Carlyle, Emer McCourt, Jimmy Coleman, George Moss, Ricky Tomlinson   Director: Ken Loach   Screenplay: Bill Jesse
Running Time: 1:36   Rated: No MPAA Rating (Profanity, brief nudity)
Theatrical Aspect Ratio: 1.66:1   In English with English subtitles

Stevie (Robert Carlyle) is an ex-con from Scotland struggling to start anew. In an attempt to change his life, he takes a construction job in North London where he meets an assortment of others who, in one

way or another, are just like him. He has no place to live, and doesn't make enough to rent a flat, so his co-workers happily appropriate a "squat" for him. Soon after, he meets Susan (Emer McCourt), an aspiring singer with a lot of heart but very little talent. The narrative moves on from there, detailing a short period in the lives of Stevie, Susan, and the workers on the construction site.

Riff-Raff is a strikingly powerful film that combines a biting sense of humor with an uncompromising, true-to-life look at the lot of England's working class. While movies like this are often maudlin and sometimes depressingly difficult to watch, that's not the case here. Director Ken Loach, with a keen sense of what makes people and relationships click, has guided his production down a narrow trail that perfectly balances comedy and drama. It's a daring move, and the film succeeds because Loach pulls it off.

Often, watching *Riff-Raff* is like viewing a home video. The realism is astonishing. Writer Bill Jesse (who died at the age of 48 and to whom the picture is dedicated) incorporated his own experience from years of construction work, and Loach cast only actors who had actually worked in construction.

Riff-Raff is in English, but Fine Line Features has chosen to subtitle the movie (in English) for American consumption. Why? Presumably because the heavy accents of the working class are occasionally difficult to understand. Personally, I found the subtitles more distracting than useful.

Riff-Raff is not a downer. There is a social message, but it doesn't bog down the film, perhaps because everything is told from the perspective of members of the lower class who view their lot pragmatically. No attempt is made to contrast the circumstances of the workers with those of the wealthy, so there isn't the seething sense of indignation and moral outrage that often accompanies films making similar statements. When one worker loses his job, instead of making an anguished display, he simply shrugs his shoulders, says goodbye to his fellows, and walks off, never to be seen again.

In *Riff-Raff,* Ken Loach has opened a window into a world that few movies dare to explore. This is not a commercial film, and therein lies one of the keys of its power — without having to pander to a certain audience, it can tell the tale on its own terms. The powerful result relies on earthy humor and a vivid depiction of reality to drive home the point **HIGHLY RECOMMENDED**

A River Runs Through It [1992]

Starring: Craig Sheffer, Brad Pitt, Tom Skerritt, Emily Lloyd
Director: Robert Redford Screenplay: Richard Friedenberg based on
the story by Norman MacLean Running Time: 2:03 Rated: PG (Nudity,
mature themes) Theatrical Aspect Ratio: 1.85:1

Watching *A River Runs Through It* is a little like leafing through an old photograph album. It conjures up feelings and images, many of them bittersweet, and all of them nostalgic. This is one of those motion pictures that truly transports you to another time and another place.

A River Runs Through It is a simple story about a typical, early-20th-century Montana family. It traces the lives of two brothers from boyhood to adulthood. Water — and a river in particular — is an important symbol for the twisting, rocky path of life, and it's never far from any scene. In fact, this may be a case of imagery being too obvious.

The two main characters, Norman and Paul MacLean, are portrayed solidly by Craig Sheffer and Brad Pitt. Tom Skerritt, as the boys' father, and Emily Lloyd, as Norman's girlfriend, lead a team of equally-solid supporting players. Skerritt especially has a daunting job, which he carries off with aplomb: showing the loving, caring man beneath the stiff, Puritanical preacher's facade.

This is a beautifully-shot film, and director Robert Redford (who also provides the voice-over narration) has paid painstaking attention to detail. The subtle humor is unforced and character-based. One of the best elements of *A River Runs Through It* is the effectively understated romance that develops. This has the feel of something genuine: sweet, touching, and sentimental. In that way, it is much like the movie as a whole.

A River Runs Through It avoids manipulating the audience's emotions, even though it has numerous chances to do so. Events happen; they aren't forced on us. Through this straightforward method of storytelling, the impact is strengthened. *A River Runs Through It* is a fine motion picture and, if it's a little slow in parts (especially the beginning), those moments are worth sitting through to experience the rest. **HIGHLY RECOMMENDED**

Rocky [1976]

Starring: Sylvester Stallone, Talia Shire, Burt Young, Carl Weathers,
Burgess Meredith Director: John G. Avildsen Screenplay: Sylvester
Stallone Running Time: 1:59 Rated: PG (Violence) Theatrical Aspect
Ratio: 1.85:1

There are essentially 3 kinds of boxing movies: those that offer a grim, tell-it-as-it-is perspective of life in the ring, those that focus (often in an exaggerated fashion) on the business aspects of things, and those that seek to uplift through a rags-to-riches story. *Rocky*, the 1977 Best Picture Oscar winner, belongs unabashedly in the third category. Although the movie contains realistic elements and is set in a believable arena, it is essentially a fairy tale about a down-and-out pugilist who gets a chance at the fight of a lifetime, and, at the same time, wins the girl. Since 1976, nearly every film featuring a big sports comeback and triumph has been inspired by and/or compared to *Rocky*, regardless of whether it involves boxing or not.

Rocky is as much a tender love story as it is about ring action. Rocky Balboa (Stallone) is a boxing bottomfeeder — someone who will fight anyone for a $50 purse. His lone ambition is to stay afloat. He lives in a one-room apartment with two turtles and a fish, and spends his days working as a collector for a South Philly loan shark. Mickey (Burgess Meredith), the crusty manager at the boxing club where he works out, is disgusted with Rocky, because he had the natural ability to become a great fighter, but threw it all away. When Rocky's attention isn't on fighting or his job, it's on wooing Adrian (Talia Shire), the painfully shy sister of his best friend, Paulie (Burt Young). Rocky is in love with her, but his inarticulate attempts to ask Adrian out frighten her off.

Rocky's fortunes change when Apollo Creed (Carl Weathers), the World Heavyweight Champion, hand picks him as an opponent. A fight scheduled for January 1, 1976 (and dubbed the "Bicentennial Match") was to feature Creed against his #1 challenger, but injuries to the opponent cause him to back out 5 weeks before the event. In an attempt to salvage something, Creed decides to give a local Philadelphia fighter a chance, and Rocky's nickname of the "Itallion Stallion" catches his attention. As a result, a boxer with no apparent future suddenly has a chance at the World Championship title. From Rocky's perspective, however, winning is secondary. He wants one thing out of the fight with Apollo: the self-respect he can earn by going the distance. Even more than that, however, he wants to win Adrian's heart.

Considering what the *Rocky* series became — popcorn action films with little heart, less intelligence, and a lot of testosterone — it's a somewhat refreshing experience to go back and re-connect with the original, which offers a lot more substance than the sequels. *Rocky* is not a flawless motion picture, but it is a feel-good classic, and well worth another look. The basic storyline has been done to death over the years; this is still one of the most effective and successful applications of the formula. **HIGHLY RECOMMENDED**

Roger Dodger [2002]

Starring: Campbell Scott, Jesse Eisenberg Director: Dylan Kidd
Screenplay: Dylan Kidd Running Time: 1:47 Rated: R (Profanity, sexual situations) Theatrical Aspect Ratio: 1.66:1

Roger Dodger is a delight for anyone who loves to absorb dialogue. The movie is almost all talk and no action, and possesses the "feel" (although not the pedigree) of a stage production translated to the screen. The plot is virtually non-existent and the character development is limited, but the longer the viewer listens to the lead character's monologues and conversations with various other individuals, the clearer it becomes that there are some fascinating philosophies being bandied about. Most of what is discussed in *Roger Dodger* pertains to sex and gender differences, and, while none of writer/director Dylan Kidd's observations are stunningly original, they are almost always interesting.

Roger (Campbell Scott) is a womanizer with ice in both his soul and his never-empty glass. His night life consists of attending parties and spending hours at bars, picking up women for one-night stands. He is currently bitter over the end of an affair with his boss, Joyce (Isabella Rossellini) — probably because he wasn't the one to break things off. Enter his 15-year-old nephew, Nick (Jesse Eisenberg), a small-town boy who is spending a few days in New York City to check out colleges. He is eager to learn the ropes about women from his uncle. It doesn't take long for Roger to warm to the idea of being a mentor, and it becomes his mission to get Nick laid before the day is over. But there's nothing altruistic in Roger's motives — he relishes the idea of destroying innocence, and the thought of stripping away Nick's naivete about sex proves to be an irresistible lure.

At first, this looks like it could be another coming-of-age story, until it becomes clear that the film is more about Roger than Nick. *Roger Dodger* does not relate how Roger's encounter with Nick causes him to reform his life. Roger may have regrets, but he is unapologetic about who he is or what he does. The film's coda — a 15-minute epilogue that seems out-of-place — is an attempt to "soften" Roger by leading us to believe that he's not beyond redemption. If there's an obvious weakness, this is it.

For Kidd, *Roger Dodger* is an auspicious debut. It won't find much of an audience outside of the art house circuit, because mainstream audiences will quickly grow tired of its talkiness. But for those who have the time and the patience to listen, Kidd's words, as delivered by Roger, have the power to weave a rare kind of magic. **RECOMMENDED**

The Rookie [2002]

Starring: Dennis Quaid, Rachel Griffiths, Brian Cox, Trevor Morgan, Beth Grant, Jay Hernandez Director: John Lee Hancock
Screenplay: Mike Rich, based on the book by Jim Morris and Joel Engel Running Time: 2:08 Rated: PG Theatrical Aspect Ratio: 2.35:1

A good baseball movie embraces the magic of baseball, and uses the game as a metaphor for life. Such is the case with *The Rookie,* and, while this outing will not challenge the likes of *The Natural* for the title of the best baseball movie ever made, it's a solid effort in its own right.

Jim Morris is a southpaw who spent parts of two seasons in the bullpen for the Tampa Bay Devil Rays. His career statistics — a 4.80 ERA, 15 IP, 13 K, and 9 BB — are hardly the stuff of which legends are made. Yet, in spite of that, Morris is the subject of Disney's *The Rookie* — not because of what he did once he reached The Show, but because he reached there in the first place. The unlikeliest of heroes, Morris became the second-oldest rookie ever to play Major League baseball when he stepped on the mound at the age of 35. A longer-than-long-shot with a story to inspire the most blasé individual, Morris' tale is a testament to the age-old saying that dreams can come true if you fight hard enough for them.

The Rookie starts out in the 1970s, as a young Jimmy Morris (Trevor Morgan) arrives in the small town of Big Lake, Texas. Jimmy's a baseball fan, but football, not baseball, is king in Big Lake. Flash forward to 1999: Jim (Dennis Quaid) is now married and has 3 kids. He's the coach for the local high school baseball team, the Big Lake Owls — a post he took after an arm injury ended his quest to break into Major League Baseball. However, while Jimmy is throwing batting practice, his players notice that his fastballs have a lot of zip on them, so they make a deal with him — if they win the district, he'll attend a big league tryout. Sure enough, when the season is over, the Owls have fulfilled their part of the bargain, so Jim throws in front of some scouts for the Tampa Bay Devil Rays. When his velocity reaches 98 mph on the radar, Jim suddenly becomes the hottest prospect around — even at age 35.

As inspirational stories go, this one is top-notch. It

satisfies without becoming cloying or going over-the-top. From a technical perspective, the film's baseball sequences are virtually flawless. This doesn't guarantee a good movie, but it helps. More important than the film's verisimilitude, however, is its structure. It manages to be uplifting without forcing us to endure a 9th-inning, come-from-behind victory. Because, when it comes down to it, *The Rookie* isn't as much about wining in a game as it is about winning in life. **RECOMMENDED**

Rosewood [1997]

Starring: Jon Voight, Ving Rhames, Don Cheadle, Bruce McGill, Loren Dean   Director: John Singleton   Screenplay: Gregory Poirier   Running Time: 2:22   Rated: R (Violence, profanity, mature themes)   Theatrical Aspect Ratio: 2.35:1

Rosewood, central Florida, 1923. The town's population numbered about 120, mostly black. It was a prosperous, happy community until a January day when one woman's lie set off a chain of events that would have devastating results. That woman was Fanny Taylor, and her false claim to have been assaulted by a black man resulted in the formation of a lynch mob that headed for Rosewood with arson and murder on their minds. Before the week was over, blood was shed and the town was in ashes.

If Singleton takes liberties with the historical account of what happened at Rosewood (and that account is murky at best — the death count differs greatly depending on which source is being consulted), it's in the name of dramatic license, and it works. This is a deeply affecting tale about the naked emotional and physical devastation that can be wrought by racial hatred. But it is also a story of hope that highlights the indomitable nature of the human spirit and the fraternity that can bind together two apparently different people. *Rosewood* does not glamorize evil, but neither does it demonize those who practice it. Singleton is careful to present a balanced and believable picture of the participants on both sides. The result presents a forceful message without ever preaching.

While *Rosewood* must be seen as a cohesive whole to be fully appreciated, there are isolated moments that stand out because of their haunting power. One of the most startling depicts white folk picnicking and frolicking while Rosewood burns in the background. In another scene, McGill's character carefully teaches his son how to make a noose for a lynching — one of the essential lessons he must learn to become a man. There are, in fact, times when *Rosewood* is reminiscent of *Schindler's List*. There's a kernel of truth that both films have in common — the theme of the duality of human nature: the capacity for great good and great evil, boundless love and infinite hatred. And, while this film is not as well-paced or tightly-structured as Spielberg's Holocaust drama, it evokes many of the same feelings and emotions. It is an important film that should not be missed. **HIGHLY RECOMMENDED**

Ruby in Paradise [1993]

Starring: Ashley Judd, Todd Field, Bentley Mitchum, Allison Dean, Dorothy Lyman   Director: Victor Nunez   Screenplay: Victor Nunez   Running Time: 1:55   Rated: No MPAA Rating (Sex, brief nudity)   Theatrical Aspect Ratio: 1.85:1

When Ruby Lee Gissing (Ashley Judd) makes it out of her Tennessee home town "without getting pregnant or beat up," she considers it quite a feat. With all her belongings in her car, she arrives in Panama City, Florida with hardly a dime to her name and little more than childhood memories to go on. Nevertheless, her pluck and determination land her a job in the off-season because Mildred Chambers (Dorothy Lyman), the owner of a souvenir shop, sees something in her. Ms. Chambers has only one rule for her employees: they don't date her son Ricky (Bentley Mitchum). So when Ruby not only goes out with him, but ends up in his bed, her troubles are about to begin.

Male coming-of-age stories are a dime-a-dozen, but the same cannot be said for the female equivalent, especially when the story is told with intelligence and sensitivity. This makes *Ruby in Paradise* a rare and welcome change of pace. Oddly enough, for something with this much insight, it's a surprise that it was written and directed by a man, Victor Nunez.

The film gives Ruby two men to choose from: the scheming, cheating Ricky, who offers her sex, gifts, and a good time; and the deep-thinking Mike (Todd Field), who offers her companionship and security. Ruby, however, is less concerned about finding a man than finding out who she really is. She came to Panama City to get something that she couldn't get back home.

Ashley Judd's performance is worth more words than I have space for. Her grasp of Ruby is such that every nuance of the character is brought out, and the subtlety with which certain emotions are brought to the fore demands appreciation from a viewer. Judd repeatedly outacts and outshines her co-stars. There isn't a moment in this movie when Judd's Ruby is upstaged, and she's in every scene.

Ruby Lee Gissing is so much like the heroines of the Jane Austen books she reads that even she recognizes the similarities. The toughness, intelligence, and resiliency are all there, and with the deft hand of Nunez replacing that of Austen, this makes *Ruby in Paradise* a surprisingly fresh and engrossing little film. **RECOMMENDED**

The Run of the Country [Ireland, 1995]
Starring: Albert Finney, Matthew Keeslar, Victoria Smurfit, Anthony Brophy Director: Peter Yates Screenplay: Shane Connaughton
Running Time: 1:49 Rated: R (Sex, nudity, violence, profanity)
Theatrical Aspect Ratio: 2.35:1

Albert Finney is one of today's best character actors, yet Finney's character is not the focus of *The Run of the Country*. His is a supporting role, presenting an opportunity for conflict with his teenage son, Danny (Matthew Keeslar). This is Danny's story — how, coping with the recent death of his beloved mother, he struggles to find independence from an overbearing father. Part of this process is moving out of his childhood home and in with his friend, Prunty (Anthony Brophy). Another part is falling in love. The object of his affection is Annagh (Victoria Smurfit), a girl from just north of the border separating Catholic South Ireland from the Protestant North.

Though it takes place in contemporary Ireland, the way in which people live — many in ramshackle huts with little evidence of modern "conveniences" — gives the story a timeless quality. Likewise, the characters would probably be equally at home in the 19th century as in the 20th. Danny and Annagh are both virgins well into their teens and Danny's father is opposed to any sort of contraceptive. Religion is a powerful force, and the penalties for premarital sex are terrible to contemplate.

The best-crafted element of the film is the love story. Director Peter Yates brings real feeling and tenderness to the interactions between Danny and Annagh, from their first furtive glances at each other to Danny's faltering attempts to address her in conversation. Annagh is somewhat more world-wise than Danny, which makes it amusing to watch her nonplussed reactions to some of his unintentional double entendres.

The relationship between Danny and his father, although of equal importance to the romance, is less developed. Drawn with broad strokes, this conflict always seems more peripheral than central, which robs a cathartic scene of emotional power. Finney does all he can with the material, creating a mild character always on the brink of an emotional eruption, but Matthew Keeslar can't keep up with him. In fact, Keeslar, who is at times flat, isn't the equal of any of his co-stars. Both Victoria Smurfit and Anthony Brophy have impressive debuts.

The script has a fair number of affecting sequences, and manages to deftly mix humor and serious issues. While the political situation and the possible involvement of the IRA are kept in the background, they are not ignored. More crucial to the story, however, are the boundaries created by religion, education, and class. Every conflict in this film has its roots in one of these three causes. So, although *The Run of the Country* has its weak spots, it nevertheless gives us a more original coming-of-age story than that which typically graces American screens. **RECOMMENDED**

The Scent of a Woman [1992]
Starring: Al Pacino, Chris O'Donnell Director: Martin Brest
Screenplay: Bo Goldman Running Time: 2:36 Rated: R (Language, mature themes) Theatrical Aspect Ratio: 1.85:1

Scent of a Woman is about Charles Simms (Chris O'-Donnell), a Boston prep school senior, and the Thanksgiving weekend he spends working as the aide and companion of Lt. Colonel Frank Slade (Al Pacino), an embittered, lonely, blind veteran. The job, which begins as an onerous task performed principally for money, becomes a tour of self-discovery when Slade decides to make an unexpected visit to New York City. There, amidst all the holiday hoopla, the lieutenant's actions force Charlie into making an emotionally painful — and potentially physically dangerous — decision.

There are certain actors that, when they appear in a film, are almost invariably indicators that the production is of high quality. They are an elite few, with names like Nicholson, Hoffman, Hackman, and Pacino. Considering some of the roles that Al Pacino has played during his celebrated career (in *The Godfather* trilogy, for example), it would be hyperbole to say that he gives the "performance of a lifetime" in *Scent of a Woman* . . . or would it? For 2 hours, he brings Frank Slade to life in a way that few others in Hollywood could. As portrayed by Pacino, there's far more to this man that a rancorous outlook on life and a couple of hearty "hoo-ha"s.

Chris O'Donnell is solid, if somewhat obscured in the more experienced man's shadow. Although the role of Charlie is understated by O'Donnell, he nevertheless manages to fashion a rapport with the audience. This is necessary for the film to succeed, since it's through his eyes that the story unfolds.

In essence, *Scent of a Woman* is another in a never-ending series of bonding pictures where each person has something unique to offer to the other. If there's anything special about the film, it's that on this occasion, the emotional realism of the characters, especially Slade, is heartwrenchingly believable. His relationship with Charlie works because Pacino won't let it fail.

Unfortunately, considering how sound the bulk of the picture is, the final moments, with their overt pandering to a Hollywood-style ending, are a severe liability. Certainly, such "triumphs" are fun to watch, but they cheapen *Scent of a Woman*. Would it have cost the production team that much to inject a little realism into the film's last reel?

The movie is as long as its storyline demands. It doesn't seem like 2½ hours, and less time with these characters would have cheated the audience. Aided by an emotive score from Thomas Newman, the picture has opportunities to soar. Hampered by the script's limitations, however, *Scent of a Woman* falls short of being a masterful production.

RECOMMENDED

Schindler's List [1993]

Starring: Liam Neeson, Ben Kingsley, Ralph Fiennes, Caroline Goodall, Embeth Davidtz Director: Steven Spielberg Screenplay: Steven Zaillian based on the novel by Thomas Keneally Running Time: 3:15 Rated: R (Violence, Holocaust images, nudity, profanity) Theatrical Aspect Ratio: 1.85:1

Schindler's List opens in September of 1939 in Krakow, Poland, with the Jewish community under increasing pressure from the Nazis. Into this tumult comes Oskar Schindler (Liam Neeson), a Nazi businessman interested in obtaining Jewish backing for a factory he wishes to build. He makes contact with Itzhak Stern (Ben Kingsley), an accountant, to arrange financial matters.

March 1941. The Krakow Jewish community has been forced to live in "the Ghetto," where money no longer has any meaning. Several elders agree to invest in Schindler's factory and the DEF (Deutsche Emailwarenfabrik) is born — a place where large quantities of pots are manufactured. To do the work, Schindler hires Jews (because they're cheaper than Poles), and the German army becomes his biggest customer.

March 1943. Germany's intentions towards the Jews are no longer a secret. The Ghetto is "liquidated," with the survivors being herded into the Plaszow Forced Labor Camp. During this time, Schindler has managed to ingratiate himself with the local commander, Amon Goeth (Ralph Fiennes), a Nazi who kills Jews for sport. Using his relationship with Goeth, Schindler begins to secretly campaign to help the Jews, saving men, women, and children from certain death.

Schindler's List gives us 3 major stories and a host of minor ones. First and foremost, it tells the tale of the Holocaust, presenting new images of old horrors. Spielberg emphasizes the brutality of the situation by not pulling punches when it comes to gore. The blood, inky rather than crimson in stark black-and-white, fountains when men and women are shot in the head or through the neck.

The second story is that of Oskar Schindler, the Nazi businessman who saved 1,200 Jews from death. Schindler starts out as a self-centered manufacturer, concerned only about making money. He hires Jews because they're cheap, not because he likes them. But his perspective changes, and he risks losing everything to save as many lives as he can. His eventual lament that he couldn't save more is heartbreaking.

The third story belongs to Amon Goeth, the Nazi commander of Krakow, a man who teeters on the brink of madness. Despite his intense hatred for Jews, he is inexplicably attracted to his Jewish housekeeper, Helen Hirsch (Embeth Davidtz). Disgusted by his feelings, he lashes out at her with a display of violence that is almost Scorsese-like in its blunt presentation. Spielberg works carefully to show unexpected depth and complexity to his character.

Despite the grisly subject matter, this movie is essentially about uncovering a kernel of hope and dignity in the midst of a monstrous tragedy. The story of Oskar Schindler's sacrifices for the Jews sets this apart from other Holocaust dramas. *Schindler's List* offers a clear view of human nature laid bare: hatred, greed, lust, envy, anger, and, most important of all, empathy and love. Because this film touches us so deeply, the catharsis has a power that few — if any — other moments in film history can match. **MUST SEE**

Searching for Bobby Fischer [1993]

Starring: Max Pomeranc, Joe Mantegna, Joan Allen, Ben Kingsley, Laurence Fishburne Director: Steven Zaillian Screenplay: Steven Zaillian based on the book by Fred Waitzkin Running Time: 1:50 Rated: PG (Mild profanity) Theatrical Aspect Ratio: 1.85:1

At the tender age of 7, Josh Waitzkin (Max Pomeranc) becomes fascinated by the game of chess. Without giving up little league baseball, he learns how to play, hanging out with Vinnie (Laurence Fishburne) and a group of speed chess hustlers who occupy nearby Washington Square. It isn't long before Josh is able to beat them all. His father, looking to take him to the next level, employs ex-chess master Bruce Pandolfini (Ben Kingsley) as a teacher. Under Pandolfini, Josh matures as a player, and, for the first time, he starts to fear losing.

Searching for Bobby Fischer is based on the true life story of Josh Waitzkin who, at the age of 16, became the highest-ranked American player under 18. It isn't just Josh's tale, however. The name and image of the mysterious chess genius Bobby Fischer infiltrate this movie. Fischer is as much an icon to this game as Babe Ruth is to baseball.

How important are games to the American way of life? Have they become so crucial that we lose sight of the people playing them? And at what point does the need to win become so important that the game ceases to be fun? These are some of the questions that *Searching for Bobby Fischer* probes. It certainly can't answer them, but the film offers fodder for thought as it explores Josh's early career and examines the relationship between the young chess master and his sports writer father, Frank Waitzkin (Joe Mantegna).

Josh starts playing chess because it fascinates him. As soon as Frank recognizes his son's gift, however, he begins to apply subtle pressure. Winning becomes important — perhaps too important — and Josh is afraid that to fail at the game is to risk losing his father's love. It's then that chess becomes a burden and he stops enjoying it.

Searching for Bobby Fischer is an intensely fascinating movie capable of involving those who are ignorant about chess as well as those who love it. The focus of the film is less on the actual game than it is on the people, emotions, and pressures surrounding Josh. It is a tale of human trials and triumph, not a sports movie that panders to a certain segment of the population. Chess may not be the most exciting activity to watch, but *Searching for Bobby Fischer* makes for engaging entertainment. **RECOMMENDED**

The Secret of Roan Inish [1994]

Starring: Jeni Courtney, Mick Lally, Richard Sheridan, Eileen Colgan, John Lynch Director: John Sayles Screenplay: John Sayles based on *The Secret of the Ron Mor Skerry* by Rosalie K. Fry Running Time: 1:43 Rated: PG Theatrical Aspect Ratio: 1.85:1

In content, setting, and cast choice, *The Secret of Roan Inish* is a departure for writer/director John Sayles. The creative force behind such memorable and diverse films as *Matewan, City of Hope, Eight Men Out,* and *Passion Fish,* has taken pen and camera across the Atlantic to Ireland, a land steeped in mystery and legend.

The Secret of Roan Inish is the story of 10-year old Fiona Coneelly (Jeni Courtney), a motherless girl living in the city who is sent to stay with her grandparents (Mick Lally and Eileen Colgan) when her father determines that his poor lifestyle is not suitable for raising a daughter. Fiona's grandparents live in a small fishing village across the waters from Roan Inish ("seal island"), the island where the Coneellys had thrived for generations until tragic circumstances forced them to the mainland. Now, however, legends about the family's connection to Roan Inish abound. Is Fiona's little brother, who drifted out to sea in a storm years ago, really dead, or have the seals nurtured and protected him? Is there any truth to the story that in Fiona's veins runs the blood of a selkie, a seal who became a woman? And what will it take to restore the ways of the past, something which inspires equal portions of longing and dread?

Geographically, Sayles may be in unfamiliar territory with *The Secret of Roan Inish,* but his inimitable style has been imprinted on this movie. Two of the director's trademarks — the ability to tell an engrossing story and the development of strong, three-dimensional characters — are in evidence. With *Roan Inish,* Sayles has found the perfect balance between the mystical and the concrete. The result is exuberant and compelling.

There's no doubt that *The Secret of Roan Inish* is a most atypical motion picture, but in many ways, this is the best kind of movie — one that takes us to a land where magic is real, and where a little girl can strive to find a lost brother and bring happiness to an entire family. The story, although straightforward, is by no means simple, and there's enough in *The Secret of Roan Inish* to delight both children and adults. **HIGHLY RECOMMENDED**

Secrets and Lies [United Kingdom/France, 1996]

Starring: Brenda Blethyn, Marianne Jean-Baptiste, Timothy Spall, Phyllis Logan, Claire Rushbrook Director: Mike Leigh Screenplay: Mike Leigh Running Time: 2:22 Rated: No MPAA Rating (Mature themes, profanity) Theatrical Aspect Ratio: 1.66:1

By wedding comedy with tragedy in intricate, realistic unions, Mike Leigh has become one of the foremost film making voices for the British working class. Yet, even though his movies bring a certain social viewpoint to the screen, this in no way limits the universality of Leigh's themes. *Secrets and Lies*, 1996's Palme D'Or winner at Cannes, represents the director at his best — unsentimental yet powerful, funny and poignant, and, in the end, undeniably satisfying.

Secrets and Lies opens with a funeral, then quickly switches to a wedding. During the former ceremony, Hortense (Marianne Jean-Baptiste), a 27-year-old black optometrist, is burying her mother. In the next scene, we meet Maurice (Timothy Spall), a 38-year-old white photographer who's taking pictures of a nervous bride. It takes nearly the entire movie before these two characters come face-to-face, but what happens during that meeting represents the climax of Leigh's beautifully-realized film. Hortense and Maurice are crucial to unraveling the entire sequence of secrets and lies.

Hortense was adopted. She has known this since she was 7 years old, but it's not until both of her parents are dead that she feels compelled to seek out her birth mother. Despite being warned by a social worker to anticipate unpleasantness or disappointment, Hortense is shocked to learn that her mother is white. Her name is Cynthia (Brenda Blethyn), and she's a 42-year-old neurotic living in a dark, gloomy rowhouse with her 21-year-old daughter, Roxanne (Claire Rushbrook). Cynthia is disliked by just about everyone who knows her, except perhaps her brother, Maurice.

Secrets and Lies chronicles Hortense's initial approach to Cynthia, their first meeting, and the development of a tentative bond. Each offers something unique to the other: Cynthia has lost her "real" daughter's love and respect, and is desperate to find a surrogate. Hortense, on the other hand, feels rootless now that the two people who brought her up are dead, and, while she doesn't look to Cynthia for parenting, she is curious about, and, ultimately, sympathetic with the disappointments that have defined her biological mother's life. There are no recriminations, at least not on Hortense's part.

Secrets and Lies exhibits the kind of breathtaking power that can be unearthed in a simple story. There's no sensationalism — Leigh has ignored stereotypes in carefully developing the situation (wealthy black professional; underprivileged, uneducated whites) to dispel racial tension. This allows the dysfunctional family dynamics to be the sole focus. What the director has accomplished with this picture is to fashion an amazingly-textured story that grips us with unexpected force on the first viewing, and is sure to reveal a new aspect each time we come back. Without a doubt, *Secrets and Lies* is worth more than one trip to the theater. **MUST SEE**

Selena [1997]

Starring: Jennifer Lopez, Edward James Olmos, Jon Seda, Constance Marie Director: Gregory Nava Screenplay: Gregory Nava Running Time: 2:05 Rated: PG (Mild profanity, mature themes) Theatrical Aspect Ratio: 1.85:1

Going into *Selena*, I didn't know or care much about the life of the late Tex-Mex singer, whose death in 1995 came just as she was attempting to break into the mainstream American pop market. As far as I was aware, Selena's tragic end was just another minor footnote in music history — I hadn't heard of her before and I didn't expect to hear of her again. Then along came this movie, and, sitting in a darkened theater, watching Selena's story unfold, my perceptions changed. I not only cared, but understood a measure of the tragedy that had stricken her fans.

It would have been easy to trivialize Selena's story, turning it into a sudsy, made-for-TV type motion picture. The details for something lurid and exploitative are there, but that was never an approach considered by writer/director Gregory Nava. It's not an original tale — movies like this abound — but Nava's point-of-view is fresh.

This is a multigenerational story, exploring not only Selena's realization of her dreams, but the importance of her father's vision to all that she accomplished. It was his belief in her that prodded her to follow her own path, and his support that convinced her that she could succeed in a field where every other Mexican American woman had failed.

Jennifer Lopez is radiant as the title character, conveying the boundless energy and enthusiasm that exemplified Selena, while effectively copying not only her look, but her mannerisms. I wonder if Selena's family, upon watching this performance, felt an eerie sense of déjà vu. It's apparent from the clips of the real performer shown at the movie's conclusion that Lopez has done a masterful job of re-creating a personality.

Nava's film flows beautifully, and the concert sequences effectively capture the electricity of such events. *Selena* achieves the perfect emotional pitch for the subject, and, though this is a celebration of life, youth, and family, our awareness of the inevitable end lends a sense of poignancy to the proceedings. It's impossible to watch Selena's triumphant Astrodome concert without remembering that her life would be snuffed out less than a month later.

Fame often follows tragedy, especially when the victim is cut down in the prime of life. James Dean. Buddy Holly. Roberto Clemente. These are just a few names in a long, long list. Now, Selena has joined that roster. This movie will serve to further elevate her name and advance her legend. *Selena* is a shining story. **HIGHLY RECOMMENDED**

A Self-Made Hero [France, 1996]

Starring: Mathieu Kassovitz, Anouk Grinberg, Sandrine Kiberlain, Albert Dupontel Director: Jacques Audiard Screenplay: Alain Le Henry and Jacques Audiard from the book by Jean-Francois Deniau Running Time: 1:45 Rated: No MPAA Rating (Mature themes, profanity, sex, brief nudity) Theatrical Aspect Ratio: 1.66:1 In French with subtitles

Have you ever wished that you could become someone else? That, without regard for the consequences, you could shed your current personality like an old shirt and slip into something more comfortable? If so, then you'll be intrigued by the premise of *A Self-Made Hero*, director Jacques Audiard's smart, fascinating, satirical meditation on the flexibility of identity.

The film opens in modern-day France, with an unseen interviewer asking questions of a seventy-something man named Albert Dehousse (Jean-Louis Trintignant). As Albert begins to talk about his past, we see it unfold on screen — his childhood in rural, pre-World War II France, his life during the German occupation, and, finally, how he rose to prominence in the wake of the Allied liberation. And, while *A Self-Made Hero*'s narrative traces Albert's life during the 1940s, a pseudo-documentary overlay offers occasional commentary and observations from those who once knew Albert.

In Lambersart, France during 1944, 26-year-old Albert (Mathieu Kassovitz) lives his life as if no war is under progress. He is content to marry a pretty blond (Sandrine Kiberlain), take a job as a salesman, and stay out of the Germans' way. Then, after the Liberation, he learns that his father-in-law was an important member of the Resistance, and, feeling overwhelmed by inadequacy, Albert flees Lambersart for Paris, where, with the help of a mysterious friend named "The Captain" (Albert Dupontel), he re-invents himself as a high-ranking member of the Resistance. Through a combination of hard work, good fortune, and brashness, Albert makes the right connections and ends up as an important player in the post-war order. But, when he falls in love with the vivacious Servane (Anouk Grinberg), he wonders about the psychological penalty of keeping the truth from her.

A Self-Made Hero has an extraordinarily perceptive script that asks a lot of complex questions but doesn't insult its audience by offering simple answers. Audiard has designed this film as part-drama, part satire, and there are times when the movie's pointed comedy is worth more than a perfunctory chuckle. And the often-ironic "documentary interview" segments, which add a layer of verisimilitude to the project, open a window onto how modern-day Parisians view their history of fifty years ago.

At the heart of *A Self-Made Hero* is a simple question: Who am I, and can I be a different person? The Captain indicates that there's no such thing as a fixed identity — losers can successfully disguise themselves as winners, cowards as heroes, and devils as saints. Albert notes that "the best lives are invented," and goes on to prove his words by actions. *A Self-Made Hero* offers an ambitious portrait of one man who used an alternative path to realize his dreams only to discover that the richest fiction can never truly supplant reality. **HIGHLY RECOMMENDED**

Seventh Heaven [France, 1997]

Starring: Sandrine Kiberlain, Vincent Lindon, Francois Berleand, Francine Berge, Leo Le Bevillon Director: Benoît Jacquot Screenplay: Jérôme Beaujour, Benoît Jacquot Running Time: 1:31 Rated: No MPAA Rating (Mature themes, sexual situations, nudity) Theatrical Aspect Ratio: 2.35:1 In French with subtitles

Seventh Heaven introduces us to Mathilde (Sandrine Kimberlain) and Nico (Vincent Lindon), a dysfunctional couple. Mathilde is not well. In addition to having kleptomaniac tendencies, she is prone to fainting spells. She wanders around with a distracted, dazed expression on her face. Her husband, who is involved in a sexual relationship with his assistant at work, cares for Mathilde as he would for a child. When he sleeps with her, he appears pleased by her passivity and lack of passion. Then Mathilde meets a mysterious hypnotist (Francois Berleand), who puts her under his influence, regresses her back to childhood, and cures her malaise. Suddenly, she is emotionally, mentally, and sexually whole. The next time she and Nico have sex, she experiences an orgasm. Oddly, this disturbs him, because his simple, well-defined home life has now been turned upside down.

At first glance, it seems that Jacquot may be going in one of two directions: exploring the power and potential for abuse inherent in hypnotism, or examining the impact of repressed memories. In reality, however, these are only red herrings — minor ideas in a tapestry whose main focus is the shifting dynamics of a marriage. Before her awakening, Mathilde is trapped in a sterile union. Her husband is more of a caregiver than a friend or a lover. He is content with the arrangement, which makes her more like a pet or a servant than an equal. She cooks his meals, cleans the house, and helps care for their child. They do not engage in lengthy conversations and their sexual relationship is limited to a few minutes of rigorous activity in the dark while he satisfies himself. Once Mathilde has shaken off her emotional lethargy, Nico feels threatened and frightened. He does not know this woman, and he isn't sure that he wants to. His most sincere desire is for things to go back to the way they were.

Jacquot is a meticulous director who relies heavily upon the performances of his actors. During one sequence in the hypnotist's office, when Mathilde is relating a childhood memory, Jacquot keeps the camera on her face, rather than yielding to the temptation of inserting a flashback. Were Kiberlain less accomplished, this could have been an unfortunate move, but the actress is capable of handling the approach. Jacquot also uses a few minor photographic tricks to emphasize the thrust of his narrative. The film opens with a freeze-frame shot of an out-of-focus Mathilde. It closes with Nico groping in the dark. Yet, as confused as the characters' needs may sometimes be, the hand of the director is never anything less than sure, and his vision is always crystal clear.

RECOMMENDED

Shanghai Triad [Hong Kong, 1995]

Starring: Gong Li, Li Baotian, Wang Xiaoxiao, Sun Chun, Fu Biao, Li Xuejian Director: Zhang Yimou Screenplay: Bi Feiyu Running Time: 1:48 Rated: R (Violence, mature themes) Theatrical Aspect Ratio: 1.85:1 In Mandarin with subtitles

Throughout the 1990s, Zhang Yimou, one of the most internationally acclaimed of all the so-called "Fifth Generation" Chinese film makers, made a series of visually striking, narratively compelling pictures, including *Raise the Red Lantern* and *To Live*. In *Shanghai Triad*, Zhang delves deeply into the workings of Shanghai's gangland during the 1930s. Reminiscent of Prohibition-era Chicago — and therefore depicting the universality of organized crime — *Shanghai Triad* is a fascinating, though imperfect, look at the lure and power of greed to corrupt and destroy.

The story is told from the point-of-view of 14-year-old Shuisheng (Wang Xiaoxiao), a country "innocent" brought by his uncle (Li Xuejian) to Shanghai to work for Boss Tang (Li Baotian). Zhang uses Shuisheng to represent the audience; everything that takes place is seen through the young boy's eyes. In fact, there are several effective first person camera shots where we see events unfold as if from Shuisheng's perspective. Like those of us watching the film, Shuisheng has no knowledge about what it means to live in Tang's circle, and his education is ours.

Shuisheng's first job for the Boss is to serve his mistress, the petulant, controlling Bijou (Gong Li). Like Shuisheng, Bijou was born and bred in the country, but, unlike her new servant, she has allowed the bright lights, easy money, and fast life of Shanghai to corrupt her innocence. A singer in the Boss' nightclub and lover to both him and one of his top men, she is trapped in a situation that is out of control. There are times when she recognizes the futility of her existence and lashes out in mingled pain and despair.

Shanghai Triad takes place over an 8-day period that chronicles Shuisheng's arrival to work for the Boss, his conflicted emotions for Bijou, a bloody attempt to kill Tang, and the subsequent flight to an island safe house. There is plenty of action, but the primary focus is on relationships and internal conflicts. The interaction between Shuisheng, Bijou, and Tang forms the central dynamic, and those three characters represent this movie's true "Shanghai triad."

With its underworld violence and straightforward narrative, *Shanghai Triad* is one of Zhang's most accessible films. It is not, however, his best work, having neither the epic scope of *To Live* nor the quiet emotional power of *Raise the Red Lantern*. Yet there is still much to like about *Shanghai Triad*, not the least of which is the production's gorgeous look (credit the director and his cinematographer, Li Xiao). *Shanghai Triad* overflows with memorable imagery and atmosphere. And, as this film verifies, a weak entry by Zhang is often far more engrossing than a strong entry by many other directors. RECOMMENDED

The Shawshank Redemption [1994]
Starring: Tim Robbins, Morgan Freeman, Bob Gunton, William Sadler, Clancy Brown, Gil Bellows Director: Frank Darabont Screenplay: Frank Darabont based on "Rita Hayworth and the Shawshank Redemption" by Stephen King Running Time: 2:22 Rated: R (Violence, language, mature themes) Theatrical Aspect Ratio: 1.85:1

With a legion of titles like *Pet Sematary, Firewalker,* and *Children of the Corn,* it's reasonable not to expect much from Stephen King-inspired motion pictures. Adaptations of the prolific author's work typically vary from mildly entertaining to virtually unwatchable. There are a few notable exceptions, however; two of which (*Stand by Me, Misery*) were crafted by widely-respected director Rob Reiner. While *The Shawshank Redemption* is not a Reiner movie per se, it is a production of Castle Rock Pictures (Reiner's film company).

Spanning the years from 1947 through 1966, *The Shawshank Redemption* takes the "innocent man in prison" theme and bends it at a different angle. Instead of focusing on crusades for freedom, the movie ventures down the less-traveled road of concentrating on the personal cost of adapting to prison life and how some convicts, once they conform, lose the ability to survive beyond the barbed wire and iron bars. As one of the characters puts it: "These [prison] walls are funny. First you hate them, then you get used to them, then you start to depend on them."

Filmed on location in a disused Ohio prison, *The Shawshank Redemption* is set in a place of perpetual dreariness. What little color there is, is drab and lifeless (lots of grays and muted greens and blues), and there are times when the film is a shade away from black-and-white (give credit to cinematographer Roger Deakins, a longtime Cohen brothers collaborator). It's ironic, therefore, that the central messages are of hope, redemption, and salvation.

Tim Robbins, as Andrew Dufresne, plays the wrongly convicted man with quiet dignity. Andy's ire is internal; he doesn't rant about his situation or the corruptness of the system that has imprisoned him. Ellis Boyd Redding (Morgan Freeman), or "Red" as his friends call him, is the self-proclaimed "Sears and Roebuck" of the Shawshank Prison (for a price, he can get just about anything from the outside). His is

the narrative voice and, for once, the disembodied words aid, rather than intrude upon, the story. Gil Bellows, in a small-but-crucial role (that was originally intended for Brad Pitt), brings the poise of a veteran to his portrayal of Tommy Williams, Andy's protege. Ultimately, the standout actor is the venerable James Whitmore. Whitmore's Brooks is a brilliantly-realized character, and the scenes with him attempting to cope with life outside of Shawshank represents one of the film's most moving — and effective — sequences.

Prison movies often focus on the violence and hopelessness of a life behind bars. While this film includes those elements, it makes them peripheral. *The Shawshank Redemption* is all about hope and, because of that, watching it is both uplifting and cathartic. HIGHLY RECOMMENDED

She's So Lovely [1997]
Starring: Sean Penn, Robin Wright Penn, John Travolta, Gena Rowlands Director: Nick Cassavetes Screenplay: John Cassavetes Running Time: 1:38 Rated: R (Profanity, violence) Theatrical Aspect Ratio: 2.35:1

The director of *She's So Lovely* is Nick Cassavetes, the son of John and actress Gena Rowlands. And, since Rowlands appears in *She's So Lovely,* this is, in a sense, a family production. The younger Cassavetes' approach to directing is different from his father's. Nick is more of a polished, traditional film maker. John relied upon improvisations from both his actors and his cinematographer; Nick scripts and choreographs everything beforehand. He may be following in his father's footsteps, but he is not attempting to copy him.

Real-life couple Sean Penn and Robin Wright Penn play Eddie and Maureen, a husband and wife who are very much in love. When we first meet them, it's the late 1970s, although only the music, hairstyles, and clothing seem to differentiate the time period from today. Both Eddie and Maureen exhibit streaks of violent, self-destructive behavior. But, although Eddie carries a gun and isn't unwilling to use his fists, he never strikes Maureen. She and the child she carries are his reason for living. Neither husband nor wife is entirely sane, and when Eddie loses it in public and shoots a mental health care worker, he is sent away to an institution for the criminally insane.

A decade passes before Eddie is given his release, but the world he returns to is far different from the one he left. His best friend, Shorty (Harry Dean Stanton), is still the same, but his wife is not. During the last 10 years, Maureen has cleaned herself up, divorced Eddie, and married a prosperous businessman named Joey (John Travolta). She lives in a big house with a swimming pool out back, and has 3 daughters (the oldest is a product of her troubled marriage to Eddie). It's an idyllic situation, yet when she learns of Eddie's release, Maureen feels the tug of long-buried feelings, and their re-emergence threatens not only her family's stability, but her own tenuous grip on sanity.

She's So Lovely is uncomfortable because it challenges our perceptions about love and family. Maureen and Joey have the American dream, but does it really mean anything? And is true love just another form of insanity? Some viewers will undoubtedly be dismayed by the film's abrupt ending but, by the time the end credits roll, we know all that we need to know to guess how things will probably turn out. *She's So Lovely* isn't a flawless production, but it's a fitting tribute to John Cassavetes, and a reminder of the many ways that a woman can be under the influence.

RECOMMENDED

Shine [Australian, 1996]

Starring: Geoffrey Rush, Armin Mueller-Stahl, Noah Taylor, Lynn Redgrave Director: Scott Hicks Screenplay: Jan Sardi based on a story by Scott Hicks Running Time: 1:45 Rated: PG-13 (Mature themes, brief nudity) Theatrical Aspect Ratio: 1.85:1

Shine is a deceptively simple title for an amazingly powerful motion picture. Based on the life story of Australian pianist David Helfgott, director Scott Hicks' film touches on themes as diverse as the nature of genius, the triumph over adversity, and the destructive power of love.

Shine has its roots in 1986, when director Scott Hicks read a newspaper story about David Helfgott, a pianist who performed a flawless classical repertoire at a Perth restaurant. Hicks' interest was piqued, and he arranged to see Helfgott in concert. For the better part of the next year, he worked to earn the man's trust with the goal of presenting his story in a motion picture. That odyssey, which is admittedly fictionalized to some degree in Jan Sardi's wonderful screenplay, became *Shine*, one of 1996's most stirring and inspirational tales.

To fully comprehend David Helfgott's story, it is necessary to understand his father, Peter Helfgott (powerfully portrayed by Armin Mueller-Stahl), a Polish Jew who settled in Australia after surviving Hitler's purge. He's a soul-sick man whose ongoing battle with private demons makes his personality erratic

and his actions unpredictable. He lost his parents and sisters-in-law to the Holocaust, and the anguish of those losses impels him to keep his family together at all costs. When we first encounter him during the 1950s, he is still rebelling against his long-dead father's influence. Peter's drive to teach his children to play instruments is a direct reaction to his own father's dislike of music.

Shine follows David's life from childhood (Alex Rafalowicz), through adolescence (Noah Taylor), to adulthood (Geoffrey Rush). When we first meet him, he's performing at a school recital. There, a music teacher, Ben Rosen (Nicholas Bell), notices his obvious talent, and offers to teach him. Eventually, after winning several competitions, David is invited to study music in the United States. His father, determined not to "let anyone destroy this family," refuses to let him go. Soon after, David's talent begins to languish as his musical progress stagnates. When he receives a scholarship to the Royal College of Music in London, an elderly writer friend (Googie Withers) encourages him to take the offer, whether his father objects or not. In following that advice, David sunders his relationship with Peter.

In London, he studies under the guidance of Cecil Parkes (John Gielgud), attempting to reach his potential. But, on the night of his crowning glory, when he plays a perfect rendition of Rachmaninoff's Third Piano Concerto, the cumulative pressure overwhelms David, and he suffers a nervous breakdown. The next time we see him, more than 10 years older, he's a pathetic, jittery individual given to incoherent, babbling monologues. Public piano performances are long behind him . . . until he enters a small restaurant.

This is unbelievably rich material, and I can say without reservation that Scott Hicks' work deserves the highest recognition. *Shine* truly does what its name says. **MUST SEE**

Short Cuts [1993]

Starring: Andie MacDowell, Bruce Davison, Jack Lemmon, Julianne Moore, Matthew Modine Director: Robert Altman Screenplay: Robert Altman and Frank Barhydt based on the writings of Raymond Carver Running Time: 3:09 Rated: R (Frontal nudity, mature themes, language) Theatrical Aspect Ratio: 2.35:1

Helicopters thunder through the air over Los Angeles, raining malathion on the city in an attempt to end the dreaded Medfly invasion. Below, in each house and apartment, an individual drama is being played out. As in any human settlement at any time in history, there is joy, sadness, jealousy, fear, reconciliation, pain, and death. With *Short Cuts*, a film by director Robert Altman based on 9 short stories and one poem by the late Raymond Carver, the audience is given a glimpse into several of those dramas.

Infidelity mars two marriages, while a tragic accident to another couple's son brings their lives to an abrupt halt. A trio of fishing buddies find a dead girl's body floating near their campsite. Another marriage is troubled by a husband's uncertainty about his wife's career choice — running a phone sex business. A man decides to teach his estranged wife a little something about the real meaning of "dividing things up," and a mother and daughter discover the pain that can come from not communicating.

Twenty-two characters and 10 tales — it would take a master to interweave all of these into a seamless whole. There are few directors who would tackle the challenge, and fewer still who could succeed. Not only has Robert Altman faced the Herculean task, but he has emerged victorious. *Short Cuts* is a magnificent triumph, an example that dramas can still be found that don't make use of the time-honored tactics of manipulation and oversentimentalization.

What is impressive about *Short Cuts* is not only that it presents so many diverse personalities and situations, but that it manages to interconnect them in a manner that doesn't leave the viewer shaking his or her head in confusion. Fans of Carver, however, should check their expectations at the door — these are not strict adaptations (as the change of setting from the Pacific Northwest to angst-riddled L.A. indicates). Altman admits that *Short Cuts* is "not a verbatim retelling of Carver's works, but rather a cinematic interpretation of their essence."

It's a genuine pleasure to find a movie with such a deep and intelligent portrayal of simple human lives, with all their minor triumphs and tragedies. *Short Cuts* is an example of a highly-respected modern director in top form. **HIGHLY RECOMMENDED**

A Short Film about Killing [Poland, 1987]

Starring: Miroslaw Baka, Krzysztof Globisz, Jan Tesarz
Director: Krzysztof Kieslowski Screenplay: Krzysztof Kieslowski and Krzysztof Piesiewicz Running Time: 1:25 Rated: No MPAA Rating (Violence) Theatrical Aspect Ratio: 1.66:1 In Polish with subtitles

A Short Film About Killing, Krzysztof Kieslowski's powerful examination of the nature of murder, was a stunning success at the 1988 Cannes Film Festival, taking home the Jury prize. In the same year, the film also captured Europe's coveted Felix award. An extended version of *Decalogue 5*, *A Short Film About Killing* was one of two features to spring from Kieslowski's 10-part television drama about applying the Ten Commandments to modern-day life (the other being *A Short Film About Love*).

Wrenching in its uncompromising indictment of capital punishment, *A Short Film About Killing* doesn't pull punches. Sitting through this film is the emotional equivalent of going through a grinder. Everything about the production is dark — from its themes and characters to the manner in which Kieslowski and cinematographer Slawomir Idiak chose to shoot the picture. Bleaker even than *Blue*, *A Short Film About Killing* captures the perfect tone for an autopsy of its subject matter.

The movie follows the activities of 20-year-old Jacek (Miroslaw Baka), a seemingly-normal young man with a sadistic streak. He goes through a day, wandering around town but rarely interacting with anyone. Then, suddenly, in a seemingly-unprovoked action, he murders a cab driver (Jan Tesarz) by garroting him then beating him to a bloody pulp with a rock. Jacek is captured and tried. Despite the best efforts of a newly-practicing, idealistic lawyer named Piotr (Krzysztof Globisz), Jacek is sentenced to die. Before the execution, the condemned man spends some time in a cell with his attorney, telling fragments of a tragic life's story and expressing his final request — to be buried in a plot alongside his father and beloved sister.

A Short Film About Killing is as grim as a motion picture gets, but the intelligence and insight applied to its themes will keep the viewer riveted despite the pervasive gloom. Whether an individual agrees or disagrees with Kieslowski's position on the issue of capital punishment, there is no denying that his case against it is powerfully made. And, while the director cannot answer the question of why men kill, his scrutiny of murder offers a bloody portrait worth repeated study. **HIGHLY RECOMMENDED**

A Short Film about Love [Poland, 1988]

Starring: Grazyna Szapolowska, Olaf Lubaszenko, Stefina Iwinska
Director: Krzysztof Kieslowski Screenplay: Krzysztof Kieslowski and Krzysztof Piesiewicz Running Time: 1:26 Rated: No MPAA Rating (Sex, mature themes) Theatrical Aspect Ratio: 1.66:1 In Polish with subtitles

A Short Film About Love, the second of Krzysztof Kieslowski's *Decalogue* episodes to be transformed into a feature film (the other being *A Short Film about Killing*), takes a unique look at the emotional latticework that interconnects love, lust, and sexual obsession. Hypnotically engrossing, this picture delves deep into the psyches of its two main characters, employing irony, humor, and drama to weave a masterful tale of human interaction that will leave an indelible imprint on all who view it.

The story begins with 19-year-old Tomek (Olaf Lubaszenko) training a telescope on the windows of an apartment opposite his. Inside, a beautiful, older woman, Magda (Grazyna Szapolowska), is undressing. Initially, we assume that Tomek is watching for the titillation value, but, as we observe him night after night, it becomes clear that he's more interested in Magda when she's fully clothed and engaged in some mundane activity than when her actions turn sexual. In fact, when she goes to bed with a man, Tomek trains the telescope away.

As his obsession deepens, Tomek is no longer content with merely watching. He begins to make phone calls and pilfer letters, then eventually works up the courage to meet Magda face-to-face. In a guilty, rushed confession, he tells all. At first, Magda is furious and seeks her own form of revenge, but eventually she finds herself drawn to the young man. One night, after the two go out on a relatively harmless date, she invites him into her apartment and proceeds to shatter his illusions. A brief, unsatisfying sexual encounter rips away Tomek's innocence and sends him fleeing Magda's apartment. Once home, he slits his wrists.

Tomek survives the suicide attempt, but while he's in the hospital, Magda is riddled with guilt. She begins to obsess over him, trying to find out everything she can about his life and friends. She uses a pair of binoculars to watch his apartment, waiting for his return. She turns away her lover, unwilling (or unable) to engage in sex while Tomek is away.

Love is probably the most commonly presented theme in all motion pictures. Most of the time, it is used as a plot device, so rarely is there a thoughtful examination of the dynamics of the emotion. *A Short Film About Love* is the exception, and what a magnificent exception it is. With actors that give finely-tuned performances and a script that is richly detailed, the movie is nothing short of a masterpiece. There is more real feeling in this brief feature than in a hundred full-length Hollywood romantic comedies. **MUST SEE**

Show Me Love (a.k.a. Fucking Amal) [Sweden, 1998]

Starring: Alexandra Dahlström, Rebecka Liljeberg, Mathias Rust, Erica Carlson Director: Lukas Moodysson Screenplay: Lukas Moodysson Running Time: 1:29 Rated: No MPAA Rating (Profanity, mature themes) Theatrical Aspect Ratio: 1.66:1 In Swedish with subtitles

Show Me Love, the feature debut of Swedish filmmaker Lukas Moodysson, is not bound by the constraints of most Hollywood-produced teen movies, with their manufactured, formulaic plots and characterizations. It's a powerful, deeply affecting depiction of the tribulations of two teenage girls who are struggling with their sexuality and identities.

Sixteen-year-old Agnes (Rebecka Liljeberg) is a loner living in the small, dead-end town of Amal. Perhaps the worst place on Earth, and certainly the most boring (or so many of the underage inhabitants believe), Amal is a backwards hamlet that always seems to be a step behind the rest of the world. Despite having attended the school in Amal for the nearly 2 years since her family moved there, Agnes has no friends. Although attractive, she does little to care for her appearance, and rumors are making their way through the classrooms and hallways that she likes girls. However, while the nature of Agnes' sexuality has yet to fully emerge, she has a deep crush on a fellow female student, the pretty and popular Elin (Alexandra Dahlström). And, like Agnes, Elin despises Amal. One night, prodded by her older sister, Jessica (Erica Carlson), Elin plays a practical joke on Agnes by kissing her on the lips. Giggling, Jessica and Elin race away, leaving a stunned and hurt Agnes behind. Later that evening, however, Elin feels remorse, and returns to Agnes' house to apologize. She arrives just as Agnes is making a halfhearted attempt to slit her wrists. The two end up spending most of the night together, talking and sharing their innermost thoughts, and their unplanned "date" ends with a real kiss. The next day, frightened by her feelings for Agnes and determined to assert her heterosexuality, Elin nabs the willing Johan (Mathias Rust) as a boyfriend and ignores Agnes, who is understandably devastated.

Show Me Love is an emotional roller-coaster ride for viewers of both genders and all sexual orientations, because the feelings it uncovers are universal in nature. No matter how far removed an individual is from high school, this film has the ability to strip away the years. And, although Moodysson is obviously sympathetic towards both of his protagonists, he does not hesitate to show the mean and selfish sides of their natures. The adults (chiefly Agnes' parents) are not presented as boorish clods; they are helpful and sensitive to the needs of their children. The script's perceptiveness provides us with a fresh, non-manufactured perspective on what it means to be a bored teenager. And it gets the details right.

Not only is this a highly dramatically sound depiction of the life struggles of adolescent girls, but it is one of the most honest and heartfelt teen dramas ever to grace the screen. HIGHLY RECOMMENDED

Sidewalks of New York [2001]
Starring: Edward Burns, Rosario Dawson, Dennis Farina, Heather Graham, David Krumholtz, Brittany Murphy, Stanley Tucci
Director: Edward Burns Screenplay: Edward Burns Running Time: 1:47
Rated: R (Profanity, sexual situations) Theatrical Aspect Ratio: 1.85:1

Sidewalks of New York feels so strongly like a Woody Allen film that the sensation couldn't be coincidental. From the setting (Manhattan, where Allen lives and breathes) to the use of hand-held cameras to the focus on a group of neurotic characters who use humor to mask their insecurities, *Sidewalks of New York* obviously owes a strong debt to New York's most famous jazz-loving movie-maker. While nothing in *Sidewalks of New York* reaches the lofty heights of an *Annie Hall* or *Manhattan*, there are plenty of moments in this film that would slide comfortably into some of Allen's less acclaimed efforts.

The 6 characters in *Sidewalks of New York* are trapped in a romantic maze of their own making. Using faux documentary interview segments with the principals to frame the narrative segments, Edward Burns seeks to make these stories seem more real and immediate. The gimmick works, primarily because there's an improvisational quality to these scenes (although I'm sure everything was carefully scripted and the guy in the background giving the finger was instructed to do so). Plus, it helps that most of the unseen interviewer's questions are about sex — a subject that few viewers will be bored by.

One practically needs a scorecard to keep all the entanglements straight. Tommy (Burns) is a 32-year-old TV show producer who has just been thrown out of his apartment by an irate girlfriend. He is immediately attracted to two women — Maria (Rosario Dawson), a school teacher, and Annie (Heather Graham), a realtor. Maria has just gotten her life together after going through a divorce, but her ex-husband, Ben (David Krumholtz), has begun stalking her, wondering if ending the marriage was a mistake. Although still hung up on his ex-wife, Ben is also attracted to Ashley (Brittany Murphy), a 19-year-old waitress at the coffee shop he frequents. He asks her out, but she rebuffs him because she's involved with Griffin (Stanley Tucci), a middle-aged man with whom she's having an affair. Griffin, meanwhile, is married to Annie.

Once fertile territory for American independent films, this sort of ensemble relationship movie has fallen out of favor of late — even Allen isn't making these any more. Despite a few easily identifiable flaws, *Sidewalks of New York* is a breezy, enjoyable motion picture that manages to be smart without demanding our undivided attention. And, during a time when New York is in need of positive portrayals, this movie functions as a postcard to the city whose skyline has changed but whose essential character has not. RECOMMENDED

A Single Girl [France, 1995]
Starring: Virginie Ledoyen, Benoit Magimel, Dominique Valadie, Vera Briole Director: Benoit Jacquot Screenplay: Benoit Jacquot, Jerome Beaujour Running Time: 1:30 Rated: No MPAA Rating (Mature themes, sexual situations, profanity) Theatrical Aspect Ratio: 1.85:1
In French with subtitles

Benoit Jacquot's *A Single Girl* isn't a typical motion picture in any sense. Narrative is curtailed in favor of pure character development, and the result is akin to suspending your own life for 90 minutes and spending that time living in someone else's skin. It's extremely unusual for a director, actress, and writer to bring an audience into such a close rapport with a character.

A Single Girl shows us 75 ordinary minutes in the life of Valerie (Virginie Ledoyen), a young woman who's beginning a new job as a room service waitress at a Paris hotel. She's 4 weeks pregnant, and has just informed her boyfriend, Remi (Benoit Magimel). Her life is at a watershed: does she continue in a strained relationship with him that may lead to discord and abandonment, or does she make a clean break now and attempt to raise the baby on her own? This is the question that preys upon her mind as she gets to know her co-workers and experiences the ups and downs of the morning room service rush.

Not once in 75 minutes does Jacquot's film transition away from Valerie or jump forward in time. It is strictly chronological, presenting a minute in real time as a minute in screen action. The camera follows Valerie's every move, no matter how mundane. She's shown walking down streets and through the halls of the hotel, riding elevators, and stealing a moment for a quick smoke. She's not just in every scene, she's in practically every frame.

The quiet, intense realism of Virginie Ledoyen's performance is one of the paramount reasons for *A Single Girl*'s unqualified success. Not only does

Ledoyen have a pleasant countenance for the camera to dote upon longingly, but she's a shrewd actress who understands the importance of details in making the character real. There are numerous occasions when we understand Valerie's mindset and intentions as a result of some subtle action: a gesture, an expression, or a mannerism. Yes, Ledoyen is beautiful, but it's her aptitude, not her comeliness, that draws us in.

When a character study fails, it is, more often than not, because the audience never really connects with the film's protagonist. This is a flaw that never plagues *A Single Girl*, because Jacquot bends all of his film making talents to forging a deep link. As a result, even though nothing much happens during the course of the movie (Valerie spends over half the running time wandering around the inside of a hotel), this is a thoroughly engrossing motion picture. HIGHLY RECOMMENDED

Sleepers [1996]

Starring: Jason Patric, Brad Pitt, Ron Eldard, Billy Crudup, Robert DeNiro, Joseph Perrino, Brad Renfro, Kevin Bacon, Minnie Driver, Dustin Hoffman Director: Barry Levinson Screenplay: Barry Levinson based on the novel by Lorenzo Carcaterra Running Time: 2:32 Rated: R (Violence, rape, mature themes, profanity, brief nudity) Theatrical Aspect Ratio: 2.35:1

Sleepers is a movie about revenge and redemption, and how, in America's darkest social corridors and backalleys, the two can be inextricably linked. It's also a condemnation of a criminal justice system that allows innocence to be callously destroyed. Yet, even though *Sleepers* is basically a vigilante motion picture, there's little thrill in watching the vengeance extracted by the protagonists of this film because *Sleepers* approaches its subject with a conscience. The movie's moral compass is Robert DeNiro's Father Bobby, a Catholic priest who recognizes that friendship and loyalty can require sacrifices of the soul.

Sleepers spans 15 years. Much of the action transpires in New York's Hell's Kitchen. During the film's era, the neighborhood was ruled by two vastly different powers: the mob (represented by gangster King Benny, played by Vittorio Gassman) and the Catholic Church (represented by Father Bobby). Every child learned to respect both, and live by a simple creed: never commit a crime against someone else in the neighborhood.

The film opens in 1966 by introducing us to four inseparable friends: Lorenzo (Joseph Perrino), Michael (Brad Renfro), John (Geoffrey Wigdor), and Tommy (Jonathan Tucker). Like most boys, they're curious about sex, enjoy playing stickball, and have an appetite for pranks. One such practical joke, gone horribly wrong, changes their lives. When their theft of a hot dog vendor's cart nearly causes a man's death, Lorenzo and his friends are found guilty of reckless endangerment and sent to the Wilkinson Reform School. There, under the watchful eye of a sadistic guard named Sean Nokes (Kevin Bacon), they are subjected to mental, physical, and sexual abuse.

Although their sentences are only for a year, those 12 months fundamentally alter their personalities. When we next meet them, in 1981, their lives have moved on, but the submerged hatred lingers. Lorenzo (now played by Jason Patric) is an aspiring reporter working for the *New York Daily News*. Michael (Brad Pitt) is an attorney in the D.A.'s office. John (Ron Eldard) and Tommy (Billy Crudup) are hardened criminals. All 4 are forced to confront their shared past when John and Tommy encounter Nokes in a restaurant. Their actions provide the catalyst for a plan that Michael devises to bring the entire Wilkinson experience into the open. So, with the help of Lorenzo; John's lover, Carol (Minnie Driver); and a burned-out lawyer (Dustin Hoffman), Michael strives to attain redemption and revenge for them all.

There has been some controversy as to whether or not *Sleepers* is based on a true story. Ultimately, however, it doesn't make much difference whether the events of *Sleepers* happened or not. The themes and messages are no less valid either way, and, even if it isn't a true story, events like these *could have* transpired. Fact or fiction, this is a memorable motion picture. HIGHLY RECOMMENDED

Sling Blade [1996]

Starring: Billy Bob Thornton, Lucas Black, Dwight Yoakam, Natalie Canderday, John Ritter, Robert Duvall Director: Billy Bob Thornton Screenplay: Billy Bob Thornton Running Time: 2:15 Rated: R (Violence, profanity) Theatrical Aspect Ratio: 1.85:1

Sling Blade is a fascinating examination of a damaged man's quest to make restitution for his past crimes. To a lesser extent, it also offers an atypical vision of the concept of "family" in modern society. Thornton has developed *Sling Blade* as a slowly-paced character study. Nearly every scene is designed to reveal something about one of characters rather than advance the minimalist story. The narrative is little more than a flimsy envelope — it's the men and women who are sealed within that make *Sling Blade* worth watching.

The best acting in the entire motion picture is by Thornton himself. He plays Karl Childers, a "mentally challenged" man who has been incarcerated in the Arkansas State Hospital for the criminally insane since the age of 9, when he butchered his mother and her lover with a sling blade. As the film opens, Karl is being released from the hospital. According to the doctors, he has been cured. By Karl's own admission, he doesn't reckon he's got a reason to kill anyone else. But we in the audience aren't so sure. His rough, gravely voice is intimidating, and his nervous mannerisms — constantly rubbing his hands together, uttering "uh-huh"s every few words, and never meeting anyone else's gaze — do not inspire confidence. Is he still dangerous, or just the "gentle, simple man" others see him to be?

Once Karl is out of the hospital, he goes to work as a mechanic in the small town where he was born (and where he committed his crime). He befriends a fatherless young boy, Frank Wheatley (Lucas Black), and, after meeting Frank's mother, Linda (Natalie Canderday), is invited to live in their garage. Frank is glad to have Karl around, not just because he yearns for a father-figure, but because he's afraid of Linda's often-drunk, abusive boyfriend, Doyle (Dwight Yoakam), and believes that Karl's presence will keep Doyle in line. Meanwhile, Linda's friend and boss, Vaughan Cunningham (John Ritter), is concerned about a stranger living with Frank and Linda, and decides to keep an eye on the newcomer.

It could be argued that the ending is predictable, but I think "inevitable" is a better word. The audience sees the resolution long before any of *Sling Blade*'s characters do, but that's because we're more removed from the situation than they are. The film builds to a perfectly-fitting, climactic moment. The key scene is not overplayed, nor are the ramifications.

Sling Blade runs for a little longer than it needs to, and there are a few scenes that border on being too cute (such as one where Karl's "date" from the previous evening gives him flowers), but, in general, it's a fine motion picture. Karl is sufficiently interesting to hold our attention for more than 2 hours, and, if the resolution of his dilemma is obvious, watching him arrive at it makes *Sling Blade* worthwhile. RECOMMENDED

The Slingshot [Denmark/Sweden, 1993]

Starring: Jesper Salen, Stellan Skarsgård, Basia Frydman, Niclas Olund Director: Ake Sandgren Running Time: 1:42 Rated: R (Violence, mature themes) Screenplay: Ake Sandgren based on the novel by Roland Schutt In Swedish with subtitles

It's interesting how almost every film out of Sweden evokes, in one way or another, impressions of Ingmar Bergman's work. *The Slingshot* is certainly not a Bergman-derivative — it's almost too lighthearted for that — but there are moments here and there when one could imagine something similar from the great director.

The Slingshot is set in the 1920s, and it explores some of the difficult realities of growing up as a boy in Sweden, especially for someone like Roland (Jesper Salen), whose mother, Zipa (Basia Frydman), is a Jew and whose father, Fritiof (Stellan Skarsgård), is devout socialist. Roland is often the target of bullying and name-calling, but the resilient lad always bounces back from whatever problems beset him, often in the most unexpected of ways. On one occasion when he needs money, Roland fashions slingshots out of scrap metal and condoms, then sells them to his schoolmates. Then there's the time when he has some fun with a few lice . . .

The Slingshot successfully navigates the turbulent waters of Roland's boyhood adventures as they turn from absurd to heartwrenching. It is a wonderful mix of tragedy, humor, and triumph. Writer/director Ake Sandgren creates a series of rich screen personalities who could easily slip into comfortable stereotypes, but don't. Take Fritiof, for example. At first, this man seems to be the typical "Swedish father figure" — someone who is stern, demanding, and distanced from his children. As *The Slingshot* progresses, however, we learn that there's a lot more to Fritiof than is initially evident.

With a trio of formidable performances (by Salen, Skarsgård, and Frydman), *The Slingshot* offers a moving, intriguing look at the difficulties faced by one child set adrift in a sea of bigotry where his own resourcefulness is the key to survival. There's more to this film than is suggested by its apparently-simple story, and it's a tribute to the ability of Ake Sandgren and his cast that so much is effectively realized. HIGHLY RECOMMENDED

Smoke Signals [1998]

Starring: Adam Beach, Evan Adams, Irene Bedard, Gary Farmer, Tantoo Cardinal Director: Chris Eyre Screenplay: Sherman Alexie based on his book "The Lone Ranger and Tonto Fistfight in Heaven" Running Time: 1:28 Rated: PG-13 (Mature themes) Theatrical Aspect Ratio: 1.85:1

Chris Eyres' *Smoke Signals*, the winner of both the Audience Award and the Filmmakers Trophy at the 1998 Sundance Film Festival, is, in essence, a road movie/buddy story. What differentiates this effort from so many others are the characters and the subtext. *Smoke Signals* is a motion picture about Native Americans made by a Native American who doesn't have an ax to grind. Sure, he deals with concerns particular to his people, but he doesn't do it from a pulpit, spewing fire and brimstone at uncomfortable audience members. The movie also features two well-rounded, interesting protagonists whose conversation is a little more memorable than the banal banter that comprises the dialogue often found in this kind of genre picture. As a result, *Smoke Signals,* while not a pillar of originality, is enjoyable and, at times, engrossing.

The movie has all the necessary ingredients of a road movie: the trip from point A to point B that turns into as much of a philosophical journey as a physical one, the oddball characters encountered along the way, and the crowd-pleasing finale. But the foundation of *Smoke Signals* isn't the plot (which, frankly, is pretty ordinary), but the central figures of Victor Joseph (Adam Beach) and Thomas Builds-the-Fire (Evan Adams), two natives of the Coeur D'Alene Reservation in Idaho. Victor and Thomas aren't friends, but they have known each other since childhood, and they share a link. On a night in 1976, Arnold Joseph (Gary Farmer), Victor's father, saved the infant Thomas from a fire that killed his parents. Now, more than 20 years later, Arnold, who abandoned his wife, Arlene (Tantoo Cardinal), and son for a life in Phoenix, has died, and Victor must make the trip to claim his ashes. Thomas, who is supplying the money for the journey, accompanies him.

While *Smoke Signals* probably wasn't the best choice to win at 1998's Sundance Film Festival, it was one of the most sincere films shown there. It doesn't manipulate, rely on contrivances, or devolve into sudsy melodrama. At a time when almost everything coming out of Hollywood seems to be getting bigger and dumber, movies like *Smoke Signals,* which are made with care and craftsmanship, are always welcome. **RECOMMENDED**

Snow Falling on Cedars [1999]

Starring: Ethan Hawke, James Cromwell, Richard Jenkins, James Rebhorn, Sam Shepard Director: Scott Hicks Screenplay: Ronald Bass, Scott Hicks based on the novel by David Guterson Running Time: 2:06 Rated: PG-13 (Violence, profanity, sex) Theatrical Aspect Ratio: 2.35:1

Seeking to do justice to the complexity of the bestselling novel by David Guterson on which *Snow Falling on Cedars* is based, Scott Hicks employs a non-linear, multi-layered structure in the movie that is characterized by flashbacks and flashbacks-within-flashbacks. Events are presented non-chronologically, with frequent, repeated jumps through time to flesh out the characters' backgrounds and reveal the truth of the mystery that lies at the film's core. This is apparently an approach that Hicks feels comfortable with — he used something similar (albeit less convoluted) in his previous movie, *Shine.* Despite the intricacy of the structure, it's not difficult to follow the progression of events. Changes in actors (characters as children versus adults), hairstyles, lighting, and weather all serve to tip us off about which era any particular scene is transpiring in.

The movie is framed as a courtroom mystery in the Pacific Northwest during the early 1950s, with a local Japanese fisherman named Kazuo Miyamoto (Rick Yune) being tried for the murder of another man, Carl Heine (Eric Thal). One foggy night, while Carl was out on his boat, the *Susan Marie,* something happened. (Only at the end of the movie do we discover what.) The next morning, he was found dead, tangled in his own fishing nets with a nasty gash on his head. Ishmael Chambers (Ethan Hawke), a reporter for the local newspaper, watches impassively as events unfold in the courtroom. Gradually, we learn that Ishmael's first and only true love is Hatsue (Youki Kodoh), the wife of the man on trial. As he begins to research background information, he discovers facts that neither the prosecutor (James Rebhorn) nor the defense attorney (Max von Sydow) are bringing out in court. But the bitterness he feels towards Hatsue for inexplicably ending their relationship years ago keeps him silent. At the same time, memories of his dead father, Arthur (Sam Shepard), one of the most respected men in the community and a pillar of integrity, haunt his thoughts.

Throughout much of the film, Ishamael is obsessed by facts. He insists that his profession, that of a reporter, is all about uncovering the truth. Not until the end does he understand what his father meant by arguing that "journalism is making choices." Indeed, only once Ishmael makes those choices — to give up his obsession for Hatsue and to embrace his father's values — is he able to find peace. Viewers who go on this excursion with him will find their time well rewarded. **HIGHLY RECOMMENDED**

A Soldier's Daughter Never Cries [1998]

Starring: Kris Kristofferson, Barbara Hershey, Leelee Sobieski, Jesse Bradford Director: James Ivory Screenplay: James Ivory, Ruth Prawer Jhabvala based on the novel by Kaylie Jones Running Time: 2:04 Rated: PG-13 (Sex, profanity, mature themes) Theatrical Aspect Ratio: 1.85:1

Merchant-Ivory (the film making team comprised of Ismail Merchant and James Ivory) is probably best known for their somewhat austere tales of life in England. One could be forgiven for the assumption that every Merchant-Ivory film features Helena Bonham Carter (*A Room with a View, Howards End*), Emma Thompson (*Howards End, The Remains of the Day*), and/or Anthony Hopkins (*Howards End, The Remains of the Day, Surviving Picasso*). As it happens, *A Soldier's Daughter Never Cries* features none of these fine actors.

These days, most movies about families deal with deep dysfunctions and hidden secrets — parents who are alienated from their children, brothers and sisters who don't get along, incestuous relationships, etc. For those looking for a change-of-pace, *A Soldier's Daughter Never Cries* offers the opportunity. This film is about a loving, united family that endures good times and hardships together. It's not an overbearing, saccharine story, but a realistic portrait of characters who are bound together by affection, respect, and shared experiences. What's even more amazing is that it transpires during the period between 1964 and 1973, when social upheaval was tearing many families apart. But not the Willis', an expatriate American clan living in Paris. In addition to adults Bill (Kris Kristofferson) and Marcella (Barbara Hershey), there are two children: Channe (short for "Charlotte Anne," and played by Luisa Conlon at an early age and Leelee Sobieski later), the couple's biological daughter, and Billy (Samuel Gruen turning into Jesse Bradford), their adopted son.

When we first meet Channe, the movie's emotional center, she's a 4th-grader who can't spell "gym." Like many foreigners who spend nearly their entire life caught between two cultures, she isn't sure whether she's French or American. The same is true of Billy, who is more introverted than his sister. We follow these two as they grow up, with the innocence of childhood giving way to the awkwardness of adolescence. When Bill's health begins to fail, he moves his family to Long Island, where he intends to live out his final years. There, in their new school, Channe and Billy are treated as outsiders. She starts having indis-

criminate sex with boys because she can't make friends. He is taunted and teased, and, instead of developing a social life, he spends his free time vegetating in front of the television.

Someone once said that the reason there are so many movies about dysfunctional families is because those are the only kinds of families capable of holding an audience's attention. *A Soldier's Daughter Never Cries* disproves that theory. It doesn't tell of anything big or earthshaking, but, in its careful portrayal of life, it offers something equally precious — an insight into the human experience.

HIGHLY RECOMMENDED

Some Mother's Son [Ireland, 1996]

Starring: Helen Mirren, Fionnula Flanagan, Aidan Gillen, David O'Hara, John Lynch Director: Terry George Screenplay: Jim Sheridan and Terry George Running Time: 1:52 Rated: R (Violence, profanity) Theatrical Aspect Ratio: 1.85:1

In 1979, when Margaret Thatcher assumed the role of England's Prime Minister, one of her stated aims was to crush the IRA and its associated "terrorism." Her "Northern Ireland Solution," as it became known, included three principles: Isolation, Criminalization, and Demoralization. Those members of the IRA captured for terrorist acts were to be treated as criminals, not soldiers. Prisons were to be used to break morale, not create martyrs.

On March 1, 1981, IRA prisoner Bobby Sands began a hunger strike which would earn him worldwide notoriety. Sands laid out 5 demands that, if met by the British government, would end the strike. Chief among these was the requirement that imprisoned IRA members would be recognized as "prisoners of war" (not common criminals), and, as such, would be allowed to wear their own clothing (instead of prison uniforms). Thatcher's government refused to negotiate, even when, on April 9, Sands was elected as the Member of Parliament from Fermanagh and South Tyrone. Sixty-six days after it began, Sands' protest ended with his death. Others followed his example, and, by the time the strike ended on October 3, ten of the more than 300 IRA prisoners in Long Kesh prison's H-Blocks had perished.

The story of Sands' hunger strike forms the background of Terry George's directorial debut, *Some Mother's Son*. However, while there is a great deal of information in the film about Sinn Fein, the IRA, and the political situation in Ireland during the early 1980s (some of which is fictionalized), this is principally a tale of sacrifice and family relationships. It's about a mother being forced to confront the very real fear that her son may die for convictions that she does not share, and that it could ultimately be her responsibility to choose life or death for him.

Make no mistake: while the core story of *Some Mother's Son* is universal in theme and deeply personal in scope, the narrative nevertheless shows evidence of a pro-Republican bias. Although the movie is arguably more balanced than Sheridan's powerful and riveting *In the Name of the Father*, the British still come off as faceless villains. Margaret Thatcher's mouthpiece is a caricature of vicious, heartless clichés. For those with an interest in the ongoing conflict in Northern Ireland, *Some Mother's Son* makes an excellent companion piece to Neil Jordan's *Michael Collins*. But, regardless of your political leanings, Terry George's picture is well worth seeing because of its intelligence and emotional depth, not to mention Helen Mirren's Oscar-caliber performance. **HIGHLY RECOMMENDED**

Sommersby [1993]

Starring: Richard Gere, Jodie Foster, Bill Pullman, James Earl Jones, Lanny Flaherty Director: John Amiel Screenplay: Nicholas Meyer and Sarah Kernochan Running Time: 1:53 Rated: PG-13 (Mature themes, sexual situations) Theatrical Aspect Ratio: 2.35:1

The United States Civil War has ended, and Jack Sommersby (Richard Gere) is returning home to a farm in ruins and a wife (Jodie Foster) who wishes he was dead. It's up to Jack to prove is that he's no longer the person he was 6 years ago when he left. Gone is the man who gambled and beat his wife, newly replaced by someone of a giving and caring nature. Yet, even as Jack begins to assemble a new beginning, questions about his identity arise. Could Jack Sommersby change this much, or is this really him at all?

Sommersby is based on the 1982 French film *The Return of Martin Guerre,* and is one of those rare remakes that does not tarnish the image of its inspiration. While *Sommersby* owes much to its predecessor, it is not a direct copy. There are differences, not only in setting, but in scripting. With the exception of a few early scenes lifted almost directly from *Martin Guerre,* only the general trajectory of the movies remains the same. The transition from 16th century France to 19th century America works effectively, and allows a few surprises for those who are familiar with *Martin Guerre.*

First and foremost, *Sommersby* is a love story. Much screen time is devoted to the relationship between Jack and Laurel. The movie takes its time with its characters; there are no sudden epiphanies. Love, and its realization, comes slowly, with a look and a touch. In many ways, this film goes against the grain of a typical Hollywood film. It has a slow, leisurely pace, and is almost (but not quite — there is one fight scene) devoid of action.

In *Sommersby,* Richard Gere gives one of his most energetic performances in recent years. Jodie Foster outdoes her Oscar-winning *Silence of the Lambs* performance, playing Laurel with equal parts strength and vulnerability. Often in period pieces such as this, forceful female characters seem anachronistic. *Sommersby* shows that, with good scripting and even better acting, that problem can easily be overcome.

Technically, *Sommersby* is a superior production. Period details abound, and the cinematography is consistently strong, and occasionally breathtaking. Virginia is shown to its best advantage. Composer Danny Elfman, best known for his *Batman* score, delivers something refreshingly different. Occasionally, the music is imperfectly matched to the scenes, but the typical Elfman repetition is absent.

Sommersby should equally entertain those who have seen *The Return of Martin Guerre* and those who have not. From start to finish, it is a well-crafted film: part love story, part mystery, and all drama. The most painful and obvious of Hollywood's contrivances are nowhere to be found. With respect to *Martin Guerre* — the spirit of the original remains intact, which is perhaps the most satisfying aspect of this production **HIGHLY RECOMMENDED**

The Son's Room [Italy/France, 2001]

Starring: Nanni Moretti, Laura Morante, Jasmine Trinca, Giuseppe Sanfelice, Sofia Vigliar Director: Nanni Moretti Screenplay: Nanni Moretti Running Time: 1:38 Rated: R (Mature themes, sexual situations, nudity) Theatrical Aspect Ratio: 1.66:1 In Italian with subtitles

The average, mainstream American feature deals with grief by employing a mixture of histrionics and melodramatic manipulation. In order to find a motion picture that offers a sensitive, intelligent examination of grief and the guilt that often accompanies it, one has to look beyond the multiplexes, to the realm of foreign and independent movies.

The Son's Room, winner of the Palm D'Or at the 2001 Cannes Film Festival, is a film from celebrated Italian director Nanni Moretti, who, at one time during his career, was known at the "Italian Woody Allen." Although he shed that moniker early last decade, Moretti still shares traits with Manhattan's best-known filmmaker. Like Allen, Moretti writes, produces, and stars in his movies, which often feature autobiographical threads and mix humor and pathos. *The Son's Room* is a departure for Moretti in many ways. It is a more straightforward drama than his other work, it is not filmed in Rome, and Moretti's character lacks the numerous neuroses that he has become known for.

The film introduces us to something very rare: a happy, well-balanced family without a hint of dysfunction. Giovanni (Moretti) is a psychiatrist who practices out of his home. He has a loving relationship with his wife, Paola (Laura Morante), and is liked and respected by his two teenage children: son Andrea (Giuseppe Sanfelice) and daughter Irene (Jasmine Trinca). For about 30 minutes, Moretti carefully develops a picture of familial bliss, keeping us uncertain where the film is going until the tragedy occurs. Once that happens, the movie moves along a more somber trajectory. Andrea dies in a diving accident, and his grieving family is left trying to pick up the pieces.

For the most part, *The Son's Room* stands as a powerful portrait of what real (as opposed to Hollywood) families go through in the wake of the loss of one of their members. There's nothing out-of-the-ordinary about Giovanni, Paola, or Irene. The difficulties they have coping with Andrea's death are easy to empathize with.

If the film has a minor weakness, it's that an outside presence is needed to bring about the necessary catharsis. It's not exactly a contrivance, but it feels less natural than all that precedes it. Moretti, perhaps aware of this flaw, provides enough of a justification in the script for us to accept things as they are. In all other areas, however, this is a superior motion picture — an example of the pleasant surprise that can result when a skilled director departs from his usual style. By daring to be honest and unsparing, *The Son's Room* is meaningful. **HIGHLY RECOMMENDED**

Soul Food [1997]

Starring: Vanessa L. Williams, Vivica Fox, Nia Long, Michael Beach, Mekhi Phifer, Irma P. Hall Director: George Tillman Jr.
Screenplay: George Tillman Jr. Running Time: 1:55 Rated: R (Profanity, sexual situations, brief violence) Theatrical Aspect Ratio: 2.35:1

When it comes to "food" movies, you know the titles: *Babette's Feast, Eat Drink Man Woman, Big Night.* You also know the advice: eat before coming to the theater or suffer a grumbling stomach for 90-plus minutes followed by a mad dash to the nearest restaurant once the end credits start to roll. And, while *Soul Food*, the first major release from director George Tillman Jr., isn't on the same level as the previously-mentioned motion pictures, there's at least one scene that's a literal feast for the eyes.

Soul Food tells the story of the trials of the Joseph family when their beloved matriarch, Mama Joe (Irma P. Hall), slips into a diabetes-induced coma. Without Mama Joe's ritual Sunday dinners to keep everyone together, the family begins to drift apart, with gaps widening between sisters and spouses. The film essentially follows the lives of Mama Joe's 3 daughters. Terri (Vanessa L. Williams), the eldest, is a driven lawyer who puts work above her neglected husband, Miles (Michael Beach). Miles is tempted away from his steady, well-paying job by the lure of his true love, music, and away from his wife by the proffered charms of Terri's cousin, Faith (Gina Ravera). Maxine (Vivica Fox) is happily married to Kenny (Jeffrey D. Sams), and spends her days caring for her husband and three children. Bird (Nia Long) is newly hitched to ex-con Lem (Mekhi Phifer), an intense, caring man whose volatile temper often proves to be his undoing.

Soul Food is told from the point-of-view of young Ahmed (Brandon Hammond), Maxine and Kenny's son. While a few of his observations are insightful, most of his voiceover narrative is superfluous and even irritating. Seventy-five percent of what he says is either needless exposition or useless trivia. Simply put, the kid won't shut up. It's one thing to open and close a film with a voiceover, but Ahmed's voice can be heard throughout, dispensing pearls of wisdom that we could have easily done without.

With a uniformly attractive cast, *Soul Food* isn't hard on the eyes. Everyone (including Vanessa Williams, who isn't known as a stellar actress) acquits themselves admirably, although it's worth noting that none of the roles are terribly complex, so there's little need for anyone to stretch their range. And, while the meals don't take on the same importance as in certain other food movies, we still get an eyeful: deep-fried catfish, chicken and dumplings, cornbread, cakes, and other assorted dishes. *Soul Food* contains enough diverse cinematic ingredients to add a little zest and flavor to the pleasant-but-familiar cinematic fare of an African American family drama.

RECOMMENDED

The Star Maker [Italy, 1995]

Starring: Sergio Castellitto, Tiziana Lodato, Franco Scaldati
Director: Giuseppe Tornatore Screenplay: Giuseppe Tornatore and
Fabio Rinaudo Running Time: 1:48 Rated: R (Nudity, sex, violence,
profanity) Theatrical Aspect Ratio: 2.35:1 In Italian with subtitles

The Star Maker is a cynical, often-grim look at cupidity and its tragic consequences. In tone, it's more like *Lamerica* than *The Postman*, and, even though director Giuseppe Tornatore previously made *Cinema Paradiso*, *The Star Maker* has little of that film's warm sense of nostalgia. This movie is designed to be disturbing, not exhilarating, and it's extremely effective at that.

Tornatore has structured his film in a most atypical fashion. *The Star Maker* starts out as a light comedy with dark undertones. Sergio Castellitto is Joe Morelli, an itinerant talent scout who is making his way across Sicily, advertising that, for 1,500 lire, anyone can film a screen test. He dangles fame and fortune before all comers, most of whom can't really afford the fee. There are numerous comic anecdotes as men and women do their own, often-absurd interpretations of Rhett and Scarlett from *Gone With the Wind*, but, lurking beneath the surface humor is a sense of growing desperation. It doesn't take long to recognize that Morelli is a con man, and his promises are as empty as the purses of those who entrust their dreams to him.

As the film progresses, Morelli becomes more reprehensible. Men and women come to him as if he was a priest, with heartfelt confessions of their past and hopes for a brighter future, but Morelli doesn't hear or care about their words — all he wants is payment, either in coin or in trade (he accepts sexual favors from one woman who doesn't have any money). He's a cruel, self-absorbed man who scavenges through life's wreckage in the small, bombed-out towns of post-World War II Sicily.

In the village of Scordizzi, a girl named Beata (Tiziana Lodato) is enraptured by Morelli and his lifestyle. To obtain the 1,500 lire for a screen test, she strips naked in front of a local bigwig, then, when Morelli leaves her town, she stows away in his van, offering him her body when he discovers her. Beata is hopelessly in the star maker's thrall, but, as usual, Morelli cares only about himself.

With *The Star Maker*, Tornatore has fashioned a powerful motion picture whose impact comes through legitimate drama, not cheap manipulation. The primary actors, Castellitto and Lodato, are both

excellent, and the film's unhurried pace allows the audience to gradually understand how much subtle damage Morelli is doing. Historically, *The Star Maker* reminds us of the deep divisions in Italy after Mussolini's fall, and how isolated Sicily is from the rest of the country. Ultimately, however, this is a study of the baser elements of human nature, and a reminder that any person's actions can have unexpectedly painful ramifications for others. **HIGHLY RECOMMENDED**

The Stars Fell on Henrietta [1995]

Starring: Robert Duvall, Aidan Quinn, Frances Fisher, Brian Dennehy
Director: James Keach Screenplay: Philip Railsback Running Time: 1:50
Rated: PG (Mild violence) Theatrical Aspect Ratio: 2.35:1

Acting is one of the keys to *The Stars Fell on Henrietta*'s success. Robert Duvall, who can give a heartfelt performance with the best, is delightful as Mr. Cox, an oil wildcatter and perennial loser roaming through Texas in the early 1930s. Equally impressive is Aidan Quinn as Don Day, a down-on-his-luck farmer with a family to provide for. The supporting cast includes Frances Fisher as Don's wife, Lexi Randall as his eldest daughter, Beatrice, and the always-delightful Brian Dennehy as Big Dave, the "richest man in Texas."

The Stars Fell on Henrietta opens with Mr. Cox, accompanied by his constant companion, Mathilda the cat, driving into town in a vintage 1930s automobile. Actually, since the car breaks down before he gets there, he ends up hitching a ride. Cox, as always, is looking for oil. He doesn't have a penny to his name, and he's never had a successful strike before, but that doesn't quell his enthusiasm, and when he thinks he locates a huge, untapped reservoir of liquid black gold in a place called Henrietta, he starts looking for investors. Cox agrees to go 50/50 with Don Day, the owner of the property where the prospective well is to be drilled, but since Don isn't rich, Cox has to raise $5,000 on his own. The only problem is, every man of means knows his fruitless track record, and isn't interested in contributing to his latest scheme. Yet, even as Cox plots to obtain the money, Don scrapes together everything he has and sinks it into the venture, with tragic consequences for himself and his family.

Don and Cox are both dreamers, and this quality binds them together in the end. Because they're such likable, well-developed characters, we root unashamedly for them. *The Stars Fell on Henrietta* doesn't race towards the inevitable; it ambles. And it's the easy, unhurried gait that makes this film worthwhile, since it gives us an opportunity to get to know the two protagonists. This film isn't about men getting rich from an oil strike; it's about visionaries who, in Cox's words, hitch their wagons to a star. Cox loves life and the freedom of the road. Whether he makes or loses money is largely irrelevant.

The Stars Fell on Henrietta functions best as a character piece, since the basic storyline is straightforward. There are some problems with the conclusion, which ties up loose ends a little *too* neatly and conveniently. Nevertheless, with excellent performances from Duvall and Quinn, and sure directing by Keach, this film offers a pleasantly engrossing and satisfying drama with underdog protagonists whose efforts everyone can applaud. RECOMMENDED

The Story of Us [1999]
Starring: Bruce Willis, Michelle Pfeiffer, Rob Reiner, Rita Wilson
Director: Rob Reiner Screenplay: Alan Zweibel & Jessie Nelson
Running Time: 1:35 Rated: R (Profanity, sexual themes) Theatrical
Aspect Ratio: 2.35:1

The Story of Us illustrates what happens when the fissure of minor differences in a marriage widens into a seemingly unbridgeable chasm. Although peppered with occasional contrivances, the film is insightful and intelligent more often than not, and paints a convincing portrait of the disintegration of a family — until the final 10 minutes, when director Rob Reiner cheats with an implausible ending.

Ben and Katie Jordan (Bruce Willis and Michelle Pfeiffer) could be Harry and Sally after the magic is gone. He's a freespirit; she's anal. She thinks he's irresponsible; he believes she should be more spontaneous. They have become incompatible. Finally, after a year of increasingly loud and acrimonious quarrels, they decide to separate as a prelude to divorce. The hardest part is telling the kids. So, instead of getting it over with, they let their son and daughter go off to summer camp without knowing the truth. As those warm, childless days pass, they attempt to cope with their new distance. A despondent Ben spends time hanging out with his two best friends, one of whom is married (Rob Reiner) and one of whom is single (Paul Reiser). Meanwhile, Katie is consoled by her gal pals, Rachel (Rita Wilson) and Liza (Julie Hagerty), and begins flirting with a dentist (Tim Matheson).

There is no doubt that *The Story of Us* falls under the "chick flick" umbrella. It is manipulative, but at least the manipulation is skillful, rather than sloppy and overwrought. For the most part, the characters are well developed and easy to sympathize with. And, even though the material is serious, Reiner keeps the tone light. There are no villains here; everyone is essentially likable.

While there are many things to appreciate about *The Story of Us,* there are problems as well. Too many of the arguments between Ben and Katie have a contrived feel. We can see them coming. While it's true that people fight about silly things in real life, rarely do they work so hard to twist each phrase into an intentional insult, and it's not this often that every minor slight is magnified into an incident of gargantuan proportions. Reiner also seems to have a problem with wringing convincing tears out of his actors.

I like the structure employed by *The Story of Us.* It ricochets back and forth between people, places, and time periods (via frequent flashbacks). Without slowing down the story, this approach allows us to get a good feeling for the various stages of Ben and Katie's marriage. We see them "meet cute," say their vows, raise their children, then drift apart. As lightweight comedy/dramas go, this one doesn't cover much new ground, but it is mostly effective as it canvasses the familiar material. *The Story of Us* is flawed, but not seriously enough to curtail its ability to function as unpretentious entertainment. RECOMMENDED

The Straight Story [United States/France, 1999]
Starring: Richard Farnsworth, Sissy Spacek, Jennifer Edwards, Barbara E. Robertson Director: David Lynch Screenplay: John Roach & Mary Sweeney Running Time: 1:51 Rated: G Theatrical Aspect Ratio: 2.35:1

David Lynch's body of work is surely one of the most recognizable of any living director. From the nightmarishness of his debut, *Eraserhead,* to the bleakness of *Blue Velvet* to the bizarrely compelling quality of his TV series, *Twin Peaks,* Lynch has defined himself as a filmmaker who relishes peeling back the façade of Americana and exposing the rot that lies beneath. *The Straight Story* is completely different from anything we have previously seen from Lynch. Here, Lynch does not attempt to dissect middle America — he celebrates it.

The Straight Story is based on a real event in the life of a real person — the kind of thing that often shows up during the final, "feel good" segment of the evening news. Veteran actor Richard Farnsworth (*The Grey Fox*), in what is arguably the best performance of a long (and somewhat uneven) career, plays Alvin

Straight, a 73-year-old man living in Laurens, Iowa with his daughter, Rose (Sissy Spacek). Alvin is not in the best of health — he has a bad hip that requires him to use two canes while walking and he has trouble with his vision. One day, Alvin receives a phone call from a family member informing him that his brother, Lyle (Harry Dean Stanton), whom he has not spoken to in 10 years, has suffered a stroke. Alvin decides that he must make the 320-mile trek to Mt. Zion, Wisconsin, and the only means of transportation available to him is his lawnmower. "I've got to go see Lyle, and I've got to make the trip on my own," he remarks. So, hitching a home-made trailer to a John Deere, he begins one of the most unusual road trips ever committed to celluloid.

The cross-state journey, which takes 6 weeks during the late summer and early fall, is chronicled episodically. Early in his trip, Alvin encounters a female hitchhiker who spends some time around a campfire with him. She has run away from home, but he gives her the following advice: "A warm bed in a house sounds a mite better than eating a hot dog on a stick with an old geezer traveling on a lawn mower." On another occasion, he encounters a woman who has just struck and killed a deer — her 13th such accident in the past 7 weeks. There's a lot of Lynchian comedy in this scene. And, while his transport is being repaired after a breakdown, he spends time reminiscing about World War II horrors with another veteran.

The Straight Story may lack the surreal, compelling quality that has defined the director's other features, but it is an example of an artist in peak form. **HIGHLY RECOMMENDED**

The Sum of Us [Australia, 1994]

Starring: Jack Thompson, Russell Crowe, John Polson, Deborah Kennedy Director: Geoff Burton and Kevin Dowling Screenplay: David Stevens based on his play Running Time: 1:40 Rated: No MPAA Rating (Mature themes, profanity)

Love is perhaps the most common theme explored by movies. It is also the most frequently misrepresented. Many Hollywood love affairs end up heavily over-romanticized, and the picture they paint is invariably far from reality. So it's refreshing to find a film like *The Sum of Us*, which is about love in all its genuine forms: sexual, platonic, and most important, familial. Given the honesty of the script, it should come as no surprise that America's film industry had nothing to do with the movie — this is yet another gem from Australia.

Not only are Harry (Jack Thompson) and Jeff (Russell Crowe) father and son, but they're best friends as well. Their relationship is relaxed and comfortable — they banter and kid around and, though they occasionally get under each other's skin, there's never any acrimony in their arguments. Harry is aware of his son's homosexual preferences and accepts them unquestioningly. The only thing he has to say on the subject is that he's disappointed Jeff will never have an opportunity to father a child. With so many dysfunctional family stories around, *The Sum of Us* serves as the perfect antidote.

Despite his good looks and outgoing personality, Jeff is actually somewhat shy, as becomes obvious when he's getting to know Greg (John Polson), a man he meets at a local gay pub. Greg is no more certain of himself than Jeff, and it's only after a lot of nervous conversation that the pair arrive at Jeff's home. No sooner have the two dimmed the lights, however, than Harry wanders into the room to greet his son's prospective lover, unintentionally but effectively dispelling the romantic atmosphere.

Meanwhile, Harry, who has been a widower for a number of years, is looking for female companionship. To that end, he enrolls in Desiree's Introduction Agency, and is set up with a middle-aged woman named Joyce (Deborah Kennedy). The two hit it off almost immediately, but, while both are interested in pursuing a serious relationship, it's unclear exactly how far each is willing to go.

The Sum of Us is delightful, by turns droll and serious. Yet even during its most dramatic moments, it retains a lighthearted tone that keeps things from becoming too grim. There's always a joke right around the corner, and none of the humor seems ill-suited to the situation.

The Sum of Us isn't exactly cutting-edge, but it takes a few chances. Jeff's homosexuality is a complete non-issue. There's nothing political or tragic in his situation. In fact, he and the other characters frequently joke about it. Also, no compromises are made to give the conclusion an extra lift, proving it's possible to have a happy ending without undermining the story's intelligence. It's production elements like this that make *The Sum of Us* such a worthwhile examination of what love is like for those whose lives don't follow traditional movie scripts.

HIGHLY RECOMMENDED

Summer of Sam [1999]

Starring: John Leguizamo, Adrien Brody, Mira Sorvino, Jennifer Esposito, Anthony LaPaglia Director: Spike Lee Screenplay: Victor Colicchio, Michael Imperioli, Spike Lee Running Time: 2:22 Rated: R (Extreme violence, sex, profanity, brief nudity) Theatrical Aspect Ratio: 1.85:1

Spike Lee's *Summer of Sam* is only tangentially about David Berkowitz, the man who, over a 4-month period, managed to paralyze New York City with terror. Actually, the movie is an exploration of '70s culture and how the paranoia fueled by the killing spree illuminated the worst aspects of human nature. Like *Boogie Nights,* this picture delves beneath the facade of glitz and glamour that was the disco era and uncovers a rotten, hollow shell. It is a dark, violent, sexually explicit motion picture that will surely offend timid viewers.

Summer of Sam focuses on a small group of Italian-American characters living in the Bronx. They aren't necessarily the most compelling individuals — Lee relies on a few too many clichés to develop them (especially those with supporting parts) — but they get the job done. There's Vinny (John Leguizamo), the slick, Travolta-like disco king who is married to the lovely Dionna (Mira Sorvino), but is constantly unfaithful. Ritchie (Adrien Brody) is Vinny's closest friend, but his punk hairdo and standoffish attitude have made him persona non grata in the old neighborhood. Other players include Luigi (Ben Gazzara), the local Mafioso; Detective Lou Petrocelli (Anthony LaPaglia), a cop investigating the Son of Sam killings; and Berkowitz himself (Michael Badalucco).

The movie begins and ends with a few brief narrative comments by *New York Post* columnist Jimmy Breslin. Soon, we're in Vinny's world, watching him light up the dance floor with Dionna on an April night. On the way home, the pair comes across a murder scene. When Vinny gets out of the car to investigate why the cops have cordoned off the area, he encounters the bodies of Valentina Suriani and Alexander Esau in the car where they were shot. They are the 4th and 5th murder victims of the ".44 Caliber Killer." Shaken, Vinny goes home, vowing to turn his life around and remain faithful to Dionna. Not surprisingly, he is unable to keep the oath.

Over the next several months, tensions run high in Vinny's neighborhood. Luigi believes that the police will be unable to prevent more murders, so he puts the word out on the streets for his boys to be on the lookout. This fosters an atmosphere in which vigilante justice takes root. After dark, people stay off the streets and out of the discos, and a July blackout results in chaos. And, for outsiders like Ritchie, who are viewed with suspicion by their neighbors, one wrong move can make them a suspect and a target for mob violence.

Although *Summer of Sam* prevails as a period piece, it works even better as an examination of how the need to assign blame can result in grave injustices. While this is one of Spike Lee's most ambitious motion pictures, it's not his angriest. Nevertheless, there's an edginess to the proceedings that makes watching the film an unsettling experience. *Summer of Sam* opens a window on the '70s that juxtaposes light pop cultural references with something dark and monstrous. The result, while not wholly successful, is compelling and disturbing. **RECOMMENDED**

Sunday [1997]

Starring: David Suchet, Lisa Harrow, Jared Harris, Larry Pine, Yeon Joo Kim Director: Jonathan Nossiter Screenplay: James Lasdun and Jonathan Nossiter Running Time: 1.66:1 Rated: No MPAA Rating (Nudity, profanity, mature themes) Theatrical Aspect Ratio: 1:33

At first glance, there's nothing extraordinary about Jonathan Nossiter's debut feature, *Sunday.* But, several hours after I had seen the movie, I was still thinking about it, and that's the mark of a film with simple, quiet power.

It's possible to classify *Sunday* as a "love story," but that would probably be a misnomer. While it's true that the main characters — Oliver, a downsized worker (played by David Suchet), and Madeleine, an aging actress for whom roles are scarce (Lisa Harrow) — go through the motions of lovers, their relationship isn't about love. It's about quenching loneliness and finding companionship in a cold, cruel world that has, in its own way, sought to crush both of them. These two have no future, but they cling desperately for a few hours to the illusion of what they have achieved.

Madeleine, once a well-known and respected British actress, has begun to register the marks of age upon her features, and her services have became less and less desired. In a moment of self-deprecating revelation, she claims that the only roles she has a shot at these days are those of zombie mutants in low-budget horror films. Her home life is a mess. She is separated from her husband, Ben (Larry Pine), but he keeps showing up at her house on the pretext of spending time with their daughter.

Oliver, meanwhile, is just as despondent as Madeleine. Like her, he's trying to uncover the meaning of life, but it's proving elusive. Since losing his job, he has sunk lower and lower on the financial and social scale. Now, he's living in a shelter by night and wandering the streets of Queens by day. Then, on one fateful Sunday, he meets Madeleine after she mistakes him for a prominent London director by the name of Matthew Delacorta. Oliver decides to play along with her, and, although their initial exchange doesn't touch upon anything that could reveal his deception, Madeleine eventually realizes the truth. Instead of challenging Oliver, however, she begins to play an elaborate game of "pretend" with him.

For the most part, *Sunday* is a poignant, powerfully-realized character study of two lonely people. As wonderfully effective as the quiet scenes are in *Sunday*, though, Nossiter takes his share of missteps. The first involves the inclusion of a small army of secondary characters. Although their purpose — to strengthen the sense of isolation — is clear, scenes with these individuals are distracting, taking time away from the interaction between the two leads and interrupting the film's flow. Secondly, there are instances when Nossiter's artsy style (point-of-view camera angles, close-up shots of dead fish, etc.) approaches pretentiousness. However, the worst these flaws can do is occasionally mute *Sunday*'s power. The best moments of the film shine through, leaving behind unforgettable images and feelings that will not evaporate when the house lights go up.

HIGHLY RECOMMENDED

Sunshine [Hungary/Germany/Canada/Austria, 1999]

Starring: Ralph Fiennes, Rosemary Harris, Jennifer Ehle, Rachel Weisz
Director: Istvan Szabo Screenplay: Istvan Szabo, Israel Horovitz
Running Time: 3:00 Rated: R (Violence, profanity, nudity, mature themes) Theatrical Aspect Ratio: 1.85:1

Istvan Szabo's *Sunshine* runs for an unapologetic 3 hours, and Szabo has lavished a great deal of time and attention on crafting a grand, beautifully shot motion picture that engages audiences for the full running length.

The film follows 3 generations of the Sonnenschein family, a close-knit clan of Hungarian Jews who live and struggle through two world wars and countless changes of government. *Sunshine* is loosely divided into 3 periods. The first spans the era from the late 1800s to the years just after World War I, and focuses on Ignatz Sonnenschein, a judge in the Austro-Hungarian Empire. The second picks up in the 1930s and concludes at the end of World War II. The central character during this segment is Ignatz's son, Adam, a fencer who represents Hungary at the 1936 Olympics, but faces persecution from the Nazis despite his fame when he refuses to live by the creed stating that "assimilation is the only possible way." Finally, the third period begins in the late 1940s and finishes around 1960. During that time frame, *Sunshine* focuses on Adam's son, Ivan, who contends with the various factions of Communism that dominate the post-World War II political climate. One of Szabo's unsubtle "tricks" is to have all 3 of the central protagonists (grandfather, father, and son) played by the same actor: the versatile Ralph Fiennes. Another character, Valerie (Jennifer Ehle as a young woman; Rosemary Harris in later years), survives virtually the entire movie, providing a glue that holds the story together.

On one level, *Sunshine* can be viewed as little more than an entertaining historical melodrama about the tribulations of a group of characters set against the backdrop of the century's most important historical events. But there's a deeper theme at work here, as well. It has to do with the repetitive cycle of history and how power inevitably corrupts, no matter who wields it. Throughout *Sunshine*, governments in Hungary rise and fall — a dictatorship, a Nazi regime, and more than one flavor of Communism — but, despite fundamental philosophical differences, they all bear remarkable similarities to each other. What begins with hope and freshness in each case quickly degenerates into something twisted and rotten. Each of the characters played by Fiennes has an opportunity to be both a hero and a criminal, depending on who is in power.

Over the course of one evening at the movies, Szabo effectively realizes more than 70 years of history, and, in the process, presents a gallery of interesting characters. Sub-themes and memorable moments abound. Ultimately, the director may have tackled a scope so vast that even 3 hours is not enough to contain it, but the result, while somewhat uneven and occasionally rushed, is still solidly entertaining and occasionally thought provoking. **RECOMMENDED**

Surrender Dorothy [1998]

Starring: Peter Pryor, Kevin DiNovis, Jason Centeno, Elizabeth Casey
Director: Kevin DiNovis Screenplay: Kevin DiNovis Running Time: 1:27
Rated: No MPAA Rating (Profanity, homosexual themes, violence)
Theatrical Aspect Ratio: 1.33:1

The fact that Kevin DiNovis' debut feature, *Surrender Dorothy*, won the Grand Jury Prize at the 1998 Slamdance Film Festival should be a warning signal to anyone expecting something even remotely mainstream. *Surrender Dorothy* is startling, gripping, disturbing, and out on the film making edge. It's the kind of movie that we don't see enough of because its commercial prospects are so limited.

The story follows a twisted, co-dependent relationship as it spirals into ever-darker territory. The lead character is Trevor (Peter Pryor), a 27-year-old busboy who lives alone in a Philadelphia apartment. His only friend is Denis (Jason Centeno), a drug dealer, and his extreme fear of women prevents him from even going out on a date, let alone having a girlfriend. So Trevor lives his solitary, stale life, nursing his loneliness until someone comes along to change it. That person is Lanh (Kevin DiNovis), a 25-year-old heroin addict. Following a drug theft, Lanh is in hiding from Denis and comes to Trevor for a place to stay. In return for shelter, Trevor exacts a price — he gradually begins to transform Lanh into his vision of the "perfect woman." To obtain a daily fix, Lanh must wear women's clothing, makeup, and high heels. And, as Trevor's need to have a "real woman" grows, his plans for Lanh become progressively more bizarre.

The core relationship between Trevor and Lanh is obviously homosexual, but *Surrender Dorothy* isn't a "gay film." The fact is, Trevor wants a woman, and is able to delude himself into believing that Lanh (who he calls "Dorothy") is (or can become) one. The real focus of DiNovis' picture is on Trevor's obsession. It's frightening to consider the kind of monster that can lurk within the psyche of someone as apparently ineffectual as Trevor.

Surrender Dorothy can also be seen as an autopsy of a universal problem: domestic abuse. Trevor is the abuser and Lanh is the victim, and, although their roles are nontraditional, the patterns are familiar. The abuse is psychological, not physical, with Lanh trapped in this dysfunctional cycle, unable to break free. The defeated, broken Lanh we see late in the film is a far different individual from the cocky man who first moves into Trevor's apartment. Likewise, Trevor has been transformed from a frightened mouse into a cruel monster.

Surrender Dorothy is part dark comedy and part (David) Lynch-inspired melodrama, although it doesn't fit neatly into either category. It's an assault on political correctness and middle class values, but the underlying message is too urgent to disregard. Ultimately, *Surrender Dorothy* isn't easy to like (in

much the same way that something in the nature of *Blue Velvet* isn't easy to like), but it is undeniably powerful. **HIGHLY RECOMMENDED**

The Sweet Hereafter [Canada, 1997]
Starring: Ian Holm, Sarah Polley, Bruce Greenwood, Tom McCamus
Director: Atom Egoyan Screenplay: Atom Egoyan based on the novel by Russell Banks Running Time: 1:50 Rated: R (Mature themes, sex, nudity, profanity) Theatrical Aspect Ratio: 2.35:1

The Sweet Hereafter is film making at its most powerful: drama capable of shaking the soul, yet free of even the slightest hint of manipulation, sentimentality, or mawkishness. Canadian director/writer/producer Atom Egoyan shows the effects of grief and anger on a community devastated by an unspeakable tragedy.

The central event of *The Sweet Hereafter* is a school bus accident that results in the death of fourteen children and the injury of many others. On a cold winter's day in the small town of Sam Dent, British Columbia, the driver loses control of the vehicle and it careens off the road onto a frozen lake which gives way beneath the weight. The scene of the bus sinking into the water — a stark, simple shot — is a painfully effective and disturbing sequence. Death has become such a cheap, bloody commodity in modern movies that viewing a scene like this is a revelation.

Since Egoyan eschews linear storytelling by allowing time to be fluid rather than fixed, we don't see the actual accident until midway through the movie. The opening scene introduces us to Mitchell Stephens (Ian Holm), an ambulance-chaser who has come to Sam Dent to persuade the victims' parents to join in a class action lawsuit. He promises financial compensation for their losses, claiming that while no one can offer an outlet for their grief, he can be the voice of their anger. But there is no clear culprit to sue for the bus accident, and Mitchell is groping for a villain who doesn't exist. Parents join him in the vain hope that money will soothe the pain or bring some sort of "closure," but the greed for compensation fractures the community.

Other players in the drama include Nicole Burnell (Sarah Polley), one of the accident survivors. She's a teenage, would-be rock star who loses the use of her legs because of the experience, and who becomes the corner stone of Mitchell's case. As the victim of incest, however, she is a damaged individual. Her parents, Sam (Tom McCamus) and Mary (Brooke Johnson), are among the lawyer's most eager clients. Two others involved in the suit are Wanda and Hartley Otto (Arsinee Khanjian and Earl Pastko), who lost an adopted child in the crash. Risa and Wendell Walker (Alberta Watson and Maury Chaykin), whose only son perished beneath the cold waters, have also signed with Mitchell. But Risa's lover, Billy Ansell (Bruce Greenwood), reject's Mitchell's advances. Having recently lost his wife, Billy is acquainted with grief, and this enables him to accept the death of his twin children, rather than wallow in denial. Finally, there's Dolores Driscoll (Gabrielle Rose), the longtime bus driver who must live with the weight of responsibility for what happened.

The most amazing thing about *The Sweet Hereafter* is not the style, the acting, or the cinematography (all of which are exceptional), but the way the film successfully juggles so many themes, persuading us to reflect upon them all before the 110-minute running time is up. This is truly a great film. **MUST SEE**

Sweet Nothing [1996]

Starring: Michael Imperioli, Mira Sorvino, Paul Calderon, Patrick Breen, Richard Bright, Billie Neal Director: Gary Winick
Screenplay: Lee Drysdale Running Time: 1:30 Rated: R (Violence, profanity, sex, mature themes) Theatrical Aspect Ratio: 1.85:1

Sweet Nothing follows a very predictable and familiar trajectory: hero becomes a drug addict, watches helplessly as his life falls apart, then seeks redemption once he has lost everything. As long as there's something new or interesting in the experience, however, it's hard to argue with exploring these themes. *Sweet Nothing* doesn't boast an outstanding script or innovative direction, but it has a pair of exceptionally strong performances, and that's enough to earn it a recommendation.

The film opens with a shot of a still-living man lying broken and beaten in a pool of his own blood. As it turns out, this is *Sweet Nothing*'s protagonist, Angel (Michael Imperioli). In terms of chronology, this is virtually the end, and, as a result, the bulk of the story is told in flashback (accompanied by an unnecessarily verbose voiceover). Angel is a crack addict and dealer who first gets into the drug world as a means of supplementing his legitimate income. With two kids and a wife, Monika (Mira Sorvino), to support, the extra $1,000 a week comes in handy. Unfortunately, while dealing, he becomes a user as well, despite the warnings of his friend and boss, Raymond (Paul Calderon).

Many "drug movies" are so dark and cynical that it's difficult, if not impossible, to care about the main characters. Not so here. Michael Imperioli plays Angel as a loving husband and father who has been seduced by the lure of getting a few more dollars for his family. It seems so easy and innocent at the beginning; everyone's doing it, Raymond advises. Even the possibility of addiction doesn't worry Angel — he falls into the common trap of believing that he can stop just as easily as he started. Imperioli makes us see Angel as a good man with a tragic flaw, and, up to the very end, we're in sympathy with him.

Oscar-winner Mira Sorvino, who made this movie before *Mighty Aphrodite*, plays Monika with the same earnestness and vulnerability that she displayed in Whit Stillman's *Barcelona*. She sees what's happening to her husband, but is powerless to stop it. And, though she loves him desperately, there are limits to what she's willing to endure. When violence threatens her children, she's had enough.

Sweet Nothing isn't going to score any points with the drug using community, even though it's more of a character study than a "message" movie. There's certainly no preaching, although the scenes of Angel scheming, dealing, and stealing to get money for his next hit don't paint an appealing picture. Ultimately, *Sweet Nothing* is simply another movie to explore the pervasive and destructive impact of drug use and drug-related crime on American society. **RECOMMENDED**

A Tale of Springtime [France, 1992]

Starring: Anne Teyssedre, Florence Darel, Hugues Quester
Director: Eric Rohmer Screenplay: Eric Rohmer Running Time: 1:47
Rated: PG Theatrical Aspect Ratio: 1.66:1 In French with subtitles

A Tale of Springtime is the first installment in French director Eric Rohmer's *Tale of Four Seasons* series. Rohmer's intention with these films is to "focus on attractive, intelligent, self-absorbed if not entirely self-aware young women who present their dilemmas with clarity and elegance and express their feelings in inspired and witty dialogue."

A Tale of Springtime tells of the budding friendship between a young woman and a girl 10 years her junior. It has a lot to say about the human condition, and does so through a small group of characters that we grow to know and care about. Occasionally, the film slips off-track with pretentious intellectual spiels on philosophy, but in general *A Tale of Springtime* progresses like real life, with superb characterization and deft acting as its hallmarks.

The film opens by introducing us to Jeanne (Anne

Teyssedre), a 30ish woman with a penchant for order and a dislike of living alone in an apartment other than her own. Since her boyfriend is away on a trip, she has decided to temporarily move out of his place, but needs somewhere to go, having lent her own rooms to a cousin. Fate intervenes in the person of Natasha (Florence Darel), a college student that Jeanne meets at a party. The two take an immediate liking to one another, and Natasha invites Jeanne to spend the night. It doesn't take long for a friendship to spring up, and Natasha begins to weigh the possibility of manipulating a relationship between her father Igor (Hugues Quester) and Jeanne.

A Tale of Springtime is a slice of heaven for anyone who enjoys solid character dramas. Those looking for action, adventure, or plots that *move* will likely be bored to tears by Rohmer's picture. The storyline is merely a playing field for Jeanne, Natasha, and Florence — an arena in which Rohmer and his actors can explore the complexities of these individuals' personalities.

Aided by tremendously natural, unaffected performances from his lead actors, Rohmer has molded three real people and created a marvelous one-hundred seven minute film about philosophy and life. *A Tale of Springtime* presents a rare and wonderful opportunity to discover a trio of multidimensional cinematic characters. Once you've been introduced, you won't want to be parted from them, whether or not *Springtime* ends. HIGHLY RECOMMENDED

A Tale of Winter [France, 1992]

Starring: Charlotte Very, Frederic Van Dren Driessche, Michel Voletti
Director: Eric Rohmer Screenplay: Eric Rohmer Running Time: 1:53
Rated: No MPAA Rating (Nudity, sexual situations) Theatrical Aspect Ratio: 1.66:1 In French with subtitles

A Tale of Winter is the second installment in French director Eric Rohmer's *Tale of Four Seasons* series. The theme of this film is love, and whatever form that love might take — friendship, companionship, passion, sex — *A Tale of Winter* examines it.

The movie opens with Felicie (Charlotte Very) engaging in a brief-but-intense "vacation affair" in the south of France with Charles (Frederic Van Dren Driessche), an itinerant chef who is on his way to America. As a result of a mistake in the address she gives him, Felicie loses touch with Charles, and is unable to contact him when she gives birth to Elise (Ava Loraschi), their daughter.

Five years later, it's winter in Paris, and even though Felicie is currently involved with two men — Maxence (Michel Voletti) and Loic (Herve Furic) — both of whom are madly in love with her, Felicie is unable to commit to a relationship with either because of a premonition that someday she will again find Charles, her one true love. Nevertheless, reality is a cruel taskmaster, and Felicie is finding it increasingly difficult to define exactly how she feels about Maxence and Loic.

A Tale of Winter is gripping and engaging, not only because of the mystery of whether Felicie will ever again encounter Charles, but in its carefully realistic portrayals of her relationships with Maxence (a beautician whom she finds physically attractive) and Loic (an "egghead" whom she finds intellectually stimulating). No matter who you are, you're likely to see some element of yourself in one of the three main characters.

As seems obligatory in any Rohmer movie, there are a number of highly-philosophical discussions, some of which run on a little long. Topics include the nature of intelligence, the relationship between the supernatural and religion, the meaning of love, and the existence of the soul. Some of these are engrossing; others are worthy of a yawn. For those to whom such intellectual interactions do not appeal, there is always the core story.

With *A Tale of Winter*, Eric Rohmer has given us a wonderful motion picture that deals with the complexities of apparently-simple themes, and utilizes genuine characters and uncontrived situations to work through them. HIGHLY RECOMMENDED

Talk to Her [Spain, 2002]

Starring: Javier Camara, Dario Grandinetti, Leonor Watling, Rosario Flores Director: Pedro Almodovar Screenplay: Pedro Almodovar
Running Time: 1:52 Rated: R (Nudity, sexual content, profanity)
Theatrical Aspect Ratio: 2.35:1 In Spanish with subtitles

Talk to Her uses the kind of offbeat premise we have come to expect from Pedro Almodovar, whose films all-but-guarantee an offbeat view of life, love, and relationships. This time, we have two men — nurse Benigno (Javier Camara) and journalist Marco (Dario Graninetti) — who spend a great deal of time in a private clinic, where the most important people in their lives are in comas. For Benigno, it's Alicia (Leonor Watling), a dancer he barely knew before she arrived at the clinic, but for whom he has unceasingly cared for years. Benigno is in love with her, and believes the feeling to be mutual. (At one point, speaking about the period during which he has nursed Alicia, he comments, "These last 4 years have been the richest of my life.") Meanwhile, Marco's girlfriend, Lydia (Rosario Flores), was a bullfighter before the fateful day when she was gored, trampled, and nearly killed. Now, she, like Alicia, lies in seeming repose, unlikely ever to awaken.

There are plenty of movies available about women talking to one another, but films that chronicle deep, meaningful conversations between men are a rarity. *Talk to Her* is one of these unusual films, with Benigno and Marco developing a powerful bond as a result of their common circumstances. They speak to their comatose women, but, with increasingly greater frequency, they begin to rely upon one another. There may be an element of homoeroticism here, at least on Benigno's part. He is a virgin and is unsure of his feelings. He is obsessed by Alicia, but there are times when his friendship with Marco seems unusually intense. Benigno is clearly a disturbed individual — he spent 20 years caring for a bedridden mother before switching his attention to Alicia. Some of the most telling scenes about him are the flashbacks, which show him spying upon the dancer from afar before working up the courage to approach her. Marco's past is less creepy, but has left deep emotional wounds.

Almodovar gets all the details right, from Alicia's dancing to Lydia's bullfighting to Benigno's nursing. As is the director's trademark, he interweaves moments of humor (of a variety that occasionally borders on the absurd) into the dramatic tapestry. *Talk to Her* is a drama of great power, yet some members of the audience will leave the theater believing they have seen a comedy. **HIGHLY RECOMMENDED**

Tango [Spain/Argentina, 1998]

Starring: Miguel Angel Sola, Cecilia Narova, Mia Maestro, Juan Carlos Copes, Juan Luis Galiardo Director: Carlos Saura Screenplay: Carlos Saura Running Time: 1:54 Rated: PG-13 (Sexual themes) Theatrical Aspect Ratio: 2.35:1 In Spanish with subtitles

It's said that the tango is a dance of passion, and nowhere is that more ably demonstrated than in Carlos Saura's involving film, *Tango*. With only the thinnest of narrative threads linking scenes and moments together, this movie becomes a celebration of the dance from which it takes its name. Approximately ¾ of the nearly 2-hour running time is devoted to expertly-choreographed performances featuring dancers of exceptional skill, sensuality, and poise.

While the music is undeniably important, this is as much a celebration of visual splendor and diversity as it is an audio feast. Saura (*Carmen, Flamenco*) uses celluloid the way a master painter uses a canvas. *Tango* is an orgy of colors and images — an intense sensory experience that stands out as one of the most memorable I have seen. The contributions of veteran cinematographer Vittorio Storaro (*Apocalypse Now*) and composer Lalo Schifrin are as significant as those made by the actors and Saura himself.

Tango is not entirely without a plot, but that's definitely not the film's forte. The main character is Mario Suarez (Miguel Angel Sola), a film maker who is in the process of producing a musical in which various episodes of Argentinean history are presented via dances. From immigrants entering Buenos Aires around the turn of the century to Argentina's recent, repressive government, Mario's film ranges over a variety of themes and topics. The leading actress/dancer is Laura Fuentes (Cecilia Narova), Mario's ex-wife. Near the beginning of *Tango*, he still carries a torch for her, but, after an explosion of jealousy and desire, he is able to move forward romantically. He falls deeply in love with a young, lithe dancer named Elena (Mia Maestro), who, as luck would have it, is the girlfriend of the gangster who is funding Mario's project.

Like Sally Potter's far less compelling *The Tango Lesson*, *Tango* refuses to be bounded by conventional storytelling techniques, and those who crave a narrative will be disappointed. Saura boldly blurs the lines between Mario's reality, his dreams, and the film within the film. On more than one occasion (especially during the climactic tango), we're unsure whether what we're watching is happening around Mario or whether it is a manifestation of his imagination. One dance in particular, which features men and women being brutally tortured then dumped into mass graves, is as evocative as any filmed nightmare.

Working in concert, Saura and Storaro use a variety of methods to tantalize the eyes: silhouettes, shadows, reflections, and hues that span the spectrum from blood red to pastel violet. The result, a sumptuous and energetic example of filmed poetry, testifies to the success of Saura's approach. **RECOMMENDED**

Tape [2001]

Starring: Ethan Hawke, Robert Sean Leonard, Uma Thurman Director: Richard Linklater Screenplay: Stephen Belber, based on his play Running Time: 1:24 Rated: R (Profanity, mature themes, drugs) Theatrical Aspect Ratio: 1.85:1

For Richard Linklater, 2001 represented a particularly fertile year, with the Texas-based director having not one, but two, films available in theaters. The first, *Waking Life*, a trippy, animated dream that rambles on about all sorts of philosophical and political subjects. The other movie, *Tape*, more conventional, but no less engrossing. A filmed (actually videotaped, since this was shot using digital video) three-character play, *Tape* never moves beyond the confines of a small motel room. Powered by the star wattage of Ethan Hawke, Robert Sean Leonard, and Uma Thurman, the project was completed in a scant three weeks (2 weeks of rehearsal and 6 days of actual filming) on a miniscule budget. Like *Waking Life*, it's a talky piece, but the subjects addressed are of a much different nature.

There isn't much of a plot. *Tape* is about the reunion of two old friends, Vince and Johnny (Hawke and Sean Leonard), at a film festival in Lansing, Michigan. As these two reminisce about past times and where their lives have gone in the 10 years since high school, one significant, unresolved issue comes to the fore — the girlfriend whom Vince dated and Johnny slept with. But was it just sex, or was it rape? When pushed, Johnny admits that they were both drunk, the sex was rough, and he held her down. Vince captures this admission on tape, then invites the woman, Amy (Thurman), to the motel to offer her own surprising recollections of the situation.

In addition to exploring the thorny topic of date rape, *Tape* examines how the passage of time can distort memories, and how no two perceptions of the same event are ever identical (remember *Rashomon*?). Along the way, a number of other issues are touched upon, but everything comes back to the central question: what is rape and was it committed in this case? The three lead actors are superlative (Hawke and Sean Leonard moreso than Thurman, who has the least amount of screen time), fully inhabiting their characters. Screenwriter Stephen Belber's words recall the cadence and content of something by David Mamet; indeed, comparisons to *Oleanna* are perhaps inevitable. For something so static, *Tape* is an amazingly dynamic motion picture — one that challenges viewers' ideas and preconceptions. **RECOMMENDED**

Temptress Moon [China, 1996]

Starring: Leslie Cheung, Gong Li, Kevin Lin, He Saifei, Zhang Shi, Lin Lianqun, Ge Xiangting, Zhou Jie Director: Chen Kaige
Screenplay: Shu Kei, based on the story by Chen Kaige and Wang Anyi
Running Time: 1:55 Rated: R (Sex, mature themes) Theatrical Aspect Ratio: 1.85:1 In Mandarin with subtitles

Farewell My Concubine, director Chen Kaige's 1992 epic drama, told a tale about sex and friendship against a turbulent political backdrop. *Temptress Moon*, the film maker's 1996 followup (which premiered with much hoopla at that year's Cannes Film Festival) has similar intentions, but less successful results. Rather than existing as a deeply-moving exploration of characters and relationships, *Temptress Moon* plunges into a sudsy, melodramatic formula that it never quite manages to escape from. The film boasts many interesting elements, but, in comparison to *Concubine*, it's a disappointing effort.

Temptress Moon opens on the Pang estate in 1911 rural China, following a lengthy opening scroll (in English) which describes the current political situation. We are introduced to the three main characters — Zhongliang, Ruyi, and Duanwu — as children, before the film skips forward in time to the 1920s. In Shanghai, we encounter an older Zhongliang (played by Leslie Cheung), who is now in the employ of one of the city's many criminal bosses. Zhongliang's specialty is blackmail — he sleeps with a wealthy woman, then threatens to go to her husband if she doesn't pay up. He's very good at his job, and the boss treats him like a son.

Meanwhile, on the Pang estate, the opium-addicted Ruyi (Gong Li) has taken command following an unfortunate "accident" in which her older brother smoked arsenic instead of his usual poison. Ruyi's cousin, Duanwu (Kevin Lin), acts as her personal servant, kowtowing to her every whim. When Zhongliang arrives from Shanghai, sent to seduce Ruyi so the boss can gain her wealth, he becomes embroiled in a more intense relationship than he anticipated. Ruyi's passionate reaction to his advances discomfits the gangster and his cold-hearted composure is shaken.

Temptress Moon requires concentration, especially at the beginning, because, as scenes change and the story makes occasionally-jarring chronological jumps, it's easy to lose track of who the characters are and how they relate to each other. Miramax has attempted to ease the burden by supplying descriptive subtitles, but it's only a minor aid. Anyone who becomes lost early during *Temptress Moon* will have a difficult and frustrating time playing catch-up.

Although *Temptress Moon* falls short of the lofty perch upon which other Chinese classics like *Farewell My Concubine* and *Raise the Red Lantern* reside, there's still something compelling about the rhythm of this film, and the ending has its own brand of power. *Temptress Moon* is a flawed motion picture, but still makes for worthwhile viewing. RECOMMENDED

The Theory of Flight [United Kingdom, 1998]
Starring: Helena Bonham Carter, Kenneth Branagh Director: Peter Greengrass Screenplay: Richard Hawkins Running Time: 1:40 Rated: R (Profanity, sex) Theatrical Aspect Ratio: 1.85:1

Subtlety, more than any other quality, is required when dealing with symbolism. In *The Theory of Flight*, Paul Greengrass' directorial debut, "flight" is not only a symbol, but an obvious and unwieldy one. In fact, it's so awkward that it dilutes the effectiveness of the central narrative, an offbeat romance between a mentally unbalanced man and a physically disabled woman.

Richard (Kenneth Branagh), a 30-something individual who doesn't really want to grow up, is obsessed with building his own flying machine. After breaking the law by taking a airborne journey off the roof of a London high rise, he is sentenced to 120 hours of community service. His "project" is to be a companion to Jane (Helena Bonham Carter), a young woman afflicted with Motor Neuron Disease/Amyotrophic Lateral Sclerosis (ALS, also known as Lou Gehrig's Disease). The two don't get along at first, but, after a while, they become friends. Only then does Jane confess to Richard that she doesn't want to die a virgin. Thus begins his quest to find a suitable sexual partner for her — a search that eventually gives him a whole new perspective on life and love.

When *The Theory of Flight* concentrates on the Richard/Jane relationship, it's in good shape. Greengrass effectively combines pathos and sentiment with some wildly offbeat comedy. The two characters are interesting, especially when they're with each other, and their interaction is credible. However, on those occasions when the film veers off into the subplot about Richard's eccentric hobby, it runs into trouble. Not only is this aspect of the movie ill-conceived, but it's not well-developed. As Jane's caretaker, Richard is a worthwhile character. As an inventor, he's pointless.

Nevertheless, since *The Theory of Flight* is primarily about the Richard/Jane relationship, it's often possible to ignore Richard's attempts to replicate the Wright Brothers' feat. Perhaps the most unexpected thing about this movie (considering, after all, that it is about a woman suffering from a terminal disease) is its occasional forays into over-the-top comedy. Many of these instances are centered on Richard's attempts to purchase the services of a gigolo to fulfill Jane's desire, and, for the most part, they are genuinely funny.

The core premise of *The Theory of Flight* — an able-bodied individual caring for and bonding with a sick person — is a standard motion picture plot, but Greengrass' approach of stirring comedy into the mix makes for a refreshingly different experience. One could almost see this movie as a romantic comedy, albeit of a very unconventional sort. *The Theory of Flight* is far from a perfect movie, but it offers enough highlights that, on balance, it's worth a recommendation. The solid acting camouflages a great many other deficiencies. RECOMMENDED

Thieves (Les Voleurs) [France, 1996]
Starring: Catherine Deneuve, Daniel Auteuil, Laurence Côte, Fabienne Babe Director: André Téchiné Screenplay: Michel Alexandre, Pascal Bonitzer, Gilles Taurand, André Téchiné Running Time: 1:57 Rated: R (Sex, nudity, profanity, violence, mature themes) Theatrical Aspect Ratio: 1.85:1 In French with subtitles

Thieves is André Téchiné's followup to his unexpectedly successful 1995 art-house entry, *Wild Reeds*. The film features riveting performances by French icons Catherine Deneuve and Daniel Auteuil as two points of a romantic triangle. The third component is essayed by the sexy Laurence Côte.

Auteuil plays Alex, a French cop with a chip on his shoulder and a penchant for keeping his emotions under lock and key. Auteuil, who does this kind of role so well (check out *Un Coeur en Hiver* for an example), is perfectly cast, and never for the briefest of moments does his portrayal ring false. Deneuve, the ageless star, is superlative as Marie, the fragile philosophy professor who falls in love often and easily. On the other hand, although Côte gives a strong performance, her character, Juliette, is more of a catalyst than a three-dimensional individual. Juliette's presence remains enigmatic and sketchily drawn, and is all-but-forgotten during the movie's final third.

The event that jump-starts *Thieves* is the murder of Alex's criminal brother, Ivan (Didier Bezace), who was the head of a car-stealing ring. Juliette is somehow mixed up in the ring, but the situation is complicated because she's sleeping with Alex, who has been trying to gather enough evidence to put his brother behind bars. Marie, Juliette's other lover, becomes involved in the investigation when Juliette disappears and Alex approaches her to see whether she has been in touch with the young woman. Through a series of flashbacks presented from 4 different perspectives

(Marie's, Juliette's, Alex's, and that of Alex's adolescent nephew, Justin), Téchiné develops both plot and characters.

Thieves' payoff occurs during the last ⅓, when Alex and Marie, ostensibly searching for Juliette, become entwined in each others' lives. This isn't love, at least not in the conventional sense, but something that is, paradoxically, less profound and more complex. As the two of them try to establish a sense of trust, the normally-open Marie finds herself shutting down while the emotionally-closeted Alex discovers, much to his surprise, that he is capable of developing feelings for a woman whom he initially treats with contempt.

Ultimately, the film's anchor is Alex, whose highest hope for life is not to feel pain, who never laughs and sees evil everywhere, and whose personality alters with brilliant-but-unmistakable subtlety. Téchiné's development of Alex and Marie is masterful; Auteuil and Deneuve keep our attention riveted to the screen whenever they're on. And, while the director doesn't succeed in plumbing the emotional depths reached by *Ma Saison Préferée*, there are elements of *Thieves* that touch us nearly as forcefully — those moments just aren't as plentiful. RECOMMENDED

Third Miracle [1999]
Starring: Ed Harris, Anne Heche, Armin Mueller-Stahl
Director: Agnieszka Holland   Screenplay: John Romano, Richard Vetere
Running Time: 2:00   Rated: PG-13 (Mature themes, profanity)   Theatrical
Aspect Ratio: 1.85:1

Polish director Agnieszka Holland is a practicing Catholic, and one of her motivations for making *Third Miracle* was to depict issues of faith and religion in a positive, but still dramatically compelling, manner. For the most part, she has succeeded. *Third Miracle* is not without flaws, however.

Holland doesn't whitewash the Church. This isn't a pro-Catholic cheerleading effort, but it treats the religion, its creeds, processes, and beliefs with fairness and respect. Nothing in *Third Miracle* could be viewed by any reasonable person as an attack on the Church. One character, a crusty archbishop with calcified views on doctrine (played by veteran actor Armin Mueller-Stahl), comes across as an antagonist, but he's not a villain in the traditional sense of the word. His opinions, despite being intractable and outdated, are legitimate, and his motivation is not malicious. This is not a gross caricature or a stereotype. There are real people in the Church like this.

Ostensibly, *Third Miracle* is about the investigation of a Catholic priest, Father Frank Morris (Ed Harris in a strong performance) — into whether a deeply spiritual, recently departed woman named Helen O'Regan should be recommended for sainthood. Morris, an avowed skeptic, researches the supposed miracles associated with Helen and discovers that the typical causes for doubt do not apply. This is really just the surface story, however. The real meat of *Third Miracle* is the way it dissects Frank's faith (or lack thereof). He has fallen into what is theologically referred to as apostasy, and now must find his way back to redemption. By promoting Helen's cause, despite stern opposition from those in power within the Church, Frank discovers the path that may lead to spiritual restoration. Of course, there are temptations along the way, including the possibility of a sexual liaison with Helen's estranged daughter, Roxanne (Anne Heche), who is attracted to Frank.

Those who have seen *Stigmata* will find elements of *Third Miracle* to be eerily familiar (especially the opening 15 to 20 minutes). Consider the following . . . Both movies open with a statue of Mary weeping blood. Both focus on supposed miracles that have no rational explanation. And both feature a priest sent to investigate such occurrences, and who is in the midst of a crisis of faith, as the protagonist. However, despite the many similarities in the initial premise, the two films are very different in tone and intent. *Stigmata* is an over-the-top thriller, while *Third Miracle* is a restrained drama. RECOMMENDED

Thirty-Two Short Films about Glenn Gould
[Canada/Portugal/Netherlands/Finland, 1993]
Starring: Colm Feore   Director: Francois Girard   Running Time: 1:33
Rated: No MPAA Rating (Nothing offensive)   Screenplay: Francois
Girard and Don McKellar

Canadian musician and composer Glenn Gould was born in Toronto in 1932. By age 3, his gifts were apparent, and he was performing professionally 9 years later. Gould became one of the world's most renowned classical performers, making more than 60 recordings, as well as working in the fields of publishing, conducting, radio and television broadcasting, and scoring feature films. His version of Bach's "Goldberg Variations" is definitive, and was included as one of the samples of humanity's best on both Voyager spacecraft. Gould died of a stroke in 1982 at the age of 50.

Thirty-Two Short Films about Glenn Gould presents a unique, impressionistic look at the offbeat musician. Instead of giving a chronological view of

Gould's life, writer/director Francois Girard has elected to present a variety of snapshots, including recreations of actual events (with Gould played brilliantly by Colm Feore) and interviews with real-life contemporaries and friends.

Give Girard credit for understanding his subject and the best method of portraying him. There are indeed 32 episodes, ranging in length from under 1 minute to just over 6. Five of these are interviews, several have no dialogue, and 3 show Colm Feore's Gould wandering a winterscape. The most original two segments are "Gould Meets McLaren," which features animated spheres dancing to Gould's music, and "Pills," which contains closeups of all the various medicines resident in the musician's bathroom.

The character and personality of Glenn Gould come across brilliantly in this film. While nothing 93 minutes in length can hope to express all the facets of a man of Gould's depth, glimpses of elements lead to an understanding of the whole.

Some of the episodes are funny; some are poignant. In "Crossed Paths," Gould's friends recall his love of talking. One man remembers falling asleep while on the phone with Gould, then waking up hours later to find that the one-sided conversation was still in progress. "Motel Wawa" presents Gould's views on the supernatural and the afterlife, which leads directly into "Forty-Nine," in which the musician expresses his fear of turning that age because the digits (4 and 9) add up to 13.

In "Lake Simcoe," one of the movie's first segments, Gould states, "I'm fortunate to have been brought up in an environment where music was always present." The same can be said of *Thirty-Two Short Films*, where Gould's recordings form a backdrop to nearly every scene. This is a movie to be savored by those who are familiar with the work of Glenn Gould, and an opportunity for those who aren't to explore the essence of a rare musical genius. It's an eclectic film, and an astonishing portrait. **HIGHLY RECOMMENDED**

This Boy's Life [1993]

Starring: Leonardo DiCaprio, Robert DeNiro, Ellen Barkin
Director: Michael Caton-Jones Screenplay: Robert Getchell from the novel by Tobias Wolff Running Time: 1:59 Rated: R (Mature themes, language, sexual situations, violence) Theatrical Aspect Ratio: 2.35:1

This Boy's Life is based on the autobiographical book by Syracuse University professor Tobias Wolff. It tells of his early life in Salt Lake City, Seattle, and Concrete, Washington. Tobias (Leonardo DiCaprio) and his mother, Caroline (Ellen Barkin), travel from place-to-place, repeatedly trying to start anew. Because of the nomadic nature of their existence, Tobias never knows the stability of a traditional home life. Then he and his mother arrive in Seattle, where Caroline meets Dwight (Robert DeNiro). With his upstanding character and resolute moral fiber, Dwight seems like the perfect choice for a husband and father. However, when Tobias spends a few months alone with Dwight and his children in advance of the wedding, he experiences firsthand his stepfather-to-be's dark side.

There isn't much that can be said about the plot of a story based on a person's boyhood adventures. No one but Tobias Wolff knows how much dramatic license was used in writing his memoirs, but, on the whole, *This Boy's Life* has the ring of truth. Every boy who has grown up in America will surely recognize parts of himself, both good and bad, in Tobias. The film is well-paced and expertly edited, allowing scenes to flow naturally into one another.

Using Dwight as its subject, *This Boy's Life* explores domination as a means of compensating for emotional inadequacy and insecurity. Dwight believes in mastery through physical and psychological force. He will insult and abuse anyone to make it clear that he is in control. He *needs* to dominate — at one time or another, he asserts his power over everyone close to him: his children, his wife, and Tobias. Since Dwight doesn't know how to react with love or tenderness, he consistently resorts to violence.

Another motif present in this film mirrors an aspect of *The Crying Game*. One of the key lines in that movie is "It's in your nature." *This Boy's Life* deals with the question of what a person's nature is and whether or not it can be changed. Tobias is forever trying to make himself into a "better person," but it becomes clear as the movie unfolds that transforming one's basic character is not a simple matter.

Ultimately, *This Boy's Life* is effective because we get to know the characters, understand their circumstances, and empathize with their dreams. Certain individual scenes don't work (too overwrought or cliched), but the film as a whole stands up relatively well. Since *This Boy's Life* is a true story, there is a sense of incompleteness, but, as coming-of-age tales go, the realism of this one gives it an edge over many overly-sentimental contenders. **RECOMMENDED**

This Is My Father [United States/Ireland, 1999]

Starring: James Caan, Aidan Quinn, Moya Farrelly, Gina Moxley, Jacob Tierney Director: Paul Quinn Screenplay: Paul Quinn Running

Time: **2:00**   Rated: **R** (Sexual situations, mature themes)   Theatrical Aspect Ratio: **1.85:1**

Paul Quinn's *This Is My Father* is clearly a family affair. Paul writes and directs, his brother Aidan has one of the starring roles, and his other brother Declan serves as cinematographer. All three are listed as executive producers. If the final result wasn't as emotionally satisfying, Quinn's "keep it in the family" approach would be an easy target for criticism.

This Is My Father is hampered by an unnecessarily cumbersome structure. The action begins in modern-day America, where Kieran Johnson (James Caan), a self-confessed "lonely history teacher [living] in rural Illinois," begins to wonder about his father, a man he never knew. He finds evidence (an old photograph wrapped in newspaper) to suggest that his mother's story about his sire's identity might not be true. And, since a recent stroke has rendered her mute and apparently senseless, he has to go to Ireland's County Galway to seek his answers. Accompanied by his nephew, Jack, he travels there and finds an elderly woman (Moira Deady) who is willing to reveal the entire story.

Caan's scenes represent a bookend for the more involving and better realized flashback sequences, which tell of the tragic love between Kieran O'Day (Aidan Quinn), a penniless farmer, and Fiona Flynn (Moya Farrelly), the only daughter of a wealthy widow. It's the spring of 1939, and Fiona has just returned from boarding school. Although she and Kieran have known each other their whole lives, they have never been close. Now, they strike up a friendship. Kieran, a loner who has little knowledge about women, tries desperately to do everything right (and usually fails). For her part, Fiona finds his efforts endearing. During one magical night they spend together at the beach, they confess their love for one another. But "times were different" in 1939, and a match between the two is frowned upon for social and religious reasons. So, as factions within the town (headed by Fiona's mother and the local priest) try to rip them apart, the two lovers fight to stay together.

This Is My Father does not startle with plot twists and unexpected revelations, but that's part of its charm. The film is always true to its simple story, and does not attempt to stray in a sensationalistic direction just to mislead the audience. It's not all that difficult to guess how things are going to end long before the cinematic punctuation is placed on Fiona and Kieran's romance. For director Paul Quinn, this is

a fine effort, and represents the kind of motion picture that lovers of well-constructed romances long for. **RECOMMENDED**

A Thousand Acres [1997]

Starring: Jessica Lange, Michelle Pfeiffer, Jennifer Jason Leigh, Jason Robards   Director: Jocelyn Moorhouse   Screenplay: Laura Jones, based on the novel by Jane Smiley   Running Time: **1:45**   Rated: **R** (Violence, profanity, mature themes)   Theatrical Aspect Ratio: **1.85:1**

When viewing a melodrama like *A Thousand Acres*, it's easy to label it as a "chick flick" or a "tearjerker." However, such a facile categorization would do the movie a disservice, since it possesses a layer of depth that most films of this sort lack. Director Jocelyn Moorhouse, working from Laura Jones' adaptation of Jane Smiley's novel (which, in turn, updated Shakespeare's *King Lear*), gives *A Thousand Acres* the emotional pitch of *Fried Green Tomatoes* (even though the stories are vastly dissimilar). Although the plot is undeniably overwrought at times, the characters remain strong and reliable, and it's their believability that pulls us through.

The story is presented from the point-of-view of 40-something Ginny Cook Smith (Jessica Lange), who burdens the film with a voiceover narrative that is occasionally useful, but more often tedious. She's the oldest of the 3 daughters of farmer Larry Cook (Jason Robards), the "most respected man in the county." Along with her husband, Ty (Keith Carradine), she still lives on her father's 1,000 acre farm. Her sister May (Michelle Pfeiffer) resides there as well, along with her husband, Peter (Kevin Anderson), and their 2 teenage daughters. Ginny and May's baby sister, Caroline (Jennifer Jason Leigh), has left the farm to become a lawyer in nearby Des Moines. Despite the distance between her and the Cook farm, Caroline is closer to her father than either Ginny or May.

Things begin happening when the son of a neighbor, Jess Clark (Colin Firth), returns home after a 13-year absence. On the day of Jess' welcome back party, Larry announces his intention to turn over control of his farm to his 3 daughters. When Caroline wonders aloud whether this is a good thing, Larry cuts her out of his plans. The entire 1,000 acres is then divided between Ginny & Ty and May & Peter. But, even though he initiated the change, losing control of the farm doesn't sit well with Larry, and he becomes angry and abusive about his lot in life. And, as his rage escalates, deeply-buried secrets begin to ooze into the open. As in David Lynch's vision of America, *A Thousand Acres* shows that green fields and crisply-painted houses can hide a festering horror.

A Thousand Acres covers a lot of ground, and raises numerous questions about the demons that some families keep buried. The land means many things in this film: a source of pride, a means of economic survival, a financial windfall, and, most importantly, a tool for revenge. This is the kind of movie that you experience more with your emotions than with your intellect. It's not a dumb film, but its undisputed strength lies in the way it tears at the heart. Moorhouse's manipulation is skillful, and that makes it easier to forgive the occasional missteps. RECOMMENDED

Three Seasons [United States/Vietnam, 1999]
Starring: Don Duong, Ngoc Hiep Nguyen, Manh Cuong Tran, Harvey Keitel, Zoe Bui Director: Tony Bui Screenplay: Tony Bui, Timothy Linh Bui Running Time: 1:53 Rated: PG-13 (Sexual themes) Theatrical Aspect Ratio: 1.85:1 In Vietnamese with subtitles

The accolades heaped upon *Three Seasons*, the debut feature of Vietnamese American film maker Tony Bui, at the 1999 Sundance Film Festival are a publicist's dream. Not only did director of photography Lisa Rinzler win the cinematography award, but Bui took home both the Best Dramatic Picture trophy and the Audience Award. *Three Seasons* is a solid and effective motion picture, however it lacks the depth and breadth one typically associates with an award winning effort.

The narrative is comprised of four different stories. One tells of the relationship between Kien An (Ngoc Hiep Nguyen), a young girl who harvests lotus flowers, and her employer, Teacher Dao (Manh Cuong Tran). He's a poet who has lost the ability to write due to the progressive degeneration of his body caused by leprosy. He lives in the past because he cannot bear the present and sees no future. Kien An, feeling pity for him (and perhaps an odd, creative kinship), agrees to function as his fingers if he will return to writing poetry. Meanwhile, in the city, a cyclo driver, Hai (Don Duong), has become infatuated with a prostitute, Lan (Zoe Bui). From the moment he first helps her out of a tight spot, he is smitten with her, but she regards his attentions as annoyances. Hai, however, is a patient man, and he saves up his money so he can afford to buy a night with her. His intention is to give her something that none of her other customers would think of offering. Elsewhere in the city, an American GI, James Hager (Harvey Keitel), has returned to Vietnam after a 30-year absence to find the daughter he fathered during the war. In his words,

"It's time to find her and maybe make some kind of peace with this place." But, as he quickly discovers, tracking down one individual can be a daunting task. Finally, there's the boy Woody (Huu Duoc Nguyen), a street peddler who makes his living selling cheap watches, flashlights, chewing gum, and cigarettes to passersby in the street. When the case containing his wares is stolen, he must face the wrath of his father and seek to find a new way to earn money.

One criticism that can be leveled against *Three Seasons* is that its vision of Vietnam is too sunny (not literally — it's almost always raining). Indeed, with the exception of a few rare moments, we fail to glimpse anything dark or depressing. Prostitution and street solicitation are sanitized so they appear almost appealing. The country itself looks like the ideal place for a vacation. Nevertheless, it is unfair to charge the movie with being a slice of pro-Vietnamese propaganda, because it's much more than that. It's an accomplished and effective piece of film making that works on many levels. RECOMMENDED

Tin Cup [1996]
Starring: Kevin Costner, Rene Russo, Cheech Marin, Don Johnson, Linda Hart, Dennis Burkley Director: Ron Shelton Screenplay: John Norville and Ron Shelton Running Time: 2:10 Rated: R (Profanity, nudity, sex) Theatrical Aspect Ratio: 1.85:1

As far as sports movies go, *Tin Cup* turns in a respectable showing, injecting some intelligence and maturity into a story that easily could have succumbed to a flood of "struggling underdog" cliches. That's not to say that elements of the formula aren't here, but they rarely threaten to overwhelm *Tin Cup*'s better aspects.

The story centers around Roy (Kevin Costner), an aging club pro who lives in a Winnebago in the lonely west Texas town of Salome. He spends his day in the company of his best friend, Romeo (Cheech Marin), working for $7 an hour at a deserted driving range. Once upon a time, Roy had a bright golfing future ahead of him, but he blew his cool on the links, went for the trick shot instead of the smart one, and failed to qualify for the tour. Since then, he has been hiding out in obscurity, picking up cash where he can, and watching bitterly as his old college partner, Dave Simms (Don Johnson), "a rich, happy, soulless" man, rises through the PGA ranks.

One day, Roy's marginal existence is turned upside down by the arrival of a woman psychologist named Molly Griswold. She wants to take golf lessons to impress her boyfriend. To the men of Salome, the concept of a female doctor is a revelation, and, in one of the film's more slyly amusing scenes, they watch eagerly as Roy teaches her the basics of hitting a golf ball, wondering how "such a pretty girl can have such an ugly swing." It doesn't take long for Roy to fall in love with Molly, so it comes as a blow when she reveals that her boyfriend is none other than Dave Simms. Roy then decides that a grand gesture is needed to win her — something like qualifying for the U.S. Open and beating Dave in front of a national TV audience.

Although this may sound like a very familiar, traditional sports movie, don't worry — director Ron Shelton applies enough tweaks and twists to the formulaic story to keep us interested and a little unsure of the outcome. *Tin Cup* isn't concerned with blazing new trails — that's beyond its scope or ambition. Instead, it's content to offer a pleasantly likable, gently comic 2 hours of simple life lessons, with golf as the obvious metaphor.

As the saying goes, you don't have to appreciate the sport to enjoy the movie. *Tin Cup* has a broad enough appeal that intimate knowledge of the joys and frustrations of playing 18 holes isn't necessary. This movie ranks as better-than-par entertainment. **RECOMMENDED**

To Live [China, 1994]

Starring: Ge You, Gong Li, Niu Ben, Guo Tao, Jiang Wu, Liu Tian Chi, Zhang Lu Director: Zhang Yimou Screenplay: Yu Hua and Lu Wei based on the novel by Yu Hua Running Time: 2:13 Rated: No MPAA Rating (Mature themes, violence) In Mandarin with subtitles

To Live explores territory that is rapidly becoming familiar to those who view the works of China's so-called "Fifth Generation" film makers. The events of the middle decades of the twentieth century, including the Communist Civil War, the "Great Leap Forward," and the Cultural Revolution, represent fertile ground for grand stories of mingled tragedy and triumph. However, this marvelously-textured movie, which is by turns funny and touching, takes a different approach from pictures like *The Blue Kite* and *Farewell My Concubine*. Instead of viewing the cultural changes on an epic scale, *To Live* gives a far more intimate, and affecting, perspective.

Fugui (Ge You), Jiazhen (Gong Li), and their 2 children are normal, hard-working Chinese citizens caught up in the chaotic changes transforming their country. Unlike many of their counterparts in other, similarly-themed films, they are not accused of acting against Mao Tse-tung's Red government, but their faithfulness to the new order doesn't keep tragedy from touching their lives. As one of the film's explanatory capsules states, few families in China were not affected by the Cultural Revolution.

Although *To Live* was banned in its country of origin because of a supposed negative portrayal of certain pro-Maoist historical events, Zhang's presentation of 3 turbulent decades of life in China seems reasonably balanced. Other films (most notably *Farewell My Concubine*) have more openly attacked the Communist Revolution and its aftermath.

The characters are powerfully developed and realized, representing some of the most "real" men and women to populate any of 1994's films. From the 1940s to the early 1970s, we follow Fugui's family through good times and bad. Zhang's skill is such that we become less a detached observer and more a passive participant. Gong and Ge (both of whom appeared in *Farewell My Concubine*), who imbue Fugui and Jiazhen with life and humanity, are perfect choices for the central characters.

Few films approach the level of honesty reached by *To Live*. This is a story whose underlying central theme is expressed in the through all the struggles, hardships, and moments of rare magic and joy, the characters continue their lives. As Jiazhen points out, no matter how bleak circumstances appear, the only choice is to go on.

With *To Live* Zhang has cemented his reputation as one of today's premier directors. It is an accolade not lightly accorded, but the filmmaker has earned it through his telling of rare stories brimming with humanity and unforced drama. **MUST SEE**

Topsy-Turvy [United Kingdom, 1999]

Starring: Jim Broadbent, Allan Corduner, Lesley Manville, Eleanor David, Ron Cook, Timothy Spall Director: Mike Leigh Screenplay: Mike Leigh Running Time: 2:40 Rated: R (Nudity, drug use) Theatrical Aspect Ratio: 1.85:1

Over the course of their famous partnership, which lasted from 1871 until 1896, the team of William Gilbert (librettist) and Arthur Sullivan (composer) produced 14 operettas, including such classics as "The Pirates of Penzance," "The Mikado," and "The Gondoliers." British filmmaker Mike Leigh (*Secrets & Lies*) has chosen to take a closer look at this duo, whose names will be forever linked. Instead of focusing on an entire quarter-century of sometimes turbulent collaboration, Leigh has limited his scope to a 14-month period between January 1884 and March 1885. *Topsy-Turvy* begins with the opening of "Princess Ida" and closes with the triumphant debut of "The

Mikado." Along the way, we learn bits and pieces about Gilbert, Sullivan, and those who loved them and worked with them.

As a history lesson, *Topsy-Turvy* is on uncertain ground, making liberal use of what is commonly termed "dramatic licence." While there is more structure to this narrative than is typical for Leigh, there are a number of sequences that have little or nothing to do with what really happened backstage at the Savoy Theater. The film is essentially divided into two parts. The first concentrates on the personal lives and ambitions of Gilbert and Sullivan, and stakes out the territory that defines their relationship. The second explores the development of "The Mikado," from Gilbert's visit to a Japanese restaurant (where inspiration struck) to its opening night performance.

Topsy-Turvy's second half is unquestionably stronger than its first. Like John Turturro's *Illuminata,* this movie takes us behind the scenes of a theatrical production around the turn of the 20th century, but Leigh's scenario and characters are better realized. In detailing the transition of "The Mikado" from idea to reality, the director shows every aspect of the process: writing, casting, costuming, developing dance steps, acting rehearsals, and musical rehearsals. Some of these episodes are highly amusing, especially a ten-minute sequence in which Gilbert puts three of his actors through their paces. Because of scenes like this, *Topsy-Turvy*'s final 80 minutes fly by. Unfortunately, the same cannot be said of the other portion of the movie, which suffers from occasional spells of torpidity.

On a certain level, this is one of Mike Leigh's most challenging productions. Not only has he produced a narrative feature based on real events and historical figures, but he has elected to stage significant portions of Gilbert and Sullivan productions. In addition to four or five numbers from "The Mikado," we are treated to songs from "The Sorcerer" and "Princess Ida." Although there are times when this movie does not seem like a "Mike Leigh Film," it is a well crafted and solidly entertaining effort that illustrates how expert filmmakers can expand their ranges while still producing movies that are worth seeing. RECOMMENDED

Total Eclipse [France/United Kingdom, 1995]

Starring: Leonardo DiCaprio, David Thewlis, Romane Bohringer, Dominique Blanc Director: Agnieszka Holland Screenplay: Christopher Hampton based on his play Running Time: 1:50 Rated: R (Nudity, sex, violence, mature themes) Theatrical Aspect Ratio: 1.85:1

The lives of tortured artists have always made for fascinating film fare, and since genius is often synonymous with self-destruction, it should come as no surprise that director Agnieszka Holland's presentation of the relationship between two 19th century poets is overflowing with grimness, grief, and anger. Yet, even though we never feel much sympathy for either Arthur Rimbaud (Leonardo DiCaprio) or Paul Verlaine (David Thewlis), the material is nevertheless strangely compelling.

Total Eclipse opens in 1871 as established poet Verlaine invites the wild 16-year-old Rimbaud to live with him. The youth, who possesses a keen intellect but little regard for conventional etiquette, astounds his host while simultaneously horrifying Verlaine's young, pregnant wife, Mathilde (Romane Bohringer). Soon, with his promises of intense experiences and new insights into life, Rimbaud seduces Verlaine from his family. The two men, now sexual partners as well as friends, bounce from Paris to Brussels to London, arguing about the existence of love and whether indeed "the only unbearable thing is that nothing is unbearable."

The story related in *Total Eclipse* is ambitious. What transpired between Verlaine and Rimbaud more than 100 years ago has influenced poetry since, but has never been dramatized for the screen until now. The relationship is complex, encompassing just about every emotion from love to hate — a profoundly unhealthy attraction that poisons not only the lives of the two principals, but that of everyone who has contact with them. What befalls the Verlaines' marriage is only the first tragedy.

As scripted by Christopher Hampton (*Dangerous Liaisons, Carrington*), the presentation of Verlaine and Rimbaud's story is erratic. At times, it's absorbing — almost hypnotic — but those stretches don't last. There are other sequences when the film becomes ponderous and pretentious, and where over-the-top acting blunts dramatic impact. The narrative also has a tendency to jump from year-to-year and place-to-place. As far as the characters are concerned, they're interesting only when they're together. During the overlong denouement, when the poets are separated, the proceedings become a little dull.

Despite its flaws, *Total Eclipse* is the kind of movie that stirs thoughts and ruminations about the nature of genius, the true meaning of art, and the unfailing capacity of great people to destroy themselves and others. This picture is a respectable examination of a fascinating historical relationship. **RECOMMENDED**

Traveller [1997]

Starring: Bill Paxton, Mark Wahlberg, Julianna Margulies, James Gammon, Luke Askew Director: Jack Green Screenplay: Jim McGlynn Running Time: 1:43 Rated: R (Profanity, sex, violence) Theatrical Aspect Ratio: 1.85:1

Traveller, the directorial debut of veteran cinematographer Jack Green, takes us into the world of blood-related grifters who pull two-bit cons as a way of life. They are the "Travellers," a close-knit band of Irish-American nomads who survive by preying on the gullibility and greed of others. This movie tells the story of one such Traveller and the forces that lead him to question his position within the society.

Bokky (Bill Paxton) is near the top of the North Carolina Traveller hierarchy. He is respected by his peers, and the local leader, Boss Jack (Luke Askew), regards him as the son he never had. One Fall day, a young man, Pat (Mark Wahlberg), arrives to bury his exiled Traveller father in a Traveller cemetery, and is met with cold stares and harsh words. As an outsider, he is regarded with suspicion, but the Traveller blood in his veins runs true and Bokky agrees to take Pat under his wing. Soon, the two have become a team and are pulling off some pretty profitable schemes. Everything is going smoothly until Bokky falls for Jean (Julianna Margulies), one of his intended victims, and his loyalties become confused.

The plot of *Traveller*, credited to Jim McGlynn, isn't all that complex or hard to follow. It's episodic in nature, with each new scam representing another chapter. The cons are fun to watch unfold. Sometimes, it's possible to see where they're going, sometimes not. The script is smart and sneaky — by never telling the audience more than is necessary, it develops a keen sense of suspense that persists until the gritty final reel.

The great strength of the film, however, is character development. The two leads, Bokky and Pat, both have clearly-defined arcs. Pat, desperate to prove himself to Boss Jack, works hard to learn the tricks of the trade. Meanwhile, Bokky, even while teaching Pat how to scam people, is starting to see his marks as human beings, and his resolve to rip them off is beginning to waver. He is suddenly reluctant to swindle a young couple out of their life's savings.

Here and there, *Traveller* takes a wrong turn. The culture of the band, which is arguably the most ab-

sorbing feature of the film, is worthy of a more thorough exploration than is offered. We're teased with a possible romantic relationship between Pat and the Boss' daughter (Nikki DeLoach), which might have uncovered another dimension of Traveller society, but this subplot is abruptly dropped during the movie's second half. Still, these are mostly small gripes, and their impact upon the viewing experience as a whole is minimal. A fine film. **RECOMMENDED**

Tumbleweeds [1999]

Starring: Janet McTeer, Kimberly Brown, Gavin O'Connor, Jay O. Sanders Director: Gavin O'Connor Screenplay: Gavin O'Connor and Angela Shelton, based on a story by Shelton Running Time: 1:44 Rated: PG-13 (Profanity, sexual situations, mature themes) Theatrical Aspect Ratio: 1.85:1

Gavin O'Connor's debut feature, *Tumbleweeds* combines elements of a road picture with a tale of mother/daughter bonding, and opens with a scene of domestic discord. Following a furious argument with her husband, Mary Jo Walker (Janet McTeer) grabs her 12-year-old daughter, Ava (Kimberly Brown), and heads west. Together, mother and child embark on the latest leg of a seemingly-endless adventure that has seen Mary Jo marry and flee 4 times — she has an uncanny knack for picking the wrong kinds of men, and, when the relationships go sour (as they seemingly must), she gets out. The next destination for the nomadic pair is Southern California, where Ava discovers a passion for acting (playing Romeo in a school play version of *Romeo and Juliet*) and finally begins to feel at home. Her sense of belonging is endangered, however, when Mary Jo embarks upon another love affair — this time with a truck driver named Jack (Gavin O'Connor). And, although Jack seems to be a good-natured, attentive man, Ava awaits the inevitable explosion with a mixture of trepidation and resignation.

The strength of O'Connor's movie, and the reason it stands above the continuum of the many similar-yet-lesser efforts, is the careful attention paid to character development and relationship building. O'Connor goes to great lengths to ensure that the bond between Mary Jo and Ava is sculpted in such a way that the audience immediately sympathizes with both individuals and recognizes the deep and powerful nature of the ties that bind them. Unlike in Wayne Wang's *Anywhere But Here*, where mother and daughter are constantly at odds, Mary Jo and Ava have a more harmonious relationship. Even though

Ava craves stability and Mary Jo shuns restraint, there's very little contention between them — they are inseparably connected by a past of shared tribulations. In fact, there are many times when they act more like sisters than a mother and daughter.

In many ways, this is not a conventional "chick flick." It is heartfelt, but does not rely on emotional manipulation to sway an audience. We feel for the characters because they seem real, not because the script has us reaching for the nearest box of Kleenexes. O'Connor and his actresses keep *Tumbleweeds* on the right course as its plot veers through a minefield of familiar situations: failed marriages, abusive menfolk, and teenage rebellion. In the end, the story may be about characters who are blown around by the winds of fate, but the way in which it is presented represents a solidly grounded effort. **RECOMMENDED**

Two Bits [1995]

Starring: Jerry Barrone, Mary Elizabeth Mastrantonio, Al Pacino, Andy Romano Director: James Foley Screenplay: Joseph Stefano Running Time: 1:25 Rated: PG-13 (Mature themes) Theatrical Aspect Ratio: 2.35:1

When you think of Al Pacino, the image that comes to mind is one of energy, intensity, and violence. Whether a cop (*Sea of Love, Serpico, Heat*) or a crook (*The Godfather, Scarface*), Pacino's characters are almost always hard-hitting, hyperactive portraits of caged fury. So it's more than a minor departure for the actor to appear in James Foley's *Two Bits* as Gitano Sabatoni, a dying, regretful old man. This is a small, understated role — character actor material — yet Pacino immerses himself so fully in the part that we forget about the performer the moment we see the performance.

Despite Pacino's presence in the cast, this isn't his movie. Nor does it belong to Mary Elizabeth Mastrantonio, who has a supporting role as Gitano's timid daughter. Instead, the focus is on Jerry Barrone, who plays 12-year-old Gennaro, the fictionalized childhood counterpart of screenwriter Joseph Stefano. This film, which Stefano first committed to paper in 1970, is autobiographical, recounting one crucial day in his life as a boy in South Philadelphia during the heat of a Depression era summer.

That day is August 26, 1933, when Gennaro first starts noticing life for what it is. It's a day of eye-opening experiences and tough lessons; of awareness, magic, and sadness. As Alec Baldwin states in his voiceover narration, it's the day La Paloma — the newest movie theater in the neighborhood — opens. Until 6 P.M., there's a special rate at the cinema: get in for only 25 cents. So Gennaro spends his time roaming the streets, looking for odd jobs that will pay enough for him to afford a matinee. This quest for two bits takes place against the backdrop of an America where the only thing more scarce than money is employment.

The story is simple, and the film's message is equally as plain: never give up wanting and striving, no matter how unattainable the dream seems. For Gennaro in *Two Bits,* that goal is watching a movie in the air-conditioned confines of La Paloma. As the film progresses, this simple theater takes on a monumental symbolic importance.

The greatest failing of *Two Bits* is a tendency to ramble. Individual episodes work well on their own, but some of the connecting material is weak, and the voiceover is often more irritating than helpful. The film is also too self-conscious about getting across its theme.

Two Bits represents an undemanding form of entertainment — a period piece that lives on nostalgia and an elemental story. Perhaps the most successful aspect of this film is that it encourages us to connect events in Gennaro's life with moments in our own, thereby enriching the emotional impact. Credit director Foley (*Glengarry Glen Ross*) for a fine, character-based piece. **RECOMMENDED**

Ulee's Gold [1997]

Starring: Peter Fonda, Patricia Richardson, Jessica Biel Director: Victor Nunez Screenplay: Victor Nunez Running Time: 1:51 Rated: R (Profanity, violence) Theatrical Aspect Ratio: 1.85:1

The title character in *Ulee's Gold* is a beekeeper who lives and works in the Florida Panhandle's tupelo marshes, and, although this is a narrative feature, not a documentary, it taught me a great deal about the difficulties of harvesting of honey. Yet, as important as honeycombs and beekeeping are to the story, they are not the central focus. This movie is about damaged characters and fractured relationships. Ultimately, it's this aspect of the film that makes it compelling; the honey-making stuff is an added bonus.

It's worth noting that Ulee (Peter Fonda, in a performance that recalls the work of his late father, Henry Fonda) is more comfortable dealing with his bees than with people. Since the death of his wife 6 years ago, he has turned into a physical and emotional recluse. He lives with his 2 granddaughters,

Penny (Vanessa Zima) and Casey (Jessica Biel), who were abandoned by their parents. Their father and Ulee's son, Jimmy (Tom Wood), is serving a sentence for armed robbery. Their mother, Helen (Christine Dunford), has dropped out of sight. One day, during the busiest time of the honey-making season, Ulee receives a call from Jimmy, who claims that a couple of his former criminal associates have located Helen, strung out on drugs, in Orlando. Reluctantly, Ulee makes the trip to bring his daughter-in-law home, and, in the process, becomes involved in a search for old robbery money.

The crime-related activities of *Ulee's Gold* represent the film's least interesting aspect, and the criminals (played by Steven Flynn and Dewey Weber) scarcely rise about the stereotype level. Fortunately, the movie offers far richer and more complex elements, such as how Ulee relates to Penny, a quiet, introverted child who misses her mother, and Casey, a rebellious teenager. Or how he struggles to mend fences with Jimmy and Helen. Or how he learns to once again trust outsiders, including the local sheriff (J. Kenneth Campbell) and Connie (Patricia Richardson), an attractive nurse renting a house across the street.

Nunez's script is thoughtful and intelligent, and it challenges his actors with fully-formed personalities for them to breathe life into (Peter Fonda, in fact, called Ulee "the best character I've ever read"). The highest compliment I can offer *Ulee's Gold* is that it plays more like real life than a movie. During the course of the film, we learn a little about the different grades of honey. And, just as the light golden Tupelo is in the top echelon, so too is *Ulee's Gold*.

HIGHLY RECOMMENDED

Un Air de Famille (Family Relations) [France, 1996]
Starring: Jean-Pierre Bacri, Agnes Jaoui, Jean-Pierre Darroussin, Catherine Frot Director: Cedric Kapisch Screenplay: Agnes Jaoui, Jean-Pierre Bacri & Cedric Klapisch Running Time: 1:47 Rated: No MPAA Rating (Mature themes) Theatrical Aspect Ratio: 2.35:1
In French with subtitles

Un Air de Famille, from French director Cedric Klapisch, is a study of a dysfunctional family on the verge of blowing apart. While this isn't exactly an original topic, Klapisch's approach is vastly different from what we have come to expect from this sort of motion picture. There's no overwrought melodrama, no sudden moment of great personal triumph, and no real catharsis. Instead, what *Un Air de Famille* offers is 110 minutes of discovery through dialogue, as the characters spar with each other, and, as the film wears on, gradually shed their carefully-erected disguises and allow their true selves to show.

The main characters are a trio of very different siblings. There's Philippe (Wladimir Yordanoff), the suave, successful one, who arrives at a family dinner immediately after finishing a television interview. The dinner, a birthday get-together for Philippe's insecure wife, Yolande (Catherine Frot), is being held at the restaurant managed by Philippe's brother, Henri (Jean-Pierre Bacri), a dour man whose wife has recently left him. Then there's Philippe and Henri's younger sister, Betty (Agnes Jaoui), whose leather jacket is just one sign of her ongoing rebellion against convention. Also in attendance for the night's "festivities" are the siblings' domineering mother (Claire Maurier), and a bartender named Denis (Jean-Pierre Darroussin), who is secretly involved with Betty.

Things don't begin well, as Betty and Henri engage in a frosty conversation before Betty unceremoniously dumps Denis. When Philippe shows up, the evening's decline accelerates. Mother's arrival exacerbates tensions as the siblings begin sniping at each other and anyone else within verbal reach. As the film progresses, it becomes apparent that first impressions aren't always accurate, and that the supposedly-affable Philippe may be far less caring and humane than his sour-faced brother. Betty begins to realize this as we do, and her attitude gradually changes. The recognition that she has been wrong about her brothers all along gives her the impetus to truly defy her family for the first time.

All of the events of *Un Air de Famille* take place over a 4-hour period, meaning that the film unfolds almost in real time. It would be interesting to see how the characters react to each other in the future, since the events of this dinner demand changes in every relationship that is explored. By the time the closing credits unfold, each member of the family has learned something new about everyone else, and we, the viewers, have come to understand and appreciate the complexities that define their interaction. In that way, *Un Air de Famille* is a wonderfully rich and intelligent exploration of family dynamics. **HIGHLY RECOMMENDED**

Un Coeur en Hiver [France, 1992]
Starring: Daniel Auteuil, Emmanuelle Beart, Andre Dussollier, Elisabeth Bourgine Director: Claude Sautet Screenplay: Yves Ulmann, Jacques Fieschi, and Jerome Tonnere Running Time: 1:45 Rated: No MPAA Rating (Mature themes) Theatrical Aspect Ratio: 1.66:1 In French with subtitles

In addition to being employer and employee, Stephane (Daniel Auteuil) and Maxime (Andre Dussollier) share an intimate friendship. Stephane works for Maxime at an exclusive Paris violin repair shop. One evening, while the two are at dinner, Maxime announces that he has fallen in love with a new client, Camille Kessler (Emmanuelle Beart). The affair is so serious that Maxime has left his wife and intends to move in with Camille. Upon meeting, Stephane and Camille are immediately intrigued by each other. Yet, even as Stephane fights to maintain his own emotional equilibrium, for the first time in her life, Camille loses hers, and her simple attraction to Stephane becomes an obsession.

Often foreign films, and French films in particular, are thought of by the average movie-goer as being exceptionally (and some would say "overly") intellectual. This could not be more true than for *Un Coeur en Hiver*, yet this picture feeds more than just the mind. The rich musical score (Ravel) is a feast for the ears, and the exceptional performances of the principals lead to several emotionally-potent moments. In the final analysis, *Un Coeur en Hiver* satisfies completely.

Distilled to its basic essence, the movie is a story that the French do so well: the romantic triangle. Beyond the premise, however, there is nothing ordinary about *Un Coeur en Hiver*. From the point that Stephane and Camille meet, much of what happens goes contrary to expectations. Theirs is definitely not a typical tale of clandestine love. Rather, it is an examination of the price of emotional honesty and emotional isolation.

Oddly enough, it's Stephane, the character with the most screen time, who remains an enigma to the audience. Even though we come to identify with him, and understand some of what he does, the depth of his emotions often remains unclear. The last scene of the movie explicitly reveals part of the truth, but for much about Stephane, the viewer must reach his or her own conclusions.

Camille is no less a complicated character, but her feelings are simpler to read. She hides nothing, and when she recognizes that she loves Stephane, there is no doubt in her mind — or ours — of the truth. Especially noteworthy is the manner in which Camille's sudden, intense passion for Stephane intertwines, and at times conflicts with, her lifelong love of music.

In *Un Coeur en Hiver*, strong characters, intelligent writing, and exquisite performances combine to draw the audience into the film's deep, churning currents. Those attracted only to Hollywood's shallow waters may find this picture too intimidating, but for anyone who enjoys a more complex cinematic experience, *Un Coeur en Hiver* offers an alternative. **MUST SEE**

Under the Sand [France, 2000]

Starring: Charlotte Rampling, Bruno Cremer, Jacques Nolot
Director: François Ozon Screenplay: François Ozon, Emmanuelle Bernheim, Marcia Romano, Marina de Van Running Time: 1:30
Rated: No MPAA Rating (Sex, nudity, profanity) Theatrical Aspect Ratio: 1.85:1 In French with subtitles

Death: it is the lone certainty in life (forget the bit about taxes). Despite that, when the end comes to a loved one, even if expected, it can be difficult to process and handle. This is the province of *Under the Sand*, from internationally celebrated French director François Ozon, whose credits include *See the Sea* and *Water Drops on Burning Rocks*.

Charlotte Rampling plays Marie Drillon, an English-born college professor who lives in France with her beloved older husband, Jean (Bruno Cremer). One summer, as usual, the couple travels to a country house near the sea to take a vacation. While Marie is lying on the beach, sunning herself and dozing off, Jean decides to take a swim. He never returns. Marie is left with a host of unanswered questions. Was Jean's death accidental or did he kill himself? Is he really dead or did he fake his death and disappear? Was there anything she could have done to prevent the tragedy? Instead of coping, she goes into deep denial, pretending that Jean is still alive and awaiting his daily return from work. Her friends worry as she continues to refer to her husband in the present tense. The one in the most difficult position is Marie's new lover, Vincent (Jacques Nolot), who knows Jean is dead and is disconcerted by Marie's seeming unwillingness to acknowledge this fact.

The film is resolutely and unflinchingly unsentimental in its depiction of Marie's situation, and this lack of melodrama is one of the most effective weapons in *Under the Sand*'s arsenal. It does not trivialize through manipulation. Instead, Ozon depicts discrete moments in Marie's life, and how they are impacted by her uncertainty: dinner with friends, dates with her lover, a teaching session with her class. When she arrives home, a specter-like Jean is there — a construct of her memories and imagination who listens quietly as she unburdens herself, only occasionally offering advice. Yet there are times when it's clear from Marie's face that she understands, at least on some level, that she is fooling herself. And, occasionally, she comes face-to-face with reality, such as when she enters Jean's home office and sees everything untouched, or when the police call to report that they may have found Jean's body.

Ozon's careful and detailed approach to the subject matter has resulted in a movie that is difficult to dismiss or forget, and is forceful in its simplicity. The ending is intentionally ambiguous, giving us the same lack of closure that defines Marie's existence. *Under the Sand* is an effective and moving account of the power of grief and denial. HIGHLY RECOMMENDED

Under the Skin [United Kingdom, 1997]

Starring: Samantha Morton, Claire Rushbrook, Rita Tushingham, Stuart Townsend Director: Carine Adler Screenplay: Carine Adler Running Time: 1:25 Rated: No MPAA Rating (Sex, frontal nudity, frank sexual discussion, profanity) Theatrical Aspect Ratio: 1.85:1

The subject matter of *Under the Skin,* while not inherently uninteresting, doesn't break barriers or attempt anything radical. The script, too, is solid and effective, but not extraordinary. The director, Carine Adler, shows promise but lacks polish, in part because her verite approach bears a resemblance to the styles of Mike Leigh and Ken Loach. But all of these things pale into insignificance in the light of *Under the Skin*'s principal performance, a stunning debut by Samantha Morton.

The film is an examination of unresolved grief, and the way it can erode a person's identity. Iris (Morton) and Rose (Claire Rushbrook) are sisters. Iris is the younger, wilder child; Rose, who is 5 years older, is happily married and pregnant. The two of them are subtle rivals for the love and attention of their aging mother (Rita Tushingham), but, when Mum dies unexpectedly, it widens the gulf between the two girls rather than bringing them together. Rose reacts to the tragedy as one might expect — she is sad and cries, then gets on with her life. Iris, however, doesn't shed a tear and shows contempt for her sister's grief, but her personality starts to disintegrate. She begins a search for *something* (comfort? affection? attention?) that throws her into a downward moral spiral of sex-and-alcohol binges.

Morton makes Iris real. Every moment she's on screen, the actress forces us to accept Iris as a living, breathing individual. This is a raw, riveting performance — deeply moving and free of artifice. Morton handles the complete range of emotions expertly, from the subtle (watch the longing in her face as she observes a choir singing) to the overt (a wrenching

breakdown). In committing herself totally to this portrayal, she gives Adler everything she has, allowing herself to be captured on camera in a state of both physical and emotional nakedness.

Adler's approach, which includes a lot of hand-held camera shots to achieve a documentary-like look, is effective in bringing out the best in Morton's performance. *Under the Skin* is emotionally potent; we are not left on the outside looking in. It's important to the director that viewers become absorbed in Iris' sordid world, and that we feel her despair and confusion. There's a note of hope at the end that keeps us from leaving the theater in a suicidal funk. *Under the Skin* is a fine movie, and features one of the best debut performances of 1997. RECOMMENDED

Unhook the Stars [1996]

Starring: Gena Rowlands, Marisa Tomei, Gerard Depardieu, Moira Kelly, Jake Lloyd Director: Nick Cassavetes Screenplay: Nick Cassavetes and Helen Caldwell Running Time: 1:44 Rated: R (Profanity, mature themes) Theatrical Aspect Ratio: 1.66:1

Unhook the Stars is the directorial debut of Nick Cassavetes, the son of acclaimed international director John Cassavetes. It is a pleasantly unsentimental character study of one woman who has difficulty letting go. Although Cassavetes may want independence from his father's name and memory, this film won't earn it, for, although the style bears only a passing resemblance to the late film maker's, Nick not only uses several members of John's crew (notably Phedon Papamichael), but has cast his mother, Gena Rowlands, in the lead role. In addition, the script has a heavy autobiographical tinge — Cassavetes is using cinema to work out his ambiguous feelings towards his famous father.

For Mildred (Rowlands), a single mother (she was widowed many years ago), her last chick is about to fly the coop. Her oldest, a son (David Sherrill), has already left home. Now, her daughter, Annie (Moira Kelly), is on her way out. Their parting is less-than-amicable. Annie finds her mother to be a controlling and interfering influence, and wants to get away as soon as possible. Mildred watches her go sadly, wondering what happened to all the aspirations she harbored for her only female offspring. But Mildred isn't destined to be alone for long. Her new neighbor across the street, Monica Warren (Marisa Tomei), has thrown her husband (David Thornton) out following a particularly nasty quarrel. Now, she's alone with her young son, J.J. (Jake Lloyd), and doesn't have the money to pay a sitter when she goes to work. Mildred offers to help, gratis, and soon becomes J.J.'s surrogate mother.

One of the more striking aspects of *Unhook the Stars* is the script's openness and honesty. It doesn't try to trick and manipulate us with melodrama. Every action has a natural consequence — nothing ever feels forced or scripted. When Monica's husband returns to town, wanting to see his son, there's no shouting match or violence. When Annie eventually comes home, there's no big, tearful reunion. And, when Mildred begins to realize that her time with J.J. is coming to a close, we're spared an emotional scene. *Unhook the Stars* is consistently low-key, and, in the context of an intelligent script and strong acting, this represents a welcome change-of-pace from most American films.

Unhook the Stars is an engaging motion picture, mixing various flavors of comedy and drama into a satisfying whole. Admittedly, there are times when Cassavetes skims lightly over subject matter that is deserving of a fuller exploration, but the quality of the finished product allows us to overlook most of these incidents. *Unhook the Stars* is a movie of many special, small moments, that, combined together, make for a shining cinematic experience. **RECOMMENDED**

Unmade Beds [1997]

Starring: Brenda Monte, Michael De Stephano, Aimee Copp, Mikey Russo Director: Nicholas Barker Screenplay: Nicholas Barker Running Time: 1:40 Rated: No MPAA Rating (Profanity, nudity, sex) Theatrical Aspect Ratio: 1.66:1

In 1995, British filmmaker Nicholas Barker decided to make a film about the personals scene in New York City. Over a span of several months, his research team interviewed more than 400 potential candidates before eventually settling upon the four who are used. Working from the actors' own versions of their life's stories, Barker wrote a screenplay. As he put it, "I'd say 90% of the script was based on behavior and language I actually observed. The rest is a pack of lies."

Unmade Beds introduces us to a quartet of unique individuals, all of whom regularly use the personals (either in print or on-line) as a means of meeting others. These are the kind of ordinary people whom we encounter on the street and rarely give much thought to. Obviously, they're not the sort of men and women who are typically featured in motion pictures.

The first is Brenda Monte, a cash-strapped ex-lap dancer who is looking for a husband. But her reasons for marrying are quite pragmatic — she's not interested in sex or love; she wants someone who's rich. In return for access to his money, she's willing to sleep with him a few times a month. Brenda is cocky, cynical, vulgar, and anti-Semitic, and isn't at all shy about displaying her size 38D chest for Barker's camera.

Michael De Stephano is an unmarried 40-year old whom most women would classify as a nice guy. He's a desperate romantic who has been using the personals for 15 years in an attempt to find a wife. For him, however, Ms. Right doesn't seem to be out there, and it's getting him down. He manages to maintain a sense of gallows humor, however, as he quips about his latest scheme to find a mate: going to a "dating coach" to learn some new pointers.

The saddest of Barker's 4 subjects is Aimee Copp, a 28-year-old woman who is overweight (225 pounds). For the most part, Aimee is the most buoyant character in the film, which makes it such a shock when she eventually breaks down, crying that "it's just so hard wanting something that you can't have." What she is referring to is the American Dream — a husband and children. Like Michael, she's a romantic, and, like him, she can't find anyone.

Finally, there's Mikey Russo, a 54-year-old security director and failed screenwriter who uses Internet dating services to find sexy women. Unlike Michael and Aimee, he's not interested in commitment. He wants an attractive woman who's willing to have a one-night stand. Still, Mikey's not as callous as he first seems. At one point, he candidly admits that "I had my chances and I blew it. She's out there somewhere. I just haven't found her yet."

Unmade Beds examines how men and women interact in a society that is constantly becoming more hostile and impersonal. Few will not find some aspect of one of the characters that they can identify with. We all have similar impulses, and something of who we are is reflected in Brenda, Michael, Aimee, or Mikey. *Unmade Beds* is an example of the kind of brilliant film making that possesses both universal appeal and subtle power. **HIGHLY RECOMMENDED**

Unstrung Heroes [1995]

Starring: Andie MacDowell, John Turturro, Nathan Watt, Michael Richards, Maury Chaykin Director: Diane Keaton Screenplay: Richard LaGravenese based on the book by Franz Lidz Running Time: 1:33 Rated: PG (Mature themes) Theatrical Aspect Ratio: 1.85:1

Unstrung Heroes opens as another coming of age story set in the early '60s. Steven (Nathan Watt) and his sister Sandy (Kendra Krull) are the children of a happily married, if somewhat unusual, non-practicing Jewish couple. It's not long, however, before we learn that Selma (Andie MacDowell), the mother of this family, is terminally ill. Sid (John Turturro), the father, doesn't handle the situation well, so when Steven asks to spend the summer with his two odd-ball uncles, there are only token objections. While living with Danny and Arthur, Steven changes his name to Franz and learns the importance of his Jewish faith.

MacDowell, playing dying wife/mother Selma Lidz, does a solid job. John Turturro, too, fills the role of Selma's husband, scientist/experimenter Sid Lidz, with his usual aptitude. As Selma fades away, Turturro's face expresses Sid's unspeakable loss with heart-breaking poignancy. Also effective is Nathan Watt as Steven, the Lidz' young son, who is forced to cope with death before he really understands what living is. On hand to teach him life's lessons are two eccentric, "black sheep" uncles: paranoid Danny (Michael Richards) and packrat Arthur (Mary Chaykin). As Steven's home life becomes increasingly unstable, Danny and Arthur are there for him, dispensing their own variety of wisdom, which includes advice never to throw away memories — like dreams, they're easily lost, and an effort must be made to preserve them.

Director Diane Keaton is on certain ground chronicling the tragedy of Selma's illness and its inevitable conclusion. While the emotional impact of *Unstrung Heroes* isn't as potent as that of Richard Attenborough's similarly-themed *Shadowlands,* the scenes showing Selma, Sid, and their children coping with impending death are well-written and effectively conveyed. Thankfully, most of this is handled with refreshing subtlety — there is no obvious audience manipulation.

Less successful is the presentation of Uncles Danny and Arthur. There's a sense that these two exist simply to populate *Unstrung Heroes* with a pair of eccentrics, and they seem more like scripted characters than real people. Their ultimate function within the context of the story — life's castoffs teaching an impressionable boy secrets of how to stay afloat — is more than a little cliched.

There's nothing especially original about *Unstrung Heroes,* but the story is told with intelligence and sensitivity. In a time when so many movies are botching promising premises, it's refreshing to see something appealing done with a retreaded subject. This film isn't a masterpiece, but it offers another view of what makes family so important, and does so with an emotional honesty that many other movies don't approach. **RECOMMENDED**

The Virgin Suicides [2000]

Starring: James Woods, Kathleen Turner, Kirsten Dunst, Josh Hartnett, Hanna Hall, Chelsea Swain Director: Sofia Coppola Screenplay: Sofia Coppola based on the novel by Jeffrey Eugenides Running Time: 1:36 Rated: R (Mature themes including suicide) Theatrical Aspect Ratio: 1.85:1

The Virgin Suicides is Sofia Coppola's directorial debut, and its effectiveness illustrates that she's better behind the camera than she is in front of it. (Most movie-goers will remember her ill-fated attempt to portray Michael Corleone's daughter in *The Godfather III.*) Tragic, haunting, and sometimes darkly comedic, this movie leaves a strong impression in its telling of a story about the destruction of innocence.

The time frame is the mid-'70s and the setting is an upper class suburban community in Michigan. The film tells the sad story of the 5 Lisbon sisters — Cecilia (age 13, played by Hanna Hall), Lux (age 14, played by Kirsten Dunst), Bonnie (age 15, played by Chelsea Swain), Mary (age 16, played by A.J. Cook), and Therese (age 17, played by Leslie Hayman) — all of whom come to a bad end before finishing high school. Unhappy, neglected Cecilia is the first to give up on life — after surviving one suicide attempt, she is successful on the second try. In the wake of that event, the atmosphere surrounding the surviving sisters becomes grim, and their parents' overprotectiveness threatens to suffocate them. For most children, mothers and fathers set boundaries; for the Lisbons, it's iron bars.

The Virgin Suicides is filmed as a memory looking back through 25 years, and the point-of-view is that of a boy who was in love with one (or perhaps all) of the girls. As a result, the events recounted here offer a filtered perspective of the sisters and the complexities of their lives.

One of *The Virgin Suicides'* strengths is its ability to effectively capture the nuances of teenage life during the '70s. Coppola gets all of the little things right: the awkwardness of a chaperoned boy/girl party, the thrill of first love, and the nervousness of the pre-dance ritual (in this case, the homecoming dance, not the prom). The film also boasts a solid soundtrack featuring a few songs that haven't been endlessly recycled in other, recent, set-in-the-'70s features. In one key scene, music provides a link between the Lisbon girls and the outside world — it becomes their only viable means of communication and free expression.

By using occasional bursts of humor and setting up the film as a collage of reminiscences, Coppola establishes a mood that is wistful and sad, but not funereal. There are a few instances when the film gets a little heavy-handed, but, for the most part, the tone is well modulated. Although Coppola almost certainly gained more than a little help from her famous father in getting the production off the ground, the talent evident in her debut argues that this is not a case of unwarranted nepotism. The apple has not fallen far from the tree. RECOMMENDED

A Walk on the Moon [1999]

Starring: Diane Lane, Liev Schreiber, Viggo Mortensen, Anna Paquin, Victoria Barkof Director: Tony Goldwyn Screenplay: Pamela Gray Running Time: 1:45 Rated: R (Profanity, sex, brief nudity) Theatrical Aspect Ratio: 1.85:1

The year is 1969. The setting is a Jewish bungalow community in the Catskills. Unlike in *Dirty Dancing*, where Jerry Orbach played a rich patriarch who could afford to spend a vacation with his family, *A Walk on the Moon* looks at the lower middle class. Instead of staying in clean, well-maintained hotel rooms, the characters in this film spend their days and nights in a ramshackle little house where the youngest child sleeps on the floor in the kitchen. Since Marty (Liev Schreiber) can't afford to take a whole week off from his job as a TV repairman (especially with the moon walk coming up — everyone wants to have a working television), he can only join his family in the mountains on weekends. That leaves his wife, Pearl (Diane Lane), alone there with the kids and her mother-in-law for the rest of the week.

The typical rhythms of Pearl's camp life are interrupted by the arrival of the "Blouse Man" (Viggo Mortensen), an itinerant salesman who travels from resort to resort in a converted bus, hawking his wares at cheap prices to eager customers. The Blouse Man, whose real name is Walker Jerome, is affable and sexy. And, when it comes to inhibitions, he's the opposite of Pearl. She's a captive in her marriage — wedded at 17 because she was pregnant, she has seen every dream die over the years. It isn't that she doesn't love her husband, but that she yearns to see where her life might have gone had things worked out differently. When it becomes obvious that Walker is attracted to her, and she to him, she embarks on a reckless affair with him as a means of breaking free from the constraints of her ordered life. They make love in his bus, share a blissful day in the wilderness, and attend Woodstock together. However, when Pearl's mother-

in-law senses what's happening, she warns her son that his marriage is in trouble.

It's easy to make a bad movie about a woman finding herself by cheating on her husband, but difficult to fashion one that hits most of the right notes. With a strong assist from Lane and Schreiber, Goldwyn has taken the nostalgia of 1969 and used it to good effect as background for a story that never loses sight of the characters. RECOMMENDED

Walking and Talking [1996]

Starring: Catherine Keener, Anne Heche, Liev Schreiber, Todd Field, Kevin Corrigan Director: Nicole Holofcener Screenplay: Nicole Holofcener Running Time: 1:30 Rated: R (Sex, profanity, mature themes) Theatrical Aspect Ratio: 1.85:1

Walking and Talking deftly portrays the dynamic of the relationship between a perpetually single young woman and her soon-to-be-wed soul-sister. By turns, it's funny, charming, and even a little touching. Director Nicole Holofcener has an ear for dialogue, and, as is often the case with the best character-centered films, a chief pleasure is simply enjoying what the participants have to say to one another. The two leading ladies represent another asset. Anne Heche and Catherine Keener are effective in both comic and dramatic scenes. Each has mastered the knack of giving a completely unforced performance. Once they step into character, they never slip out.

Walking and Talking successfully navigates a minefield of familiar territory. The storyline, which is essentially a slice-of-life, doesn't attempt anything big, but it offers a number of small surprises. Just when you think you know how one romantic entanglement is going to turn out, Holofcener throws in a little twist. That's not to say that the plot is masterful (in fact, it's rather simple), but there's enough there to hold the viewer's interest.

While *Walking and Talking* is pretty light fare, it's not without substance, too. Both Amelia and Laura are confused about the future, albeit in different ways. They're afraid of change, even though they recognize it's inevitable, and each suffers from the typical Generation X lack of self-esteem. Amelia sits alone in her room, stroking her cancer-riddled cat and listening to "music to slit your wrists by," and Laura bemoans her career choice, saying that she's not a good therapist because she makes her patients worse. Even though these two don't need each other the way they once did, their mutual importance is still apparent.

Walking and Talking ends by giving us closure

without wrapping everything up in a neat package. Because the main characters are both women, the writer/director is a woman, and the themes relate to female bonding, this will inevitably be pegged as a "chick flick." That's an unfortunate appellation, because *Walking and Talking* has universal appeal. Many of the issues it approaches have less to do with gender than with the simple condition of living in the '90s. **RECOMMENDED**

The War [1994]

Starring: Elijah Wood, Kevin Costner, Mare Winningham, Lexi Randall, LaToya Chisholm Director: Jon Avnet Screenplay: Kathy McWorter Running Time: 2:04 Rated: PG-13 (Violence, profanity) Theatrical Aspect Ratio: 1.85:1

The primary theme of *The War* is that violence, irrespective of its motivation, is never justified. To illustrate this point, the movie takes us to 1970 Mississippi and introduces Stephen Simmons (Kevin Costner), a Vietnam Vet who lost pieces of his soul halfway across the world when, to save his own life, he left behind a dying friend. Since then, he has attempted to reconstruct a shattered life, encouraging his two children, Stu (Elijah Wood) and Lidia (Lexi Randall), to follow his pacifist example. At the same time, he has been searching to re-establish a bond with his wife, Lois (Mare Winningham).

Stu and Lidia, however, aren't sold on the non-violent way, especially as it applies to their ongoing feud with the Lipnicki clan, a group of local bullies who delight in picking on those less physically gifted. When the Lipnickis decide to claim a tree fort built by Stu, Lidia, and their friends, their actions precipitate an all-out battle.

The anti-war stance of *The War* works primarily because of a tremendous performance from an unlikely source: Kevin Costner. As was the case in *A Perfect World,* the actor impresses by underplaying his less-than-heroic role. As long as Stephen is on screen, the message never threatens to overwhelm the story. The character, rendered by Costner with subtlety and care, is searching for redemption; he wants his children to learn life's harsh truths before they reach the point that he's at.

Both the strength and the weakness of *The War,* however, is its inability to let pass an opportunity to teach a lesson. At times, to the film's benefit, this sermonizing is seamlessly integrated into the story. On other occasions, it sticks out like a proverbial sore thumb, since there's nothing more uncomfortable or obvious than when a moral calls attention to itself.

To a lesser degree, *The War* imparts an anti-racist message. Unfortunately, it does this in a heavy-handed manner by having Lidia come to the defense of her black friend (LaToya Chisholm) when a teacher tries to relegate the "colored" children to the back of the classroom. The young white girl gives an impassioned, and obviously scripted, speech about ignorance. While it's impossible to argue with the sentiment, the presentation is flawed.

Whatever failings *The War* may exhibit, though, it is still solid entertainment, and there are moments of sublime beauty and rare power. Even at its most affecting and manipulative, the film never strays from its message or allows its high production values to decline, and that's a lot more than can be said of a great deal of other recent theatrical releases. **RECOMMENDED**

The War Zone [United Kingdom, 1999]

Starring: Ray Winstone, Tilda Swinton, Lara Belmont, Freddie Cunliffe Director: Tim Roth Screenplay: Alexander Stuart, based on his novel Running Time: 1:38 Rated: No MPAA Rating (Sex, nudity, graphic rape, profanity, mature themes) Theatrical Aspect Ratio: 2.35:1

Despite the title, this stunningly accomplished feature debut from Tim Roth has nothing to do with traditional battlefields, yet it is every bit as harrowing as the first 30 minutes of *Saving Private Ryan* or the whole of *Schindler's List*. The destruction presented in this film is as graphic and shocking as anything depicted in the most unsparing war movie, except that the victims are not soldiers trained for combat, but children placed in harm's way.

The film takes place in the rural Devon countryside, where a family of 4 has just moved from London. Events are related from the perspective of 15-year old Tom (Freddie Cunliffe), who is unhappy with life away from the city. His 18-year-old sister, Jessie (Lara Belmont), has apparently adjusted better than he has. His parents (Ray Winstone, Tilda Swinton) seem happy and comfortable in their new home, and his mother is on the verge of delivering her third child. Then, shortly after the baby is born, Tom's world is turned upside down when he spies a covert sexual encounter between Jessie and his father. Tom confronts Jessie about the incident, but she denies it, accusing him of having an overactive imagination. He is not convinced, however, and sets out to learn the facts. The truth he must face, and its ramifications upon every member of the family, form *The War Zone*'s core drama.

In his handling of the material, Roth shows more

ability than many accomplished, veteran filmmakers. He paints Devon as a grim, rainy place where darkness and grayness are always enroaching upon the light. There is much ambiguity to be found here. While one key rape is graphically depicted, the depth of the father's depravity and the question of how much the mother knows are left up to the individual to determine. Roth freely admits that, with *The War Zone,* he has pushed the envelope as far as it can go — had he attempted more, the movie would have become too painful for anyone to watch. There is no comic relief and no happy ending (although there is a catharsis of sorts).

The War Zone is a devastating motion picture; it's the kind of movie that stuns an audience so absolutely that they remain paralyzed in their seats through the end credits. It does not deal in euphemisms nor does it hide the physical and emotional brutality of the act from viewers. In my lifetime, I have seen thousands of films, but none has been as unflinching in its approach to this issue as *The War Zone.* For his courage and ability, Tim Roth deserves praise and recognition. **MUST SEE**

Washington Square [1997]

Starring: Jennifer Jason Leigh, Albert Finney, Ben Chaplin, Maggie Smith Director: Agnieszka Holland Screenplay: Carol Doyle based on the novel by Henry James Running Time: 1:55 Rated: PG (Mature themes, mild profanity) Theatrical Aspect Ratio: 1.85:1

While most films are content to explore the lighter, romantic side of love, *Washington Square* takes a cold, hard look at the painful, destructive aspect of the same emotion.

Washington Square is actually the second film to be made from the James novel of the same name. The first, 1949's *The Heiress* (directed by William Wyler and starring Olivia De Havilland), was based on a stage play version of the book that eliminated many of the more subtle aspects of James' text. For this interpretation of *Washington Square,* director Agnieszka Holland and screenwriter Carol Doyle have returned to James' original story and created a quiet, thoughtful examination of the author's favorite theme: the difficulty of balancing love and money, and the pernicious influence of the latter upon the former.

As *Washington Square* opens, we are greeted with a tragic scene: a young woman lying dead in the aftermath of childbirth. Her husband, Austin Sloper (Albert Finney), barely looks at his newborn daughter, Catherine, as she is presented to him. Flash-for-ward several years. Catherine, an awkward adolescent, is shown trying to please her father on his birthday. But, despite her best efforts, everything goes wrong, and she is forced to flee from his party in embarrassment. When we next meet Catherine (now played by Jennifer Jason Leigh), she is an adult, but is still slavishly trying to win her father's adoration. However, in his characteristically brusque manner, he finds fault with nearly everything she does.

The domestic tranquillity of the Sloper household changes dramatically on the day that Catherine meets Morris Townsend (Ben Chaplin), an adventurer and wanderer who has just returned to America from abroad. Catherine falls in love with him, and, although he apparently returns her feelings, Austin is suspicious of his motives. Morris is penniless and Catherine is wealthy, and all Austin sees in the young man is a fortune hunter. He refuses to sanction a marriage and indicates that if Catherine defies him, he will disown her.

Washington Square deftly draws us into the world of the characters and challenges us to understand them and question their views and motivations. The film is emotionally effective without going overboard. Director Agnieszka Holland (whose previous efforts include *Europa Europa* and *Olivier Olivier*) opts to avoid the temptation of reducing *Washington Square* to the level of a costume melodrama. Her careful, modulated handling of the material makes this resemble Merchant-Ivory's better work (like *The Remains of the Day*). *Washington Square* is faithful representation of James' text, and a moving and satisfying portrait of one woman's struggle for independence in a society where everything is defined by love, money, or both. **RECOMMENDED**

Welcome to the Dollhouse [1996]

Starring: Heather Matarazzo, Victoria Davis, Christina Brucato, Christina Vidal Director: Todd Solondz Screenplay: Todd Solondz Running Time: 1:27 Rated: R (Profanity, mature themes) Theatrical Aspect Ratio: 1.85:1

Welcome to the Dollhouse, which won the Grand Jury Prize at the 1996 Sundance Film Festival, is Todd Solondz' counterattack against the *Wonder Years* nostalgia that clouds movie memories of adolescence. After all, junior high school isn't the endless series of halcyon days that television and films would have us believe. Especially for those who aren't members of the "in" crowd, the pre-teen and early teen years can be an extremely painful time. In this impressive debut, Solondz doesn't pull any punches in conveying the side of junior high that *The Wonder Years* never depicted: the naked cruelty that some boys and girls suffer at the hands of their classmates, their teachers, and even members of their own family.

This is the story of Dawn Weiner (Heather Matarazzo), or "Dogface Weiner," as just about everyone at school calls her. Bespectacled and not blessed by perfect features or a good complexion, Dawn is not a popular girl. A loner by nature, she has only one friend — a sickly elementary school boy who is as much an object of derision as she is. At school, she is pelted by spitballs and epithets. When she asks a classmate "Why do you hate me?," the response is simple and succinct: "Because you're ugly." The teachers at Benjamin Franklin Junior High seem to go out of their way to humiliate Dawn, accusing her of grade-grubbing and forcing her to write essays about the meaning of dignity. At home, as the middle child, she is the most frequently neglected. Her older brother is a nerdy computer whiz and her younger sister is her parents' favorite. The only time Mom and Dad take notice of Dawn is when she does something wrong.

Despite its grim subject matter, *Welcome to the Dollhouse* isn't a complete downer. Dawn is resigned to her fate, and, though her dearest wish is to be popular, she's able to accept her lot. Solondz has injected a fair amount of natural humor into his script. Some of the audience's laughter will be in response to uneasy situations, but there are a few genuinely funny situations, such as when Dawn avenges herself against her fairy princess sister (who often appears on screen to the strains of "The Nutcracker") by taking a saw to a doll's neck.

Welcome to the Dollhouse is sort of like *Angus*, but without the false Hollywood sheen and forced happy ending. Solondz's perceptiveness is acute, and, at one time or another, it will make most viewers feel uncomfortable. It's not a perfect motion picture, but, as far as taking a cold look at an over-romanticized period of childhood, it's uncompromising. *Welcome to the Dollhouse* won't make you wistful for your lost junior high years; it will make you glad you grew up.
RECOMMENDED

What Dreams May Come [1998]

Starring: Robin Williams, Annabella Sciorra, Cuba Gooding Jr., Max von Sydow Director: Vincent Ward Screenplay: Ron Bass based on the novel by Richard Matheson Running Time: 1:48 Rated: PG-13 (Mature themes, images of hell, mild profanity) Theatrical Aspect Ratio: 2.35:1

If I wanted to be cynical about this film, I could say that the moral is not to get out of the car and help at the scene of an accident. That's what gets Chris Nielsen (Robin Williams) killed. Of course, I'm not giving anything away here, since this happens at the beginning of the movie, after a short prologue that offers glimpses of Chris' marriage to his wife, Annie (Annabella Sciorra). In more than a decade of bliss, there was only one dark period. Four years ago, Chris and Annie's two children, Marie (Jessica Brooks) and Ian (Josh Paddock), died in a car crash and now, tragically, Chris has joined them. One moment, he's trying to help someone trapped in a wreck; the next, he's making his way into the light.

As it turns out, the afterlife isn't what Chris expected. To begin with, he has a guide — an old mentor named Albert (Cuba Gooding Jr.). He spends some time wandering around on Earth — looking in at his funeral, checking on his grief-stricken wife, and generally seeing how the world is progressing without him. Eventually, when he realizes that his continued ghostly presence is causing Annie pain, he quits this realm and heads into heaven, a place of colors, light, and beauty. But Chris is not content. Even the realization that he can again meet with his children is not enough. Then an event occurs that threatens to sever his connection with Annie forever.

What Dreams May Come has the sensibilities of an art film placed into a big-budget feature with an A-list cast. A tear-jerker, its offbeat storyline, which has Chris relishing the serenity of heaven before taking a trip through hell, is compelling, even if the ending is a little too cute. Part of the reason the movie works is that the characters are likable. Most of us would love to have the kind of relationship that Chris and Annie enjoyed, so it's not hard to root for them to somehow find each other again, even with the chasm of death dividing them.

Many movies have offered representations of heaven and hell, but few with as much conviction and creativity as *What Dreams May Come*. The plot, which focuses on the sacrifices one man will make for true love, is neither complicated nor original, but, bolstered by the director's incredible visual sense, it becomes an affecting piece of drama. While not as sickly sweet as *Ghost*, *What Dreams May Come* shares an important trait with the Demi Moore/Patrick Swayze melodrama — namely, that love does not end with death. Those who embrace this belief and don't mind a somewhat artistic approach are likely to enjoy Vincent Ward's movie. RECOMMENDED

What Happened Was [1994]

Starring: Tom Noonan, Karen Sillas Director: Tom Noonan
Screenplay: Tom Noonan Running Time: 1:30 Rated: No MPAA Rating
(Language, mature themes) Theatrical Aspect Ratio: 1.85:1

What Happened Was is not a date movie, especially if it's a first date. Oh, it will give you an endless source of conversational topics, all right, but it's almost guaranteed to warp your view of the entire experience. The Samuel Goldwyn Company is advertised this as "an adventure in romance." More often, however, it feels like some sort of insidious means of torture.

Based on director Tom Noonan's stage play, this two-person film is a simple character study that finds its dynamics through the interplay of a very unpleasant first date. Jackie (Karen Sillas) and Michael (Tom Noonan) know each other from the office, but on a personal level, they discover that they're both basically clueless. Jackie's image of Michael is far from reality, and Michael doesn't even recognize Jackie's attraction to him. In that sense, this is a true "blind" date.

The intense feeling of discomfort generated by *What Happened Was* is the result of the movie's careful attention to detail. Everything seems true-to-life, distorted only slightly by director Tom Noonan's use of camera angles and lighting. The conversation is frequently interrupted by awkward pauses, and the two principals are constantly on edge, each of them trying to come up with words to fill the aching void between them.

At the start of *What Happened Was* Michael's character is the most interesting. He's smart, witty, and seems to have it all together. His opposite, on the other hand, is nervous, flustered, and indecisive. During the course of the film, however, a role-reversal takes place, causing our attention to shift more and more towards Jackie as the layers of her personality are peeled back, onion-like. The psychological revelations about these two, and the manner in which they are uncovered, illustrates a willingness on Noonan's part to take his story in a refreshingly unorthodox direction.

The key sequence in the film involves Jackie opening up through a disturbing "children's story" that she reads to Michael. It's here that the audience starts to see the genuine people behind the carefully-constructed, socially acceptable masks. All sorts of unsettling things happen during this scene, and the overall tone undergoes a palpable shift from offbeat comedy to drama. Nervous or not, the laughter is over. Circumstances have become a little too poignant.

For something billed as a lightweight romantic comedy, *What Happened Was* wades through some surprisingly deep waters. There's an ending, but no conclusion, and the most obvious unanswered question has more to do with what is yet to come than with what has already happened. RECOMMENDED

When a Man Loves a Woman [1994]

Starring: Meg Ryan, Andy Garcia, Tina Marjorino, Mae Whitman, Ellen Burstyn Director: Luis Mandoki Screenplay: Ronald Bass and Al Franken Running Time: 2:06 Rated: R (Profanity, mature themes)
Theatrical Aspect Ratio: 1.85:1

Luis Mandoki's *When Man Loves a Woman* film succeeds not because it tackles alcoholism, but because it faces up to the trauma that eats away at the lives of the non-alcoholics in the family.

When a Man Loves a Woman centers on a seemingly-happily married couple. Michael Green (Andy Garcia) and his wife Alice (Meg Ryan) have, at first glance, the perfect relationship. But take a peek beneath the veneer, and there are problems. Alice is a habitual drinker, and her periods of sobriety are getting fewer and fewer. Meanwhile, Michael's duties as an airline pilot take him away from home for weeks at a time, keeping him ignorant of the extent of his wife's problem

Completing the family unit are Jess (Tina Marjorino), Alice's daughter by another man whom Michael has adopted as his own, and Casey (Mae Whitman), the 4-year-old child of the Greens. The presence of these children, and their importance to the development of the story, is what elevates *When a Man Loves a Woman*. As potent as some of the scenes between Michael and Alice are, those featuring Jess or Casey invariably have greater impact. It helps that both young actresses are believable.

One failing of the script is that it assumes an unlikely level of ignorance from its audience. Alcoholism is such a pervasive social problem that it's hard to accept that anyone likely to see *When a Man Loves a Woman* wouldn't have a better understanding of the disease than the movie gives them credit for. After all, everything from high school health classes to *Oprah* have, at one point or another, addressed the issue. Unlike AIDS, alcoholism is not a new disease that the public needs to be educated about.

The ending is too facile, and *When a Man Loves a Woman* may take longer than necessary to arrive at its resolution. There are moments throughout when the script is apt to strike a raw nerve with some, as is often the case when a "real" issue is probed with any degree of sincerity. Whatever else it may do, this film does not play it safe, and the risks it takes keep the audience engaged by the drama.

When a Man Loves a Woman is about pain. This is not an original topic for a movie — especially one about alcoholism — but the script does a good enough job establishing the dynamics of the Green family that we never doubt that the story deserves to be told. The film's poignancy is its strength, even as occasional didactic tendencies are its weakness. In balance, the former by far outweighs the latter, making this a worthwhile picture. **RECOMMENDED**

Where the Heart Is [2000]

Starring: **Natalie Portman, Ashley Judd, Stockard Channing, Joan Cusack, James Frain** Director: **Matt Williams** Screenplay: **Lowell Ganz & Babaloo Mandel, based on the novel by Billie Letts** Running Time: 1:58 Rated: PG-13 (Profanity, mature themes, violence, sexual situations) Theatrical Aspect Ratio: 1.85:1

Natalie Portman isn't just the foundation upon which *Where the Heart Is* is built; she's the glue that holds it together. Portman plays Novalee Nation, a frightened, 7-month pregnant teenager on the road from Tennessee to California with her self-centered boyfriend, Willy Jack Pickens. When the couple stops at a Wal-Mart in Oklahoma so that Novalee can take a bathroom break, Willy Jack sees his chance to get away, so he abandons her with nothing more than a Polaroid camera and $5.55 in change. Novalee, homeless and alone, begins to establish a life in the community of Sequoyah, befriending the open-hearted Sister Husband and spending time at the library, where she captures the attention of the librarian, Forney. From dusk till dawn, she hides out in Wal-Mart, carefully recording every dollar and cent that she owes the company for food, clothing, and bed materials. Then, one rainy night, she goes into labor, and, with the help of Forney (who arrives on the scene after following her), she gives birth to a healthy baby girl. When she wakes up, she's in the hospital, being cared for by a perky nurse, Lexie, who tells her that she's an instant celebrity: the mother of "the Wal-Mart baby."

Where the Heart Is is as obvious a "chick flick" as they come. All of the typical elements are in place: the strong-willed heroine dealt a bad hand by life, the abusive and selfish men, and the supportive women. However, by subduing the melodrama to a tolerable level, the filmmakers have crafted a motion picture that should appeal to members of both sexes.

Where the Heart Is is the story of someone who overcomes life's hardships despite overwhelming odds. She does not become famous, wealthy, or successful, but attains family and love — two things which were robbed from her as a child and which she has craved ever since. We spend 5 years in Novalee's company, but the time goes by quickly. *Where the Heart Is* is not perfect, but it works in almost every way that a character-based drama is supposed to. It is a simple pleasure. **RECOMMENDED**

Three Colors: White [France/Switzerland/Poland, 1994]

Starring: **Zbigniew Zamachowski, Julie Delpy, Janusz Gajos, Jerzy Stuhr** Director: **Krzysztof Kieslowski** Screenplay: **Krzysztof Kieslowski and Krzysztof Piesiewicz** Running Time: 1:32 Rated: R (Sexual situations, mature themes, violence) Theatrical Aspect Ratio: 1.85:1 In French and Polish with subtitles

White, the second chapter of Krzysztof Kieslowski's *Three Colors* trilogy, is different from *Blue* in more ways than the color it centers on and the ideals represented. Instead of the dark, somber tone adopted *Blue*, this film aims for something lighter. Additionally, while *White* possesses a sardonic quality never sought after by its predecessor, the emotional tapestry of this picture is not the other's equal.

Although *White* is self-contained, there is an intersection with *Blue*. In the previous film, the stars of this one, Julie Delpy and Zbigniew Zamachowski, make brief appearances; likewise, Juliette Binoche sticks her head through a courtroom door near the beginning of *White* (blink and you may miss her). Delpy, Zamachowski, and Binoche all turn up at the conclusion of *Red*, along with the featured performers of that movie, Jean-Louis Trintignant and Irene Jacob.

White begins in a Parisian courtroom with the arrival of a lonely, dejected Karol Karol (Zamachowski), clutching a summons and looking downtrodden. Shortly thereafter, his marriage has been dissolved by the court because of his inability to consummate the union, and his beautiful young wife Dominique (Delpy) has claimed that she no longer loves him. Karol is devastated, and decides to quit Paris for his native Poland.

To make matters worse, he has no passport and no money to obtain one, and after Dominique sets fire to a beauty shop that he and she owned together, the police want him for arson. Fate, however, is not entirely working against Karol, and he finds a friend in his fellow countryman Mikolaj (Janusz Gajos), who helps him back to Warsaw, where he begins rebuilding his life and planning revenge against the woman he still loves.

White focuses mainly on Karol's life, and that's one of its possible flaws. While we are presented with a well-rounded picture of the Polish hairdresser, we see so little of his wife that the eventual resolution falls a little flat. The few glimpses we are afforded of Dominique reveal an intensely interesting character who is quite simply never given enough screen time.

Kieslowski understands human nature, and his ability to breathe life into that understanding through these characters is what sets his films apart from those of many others. As *Blue* did for liberty, so *White* does for equality, giving a face to an abstract concept. RECOMMENDED

The White Balloon [Iran, 1995]

Starring: Aida Mohammadkhani, Moshen Kalifi, Fereshteh Sadr Orfani, Anna Bourkowska Director: Jafar Panahi Screenplay: Abbas Kiarostami Running Time: 1:25 Rated: No MPAA Rating (nothing offensive) Theatrical Aspect Ratio: 1.85:1 In Farsi with subtitles

The White Balloon, written by Abbas Kiarostami and directed by one of his protégés, Jafar Panahi, has the characteristic slow, stately tone that dominates Iranian efforts, but, at least in terms of its minimalist narrative, it's reminiscent of Vittorio De Sica's Italian classic, *The Bicycle Thief.*

The White Balloon is told in real time through the eyes of its 7-year-old, female protagonist, the feisty Razieh (Aida Mohammadkhani). Our impressions of other characters are filtered through Razieh, so we see them as she does, whether they're strange, frightening, indifferent, or helpful. All the facets of humanity are represented, from a generous-but-ineffectual old woman to a sinister soldier who tells lies to gain the young girl's confidence.

It's New Year's Day in Tehran, and, in 90 minutes, all the shops will close for a week-long holiday. Before that happens, Razieh desperately wants to buy a plump, white goldfish with elaborate fins. She has her heart set on this prize and refuses to give up even when her mother says "no." So, with the help of her brother (Moshen Kalifi), she eventually wears down all resistance, and, armed with her mother's last 500 tomans bill, heads into the marketplace on her own. Between home and the fish store, however, she loses the money down a street grate, where the metal bars keep it within sight, but out of reach.

In addition to its account of a girl's first venture into the adult world on her own, *The White Balloon* gives Western viewers a rare glimpse into the real Iran. Here, freed of political shading, we meet the genuine inhabitants of Tehran, and, unsurprisingly, find that they're not all that different from us. *The White Balloon* certainly isn't everyone's kind of film, but those with the patience to sit through all 85 minutes will uncover a sublime, unconventionally engrossing story. RECOMMENDED

The Whole Wide World [1996]

Starring: Vincent D'Onofrio, Renee Zellweger Director: Dan Ireland Screenplay: Michael Scott Myers based on the novel *One Who Walked Alone* by Novalyne Price Ellis Running Time: 1:45 Rated: PG (Mild profanity, mature themes) Theatrical Aspect Ratio: 2.35:1

During the course of his short, stormy life, Depression era writer Robert E. Howard created more than two dozen pulp heroes, and wrote hundreds of short stories. His best-known creation, Conan the Barbarian, became so popular during the 1970s and '80s that he spawned comic books, more than fifty original novels (far outstripping Howard's original output), and two motion pictures (*Conan the Barbarian* and *Conan the Destroyer,* both starring Arnold Schwarzenegger). It's said that the best way to know an author is to read his writing, and, as Dan Ireland's *The Whole Wide World* shows, Howard was a man who gave his all to his work.

During Conan's resurgence in the 1970s, a lot of things — many of them profoundly uncomplimentary — were written and said about the author, who had died some 40 years earlier from a self-inflicted gunshot wound. Novalyne Price Ellis, a woman who had enjoyed a special relationship with Howard, decided to set the record straight by revealing "the real Bob Howard." The result was *One Who Walked Alone,* which was published in 1985. This memoir became the basis of *The Whole Wide World.*

The film opens during 1933 in Brownwood, Texas, with the meeting of Novalyne (Renee Zellweger), a would-be author, and Robert (Vincent D'Onofrio). The two hit it off almost immediately, despite the difference in their life-views. Over the course of the next three years, their relationship ebbs and flows, with Novalyne falling for Robert in a way that is never reciprocated. It's clear that he cares for her, but he is emotionally unable to commit to a relationship.

There's nothing earthshaking about *The Whole Wide World,* a film that is, by the director's own admission, very small. Nevertheless, it successfully accomplishes what it sets out to do, and the result is affecting and involving. So, while it may be true that the best way to get into the mind of Robert E. Howard is to read his stories, seeing *The Whole Wide World* will give you an appreciation of a side of him that was never revealed in any Conan yarn. **HIGHLY RECOMMENDED**

Why Do Fools Fall in Love [1998]

Starring: Halle Berry, Vivica A. Fox, Lela Rochon, Larenz Tate, Paul Mazursky Director: Gregory Nava Screenplay: Tina Andrews Running Time: 1:55 Rated: R (Profanity, drug use, sex, violence) Theatrical Aspect Ratio: 1.85:1

It was in the mid-'50s when, at the tender age of 13, Frankie Lymon burst onto the pop music scene with the Top 10 hit, "Why Do Fools Fall in Love?" Frankie and the Teenagers, as the group was called, became an instant success story. Soon, prodded by an unscrupulous manager, Frankie went solo, and his fall from grace was as spectacular as his meteoric rise. By the age of 20, he was a washed-up has-been whose only gigs were nostalgia shows. Seven years later, he was dead of a drug overdose. But, even in death, Frankie Lymon's story continued. In 1981, Diana Ross' cover of "Why Do Fools Fall in Love?" became a financial success, and this led to an unusual court case over music rights. During his lifetime, Frankie had married 3 women, but he never divorced any of them. Now, they all wanted a piece of his legacy and the decision was left up to a court of law as to who was legally entitled to be called Mrs. Frankie Lymon.

These are the essential facts behind Gregory Nava's spotty-but-entertaining biopicture of the '50s singing star. Actually, while Frankie (played by Larenz Tate) has more screen time than any other character, *Why Do Fools Fall in Love* is more about his wives, and the hardships they endured while with him, than about him. By the end of the film, we have a clearer picture of Zola Taylor (Halle Berry), Elizabeth Waters (Vivica A. Fox), and Emira Eagle (Lela Rochon) than we do of the self-destructive singer. Frankie may be at the center of the movie, but his wives represent its heart, soul, and funny bone.

Why Do Fools Fall in Love has a nearly 2-hour running length, but the manner in which Nava has structured it, with frequent leaps backward and forward through several decades, keeps the viewer involved for the entire time. The focus on the women and the different points-of-view used to piece together the story give *Why Do Fools Fall in Love* an edge. Despite employing the familiar motion picture

elements of sex, greed, and music, this is not a run-of-the-mill biopic. **RECOMMENDED**

Wide Awake [1998]

Starring: Joseph Cross, Denis Leary, Dana Delany, Robert Loggia, Antoine McLean, Rosie O'Donnell Director: M. Night Shyamalan Screenplay: M. Night Shyamalan Running Time: 1:30 Rated: PG (Profanity, mature themes) Theatrical Aspect Ratio: 1.85:1

In this age of cynicism, it's unusual to find a film like *Wide Awake*. The movie is Capra-esque in its outlook on life and death. And, while the ultimate result is somewhat uneven, there's no denying that *Wide Awake* contains its share of affecting moments, and the production as a whole offers enough solid drama and legitimate emotion to earn it a recommendation not only for adults, but for older children as well, who will relate to the protagonist and narrator. It's definitely a two hankie movie, though.

Joseph Cross is 10-year-old Joshua Beal, a 5th-grader who attends a Catholic school for boys in suburban Philadelphia. Josh lives with his father (Denis Leary), mother (Dana Delany), and sister (Julia Stiles), but a key member of the family is absent. Josh's grandfather (Robert Loggia) recently died of bone marrow cancer, and his death has hit the young boy hard. The sudden void causes Josh, an extremely intelligent child, to begin questioning many aspects of life, truth, and religion. His quest for answers leads him to begin a year-long search for God.

Wide Awake creates likable characters who engage the audience, and the storyline addresses sensitive, emotionally-compelling issues without becoming cloying. At times, the movie is manipulative, but it's a gentle, rather than forced, approach.

While it's true that the script for *Wide Awake* isn't all that ambitious, too often relies on the exposition of an overly-verbose narrator, and includes a few necessary contrivances, what makes the film special are the numerous individual moments that shine. And, although the dialogue is too sophisticated for the way children really talk, it is intelligent enough not to leave us shaking our heads in dismay and disbelief. I left *Wide Awake* feeling the same way I did after seeing a number of Frank Capra's movies — I was aware of the problems, but that didn't diminish the warm, fuzzy glow I was experiencing. **RECOMMENDED**

The Widow of St. Pierre [France, 2000]

Starring: Juliette Binoche, Daniel Auteuil, Emir Kusturica Director: Patrice Leconte Screenplay: Claude Faraldo Running

Time: **1:52** Rated: **R** (Violence, sex, mature themes) Theatrical Aspect Ratio: **2.35:1** In French with subtitles

The Widow of St. Pierre is a costume drama with a distinct anti-death penalty flavor. Thankfully, its intent is not to preach but to demonstrate by example. *The Widow of Saint-Pierre* asks two complex questions: what does it take to redeem a murderer and which path should an individual choose when morality conflicts with the law?

To play out this tale, which transpires during the 1850s in the French territory of Saint-Pierre, an island off the coast of Newfoundland, Leconte has brought together two of his country's best-known actors. Juliette Binoche plays Madame La and Daniel Auteuil is her husband, the captain in charge of the French military stationed on the island. The third player in the drama is Neel Auguste (Yugoslavian director Emir Kusturica in his acting debut), a convicted killer. The court sentences Neel to death for his act, but there's a problem. French law demands execution by guillotine, and there isn't one on the island, nor is there an executioner. So, while the islanders of Saint-Pierre await the arrival of the instrument from Martinique (a several month delay), Neel is allowed a degree of freedom by the Captain and Madame La. A series of good deeds on his part make him a beloved member of the community, and, when the guillotine eventually arrives, no one is willing to wield it. Meanwhile, the Captain, having decided that it would be unjust to execute Neel given his reformed character, informs the local government that his troops will not aid in the beheading — a stance that places him in a dangerous, possibly treasonous position.

Leconte's point is that not all criminals are beyond rehabilitation and redemption. Neel commits a brutal, senseless crime, but his actions afterward prove that his transformation is one of the heart and soul. In truth, he believes that he deserves his sentence, and is unwilling to put others at risk to flee from it. *The Widow of Saint-Pierre* points out one of the key flaws inherent in the death penalty — the possibility that a man's nature can be re-shaped.

If there's a flaw in the film, it's Leconte's cool, detached perspective of the characters, which dissuades emotional involvement. It's as if the starkness of the film's setting has seeped into the heart of the production. Leconte's film will not be remembered alongside his masterworks, but it is nevertheless a worthy effort. **RECOMMENDED**

Wild Reeds [1995]

Starring: Elodie Bouchez, Gael Morel, Stephane Rideau, Frederic Gorny Director: André Téchiné Screenplay: André Téchiné, Gilles Taurand, Olivier Massart Running Time: **1:50** Rated: No MPAA Rating (Frank sexual themes, language, brief nudity) In French with subtitles

Winner of four 1994 Cesar awards (best picture, best director, best screenplay, and best female newcomer), *Wild Reeds* beat out such big-name, high-budget productions as *Queen Margot*. Originally commissioned by French television, but first released theatrically, this story of 4 youths struggling with the pressures of becoming adults in 1962 France presents an honest look at all the angst and uncertainty of finding oneself.

If *Wild Reeds* was just another coming-of-age story, it wouldn't be worth more than a cursory glance. However, André Téchiné's semi-autobiographical look back at his final year in boarding school possesses more depth and realism than many similar films. Nostalgia does not tint this narrative with its warm sepia tones. Essentially a character study of the four corners of a romantic quadrangle, *Wild Reeds* examines adolescence from the point-of-view of those who feel themselves to be "outsiders," and shows that while the political and social climate may affect a person's development, other factors — such as friendship and love — are often more dominant.

Maite (Elodie Bouchez) is the only girl in the group of four. Descended from a Spanish family (her last name is Alvarez), she's the daughter of the school's French teacher. She is also a devout Communist, at a time when Communism is in vogue. Fiercely loyal to her beliefs and hopelessly in love with the intellectual François (Gael Morel), Maite is nevertheless frightened of a sexual relationship. Not that one is likely with François in any case, since he's in the process of recognizing and coping with his homosexuality. An experimental relationship with Serge (Stephane Rideau) confirms François' beliefs, but Serge views their coupling as a moment of experimentation best forgotten. François, however, is unwilling to give up his newfound friend/lover, but Serge is more interested in pursuing Maite.

Into this mix comes Henri (Frederic Gorny), a 21-year-old intellectual French national expelled from Algeria. Branded a fascist by Maite, Henri arrives steeped in bitterness and anger at just about everyone and everything. Gradually, through patience and effort, François breaks through Henri's facade. But it is the tempestuous relationship that develops between Henri and Maite that leads to one of the film's defining moments.

Ultimately, *Wild Reeds* is a slice of life with an imperfect beginning and conclusion, but what transpires between those two endpoints is strong enough to leave an impression on anyone with the patience to commit to a movie of such unhurried temperament. **HIGHLY RECOMMENDED**

Wilde [United Kingdom, 1997]

Starring: Stephen Fry, Jude Law, Vanessa Redgrave, Jennifer Ehle, Gemma Jones Director: Brian Gilbert Screenplay: Julian Mitchell based on the book by Richard Ellmann Running Time: 1:57 Rated: R (Homosexual themes, sex, nudity, profanity) Theatrical Aspect Ratio: 1.85:1

Oscar Wilde — satirist, playwright, and novelist — was one of the great figures of the late 19th century. Born in Dublin in 1854, Wilde was schooled at Oxford, where he became a free-thinker and settled into the lifestyle of an aesthete. In 1881, he published his first volume of poems and in 1882, his debut stage production, *Vera, or the Nihilists* was performed. Thereafter, for the next 13 years, Wilde's reputation was in a constant state of ascension. He published his lone novel, *The Picture of Dorian Gray,* in 1891, but is best known for 4 plays: *Lady Windermere's Fan* (1892), *A Woman of No Importance* (1893), *An Ideal Husband* (1895), and *The Importance of Being Earnest* (1895). In 1895, Wilde, a known homosexual, was arrested and convicted of sodomy in association with his relationship with Lord Alfred ("Bosie") Douglas. He served 2 years of hard labor, but, after his release, never fully recovered his health and died of meningitis in 1900.

Brian Gilbert's *Wilde* is a fairly straightforward biographical tale that chronicles the title character's life from 1882, when he visited a silver mine in Colorado, until 1897, when he was released from prison. Despite an uneven script and a rather mundane, occasionally-plodding narrative, the movie is compelling, largely because Wilde's life was fascinating. Throw in a number of top-notch performances and, even without any flourishes, the film offers a solid 2 hours of entertainment, and, for anyone unfamiliar with Wilde or his work, perhaps education.

Like many artistic figures throughout history, Wilde's reputation has waxed and waned with the mutation of the social climate. During the 1880s and early 1890s, he was the toast of England. Following his trial, he was persona non grata, and had to eke out an existence using a pseudonym for the rest of his life. Into the early 20th century, his name was reviled, but, as the years passed and critics looked back at Wilde's work from a more detached perspective, his sullied reputation became rehabilitated. Today, he is regarded as a literary giant, and perhaps the best playwright of the second half of the 19th century.

One of the many things *Wilde* does right is to convey a sense of the man apart from his work. During the course of the film, Wilde is often compared to some sort of literary prophet (he has "disciples"), and it's easy to see how young men would be attracted to this charming, erudite man who uses his "wit as a foil." **RECOMMENDED**

The Wings of the Dove [United Kingdom, 1997]

Starring: Helena Bonham Carter, Linus Roache, Alison Elliott, Charlotte Rampling Director: Iain Softley Screenplay: Hossein Amini Running Time: 1:48 Rated: R (Sexual situations, mature themes) Theatrical Aspect Ratio: 2.35:1

When adapting classic novels (such as *The Wings of the Dove*) into movies, there are generally two approaches that film makers consider. The first is a straightforward, literal translation that leaves the characters, narrative, and dialogue intact. The second is to opt for a more "free" adaptation that allows condensation, change, and, in some cases, "modernization." Sometimes it works (*Sense and Sensibility*), sometimes it doesn't (*Anna Karenina*). At any rate, the latter method is the one chosen by director Iain Softley and screenwriter Hossein Amini for *The Wings of the Dove*. While leaving the general storyline and basic themes of the novel intact, these 2 men elected to alter certain key aspects of James' book to make it more cinematic and to give it greater appeal for a contemporary audience.

As might be expected, the basic plot of the movie and the book is the same (although the time line has been shifted by 10 years to 1910 in the film). *The Wings of the Dove* opens with Kate Croy (Helena Bonham Carter) going to live with a wealthy, cultured aunt (Charlotte Rampling) shortly after the death of her mother. Kate's aunt has every intention of setting up her niece in a comfortable, socially-acceptable marriage. But Kate, who has fallen in love with Merton Densher (Linus Roache), a poor journalist far below her social station, has other ideas. But when her aunt threatens to disinherit her if she doesn't break off the illicit relationship, Kate is faced with a moral dilemma. Her singular solution proves to be damaging to all involved.

Kate befriends a wealthy young American, Milly Theale, who has come to Europe for health reasons. Milly is seriously ill, and her state of health suggests a plan to Kate, who contrives for Milly to meet Merton. Soon, Milly is hopelessly in the thrall of the handsome journalist, and, with Kate's aid, Milly makes a play for him while all 3 are on a holiday in Venice. It is only then that Merton divines the nature of Kate's plot: that he should marry Milly for her money, then, upon her death when he would be rich, he could marry Kate.

Much as he did with his adaptation of Thomas Hardy's *Jude the Obscure*, screenwriter Amini focuses on the emotional aspects of the story, detailing how the consequences of each of the characters' actions tears at their psyches. Like *Jude*, *The Wings of the Dove* is not a happy tale, but it is a vivid and unforgettable one, featuring multi-dimensional characters, beautiful cinematography, impressive set design, and accomplished acting. *The Wings of the Dove* is an impressive motion picture adaptation of a classic novel. **HIGHLY RECOMMENDED**

The Winslow Boy [1999]

Starring: Nigel Hawthorne, Rebecca Pidgeon, Jeremy Northam, Gemma Jones Director: David Mamet Screenplay: David Mamet, based on the play by Terence Rattigan Running Time: 1:44 Rated: G Theatrical Aspect Ratio: 1.85:1

The Winslow Boy is set in the Edwardian era of pre-World War I England. It seems better suited to the style of Merchant-Ivory than to that of the man who is best-known for writing the 4-letter word tirades of *Glengarry Glen Ross* and *American Buffalo*. Yet the job David Mamet has done here should silence his critics. *The Winslow Boy* remains true to playwright Terence Rattigan's source material; at the same time, it retains an element of Mamet's singular style as a filmmaker — the characters frequently speak in clipped, staccato sentences.

Loosely based on a true event, *The Winslow Boy* tells the story of 14-year-old Ronnie Winslow (Guy Edwards), a young cadet who was expelled from Britain's Osbourne Naval College in 1908, and his family's arduous struggle to exonerate him of theft and fraud charges. After being found guilty of forging another student's signature in order to steal a 5-shilling postal order, Ronnie is thrown out of the college and dejectedly returns home. His mother, Grace (Gemma Jones); older sister, Catherine (Rebecca Pidgeon); and brother, Dickie (Matthew Pidgeon) all express sympathy and support. His father, Arthur (Nigel

Hawthorne), asks one question of his son: Did you steal this postal order? When Ronnie looks his father in the eyes are responds, "No," that's good enough for Arthur to begin a campaign to prove his son's innocence. Arthur's long battle drains his financial resources, saps his strength, and causes everyone in his family to sacrifice. Grace must give up her comfortable lifestyle. Dickie must leave Oxford and go to work. And Catherine loses her fiancé and is forced to contemplate a loveless marriage. Even Sir Robert Morton (Jeremy Northam), the famous lawyer hired by the Winslows to argue their case, turns down a prestigious honor to continue the fight.

The Winslow Boy asks two pointed questions. The first penetrates to the heart of human altruism by examining the point at which the quest for justice turns into an exercise in pride and self-interest. How much of Arthur's fight is really to remove the blight from his son's record and how much is because of his own stubbornness and intransigence? It's clear that Ronnie really doesn't care about the results and everyone else in the family is being hurt, yet Arthur doggedly pushes onward. The second question reiterates a common theme in legal dramas: how does what's right differ from what justice demands?

Despite a few failings, *The Winslow Boy* is a solidly engaging movie. What it lacks in emotional involvement, it makes up for in intelligence and, at times, wit. It's to Mamet's credit that he keeps the tone low-key; in another director's hands, the finale might have turned into the overblown melodrama of a *Scent of a Woman*. **RECOMMENDED**

The Winter Guest [United States/United Kingdom, 1997]

Starring: Phylida Law, Emma Thompson, Gary Hollywood, Arlene Cockburn, Sheila Reid Director: Alan Rickman Screenplay: Sharman Macdonald and Alan Rickman Running Time: 1:50 Rated: R (Profanity, mature themes, brief nudity) Theatrical Aspect Ratio: 1.85:1

The Winter Guest does not tell a traditional tale, nor does it ascribe to a conventional narrative structure — there is no real beginning or end. Instead, we are given an opportunity to observe one day in the lives of eight humans. They represent both sexes, multiple generations, and a variety of relationships — male and female; young, middle-aged, and elderly; friends, would-be lovers, and kin. We see expectations fulfilled and disappointed, emotional boundaries eroded, and truths unveiled.

The setting is a small town in Scotland on the coldest day of the year. It's so frigid that the sea has begun to freeze over. The onshore wind cuts like a knife and snow blankets the beach, giving the terrain an alien appearance. It is against this backdrop that the relationships of the film are captured. There are four pairings, and, although there is some interaction between the different twosomes, *The Winter Guest*'s focus is on the dynamics internal to each relationship.

The first, meatiest pairing is that of Elspeth (Phylida Law) and her recently-widowed daughter, Frances (Emma Thompson). These two have a stormy relationship. They love each other deeply, but both are stubborn and willful, and neither is willing to admit that they need the other. Much of their interaction is argumentative, but, during the course of a long walk to the frozen shoreline, they come to an unspoken understanding of how much each means to the other.

Frances' adult son, Alex (Gary Hollywood), is a lonely young man who has been caring for his mother since the death of his father. On this day, he meets a girl, Nita (Arlene Cockburn), who has secretly been spying on him for weeks. Although their first encounter is antagonistic, both quickly become aware of an undeniable attraction. Once they retire to a place where they can be alone, however, things don't go exactly as planned.

Lily (Sheila Reid) and Chloe (Sandra Voe) are a couple of old friends who are frequent funeral attendees. Death is a topic of endless fascination for them, perhaps because they are so close to it, and they spend their spare time scanning the obituaries, looking for the next funeral or cremation in the area. It doesn't matter whether or not they knew the deceased. It's the ceremony that they're interested in.

Sam (Douglas Murphy) and Tom (Sean Biggerstaff), a pair of schoolboy chums, are spending this cold February day cutting classes and hanging out at the beach, horsing around, building a small fire for warmth, and walking on the frozen water. Unlike Lily and Chloe, these two have their entire lives ahead of them. They are young enough to still believe in magic, but old enough to recognize that the process of crossing into adulthood robs life of the simple joy that only children can experience.

If you appreciate character studies, *The Winter Guest* is a solid effort with staying power. RECOMMENDED

Without Limits [1998]

Starring: Billy Crudup, Donald Sutherland, Monica Potter, Jeremy Sisto Director: Robert Towne Screenplay: Robert Towne, Kenny Moore Running Time: 1:57 Rated: PG-13 (Profanity, sexual situations) Theatrical Aspect Ratio: 235:1

During the late '60s and early '70s, Steve Prefontaine singlehandedly revitalized the sport of track, transforming it from a second-tier college activity to a major national interest. Prefontaine became something of a hero, the James Dean of running. His competitive spirit was so fierce that he could not accept being anything worst than first, and he refused to pace himself to allow a victory with anything less than a full effort. At one point, when asked how he could win against men who arguably possessed more pure talent, Prefontaine's response was, "I can endure more pain than anyone you've ever met." For him, each race was a work of art, which made his poor placing in the 1972 Olympic Games galling.

Munich was the culmination of Prefontaine's amateur track career. After setting countless American and collegiate records, Pre (as he was commonly known) was ready for the world stage. There, although the off-field murder of the Israeli athletes overshadowed any on-field activity, the race was held, with Prefontaine coming in a disappointing fourth. Following the loss, Pre went into an extended tailspin. He eventually recovered, and was preparing for the 1976 Olympics, when, at the age of 24 in 1975, he was killed in a single-car accident.

As far as true sports movies go, Prefontaine's story has all of the elements necessary for an engaging motion picture (except a happy ending), and Towne does the best he can with the material at his disposal. Consequently, *Without Limits* makes for an engrossing examination of the will to win, the importance of icons in American sports, and the interference of money in amateur athletics. Above all, however, this film is an effective character study of a figure who has attained an almost-mythical status among track-and-field followers. RECOMMENDED

Wonder Boys [2000]

Starring: Michael Douglas, Tobey Maguire, Frances McDormand, Katie Holmes, Robert Downey Jr. Director: Curtis Hanson Screenplay: Steve Kloves, based on the novel by Michael Chabon Running Time: 1:48 Rated: R (Profanity, drugs, homosexual themes) Theatrical Aspect Ratio: 2.35:1

Wonder Boys uses a standard premise — the older, wiser father figure who both teaches and learns from his protégé — as a starting-off point. While it's true that familiarity can breed contempt, and too many movies of this sort veer into overly-sentimental melodrama, *Wonder Boys* manages to keep audiences involved despite its less-than-original underlying idea. There are two obvious reasons for this. The first is tone — the film successfully shifts from comedy to poignancy without the awkwardness that often mars such transitions, and it never goes overboard in either category. The second is characters. The men and women inhabiting this film feel like real people, not recycled caricatures from other, similar motion pictures.

Grady Tripp (Michael Douglas, looking worn out and unkempt) is a celebrated English professor at a small university. Once upon a time, Grady was regarded as a literary luminary, but it has been seven years since his critically acclaimed *Arsonist's Daughter* was published. His editor, Terry Crabtree (Robert Downey Jr.) is itching to release the much anticipated follow-up, but the author keeps putting him off. It isn't that Grady is suffering from writer's block, but he can't figure out how to end his lastest novel — an epic endeavor that is at least twice the length of *War & Peace*. Meanwhile, Grady's personal life is a mess. His wife has left him. His married girlfriend, Sarah Gaskell (Frances McDormand), who also happens to be the college's chancellor, is pregnant with his child. And a student named Hannah (Katie Holmes), who rents a room in his house, has a huge crush on him. Then there's the strange case of James Leer (Tobey Maguire), a brooding young man with unlimited writing potential. Grady decides to take James under his wing and teach him a little about life. The experience turns out to be much different than Grady anticipated.

Wonder Boys is about the relationship between Grady and James, and the importance of storytelling to both of them. The film's other characters are secondary, and often serve little purpose beyond acting as catalysts. In fact, Grady's wife is so unimportant that she never makes an appearance in the flesh (although we do catch a glimpse of her in a photograph). *Wonder Boys* explores themes that most of us can relate to: chasing the dreams of youth, taking risks and making a commitment, and finding and pursuing something of meaning.

Wonder Boys is not as accomplished a feature as *L.A. Confidential,* but it's a strong follow-up for Hanson, especially since it shows that he is not afraid to broaden his horizons. With vivid characters, an ironic voice-over narrative, and a solidly written screenplay, *Wonder Boys* provides its share of small pleasures.

RECOMMENDED

Wonderland [United Kingdom, 1999]

Starring: **Shirley Henderson, Gina McKee, Molly Parker, Ian Hart, John Simm, Stuart Townsend** Director: **Michael Winterbottom** Screenplay: **Laurence Coriat** Running Time: 1:48 Rated: R (Profanity, sex, nudity) Theatrical Aspect Ratio: 2.35:1

Wonderland covers 4 days (Thursday through Sunday) in the lives of several characters as their paths intersect, merge, and diverge. The film is not constructed using events of momentous dramatic importance — almost everything that transpires is the kind of everyday incident that a typical viewer can relate to. The circumstances and situations take on an added importance because of the bond that Winterbottom creates between the protagonists and the audience. Only a few scenes into the movie, we have a strong sense that these are real people and that everything they do matters, if not to anyone else, then at least to them (and, by extension, to us).

Wonderland's three primary characters are sisters: single mother Debbie (Shirley Henderson), whose 11-year-old son is spending the weekend with his dad; lonely Nadia (Gina McKee), whose quest for a worthwhile companion has led her to place an ad in the personals; and pregnant Molly (Molly Parker), who is only days away from giving birth. There are men here, too, although they play secondary roles. There's Molly's husband, Eddie (John Simm), who is becoming unnerved by the possibility of fatherhood. Debbie's ex, Dan (Ian Hart), uses a VCR to babysit his son while he goes out to the pub. And quiet Tim (Stuart Townsend) allows Nadia to believe that not all the men responding to her ad are creeps. Finally, to round out things out, we're given a look into the unhappy married existence of Eileen (Kika Markham) and Bill (Jack Shepherd), an older couple whose feelings for each other are as empty as the rooms in which their children once lived.

Watching *Wonderland* is like stripping away the public anonymity offered by the crowd, separating the individual from the vast human continuum that forms an ever-changing background. There's nothing extraordinary about any of the characters whose lives unfold during the course of Winterbottom's 108-minute film, so it's the essential truth of the material that makes *Wonderland* a compelling and rewarding experience. **RECOMMENDED**

Xiu Xiu: The Sent-Down Girl (Tian Yu) [United States/Hong Kong/China, 1998]

Starring: **Lu Lu, Lopsang** Director: **Joan Chen** Screenplay: **Joan Chen, Yan Geling** from her novella "Tian Yu" Rated: No MPAA Rating (Sex, nudity, gore) Running Time: 1:40 Theatrical Aspect Ratio: 1.85:1 In Mandarin with subtitles

Xiu Xiu is a devastating and unforgettable portrait of hopeless love and the corruption of innocence set against the backdrop of the Cultural Revolution.

The director of *Xiu Xiu* is Chinese-born actress Joan Chen, who established herself in the West with a key role in *The Last Emperor* and a recurring part in David Lynch's offbeat TV series, *Twin Peaks*. Chen wears many hats for this motion picture, which is obviously a labor of passion. In addition to making her directorial debut, she functions as co-producer and co-writer. The result is one of the most stunning first features from any film maker since Quentin Tarantino burst upon the scene with *Reservoir Dogs*.

The movie takes place in mainland China near the city of Chengdu during the mid-1970s. A 15-year-old girl, Wen Xiu (nicknamed Xiu Xiu, and played by Lu Lu), is joining the core of youths who are sent into the country to be properly "educated" (through hard labor) in service to their country. After an exemplary record on her first assignment, Wen is transferred to the Tibetan borderlands to study under the tutelage of Lao Jin (Lopsang), a master horse herder. She is supposed to be there for 6 months. Lao proves to be a gentle man who is at home with animals and nature, but uncomfortable around humans. Gradually, he develops a deep affection for the girl under his care, and, because he is unable to function sexually, there is no danger that the relationship will become inappropriate.

The months pass, with Wen Xiu and Lao Jin living in easy communion, but she makes no secret of the fact that when her tour of duty is up, she intends to return home to Chengdu. To her, life in isolation is worse than death — it is endurable only for a short time. But 6 months pass and she is not recalled. Shortly thereafter, a peddler from the city visits Lao Jin and hints that, in return for sexual favors, he might be able to pull a few strings to get Wen Xiu home. He becomes the first of many male visitors to share her bed. All promise results; none are able to deliver them. And, through all of this, Lao Jin must sit by and watch. He knows that none of the men are sincere, but Wen Xiu is so blinded by her desire to leave that she cannot see what is obvious: she has become a whore, and is being paid with worthless promises.

The film's condemnation of the Cultural Revolution is overt. Although it only explicitly depicts the downfall of one girl, it hints at a widespread corruption that is terrible to contemplate. Unlike movies such as *Farewell My Concubine* and *To Live, Xiu Xiu* is not a product of the Chinese film industry, so there is no danger of it being suppressed. It is a forceful, emotionally-riveting experience that only the most accomplished motion pictures can offer. **MUST SEE**

You Can Count On Me [2000]

Starring: Laura Linney, Mark Ruffalo, Rory Culkin, Matthew Broderick
Director: Kenneth Lonergan   Screenplay: Kenneth Lonergan   Running Time: 1:49   Rated: R (Profanity, drug use, sex)   Theatrical Aspect Ratio: 1.85:1

Kenneth Lonergan's directorial debut, *You Can Count On Me*, is one of those movies that straddles a number of fences. It functions well as either a comedy or a drama. It tells a straightforward story, but does so in a slightly off-kilter manner. It's bold enough to appeal to aficionados of independent cinema, but conventional enough not to drive away mainstream audiences.

You Can Count On Me is a seemingly simple family drama that turns out not to be so simple. The film opens with a short sequence in 1982 that shows two young children attending the funeral of their parents, who were killed in a car accident. Fast forward 18 years. Sammy (Laura Linney) is now a single mother, trying to cope with raising a precocious 8-year old, Rudy (Rory Culkin), and holding down her job at the local bank. Brian (Matthew Broderick), the new manager, has come aboard with Gestapo-like tactics that are driving Sammy crazy. Out of the blue, Sammy's brother, Terry (Mark Ruffalo), decides to visit his sister. She is overjoyed, but he has an ulterior motive for coming home — he needs money. And his arrival in the small upstate New York town where he grew up causes a few minor waves.

In terms of broad plot, *You Can Count On Me* doesn't offer much that's new. The film uses some fairly standard building blocks: the brother/sister angle, the single mother struggling to raise a child on her own, and the contentious at-work relationship between two people who are simultaneously attracted to and repelled by one another. However, instead of relying exclusively on formulas, Lonergan gives his characters and their circumstances some room in which to breathe. He is also a talented screenwriter. The dialogue in this film is not written for a least-common-denominator audience, and there's plenty of humor (some of it laugh-aloud funny) peppered in between the dramatic episodes. Lonergan also brings religion into the mix in a way that is not condescending or preachy — a difficult thing for any filmmaker to accomplish.

On the whole, *You Can Count On Me* is a pleasant motion picture, offering a solid evening's worth of entertainment. The film probably wouldn't have suffered had a few minutes been trimmed from the running length — the final cut seems a little protracted. As far as dramatic comedies (or comedic dramas) go, this one offers everything one might expect from a successful entry into the genre, delivering laughs and some genuinely moving instances of character interaction. RECOMMENDED

Your Friends and Neighbors [1998]

Starring: Jason Patric, Ben Stiller, Catherine Keener, Aaron Eckhart, Amy Brenneman, Nastassja Kinski Director: Neil LaBute
Screenplay: Neil LaBute Running Time: 1:35 Rated: R (Sex, profanity)
Theatrical Aspect Ratio: 2.35:1

Those looking for something lightweight or feel-good need not bother with *Your Friends and Neighbors,* a slow-moving, often disturbing look at miscommunication between the sexes, dysfunctional personalities, and the disintegration of relationships. The film contains enough humor to qualify it as a black comedy, but, underneath all the dialogue, *Your Friends and Neighbors* offers a bleak message about life and love in an era of growing emotional isolation.

The characters in *Your Friends and Neighbors* are well-defined, but there isn't much growth. We know who they are, but not who they have been or who they will become. That's really the point, though, since *Your Friends and Neighbors* is designed as a voyeuristic peek behind the drapes and blinds of suburban bedrooms, not a drama with character arcs. With a sparse narrative that does little more than move the protagonists from situation to situation, the movie lives and dies on the basis of two primary characteristics: acting and dialogue. Both, fortunately, are strengths.

The first person we're introduced to is Cary (Jason Patric), an egotistical womanizer who uses sex as a weapon. Those who saw *In the Company of Men* will recognize similarities between Cary and that film's vicious protagonist, Chad. Cary doesn't really have women problems, because he never lets anyone get close to him. He sleeps with them, then discards them. On the other hand, Cary's two friends, Jerry (Ben Stiller) and Barry (Aaron Eckhart), are embroiled in problematic relationships. Jerry, a college drama professor, is having increasing difficulties with his girlfriend, Terri (Catherine Keener), who wants him to be quiet during sex. Barry is unable to perform with his wife, Mary (Amy Brenneman), leaving them both sexually frustrated. Meanwhile, there's the wild card, Cheri (Nastassja Kinski), an artist's assistant who, in her quest to have meaningful human contact, meets the other characters one-by-one as they stop by the gallery where she works.

There isn't one healthy male/female relationship in *Your Friends and Neighbors.* Jerry and Terri are at each other's throats from the beginning, and are cheating on one another before the movie is half over. Barry and Mary, despite having what looks to outsiders like the ideal marriage, are miserable because their attempts at sexual intimacy turn into sessions of ego-bruising failure. Then, when Mary tries to have an affair, the experience is an unmitigated disaster, destroying what little self-confidence she has about her ability in bed. As for the other two characters, Cary rejects the concept of intimacy, and Cheri craves it like a drug.

As was true for *In the Company of Men,* LaBute doesn't care if viewers are offended. Supported by a fine group of actors, he tells the story without compromises, and that gives us a refreshing alternative to multiplex fare. RECOMMENDED

The Adventures of Huck Finn [1993]

Starring: Elijah Wood, Cortney B. Vance, Robbie Coltrane, Jason Robards Director: Stephen Sommers Screenplay: Stephen Sommers, based on the novel by Mark Twain Running Time: 1:48 Rated: PG (Mature themes, violence) Theatrical Aspect Ratio: 1.85:1

Whenever a book is adapted into a movie, there are sacrifices and interpretations that must be made because the totality of the written work cannot possibly be translated to the screen. These choices can become exceptionally difficult when the work is one as widely-read and well-beloved as Mark Twain's *The Adventures of Huckleberry Finn*. For this latest filmed version, Stephen Sommers' script is faithful in spirit — if not in all the details — to the original. Much of Twain's keen insight into human nature, as well as his finely-tuned sense-of-humor, is kept intact in Disney's 1993 *The Adventures of Huck Finn*.

Young Huck Finn (Elijah Wood) has a penchant for getting into mischief. He spends the bulk of his days playing truant from school, getting into fights, and lying to his two female guardians about how he got black eyes. One day, Huck's drunken, good-for-nothing father (Ron Perlman) arrives and takes his son away with him, looking for a way to get his hands on $600 left to Huck by his late mother. Huck escapes from his father's clutches, and, in the company of a runaway slave named Jim (Cortney B. Vance), sets off on a journey by boat down the Mississippi with the goal of getting Jim's freedom. Along the way, the duo meet a number of interesting people and become involved in several adventures.

One of the things that impressed me the most about this movie is the realism of the river scenes. Of necessity, less of the movie takes place on the Mississippi than in the book, but the river remains an important part of the plot. It's genuinely awe-inspiring, and a little frightening, to see a giant steamboat bearing down on a little raft.

Some will doubtless argue that this latest updating is unnecessary. They may be right, but rarely has the existence of a perfectly good adaptation prevented film makers from doing their own version. In the case of *The Adventures of Huck Finn*, at least Disney has produced a film of some quality. It's not a milestone, nor can it be considered the definitive adaptation of Twain's work but, on the whole, it deserves some recognition and credit. **RECOMMENDED**

Babe [1995]

Starring: James Cromwell, Magda Szubanski, Christine Cavanaugh (voice) Director: Chris Noonan Screenplay: George Miller & Chris Noonan, based on Dick King-Smith's book, *Babe: The Gallant Pig* Running Time: 1:29 Rated: G Theatrical Aspect Ratio: 1.85:1

At first glance, a movie about the adventures of a piglet who thinks he's a sheepdog doesn't appear to be the perfect entertainment recipe for those beyond puberty. However, through a mixture of imaginative storytelling, impressive animatronics, and irresistible cuteness, *Babe* casts a spell over all viewers — young, old, or somewhere in between.

Babe is a small pig whose parents have gone to hog heaven. Abducted from the pork penitentiary, he ends up as the lone representative of his kind on the property of Farmer Hoggett (James Cromwell), a kindly man of few words who knows far more about sheep than pigs. On the farm, Babe makes a few enemies, but many more friends, including a talkative duck who wants to be a rooster and a dog willing to play the role of substitute mother. Unfortunately, one of those not in the pig's corner is Mrs. Hoggett (Magda Szubanski), who has visions of a roast pork Christmas dinner dancing in her head.

Babe is a new twist on the traditional story of the underachiever attaining greatness. It's a buddy film, about a man and his best friend (who, in this case, happens to be pink), and an adventure-comedy. Above all, it teaches the lesson of how easy it is to fall back on "comfortable" prejudices. Babe triumphs because his first thought is always of bridging gaps, not building walls. Unlike in George Orwell's *Animal Farm*, here the pig is the instrument of unity and mediation.

Babe's greatest asset (besides the pig) is director Chris Noonan, who finds the right tone for this modern fable. Most animal movies come across as unbelievably cloying or simply unbelievable, but Noonan makes his picture work. And, by using the talents of the men and women of Jim Henson's workshop, Noonan has assured that when the animals' lips move, they don't look like *Mr. Ed*. Thought was put into the adaptation of Dick King-Smith's book. Even the narrative voiceovers, laced with subtle irony and understated revelations, are effective in this context.
RECOMMENDED

Babe: Pig in the City [1998]

Starring: Magda Szubanski, James Cromwell, Mary Stein, Mickey Rooney, E.G. Daily (voice) Director: George Miller Screenplay: George Miller, Mark Campbell, Judy Morris, based on *The Sheep Pig* by Dick King-Smith Running Time: 1:32 Rated: G Theatrical Aspect Ratio: 1.85:1

Pig in the City has a slightly darker tone than *Babe*, but it's by no means grim or frightening. The G-rating is still deserved; only the smallest of children will be disturbed by some of the movie's most disconcerting images. *Pig in the City* has been designed with the goal of recapturing the enchanting feel of the original while taking the story in new and different directions. It succeeds at both aims, standing as a worthy sequel to one of the decade's most innovative family features.

Pig in the City opens on "a place just a little to the left of the 20th century" — the farm of "Boss" Arthur Hoggett (James Cromwell), who has returned home triumphant with his world-renowned sheep-pig, Babe. However, Babe's time to bask in the glow of his fame is short-lived. After the farmer suffers an accident and is laid up in bed, his wife (Magda Szubanski), needing to raise money to keep the bank men at bay, takes the pig with her on a trip, hoping to get a generous appearance fee by showing up at a county fair. (Apparently, she's no longer obsessed with the thought of a pork dinner.) After missing a connecting flight, however, Mrs. Hoggett and Babe end up stranded in the unfamiliar land of the Big City, where a series of astounding adventures awaits them.

This is essentially a fractured fairy tale. The unnamed city is a fantasyland mixture of cultures, eras, and places — a visually tantalizing display of all that is grand and intimidating about the world's largest population centers. In the city's vast canyon of buildings can be found the "Hollywood" sign, the World Trade Center, the Space Needle, the Statue of Liberty, the Golden Gate Bridge, the Eiffel Tower, and dozens of other famous landmarks, all nestled together. Much of the action takes place in and around a quaint, old hotel in a section of the city that looks like a romanticized slice of Venice (canals, bridges, etc.).

George Miller, who co-wrote and co-produced *Babe*, takes over for Chris Noonan in the director's chair. The transition is relatively seamless. All the elements that made the first film successful are here — comedy, adventure, fantasy, and a happy ending. Even though the title character is adorable, *Pig in the City* is careful not to overdo the cuteness factor (at times, the tone seems almost gothic). The film's underlying sense of sophistication will satisfy adults, while the nearly nonstop adventure will grab kids' attention. **RECOMMENDED**

Black Beauty [1994]

Starring: Justin, Rat, Alan Cumming, David Thewlis, Andrew Knott, Peter Davison Director: Caroline Thompson Screenplay: Caroline Thompson, based on the book by Anna Sewell Running Time: 1:28 Rated: G Theatrical Aspect Ratio: 1.85:1

Even though it's eminently suitable for family viewing, the latest adaptation of Anna Sewell's *Black Beauty* could be a film in search of an audience. Adults may avoid this movie because it's G-rated, based on a children's book, and has actors speaking with British accents. Children, on the other hand, may stay away because there are no musical numbers with singing animals, no McDonald's Happy Meals, and the actors speak with British accents.

In many ways, *Black Beauty* is almost more of an adult movie than one for children. Restless kids are going to have difficulty sitting through several of the slower portions, and the overall tone is more somber than anything put out by Disney. Even *The Lion King,* with its Shakespearean leanings, is ultimately lighter than *Black Beauty.*

Not the first adaptation of the classic story, Caroline Thompson's is the most faithful. Told from the perspective of Black Beauty (played by the stallion Justin, with a voice supplied by Alan Cumming), the film follows the horse's adventures as he serves masters both kind and cruel. It's a tale of friendship, abuse, betrayal, and redemption. The setting moves from the verdant pastures of rural England to the crowded streets of 19th-century London.

Tremendous camerawork by Alex Thomson and an effective score from Danny Elfman (this sounds nothing like his *Batman* music) add to *Black Beauty's* luster. The film has the look and feel of something out of Dickens, with a theme to match.

Black Beauty has a lot more to offer than the typically available, brainless family entertainment. It's worth the price of admission (or a rental) even if you don't have a kid to bring with you. Entertainment of this sort knows no age limits. RECOMMENDED

Fairytale: A True Story [United Kingdom/United States, 1997]
Starring: Florence Hoath, Elizabeth Earl, Paul McGann, Peter O'Toole, Harvey Keitel Director: Charles Sturridge Screenplay: Ernie Contreras Running Time: 1:38 Rated: PG (Mild profanity) Theatrical Aspect Ratio: 1.85:1

Fact or fiction, *Fairytale: A True Story* is a fine motion picture. While the movie is likely to make smaller children fidget, those who are old enough to grasp the themes and issues addressed will find themselves enchanted by the story. And grown-ups will discover that there's enough depth in the material to arrest their attention.

The chief truth explored by *Fairytale* is that the process by which a child becomes an adult destroys innocence and robs life of its magic. Paradoxically, the older one gets, the more he or she craves the wonders that only boys and girls can believe in. In *Fairytale,* children are the ones with insight, who can never be fooled because "the expect nothing, and so see everything." Adults, on the other hand, "don't know how to believe." They have lost the capacity to accept what they cannot see.

Fairytale takes place in the English countryside around the end of World War I. Eight-year old Frances Griffiths (Elizabeth Earl) has come to live with the family of her 12-year-old cousin, Elsie Wright (Florence Hoath), after her father has been declared missing in action. Almost immediately, Frances and Elsie find that they have a great deal in common, chief of which is a fascination with fairies — the tiny spirits of the air that only children can see. One day, while the girls are playing near a local stream, they experience their first sighting of one of the small creatures.

Soon, Elsie and Frances have procured Elsie's father's camera. Using it, they take two pictures of the fairies, and, when it has been confirmed that no photographic trickery has been used, the snapshots come to the attention of none other than Sir Arthur Conan Doyle (Peter O'Toole) and his friend, Harry Houdini (Harvey Keitel). Soon, these two luminaries make a trip to meet the girls, each with a different opinion of what they have seen. Houdini, a master of illusion himself, claims that the pictures are fakes. Conan Doyle, on the other hand, is willing to take the photos at face value. Meanwhile, Elsie's parents don't know what to think. As her mother says, "I'm not sure which frightens me more — that the children are lying to us or that they're telling the truth."

Fairytale is extraordinarily intelligent and insightful in its approach to the story, blending images of illusion and reality while playing the two off against one another. The film, which is presented from a child's point-of-view, also examines the mysteries of growing up. The manner in which this subject is approached will have many audience members thinking back to when they first realized they had crossed the invisible barrier separating childhood from adulthood. HIGHLY RECOMMENDED

Fly Away Home [1996]
Starring: Anna Paquin, Jeff Daniels, Dana Delany, Terry Kinney Director: Carroll Ballard Screenplay: Robert Rodat & Vince McKewin Running Time: 1:47 Rated: PG (Nothing offensive) Theatrical Aspect Ratio: 1.85:1

Fly Away Home starts with one of the most disconcerting scenes I've seen in a recent motion picture: a silent car accident that takes place during the opening credits while a soft, gentle melody plays in the background. The effect created by this juxtaposition of tragic and hopeful elements is sufficient to arrest anyone's attention. And, while the film never again attains this level of artistry, there are a few scenes that come close. Caleb Deschanel's photography is one of the movie's highlights.

The opening crash occurs in New Zealand, where

Amy Alden (Anna Paquin) and her mother live. Amy's mother dies in the accident, and the 13-year-old is forced to move to Ontario, Canada, where her father, Thomas (Jeff Daniels), has a home. Thomas, a sculptor and wilderness conservation activist, doesn't understand his daughter, and his earnest attempts to get close to her are rebuffed. When asked why he didn't visit her more often when she was younger, he says that New Zealand is a long way off. Her response to that: "That's a lame excuse, Dad." And, of course, it is.

While Thomas is busy with his work, Amy plays mother to 16 goose eggs that she finds abandoned in their nest. After constructing a makeshift incubator, Amy awaits the big moment. One day, when she comes home from school, a brood of newly-hatched birds are waiting to greet her. The story then shifts to the question of how Amy, recognized by the geese as their mother, can teach them certain basic necessities of survival — namely, how to fly and migrate. Thomas comes up with the answer: instruct Amy to pilot an ultra-light plane, then accompany her in his own craft on a 600-mile, 4-day aerial flight to North Carolina, with the geese tagging along behind.

As a family film, *Fly Away Home* has something for members of every temperament and age group: adventure, pathos, technical detail about the design of the aircraft, cute animals, and human drama. There's a subplot involving attempts to clip the birds' wings, a look at how the media covers Amy's flight, and a sequence where Amy and Thomas' crafts are mistaken for UFOs by the U.S. military. There's also a pro-conservation message that, while laudable in intent, comes across as simplistic and heavy-handed (land developers = bad; geese = good). Ballard uses this as the backdrop for a warm drama that's more about love and trust between a father and daughter than inter-species connections. The result, even for geese-haters, is charming. **RECOMMENDED**

Harriet the Spy [1996]

Starring: Michelle Trachtenberg, Vanessa Lee Chester, Gregory Smith Director: Bronwen Hughes Screenplay: Theresa Rebeck & Dogulas Petrie, based on the novel by Louise Fitzhugh Running Time: 1:41 Rated: PG (Some potentially disturbing sequences) Theatrical Aspect Ratio: 1.85:1

Harriet the Spy, based on the popular novel by Louise Fitzhugh and directed by feature newcomer Bronwen Hughes, is the premiere theatrical film from the popular cable TV channel, Nickelodeon. Harriet Welsch (Michelle Trachtenberg) is an unusual 6th-grader.

Instead of spending her time playing "tag" or "spin the bottle" with her schoolmates, she dons a yellow slicker, carries a notebook and pencil, and spies on people. From her vantage point in a tree, on a rooftop, outside a window, or even in a dumbwaiter, she watches, then jots down comments in her notebook about those she observes. There are even entries about her two best friends, Janie (Vanessa Lee Chester), a budding chemist, and Sport (Gregory Smith), a motherless boy who lives just above the poverty line. Harriet has been raised by a nanny named Golly (Rosie O'Donnell), who encourages her creativity. However, when Golly leaves, Harriet feels lost. And things go from bad to worse when the most popular girl in Harriet's class, Marion (Charlotte Sullivan), finds the notebook and reads the most damning passages aloud. As a result, Harriet becomes a pariah, shunned by even her friends. She plots revenge, but learns that vengeance can have a bitter taste.

To heighten its appeal for the under-12 crowd, *Harriet the Spy* uses MTV-like camera movements. The cinematography is kinetic, almost to the point of being distracting, with strange angles and numerous quick cuts. This, however, is what children are used to, and, admittedly, it keeps the film's energy level high. But the subtlety absent from the picture's visual aspect is more than compensated for on an emotional plane. As Harriet travels the long road from isolation to bittersweet revenge to redemption, we can see and feel her every change in emotion. This is a real person acting believably as dictated by a script that remains low-key. The ending is a little saccharine, but, considering the target audience, it's reasonable.

Certainly, one of the reasons *Harriet* effectively captures our sympathy is the fine performance by Michelle Trachtenberg (Nickelodeon's *The Adventures of Pete & Pete*), who exhibits the charisma of a younger Christina Ricci. Trachtenberg is very good in the title role, embodying all of Harriet's traits from youthful exuberance to petulance. As the cliché goes, good things do indeed come in small packages. **RECOMMENDED**

How the Grinch Stole Christmas [2000]

Starring: Jim Carrey, Taylor Momsen, Jeffrey Tambor, Christine Baranski, Molly Shannon Director: Ron Howard Screenplay: Jeffrey Price & Peter S. Seaman, based on the book by Dr. Seuss Running Time: 1:38 Rated: PG (Nothing offensive) Theatrical Aspect Ratio: 1.85:1

For more than 3 decades, *How the Grinch Stole Christmas* has been a holiday season television staple. The 22-minute cartoon, based on the book by Dr. Seuss and narrated by Boris Karloff, has enchanted multiple generations of children (not to mention adults), and, even with its ready availability on video, it still draws a sizable viewing audience every time it is broadcast. With the possible exception of the Peanuts Christmas Special, no other seasonal program is as beloved and respected as this venerable classic. So, in deciding to transform it into a 90-minute, live action motion picture, director Ron Howard has taken a sizable risk. To Howard's credit, he has worked hard to keep the spirit of the animated *Grinch* intact. The text of the Dr. Seuss book is in place, although a great deal has been added to pad out the running time.

The movie opens with nearly one hour of background material about the Grinch and Whoville that was not in either Seuss' book or the TV special. We learn all sorts of interesting tidbits designed to fill in supposed "holes" in Grinch lore (not that anyone really noticed). We come to understand why the Grinch hates Christmas (it has more to do with bad childhood experiences than with a heart that's 2 sizes too small), why he has it in for the Mayor of Whoville, and why Little Cindy Lou-Who finds his soft spot so easily. Finally, at about the film's two-thirds point, the narrative switches over to following the book letter-for-letter, and we get a strikingly faithful re-creation of the cartoon. There is a difference in tone between the two portions of the film — the part that follows the book is smoother, has considerably more narration, and consistently rhymes, while the remainder has a "tacked on" feel. Children, however, won't notice, and the shift isn't glaring enough that it will bother most adults — even those who have sat through the TV special countless times.

Of course, *How the Grinch Stole Christmas'* big selling point isn't nostalgia or great production values — it's Jim Carrey. Buried beneath Rick Baker's flexible makeup, he's a dead ringer for the cartoon creature, but, although he isn't physically recognizable, there's no doubt who's under all of the green latex and hair. For Carrey, whose caged energy is released, this falls just short of a tour de force. He brings animation to the live action, and, surrounded by glittering, fantastical sets and computer-spun special effects, Carrey enables Ron Howard's version of the classic story to come across as more of a welcome endeavor than a pointless re-tread. RECOMMENDED

The Indian in the Cupboard [1997]

Starring: Hal Scardino, Litefoot, Lindsay Crouse, Richard Jenkins, Rishi Bhat, David Keith Director: Frank Oz Screenplay: Melissa Mathison, based on the book by Lynne Reid Banks Running Time: 1:37 Rated: PG (Mild violence) Theatrical Aspect Ratio: 1.85:1

Omri, played with charm and enthusiasm by Hal Scardino, is an average 9-year-old with a very unusual cupboard in his room. Whenever he places a figurine in it, turns the key in the lock, then opens the door, a living, breathing, four-inch high creature emerges. Omri's first transformation is the Onondaga warrior Little Bear (Litefoot), whose reaction upon seeing the "giant" boy is a mixture of awe and fear. Gradually, however, Little Bear realizes that his caretaker is no god, and Omri learns that his newfound friend is a human being, not just a plaything.

As *The Indian in the Cupboard* progresses, other things get animated, including a cranky Texas cowboy (David Keith), a wartime British medic, Darth Vader, and Robocop. The visual effects that mix 4-foot actors with their miniature companions are effective, but not ostentatious, and the lack of flash keeps the focus on the characters and their story. Suspension of disbelief in *The Indian in the Cupboard* is surprisingly easy.

This film is about friendships, responsibility, and ethics. The bond between Omri and Little Bear illustrates that, regardless of size, shape, or race, any friendship is a rare and special thing. *The Indian in the Cupboard* also enforces the truth that everyone — even a child — must be responsible for his or her actions. When Omri begins capriciously to give life to figurines, Little Bear reprimands him: "You should not use magic that you do not understand." This prefaces a tragic epiphany for the young boy.

Frank Oz, a director who always seeks original and challenging projects, brings an uplifting sense of fun to this film. *The Indian in the Cupboard* moves along at a nearly-perfect pace: slowly enough to capture the nuances of the characters' relationships, but quickly enough to avoid stagnation. Hopefully, the double-edged classification of being a "family feature" will not destroy *The Indian in the Cupboard*'s chances at the box office. It deserves a better fate than that normally reserved for similar fare because, ultimately, this movie is not only about magic — it is magical. HIGHLY RECOMMENDED

The Jungle Book [1994]

Starring: Jason Scott Lee, Cary Elwes, Lena Headey, Sam Neill, John Cleese Director: Stephen Sommers Screenplay: Stephen Sommers and Ronald Yanover; based on characters from *The Jungle Book* by Rudyard Kipling Running Time: **1:51** Rated: **PG** (Violence) Theatrical Aspect Ratio: **2.35:1**

Beautifully photographed and tightly paced with a spate of solid performances, this latest Kipling-inspired motion picture is an enjoyable and exuberant film-going experience. Where Disney's animated *The Jungle Book* was a light-hearted affair, this rendition is more of a straightforward adventure. That's not to imply that it's in any way stodgy or somber; comic relief is provided by an orangutan called King Louie and a human named John Cleese.

Taking place in late 19th-century, British-occupied India, *The Jungle Book*'s story is uncomplicated: a human boy who has grown up in the jungle is lured back to civilization by the sight of a beautiful young woman. There, surrounded by a few who wish to help him and many whose motives are less pure, he learns to speak and act like a man. Eventually, his enemies, motivated by jealousy, ill-will, and greed, drive him back into the wild. Once there, the battle for life becomes a struggle of man's guns against the Law of the Jungle.

Those familiar with the animated feature will recognize some non-human characters, including King Louie, Baloo the bear, Bagheera the panther, and, of course, Shere Khan, the tiger king. Mowgli, the "wild boy" of the Black Jungle, is portrayed by Jason Scott Lee. This performance, while not of award-winning caliber, is characterized by a number of nice little "man/beast" touches. Lena Headey, as Katherine, is the object of Mowgli's love, but she's engaged to a British officer (Cary Elwes) who kills wild animals for sport. Sam Neill plays Katherine's father, and John Cleese is the kindly Dr. Julius Plumford.

There are moments when *The Jungle Book* may be too intense for small children. Animal maulings, while shown obliquely, occur on screen. Those old enough not to be disturbed by such things should enjoy this movie, regardless of whether they consider themselves adults, kids, or something in-between. *The Jungle Book* doesn't offer any thought-provoking philosophical messages, and its view of good and evil is simplistic, but that lack of complexity is part of its charm. **RECOMMENDED**

The Leopard Son [1996]

Director: **Hugo Van Lawick** Screenplay: **Michael Olmert** Running Time: **1:25** Rated: **G** Theatrical Aspect Ratio: **1.85:1**

Even frequent viewers of made-for-TV nature specials won't be fully prepared for the majesty of *The Leopard Son*. This is a singularly cinematic experience that will lose much when cropped for television viewing. And, because the cinematography is by far the most important aspect of this movie, the high aptitude level evidenced by directors of photography Hugo Van Lawick and Matthew Aeberhard makes this a rewarding motion picture experience.

Van Lawick is a Dutch photographer and naturalist who has spent most of his adult life living on the plains of the Serengeti. In his own words, "To be as close as possible to nature as I could — that was my dream." *The Leopard Son* is his filmed journal of 2 years in the life of a young male leopard. Van Lawick's camera first captures the cub when he's only a few weeks old, then follows him through youth and adolescence to adulthood. Along the way, we observe his relationship with his mother, his first attempts at hunting his own meals, and the harsh lessons that identify his place in the food chain. And, in a film which has a leopard as the central character, there are supporting appearances by all manner of other African wildlife, including baboons, elephants, giraffes, hyenas, rhinos, cheetahs, and lions. Some children may rightfully see this as a kind of live action *Lion King*.

What's unusual about *The Leopard Son* is that it's a nature film with characters and a plot. We are drawn into the drama of the title creature's life, and find ourselves rooting for him to hunt down a meal, rediscover his mother, make peace with his half-siblings, and, in the end, find a mate. As in any well-constructed motion picture, there's humor, pathos, passion, and danger. Unfortunately, however, we are subjected to an irritatingly repetitive and superfluous voiceover provided by Sir John Gielgud. This would have been a better film without it. *The Leopard Son* is so well-crafted visually that it doesn't need a narrator. **HIGHLY RECOMMENDED**

The Little Princess [1995]

Starring: **Liesel Matthews, Eleanor Bron, Liam Cunningham, Vanessa Lee Chester** Director: **Alfonso Cuaron** Screenplay: **Richard LaGravanese and Elizabeth Chandler** based on the novel *Sara Crewe* by Frances Hodgson Burnett Running Time: **1:38** Rated: **G** Theatrical Aspect Ratio: **1.85:1**

The film is based on the popular 1888 children's book *Sara Crewe* by Frances Hodgson Burnett. This is the third filmed version, following 1917's *A Little Princess* with Mary Pickford and 1939's, which featured Shirley Temple. This new version can more than hold its own in a sea of overly-commercial attempts to grab children's hard-earned money. Unfortunately, since it actually takes the time to develop characters and a story while eschewing explosions, it's unlikely to garner much at the box office. Witness the performance of similar recent films if you doubt that.

The main character is Sara, played delightfully by newcomer Liesel Matthews. The motherless girl has grown up in India, a land where "the air is so hot you can taste it." In fact, the scenes there are filmed with warmth and color to emphasize the beauty as seen through Sara's eyes. The year is 1914, and World War I is in full swing. When Sara's father (played by Liam Cunningham), a British army captain, decides to rejoin his regiment, he deposits Sara in an exclusive girls' school in New York City. Run by the nasty Miss Minchin (Eleanor Bron), this is a place that stifles creativity in favor of etiquette and strict rules. Sara is immediately unhappy there, but her fortunes go from bad to worse when her father is declared dead in Europe and all his assets are seized by the Indian government. Sara is left penniless and forced to work as a servant to earn her keep.

A Little Princess is an engaging tale about self-respect and the importance of imagination. In India, Sara is told that "all girls are princesses," and this is a lesson she clings to when forced to mop floors and serve meals. Even dressed in rags and living in a bare attic room, she is special — and so are all the others around her, regardless of whether they're nice, snobbish, or bossy. Princess or pauper, there's no difference in Sara's eyes.

She also accepts magic. In her father's words, "Magic has to be believed — that's the only way it's real." Her stories about Princess Sita and Prince Rama not only enchant her schoolmates, but they give Sara an escape route once her father has been declared dead. She uses fantasy as a tonic for her bleak reality without ever losing sight of what's happening around her. Together with her friend Becky (Vanessa Lee Chester), she ventures to amazing places without leaving her room. **RECOMMENDED**

Madeline [United States/France, 1998]

Starring: Frances McDormand, Nigel Hawthorne, Hatty Jones, Ben Daniels Director: Daisy von Scherler Mayer Screenplay: Mark Levin & Jennifer Flackett based on the book "Madeline" by Ludwig Bemelmans Running Time: 1:35 Rated: PG (A few mildly scary moments) Theatrical Aspect Ratio: 1.85:1

Madeline is based on the popular series of illustrated children's books by Ludwig Bemelmans, whose first volume, *Madeline,* was written in 1939. The movie version of the tiny heroine's adventures, scripted by husband-and-wife Mark Levin and Jennifer Flackett, incorporates elements from four Madeline tales — "Madeline," "Madeline and the Bad Hat," "Madeline's Rescue," and "Madeline and the Gypsies" — into an entirely new story that is sure to please those familiar with Bemelmans' work and delight those for whom this is a first exposure.

Madeline transpires in Paris during the 1950s, where we're introduced to the sturdy, reliable Miss Clavel (Frances McDormand), a nun who runs a French school for girls. Madeline (Hatty Jones) is the smallest and most outspoken of the 12 children in Miss Clavel's care. Unlike her 11 friends, Madeline is not at the school merely to earn an education — she's an orphan, and Miss Clavel and her friends are the closest thing she has to a family. When the owner of the school, Lady Covington (Stephane Audran), dies, her bereaved husband, Lord Covington (Nigel Hawthorne), decides to sell the house where the girls live and learn. Madeline, unwilling to bear this nasty twist of fate passively, recruits the aide of a local boy troublemaker, Pepito (Kristian De La Osa), in her attempts to fight back.

Director Daisy von Scherler Mayer wisely develops the film in such a way that adults will observe things a little differently than children. For example, grown-ups will see Lord Covington as a sly caricature of British nobility; children will view him as a nasty man determined to take away Madeline's home. It's this kind of layering that makes a movie of this sort a true "family film" rather than 95 minutes with kids-only appeal. Of course, there are sequences, such as one in which Madeline and Pepito seek to foil a kidnapping, that are enjoyed by everyone for the same reason — they're fun and exciting. **RECOMMENDED**

Matilda [1996]

Starring: Mara Wilson, Danny DeVito, Rhea Perlman, Embeth Davidtz Director: Danny DeVito Screenplay: Nicholas Kaza & Robin Swicord, based on the book by Roald Dahl Running Time: 1:33 Rated: PG (Scary situations) Theatrical Aspect Ratio: 2.35:1

Matilda contains numerous elements of traditional fairy tales — a wicked step-aunt, a true friend with a pure heart, and more than a little magic — but "traditional" is about the last word that comes to mind when describing this quirky film. The basic material may seem odd for a family film, dealing as it does with issues of child neglect, abuse, and revenge. By removing the story from conventional reality, however, director Danny DeVito pulls it off. This is a world where adults (except two) are bad and children (except one) are good. It's a place where television is a force of mind-numbing evil and where books represent escape and solace. And, most importantly, empowerment is genuine, not just a slogan.

Matilda (Mara Wilson) is the youngest child, and only daughter, of Harry and Zinia Wormwood (Danny DeVito and Rhea Perlman), who are described as living "in a very nice neighborhood in a very nice house," but not being very nice people. Mr. Wormwood is a used car salesman with the police tracking his every move, and Mrs. Wormwood is obsessed with bingo parlors and television game shows. Both parents are extremely neglectful of their little 6½-year-old daughter, even though she shows signs of amazing intelligence and various remarkable powers.

Eventually, Mr. Wormwood notices his daughter long enough to send her off to Crunchem Hall, an elementary school lorded over by the ogre-like Miss Trunchbull (Pam Ferris), whose motto is "Use the rod, beat the child." She practices what she preaches, taking delight in punishing her charges and informing them mercilessly that her idea of a perfect school is one where there are no children. Fortunately for Matilda, her 1st grade teacher, Miss Honey (Embeth Davidtz), is kind and good-hearted, and immediately recognizes her new student's amazing gifts.

Matilda is not politically correct — it is, after all, a pint-sized revenge fantasy — but, in this case, that's a definite plus. Besides, for those who want bland, "wholesome" family entertainment, there's always Disney. Children aren't likely to understand much of the black comedy and satire here, but they'll be so involved in the story that they won't notice that a lot is going over their heads. Hardly a moment of *Matilda* can be described as either juvenile or condescending, and, compared with many of this summer's so-called "mature" features, that makes for a delightfully refreshing change-of-pace. RECOMMENDED

The Mighty [1998]

Starring: Elden Henson, Kieran Culkin, Sharon Stone, Gena Rowlands, Harry Dean Stanton Director: Peter Chelsom Screenplay: Charles Leavitt, based on the book *Freak the Mighty* by Rodman Philbrick Running Time: 1:46 Rated: PG-13 (Mild violence, mild profanity) Theatrical Aspect Ratio: 1.85:1

The Mighty, which is based on the book *Freak The Mighty* by Rodman Philbrick, tells the story of two phenomenally mismatched children who complement each other so well that, together, they form one complete (not to mention formidable) individual.

The film's narrator, Max Kane (Elden Henson), is a hulking 7th-grader who makes up for his limited intellectual prowess with an imposing physical presence. But, because Max is a gentle giant — slow to anger and even slower to retaliate — he has become the target of taunts and teasing. But that all changes when Kevin Dillon (Kieran Culkin) moves in next door. Kevin is Max's opposite: frail in form, but a giant in intelligence. Crippled by a disease that eats away at his body, Kevin has devoted himself to developing a powerful world of imagination where he is a knight in King Arthur's court and the braces on his legs do not affect his ability to do great deeds (slay dragons and save damsels). Now, in concert with Max, these things become possible in the real world, even if the dragons are just local bullies and the damsels are not maidens of virtue.

At the center of *The Mighty* is the friendship between Max and Kevin, two constant outsiders who discover the joy of finding someone else in the same predicament. Their relationship is presented with such insight and sensitivity that we feel the strength of their bond. The film is also a salute to the power of imagination and creativity. Kevin introduces Max to his magical world of the mind, and soon both boys are employing it as a refuge. They do not use it as a means of denying reality, but as a way to help them struggle through the most difficult times. Reassured that they are Knights of the Round Table, and knowing that "a knight proves his worthiness through his deeds," each can face his most daunting opponent.

Although the list of good, live-action family features is small, the list of great ones is microscopic. *The Mighty* deserves a place on the exclusive roster of the latter. Seeing a film like this does more than simply entertain; it fills the viewer with optimism that the future of motion pictures might not be as bleak as it sometimes seems. If something like *The Mighty* can be produced, then the monsters haven't yet won, and the knights still have a chance. HIGHLY RECOMMENDED

Muppet Treasure Island [1996]

Starring: Tim Curry, Kevin Bishop, Kermit the Frog, The Great Gonzo, Rizzo Rat, Fozzie Bear, Miss Piggy Director: Brian Henson Screenplay: Kirk R. Thatcher, Jenny Juhl, and James V. Hart, based on the novel by Robert Louis Stevenson Running Time: 1:39 Rated: G Theatrical Aspect Ratio: 1.85:1

There have been over a half-dozen movie adaptations of Robert Louis Stevenson's *Treasure Island.* Of course, none before now have featured singing crocodiles, warbling lobsters, talking frogs, and high-kicking pigs. As usual, a few human actors get in on the fun, including Tim Curry and Kevin Bishop. *Muppet Treasure Island* doesn't exactly re-invent the classic story, but it takes a few liberties with it. Young Jim Hawkins (Bishop) is on board the ship of Captain Smollett (Kermit the Frog), bound for the Caribbean and buried pirates' treasure. The crew, a mutinous group of thugs and cutthroats, are led by the one-legged bandit Long John Silver (Tim Curry). Once land is sighted, Silver makes his power-play, nabbing Jim and his treasure map and seizing control of the ship. The only obstacle still remaining between the rogue and unlimited wealth is an army of wild boars and their leader, Benjamina Gunn (Miss Piggy).

One of the chief pleasures of *Muppet Treasure Island* is watching Tim Curry essay Long John Silver. Curry, who no one would ever call subtle, creates one of the most memorable human characters in any Muppet film. Kevin Bishop makes an appealing Jim Hawkins, the young protagonist in search of a family. Jennifer Saunders and Billy Connolly have suitably overt-the-top cameos.

As has always been true in Muppet movies, set design is superb. *Muppet Treasure Island* is an impressive-looking motion picture, rich in color and contrast, and featuring some impeccable matte paintings. There are the usual musical numbers — seven jaunty tunes that will be forgotten the moment you leave the theater. They may not be memorable, but at least they're not irritating.

There have been many great on-screen/off-screen couples — Bogart and Becall, Tracy and Hepburn, Branagh and Thompson — but none are quite as intriguing as Kermit and Piggy. A match made in Jim Henson's workshop, these two have gone through some tough times in the last 20 years, but they have endured. And, although they don't have many scenes together in *Muppet Treasure Island* (Piggy doesn't show up until the film is 2/3 over), it's clear that the chemistry is still there. RECOMMENDED

The Pagemaster [1994]

Starring: Macaulay Culkin, Christopher Lloyd, Ed Begley Jr., Mel Harris
Directors: Maurice Hunt (animation) and Joe Johnston (live action)
Screenplay: David Casci, David Kirschner & Ernie Contreras Running
Time: 1:16 Rated: G Theatrical Aspect Ratio: 1.85:1

At a time when children are reading less, opting instead for such fast, furious, and empty entertainment as video games and MTV, it falls to a movie, *The Pagemaster*, to make the case for books. This clever, often engaging, and always fast-paced motion picture uses the visual medium to encourage its viewers to reach out with their imagination. They may not be as visibly transformed as Macaulay Culkin's Richard Tyler, but through the magic of page-turning, they can enter different worlds — or at least that's the message this release is trying to convey.

Richard Tyler is a child with so many phobias that they've run out of names for them all. His father (Ed Begley Jr.) despairs that his son will ever shed his cloak of fear, especially when Richard's response to an invitation to climb into a tree house is that he can't because "7% of all accidents involve ladders." So, instead of joining Dad up in the branches, Richard is sent off to the store on a quest for a box of nails. Instead, he finds something he never dreamed possible.

Along the way, a sudden thunderstorm necessitates Richard to seek shelter in the nearest building — a mysterious library run by the prescient Mr. Dewey, aka The Pagemaster (Christopher Lloyd). During his stay amidst the thousands of books, Richard is transformed into a cartoon character and forced to make his way through several lands of fiction, guided by a trio of genres-come-to-life: adventure (voice of Patrick Stewart, lustily belting out his lines like a refugee from *Pirates of the Caribbean*), fantasy (Whoopi Goldberg, all sugar-and-starch), and horror (Frank Welker, doing his best "Igor" imitation).

Titles as diverse as *Atlas Shrugged, Dr. Jekyll and Mr. Hyde, Treasure Island, Moby Dick, Gulliver's Travels, Alice in Wonderland,* and *Jack and the Beanstalk* are either alluded to or represented. If the sight of Culkin's animated image making his way through these adventures isn't enough to pique the reading curiosity of the average youngster, it's hard to imagine what will.

With its plain sense of fun, *The Pagemaster* represents the least-annoying and most enjoyable contribution Culkin has made to the industry since *Home Alone*. Grownups who often feel insulted by the too-juvenile tone of most so-called "family features" will likely find this movie long enough to catch their attention, but short enough not to lose it — in essence, a surprisingly affable (and occasionally even sophisticated) movie-going experience. RECOMMENDED

The Secret Garden [United Kingdom/United States, 1993]

Starring: Kate Maberly, Heydon Prowse, Andrew Knott, Maggie Smith,
John Lynch Director: Agnieszka Holland Screenplay: Caroline
Thompson, based on the novel by Frances Hodgson Burnett Running
Time: 1:39 Rated: G Theatrical Aspect Ratio: 1.85:1

Orphaned in India, where her transplanted English parents lived before falling victim to an earthquake,

Mary Lennox (Kate Maberly) comes to the cold, aloof household of her uncle, the widower of her mother's twin sister. There, she is viewed as a meddlesome nuisance by the housekeeper, Mrs. Medlock (Maggie Smith), and is ordered to stay in her room. Mary doesn't obey, of course, and, during one of her unauthorized explorations, she discovers the room of her sickly cousin, Colin (Heydon Prowse). Outside, she finds something even more wondrous: the secret garden of her late aunt. With the help of Dickon (Andrew Knott), a local boy who can talk with animals, Mary sets to work reclaiming the garden from the weeds and brambles that had overrun it.

The Secret Garden is based on Frances Hodgson Burnett's 1911 novel, and director Agnieszka Holland has taken care that the screenplay follows the book. Holland is an avowed fan of the story, having read it over and over again as a child. The care and effort she poured into this, her first English-language effort, is proof enough of that, resulting in a picture that is magical for viewers of all ages.

The story is essentially about the redemption of two damaged children. Mary, while hale of body, is an emotional cripple. She grew up unloved in a household where her selfish parents handed her off to the servants. Colin is neither physically nor emotionally whole. His father, never having recovered from the death of his wife, rarely visits Colin in the sickroom, leaving the boy's care to the implacable and unaffectionate Mrs. Medlock. The secret garden is a place of rare and wondrous beauty, and it becomes the emotional balm that heals all wounds, both physical and psychological.

I'm not sure how younger viewers will react to this film. Many will miss the subtle nuances that Agnieszka Holland brings to the screen (which are aimed at adults), but the story, centering as it does around children, will captivate many. By any standard, this is an excellent family film for those willing to immerse themselves in its leisurely pace — the picture proceeds just fast enough to keep the audience's attention while exhibiting a great attention to detail. RECOMMENDED

Shiloh [1997]

Starring: Blake Heron, Michael Moriarty, Scott Wilson, Ann Dowd, J. Madison Wright, Rod Steiger Director: Dale Rosenbloom
Screenplay: Dale Rosenbloom, based on the novel by Phyllis Reynolds Naylor Running Time: 1:33 Rated: PG (Mild violence) Theatrical Aspect Ratio: 1.85:1

I have never been a big fan of "animal in danger" tales, but *Shiloh* is far better than most. Not only does it show the animal, a 1-year-old beagle, being abused (although not graphically), but it doesn't turn the dog into some sort of living cartoon character. Likewise, the young protagonist, 11-year-old Marty Preston (Blake Heron), doesn't have all the answers and isn't constantly outsmarting his parents. And the film's villain, Judd Travers (Scott Wilson), isn't just inherently evil — there's a legitimate reason why he's so nasty, as Marty comes to find out during the movie's second half.

Shiloh takes place in the tiny town of Friendly, West Virginia. It's a lazy summer and Marty is wandering around town looking for odd jobs to earn a little cash. On his way home one day, he encounters a beagle with a cut over its eye. It follows him, and Marty, a loner by nature, develops an immediate attachment to the injured animal. He even gives it a name — Shiloh — after the bridge where he encountered it. His father (Michael Moriarty) recognizes Shiloh as the new hunting dog of the reclusive Judd Travers, and Marty reluctantly agrees to return it, even though he suspects Judd of mistreating the animal. Several days later, Shiloh again runs away from Judd, and this time, when the dog seeks him out, Marty decides not to tell his parents. So, with the help of his friend Samantha (J. Madison Wright), he hides the beagle in a fort and sneaks food to it every night. But it's only a matter of time before someone else learns his secret.

The strength of *Shiloh* is that it approaches its subject matter intelligently. There are no easy answers to Marty's dilemma — the Law is on Judd's side, but the boy believes his position is morally defensible. At one point, when his father accuses him of not doing the right thing, Marty's response is a simple question: "What's right?" Later, the kindhearted town doctor (played by Rod Steiger) tells him that if he wants to keep Shiloh, he may be forced to fight for the dog.

Shiloh, which is adapted from a Newberry Award winning book, fits nicely into the class of better animal-related family films, joining the ranks of *Lassie* and *Black Beauty*. And, while the primary target audience is undeniably children, few adults who sit through this motion picture will wish they had done otherwise. RECOMMENDED

Small Soldiers [1998]

Starring: Gregory Smith, Kirsten Dunst, Kevin Dunn, Phil Hartman, Denis Leary, Ann Magnuson Director: Joe Dante Screenplay: Ted

Elliot, Zak Penn, Adam Rifkin, Terry Rossio, Gavin Scott Running Time: 1:48 Rated: PG-13 (Action figure violence, mild profanity) Theatrical Aspect Ratio: 2.35:1

Critics often say that a movie works on multiple levels, and never has this been more true than with Joe Dante's *Small Soldiers*, a veritable treasure-trove of in-jokes and sly humor that will go over the heads of most children. Of course, missing that aspect of the film won't prevent anyone from enjoying the action/adventure and special effects elements. A sort of *Gremlins* meets *Toy Story*, this picture investigates what might happen if a group of homicidal, xenophobic commando action figures were able to move around on their own. As absurd as the premise might seem, *Small Soldiers* works for two primary reasons: the visual effects are entirely convincing and the script never takes its tongue out of its cheek.

The weakest aspect of *Small Soldiers* is the back story, which isn't all that convincing. *Small Soldiers* opens in the offices of Hartland Play Systems, a toy company that has just been acquired by Globotech, a conglomerate specializing in military contracts. Globotech's owner and CEO, Gil Mars (Denis Leary), wants Hartland to come up with a revolutionary new toy. So designers Larry Benson (Jay Mohr) and Irwin Wayfair (David Cross) create a series of foot-high soldiers and monsters containing a computer chip that allows them to move and speak on their own. There is a problem, however — the chip is a top-secret military release that allows artificial intelligence and encourages potentially violent behavior.

Cut to small-town America, where teenager Alan Abernathy (Gregory Smith), who is temporarily running his father's toy store, receives a shipment of "The Commando Elite" and their enemies, "The Gorgonites." Before they are placed on display, the toys escape from their boxes. The militant commandos, led by the grizzled veteran Chip Hazard (voice of Tommy Lee Jones), declare war on the gentle-but-hideous Gorgonites and their leader, Archer (voice of Frank Langella). Alan, his would-be girlfriend, Christy (Kirsten Dunst), and the kids' parents involuntarily become involved in the battles between these tiny opponents.

Although *Small Soldiers* lacks the simple brilliance and magic of *Toy Story*, it works for many of the same reasons, chief of which is the human fascination with toys and gadgets. The film treads a fine line between cartoonish and excessive violence, and finds the best compromise by limiting the most graphic images to the bloodless dismemberment and evisceration of plastic action figures. Through it all, Dante maintains a sense of humor that is neither too sophisticated for children nor too juvenile for adults. The result is a fine piece of entertainment for all but the youngest viewers. RECOMMENDED

Spy Kids [2001]

Starring: Antonio Banderas, Carla Gugino, Alexa Vega, Alan Cumming, Daryl Sabara Director: Robert Rodriguez Screenplay: Robert Rodriguez Running Time: 1:28 Rated: PG (Violence) Theatrical Aspect Ratio: 1.85:1

The storyline isn't terribly complex, and the movie develops in a cartoonish, tongue-in-cheek fashion that promises never to take anything too seriously. *Spy Kids* isn't exactly a parody, but it doesn't mind occasionally poking fun at staples of the espionage genre. Gregorio and Ingrid Cortez (Antonio Banderas and Carla Gugino) are retired spies who gave up their secret agent duties to act as "consultants" while raising two kids: Carmen (Alexa Vega) and Juni (Daryl Sabara). But Gregorio and Ingrid still have adventure in their blood, and, when a mission calls, they can't resist. Unfortunately, they're rusty, and end up being captured by the diabolical Fegan Floop (Alan Cumming), a children's TV show host who is planning to use an army of robot children to take over the world. So it's Carmen and Juni to the rescue. After paying their dour Uncle Machete (Danny Trejo) a visit, they load up on cool gadgets and head for Floop's castle to save their mom and dad.

One common failing of the generic family film is to make everyone over the age of 12 terminally stupid. Another is to make the child protagonists either (a) unbearably cute or (b) irritatingly obnoxious. These are pitfalls that Rodriguez consciously avoids. Carmen and Juni are cute, likable kids — but not too cute or cloyingly likable. And, although the adults are occasionally prone to doing dumb things, they are presented sympathetically. They're not all ogres with pea-sized brains, à la the crooks in *Home Alone*.

The film moves at a brisk pace that never threatens to bog down. In addition to the humor, which surfaces on a consistent basis, there's a lot of adventure and action. Several of the creatures living in Floop's castle look like refugees from the *Star Wars* cantina, and there is a race of human-sized thumbs that are, predictably, clumsy ("all thumbs"). Since the film was made on a modest budget, digital effects were used liberally to spruce up the look. Their incorporation is sometimes a little too obvious, but there are times when they work. There are also numerous neat gadgets — everything from a super-fast, single-passenger spy plane to bubble gum that packs a real punch.

For Robert Rodriguez, who began his career with great promise as the hotshot director of *El Mariachi*, it has been a while since he has been embraced by the critics or the public. *Spy Kids* proves that he can be as adept at the family genre as he is at making ultra-gory revenge and horror films. With this charming and unpretentious effort, Rodriguez has successfully put the "family" back into the term "family film." **RECOMMENDED**

Spy Kids 2: The Island of Lost Dreams [2002]
Starring: Antonio Banderas, Carla Gugino, Alexa Vega, Daryl Sabara, Steve Buscemi Director: Robert Rodriguez Screenplay: Robert Rodriguez Running Time: 1:38 Rated: PG (Cartoon violence, mild profanity) Theatrical Aspect Ratio: 1.85:1

With his tongue planted firmly in his cheek, Robert Rodriguez sets out to lampoon the spy genre while still providing a breezy, fast-paced ride full of bumps and jolts. The movie has the sensibility of a cartoon, with larger-than-life bad guys, a thoroughly implausible plot, and enough nifty gadgets and vehicles to impress Q.

Once again, our heroes are Carmen Cortez (Alexa Vega) and her younger brother, Juni (Daryl Sabara). They are the children of ace spies Gregorio and Ingrid Cortez (Antonio Banderas and Carla Gugino) and the grandchildren of two legendary agents (Ricardo Montalban and Holland Taylor). As the film begins, Carmen and Juni, now junior members of the OSS, are out to save the President's daughter, Alexandra (Taylor Momsen), who is in danger at an extreme amusement park. Rival spy kids Gary and Gerti Giggles (Matthew O'Leary and Emily — sister of Haley Joel — Osment) arrive in time to complicate the rescue. But this is only a prelude to the real adventure. Soon, all 4 kids end up on a mysterious island, fighting bizarre creatures while looking for the mysterious Romero (Steve Buscemi) and his dangerous creation, the "Transmooger Device," which can be used to control (or destroy) the world.

Boiled down to its basics, *Spy Kids 2* is just good, clean fun. It works as well for kids as it does for adults, due in large part to two things: (1) its refusal to talk down to the audience, and (2) an unflagging pace. There are opportunities for character expansion — Carmen has a "thing" for Gary, Juni develops a crush

on the President's daughter, and Gregorio has to deal with insecurities regarding his in-laws and the consideration that his son may be outgrowing him. And, as a mad scientist creator, Romero finds himself asking surprisingly deep philosophical questions like, "Do you think God stays in heaven because he fears what he has created?"

Spy Kids 2 is a worthy successor to the original, and an enjoyable romp in its own right. **RECOMMENDED**

Stuart Little [United States, 1999]
Starring: Geena Davis, Hugh Laurie, Jonathan Lipnicki, Michael J. Fox (voice), Nathan Lane (voice) Director: Rob Minkoff Screenplay: Gregory J. Brooker and M. Night Shayamalan, based on the book by E.B. White Running Time: 1:20 Rated: PG (Mild profanity, mouse in danger) Theatrical Aspect Ratio: 1.85:1

Stuart Little has been inspired by E.B. White's book, a classic that almost every child is familiar with. The picture is quiet, gentle, and family-friendly — 3 qualities that rarely apply to the form of entertainment that kids crave. The story begins in a New York City orphanage, where Mr. And Mrs. Little (Hugh Laurie and Geena Davis) have come to adopt a baby brother for their only son, George (Jonathan Lipnicki). However, while observing the children at play, their attention is arrested by a mouse (voice of Michael J. Fox) who approaches them and offers tips about which girls and boys might make the best daughters or sons. When it comes time to make a choice, the Littles select the mouse and name him Stuart. George is at first unimpressed, but, after a few false starts, he bonds with his "brother." The only one displeased by the new arrival is the cat, Snowbell (voice of Nathan Lane), who is upset by the idea of being placed lower in the family pecking order than someone who should be below him on the food chain. So Snowbell enlists the aid of a pair of other felines: the hyperactive Monty (voice of Steve Zahn) and the dangerous Smokey (voice of Chazz Palminteri). Together, the 3 of them plan a way to "scratch" Stuart from the Little family album.

Stuart Little is not a film of great performances, but it is one of subtle-but-impressive special effects. Without a doubt, Stuart is the most real and sympathetic character in the film. From a visual standpoint, he is also consistently believable. Equally impressive are the cats. One of the reasons for this is that, at least most of the time, Snowbell, Monty, and Smokey are living, breathing animals, but the manipulation of their mouths (when they talk) is executed flawlessly.

The vocal talents fit into the category of "familiar,

but not necessarily recognizable without a credits list." Another high-profile name involved with the project is M. Night Shyamalan, who co-wrote the screenplay. (Shyamalan is, of course, a suddenly hot property in the wake of the success of *The Sixth Sense*, which he wrote and directed.) Of course, all of this talent would mean little if the final product wasn't worthwhile, but, in the case of *Stuart Little*, the results are favorable. Hopefully, parents and children seeking theatrical fare will give this movie a chance before seeking out something that's louder, flashier, and lobotomized. **RECOMMENDED**

Stuart Little 2 [2002]

Starring: Geena Davis, Hugh Laurie, Jonathan Lipnicki, Michael J. Fox (voice), Nathan Lane (voice) Director: Rob Minkoff Screenplay: Bruce Joel Rubin Running Time: 1:16 Rated: PG (Mildly frightening images) Theatrical Aspect Ratio: 1.85:1

Stuart Little 2 brings back all of the elements that made its predecessor so successful, including most of the original cast (both live-action and computer generated) and director Rob Minkoff. The screenplay, freed from the constraints of having to introduce everyone, can go off in more interesting directions. In this case, the story involves a wounded bird befriended by Stuart and a dangerous falcon who is hunting her. There are also issues of sibling separation, or what happens when the older child outgrows the younger one and starts spending more time with his school friends. This is a theme that many children, and more than a few adults, will be able to relate to: the point at which the younger brother or sister ceases to be a playmate and starts to be a pest. (In this case, however, Stuart literally is a "pest," although no one refers to him in those terms.)

The talking animals are all back, and the digital technology that allows their lips to seemingly move is as effective as it was 3 years ago. Michael J. Fox picks up where he left off providing the voice of the lead character. Nathan Lane returns as the scene-stealing Snowball, the Littles' disgruntled cat. (About 90% of the best lines all go to Snowball, and Lane utters them with relish.) Newcomers include James Woods as the dangerous Falcon and Melanie Griffith as Margalo, Stuart's new flying friend. The live-action actors are Geena Davis and Hugh Laurie as Stuart's mom and dad, and Jonathan Lipnicki as George Little.

As was true of the first film, the special effects will have kids thinking Stuart and Margalo are real. Indeed, the computer animators went to great lengths to put a lot of the real actions of mice and birds into the way the characters look and act. Meanwhile, the humans are unreal, taking everything in with a cheerful seriousness that pokes gentle fun at old TV programs like *Father Knows Best* and *My Three Sons*. And no one thinks its odd that George's little brother is actually a mouse. Watching the blasé reactions of everyone to a talking mouse is worth a smile and a chuckle, but that's only one of many reasons to see, and enjoy, *Stuart Little 2*. **RECOMMENDED**

Tuck Everlasting [2002]

Starring: Jonathan Jackson, Alexis Bledel, Ben Kingsley, Sissy Spacek, William Hurt Director: Jay Russell Screenplay: Jeffrey Lieber & James V. Hart, based on the novel by Natalie Babbitt Running Time: 1:29 Rated: PG (Mature themes) Theatrical Aspect Ratio: 2.35:1

"Do you want to live forever?" That question has become a prominent "payoff" line for movies and television shows, but, underneath the flip tone in which it is often asked hides a query that expresses humankind's greatest longing — immortality. The first reaction of most people when asked that question would be to answer "yes." After all, immortality (with invulnerability and eternal youth thrown in at no extra charge) is a heady possibility. Unquestionably a blessing . . . or is it? Think about the price. It's not immediately apparent, but it is an unpleasant one. Never dying means *never*. Life will go on and on and on, until, inevitably, one is almost guaranteed to wish and hope and pray for some way to end it all.

No one asked the Tuck family if they wanted to live forever. In the early years of the 19th century, they came upon a small spring in the woods in upstate New York. Unbeknownst to them, it was the fountain of youth — the water for which Ponce de Leon had so aggressively sought. Drinking froze all 4 Tucks at their current ages. The parents, Mae and Angus (Sissy Spacek and William Hurt), remained middle-aged but spry. Miles (Scott Bairstow) was trapped in the prime of his life. And Jesse (Jonathan Jackson) was fated to exist through eternity in a 17-year-old body.

Nearly 100 years later, on the eve of the United States' entrance into the Great War, a teenage girl, Winnie Foster (Alexis Bledel), stumbles upon the Tucks' house while running away from home. After living with the Tucks for a while, Winnie learns their secret. Meanwhile, she and Jesse fall in love. Then she must face a choice — drink from the fountain and gain the promise of everlasting life and love with Jesse, or refuse and live for the normal span of human years.

The romantic aspect of *Tuck Everlasting*, which is

clearly the element that will attract pre-teen and teenage girls, is nicely developed, although it follows the familiar arc of the overprotected rich girl falling for the poor, free-spirited boy. For younger viewers, the immortality question probably won't mean much, but, for those who have lived long enough, it represents the film's true strength. We know from early in the proceedings that Winnie will have to choose — and it won't be an easy choice.

Viewed on its own terms, this is a gently engaging and thought-provoking motion picture. *Tuck Everlasting* is suitable for children, but the material is designed more for those with longer attention spans. The cartoonish buffoonery and mindless action of many family films is entirely absent. Disney's live-action division has a history of releasing cinematic flotsam, but this is one occasion when they have unearthed a rare gem. **HIGHLY RECOMMENDED**

Horror

An American Werewolf in London [United States/ United Kingdom, 1981]

Starring: David Naughton, Griffin Dunne, Jenny Agutter
Director: John Landis Screenplay: John Landis Running Time: 1:37
Rated: R (Violence, gore, nudity, sex, profanity) Theatrical Aspect Ratio: 1.85:1

In terms of storyline and plot structure, there's nothing new or surprising about *An American Werewolf in London*. What makes this film different (if not unique) is its successful marriage of comedy and horror. The humorous sequences are funny enough to laugh at, while the gruesome scenes retain the power to shock. From time-to-time, director John Landis strays close to the line of camp, but never quite crosses over. This is in large part due to our identification with the main character, whom we hope against hope will find some way out of an impossible predicament.

The movie opens in the wild countryside of North England, where 2 Americans, David Kessler (David Naughton) and Jack Goodman (Griffin Dunne), are on a backpacking trip. By the time they reach a small village near the onset of nightfall, they are cold and hungry, so they decide to stop in at the local pub, a place with the odd and ominous name of "The Slaughtered Lamb." Their reception there is decidedly frosty, with angry glares from the patrons and the barmaid. After they ask one too many questions, they are rudely told to leave, although, before departing, they are given a warning to stick to the road and not wander onto the moors — a warning they ignore, much to their regret.

When it comes, the attack is swift and merciless. A huge, wolf-like creatures leaps from the shadows, killing Jack and injuring David before several of the townspeople, armed with guns, subdue it. The next thing David knows, he is recovering in a London hospital under the tender ministrations of an attractive nurse named Alex Price (Jenny Agutter) and the pragmatic Dr. Hirsch (John Woodvine). Despite a series of harrowing nightmares, David seems to be progressing — until he receives an unsettling visit from his zombified friend, Jack, who informs him that he has become one of the walking dead and that David, on the night of the next full moon, will exhibit the curse of lycanthropy and be transformed into a werewolf.

Over the years, there have been so many bad werewolf movies that one is almost tempted to disbelief one's eyes when the rare good one comes along. For atmosphere and effect, *An American Werewolf in London* doesn't match the classic *The Wolf Man*, but it's the earlier film's equal in many other areas. Considering its often campy competition, it's hard to argue that, if your in the mood for lycanthropy, London is the place to go. (Avoid Paris, however. The sequel is a horrible bust.) **RECOMMENDED**

Army of Darkness [1993]

Starring: Bruce Campbell, Embeth Davidz, Marcus Gilbert
Director: Sam Raimi Screenplay: Sam & Ivan Raimi Running Time: 1:21
Rated: R (Violence, gore, language) Theatrical Aspect Ratio: 1.85:1

Ash (Bruce Campbell) is a housewares salesman at an S-Mart department store before a venture to the house from *Evil Dead 1* and *2* sends him through a time tunnel into the Middle Ages. Suddenly, as the "Promised One" of prophesy, he is expected to save the locals from an upsurge in evil. Armed with a chainsaw and a 12-gauge shotgun, Ash sets out to put down an army of skeletons and woo one of the locals (Sheila, played by Embeth Davidz), all the while trying to find a way back home.

Army of Darkness is openly campy — and proud of it — blending a unique mix of horror, swords-and-sorcery, and the Three Stooges. Bruce Campbell, returning after the two *Evil Dead* films, is in top form, delivering ridiculous lines with a deadpan seriousness that would make Leslie Nielsen take notice. As the reluctant hero, he's a walking anachronism who shoots up ghouls, turns his Chevy into a tank, and can't remember how to pronounce a series of magic words that pay homage to Robert Wise's *The Day the Earth Stood Still*.

There are some very memorable Three Stooges-type moments, complete with sound effects (pops, zings, and so forth). There's eye-poking, headshaking, and other slapstick standards. What makes these moments especially bizarre — and effective — is that most of the time, Larry, Curly, and Moe are represented by ghouls and animated skeletons. Every ounce of fat has been trimmed from this production. It's a comic book brought to life, with no time for characterization, exposition, or subplots. *Army of Darkness* moves with breakneck speed, but its direction is straight, so there's little chance of anyone getting lost on the way. Those who like this kind of thing — lots of action and gore, silly dialogue, over-the-top acting, and a self-mocking campiness that permeates all eighty-one minutes — will love this movie. Anyone who prefers a more "traditional" motion picture will probably do best to stay away. Then again, you never know . . . **RECOMMENDED**

Beloved [1998]

Starring: Oprah Winfrey, Danny Glover, Thandie Newton, Kimberly Elise Director: Jonathan Demme Screenplay: Adam Brooks, Akosua Busia, Richard LaGravanese, based on the novel by Toni Morrison Running Time: 2:55 Rated: R (Violence, sexual violence, frontal nudity, sex) Theatrical Aspect Ratio: 1.85:1

Beloved, Jonathan Demme's much-anticipated adaptation of Toni Morrison's novel, is a powerful and disturbing motion picture that is likely to leave many movie-goers unsettled as they file out of the theater. *Beloved* is a ghost tale. It's about a woman's sins literally coming back to haunt her. The main story transpires in Ohio during 1865, but there are numerous flashbacks to pre-Civil War times. Like many other motion pictures set during this era, *Beloved* is about the pernicious influence of slavery, but the approach taken by Morrison's novel attains its uncommon power through originality. Some of what happens in *Beloved*, you will expect. Other things, you will not.

The film opens on a peaceful summer afternoon in Ohio, when a lonely traveler named Paul D (Danny Glover) arrives at the house at 124 Bluestone Road. Living there is Sethe (Oprah Winfrey), a woman Paul D knew many years ago when they were both slaves on a Kentucky farm named Sweet Home. ("It wasn't sweet and it wasn't home.") Sethe is not alone in her house. Her daughter, Denver (Kimberly Elise), a virtual shut-in, also lives there. However, her 2 sons have long since gone, scared away by the ghost of another child that haunts the premises. ("It ain't evil, just sad.") No sooner has Paul D arrived than he meets the spirit, and, in a struggle of wills, appears to dispel it. But Denver doubts his success, thinking that the dead baby is planning something.

Soon after, Paul D, now Sethe's lover, has moved in, and is setting his sights on winning Denver's trust. One afternoon, on the way back from a carnival, Denver and Sethe encounter a nearly-mute young woman (Thandie Newton) who has been overcome by heat exhaustion. They bring her home and revive her. The only name she gives them is "Beloved." Thereafter, Denver makes Beloved her special project, teaching her things about life, and how to speak. But, while Denver and Sethe are infatuated with this strange, wild woman, Paul D is suspicious. Something about Beloved strikes him as dangerous.

Beloved is one of those films that won't work for someone in search of light entertainment. The movie deals with difficult subjects without flinching or sugar-coating the truth. *Beloved* is for those who want substance from a movie, and don't mind facing uncomfortable truths in the process. **HIGHLY RECOMMENDED**

Below [2002]

Starring: Matt Davis, Bruce Greenwood, Holt McCallany, Olivia Williams Director: David Twohy Screenplay: Lucas Sussman, Darren Aranofsky and David Twohy Running Time: 2:55 Rated: R (Violence, profanity) Theatrical Aspect Ratio: 1.85:1

Although it's hard to imagine a better match than ghosts and submarines, this story has never previously been told. Consider all of the natural claustrophobia and tension inherent in a movie about men trapped in the bowels of a submerged sub, and add in the possibility that the boat might be haunted. The result would seem to be the formula for a superior horror/thriller. And, while director David Twohy arguably doesn't mine the premise for all it's worth, he gets enough out of it to make it an effective Halloween treat.

The film, which transpires during World War II, begins with a rescue mission, as the crew of the *Tiger Shark* brings on board 3 survivors of a torpedoed British hospital ship. All is not well aboard the *Tiger Shark,* however. Morale has been at a low ebb since the death of the captain. The current commander, Lt. Brice (Bruce Greenwood), seems unsure of his position. When the *Tiger Shark* is attacked soon after the British are brought on board, Brice reacts by accusing a female nurse, Claire (Olivia Williams), of being a collaborator. Ensign Douglas O'Dell (Matt Davis) watches all of this transpire with unease, sensing that Brice may know more about the captain's death than he is willing to acknowledge. Meanwhile, supernatural occurrences begin plaguing the boat, starting with a record player that turns itself on at will.

Twohy understands the importance of atmosphere, and allows it to suffuse *Below*. Nearly every scene is shot in dim lighting, and the camera moves in such a way that we think, but are not certain, that something out-of-the-ordinary is happening. There are a few "boo!" moments, but not as many as there could have been. Twohy uses sound to good effect, as the men trapped in the sub hear the eerie, expected echoes of whale songs and sonar pings, as well as some chilling noises that they cannot identify.

Below is a psychological horror movie that emphasizes tension over the macabre. And, in the end, the protagonists must determine whether they have more to fear from the spirits haunting the sub, the Germans prowling the waters above, or the men who will do almost anything to keep their secrets buried. **RECOMMENDED**

The Blair Witch Project [1999]
Starring: Heather Donahue, Michael Williams, Joshua Leonard Directors: **Eduardo Sanchez and Daniel Myrick** Screenplay: **Eduardo Sanchez & Daniel Myrick** Running Time: 1:27 Rated: R (Profanity, terror) Theatrical Aspect Ratio: **1.33:1 & 1.66:1**

The Blair Witch Project is, in a word, brilliant — and is even more impressive considering that it's the debut effort from filmmakers Eduardo Sanchez and Daniel Myrick. Watching this film is a harrowing experience because we accept the characters as completely real and become engaged in their ordeal. In one corner of my mind, I knew this was all fictional, but the verisimilitude is impressive, and results in an experience that is as fascinating as it is involving and creepy.

The Blair Witch Project is presented as a documentary within a documentary. Aspiring director Heather Donahue, a film student at Montgomery College, has decided to chronicle the legend of the supposed "Blair Witch" — a mythical figure that has supposedly haunted Maryland's Black Hills Forest since the late 18th century and is credited for numerous, heinous murders. Accompanying Heather are camera man Joshua Leonard and sound operator Michael Williams. In addition to making a 16mm black-and-white film, Heather is capturing virtually everything on High 8 video with the intention of assembling a behind-the-scenes look at how her movie, "The Blair Witch Project," was made.

The element that makes *The Blair Witch Project* unusually compelling is the atypical manner in which it is presented. Every scene is a point-of-view shot, shown exactly as one might expect from someone carrying around a video camera. The transitions are unexpected and often jarring — the kind of thing that would result from turning the camera off at one point, then turning it back on later. Some of the most chilling sequences occur at night, when the darkness foils the video. There are instances when the screen is black and all we have to rely on is the audio — the near-panicked voices of the protagonists in the foreground and strange, unearthly noises in the background. At other times, the action depicted is chaotic and difficult to piece together, often because the person doing the filming is running or unsure what to capture.

It's not hard to understand why these segments work so well — they rely on the imagination to fill in the pictures, and what our minds conjure up is always more horrifying than anything the filmmakers can put on screen. Also, this seemingly haphazard and "unprofessional" approach gives the audience a "you are there" feeling that draws them into the experience, making everything that transpires more shocking and immediate that it would seem in a conventional format. Sanchez and Myrick deserve credit not only for attempting something different, but for succeeding so brilliantly at it. **HIGHLY RECOMMENDED**

The Evil Dead [1982]
Starring: Bruce Campbell, Ellen Sandweiss, Hal Delrich, Betsy Baker, Sarah York Director: **Sam Raimi** Screenplay: **Sam Raimi** Running Time: 1:25 Rated: NC-17 (Extreme gore, violence, profanity, brief nudity) Theatrical Aspect Ratio: **1.85:1**

Long before *Scream* came along to simultaneously parody the horror genre while participating in it, there was Sam Raimi's *Evil Dead* trilogy (the third entry into the series, *Army of Darkness,* was released in 1993). Equal parts suspense, camp, comedy, and over-the-top gore, the first two *Evil Dead* movies didn't take long to attain the status of cult classics. Today, while relatively few mainstream movie viewers have heard of these movies, they have garnered a small but loyal gathering of fans who can recite every one liner delivered by the ultra-cool hero, Ash.

The Evil Dead follows the ill-fated expedition of 5 20-somethings who decide to spend a weekend at an isolated cabin in the middle of the woods. They are Ash (Bruce Campbell); his girlfriend, Linda (Betsy Baker); his sister, Shelly (Sarah York); and his friends, Cheryl (Ellen Sandweiss) and Scotty (Hal Delrich). At the cabin, the 5 discover a strange book whose pages are made out of human skin and whose writing is done in human blood. This is the Necronomicon, or the "Book of the Dead," which "speaks of a spiritual presence — a thing of evil — that roams the forests and dark bowers of man's domain." It also includes incantations to raise demons — spells that are invoked when a tape recording of a man reading them is played. Soon, Ash and his compatriots are the unfortunate targets of an implacable force that lurks in and around their little cottage and, one-by-one, they are possessed or killed.

The Evil Dead is much more of a straightforward horror endeavor than its sequel, containing little in the way of overt comedy. Its humor comes through accentuating traditional elements of the thriller/horror genre, including drenching the screen in copious amounts of fake blood, allowing the actors to give over-the-top performances, and intentionally placing characters in positions where they do stupid things.

One of the most remarkable things about *The Evil Dead* is how much it was able to accomplish on such a small budget (reportedly around $50K). Of course, it could be argued that many of the best horror films, including *Halloween* and *The Blair Witch Project,* have come cheaply, with the lack of funding forcing the filmmakers to rely more on innovation than special effects. *The Evil Dead* is at times genuinely creepy, due in no small part to the imaginative camerawork devised by Raimi and cinematographer Tim Philo. Also, the evil force inhabiting the forest is never shown in *The Evil Dead,* leaving all the details to our imagination. **RECOMMENDED**

Evil Dead II [1987]

Starring: Bruce Campbell, Sarah Berry, Dan Hicks, Kassie Wesley, Denise Bixler Director: Sam Raimi Screenplay: Sam Raimi, Scott Spiegel Running Time: 1:25 Rated: R (Extreme gore, violence, profanity) Theatrical Aspect Ratio: 1.85:1

What do you get when you cross George Romero with The Three Stooges by way of the director of *A Simple Plan* and *The Gift*? Something offbeat, to be sure. Something grotesque, without a doubt. Something . . . groovy.

To say that the *Evil Dead* movies are not for everyone is an understatement. A strong stomach is required. If you can't take copious amounts of blood and gore, this is not your movie. Both *The Evil Dead* and *Evil Dead II* have enough vile colored liquids to fill a small swimming pool. Plus, there are assorted body parts (decapitated heads, bodiless hands, etc.). Of course, the extreme nature of the gore isn't beside the point — it *is* the point. Raimi goes so far over the top in presenting these displays that they take on a campy, almost humorous appearance. It's impossible to take all this blood seriously. So, instead of being sickened, we're strangely amused — and this is all intentional.

Evil Dead II can be seen as a sequel to *Evil Dead,* a remake, or a little of both. Rather than starting off where its predecessor finished, *Evil Dead II* goes back to the beginning — sort of. The first 10 minutes of the second film essentially recap what occurred in *The Evil Dead.* Ash heads up to the cabin, although, in this movie, his only companion is Linda (played here by Denise Bixler). The two discover the Necronomicon, and, in no time, Linda is a zombie and Ash is forced to chop her up to save himself. Before long, Ash is possessed, but he manages to fight off the demonic influence. He is joined by a group of 4 additional characters: Annie Knowby (Sarah Berry), whose father owns the cabin; her boyfriend, Ed (Richard Domeier); a redneck named Jake (Dan Hicks); and his girlfriend, Bobbie Joe (Kassie Wesley). Predictably, these characters are dispatched one-by-one, leaving Ash as the last one standing. The ending of *Evil Dead II* leads directly into *Army of Darkness.*

That brings us to the Three Stooges. Raimi is on record as being an avid Three Stooges fan, and his appreciation of the old-time comics shows clearly in a variety of slapstick homages that appear throughout both *Evil Dead II* and *Army of Darkness.* While the Stooges' routines might not seem to be ripe for incorporation in a horror movie, Raimi's use of this material works, primarily because the tapestry into which it is woven already has a highly satirical/ comedic aspect. It's also interesting to note that, while the role of one of the Stooges is occasionally played by the human Ash, there are occasions when a zombie takes on the part of Larry, Curly, or Moe. **RECOMMENDED**

The Exorcist [1973]

Starring: Ellen Burstyn, Max von Sydow, Lee J. Cobb, Kitty Winn, Jack MacGowran Director: William Friedkin Screenplay: William Peter Blatty Running Time: 2:02 Rated: R (Violence, profanity, horror elements) Theatrical Aspect Ratio: 1.85:1

During the cold months of the winter of 1973-74, the release of a horror film called *The Exorcist* became a national phenomenon. Would-be viewers stood outside for hours in bad weather to get a ticket, and the lines in New York City were said to circle entire blocks. Although this kind of fervor was not unprecedented, it was unexpected. As recently as several months before the movie's release, Warner Brothers had been discussing shelving the entire project. The distributor's ultimate willingness to take a chance returned huge financial dividends and established one of the most frequently copied films about demonic possession.

The Exorcist's strength is that it places character development on the same level as the horror elements, but it is not a ground-breaking motion picture. It is also too long, with a setup that could have accomplished the job with equal effectiveness in about ⅔ the time. There are instances when the first hour of *The Exorcist* noticeably drags, and there will always be a debate about whether the prologue (featuring Max von Sydow's Father Merrin at an archeological dig in North Africa) is necessary (or even useful).

The story is based on a series of true events that occurred in 1949 and were later fictionalized by author William Peter Blatty in his novel. It tells of the demonic possession of 12-year-old Regan MacNeil (Linda Blair), the daughter of popular actress Chris MacNeil (Ellen Burstyn). When we first meet Regan, she seems like any happy, well-adjusted girl. Soon, however, she is hearing strange noises, uttering obscenities, and experiencing violent tantrums and seizures. As her condition worsens and she begins speaking in an inhuman voice (provided by Mercedes McCambridge), the army of attending doctors advises calling in spiritual help. So Chris consults a local priest (who also happens to be a psychiatrist), Father Damien Karras (Jason Miller). After examining

Regan, he agrees to assist in an exorcism, which will be performed by the respected and mysterious globe-trotting priest, Father Merrin (von Sydow).

Friedkin has crafted an atmospheric motion picture that is creepy from its early scenes in Georgetown (one of which shows Chris casually walking home on a Halloween afternoon). The film includes one of the most evocative and memorable images in a modern horror film, with Father Merrin emerging from a taxi and standing, in silhouette, under a street lamp as he faces the house where his latest struggle with the Devil will transpire. Moments like these, peppered throughout the production, give *The Exorcist* an artistic edge. **RECOMMENDED**

From Dusk Till Dawn [1996]

Starring: George Clooney, Harvey Keitel, Quentin Tarantino, Juliette Lewis Director: Robert Rodriguez Screenplay: Quentin Tarantino Running Time: 1:48 Rated: R (Gore, violence, gore, profanity, gore, nudity, gore) Theatrical Aspect Ratio: 1.85:1

It's great fun, but certainly not great art. *From Dusk Till Dawn*, a special effects blood-and-gore extravaganza from director Robert Rodriguez (written by Quentin Tarantino), follows in the footsteps of such cult classics as Sam Raimi's *Evil Dead* series, thumbing its nose at conventional film expectations and gleefully embracing the campiness of the B-movie genre. With its palette of hideous monstrosities, decapitations, dismemberments, eviscerations, topless dancers, profane dialogue, and bare foot licking, this motion picture pushes the R-rating to the edge.

Yet the reason *From Dusk Till Dawn* entertains is because it never takes itself seriously. The film is steeped in wit, parody, and offbeat humor. There aren't any characters here — only caricatures. The movie has been designed as a burst of high energy, and that's exactly what it turns out to be. *From Dusk Till Dawn* will appeal to only a small portion of the cinema-visiting population, but for those who enjoy this kind of tongue-and-cheek horror story, the film has a lot to offer.

In *From Dusk Till Dawn*, the setup is as long as the main story. The film opens by introducing us to two bank robbers on the run — Seth Gecko (George Clooney) and his nutcase brother Richie (Tarantino). They're on their way to Mexico, but they need a cover to get across the border. So, to that end, they hijack the mobile home of ex-preacher Jacob Fuller (Harvey Keitel) and his two kids (Juliette Lewis and Ernest Lieu), and force them, at gunpoint, to help. Once in

Mexico, the 5 stop at an all-night bar for a little R&R. Only one problem: the place is run by vampires, and, after a little topless dancing, it's feeding time.

The film isn't for everyone, but, if you're in the target audience, you'll get what you want: a stylish, ultra-hip twist to one of humanity's oldest, darkest legends. Vampires will never live this one down. RECOMMENDED

From Hell [2001]

Starring: Johnny Depp, Heather Graham, Ian Holm Directors: Albert and Allen Hughes Screenplay: Terry Hayes & Rafael Yglesias, based on the comic book series by Alan Moore & Eddie Campbell Running Time: 2:01 Rated: R (Violence, gore, drug use, sex) Theatrical Aspect Ratio: 2.35:1

There is no more famous serial killer than Jack the Ripper. Since his infamous 1888 killing spree in London's Whitechapel district, there have been more sophisticated psychopaths, and those who have slaughtered far more victims, but Jack the Ripper remains at the top of the totem pole. His exploits are the stuff of legends. With *From Hell*, the brotherly team of Albert and Allen Hughes have not attempted to do much in the way of a factual exploration of the Ripper's spree. Instead, working from Alan Moore and Eddie Campbell's graphic novel of the same name, they have used a few facts as the foundation for an entirely fictional murder mystery/horror movie that has the opium-addicted Scotland Yard Inspector Abberline (Johnny Depp) tracking down the Ripper while falling in love with a potential victim, street whore Mary Kelly (Heather Graham). Also thrown into the mix are a syphilis-infected Prince of England, doctors eager to perform lobotomies, and the Order of Freemasons, members of which act with impunity. In keeping with the tone and nature of their source material, the Hughes Brothers have converted *From Hell* to the cinema with an edgy, blood-soaked, comic book-like flair.

From the Ripper's butchery to Abberline's opium trips, watching *From Hell* is certainly a grim experience, but it's not without its rewards for those who can stomach the level of graphic gore. The movie is a macabre and intense experience whose pace and tone remain consistent throughout. The acting, especially that by Depp, Ian Holm (as a doctor who assists in the Inspector's investigation), and Robbie Coltrane (as Abberline's right-hand man), never fails to convince. Even Heather Graham, in a part one would not immediately connect with the normally two-dimensional actress, isn't all that bad. The plot isn't the stuff

of literary greatness, but the mystery is effectively developed and it's not immediately evident how things will turn out and who will be unmasked as the Ripper.

From Hell is a good deal better than Depp's last atmospheric horror story, *Sleepy Hollow*. This movie has more realized potential, including a storyline that goes somewhere. And, while we may never find ourselves truly liking Abberline, the Hughes Brothers' mastery of the screen is such that we can imagine ourselves winding our ways through the fog-enshrouded, cobbled streets of London with something lurking in the shadows just behind us . . . RECOMMENDED

The Gift [2000]

Starring: Cate Blanchett, Katie Holmes, Keanu Reeves, Giovanni Ribisi, Greg Kinnear Director: Sam Raimi Screenplay: Billy Bob Thornton & Tom Epperson Running Time: 1:51 Rated: R (Violence, nudity, sex, profanity) Theatrical Aspect Ratio: 1.85:1

The Gift is an example of how superior craftsmanship can transform a ho-hum genre entry into a sporadically gripping thriller. On the surface, there's nothing special about this movie — it's a run-of-the-mill supernatural murder mystery with all of the elements one expects from this sort of a motion picture: ghostly apparitions, courtroom drama, red herrings, and an "unexpected" twist at the end. Yet, while the script, credited to Billy Bob Thornton and Tom Epperson, is strictly generic, the direction by Sam Raimi and the performances of a stellar cast are anything but that. As a result of their contributions, a film that might originally have been strictly palatable for late-night cable viewing has turned into something worthy of theatrical consumption.

The Gift tells the story of Annie Wilson (Cate Blanchett), a widowed psychic scraping out a meager living by telling fortunes. Having lost her husband a year ago, she must provide for herself and her 3 young boys. There are plenty of people in the backwater Southern town who don't approve of what Annie does — they think she's a fraud or in league with the devil. Chief among them is Donnie Barksdale (Keanu Reeves), the abusive husband of one of Annie's clients, Valerie (Hilary Swank). One of Annie's few defenders is Buddy Cole (Giovanni Ribisi), the emotionally disturbed owner of a local garage. And, although Annie isn't looking for romance, there's clearly a connection between her and clean-cut Wayne Collins (Greg Kinnear), the principal at her sons' school. But a relationship doesn't look likely — Wayne is set to marry Jessica King (Katie Holmes), whose father is one of the most respected men in town. Then, one night, Jessica turns up missing and Annie experiences visions that implicate Donnie in her murder. Unwilling to credit the genuine nature of Annie's talent, the police are reluctant to believe her, but when the investigation uncovers a body, Annie becomes a star witness in a sensational trial.

Cate Blanchett, who can play any part from the Queen of England to a denizen of J.R.R. Tolkien's Middle Earth, proves that a gritty, unglamorous role like that of Annie does not challenge her range. Blanchett is wonderful as the uncertain, tortured psychic, and her performance brings Annie's humanity to the surface in a manner that a less gifted actress might not be able to manage. Katie Holmes is suitably saucy and sassy (and exhibits in graphic terms that she is willing to take roles that require nudity), and Greg Kinnear is intentionally bland. Finally, there's Keanu Reeves, who surprises with the pure evil he radiates. Maybe it takes a tough role like this to bring out the actor in Hollywood's original bogus adventurer. **RECOMMENDED**

Halloween [1978]

Starring: Jamie Lee Curtis, Donald Pleasance, Nancy Loomis, P.J. Soles Director: John Carpenter Screenplay: Debra Hill & John Carpenter Running Time: 1:33 Rated: R (Violence, profanity, sex, brief nudity) Theatrical Aspect Ratio: 2.35:1

Because of its title, *Halloween* has frequently been grouped together with all the other splatter films that populated theaters throughout the late-1970s and early-1980s. However, while *Halloween* is rightfully considered the father of the modern slasher genre, it is not a member. This is not a gruesome motion picture — there is surprisingly little graphic violence and almost *no* blood. *Halloween* is built on suspense, not gore, and initiated more than a few of today's common horror/thriller cliches. The ultimate success of the movie, however, encouraged other film makers to try their hand at this sort of enterprise, and it didn't take long for someone to decide that audiences wanted as many explicitly grisly scenes as the running length would allow.

The film opens with a long, single-shot prologue that takes place on Halloween night, 1963. A young Michael Myers watches as his older sister, Judith, sneaks upstairs for a quickie with a guy from school. After the boyfriend has departed, Michael takes a knife out of the kitchen drawer, ascends the staircase, and stabs Judith to death. The entire sequence employs the subjective point-of-view, an approach that writer/director John Carpenter returns to repeatedly throughout the movie. Only after the deed is done do we learn that Michael is only a grade-schooler.

The bulk of the movie takes place 15 years later. Michael, confined to an asylum for the criminally insane for more than 10 years, escapes on the night before Halloween. His doctor, Sam Loomis (Donald Pleasance), believing Michael to be the embodiment of evil, tracks the killer back to his hometown of Haddonfield. From there, it's a race against time as Loomis seeks to locate and stop Michael before he starts again where he left off in 1963.

The final body count in *Halloween* is surprisingly low, but the terror quotient is high. This is the kind of impeccably crafted motion picture that burrows deep into our psyche and connects with the dark, hidden terrors that lurk there. *Halloween* is not a perfect movie, but no recent horror film has attained this pinnacle (as evidenced by the plaudits heaped upon it in Wes Craven's recent *Scream*). Likewise, John Carpenter has never come close to recapturing *Halloween*'s artistic or commercial success, though he has tried many times. *Halloween* remains untouched — a modern classic of the most horrific kind. **MUST SEE**

Interview with the Vampire [1994]

Starring: Tom Cruise, Brad Pitt, Kirsten Dunst, Antonio Bandaras, Christian Slater Director: Neil Jordan Screenplay: Anne Rice Running Time: 2:02 Rated: R (Violence, gore, mature themes, nudity) Theatrical Aspect Ratio: 1.85:1

Interview with the Vampire, based on the hugely successful novel by Anne Rice, begins and ends in present-day San Francisco, with Louis (Brad Pitt), a 2-century old vampire, telling his story to a fascinated interviewer (Christian Slater). His tale opens in 1791 Louisiana, just south of New Orleans, where Louis falls victim to the vampire Lestat (Tom Cruise). Given a choice between death and eternal life as one of the undead, Louis chooses the latter, a decision he will forever regret.

Louis cannot kill with the impunity of Lestat, but, to sate his hunger, he must feed, and the blood of animals is not enough. Eventually, he pierces the neck of a grief-stricken young girl named Claudia (Kirsten Dunst), whom Lestat then curses with his unholy form of resurrection so that she can be a surrogate daughter to both himself and Louis. For a while, they are one "big, happy family." But all things end, and

Claudia's growing resentment of Lestat fuels a bloody confrontation.

When *Interview with the Vampire* works, it's as compelling and engrossing a piece of entertainment as is available on film today. When it falters, the weaknesses seem magnified. Fortunately, under the care of director Neil Jordan, instances of the former are more frequent that those of the latter, although the film noticeably stumbles during two key sequences (a needlessly drawn-out exploration of life as a vampire in Paris and the illogical, dumb conclusion). Despite the ups and downs of the second half, however, the first hour is classic horror at its most grotesque. In the best tradition of the *Grand Guignol*, *Interview with the Vampire* revels in its graphic and horrifying bloodiness. **RECOMMENDED**

Mary Reilly [1996]

Starring: **Julia Roberts, John Malkovich, George Cole, Glenn Close**
Director: **Stephen Frears** Screenplay: **Christopher Hampton**, based on the novel by **Valerie Martin** Running Time: **1:48** Rated: **R** (Violence, mature themes) Theatrical Aspect Ratio: **1.85:1**

Mary Reilly, brought to the screen by *Dangerous Liaisons* director Stephen Frears and *Liaisons* screenwriter Christopher Hampton, may be the most thought-provoking, intelligent, and disturbing motion picture version of Robert Louis Stevenson's *The Strange Case of Dr. Jekyll and Mr. Hyde* ever to be produced. Telling the classic split-personality story from the point-of-view of Dr. Jekyll's (John Malkovich) maid, Mary Reilly (Julia Roberts), this movie is an engrossing examination of the elemental forces that define human nature.

Any serious film interpretation of *Dr. Jekyll and Mr. Hyde* must, first and foremost, explore the meaning of Jekyll's split personality. As *Mary Reilly* interprets it, this is not a classic conflict between good and evil — life isn't that simple. Hyde does not represent the distillation of pure evil, just as Jekyll is not a paragon of righteousness. Each has virtues and flaws, and only together do they represent a whole person. Hyde is raw emotion — the animal side of humanity. His passion, twisted though it may be, gives Jekyll the will to live. Through the dichotomy presented by these two characters, we are challenged to consider that perhaps it's the combination of good and evil, control and liberation, and restraint and passion that makes each of us who we are. *Mary Reilly* has the power to disturb because it forces us to look inside and recognize our own Jekylls and Hydes.

By using Mary as the main character, this film is also able to illustrate the transforming power of love. To be sure, *Mary Reilly* isn't a conventional romance, but it's a love story nevertheless. Mary loves Jekyll for his goodness, and Hyde for what she sees of herself mirrored in him. When Jekyll speaks of having a fractured soul, Mary understands his pain. Her own spirit has been crippled by her childhood torture at the hands of an abusive father (Michael Gambon). Moreover, Hyde's feelings for Mary prove to be his undoing. In the end, her gift to him is indescribably precious.

I suspect that many who see *Mary Reilly* will get a completely different movie than they're expecting. Instead of murder and mayhem (although both of these are evident), we are presented with a beautifully-textured motion picture tapestry that focuses on characters and themes rather than gory special effects. *Mary Reilly* is haunting, not only because of its foggy, shadowy settings, but because of the questions it encourages us to ask about ourselves and others. **HIGHLY RECOMMENDED**

A Nightmare on Elm Street [1984]

Starring: **John Saxon, Ronee Blakley, Heather Langenkamp, Johnny Depp, Robert Englund** Director: **Wes Craven** Screenplay: **Wes Craven** Running Time: **1:31** Rated: **R** (Violence, gore, sexual situations) Theatrical Aspect Ratio: **1.85:1**

The primary element that elevates *A Nightmare on Elm Street* above many of its contemporaries is that the storyline invites intellectual participation. In addition to offering the visceral thrills that are necessary in a genre entry, Wes Craven's screenplay works on another level. He wants viewers to think about the division between dreams and waking, between fantasy and reality, between other worlds and this one. He also warps expectations — at times, we're aware that the characters are trapped in a dreamscape, but there are times when we're not. And there are occasions when we think they're dreaming and they're actually awake.

In the first *A Nightmare on Elm Street*, Freddy Krueger (Robert Englund) is the demon in the background. His popularity, however, mandated that subsequent sequels center increasingly upon his character. He has a backstory, only part of which is revealed in the first film, and many of the later *Elm Street* chapters focus on the events that led to Freddy's becoming the monster of dreams that he is. Unfortunately, the more we learn about Freddy, the less imposing he is, which is the reason the he's the most frightening in this installment, where he's a new, and entirely unknown, danger.

A Nightmare on Elm Street isn't principally about Freddy. It's about Nancy Thompson (Heather Langenkamp), a typical teenager with the usual teenage problems — divorced parents, gossipy friends, and a boyfriend who wants a little more than she's willing to offer. Nancy lives in an average house in an average middle America town. In keeping with the theme that sex equates to death in horror movies, the first one to fall victim to Freddy is Nancy's best friend, Tina (Amanda Wyss), who is ripped to shreds shortly after enjoying an athletic evening under the covers with her boyfriend, Rod (Nick Corri). In the wake of the massacre, Rod ends up in jail for murder, but Nancy isn't sure of his guilt. Freddy begins appearing in her nightmares and she becomes convinced that he, not Rod, is responsible for Tina's death. Shortly after that, Freddy strikes again, eliminating Rod. Nancy realizes that either she or her boyfriend, Glen (Johnny Depp), will be next, so she decides to take the offensive and attempt to bring Freddy out of the dream world.

A Nightmare on Elm Street is tailor made for those who like their gore leavened with thought-provoking ideas — something that is a rarity in this genre. Sequels dumbed down the series to a regrettable degree, but the first movie still stands on its own as an intriguing and chilling example of how horror works best when the characters and the audience don't have to be lobotomized. **HIGHLY RECOMMENDED**

Nosferatu the Vampyre [Germany, 1979]

Starring: Klaus Kinski, Isabelle Adjani, Bruno Ganz Director: Werner Herzog Screenplay: Werner Herzog, based on *Dracula* by Bram Stoker Running Time: 1:47 Rated: PG (Ghoulish images, sexual innuendo) Theatrical Aspect Ratio: 1.85:1

Werner Herzog approached *Nosferatu the Vampyre* with fewer preconceptions than many directors who tackle the tale of Count Dracula. The image of Dracula burned into his memory was of the gaunt, predatory Max Schreck. It's no surprise, therefore, that Schreck's appearance served as a blueprint for Klaus Kinski's count.

Kinski's Dracula is unlike any other interpretation of the character. Visually, he resembles Schreck, with a bald pate, pointed ears, rat-like fangs, clawed hands, and a stiff gait — but that's where the similarity ends. This version of the count is neither a cultured nobleman, a sadistic monster, nor a romantic lead. Instead, he is a twisted wretch — monstrous yet sad; indomitable yet tragic. He is undone not by hubris or carelessness, but by the yearning to steal a few moments extra pleasure in the arms of a woman.

That woman is the gorgeous Isabelle Adjani, who plays Lucy Harker, the object of the count's obsession. As in the original *Nosferatu,* Lucy and Dracula share a psychosexual connection, and he is drawn to her like a moth to a flame, with equally traumatic results.

The third member of the main acting trio is Bruno Ganz, who plays the unfortunate Jonathan Harker. The film opens with Harker leaving behind his young wife, Lucy, and venturing into the Carpathian Mountains on the way to Castle Dracula, where he is to finalize a real estate deal with the mysterious and elusive Count Dracula. Once there, he becomes the Count's prisoner. Later, after escaping from the castle, he races Dracula back to Wismar, but, by the time he arrives, brain fever has struck and he can no longer remember his friends, his wife, or his ordeal in Transylvania.

Unlike most vampire films, *Nosferatu the Vampyre* rejects the expected frantic tone in favor of a deliberate, relentless pace. Some find that the film moves too slowly, but Herzog's unwillingness to rush things allows the images and music to work their magic, building a powerful and foreboding sense of atmosphere. Jonathan's journey through the Borgo Pass is a perfect example of this. Another director might have edited this 10-minute sequence to a fraction of its running length, but, by keeping it intact, the striking visuals and haunting score heighten suspense and build anticipation.

Nosferatu the Vampyre will not be to everyone's taste. This film, like its silent inspiration, concentrates on tone and atmosphere. The result is a superior horror film that offers a greater sense of disquiet than any other Dracula motion picture. *Nosferatu the Vampyre* may not be scary in a traditional sense, but it is not easily forgotten. **HIGHLY RECOMMENDED**

Scream [1996]

Starring: Neve Campbell, Rose McGowan, Skeet Ulrich, Courteney Cox, David Arquette Director: Wes Craven Screenplay: Kevin Williamson Running Time: 1:50 Rated: R (Violence, gore, profanity) Theatrical Aspect Ratio: 2.35:1

Scream is a rarity: a horror movie spoof that succeeds almost as well at provoking scares as laughs. That's because director Wes Craven, in addition to having a genuine affection for the genre, understands how wildly improbable and easy to lampoon it is. And, with *Scream,* he skewers it at every corner, using self-referential humor and a flood of in-jokes (some subtle, some obvious).

Scream opens with a 12-minute prologue that introduces us to Casey (Drew Barrymore), an all-American girl who's popping popcorn in preparation for watching a video. The phone rings, and there's a mysterious voice on the other end. He asks her what her favorite scary movie is, and she replies that it's *Halloween*. He then invites her to play a game, but she gets freaked out and hangs up. When he calls again and she demands to know what he wants, his response is simple and succinct: "To see your insides." The cat-and-mouse game continues until both Casey and her boyfriend (who has the misfortune to stop by) are gutted like fish.

This double murder is only the beginning, however. It appears that the killer's real target is Sidney Prescott (Neve Campbell, from TV's *Party of Five*), a high school girl with a troubled past. One year ago, Sidney's mother was raped and murdered in a highly-publicized case. Now, when Sidney is attacked by someone wearing a Grim Reaper mask and her boyfriend, Billy (Skeet Ulrich), is arrested, her life is turned upside down. From the bathrooms at school to a friend's house, the stalking continues. Meanwhile, an aggressive tabloid reporter (Courteney Cox) begins harassing Sidney for a story.

Scream never stops poking fun at itself. Craven and screenwriter Kevin Williamson allow their characters to make all sorts of disparaging remarks about the horror movie clichés they're living (and dying) through. Craven couldn't have made this movie if he didn't understand both his craft and what his fans expect. Of all the mainstream horror directors, he has been the one most willing to take chances. This is a horror film designed with movie-lovers in mind. Beneath all the gore and violence (and there's a lot of both), there's a keen sense of wit and intelligence which sophisticated viewers are likely to appreciate. And that makes this much more than a common slasher flick. Have fun, and remember that "movies don't create psychos; movies make psychos more creative." RECOMMENDED

Scream 2 [1997]

Starring: Neve Campbell, Courtney Cox, David Arquette, Jamie Kennedy, Liev Schreiber Director: Wes Craven Screenplay: Kevin Williamson Running Time: 2:00 Rated: R (Violence, gore, profanity) Theatrical Aspect Ratio: 2.35:1

Scream 2 isn't quite as clever as its predecessor, but it fills the gap with a cutting wit. Death — even gruesome, bloody death — can be funny if handled the right way. As stipulated by one of the "rules of sequels" uttered by a movie-obsessed character in the film, the body count in *Scream 2* is higher than that in the original. Paradoxically, there's a lot less gore. Craven has remembered that scares are more important that graphic displays of human insides and bodily fluids. A second strength of *Scream 2* is that it features a gallery of legitimate characters rather than a group of cardboard cut-out stereotypes lined up for slaughter.

Scream 2 opens approximately 2 years after the original. As in the first picture, there's a slick, self-mocking prologue. This time, the victims are Jada Pinkett and Omar Epps, whose characters are visiting a local theater for a preview screening of the movie *Stab* (which is based on the "true life" events of *Scream*).

Following the prologue, we are re-introduced to Sidney Prescott, who has left her sleepy hometown to go to Windsor College. Her friend Randy (Jamie Kennedy) is a student there as well, and he's just as knowledgeable about horror films as ever. Once the double murder at *Stab* becomes big news, the media converges on Windsor, looking to interview the original victim. At the head of the flock of vultures is Gale Weathers (Courtney Cox), who has a little surprise for Sidney. She has brought Cotton Weary (Liev Schreiber), the man Sidney falsely accused of murder, with her. Also arriving at the college is Deputy Dewey (David Arquette), who is there to act as a big brother to Sidney during this latest round of tribulations.

From the *Stab* scenes to lines like "Brothers don't last long in situations like this," Craven and Williamson are clearly having a lot of fun with *Scream 2*, and the movie is enjoyable, if overlong (the livelier first hour is better than the second). Their resolution to the obligatory "whodunit?" is less of a letdown than it could be, and knowingly offers a wink and nod at past unmasking scenes. One senses, however, that by the end of this picture, the overall concept of a hip, self-referential slasher film has been played out. RECOMMENDED

Shadow of the Vampire [United States/United Kingdom, 2000]

Starring: John Malkovich, Willem Dafoe, Cary Elwes, Eddie Izzard, Udo Kier Director: E. Elias Merhige Screenplay: Steven Katz Running Time: 1:30 Rated: R (Violence, sexual situations, brief nudity) Theatrical Aspect Ratio: 1.85:1

Nosferatu. For movie-lovers, that one-word title conjures a whirlwind of indelible images forever imprinted in the mind's eye, with none more stark than the harrowing sight of the gaunt, horrific Count Orlock. E. Elias Merhige's sophomore feature offers a compelling, fictionalized account of the filming of the seminal 1922 film. As Merhige and screenwriter Steven Katz have imagined things, the pointy-eared, bald star of *Nosferatu,* Max Schreck, didn't just play a vampire — he was one in real life.

John Malkovich gets top billing, being Murnau. However, the standout is an unrecognizable Willem Dafoe, whose eerie turn as the bloodthirsty Schreck should earn him an Oscar nomination. Dafoe is the spitting image of Schreck, from the unmistakable look to the mannerisms.

The simple story follows the movie's production history, which runs into trouble early when Bram Stoker's widow refuses Murnau the rights to *Dracula* and certain substitutions have to be made. The director also is forced to deal with a temperamental leading lady (played by Catherine McCormack). Then there's the casting of the mysterious Schreck as Count Orlock. Murnau introduces the reclusive performer to his co-workers as the ultimate method actor, and they all marvel at his dedication (staying in character all the time). Soon after, various cast and crew members inexplicably begin to fall ill. Murnau knows Schreck's nasty little secret — the two have made a pact — but his conscience is clear. He is willing to do almost anything in the name of making a great movie.

Based exclusively on the concept, one might easily assume that *Shadow of the Vampire* is a horror film, and, to a degree, it is. But Merhige's intention is not to scare the daylights out of his audience. The amount of comedy — good, genuinely funny comedy — to be found in this movie surprised me. Great one-liners abound, many of which are delivered by Dafoe's Schreck in a delightfully deadpan manner. And some of his bemused expressions are priceless. Obviously, those who have seen *Nosferatu* are going to get a lot more out of this movie than those who are unfamiliar with it, but *Shadow of the Vampire* stands up well enough on its own that viewers who haven't even heard of Murnau's original will not feel set adrift in an unfamiliar cinematic landscape. The idea of a real-life vampire playing one in a movie should appeal to wider crowd than silent movie buffs and film historians. **HIGHLY RECOMMENDED**

Stigmata [1999]

Starring: Patricia Arquette, Gabriel Byrne, Jonathan Pryce Director: Rupert Wainwright Screenplay: Tom Lazarus Running Time: 1:42 Rated: R (Blood, mature themes, profanity, brief sex & nudity) Theatrical Aspect Ratio: 2.35:1

Stigmata are bleeding injuries that represent the 5 wounds received by Jesus when he was crucified:

nails through the wrists & feet, lashes on the back, scratches on the scalp from the crown of thorns, and a spear through the side. The phenomena of stigmata is neither well understood nor extensively studied, but those afflicted with it are invariably deeply religious and view their condition as a gift of God. Director Rupert Wainwright and screenwriter Tom Lazarus have chosen to use this as the jumping-off point for an unconventional thriller.

At the center of the story, providing a human perspective on issues with vast and far-reaching implications, are Frankie Page (Patricia Arquette), a 23-year-old Pittsburgh hairdresser who is a confessed athiest, and Father Andrew Kiernan (Gabriel Byrne), a Roman Catholic Priest who investigates (and disproves) miracles. When *Stigmata* begins, Frankie is just one of Pittsburgh's many anonymous citizens. That all changes when she receives a package from her globe-trotting mother, who has recently been vacationing in Brazil. Included in a box of odds and ends is an old rosary. Within 24 hours of touching the elegant circlet of black beads, Frankie is in the hospital with a deep puncture wound in each wrist — the first of the 5 stigmata. She receives the second, a crisscrossing of her back with the lashes of a whip, while on a subway train, and in plain view of a priest, who contacts Rome about the strange occurrence. Cardinal Houseman (Jonathan Pryce), the head of the Vatican's "Sacred Congregation for the Causes of Saints," sends Andrew Kiernan, his best investigator, to Pittsburgh to meet the woman and determine what's going on. What Andrew finds not only tests his own belief system, but threatens the authority of the modern church.

Stigmata is an unusually intelligent and original thriller. While it loosely resembles end-of-the-world efforts like *The Seventh Sign,* the plot is more thoughtful and restrained. *Stigmata* takes an unflinching look at the power of and the capability for corruption in organized religion. Yet *Stigmata* is not an attack; it does not hurl cruel or thoughtless barbs at Catholicism, and its view of religion in general and Christianity in particular is almost reverent. **RECOMMENDED**

Stir of Echoes [1999]

Starring: Kevin Bacon, Kathryn Erbe, Illeana Douglas, Kevin Dunn, Zachary David Cope Director: David Koepp Screenplay: David Koepp, based on the novel by Richard Matheson Running Time: 1:40 Rated: R (Violence, profanity, nudity, sex) Theatrical Aspect Ratio: 1.85:1

Stir of Echoes belongs to one of the oldest genres of horror films: the ghost story. And, unlike a multitude of subpar entries that have borne this appellation over the years, it's mostly effective. Like all good ghost stories, it understands that the intent is to build suspense through atmosphere and a strong narrative, not through a barrage of sudden shocks and copious gore.

The main characters are both normal, likable people — husband and wife Tom (Kevin Bacon) and Maggie (Kathryn Erbe). Both are hard workers, and, with their combined incomes, they can just about make ends meet for their family, which includes a 5-year-old boy named Jake (Zachary David Cope) and another baby on the way. One night, at a party, Tom allows himself to be hypnotized by Maggie's new-agey sister, Lisa (Illeana Douglas). While she's in his mind, she leaves a suggestion for him to "open up." This results in Tom beginning to experience paranormal experiences, including seeing the ghost of a teenage girl (Jenny Morrison) in his living room. He becomes obsessed with initiating a second contact with the ghost, losing his job and neglecting his friends and family in the process. Only his son understands — because, like Tom, Jake also has strange visions of dead people.

Director David Koepp does an excellent job of creating atmosphere. *Stir of Echoes* is an eerie movie; Koepp gets us into Tom's unstable mindset through a series of tight closeups and distorted point-of-view shots. As a study of obsession, the film is first-rate. Tom's tunnel vision focuses on the ghost to the virtual exclusion of all else. Maggie desperately wants to support him, but, not being able to share the experience with him, she is unable to understand the forces that are driving him.

The film is intelligent, but not so talky or esoteric that it could be labeled as an art house attraction. And, while *Stir of Echoes* isn't as downright disturbing as some horror movies, it's still the kind of film that may give you pause the next time you walk into a dark room by yourself. RECOMMENDED

Wes Craven's New Nightmare [1994]
Starring: Heather Langenkamp, Robert Englund, Miko Hughes Director: **Wes Craven** Screenplay: **Wes Craven** Running Time: **1:52** Rated: **R** (Violence, gore, language) Theatrical Aspect Ratio: **1.85:1**

Wes Craven's New Nightmare focuses on the lives of some of the actors who appeared in the 1984 original (Heather Langenkamp, Robert Englund, and John Saxon, all of whom play themselves). Langenkamp is having dreams about Freddy, and Englund is painting

some very strange pictures. For his part, Craven (who also appears in the film) is writing a new script (which turns out to be the screenplay for *this* picture). All of them realize that something is very wrong.

Then, Langenkamp's young son, Dylan (Miko Hughes), starts having catatonic episodes where he speaks in Freddy's voice, and her husband, Chase (David Newsom), is involved in an accident that appears to involve razor-sharp claws. Freddy, according to Craven (who is called upon to provide an explanation for everything that's going on) is a being of mythical evil whose essence was captured by the *Nightmare* films. Now that the series is complete, he is seeking a gateway into the real world.

Whereas the other *Nightmare on Elm Street* films delighted in blurring the lines between waking and dreaming, this one adds another layer — that of pseudo-reality versus fantasy. Craven has given himself a wonderful new playground to fool around in, and he clearly relishes the opportunity. Those who can accept the basic premise are likely to have nearly as much fun. The only argument against Craven's vision is that he perhaps didn't push the envelope far enough.

Of course, the centerpiece of *Wes Craven's New Nightmare* is Freddy Krueger (once again played by Englund, even though the end credits ascribe Freddy's role to "himself"). This time around, the dream demon has been given a newer, meaner look and a set of nastier claws. The visual and gore effects, while not top-of-the-line, are believable and occasionally downright chilling. The entire production is steeped in an unsettling atmosphere. RECOMMENDED

The Wicker Man [United Kingdom, 1973]
Starring: Edward Woodward, Christopher Lee, Diane Cilento, Britt Ekland Director: **Robin Hardy** Screenplay: **Anthony Shaffer** Running Time: **1:40** Rated: **R** (Nudity, sexual situations, violence) Theatrical Aspect Ratio: **1.85:1**

The Wicker Man is an early '70s British export that criss-crosses genres as easily as it confounds audience expectations. A film that defies categorization, *The Wicker Man* can be considered to be a horror film, a psychological thriller, a musical, or a melodrama. In reality, since it includes elements of each of those types, it literally has something for just about everyone. And, because there's a richness and intelligence to the story that leads to an unexpected climax, few viewers leave *The Wicker Man* unshaken.

Edward Woodward has the lead role of Sergeant Howie, a humorless policeman whose devout religious views cause him to look dimly upon any kind of heathen activity. When Howie receives an anonymous letter informing him that a young girl is missing on the remote Scottish island of Summerisle, he flies out to investigate. What he discovers shocks him — a community of pagans who worship the old Celtic gods and have rejected Christianity. The leader of the island, Lord Summerisle (Christopher Lee), explains to Howie that the citizens of the island are not irreligious — they just worship different gods. And Howie's faith comes under assault when Willow (Britt Ekland), the sensual daughter of the local innkeeper, offers herself to him. But, under it all, there is the mystery of the missing girl, and, as Howie uncovers clues, he begins to suspect a terrifying possibility.

The Wicker Man places us in Howie's shoes, although his dour disposition and puritanical outlook on life makes it difficult to sympathize with him entirely. Like Howie, we suspect that there's something rotten at the core of the community, and, also like the dauntless police officer, we don't figure out what it is until it's far, far too late. The brilliance of the writing is such that we don't seen the twist coming until it's nearly upon us. And that's when *The Wicker Man*'s uneasy undertow turns into a riptide of roiling dread.

Woodward's approach to the final scenes is critical to their being as unsettling as they are. His broken cry of "Oh my God!" is unnerving. Hardy's meticulous approach to filming the final scenes leaves us more than a little shaken and disturbed. By a combination of careful planning and happenstance, he chooses all the right shots to send *The Wicker Man* out with a bang. The story is told, although there are questions than linger. **HIGHLY RECOMMENDED**

Musical

Chicago [2002]

Starring: Renee Zellweger, Catherine Zeta-Jones, Richard Gere, John C. Reilly, Queen Latifah Director: Rob Marshall Screenplay: Bill Condon, based on the play by Fred Ebb & Bob Fosse Running Time: 1:52 Rated: PG-13 (Sensuality, profanity, violence) Theatrical Aspect Ratio: 1.85:1

Chicago represents good, solid entertainment. It's not nearly as rousing as the Broadway revival (then again, it's rare that the cinematic version of a musical comes close to the stage incarnation), but, for those unable or unwilling to see a live production, it represents a sparkling replacement. The film strikes a nice balance between the lavishly overproduced likes of Baz Luhrmann's *Moulin Rouge* and the less openly flamboyant movies from the '50s. The style, by intention, echoes that of the late, great choreographer Fosse.

The film's central characters are Roxie Hart (Renee Zellweger), a housewife who fantasizes becoming a vaudeville star, and Velma Kelly (Catherine Zeta-Jones), a chorus girl who dreams of greater fame than she currently has. Both women find themselves in the Cook County Jail on "Murderers' Row." Roxie shot her lover after discovering that he had lied to her about working to further her singing career. Velma eliminated her husband and sister after finding them together in bed. Both women are being represented by slick lawyer Billy Flynn (Richard Gere), who has never lost a case. His approach is to set up his clients as media darlings, then use that exposure to swing the trial in their favor. "In this town, murder's a form of entertainment," he comments. He refers to courtrooms as "three-ring circuses" and assures Roxie that justice can be blinded by the "razzle dazzle" he will employ.

Their notoriety sets up Roxie and Velma as rivals for the public spotlight. The lurid details of their lives and crimes make them instant celebrities. But neither stays on top for long, and it becomes a difficult task to recapture the interest of the public once another sensational crime has been committed. There's an insatiable appetite for fresh blood, and, unless Roxie and Velma can come up with new revelations to keep them on the front page, they will be quickly forgotten — not only by the general populace, but by their camera-loving lawyer, as well.

Even though the movie's original source material is 75 years old, the issues addressed by this film will be familiar to everyone in the audience, proving the point that technology may evolve, but human nature remains the same. The social commentary and attacks on the American system of jurisprudence are as stinging as they are valid. The 9 or 10 song-and-dance numbers allow us to enjoy *Chicago* on a less cerebral, more visceral level than might be the case if this was not a musical, but there's still a fair amount of substance to be considered. It's a pleasure to note that the return of the movie-adapted stage musical is such an unqualified success. **HIGHLY RECOMMENDED**

Everyone Says I Love You [1996]

Starring: Woody Allen, Natasha Lyonne, Julia Roberts, Goldie Hawn, Alan Alda Director: Woody Allen Screenplay: Woody Allen Running Time: 1:41 Rated: R (Profanity, angst) Theatrical Aspect Ratio: 1.85:1

With *Everyone Says I Love You*, Woody Allen is paying homage to the way musicals used to be made, back in the era when stars who didn't have great voices were occasionally forced to sing. The plot, which centers loosely around one sprawling, extended family, is extremely complicated, primarily because there are so many characters. For most of the film, Allen makes effective use of his ensemble cast; only near the end does the crowd of people vying for screen time turn into a detriment. That's not a surprise, however, considering that the last 15 minutes of the movie are its weakest, in spite of a wonderful song-and-dance number featuring Allen and a feather-light Goldie Hawn (who *can* sing).

The story is told from the point-of-view of DJ (Natasha Lyonne), the college-age daughter of Joe (Allen) and Steffi (Hawn). DJ's parents have been divorced for a decade-and-a-half, but they get along well. In fact, Joe considers Steffi and her husband, Bob (Alan Alda), to be his best friends, and, when his latest girlfriend dumps him, he flies from his home in Paris to New York to commiserate. DJ also has a stepsister, Skylar (Drew Barrymore), who is about to become engaged to a proper, upright guy in a suit (Edward Norton). Her stepbrother, Scott (Lukas Haas), has shocked the entire family by stating that he has joined the Young Conservatives. And her 2 half-sisters, Lane (Gaby Hoffman) and Laura (Natalie Portman), are trying to summon the courage to speak to a boy whom they both find attractive. Meanwhile, it's not long before Joe finds himself drawn to a younger woman (Julia Roberts), but it takes all of DJ's considerable powers of persuasion to get him to overcome his angst and pursue her.

When it comes to humor, *Everyone Says I Love You* is overflowing with genuinely funny moments that span the spectrum from physical comedy to sly, sophisticated wit. Allen gets in a number of terrific one-liners, and his comic sense extends to the musical numbers, many of which are done tongue-in-cheek. There's one sequence where ghosts rise from the grave to dance around and another where doctors and patients form a chorus line. It's difficult not to be impressed by what Allen has achieved with this film: successfully reviving the musical comedy in such a thoroughly delightful fashion. The production may be uneven, but it's still wonderful to behold, even at the end, when the structure frays around the edges.

HIGHLY RECOMMENDED

Evita [1996]

Starring: Madonna, Antonio Banderas, Jonathan Pryce Director: Alan Parker Screenplay: Alan Parker and Oliver Stone Running Time: 2:14 Rated: **PG** (Minor violence) Theatrical Aspect Ratio: **2.35:1**

As bold and dazzling a spectacle as *Evita* is, it's missing a soul. This brash, glitzy, energetic entertainment has the power to hold an audience enraptured, but, at the same time, there's a sense that what we're experiencing is just candy for the eyes and ears. In its own way, *Evita* is much like this past summer's blockbusters — lots of flash and pizzazz, but very little beneath the surface. Anyone expecting more than loud music and boisterous musical numbers will be disappointed. *Evita*, even more than the stage show upon which it is based, is light on characters and even lighter on historical facts.

Only the bare facts of Evita Peron's life have been retained for the film. As in the stage musical, she is represented as an heroic figure — sometimes vain and self-serving, but rarely harsh or manipulative. This doesn't necessarily agree with the historical record, but it makes for better cinema. Likewise, Jonathan Pryce's Juan Peron is played as far more amiable than the actual dictator who took control of Argentina during the mid-'40s.

Eva Duarte (or, as she was better known, Evita) was born in 1919, the bastard child of a man who perished when she was 7. Thirty-three years after her birth, Evita, then the wife of Argentina's President, Juan Peron, died of cancer. The film, which opens with a flash forward to Evita's funeral, takes us from the day in 1926 when she places flowers upon her father's casket to the time when thousands of mourners file past her own still form. In between, she uses an affair with a singer (Jimmy Nail) to enable a move from her family's rural home to Buenos Aires, where she eventually becomes Peron's wife. Once he takes over the country, she attempts to apply her newfound power to the task of bettering the lot of Argentina's women and lower classes.

Evita tells Evita's story almost entirely in song (spoken lines are few and far between), making it more of an opera than a traditional musical. There are several familiar tunes (most notably, "Don't Cry for Me, Argentina"), but much of the dialogue is delivered in recitatives, which occasionally seem awkward. Nevertheless, in those instances when *Evita* reaches its musical stride, with a full orchestra accompanying Madonna's strong, clear voice, this movie soars. Unfortunately, in the end, it always comes back to Earth.

RECOMMENDED

Fiddler on the Roof [1971]

Starring: Topol, Norma Crane, Leonard Frey, Molly Picon, Paul Mann
Director: Norman Jewison Screenplay: Joseph Stein, adapted from his
stage play and based on "Tevye and His Daughters" by Sholom
Aleichem Running Time: 3:00 Rated: G Theatrical Aspect Ratio: 2.35:1

Fiddler on the Roof takes place around 1910 in a small Ukranian village. It is an uncertain time. Unrest grips the country — unrest caused by the Pogroms (when Jews were driven en masse from their homes), rising anti-Tsarist sentiment, and the approach of World War I. The historical realities of the time do not simply provide a colorful backdrop to this story; they are central to all that transpires. A central theme is how the old traditions are disintegrating under the pressure of a world culture that is being re-shaped by industrialization and mechanization.

One of those traditions is the means by which Jews have been married: a matchmaker chooses a wife for a man, the girl's father approves the match, and the ceremony is held. That's how Tevye (Topol) and his wife, Golde (Norma Crane), were united, and that's how the hard-working milkman believes his 5 daughters should find their husbands. But Tzeitel (Rosalind Harris) has other, modern ideas. She spurns Tevye's selection of a mate, the wealthy butcher Lazar Wolf (Paul Mann), in favor of her childhood sweetheart, the poor tailor Motel (Leonard Frey). Reluctantly, Tevye eventually assents to her choice, but, in doing so, he acknowledges the freedom of all his children. Subsequently, his second daughter, Hodel (Michele Marsh), decides to marry a young revolutionary, Perchik (Paul Michael Glaser). And Tzeitel and Hodel's younger sister, Chava (Neva Small), falls in love with a non-Jew by the name of Fyedka (Raymond Lovelock). This is one match that Tevye cannot countenance, and he warns of dire consequences if Chava goes through with the marriage.

As with any musical, the focus never strays far from the songs, and *Fiddler on the Roof* contains a number of instantly recognizable numbers, from the lively and uplifting "Tradition," "If I Were a Rich Man," and "To Life" to the delightful "Matchmaker" and the sublime "Sunrise, Sunset." In all, the film contains more than a dozen songs. Jewison does his best to incorporate them seamlessly into the storyline, which causes "Matchmaker" and "Sunrise, Sunset" to be more subdued than in many stage productions. However, those in search of a particularly rousing rendition need look no further than "If I Were a Rich Man."

Fiddler on the Roof is not a perfect motion picture — it is too long and there are times when it's obvious that the musical numbers have been prerecorded then lip-synched — but it represents an enjoyable 3 hours. Jewison's attention to detail is undeniable, and it's obvious that he immersed himself in the material, creating an effective and enduring cinematic representation of a great play.

HIGHLY RECOMMENDED

Grease [1978]

Starring: John Travolta, Olivia Newton-John, Stockard Channing,
Jeff Conaway Director: Randal Kleiser Screenplay: Allan Carr,
Bronte Woodward based on the play by Warren Casey and
Jim Jacobs Running Time: 1:50 Rated: PG (Sexual innuendo,
mild profanity) Theatrical Aspect Ratio: 1.85:1

Grease boasts what all successful motion picture musicals have: likable stars, a simple but not trivial plot, and a lot of enjoyable music. Familiarity with the soundtrack is undoubtedly one of the reasons for the film's popularity — several of the songs have achieved pop hit status. Who can't recognize "Grease," "Hopelessly Devoted to You," "You're the One that I Want," "Greased Lightning," and "Summer Nights"? These may not represent great music, but they're a lot of fun to listen to, as their abiding appeal proves. (Incidentally, 3 of those, "Grease," "Hopelessly Devoted," and "You're the One" were penned specifically for the movie; the others are leftovers from the stage show.)

The plot, such as it is, opens during the summer of 1958 when, to the tune of "Love is a Many Splendored Thing," Danny (Travolta) and Sandy (Newton-John) fall in love. After pledging their undying affection, they go their separate ways, returning to the reality that every teenager must face after Labor Day — high school. The two are in for a surprise, however. Sandy has changed schools, and, unbeknownst to Danny or her, they are now both in Rydell High's Senior Class. Their eventual reunion, however, is anything but joyous. Although Danny is secretly delighted to see Sandy, he realizes that an overt display of joy will look bad in front of his tough friends, so he plays it cool. To Sandy, the reaction is like a slap in the face. The two then spend the rest of the movie dancing around each other, eventually getting together for the musical finale.

In addition to the songs, highlights of *Grease* include Travolta's daffy, limber performance as Danny, Newton-John's sexy-but-sweet Sandy, and a cast of adults trying vainly to pass themselves off as high-schoolers. Despite all of the silliness and singing, the exuberance of youth lies at the core of *Grease*, and, although everything is greatly exaggerated here, the film brings back memories of what it was like to hang out in the school yard, take a date to a drive-in movie, and attend a prom. *Grease* works as a musical, a comedy, a light romance, and a gentle satire of teenage life during the '50s. RECOMMENDED

Hedwig and the Angry Inch [2000]

Starring: John Cameron Mitchell, Michael Pitt, Miriam Shor, Stephen Trask Director: John Cameron Mitchell Screenplay: John Cameron Mitchell, based on the play by John Cameron Mitchell and Stephen Trask Running Time: 1:35 Rated: R (Sexual situations, profanity, nudity) Theatrical Aspect Ratio: 2.35:1

In many ways, *Hedwig and the Angry Inch* is the most far afield of any recent musical. The subject matter is certainly edgy: a transvestite singer, who, as a result of a botched sex-change operation only has an "angry inch" left between his legs, strives for the same stardom accorded to his successful former gay lover and protégé. Hedwig (John Cameron Mitchell) grew up behind the wall in East Berlin. Living in a cramped apartment with an unloving mother, Hedwig (nee Hansel) led an unhappy childhood and, by late adolescence, he was confused about his sexuality. His chance for freedom arrived when a U.S. serviceman offered to marry him and take him to the United States — provided he obtained the sex-change operation. Eventually, Hedwig ended up alone and penniless in the U.S. midwest, where he met Tommy Gnosis (Michael Pitt), who became Hedwig's musical collaborator. After a rift developed between Tommy and Hedwig, the former hit paydirt and started playing in front of arena crowds while Hedwig and his band continued to toil in small clubs and bars. Now, shadowing Tommy on his U.S. tour, Hedwig is determined to get what he believes to be rightfully his — a piece of Tommy's action.

Although *Hedwig and the Angry Inch* features an array of over-the-top costumes and a strong central performance by writer/director/star John Cameron Mitchell, the movie's selling point is its music. While none of *Hedwig*'s half-dozen numbers are likely to become Top 40 radio hits, they aren't as outrageous as one might expect from a film with this title. A mix of rock and pop, there's nothing in any of these tunes that couldn't be ascribed to the likes of a Phil Collins or an Elton John (with the exception of one song that could have been written by the Sex Pistols). The mu-

sical numbers are gaudily presented and exhibit a lot of toe-tapping energy.

Hedwig deals with issues of duality and healing. The aim of the film is to show how Hedwig became the confused, conflicted individual he is and to illustrate the healing process he undergoes to again become whole. At the movie's beginning, Hedwig believes he has already become a butterfly; we learn that he's still in the chrysalis. In addition to the high level of energy imparted by the musical numbers, *Hedwig* boasts a darkly funny screenplay that is littered with instances of self-deprecating humor. The film wants us to take something away from it, but it also doesn't want us to take it *too* seriously. RECOMMENDED

Jeanne and the Perfect Guy [France, 1998]

Starring: Virginie Ledoyen, Mathieu Demy Directors: Olivier Ducastel, Jacques Martineau Screenplay: Olivier Ducastel, Jacques Martineau Running Time: 1:38 Rated: Not rated (Sex, nudity, mature themes) Theatrical Aspect Ratio: 2.35:1 In French with subtitles

At first glance, *Jeanne and the Perfect Guy* appears to be a relatively traditional French melodrama — well acted and intelligently written, but nothing special. Then a group of janitors breaks into song and the cinematic landscape has changed. Approximately 50% of this movie is told through its music, with a significant portion of the dialogue being presented in the lyrics.

Jeanne (Virginie Ledoyen) is a sexually promiscuous young woman. By days, she toils as a receptionist at a travel agency; by nights, she plays musical beds with her many lovers, one of which is a supervisor at work (portrayed as a self-centered cad by Frédéric Gorny). Even her sister, Sophie (Valérie Bonneton), thinks she's a slut. But Jeanne is simply looking for Mr. Right — someone she's not sure really exists. Then, one Sunday morning on a train, she locks eyes with Olivier (Mathieu Demy), and it's love at first sight. The two are so drawn to each other that, once the car has emptied, they have sex there and then. Jeanne has found her perfect man, but there's a problem: Olivier is HIV+ (acquired from his days as a heroin user), and the AIDS virus is already taking its toll on his health. By entering into a relationship with him, Jeanne risks the inevitable pain of a permanent separation — but she is powerless to control her feelings for Olivier. And, although he feels terrible guilt for subjecting her to such an unfair ordeal, he cannot deny the strength of the attraction.

Presenting *Jeanne and the Perfect Guy* as a musical gives the film a fresh perspective (the story alone certainly isn't unique). Co-directors Olivier Ducastel and Jacques Martineau, making their motion picture debuts, sail smoothly through potentially treacherous waters. Done incorrectly, this movie could have turned into an awkward experience, but Ducastel and Martineau are in control of the material. The movie is also characterized by genuine emotional depth and the refreshingly open attitude that the French have towards sexuality. One of the best scenes features a naked Jeanne and Olivier in bed, singing heartfelt (and somewhat bittersweet) endearments to each other.

Jeanne and the Perfect Guy is not a perfect movie. The final cut is a little unpolished, but the compensation for this is a raw, infectious energy, and, as offbeat fare, it's difficult to beat. Even for those who don't consider themselves to be fans of musicals, there's plenty about this movie to applaud. **RECOMMENDED**

Little Shop of Horrors [1986]

Starring: Rick Moranis, Ellen Greene, Vincent Gardenia, Steve Martin Director: Frank Oz Screenplay: Howard Ashman, based on the screenplay by Charles B. Griffith Running Time: 1:34 Rated: PG (Cartoon violence, mild profanity) Theatrical Aspect Ratio: 1.85:1

The 1986 version of *Little Shop of Horrors* is a celebration of two beloved motion picture genres: the musical and the cheesy science fiction flick. Before making it to the screen in its final form during the '86 Christmas season, *Little Shop of Horrors* had a long and colorful history. It is based on an off-Broadway play that soared to popularity during the early '80s. That, in turn, was loosely adapted from Roger Corman's infamous 1960 B-grade monster movie of the same name

Little Shop of Horrors tells the story of a downtrodden nerd named Seymour Krelborn (Rick Moranis) who lives in the basement of his workplace, Mushnik's Flower Shop. Mr. Mushnik (the late Vincent Gardenia) treats Seymour like dirt, causing Seymour to bemoan his fate: "I keep askin' God what I'm for, And He tells me 'Gee, I'm not sure.'" The other employee at the "God — and customer — forsaken store" is the platinum blond bimbo Audrey (Ellen Greene, reprising the role she played on stage in New York and London), with whom Seymour is hopelessly in love. Audrey secretly fantasizes about living a life with Seymour as her husband, but doesn't reveal her dreams because her boyfriend, a sadistic dentist named Orin Scrivello, D.D.S (Steve Martin), wouldn't like it.

For Seymour, everything is about to change. A strange and exotic plant he recently bought is beginning to blossom into something the likes of which no one has ever before seen. It's a sickly thing, however, because it responds only to one kind of food: fresh blood. After draining himself on a daily basis via cuts in his fingers, Seymour is rewarded by a spurt of growth from Audrey II. Suddenly, the plant is the talk of the city, Seymour is famous, and Mushnik's Flower Shop is flooded with customers. But, when Seymour cannot keep up with the plant's insatiable appetite, Audrey II makes a suggestion (yes, it can talk, using the voice of the Four Tops' Levi Stubbs): ice the nasty, abusive Orin and use him as food.

Little Shop of Horrors is one of those musicals where it benefits the viewer to pay attention to the lyrics, because they're saturated with humor and in-jokes. This is the kind of charming motion picture that can be viewed repeatedly without ever wearing out its welcome. With several triumphant musical numbers, an original villain, a smart and witty script, a cute romance, and a new, upbeat ending, this *Little Shop of Horrors* offers countless delights during its 94-minute running time. **HIGHLY RECOMMENDED**

Love's Labour's Lost [United States/United Kingdom, 2000]

Starring: Kenneth Branagh, Alicia Silverstone, Alessandro Nivola, Natascha McElhone Director: Kenneth Branagh Screenplay: Kenneth Branagh, based on the play by William Shakespeare Running Time: 1:35 Rated: PG-13 (Sensuality) Theatrical Aspect Ratio: 2.35:1

Love's Labour's Lost is about 1/3 Shakespeare, 1/3 song-and-dance, and 1/3 ribald slapstick. At times, the wedding of these elements is awkward, but the overall result is strangely appealing. Kenneth Branagh has envisioned the film as a romantic musical comedy, with an emphasis on the final two words of the term. Branagh has elected to liven up the story by including about 10 musical numbers, often replacing lengthy verse-laden soliloquys with elaborate production numbers. But there's a catch. The play has been time-shifted into the late-1930s, allowing Branagh to incorporate standards of the era. As a result, we hear such familiar tunes as "The Way You Look Tonight," "Cheek to Cheek," and "There's No Business Like Show Business."

The story is undoubtedly the movie's weakest point, and does not stand out as one of Shakespeare's high points. We are introduced to the 4 male leads: King Ferdinand of Navarre (Alessandro Nivola), and his 3 best friends, Berowne (Branagh), Longaville (Matthew Lillard), and Dumain (Adrian Lester). In concert, these 4 have agreed to sign a ridiculous pact: for 3 years while students at a university, they will fast, sleep only 3 hours per day, and forego women. Berowne warns that the oath is not one that any of them will be able to keep, and his words prove to be prophetic. When the Princess of France (Alicia Silverstone) arrives with her 3 lady attendants, Rosaline (Natascha McElhone), Maria (Carmen Ejogo), and Katherine (Emily Mortimer), all of the men are smitten. But complications ensue when Berowne entrusts a love letter to the king's clown, Costard. At the same time, Don Adriano de Armado gives the fool a missive professing his love for a local wench, Jaquenetta (Stefania Rocca) — and Costard mixes the letters up.

Although *Love's Labour's Lost* does not score the kind of complete success that Branagh has achieved with his other Shakespeare adaptations, it is a welcome addition, not only because it represents the first time the play has been brought to the screen, but because it shows the lengths to which the director is willing to stretch the envelope. Flaws (most of which are minor) aside, *Love's Labour's Lost* is an enjoyable trifle, especially for those who don't take their Shakespeare *too* seriously and those who love the old Hollywood musicals as much as Branagh obviously does. **RECOMMENDED**

Madame Butterfly [France, 1995]

Starring: Ying Huang, Richard Troxell, Ning Liang, Richard Cowan, Jing-Ma Fan Director: Frederic Mitterrand Screenplay: Giuseppe Giacosa and Luiji Illica Running Time: 2:14 Rated: Not rated (Mature themes) Theatrical Aspect Ratio: 1.66:1 In Italian with subtitles

For his 1995 version of Puccini's *Madame Butterfly*, Frederic Mitterrand chose not to film a live performance or craft a set-bound, stagy motion picture. Instead, he took his cast and crew on location, giving this rendition of the opera a decidedly cinematic quality. From a technical standpoint, Mitterrand's approach to *Madame Butterfly* is unique, and it reaps dramatic dividends.

For those unfamiliar with the story, Puccini's opera tells of a self-absorbed American naval officer named Benjamin Franklin Pinkerton (Richard Troxell) who buys a 15-year-old geisha, Cio-Cio-San (a.k.a. "Butterfly," played by Ying Huang), to be his "Japanese wife." From the beginning, Pinkerton has no intention of staying with Butterfly — he is using her as temporary amusement, a bit of comfort in a foreign port. Despite being enchanted by her quiet, fragile beauty, he has no difficulty abandoning her at the first opportunity. Yet, even after Pinkerton has been

gone for 3 years, Butterfly awaits his return, confident that he loves her as much as she loves him.

Madame Butterfly takes place in 1904 Japan, just outside of Nagasaki, and, in addition to being a tragedy of Shakespearean proportions, it also illustrates a common international perception of American imperialist attitudes. Pinkerton isn't just a good-looking, dislikable cad who abandons a young, innocent girl — he's a personification of his entire nation, and, by extension, Butterfly represents the countries that the United States ruthlessly plundered and left behind. Using archival footage of the time, Mitterrand brings home the film's historical perspective far better than a live version ever could.

For the most part, operas, like musicals, improve with familiarity. It's difficult to guess how Puccini diehards will react to some of Mitterrand's creative choices, but the result is a cinematic success — powerful, passionate, and memorable. It's a daring way for the director to present *Madame Butterfly*, and I applaud his decision to try something different than a traditional, formal version. I have little doubt that my appreciation will increase with successive viewings. **HIGHLY RECOMMENDED**

Moulin Rouge [United States/Australian, 2001]

Starring: Nicole Kidman, Ewan McGregor, John Leguizamo, Jim Broadbent, Richard Roxburgh Director: Baz Luhrmann Screenplay: Baz Luhrmann & Craig Pearce Running Time: 2:06 Rated: PG-13 (Mature themes, double entendres) Theatrical Aspect Ratio: 2.35:1

Moulin Rouge subjects its viewers to a sensory overload with gaudy, gloriously overproduced musical numbers that pay homage to the greats of the past while simultaneously outdoing them. When Ewan McGregor and Nicole Kidman are dancing on the clouds, they're doing so with digitally-created stardust falling all around them. Splashed with garish colors that span the spectrum, *Moulin Rouge* is bright, brash, and wildly entertaining. It modernizes the musical in a way that may give younger movie-lovers a sense of why this genre was once so popular. The production numbers are presented with so much energy and gusto that it's impossible not to be sucked in — and also impossible not to feel a moment's letdown on each occasion when one is over and it's time to get back to moving the paper-thin narrative forward.

The film's protagonist and narrator is Christian (Ewan McGregor), a penniless writer who hooks up with a group of bohemians putting together a play to be performed at the Moulin Rouge. His goal: "to write about truth, beauty, freedom, and love." When the group's leader, the dwarf Toulouse Lautrec (John Leguizamo), likes Christian's work, he decides to get him a one-on-one interview with the star of the Moulin Rouge's racy revue, the courtesan Satine (Nicole Kidman, who keeps her clothes on throughout — much to the chagrin of male viewers). He is immediately smitten, and, to her surprise, so is she. But she is also being pursued by a wealthy duke (Richard Roxburgh), whose investment in the Moulin Rouge will make the club's owner, Zidler (Jim Broadbent, who keeps his clothes on throughout — much to the relief of all viewers), a wealthy man. And there's another factor — Satine is afflicted with tuberculosis (her fate is revealed in the film's first scene, but I won't give it away here).

Despite all of the bombastic musical numbers, or perhaps because of them, the love story in *Moulin Rouge* works. At times, it's even touching. Some of this has to do with the actors. Ewan McGregor plays his role with a puppydog likability and naïve romanticism, and Nicole Kidman positively smolders. Their voices are strong and clear (although occasionally drowned out by the instruments). Historical purists and those who enjoy only sedate films are likely to be infuriated by what Luhrmann has done here, but who cares? We live in an age of excess, and Luhrmann takes it to the hilt. **RECOMMENDED**

Stop Making Sense [1984]

Starring: David Byrne, Tina Weymouth, Chris Frantz, Jerry Harrison
Director: Jonathan Demme Running Time: 1:28 Rated: Not Rated
(Nothing offensive) Theatrical Aspect Ratio: 1.85:1

Upon its release in 1984, Jonathan Demme's *Stop Making Sense* was hailed by many critics as the "greatest concert film of all time." The picture, which captured a live concert performance given by the Talking Heads, used state-of-the-art direct-to-digital re-recording and non-intrusive camera positioning and movement to capture the kinetic energy of the experience and replicate it for nationwide theatrical viewing. Demme's greatest ally is simplicity. He understood that the Talking Heads put on a strong enough show that there was no need for the cameras to artificially enliven things. Consequently, we are not subjected to the barrage of irritating quick cuts that have become the norm in the MTV era of concert footage.

Despite being a concert film, *Stop Making Sense* possesses the skeleton of dramatic structure. It takes

6 numbers for the entire band to assemble in front of the audience. For the first song, "Psycho Killer," David Byrne takes the barren stage alone, using a boom box and acoustic guitar as his only accompaniments. Tina Weymouth joins Byrne for "Heaven," followed by Chris Frantz for "Thank You For Sending Me An Angel," Jerry Harrison for "Found A Job," and the supporting band members for "Slippery People." Not until "Burning Down the House" are all the pieces in place.

The Talking Heads capture their audience through music and shared energy, not through pyrotechnics and violent/sexual imagery. The set design is stark and the lighting simplistic. Sex might normally sell rock-and-roll, but not in this case. For the most part, the Talking Heads don't do love songs — they sing about simple things in life. In fact, David Byrne, with his herky-jerky movements that resemble a man undergoing electric shock treatment, is almost anti-sexual. He is also the consummate showman. At various times during the concert, he jogs in place, runs from one side of the stage to the other, appears ready to devour the microphone, bobs his head like a chicken, dances with a floor lamp, falls on his back and sings from a prone position, and seems to lose complete control of his body. This movie is pure fun and sheer exuberance transferred onto celluloid and perfectly re-created at the other end. Experiencing what Demme and the Talking Heads have crafted with this motion picture makes perfect sense. **MUST SEE**

The Umbrellas of Cherbourg [France, 1964]

Starring: Catherine Deneuve, Nino Castelnuovo, Anne Vernon, Marc Michel, Ellen Farner Director: Jacques Demy Screenplay: Jacques Demy Running Time: 1:27 Rated: Not Rated (Mature themes)
Theatrical Aspect Ratio: 1.66:1 In French with subtitles

The Umbrellas of Cherbourg was initially released in 1964, and, amongst other things, helped catapult Catherine Deneuve to stardom. In filming *The Umbrellas of Cherbourg*, director Jacques Demy opted to sacrifice print longevity for vibrant color. The stock he used yielded brilliant hues, but degraded quickly. By the mid-'70s, the only remaining copies of the film were in terrible condition. But Demy, anticipating this problem from the outset, had archived multiple monochromatic negatives that, when properly combined with each other, allowed re-creation of the original color. With Demy's widow, Agnes Varda, supervising the re-mastering, *The Umbrellas of Cherbourg* was recently brought back to life, and is now available in its previous splendor.

As a musical, *The Umbrellas of Cherbourg* is unusual in several ways. First, unlike most big American productions of the time, there are no show-stopping production numbers. There's no dancing, no chorus, and no duets. Secondly, there are *no* spoken lines of dialogue — everything, from the mundane to the important, is sung. Finally, *The Umbrellas of Cherbourg* isn't a lightweight bon-bon with a happily-ever-after ending. While the film has its share of effervescent moments, there's also an element of undeniable poignancy.

The two main characters, 17-year-old Genevieve (Deneuve) and 20-year-old Guy (Nino Castelnuovo), are star-crossed lovers. Despite the stringent objections of Genevieve's mother (Anne Vernon), who thinks a gas station mechanic is beneath her daughter, the two continue their clandestine meetings, and eventually consummate their relationship. Soon after, Guy has to serve a stint away from France in the army. Following his departure, Genevieve learns that she is pregnant, and must decided whether to wait for Guy's uncertain return or marry the rich, cultured Roland Cassard (Marc Michel), who offers stability, undying love, and the promise of raising her child as his own. Genevieve's choice irrevocably alters the lives of at least four people.

Agnes Varda's recent reconstruction has done the film justice. The colors, which include bright pinks, reds, purples, and oranges, look great, and the cleaned-up soundtrack is better than ever. Although *The Umbrellas of Cherbourg* lacks song-and-dance numbers, there is one tune that recurs throughout. This song, beautifully composed by Michel Legrand, radiates longing and loss, and forms the movie's core. It, like the film, is far more powerful than one would initially suppose. **HIGHLY RECOMMENDED**

West Side Story [1961]

Starring: **Natalie Wood, Richard Beymer, Russ Tamblyn, Rita Moreno**
Directors: **Robert Wise & Jerome Robbins** Screenplay: **Ernest Lehman** based on the play by Arthur Laurents and Jerome Robbins Running Time: **2:32** Rated: **Not Rated (Mild violence)** Theatrical Aspect Ratio: **2.35:1**

The movie transpires in New York's Upper West Side during the late 1950s. The feuding Montagues and Capulets are represented by rival gangs: the Jets and the Sharks. The former group is comprised of first-generation New Yorkers whose parents came across on boats during the early decades of the century. Their rivals are Puerto Rican immigrants who are newly arrived in the United States. The constant skirmishing of the Jets and the Sharks is primed to explode into an open war, but not before Tony (Richard Beymer), a founder of the Jets (who is no longer with the gang — he has gotten a job), falls in love with Maria (Natalie Wood), the sister of the Sharks' leader. In true *Romeo and Juliet* fashion, these two defy conventions and risk everything, including their lives, to be with one another. And, also as in Shakespeare's play, there are no happy endings.

To its credit, *West Side Story* does not shy away from difficult issues. It explores both the senselessness of gang strife and the prejudice faced by immigrants. Yet, by today's standards, its views on both seem a little naïve. However, the film's approach to violence is unique. *West Side Story* is almost bloodless — even the stabbing and gunshot scenes are sanitized. All the fights are highly stylized and divorced from reality. The characters dance around each other while in the process of stalking and attacking. Yet there's a real sense of menace to some of these scenes, due in large part to the choreography and Bernstein's dissonant score. We end up feeling the violence more than seeing it. It doesn't always work — the power of the scenes in which characters die is arguably lessened by this approach — but it enables a grittier story to be told within the musical framework.

Until Baz Luhrmann attempted a highly unusual take of *Romeo + Juliet* using snatches of Shakespeare's original dialogue in a radical setting, *West Side Story* remained the best known and most atypical modernization of the Bard's tale. And, even though the movie version of the stage production does not play quite as well today as it once did, it still represents a brave and effective fusion of serious and fantasy elements, and offers 2½ hours of solid entertainment. Admittedly, there are times when *West Side Story* strikes a campy or discordant note, but those instances are overbalanced by the more frequent moments when it offers its own brand of cinematic magic. **HIGHLY RECOMMENDED**

Romance

10 Things I Hate About You [1999]

Starring: Heath Ledger, Julia Stiles, Joseph-Gordon Levitt, Larisa Oleynik Director: Gil Junger Screenplay: Karen McCullah Lutz & Kirsten Smith Running Time: 1:38 Rated: PG-13 (Sexual themes, double entendres, profanity) Theatrical Aspect Ratio: 1.85:1

10 Things I Hate About You is a modern-day, souped-up version of William Shakespeare's *The Taming of the Shrew*. What sets this apart from its many competitors for teen dollars is that not only does the movie feature a surprisingly edgy and intelligent script, but it offers a group of characters capable of holding an audience's interest for more than 90 minutes.

Kat (Julia Stiles) and Bianca (Larisa Oleynik) are sisters, but, despite sharing the same parents, their personalities are polar opposites. Bianca, the younger, is pretty, popular, and shallow. Kat, the older one, is a rebel without a cause, a girl who is described kindly as being "incapable of human interaction." Kat and Bianca's father, Walter (Larry Miller), has one hard and fast rule for his daughters: Bianca cannot begin dating until her sister does. This represents a major problem for the socially-adept Bianca, since Kat shows no inclination whatsoever to date. As the prom approaches, Bianca finds herself as the object of two boys' affections: cool, vain Joey Donner (Andrew Keegan) and kind, somewhat shy Cameron James (Joseph Gordon-Levitt). Working as reluctant allies, Joey and Cameron pick out a potential date for Kat: Patrick Verona (Heath Ledger), the local bad boy. They reason that Kat might find him too great a challenge to refuse, and, once she starts going out with him, Bianca will be free to date one of them. But getting Kat and Patrick

together proves to be a difficult chore, and, when he realizes that he genuinely likes her, Patrick must go to extraordinary lengths to tame the shrew.

The dialogue in *10 Things I Hate About You* is peppered with sexual references and double entendres. Kat has all of the best lines, and Stiles utters them with relish. Smart, sharp dialogue may not be the foundation of a good movie, but it certainly is a key ingredient, and one of the reasons why *10 Things I Hate About You* succeeds. The comedy (and there's plenty of it) is of the hit-and-miss variety, sometimes trying too hard to get laughs instead of letting them come naturally. Some of it is genuinely funny, while other examples (the buffoonery of Kat and Bianca's father) miss the mark by a wide margin. The love stories are frothy, although the plot is littered with the debris of several unfortunate romantic comedy devices. However, if we accept that these elements are a necessary part of the genre, then *10 Things I Hate About You* ranks as one of the strongest entries in the recent wave of teen-oriented films — a pleasant blend of Shakespeare and John Hughes. **RECOMMENDED**

Addicted to Love [1997]

Starring: Meg Ryan, Matthew Broderick, Kelly Preston, Tcheky Karyo Director: Griffen Dunne Screenplay: Robert Gordon Running Time: 1:41 Rated: R (Sexual content) Theatrical Aspect Ratio: 1.85:1

Maggie (Meg Ryan) is a bad girl, although not quite as bad as she'd like everyone to believe. She wears her hair short and unkempt, travels around the streets of New York on a motorcycle, and prefers donning anything in black that exposes her navel. She talks tough and her eyes are hard little agates, except when she's alone and a softer side comes to the surface (Ryan does a good job showing this in mostly-subtle ways, such as the set of Maggie's shoulders). Why is she so abrasive? Because her currently mission in life is revenge — revenge against the ex-fiancée, Anton (Tcheky Karyo), who cast her aside when he found his latest paramour, Linda (Kelly Preston).

Linda happens to have been the lifelong love of small-town astronomer Sam (Matthew Broderick). When *Addicted to Love* opens, we're shown a slice of his idyllic life (complete with a number of irritating technical inaccuracies about the abilities of a telescope) — how he has a job he loves and a woman he adores. But Linda is restless, and she decides to take a 2-month trip to New York City. While there, she meets Anton, falls in love, and moves in with him. When Sam learns the truth via a "Dear John" letter, he gets on the next flight to the Big Apple.

In New York, he sets up home in abandoned building across the street from the apartment shared by Linda and Anton, and constructs a camera obscura to watch their every movement (his voyeurism recalls the likes of *Rear Window* and *Stakeout*). Soon, Maggie joins him in his "bohemian hellhole," bringing along bugging equipment so they can have sound in addition to video. Together, the two hatch a plan to break apart the new lovers — Sam, so he can win back Linda, and Maggie, so she can see Anton "in pain, hopeless, and finished off."

It's kind of fun seeing Meg Ryan suppress her usual mannerisms and do the grunge thing, but not nearly as enjoyable as it is immersing oneself in director Griffen Dunne's bizarre-yet-oddly-engaging romantic comedy about voyeurism, moldy strawberries, and monkeys wearing lipstick. *Addicted to Love* is for those who don't mind a world view that's a little askew, yet who can still accept that love conquers all. **RECOMMENDED**

As Good as It Gets [1997]

Starring: Jack Nicholson, Helen Hunt, Greg Kinnear, Cuba Gooding Jr. Director: James L. Brooks Screenplay: Mark Andrus and James L. Brooks Running Time: 2:18 Rated: PG-13 (Nudity, profanity, mature themes, violence) Theatrical Aspect Ratio: 1.85:1

As Good as It Gets is really two related movies in one, which explains the surprisingly long running time. While 138 minutes is fine for an epic adventure or a weighty drama, it makes a lightweight effort like this seem a little bloated. The film is ambitious: it tries to wed the modern-day, non-supernatural *A Christmas Carol* with a traditional romantic comedy. Director

James L. Brooks, who does these kinds of movies as well as anyone in Hollywood, has moderate success. *As Good as It Gets* is not a positive triumph, but it does bring a smile to the face and, perhaps in some cases, a tear to the eye.

Jack Nicholson plays Melvin, a successful author who lives the life of a recluse. He's a homophobic, anti-Semitic racist with an intense dislike of dogs and people. The neighbors in his Greenwich Village apartment building all avoid him, and the waitress at his favorite restaurant barely tolerates his presence. To make matters worse, Melvin is afflicted with an obsessive/compulsive disorder that makes his behavior seem even more strange.

Then something happens to change Melvin's life. One of his neighbors, a gay artist named Simon (Greg Kinnear), is beaten up by a group of robbers. Simon's dealer, Frank (Cuba Gooding Jr.), forces Melvin to care for Simon's dog. Gradually, Melvin comes to love the little animal, and, after discovering a previously-unsuspected wellspring of humanity deep within himself, he begins exercising it in other ways: paying a doctor to care for the sick son of his regular waitress, Carol (Helen Hunt), and offering Simon support when he comes home from the hospital.

Ultimately, it's the quirks and details of *As Good as It Gets*' script (by Brooks and co-writer Mark Andrus), rather than the broad strokes, which make the film enjoyable. Essentially, this is a formulaic, connect-the-dots tale which offers few, if any surprises. Fifteen minutes into the movie, you'll be able to guess exactly how it will all work out. As a result, the chief pleasure for the next 2 hours is watching the characters grow and interact as they traverse the familiar path. *As Good as It Gets* may not quite live up to its title, but it doesn't fall unacceptably short of the mark. **RECOMMENDED**

Bed of Roses [1996]

Starring: Mary Stuart Masterson, Christian Slater, Pamela Segall, Josh Brolin Director: Michael Goldenberg Screenplay: Michael Goldenberg Running Time: 1:27 Rated: PG (Mature themes) Theatrical Aspect Ratio: 1.85:1

Bed of Roses follows the expected pattern of a conventional romance: two characters meet and fall in love, complications arise, causing a breakup, then there's a reunion just in time for the end credits. Although the film offers few surprises in its formulaic progression of events, the tale is told with heartfelt tenderness, and, for once, the circumstances that threaten the pair's happiness have nothing to do with re-appearing old flames.

In some romances, couples must cross a generational gap to be together. Other times, the barrier may be cultural or racial. In *Bed of Roses,* each of the protagonists — Lisa (Mary Stuart Masterson) and Lewis (Christian Slater) — must overcome their own emotional dysfunctions in order to enter into a relationship. As a result of tragic pasts, neither is confident about expressing feelings, and, while both are emotionally needy, they discover that receiving is often as hard as giving.

Lewis was a happily married Wall Street mover and shaker when he lost both his wife and baby to childbirth. Since then, he has devoted his life to his new job: delivering flowers from the shop he owns. Lisa had a sad, lonely childhood that she never recovered from. Now, to compensate for the emotional gulf in her life, she has thrown herself fully into her career. One night while Lewis is out for a walk, he looks up and sees Lisa standing by her window, crying. Moved, and not understanding why, he sends her an anonymous flower arrangement. Eventually, after being pressed for the sender's name, Lewis admits the truth, then follows up by inviting Lisa to spend the day with him, delivering flowers and watching people's faces.

Bed of Roses probably wants to be more literate than it succeeds at being. The film belabors the symbolism of flowers, which, at one point or another, stand for everything from life and love to the fragility of emotions. There are also messages about the importance of family and how the traumas of childhood affect a person's behavior as an adult. Not all these themes are effectively explored. Better, however, for *Bed of Roses* to be overambitious than for it to "dumb up" its script. Although the overall story claims little in the way of originality, it at least approaches its material with charm, which is more than can be said of many so-called love stories. RECOMMENDED

Before Sunrise [1995]

Starring: Ethan Hawke, Julie Delpy Director: Richard Linklater Screenplay: Richard Linklater and Kim Krizan Running Time: 1:41 Rated: R (Mature themes, language) Running Time: 1:41 Theatrical Aspect Ratio: 1.85:1

Richard Linklater has succeeded where many before him have failed — in fashioning a modern-day romance that is both original and enthralling. *Before Sunrise* is nothing short of movie magic. Even the best romantic comedy/dramas tend to be formula-driven, frequently relying more upon actor chemistry than plot. Surprises are about as foreign to this genre

as a pacifist hero is to a shoot-'em-up. Somewhere along the way, a storyteller originated the basic love story structure. Film makers have religiously followed this roadmap, rarely taking more than an occasional minor detour. With *Before Sunrise,* however, Linklater not only travels an entirely different route, but heads for a new destination.

Jesse (Ethan Hawke) meets Celine (Julie Delpy) on a train traveling through Europe. His destination is Vienna, where a flight back to America awaits him the next morning. She's on her way to Paris, where she starts classes at the Sorbonne next week. From their first moment of eye contact, they're drawn to each other. They share a meal in the lounge car, savoring the conversation more than the food, and when they arrive in Vienna, Jesse persuades Celine to disembark with him and keep him company wandering the streets until the time comes for his plane to depart. Thus begins an unforgettable screen romance.

One of the first things to notice about *Before Sunrise* is how completely natural it all seems. Credit both director Linklater and his two leads. The rapport between Jesse and Celine is so lacking in artifice that at times the viewer feels like a voyeur. We are privy to everything, including the sort of "unimportant" dialogue that most films shy away from. Here, its inclusion is just one of many fresh elements. *Before Sunrise* is about life, romance, and love. It magnifies the little things, paying scrupulous attention to the subtleties and mannerisms of body language. There are moments of unforced humor, and times of bittersweet poignancy. *Before Sunrise* speaks as much to the mind as to the heart, and much of what it says is likely to strike a responsive chord — a rare and special accomplishment for any motion picture. MUST SEE

Belle Epoque [Spain, 1992]

Starring: Jorge Sanz, Fernando Fernan Gomez, Penelope Cruz, Maribel Verdu, Ariadna Gil Director: Fernando Trueba Screenplay: Rafael Azcona Running Time: 1:48 Rated: R (Sexual situations, brief nudity, language, mature themes) Theatrical Aspect Ratio: 2.35:1 In Spanish with subtitles

Belle Epoque, the winner of 9 Goyas (Spanish Oscars), is a charming motion picture that requires only enough thought and concentration to read the subtitles. As a diversion, the film is fabulous.

It is 1931 Spain and the country's monarchy is facing its final days. During this time of confusion and conflicting loyalties, Fernando (Jorge Sanz), whose allegiance is to the republic, deserts from the army and goes on the run into the Spanish countryside. There, he meets Manolo (Fernando Fernan Gomez), a painter who shares his political beliefs. The two quickly become friends and Fernando spends a night at the older man's house, listening to his stories and cooking for him. Then, in the morning when Fernando is to leave, Manolo's 4 young, beautiful daughters — Luz (Penelope Cruz), Rocio (Maribel Verdu), Violeta (Ariadna Gil), and Clara (Miriam Diaz-Aroca) — arrive. Fernando takes one look at them and decides to prolong his stay with Manolo for a while longer.

Some of issues presented by the tumultuous political climate and the churning waters of religious uncertainty keep *Belle Epoque* from being a completely brainless endeavor. Nevertheless, anything serious is kept strictly in the background, and even the most dismal scenes are presented with enough playfulness to avoid betraying the giddy tone.

All 6 major characters are nicely-developed. Despite the numerous sexual trysts he engages in, Fernando is still something of an innocent, and Jorge Sanz plays him to wide-eyed perfection. The most complex character of all is Manolo, who is based on a real-life acquaintance of producer/director Fernando Trueba. The character's own words describe him best: "I am a rebel, an infidel, and a libertine by nature, living life like a scared old bourgeois."

Very little of the humor in *Belle Epoque* is "intellectual" — in fact, much of it is quite earthy. More important than the nature of the comedy, however, is that it is legitimately funny. As was Trueba's intention when he crafted the film, the viewer's most likely reaction is a smile. Despite the subtitles, this is less art than fun. *Belle Epoque* is an enchanting, unpretentious, 2-hour vacation from the rigors of real life. **RECOMMENDED**

Born Romantic [United Kingdom, 2000]
Starring: Craig Ferguson, Ian Hart, Jane Horrocks, Adrian Lester, Catherine McCormack   Director: David Kane   Screenplay: David Kane   Running Time: 1:36   Rated: R (Profanity, sex)   Theatrical Aspect Ratio: 1.85:1

The light, frothy, and likeable *Born Romantic* is from theater and TV director David Kane (who has made motion pictures before, none of which have been released on this continent). He has gathered a reasonably high profile cast for this project, including such notable names as Craig Ferguson, Ian Hart, Jane Horrocks, Adrian Lester, Catherine McCormack, Olivia Williams, Jimi Mistry, and David Morrissey. *Born Ro-*

mantic essentially tells three loosely connected romantic stories set against the backdrop of a salsa club that is visited by all of the principals.

Fergus (Morrissey) is an ex-musician who is scouring London for his One True Love (Jane Horrocks), a woman he jilted 8 years ago. Eddie (Mistry), an inept thief, unexpectedly falls for shy Jocelyn (McCormack), who has a fetish for morbidity. And Frankie (Ferguson) is hot for the aloof Eleanor (Williams), who seems to have no interest in him whatsoever. In the background are a group of cab divers who act almost like a Greek chorus, offering differing opinions on such diverse subjects as life, love, and blowjobs.

Kane keeps things moving, and it doesn't hurt that there's a great deal of lively salsa music to elevate the energy level. All of the characters are affable; it's virtually impossible not to wish for them to hook up with their soul mates. The screenplay is a shade smarter than that of the average romantic comedy, and there are plenty of funny lines and scenes. And, unlike in many British films, Kane doesn't seek any dark tangents for his characters to explore. This is a straightforward film — enjoyable and fresh, but not terribly deep. **RECOMMENDED**

Bounce [2000]
Starring: Ben Affleck, Gwyneth Paltrow   Director: Don Roos   Screenplay: Don Roos   Running Time: 1:45   Rated: PG-13 (Profanity, sensuality)   Theatrical Aspect Ratio: 1.85:1

Bounce is a solid romance with 3 things going for it. In the first place, Don Roos' dialogue is a cut above the norm. Secondly, stars Ben Affleck and Gwyneth Paltrow connect in a credible manner. Finally, the film touches on a few intriguing philosophical issues, such as the guilt an individual feels when someone close to him or her unexpectedly dies.

The setup is not complicated. It's a few days before Christmas and a group of strangers is stranded at a bar in Chicago's O'Hare Airport. Buddy (Ben Affleck), an ad man, has a first-class ticket back to Los Angeles. Mimi (Natasha Henstridge) has been forced to take a room at the airport hotel because her flight has been canceled. And Greg (Tony Goldwyn) has allowed himself to be bumped from an L.A.-bound flight in order to get 2 free round-trip tickets to anywhere in the U.S. plus $200. So he's waiting for a spot to open up on a later flight. However, when Mimi makes it clear to Buddy that she wouldn't mind it if he shared her hotel room, he gives his ticket to Greg.

Hours later, Flight 82 from Chicago to Los Angeles has crashed and Greg is dead, leaving behind a wife, Abby (Gwyneth Paltrow) and two children (Alex D. Linz and David Dorfman).

It takes Buddy a year and a stay in an alcohol rehab clinic before he can overcome his feelings of guilt and re-emerge into the real world. One of his first actions is to seek out Abby. Even though he has never met her, he feels responsible for her circumstances and wants to make sure she's okay. She's working as a real estate agent and he pretends to be a client. After arranging for his company to buy an expensive property through her, Buddy believes he has paid his karmic debt. But Abby is attracted to him, and keeps contriving ways to meet him. Before long, Buddy finds himself falling in love — not only with Abby, but with her kids as well. And, as this relationship transforms him from a self-serving hotshot into a caring individual, he is aware that, sometime, somewhere, his secret must emerge.

Effective romances are difficult to craft. They must be sentimental and endearing without going overboard. Low-key love stories run the risk of coming across as cold and unemotional. Conversely, going too far in the other direction can result in a cloying, mawkish production. Roos has landed safely on the middle ground. He gives us characters worth caring about and a situation we can feel comfortable with. **RECOMMENDED**

Bread and Tulips [Italy, 2000]
Starring: Licia Maglietta, Bruno Ganz, Marina Massironi, Giuseppe Battiston Director: Silvio Soldini Screenplay: Silvio Soldini, Doriana Leondeff Running Time: 1:52 Rated: PG-13 (Mature themes, profanity) Theatrical Aspect Ratio: 1.85:1 In Italian with subtitles

Bread and Tulips is a light, uncomplicated venture into standard romantic comedy territory. That should not necessarily be seen as a bad thing. This frothy, charming parfait of a motion picture will endear itself to many of those who seek it out.

As the story begins to unfold, Rosalba (Licia Maglietta) is on vacation with her indifferent husband and two sons. When she spends too much time in a bathroom at a rest stop, the tour bus leaves without her and she is stranded. She initially decides to hitchhike home, but, along the way, changes her mind and elects to visit Venice, where she has never before been. Once there, she is so enamored with the setting and her newfound freedom, that she gets a job at a flower store and rents a room from a local restaurateur, Fernando (Bruno Ganz). She becomes close

friends with a neighbor, a flighty masseuse named Grazia (Marina Massironi), who has a history of bad relationships with men. For her part, Rosalba is gradually drawn to the quiet Fernando, and he to her. Meanwhile, Rosalba's husband, unable to cope with cleaning duties around the house, hires an inept private investigator, Costantino (Giuseppe Battiston), to seek out his absent wife.

Strong acting is *Bread and Tulips'* greatest asset. It enables us to identify with the characters and, as a result, to root for their well-being and a happy ending. The lion's share of the screen time belongs to the luminous Licia Maglietta, who reminds us that it's possible for a 40-something woman to effectively function at the epicenter of a romantic comedy. Maglietta's performance is flawless, and, since the story isn't solely focused upon Rosalba's romantic entanglement with Fernando, but is also about how she changes when liberated from the constraints of an unhappy marriage, she presents us with a memorable transformation. Bruno Ganz, perhaps best known for his part in Wim Wenders' *Wings of Desire,* nicely underplays Fernando. The chemistry between Maglietta and Ganz is low-key, but palpable.

Director Silvio Soldini has a clear understanding of what audiences want from a motion picture like this, and he delivers it without hesitation — a strong female protagonist, a mature love story that isn't bogged down by saccharine or melodrama, and some effectively realized moments of comedy. *Bread and Tulips* doesn't offer much in the way of substance, but that doesn't prevent it from having a high enjoyability quotient. **RECOMMENDED**

Brown Sugar [2002]
Starring: Taye Diggs, Sanaa Lathan, Mos Def, Ralph E. Tresvant, Nicole Ari Parker Director: Rick Famuyiwa Screenplay: Michael Elliot and Rick Famuyiwa Running Time: 1:48 Rated: PG-13 (Sexual situations, profanity) Theatrical Aspect Ratio: 1.85:1

Those looking for a concise description of *Brown Sugar* could refer to it as the "African American *When Harry Met Sally.*" After all, it is a romantic comedy that asks the popular movie question of whether a man and woman can be platonic friends without sex becoming an issue.

Music producer Dre (Taye Diggs) and magazine editor Sidney (Sanaa Lathan) have known each other since childhood, when they became friends as a result of their mutual love for hip-hop music. That love led both of them to their respective careers. Dre makes records and Sidney reviews the music. Over the years, neither of them has seriously considered the other as a potential romantic partner, until something happens to upset the chemistry — Dre falls in love with the willowy Reese (Nicole Ari Parker), and decides to get married. Despite feigning delight, Sidney is less-than-happy with the prospect of her friend tying the knot, and, after she and Dre share a kiss on the night before his nuptials, he is left with his own doubts — doubts that are deepened when Sidney begins dating a star New Jersey Nets basketball player (Boris Kodjoe).

The backdrop of *Brown Sugar* is the world of hip-hop music, and rapper Mos Def has a role as an artist that Dre decides to back. The soundtrack is loaded with hip-hop numbers, and will prove to be a "must have" for fans. However, although hip-hop provides form, color, and a rather obvious metaphor (Dre and Sidney's love for music represents their love for one another), it is not *Brown Sugar*'s focal point. The key to unlocking the film's enchantment is to uncover the unforced romance. We know how this is going to play out, but, as in any worthwhile comedy about love, the pleasure is derived not from the destination, but from the road taken to get there.

Despite having an all-black cast, *Brown Sugar* is essentially color-blind. Or, to put it another way, the film's intrinsic appeal is not confined to African American audiences. There are undoubtedly some who will complain that *Brown Sugar*'s screenplay has been homogenized for mass-market consumption, but it doesn't seem to me that there's anything wrong with making a movie that can attract both black and white viewers. And, if you want edgy, looking to a romantic comedy to provide it is ill-advised. *Brown Sugar* is undemanding fun capable of providing 2 hours of entertainment for anyone who enjoys a smart story with plenty of romantic tension. **RECOMMENDED**

Chasing Amy [1997]

Starring: Ben Affleck, Joey Lauren Adams, Jason Lee Director: Kevin Smith Screenplay: Kevin Smith Running Time: 1:55 Rated: R (Profanity, frank sexual discussion) Theatrical Aspect Ratio: 1.85:1

With *Chasing Amy*, it's easy to anticipate a certain degree of inventive humor, but what's a bit unexpected is the solid drama, effective romance, and strong characters. *Clerks* worked because the dialogue sparkled, but Smith has honed his screenwriting and film making skills since then. While *Chasing Amy*

boasts the same keen interplay, that quality, along with first-rate character development, acts as a supplement to the smart, surprisingly original plot. The movie starts out as light as a feather, but it doesn't take long for us to realize that *Chasing Amy* isn't just another lark for Smith. This movie is *about* something, and the deeper we get into it, the more we realize how emotionally on-target the script is.

Holden McNeil (Ben Affleck) and Banky Edwards (Jason Lee) are comic book authors. Their *Bluntman & Chronic* magazine is a big-seller, and, when they attend a comic book convention in New York, they attract long lines for autograph signings. At that convention, Holden meets fellow comic writer/artist Alyssa Jones (Joey Lauren Adams). Alyssa's project is the less testosterone-oriented *Idiosyncratic Routine*. She and Holden hit it off almost immediately. They go out for a few drinks and play darts. Later, when talking to best friend Banky, he claims that he and Alyssa "shared a moment" and confesses that he has fallen for her. But, whether or not it's really love, Holden is in for a big surprise because Alyssa is a lesbian. So, while she wants to be friends and pal around with him, Holden finds himself helplessly, hopelessly smitten.

Smith clearly has his hand on the pulse of his generation ("X" marks the spot). His observations about comic books, video games, and other aspects of life in the '90s are as insightful as they often are scathing. But this is nothing new — it was evident in both *Clerks* and *Mallrats*. What's different here is that Smith has crafted a touching, nuanced romance. There are real human feelings and problems involved in Holden and Alyssa's relationship, and, every time the storyline threatens to devolve into a cliché, it somehow avoids the trap. There's also a rich subtext pertaining to the difficulty that many individuals face in attaining a level of comfort with their sexual identity. **HIGHLY RECOMMENDED**

City of Angels [1998]

Starring: Nicolas Cage, Meg Ryan, Denis Franz, Andre Braugher Director: **Brad Silberling** Screenplay: **Dana Stevens** based on *Wings of Desire* Running Time: 1:56 Rated: PG-13 (Occasional profanity, discreet sex, brief male nudity) Theatrical Aspect Ratio: 2.35:1

City of Angels is based, not unexpectedly, in Los Angeles, which here is a literal "City of Angels," with the invisible celestial agents sitting high atop billboards and skyscrapers. Dressed like Heaven's Men in Black, the angels are an odd bunch. They spend their days and nights observing and occasionally offering comfort to select humans. They cannot touch, taste, or smell. They are immortal and ethereal. They live in a library and spend time at the beach in a kind of wordless communion.

Seth (Nicolas Cage) is just one of many angels assigned to Los Angeles. But, unlike most of his brethren, he has a strong desire to experience what it's like to be human. He seems to share the sentiment of a comment that he relates to fellow angel Cassiel (Andre Braugher): "What good would wings be if you couldn't feel the wind on your face?" One day, Seth is in a hospital to guide a dying man to the next life. His attention is captured by the determination of a doctor, Maggie Rice (Meg Ryan), to save the patient's life. Later, he returns with the intention of soothing Maggie's distress, but it proves to be a difficult task. Soon, he is spending hours on end watching her, eventually revealing himself as a benevolent stranger. Seth has fallen in love with Maggie, but he thinks it's a doomed proposition until a angel-turned-human (Denis Franz) reveals that God gives all of his creations free will, and, if Seth wants it enough, he can shed his wings for a human body. But, just because Seth loves Maggie, there's no guarantee that she will reciprocate his feelings, and if he gives up his immortality for a romantic illusion, what then?

When it comes to heavenly matters, *City of Angels* doesn't offer any particular insights. The movie does not ponder the meaning of life; rather, it shamelessly celebrates the human experience by demonstrating the monotony of endless voyeurism. On a somewhat less-intellectual level, it's also about sacrifice. *City of Angels* is more romantic than profound, but Dana Stevens' script is thoughtful and intelligent, and I never felt insulted by what the characters said, did, or thought. It's a subdued motion picture, but the lack of overt melodrama makes for a moving and involving story. **RECOMMENDED**

The Closer You Get [Ireland, 2000]

Starring: Ian Hart, Sean McGinley, Niamh Cusack, Ruth McCabe
Director: Aileen Ritchie Screenplay: William Ivory, based on a story by Herbie Wave Running Time: 1:32 Rated: PG-13 (Occasional profanity, mild violence, sexual themes) Theatrical Aspect Ratio: 1.85:1

The Closer You Get, the feature debut of director Aileen Ritchie, is one of those feather-light romantic comedies that's pleasant to watch but not likely to stick in the mind long after the end credits have rolled. It's a welcome distraction, but not much more.

The film takes place in Ireland, and some of its charm comes from the culture and countryside. Of course, all of the characters in this film are eccentrics, but that's only to be expected, since a movie featuring normal Irish folk wouldn't be as quirky.

The Closer You Get focuses on the romantic trials and tribulations of a group of young men living in a small, out-of-the-way village. They meet every night in the pub to bemoan the lack of attractive, eligible women in their town. Of course, this sort of talk doesn't go over well with the members of the opposite sex. Oddly, with the exception of the pub owner, no one seems to be married. In fact, the local priest, who is new to the district, has never performed a wedding. Eventually, bitten by the romance bug, the men take an action out of desperation. Led by their ring-leader, Kieran O'Donnagh (Ian Hart), who is said to have "the constitution of an ox and the wits to match," they decide to place an ad in a Miami newspaper trumpeting the assets of their village and its men for any adventurous American women who would like to cross the ocean and get married. Then, to the amusement of the local womenfolk, they sit back and await the arrival of their potential brides.

The romantic fantasy employed here is a common one — that we often miss true love because we're busy looking in the distance while it's right under our nose. That's where the title comes from: "The closer you get to something, the harder it is to see." With a single exception (the pub keeper), everyone in *The Closer You Get* is likable. Kieran may be a bit dense, but he's the kind of dullard who's easy to like. As was true of the characters in *The Full Monty,* we find ourselves rooting for these men, even though they're not traditional hero material. While Irish films have yet to become a staple of American cinema, they are gradually gaining in popularity. **RECOMMENDED**

The Cutting Edge [1992]

Starring: D. B. Sweeney, Moira Kelly, Roy Dotrice, Terry O'Quinn
Director: Paul M. Glaser Screenplay: Tony Gilroy Running Time: 1:40
Rated: PG (Mature themes, profanity) Theatrical Aspect Ratio: 1.85:1

Romantic comedies are a dime-a-dozen, and most of them fail because they pursue slapstick while losing sight of the characters. Because *The Cutting Edge* doesn't fall into that trap, it results in an enjoyable lark. Despite a recycled plot, this appealing motion picture is likely to be embraced by everyone who enjoys a little romance.

It's "The Taming of the Shrew" on ice, even down to the name of the female lead. Kate Mosely (Moira Kelly) has been a pairs skater for most of her life, and her ultimate goal has always been an Olympic gold medal. But, despite her talent, she has an attitude problem that drives partner after partner away until even the least experienced skaters would rather "sleep with [a] cross and wear garlic" than join Kate on the ice. So, when her coach (Roy Dotrice) becomes desperate, he tries something unconventional — seeking out ex-Hockey star Doug Dorsey (D.B. Sweeney), who's spending his days working at his brother's sports bar while coming to grips with the reality that an eye injury has ended his professional dreams.

The Cutting Edge is not built on storyline. From the opening scene to the closing credits, there is not one new plot element in this entire movie. Zip. Nada. Zilch. We've seen it all before, whether in sports films or romantic comedies. Those looking for originality had best search somewhere else. However, there are some movies where plot has to play second string to characters, and this is one of them. Kate and Doug are refreshingly real and immensely likable. Their love/hate relationship is played out perfectly, recalling the Bruce Willis/Cybill Shepherd sparring matches of *Moonlighting,* albeit without all the teasing. It's the romantic tension, not the skating story, that holds *The Cutting Edge* together.

Anyone expecting a movie dominated by figure skating will be disappointed. *The Cutting Edge* concentrates on its characters, with the skating limited to a supporting role. This is not a movie for cynics, nor for those who don't occasionally like to sit back and enjoy an undemanding, "comfortable" film. For unadulterated fun, *The Cutting Edge* may not earn a gold medal, but it's worth at least a bronze. RECOMMENDED

Déjà Vu [1997]

Starring: Stephen Dillane, Victoria Foyt, Vanessa Redgrave, Glynis Barber Director: Henry Jaglom Screenplay: Henry Jaglom & Victoria Foyt Running Time: 1:57 Rated: PG-13 (Profanity, brief sexuality) Theatrical Aspect Ratio: 1.85:1

Is there such a thing as love at first sight? It's a question that cynics and romantics have debated endlessly for as long as there has been a common language. Film maker Henry Jaglom, who is known for his languidly-paced, verbose movies, is obviously a believer, and he uses his latest work, *Déjà Vu,* as a platform to examine not only the phenomenon of love at first sight, but the consequences of accepting

it, and the role that fate and coincidence play in all of our lives.

Déjà Vu opens in Tel Aviv, where Dana (Victoria Foyt), an American, is making purchases for her business. There, in a café, she meets an elderly woman (Aviva Marks), who tells her a sad story of love, then leaves a pin of great sentimental value in Dana's possession before disappearing. Knowing the woman's approximate address in Paris, Dana flies there, and, while in a jewelry shop, she spots Sean (Stephen Dillane) for the first time. Their eyes lock and there is an immediate attraction. She soon encounters him again, this time in Dover, and they speak, acknowledging the difficult-to-fathom electricity that exists between them. It's an uncomfortable situation, because he is married and she is engaged. Nevertheless, he offers to drive her to London and she accepts. Once there, they discover that they're both staying at the same house for the weekend.

There are so many coincidences in *Déjà Vu* that the plotline has an artificial feel to it, as if every action is choreographed to serve a purpose or emphasize a point. In many films, so many contrivances would wreck the drama, but since one of the primary themes of *Déjà Vu* relates to the mysterious working of fate to bring men and women together, Jaglom's approach makes perfect sense. By the end of the movie, when the script reveals one final twist, we're no longer surprised; it's a fitting way to bring closure to the situation.

I enjoyed *Déjà Vu* because it made me think, remember, and consider the appealing notion that there is *someone* out there for each of us. *Déjà Vu* is for romantics, not cynics, and those who pooh-pooh the notion of love at first sight may find Jaglom's approach hard to swallow. For the rest of us, however, it's a hopeful look at a philosophy that is wonderful to mull over, and even more pleasant to believe in. RECOMMENDED

Don Juan De Marco [1995]

Starring: Marlon Brando, Johnny Depp, Faye Dunaway, Rachel Ticotin Director: Jeremy Leven Screenplay: Jeremy Leven Running Time: 1:37 Rated: PG-13 (Mature themes, nudity, profanity) Theatrical Aspect Ratio: 1.85:1

The title character, a modern day Don Juan (with the Italian last name of DeMarco), is played by Johnny Depp. At the age of 21, he claims to have made love to more than 1,500 women. He has been rejected only once, by the enchanting and innocent Ana (Geraldine Pailhas), but, as is so often the case, she was "the only one who really mattered." So, with no possibility of a life with his true love, Don Juan decides to kill himself. He climbs high atop a billboard and demands that the police send him the greatest living swordfighter so he can die in a duel. What he gets instead is Dr. Jack Mickler (Marlon Brando), a massively-overweight, near-to-retirement psychiatrist who pretends to be Don Octavio de Flores and talks Don Juan down from his perch. Then, at Woodhaven State Hospital, where the young man is temporarily held, Jack petitions his boss (Bob Dishy) for the right to supervise the newcomer's treatment.

Don Juan DeMarco is a lighthearted, frothy fable about romance and the way a patient's fantasies affect his doctor's reality. Despite several astute lines which give the film an intellectual appeal, this is not an exceptionally deep movie. The playful, often humorous tone, coupled with Don Juan's accent, suggests *The Princess Bride*. Writer/director Jeremy Leven takes pleasure in clouding the division between what's real and what isn't, but he never stretches matters to such an extreme that *Don Juan DeMarco* is reduced to a mindless farce.

Don Juan DeMarco has a seductively sensual veneer, but the full complement of the title character's sexual conquests lacks the romance of the low-key relationship between Jack and his wife (Faye Dunaway). These two act like they've been married for 32 years, and her wonder at his sudden re-awakening is charmingly unaffected. There is proof here — as if any is really needed — that couples don't have to be under thirty to capture an audience's heart.

With so much blurring between reality and fantasy, there are bound to be a few missteps, but Leven keeps these to a minimum, and the film is mostly a success in its approach to its themes. Don Juan asks the four essential questions about existence: "What is sacred?," "Of what is the spirit made?," "What is worth living for?," and "What is worth dying for?" The proposed answer to all is "love," that singular emotion which pervades this disarming motion picture. **RECOMMENDED**

Emma [1996]

Starring: Gwyneth Paltrow, Toni Collette, Jeremy Northam, Alan Cumming, Ewan McGregor Director: Douglas McGrath
Screenplay: Douglas McGrath based on the novel by Jane Austen Running Time: 2:01 Rated: PG (Nothing offensive) Theatrical Aspect Ratio: 1.85:1

It's the romantic buried inside each of us that responds to movies like *Emma*. Sure, the film, like the

Jane Austen novel upon which it is based, is laced with wit and sophistication. And, although it contains enough social commentary and character development to lift it well above the plane of genre romances, *Emma* is still primarily about lovers finding each other during a simpler age (Austen published her novels in the early 19th century).

Emma details the matchmaking attempts of 21-year-old Emma Woodhouse (Gwyneth Paltrow), an incorrigible meddler who believes that "there is nothing more beautiful than a match well made." After successfully marrying her governess (Greta Scacchi) to a widower (James Cosmo), Emma sets her sights on pairing her plain, uncultured friend, Harriet Smith (Toni Collette), with the local vicar, Reverend Elton (Alan Cumming). Elton, however, has other ideas, as does Emma's closest male friend, Knightley (Jeremy Northam), who describes her activities as "vanity working on a weak mind [that] produces every kind of mischief." Emma herself is unattached, but, since this is a Jane Austen story, it's obvious that won't last for long. Indeed, before the 2 hours are up, the title character has become enmeshed in a number of romantic entanglements, and it doesn't take a genius to uncover the identity of Emma's true soul-mate.

Emma lacks the depth of passion present in the other Austen films, but, in large part because it's trying for something lighter and breezier, it's still fun. The film runs a little longer than seems necessary, and gets off to a slow, fitful start (Douglas McGrath's screenplay is not the equal of the other Austen adaptations), but Paltrow keeps us interested until the story's inherent romantic magic begins to weave its spell. **RECOMMENDED**

The Englishman Who Went Up a Hill but Came Down a Mountain [United Kingdom/United States, 1995]

Starring: Hugh Grant, Colm Meaney, Tara Fitzgerald, Ian McNeice Director: Christopher Monger Screenplay: Christopher Monger
Running Time: 1:39 Rated: PG (Mature themes) Theatrical Aspect Ratio: 1.85:1

The title of this film, *The Englishman Who Went Up a Hill but Came Down a Mountain*, is so long that it can function as a plot synopsis in its own right. "The Englishman" in question is British cartographer Reginald Anson, played by Hugh Grant with his usual aw-shucks charm, and "the hill/mountain" is Ffynnon Garw, a 984-foot high protuberance in the Welsh terrain. In 1917, as World War One is winding to a conclusion, Anson arrives in Wales with his commanding officer, George Garrad (Ian McNeice), to survey Ffynnon Garw's height. When the mountain is measured at less than the 1,000 feet necessary for official recognition as more than a hill, the locals are up in arms. Horrified by the thought that the "first mountain in Wales" might be considered anything less than grand, they decide to build a 20-foot high dirt mound at the summit, then get the measurement repeated. As an inducement to keep the two Englishmen in town until the construction is complete, a young woman, Betty of Cardiff (Tara Fitzgerald), is called upon to use all her wiles and charms. And, just in case Betty isn't persuasive enough, the visitors' car is sabotaged.

It's rare that a movie owes this much of its success to its director and stars. The storyline for *The Englishman* isn't all that dynamic and the screenplay is rather bland. However, using the acting skills and natural charisma of Hugh Grant, Tara Fitzgerald, and Colm Meaney, director Christopher Monger has compiled a wonderfully droll comedy. For the most part, the humor is witty, not laugh-aloud funny. Chuckles and smiles can be expected, but not explosive guffaws. *The Englishman* is low-key in all aspects, from the comic elements to the love story.

The Englishman is framed as a true story told to a child and, as was the case with *The Princess Bride*, this is the best way to establish the somewhat fanciful narrative. The picture has some things to say about the importance of community and the desultory effects of war, but its primary concern is lightening the heart's burden — a job at which it is eminently successful, regardless of how mountainous the task proves to be. **RECOMMENDED**

Ever After [1998]

Starring: Drew Barrymore, Dougray Scott, Anjelica Huston, Megan Dodds Director: Andy Tennant Screenplay: Susannah Grant and Andy Tennant & Rick Parks Running Time: 2:00 Rated: PG-13 (Mild violence, mild profanity) Theatrical Aspect Ratio: 1.85:1

Ever After's twist is that it's telling the "real" Cinderella story from which the Brothers Grimm fable was derived (the two famous fairy tale scribes make a brief appearance in a prologue that also features a cameo by the incomparable Jeanne Moreau). Consequently, there are no pumpkins, mice, magic spells, or fairy godmothers. The love story between a peasant girl and a prince is still at the core, although, in this case, "Cinderella" (whose name is Danielle), has the kind of progressive attitude that would be more at home in the 1990s than in the 1500s.

The broad strokes of the story are certainly familiar. After the tragic death of her father (Jeroen Krabbe), Danielle (played by Anna Maguire as a little girl, and Drew Barrymore thereafter) is consigned to a life of servitude for her cruel stepmother, Rodmilla (Anjelica Huston), and vain step-sister, Marguerite (Megan Dodds). Danielle has an ally in the household, her second step-sister, Jacqueline (Melanie Lynskey), but she's too meek to stand up to her mother. While Rodmilla, Marguerite, and Jacqueline enjoy as much luxury as their farm house provides, Danielle (dubbed "Cinderella" by Marguerite for the cinders that always stain her clothing) is forced to scrub the floors, cook the meals, and feed the animals.

One day, when Danielle is picking apples, she spies a man stealing one of her step-mother's horses. It's actually Prince Henry (Dougray Scott), the heir to the throne of France, in the process of running away from his father because he is unwilling to be trapped in a loveless, arranged marriage. Mistaking Henry for a common thief, Danielle knocks him from the horse with a well-aimed apple. After she realizes who he is, she is apologetic, but the meeting leaves an impression on both of them. At the time of their next encounter, Danielle is posing as a countess in order to rescue a family retainer from debtors' prison. She engages the Prince in a spirited debate, and, although he thinks he recognizes her, he can't put a name to the face. Soon, he is scouring the countryside looking for her, and, although Danielle is attracted to him, she avoids contact, fearing that if he learns that she isn't a member of the nobility, he will shun her. Through all of this, there is a fairy godmother of sorts — Leonardo da Vinci (Patrick Godfrey), who uses science, not magic, to smooth the path of true love.

Tennant, who showed skill at the helm of a romance with *Fools Rush In*, has found the right tone for this effort. The love story is wrapped around interludes of comedy, adventure, and drama. It never seems to matter that we know the entire story from the beginning — the characters, not the plot, capture our attention. **RECOMMENDED**

Fools Rush In [1997]

Starring: Matthew Perry, Salma Hayek Director: Andy Tennant Screenplay: Katherine Reback from a story by Joan Taylor and Katherine Reback Running Time: 1:46 Rated: PG-13 (Mature themes, sex) Theatrical Aspect Ratio: 1.85:1

Done well, a romantic comedy can be an enchanting experience — something guaranteed to bring a smile to the lips of all but the most hardened cynic. Done poorly, a film in that genre can be sickening and unbearable. It's all a matter of style, tone, and chemistry. Some films have it; many don't. Fortunately for those who venture out to *Fools Rush In,* it's camped in the former category. If you want daring or original, *Fools Rush In* isn't the movie to see. Like 90% of all romantic comedies, it follows a time-honored formula that allows little room for variation. For those who don't know it, it goes something like this: boy meets girl, boy and girl fall in love, boy loses girl, boy goes after girl, boy and girl get together and live happily ever after.

The "boy" in this scenario is Alex Whitman (Matthew Perry), a WASP construction manager for a chain of nightclubs popping up all over the United States. His latest gig has landed him in Las Vegas, where he runs into the "girl." She's Isabel Fuentes (the radiant Salma Hayek), a strict Mexican American Catholic who has just broken off an engagement to longtime boyfriend Chuy (Carlos Gomez). She and Alex have a one night stand, then, 3 months later, she shows up at his home and tells him that she's pregnant. Twenty-four hours later, they're married, but it takes the rest of the movie before they attain wedded bliss.

Between falling in love and finding happiness come The Complications. Depending on the romantic comedy, these can be (guess the movie): deciding whether men and women can be just friends, claiming to be engaged to an unconscious man, trying to split up the winnings from a lottery ticket, arranging a meeting atop the Empire State Building, skating into the Olympics, and so on . . . In *Fools Rush In,* The Complications arrive in the form of a culture clash. Mexico-born Isabel and Connecticut-born Alex are from two different worlds, and the impending birth of a baby doesn't suddenly sweep away all differences. While *Fools Rush In* isn't going to win any awards, it should please most audiences, which is about the most anyone can ask for from this kind of effervescent, unambitious project. RECOMMENDED

Forces of Nature [1999]

Starring: Sandra Bullock, Ben Affleck, Maura Tierney, Steve Zahn
Director: Bronwen Hughes Screenplay: Marc Lawrence, Ian Bryce, Donna Roth Running Time: 1:46 Rated: PG-13 (Mild profanity, sexual themes) Theatrical Aspect Ratio: 1.85:1

Murphy's Law states that anything that can go wrong will go wrong, and that's exactly what happens to Ben Holmes (Affleck) with the approach of his wedding day. Ben, who earns his living by writing blurbs for book jackets, and his fiancée, Bridget (Maura Tierney), live in New York City, but the big event is being conducted in Savannah, Georgia. So, a couple days before he's due to tie the knot, Ben, who's terrified of flying, reluctantly boards a southern-bound plane at JFK. Shortly thereafter, the plane has crashed (actually, it never gets off the ground), and Ben is trying to find an alternative means of transportation to Savannah. Coming to his rescue is Sarah (Sandra Bullock), an attractive freespirit he helped during the crash. She gets them both a ride in a rental car with a guy named Vic. It's only the first of many segments of a wild and unpredictable trip down the East Coast that includes planes, trains, and automobiles. Along the way, Ben starts to fall for Sarah, and is forced to examine whether he *really* wants to marry Bridget after all.

Affleck and Bullock share an effective chemistry that enhances their scenes. Although *Forces of Nature* isn't really about sex — it's more about love, romance, and taking chances — there's an element of eroticism in Ben and Sarah's interaction, and it's never overplayed. Affleck also connects with his other female co-star, Maura Tierney, in a palpable way, which makes it difficult to determine which lovely lady Ben will finish the film with. Because Affleck and Bullock spend the lion's share of the screen time in each other's company, it's only natural to root for them to end up together. On the other hand, there's a sense of genuine affection and tenderness between Ben and Bridget. This conflict heightens the limited dramatic aspect of *Forces of Nature.* There's a realization that, no matter what happens, someone is going to get hurt — if only a little bit.

In many ways, the romance is just a backdrop for a series of crazy misadventures. While *Forces of Nature* doesn't go for the all-out zaniness of *Planes, Trains, and Automobiles* (there are no pillows), the 1986 film is clearly an inspiration. During the course of their trek, Ben and Sarah are arrested, end up on a train going in the wrong direction, lose all their money (a necessary plot device), masquerade as a rich, married couple, are chased by the police, and are waylaid by a hurricane. Towards the end of the trip, as the couple watches a building go up in flames, Ben jokes, "Let's just sit here and wait for the locusts to come." *Forces of Nature* represents a pleasant movie-going experience — one that replaces cloying romance with something breezier while remaining true to the appeal of the leads. RECOMMENDED

The Girl on the Bridge [France, 1999]

Starring: **Vanessa Paradis, Daniel Auteuil** Director: **Patrice Leconte**
Screenplay: **Serge Frydman** Running Time: **1:30** Rated: **R (Sex)**
Theatrical Aspect Ratio: **2.35:1** In French with subtitles

The Girl On the Bridge follows standard romantic comedy guidelines with some interesting variations and rhythms. There are those who will immediately assume that because the film is French, it must contain deep philosophical musings, but that's not really the case. Leconte, working from a script by Serge Frydman, tickles the underbelly of things like fate and chance, but he never does much with these weighty issues. They are present as plot devices; this is not a deep exploration of the existential aspect of humanity's nature. Instead, it's a quirky love story that appeals more to the emotions than to the intellect.

With the exception of a few supporting characters who make brief appearances, this is essentially a two-character movie. Adele (Vanessa Paradis) is a down-on-her-luck young woman who is convinced that she is afflicted with a Midas Touch in reverse. She's as unlucky in love as she is in life in general. A compulsive sex addict, she sleeps with almost any man she has eye contact with, but she falls in love easily and has had her heart broken on multiple occasions. Eventually, after deciding that things aren't going to get better, she walks out on a bridge crossing the Seine and prepares to jump. That's when she meets Gabor (Daniel Auteuil), who changes the course of her life.

Gabor is a professional knife-thrower, and he offers Adele an alternative to suicide: become his assistant (a position which, he insists, might lead to the same end). She agrees, and the two begin a successful partnership. Of course, they fall in love, but neither admits it. Adele continues her trysts with attractive men, and, although she and Gabor never consummate their relationship, they develop a deep psychic bond (they can hold conversations over long distances) and their knife-throwing exhibitions mimic sex in every way possible (except that they're not touching). Best of all, when they're together, they have tremendously good luck. But, when their paths diverge, their fortunes begin a downward spiral.

If subtitles were not so feared in the United States, *The Girl On the Bridge* might have been a big hit — an unpretentious romantic comedy that revels in the exuberance of new love. However, because it is not in English, the movie never reached a wide American audience. But, for those who aren't scared off by the thought of entertainment in a different language, a rewarding experience awaits. *The Girl On the Bridge* is an appealing diversion. **RECOMMENDED**

Go Now [United Kingdom, 1996]

Starring: **Robert Carlyle, Juliet Aubrey, James Nesbitt, Sophie Okonedo** Director: **Michael Winterbottom** Screenplay: **Paul Powell and Jimmy McGovern** Running Time: **1:26** Rated: **R (Mature themes, profanity, sex)** Theatrical Aspect Ratio: **1.85:1**

Few screen romances are as touching, as tragic, and as life affirming as the one shared by Nick (Robert Carlyle) and Karen (Juliet Aubrey) in director Michael Winterbottom's *Go Now*. While the film is ultimately about the effects of multiple sclerosis upon both a body and a relationship, *Go Now* is not the exercise in depression the material might make it seem to be. By including a copious amount of lowbrow humor and occasionally using black-and-white freeze-frames with amusing captions, director Michael Winterbottom never allows *Go Now* to become too much of a downer.

The film starts at the beginning — the beginning of Nick and Karen's relationship, that is. They meet one night at a pub, then, after a few chance meetings on the street following their initial encounter, they start dating. The relationship quickly becomes serious, and the two move in together. Only then does Nick's disease begin to assert itself. In this way, Winterbottom allows us to get to know the characters before introducing complications.

It starts slowly, with minor symptoms: double vision, numbness of the hands, and a lack of bladder control. Nick goes for tests and is diagnosed to have MS. *Go Now* doesn't use a didactic, "movie of the week" approach to the subject. It doesn't explain what MS is, why people get it, or how they can live with it. Instead, the film concentrates on showing the condition's debilitating effects on Nick, and, equally important, on his perfectly-healthy partner. It's rare for any motion picture about a disease to take such a blunt, uncompromising look at how it can erode the foundation of even the most loving relationship. Sunk in frustration and self-pity, Nick frequently lashes out at Karen, torn between wanting her to leave him alone in his misery and needing her to help him. For her part, Karen loves Nick dearly, but his moodiness threatens to drive her into the arms of another man, if only for a brief respite from Nick's rancor.

With its rich and varied emotional texture, *Go Now* is a movie that you feel deep in the heart, with a pair of characters, Nick and Karen, who are so vivid that they stay with you long after the theater lights have gone on. *Go Now* illuminates the director's keen, unerring insight into the complexity of emotions and situations that movies too often reduce to familiar clichés. Wrenching, passionate, and unforgettable, *Go Now* hardly makes a misstep from beginning to end. **HIGHLY RECOMMENDED**

Innocence [Australia, 2000]

Starring: Charles Tingwell, Julia Blake, Terry Norris   Director: Paul Cox   Screenplay: Paul Cox   Running Time: 1:38   Rated: R (Sex, nudity, profanity, mature themes)   Theatrical Aspect Ratio: 1.85:1

Innocence is little more than a solid, old-fashioned romance. In essence, the movie doesn't do anything more ambitious than chronicle the ebb and flow of a romantic relationship between two characters. The emotions they feel are familiar to all of us — young and old, male and female, gay and heterosexual. The plot doesn't do anything extraordinary, and, if it's given to occasionally slipping into melodrama, we must forgive it — after all, that's a characteristic of even the best romances. And, if the dialogue occasionally becomes somewhat stilted and esoteric, we must forgive that, as well — better characters saying these kinds of things than spouting the dumbed-down lines that permeate big-budget features. To a degree, *Innocence* doesn't sound that far afield from many motion pictures that arrive in theaters every year, but there is one important difference: the lovers in this romance are both around 70 years of age, and have far less of their lives ahead of them than behind them.

Innocence tells of the affair between Andreas (Charles Tingwell), a widower, and Claire (Julia Blake), a woman trapped in a comfortable but loveless marriage. Fifty years ago, Andreas and Claire were deeply in love, but circumstances separated them. They both married, had children, and lived their lives. Now, in their twilight years, they have found each other again, and, even though their bodies have aged, their passion is as strong as it ever was. Of course, there are complications — Andreas is afflicted with terminal cancer and Claire's husband (Terry Norris) reacts in an expectedly negative manner to the news of his wife's late-life infidelity. But Paul Cox's script remains thought-provoking, even when it veers into melodrama.

Is *Innocence*'s appeal generation-based? While older viewers are more likely than younger ones to identify intimately with the characters, the central emotions are universal. There's nothing in *Innocence*

that will confound or alienate an 18-year old. It has been suggested that the idea of depicting two 70-year olds having sex (the scenes are not graphic, but they are present) is somehow revolutionary, but that would imply that 70-year olds don't have sex — an idea that is ludicrous. The only thing *Innocence* has done is to face up to a fact of life that some people, for whatever reason, aren't comfortable acknowledging. In the end, *Innocence* speaks to the romantic in all of us, and it doesn't take long before we don't care about age. Cox works his magic on us, and we are drawn in. **RECOMMENDED**

Italian for Beginners [Denmark, 2000]

Starring: Anders W. Berthelsen, Ann Eleonora Jørgensen, Anette Støvelbæk   Director: Lone Scherfig   Screenplay: Lone Scherfig   Running Time: 1:52   Rated: R (Profanity)   Theatrical Aspect Ratio: 1.66:1   In Danish with subtitles

Based on the title, one might mistakenly assume that *Italian for Beginners* is a saucy Italian romp; in point of fact, it comes from Denmark. It is a comedy, and there is romance involved, but the film also has a bit of an edge. There are several truly loathsome characters — an aging mother and father and a deposed pastor, to name a few — which keep the movie from turning light and frothy. And the film earns its R-rating simply because characters occasionally use profanity, not because of a litany of 4-letter words or the presence of explicit sex and/or violence.

Italian for Beginners is 3 romances bundled into one. The connecting thread is that all of the principals live in the same Danish town and, at one time or another, they all attend the same adult education night class: Italian for Beginners. Andreas (Anders W. Berthelsen) is the new pastor, and is desperately uncertain of himself. He becomes interested in shy, clumsy Olympia (Anette Støvelbæk), who works at a baker's shop and lives with a despot of a father. Because the former pastor has not yet vacated the living quarters, Andreas is forced to stay at a hotel. The desk manager there, Jorgen Mortensen (Peter Gantzler), befriends the minister. Jorgen, who hasn't had sex in 4 years, is beginning to despair that he'll ever find a woman who excites him, although there is an attraction between him and Giulia (Sara Indrio Jensen), a waitress at a local restaurant. The restaurant is managed by the sharp-tongued Halvfinn (Lars Kaalund), who also happens to be Jorgen's best friend. He is drawn to Karen (Ann Eleonora Jørgensen), who runs a hair-cutting salon. These characters engage in an elaborate courtship dance until, during a vacation they take together in Venice, each relationship is clarified — one way or another.

Director Lone Scherfig has the benefit of a well-written script (which she penned) that throws a few surprises the viewer's way and doesn't tie up all the loose ends to the degree that a Hollywood production might. She also has an expert cast portraying characters that are not lifted off of a stereotype shelf. There is far more going on than one might expect to see in a traditional romantic comedy, and *Italian for Beginners* is all the more rich for it. RECOMMENDED

Jerry Maguire [1996]

Starring: Tom Cruise, Cuba Gooding Jr., Renee Zellweger
Director: Cameron Crowe Screenplay: Cameron Crowe Running
Time: 2:18 Rated: R (Profanity, sexual situations, nudity) Theatrical
Aspect Ratio: 1.85:1

Jerry Maguire is magic on celluloid — fresh, funny, romantic, and upbeat. As the movie opens, super sports agent Jerry Maguire is facing a crisis of conscience (that he still possesses one after working in such a cynical, materialistic business is something of a miracle). He wonders what he has become — "Just another shark in a suit?" He realizes that he hates himself and his place in the world, and laments that, although he has a lot to say, no one will listen. So, late one night, he writes a Mission Statement called "The Things We Think and Do Not Say: The Future of Our Business." The essay attacks the sports agency business, advocating a more humane approach. The next day, a copy is distributed to everyone in the office. And, although Jerry's co-workers applaud his courage ("Somebody finally said what had to be said"), his bosses are offended, and he loses his job. Only one client, unremarkable Arizona Cardinals wide receiver Rod Tidwell (Cuba Gooding Jr.), elects to remain with Jerry as he strikes out on his own. Also joining him is a 26-year-old single mother, Dorothy Boyd (Renee Zellweger), who is so moved by Jerry's Mission Statement that she's willing to throw away a safe job to be part of his new venture.

Jerry Maguire is about redemption and love. It's about finding one's heart and soul in a business climate that attempts to rip both away. Writer/director Cameron Crowe brings both a strong sense of verisimilitude and a lively wit to his film. Even as *Jerry Maguire* reaches out to the heart, it tickles the funny bone. Not only does Crowe have a knack for creating multi-dimensional personalities for secondary characters with minimal screen time, but he uses traditional formulas in unique ways to serve his themes.

While the budding romance between Jerry and Dorothy is *Jerry Maguire*'s most enchanting element, the remainder of the film has the necessary appeal to keep our attention when Zellweger isn't around (Cruise, on the other hand, is in just about every scene). Crowe, who doesn't have a subpar entry on his short resume, has crafted another winner here. For anyone who has forgotten the feelings that a wonderful movie can trigger, *Jerry Maguire* provides a welcome reminder. HIGHLY RECOMMENDED

Kate & Leopold [2001]

Starring: Meg Ryan, Hugh Jackman, Liev Schreiber Director: James
Mangold Screenplay: James Mangold and Steven Rogers Running
Time: 2:00 Rated: PG-13 (Profanity) Theatrical Aspect Ratio: 1.85:1

In an attempt to add some freshness to the romance, *Kate & Leopold* throws a little science fiction flavoring into the cinematic stew. As it turns out, however, while this aspect of the film spices things up, it doesn't lead to anything ground-breaking. The Twilight Zone is kept at bay. It's more of a means to create a fish-out-of-water subplot than to investigate the paradoxes of time travel. Ultimately, however, the love story aspect works better than the science fiction one.

Leopold, the Duke of Albany (Hugh Jackman), lives a life of privilege in 1876 until the night when he spies a stranger in his uncle's house. He pursues the man and ends up in 2001 New York City, in the apartment of Stuart (Liev Schreiber), his great-great-grandson. When Stuart is involved in an elevator accident that lands him in the hospital before he can send Leopold back to 1876, the Duke comes under the care of Stuart's ex-girlfriend and downstairs neighbor, Kate (Meg Ryan), and her actor brother, Charlie (Breckin Meyer). Kate knows the truth about Leopold, but doesn't believe it, and she bears her obligation of looking after him like a burden — until she realizes that he would be the perfect spokesperson for an advertising campaign her marketing company is working on. Suddenly, hard-bitten, unromantic Kate and Leopold, the "psychotic escapee from a Renaissance Fair," are spending quite a bit of time together and falling in love. But there's an obvious problem in the form of a 125-year age gap.

One could argue that the dialogue in *Kate & Leopold* is a cut above that from many of Ryan's previous romantic comedies (except perhaps *When Harry Met Sally*), but if this film is relying on its occasional zingers and smart bits of conversation to get bodies in theater seats, it's in trouble. People will go to see Ryan, who's as cute at age 40 as she was in her late 20s, and Jackman, who continues to prove that his range extends beyond that of playing Wolverine in *X-Men*. The chemistry between these 2 bubbles pleasantly. There's no powerful sexual attraction, but this movie is more about innocent romance than passion, so it works. Like most of Ryan's films, *Kate & Leopold* succeeds as a diversion (although, at 2 hours in length, it's too long). It is cinematic cotton candy — insubstantial perhaps, but ultimately sweet and pleasant to the taste. **RECOMMENDED**

Kissing Jessica Stein [2002]

Starring: Jennifer Westfeldt, Heather Juergensen, Scott Cohen, Tovah Feldshuh Director: Charles Herman-Wurmfeld Screenplay: Heather Juergensen & Jennifer Westfeldt, based on their play "Lipschtick" Running Time: 1:34 Rated: R (Profanity, sexual situations) Theatrical Aspect Ratio: 1.85:1

Without resorting to hyperbole, I can state that *Kissing Jessica Stein* may be the best same-sex romance I have seen. The screenplay is written with a thinking audience in mind, the dialogue sparkles, the characters leap off the screen in full three-dimensionality, and the clichés are kept to a bare minimum. Plus, unlike the average romantic comedy, this one deals with thought provoking issues. To wit: if a person is not gay, but is in love with someone of the same sex, how do they display that emotion? Is it possible to have romantic love without a physical expression of it?

Neither of the 2 principles in this movie is a lesbian. Jessica (Jennifer Westfeldt) is straight. Her entire sexual history has been one of pairing with men, and the very thought of having a sexual relationship with another woman is . . . well . . . a little weird. Helen (Heather Juergensen), on the other hand, is bisexual. Her primary partners are men, but there are times when she feels in the mood for female companionship, and usually has no difficulty procuring it. When Jessica and Helen meet, Helen is on the prowl. The two do not immediately connect romantically, but there is a spark, and it doesn't take long for their new friendship to begin straying into the sexual realm. Jessica is nervous about sleeping with Helen, but Helen is patient. She knows that Jessica loves her, but that crossing the line is difficult. Meanwhile, at her office, where Jessica works as a proofreader, she has to deal with her ex-lover (Scott Cohen), whose frequent put-downs and pugnacious nature may hide feelings that he is unwilling to admit.

Kissing Jessica Stein has been called a "lesbian *Annie Hall*," and, while such a description is too facile, it's easy to understand its origins. Like Woody Allen's classic romantic comedy, this movie chronicles the entire arc of a relationship, not just the beginning. Both films effectively wed comedy and drama, never veering too much in one direction or another. Each is set in the shadow of the towering skyscrapers of Manhattan. Finally, *Annie Hall* and *Kissing Jessica Stein* display an understanding of human nature that far, far too many motion pictures ignore. The average romantic comedy relies almost exclusively on the chemistry between the leads; the plot is usually a throw-away. In this case, we are fortunate to have both an interesting storyline and actresses who interact with each other in a pleasant, unforced manner. **HIGHLY RECOMMENDED**

Loser [2000]

Starring: Jason Biggs, Mena Suvari, Greg Kinnear Director: Amy Heckerling Screenplay: Amy Heckerling Running Time: 1:35 Rated: PG-13 (Sexual situations, drug use, mild profanity) Theatrical Aspect Ratio: 1.85:1

Loser is a straightforward romantic comedy where the relationship between two unlikely friends develops into something deeper than a casual acquaintanceship. The film's romantic complications are restrained — they neither stretch the viewer's credulity nor make the characters seem airheaded, vindictive, or blind. Most importantly, the protagonists — a geek's geek named Paul (Jason Biggs) and a gothic grunge girl named Dora (Mena Suvari) — are presented as real people with genuine problems. These two seem less like the product of a writer's invention than the type of individuals one meets on a college campus. Of course, there are limits to the level of verisimilitude that can be employed, since a truly satisfying ending requires a heavy dollop of fantasy.

Paul is a hopeless loser, but he's also the nicest guy attending a prestigious New York City university. He won't accept money from his grandfather, is nice to his little sister, and willingly hangs out with his dad (a cameo appearance by Dan Aykroyd). However, in a city populated by cynics, he is viewed as a living caricature. His three party-animal roommates (played by Thomas Sadoski, Zak Orth, and Jimmi Simpson) find his presence so restricting that they have him kicked out of the dorm. The school relocates him to a small room in a local veterinary clinic. Meanwhile, Dora is trying to balance her financial difficulties with her studies and a torrid affair she's having with her European Lit professor, Edward Alcott (Greg Kinnear). She works nights as a waitress at a topless bar, but her commute is running her down. One night at a party held by Paul's ex-roommates in the veterinary clinic, someone slips something into her juice, and she wakes up in Paul's care.

Romantic comedies, especially those set in high schools and colleges, have suffered from overexposure in the past few years. Most have been cliché-riddled pabulum — endless, thinly-veiled reworkings of *Pygmalion* and *The Taming of the Shrew*. The danger is that *Loser* will suffer from guilt by association at the box office. That would be a shame, because Heckerling's movie is smarter and breezier than anything that has recently traveled this well-trodden path. While *Loser* never quite breaks free of the romantic comedy envelope, it occasionally tests the boundaries. With one exception, the film earns its laughs without turning its characters into buffoons or endangering their dignity. And it's a pleasure to watch a movie in which the protagonists speak and act like individuals who have more on their minds than who they're going to take to the big dance. **RECOMMENDED**

Love and Sex [2000]

Starring: Famke Janssen, Jon Favreau Director: Valerie Breiman Screenplay: Valerie Breiman Running Time: 1:22 Rated: R (Sexual situations, profanity) Theatrical Aspect Ratio: 1.85:1

It is said that first-time filmmakers should stick to what they know, and that's one rule Breiman has taken to heart, jokingly referring to *Love and Sex* as "my sex life on screen." And, although Breiman's admission is designed more as a sound bite than anything else, there's probably some truth to it. Of course, there's a happy ending, but the route to get to that point takes a few refreshing detours from the expected path.

Love and Sex's main character is Kate Welles (Janssen), a writer for *Monique* magazine, where she pens "happy, perky [pieces] on how to find and keep that perfect man." She spends the early part of the film ruminating over a number of failed relationships; in fact, like the female lead in every romantic comedy, she's looking for Mr. Right, but having a hard time finding him. In her words, "It hurts so much to be alone that we'd all rather blow up than be single" — a sentiment that explains her predilection for becoming involved with inappropriate men. Then Adam (Favreau), an artist who creates bizarre paintings, bulldozes his way into her life and heart. "We were instant best friends," Kate rhapsodizes as she recounts the early stages of their relationship — the so-called "honeymoon period" when love rules by day and sex by night. Unfortunately, no two people who

remain together can stay in that wonderful place, and things settle down into a dull routine. "The more you're with someone, the more annoying they'll become." Eventually, Adam decides that he is bored with the relationship's stasis and wants to move on. Of course, it's only once the two have separated that they realize how right they were for each other.

In person, Breiman is a bundle of barely contained enthusiasm, and some of that energy comes across in her film. There's also a little Woody Allen at work here. Bits and pieces of *Love and Sex* may remind viewers of some of Allen's earlier, lighter work. It's a refreshing, unpretentious romantic comedy that works for what it is, and doesn't try to be more than it is capable of being. Favreau and Janssen both show themselves to be capable in the comedy arena, and, while there isn't much heat between them, they are playful and cute as a couple, and the fact that they were having a good time making the film shines through. **RECOMMENDED**

Love Jones [1997]

Starring: Larenz Tate, Nia Long, Isaiah Washington, Lisa Nicole Carson Director: Theodore Witcher Screenplay: Theodore Witcher Running Time: 1:48 Rated: R (Sex, profanity, brief nudity) Theatrical Aspect Ratio: 1.85:1

Love Jones' main characters are Darius Lovehall (Larenz Tate), a soulful poet with a roving eye, and Nina Mosley (Nia Long), a would-be photographer on the rebound from a long-term relationship. He has only once been with a woman for more than 6 months; she's through with love, saying that it's "played out like an 8-track." Needless to say, the two meet each other, sparks fly, and they end up in bed. And, even though the truth is obvious to their friends and everyone in the audience, they assert that they're not in love, they're "just kickin' it." So, when complications arise, as they must in any motion picture romance, the question (which in this sort of movie isn't that hard to answer) is whether their relationship can survive the stormy waters.

There are several reasons why this film works better than the common, garden-variety love story. To begin with, the setting and texture are much different than that of most mainstream romances. The culture, in which post-college African Americans mingle while pursuing careers and relationships, represents a signficant change from what we're used to. The Sanctuary, the intimate Chicago nightclub where Darius and Nina meet, is rich in its eclectic, bluesy atmosphere. And *Love Jones*' dialogue is rarely trite. When the characters open their mouths, it usually because they have something intelligent to say, not because they're trying to fill up dead air with meaningless words.

Larenz Tate (*Dead Presidents*) and Nia Long (*Boyz 'N the Hood*) invest their portrayals with a great deal of energy. The chemistry between Darius and Nina alternately sizzles and smolders, resulting in a relationship that varies from playful to hot. While the romantic dynamic between these two is familiar, the performances add a refreshing dimension to the often-stale choreography of motion picture love affairs. And, in a surprising move, while Witcher ends the film on an upbeat note, there's no "happily ever after" promise. **RECOMMENDED**

Lovers of the Arctic Circle [Spain, 1998]

Starring: Najwa Nimri, Fele Martínez, Nacho Novo, Maru Valdivieso, Kristel Díaz Director: Julio Medem Screenplay: Julio Medem Running Time: 1:54 Rated: R (Sex, nudity, profanity) Theatrical Aspect Ratio: 1.85:1 In Spanish with subtitles

The first hour of *Lovers of the Arctic Circle* comes close to being a perfect romance. The characters are meticulously developed as their relationship is explored, starting from their initial meeting as schoolmates to the clandestine sexual trysts they engage in behind their parents' backs. In many ways, Otto and Ana share the kind of love we all strive for. Yet, once fate has brought them together, it shows its fickle nature by seeking to tear them apart. For much of the weaker second half, Otto and Ana are seeking to find themselves (metaphorically) and each other (literally). *Lovers of the Arctic Circle* allows the lovers to be in close physical proximity (as when they sit nearly back-to-back in an outdoor café) without recognizing it. Of course, we know they'll meet once again in the end . . . or will they?

The script for *Lovers* relies heavily on coincidence. Writer/director Julio Medem gets around this by making fate a significant theme in the film. He sets the tone early, during the scene when Otto and Ana first meet. In a voiceover, Otto remarks that if a ball had been kicked straight, he wouldn't have chased it, and if he hadn't run after it, he never would have encountered Ana. Throughout the film, coincidence builds upon coincidence. By acknowledging it, however, Medem keeps us from shaking our heads and muttering, "Give me a break!"

Lovers of the Arctic Circle touches on several intriguing and potentially-controversial issues, but avoids the trap of becoming obvious or moralistic. One is incest — when Otto's father marries Ana's mother, the two become step-brother and step-sister. However, instead of circumstances cooling their ardor, things heat up. Now, the two teenagers are living under the same roof, just a bedroom apart. The ending is likely to polarize viewers. Some will hate it, and I admit that the impact is a little like being kicked in the stomach. Nevertheless, there's also something poetic about the cosmic irony of the resolution, and the way Medem elects to present it. *Lovers of the Arctic Circle* is a moving film that touches the heart without insulting the mind. **HIGHLY RECOMMENDED**

Much Ado About Nothing [United Kingdom/United States, 1993]

Starring: Kenneth Branagh, Emma Thompson, Denzel Washington, Robert Sean Leonard, Kate Beckinsale Director: Kenneth Branagh Screenplay: Kenneth Branagh based on the play by William Shakespeare Running Time: 1:51 Rated: PG-13 (Mature themes, nudity) Theatrical Aspect Ratio: 1.66:1

Much Ado about Nothing is Kenneth Branagh's adaptation of one of Shakespeare's better-known comedies. Centered around two romances — Hero (Kate Beckinsale) and Claudio (Robert Sean Leonard), and Benedick (Kenneth Branagh) and Beatrice (Emma Thompson) — the story follows these very different courtships. For Hero and Claudio, it's love at first sight and, as with any immediate attraction, they have a lot to learn about each other. Beatrice and Benedick, on the other hand, have known each other for quite some time and it takes a little none-too-subtle prodding from their friends to help them realize and admit their feelings.

For those who don't find Shakespeare's comedies funny, this is the film to see, because it's hilarious. It isn't just the lines that create laughter, but the manner in which they're set up and delivered. Expressions and actions often play a large part in the comedy, some of which is decidedly physical. These are the kinds of things that don't appear on the written page. The film also contains its share of drama, and the pathos and poignancy come as easily and naturally as humor.

The life and vitality of this production are amazing. Things move along with a breezy energy that makes it impossible not to get caught up in the experience. Cuts and edits to the unabridged play are partly responsible for the uptempo pace. However, while Branagh is not entirely faithful to the original text of *Much Ado about Nothing*, his film takes pains to capture the play's spirit. Only Shakespearean purists are likely to recognized what has been excised.

Much Ado about Nothing is a gem of a movie. Branagh has successfully used a mixed cast of "names" and "unknowns" to breathe life into this lavish production, and never has Shakespeare been more warmly received. I'm not sure if "feel good" has ever been used to describe a picture based on the Bard's work, but the expression fits. **MUST SEE**

My Best Friend's Wedding [1997]

Starring: Julia Roberts, Dermot Mulroney, Cameron Diaz, Rupert Everett Director: P.J. Hogan Screenplay: Ronald Bass Running Time: 1:45 Rated: PG-13 (Mature themes, profanity) Theatrical Aspect Ratio: 2.35:1

As in any romantic comedy, the two most important elements are in place: the couples and the complications. Couple #1 consists of the soon-to-be married groom, Michael O'Neal (Dermot Mulroney) and his perky bride, Kimmy (Cameron Diaz). Couple #2 comprises food critic Julianne Potter (Julia Roberts) and her gay editor, George Downes (Rupert Everett). They're not really together, but they pretend to be to make Michael jealous. Because, for the past 9 years, since they had a one-month fling in college, Julianne has carried a torch for Michael. They've been best friends, but only now, when she's about to lose him to another woman, does Julianne realize that she wants to be the bride. And, to get her man, she's willing to do almost anything, including play dirty. So, when Kimmy opens her arms to Julianne and offers her the position of maid of honor, Julianne accepts, all the while plotting the best way to break up the happy couple.

Because *My Best Friend's Wedding* features a smart script and deft direction, it manages to keep alive the mystery of who will end up with whom. Things aren't as clear-cut as they initially seem to be, and, with every passing minute, they get murkier. The film has a high energy level and features a number of standout scenes, some of which are designed to cull laughter from the audience, others which go for the tear ducts. The best is arguably a restaurant episode where an impromptu sing-along gets everyone in the place to join in. It's clever, irreverent, and fun.

Although *My Best Friend's Wedding* is intended to be relatively light entertainment, it briefly addresses some interesting, serious issues regarding the nature of friendship, jealousy, and love (real and idealized). There's a wonderfully evocative scene that suggests "a moment passing by," which will undoubtedly cause a portion of the audience to reflect on similar occasions in their own lives. In the final analysis, *My Best Friend's Wedding* represents 2 hours of fine entertainment not because it offers a feel-good love story but because the film makers understand that it's possible for a romantic comedy to appeal not only to the heart, but to the mind as well. **RECOMMENDED**

Paperback Romance [Australia, 1994]

Starring: Gia Carides, Anthony LaPaglia, Rebecca Gibney Director: Ben Lewin Screenplay: Ben Lewin Running Time: 1:27 Rated: R (Sexual situations, nudity) Theatrical Aspect Ratio: 1.66:1

The phrase "paperback romance" generates all sorts of vivid images: lusty, well-endowed women; men with "ruggedly handsome features" and "well-chiseled muscles"; exotic locations; and, most importantly, plenty of steamy sex. The purple prose of these so-called bodice-rippers is appreciated and admired by millions, yet, by its very nature, it's ripe for the kind of satire evident in *Paperback Romance*. This film can be considered a legitimate romantic comedy, although it's a little too quirky to be lumped in with most of the run-of-the-mill entries.

Our heroine is Sophie (played by the delightful Gia Carides), an author of romance novels. She's a dreamer who takes refuge in her writing; since her love life is barren, she kisses through her characters. One day at a library, as Sophie is reading aloud while she pens an erotic passage, her voice and words captivate Eddie (Anthony LaPaglia), a high-stakes jewel dealer who is browsing nearby. He is so taken with Sophie's beauty and charm that he asks her out on the spot, but she refuses. A childhood victim of polio, Sophie cannot walk without a leg brace, and she doesn't want Eddie to see her disability. He leaves, convinced that she's the perfect woman. (Why? Because she rejected him.)

For Sophie, out of sight does not mean out of mind. Unable to dismiss Eddie from her thoughts, she finds out where he works, then goes to spy on him, watching him with his fiancée, Gloria (Rebecca Gibney). When she's afraid that Eddie is about to notice her, brace and all, Sophie hurries to get out of sight. In the process, she takes a nasty spill and breaks her leg. Now, with her stricken limb in a cast, she can pretend that she's normal and that the injury is the result of a skiing accident. Freed from her fear that Eddie will reject her because she's disabled, she is able to pursue a relationship with him — at least temporarily.

The tone of *Paperback Romance* is erratic; you can be laughing one minute and wincing the next. On at least two occasions, the slapstick, while admittedly funny in a sophomoric way, is so overblown that it seems out of place. In general, however, *Paperback Romance* manages to successfully navigate such choppy waters, and the result is a pleasant, if uneven, hour and a half. RECOMMENDED

Persuasion [United Kingdom, 1995]
Starring: Amanda Root, Ciaran Hinds, Sophie Thompson, Samuel West Director: Roger Michell Screenplay: Nick Dear based on the novel by Jane Austen Running Time: 1:44 Rated: PG (Mild language) Theatrical Aspect Ratio: 1.85:1

Persuasion, based on the Jane Austen novel, opens in early 19th century England (1814, to be precise), in the wake of war with France. Across the Channel, Napoleon has abdicated and been confined to Elba, and British servicemen are returning home. Among them is Captain Frederick Wentworth (Ciaran Hinds), a navy officer who has been away for more than 8 years since his marriage proposal to then-19-year-old Anne Elliot (Amanda Root) was refused. Now, almost a decade later, Anne lives in a state of constant regret, attempting to fill an empty life through her selfless devotion to family and friends. However, although she remains without either husband or suitors, circumstances have decreed that she has not seen the last of the one true love of her life.

Even though the subject material of the film might sound like the stuff of a Harlequin romance, *Persuasion* has far greater depth than any dime store soap opera. The movie offers not only keen insights on the lasting, and agonizing, effects of love, but explores the theme of consequences. While the hand of fate can be seen working throughout, the characters' circumstances are ultimately the result of their own choices and actions. Anne is responsible for her unhappiness, and, when an opportunity arises to redress her past error, she must seize it or lose Frederick forever. The barrier to overcome is the deep emotional scarring created by her decision of eight years ago.

To a lesser extent, *Persuasion* also works as a social commentary. The film takes aim at the pre-Victorian society in which it is set — a social structure that encouraged the empty words of sycophants over true expressions of friendship. Many of the characters are cloaked in artifice, and it's only as their real motives are uncovered that we learn of their duplicity and superciliousness. Michell uses some of this shallowness to comic effect through the fatuous presentation of characters like Anne's father (Corin Redgrave) and sister Elizabeth (Phoebe Nichols). It's men and women like this that draw our sympathy towards those who are honest and straightforward, like Anne and Frederick.

Like so many British costume dramas, this one boasts impeccable production values. Its faithfulness to the source material results in a few slow spots, but *Persuasion* is nevertheless fine entertainment. And, at a time when most love stories involve copious displays of skin, it's a rare pleasure to see so much emotion brought to the screen by a single kiss. HIGHLY RECOMMENDED

The Pillow Book [United Kingdom, 1996]
Starring: Vivian Wu, Ewan McGregor Director: Peter Greenaway Screenplay: Peter Greenaway Running Time: 2:06 Rated: Not Rated (Nudity, sex, mature themes) Theatrical Aspect Ratio: 1.66:1 and 2.35:1

Calligraphy is one subject that not many movies have explored, and none has approached it in quite the way that British director Peter Greenaway does in *The Pillow Book*. To use the film's own words to describe it, this is about the "two things in life that are dependable: the delights of the flesh and the delights of literature" and how they can be melded into one. While there's nothing especially groundbreaking or difficult to grasp in *The Pillow Book,* Greenaway's experimentation here still has the power to alienate audiences who aren't prepared for what the film offers. As has been true in his past efforts, there are copious amounts of full frontal nudity, and it seems that lead actors Vivian Wu and Ewan McGregor perform half of their scenes without any clothes on. Nevertheless, by keeping the audience at arm's length, Greenaway manages the impressive feat of de-eroticizing the nudity.

For the most part, the director seems more concerned about technique than narrative and character development. The plot functions more as a series of markers for Greenaway's stylistic riffs than a necessary aspect of the movie. Indeed, *The Pillow Book* is so visually arresting that it's capable of holding our attention for 2 hours largely on the strength of its images. The only character of any real importance in *The Pillow Book* is Nagiko (Vivian Wu), a Japanese-born fashion model with obsessions for calligraphy, physical pleasure, and revenge. When she was little, Nagiko's aunt would read her excerpts from the *Pillow Book of Sei Shonagon,* the 1,000-year old diary of a courtesan. In Hong Kong, Nagiko begins her own pillow book, but, instead of writing on paper, she uses the bodies of her lovers. They, in turn, utilize her flesh for their calligraphy. Nagiko's quest is for the perfect lover/calligrapher combination, but it becomes a difficult search. As she says, the older men are not interested in the pleasure she can provide, and the younger men are easily distracted. Then she meets Jerome (Ewan McGregor), an Englishman in Hong Kong, who proves not only to be her artistic match, but offers the means by which she can enact a long-dormant plan of vengeance against her father's publisher.

The great irony of this film, which is (at least on one level) about the power of writing, is that the words are of secondary importance to the overwhelming visual presentation. The camera, not the script, dominates our response to Greenaway's film. In the final analysis, *The Pillow Book* has much more to show than it has to say. **RECOMMENDED**

Polish Wedding [1998]

Starring: Lena Olin, Gabriel Byrne, Claire Danes, Adam Trese
Director: Theresa Connelly Screenplay: Theresa Connelly Running Time: 1:48 Rated: PG-13 (Profanity, sex) Theatrical Aspect Ratio: 1.85:1

In an age during which the traditional family is disintegrating under the pressure of modern-day existence, Theresa Connelly's debut feature, *Polish Wedding*, illustrates that there are still some households in which blood-ties are the most important thing. The film opens a window into the ongoing chaos that marks the day-to-day activities of the Pzoniaks, a lower middle class Polish American clan living in Detroit. The Pzoniaks all live together in two adjoining single-family units. The walls are paper thin and there's no privacy. Space is at such a premium that the 4 unmarried children (3 boys and 1 girl) must all sleep in the same room. The matriarch and patriarch of the clan are Jadzia (Lena Olin) and Bolek (Gabriel Byrne), who have been married for more than 20 years. Over the span of their union, they have had 5 children (4 boys), the oldest of which is now married and has his own son.

Jadzia and Bolek's only daughter is Chala (Claire Danes), a carefree and sensual teenager who finds subtle ways of rebelling. She's very close to her father, but there's an emotional gulf between her and her mother. This year, Chala has been selected to lead the annual procession for the Feast of the Virgin, an honor reserved for girls of the highest moral caliber. Ironically, it's around this time that Chala elects to lose her virginity with Russell (Adam Trese), a local policeman. The brief tryst, which begins with smoldering looks, results in a pregnancy.

Theresa Connelly, who clearly has a great deal of affinity for these characters, presents them in warts-and-all fashion, rightfully certain that we will sympathize with them in spite of (or perhaps because of) their faults. Connelly displays the skill of a veteran in the unforced manner in which she weds comedy and pathos throughout the film.

Certainly, the American film industry has produced a large number of first-and second-generation immigrant family stories. This is only natural, considering the ethnic diversity of our society. *Polish Wedding* uses the Pzoniaks' cultural heritage as more than a colorful backdrop — it's an integral part of the plot, and that's one of the things that makes the film enjoyable. By offering a slightly different flavor of the immigrant experience, *Polish Wedding* carves out its own small niche in a crowded genre, and manages to entertain in the process. **RECOMMENDED**

Possession [2002]

Starring: Gwyneth Paltrow, Aaron Eckhart, Jeremy Northam, Jennifer Ehle Director: Neil LaBute Screenplay: David Henry Hwang and Laura Jones and Neil LaBute, based on the novel by A.S. Byatt Running Time: 1:42 Rated: PG-13 (Sexual situations) Theatrical Aspect Ratio: 2.35:1

Roland Michell (Aaron Eckhart) is an American researcher who has come to London to further his investigations into the life of his favorite author, Randolph Henry Ash (Jeremy Northam), who once served as Queen Victoria's poet laureate. After discovering two previously unknown letters, Michell believes that Ash may have had contact with an obscure female poet named Christabel LaMotte (Jennifer Ehle). This discovery leads him to collaborate with England's foremost authority on Christabel, Maud Bailey (Gwyneth Paltrow), who is initially unimpressed by Michell's findings. However, as the two begin to delve more deeply into the potential Christabel/Ash connection, they learn that not only did the two know each other, but they may have been lovers. And, as they unravel the story of Christabel and Ash's relationship, Michell and Maud find their own interaction becoming increasingly intimate.

Neither romance in *Possession* represents a timeless love story (one could argue there's not enough tear-inducing melodrama for that), but, in large part because of credible performances and Neil LaBute's workmanlike helmsmanship, we come to care about the characters and their interactions. The relationships of the two couples are very different, even though one would not exist without the other. Ash and Christabel have a short-lived, fiery affair, preceded by a long period of written correspondence and succeeded by a series of personal tragedies. Michell and Maud are attracted to each other almost from the beginning, but both have erected heavy emotional barriers that have to be overcome, and their mutual fear of commitment nearly prevents them from getting together at all. Nevertheless, the more they learn about the connection between the 19th century lovers, the more they become open to possibilities that neither has been previously equipped to deal with. For a while, the progression of their relationship echoes the discoveries they unearth about Ash and Christabel.

Although LaBute goes to some lengths to emphasize the connections between the two love stories, he also stylistically italicizes the differences. It's interesting to note that the present-day romance is developed primarily through words while the past-tense one is defined though gestures and images (Northam and Ehle don't have many lines). Yet the words of those two poets, written more than 100 years earlier, resonate with the man and woman investigating their liaison. *Possession* is compelling material, especially for those who believe that the lives and loves of the dead can impact the trajectory of the existences of the living. RECOMMENDED

Prelude to a Kiss [1992]

Starring: Alec Baldwin, Meg Ryan, Sydney Walker Director: Norman René Screenplay: Craig Lucas, based on his play Running Time: 1:45 Rated: PG-13 (Sexual situations, profanity) Theatrical Aspect Ratio: 1.85:1

Prelude to a Kiss opens with one of the most delightfully romantic half-hours of any recent motion picture. Not only is the aura intoxicating, but it gives us an almost-immediate investment into the main characters and their relationship. René offers a striking portrait of the "psychotic bliss" of love's early stages. Bartender Rita Boyle (Ryan) and publishing executive Peter Hoskins (Baldwin) are attracted to each other from the moment they first meet at a party. Their romance progresses quickly, from dancing in a crowded room to a coy exploration of each other's feelings to uninhibited sex, all punctuated by smartly written dialogue. Eventually, despite their differences on key issues (he wants children; she doesn't), Peter asks Rita to marry him, and she accepts. Meanwhile, we are briefly introduced to Julius (Sydney Walker), an old man who spends most of his time vegitating in his bedroom. One morning, he dresses up in his best clothing and walks to the train station. There, he buys a ticket to Lake Forest. The next time we see him, he

is wandering into Peter and Rita's wedding, an uninvited but apparently unthreatening interloper. After the ceremony, Julius approaches Rita and asks to kiss her as a means of congratulations. She agrees, and, when their lips meet, a transference takes place. Suddenly, Rita finds herself in the old man's body while his essence inhabits her form.

One can successfully argue that, in a strange way, *Prelude to a Kiss* follows the traditional pattern of a romance: the characters meet, fall in love, are torn apart by plot complications, then find their way back to each other in the end. The difference here is that the "plot complications" are far from the norm, and give the film a rich subtext that more conventional motion pictures lack. The intelligence of what the characters say also elevates the production. Like most plays-turned-into-movies, this one is a little talky, but that's not much of a problem, because what the characters have to say is absorbing.

I have always considered *Prelude to a Kiss* to be one of 1992's most underrated motion pictures. It was one of the most original romances to grace the screen that year, yet it was swallowed up in a summer season where audiences weren't interested in intelligent, penetrating dramas that ask provocative questions about substantive issues. The film doesn't have many holes and offers an ending that is satisfying, cathartic, and poignant. In the final analysis, it can be said that *Prelude to a Kiss* explores the issue of love in a way that will encourage many viewers to examine what the emotion means to them. Too few motion pictures cause us to think and feel this deeply. HIGHLY RECOMMENDED

The Promise [Germany, 1995]

Starring: Meret Becker, Corinna Harfouch, Anian Zollner, August Zimer Director: Margarethe von Trotta Screenplay: Peter Schneider Running Time: 1:59 Rated: R (Mature themes, sex, profanity) Theatrical Aspect Ratio: 1.66:1 In German with subtitles

Sometimes lovers are separated by race. Other times, it's age. On still other occasions, it's religion. But in *The Promise*, Sophie and Konrad are the same nationality, the same age, and the same faith. What divides them is an ugly construct of stone and barbed wire that becomes a symbol of the cold war. In Berlin during the 1960s, nothing was more tragic than the reality of families, friends, and lovers kept apart by what became known simply as "the Wall."

The Berlin wall was erected in the summer of 1961. In the early days, a crossing was less difficult than it eventually would become. As *The Promise* opens, Sophie (Meret Becker), Konrad (Anian Zollner), and two friends have planned an escape to the West. When the time arrives to climb through a manhole and a passing guard troop passes dangerously near to the escape route, Konrad stays behind to cover the others' tracks. He promises to join his girlfriend and her pals later, but he never does. By 1968, Konrad has become a respected astronomer, and is allowed to travel to Prague for a seminar. After receiving his letter, Sophie meets him there. Shortly after Sophie becomes pregnant, however, events split the couple, with Konrad again in the East and Sophie in the West.

Their next meeting occurs 12 years later. This time, the lead actors have been seamlessly switched (Corinna Harfouch now plays Sophie; August Zimer, Konrad). By now, Konrad is married and has a daughter, and Sophie is living with someone. Their common link is their son, Alexander, and Konrad, as a top-level scientist, is allowed visitation privileges. The final segment is in November 1989, at the fall of the Wall. Equally full of promise and poignancy, this sequence gives the film closure. *The Promise* ends on an ambiguous note, allowing the viewer to draw his or her own conclusions about what comes next.

Director Margarethe von Trotta effortlessly weaves history and personal events into a tapestry full of emotion and irony. Sophie and Konrad are likeable and we, as an involved audience, can't help but root for them to reach each other, even while recognizing that their different values and goals make a lasting union unlikely. Von Trotta doesn't cheat either side of her story, West or East. People and politics mix, but nothing is black or white in exploring one of many tales about the Wall. **HIGHLY RECOMMENDED**

Punch Drunk Love [2002]

Starring: Adam Sandler, Emily Watson Director: Paul Thomas Anderson Screenplay: Paul Thomas Anderson Running Time: 1:29 Rated: R (Profanity, sexual dialogue, violence) Theatrical Aspect Ratio: 2.35:1

Punch Drunk Love is quirky and stylish, but not in a manner that comes across as overly artsy or pretentious. Writer/director Paul Thomas Anderson, whose previous outings (*Boogie Nights* and *Magnolia*) were challenging, compelling, and deep, has not abandoned his affinity for trying new things, even though he's working in a vastly different genre.

In Anderson's crosshairs is Barry Egan (Sandler), a grown man with serious emotional issues. In addition to being socially retarded and borderline agoraphobic, he is subject to frequent emotional outbursts that can

alternately result in an explosion of anger or an unrestrained bout of crying. Then he meets Lena (Emily Watson), the shy and secretive British friend of one of Barry's seven sisters. She is smitten with him, and he with her, and they begin a tentative relationship. When she goes to Hawaii on a business trip, Barry elects to follow her. Meanwhile, he is feuding with a phone sex girl whose services he once employed. She has decided to extort money from Barry, and, when he refuses to pay, she gets her boss (Philip Seymour Hoffman) to arrange to have him roughed up.

Some will probably trumpet *Punch Drunk Love* as an opportunity for Adam Sandler to show his range. And, while it's true that Sandler has unquestionably ventured into virgin territory, he's not doing things significantly different from what he usually does. Barry is the quintessential Sandler character — an angry man stuck in a state of arrested emotional and social development — with the humor siphoned off. This is Happy Gilmore or Billy Madison with the comedy button on mute. It's interesting to see how genuinely disturbed Sandler's screen alter-egos can be when they are no longer viewed through the distorted lens of mirth.

In the end, *Punch Drunk Love*'s real strength is its willingness to take off on some unexpected tangents. Anderson has created the kind of unconventional "romantic comedy" we might expect from him. And, while it could be a disappointment to die-hard Sandler fans (who don't get even a sampling of their hero's usual lowbrow humor) and lovers of traditional romance, *Punch Drunk Love* offers a lot to those who appreciate motion pictures that embrace a journey into relatively new territory. **RECOMMENDED**

Return to Me [2000]

Starring: David Duchovny, Minnie Driver Director: Bonnie Hunt Screenplay: Bonnie Hunt & Don Lake Running Time: 1:55 Rated: PG-13 (Mature themes, profanity) Theatrical Aspect Ratio: 1.85:1

Return to Me is the cinematic child of actress-turned-filmmaker Bonnie Hunt. This is the directorial debut for Hunt, who has an affinity and aptitude for this kind of material, rarely striking a sour note even though there are plenty of opportunities to do so. Hunt manages the tricky task of balancing drama, comedy, and romance, and, as a result, avoids unnecessary silliness, lugubriousness, and moments of extreme sugar shock.

The film opens with parallel stories, both taking place in Chicago. In one, a happily-married couple, Bob and Liz Rueland (David Duchovny and Joely

Richardson), are attending a fund-raiser being held for the Lincoln Park Zoo. In the other, a young woman, Grace (Minni Driver), is lying sick in a hospital bed awaiting a heart transplant while her sister, Megan (Hunt), looks on anxiously. What happens next is a tragic irony: Grace's life is saved when Liz is killed in an accident. Within months, she is at home, leading a normal life. The same cannot be said of Bob, whose entire world has crumbled around him.

Skip ahead a year. Grace is fully recovered from the operation and is working as a waitress at her grandfather's place, "O'Reilly's Italian Restaurant." Bob, trying to get his life back on track, goes there on a blind date, but loses interest in his companion when he spies Grace. The attraction between them is as mutual as it is immediate. Of course, neither realizes that Liz's heart beats in Grace's breast, and the question of how the characters will react when they learn this truth (as they surely must) provides a little suspense, since there's no uncertainty about whether these two will end up together. That is, after all, what the formula demands.

These days, an increasing number of romantic comedies feature teenagers, leaving a void for those who enjoy these kinds of stories with slightly older characters. *Return to Me* fills that breach, and does so with admirable restraint. There's enough emotion in the interaction of the characters that there's no need for a big, over-the-top finale or the inclusion of an old boyfriend or girlfriend to provide romantic complications. Watching *Return to Me* is not a trailblazing experience, nor is it intended to be, but Bonnie Hunt proves to be an expert tour guide through this familiar terrain. Despite sticking pretty much to the expected formula, *Return to Me* manages to disarm with its charm and delight with its bite. **RECOMMENDED**

The Road Home [China, 1999]

Starring: Zhang Ziyi, Sun Honglei, Zheng Hao, Zhao Yuelin Director: Zhang Yimou Screenplay: Bao Shi, based on his novel, *Remembrance* Running Time: 1:30 Rated: PG (Mature themes) Theatrical Aspect Ratio: 2.35:1 In Mandarin with subtitles

For celebrated Chinese director Zhang Yimou, *The Road Home* represents a short journey on a path not previously taken in his career. This simple love story, which is poignant, sensitive, and emotionally-satisfying, lacks Zhang's characteristic hard edge and political subtext. *The Road Home* is a chaste romantic melodrama that engages, but does not challenge, viewers. The movie features emotional intensity, but not breadth, and offers little in the way of subject

matter that could be considered controversial. *The Road Home* works, but may not offer followers of Zhang's work the kind of experience they have come to expect from his outings.

The movie transpires in two eras. The framing story, which comprises *The Road Home*'s first 15 minutes and final 15 minutes, is presented in stark black-and-white and takes place in a modern-day village in north China. The bulk of the film occurs in the same village 40 years ago, and is photographed in color. In the bookends, Yusheng Luo (Sun Honglei), a successful businessman in his late-30s, returns to his native village to help his aging mother, Di (Zhao Yuelin), bury his recently deceased father. The extended flashback details the fairy-tale courtship of 18-year-old Di (Zhang Ziyi) and 20-year-old Yusheng Luo (Sun Honglei), who broke with tradition and married for love rather than based on an arrangement.

Zhang has developed *The Road Home* as a pure romantic fable. In the director's canon, this must be considered a lesser effort (especially when compared to some of his great movies, like *Raise the Red Lantern* and *To Live*). It's also very much a change-of-pace. However, in the hands of someone with Zhang's talent, even a minor motion picture can be fundamentally satisfying, warts and all. That is the case with *The Road Home*. It's certainly not perfect, but it is a nicely realized love story and will find an audience in those who appreciate Chinese cinema and the poetry of a simple, well-developed romance. **RECOMMENDED**

Romeo + Juliet [1996]

Starring: Leonardo DiCaprio, Claire Danes, Brian Dennehy, John Leguizamo Director: Baz Luhrmann Screenplay: Craig Pearce and Baz Luhrmann based on the play by William Shakespeare Running Time: 2:00 Rated: PG-13 (Mature themes, violence) Theatrical Aspect Ratio: 2.35:1

In *Looking for Richard*, actor/director Al Pacino expresses his great hope for his film — to extend his enthusiasm for the Bard's plays to a broader audience. In a very different way, that's what Baz Luhrmann (*Moulin Rouge*) is attempting to do with this radical approach to *Romeo and Juliet*. Luhrmann hasn't fashioned this motion picture with the stodgy, elitist Shakespeare "purist" in mind. Instead, by incorporating lively, modern imagery with a throbbing rock soundtrack and hip actors, he has taken aim at an audience that would normally regard Shakespeare as a chore to be endured in school, not a passionate drama to ignite the screen.

Make no mistake, this *Romeo + Juliet* isn't the match of Franco Zeffirelli's unforgettable 1968 classic. While Leonardo DiCaprio and Claire Danes make an effective couple, their romance doesn't burn with the white-hot intensity of Leonard Whiting and Olivia Hussey's. For those who aren't aware, *Romeo and Juliet* tells the tale of two "star-cross'd" teenage lovers who secretly fall for each other and marry. Their families, the Montagues and Capulets, have been fierce enemies for decades, and, even as Romeo and Juliet say their wedding vows, new violence breaks out between the clans. In the end, their love is doomed. When Romeo mistakenly believes Juliet is dead, he poisons himself. And, when Juliet discovers that he is dead, she too commits suicide.

Ultimately, no matter how many innovative and unconventional flourishes it applies, the success of any adaptation of a Shakespeare play is determined by two factors: the competence of the director and the ability of the main cast members. Luhrmann, Danes, and DiCaprio place this *Romeo + Juliet* in capable hands. And, while such a loud, brash interpretation may not go down in cinematic history as the definitive version of the play, hopefully it will open a few eyes and widen the audience willing to venture into any movie bearing the credit "based on the play by William Shakespeare." **RECOMMMENDED**

Sabrina [1995]

Starring: Harrison Ford, Julia Ormond, Greg Kinnear Director: Sydney Pollack Screenplay: Barbara Benedek & David Rayfiel Running Time: 2:07 Rated: PG (Sexual innuendo) Theatrical Aspect Ratio: 1.85:1

In general, I approach romances with a great deal of skepticism, principally because it's so easy to mess up this kind of movie. Love is a difficult emotion to effectively capture on film, and, too often, screen romances look like two actors going through the motions. Happily, with *Sabrina*, that's not the case. Despite the unambitious, formula-driven plot, wonderful performances by Julia Ormond and, especially, Harrison Ford keep this remake afloat.

The title character, Sabrina Fairchild (Ormond), is the daughter of the Larrabee family's chauffeur (John Wood). Since she was little, Sabrina has had a crush on the youngest Larrabee son, David (Greg Kinnear), a dashing playboy. Unfortunately for her, David doesn't really know she exists. So, when Sabrina goes off to Paris to change her life (and appearance), she still harbors her passion in secret. When, after "finding herself" abroad, she returns home and dazzles David with her new glamour and self-possession, she sees a chance for her dreams to become real. But complications arise — David is engaged to a wealthy pediatrician (Lauren Holly), and the marriage will seal a major merger between the Larrabee Corporation and Tyson Electronics. David's older brother, Linus (Harrison Ford), the "living heart donor" head of the corporation, won't allow his brother's flirtation with Sabrina to endanger the deal, so, in the best interests of business, he makes a play for her. Unfortunately, Linus gets in over his head and the cold, calculating businessman discovers that he does indeed have a heart.

In 1954, Audrey Hepburn was Sabrina. While Julia Ormond is no Hepburn, she possesses the kind of luminous screen presence which allows us to accept her part in this modern-day fairy tale. Harrison Ford, taking over for Humphrey Bogart, is very good as Linus, carefully mixing pathos, cruelty, and compassion into a surprisingly complex personality. The weakest of the main performers is Greg Kinnear (in the William Holden part), who is more of a personality than an actor — and, at times, this shows. Of the supporting players, only veteran actor John Wood is worthy of special note. The rest of the cast do adequate, but not noteworthy, jobs.

It's not really that difficult to defend *Sabrina*, despite its numerous faults. Even though it isn't as good as the original 1954 version, this movie, brought to the screen by director Sydney Pollack (*Out of Africa*), simply has too much romantic appeal and on-screen chemistry to be dismissed as "just another" in the ever-growing pool of remakes. **RECOMMMENDED**

Say Anything [1989]

Starring: John Cusack, Ione Skye, John Mahoney Director: Cameron Crowe Screenplay: Cameron Crowe Running Time: 1:40 Rated: PG-13 (Profanity, sexual situations) Theatrical Aspect Ratio: 1.85:1

Say Anything is one of the best in a long line of teen romance movies, if not *the* best. Unlike many of its fellow genre entries, it is not filled with crude sex jokes, nudity, a lobotomized population, and poorly-defined subplots. And, while the broad strokes of the storyline are familiar, the details are what make this movie special — smart, well-developed characters, believable situations, and a solid emotional investment for us in the film's people and circumstances

Lloyd Dobler (John Cusack) is an average high school senior. As *Say Anything* begins, he's getting ready for graduation, even though his future is wide open. His father wants him to join the army, but Lloyd doesn't think that's for him. The object of Lloyd's high school affection is Diane Court (Ione Skye), the class valedictorian. Lloyd has yearned for her from afar, but, after graduation, he finally works up the courage to ask her out. Much to his delight, she accepts, and he takes her to an all-night, post-graduation bash. She discovers that she genuinely likes Lloyd, even though he and she have virtually nothing in common.

Diane's parents are divorced, and she lives with her father, James (John Mahoney), a businessman who runs a nursing home. He loves his daughter dearly, and enjoys showering her with expensive gifts. His high expectations also place a great deal of pressure on Diane. He is also profoundly distrustful of Lloyd, especially when the young man describes his career aspirations as being "to spend as much time as possible with your daughter." Then, with the arrival of a pair of tax men at the door, James' entire world is turned upside down.

In one sense, *Say Anything* is a romantic comedy, but it's firmly grounded in reality (rather than the fantasy world of hearts and candies where many love stories exist). The film isn't overly-intellectual in its approach, but it is smart. It doesn't demand anything from its audience except a willingness for each viewer to turn over a couple of hours to these two characters and the special magic they weave while together. *Say Anything* hardly has a misstep, and, despite the passage of a decade since its release, it's just as hip today as it was at the time of its theatrical run. **HIGHLY RECOMMMENDED**

Sense and Sensibility [United Kingdom, 1995]

Starring: Emma Thompson, Kate Winslet, Alan Rickman, Hugh Grant Director: Ang Lee Screenplay: Emma Thompson based on the novel by Jane Austen Running Time: 2:15 Rated: PG (Nothing offensive) Theatrical Aspect Ratio: 1.85:1

Sense and Sensibility is a wonderful motion picture, even given the weaknesses of the source material. Emma Thompson's screenplay has remained faithful to the events and spirit of Jane Austen's novel, while somehow managing to plug a few holes and infuse the tale with more light humor than is evident in the original text. The resulting product is a little too long (135 minutes), but still represents a fine time at the movies, especially for those with a bent towards historical romantic melodramas.

We're introduced to the three Dashwood sisters: Elinor (Emma Thompson), the eldest — a old maid past marriageable age who keeps her emotions bottled up in favor of a constant show of public decorum; Marianne (Kate Winslet), the middle child, who is Elinor's opposite in temperament and attitude; and

Margaret (Emilie Francois), an 11-year-old who seems to be following in Marianne's uninhibited footsteps. The girls live with their mother (Gemma Jones) in a small country cottage to which they are "exiled" after their half-brother inherits their father's estate and decides there's not enough room for everyone.

During the course of *Sense and Sensibility,* three men come in and out of the Dashwoods' home: Edward Ferrars (Hugh Grant), a charming, if somewhat inept, young gentleman who captures Elinor's heart; Colonel Brandon (Alan Rickman), a gallant neighbor who is hopelessly smitten by Marianne; and the dashing Willoughby (Greg Wise), who is the living embodiment of Marianne's every fantasy. The story of who ends up with whom, and how they get that way, is told with deft skill and a pleasantly humorous romantic touch.

The novel's flaws guarantee that *Sense and Sensibility* cannot be a perfect motion picture, but it would be difficult, I think, to do much better with the material than Emma Thompson and director Ang Lee have here. **HIGHLY RECOMMMENDED**

Shadowlands [United Kingdom, 1993]

Starring: Anthony Hopkins, Debra Winger Director: Richard Attenborough Screenplay: William Nicholson based on his stageplay Running Time: 2:10 Rated: PG (Mature themes) Theatrical Aspect Ratio: 2.35:1

Richard Attenborough's *Shadowlands* stays remarkably close to the true story of C.S. Lewis' relationship with Joy Gresham, taking only occasional liberties with the material for reasons of pacing, not over-sentimentalization. Joy's two sons are "combined" into a single boy, young Douglas (Joseph Mazzello). The film ignores Lewis' professorship at Cambridge, preferring instead to keep him at Oxford, and Joy's final days are shown spent at Lewis' house rather than in a hospital.

It's hard to imagine a better choice than Anthony Hopkins for the lead role. Chad Walsh, one of Lewis' close associates, described his friend this way: "In manner, he was straight to the point. He was not given to the sort of chitchat that simply fills in time, though in some moods he could delight in a battle of verbal wit . . . To him, an ideal conversation was an intellectual fencing match, and may the man with the best dialectic win. The few times I crossed swords with him, he won. I also noticed that he seemed singularly uninterested in introspection." This is the C.S. Lewis that Hopkins brings to life; the man that we follow from beginning to end in *Shadowlands.*

It's hard not to be eclipsed when playing opposite

Hopkins, but Debra Winger avoids being swallowed in his shadow. She brings a gritty worldliness to Joy Gresham that compliments perfectly Lewis' intellectual spirituality. Where he is reserved, she is frank and honest, going so far to remark to a friend of Lewis', "Are you trying to be offensive, or just merely stupid?"

Best of all is the chemistry between Winger and Hopkins. There is no smouldering sensuality, but they seem very much like a real couple, and there is no phase of their relationship that doesn't strike a true chord. Richard Attenborough knows how to keep the film's tone appropriate to the subject matter, and the scenes flow together

The initial impression of *Shadowlands* presented equally by its creative team and title, may be one of somber austerity, but there is a great deal of humor, energy, and life to be discovered beyond the drizzly, often-dreary Oxford landscape. The photography is beautiful, but rarely do green vistas upstage the actors.

To be captivated by *Shadowlands,* it isn't necessary to have read Lewis' writings. The story is self-contained, and William Nicholson's screenplay (adapted by the author from his own stage play) brings characters and situations into bas-relief. The tapestry of this film successfully weaves together emotion, intellect, and narrative into a pleasing, but never cloying, whole. **MUST SEE**

Shakespeare in Love [United Kingdom/United States, 1998]
Starring: Gwyneth Paltrow, Joseph Fiennes, Geoffrey Rush, Colin Firth
Director: John Madden Screenplay: Marc Norman and Tom Stoppard
Running Time: 2:03 Rated: R (Sex, nudity, brief profanity) Theatrical
Aspect Ratio: 2.35:1

At first glance, the film appears to be little more than a period piece romantic comedy. The main character, Will Shakespeare (Joseph Fiennes), is a struggling writer in 1593 England. Currently, he's having trouble with his latest play, a comedy called *Romeo and Ethel the Pirate's Daughter.* His problem is that he needs a muse to inspire him. He finds her in Viola (Gwyneth Paltrow), the daughter of a rich man. Viola, one of the few theater-goers who prefers Shakespeare to Christopher Marlowe, is equally smitten with Will, but she is engaged to the cold, loveless Lord Wessex, who wants her for her money. To fulfill a lifelong dream to be on stage, Viola dresses as a man and auditions for the role of Romeo, a part that she wins. With Viola's inspiration, Will begins writing a great play, which he retitles *Romeo and Juliet,* while simultaneously trying to find a way to make his impossible romance work.

Although *Shakespeare in Love* offers its share of belly laughs, most of the humor — and there is quite a bit of it — falls more into the "wit" category. For example, while the scene of Will undergoing a primitive form of psychoanalysis is amusing, it's not likely to cause anyone to roll in the aisles. The romance between Will and Viola is not one of the great pairings of the decade (or even of the year, for that matter), but there's enough chemistry between Paltrow and Fiennes to make it work. For admirers of Shakespeare, however, there's a great deal more to appreciate. Numerous aspects of the script are peppered with elements from the Bard's plays: mistaken identities, transvestites, ghosts, poetry, and significant chunks of dialogue from *Romeo and Juliet.*

Shakespeare in Love is about 10 minutes too long, but, for most of the 2-hour running length, Stoppard and Norman's script seamlessly blends comedy, romance, and light drama. An added bonus is that, unlike in most romantic comedies, the ending isn't a foregone conclusion. Plus, for those who like *Romeo and Juliet,* there's an opportunity to see how scenes from the play look with Gwyneth Paltrow alternately playing *both* of the title roles. *Shakespeare in Love* is not a great film, but it's an excuse to have an evening of pure enjoyment with a little culture painlessly mixed in. **RECOMMENDED**

Shall We Dance? [Japan, 1996]
Starring: Koji Yakusyo, Tamiyo Kusakari, Naoto Takenaka, Eriko Watanabe Director: Masayuki Suo Screenplay: Masayuki Suo Running Time: 2:06 Rated: PG-13 (Mature themes) Theatrical Aspect Ratio: 1.85:1 In Japanese with subtitles

In Japan, where public displays of affection between a husband and a wife is considered scandalous behavior, the concept of two unmarried people holding each other close in a dance is "beyond embarrassing." For that reason, ballroom dancing is not popular, and anyone caught engaging in it risks being labeled as depraved and lecherous. Nevertheless, for some men and women trapped in such a restrictive culture, dancing offers the seductive, forbidden allure of slipping the confining boundaries of what is socially acceptable and finding a measure of liberty.

Shohei Sugiyama (Koji Yakusyo) is a 42-year-old Japanese businessman who lives in a comfortable house with a loving wife and an adolescent daughter. But all is not right in his world. Now that he has attained his goals (a home, a family, and a successful career), his life feels empty. His wife notices his growing depression, commenting that "he really should get out and enjoy himself more often." One day, while riding the train home from work, Sugiyama spies the figure of a sad, beautiful woman (Tamiyo Kusakari) gazing out a dance school window. Day after day passes, with Sugiyama watching for this mysterious woman on each trip home. Eventually, he summons all his courage, exits the train at the stop nearest to the dance school, and enrolls for lessons. However, what begins as an attempt to get to know a pretty woman turns into the cure for Sugiyama's soul-sickness.

The parts of *Shall We Dance?* that are done well, are done *very* well, muting the negative impact of certain less successful elements. One of the most interesting aspects of the film for a Western viewer is that we're offered an opportunity to peer through an open window into Japanese society, especially as it addresses issues of intimacy. For those of us who are used to the idea that dancing is an integral part of the cultural fabric, understanding how the Japanese view this activity can cause a shift in perspective. The pleasant emotional aftereffects are a testimony to Suo's ability to fashion a story whose appeal reaches far beyond the shores of his native country. *Shall We Dance?* promises a convivial evening at the movies, and a rare chance to mix culture with pleasure. **RECOMMENDED**

Sleepless in Seattle [1993]

Starring: Tom Hanks, Meg Ryan Director: Nora Ephron Screenplay: Nora Ephron, David S. Ward, and Jeff Arch Running Time: **1:45** Rated: **PG** (Mature themes, language) Theatrical Aspect Ratio: **1.85:1**

Eight-year-old Jonah Baldwin (Ross Malinger) misses his mother, who died from cancer 18 months ago. More than that, however, he recognizes that his father, Sam (Tom Hanks), is desperately lonely. So, on Christmas Eve, Jonah calls a radio talk-show psychologist and asks for help. Forced onto the phone by his son and identified as "Sleepless in Seattle," Sam reluctantly (at first) opens up and talks about his love for his dead wife and the things that made her special. Across the country in Baltimore, Annie Reed (Meg Ryan) is listening to the syndicated program, and Sam's testimonial of love brings tears to her eyes. Even though she is engaged to Walter (Bill Pullman), Annie begins to wonder what it would be like to meet Sam. She even becomes one of thousands to write a letter to him. But, when circumstances make an assignation possible, the question is whether either Sam or Annie will have the courage to follow through with it.

There are those who will claim that *Sleepless in Seattle* is too corny, with sugar-coated cuteness filling in for the lack of a strong plot. And, while they have a point, there's something that the cynics are missing — it's meant to be that way. By its own admission, this film is intended as a throwback to the screen romances of the past (*An Affair to Remember* in particular, which is cited numerous times, and borrowed from explicitly and implicitly). Anyone expecting a tale of stark modern life from *Sleepless in Seattle* has walked into the wrong theater. This is a dreamy, romantic fantasy whose mood falls somewhere between magic and reality.

Coincidence is the backbone of Nora Ephron's story, wending its way through the plot with uncanny repetitiveness. The concept of destiny is an important thematic element. At the beginning of the film, Annie is a realist who dismisses the idea of a supernatural sign as nothing more than a random occurrence. By the end of *Sleepless*, she has become a believer in fate. Considering the unusual nature of the bond she develops with Sam, how could she not? **RECOMMENDED**

A Summer's Tale [France, 1996]

Starring: Melvil Poupaud, Amanda Langlet, Gwenaëlle Simon, Aurelia Nolin Director: Eric Rohmer Screenplay: Eric Rohmer Running Time: **1:53** Rated: **Not Rated** (Mature themes) Theatrical Aspect Ratio: **1.66:1** In French with subtitles

With this outing, director Eric Rohmer once again proves something he has been doing for his entire career: movies don't have to be about momentous events or larger-than-life characters to be entirely absorbing. *A Summer's Tale* works because the characters are so real and their circumstances presented in such a natural, unforced manner that we cannot help but be drawn into their lives. When it comes to traditional plot development, very little happens during the course of *A Summer's Tale*. The film is all about characters interacting. What they say — and, in some cases, don't say — forms the framework of the story.

Gaspard (Melvil Poupaud) is a young mathematician/musician vacationing by the seaside in Brittany, France before starting a new job. The film covers roughly 3 weeks in his life and introduces us to the trio of women he encounters during that time. First is Margot (Amanda Langlet), a cheerful waitress who enjoys spending time with Gaspard, but isn't interested in more than a friendship. Solene (Gwenaëlle Simon) is more affectionate and sensual — she's willing to have a relationship with Gaspard if he will commit to only her. Then there's Łena (Aurelia Nolin), Gaspard's longtime semi-girlfriend whose ambiguous romantic attitude towards him keeps him in a state of constant consternation. As the summer wears on, Gaspard finds himself increasingly torn between the 3 women, finding each the most appealing when he's with her, and recognizing that the day is fast approaching when he will have to choose.

As is often the case with Rohmer, the director has chosen a completely natural group of young actors to portray his protagonists. Melvil Poupaud, who plays Gaspard, has a fairly long resume, stretching back to the mid-'80s. Amanda Langlet, who worked with Rohmer 13 years earlier as the title character in *Pauline At the Beach*, is flawless as Margot — it's impossible to see how any man wouldn't be mesmerized by her charm. Both Gwenaëlle Simon and Aurelia Nolin, making their feature debuts, show amazing poise for a first film.

Of the 4 films that comprise Rohmer's *Tale of Four Seasons, A Summer's Tale* is arguably the lightest. But, as is always true of the director's work, there's far more going on than is initially apparent. What might at first seem to be a pleasant-but-inconsequential motion picture conceals deep (but not dark) emotional currents. Rohmer has always enjoyed exploring the lighter side of the human psyche, with a special affinity for love. *A Summer's Tale* finds him plumbing that familiar well one more time with results that are likely to please anyone who isn't averse to a movie where character development and dialogue take precedence over plot contortions and mindless action. **HIGHLY RECOMMENDED**

The Tao of Steve [2000]

Starring: Donal Logue, Greer Goodman, Kimo Wills Director: Jenniphr Goodman Screenplay: Duncan North, Greer Goodman and Jennifphr Goodman Running Time: 1:27 Rated: R (Sexual situations, profanity, drug use) Theatrical Aspect Ratio: 1.85:1

So what is the Tao of Steve? Some ancient Buddhist practice that allows the practitioner to better confer with eternity? A means to come closer to god? Actually, it's a way to pick up babes. Just ask Dex (Donal Logue), whose entire sex life is defined by it. As Jack Palance once declared in a TV commercial (and as Dex would no doubt agree), "Confidence is sexy." In this philosophy, "Steve" isn't just a name, it's a state of mind. "Steve" represents the kind of man who never tries to impress a woman but ends up getting the girl in the end. Think Steve McGarrett (of *Hawaii 5-0*). Or Steve Austin (*The Six Million Dollar Man*). Or especially Steve McQueen, the "ultimate Steve." James Bond is a "Steve." And so is Dex.

Back in high school, Dex was voted most likely to succeed. By the time his 10-year reunion comes around, however, the only thing he has succeeded at is perfecting the life of a slacker. But, when it comes to women, he's a veritable babe magnet. No one, married or unmarried, can seemingly resist his dubious charm. Even someone like Dex can't hide forever from love, and he's smitten from the first time he sees Syd (co-writer Greer Goodman, the director's sister) playing drums for the band at the high school reunion. She remembers him — he was the smartest guy in her philosophy class — but he can't place her. Nevertheless, whatever he may have thought of her during their time together in school, he is definitely intrigued now. And, while his life has stagnated, she has moved on to become the set director for the Santa Fe opera. She has a boyfriend and a lifestyle she enjoys, and Dex's charisma seemingly has no effect upon her.

The most enjoyable romantic comedies focus on characters, ideas, and dialogue (plotting is never a big issue, due to obvious constraints). *The Tao of Steve* is strong in all three areas. Admittedly, the men and women populating this movie do not talk the way real people talk, but since what they have to say is so interesting, we're willing to forgive the cinematic conceit. *The Tao of Steve* will be remembered for its fresh, breezy approach and its easy mingling of pop culture and spiritualism. **RECOMMENDED**

Trick [1999]

Starring: Christian Campbell, John Paul Pitoc, Tori Spelling, Stephen Hayes Director: Jim Fall Screenplay: Jason Schafer Running Time: 1:30 Rated: R (Sexual situations, gay themes, nudity, profanity) Theatrical Aspect Ratio: 1.85:1

Trick is one of the few gay romantic comedies with the potential to be appreciated by a more diverse audience than those who typically explore this niche of the motion picture market. And the film's quintessential appeal is not diminished by the assertion of first-time director Jim Fall that he made the film with the primary intention of appealing to homosexual viewers. There is enough charm and tenderness on the screen that it's virtually impossible not to sympathize with the characters on some level. Unlike many gay-themed motion pictures, *Trick*'s central focus isn't sex. Sure, that's what it's superficially about, but it doesn't take much digging to determine that the movie is really concerned with issues of intimacy and commitment — and these will strike a chord with any viewer, regardless of his or her sexuality. That's where Fall's picture works, and the reason why it has crossover potential.

Gabe (Christian "brother of Neve" Campbell) is a would-be Broadway songwriter whose inability to pen believable lyrics can be traced to a lack of experience in meaningful relationships. After meeting Gabe, we are soon introduced to those who inhabit his inner circle of friends and acquaintances. There's his straight roommate, Rich (Brad Beyer), who often makes Gabe sleep in the hall so he can be alone with a girl. His best friend is Katherine (Tori Spelling), who isn't nearly as good a singer/actress as she thinks she is. And his #1 supporter is Perry (Stephen Hayes), a semi-successful member of his desired trade who spends his evenings playing tunes at a New York City piano bar. One night while passing his time at an all-males strip joint, Gabe catches the eye of Mark (John Paul Pitoc), and it's lust at first sight. Later, on the subway, the two meet again and, without preliminaries, Mark asks Gabe if he knows of a place where they can be alone. For the rest of the movie (and the rest of the night), Gabe and Mark undergo a series of comic misadventures as they pursue this goal.

Despite not being graphic in its depiction of certain acts, the movie is frank in the way it deals with the characters' sexuality. The dialogue is not brilliant, but it gets the job done. Once in a while, screenwriter Jason Schafer resorts to saccharine platitudes, but, for the most part, he sticks to well-written lines and occasionally hits paydirt. But the strength of the script is not in what the characters say nor in the way it throws contrived obstacles in their paths. Instead, it's in the believable nature of the central relationship — a key element that many big budget, mainstream romantic comedies lose sight of. This movie gets that trick (and a few others) right. RECOMMENDED

The Truth About Cats and Dogs [1996]

Starring: Janeane Garofalo, Uma Thurman, Ben Chaplin
Director: Michael Lehmann Screenplay: Audrey Wells Running
Time: 1:37 Rated: PG-13 (Profanity, phone sex) Theatrical Aspect
Ratio: 1.85:1

Since Edmond Rostand first committed the play to paper in 1897, *Cyrano De Bergerac* has become a reliable romantic formula. With a standout performance by Janeane Garofalo, this loose reworking makes for solid, if feather-light, entertainment.

The story, which starts out as upbeat variation of *Cyrano* before moving in another direction, introduces Garofalo as radio pet doctor Abby Barnes. Her show, *The Truth About Cats and Dogs,* has made her a household voice, but, as is often true for radio personalities, her face is less familiar. One day, a British-accented photographer named Brian (Ben Chaplin) calls up with a problem: he has an angry dog on roller skates ruining his studio. Abby talks him through the process of pacifying the dog, and, in gratitude, Brian invites her out for a drink. She accepts, but, afflicted with low self-esteem, lies about her appearance. Although Abby is a 5' 1" brunette, she tells Brian to look for someone 5' 10," blond, and "hard to miss" — an exact description of her airhead actress/model neighbor, Noelle (Uma Thurman).

When Abby explains her deception to Noelle, the statuesque beauty agrees to help, but it doesn't take long for things to get out of hand. Inevitably, Noelle becomes attracted to Brian, and the two women vie for his attention — Noelle using her body and Abby, her voice. Brian doesn't realize that the face of his dreams isn't that of the woman with whom he has a 7-hour telephone conversation that culminates in phone sex.

Buying into the premise of *The Truth About Cats and Dogs* — that any man could mistake a ditz like Noelle for Abby — requires a huge suspension of disbelief, but, once you get past that stumbling block, the film is disarmingly charming, and even offers a few flashes of substance. Nothing in the screenplay is groundbreaking, but there are some observations about low self-confidence. Brian gets tongue-tied around women. Abby is unsure of herself because she thinks she's ugly. And Noelle has self-esteem problems because she believes herself to be stupid. The requisite chemistry between Chaplin and Garofalo is present, and the story follows an unthreateningly predictable route. RECOMMENDED

Two Family House [2000]

Starring: Michael Rispoli, Kelly MacDonald, Kathrine Narducci
Director: Raymond De Felitta Screenplay: Raymond De Felitta Running
Time: 1:54 Rated: R (Profanity, sex) Theatrical Aspect Ratio: 1.85:1

The time is 1956. The place is Staten Island. Buddy Visalo (Michael Rispoli), his head bursting with grand plans of self-employment and wealth, has just bought a dilapidated two family house with the intention of turning the downstairs into a tavern and using the upstairs as an apartment for him and his shrewish wife, Estelle (Kathrine Narducci). There are a few complications, however. In the first place, Estelle hates the idea of her husband running a bar. Convinced that the venture will fail, she does everything in her power to accelerate that failure. In the second place, the upstairs is occupied by a belligerent, perpetually drunk Irishman (Kevin Conway) and his pregnant wife, Mary (Scottish actress Kelly

MacDonald), who are unwilling to give up their tenancy and have the law on their side.

Things change when Mary gives birth, and the child turns out to have much darker skin than his supposed father. Mary's husband leaves her, and Buddy, pressured by his wife, evicts her. Feeling remorse, however, he rescues Mary from the dive where she is forced to go and sets her up in a cozy, low-rent apartment where she and the baby can live in relative peace. Finding Mary's company more pleasant than his wife's, Buddy becomes a regular visitor, and, although their friendship begins platonically, circumstances force them closer together until the inevitable happens.

Two Family House is thoroughly charming. The romantic relationship that forms the film's core is presented on a level that's a notch above what we usually see in movies. There are some serious cultural and social elements that De Felitta has to juggle, and he does so without sweeping them under the table. Mary is ostracized by almost every segment of society because her baby is biracial. The closer Buddy gets to her, the more he risks. He admires her strength and spirit, and, most importantly, she supports and encourages his dreams while his wife is interested only in shooting them down.

One of the most refreshing aspects of *Two Family House* is that it doesn't feel the need to go through all of the obligatory (and predictable) plot contortions mandated by most romances. Buddy and Mary don't endure the Big Breakup caused by the Big Misunderstanding, which, in turn, is followed by the Bigger Reunion. Their relationship has its share of complications, but they're not the run-of-the-mill stumbling blocks that we see in 9 out of 10 mainstream films. That's only one of many reasons why *Two Family House* is worth seeing. **RECOMMENDED**

What Women Want [2000]

Starring: Mel Gibson, Helen Hunt, Marisa Tomei, Bette Midler
Director: Nancy Meyers Screenplay: Josh Goldsmith and Cathy Yuspa
Running Time: 2:05 Rated: PG-13 (Sexual humor, sexual situations, profanity) Theatrical Aspect Ratio: 1.85:1

Most of the credit for the film's success has to be laid at the feet of Mel Gibson, who exudes energy and oozes charm. Gibson's dynamic personality elevates the film. His co-star, Helen Hunt, seems content to remain largely in the background, although, during the course of her low-key performance, she does a nice job of developing her character into the semblance of a rounded individual.

What Women Want has a simple premise that it exploits to a point, although not to the fullest. Nick Marshall (Gibson) is a "man's man" — the kind of politically incorrect charmer whom women fall for instantly. But there's a drawback to all of that machismo. Despite being the most accomplished ad man at Chicago's Sloane Curtis agency, Nick is passed over for the job of Creative Director, a position everyone in the office assumed he would get — everyone except the boss, Dan Wanamaker (Alan Alda), who patiently explains that, with the increase in female buying power, Sloane Curtis needs someone who understands that "it's a woman's world out there." That person isn't Nick; it's Darcy Maguire (Helen Hunt), the queen of female-driven marketing. And the moment she gets the job, Nick is determined to unseat her at all costs.

Then, suddenly, the King of Testosterone gets an unexpected infusion of estrogen. A home accident gives him the unlikely ability to hear what women are thinking. At first, he believes it's a curse, but then a psychologist (Bette Midler in a cameo) convinces him that it's a gift. So he begins to employ his powers for personal gain, both in bed and at the office, where he shamelessly pilfers Darcy's ideas and passes them off as his own. But, along the way, two things start happening. First, Nick begins to actually empathize with women. Secondly, he develops feelings for Darcy.

A fair amount of the comedy, like the romance, works. Some of the humor is pretty raunchy, but there are enough solid laughs to make up for when things fall flat. When the film strays into dramatic territory, it's on less certain ground. Director Nancy Meyers has fashioned cinematic cotton candy — all sugar and air. She understands the essence of the formula, and applies it in a manner that is infectious. In an era of largely disposable and forgettable motion pictures, there are far worse ways to spend a couple of hours. **RECOMMENDED**

When Harry Met Sally [1989]

Starring: Billy Crystal, Meg Ryan, Carrie Fisher, Bruno Kirby
Director: Rob Reiner Screenplay: Nora Ephron Running Time: 1:36
Rated: R (Profanity, sexual situations) Theatrical Aspect Ratio: 1.85:1

The thing that *When Harry Met Sally* does best is to keep the focus firmly on the relationship between the two title characters, never wandering off on unwelcome tangents. There are subplots, to be sure, but even those are crucial to the evolution of Harry and Sally's friendship. And the film is not hamstrung by a litany of familiar romantic comedy clichés. *When Harry Met Sally* offers an often humorous, occasionally poignant view of men, women, sex, love, and friendship.

When Harry Burns (Billy Crystal) and Sally Albright (Meg Ryan) first meet, it's 1977. Both are leaving the University of Chicago for New York City, and they share the drive. Along the way, they discover that they have little in common. At one point, Harry makes a pass at Sally, but she demurs, saying that they'll have to settle for being friends. That's when he makes his famous comment. They part in Manhattan, and it's 5 years before they bump into each other again, this time in an airport. By then, Harry is engaged to be married and Sally is in the midst of a serious relationship. They spend some time together on a plane, then separate amicably when they reach their destination. Their next encounter occurs in the late-'80s. They are both newly single (Harry's wife has recently left him and Sally has broken off a long-term, dead-end affair), and this mutual bond of loss draws them into a close friendship. When events push their relationship over the sexual line, things don't go smoothly.

Ultimately, *When Harry Met Sally* works because it dares to be *slightly* different from most romantic comedies. While there's nothing radical in the trajectory of Harry and Sally's romance, it's not entirely conventional, either. The two main characters are well-written, with both easily transcending the level of stereotyping they could have easily fallen into. The dialogue is smart and witty, offering numerous quotable passages. However, although the film poses some intriguing questions about the nature of male/female relationships, it never really answers them, instead using this material as little more than a jumping-off point for the interaction between Harry and Sally. For those who appreciate romantic comedies for both aspects of the genre (the "romance" and the "comedy"), *When Harry Met Sally* is a treat. **HIGHLY RECOMMENDED**

You've Got Mail [1998]

Starring: Tom Hanks, Meg Ryan, Greg Kinnear Director: Nora Ephron
Screenplay: Nora Ephron & Delia Ephron Running Time: 1:57
Rated: PG (Mature themes, mild profanity) Theatrical Aspect
Ratio: 1.85:1

Joe Fox (Tom Hanks), part owner of the Fox Books Superstore chain (a Barnes & Noble clone), is a cold businessman who puts the competition out of business without a second thought. As things develop, Joe's character follows a Scrooge-like arc. He isn't haunted by ghosts, but events gradually open his eyes to the evil of his ways, and he undergoes an attitude change. By the final reel, Joe gives us exactly the kind of Jimmy Stewart personality we expect from someone played by Hanks. Kathleen Kelly, on the other hand, is pure Meg Ryan, from her chirpy pep to the tilt of her head. And can anyone cry quite like Ryan? Kathleen, who owns a small children's bookstore called The Shop Around the Corner, finds herself in direct conflict with Joe, whose nearby superstore is stealing all of her customers. But that's not the whole story. To this standard rivals-who-fall-for-each-other tale, Ephron adds a great opening credits sequence (a view of "cyberManhattan") and a heavy dose of fate. For, while Joe and Kathleen are locking horns in business, their on-line alter-egos are falling in love.

You've Got Mail is appropriately rated PG, because, while Hanks and Ryan play well off of one another, there are no sparks. This film is about pure, old-fashioned romance, unsullied by things like lust and sex. *You've Got Mail* is peppered with Ephronisms (the kind of exchanges that characterized both *When Harry Met Sally* and *Sleepless in Seattle*). In *Sleepless,* the movie that embodied a woman's fantasies was *An Affair to Remember*; for men, it was *The Dirty Dozen*. Here, the approach is the same, but the text is different. For Kathleen, *Pride and Prejudice* is the Bible. In Joe's case, *The Godfather* is "the sum of all wisdom." For the most part, the script, despite being predictable, is smart and quirky, although the final line of the film, delivered by Ryan to Hanks, is a miscalculation. The punctuation mark would have been there without the neon sign to point it out.

You've Got Mail has the virtue of delivering *exactly* what's expected from it. It's a feel-good movie that offers enough comedy and romance to warm the heart without risking a sentimental overdose. Fans of *Sleepless in Seattle* will almost certainly fall in love with the similar-yet-different nature of the production; only die-hard cynics will be turned off by all of the unabashed good will. If there are messages to be found here, they're that romance is still thriving in our technological era, and that well-written romantic comedies starring Hanks and Ryan don't represent much of a gamble for the financing studio. **RECOMMENDED**

Science Fiction/Fantasy

A.I. [2001]

Starring: Haley Joel Osment, Jude Law Director: Steven Spielberg
Screenplay: Steven Spielberg, based on the screen story by Ian
Watson Running Time: 2:25 Rated: PG-13 (Profanity, sexual situations)
Theatrical Aspect Ratio: 1.85:1

A.I. is a science fiction re-interpretation of *Pinocchio* (a story the film frequently references) crossed with *Frankenstein*. Events take place in a futuristic setting, where the rise of the oceans has swallowed up seaside cities like New York and Amsterdam, where New Jersey resembles an Amazon rain forest, and where the sin-and-sex center of the planet is a place called Rouge City, which resides across the Delaware from New Jersey. This future, as imagined by Spielberg and his set designers, is every bit as awe-inspiring as what Ridley Scott brought to the screen in *Blade Runner* and what Luc Besson crafted for *The Fifth Element*. Rouge City is stunning, and the waterlogged ruins of Manhattan are hauntingly beautiful.

The story centers around David (Haley Joel Osment), a child substitute "mecha" who represents the first of his type — a synthetic who can actually love. In this case, the object of his incompletely-understood emotion is his "mother," Monica Swinton (Frances O'Connor). Monica's husband, Henry (Sam Robards), who brought David home as a pilot project from his workplace, Cybertronics of New Jersey, is more wary of the robot child. And, when one of David's actions endangers Monica and Henry's natural son, Martin (Jake Thomas), Monica is forced to take David into the woods and "lose" him. He is quickly found by a group of anti-robot fanatics, and, while being held captive by them, he befriends Gigolo Joe (Jude Law), who becomes an invaluable ally in his escape.

Like the real-life science surrounding the development of Artificial Intelligence, the movie is top-heavy with moral and ethical questions. What is life and where is the line that divides sentience from a programmed response? If a robot can genuinely love a person, what responsibility does that person bear in return? How can an immortal robot cope with outliving its organic creators? Writers from Mary Shelley to Isaac Asimov have been fascinated by these dilemmas. Perhaps Spielberg attempts too much with *A.I.* To some degree, by trying to tackle all of these issues, he fails to effectively present any of them.

A.I. is an ambitious film that, when it misses its mark, does so because it strives for so much. The script does not insult the audience's intelligence, and it gets us thinking about "big issues," such as love, life, god, and our place in the universe. It's unfortunate that as much thought didn't go into structuring the narrative as went into crafting the movie's thematic content. And those who have come to equate science fiction with action will be disappointed. *A.I.* is a drama with little in the way of adrenaline-boosting sequences. Spielberg has consciously slowed things down, relying on viewers' curiosity about the ideas and identification with the characters to keep them involved in the proceedings. **RECOMMENDED**

Alien [1979]

Starring: Tom Skerritt, Sigourney Weaver, Ian Holm, John Hurt
Director: Ridley Scott Screenplay: Dan O'Bannon Running Time: 1:56
Rated: R (Violence, gore, profanity) Theatrical Aspect Ratio: 2.35:1

In many ways, *Alien* was the first of a kind. True — it wasn't the first space movie to feature a homicidal monster, nor was it the first time a group of characters were hunted down one-by-one in dark, dank spaces. However, this "haunted house in space" film was one of the first to effectively cross-pollinate these two genres. In addition to blending graphic horror with science fiction, *Alien* has another distinction — it is one of the first films to feature a female action hero. Even today, on those rare occasions when a woman takes the lead in an action/adventure movie, she is typically measured up to Sigourney Weaver's Ellen Ripley.

Alien begins slowly and calmly by introducing us to the crew of the *Nostromo,* a commercial towing space vehicle on a return course for Earth. They number 7 — the relatively laid-back captain, Dallas (Skerritt); his second-in-command, Ripley (Weaver); Lambert (Veronica Cartwright), the ship's highly-strung navigator; science officer Ash (Ian Holm), who seems to have ice water for blood; Kane (John Hurt), who is possessed of a gallows humor; and grunts Brett (Harry Dean Stanton) and Parker (Yaphet Kotto), who spend their time grumbling about not getting full bonuses.

After receiving a possible distress signal from a seemingly uninhabited planet, Dallas, Kane, and Lambert head down to investigate. On the inhospitable surface, they come across what appears to be a downed space ship. Inside, they find a chamber full of egg-like objects. As Kane is examining one, it opens and a leathery creature emerges, launches itself at Kane, and forces a proboscis down his throat. Kane is taken to the medical lab, where Ash determines that it would be too dangerous for the life form to be removed from his face. Eventually, however, it falls off on its own, apparently dead. Kane returns to consciousness and all seems to be well. Then comes the fateful dinner. The normal mealtime chit-chat of the crew is interrupted when Kane begins gagging and choking. Before anyone can help him, a creature bursts through his chest and scampers into the air ducts, leaving behind Kane's bloody, dead husk. The rest of the crew mounts a search through the *Nostromo's* dark, claustrophobic passageways, with the alien picking them off one-by-one. And, with each new victim, it grows larger and stronger.

Alien contains its fair share of genuine scares. These aren't mere "boo" moments, where something benign jumps out of the shadows accompanied by a loud noise and a musical crescendo, but legitimate shocks. The level of suspense during the film's final 30 minutes becomes almost unbearable. What started as a seemingly low-key motion picture turns into a real white-knuckler. *Alien* may not have been totally original in its approach, but the film's widespread acceptance made it a blueprint for an entire sub-genre.

HIGHLY RECOMMENDED

Aliens [1986]

Starring: Sigourney Weaver, Carrie Henn, Michael Biehn, Paul Reiser Director: James Cameron Screenplay: James Cameron Running Time: 2:17 Rated: R (Violence, gore, profanity) Theatrical Aspect Ratio: 1.85:1

Perhaps the best single word to describe James Cameron's *Aliens* is relentless. Tautly paced and expertly directed, this roller coaster ride of a motion picture offers a little bit of everything, all wrapped up in a tidy science fiction/action package. From the point when the opening half-hour of exposition ends and the real movie begins, Cameron barely gives viewers a chance to catch their breaths or ease their grips on their armrests as he plunges his characters from one dire situation to the next. This is one of those rare motion pictures that involves the audience so completely in the story that we're as worn out at the end as our on-screen counterparts.

Aliens takes place a half-century after the events in *Alien.* Ellen Ripley (Sigourney Weaver) has been in cryogenic sleep in outer space until a salvage ship discovers her and brings her back to Earth. There, she finds herself facing serious charges of official misconduct and her claims about the alien are greeted with skepticism. She is stripped of her pilot's license and left to cope on her own with life in the future. Then, all contact is suddenly lost with the terraforming colony on LV-426 — the planet on which Ripley's crew discovered the alien. A corporation executive, Carter Burke (Paul Reiser), approaches Ripley with a proposition: accompany a military team to LV-426 as an advisor and have her pilot's license restored. She agrees, but with a proviso: they are going there to destroy the aliens, not to harvest them or bring them back. Burke agrees.

Ripley's new companions are a tough-talking, hard-bitten bunch: Ground Troop Commander Apone (Al Williams), wisecracking Private Hudson (Bill Paxton), somber Corporal Hicks (Michael Biehn), unflappable Vasquez (Jenette Goldstein), quiet android Bishop (Lance Henriksen), and several others. Only Gorman (William Hope), the squadron commander, is cut from a different cloth — he's by-the-book and does not react well to unexpected developments, especially in combat. Of course, when faced with the plethora of aliens on LV-426, the others don't know what to do either, as the insect-like creatures decimate their ranks and trap them in an abandoned operations center. There, they encounter Newt (Carrie Henn), a young girl who is the only survivor of the aliens' attack on the colony. Newt is unconvinced that a small group of armed soldiers will be able to stop the ever-growing army of aliens. Soon, they are fighting the clock as well as the creatures, as the plant's nuclear reactor starts on a countdown to going critical.

For James Cameron, who would go on to direct two of the 1990s most memorable motion pictures (*Terminator 2* and *Titanic*), *The Terminator* may have been the movie to put him on the map, but *Aliens* announced him as a force to be reckoned with. When it comes to the logical marriage of action, adventure, and science fiction, few films are as effective or accomplished as *Aliens*. MUST SEE

The Arrival [1996]

Starring: **Charlie Sheen, Lindsay Crouse, Teri Polo, Ron Silver** Director: **David Twohy** Screenplay: **David Twohy** Running Time: **1:55** Rated: **PG-13** (Violence, mature themes) Theatrical Aspect Ratio: **1.85:1**

When aliens can disguise themselves as humans, as in *The Arrival,* we're never sure who's a friend and who's a foe, and the best science fiction/horror films of this ilk continuously keep us guessing. Conspiracy lovers will have fun sorting through the layers of cover-up and treachery here. And those who crave scary-looking, otherworldly creatures will get their fill from the aliens in their natural forms.

The premise is rather simple. The aliens hail from a planet orbiting Wolf-336, an unstable star located 14.6 light years from Earth. A colonizing force has arrived here incognito with the goal of readying this world for inhabitation. That process involves accelerating the greenhouse effect — intentionally polluting the atmosphere so that the global temperature rises, causing the polar ice caps melt.

Zane (Charlie Sheen) and Calvin (Richard Schiff), a pair of SETI radio astronomers, intercept communications between Wolf-336 and Earth. When they report this to their boss, Phil Gordian (Ron Silver), Zane is fired and Calvin suffers an unfortunate accident. With the help of Kiki (Tony T. Johnson), a neighborhood boy, Zane begins investigating on his own, ignoring his girlfriend (Teri Polo) in his quest to deter-

mine who's out there. But Zane isn't the only one observing strange goings-on. A UCLA environmentalist (Lindsay Crouse) has noticed the alarming increase in global warming, and it's only a matter of time before she and Zane meet each other and compare notes.

The Arrival is low key, which is refreshing, and it's as much horror as pure science fiction. This is the kind of movie that a director like John Carpenter might have made during his late-70s/early-80s heyday. It's creepy and atmospheric, and, after a rather protracted opening 40 minutes, well-paced. RECOMMENDED

The City of Lost Children [France, 1995]

Starring: **Daniel Emilfork, Ron Perlman, Judith Vittet, Dominique Pinon** Directors: **Jean-Pierre Jeunet and Marc Caro** Screenplay: **Jean-Pierre Jeunet, Marc Caro, Gilles Adrien** Running Time: **1:52** Rated: **R** (Mature themes, profanity) Theatrical Aspect Ratio: **1.85:1** In French with subtitles

In *The City of Lost Children*, directors Jeunet and Caro have presented a gloomy world where "normal" life is no more. The film is saturated with atmosphere and features imaginative set construction. The picture works in part because the film makers have taken the time and effort to frame a strange land where all their quirky characters can live and operate. *The City of Lost Children* is characterized by dark, twisted humor, yet this movie is more of a fantasy than a macabre comedy.

The City of Lost Children relates dreams to creativity, youth, and wonder. The capacity to escape the rational world through imagination fuels not only the desire to continue living, but the need to make something out of one's life. In this film, we are introduced the brilliant-yet-warped mad scientist Krank (Daniel Emilfork), who is aging prematurely because he cannot dream. In an effort to stay alive, he has begun capturing children to steal their dreams. One of the toddlers abducted by Krank is little Denree (Joseph Lucien), the brother of a simpleminded circus strongman named One (Ron Perlman). One is joined in his search for his brother by Miette (Judith Vittet), the 9-year-old, wise-beyond-her-years leader of an orphan gang. Together, One and Miette seek to penetrate Krank's fortress; elude his 6 cloned henchmen (all played by Dominque Pinon), the deadly Miss Bismuth (Mireille Mosse), Irvin the talking brain (voice of Jean-Louis Trintignant), and the scientist himself; and rescue Denree. It proves to be a difficult task.

While much of *The City of Lost Children* is surreal

and strange, the film's emotional center — the relationship between One and Miette — is nurtured with care and genuine feeling. Miette sees in One and Denree the chance for the family she has never known, although there are times when her intentions towards the older, child-like man seem more romantic than sisterly. It's to Jeunet and Caro's credit that they are able to present the ambiguities of this relationship tenderly, without ever injecting a hint of the sordid or perverse. **HIGHLY RECOMMENDED**

Conan the Barbarian [1982]

Starring: Arnold Schwarzenegger, James Earl Jones, Max von Sydow, Sandahl Bergman Director: John Milius Screenplay: John Milius and Oliver Stone, based on the stories by Robert E. Howard Running Time: 2:08 Rated: R (Violence, nudity, sex) Theatrical Aspect Ratio: 2.35:1

The plot of *Conan the Barbarian* is broad and adventurous, with plenty of the elements that have made Conan popular: voluptuous women, brawny men, a vile wizard, grotesque monsters, faithful sidekicks, and plenty of violent, bloody battle action. Those who have an inherent distaste for this sort of entertainment will appreciate *Conan the Barbarian*'s impeccable production values without enjoying the story; most everyone else will be swept away by the film's spectacle. *Conan* is not designed to have broad appeal. It is a well-made motion picture, but it is constricted by the constraints of the genre.

As the movie opens, Conan (Jorge Sanz), is a boy learning the "Riddle of Steel" from his father. Shortly thereafter, the young barbarian is in chains, a prisoner of the wizard Thulsa Doom (James Earl Jones) and his henchman, Rexor (Ben Davidson), who have burned down his village and killed his parents. Conan grows up as a slave, and, once he is an adult (now played by Arnold Schwarzenegger), he becomes a gladiator champion and is used to breed prime slave stock. Eventually, his owner, fearing Conan's physical prowess, sets him free. After stealing a sword from a crypt and picking up a thief sidekick named Subotai (Gerry Lopez), he heads for the riches of civilization. In the city of Zamora, he meets Valeria, Queen of the Thieves (Sandahl Bergman), and, with her help, robs the Tower of the Serpent. He and Valeria become lovers, but Conan is only temporarily sated by gold, drink, and sex. The flame of revenge burns within him, and he is given valuable information to find Thulsa Doom when King Osrik (Max von Sydow), the ruler of Zamora, summons him to the palace with a proposition.

To date, *Conan the Barbarian* has been one of the few successful Swords and Sorcery movies. The reasons for this film's effectiveness are not difficult to understand. It treats its characters and subject matter seriously without becoming lugubrious. There is some humor, but it is mostly underplayed, and Milius avoids any overt suggestions of camp. *Conan the Barbarian* is also adult in nature — the battles are bloody and the women take their clothes off. Instead of the slightly overblown epic aura of *Conan*, most other films adopt a jokey tone. Years after its release, *Conan the Barbarian* still weaves a spell capable of ensorcelling fans of fantasy adventure. **RECOMMENDED**

Contact [1997]

Starring: Jodie Foster, Matthew McConaughey, James Woods, Tom Skerritt Director: Robert Zemeckis Screenplay: James V. Hart and Michael Goldenberg based on a story by Carl Sagan and Ann Druyan Running Time: 2:30 Rated: PG-13 (Profanity, mature themes) Theatrical Aspect Ratio: 2.35:1

Contact opens with an unforgettable sequence that takes the viewer on a tour of the universe. After this eye-popping trek, we return to Earth during the early 1970s, where we meet 9-year-old Ellie Arroway (Jena Malone), a budding scientist with a fascination for short wave radio (she likes hearing messages from far away) and astronomy. Her father, Ted (David Morse), is an English teacher, and has schooled Ellie in the beauty of the stars. Following his sudden death, an event that leaves Ellie orphaned, she decides to devote her entire life to pursuing the mysteries that her father opened her eyes to.

When we next encounter Ellie (now played by Jodie Foster), she's a promising researcher for the SETI (Search for Extraterrestrial Intelligence) Institute, working on a giant radio telescope in Puerto Rico. Ellie's obsession is to find evidence of life on another planet. Despite the scorn of her colleagues, she spends hours on end listening for that proof. While in Puerto Rico, she becomes involved with a religious scholar, Palmer Joss (Matthew McConaughey). The two have a short, passionate affair that ends when Ellie's former mentor (and the President's national science advisor), David Drumlin (Tom Skerritt), pulls the plug on the SETI project in Puerto Rico. To maintain her work, Ellie is forced to seek private funding, which she receives from a multi-billionaire eccentric named S.R. Hadden (John Hurt). Armed with as much money as she needs, Ellie rents time on New Mexico's VLA (very large array) radio telescope range, and, while there, discovers a message from the star

Vega that indicates intelligent life. Once the signal is confirmed, the VLA becomes the center of a media blitz, and, along with the reporters, National Security Advisor Michael Kitz (James Woods) arrives, ready to militarize the project and push Ellie out.

In its own unique way, *Contact* offers a little bit of almost everything: drama, romance, suspense, and science fiction. It touches the emotions and the intellect. There are glorious special effects, wonderful acting, and a couple of impressive pyrotechnic displays. The plot contains the most believable approach to this subject matter ever presented in a movie. In addition to the scientific aspect, there's the media feeding frenzy, the fierce in-fighting to gain control of the project, the international ramifications of the U.S. taking charge, and the religious implications of life on another planet. One of the key, recurring struggles presented in *Contact* is that of science versus religion, and how the conflict between these two seemingly-divergent disciplines reveals the importance of both faith and facts to human well-being. **MUST SEE**

Dark City [1998]

Starring: Rufus Sewell, Kiefer Sutherland, Jennifer Connelly
Director: Alex Proyas Screenplay: Alex Proyas and Lem Dobbs and
David S. Goyer Running Time: 1:43 Rated: R (Violence, nudity,
profanity) Theatrical Aspect Ratio: 2.35:1

No movie can ever have too much atmosphere, and *Dark City* exudes it from every frame of celluloid. Alex Proyas' world isn't just a playground for his characters to romp in — it's an ominous place where viewers can get lost. We don't just coolly observe the bizarre, ever-changing skyline; we plunge into the city's benighted depths, following the protagonist as he explores the secrets of this grim place where the sun never shines. *Dark City* has as stunning a visual texture as that of any movie that I've seen. Visually, this film isn't just impressive, it's a tour de force.

Dark City opens by immersing the audience in the midst of a fractured, nightmarish narrative. The protagonist, who later learns that his name is John Murdoch (Rufus Sewell), has amnesia. He begins his "new life" as a full-grown adult naked in a bath tub, uncertain of how he got there. His only company in the grungy hotel suite is the nude body of a dead prostitute. Did he kill her or not? He doesn't know. Suddenly, Murdoch receives a phone call from someone named Dr. Schreber (Kiefer Sutherland), who claims to have his best interests at heart. Schreber warns him to get out of the hotel immediately. Soon, without a clue about his identity, Murdoch is fleeing from

corpse-like creatures with incredible mental powers. But it turns out that Murdoch is not defenseless against his enemies — his mind, like theirs, can shape reality, although he doesn't understand how to harness his abilities. Soon, his quest to unearth his past links him up with Emma (Jennifer Connelly), a woman who is supposedly his wife, and Police Inspector Bumstead (William Hurt), who believes Murdoch to be innocent of the prostitute's murder. But Murdoch's small group of allies offer little help when it comes to dealing with his powerful, ghoulish adversaries, the amoral Mr. Book (Ian Richardson) and Mr. Hand (Richard O'Brien).

Thankfully, *Dark City* doesn't have an "all style, no substance" problem, because there's a mind-challenging story to go along with the eye candy. Proyas hasn't written this film for the passive viewer. To become involved in *Dark City*, thinking is mandatory. Unless you're puzzling out the answers alongside Murdoch, you're going to miss more than one revelation. Very little is spelled out in this movie; the answers are all there, but you have to recognize them for what they are. How often do we get features like this, that don't pander to the least common denominator? **HIGHLY RECOMMENDED**

Donnie Darko [2000]

Starring: Jake Gyllenhaal, Jena Malone, Drew Barrymore
Director: Richard Kelly Screenplay: Richard Kelly Running Time: 2:00
Rated: R (Profanity, drug use, violence) Theatrical Aspect Ratio: 2.35:1

Donnie Darko, the debut feature from writer/director Richard Kelly, is part psychological thriller and part science fiction mystery. The title character (Jake Gyllenhaal), a teenager in his last year of high school, is suffering from all manner of delusions and hallucinations. He sees and does the bidding of a 6-foot high rabbit wearing an insect mask, and, at times, appears completely dissociated from his surroundings. He is visiting a therapist and taking medication, but neither solution is working. Donnie is getting worse, but is it because he's descending deeper into a web of mental instability or because he's really seeing and experiencing these things? These are questions that the movie leaves unanswered until the end.

For much of the running length, *Donnie Darko* focuses more on Donnie's relationships with his sisters, parents, and girlfriend than on the science fiction aspects. This is meant to humanize a non-traditional protagonist and make him more "accessible" to viewers. It also allows the climax to have an emotional component (in addition to explaining the storyline's assorted, convoluted weirdness). *Donnie Darko* has a slow, methodical pace that allows the narrative to breathe; unfortunately, there are times when Kelly falls prey to the easy trap of self-indulgence. Selective edits would have made *Donnie Darko* tighter and more gripping, and, as a result, a better motion picture. As it is, there's a little too much redundancy in what's on screen.

One aspect of *Donnie Darko*'s production that's definitely worth mentioning is the special effects. The movie was made on the kind of low budget typically associated with independent films, yet the visual effects are first-rate. *Donnie Darko* proves that it's possible to do science fiction with visual effects in the independent film arena. This is just another area where the line between mainstream and indie movie-making has become increasingly blurred. Perhaps the only remaining difference is that smaller efforts like *Donnie Darko* use effects in service of an interesting story, while too many Hollywood productions think of the plot as a bothersome adjunct to their CGI eye candy. RECOMMENDED

E.T.: The Extra-Terrestrial [1982]

Starring: Dee Wallace, Henry Thomas, Peter Coyote Director: Steven Spielberg Screenplay: Melissa Mathison Running Time: 1:57 Rated: PG (Mature themes, mild profanity) Theatrical Aspect Ratio: 2.35:1

Steven Spielberg has always harbored a more benevolent view of space aliens than most of his Hollywood brethren. In *E.T.*, he postulates what might happen if a cute-but-strange-looking alien is marooned on Earth. "E.T.," as he is dubbed, chances upon a boy named Elliot (Henry Thomas). After their initial encounter, in which they frighten one another, they meet again, and form a tentative bond. Elliot invites E.T. into his house and hides him in his closet. He tells his older brother, Michael (Robert MacNaughton), and his younger sister, Gertie (Drew Barrymore), about his new friend. But, under the influence of Earth's unfamiliar climate, E.T. begins to show symptoms of a wasting sickness. Using household items, the strange little alien builds a communication device that allows him to "phone home" by sending a signal into space. Elliot's mother, Mary (Dee Wallace), learns about E.T. when government operatives, led by agent Keys (Peter Coyote), arrive at her house and place it under quarantine. But E.T. is dying, and Elliot, who is psychically bonded to him, is seriously ill.

E.T. is a tear-jerker and a feel-good experience

rolled into one. It plays best to the child inside all of us, and is most effective when fitted into the family film niche. Members of the under-10 crowd are guaranteed to fall under its spell, but there's enough intelligence in the story (written by Melissa Mathison) to enchant adults, as well. Strip away 20 years of hype, all the hyperbole and overblown praise, and *E.T.* comes across as a very pleasant diversion, but little more. The movie has (perhaps unfairly) been saddled with the mantle of "masterpiece," a title for which it is ill-suited. *E.T.* earned its reputation by capturing the imagination of movie-going audiences across the nation and holding it for an entire summer. Parents could take children. Teenagers could take dates. And older viewers were pleased to find a movie with old-fashioned values. Over the years, *E.T.*'s strengths have been magnified and its weaknesses diminished. In its latest re-release, it will draw crowds for the same reasons it did in 1982 (in addition to the nostalgia factor).

Even considering its mawkish tendencies and unsubtle manipulation, *E.T.* represents effective storytelling. It's a fairy tale with a heart, an allegory whose themes of peace and anti-prejudice will not be lost on those who don't recognize the allusions. For those who have previously seen *E.T.*, this is a chance to recapture something. And for those who haven't, this is an opportunity to see a movie that, at its best, is almost as special as its reputation indicates. RECOMMENDED

Galaxy Quest [1999]

Starring: Tim Allen, Sigourney Weaver, Alan Rickman, Tony Shalhoub Director: Dean Parisot Screenplay: Robert Gordon, David Howard Running Time: 1:42 Rated: PG (Mild violence) Theatrical Aspect Ratio: 1.85:1

Since its cancellation in 1982, *Galaxy Quest* has developed a loyal and fanatical following. However, none of the actors who appeared in the series have gone on to greater glory. Instead, they continue to earn a living by taking bit parts and appearing in costume at *Galaxy Quest* conventions. Jason Nesmith (Tim Allen), who played Commander Peter Quincy Taggart, seems to enjoy being associated with his character, but his opinion is not shared by his fellow cast members. Gwen DeMarco (Sigourney Weaver), Fred Kwan (Tony Shalhoub), and Tommy Webber (Daryl Mitchell) regard their lot in life with resignation, but Alexander Dane (Alan Rickman), who played the alien Dr. Lazarus, is resentful. Then, during one *Galaxy Quest* convention, Nesmith is approached by a group of fans dressed up (or so he thinks) as aliens. Their leader, Mathesar (Enrico Colantoni), explains that his people, the Thermians, need Commander Taggart's help. In short order, thinking they're going to some sort of low-level acting gig, Nesmith and his fellow actors find themselves transported to a space ship where they are expected to dispatch an intergalactic tyrant. It seems that the Thermians have picked up the *Galaxy Quest* TV show broadcasts and have mistaken the program for a series of "historical documents." So, believing Nesmith to be Taggart, they expect him to save the day.

In terms of parodying all things *Star Trek*, *Galaxy Quest* is often inventive, hitting both obvious and not-so-obvious targets. Fandom receives the sharpest edge of director Dean Parisot's satirical blade, although he and his screenwriters (Robert Gordon and David Howard) are never overtly vicious or cruel in their thrusts. What we see of the *Galaxy Quest* TV show looks an awful lot like *Star Trek* — right down to the indoor planet sets with styrofoam rocks. Taggart is a Kirk clone, and there's more than a passing likeness between Dr. Lazarus and Spock. The tempestuous relationships among the *Galaxy Quest* actors also recall those of the *Trek* cast members. Nesmith's colossal ego is undoubtedly supposed to echo the personality trait for which Shatner became best known after the original program went off the air.

Galaxy Quest has a good time playing with different aspects of science fiction in general, and *Star Trek* in particular. And, although it isn't necessary to come armed with an encyclopedic knowledge of the original *Star Trek* TV series to enjoy this movie, the better you know *Galaxy Quest*'s inspiration, the more you will get out of this picture. RECOMMENDED

Gattaca [1997]

Starring: Ethan Hawke, Uma Thurman, Alan Arkin, Jude Law
Director: Andrew Niccol Screenplay: Andrew Niccol Running
Time: 1:52 Rated: PG-13 (Violence, mature themes, profanity)
Theatrical Aspect Ratio: 2.35:1

Welcome to the 21st Century, an era when things aren't that much different, but people are. No longer is standard procreation the accepted way to reproduce. While it would be unreasonable to outlaw sex for the purpose of producing offspring, be aware than any children so conceived are almost certain to be "in-valids" — genetically imperfect and ill-suited to be productive members of society. There is a better, more rational way. Let science do a little tinkering with the DNA.

Andrew Niccol's oppressive future, which contains more than an element of Orwell's "Big Brother is watching" mentality, isn't just a clever backdrop against which to set a thriller. Instead, it's an integral part of the story. While it's true that there is a murder mystery, that's just a subplot. The main focus of *Gattaca* is the struggle of a genetically inferior man, Vincent Freeman (Ethan Hawke), to survive and prosper in a world where his kind is routinely discriminated against.

Shortly after they were married, Vincent's parents decided to start a family the old-fashioned way, without any help from doctors and test tubes. The result was a boy who was diagnosed as 99% likely to have a serious heart defect. That rendered Vincent ineligible for all but the most menial of jobs. But his dream was to one day work at The Gattaca Aerospace Corporation and participate in the first-ever manned flight to the moons of Saturn. For most "in-valids," this would have remained a fantasy, but Vincent possessed the determination and drive to make it real.

With the help of a shady middle-man, Vincent locates Jerome Morrow (Jude Law), a genetically superior individual who was paralyzed as the result of an accident. He agees to sell Vincent his identity (including blood and urine on demand, fingerprints, hair and other body debris, etc.). So, equipped with Jerome's genetic resume, which guarantees him work anywhere, Vincent applies for a position at Gattaca. He is accepted and quickly proves his worth to everyone. But, a week before he is to attain his life-long ambition of making a space flight, he becomes a suspect in a murder investigation and his carefully-guarded secret is in danger of being exposed.

One of the things that impressed me the most about *Gattaca* is its ability to keep the level of tension high without compromising the script's intelligence or integrity. First-time director Andrew Niccol, a New Zealander working in Los Angeles, displays a sure hand in his execution of the material. HIGHLY RECOMMENDED

Godzilla 2000 [Japan, 1999]

Starring: Takehiro Murata, Naomi Nishida, Mayu Suzuki
Director: Takao Okawara Screenplay: Hiroshi Kashiwabara, Wataru
Mimura Running Time: 1:37 Rated: PG (Monster movie violence, mild
profanity) Theatrical Aspect Ratio: 2.35:1 Dubbed into English

Godzilla 2000 represents Toho's attempt to reclaim their most durable, bankable product and re-package it for a new series of movies whose special effects are sporadically good enough to stand toe-to-toe with the American version. As is typical of a Godzilla movie, the plot is extremely silly, but one sort of has to take that as a given and sit back to enjoy the film on its own terms. Seen in that light, *Godzilla 2000* represents solid, campy, escapist entertainment.

The basic story will sound pretty familiar to those familiar with any of the other Godzilla movies. The Not-So-Jolly Green Giant (who actually seems a little shorter in this version than in his previous incarnations) goes on a rampage, gleefully stomping a Japanese city while humans try in vain to stop him. Meanwhile, an alien spacecraft has surfaced after an extended period under the sea. It eventually comes into contact with Godzilla, which results in a short-but-sweet battle sequence. Later, after a half hour's worth of Godzilla-less exposition and action scenes, the spacecraft metamorphoses into an ugly monster of about Godzilla's size and engages our hero in a no-holds-barred grudge match. In the end, when one character philosophically wonders about why Godzilla always seems to help humanity, his conclusion (the last line in the movie) is enough to send even the most dour viewer into paroxysms of laughter.

Godzilla 2000 uses the Godzilla formula effectively. The human beings are rather inconsequential, the dubbed, Americanized dialogue is frequently hilarious, the battle sequences are impressive, and the expository/character building sequences are kept to a minimum. Godzilla is more majestic than ever (although he's still a guy in a monster suit). In fact, his introductory scene, where he chomps on a ship then menaces a car in a tunnel, is handled impressively. The special effects are a leap forward for Toho. Although there are still some cheesy instances when it's obvious that models are being used, there are enough impressive moments to counterbalance the sillier ones. As for Godzilla himself, he is presented as more of the force of nature he represented in the first movie than the champion of Earth he eventually turned into. This Godzilla isn't out to save humanity; he's trying to ensure his own survival. If you have enjoyed any of the previous Godzilla outings, it's a pretty good bet that *Godzilla 2000* will be up your ally. If not, this is one big green lizard to avoid. RECOMMENDED

Harry Potter and the Sorcerer's Stone [United States/United Kingdom, 2001]

Starring: Daniel Radcliffe, Rupert Grint, Emma Watson, Richard Harris, Robbie Coltrane Director: Chris Columbus Screenplay: Steve Kloves, based on the novel by J.K. Rowling Running Time: 2:32 Rated: PG (Mild violence) Theatrical Aspect Ratio: 2.35:1

The movie opens in modern-day England, where 11-year-old Harry Potter (Daniel Radcliffe) dwells with his aunt, uncle, and cousin. Harry has lived with his mother's sister's family since shortly after birth, when his parents were murdered by the evil wizard Voldemort. On his birthday, Harry is visited by the imposing Rubeus Hagrid (Robbie Coltrane), who has come to bring Harry to Hogwarts School of Witchcraft and Wizardry, where he will study to fulfill his true calling as a wizard. Once at Hogwarts, he meets classmates who will become close friends, such as red-haired Ron Weasley (Rupert Grint) and bossy Hermione Granger (Emma Watson), and antagonists, such as the arrogant Draco Malfoy (Tom Felton). Then there's the headmaster of Hogwarts, the venerable wizard Albus Dumbledore (Richard Harris), and his staff — Professor Minerva McGonagall (Maggie Smith), who teaches Transfiguration; Professor Quirrell (Ian Hart), whose course is Defense Against the Dark Arts; Professor Flitwick (Warwick Davis), who teaches Charms; and Professor Snape (Alan Rickman), master of Potions. For Harry, however, there's more to attending Hogwarts than studying, as he begins to suspect one of the teachers of being in league with a dark force lurking in the forest.

Harry Potter and the Sorcerer's Stone is a rigorously faithful adaptation of the novel. With the exception of occasional details, short scenes, and a poltergeist, everything in the book is in the movie. For Harry Potter fans looking to see how their favorite scene appears on screen, this is a boon. But there's something almost workmanlike about Columbus' approach to the project. Movies and books are different media, and the best approach for adapting the latter into the former is not always an unvarnished translation. Columbus doesn't use any imagination beyond that which J.K. Rowling previously supplied for her book. There's no denying that the film is diverting, but it isn't *inspired*.

Harry Potter and the Sorcerer's Stone delivers as promised — a herd of colorful characters, fast-paced, inventive adventure, liberal doses of comedy, and even a little pathos. The film runs 2½ hours, but doesn't seem that long, and all but the youngest children should be able to sit through it without becoming restless. Just as the Harry Potter books have reached a wide audience, so too does the movie appeal to audience members of all ages. The film's spell may not be as potent as that of the book, but there's still some magic in what Columbus and his crew have wrought. RECOMMENDED

Harry Potter and the Chamber of Secrets
[United States/United Kingdom, 2002]
Starring: Daniel Radcliffe, Rupert Grint, Emma Watson, Richard Harris, Kenneth Branagh Director: Chris Columbus Screenplay: Steve Kloves, based on the novel by J.K. Rowling Running Time: 2:41 Rated: PG (Mild violence) Theatrical Aspect Ratio: 2.35:1

Harry Potter and the Chamber of Secrets opens up with Harry (Daniel Radcliffe) joining his friends, Hermione (Emma Watson) and Ron (Rupert Grint), and his nemesis, Draco (Tom Felton), as they prepare to begin their sophomore year at Hogwarts School for Witchcraft and Wizardry. Many of the old professors and administrators are back, including headmaster Albus Dumbledore (Richard Harris in his final role), the strict Professor McGonagall (Maggie Smith), and the dark, unwelcoming Professor Snape (Alan Rickman). There's also a newcomer — the charismatic, self-absorbed Gilderoy Lockhart (Kenneth Branagh), who is more concerned with answering fan mail than teaching how to defend against the dark arts. But all is not well at Hogwarts. A dark plot is brewing, with someone planning to break into the legendary "Chamber of Secrets" and unleash a monster that can petrify or kill with a look. It's up to Harry and his two friends to uncover the individual behind the plot and foil him or her before Hogwarts is closed.

All of the true inspiration underlying *Harry Potter and the Chamber of Secrets* lies in J.K. Rowling's writing. The Harry Potter books don't break new barriers, but they mix long-accepted fantasy formulas into a mélange that is fresh, easygoing, and infectious. Some of that comes across in the movies, but there are times when director Chris Columbus' pedestrian filmmaking lacks the spark that would truly ignite a movie. Columbus doesn't take a single chance. As a result, there are times when *Harry Potter and the Chamber of Secrets* seems more like a pre-packaged product than a living, breathing motion picture. It satisfies, but does not overwhelm.

The film's high octane second half is vastly better than the fitfully entertaining opening 75 minutes. All of the memorable scenes occur late in the movie, including an amazingly realized sequence featuring a bunch of large, unfriendly spiders and an equally eye-popping battle with a giant snake. As a companion piece to *Harry Potter and the Sorcerer's Stone*, *Harry Potter and the Chamber of Secrets* makes for ef-fective viewing. The second film may be a little darker than the first, but the two pictures mesh perfectly — not surprising, considering that many of the same people were responsible for both. RECOMMENDED

Jurassic Park [1993]
Starring: Sam Neill, Jeff Goldblum, Richard Attenborough, Laura Dern Director: Stephen Spielberg Screenplay: Michael Crichton and David Koepp based on the book by Michael Crichton Running Time: 2:06 Rated: PG-13 (Violence) Theatrical Aspect Ratio: 1.85:1

On a small island off the coast of Costa Rica exists a most unusual animal preserve by the name of Jurassic Park. Operated by dinosaur lover John Hammond (Richard Attenborough), Jurassic Park is the first of its kind. Its population of creatures includes brachiosaurs, dilophosaurs, triceratops, velociraptors, and a Tyrannosaurus Rex, each of which has been cloned using the latest technology that takes DNA from dinosaur-biting prehistoric insects preserved in amber, and uses that DNA for the re-creation. When the consortium funding Jurassic Park become concerned that all is not as it should be, Hammond is forced to call in 3 experts: paleontologist Dr. Alan Grant (Sam Neill), his partner, paleo-botanist Dr. Ellie Sattler (Laura Dern), and the brilliant-but-cynical mathematician Dr. Ian Malcolm (Jeff Goldblum). When the trio arrives at Jurassic Park, they are astonished by what it represents. It doesn't take long, however, for astonishment to turn to horror.

The apparent realism of some of Crichton's pseudo-science imbues *Jurassic Park* with a grounding that is acceptable in our high-tech world. After all, to weave a dinosaur fable in this day and age, it helps if science, not fantasy, is the driving force. Of course, the special effects help immensely. They are so good, in fact, and the dinosaurs look so real, that I half expected to see "dinosaur trainer" during the closing credits. Instead, however, plaudits go to the creators of *Jurassic Park*'s primary screen presences (all apologies to the actors).

I doubt there are many who will go to *Jurassic Park* for its characters or story. Rightly so, viewers will see this movie so they can ooh and aah, jump in their seats, and root for the overmatched humans against the big, bad dinosaurs. Even those familiar with the written work can't help being drawn in to the pulse-pounding exhilaration of the chase as the Tyrannosaurus menaces two powerless electric cars and the trapped humans inside. In the end, *Jurassic Park* succeeds because it's good entertainment. RECOMMENDED

Jurassic Park: The Lost World [1997]

Starring: Jeff Goldblum, Julianne Moore, Vince Vaughn
Director: Stephen Spielberg Screenplay: David Koepp based on the novel by Michael Crichton Running Time: 2:13 Rated: PG-13 (Violence) Theatrical Aspect Ratio: 1.85:1

Like its predecessor, *The Lost World* is basically a big-budget monster movie of the sort that has been popular ever since the dawn of motion pictures. Unfortunately, like many entries into the genre, it falls into expected patterns. As a result, much of this movie seems like a retread of *Jurassic Park* (with a little *King Kong* thrown in at the end), not because director Steven Spielberg is intentionally copying himself, but because there's really not much more that he can do with the premise. If there's a third movie in the series, it will probably follow pretty much the same storyline as the first and second installments.

Returning from the first film is Jeff Goldblum as Dr. Ian Malcolm, a mathematician with an analytical mind and a wry sense of humor. This time, he has an adolescent daughter, Kelly (Vanessa Lee Chester), and a paleontologist girlfriend, Sarah Harding (Julianne Moore). Ian gets pulled back into the dinosaur game when Sarah joins an expedition to the island of Isla Sorna, which is populated by a wide variety of genetically-engineered extinct species. John Hammond (Richard Attenborough), older and wiser after his *Jurassic Park* experience, no longer intends to open an amusement park; he simply wants to study dinosaurs in a natural environment. So, a reluctant Ian, along with Sarah, a nature photographer named Nick Van Owen (Vince Vaughn), and a gadgets expert, Eddie Carr (Richard Schiff), begins a "look-but-don't-touch" foray. Little do they know, however, that Hammond's nephew (Arliss Howard) is on his way to the island with far less benevolent intentions. He wants to bring dinosaurs back to San Diego for a prehistoric zoo. Accompanying him is big game hunter Roland Tembo (Pete Postlethwaite), whose goal is to bag a male T-Rex.

The differences between *Jurassic Park* and *The Lost World* can be summed up relatively simply: more dinosaurs, fewer legitimate thrills. Although *The Lost World* has its share of problems, chief of which is the familiarity factor, it still offers a couple hours of glitzy, hi-tech fun. And that's just about all that anyone can reasonably expect from this kind of blockbuster.

RECOMMENDED

The Lord of the Rings: The Fellowship of the Ring [New Zealand/United States, 2001]

Starring: Elijah Wood, Ian McKellen, Viggo Mortensen, Sean Astin
Director: Peter Jackson Screenplay: Fran Walsh & Philippa Boyens & Peter Jackson, based on the novel by J.R.R. Tolkien Running Time: 2:58 Rated: PG-13 (Violence, mature themes) Theatrical Aspect Ratio: 2.35:1

The Fellowship of the Ring begins in the quiet countryside of the Shire, where Bilbo Baggins of Bag End (Ian Holm), a hobbit, is celebrating his 111th birthday. In attendance, among other people, are Bilbo's young heir, Frodo (Elijah Wood), and the wizard Gandalf (Ian McKellan). Gandalf informs Bilbo that the time has come for him to leave Bag End and go on a journey. To Frodo, he leaves his home and his most beloved possession, a magical ring that turns the wearer invisible. But this isn't just any magical ring — it is the One Ring, forged by the Dark Lord, Sauron, and capable of corrupting the wearer. Sauron's servants, the Ring Wraiths, are scouring Middle Earth for it, since, when it is returned to their master, nothing will be able to stop him. All of the world is about to be plunged into war, and the only way to stop the evil will be to destroy the ring by casting it into the fire where it was forged — in Mordor, on the Dark Lord's doorstep. That unenviable task falls to Frodo, the ring bearer.

Frodo starts his journey in the company of 3 other hobbits — his faithful servant, Sam (Sean Astin), and his cousins, Merry (Dominic Monaghan) and Pippin (Billy Boyd). Later, as the dangers mount and Frodo faces even greater challenges, others join his company: the humans Aragorn (Viggo Mortensen) and Boromir (Sean Bean), the wizard Gandalf, the elf Legolas (Orlando Bloom), and the dwarf Gimli (John Rhys-Davies). Together, these 9 individuals must face Ring Wraiths, orcs, and worse; travel through strange lands and the dreaded mines of Moria; and face mistrust within their fellowship. And this is all just the first of 3 cinematic chapters . . .

Lord of the Rings devotees will be delighted to learn that the motion picture adaptation is as faithful as one could imagine possible. Jackson and his co-screenwriters (Fran Walsh & Philippa Boyens) do an excellent job condensing more than 500 pages of text into a script that never feels choppy, uneven, or rushed. *The Fellowship of the Ring* moves fluidly and, in the process, exhilarates. Certain scenes have been cut or condensed in the name of pacing, and the role of one character (Arwen) has been expanded to enhance a romantic angle, something that was largely absent from Tolkien's work.

First and foremost, *The Lord of the Rings* is an

adventure, and, in that, it is relentlessly successful. One does not need to have read the books to appreciate the movie. The background is explained concisely in a voiceover prologue, and the action proceeds in a straightforward manner. As long as one enjoys a well-crafted adventure yarn set against the backdrop of a mythical clash between good and evil, *The Lord of the Rings* will satisfy. At last, someone has figured out how to do an epic fantasy justice on the big screen. **MUST SEE**

Lord of the Rings: The Two Towers [United States/ New Zealand, 2002]

Starring: Elijah Wood, Ian McKellen, Viggo Mortensen, Sean Astin Director: Peter Jackson Screenplay: Fran Walsh & Philippa Boyens & Stephen Sinclair & Peter Jackson, based on the novel by J.R.R. Tolkien Running Time: 2:59 Rated: PG-13 (Violence, mature themes) Theatrical Aspect Ratio: 2.35:1

In nearly every way that counts, *The Two Towers* is *The Fellowship of the Ring*'s equal. In terms of tone, pacing, character development, plot advancement, and visual splendor, there is no drop-off. More importantly, the continuity is seamless, allowing a viewer familiar with the first movie to flow effortlessly into the second. Of course, therein lies a drawback, as well. *The Two Towers* cannot stand on its own. Familiarity with *The Fellowship of the Ring* is not just advisable, it is mandatory.

The Two Towers essentially picks up where *The Fellowship of the Ring* concludes, albeit following a short flashback to the battle between the wizard Gandalf (Ian McKellan) and the Balrog. In the wake of his victory over his foe, Gandalf is reborn as a white wizard, and returns to the world above to re-unite with his former companions. In the company of Aragorn (Viggo Mortensen), Legolas the elf (Orlando Bloom), and Gimli the dwarf (John Rhys-Davies), the wizard heads for the city of Rohan, where he hopes to convince the king, Theoden (Bernard Hill), that war is upon his kingdom. At the same time, the hobbits Merry (Dominic Monaghan) and Pippin (Billy Boyd), having escaped from their orc captors, flee into the forbidding Fanghorn Forest, where they encounter Treebeard the Ent (voice of John Rhys-Davies).

Meanwhile, to the East, Frodo (Elijah Wood) and Sam (Sean Astin) find themselves lost on their way to Mount Doom. And, in addition to suffering from the physical difficulties of such an arduous journey, Frodo is beginning to show the strain of bearing the ring, with the Dark Lord Sauron's baleful glare constantly seeking him. The creature Gollum (Andy Serkis), who has been following the hobbits, attempts to steal the ring from Frodo, but is subdued and captured. Thereafter, he reluctantly agrees to serve as Frodo and Sam's guide and take them to Mordor.

The stunning climax of *The Two Towers* is the battle of Helm's Deep — a 30-minute spectacle that features the siege of a seemingly impregnable stone fortress by an army of 10,000 creatures of Sauruman (Christopher Lee). Inside that fortress is a small force of several hundred humans and elves, led by Aragorn, Theoden, Legolas, and Gimli. While a huge special effects contribution is needed to make the battle such an awesome feast for the eyes, Jackson never lets the CGI work overwhelm the human element of what's going on.

The Two Towers starts out a little slowly, but the rousing second half, which gathers momentum like a boulder racing downhill, will leave audiences craving more when the end credits roll. Combined, *The Fellowship of the Ring* and *The Two Towers* represent one of the most engrossing and engaging six-hour segments of cinema I have ever enjoyed. Like its predecessor, *The Two Towers* is a great motion picture, and not to be missed by anyone who appreciates fantasy adventure. **MUST SEE**

The Matrix [1999]

Starring: Keanu Reeves, Laurence Fishburne, Carrie-Anne Moss, Joe Pantoliano, Hugo Weaving Directors: Andy Wachowski, Larry Wachowski Screenplay: Andy Wachowski, Larry Wachowski Running Time: 2:15 Rated: R (Violence) Theatrical Aspect Ratio: 2.35:1

Thomas Anderson (Keanu Reeves) is leading a double life. To most people, he's a hard-working computer programmer who holds down a 9-to-5 job for a major software corporation. But, in the privacy of his home, he's a hacker named Neo who is "guilty of virtually every computer crime [there's] a law for." Neo is dissatisfied with his existence, and, while he's groping for a meaning to it, he is contacted by a mysterious computer presence known as Morpheus. "Wake up Neo," a printout on his monitor screen reads. "The Matrix has you. Follow the white rabbit." And so begins an amazing odyssey for both Neo and the audience.

It turns out that Morpheus (Laurence Fishburne) is the captain of a small space ship, and he believes that Neo is a messianic figure. When the two finally meet, Morpheus explains to Neo that all is not as it seems. The reality he is used to is a fabrication, the product of a sinister race of intelligent machines that use human beings as power supplies, to be discarded at will. Neo is dubious, and Morpheus sets out to show him the truth. Soon, he is learning how to manipulate the Matrix: a computer-generated dreamworld built by the machines to control human minds. But danger lurks ahead for Morpheus and his small band of followers. The goal of the machines is to eliminate all free humans, and their most powerful weapons, the Sentient Agents (who look like Men in Black), are closing in. Led by Agent Smith (Hugo Weaving), their goal is to capture Morpheus and pry the secrets from his brain.

The Matrix offers a little something for everyone. The die-hard science fiction fan will discover a plot that mixes and matches both new and old conventions of the genre in a compelling fashion. Action aficionados will find that there's no shortage of electric excitement, whether it's in the form of hand-to-hand kung fu-type fights or shoot-outs with seemingly limitless ammunition. There's also betrayal, a little romance, some humor, and a moral dilemma or two, all wrapped into a well-produced package. The way in which the Wachowskis choose to resolve everything seems slightly contrived, but, in the overall scheme of things, that's a small price to pay for one of the most enjoyable science fiction thrillers to reach the screen in months. HIGHLY RECOMMENDED

Men in Black [1997]

Starring: Tommy Lee Jones, Will Smith, Linda Fiorentino
Director: **Barry Sonnenfeld** Screenplay: **Ed Solomon** based on the comic book by Lowell Cunningham Running Time: **1:35** Rated: **PG-13** (Violence, profanity) Theatrical Aspect Ratio: **1.85:1**

As Jay, Will Smith is the latest recruit of the ultra-secret sixth division of the INS (the "Men in Black" of the title) — a group of government workers in charge of licensing and regulating the presence of non-Earth-born aliens. His partner, Kay (Tommy Lee Jones), is a venerable agent who knows the ropes and is willing to give lessons. Together, the pair go in search of an intergalactic assassin (played in human form by Vincent D'Onofrio) whose unauthorized activities on Earth could result in the planet's destruction.

Men in Black is a snappy, clever, often-funny motion picture that provides the perfect blend of science fiction-style action with comic dialogue. The screenplay, credited to Ed Solomon (and based on the Marvel comic book by Lowell Cunningham) has a sly, sophisticated edge that many blockbuster scripts lack. Sonnenfeld's direction is crisp and the editing is tight, resulting in a film that clocks in at a mere 95 minutes, which proves to be a nearly-perfect length.

The chief pleasure of *Men in Black* isn't being dazzled by the special effects, but enjoying the deadpan performances of Tommy Lee Jones (whose offhand attitude towards the most bizarre events would make Jack Webb proud) and Will Smith. This is a rare case when the multi-million dollar, computer-generated creatures don't upstage their real-life co-stars. Smith and Jones are a fine pair, and the film's focus on them never wavers.

Men in Black is an outright comedy, not a pastiche of worn sci-fi/adventure elements, and there's no big space battle to be found. In fact, from the opening credits to the closing ones, our heroes stay firmly rooted on terra firma. Those accepting *Men in Black* for what it is will likely agree that this is a satisfying big-budget offering. RECOMMENDED

A Midsummer Night's Dream [1999]

Starring: Kevin Kline, Michelle Pfeiffer, Rupert Everett, Stanley Tucci
Director: **Michael Hoffman** Screenplay: **Michael Hoffman, based on the play by William Shakespeare** Running Time: **1:58** Rated: **PG-13** (Sensuality, nudity) Theatrical Aspect Ratio: **2.35:1**

A Midsummer Night's Dream is arguably the best loved and most frequently performed of Shakespeare's comedies. The text shows its great versatility with each new interpretation — depending on the director's vision, *A Midsummer Night's Dream* can be a light fantasy, a dark nightmare, a slapstick comedy, or a semi-serious melodrama. One might understandably wonder whether there's a pressing reason for a new motion picture version. But director Michael Hoffman deflects such criticism by presenting a rendering that is sufficiently contemporary and fresh.

Hoffman has elected to shift the setting from 16th century Greece to Tuscany in the late 1800s. The bicycle — a relatively new invention at the time — becomes a key prop, allowing characters to pedal after each other instead of chasing around on foot. Understandably, the basic story has not changed, even though the locale and time period have. *A Midsummer Night's Dream* opens by introducing Duke Theseus (David Strathairn), who is preparing for his wedding to the reluctant Hippolyta (Sophie Marceau). Theseus is called in to resolve a dispute centering on the romantic inclinations of Hermia (Anna Friel), the daughter of Egeus (Bernard Hill). While the girl wants to marry the dashing Lysander (Dominic West), whom she loves, her father has betrothed her to Demetrius (Christian Bale). When Theseus' ruling goes against them, Hermia and Lysander resolve to elope. Meanwhile, Demetrius is being pursued by Helena (Calista Flockhart), who is willing to suffer any number of humiliations to be with him. These four, along with an actor named Bottom (Kevin Kline), end up in a nearby forest on a night when the nymphs, satyrs, and fairies are out and about. The King of the Fairies, Oberon (Rupert Everett), is quarreling with his queen, Titania (Michelle Pfeiffer). To untangle matters, Oberon enlists his servant, Puck, to procure a love potion, of which he says, "The juice of it on sleeping eyelids laid will make or man or woman madly dote upon the next live creature that it sees." However, not everything goes according to plan, resulting in some unexpected romantic pairings.

Although set design and atmosphere are critical to Hoffman's vision of the play (and represent the primary cues by which this version can be differentiated from its predecessors), Shakespeare's text still lies at the movie's heart. In a fantasy setting such as this, the flowery language works exceptionally well. This thoroughly enjoyable piece of cinema does credit to its director, cast, and writer. **HIGHLY RECOMMENDED**

Mighty Joe Young [1998]

Starring: Charlize Theron, Bill Paxton, Rade Sherbedgia, Peter Firth
Director: Ron Underwood Screenplay: Mark Rosenthal & Lawrence Konner Running Time: 1:50 Rated: PG (Violence, mild profanity)
Theatrical Aspect Ratio: 1.85:1

Mighty Joe Young begins in Africa during the mid-1980s, when Jill Young (Mika Boorem) loses her mother (Linda Purl) to a gunshot fired by a ruthless big-game hunter, Strasser (Rade Sherbedgia). Strasser is a major player in the black market selling of endangered species, and he has come to Jill's part of Africa in search of new inventory. Another of his bullets finds a female gorilla, the mother of Jill's simian friend, Joe. Bonded by their mutual orphanage, the two become inseparable as they grow up together. But Joe is no ordinary gorilla — by the time he reaches adulthood, he's 15 feet tall and weighs 2000 pounds.

The next time we meet Joe and Jill (now played by Charlize Theron), it's 12 years later. Poachers are threatening Joe's existence and Gregg O'Hara (Bill Paxton), an adventurous zoologist who works for the California Animal Conservatory, has arrived with an offer of sanctuary for Joe if Jill is willing to bring him to a preserve in America. Reluctantly, she agrees. Soon, Joe is acclimating to his new home, but all is not well. The Conservatory, anxious to use their new attraction as a fund-raising tool, has put Joe in the media spotlight, and Strasser is eager to capture him. Eventually and inevitably, Joe escapes from the preserve and begins romping around Hollywood.

Plot-wise, there's not much going on here. *Mighty*

Joe Young is like a low-rent *King Kong* with a little more emphasis on the humanity of the primate. In fact, a great deal of effort is undertaken to make Joe a likable character — he is shown to be intelligent, childlike, and gentle (except when provoked). Although Joe's size makes him a monster, his disposition makes him cuddly. The movie contains elements of comedy and romance (between Gregg and Jill, although Joe is jealous), but the silliest aspects of the original 1949 film have been eliminated. Despite not being daring in style or story, *Mighty Joe Young* is nevertheless a charming and enjoyable adventure, and a rare remake that's better than the original. **RECOMMENDED**

Minority Report [2002]

Starring: Tom Cruise, Max von Sydow, Colin Farrell, Samantha Morton
Director: Steven Spielberg Screenplay: Scott Frank and Jon Cohen, based on the short story by Philip K. Dick Running Time: 2:31
Rated: PG-13 (Violence, mature themes, drug use) Theatrical Aspect Ratio: 2.35:1

For those that must classify *Minority Report*, the primary category is science fiction. But *Minority Report* can also be viewed as an action thriller or a futuristic film noir. It owes a debt to Dashiel Hammitt and Raymond Chandler. And *Minority Report* plays like a different film to different audiences. Those in the mood for the action and adrenaline rush will find something to their taste here. Yet there are richer rewards for viewers who are willing to engage their brains. Anyone who wants to think through the mysteries and paradoxes presented herein will discover a multi-course cinematic buffet that can keep the gray matter occupied for days to come.

The year is 2054. Washington D.C., once the murder capital of the union, is now the safest place to live — thanks in large part to the Department of Pre-Crime, an elite taskforce of law officers who, by using the predictive capabilities of 3 captive "precogs," know that a murder is going to happen before it takes place. Armed with that knowledge, they can arrest someone before he actually kills, saving the victim(s) and preventing the crime. The head of the Department is Director Burgess (Max von Sydow), a dispassionate man who has shepherded the group through eight years of growing pains and is now on the verge of losing control of it as the program goes national. His right hand man, Detective John Anderton (Tom Cruise), is in an equally precarious position.

The first part of the movie introduces us to the Pre-Crime squad and shows how they operate by illustrating their attempts to solve Case #1108 — a crime of passion in which a man discovers his wife's infidelity and kills both her and her lover. Once that is successfully wrapped up, *Minority Report* moves on to Case #1109 — the pre-meditated murder of a man by none other than Anderton. Within moments of recognizing that he has run afoul of the system he works for, Anderton is in full flight, certain that he is being set up by Detective Ed Witwer (Colin Farrell), a federal agent who is after his job. Anderton's belief in his own innocence is so strong that he even risks breaking into the Pre-Crime building and kidnapping Agatha (Samantha Morton), the most gifted of the 3 Precogs. He suspects that, with her help, he can clear himself.

Predestination or free will? It's a question that has obsessed philosophers and religious scholars throughout the years. Now, it is the underlying subject material of a major motion picture made not for deep thinkers but for a mass audience. Action fans have plenty to engage their attention. *Minority Report* features its share of shoot-outs, fights, and chase scenes, some of which are quite spectacular. And the special effects serve the ingenuity of the script, not the other way around. These days, many blockbusters offer eye candy without substance. Not so in here, where both are available in equal proportions. **MUST SEE**

Π (Pi) [1998]

Starring: **Sean Gullette, Mark Margolis, Ben Shenkman, Pamela Hart**
Director: **Darren Aronofsky** Screenplay: **Darren Aronofsky** Running Time: **1:25** Rated: **Not Rated (Violence, profanity)** Theatrical Aspect Ratio: **1.66:1**

π, the letter, is a character in the Greek alphabet roughly equivalent to the English "p." π, the mathematical notation, is commonly used to represent the ratio of the circumference of a circle to its diameter. π, the movie, is Darren Aronofsky's debut feature, an independent science fiction thriller that combines questions about God and infinity with the personal struggle of one man to regain control of his life.

π is the story of Max Cohen (ably portrayed by Sean Gullette), a computer geek with a genius for mathematics. Socially, Max is completely inept. Aside from occasionally showing off his arithmetic abilities to a girl who lives in his apartment building, he avoids all human contact, including any interaction with his attractive next door neighbor (Samia Shoaib), who shows an interest in him. Max lives by 3 basic principles: (1) mathematics is the language of nature, (2) everything can be represented and understood through numbers, and (3) there are patterns in nature. His objective is to use his home-built supercom-

puter, Euclid, to analyze the patterns in the financial markets to predict the exact performance of every stock. During the course of his studies, he encounters a mysterious string of 216 digits, and, when a Jewish numerologist (Ben Shenkman) becomes aware of this, he confides in Max that "the pattern in the Torah is 216 digits," and this discovery may hold the key to unlocking God's true name. Max, who doesn't believe in God, is more interested when his mentor (Mark Margolis) reveals that he once encountered a "bug" of 216 digits when he was investigating π.

Max's mathematical brilliance comes at a price, however: he has frequent, debilitating headaches and seizures that send him into a bizarre state of consciousness. During those episodes, he encounters people who stalk him then disappear, and, on one occasion, he discovers a brain lying on the ground in a New York City subway station. The key to Max's genius and pain appears to be a mark on his skull, and, perhaps in order to eliminate the one, he must sacrifice the other.

Although the plot of π is eccentric (even for a science fiction effort), Aronofsky's message is actually quite simple: life does not fit into neat patterns, and complete control is impossible. In addition to all of its intellectually-stimulating aspects, π also works as a character study of an obsessed individual whose single-minded goal blinds him to everything else, including health, friendship, love, and even sanity. π transports us to a world that is like yet unlike our own, and, in its mysterious familiarity, is eerie, intense, and compelling. Reality is a fragile commodity, but, because the script is well-written and the central character is strongly developed, it's not hard to suspend disbelief. **RECOMMENDED**

Pitch Black [2000]

Starring: **Vin Diesel, Radha Mitchell, Cole Hauser, Keith David**
Director: **David Twohy** Screenplay: **Jim Wheat & Ken Wheat and David Twohy** Running Time: **1:47** Rated: **R (Violence, gore, profanity, scary aliens, bad science)** Theatrical Aspect Ratio: **2.35:1**

Pitch Black can be viewed as a slick, stylish version of the kind of outer space creature feature that is typified best by the *Alien* movies. At its best (which is quite often), *Pitch Black* is an entertaining effort. On the down side, there are times when various largely anonymous characters wander around in the dark and do incredibly stupid things while being stalked by vicious alien creatures. As they get picked off one-by-one, the only question is who's going to be *next*.

The movie begins with the crash, a violent concussion that leaves most of the crew and passengers dead. Among the handful of survivors are Fry (Radha Mitchell), the pilot; Johns (Cole Hauser), a police officer; Riddick (Diesel), a convicted murderer who is being transported in chains; and Inam, a holy man (Keith David). The planet is an apparently lifeless wasteland — a desertscape where 3 suns assure that there is no night and possibly no water. Shortly after the rough landing, Riddick escapes, but, while the survivors are looking for him, they too are being hunted — by a species of alien that shuns the daylight but is lethal in the dark. Soon, with the realization that the world is about to be plunged into blackness by an inconvenient total eclipse, everyone must learn to trust Riddick, who can see in the dark, if they are to survive. Meanwhile, it's unclear whether Riddick's primary goal is self-preservation or redemption.

Pitch Black has a stylish look. The outdoor sequences, which are nearly monochromatic to emphasize the color-leaching power of the multiple suns, are effectively photographed. After the eclipse occurs, there are some genuinely creepy sequences featuring packs of aliens honing in on the protagonists, who are only able to keep them at bay by waving around lights. For the most part, the special effects are first-rate — I was impressed by the scene of a ringed planet sliding across the sky on its way to block out the sun. These strong visuals complement a workmanlike script, resulting in a consistently engaging science fiction/horror excursion. RECOMMENDED

Pleasantville [1998]

Starring: Tobey Maguire, Reese Witherspoon, Jeff Daniels, Joan Allen
Director: Gary Ross Screenplay: Gary Ross Running Time: 1:56
Rated: PG-13 (Mature themes, sexual situations, mild profanity)
Theatrical Aspect Ratio: 1.85:1

Pleasantville opens in the comfortable familiarity of the '90s, with a common '90s family — David (Tobey Maguire) and Jennifer (Reese Witherspoon) are the twin children of a broken marriage. They live with a mother who's never around. One night, a mysterious television repair man (Don Knotts) shows up at the door and gives David a "special" remote control for the set. Later, as he's settling down to watch a 24-hour marathon of his favorite show, *Pleasantville,* he and his sister struggle over the remote. In the process, something very strange happens.

Suddenly, they are no longer in their home. In fact, they're no longer in color. They have entered the black-and-white world of '50s television, where the temperature is always 72 degrees, it never rains, pro-

fanity is never spoken, sex is taboo, there are no toilets, and words like "swell," "gee-whiz," and "keen" are part of the regular vocabulary. David is thrilled with the change in events. After all, *Pleasantville* is his favorite program. Jennifer, on the other hand, is horrified ("I'm pasty!" she screams upon seeing her gray complexion). She wants to go back immediately. She doesn't like the idea of having a perfect Dad in George (William H. Macy) and a perfect Mom in Betty (Joan Allen). But the gateway the two teens entered appears to be one-way, so they have to make do with their new world. Soon, however, David and Jennifer's "radical" ideals are bringing about changes in their environment. Perfection begins slipping away. Colors start to dot the black-and-white vistas. Jealousy, anger, and passion make appearances. The stale utopia of family values begins evolving.

The most stunning thing about *Pleasantville* is the film's look. Color is used purposefully and impressively; it's hard to describe the impact of seeing one red rose amidst the black and white, or one monochromatic person in a sea of green grass. Ross has a reason for every change in hue, and the way he gradually evolves the film from pure black and white to a vibrant cacophony of colors is stirring.

One of the things I liked best about *Pleasantville* is that, while it entertains with its quirky plot and stunning visuals, it also made me think. Too few movies manage to be both thought-provoking and thoroughly entertaining. *Pleasantville* is a tour de force — it's a magical, modern-day fairy tale that invites us to explore who we are, and, like *The Wizard of Oz* and *It's a Wonderful Life* (heady company indeed), it trumpets the messages that the individual can make a difference, and that life in an alternate reality isn't necessarily better, just different. Not only is *Pleasantville* a satire, a fantasy, and a visual marvel, but it's the best kind of feel-good movie. HIGHLY RECOMMENDED

Reign of Fire [2002]

Starring: Matthew McConaughey, Christian Bale, Izabella Scorupco
Director: Rob Bowman Screenplay: Gregg Chabot & Kevin Peterka and Matt Greenberg Running Time: 1:45 Rated: PG-13 (Violence) Theatrical Aspect Ratio: 2.35:1

The film begins with a short prologue in modern-day London, where a construction crew working underground awakens a huge fire-breathing dragon. Skip ahead to 2020, where most of civilization is a blackened cinder — reduced to ashes by a scourge of countless flying reptiles. The few remaining humans have banded together into small refugee camps, trying to eke out an existence while staying out of the way of the dragons, who, in their hunger, are starting to feed on one another. Quinn (Christian Bale) is the leader of one such settlement, and his world is turned upside down by the arrival of Van Zan (Matthew McConaughey), Alex (Izabella Scorupco), and their group of gung-ho American military men, who are hunting dragons. They have come all the way to England in search of the big prize — the lone male dragon, the most fearsome creature on Earth. Kill it, they reason, and the dragons will die out. With no means of fertilizing their eggs, they will disappear within a generation.

The dragons look much more impressive than any of their past kin in other films. Sleek, deadly, and lightning fast, they strike quickly, then move on. There are times when the dragons, especially the bull, are imposing enough to be a little frightening. This is an instance when a filmmaker uses CGI to good effect. The visuals are not the least bit cheesy, and the dragons blend in well enough with the live-action actors that suspending disbelief is not difficult.

To say that the casting is a bit unusual is to understate matters. Christian Bale, the British actor who has had a smattering of success on both sides of the Atlantic, and Matthew McConaughey do not fit the mold of traditional action heroes, yet they acquit themselves admirably. Both have bulked up and tossed aside their pretty-boy images in an effort to get down and dirty. With his shaved head, beefy physique, and wild gaze, the cigar-chomping McConaughey is virtually unrecognizable, and entirely believable as a madman who will play chicken with a dragon.

I certainly wouldn't want every movie to be like *Reign of Fire,* but this sort of picture has just as much of a place in theaters as an adaptation of a Henry James novel. The key to the success of either is for the production to be well done, which, in this case, it is. *Reign of Fire* has no pretentions (which is refreshing in a way). It's about kicking butt, killing big, ugly monsters, and saving the human race. Bowman believes in it, and, because of his conviction, so do we. RECOMMENDED

Screamers [1996]

Starring: Peter Weller, Roy Dupuis, Jennifer Rubin Director: Christian Duguay Screenplay: Dan O'Bannon and Miguel Tejada-Flores Running Time: 1:47 Rated: R (Violence, profanity) Theatrical Aspect Ratio: 1.85:1

Screamers oozes atmosphere. It's a dark film that borrows heavily from the likes of the *Alien* films, *Dune, Blade Runner,* and John Carpenter's updated *The Thing.* From start to finish, *Screamers* is shot in a manner intended to convey paranoia and claustrophobia. Set design is always impressive, if bleak, and consists primarily of ruined buildings and underground bunkers. Matte paintings of wrecked bridges and smashed cities form an ominous backdrop to much of the movie's action.

The film opens with several paragraphs of background text. The year is 2078 and the place is Sirius 6B. Once a paradise, it has been reduced to a radioactive wasteland as the result of mining toxic Berynium (the "solution" to Earth's energy crisis) and a war that has lasted more than a decade. Peace may be close at hand, however, and it's up to Commander Hendricksson (Robocop himself, Peter Weller) to decide the legitimacy of his enemies' appeal for an armistice.

Along with fresh-out-of-training rookie Ace (Andy Lauer), Hendricksson heads into the wasteland, traveling to the opposition's control bunker. Along the way, he meets several other Sirius 6B survivors, all eking out a nomadic existence: bootlegger Jessica (Jennifer Rubin), a woman who wants nothing more than to go to Earth; Ross (Charles Powell), the sole survivor of a massacre; and Becker (Roy Dupuis), a hardened cynic who prefers killing to asking questions.

As these five trek across the surface of Sirius 6B, they encounter a new, deadly adversary: the screamers (so nicknamed because of the squeal they make when attacking). Originally created as "autonomous mobile swords" by Hendricksson's side, the electronic, buzz-saw-like creatures have evolved, shaking off the yoke of slavery. With the ability to form a human shape and mimic human behavior, little appears beyond their capabilities, including infiltrating Hendricksson's small group.

Screamers emphasizes that science fiction doesn't have to be upbeat to succeed. This "sci-fi noir" style has led to a crop of films that hopefully heralds a new trend in the industry. If nothing else, *Screamers* underlines an important truth: you don't need a big budget or big-name stars to make this sort of motion picture succeed. RECOMMENDED

Signs [2002]

Starring: Mel Gibson, Joaquin Phoenix, Rory Culkin, Abigail Breslin Director: M. Night Shyamalan Screenplay: M. Night Shyamalan Running Time: 1:48 Rated: PG-13 (Mature themes, profanity, violence) Theatrical Aspect Ratio: 1.85:1

Mel Gibson, whose salary probably represents a significant portion of *Signs'* budget, plays Father Graham Hess, a widower who is caring for his two children, Morgan (Rory Culkin) and Bo (Abigain Breslin), on a Bucks County (Pennsylvania) farm. Following his wife's death 6 months ago, Graham has done his best to keep his family together. He is aided by his younger brother, Merrill (Joaquin Phoenix), who moved to the farm following the tragedy. But Graham has lost his faith in God and has renounced his vocation. Then, one morning, he awakens to an amazing discovery — crop circles in his fields. At first, he is inclined to believe it's all a hoax, but, as evidence mounts that this may not be the case, he and his family realize that what has happened in their fields may be the first signs that Earth is about to have a close encounter.

While much of Shyamalan's setup is familiar, the meat of the story has an exotic flavor. Taking a page from Steven Spielberg's *Jaws,* the director keeps the aliens hidden from our view. We catch occasional, brief glimpses — a leg in the corn field, a hand under a door, and a flash of green on a television screen. With today's special effects being so convincing, it's unusual for a filmmaker to fall back on the old, tried-and-true technique of "less is more." In the case of *Signs,* it creates a level of tension that a full revelation would have spoiled.

Then there's the added mystery of whether the aliens are benevolent or aggressive. Shyamalan obscures their intentions for most of the movie, concentrating instead upon the fears and concerns of the characters when they don't know the truth. Graham gives a speech in which he talks about how some humans will view first contact as a miracle that gives them hope, while others will see it as a cause for anxiety and uncertainty. In other words, is Earth about to be subjected to a *Close Encounters* or an *Independence Day*? For quite some time, Shyamalan doesn't tip his hand, and, when he does so, it isn't in a predictable manner. RECOMMENDED

Solaris [2002]

Starring: George Clooney, Natascha McElhone, Jeremy Davies, Viola Davis Director: Steven Soderbergh Screenplay: Steven Soderbergh, based on the novel by Stanislaw Lem Running Time: 1:38 Rated: PG-13 (Mature themes, sexual situations, brief nudity) Theatrical Aspect Ratio: 2.35:1

Solaris may be the first big budget science fiction motion picture that belongs in an art house rather than a multiplex. The movie bears a stronger resemblance to *2001: A Space Odyssey* than to *Star Wars,* with an emphasis on ideas over action. Those expecting to see space battles and bug-eyed aliens will be disappointed. There's nothing like that here. The experi-

ence of watching *Solaris* doesn't just invite thought and rumination; it demands it.

Solaris transpires at an unspecified time in the near future. Therapist Chris Kelvin (George Clooney) travels to a space station orbiting the distant planet of Solaris after a friend requests his help analyzing a problem that the crew of the station has encountered. When Chris arrives, he finds that his friend is among the dead, and there are only 2 survivors — the laid-back Snow (Jeremy Davies) and the paranoid Dr. Gordon (Viola Davis). Although neither Snow nor Gordon provides helpful information, Chris soon discovers on his own what's transpiring when he receives a visitation from his dead wife, Rhea (Natascha McElhone). Rhea does not appear to be a hallucination or a ghost, and that leaves Chris with a serious issue to resolve: Is she real or not, and, if she is, *what* is she?

Solaris examines weighty issues like the power of guilt, the nature of life, and the importance of memory. There are no traditional antagonists in this film; Chris' greatest enemy is a burden of conscience that he carries with him, the presence of which weighs down his soul and clouds his judgment. Initially, he doesn't believe his visitor is Rhea. Later, he no longer cares. The presence of someone who looks, feels, and sounds identical to his dead wife gives him an opportunity to assuage the pain of misplaced responsibility.

The number of "thinking" science fiction films is small, and most are produced on small budgets for start-up directors. The first-rate production values and A-list star make *Solaris* an exception — and a rewarding one, at that. This is the first film I have seen in a long time to make me feel some of the things I experienced while watching *2001. Solaris* is neither as effective nor as ambitious as Kubrick's masterpiece, but it's still a compelling cinematic experience for those who are willing to abandon themselves to the unforced, measured rhythms of an issues-based motion picture. RECOMMENDED

Star Trek: The Motion Picture — Director's Edition [2001]

Starring: William Shatner, Leonard Nimoy, DeForest Kelley Director: Robert Wise Screenplay: Alan Dean Foster and Harold Livingstone Running Time: 2:16 Rated: PG (Science Fiction action) Theatrical Aspect Ratio: 2.35:1

In 1979, the release of *Star Trek — The Motion Picture* represented the climax to every *Star Trek* fan's wet dream. The date, December 7, lived in infamy for the entire production crew. Paramount Pictures etched this date into their release calendar and informed everyone involved that the film *would* be ready on that day. Despite the Herculean effort by legendary director Robert Wise and his army of post-production assistants, the version of *Star Trek — The Motion Picture* that reached theaters was not complete. Now, more that 20 years later, Robert Wise has had the opportunity to return to the film and complete it in the manner he had originally envisioned.

The film opens with the destruction of three Klingon warships by a mysterious energy cloud that is on a direct heading for Earth. The newly redesigned *U.S.S. Enterprise* is the only ship available to intercept the cloud, and it hasn't undergone its shakedown cruise. Admiral James T. Kirk (William Shatner), restless after 2½ years behind a desk, uses the crises to once again take command of the *Enterprise,* forcing the ship's expected captain, Will Decker (Stephen Collins), into the role of Executive Officer. Most of the crew is re-united, including the irascible Dr. McCoy (the late DeForest Kelley) and the half-Vulcan Mr. Spock (Leonard Nimoy). Spock senses a kinship with the vast consciousness that exists at the heart of the cloud. Also on board are Chief Engineer Scotty (James Doohan), Security Chief Chekov (Walter Koenig), Helmsman Sulu (George Takei), Communications Officer Uhura (Nichelle Nichols), and a newcomer, Navigator Ilia (Persis Khambatta).

After battling several systems failures, including a malfunctioning transporter that kills two crewman and a propulsion system that becomes unstable and creates a wormhole, the *Enterprise* makes contact with the entity within the cloud, called V'ger. The journey to the center of the alien ship is a strange and bizarre one. Ilia is killed when a probe invades the *Enterprise* bridge, and V'ger later sends a second probe to the ship in the form of a mechanism that mimics Ilia's body and features. Kirk learns that V'ger is a living machine traveling to Earth to make contact with its "Creator." If this contact is not made, V'ger intends to wipe out all of the human beings "infesting" the planet. It is up to the crew of the *Enterprise* to prevent that eventuality.

Re-visiting *Star Trek — The Motion Picture* via this director's cut is like seeing a familiar story unfold in a new way. Wise's picture was an ambitious effort from the beginning, striving for a greatness that it never attained. In this new version, it still falls short, but not by as much. It has taken more than 20 years for Robert Wise to return to his chapter of the *Star Trek*

saga and fulfill his vision. With no hesitation, I can say that it has been worth the wait. *Star Trek — The Motion Picture: Director's Edition* vaults this movie from a position as one of the weakest entries in the long-running film series to a perch as one of the strongest. **RECOMMENDED**

Star Trek II: The Wrath of Khan [1982]

Starring: William Shatner, Leonard Nimoy, DeForest Kelley, Ricardo Montalban Director: Nicholas Meyer Screenplay: Harve Bennett and Jack B. Sowards Running Time: 1:50 Rated: PG (Violence) Theatrical Aspect Ratio: **2.35:1**

The film is a sequel to a first season episode of the series ("Space Seed"). Here, the evil genius Khan (Ricardo Montalban, in a deliciously over-the-top performance) and his followers have escaped from the barren planet where then-Captain Kirk (William Shatner) stranded them some 15 years ago. Khan, once a brilliant, charismatic leader, has become an embittered maniac, dedicated only to revenge. He blames Kirk for the death of his wife and the waste of his own life, and intends to extract payment — in blood. After hijacking a Federation starship, Khan steals Genesis, a potential doomsday weapon created by Kirk's son, David (Merritt Butrick), and ex-lover, Carol (Bibi Besch), and lures the *Enterprise* into a carefully-orchestrated trap.

The *Star Trek* regulars do what's expected of them. William Shatner, not generally regarded as a top-flight actor, fits comfortably into this role, mixing heroic arrogance with surprising vulnerability. Of the seven *Star Trek* features in which he has appeared, Shatner does his best work here. Leonard Nimoy, as usual, plays Spock with a touch of sardonic wit, and DeForest Kelley proves to be his perfect, illogical foil. Familiar faces James Doohan (Scotty), Walter Koenig (Chekov), George Takei (Sulu), and Nichelle Nichols (Uhura) are all on hand, although only Koenig has more than a few token scenes.

The Wrath of Khan is a top-notch, fast-paced adventure that can be enjoyed equally by fans of the series and those who have never seen an episode. There are several tense, well-executed battle sequences that feature impressive special effects and a soaring score by James Horner. The ending, which I won't reveal (although everyone probably knows it by now) is tender and poignant — proof that *Star Trek* can still touch the heart. *The Wrath of Khan* shows the potential inherent in the *Star Trek* concept as applied to the big screen. It's unfortunate that none of the other films in this long-running series have come close to the level achieved by this marvelous example of entertainment. **HIGHLY RECOMMENDED**

Star Trek III: The Search for Spock [1984]
Starring: William Shatner, DeForest Kelley, Christopher Lloyd Director: Leonard Nimoy Screenplay: Harve Bennett Running Time: 1:45 Rated: PG (Violence) Theatrical Aspect Ratio: 2.35:1

With a title like *The Search for Spock*, did anyone really expect that they wouldn't find the erstwhile first officer? So, with the resolution never in doubt (especially considering that Leonard Nimoy was directing), the *real* question to ask is: Is the search fun? The answer, for the most part, is "yes," at least once the story kicks into high gear. *Star Trek III* takes nearly 40 minutes, much of which is filled with silly, mystical exposition about the current state of Spock's soul, before things start moving. The last 20 minutes are equally slow, but the stuff in between is quite enjoyable.

The Search for Spock opens where *The Wrath of Khan* left off — with Spock's death and funeral. Days later, the *Enterprise* is limping home, ready to be decommissioned, with the crew awaiting reassignment. Dr. McCoy (DeForest Kelley) is suffering from some sort of unexplainable trauma — he hides out in dark rooms speaking in Spock's voice and tries to hire a ship to take him back to the Genesis planet, which has been classified as "off limits" for all space travel. A visit by Spock's father (Mark Lenard) to Kirk (William Shatner) reveals that McCoy carries Spock's soul within him, and must be taken to Vulcan to have it exorcised. For the ritual, Kirk must also retrieve Spock's body from Genesis — a task impeded by Starfleet's policy regarding the new planet. Undaunted, the Admiral, accompanied by his crew, steals the soon-to-be-mothballed *Enterprise*, and heads into a confrontation with a ship of belligerent Klingons who are trying to steal "the secret of Genesis."

Like *Star Trek II, Star Trek III* is about sacrifice. In *The Wrath of Khan*, Spock gave his life for his shipmates. Here, Kirk loses just about everything except his life so that his friend can have a chance at a future. It's this sort of thing — placing characters and themes above battles and special effects — that has always distinguished *Star Trek*. While the absence of Spock leaves a vacuum in character interaction (there is none of the witty repartee that defines the Kirk/Spock/McCoy relationship), expectations about his return create a palpable sense of anticipation. So,

while the sluggish beginning and ending mar this *Star Trek* outing somewhat, there's still enough here to please fans of the series, and, to a lesser extent, movie-goers in general. **RECOMMENDED**

Star Trek IV: The Voyage Home [1986]
Starring: William Shatner, Leonard Nimoy, DeForest Kelley, Catherine Hicks Director: Leonard Nimoy Screenplay: Harve Bennett, Peter Krikes, Steve Meerson, and Nicholas Meyer Running Time: 1:59 Rated: PG (Mild profanity) Theatrical Aspect Ratio: 2.35:1

Star Trek IV picks up where *Star Trek III: The Search for Spock* left off, and forms the final segment of the motion picture trilogy begun in *Star Trek II: The Wrath of Khan*. The crew of the destroyed starship *Enterprise* has been in exile on Vulcan while their resurrected shipmate, Captain Spock (Leonard Nimoy), is re-trained in the ways of logic. Once Spock has recovered sufficiently to travel, Admiral Kirk (William Shatner) and his fellow officers must go back to Earth to answer a battery of charges leveled against them for stealing the *Enterprise* and nearly provoking a war with the Klingon Empire.

However, before Kirk and company can return home, a mysterious probe enters orbit around Earth and wreaks havoc on the planet's climate. Nothing seems capable of stopping the probe, and a planetary distress call is issued. Spock, analyzing the probe's transmissions, determines that they match the songs of humpback whales, an extinct species of ocean-dwelling life. For Earth to survive, the crew of the former *Enterprise* must travel back in time to 20th Century Earth, capture a humpback whale, confine it in their stolen Klingon spaceship, then return to the future. Soon, Kirk and his friends are wandering around 1986 San Francisco, every bit out-of-place as Crocodile Dundee was in New York City.

The tone of *The Voyage Home* is considerably lighter than that of its predecessors; in fact, this is as close as *Star Trek* gets to being a straight comedy. At times, the proceedings become overly silly to garner cheap laughs, and the characters suffer as a result. Kirk, McCoy, and especially Spock, flicker back and forth between resembling the heroic figures we know and acting like caricatures of themselves. There's a running gag about Spock's inability to master profanity that, while undeniably amusing, is a little too cute.

Star Trek IV: The Voyage Home marked the end of the "golden age" of *Star Trek* movies, such as it was (three straight quality outings). *Star Trek IV*, while not a superior effort, is an effective and enjoyable sample of entertainment — not good science fiction, but a lightweight piece of comic fantasy utilizing characters so familiar that they feel like old friends. RECOMMENDED

Star Trek: First Contact [1996]

Starring: Patrick Stewart, Jonathan Frakes, Brent Spiner, LeVar Burton Director: Jonathan Frakes Screenplay: Rick Berman, Brannon Braga, and Ronald D. Moore Running Time: 1:51 Rated: PG-13 (Violence, profanity, sexual innuendo) Theatrical Aspect Ratio: 2.35:1

For the first time in the 17-year run of the successful *Star Trek* movie franchise, there is no Captain Kirk. *Star Trek: First Contact*, the 8th entry into the motion picture series, is the first to rely exclusively on the crew of *The Next Generation*. First time director Jonathan Frakes (who also plays Riker, the *Enterprise*'s second-in-command) injects some badly-needed energy and inventiveness into a series that, prior to this effort, was sinking under its own weight and boldly going nowhere.

The highlight of *First Contact* is the first reel, a recklessly-paced, dazzling display of special effects that is exhausting in its intensity. For the first time in eight films, there's no "getting to know you" period. Five minutes after the opening credits have ended, we're right in the middle of the action. And what action it is — the most spectacular space battle ever to grace the screen in a *Star Trek* film. It's clear that this sequence, with dozens of starships doing battle with the enemy — a cube-like Borg vessel — ate up a considerable portion of the budget.

The Borg, undoubtedly *The Next Generation*'s most popular foe, appeared in about a half-dozen TV episodes, but created a legacy that made them a natural choice for a big screen appearance. Half-organic, half-robot, the Borg all share one mind, and have proven to be the most difficult foe for the Federation to overcome. In *First Contact*, when an attack of Earth during the 24th century fails, the Borg travel back in time to change history. The *USS Enterprise-E*, helmed by Captain Jean-Luc Picard (Patrick Stewart), must follow them to the mid-21st century to save the future. But the Borg are on board the *Enterprise*, and a battle for control of the ship soon develops.

As a species, the Borg are effective, cinematic villains, although, on an individual level, their "queen" (played by Alice Krige) is probably the least menacing of them all. The Borg's natural implacability enhances their sinister aura. There's something eerie about creatures that kill matter-of-factly and don't make a sound when they're injured. The Borg's hive — actually the corridors of the *Enterprise*'s lower decks —

bears more than a passing resemblance to the nest of the Alien queen in James Cameron's *Aliens*.

The script is cleverly written so that non-fans will be able to follow and enjoy the plot while aficionados will get all the little "in" references. *First Contact* effortlessly negotiates a number of potential problem areas (such as time travel), which is a credit to the screenwriting team of Brannon Braga, Ronald Moore, and producer Rick Berman. *First Contact* ensures that *Star Trek* continues to live long and prosper. RECOMMENDED

Star Trek: Insurrection [1998]

Starring: Patrick Stewart, Jonathan Frakes, Brent Spiner, LeVar Burton Director: Jonathan Frakes Screenplay: Michael Piller based on a story by Michael Piller & Rick Berman Running Time: 1:43 Rated: PG (Violence) Theatrical Aspect Ratio: 2.35:1

Insurrection begins with a puzzle. Lt. Commander Data (Brent Spiner), on a routine mission to study the Ba'ku, a seemingly-backward people living on an idyllic planet, turns against the other members of his team, including Federation officers and members of the alien Son'a race. Admiral Dougherty (Anthony Zerbe), the officer in charge of the mission, orders Captain Picard (Patrick Stewart) and his crew to retrieve Data within 12 hours or destroy him. However, what starts out as a simple rescue mission causes Picard to stumble unwittingly into the midst of a conspiracy that involves Dougherty, the Son'a leader, Ru'afo (F. Murray Abraham), and the Federation High Council in a plot to violate the Prime Directive (which states that the Federation cannot meddle in the natural development of other civilizations) in the name of the "greater good." They want to forcibly remove the Ba'ku from their world so that the restorative properties of the planet can be strip-mined for distribution across the galaxy. Picard must choose whether to obey orders and head for home or risk his career, his ship, and his life by defying Dougherty and defending the Ba'ku against Federation and Son'a interference.

The message in *Star Trek: Insurrection*, which has to do with the immorality of displacing a populace and destroying a way of life in the name of progress (i.e., what the European settlers did to the Native Americans), is somewhat more esoteric than the one in *Star Trek IV* (save the whales), but no less difficult to spot. The best *Star Trek* stories are allegorical — in addition to telling an involving story, they're about something other than going into space and blowing up enemy ships. *Insurrection* continues that tradition.

From a visual standpoint, this is easily the most

impressive *Star Trek* film to date. With location shooting done in the Sierra Nevada mountains, cinematographer Matthew Leonetti has captured a series of gorgeous vistas. The special effects, which rely more on computer generated images than anything previously attempted in a *Star Trek* movie, look especially crisp, and give the space sequences a polish that they never before achieved. Meanwhile, in two outings as director, Jonathan Frakes has proven that he understands what makes *Star Trek* work on the big screen. RECOMMENDED

Star Wars Episode I: The Phantom Menace [1999]
Starring: Liam Neeson, Ewan McGregor, Natalie Portman, Jake Lloyd
Director: George Lucas Screenplay: George Lucas Running Time: 2:15
Rated: PG (Mild violence) Theatrical Aspect Ratio: 2.35:1

Jedi Master Qui-Gon Jinn (Liam Neeson) and his apprentice, Obi-Wan Kenobi (Ewan McGregor), are on a diplomatic mission to the planet Naboo, where they hope to negotiate the end to a blockade of the planet organized by the Trade Federation. When they arrive, however, they find themselves caught in a trap sprung by the mysterious Darth Sidious (Ian McDiarmid), who is making a play to take control of the Galactic Republic. After surviving an attempt on their lives in a planet-orbiting space station, Qui-Gon and Obi-Wan end up on the ground in the midst of an invasion by an army of droids. After meeting the amphibious Jar Jar Binks (Ahmed Best), they move to save Naboo's teenage ruler, Queen Amidala, from possible execution. That involves taking her and her retinue (including her favorite squat droid, R2-D2) into space. From Naboo, the action moves to the desert planet of Tatooine, where the two Jedi encounter young Anakin Skywalker (Jake Lloyd), a slave child with amazing potential in the Force, then to the capital world of the Republic, and finally back to Naboo. Meanwhile, Darth Maul (Ray Park), Sidious' minion, is tracking the Jedi with dire intentions.

Plot-wise, the film borrows a lot, at least in terms of structure, from *Return of the Jedi*. After a rousing opening sequence, things slow down for a while. Then, on Tatooine, there's an amazing racing sequence featuring "pod" space ships. Finally, the film concludes with three separate, simultaneous story threads all building to a climax. The martial arts-influenced light saber duel between Darth Maul and Qui-Gon & Obi-Wan is the best that *The Phantom Menace* has to offer — a virtuoso action sequence directed with skill and understanding of what an audience craves from this sort of confrontation.

The *Star Wars* movies have always relied on the nobility of heroes and the nastiness of villains, and *The Phantom Menace* is no exception. As Qui-Gon, Liam Neeson brings an unforced nobility to his performance, while Ewan McGregor injects a sense of recklessness into his portrayal of Obi-Wan. On the other side of the Force is Ray Park's Darth Maul, who doesn't say much, but compensates with menacing stares and quick reflexes. Ian McDiarmid makes for a more chilling villain, even though his Darth Sidious stays in the shadows.

Plainly, this is not an actors' movie and the director, George Lucas, is not an actors' director. Lucas' forte is in creating worlds and pushing the special effects envelope, and, in both of those areas, *The Phantom Menace* doesn't just meet expectations — it exceeds them. For the most part, Lucas' vision isn't limited to putting spectacular visuals on screen for the purpose of creating a momentary sense of awe. His intention is to craft a wonderful, weird, vast universe that we can experience in a way that no other movie has been able to offer. HIGHLY RECOMMENDED

Star Wars Episode II: Attack of the Clones [2002]
Starring: Ewan McGregor, Natalie Portman, Hayden Christensen, Christopher Lee Director: George Lucas Screenplay: George Lucas and Jonathan Hales Running Time: 2:18 Rated: PG (Science fiction violence) Theatrical Aspect Ratio: 2.35:1

Middle episodes in trilogies have the potential to be fundamentally dissatisfying. Thankfully, George Lucas has managed to avoid that pitfall for Episode II of the *Star Wars* saga, *Attack of the Clones*. Admittedly, the primary purpose of this film is to advance the overall story, bridging the gap between the lightweight, heroic antics of *The Phantom Menace* and the overwhelming darkness of the as-yet unnamed *Episode III*. *Attack of the Clones* has a starting point and a stopping point, but no true beginning or end.

Attack of the Clones opens approximately 10 years after the events of *The Phantom Menace*. Anakin Skywalker (Hayden Christensen), having spent a decade under the tutelage of his mentor, Obi-Wan Kenobi (Ewan McGregor), is anxious to take the tests that will mark him as a full-fledged Jedi, although Obi-Wan advises patience. Senator Amidala (Natalie Portman), formerly the Queen of Naboo, has arrived on the planet of Coruscant, the Republic's capital, to let her voice be heard on the key issue of what to do with seceding systems. When an attempt is made on her life, Jedi Master Mace Windu (Samuel L. Jackson) assigns Obi-Wan and Anakin to protect her. This mission leads them in different directions — Obi-Wan pursues the assassin, a bounty hunter named Jango Fett (Temeura Morrison), while Anakin accompanies Amidala to Naboo. While there, the would-be Jedi and the Senator fall in love. Soon after, Anakin and Amidala leave Naboo for Tatooine to discover what has become of Anakin's mother. Meanwhile, Obi-Wan begins to unravel a sinister plot that leads to the mysterious Count Dooku (Christopher Lee) and the Sith Lord Dark Sidious (Ian McDiarmid), who is manipulating everything from behind the scenes.

Episode II opens with a bang — literally. There are some early action scenes, including an impressive chase sequence through the air and streets of Coruscant, then exposition takes over. In fact, the middle section of *Attack of the Clones* is so bogged down with setting up current and future plotlines that the pace starts to flag. It's difficult to decide how Lucas could have done this differently, but the reality is that parts of the film border on being too talky. Nevertheless, from a dramatic standpoint, the screenplay holds up better than that of *The Phantom Menace*. The film's highlight is a rousing battle sequence that consumes the final 40 minutes and includes, among other things, a massive conflict between Jedi, clones, and battle androids; a two-on-one lightsaber duel; and our first opportunity to see why Yoda (Frank Oz) is considered the greatest of all Jedi. *Attack of the Clones* closes with a series of scenes that presage what will happen in Episode III. HIGHLY RECOMMENDED

Star Wars Episode IV: A New Hope [1977]

Starring: Mark Hamill, Harrison Ford, Carrie Fisher, Alec Guinness
Director: George Lucas Screenplay: George Lucas Running Time: 2:09
Rated: PG (Science fiction violence) Theatrical Aspect Ratio: 2.35:1

When one examines the roster of the tens of thousands of motion pictures produced since the late 1800s, not many stand out as trailblazers. One of the few inarguable members of that select cadre is George Lucas' soaring 1977 space opera, *Star Wars* (or, as it has since become known, *Star Wars: A New Hope*). Not only is this film a rousing adventure, but, upon its initial release, it revived science fiction as a viable movie medium, and, most importantly, began a special effects revolution that is still going on

By now, the heroes — Luke Skywalker (Mark Hamill), Han Solo (Harrison Ford), Princess Leia (Carrie Fisher), Obi-Wan Kenobi (Alec Guinness), Chewbacca (Peter Mayhew), C-3P0 (Anthony Daniels), and R2-D2 (Kenny Baker) — are household

names. Equally well-known are the villains — Governor Tarkin (Peter Cushing) and, of course, the Dark Lord of the Sith, Darth Vader (David Prowse; voice courtesy of the inimitable James Earl Jones). These characters, familiar types with enough unique personality traits to brand them as individuals, have become so universally recognized that the mere mention of their names almost anywhere in the world will spur a reaction.

At its heart, *Star Wars* is about Luke's quest to join the battle against evil. He doesn't want to be just another bystander while the struggle for freedom goes on all around him — he wants to be a participant. And, when two droids carrying a secret message from a beautiful rebel princess fall into his hands, his chance arrives. Amidst of the dunes of Luke's home planet of Tatooine, the young man meets the aging Jedi Knight, Obi-Wan Kenobi, who teaches of the mysterious Force, a mystical energy field that binds together all things in the universe. Obi-Wan convinces Luke to join the droids and him on a mission to rescue the princess. Accompanied by a cynical smuggler, Han Solo, and his first mate, the hairy Chewbacca, the odd little group blasts off into space with agents of the corrupt Galactic Empire in pursuit. Their destination: the dreaded Imperial Death Star, a confrontation with the evil Darth Vader, and motion picture immortality.

Since 1977, there have been many science fiction movies, but none has managed to equal *Star Wars'* blend of adventure, likable characters, and epic storytelling. Like some indefatigable King of the Hill, it stands alone and triumphant, regardless of the many imitators that assail its position. *Star Wars* will endure long after its creators are gone. And watching it today is like coming home after a long journey and finding everything just as you remember it — if not better. MUST SEE

Star Wars Episode V: The Empire Strikes Back [1980]

Starring: Mark Hamill, Harrison Ford, Carrie Fisher, Billy Dee Williams
Director: Irvin Kershner Screenplay: Leigh Brackett and Lawrence Kasdan, based on a story by George Lucas Running Time: 2:06
Rated: PG (Science fiction violence) Theatrical Aspect Ratio: 2.35:1

Although it lacks the pioneering "newness" of *Star Wars, The Empire Strikes Back* is in many ways a superior motion picture. The storyline is more interesting and ambitious, the characters — little more than appealing types in the original — are allowed to grow and develop, the special effects are more mature, and the tone is deliciously dark and downbeat. It's the latter quality that has made *The Empire Strikes Back* the least favorite among young *Star Wars* fans — excepting Yoda, there's nothing cute to be found, and the film definitely doesn't leave viewers with a warm, fuzzy feeling. In the first film, good triumphed decisively over evil; here, it's almost the other way around.

The movie does not pick up where *Star Wars* left off. The Death Star's destruction is a thing of the past; Luke Skywalker (Mark Hamill) and Han Solo (Harrison Ford) have been with the Rebellion for quite some time. There's a love triangle involving the two friends and Princess Leia (Carrie Fisher), although Han, the perpetual scoundrel, has the upper hand. When an Imperial Probe Droid turns up on the ice world Hoth, where the current Rebel base is located, it's time for a quick evacuation. Darth Vader (David Prowse, voice of James Earl Jones) detects his quarry, Luke, there, and orchestrates a full-scale invasion. Suddenly, the Rebels are on the run, with Han taking the princess, Chewbacca (Peter Mayhew), and C-3P0 (Anthony Daniels) on board the *Falcon* and into an asteroid field to avoid pursuing TIE fighters. Meanwhile, Luke, along with the faithful R2-D2 (Kenny Baker), heads for the swamp planet of Dagobah to learn from the wizened Jedi Master, Yoda (Frank Oz).

The defining moment of *The Empire Strikes Back* occurs in the final 15 minutes, and, during screenings in 1980 (before the nature of the secret became public knowledge), one particular scene provoked collective gasps. In terms of the mythological antecedents that Lucas based much of his *Star Wars* trilogy on, there was nothing startling about Vader's origins, but, considering the darkness it would inevitably inject into the series, it was a bold stroke.

Seventeen years after its intial release, *The Empire Strikes Back* is still as thrilling and involving as ever. Because of the high quality of the original product, it doesn't show a hint of dating. Neither the first nor the third chapters (or, properly, the "fourth" and "sixth") of the *Star Wars* saga were able to match the narrative scope of *Empire*, which today remains one of the finest and most rousing science fiction tales ever committed to the screen. **MUST SEE**

Star Wars Episode VI: Return of the Jedi [1983]

Starring: Mark Hamill, Harrison Ford, Carrie Fisher, Billy Dee Williams, Ian McDiarmid Director: Richard Marquand Screenplay: Lawrence Kasdan and George Lucas, based on a story by George Lucas Running Time: 2:15 Rated: PG (Science fiction violence) Theatrical Aspect Ratio: 2.35:1

There's an old saying that states something about leaving the best for last. George Lucas certainly didn't follow that adage when crafting the original *Star Wars* trilogy. *Return of the Jedi,* the final installment of the series, is easily the least innovative and most hokey of the three films. In fact, most of the enjoyment derived from this motion picture comes from the simple act of getting together with old friends and enemies one more time.

Cuteness is the watchword here. The dark, eerie atmosphere that oozed from every frame of *The Empire Strikes Back* is gone. Instead, for *Return of the Jedi,* we have good triumphing decisively over evil, a too-pat resolution to a love triangle, and walking teddy bears. Even Darth Vader doesn't seem very daunting this time around. With the arrival of the Emperor (a gaunt-looking Ian McDiarmid), Vader has turned into a second fiddle. It's decidedly unsatisfactory to watch him engage Luke in a civilized conversation.

Return of the Jedi picks up an unspecified time after the conclusion of *The Empire Strikes Back.* Luke (Mark Hamill), Leia (Carrie Fisher), Lando (Billy Dee Williams), Chewbacca (Peter Mayhew), and the droids (Anthony Daniels and Kenny Baker) are on a rescue mission to Luke's home planet of Tatooine. Their aim: to save Han (Harrison Ford) from the clutches of Jabba the Hutt. Once this goal is attained, it's back to outer space, where the Rebel alliance is about to face the Empire's newest threat: a second, more powerful Death Star, that, if activated, could spell doom for anyone who stands against the Emperor. So, while the fleet prepares for the final battle, Luke and company travel to the forest moon of Endor to knock out the shield that defends the Death Star against all attacks. There, they are befriended by the Ewoks, the teddy bear-like indigenous race, and Luke, fearing that his presence is endangering the group, turns himself over to Vader.

Return of the Jedi has some interesting elements. The Luke/Vader/Emperor scenes are suitably tense and well-acted, and, if the resolution isn't a complete surprise, at least it's a little more original that it could have been. From a technical point-of-view, the space battles are amazing, easily dwarfing anything depicted in the previous films. Not only are there many, many more ships, but their speed and range of movement have been dramatically improved. Despite its flaws, this is still *Star Wars,* and, as such, represents a couple of lightly-entertaining hours spent with characters we have gotten to know and love over the years.

Return of the Jedi is easily the weakest of the series, but its position as the conclusion makes it a must-see for anyone who has enjoyed its predecessors. **RECOMMENDED**

Starship Troopers [1997]

Starring: Casper Van Dien, Dina Meyer, Denise Richards, Jake Busey, Neil Patrick Harris Director: Paul Verhoeven Screenplay: Ed Neumeir based on the novel by Robert A. Heinlein Running Time: 2:09 Rated: R (Extreme violence, profanity, nudity) Theatrical Aspect Ratio: 1.85:1

Probably the best way to approach *Starship Troopers* is to divorce it from its intelligent and gripping pedigree. Many of the most intellectually stimulating aspects of the book have been stripped away, and those that remain are only shadows of their former selves. Nevertheless, taken on its own terms, the movie entity *Starship Troopers* offers an enjoyable 2 hours. At its best, the film recaptures the kind of taut, visceral thrills offered by James Cameron's *Aliens*. At its worst, it replicates the feel of a futuristic episode of TV's *Beverly Hills 90210*.

The story begins sometime in the future on Earth, where society has evolved into what producer Jon Davison calls a "fascist utopia." It's there, in the city of Buenos Aires, that we meet *Starship Troopers'* protagonist, Johnny Rico, played by relative newcomer Casper Van Dien. Rico, along with classmates Carmen Ibanez (Denise Richards), Carl Jenkins (Neil Patrick Harris, TV's Doogie Howser), and Dizzy Flores (Dina Meyer, from Dragonheart), is preparing for the future as high school graduation approaches. All 4 friends are considering joining the Federal Service — the futuristic equivalent of today's military. Carmen wants to be a pilot, Carl wants to enter the intelligence ranks, and Rico and Dizzy are headed for the infantry. To add a little spice to their interaction, a romantic triangle has developed between Rico, Carmen, and Dizzy.

While the early sequences of *Starship Troopers* can seem like a prime time soap opera, complete with cheesy dialogue and unconvincing character development, it's clear that Verhoeven knows what he's doing. None of this is played completely straight; at times, *Starship Troopers'* first half-hour treads a line between overblown melodrama and parody.

Eventually, we get to the action. Humanity is at war with a race of lethal bugs who hail from the planet Klandathu, located halfway across the galaxy. They nuke an Earth city and mankind retaliates by launching an invasion of their homeworld. Rico and Dizzy are members of the invading army, and Carmen pilots the ship taking them there, but the campaign turns into a debacle. The death toll is phenomenal and the enemy scores a clear victory. The war, however, is just beginning.

In the final analysis, *Starship Troopers* is flawed but fun. And, while the outline of Heinlein's story and many of the characters remain intact, only echoes of the rich and controversial political subtext have survived. If you want content, read the book. If you want a skillfully-directed, fast-paced ride through space and into war, see the movie. **RECOMMENDED**

Strange Days [1995]

Starring: Ralph Fiennes, Angela Bassett, Juliette Lewis, Tom Sizemore Director: Kathryn Bigelow Screenplay: James Cameron and Jay Cocks Running Time: 2:25 Rated: R (Violence, sex, nudity, profanity) Theatrical Aspect Ratio: 2.35:1

December 30, 1999: the penultimate day of the penultimate year of the century (the 20th century doesn't officially end until the close of 2000). In Los Angeles, the "biggest party of all time" is already underway. Crime is flowing as freely through the streets as champagne at the high-class galas. Ex-cop Lenny Nero (Ralph Fiennes) is in his element: a world where his former colleagues are too busy with serious matters, like the roadside shooting of rapper/black activist Jeriko One (Glenn Plummer), to harass small-time dealers like him. What Nero sells, however, isn't traditional dope, although it's just as addictive and arguably more dangerous. He's the magic man, not the candy man, and his bag of goodies contains disks full of memories and experiences. Once plugged into the appropriate player, one disk allows the user to relive its contents, which could be something as innocent as taking a shower, something as raunchy as participating in an orgy, or something as grotesque as committing a murder.

This is the premise of James Cameron's script for *Strange Days,* the technologically slick action/thriller directed by his ex-wife, Kathryn Bigelow (*Point Break*). Where *Total Recall* underused a similar concept, *Strange Days* takes the subject matter and runs with it. The picture does not attempt to mix, mingle, or confuse fantasy and reality. Instead, it uses these ideas as a launching pad for a murder mystery conspiracy that involves a car chase, shoot-outs, and a fight-to-the-death climax — all the things expected from this sort of motion picture. One of the most fascinating elements of *Strange Days* is the subculture that has developed around Superconductor Quantum Interference Device (SQUID) users. Even though it's illegal to buy or own these machines, their availability has created a thriving black market for disks to run in them.

While *Strange Days* is accomplished in choreographed action, character development, pacing, and visual effects, it displays serious flaws as a murder mystery. Not only is the killer's identity telegraphed far too early, but one of the worst clichés of the genre is reproduced here: while holding the good guy at gun point, the bad guy describes his entire plan. Even the slight twist Cameron employs isn't enough to camouflage this contrivance. Overall, however, *Strange Days* is a thriller first and a mystery second. It's big, explosive entertainment and, although not directed by Cameron, is very much in the vein we've come to expect from him. HIGHLY RECOMMENDED

Superman [1978]

Starring: Marlon Brando, Gene Hackman, Christopher Reeve Director: Richard Donner Screenplay: Mario Puzo and David Newman and Leslie Newman & Robert Benton Running Time: 2:23 Rated: PG (Violence, disaster sequences) Theatrical Aspect Ratio: 2.35:1

To date, the 1978 theatrical version of *Superman* remains the only motion picture based on a comic book to have a lush, epic feel. Developed by *Godfather* scribe Mario Puzo with reverence for the venerable superhero, *Superman* pays homage to the legend's mythology without losing sight of the character's essential humanity.

Superman opens in deep space on the planet Krypton, where respected citizen and elder Jor-El (Marlon Brando) warns that evidence indicates the world's destruction is at hand. The leaders, who disagree with his conclusions and are concerned about a widespread panic, extract a promise that he will keep silent and that neither he nor his wife, Lara (Susannah York), will leave Krypton. Nothing, however, is said about Jor-El's son, Kal-El, and, when the end begins, the child's parents bundle him into a small spacecraft bound for Earth. Once he crash-lands on Earth, he is adopted by the Kents (Glenn Ford and Phyllis Thaxter), who raise him as their own.

Clark (Jeff East as a teenager; Christopher Reeve as an adult) grows up as a clean-cut, all-American type boy, but he knows his origins are not of this planet. Following the death of his adopted father, he goes on a journey to the arctic circle to find himself. There, in a fortress of solitude made out of crystal and ice, he spends 13 years learning about the histories and cultures of Krypton and Earth. When he emerges, wearing the unmistakable blue spandex suit, Superman has been born.

However, even as Metropolis' first superhero makes his presence known, the man who will become his arch enemy is planning. Lex Luthor (Gene Hackman) has hatched a plan that will make him the wealthiest man in the world. By detonating a nuclear warhead in the San Andreas Fault, Luthor will cause California to sink into the ocean. While Luthor plots, Superman, using his secret identity as the mild-mannered Clark Kent, begins working as a reporter for Metropolis' largest newspaper, *The Daily Planet*. As Clark, he befriends co-worker Lois Lane (Margot Kidder). Unfortunately, she only has eyes for Superman. Thus begins one of the oddest romantic triangles ever to grace the screen.

Taking *Superman* as a whole, there's no doubt that it's a flawed movie, but it's one of the most wonderfully entertaining flawed movies made during the 1970s. It's exactly what comic book fans hoped it would be, and it never apologizes about its origins. There are numerous sly nods to many aspects of Superman lore — a young Clark Kent outracing a train, Clark stopping a speeding bullet, the race to find a place to change into the Superman costume when a telephone booth has been replaced by a kiosk, and the reference to "truth, justice, and the American way." Perhaps most heartening of all, however, is the message at the end of the credits announcing the impending arrival of *Superman II*. HIGHLY RECOMMENDED

Superman II [1980]

Starring: Gene Hackman, Christopher Reeve, Terence Stamp, Margot Kidder Director: Richard Lester Screenplay: Mario Puzo & David Newman & Leslie Newman Running Time: 2:07 Rated: PG (Mild profanity, violence) Theatrical Aspect Ratio: 2.35:1

Superman II opens with a visual recap of the first movie during the opening credits. This is intended to refresh the memories of those who saw *Superman*, not to provide a primer for those who did not. Almost all of the surviving characters from *Superman* are back, some for cameos and some for more substantive screen time. The comically villainous Lex Luthor (Gene Hackman) once again provides a thorn in Superman's side. The 3 villains from Krypton — General Zod (Terence Stamp), Ursa (Sarah Douglas), and Non (Jack O'Halloran) — have greatly expanded roles. Everyone on the Daily Planet staff has returned: Perry White (Jackie Cooper), Jimmy Olsen (Marc McClure), and, of course, Lois Lane (Margot Kidder).

The film opens with Superman (Christopher Reeve) flying to Paris to stop a group of terrorists from blowing up the Eiffel Tower with a hydrogen bomb. Hurling the device deep into space before it can explode, Superman saves the planet from nuclear devastation. Unbeknownst to him, however, he creates a bigger problem. Shock waves from the bomb rip open the "Phantom Zone" in which Jor-El had imprisoned Zod and his two cronies. Free, they make their way to Earth, intent upon conquest. Meanwhile, Clark and Lois end up in Niagara Falls doing a piece of investigative journalism. While there, things heat up between the two of them as Lois finally realizes that Clark and Superman are one and the same. Once she has confessed her love for him, and he for her, they fly to his Fortress of Solitude, where he uses a supposedly irreversible process to strip away his superpowers so he can share his life with a mortal. Unfortunately, after returning to the real world and getting a rude awakening about his new physical limitations, Clark learns that, without Superman, the world is doomed to be ruled by Zod, Ursa, Non, and perhaps Luthor (who only wants Australia). So, leaving Lois to return to Metropolis by herself, he heads back to the Fortress, hoping to find some way to resurrect his powers.

As with the original *Superman*, *Superman II* is a comic book come to life. It is a fantasy, and, as a result, the more deeply you apply rational thought to what's transpiring on screen, the more quickly everything will unravel. Fortunately, the rapid pacing and strong character identification makes suspension of disbelief a relatively easy task, even during the most preposterous of moments. *Superman II* delivers on the promise hinted at in *Superman*. *Superman* acquaints us with the characters and sets up the scenario; *Superman II* takes the plot threads introduced in the original and resolves them. Viewed together, the two movies tell the entire story and allow anyone to understand why Superman is the comic book superhero with the greatest longevity. **HIGHLY RECOMMENDED**

The Truman Show [1998]

Starring: Jim Carrey, Laura Linney, Ed Harris, Noah Emmerich, Natascha McElhone Director: Peter Weir Screenplay: Andrew Niccol Running Time: 1:43 Rated: PG (Mild profanity) Theatrical Aspect Ratio: 1.85:1

Truman Burbank (Jim Carrey) is the star of the most popular show in the history of television. For 10,909 days, it has been on the air, using 5,000 cameras to show every moment in every day of the life of one man. The public loves it — there are Truman addicts who go to sleep with the TV on and who have sets installed in the bathroom so they don't miss anything when they're taking a bath. Every individual in "The Truman Show" is an actor with one important exception: the lead character himself. For, while everyone around Truman is playing a part, he is cheerfully ignorant about the truth. He thinks this is all real, and his obliviousness to the situation gives the program its core appeal — that there's nothing counterfeit about Truman. One day, however, when a former member of the cast sneaks back onto the set with a warning for the star, Truman begins to suspect that appearances can be deceiving.

For Carrey detractors who are easily turned off by the comic's rubber-faced antics, *The Truman Show* proves to be an eye-opener. Not only does Carrey remain rigidly-controlled and reigned in, but it would be fair to call his performance both understated and effective. Exhibiting the charm and charisma of a Tom Hanks or even a young Jimmy Stewart, Carrey develops the sort of likable personae that a movie of this sort needs to succeed. He is ably supported by a cast that includes Laura Linney as Truman's TV wife, Natascha McElhone as his one true love, Noah Emmerich as his best friend, and Ed Harris as "God," the TV program's creator and director.

As an intriguing, well-written piece of entertainment and a mild social commentary, *The Truman Show* deserves high marks. Not everything in the film works, and the script isn't perhaps as deep or incisive as it would like us to believe, but there's enough here to mark *The Truman Show* as a worthwhile motion picture — an appealing, offbeat, one-hundred minute diversion for those who really are tired of monsters tearing down buildings and action heroes saving the world. **RECOMMENDED**

Twelve Monkeys [1995]

Starring: Bruce Willis, Madeleine Stowe, Brad Pitt, Christopher Plummer Director: Terry Gilliam Screenplay: David Peoples and Janet Peoples, inspired by the film *La Jetee* Running Time: 2:09 Rated: R (Violence, profanity, nudity) Theatrical Aspect Ratio: 1.85:1

On December 13, 1996, in Philadelphia, a malignant virus is let loose. Months later, 5 billion worldwide are dead. The few survivors are relegated to living underground in germ-free cellars and tunnels. On the surface, Earth is ruled by animals, insects, and vegetation. Mankind's legacy to the planet is its slowly-decaying cities.

James Cole (Bruce Willis) is a 21st century convict

living in a hellhole prison sometime in the 2020s. In order to reduce his sentence, or even obtain a full pardon, he "volunteers" to travel back in time to the 1990s to obtain a pure sample of the virus so that modern science can analyze it. Cole's trip takes him to 1990, where he is incarcerated in a Maryland asylum under the care of psychiatrist Kathryn Railly (Madeleine Stowe). One of Cole's fellow inmates is a totally off-the-wall nutcase named Jeffrey Goines (Brad Pitt), the son of renowned virologist Leland Goines (Christopher Plummer), a man whose name is featured prominently in future headlines.

Twelve Monkeys spans four time periods: 1917 in the trenches of World War One, 1990 in Maryland, 1996 in Maryland and Philadelphia, and the 2020s deep beneath Philadelphia. Like director Terry Gilliam's previous efforts *Brazil* and *Time Bandits,* this movie is saturated with atmosphere. The grim, gray film has two tones: somber and apocalyptic. For the most part, *Twelve Monkeys* is a maze of plot twists and turns. Yet, despite all the hiccuping through time, the story is neither exceptionally obtuse nor hard to follow. In fact, it's possible to make shrewd guesses about some of what's going to happen. Even a movie as complex as this doesn't want to lose its audience along the way — at least not for too long.

Although the movie as a whole is open to interpretation, certain elements of Gilliam's film are straightforward. *Twelve Monkeys* uses a rapier-sharp wit to skewer both sides of the animal rights' movement, as well as the general conscience of society. The scenes of wild animals running amok might recall *Jumanji* to some, but Gilliam's sense of style makes for more startling and lasting images. If anything, these sequences underline the ephemeral nature of humanity's supremacy on this planet. **HIGHLY RECOMMENDED**

Waterworld [1995]

Starring: Kevin Costner, Dennis Hopper, Jeanne Tripplehorn, Tina Majorino Director: Kevin Reynolds Screenplay: Peter Rader and David Twohy Running Time: 2:15 Rated: PG-13 (Violence, brief nudity) Theatrical Aspect Ratio: 1.85:1

It's an unspecified date in the future. As we're told in a quick voiceover intro, the polar ice caps have melted and Earth's continents are buried under water. Humanity has been relegated to a tenuous existence on shakily-constructed floating fortress-cities. There is no land, and pure water and dirt have become exceptionally valuable commodities. There are three kinds of survivors: those who try to live in orderly societies, nomads who roam the seas in their own vessels, and members of an outlaw band called the "Smokers." Headed by the larger-than-life Deacon (Dennis Hopper), these criminals amuse themselves by raping and pillaging while on a quest for the mythical Dryland — a paradise that no one has seen, yet everyone believes exists.

The Mariner (Kevin Costner) becomes one of the Smokers' targets when he rescues the girl Enola (Tina Majorino) from a raid on a fortress-city. She is no ordinary child — on her back is a tattoo which supposedly identifies the location of Dryland. The Mariner, a mutant man who has developed working gills and webbed feet, has little use for Enola or her older companion, Helen (Jeanne Tripplehorn), but he owes them his life and intends to pay the debt. Once the scales are even, however, they become expendable.

Waterworld follows two parallel paths. The first sets the Mariner's personality on a course of transformation from self-centered to heroic. The other is the more tangible search for Dryland, which we instinctively know is going to appear during the film's last act. After all, how often do movie quests go unfulfilled? The script doesn't do a great job with either the spiritual or the physical trek, but the spectacular action sequences occur with enough regularity that strong writing isn't necessary to keep *Waterworld* afloat. A little adrenaline can obscure quite a few holes. In the tradition of the old Westerns and Mel Gibson's Road Warrior flicks, this film provides good escapist fun. Everyone behind the scenes did their part with aplomb, and the result is a feast for the eyes and ears. **RECOMMENDED**

The X-Files [1998]

Starring: David Duchovny, Gillian Anderson, Martin Landau, Blythe Danner Director: Rob Bowman Screenplay: Chris Carter Running Time: 1:58 Rated: PG-13 (Violence, gore, mature themes) Theatrical Aspect Ratio: 2.35:1

In interviews, writer/producer/series creator Chris Carter has stated that his goal with *The X-Files* was to make a movie that could stand on its own. There's no question that he has succeeded. The script can be followed by someone with literally no previous knowledge of the characters or situations. FBI special agents Fox Mulder (David Duchovny) and Dana Scully (Gillian Anderson) are introduced as any film protagonists might be, and we're presented with bits and pieces of information about their background through cleverly constructed dialogue.

As the film opens, the X-Files special unit of the FBI has been disbanded. Mulder and Scully have exchanged their investigations of things paranormal and extraterrestrial for more mundane matters such as terrorism. But, when an Oklahoma City-like bomb explosion destroys a $45 million building in Dallas, Mulder and Scully appear to be the FBI's first choice for fall guys. Their research to clear their names reveals what could be the tip of a massive cover-up of alien activity on Earth. And, as their search stretches from Texas to Washington D.C. to Antarctica, they come face-to-face with the dark secret that endangers the future of the human species.

It's not hard to understand the appeal of Mulder and Scully. Both are competent, intelligent, and re-

sourceful, and their different approaches to their jobs (he's a believer; she's a skeptic) enable them to complement one another. It also doesn't hurt that they're both likable and neither is hard on the eyes. Actors David Duchovny and Gillian Anderson are both accomplished and entirely believable in these roles.

Having seen the movie, it's easy for me to comprehend why so many people are enamored with the series. Although a lot of the material explored in *The X-Files* isn't new or revolutionary, the style of presentation and the quality of the writing set this above most other conspiracy theory/alien invasion pictures. **RECOMMENDED**

Thriller

2 Days in the Valley [1996]

Starring: Danny Aiello, Greg Cruttwell, Jeff Daniels, Teri Hatcher
Director: John Herzfeld Screenplay: John Herzfeld Running Time: 1:47
Rated: R (Violence, sex, profanity, nudity) Theatrical Aspect
Ratio: 1.85:1

The film opens with two hitmen, Desmo (Danny Aiello), an old-timer who's washed up, and Lee (James Spader), a cool-as-a-cucumber sociopath, staking out the house where a notorious womanizer, Roy Foxx (Peter Horton), is making the moves on his ex-wife, Becky (Teri Hatcher). Desmo and Lee have a contract to kill Roy, but who's paying the bill? Meanwhile, a wealthy art dealer, Allan Hopper (Greg Cruttwell), suffering from an acute case of kidney stones, has to be rushed to the hospital. His personal assistant, Susan (Gleanne Headly), brings him home afterwards. Two vice cops, Alvin (Jeff Daniels) and Wes (Eric Stoltz) are staking out a Japanese massage parlor, intending to bust the employees for illegal sexual activities. However, when Wes goes inside to get a first-hand experience, he feels sorry for the girl who services him, and walks out without making an arrest. Finally, there's Teddy Peppers (Paul Mazursky), the Emmy-Award winning director of *Arthur's Last Hope*. But that was 4 years ago, and, since then, he's had nothing but bombs. His life is a wasteland and his finances are in disarray. So, after finding a woman (Marsha Mason) who's willing to take responsibility for locating a new home for his beloved dog, he decides to end it all with a gun. Fate intercedes, however — but not just in Teddy's life. In one way or another, the wheels of destiny bring nearly all of these characters together, although not always at the same time and in the same place.

2 Days in the Valley has a penchant for the outrageous, with generous helpings of dark and ironic humor. There are a number of laugh-aloud lines, but the film works best when the comedy is of the "wink-wink-nudge-nudge" variety. I enjoyed *2 Days in the Valley*. It's pure entertainment — nothing too serious, nothing too deep — with an artistic sensibility. It's rare for movies these days to recognize that their audience has an intelligence, and even more unusual for them not to talk down to us. *2 Days* does both. So, if you're looking for some smart fun, John Herzfeld's feature is a worthy choice. And you don't need 2 days — just 2 hours. **RECOMMENDED**

Absolute Power [1997]

Starring: Clint Eastwood, Gene Hackman, Ed Harris, Laura Linney
Director: Clint Eastwood Screenplay: William Goldman based on the novel by David Baldacci Running Time: 2:02 Rated: R (Violence, sex, profanity) Theatrical Aspect Ratio: 2.35:1

Luther Whitney (Clint Eastwood) is a master thief; he's one of only 6 people who can defeat the Sullivan mansion's alarm system. Once inside, he makes his way into the bedroom, finds the hidden vault, and proceeds to fill his bag with cash and jewelry. But this isn't Luther's night. Just as he's finishing up the robbery, the lady of the house (Melora Hardin) arrives home with a gentleman guest. Luther is forced to hide in the vault, behind a one-way mirror. What he sees next not only shocks him, but makes him the target of a hit man, the Secret Service, and the Washington D.C. police. Christy Sullivan's inebriated escort is none other than Alan J. Richmond (Gene Hackman), the President of the United States. And, after some rough foreplay, she's dead and a cover-up is underway. Luther witnesses all this from his hiding place, but it's not long before the detective leading the murder investigation, Seth Frank (Ed Harris), realizes that the aging thief was in the house when the crime occurred. But was he a witness or a participant?

Absolute Power, adapted by veteran screenwriter William Goldman from the novel by David Baldacci, is an intriguing story told in an effective manner. It's entertaining for the most part, sporadically clever, and occasionally gripping, but thoughtful viewers will easily recognize a number of sizable plot holes. This is one movie that looks better while you're watching it than when you reflect upon it afterwards. Ultimately, the reason to see *Absolute Power* is for the pleasure of the cat-and-mouse game between Luther and everyone who's out to get him. The end isn't the fun part; getting there is. At the appropriate moments, Eastwood ratchets up the level of tension to keep us involved.

In the wrong hands, *Absolute Power* could have resulted in a splashy, inept film. For, while the material here is inherently better than that of *Shadow Conspiracy*, it takes strong performances and a sure, steady hand at the helm to lift the production above the level of its uneven script. Eastwood's approach is slow and deliberate; he develops characters and relationships and doesn't rely on cheap gimmicks to generate tension. The favorable result speaks for itself. **RECOMMENDED**

Albino Alligator [1996]

Starring: Matt Dillon, Faye Dunaway, Gary Sinise, William Fichtner
Director: **Kevin Spacey** Screenplay: **Christian Forte** Running Time: 1:43
Rated: R (Violence, profanity) Theatrical Aspect Ratio: 1.85:1

Albino Alligator, the directorial debut of Oscar winner Kevin Spacey, is a cagey, claustrophobic noir thriller highlighted by a few clever plot twists, some nicely-honed dialogue, and a half-dozen top-notch performances. Spacey's picture doesn't feature anything new or startling, but it's competently constructed, and, with the possible exception of a stale patch in the middle, keeps the tension at a consistently high level. Built around a pyramidal series of coincidences, *Albino Alligator* is rich in irony and occasionally darkly humorous. The characters, who all start out as familiar types, are allowed to grow and develop

in sometimes-unexpected directions. Even the viewer who recognizes *Albino Alligator*'s flaws is still likely to be intrigued and captivated by the increasingly-desperate proceedings.

Dova (Matt Dillon), Milo (Gary Sinise), and Law (William Fichtner) are 3 crooks on the run in New Orleans. A failed robbery combined with a police mix-up leads to a high-speed car chase, 3 dead bodies, and a tense situation in a place called Dino's Last Chance Bar. With the police gathering outside, the trio takes everyone in the small joint hostage, including the bartender (M. Emmet Walsh), a waitress (Faye Dunaway), and several customers (Skeet Ulrich, John Spencer, and Viggo Mortensen). Outside, the cops' actions are directed by a goateed Joe Mantegna, who's irritated at the growing media presence on the scene.

The core of *Albino Alligator* is atmosphere and dialogue. The characters do a lot of talking, and, although few of their lines are memorable, almost all of what they say rings true. There are occasions, however, when the film's talkiness eats into the tension, especially towards the midpoint. *Albino Alligator* doesn't flow as smoothly as it might; there are times when it surges forward, and other instances when it drags a little.

In an era when Tarantino-flavored crime thrillers are becoming more commonplace, *Albino Alligator* manages to distinguish itself. For the most part, Christian Forte's script is smart, even if the characters aren't, and Spacey's direction is sure-handed. There's something darkly delightful about watching a movie like this, which, despite occasionally falling back on formulaic conventions, still manages to surprise its audience from time-to-time. **RECOMMENDED**

Amateur [1995]

Starring: Isabelle Huppert, Martin Donovan, Elina Lowensohn
Director: **Hal Hartley** Screenplay: **Hal Hartley** Running Time: 1:45
Rated: R (Violence, profanity, sex) Theatrical Aspect Ratio: 1.85:1

As it develops, *Amateur* is a joint homage to/parody of film noir. And, as with the most reverent satires, the movie contains enough legitimate elements of the genre to be recognized as an entry. Unfortunately, this is far from a great thriller. The plot is rather stale, and, story-wise, there isn't a whole lot to hold the viewer's attention. The noir framework serves its purpose, but there's nothing great about it.

For his main character, Hartley has chosen an amnesiac. Thomas (Martin Donovan) wakes up in a cobblestoned New York City back alley with shattered glass all around him, a gash on the back of his head, and no memory of how he got in that predicament. When he wanders into a nearby café, a woman (Isabelle Huppert) notices the blood and comes to his rescue. Isabelle is a 33-year-old ex-nun who believes herself to be a nymphomaniac even though she's still a virgin. When Thomas asks her to explain this apparent contradiction, she says she's choosey. Also folded into *Amateur* is Sofia (Elina Lowensohn), the world's hottest porn star, whose connection to Thomas is nebulous at the start. Then there are hitmen Jan (Chuck Montgomery) and Kurt (David Simonds), who have been hired by the mysterious Mr. Jacques to rub out anyone who knows too much about certain floppy disks.

Hartley's witty dialogue is a pleasure to absorb. There are times when the delivery is more important than the actual lines. The hit men discuss cellular phones like they're in the midst of a TV commercial. Stilted statements are made in the most melodramatic fashion possible, and half-baked dialogue is spoken with somber pretentiousness. To enforce the impact of this unique style, the director culls over-the-top performances from his actors, sometimes to an intentionally hilarious effect.

Amateur is a curious mixture of high art and delicious campiness, and the result is a funny, insightful, and almost-hypnotic motion picture. As the film progresses, you could care less what happens to Thomas and Isabelle, but the lure of what they'll say next draws the viewer on. Certainly, the script fails to do much with the issue of confused identities, its ostensible theme, but Hartley's style is such a pleasure to watch that it isn't a major disadvantage for the substance to be weak. RECOMMENDED

Amongst Friends [1993]

Starring: Steve Parlavecchio, Patrick McGaw, Joseph Lindsey, Mira Sorvino Director: Rob Weiss Screenplay: Rob Weiss Running Time: 1:27 Rated: R (Language, mature themes, violence) Theatrical Aspect Ratio: 1.85:1

Andy (Steve Parlavecchio), Trevor (Patrick McGaw), and Billy (Joseph Lindsey) have grown up together in the Long Island community of Five Towns. By their own admission, their friendship started almost from birth. However, relationships that were once strong begin to fracture with the onset of adulthood. A drug bust gone bad sends Trevor to prison and he emerges bitter and disillusioned. Billy becomes a big-time hood using Andy as his gopher, a role from which

the somewhat-timid 23-year-old is desperate to escape.

Amongst Friends is another story about crime in America, but instead of telling about the "have nots" of society, the film focuses on 3 boys who come from wealthy, respectable families. Bored and dissatisfied with comfortable lives where all their conventional wants are met, they crave something different and exciting. Andy's grandfather, who built his fortune as a bookie, and his gangster friends become inspirations and role models.

The 3 main characters couldn't be more different. Trevor is a dreamer and a romantic, a man to whom freedom and love mean more than all the money in the world. His feelings for Laura (Mira Sorvino) bring him back to Five Towns following a lengthy absence, and his return sets in motion the film's events. Billy is, plain and simple, a thoroughly unlikable bully. In fact, if there's an obvious flaw in any of the characters, it's that he has absolutely no redeeming characteristics. Of the 3, Andy is the most discontented. Each of his friends has something while he's still striving for that one big score to fill the gaping void. It isn't that he needs the money — he can get that from his parents any time he wants it — but the cash is a way of proving that he can hit the big time, even if it is gained through drug deals.

In the final analysis, *Amongst Friends* works not because it's an expose of upscale, suburban violence and drug use, but because it takes the time to develop its characters so that the events which swirl around them involve us. Emotional honesty is difficult for many films, but this one attains it, and when something devastating happens on screen, the reverberations shake the theater and the people sitting in it. HIGHLY RECOMMENDED

Amores Perros [Mexico, 2000]

Starring: Emilio Echevarría, Gael García Bernal, Goya Toledo, Álvaro Guerrero Director: Alejandro González Iñárritu Screenplay: Guillermo Arriaga Jordan Running Time: 2:31 Rated: R (Violence, profanity, sex, nudity) Theatrical Aspect Ratio: 1.85:1 In Spanish with subtitles

Amores Perros introduces us to a veritable Rogues Gallery of individuals. Of the 7 or 8 significant characters traversing Alejandro González Iñárritu's terrain, only one could be considered sympathetic. The others comprise a web of corruption and deceit. There are hit men, murderers, philanderers, thieves, betrayers, and other assorted riff-raff. Tarantino's anti-heroes are cool and suave, with always the right one-liner to offer. Iñárritu's are brutal and lacking even a modicum of charisma.

The first two we meet are Octavio (Gael García Bernal) and Susana (Vanessa Bauche). She's his sister-in-law, but that doesn't stem his ardor for her, and, because he treats her with a degree of kindness that her brutish husband, Ramiro (Marco Pérez), never shows, she can't help but be attracted to him. Octavio is determined to make enough money so that he and Susana can run away together (along with her infant son), but, in Mexico City, where poverty abounds, clean money is hard to find. Meanwhile, a couple of rungs higher on the social ladder are Daniel (Álvaro Guerrero) and Valeria (Goya Toledo). She's a world-class model who has hit the big time. Her face and body are plastered all over billboards throughout Mexico City. He's a magazine publisher who has left his wife and two children to be with her. Together, they make the perfect couple — young, good-looking, and in love — until tragedy strikes. Valeria is seriously injured in a car accident and Daniel must cope with living with a mentally and physically crippled woman whose modeling career is at an end. Finally, there's Chivo (Emilio Echevarría), a mysterious, wild-looking figure who hovers around the periphery of the other stories until his tale is finally told. Chivo is an ex-guerilla who abandoned his wife and daughter for The Cause. Now, many years later, he lives with regrets.

Amores Perros won an impressive number of awards in film festivals across the globe. Watching the film, it's not hard to understand why. Iñárritu's style contains elements of Tarantino, Peckinpah, and others, but, ultimately, the synthesis is all his own. Even though there's really no one in this film we can like, root for, or sympathize with, the intricacies of the narrative and the its themes are strong enough to ensure that we will not lose interest. *Amores Perros* is more than just a strong debut; it's good, gritty filmmaking. RECOMMENDED

Before the Rain [France/United Kingdom/Macedonia, 1994]

Starring: Rade Serbedzija, Katrin Cartlidge, Gregoire Colin
Director: Milcho Manchevski Screenplay: Milcho Manchevski
Running Time: 1:53 Rated: R (Violence, nudity, mature themes)
Theatrical Aspect Ratio: 2.35:1

"Time never dies. The circle is not round." As well as being a repeated line in *Before the Rain*, this statement clarifies director Milcho Manchevski's perspective. The film is an exploration of the vicious circle that is violence in the Balkans, and the way tribal and ethnic bloodshed in that part of the world can spill over into more "civilized" countries.

Before the Rain opens and closes in Macedonia. The middle section — an interlude of sorts — takes place in England. The structure of the movie is non-chronological with the conclusion actually occurring about 40 minutes into the film. The flow of the narrative follows the "imperfect circle" pattern. Beginning and end meet and merge, but the closure is broken by one very disconcerting (and not so obvious) flashforward.

What at first appears to be several disparate stories resolves itself into a cohesive single entity, and the characters who start out as *Before the Rain*'s central figures (including a monk played by Gregoire Colin) are ultimately reduced to supporting roles. Most of the film is about — in one way or another — Pulitzer Prize-winning photographer Aleksandar (Rade Serbedzija), who became involved in the war in Bosnia by taking sides. Now, back from that war-torn place and wracked with guilt for having caused a man's death, he intends to leave England (and his English lover, played by Katrin Cartlidge) for Macedonia in hopes of making a positive difference in the violently unstable country of his birth.

The film is as rich in symbols as in narrative. Circles are everywhere, and water takes on its age-old meaning of purification. The titles of *Before the Rain*'s three chapters — "Words," "Faces," and "Pictures" — reveal aspects of the 35-odd minutes they each represent.

The visceral effectiveness of *Before the Rain* is undeniable — it brings home the global reality of violence without ever glorifying or glamorizing it. The film is loaded with chilling little touches of how this particular circle has trapped humanity. *Before the Rain* doesn't offer hope. As "Words" reminds us, communications problems are often more fundamental than language differences. In Manchevski's world, when peace exists, it's an exception, and redemption is perhaps a futile gesture. RECOMMENDED

Best Laid Plans [1999]

Starring: Alessandro Nivola, Reese Witherspoon, Josh Brolin
Director: Mike Barker Screenplay: Ted Griffin Running Time: 1:32
Rated: R (Violence, profanity, sexual situations, mature themes)
Theatrical Aspect Ratio: 1.85:1

Mike Barker's *Best Laid Plans* is a slightly overplotted, but nevertheless entertaining thriller that works primarily because it concentrates on developing characters and building relationships instead of throwing a series of improbable twists at the audience. That isn't to say there aren't a few unexpected turns in the story, but *Best Laid Plans* would still be effective without them. This is also a rare thriller that doesn't soak the screen with blood, violence, sex, and profanity. There's a little of each, but nothing compared to what we have come to expect in the post-Tarantino era.

Nick (Alessandro Nivola) and Lissa (Reese Witherspoon) are young, in love, and willing to do almost anything to get out of the dying rural town of Tropico. Nick thinks his boat has come in when his father dies, but the supposedly substantial estate evaporates when it turns out that Nick's father owed the IRS. With his finances in disarray, Nick looks for an alternative method to secure the means for his trip away from Tropico. When a co-worker at the local recycling plant offers a $10,000 opportunity for acting as a driver in a drug scam, Nick can't refuse. Unfortunately, things go bad, and Nick finds himself owing a drug dealer $15,000. His grace period to pay is a scant 5 days. With time running out, Nick and Lissa hatch a scheme to bilk Bryce (Josh Brolin), an old high school buddy of Nick's, out of the money. The plan looks foolproof — until Bryce doesn't react as expected.

Best Laid Plans is not presented linearly, but it doesn't play too many games with the chronology. The film begins in the present with a 10-minute introductory sequence designed to hook the viewer. The next hour is an extended series of flashbacks that introduce the characters and set up the situation. Finally, we're back in the present with 20 minutes to wrap things up. *Best Laid Plans* offers one surprise near the end (as seemingly all thrillers must), but it comes from an unexpected source.

These days, most thrillers are loud, brazen, and filled with MTV-style quick cuts. It's refreshing to come across a small film like *Best Laid Plans* that emphasizes story, characters, and acting over style and adrenaline (not that those qualities don't have their place). The dialogue snaps and crackles, but doesn't get carried away with its own cleverness (a flaw in too many movies like this). *Best Laid Plans* isn't the kind of motion picture that's going to linger in the mind or the memory, but, while you're in the theater watching it, the movie offers 90 minutes of solid, unpretentious entertainment. **RECOMMENDED**

Bloody Sunday [United Kingdom/Ireland, 2002]

Starring: James Nesbitt, Tim Pigott-Smith, Nicholas Farrell, Gerard McSorley Director: Paul Greengrass Screenplay: Paul Greengrass, based on the book *Eyewitness Bloody Sunday* by Don Mullan Running Time: 1:47 Rated: R (Violence, profanity) Theatrical Aspect Ratio: 1.85:1

It is said that every story has two sides, and the 1972 Bloody Sunday is no exception. The two sides — the citizens of Derry (Ireland) and the British army — have differing perspectives on what happened that afternoon. According to the latter, the military did not initiate the shooting, but returned fire after IRA members began firing at them. According to the former, the British attacked without provocation, and the resulting casualties were innocents caught in the line of fire. Official inquiries and investigations have failed to provide a clear path of culpability, and, while the evidence weighs slightly in favor of the version offered by the residents of Derry, there is no way to make a clear-cut determination of what is "the truth."

For *Bloody Sunday,* Greengrass has elected to tell the story using the citizens' version of events. Aside from this representing his personal conviction of what transpired, it is the more dramatically compelling interpretation. Greengrass' approach attempts a sort of balance — he builds to the confrontation by presenting the view from both sides. In addition to spending time with key individuals participating in the Civil Rights march, he introduces the audience to a number of British officers, including one conflicted, sympathetic man, Brigadier Maclellan (Nicholas Farrell), who tries unsuccessfully to curb the excesses of his men.

Bloody Sunday takes us through the day of January 30, 1972, beginning in the wee hours of the morning and extending until after sunset. The film's focus is on several characters. Ivan Cooper (James Nesbitt), a local Member of Parliament, is the organizer of the Civil Rights March. He believes that peaceful assembly is the route through which change can be affected. "We will march peacefully," he declares, "Until Unionist rule is put in place." Another goal is to keep the IRA out of the march, since violence begets violence. However, many of the younger marchers, such as Gerry Donaghy (Declan Duddy), are prone to rioting, needing only a spark to set them off. The British are ready for the day's activities — which are illegal under current rules that prohibit marching. Major General Ford (Tim Pigott-Smith) has decided to take a hard line, commanding Maclellan to arrest hundred of "hooligans." Troops are deployed, ready to move into position if things get out of hand. And, although the march starts out calmly enough, with between 5,000 and 20,000 citizens participating, it doesn't take long before things go badly wrong. And, in the midst of the chaos, a group of overzealous soldiers starts shooting using live ammunition, and the result is bloody carnage.

Although Greengrass brings his own perspective of the day's events to this film, he avoids the pitfalls of sermonizing, lionizing the dead, and demonizing the British. The result is a grim, startling motion picture. **RECOMMENDED**

Blow [2001]

Starring: Johnny Depp, Penélope Cruz, Franka Potente, Rachel Griffiths
Director: Ted Demme Screenplay: David McKenna and Nick Cassavetes, based on the book by Bruce Porter Running Time: 2:00
Rated: R (Pervasive drug use, profanity, violence, brief nudity)
Theatrical Aspect Ratio: 2.35:1

Blow is an effective and powerful motion picture that follows the rise and fall of drug dealer George Jung (Johnny Depp) as his story plays out against the ever-shifting tapestry of the '60s, '70s, and '80s. Based on a true story (as related in Bruce Porter's book and adapted for the screen by David McKenna and Nick Cassavetes) and employing a voiceover narrative, *Blow* shows how George's insatiable desire for material possessions leads him to betray, or be betrayed by, nearly everyone he knows or loves.

The film opens with a brief segment set in George's childhood. His hard-working father, Ray (Ray Liotta), and materialistic mother (Rachel Griffiths) are forced to declare bankruptcy when they can't make ends meet. Ray gives George some advice: "Money isn't real. It doesn't matter; it only seems like it does." That's a lesson George doesn't take to heart; by the late '60s, he's on his own and determined not to end up in the dire financial straits that paralyzed his parents. So he heads out to California with his best friend, Tuna (Ethan Suplee), to make his fortune. There, he meets the love of his life, Barbara (Franka Potente), and, with the help of Barbara's friend, Derek (Paul Reubens), gets established selling pot. Soon, "Boston George" is the King of the Beach, but he realizes that the real money is in transporting the drug to the East Coast, where college students will pay top dollar. So, using the services of Barbara, who is a stewardess (and whose bags are not checked at airports), he sets up a distribution network that nets both him and Derek $15,000 a week — until he gets caught.

While in prison, George's Colombian cellmate (Jordi Mollà) suggests that he change his product from marijuana to cocaine. After being freed from jail, George goes to Colombia, where he is introduced to the most powerful drug lord in South America, Pablo Escobar (Cliff Curtis). Escobar likes what he sees, and soon George and his new wife, Mirtha (Penelope Cruz), are supplying roughly 85% of the United States' coke. But it's a risky business, especially when the dealer is also a user.

Ultimately, the film isn't as much about drugs as it is about generational dynamics — fathers and children. The two relationships that form *Blow*'s emotional foundation are those of George and his father and George and his daughter. The tragedy of the film is that, in one way or another, George manages to betray the two people he loves the most. His failure in these relationships is the thing that haunts him and reduces him to a shadow of the man he once was. In depicting George's relationships with his father and daughter, *Blow* does an excellent job with an economy of scenes. **HIGHLY RECOMMENDED**

Boiler Room [2000]

Starring: Giovanni Ribisi, Vin Diesel, Ben Affleck, Jamie Kennedy
Director: Ben Younger Screenplay: Ben Younger Running Time: 1:57
Rated: R (Profanity) Theatrical Aspect Ratio: 1.85:1

Those who work in boiler rooms are participating in scams that routinely break SEC regulations and bilk investors out of huge amounts of money. Boiler room employees are the ultimate high-pressure salesmen. They do all their work on the phone, promising untold riches, confiding ultra-confidential "tips," and preying on the investor's greed and fear of missing out on a great opportunity. "No" is not in their vocabulary, and the only way to get rid of them is to hang up on them. Ultimately, the commodity they are offering tends to be worthless — some of the companies they sell stocks in don't exist. Boiler room brokers have two goals on any given day: make as much money as possible and avoid being arrested.

The lure of quick money is what attracts Seth Davis (Giovanni Ribisi) to the boiler room of J.T. Marlin, a "chop shop" brokerage firm located on Long Island, not on Wall Street. For all of Seth's life, he has wanted only two things: to become a millionaire and to earn his father's respect. In his quest to attain the former, however, he has endangered his chances for the latter. A 19-year-old college drop out, Seth is running a small-time illegal casino out of his apartment — a business that his dad (Ron Rifkin), a New York City judge, disapproves of. So, in an attempt to go legit, Seth joins J.T. Marlin as a trainee. But, even as he's on the fast track to wealth and success, he suspects that everything may not be on the up-and-up, and his conscience begins to prick him when he realizes he is cheating hard-working family men out of their life's savings just to earn himself a few thousand dollars in commissions.

First time writer/director Ben Younger crafted this screenplay from an insider's perspective. The attention to detail allows *Boiler Room* to achieve the same sort of insight into stock brokering that *Glengarry Glenn Ross* offered into sales. In fact, this aspect of the film is what makes *Boiler Room* a compelling moviegoing experience. The characters and plot become secondary to the setting and atmosphere. There's a familiarity to the attitudes and ideas encountered here. As Seth notes, too few of us want to work hard for our money; instead, we seek the quick, easy path to excess. Also apropos, however, is an old proverb: "If it seems too good to be true, it is." And that simple adage encapsulates a philosophy that no one in this film has learned. RECOMMENDED

The Bone Collector [1999]

Starring: Denzel Washington, Angelina Jolie, Queen Latifah, Michael Rooker Director: Phillip Noyce Screenplay: Jeremy Iacone, based on the book by Jeffery Deaver Running Time: 1:57 Rated: R (Disturbing images of violence & gore, profanity) Theatrical Aspect Ratio: 2.35:1

The Bone Collector is a dark mystery/thriller that takes its characters and its audience on a twisted trek into benighted venues and disused tunnels where the sun has never shone. Director Phillip Noyce, best known for helming the two Harrison Ford/Tom Clancy films, opts to follow in David Fincher's footsteps. Those who have seen *Seven* will recognize the similarities — pervasive shadows, few daytime shots, and some interesting camera angles. The technique is used to develop a growing sense of menace, and is effective to that end.

Police detective Lincoln Rhyme (Denzel Washington) is widely considered to be a genius of forensic science. During his heyday, Rhyme was called on as an expert witness in hundreds of trials and he is said to have investigated about half the crime scenes in the city. Then 4 years ago, a tragic accident all but ended his career. In its aftermath, he is paralyzed and bedridden, able only to use one finger and everything above the shoulders. Although he is still officially a member of the force, his former colleagues have pre-

dominantly left him alone — until a new, troubling case forces them to seek his help. This case concerns the murder of a wealthy, powerful New York City businessman, whose half-buried body was discovered near a railroad track. The patrolwoman responding to the call, Amelia Donaghy (Angelina Jolie), used a disposable camera to photograph the crime scene before an approaching rainstorm washed away the evidence. Rhyme, after looking at her handiwork, decides that she has a "natural talent for forensics," and wants her on the case.

Despite its grim and explicit nature, *The Bone Collector* contains a strong element of the old-fashioned detective mystery story. And, as is often the case in such yarns, there are some astounding leaps in logic. Throughout the picture, Rhyme lies immobile in bed, puzzling over clues and attempting to determine where the killer is going to strike next. There's more than a little Sherlock Holmes in his makeup, and his rival is the perfect Moriarty — intelligent, demented, and dangerous. Seen from this perspective, Amelia could almost be considered Rhyme's Doctor Watson. Overall, the atmosphere and suspense, coupled with strong lead performances and an interesting central relationship, allow *The Bone Collector* to work despite a storyline that no one would consider airtight. RECOMMENDED

Bound [1996]

Starring: Jennifer Tilly, Gina Gershon, Joe Pantoliano Director: The Wachowski Brothers Screenplay: The Wachowski Brothers Running Time: 1:49 Rated: R (Violence, sex, nudity, mature themes) Theatrical Aspect Ratio: 1.85:1

Bound appears to be ripe with all the elements necessary for a top-notch exploitation flick: leather, guns, gangsters, blood, and a couple of hot-to-trot lesbians. From the first scene, however, it's obvious that the writing/directing team of Andy and Larry Wachowski are aiming for something considerably higher than rudimentary titillation. And, by taking chances and twisting conventions, they have hit paydirt. *Bound* is among the best film noir entries of the decade; from beginning to end, it's solidly entertaining.

Ceasar (Joe Pantoliano) is a money launderer for the mob (sometimes in a very literal fashion — watch how he cleans up a sack of bloody bills). His live-in girlfriend, Violet (Jennifer Tilly), a closet lesbian, is itching to get free of him ("I want out! I want a new life!"). She sees her chance when an ex-con named Corky (Gina Gershon) moves in next door. Methodically, Violet seduces Corky, then, after a heated sexual encounter, the two plot how to liberate Violet along with $2 million of the mob's money that's currently in Ceasar's possession.

Saying more than that about *Bound* would be unfair, because the plot is loaded with the unexpected. For most thrillers, I'm able to predict the so-called "surprises" far in advance, but this film's well-orchestrated twists kept me off balance. Until the final scenes, it's impossible to be sure of anyone or anything. The biggest question, which is raised by the characters and stays with us, is who can be trusted? We're never sure who's on the level and who's lying. Since the Wachowskis don't feel bound by the conventions of the genre, they freely violate our expectations. Best of all, everything that transpires in *Bound* makes perfect sense — the film doesn't demand unreasonable leaps of logic to tie everything together. From the opening moments, ripe with sexual tension, to the closing shot, *Bound* offers an edge-of-the-seat experience. **HIGHLY RECOMMENDED**

Buffalo '66 [1998]

Starring: Vincent Gallo, Christina Ricci Director: Vincent Gallo
Screenplay: Vincent Gallo and Alison Bagnall Running Time: 1:50
Rated: R (Profanity, nudity, sexual situations, violence) Theatrical
Aspect Ratio: 1.85:1

Weird and darkly comic, *Buffalo '66* is the story of the redemption of one almost unbearable character afflicted with a phobia about everything. Played by Vincent Gallo, who often essays lowlife individuals, Billy Brown is at the bottom of the human totem pole. He's violent, boorish, obsessive, angry, self-deluded, and unable to deal with intimacy. He has what are euphemistically called "issues," and, unlike many similar characters, he's not the least bit endearing.

The film opens with a disheveled Billy walking out the door of the prison where he has been incarcerated for the past 5 years. Back in 1991, when the Buffalo Bills lost a nailbiter Superbowl to the New York Giants, Billy made the tactical error of betting $10,000 he didn't have on the game. So, when the kicker missed a last-second field goal, Billy found himself in a serious hole. To pay off the bookie (Mickey Roarke), he agreed to confess to a crime he didn't commit to let one of the gangster's friends off the hook. Now, with his time served, Billy finds himself on the outside again, unsure of what to do with himself.

He eventually ends up in Buffalo, looking for somewhere to go to the bathroom. His quest for a toilet leads him into a dance studio, where, in a moment of blind irrationality, he kidnaps a young student named Layla (Christina Ricci), who doesn't put up that much of a struggle. It seems that Layla, while sullen about the experience, really doesn't mind being kidnapped. Her level of self-esteem is so low that, on a certain level, she actually relishes the experience. The rest of the film is about the two bonding as Billy contemplates whether or not he's going to put a bullet into the head of the former Bills' field goal kicker who lost the Superbowl.

There's no doubt that Gallo's approach is uneven. The film's high level of energy is undeniable, but several of the director's flourishes seem gratuitous and unnecessarily flamboyant. The movie has a grungy look that suits the characters; however, this is not the kind of film that does much for promoting tourism in Buffalo. The city comes across as gray, cold, and unpleasant. Gallo's script is quirky and filled with a number of hilariously strange comic moments. Ultimately, it's *Buffalo '66*'s tone, not the reprehensible main character, that makes this an engaging motion picture. **RECOMMENDED**

The Business of Strangers [2001]

Starring: Stockard Channing, Julia Stiles, Frederick Weller
Director: Patrick Stettner Screenplay: Patrick Stettner Running
Time: 1:24 Rated: R (Profanity, sex) Theatrical Aspect Ratio: 1.85:1

Patrick Stettner's *The Business of Strangers* takes an unusual tack in addressing the issue of date rape. In the movie, Stockard Channing plays Julie, a successful business woman who is at the end of a long business trip and is looking to let off a little steam. Julia Stiles is Paula, a young woman she meets at a bar. Using alcohol as a lubricant, the two bond. Enter Nick (Frederick Weller), a head hunter whom Julie has casually known for years. Paula's reaction to Nick — one of horror and revulsion — is unexpected. She later confesses to Julie that Nick raped a friend of hers years ago at college. So, with their inhibitions loosened by too much booze, the women plot a form of revenge.

For most of its running length, *The Business of Strangers* is a sharp, compelling film that walks a tightrope between thriller and drama. The psychological interplay between Julie and Paula lies at the movie's core, and Stettner gives us about 45 minutes of it. For the most part, the movie works because the dialogue is insightful and meaningful. The conflict between the two leads is entirely verbal, but it is every bit as tense as any cinematic physical confrontation.

Only at the end, when the director employs a cheat to offer one final plot twist, do things start to unravel. While the film's final turn shines a different light on many of the events that preceded it, it also significantly reduces the complexity of Paula, transforming her into little more than a plot device.

Channing and Stiles are marvelous. Channing, a veteran performer who has had plenty of opportunities to shine, is completely at home as Julie, a woman who has become hard-as-nails to survive in a man's world. Stiles, an up-and-coming actress who is already known because of fine performances in pictures like *Save the Last Dance* and *O*, has no problem with the complexities and contradictions of Paula's character. *The Business of Strangers* is one of those films where the acting can either enhance or torpedo the storyline; Channing and Stiles ensure that the former is the case.

Disappointing though the conclusion of *The Business of Strangers* may be, it does little to blunt the film's overall impact. Stettner's screenplay still makes its point and there's plenty of material to ponder and discuss once the end credits have finished rolling. **RECOMMENDED**

Café Society [1997]

Starring: Frank Whaley, Peter Gallagher, Lara Flynn Boyle
Director: Raymond De Felitta Screenplay: Raymond De Felitta Running Time: 1:24 Rated: Not Rated (Sex, nudity, profanity, mature themes) Theatrical Aspect Ratio: 1.85:1

Café Society transpires in New York during the 1950s, focuses on the lurid sex-for-sale trade, and, most strikingly, delves into the incestuous relationship between the police and the tabloid reporters. Mickey Jelke (Frank Whaley) is a playboy. Going out on the town, drinking, and picking up girls are his life — they're about the only things he's good at. And, as another character puts it, he's addicted to the lifestyle (it's called "night club-itis"). One night, Mickey is beguiled by a beautiful woman (Lara Flynn Boyle) who shows up at one of his favorite spots. She spins him a yarn about being Pat Ward "of Newport, by way of Philly." Mickey, who has been unlucky in love, is all too willing to believe Pat, even though common sense tells him that she's hiding something. And she's not the only one who's playing him false. His newfound friend, Jack Kale (Peter Gallagher), is an undercover cop whose assignment is to bring to light evidence that Mickey heads a prostitution ring.

One of the most interesting aspects of *Café Society* is the way it examines the relationship between the police and the press. Mickey becomes the cops' target because he's a rich guy with a high profile. Other, more deserving pimps are passed over because the reporters aren't interested in them. The police want headlines, and the papers are willing to comply if they deliver Mickey. And, given a chance, the tabloids are capable of turning an unsavory party girl like Pat Ward into an overnight sensation.

For approximately ⅔ of its 106-minute running length, *Café Society* is on solid ground. Only towards the end does it begin to fray around the edges with a spate of moralizing that is layered on a bit too thickly. But, although the movie's weak conclusion includes a painfully predictable, melodramatic courtroom scene, the unevenness of the final half hour does little to lessen the impact of what preceded it.

Café Society oozes style with as much conviction as an *L.A. Confidential*, but at a significantly lower budget. In fact, one of the most impressive aspects of this film is how writer/director Raymond De Felitta managed to create such a rich, believable atmosphere without breaking the bank. This is a great looking motion picture, and, while visual appeal can't save a bad movie, it can (and does) help a good one like this. **RECOMMENDED**

Catch Me if You Can [2002]

Starring: Leonardo DeCaprio, Tom Hanks, Christopher Walken, Nathalie Baye, Amy Adams Director: Steven Spielberg Screenplay: Jeff Nathanson, based on the book by Frank Abagnale Jr. and Stan Redding Running Time: 2:20 Rated: PG-13 (Profanity, sexual situations) Theatrical Aspect Ratio: 1.85:1

Catch Me if You Can details the somewhat fictionalized tale of Frank Abagnale Jr. (Leonardo DiCaprio), who, between the ages of 16 and 21, was the world's most successful con artist. Not only did he successfully pose as an airplane pilot, a doctor, and a lawyer, but he cashed more than $2.5 million worth of fraudulent checks. Now, nearly 4 decades after being brought down, Abagnale is one of the foremost authorities on corporate security.

Soon after beginning his life of crime, Frank finds himself being pursued by FBI agent Carl Hanratty (Tom Hanks). For years, the two engage in a cat-and-mouse game, with Carl always a few steps behind Frank. But, despite his numerous failures in just missing Frank, Carl never gives up. Meanwhile, Frank frequently re-invents himself, sometimes because he needs a new cover to escape capture and sometimes out of sheer boredom. But, despite his wealth and success, he is a lonely person. His deepest connection is with his father, Frank Sr. (Christopher Walken, in a low-key and moving portrayal), whom he deeply respects. He harbors feelings of resentment towards his self-absorbed mother, Paula (Nathalie Baye), who dumped his father for a more successful man (James Brolin). His loneliness makes him vulnerable to the sweet naïveté of Brenda Strong (Amy Adams), a nurse he meets in an Atlanta hospital where he is posing as a doctor. He genuinely falls in love with her, but, when Hanratty closes in, he is forced to run . . . again.

Catch Me if You Can crosses several genres without abandoning its overall tone. There are several deeply affecting scenes, including an exchange in a bar between Frank and his father and a sequence on an airplane when Carl delivers some sad news. There are also elements of a thriller, albeit a light one, with the authorities often nearly cornering Frank, only to have him slip away. There is no question that, despite Frank's illicit behavior, he is the movie's protagonist, and we are intended to root for him. Leonardo DiCaprio's charm serves him well; Frank is charismatic and easy to like. On the other hand, Tom Hanks does not play a bad guy. By intent, Carl is not a very interesting man, and his personal life is left largely unexplored. But he becomes a confidant for Frank, and, eventually, even though the two are on opposite sides of the law, they develop a bond.

Catch Me if You Can is not the kind of movie that was made to garner Oscar nominations. Instead, it was developed as an exercise in pure entertainment. To that end, it succeeds admirably. RECOMMENDED

The Cell [2000]

Starring: Jennifer Lopez, Vince Vaughn, Vincent D'Onofrio Director: Tarsem Singh Screenplay: Mark Protosevich Running Time: 1:45 Rated: R (Violence, nudity, profanity, child abuse) Theatrical Aspect Ratio: 2.35:1

Visually enticing and intellectually demanding, *The Cell* takes viewers deep into the nightmarish realm of a killer's mind, exposing audiences to a cacophony of dissonant scenes and images that are at times horrific and disturbing, but are never gratuitous. And, although the film has a clear narrative trajectory, its most compelling aspects are those that are the most disjointed.

At the heart of *The Cell* lies a new kind of technology that allows one person to enter the subconscious of another. The intent of the procedure is to facilitate the psychological analysis of deeply disturbed individuals who are unable to participate in traditional sessions due to catatonia. A team of two scientists,

Miriam Kent (Marianne Jean-Baptiste) and Henry West (Dylan Baker), and one psychotherapist, Catherine Deane (Jennifer Lopez), are the only ones skilled in using the equipment — they have been experimenting on a young boy for the past 18 months. But, when approached by a pair of FBI agents, Peter Novak (Vince Vaughn) and Gordon Ramsey (Jake Weber), with a proposal, they find the challenge impossible to resist. Novak and Ramsey have just captured serial killer Carl Stargher (Vincent D'Onofrio), who has murdered seven times and has recently kidnapped an eighth victim. When the FBI locates Stargher, he has suffered some sort of massive psychological collapse and is in a coma. The location of his newest captive is unknown, but the FBI is aware that she has been placed in a glass tank that will automatically fill with water in 40 hours and drown her — unless Catherine can enter Stargher's mind, make contact with him, earn his trust, and learn the location of victim #8.

The Cell becomes the first serial killer feature in a long time to take the genre in a new direction. Not only does it defy formulaic expectations, but it challenges the viewer to think and consider the horrors that can turn an ordinary child into an inhuman monster. There are no easy answers, and *The Cell* doesn't pretend to offer any. Instead, director Tarsem Singh presents audiences with the opportunity to go on a harrowing journey. For those who are up to the challenge, it's worth spending time in *The Cell*. RECOMMENDED

Changing Lanes [2002]

Starring: Ben Affleck, Samuel L. Jackson, Toni Collette, Amanda Peet Director: Roger Michell Screenplay: Chap Taylor and Michael Tolkin Running Time: 1:40 Rated: R (Profanity) Theatrical Aspect Ratio: 2.35:1

Changing Lanes doesn't get the adrenaline pumping — but that's not a bad thing, because that isn't its goal. This is a character-centered movie — a film that makes a bold statement about societal pressures and the human condition, and how external influences can cause an otherwise decent human being to do things that are despicable. Those who go to *Changing Lanes* expecting to see a revenge thriller will probably be moderately entertained; those who look for more will find that there are greater rewards to be had.

On the one hand, we have Gavin Banek (Ben Affleck), a new partner in a high-profile Wall Street law firm that views ethics as a distraction. Unfortunately, Gavin has a conscience of sorts, and, while he doesn't mind engaging a little lying and cheating, he feels exceedingly uncomfortable about going much further. On the other hand, we have Doyle Gipson (Samuel L. Jackson), a reformed alcoholic who is trying to put his life back together. His soon-to-be-ex-wife wants custody of their son, and intends to move to Oregon, far away from Doyle. In a last-ditch effort to prove that he can be a worthy father, Doyle is working hard to control his volcanic temper and play the part of a model citizen. Things seem to be lining up in his favor when an event brings him into contact with Gavin.

The event is a car accident which occurs when both men are in a rush to get to court — Gavin to present a judge with a Power of Appointment and Doyle to participate in a custody hearing. At the scene of the accident, Gavin doesn't want to wait around for the police — he's in too much of a hurry. So, wishing Doyle "Better luck next time," Gavin gets in his car and takes off — leaving behind Doyle and his non-functional vehicle, and (accidentally) the Power of Appointment Gavin is so eager to file. Now Doyle has something that Gavin desperately needs, and he's in no mood to return it. What follows is a cat and mouse game of one-upsmanship, as Doyle and Gavin go to increasingly unfriendly lengths to gain the upper hand. When Doyle won't give up the Power of Appointment, Gavin pays someone to hack into his financial records and bankrupt him. Doyle's response to this is potentially lethal.

The intriguing aspect of *Changing Lanes* is that both Gavin and Doyle are basically average guys caught in an extreme situation. In other circumstances, while they might not be friends, they would never be at each other's throats. Yet events drive Doyle to turn into an uncontrolled lunatic, while Gavin reflects on his misdeeds with growing disbelief: defrauding a charity, bankrupting a man, leaving the scene of an accident, forging a legal document, etc. Yet, in being brought to the edge, these men recognize things about themselves that they might otherwise not have understood. RECOMMENDED

Chopper Australia [2000]

Starring: Eric Bana, Simon Lyndon, Vince Colosimo Director: Andrew Dominik Screenplay: Andrew Dominik Running Time: 1:33 Rated: R (Violence, profanity, sexual situations) Theatrical Aspect Ratio: 1.85:1

The energetic and visceral *Chopper* is an Australian import that offers a somewhat fictionalized account of events in the life of Mark "Chopper" Read, a ruthless killer who has become a best selling author in his native country. Using the same kind of blood-and-vi-olence-drenched mixture of comedy and suspense that enlivened well-known productions like *Pulp Fiction* and *Lock, Stock and Two Smoking Barrels,* neophyte director Andrew Dominik brings Read to life with all the fury he can muster.

In Australia, Read is a hugely controversial and immensely popular figure (his first novel sold over 250,000 copies). Dominik's intention with this movie is to present a picture of a man who is so unpredictable that no one — not the audience, not other characters in the movie, perhaps not even himself — can predict his next action. It's this kind of spontaneity that gives *Chopper* its edge. As it follows Read from a mid-'70s incarceration in a maximum security prison to another time in jail during the early '90s, *Chopper* never lets the viewer feel completely comfortable. Dominik's direction is fresh and lively, and the camerawork is exceptional.

With a movie like this, in which the main character often seems to inhabit the realm of tall tales, it's easy to question how far from the established facts *Chopper* strays. Dominik gets a preemptive strike against those who would criticize the movie on those grounds by mentioning in a pre-credits disclaimer that certain events in the film have been enhanced to generate a better narrative. It's also worth mentioning that the movie is based on a book by a man who's motto is "Never let the truth get in the way of a good story." So, although the events portrayed in *Chopper* are purportedly all true, one has to take just about everything with a grain of salt. As far as I'm concerned, it's irrelevant — the movie works, regardless of its factual accuracy or lack thereof.

The best thing about *Chopper* is the lead performance by Eric Bana, who powerfully inhabits Read's huge boots. More than anything else, he is the reason that *Chopper* is such a compelling motion picture. An hour after the end credits have rolled, he's the one — perhaps the *only* one — we remember. The film certainly isn't for everyone — those who shrink away from cinematic depictions of extreme violence will immediately be turned off — but, for those who don't mind this type of fare, *Chopper* will not be easily dismissed or forgotten. RECOMMENDED

City by the Sea [2002]

Starring: Robert De Niro, Frances McDormand, James Franco, Eliza Dushku Director: Michael Caton-Jones Screenplay: Ken Hixon, based on the article "Mark of a Murderer" by Michael McAlary Running Time: 1:48 Rated: R (Violence, profanity, drug use) Theatrical Aspect Ratio: 2.35:1

The City by the Sea of the title is Long Beach, New York — once a resort town like so many others, now a classic portrait of urban decay. It's a story that has been repeated in lakeside and oceanfront locales all around the country. A generation ago, certain beaches were crammed with happy families; now, many of those places have grown desolate and forgotten as vacationers have moved on to the newest trendy spot.

Homicide detective Vincent LaMarca (Robert De Niro) is a Manhattan cop investigating the death of a low-level drug dealer who went by the street name of "Picasso." Aided by his stalwart partner and friend, Reg (George Dzundza), Vincent returns to his old stomping grounds of Long Beach, from which the dead man hailed. To Vincent's shock, it appears that his son, Joey (James Franco), may be Picasso's killer. This revelation forces him to make a choice between being a cop (a job at which he has been inarguably good) and being a father (a job at which he has been inarguably bad).

Director Michael Caton-Jones employs an unhurried style atypical of cop movies. The reason for this is that the thriller/mystery elements are secondary to the film's deeper aspects — those of how fathers and sons relate to one another and how the lives of individuals can echo the life of a community. One could argue that Caton-Jones overplays the link between Vincent and Long Beach, but his depiction of the lost town is powerful and leaves a lasting impression.

If there's a weakness in *City by the Sea*, it's that the ending is too pat, the resolution too facile. But, until the closing moments, this is a motion picture of real character — a film that tells a compelling story in a way that raises issues and questions beyond what one expects from a genre picture. Those who venture into *City by the Sea* will find their 2 hours well spent. **RECOMMENDED**

A Civil Action [1998]

Starring: John Travolta, Robert Duvall, Tony Shalhoub, William H. Macy Director: Steven Zaillian Screenplay: Steven Zaillian based on the book by Jonathan Harr Running Time: 1:52 Rated: PG-13 (Profanity, mature themes) Theatrical Aspect Ratio: 1.85:1

A Civil Action does not enter groundbreaking territory, but it tones down the inherent melodrama of courtroom scenes to tolerable levels and does not offer any shock testimony or dramatic legal maneuvers. Indeed, the film isn't as much about a court case as it is about the legal system in general and how a sudden empathy with human suffering changes the person-ality of an ambulance chaser. The problem with the movie is that the transition of Jan Schlichtmann (John Travolta) from money-grubbing bottom feeder to champion of human rights happens too suddenly and without proper motivation. One moment, he's telling a group of citizens that he'll only take the case if there's a big payout; shortly thereafter, he's refusing a $25 million settlement because he wants to send a message.

Jan is the shining star at the small Boston law office comprised of him, Kevin Conway (Tony Shalhoub), and Bill Crowley (Zeljko Ivanek). They work in close concert with their accountant and financial wizard, James Gordon (William H. Macy). When Jan is offered a case in which eight children in the small town of Woburn, Massachusetts have died of leukemia, he decides to turn it down, even though he can "appreciate the theatrical value of several dead kids." The theory is that spilled chemicals from a local factory and tanning plant tainted the water and caused the cancer. Then a cursory investigation reveals that a pair of extremely wealthy corporations, W.R. Grace & Co. and Beatrice Foods, may be involved. Their deep pockets and the potential for a huge pay day cause Jan to change his mind. Soon, he is squaring off in court against William Cheeseman (Bruce Norris), the inept lawyer representing Grace, and Jerome Facher (Robert Duvall), the wily and dangerous attorney for Beatrice.

Unlike many courtroom dramas, which are grim and filled with dark tragedies and triumphant revelations, *A Civil Action* doesn't take itself too seriously, nor does it rely on the crutch of inane action sequences. There's plenty of comedy in the script. The other interesting element is that Zaillian offers some atypical insights into the workings of the legal system. *A Civil Action* does not function as an attack against lawyers, but as a hard, bitterly humorous look at the realities of the legal system. Combining a few good performances with an engaging and intelligent script, *A Civil Action* marks a rare worthwhile entry into a genre that has worn out its welcome. **RECOMMENDED**

Clockers [1995]

Starring: Harvey Keitel, Mekhi Phifer, Delroy Lindo, John Turturro Director: Spike Lee Screenplay: Richard Price and Spike Lee based on the novel by Richard Price Running Time: 2:08 Rated: R (Violence, profanity) Theatrical Aspect Ratio: 1.85:1

Clockers focuses on young Ronald "Strike" Dunham, played with impressive intensity by Mekhi Phifer. Uneducated-but-streetwise, Strike is a low-level drug-dealer (a "clocker") and possibly a murderer. His life revolves around a few simple truths: his friendship with his father-figure mentor, Rodney (Delroy Lindo), the support he offers to his own young protégé (Pee Wee Love), and his prized model train collection. Strike follows Rodney's code: don't snitch on your friends, pay off the cops to keep them happy, and never sample the drugs you deal.

The walls of Strike's life begin to crumble when Rodney asks him to eliminate a "problem." Hours later, the night manager of Ahab's fast food is dead, shot four times, and Strike's brother Victor (Isaiah Washington) has confessed to the murder, even though he can't give a coherent account of what happened and no one on the streets thinks he did it. It's up to Detective Rocco Klein (Harvey Keitel) and his partner (John Turturro) to uncover the truth, and the deeper they dig, the more they become convinced that Strike, not his brother, is guilty.

The script, written by Richard Price and Spike Lee (and based upon Price's novel), is less clichéd than the average New York-based crime story. All of the characters — drug dealers and men in uniform — are given enough depth to circumvent stereotypes. *Clockers* is about people trapped by circumstances, and with all the ambivalent personalities, there are no "good guys" or "bad guys" in the traditional sense.

Although racism is only a subtle part of *Clockers*, the movie nevertheless has a strong anti-racist theme. This is most eloquently expressed when Rocco offers no verbal response to a key question: Why would a white cop care about justice in a case of a black-on-black murder? While some of *Clockers'* characters may not understand this, the viewer does, and that's why Keitel's role, although tangential to the primary story, is crucial to the film's success. While Lee doesn't shy away from violence, his methods are less straightforward. *Clockers* uses unexpected narrative turns to accentuate the themes of lost innocence and uncultivated potential, and affirms that tragic melodrama is not a prerequisite for emotional impact. RECOMMENDED

The Contender [2000]

Starring: Joan Allen, Jeff Bridges, Gary Oldman Director: Rod Lurie Screenplay: Rod Lurie Running Time: 2:05 Rated: R (Profanity, sexual situations, nudity) Theatrical Aspect Ratio: 1.85:1

The story opens several weeks after the death of the Vice President. President Jackson Evans (Jeff Bridges) has narrowed his selection of candidates to a short list. The party favorite is up-and-coming Democratic star, Jack Hathaway (William Petersen), the popular governor of Virginia. Evans, however, is pursuing his own agenda. Midway through his second term, he is in search of a means to secure his legacy, and he believes that putting a woman in the Vice President's position is unique enough to earn him a spot in the history books. So, bucking the advice of even his key advisors, he names Ohio Senator Laine Hanson (Joan Allen) as his choice. However, his hopes for smooth sailing run afoul of Congressman Sheldon Runyon (Gary Oldman), the Republican chairman of the confirmation hearings. Runyon wants Hathaway, and will stop at nothing to derail Hanson's chances, including dredging up a 25-year-old sex scandal. Hanson finds herself embroiled in a battle where she is hampered by her own high ethical standards while her opponents have no such handicaps.

For most of its running length, *The Contender* offers a fairly straightforward account of the moves and counter-moves made by Runyon and Evans as they maneuver against one another. For either of them, a defeat means absorbing a political blow, but for Hanson, the pawn in the middle, everything is at stake — her credibility, her reputation, and her future. *The Contender* turns Hanson's confirmation process into a high-stakes game of strategy, where there are no rules. In the end, *The Contender* asks a key question: can someone with a moral code survive in the national political forum?

The Contender is not without hiccups. A subplot featuring a female FBI agent is clumsily grafted onto the main story. Although it serves a purpose — to soften the deus ex machina aspect of a key twist — Lurie never integrates it seamlessly into *The Contender's* fabric. As a result, it remains an appendage. Additionally, the way everything is wrapped up into a nice, neat package at the end seems a little too convenient. Finally, although I'm not a big fan of using grandstanding speeches to offer a catharsis, at least in this case the speech fits the circumstances and is delivered in a suitably convincing manner. RECOMMENDED

Copland [1997]

Starring: Sylvester Stallone, Harvey Keitel, Ray Liotta, Robert DeNiro Director: James Mangold Screenplay: James Mangold Running Time: 1:44 Rated: R (Violence, profanity, mature themes) Theatrical Aspect Ratio: 1.85:1

In *Copland*, action megastar Sylvester Stallone plays Freddy Heflin, the shy, overweight, rather dumb sheriff of the tiny town of Garrison, New Jersey. The most noticeable thing about Freddy isn't the caliber of his gun, it's the size of his paunch. And, every time Freddy confronts *Copland*'s villain, Ray Donlan (Harvey Keitel), something extraordinary happens: he meekly backs down. It's a strange thing to see Stallone playing someone whose primary characteristic is impotence.

Ultimately, *Copland* is just another story of police corruption in New York City — a Western transposed into modern times. The film takes place in Garrison, a tiny northern New Jersey town (population 1,280) that has been dubbed "Copland" because of the number of NYPD officers who live there with their families. Ray and his cronies basically own Garrison, due in large part to Freddy's passivity. He's "a wannabe who couldn't get on the force because of his bad ear," and who isn't willing to do anything to rock the boat. But Ray is a bad cop — he has his fingers in a number of illegal pies, and he has connections so high up that not even an internal affairs officer, Moe Tilden (Robert DeNiro), can touch him without concrete evidence.

In addition to the high caliber of acting, another thing that sets *Copland* apart from an average entry into the genre is Mangold's dialogue, which sparkles with intelligence. The director may not have Tarantino's gift for words, but his characters speak reasonably, not like they're reading from a sheet of paper. Even the supporting players, like Janeane Garofalo's officer Cindy Betts, say and do things in a believable manner. The overall story has problems, but Mangold is a master of the moment, and he gets us to care about the characters enough that we don't spend one-hundred minutes obsessing over flaws. As a result, *Copland* is a compelling, if imperfect, motion picture. **RECOMMENDED**

Copycat [1995]

Starring: Sigourney Weaver, Holly Hunter, Dermot Mulroney
Director: **Jon Amiel** Screenplay: Ann Biderman and David Madsen
Running Time: 2:03 Rated: R (Violence, post mortem photographs)
Theatrical Aspect Ratio: 2.35:1

Copycat opens in a college lecture hall. Dr. Helen Hudson (Sigourney Weaver), a psychiatrist who specializes in serial killers, is giving a talk on her pet subject. Her words drive home the point: these people get turned on by what they do. They feel no remorse — only anticipation of the next kill. After finishing the seminar, Helen heads for the restrooms, where she comes face-to-face with Daryll Lee Cullem (Harry Connick Jr.), a man with murderous intentions who has been stalking her.

Thirteen months later, Helen is an agoraphobiac recovering from a nervous breakdown. She hides inside her apartment, connected to the Internet while downing pills and booze in roughly equal quantities. She's useless to herself or anyone else. Then the police, led by Mary Jane Monahan (Holly Hunter) and Reuben Goetz (Dermot Mulroney), arrive at her door. They need help tracking a serial killer who has been terrorizing young women in the San Francisco area, and who better to go to than an expert with 20 years of having "serial killers on the brain"? Although at first reluctant, Helen eventually relents and lends her experience to the investigation. Her first contribution is to identify the killer as a copycat. He is mimicking the great serial killers — the Boston Strangler, Son of Sam, the Hillside Strangler, Dahmer, and Bundy — and there's no way to tell who or how he will murder next. On top of everything, he has decided to play Internet games with Helen, the "Muse of Serial Killers."

It's a difficult task to perfect this sort of story. There are so many areas where the script can fail that it's astounding how seamlessly *Copycat* overcomes all obstacles. There are no stupid characters, contrived resolutions, or deus ex machinas. The police are smart, but so is the killer. And the movie doesn't play games with the villain's identity — we aren't left wondering whether he's one of the supposed "good guys."

The worst thing that can happen in a movie like this is for the characters to be a step behind the audience. That's not the case in *Copycat,* where the viewer is in synch with what's occurring on-screen. Tension and atmosphere are excellent, and director Jon Amiel pays careful attention to detail. Parts of this film are frightening, and will have many viewers either on the edge of their seat or hiding their eyes. And, unlike in many so-called thrillers, the ending is not a let-down. **RECOMMENDED**

Crimson Tide [1997]

Starring: Denzel Washington, Gene Hackman, George Dzundza, Viggo Mortensen Director: **Tony Scott** Screenplay: **Michael Schiffer** Running Time: 1:55 Rated: R (Violence, post mortem photographs) Theatrical Aspect Ratio: 2.35:1

There's a lot happening in this film. It opens with a quick synopsis of the current political situation: Russia is in the midst of a civil war and the anti-American rebels have taken control of a nuclear base. The *USS Alabama,* commanded by Captain Ramsey (Gene Hackman), is ordered off the Asian coast as the "front line and the last line of defense." Since Ramsey's usual XO has appendicitis, he must choose a new right-hand man. At the top of a short list is Ron

Hunter (Denzel Washington), an officer who doesn't necessarily agree with his captain's no-thought, gut reaction method of commanding. Tension builds as orders from land make it apparent that war is imminent. A Russian sub — possibly hostile — is sighted nearby, and the crew is ready to mutiny when a fissure develops between the two men who must co-authorize a nuclear launch.

Michael Schiffer's script (as doctored by an uncredited Quentin Tarantino) works hard to incorporate elements from the likes of *The Hunt for Red October* and *Das Boot,* weaving them into his story of mutiny on a nuclear vessel. In some ways, trying to do all these things almost overburdens *Crimson Tide.* So much is going on that no single element gets the screenplay's full attention.

Denzel Washington and Gene Hackman are both in top form, and their multiple confrontations are some of *Crimson Tide*'s best moments. With these two actors going toe-to-toe, everything else fades into the background. There's little doubt that Hunter is the hero — the guy the audience is supposed to identify with — but he's shown to have a fault or two. And, while Ramsey is the obligatory human antagonist, he has his redeeming qualities, and his position on the to-launch-or-not-to-launch issue is not without merit.

Because of the contained environment, submarines make great settings for thrillers, with the throbbing of the engines sounding like a pulse. *Crimson Tide* is no exception — the atmosphere alone is sufficient to keep the audience on edge. There's not a lot that's remarkable, ground-breaking, or earth-shattering about the production, but director Tony Scott (*Top Gun, True Romance*) shows a flair for the visual. This is great, light entertainment. RECOMMENDED

Croupier [United Kingdom, 1998]

Starring: Clive Owen, Gina McKee, Alex Kingston Director: Mike Hodges Screenplay: Paul Mayersberg Running Time: 1:31 Rated: R (Nudity, sex, violence, profanity) Theatrical Aspect Ratio: 1.85:1

The world of the croupier (casino dealer) is seen through the eyes of Jack Manfred (Clive Owen), a writer who's looking for material to put into a new novel. By nature, Jack is an observer, not a participant. He doesn't gamble, because he knows the odds aren't good. For the most part, he likes to play by the rules. And he has a perverse addiction — he likes watching people lose. He drinks in defeat like a stimulant, and the experience of dealing often leaves him shaking afterwards. As the story unfolds, Jack begins to blur the lines between his real-life self and his fic-

tional alter-ego, Jake. Sometimes, it's Jake, not Jack, who steps behind the tables and begins to shuffle the cards. However, while Jack is cold and detached, Jake believes in taking risks and getting involved — two things that lead to trouble.

Croupier is an unconventional thriller because it does not feature the staples of most such movies. There's some violence, but not much, and there's not a car chase to be found (in fact, for most of the film, the lead character doesn't own a car). All of the suspense is internalized — it builds slowly but consistently as we begin to understand the kinds of underhanded deeds that occur at the casino. Jack may have "the hands of a conjurer (or a cardshark)," but he'll need a peculiar kind of magic to extricate himself from a situation he agrees to be party to. His girlfriend (Gina McKee) is supportive of his writing career but despises the kind of person his casino work is turning him into. And there's a femme fatale (played by Alex Kingston), who plays on Jack's sympathies to get her way.

One of the biggest problems with modern-day thrillers is that they think a quick burst of adrenaline is a good substitute for solid plotting and intelligent dialogue. *Croupier* proves how flawed this philosophy is. The best antidote to the dumbing-down of motion pictures is to see something smart, savvy, and unpredictable — three qualities that this movie possesses in abundance. HIGHLY RECOMMENDED

The Crying Game [United Kingdom, 1992]

Starring: Stephen Rea, Jaye Davidson, Forest Whitaker, Miranda Richardson Director: Neil Jordan Screenplay: Neil Jordan Running Time: 1:50 Rated: R (Language, nudity, violence, mature themes) Theatrical Aspect Ratio: 2.35:1

The Crying Game, the creation of Irish director/writer Neil Jordan, loosely fits into the category of a "thriller," although to saddle it with such a label is perhaps to do it a great injustice, since this immediately causes images of the *Die Hard* series to spring to mind, and it would be hard to imagine two movies more dissimilar than *Die Hard* and *The Crying Game.*

Jordan has managed to find another dimension to the thriller, giving us not only the requisite tension and action, but a healthy — and heavy — dose of drama as well. As is typical for non-mainstream films, *The Crying Game* demands the audience's attention and moves at its own pace, never knuckling under to the pressure of its "genre." Some might complain that the first portion of the movie, where British army officer Jodi (Forest Whitaker) is held prisoner by Fergus

(Stephen Rea) and his IRA cronies (including Miranda Richardson and Adrian Dunbar), is too long. If you're waiting for something explosive to happen, that may be the case, but if you're absorbing the meticulous and subtle character interaction, the pacing is perfect. There's excitement and gunplay in *The Crying Game,* but those things are almost incidental to the themes that the movie explores. The two most basic (and potent) deal with the nature of the individual and the meaning of love.

As is often the case with European films, the acting is superlative. Stephen Rea is rock-solid throughout, giving the audience a character that we can relate to and sympathize with. Forest Whitaker, the only American in the film, is credible as Jodi, and he has surprisingly little trouble with a British accent. Miranda Richardson and Adrian Dunbar are strong in supporting roles. The real standout, however, is newcomer Jaye Davidson, whose performance is, without exaggeration, stunning.

The Crying Game is not to be missed. The script isn't especially convoluted or filled with twists and turns, but the less said the better. The film contains one surprise revelation that is central to *The Crying Game*'s resolution. Regardless of what is known — or not known — about plot details, however, the movie will still reward its viewers with a thought-provoking, superbly-rendered 110 minutes. **HIGHLY RECOMMENDED**

Dead Again [1991]

Starring: Kenneth Branagh, Emma Thompson, Derek Jacobi, Andy Garcia Director: Kenneth Branagh Screenplay: Scott Frank Running Time: 1:47 Rated: R (Profanity, violence) Theatrical Aspect Ratio: 1.85:1

Over the course of 107 minutes, director Kenneth Branagh fashions a fascinating puzzle that contains its share of action, romance, dry wit, and (of course) twists & turns. And, unlike most thrillers, there's a distinct element of unpredictability to the latter. *Dead Again* contains two significant plot contortions. While it's possible, and even reasonable, for an intelligent viewer to surmise the second, the first is almost unguessable.

Dead Again is a tale of parallel stories in different time frames. The first, which transpires in post-World War II Los Angeles and is presented entirely through black-and-white flashbacks, relates the tragic romance of Roman and Margaret Strauss (Branagh and his then-wife, Emma Thompson). Roman is a world-famous composer and conductor, and Margaret is an up-and-coming musician. They meet when Roman

conducts Margaret's orchestra, and it's love at first sight. They are soon married, but their fairytale existence begins to fray. Margaret is suspicious that Roman's housekeeper, Inga (Hanna Schygulla), and her son, Frankie (Gregor Hesse), may be stealing from Roman. He, in turn, is wary of her relationship with a reporter named Gray Baker (Andy Garcia), who appears to be exceeding the bounds of friendly propriety. This all leads to murder. Margaret is stabbed to death using a pair of scissors, an expensive anklet is stolen, and Roman is arrested and convicted. He goes to the electric chair claiming to be innocent.

The other part of the story occurs in 1991 Los Angeles, where a solitary private investigator, Mike Church (Branagh), has been requested by a local priest to uncover the identity of a pretty woman (Thompson) who has lost her voice and her memory. Mike's friend, newspaper man Pete (Wayne Knight), puts her photograph in the local paper, and the only respondent is a hypnotist/junk dealer named Franklyn Madison (Derek Jacobi), who believes that a trauma from the woman's past life may be causing her mute amnesia.

Although *Dead Again*'s story is complicated, Branagh presents it in a clear, straightforward manner that leaves little room for confusion. Each of the plot twists is exposed with suitable buildup, maintaining viewer interest. One of the reasons for *Dead Again*'s strong resonance and appeal is the way it toys with two issues that fascinate almost everyone: chance and fate.

Rhythm is a critical element of any psychological thriller, and *Dead Again* is no exception. However, unlike most Hitchcock wannabes, this one has it. High points and shock revelations are interspersed with exposition, and the characters are not permitted to degenerate into walking clichés. Branagh has combined all of the cinematic elements into an achievement that rivals Hitchcock's best work and stands out as one of the most intriguing and memorable thrillers of the 1990s. **MUST SEE**

Dead Presidents [1995]

Starring: Larenz Tate, Keith David, Rose Jackson, N'Bushe Wright, Chris Tucker Director: Allen & Albert Hughes Screenplay: Michael Henry Brown Running Time: 2:00 Rated: R (Violence, profanity, sex) Theatrical Aspect Ratio: 2.35:1

Although ¾ of *Dead Presidents* (the title refers to the portraits on money) takes place in the Bronx, it's the segment away from New York that drives the story. There have been any number of Vietnam tales —

Oliver Stone has made a career out of that time and place — but none with quite the perspective of the Hughes Brothers'. This is the story of a black man who goes off to war as a relative innocent, and returns a decorated hero whose only scars are inside. His re-acclimatization to civilian life is difficult, but, unlike some of his friends, he never turns to drugs, and isn't averse to working hard to earn a living. Sometimes, however, good intentions and a valiant effort aren't enough. In detailing one man's actions and their consequences, *Dead Presidents* isn't just an African American tragedy — its impact is universal. People of any color can sympathize with the plight of Anthony Curtis and understand, if not agree with, the eventual choices life forces him to make.

Dead Presidents opens in 1969, as Anthony (Larenz Tate) is about to graduate from high school. Not wanting to go to college, but needing to get away from home to find himself, he enrolls in the Marine Corps, and heads off to Vietnam, leaving behind a middle-class family, a pregnant girlfriend (Rose Jackson), and a mentor/small time crook, Kirby (Keith David), who is like a second father. Joining Anthony in the military are two of his close friends, Skip (Chris Tucker) and Jose (Freddy Rodriguez). When Anthony finally comes back to the Bronx in 1973, after two tours of duty, he discovers that returning to "normal" life isn't easy or pleasant.

Even though *Dead Presidents* is more about the effects of poverty than those of racism, only the most naïve viewer could completely dissociate the two. Nevertheless, the Hughes Brothers don't overtly introduce race as an issue. Instead, this is about the failure of society, and how desperation, more than greed, can lead to radical and violent acts. The film is not perfect — certain sequences are awkward or drawn from stock, and many of the supporting characters are stereotypes — but solid storytelling and tight pacing push *Dead Presidents* through its weak spots. The result not only reaffirms the Hughes Brothers' ability as film makers, but shows they can go beyond the limits of the urban street drama they presented so forcefully in *Menace II Society*. RECOMMENDED

Deceiver [1997]

Starring: Tim Roth, Chris Penn, Michael Rooker Director: Jonas & Josh Pate Screenplay: Jonas & Josh Pate Running Time: 1:42 Rated: R (Profanity, violence) Theatrical Aspect Ratio: 2.35:1

It's Wednesday, March 27, and a murder investigation is underway in Charleston, South Carolina. The crime: a young prostitute, Elizabeth (Renee Zell-weger), has been brutally slain. One half of her severed body was found in a bag at the train station. The other half was discovered in a trunk at the harbor authority, miles away. The police duo of Braxton (Chris Penn) and Kennesaw (Michael Rooker) are strapped for leads. At the moment, they have only one possible suspect: Wayland (Tim Roth), a wealthy, unemployed genius who graduated Summa Cum Laude from Princeton and appears to be the least likely character to commit such a heinous act.

That's the premise for *Deceiver*, a thriller from the Pate Brothers, Jonas and Josh. *Deceiver* plays out like a mind game between the intellectually superior Wayland and the two not-so-bright cops (captions early in the proceedings let us know that Wayland's IQ is 151; by contrast, Kennesaw's is 122 and Braxton's is 102). The setting is a police interrogation room where a lie detector test is about to be administered. Over three days, as Wayland returns to answer more questions, the drama and tension among these three characters gradually escalates until, inevitably, it boils over.

The movie, obviously fashioned in the manner of classic film noir, drips atmosphere. There are some fascinating stylistic touches; for example, although the setting is contemporary, all of the telephones are old-fashioned, rotary models. Cinematographer Bill Butler is given an opportunity to use unconventional camera work to liven up *Deceiver*'s look. Some of the things he tries (mostly those that involve the contrast between light and shadow) work exceptionally well, while others (like any of several Lazy Susan shots) seem more like unnecessary visual tricks.

One of the best things about *Deceiver* is that it never talks down to the audience. Plot points aren't hammered home, and, although the ending has its weaknesses, everything isn't spelled out in bold letters. The Pates give audience members credit for having brains, which is an increasingly rare characteristic for film makers. Occasionally gripping and never uninteresting, *Deceiver* is a fine noir effort. RECOMMENDED

The Deep End [2001]

Starring: Tilda Swinton, Goran Visnjic, Jonathan Tucker, Peter Donat Directors: Scott McGehee, David Siegel Screenplay: Scott McGehee, David Siegel, based on the novel "The Blank Wall" by Elisabeth Sanxay Holding Running Time: 1:39 Rated: R (Violence, mature themes, profanity) Theatrical Aspect Ratio: 2.35:1

The Deep End is an exceptionally involving and intelligent thriller, and, unlike many of its commercially-driven cohorts in the genre, it does not rely overmuch on narrative twists and turns. The complexity lies more in the characters than in the plot. Using one of Hitchcock's favorite devices — the "wrong man" theme — co-writers/producers/directors Scott Mc-Gehee and David Siegel have crafted a motion picture that the Master would be proud of. With each scene, McGehee and Siegel tighten the screws, heightening suspense without benefit of such cheap theatrics as gunfights or chases. The presence of so many mindless movies makes the experience of watching *The Deep End* all the more worthwhile.

Events in this film take place in and around Lake Tahoe, where Margaret Hall (Tilda Swinton) and her three children, Beau (Jonathan Tucker), Paige (Tamara Hope), and Dylan (Jordon Dorrance) live in a nice house on a wooded parcel of lakefront property. Also in residence is Margaret's father-in-law, Jack (Peter Donat). Her husband, Tom, an officer in the Navy, is away (as is often the case) at sea. Domestic problems are brewing on the homefront. Beau, a newly self-aware homosexual, is carrying on an affair with a man 12 years his senior, the rather sleazy Darby Reese (Josh Lucas). Margaret wants Darby to leave her son alone — she doesn't trust Darby and doesn't want him around. He agrees, but for a price of $5,000. When she refuses to pay, he shows up at night and encourages Beau to sneak outside so they can have sex. But Margaret has told Beau about Darby's proposal, and a fight breaks out between the two lovers. Soon, there's a dead body, a mysterious black-mailer (Goran Visnjic), and a police murder investigation. Margaret finds herself covering up for what she believes to be her son's crime, but we in the audience know a critical clue that she is unaware of.

It would be impossible to talk about why *The Deep End* succeeds without gushing rapturously about the performance of Tilda Swinton. There's Oscar buzz already for the red-haired actress, and with good reason. This is the kind of acting job that people remember all year long. Swinton's down-to-earth portrayal of Margaret is what draws us into this story and allows us to accept the coincidences and contrivances that the storyline occasionally throws in our direction. We buy into Margaret, and, through her, into everything that happens.

The Deep End is unquestionably a thriller, but, in an odd way, it's also a love story. At the film's emotional center is the question of what a mother will sacrifice for her son — what lies she will tell and what blame she will accept to keep him safe. It is said that maternal love is the fiercest kind of all, and

nowhere is this more apparent than in *The Deep End*.
HIGHLY RECOMMENDED

Devil in a Blue Dress [1995]

Starring: Denzel Washington, Jennifer Beals, Tom Sizemore, Don Cheadle Director: Carl Franklin Screenplay: Carl Franklin based on the novel by Walter Mosley Running Time: 1:41 Rated: R (Violence, sex, profanity) Theatrical Aspect Ratio: 1.85:1

Beneath all the trappings — a sultry woman in blue, dead bodies, smoky back rooms, shoot-outs, and blackmail — *Devil in a Blue Dress* addresses the kind of subject matter that most crime thrillers, in their quest for pure (often prurient) entertainment, avoid. Easy Rawlins (Denzel Washington), the lead character, is black, and this is 1948 Los Angeles, where segregation and racism are the accepted way of life. As the film progresses, it becomes evident that skin color is more than a background issue — it's the first thing anyone notices, and can break careers, shatter marriages, and end lives.

Easy's not a typical private investigator — he's a bit naive and doesn't own a gun. He's not a detective by trade, but he's out of work and has a mortgage to pay (he's one of the few property-owning blacks in this time and place), so when a man of dubious connections named DeWitt Albright (Tom Sizemore) offers him $100 to locate Daphne Monet (Jennifer Beals), Easy agrees. He doesn't realize what he's gotten himself into. Daphne is the girlfriend of the richest man in L.A. (Terry Kinney), and there are a lot of people — including one talented knife-wielding gangster — looking for her. In a short time, Easy has become implicated in two murders, has been offered money by just about everyone involved, and has become a key player in a political contest where the path to victory is paved with dirty tricks and smoking guns.

If the resolution of *Devil in a Blue Dress* is a little flat, the lack of startling revelations or unexpected twists can be forgiven considering the material's depth. Capable of being viewed on more than one level, this picture has narrative texture. While *Devil in a Blue Dress* never develops the taut momentum of Franklin's previous effort, *One False Move*, it maintains audience involvement, especially after the first, somewhat slow, half-hour. And, to keep the noir elements from becoming too pervasive, the movie is sprinkled with humor.

The most interesting element of *Devil in a Blue Dress* is not the whodunit, but the "whydunit." Finding the guilty parties isn't as involving as learning their motivation, which is buried in society's perception of racial interaction. By uncovering the truth behind this mystery, Franklin illustrates that some attitudes have indeed changed for the better over the last forty years. RECOMMENDED

The Devil's Advocate [1997]

Starring: Al Pacino, Keanu Reeves, Charlize Theron Director: Taylor Hackford Screenplay: Jonathan Lemkin and Tony Gilroy, based on the novel by Andrew Niederman Running Time: 2:25 Rated: R (Profanity, sex, violence, nudity) Theatrical Aspect Ratio: 2.35:1

Taylor Hackford's *The Devil's Advocate* has many laudable qualities, but subtlety is not among them. The story, which postulates that the devil is walking among us today, gives Satan's human alter-ego a truly obvious name: John Milton. And, in what is arguably the most believable aspect of the movie, *The Devil's Advocate* takes lawyer-bashing to its logical extreme by making Lucifer the head of a prestigious law firm. That being said, *The Devil's Advocate* is a highly-enjoyable motion picture that's part character study, part supernatural thriller, and part morality play. Although the film isn't a landmark combination of unique elements, it has a lot of energy and the rather long 145-minute running time passes quickly.

The Devil's Advocate's protagonist is Kevin Lomax (Keanu Reeves), a Florida prosecutor-turned-defense attorney who has never lost in more than 60 cases. Kevin's approach to a trial isn't that it's a forum for justice, but a game to be won or lost — and he is willing to do anything for victory, even if he knows that his client is guilty (the official term for this kind of person is a "sleazeball"). When he successfully gains an acquittal for an accused child molester in a difficult-to-win case, he attracts the attention of a big-time New York lawyer (Ruben Santiago-Hudson), who invites Kevin and his beautiful wife, Mary Ann (Charlize Theron), to Manhattan to meet the head of his firm. Once there, Kevin finds himself being offered a very attractive job by the charismatic John Milton (Al Pacino). But John isn't just a very powerful attorney and astute businessman — he's the devil incarnate — and he has special plans for Kevin.

Aside from Pacino's performance, the greatest strength of the film is its delicious build-up to an operatic climax. And, although huge parts of *The Devil's Advocate* are overblown and overplayed, it's never as silly as it has the potential to be — and this quality consistently keeps the picture out of the dangerous realm of self-parody. The movie's greatest weakness is its ending, which, by trying to be too clever, ends up cheating the audience of a legitimate conclusion.

While there's a sense of closure, it's not an especially satisfying one. *The Devil's Advocate* certainly has problems, chief of which is the subtlety thing, but Pacino's performance is so fun to watch that it eclipses the most significant of them. RECOMMENDED

Disclosure [1994]

Starring: Michael Douglas, Demi Moore, Donald Sutherland Director: Barry Levinson Screenplay: Paul Attanasio based on the novel by Michael Crichton Running Time: 2:08 Rated: R (Language, sex, mature themes) Theatrical Aspect Ratio: 2.35:1

As a thriller, this movie is effective and gripping, if occasionally contrived as a result of overplotting. However, as an examination of a pervasive societal problem, *Disclosure*'s success is questionable. The woman-sexually-harassing-the-man situation seems suspiciously like a male knee-jerk reaction to the issue rather than the unique "twist" it is set up to be (imagine the likely differences in a *Disclosure* penned by a female author). An incident of relatively "benign" harassment of a woman by a man is thrown in almost gratuitously.

Tom and Susan Sanders (Michael Douglas and Caroline Goodall) are a well-matched couple. Affluent and co-supportive, they have a nice house, two children, and prosperous careers. Tom is expecting a promotion when his company, Digicom, enters into a corporate merger — a merger made possible in large part because of one of Tom's projects: Arcamax, a stand-alone CD-ROM player that works twice as fast as any commercially-available product.

Tom doesn't get the raise, however. Instead, his prospective position is given to Meredith Johnson (Demi Moore), an outsider who coincidentally used to be Tom's lover. Worried that his job might be eliminated, Tom agrees to an evening meeting alone with his new boss. Once there, he discovers that she's more interested in renewing a personal relationship than discussing work. Apparently unwilling to take "no" for an answer, Meredith threatens that if Tom leaves her unsatisfied, she'll ruin him.

Disclosure is a great crowd-pleaser, scripted by men who understand exactly how a typical audience likes to be entertained. Together, Crichton, Levinson, and screenwriter Paul Attanasio create a situation, present a sympathetic protagonist and a thoroughly-dislikeable villain, bend and twist the plot, then come up with a resolution that has everyone clapping. At 128 minutes, the film is long, but its crisp pacing keeps it moving through the entire length. And the use of sexual harassment serves the dual purpose of giving Meredith her fangs and getting the audience on Tom's side. On its own terms — the fear of lost security that many thrillers prey upon — *Disclosure* works, and that's all that anyone can reasonably ask from this kind of motion picture. RECOMMENDED

Enemy of the State [1998]

Starring: Will Smith, Gene Hackman, Jon Voight Director: Tony Scott Screenplay: David Marconi Running Time: 2:08 Rated: R (Profanity, violence) Theatrical Aspect Ratio: 2.35:1

Enemy of the State is the latest entry into the suddenly-hot thriller subgenre of films that, because of convoluted plots characterized by bursts of action and unexpected twists, are fun to watch even if they defy logic. In addition to being an in-your-face experience, this kind of movie exudes self-confidence, never doubting for a moment that the viewer will buy into the premise (no matter how ludicrous it might be) and come along for the sheer exhilaration of the ride.

Robert Dean (Will Smith) is a hotshot young attorney on the fast track to prominence. There's little he won't do for a client, including tangling with known mobsters. Robert's wife, Carla (Regina King), is also a lawyer, but, unlike her husband, she's strictly by-the-book. Her passion is the Constitution, and she doesn't like what she sees in a new piece of legislation up for a vote on Capitol Hill that will give the National Security Agency (NSA) the power to use any kind of advanced, electronic surveillance equipment without previous permission or authorization. Robert essentially ignores Carla's gripes, figuring that this kind of law will never affect him. He's wrong. The wheels are already in motion. An incriminating digital tape passed on to him without his knowledge is about to put his life and family in danger as government agents seek to clean up all evidence of a sanctioned murder.

The victim was a United States congressman. The culprit was Thomas Reynolds (Jon Voight), a high-ranking State Department official on loan to the NSA who felt that the congressman's opposition to the surveillance bill would ground it. Unfortunately for Reynolds, the killing was captured on camera by a naturalist (Jason Lee) studying geese migration. Before Reynolds' team can eliminate the witness, he slips a copy of the tape into one of Robert's shopping bags. The NSA realizes this, although Robert doesn't, and he suddenly finds himself in the crosshairs without understanding why. With his life being systematically dismantled (credit cards canceled, wife thinking he's having an affair, fired from his job), he seeks out the mysterious Brill, a shady contact who may hold the key to his situation. But who is Brill? A tough-talking stranger (Gabriel Byrne) who corners him in a lavatory? A pugnacious nerd (Gene Hackman) who threatens him with bodily harm? Or someone else?

Enemy of the State is a kinetic movie, with very few slow moments. The climax, which features an improbable standoff, is both too convenient and a little silly, but it has the virtue of wrapping everything up into a neat package. There are also more than a few gaping holes in the story's plausibility, although these generally don't become evident until long after the end credits have rolled. RECOMMENDED

Enigma [Germany/United Kingdom/United States, 2001]

Starring: Dougray Scott, Kate Winslet, Jeremy Northam, Saffron Burrows Director: Michael Apted Screenplay: Tom Stoppard, based on the novel by Robert Harris Running Time: 1:57 Rated: R (Profanity, sexual situations) Theatrical Aspect Ratio: 2.35:1

The action takes place at Bletchley Park, 60 miles north of London, where the heart of England's World War II decoding operation was located. Tom Jericho (Dougray Scott) was one of the best in the business until he suffered a nervous breakdown after being dumped by his girlfriend, Claire Romilly (Saffron Burrows). Now, a shell of the man he once was, Jericho is back at work — the decoders need him because the Germans have altered their encryption methods, blacking out the Allies at a crucial time (a huge convoy crossing the Atlantic may be headed into a German U-boat trap). Meanwhile, Claire has vanished, and Tom, aided by her flatmate, Hester Wallace (Kate Winslet), begins to investigate her disappearance. The deeper they dig, the more their activities attract the attention of the mysterious Wigram (Jeremy Northam).

Enigma is an imperfect but entertaining thriller that probably would have been more engaging had it been allowed to expand well beyond the 2-hour running length. Parts of the film, especially during the last 45 minutes, feel rushed, as if Apted was under pressure to tell the story as quickly as possible. Economy of screen time is typically an asset in motion pictures (these days, it's also an increasingly rare commodity), but Apted cuts a few too many corners. For example, Tom Stoppard's screenplay never gives us real insight into how the codebreaking is accomplished. An attempt is made to reduce the complex procedure into layman's terms, but the analogy (which involves the name on a tombstone) is neither lucid nor effective.

Nevertheless, *Enigma* does a good job of depicting the wild energy that drives the codebreakers, as well as the strain they're under from all sides. Lives depend on their actions and the politicians and military men can't understand why the process takes so long. With its combination of intrigue, romance, and adventure set against a World War II backdrop, the movie has an undeniable appeal. Flaws aside, *Enigma* is engaging and ambitious. **RECOMMENDED**

Erin Brockovich [2000]

Starring: Julia Roberts, Albert Finney, Aaron Eckhart Director: Steven Soderbergh Screenplay: Susannah Grant Running Time: 2:10 Rated: R (Profanity) Theatrical Aspect Ratio: 1.85:1

The film opens with a car accident. The vehicle driven by Erin Brockovich (Roberts), an unemployed single mother of 3, is broadsided by a speeding car at an intersection. She takes her case to lawyer Ed Masry (Finney), who agrees to represent her on a contingency basis. However, in court, Erin's surly manner and profane vocabulary do not endear her to the jury, which finds in the defendant's favor. Both Erin and Ed go home empty-handed. Still without work and needing to pay her bills, Erin tries an unusual approach to get a job: half-bullying, half-pleading with her former attorney for a position as a file clerk. With grave reservations, Ed relents.

When a pro bono real estate case file comes across her desk, Erin becomes intrigued and begins investigating. She soon learns that the water supply of the property in question may have been contaminated with hexavalent chromium, a "highly toxic, highly carcinogenic" compound that can get into a person's DNA. Erin's efforts uncover hundreds of potential victims of Pacific Gas & Electric's illegal dumping policy, and the information she puts together is convincing enough that Ed agrees to pursue the case. But fighting a $28 billion corporation in court is a daunting and expensive prospect, and Ed isn't sure he has the resources to see it through to the end. Meanwhile, the amount of time Erin is spending working is putting a strain on her relationship with her boyfriend (Aaron Eckhart) and keeping her away from her 3 children for lengthy periods of time.

Erin Brockovich is a unique legal thriller in that, during an era when overplotted and contrived stories like those of John Grisham define the genre, this movie is not littered with throw-away plot devices designed exclusively to generate tension. With only a minor exception, Erin is not followed by shadowy figures. She does not become the target of violence and terroristic threats. *Erin Brockovich*'s suspense does not arise from the likelihood that someone will do something to harm her or her family (although the possibility certainly exists), but from the question of whether a David can succeed in today's legal world against "[Goliath's] whole family." This is the story of someone on the moral high ground fighting for what is right in a legal arena that too often favors those who have money to burn. *Erin Brockovich* is a winner — a reminder of the impact that a truly good motion picture can have. **HIGHLY RECOMMENDED**

Extreme Measures [1996]

Starring: Hugh Grant, Gene Hackman, Sarah Jessica Parker, David Morse Director: Michael Apted Screenplay: Tony Gilroy based on the novel by Michael Palmer Running Time: 1:58 Rated: R (Violence, profanity, mature themes) Theatrical Aspect Ratio: 2.35:1

Gramercy Hospital's emergency room is a picture of overcrowded chaos. Only one operating room is available, and Dr. Guy Luthan (Hugh Grant) has to make a decision: operate immediately on an injured cop whose vital signs are stable or on the drugged-out junkie who shot him, whose condition is worse. Luthan elects the former, and, while both patients survive, he's never wholly satisfied with his choice, as he later confides to Jodie (Sarah Jessica Parker), a sympathetic ER nurse.

It's moral questions like these that lift *Extreme Measures* above the level of a routine, paranoia-driven thriller. True, when you get right down to it, this movie is about a guy trying simultaneously to survive, clear his name, and bring the bad guys down, but there are more shades of gray here than in most modern-day Hitchcockian efforts. *Extreme Measures* never portrays guilt as clear-cut, and its easy to see how, by telling the same story with a script slanted towards another character's perspective, the roles of protagonist and antagonist could be reversed.

Extreme Measures is also about a doctor who crosses the line. Dr. Lawrence Myrick (Gene Hackman) is a world renowned neurosurgeon who believes he has discovered the means to heal severed spines and allow paralyzed people to walk again. Frustrated by the laws that constrain medical experimentation, he sets up an underground complex and begins to kidnap homeless people from hospital ERs to involuntarily assist him. His goal is to be known as the man who enabled the lame to walk — a very god-like ambition.

Luthan becomes involved when lab tests on one of his dead patients reveal some very strange things.

Stonewalled by his bosses, who tell him to forget it or risk his promising career, he begins his own investigation. Soon, pressure is being brought to bear on him, and he discovers the price of ignoring others' warnings. Now, desperate to clear himself of a crime he didn't commit, he ends up wandering through New York City sewers and subway tunnels, dodging bullets and searching for the mysterious place where Myrick conducts his experiments.

The question that Luthan eventually has to confront is whether the ends do indeed justify the means. There's no court scene here, but, in an extended, well-played confrontation between the two leads, the morality of the entire medical profession (not to mention the validity of the Hippocratic Oath) is put on trial. The resolution is perhaps not as powerful or satisfying as we might hope, but it's not a cop-out, either. RECOMMENDED

Eyes Wide Shut [1999]

Starring: Tom Cruise, Nicole Kidman, Sydney Pollack Director: Stanley Kubrick Screenplay: Stanley Kubrick & Frederic Raphael Running Time: 2:40 Rated: R (Graphic sex, frequent nudity, profanity) Theatrical Aspect Ratio: 1.85:1

Eyes Wide Shut is Kubrick through and through, from the frequent long, unbroken takes to the camera's refusal to remain static. Kubrick's style, which became increasingly personalized with every new project, is one of Eyes Wide Shut's most recognizable traits. Every shot and camera angle was selected with great care. There were no happy accidents — each moment of screen time was meticulously plotted, with many scenes being re-done at a later date when the initial version did not meet with the director's approval.

The story, which deals with the various faces of sex and love, is adult in nature. The curtain rises on Dr. Bill Harford (Tom Cruise) and his wife, Alice (Nicole Kidman), as they prepare for a glamorous Christmas party given by one of Bill's friends, Victor Ziegler (Sydney Pollack). Alice isn't happy about attending, and, when her husband abandons her so he can chat with an old medical school buddy-turned-pianist (Todd Field) and flirt with a pair of models, she imbibes a few too many glasses of champagne. This makes her susceptible to the suave advances of a debonair party guest who suggests, "Don't you think that one of the charms of marriage is that it makes deception a necessity for both parties." Alice eventually fends off this seduction, but it causes her to consider fidelity in marriage — both hers and her husband's.

The next night, following a heated argument, Alice admits to Bill that she almost cheated on him once, and, had the circumstances been slightly different, she would have thrown her entire life away for one night with the man she had lusted after. This revelation shatters the stability of Bill's world; he had been confident that, no matter what, he could be sure of his wife's faithfulness. He leaves their home to visit a patient, but, instead of coming straight back, he wanders the streets of New York. A series of chance encounters leads him on an unexpected path of discovery into a sexual underworld where he finds not only perversion and pleasure, but death and danger. Soon, he is being followed and has reason to fear for his safety as well as that of his wife and his young daughter.

The key theme in Eyes Wide Shut is one near and dear to Kubrick's heart: the dehumanization of society. This is a concept he has returned to repeatedly during his career (most obviously in 2001, A Clockwork Orange, and Full Metal Jacket). Here, Kubrick has something to say about the causes and effects of depersonalized sex. There is freedom in anonymity, but also isolation and a complete dearth of emotion. In terms of power and effect, Eyes Wide Shut approaches (but does not surpass) Kubrick's vintage work — it is thought-provoking and unsettling. Impressions and images linger long after the projector has finished weaving its peculiar magic. HIGHLY RECOMMENDED

Fallen [1998]

Starring: Denzel Washington, John Goodman, Donald Sutherland, Embeth Davidtz Director: Gregory Hoblit Screenplay: Nicholas Kazan Running Time: 2:03 Rated: R (Violence, profanity) Theatrical Aspect Ratio: 2.35:1

A serial killer (Elias Koteas) has been on the loose in Philadephia, but Detective John Hobbes (Denzel Washington), the noblest man on the police force, has brought him to justice. Now, during his last hours on death row awaiting his inevitable date with the gas chamber, the mass murderer cryptically tells Hobbes, "What goes around really goes around." Shortly thereafter, he begins to sing "Time Is on My Side" as he's taken on his last walk. Minutes later, the State of Pennsylvania has carried out the execution and Edgar Reese is dead. But for Hobbes, the nightmare is just beginning, because Reese wasn't a normal psychopath — he was the host body for a mythical dark angel named Azazel. And, with Reese's death, Azazel is free to hop from body to body, murdering and wreaking havoc at will. Only Hobbes and a pretty, female theology teacher (Embeth Davidtz) have an inkling of what they're up against. The rest of the cops, including Hobbes' partner, Jonesy (John Goodman); Lou (James Gandolfini), a newcomer to the department; and Lieutenant Stanton (Donald Sutherland), don't have a clue, and, as a result, they are in mortal danger.

Fallen's plot is brimming with potential, not all of which is realized. Somehow, I would have expected a more frightening tale to emerge from something with this kind of premise. But the level of terror, like that of gore, is kept in check. Nevertheless, there are several creepily effective scenes as the spirit of Azazel moves from body to body when people bump against each other on crowded city sidewalks. The film also boasts a chase sequence of a kind that can best be described as unusual.

However, despite the negatives, I'm still recommending *Fallen* on the strength of its complex plot and especially its ending, which I loved. The final scenes are startling, audacious, and unexpected. It's not often that a plot development takes me by surprise the way this one did. At a time when most movies fall apart in the last 10 minutes, *Fallen* manages to buck the trend and redeem itself. RECOMMENDED

Fargo [1996]
Starring: William H. Macy, Steve Buscemi, Frances McDormand Director: Joel Coen Screenplay: Joel and Ethan Coen Running Time: 1:38 Rated: R (Violence, profanity) Theatrical Aspect Ratio: 1.85:1

Fargo opens, appropriately enough, in Fargo, North Dakota, with a meeting between Minnesota car salesman Jerry Lundegaard (William H. Macy) and two local thugs, Carl Showalter (Steve Buscemi) and Gaear Grimsrud (Peter Stormare). Jerry wants this pair to kidnap his wife, then ransom her for $80,000. While Jerry doesn't have that kind of money (in fact, he's strapped for cash), his father-in-law, Wade Gustafson (Harve Presnell), does. When the cash is paid out, Jerry is supposed to receive a 50% cut, as well as the safe return of his wife. That way, everyone except Wade comes out ahead. Unfortunately, with two such incompetent crooks, things are bound to go wrong, and Carl and Gaear are soon leaving a trail of dead bodies behind them. A local cop, Marge Gunderson (Frances McDormand), is given the task of investigating the murders, and it's only with an amazing assist from fate that she ends up on the right track.

A current of absurd humor runs through *Fargo*. Like David Lynch, the Coens are fascinated with what lurks behind the white picket fences of middle America. In *Fargo*, everyone falls into one of two categories — the motivated (who are greedy, duplicitous, or homicidal) or the simpleminded (everyone else).

Born and raised in Minnesota, the Coens know their home state, which accounts for their ability to reflect reality there (which is like *un*reality for most of the rest of the country). People say things like "You're darn tootin'," "aw, geez," and "what the heck." Knowing how strange the talk of Minnesotans will seem to the rest of the world, the Coens intentionally play it for deadpan comic effect.

It's easy to admire what the Coens are trying to do in *Fargo*, but more difficult to actually *like* the film. The absence of viable characters limits any dramatic impact, making this more of a laid back, lightly entertaining experience than a fully immersive one. **RECOMMENDED**

Fifteen Minutes [2001]
Starring: Robert De Niro, Edward Burns, Vera Farmiga Director: John Herzfeld Screenplay: John Herzfeld Running Time: 2:00 Rated: R (Violence, profanity, nudity, sex) Theatrical Aspect Ratio: 2.35:1

Thematically, John Herzfeld's *Fifteen Minutes* has nothing new to offer. Its various elements of social commentary — about the power of the media; the country's love of violent, lurid, "real-life" TV fare; and the cult of stardom — have all been tackled before. Yet, despite its occasional lapses, the movie still works — primarily because it has the audacity to do the unexpected. Some of the concepts may be recycled, but there's something fresh and ambitious about the way they are presented. Best of all, *Fifteen Minutes* manages to develop some genuine tension, especially during the closing sequence, by which time we're convinced that *anything* can happen.

Robert De Niro plays Eddie Flemming, a New York City homicide detective (undoubtedly a big stretch for the actor). Not only is Eddie a good cop, but he's also well-liked, especially by the media. He always seems to have a statement or a scoop for the cameras, and his accessibility has made him a local celebrity. Plus, he's good friends with Robert Hawkins (Kelsey Grammer), the host of the TV tabloid show *Top Story* and is involved in a serious relationship with a newswoman (Melina Kanakaredes). Eddie's latest case brings him onto the turf of fireman Jordy Warsaw (Edward Burns), who is investigating a fire that was used to cover up a double murder. Together, Eddie and Jordy begin to piece together the puzzle, which leads them to an odd-couple of Eastern European immigrants, Oleg (Oleg Taktarov) and Emil

(Karel Roden), who are killing people and making home movies of their acts. Their ultimate goal is to elminate someone famous, plead temporary insanity, then make a ton of money by selling the video tape and book rights to their story. And Eddie becomes their choice for a victim.

Fifteen Minutes takes its share of chances, not all of which work. But it doesn't feel like a cookie-cutter cop thriller, and, on top of that, it's actually about something — a trait that is becoming increasingly rare in mainstream motion pictures. *Fifteen Minutes* probably won't get you to think hard about the thin line between entertainment and exploitation, but it makes its point, and does so in a compelling way. RECOMMENDED

Fight Club [1999]

Starring: Brad Pitt, Edward Norton, Helena Bonham Carter
Director: David Fincher Screenplay: Jim Uhls, based on the novel
by Chuck Palahniuk Running Time: 2:19 Rated: R (Graphic violence,
sex, nudity, profanity) Theatrical Aspect Ratio: 2.35:1

With its kinetic style, visceral approach, compelling storyline, and powerful social message, *Fight Club* makes a commanding case to be considered the '90s version of *A Clockwork Orange*. In a time when so few motion pictures leave an impact, *Fight Club* refuses to be ignored or dismissed. The experience lingers, demanding to be pondered and considered, and, unlike 95% of modern-day thrillers, there is a great deal here to think about and argue over. *Fight Club* presents an overload of thought-provoking material that works on so many levels as to offer grist for the mills of thousands of reviews, feature articles, and post-screening conversations.

The film begins by introducing us to our narrator, Jack, who is brilliantly portrayed by Norton. Here, the actor flows fluidly into the part of a cynical but mild-mannered employee of a major automobile manufacturer who is suffering from a bout of insomnia. When he visits his doctor for a remedy, the disinterested physician tells him to stop whining and visit a support group for testicular cancer survivors if he wants to meet people who really have problems. So Jack does exactly that — and discovers that interacting with these victims gives him an emotional release that allows him to sleep. Soon, he is addicted to attending support group meetings, and has one lined up for each night of the week. That's where he meets Marla Singer (Helena Bonham Carter), another "faker."

Then, on what can be described as the worst day of his life (an airline loses his luggage and his apartment unit explodes, destroying all of his possessions), Jack meets the flamboyant Tyler Durden (Brad Pitt), a soap salesman with an unconventional view of life. Since Jack is in need of a place to live, Tyler invites him to move in, and the two share a "dilapidated house in a toxic waste part of town." Tyler teaches Jack lessons about freedom and empowerment, and the two begin to physically fight each other as a means of release and rebirth. Soon, others find out about this unique form of therapy, and Fight Club is born — an underground organization that encourages men to beat up each other. But this is only the first step in Tyler's complex master plan.

Told in a conventional fashion, *Fight Club* would still have been engaging. However, Fincher's gritty, restless style turns it into a visual masterpiece. The overall experience is every bit as surreal as watching Kubrick's *A Clockwork Orange*. This is a tale that unfolds in an eerie alternate universe where the melodies of life have the same rhythm as in ours but are in a different key. Fincher also shows just enough restraint that his flourishes seem like important parts of the storytelling method instead of gimmicks. *Fight Club* is a memorable and superior motion picture — a rare movie that does not abandon insight in its quest to jolt the viewer. MUST SEE

Flesh and Bone [1993]

Starring: Dennis Quaid, Meg Ryan, James Caan, Gwyneth Paltrow
Director: Steve Kloves Screenplay: Steve Kloves Running Time: 2:05
Rated: R (Violence, language, sexual situations, nudity) Theatrical
Aspect Ratio: 1.85:1

One night in the early 1960s, a young boy is taken in by a West Texas family. He claims that he's lost, and, being the decent folk that they are, his benefactors decide that it's their responsibility to see that he's fed, bathed, and given a place to sleep. But this guest turns out not to be the homeless waif the family believed him to be, and, when he's discovered letting his criminal father, Roy (James Caan), into the house to rob it, a bloodbath ensues. The sole surviving member of the family is a baby girl. Father, mother, and son are all brutally gunned down — two of them in cold blood.

Thirty years later, the boy has grown into the man, Arlis Sweeny (Dennis Quaid), a vending machine stocker who roams from town-to-town following a set routine that gives him comfort and helps shield him from memories better left buried. Then, into his life comes Kay (Meg Ryan), a woman whose future is as bleak as her past, and suddenly Arlis' deeds of 30 years ago return to haunt him anew.

Flesh and Bone is film noir, complete with the characters and settings expected from the genre. It's a thriller that doesn't rely on action for its suspense. Drama — occasionally spilling over to melodrama — is the backbone. The story isn't overplotted; the only real twist is easily guessed, and, while the entire script turns on one massive coincidence, that event is so expertly buried within the context of a gripping tale that it doesn't seem so implausible when it happens. Chock it up to fate's bitterly ironic sense of humor.

Perhaps, ultimately, *Flesh and Bone* is mostly-static, and maybe its central plot element is hard to swallow. But these characters are so impressive, and their circumstances so compelling, that I didn't care about shortcomings in the story. *Flesh and Bone* is all suspenseful buildup without shoot-outs, chases, and explosions, and its conclusion doesn't demand a neatly packaged resolution. RECOMMENDED

Freeway [1996]

Starring: Reese Witherspoon, Kiefer Sutherland Director: Matthew Bright Screenplay: Matthew Bright Running Time: 1:42 Rated: R (Profanity, violence, sexual situations) Theatrical Aspect Ratio: 1.85:1

What happens when you cross The Brothers Grimm with David Lynch, and throw in a little Quentin Tarantino for good measure? The result, or something very much like it, can be found in Matthew Bright's brilliant, incisive satire, *Freeway*, which updates the children's story "Little Red Riding Hood" in new, surprising, and very adult ways. Anyone who never appreciated this fable may revise their opinion after watching *Freeway*.

The film works — and does so manifestly — because its intentions are clearly delineated. Using black humor, blood, and a pair of tremendous performances, *Freeway* hones in on its targets and calculatedly skewers them one-by-one. First up is America's welfare system. Then the judicial system. Then the penal system. And, when you put all the pieces together, you realize that *Freeway* is making a penetrating statement about the general populace's endless fascination with the lurid and violent. This movie is both grimly funny and thought-provoking.

Reese Witherspoon plays a modern-day, white trash Red Riding Hood by the name of Vanessa. She has what might be termed "domestic problems." Her mother (Amanda Plummer) is a prostitute and her stepfather (Michael T. Weiss) is a drug addict. When the cops bust both of them, Vanessa faces another round of foster care. So, instead, she runs off to find her paternal grandmother, who lives in Northern California. Her boyfriend (Bokeem Woodbine) gives her a gun as a going-away present. Shortly after she gets on I-5, her clunker of a car breaks down. A passing motorist by the name of Bob Wolverton (Kiefer Sutherland, the wolf — or Wolverton — in sheepish clothing) gives her a lift. As they drive north, she starts opening up to him, relating her sad life's story. His intentions are anything but altruistic, however, and their little trip leads to a violent off-highway confrontation. This critical event takes place well before *Freeway*'s halfway point, and opens the door for a number of surprising plot developments.

Red Riding Hood references abound, from the opening credits (which depict the Grimm story in drawings) and a TV cartoon to one of the film's last lines ("what big teeth you have"). In addition to already-noted differences between the fairy tale and *Freeway*, there's one other factor that deserves mentioning. In this "Little Red Riding Hood," the wolf makes one huge mistake — he picks a girl who certainly doesn't need a woodcutter to do her butt-kicking for her. HIGHLY RECOMMENDED

The Game [1997]

Starring: Michael Douglas, Sean Penn, Deborah Kara Unger Director: David Fincher Screenplay: John D. Brancato, Michael Ferris, Andrew Kevin Walker Running Time: 2:15 Rated: R (Profanity, violence) Theatrical Aspect Ratio: 2.35:1

This is Michael Douglas' movie. Sean Penn and Deborah Kara Unger, who receive second and third billing, respectively, are supporting performers in the truest sense of the word, since neither has more than 15 to 30 minutes of screen time. Douglas, however, is omnipresent. He's in nearly every scene, and the film is told from his character's point-of-view. And Nicholas Van Orten is the kind of man that Douglas plays best — initially cool and reserved, then gradually less and less sure of himself and his circumstances. The actor's intensity in his approach to this character is palpable.

Nick is a very wealthy man. He lives in a huge mansion equipped with every creature comfort available, but, aside from his housekeeper, he is alone. His wife left him after he elevated the priority level of his work over that of his family. Now, for his 48th birthday, his brother, Conrad (Sean Penn), comes up with the perfect gift for the man who has everything: the game. Developed by a company called "Consumer Recreation Services," the game is "a profound life experience" that "provides whatever is lacking" in a person's existence. Beyond making obtuse statements like it's "an experiential book-of-the-month club," no one is willing or able to describe the game in any detail to Nick. Despite his misgivings, he agrees to participate, but events conspire to raise a vital question: is it really all a game, or is it in deadly earnest?

Figuring out all the ins and outs of *The Game* is like piecing together a jigsaw puzzle. We struggle alongside Nick to determine what's really going on, and, just when we think we have it, something happens to make us doubt our conclusion. The script has its clever moments, and it's easy to mistake this for a smart movie. However, that intelligence is only surface-deep — the seams in the plot are quite visible if you look hard enough. Nevertheless, for anyone who is willing to suspend their disbelief (which, admittedly, isn't all that hard to do), *The Game* offers the kind of taut, unpredictable ride that Hitchcock would have approved of. **RECOMMENDED**

Gangs of New York [2002]

Starring: Leonardo DiCaprio, Daniel Day-Lewis, Cameron Diaz, Jim Broadbent Director: Martin Scorsese Screenplay: Jay Cocks and Steven Zallian and Kenneth Lonergan Running Time: 2:44 Rated: R (Violence, profanity, sex, nudity) Theatrical Aspect Ratio: 2.35:1

Gangs of New York is a bold, epic spectacle brought to the screen using more of the old-fashioned Hollywood techniques (elaborate sets, large groups of extras) than the new ones (CGI). Visually, it is stunning, and the storyline encompasses a grand scope, using a fascinating and turbulent period of American history as the canvas upon which master cinematic painter Martin Scorsese crafts his images. Yet, despite all of this, *Gangs of New York* doesn't come close to masterpiece status. There are some great individual scenes and a tremendous performance by Daniel Day-Lewis, but the connecting material is mediocre, leading to the occasional twinge of dissatisfaction.

Following a short prologue in 1846 New York, the time line jumps ahead to the 1860s, where, set against the background of the American Civil War, the bulk of the story unspools. Amersterdam Vallon (Leonardo DiCaprio) has returned to the Five Points in lower Manhattan to settle a score. When he was a boy, he saw his father murdered in a gang war by Bill the Butcher (Daniel Day-Lewis). Bill, the head of the powerful New York "Nativists" (who are anti-black and anti-immigrant), now rules the Five Points with an iron fist, and Amsterdam has returned to extract revenge. With the help Johnny Sirocco (Henry Thomas), the only one to recognize Amsterdam as the son of the dead Priest Vallon (Liam Neeson), the

young man worms his way into Bill's inner circle. But his resolve to kill Bill wavers when the flamboyant butcher takes him under his wing and treats him like a son. Meanwhile, his friendship with Johnny frays when he becomes involved with Jenny Everdeane (Cameron Diaz), an ex-flame of Bill's with whom Johnny is infatuated.

With *Gangs of New York*, Scorsese has both hit and missed. This is inarguably the most ambitious motion picture of his long career, the first time he has attempted a pure epic. There is much to appreciate about the spectacle, and about the meticulous manner in which the director has brought to life the turbulence of New York in the mid-1800s. We see here the birth pangs of the greatest American city in all of its ugliness. Yet, in presenting such a large tapestry, Scorsese occasionally seems to lose control of the flow. There are times when the movie meanders and the psychological depth of 2 of the 3 principal characters falls far below what we have come to expect from the director of the masterworks *Taxi Driver*, *Raging Bull*, and *Goodfellas*. *Gangs of New York* is an example of a production in which the whole is less than the sum of its elements. Despite some reservations, however, the movie never lost my interest, and I consider it to be worth seeing. **RECOMMENDED**

The General [Ireland, 1998]

Starring: Brendan Gleeson, Jon Voight, Adrian Dunbar, Maria Doyle Kennedy Director: John Boorman Screenplay: John Boorman based on the novel by Paul Williams Running Time: 2:00 Rated: R (Profanity, violence) Theatrical Aspect Ratio: 1.85:1

Gangster movies generally come in two flavors: those that portray mob personalities as vicious figures and those that dwell on the charismatic, family-oriented side of such men. *The General*, a black-and-white, cinematic biography of the recently-assassinated Irish criminal, Martin Cahill (Brendan Gleeson), falls into the latter category. Veteran director John Boorman weaves together real-life incidents and fictional anecdotes to create a fascinating portrait of a man who was both more human and more humane than the legends about him indicate.

The real Martin Cahill was at the pinnacle of Dublin's organized crime structure during the late-'80s and early '90s. Cahill was reputed to have been heavily involved in the drug trade (an assertion that Boorman's film disputes) and was known for nailing men's hands to a pool table when they wouldn't talk. By all accounts, he was also a lively, fun-loving man who could charm with a smile. Unlike American gangsters, Cahill did not leave a trail of bodies in his wake — his criminal activities were more in the line of burglary and theft than murder. Eventually, perhaps for selling rare artwork to members of the Ulster Volunteer Force, Cahill ran afoul of the IRA, and, in 1994, they assassinated him. That event bookends *The General*; the movie begins and ends with it. The film is not about Cahill's death, but about his life. 90% of *The General* focuses on Cahill as an adult, showing him plotting various crimes, carrying them out, and feuding with the local cops.

Gleeson's portrayal of Cahill is nothing short of brilliant. The actor, who is largely unknown in North America, effectively displays the numerous complex facets of his character, including the cold-hearted torturer and the loving father. Cahill is depicted as being apolitical, stealing not to fund a cause, but for his own enjoyment. And he routinely shows his contempt for all forms of "the establishment," regardless of whether they're the police, the Church, or the IRA. It's fair to say that Boorman has romanticized Cahill's life, but he and Gleeson make much more out of this character than a likable rogue. By culling a career performance from Gleeson, Boorman has crafted a memorable portrait of a man who, in his homeland, was known as both a modern-day Robin Hood and a vile gangster, and who, on screen, can be seen as either. RECOMMENDED

The General's Daughter [1999]

Starring: John Travolta, Madeleine Stowe, James Cromwell, Timothy Hutton Director: Simon West Screenplay: Christopher Bertolini and William Goldman, based on the novel by Nelson DeMille Running Time: 2:00 Rated: R (rape, violence, nudity, kinky sex, profanity) Theatrical Aspect Ratio: 2.35:1

The General's Daughter is for all those who enjoy mystery/thrillers that neither attempt to break new ground nor are afraid to employ familiar plot devices. However, while originality isn't one of the film's hallmarks, it is a consistently involving effort, due in large part to solid acting by an A-list cast and effective storytelling by director Simon West, working from a script by Christopher Bertolini and the legendary William Goldman. And, even though the overall arc of the movie travels some well-trodden roads, there are enough small twists and surprises to prevent *The General's Daughter* from seeming like a pale copy of other, similar efforts.

The film does not begin in a promising fashion. When we first meet John Travolta's Warrant Officer Paul Brenner, he's chomping on a cheap cigar and using his worst Bill Clinton accent. Fortunately, we soon learn that the accent is fake and the cigars are for show. He's an army cop working under cover to expose a soldier who's selling arms to a private citizen. Soon, Brenner has been called in to investigate the brutal rape, torture, and murder of Captain Elizabeth Campbell (Leslie Stefanson), the beautiful daughter of 3-star General Joe Campbell (James Cromwell), who's retiring from the army to pursue a vice presidential nomination. Paired with a former flame, rape investigator Sarah Sunderland (Madeleine Stowe), Brenner delves into the investigation, turning Fort MacCallum upside down in his quest for a suspect. He meets Elizabeth's mentor, Colonel Moore (James Woods), who enjoys playing mind games, and learns that not only was the murder victim involved in some unsavory sexual activities, but there's a skeleton in her closet.

Flow is exceptionally important to a narrative like this, and West generates a nearly perfect pace, keeping things moving despite the need to provide a fair amount of exposition. *The General's Daughter* is the exception to the rule: a rare film that earns its 2-hour running time (as opposed to being stretched to that length by having extraneous material inserted). This isn't a masterpiece, but it is consistently entertaining (although those who are offended by strong sexual content or the depiction of sexual violence will find several scenes tough to watch). As far as mystery/thrillers go, *The General's Daughter* supplies what most viewers want and expect from this kind of motion picture. RECOMMENDED

Get Shorty [1995]

Starring: John Travolta, Gene Hackman, Rene Russo, Danny DeVito Director: Barry Sonnenfeld Screenplay: Scott Frank based on the novel by Elmore Leonard Running Time: 1:45 Rated: R (Profanity, violence) Theatrical Aspect Ratio: 1.85:1

John Travolta is Chili Palmer, a loanshark on a mission to Los Angeles to recover $300,000 gained through an insurance fraud. Once near Hollywood, however, Chili, an avowed movie-lover (he has the lines from *Touch of Evil* memorized and can recognize *Rio Bravo* from a sound bite), becomes seduced by the thought of producing a film. So he hooks up with schlock director Harry Zimm (Gene Hackman) and scream queen Karen Flores (Rene Russo). And when Chili starts to pitch an idea, none other than big time actor Martin Weir (Danny DeVito) shows interest. Nevertheless, even as things start looking up for Chili's movie, a host of gangsters try to muscle in on his action — one way or another.

One of the great pleasures of watching *Get Shorty* is that you don't have to turn off your brain while the film is on screen. The script is smart, and makes few concessions to mentally challenged audience members. There's a lot going on beyond the obvious. Take role reversals, for example. As Chili is seduced from a criminal lifestyle by movies, his motion-picture colleagues are drawn away from film by the lure of the gangster experience. Ultimately, it turns out that the common denominator for success in either career is attitude — a quality which Chili possesses in abundance.

The ending is a little reminiscent of that of *The Player*, with a couple of big name cameos. It's a clever way to conclude a wonderfully entertaining romp. *Get Shorty* may be compared to *Pulp Fiction*, but this less profane film is likely to find wider acceptance. It's certainly more mainstream, but, at least in this case, that's not a bad thing. With *Get Shorty*, director Barry Sonnenfeld has shown that broad appeal doesn't necessarily equate with stupidity. That's a lesson Hollywood should learn. **HIGHLY RECOMMENDED**

The Gingerbread Man [1998]

Starring: Kenneth Branagh, Embeth Davidtz, Robert Downey Jr., Robert Duvall Director: Robert Altman Screenplay: "Al Hayes" (Robert Altman) based on an original story by John Grisham Running Time: 1:55 Rated: R (Profanity, nudity, violence) Theatrical Aspect Ratio: 1.85:1

Kenneth Branagh, stepping into a rare contemporary role, is Rick Magruder, a top-notch Savannah-based defense attorney who hasn't lost a case in 8 years. Since his successful record has resulted in part from his ability to chew cops apart on the stand, he's not one of the police department's favorite citizens. One night, following a big victory celebration, as Rick is making his way through a torrential downpour, he encounters Mallory Doss (Embeth Davidtz), a waitress whose car has just been stolen. Rick offers her a lift home and a shoulder to cry on. Soon, her whole sad story pours out: her deranged father, Dixon (Robert Duvall), has been stalking her, and she's afraid for her life. Rick, instantly sympathetic because of his infatuation, agrees to help her get an order of commitment for Dixon. But the wily old man proves to be more dangerous than the lawyer expected, and soon his 2 children are in peril. And, on top of everything else, Hurricane Geraldo is bearing down on Savannah.

The Gingerbread Man starts out strongly by defining the characters, establishing the setting, and anchoring the somewhat convoluted storyline. One of Altman's strengths is character development, so it's no surprise that we are introduced to a gallery of interesting individuals. Past the setup, as the plot gathers steam, the movie takes on the characteristics of a traditional thriller, with such familiar elements as a mysterious car that tails Nick, a drunk private investigator (Robert Downey Jr.), a damsel in distress, and children in jeopardy. Altman ratchets up the tension during this section of the film, providing a few genuine edge-of-the-seat moments.

At its best, *The Gingerbread Man* evokes memories of Alfred Hitchcock, the master of suspense who used every tool at his disposal to trick, cajole, and manipulate the audience into a state of heightened anxiety. One of the mechanisms employed here by Altman is the weather — it always seems to be raining, and the approach of the hurricane promises even more wind and water. Fortunately, the storm sequences are impressively filmed and serve to enhance the atmosphere, rather than drown it.

Although *The Gingerbread Man* has its faults, there are enough fine moments and solid performances to more than balance them out. While Altman aficionados may be disappointed by the conventional nature of the production, fans of writer John Grisham (who gets story, but not screenplay, credit) will probably feel right at home. The legal thriller has become Grisham's home field, and *The Gingerbread Man*, with an accomplished director at the helm, is as worthwhile as anything he has helped bring to the screen. The result is an entertaining and sporadically engrossing 2 hours. **RECOMMENDED**

Hard Eight [1997]

Starring: Philip Baker Hall, John C. Reilly, Gwyneth Paltrow, Samuel L. Jackson Director: Paul Thomas Anderson Screenplay: Paul Thomas Anderson Running Time: 1:41 Rated: R (Profanity, violence, sex) Theatrical Aspect Ratio: 2.35:1

Inertia. The dictionary defines it as "a property of matter by which it remains at rest or in uniform motion," and this is an apt descriptor for Paul Thomas Anderson's debut feature, *Hard Eight*. During the first half, virtually nothing happens — the characters are stuck in a stasis from which escape seems impossible. Then, during the second half, momentum carries the story to its inescapable conclusion. The dualistic nature of *Hard Eight* makes it a difficult picture to size up. At times, it's engrossing, but, on other occasions, it's a lesson in frustration.

Hard Eight opens with a fascinating, 20-minute prologue. A dapper, elderly gentleman named Sydney (Philip Baker Hall), approaches a disheveled, younger man, John (John C. Reilly), outside a roadside diner. Sydney invites John to join him for a cup of coffee and a cigarette. Inside, they talk. John's on his way back from Vegas, where he lost all his money trying to win enough to bury his mother. Sydney thinks his intentions are admirable, and offers him an opportunity: come back to Vegas and learn how to get a free room and maybe even win a little extra cash. Sydney's scam is deceptively simple and undeniably effective, and Anderson presents it with flair and an undercurrent of wry humor.

The rest of *Hard Eight* takes place 2 years later in Reno, when Sydney and John are good friends. Theirs is a father/son relationship, with John never far from Sydney's side. As John's girlfriend, waitress/prostitute Clementine (Gwyneth Paltrow), observes to the older man, "He follows you and worships you like you're a captain." Clementine's actions soon introduce new obstacles in Sydney and John's friendship, as do those of a seedy security advisor named Jimmy (Samuel L. Jackson).

Hard Eight borrows its share of conventions from noir thrillers, but this is more of a character drama than anything else. Sure, there's some violence, gunplay, and a few plot twists, but everything keeps coming back to the relationship between Sydney, an aging man with an opaque past, and John, the damaged and none-too-bright individual he takes under his wing. Clementine too is one of life's castoffs, but Sydney's interest in her is primarily as a companion for his surrogate son. As much as Sydney likes Clementine, however, that's how much he dislikes Jimmy, whose vulgar, arrogant manner marks him as trouble from the beginning. There's something almost hypnotic about the way *Hard Eight* develops — even in its slowest moments, it keeps our attention. **RECOMMENDED**

Heavenly Creatures [New Zealand, 1994]

Starring: Melanie Lynskey, Kate Winslet Director: Peter Jackson
Screenplay: Peter Jackson and Frances Walsh Running Time: 1:38
Rated: Not Rated (Mature themes, sexual themes, violence) Theatrical Aspect Ratio: 2.35:1

Heavenly Creatures is based on the true story of Pauline Rieper (Melanie Lynskey) and Juliet Hulme (Kate Winslet) set in Christchurch, New Zealand from 1952 to 1954. These two teenagers (Pauline was 15 in 1954; Juliet was 17) formed an intense and, some argued, unhealthy friendship. They were inseparable, and when a case of tuberculosis forced Juliet into quarantine, they wrote voluminous letters to each other, both as themselves and as fantasy characters

they created. Eventually, their parents became concerned about the nature of this friendship, and attempted to prevent Pauline and Juliet from seeing each other. The tragic ramifications of this action, as described in the real Pauline's journal, are related in Peter Jackson's original motion picture.

This uniquely powerful film accrues much of its momentum through character interaction. Pauline and Juliet are so well-scripted and solidly portrayed that the viewer cannot help but be captivated by their relationship. While it is intentionally left ambiguous whether either of these girls is a lesbian (one sexual encounter does not define a lifestyle), no such uncertainty accompanies the exploration of how hopelessly tangled their lives and emotional well-being have become.

Fantasy plays a crucial role in *Heavenly Creatures*. It's up to the individual viewer to decide how psychotic Pauline and Juliet are (they share visions of the "4th World," a "heaven without Christians" inhabited by clay people, where the tunes of Mario Lanza perpetually fill the air). Certainly, these two are more at home living in a world apart from our own, where romance and happiness reign.

As a dysfunctional family tale, the disturbing *Heavenly Creatures* offers no facile answers as to what might have been done differently to prevent circumstances from degenerating as they did. Revealed in unforgettable fashion by a capable director, the events that unfold in this film are not easily forgotten.
HIGHLY RECOMMENDED

Heist [2001]

Starring: Gene Hackman, Danny DeVito, Delroy Lindo, Sam Rockwell
Director: David Mamet Screenplay: David Mamet Running Time: 1:49
Rated: R (Profanity, violence) Theatrical Aspect Ratio: 1.85:1

Heist is a wonderfully written excursion into criminal activity that throws us into the deep end and asks us to sink or swim. With dizzying speed, we are shuttled through a series of double-crosses and triple-crosses, and all is not revealed until the very end. One could argue that there's one twist too many, but it works brilliantly, so who cares? *Heist* begins with a meticulously planned and flawlessly executed jewelry store robbery, proceeds to the plotting of an even bigger crime, and ends with an apparent falling out between thieves. It's fast-paced and wildly entertaining.

Dialogue has always been one of Mamet's trademarks — especially the staccato beat with which it is delivered. However, while *Heist* contains its share of brilliant one-liners (including one or two that Arnold

Schwarzenegger would be proud to utter), the words are spoken in a much more "natural" manner than in any previous Mamet-directed effort. There are no strange pauses and there is no odd rhythm. Admittedly, I missed it a little, but it's the right approach for this movie.

The cast is stellar. Gene Hackman plays Joe Moore, the veteran thief who is looking for one final score to finance his exit from the business. His team is comprised of Rebecca Pidgeon, Ricky Jay, Delroy Lindo, and Sam Rockwell as the cocky newcomer. Danny DeVito shows his vicious side as Joe's fence, who suddenly wants a bigger piece of the action. Admittedly, this is not a character-driven motion picture, so none of these performers have to take their alter-egos through anything more dramatic than a perfunctory arc, but they all do solid jobs inhabiting their characters' skins.

To say anything more about the specifics of *Heist* would be to ruin the fun of discovery. It's consistently fun, occasionally funny, and will have viewers on the edges of their seats on more than one occasion. Once again, playwright-turned-filmmaker David Mamet has crafted a motion picture worth seeking out. **HIGHLY RECOMMENDED**

In the Company of Men [Canada, 1997]
Starring: Aaron Eckhart, Matt Malloy, Stacy Edwards Director: Neil LaBute Screenplay: Neil LaBute Running Time: 1:33 Rated: R (Mature themes, profanity) Theatrical Aspect Ratio: 1.85:1

In the Company of Men is one of those rarest of rare breeds — a movie that doesn't just ignore Hollywood conventions, but openly flouts them. The picture begins as something much different than what it concludes as, and the metamorphosis occurs so gradually that it only becomes apparent in retrospect. Shortly after *In the Company of Men* opens, the intent appears to be to center on the conflict between the sexes. Ultimately, however, this only a small piece of the much larger pie into which Neil LaBute's directorial debut slices. *In the Company of Men* widens its focus to encompass the falseness and gamesmanship that underlies many aspects of everyday human interaction. It's a cynical perspective that's all the more disturbing because it's grounded so deeply in reality. The characters here aren't cardboard cut-out stereotypes — they're the kind of people you can find anywhere inside or outside of the workplace.

Chad (Aaron Eckhart) and Howard (Matt Malloy) are two very different guys with a great deal in common. They attended the same college, work for the

same corporation, and have a history of bad relationships with women. Their combined romantic record reads like a litany of injustices perpetrated on them by females. They have been duped, rejected, neglected, and intentionally misunderstood. Chad, ready to go to war against the entire gender to "restore a little dignity," has a simple, vicious suggestion for revenge. They will find a woman who has trouble getting dates, both take her out, then, after duping her into falling in love with one or both of them, they'll dump her at the same time. Howard is initially reluctant, but Chad talks him into it before locating the perfect target: an attractive-but-deaf typist named Christine (Stacy Edwards), whose disability has caused her self-esteem to erode.

Much of LaBute's script is about manipulation and deceit, but he's smart enough to show the characters manipulating each other without turning that manipulation on the audience. Nevertheless, because we become so involved in the interaction between these people, it's impossible for us not to be enflamed by what's transpiring, or to hope that justice comes from heaven in the form of a lightning bolt.

In the Company of Men doesn't take prisoners, and "feel good" is a term *no one* will ever use to describe it. But the movie deserves high praise because what it does, it does extraordinarily well. Finally, here's a film with the guts to tell this kind of the story without turning it into a fairy tale. It's rare for any motion picture to generate such a profound sense of disquiet, but the path traversed by LaBute's characters is so bold that it's impossible not to be affected. **MUST SEE**

Insomnia [Norway, 1997]
Starring: Stellan Skarsgård, Sverre Anker Ousdal, Bjorn Floberg Director: Erik Skjoldbjærg Screenplay: Nikolaj Frobenius, Erik Skjoldbjærg Running Time: 1:37 Rated: R (Violence, profanity, nudity, sex) Theatrical Aspect Ratio: 1.85:1 In Norwegian with subtitles

Most murder mysteries take place in the dark. *Insomnia*, a compelling thriller from first-time Scandinavian director Erik Skjoldbjærg, occurs in a state of perpetual light. The setting is north of the Arctic circle in the middle of summer. At that time and place, we have entered the land of the midnight sun, a strange world where daylight holds court 24 hours a day. Yet, even in such bright circumstances, the darkest impulses of the human soul can not always be held at bay.

Jonas Engstrom (Stellan Skarsgård) and his partner, Erik Vik (Sverre Anker Ousdal), are cops from Oslo brought in to a small town to help with a murder investigation. A 17-year-old girl, Tanja (Maria Mathiesen), has been found naked and dead, and the killer has carefully removed all traces of his presence by washing her hair and scrubbing under her fingernails. Engstrom and Vik, who have a reputation as Scandinavia's most effective and tenacious investigators, are on the case immediately, and an early break allows them to set a trap for the suspect. But things go wrong, and, in the confusion of a shoot-out, Engstrom kills Vik. He is about to confess this career-damaging act to the local police chief when the man gives him an unexpected way out. From that point onward, Engstrom finds himself trapped in an increasingly-complex web of deceit as he attempts to solve the crime while covering up his own misdeed. And, as his guilty conscience and the never-ending light keep him awake at night, the lack of sleep makes him increasingly desperate and prone to error.

Although *Insomnia* is not without its share of surprises and unexpected plot twists, it does not offer the red herrings of a whodunit. Instead, it's a dissection of moral decay — of a once-decent man whose circumstances cause him to contemplate actions that place him in an increasingly indefensible situation. Along the way, he engages in the sexual molestation of a teenager and mistakes the flirtatious advances of a pretty hotel receptionist for something more serious. Engstrom is the kind of darkly complex, morally ambiguous character that American movies rarely highlight.

Insomnia works as a noir thriller of a different sort, where circumstances gradually warp a hero into a villain. Mysteries typically focus so intently on plot that there's little room for a detailed character arc, but *Insomnia* manages to balance both aspects.

HIGHLY RECOMMENDED

Insomnia [2002]

Starring: Al Pacino, Robin Williams, Hilary Swank
Director: Christopher Nolan Screenplay: Hillary Seitz, based on the
1997 screenplay by Nikolaj Frobenius and Erik Skjoldbjærg Running
Time: 1:57 Rated: R (Violence, profanity, nudity, sexual situations)
Theatrical Aspect Ratio: 2.35:1

One of the most breathtaking scenes in Christopher Nolan's *Insomnia* occurs early in the film as a small plane flies over the barren wasteland of jagged mountains and broken ice that makes up so much of the rugged terrain of America's northernmost state. For this thriller, which unites 3 Academy Award-winning actors (Al Pacino, Robin Williams, Hilary Swank) with the director of *Memento*, we're up above the Arctic Circle in the Land of the Midnight Sun. Call it *film blanche*.

For Los Angeles police detectives Will Dormer (Al Pacino) and Hap Eckhart (Martin Donovan), their latest murder investigation isn't business as usual. They have come to Alaska not only to aid the authorities of the small town of Nightmute in finding a killer, but to temporarily escape the spotlight of an Internal Affairs investigation. Will is greeted like a legend in Nightmute, especially by Officer Ellie Burr (Hilary Swank), who hero-worships him. After examining the body and getting a rundown on some basic facts about the case, Will and Hap retire to their hotel, where Hap drops a bombshell on Will — he's going to cut a deal with I.A. Will is livid, claiming that if Hap does that, all of the criminals they put away will get out. But Hap is adamant.

The next day, Will sets a trap for the killer, an author named Walter Finch (Robin Williams), who falls into it. There's a chase along a foggy shoreline, and, when Will fires his gun at a shape in the mist, he accidentally kills his partner, whose dying words are that Will did it on purpose to stop him from testifying. Walter, concealed nearby, sees and hears everything. Later, Will decides to cover things up, pretending that their quarry shot his partner. Everyone believes Will, so it isn't difficult for him to tamper with the evidence. But Walter knows the truth, and he believes that gives him power over Will. In his mind, they're partners, and, as sleep deprivation caused by insomnia clouds Will's ability to think clearly, he is drawn into Walter's web.

For those who have not seen the earlier *Insomnia*, this motion picture delivers the goods. It's smart, well-acted, beautifully shot, and suspenseful. For those who are familiar with the source material, while there may be a sense that something is lacking, the movie still has the capacity to engage for 2 hours. *Insomnia* does not become one of those rare remakes to eclipse the original, but it doesn't disgrace it, either. Under the relentless glare of the Midnight Sun, the only darkness is in the hearts and actions of the characters. **RECOMMENDED**

The Interview [Australia, 1998]

Starring: Hugo Weaving, Tony Martin, Aaron Jeffrey Director: Craig
Monahan Screenplay: Craig Monahan, Gordon Davie Running
Time: 1:43 Rated: Not Rated (Profanity) Theatrical Aspect Ratio: 1.85:1

What starts out as a seemingly straightforward police thriller develops into something far less conventional, where even the most seasoned movie-goer will find himself or herself re-assessing the characters and the storyline that defines their interaction. *The Interview* becomes a meditation upon police procedure, justice, truth, and the (un)reliable narrator. It isn't until the final frame of the motion picture that first-time director Craig Monahan answers the question that preys upon the mind of every viewer (and, even when he does so, there's still room for interpretation).

The film opens with an unkempt man, Eddie Fleming (Hugo Weaving), being rousted out of bed when the police break down his front door. As is cursorily explained to him by Detective Sergeant John Steele (Tony Martin) and his thuggish associate, Detective Senior Constable Wayne Prior (Aaron Jeffrey), he is wanted in association with a stolen car. After being cuffed, terrorized, and humiliated, Fleming is taken to the police station to be interviewed. That segment of the movie, which comprises most of the running length, turns into a cat-and-mouse war of wills between Fleming and Steele.

For his part, Steele believes that Fleming may be connected to a series of seemingly unrelated murders, and he uses every trick in the book to get Fleming to reveal something. Along with Prior, he plays "good cop/bad cop," all the while unaware that he is under surveillance by Internal Affairs. Meanwhile, Fleming regains the composure he lost when the police broke into his home, but is his calm demeanor merely his way of reacting to circumstances, or does he have a deeper motive? And, when he appears to let something slip by the way of a confession, is he weaving a story or recounting the facts?

In essence, Monahan is examining one of the trickiest questions of law and justice — something that applies not only in Australia, but in every society with its roots in English jurisprudence. Is it better for a guilty man to go free in order to protect against the possibility of an innocent man being sent to prison? If Fleming is blameless, then he is being horribly mistreated by the police, but if he is a serial killer, then Steele's methods seem justified — perhaps even lenient. And, because Monahan doesn't tip his hand, viewers teeter from one point-of-view to the other. **HIGHLY RECOMMENDED**

Interview with the Assassin [2002]

Starring: Raymond J. Barry, Dylan Haggerty Director: Neil Burger
Screenplay: Neil Burger Running Time: 1:34 Rated: Not Rated (Profanity, violence) Theatrical Aspect Ratio: 1.85:1

Interview with the Assassin is a valentine to conspiracy theorists. It is also an intelligent and gripping thriller — one that uses the first-person, pseudo-

documentary approach to an effective end. *Interview with the Assassin* plays with reality in such a way that it's easy to forget that what you're watching is a cleverly constructed fabrication, not a representation of something that actually happened.

There have been more conspiracy theories devised about the situations and circumstances of November 22, 1963 than about any other event in American history. According to ex-military operative Walter Ohlinger (Raymond J. Barry), Lee Harvey Oswald did not act alone. There was a second gunman on the so-called "grassy knoll" in Dealey Plaza, and that man fired the fatal head shot. How does Walter know this? Because, he claims, he was that individual. He makes this revelation in a videotaped confession to out-of-work news cameraman Ron Kobeleski (Dylan Haggerty). Dying of cancer, Walter has decided to come clean. The two take a trip to Dallas, where Walter lays out in meticulous detail his every movement during the early afternoon of November 22, 1963. Thereafter, he and Ron embark upon a journey to find the one man who may be able to verify Walter's claim and answer Ron's paramount question: Why was President Kennedy shot?

Is Walter telling the truth or is he an insane delusional who has lost touch with reality to the point where he believes his story? Are there men following Ron and Walter, or is this paranoia? These are questions viewers will ask themselves as the film unfolds. Writer/director Neil Burger, making his feature debut, does not tip his hand early — in fact, some might argue that he doesn't tip it at all. It should be noted, however, that although the film starts out to be chillingly plausible, it grows progressively less so during the course of the proceedings. But, by the time *Interview with the Assassin* begins to strain our credulity, we're already hooked. **RECOMMENDED**

Jackie Brown [1997]

Starring: Pam Grier, Samuel L. Jackson, Robert Forster, Bridget Fonda, Robert De Niro Director: Quentin Tarantino Screenplay: Quentin Tarantino, based on the book *Rum Punch* by Elmore Leonard Running Time: 2:35 Rated: R (Profanity, violence, sex, drug use) Theatrical Aspect Ratio: 2.35:1

The story of *Jackie Brown*, which starts out slowly, develops into a twisty affair, with double-crosses and triple-crosses. And the movie is littered with occasional Tarantino trademarks: witty dialogue, unexpected gunfire, '70s pop tunes, and close-ups of womens' bare feet. Yet, for all of that, the production is something of a letdown. The sheer, in-your-face exuberance that marked *Reservoir Dogs* and especially *Pulp Fiction* is absent. The mostly-straightforward chronology of *Jackie Brown* doesn't match up favorably to the non-linear style of Tarantino's previous efforts — an approach that added tension and edginess to the narratives. And there aren't nearly as many deliciously offbeat conversations this time around. There's a Samuel L. Jackson monologue about guns, a Jackson/Chris Tucker argument regarding the merits of hiding in a car trunk, and a Jackson/Robert De Niro exchange that recalls some of the Jackson/Travolta material from *Pulp Fiction*, but that's about it.

Pam Grier is Jackie Brown, a flight attendant who gets caught transporting drugs and money into the United States. She's working for gun dealer Ordell Robbie (Samuel L. Jackson), but she keeps her mouth shut under questioning, despite pressure from Ray Nicolet (Michael Keaton), a Federal official. No longer sure whether or not he can trust Jackie, Ordell arranges for a bail bondsman, Max Cherry (Robert Forster, TV's "Banyon") to post the necessary $10,000, then plans to shoot Jackie if she proves disloyal. Jackie passes Ordell's test, however, and soon the two of them are plotting a way to smuggle $500,000 of Ordell's money into the United States without tipping off the Feds. Soon, just about everyone is after that money, including Jackie, Max, Ray, Ordell's perpetually oversexed and drugged-out girlfriend, Melanie (Bridget Fonda), and his right-hand man, Louis (Robert De Niro).

The film, which clocks in at several minutes over the 2½ hour mark, is probably too long for the material, but the plot is convoluted enough to keep us guessing throughout (although the payoff is a letdown). Tarantino keeps things moving along nicely, with a heavier dose of humor and less violence than in *Pulp Fiction*, but, on the whole, this movie seems more like the work of one of his wannabes than something from the director himself. When it comes to recent caper films, *Jackie Brown* is a second-tier effort. It's an entertaining diversion, but not a masterpiece. **RECOMMENDED**

Jagged Edge [1985]

Starring: Jeff Bridges, Glenn Close, Peter Coyote, Robert Loggia
Director: Richard Marquand Screenplay: Joe Eszterhas Running Time: 1:50 Rated: R (Violence, mature themes, sex, language, brief nudity) Theatrical Aspect Ratio: 1.85:1

At first glance, it might appear that *Jagged Edge* is a cleverly-scripted mystery that asks not the question

"Whodunnit?" but "Did *he* do it?" However, upon closer examination, it becomes clear that the screenplay for this film is rather pedestrian: filled with clichés, formulas, and typical red herrings, and with twists that aren't as unexpected as they initially seem. Instead, what success this movie achieves is due more to solid direction and competent acting than to what spilled out of Joe Eszterhas' pen.

The chief suspect in the brutal murder of Page Forrester is her husband, Jack (Jeff Bridges), the person who stood the most to gain. Page was rich, and Jack inherits everything, making him the lone target of an investigation launched by D.A. Thomas Krasny (Peter Coyote). When a witness claims to have seen the possible murder weapon in Jack's gym locker, the widowed newspaper executive is arrested.

For his defense, Jack wants Teddy Barnes (Glenn Close), a one-time assistant under Krasny. Teddy hasn't practiced criminal law for 4 years since procedural violations allowed her to convict an innocent man. The thought of acquitting Jack — whom she believes to be innocent — seems an appropriate salve to her conscience. With the help of her investigative friend Sam Ransom (Robert Loggia), she constructs a defense, unaware that neither her client nor the DA are being straight with her.

The plot isn't all that complex, and the only reason it isn't possible to discover the truth before the climax is that the script doesn't offer enough clues. Fortunately, director Richard Marquand and his actors are up to the challenge of transforming a mediocre script into an entertaining film.

Like many entries into the genre, *Jagged Edge* works best when it's watched with a minimum of analysis. There are a fair number of gaffes, flaws, and other assorted problems, and the plot looks progressively less substantial the more closely it's examined. However, the bottom line is that the crux of the story — whether or not Jack is guilty — is engrossing, and it isn't until we know the answer that the movie really seems to let us down. **RECOMMENDED**

K-19: The Widowmaker [United States/United Kingdom, 2002]

Starring: Harrison Ford, Liam Neeson, Peter Sarsgaard
Director: Kathryn Bigelow Screenplay: Christopher Kyle Running Time: 2:15 Rated: PG-13 (Mature themes, disturbing images) Theatrical Aspect Ratio: 2.35:1

K-19: The Widowmaker is a war movie without a war, or at least without a hot war. The film uses the backdrop of a potential nuclear holocaust to generate a powerful sense of escalating tension. Most submarine pictures use the claustrophobic setting of the submerged vessel as an opportunity to ratchet up the suspense level during battle scenes. However, in *K-19*, there are no battles — neither of the sub-to-sub nor the sub-to-surface variety. The movie finds other ways to fray our nerves, such as setting up a situation in which there is a leak in the boat's nuclear reactor, and, if the men can't find a way to repair it or get off the ship, they will all die of radiation poisoning. And, as long as the reactor is non-functional, their engine is down and they can't move fast enough to reach a safe harbor.

Harrison Ford, whose stern demeanor is perfect for this part, is Captain Alexi Vostrikov, the man brought in to command the flagship of the Soviet submarine fleet, K-19. It's 1961, and the USSR is convinced that America is planning a first strike. By situating K-19 off the North American eastern seaboard, the Soviets believe they can nullify the United States' superior weapons advantage. Vostrikov has a difficult assignment. K-19 has been rushed into action, so all of its systems are not in perfect working order. And the crewmembers, except for one officer, Vadim Radtchenko (Peter Sarsgaard), are loyal to the former Captain, Polenin (Liam Neeson), who remains on board as the Executive Officer. When Vostrikov's fondness for taking seemingly unnecessary chances creates unrest amongst the crew, rumbles of a mutiny begin.

K-19 contains a number of scenes that are obligatory in any submarine movie — a dive to crush depth, an uncontrolled rise to the surface, and exercises that presage real emergencies (in particular, fire fighting drills). The strained relationship between Vostrikov and Polenin is as important as any other aspect of the movie. Their interaction undergoes a number of shifts and changes, some of which seem motivated more by a necessity of the plot than by an element of one or both of their personalities. Nevertheless, they progress from wariness to open distrust to respect — a fairly common arc in movies of this nature. *K-19* will not go down in the annals of cinema as one of the great submarine stories, but it is an engaging and exciting narrative of Man confronting the Demons of his own fear and paranoia. **RECOMMENDED**

Kiss the Girls [1997]

Starring: **Morgan Freeman, Ashley Judd, Cary Elwes, Tony Goldwyn**
Director: **Gary Fleder** Screenplay: **David Klass**, based on the novel by

James Patterson Running Time: 2:00 Rated: R (Violence, profanity, mature themes) Theatrical Aspect Ratio: 2.35:1

Kiss the Girls wouldn't be nearly as involving without the two strong performances of the leads. Morgan Freeman plays Dr. Alex Cross, a Washington, D.C. forensic pathologist who travels to Durham, N.C., when his niece, Naomi (Gina Ravera), disappears. Freeman plays Alex as an insightful, confident investigator with powerful emotions bubbling just beneath his calm, carefully-controlled exterior. Despite a less-than-enthusiastic greeting by Durham's chief of police, Alex learns that Naomi is the eighth young woman to disappear recently, all of whom fit the same description: intelligent, strong-willed, college-age, attractive, and talented. Three are already dead, but Alex suspects that the primary interest of the killer (who calls himself "Casanova") is not murder. Instead, the doctor sees him as "a collector."

Disappearance #9 is Dr. Kate McTiernan (Ashley Judd), an intern at the Carolina Regional Medical Center. As Kate, Judd adds another impressive performance to a growing resume. The actress plays her character as outwardly-tough and self-sufficient with an inner core of vulnerability. She may be a target, but she refuses to be a victim, and it's hard to miss the fire in her eyes. Nevertheless, vulnerability, whether emotional or physical, is something she has a hard time coping with. One night, Kate is abducted from her house and brought to a lightless room where she is bound and drugged. But, by taking her masked captor unawares, she escapes in what is one of *Kiss the Girls'* best filmed-sequences. Later, after surviving a fall into a river where she nearly drowns, Kate joins forces with Alex for one purpose: to bring Casanova to justice.

One thing I appreciate about *Kiss the Girls* is its willingness to spend time developing the characters before jumping into the main story. During the first 20 minutes, we gather information about both Alex and Kate. Later, the relationship between these two is developed in an intentionally ambiguous manner. There are times when it manifests itself almost as a father/daughter bond, but, on other occasions, there's a sense of latent romance. However, the film underplays this dynamic to avoid wandering off on a tangent.

The film makers, with a nod to the success of *Seven*, have apparently decided to mimic the grim atmosphere and in-your-face cinematography of that movie (light, darkness, and shadow are used to great effect here). Stylistically, *Kiss the Girls* is very similar, and the presence of Morgan Freeman only heightens the connection. Even though there are vast plot differences between the two, both are well-made and are likely to appeal to the same kind of audience. So, much like *Seven*, *Kiss the Girls* makes for a suspenseful, if somewhat bleak, 2 hours. RECOMMENDED

L.A. Confidential [1997]

Starring: Kevin Spacey, Russell Crowe, Guy Pearce, James Cromwell
Director: Curtis Hanson Screenplay: Curtis Hanson and Brian
Helgeland based on the novel by James Ellroy Running Time: 2:20
Rated: R (Profanity, violence, sex, nudity) Theatrical Aspect
Ratio: 2.35:1

Crooked cops. The mystery and allure of Hollywood in the '50s. Death, double-crossing, and secret alliances. Paparazzi waiting to get that one breakthrough picture. These are just some of the elements that make Curtis Hanson's *L.A. Confidential* one of the most exhilarating noir thrillers to reach the screen in recent memory. It's 1953, and the City of Angels is in the grip of an unprecedented wave of violence. Cops on the take turn their backs on crimes. The jailing of a major mob boss leaves a vacuum of power that leads to a turf war. Then comes the Night Owl Massacre, where 6 victims (including an ex-cop) are brutally gunned down at the Night Owl Café. The police begin routine investigations, but it quickly becomes apparent that this is no ordinary multiple homicide.

There are 3 cops on the job. The first, Bud White (Russell Crowe), is a "muscle" guy who believes that violence solves almost everything and is willing to bend (or even break) the rules to obtain results. The second, Jack Vincennes (Kevin Spacey), is the kind of officer who prefers the spotlight to a down-and-dirty lifestyle. He's the high-profile technical advisor to the hit TV series, *Badge of Honor*, and has a clandestine agreement with the editor (Danny DeVito) of *Hush Hush* magazine, a sleazy tabloid that publishes photos and stories showing Jack arresting celebrities in compromising positions. Finally, there's Ed Exley (Guy Pearce), a by-the-book cop who thinks he can rise through the ranks without resorting to Bud's boorish methods. Obviously, the tactics used by these 3 differ greatly, but, as they delve deeper into the murky mysteries of the L.A. police force, it becomes clear that their survival depends on working together.

The difference between *L.A. Confidential* and numerous other, more routine films of the genre begins with the script. Smart, insightful, and consistently engaging, Hanson and Brian Helgeland's faithful adaptation of James Ellroy's novel is a real treat for anyone who views film as a medium for both art and entertainment. The movie is filled with small twists and turns, but not so many that the plot becomes difficult to swallow or to follow. The subplots — and there are several — are as well-developed as the main story, and the supporting characters are presented as more than mere colorful misfits decorating the background. It takes *L.A. Confidential* nearly 2½ hours to spin its tale, but the time passes remarkably quickly. There's hardly a wasted moment in the entire movie, and director Hanson maintains tight control of every scene. HIGHLY RECOMMENDED

Lantana AUSTRALIAN [2001]

Starring: Anthony LaPaglia, Geoffrey Rush, Barbara Hershey, Kerry
Armstrong Director: Ray Lawrence Screenplay: Andrew Bovell, based
on his play "Speaking in Tongues" Running Time: 2:00 Rated: R
(Violence, profanity, sex) Theatrical Aspect Ratio: 2.35:1

For the briefest of moments, someone not paying attention might mistake *Lantana* for a mystery. After all, there is a body, a missing person, indications of foul play, and several police detectives. But don't be fooled — all of that is little more than a hook upon which the film's real meat can be hung. So there's a reason why *Lantana* can be considered an "unconventional murder mystery" — because it's not really a murder mystery at all. And, while the title sounds like some kind of new Latin dance, *Lantana* is actually an examination of human interaction.

Leon Zat (Anthony LaPaglia) is an Australian cop whose marriage to Sonja (Kerry Armstrong) is in the doldrums. He claims to have become emotionally numb, while she laments that she's looking for a relationship that is "passionate, challenging, [and] honest." While Leon engages in an affair with Jane O'May (Rachael Blake), Sonja emotionally unburdens herself to her psychiatrist, Valerie Somers (Barbara Hershey), stating that she believes Leon is unfaithful. She goes on to say that she doesn't mind that he's sleeping with someone else — the betrayal is that he hasn't told her. That claim will be put to the test. Meanwhile, Valerie's own marriage is on uncertain ground. Her husband, John Knox (Geoffrey Rush), has been emotionally detached from her since the death of their daughter over a year ago. Valerie's means of dealing with the death was to write a book — a project John does not agree with. Also entering the story are Jane's estranged husband, Pete (Glenn Robbins), the O'Mays' next-door neighbors, Nik and Paula Daniels (Vince

Colosimo and Daniella Farinacci), and Michael (Rusell Dyskstra), a gay patient of Valerie's whom she believes may be having an affair with John. Then, one night, one of these characters vanishes, another one witnesses something, and several of the others become suspects.

Lantana argues that inertia may be the natural state of the human condition. Sometimes, only a tragedy of significant magnitude has the power to shake us out of our state of slumber, and, in some cases, even that may not be enough. Being alive and living are not the same. Through their characters, director Ray Lawrence and writer Andrew Bovell show that many humans, once happiness has evaporated, move through life in a stupor — people so easily embrace comfortable routines, giving up any hope of leading dynamic lives and instead becoming reactive. Ultimately, the achievement of sophomore director Lawrence is not what he has to add to the "whodunnit?" genre, but the observations he has to make about how people connect considering the emotional armor with which we gird ourselves. RECOMMENDED

The Last Seduction [1994]

Starring: Linda Fiorentino, Peter Berg, Bill Pullman Director: John Dahl Screenplay: Steve Barancik Running Time: 1:50 Rated: R (Sex, language, nudity, violence, mature themes) Theatrical Aspect Ratio: 1.85:1

Linda Fiorentino's Bridget Gregory does things to men that most of us wouldn't consider for what we scrape off the sidewalk. Using the word "bad" to describe her is as mammoth an understatement as calling the Sistine Chapel "nice" or the Grand Canyon "big." It has been decades since someone the likes of Bridget has graced the screen (Barbara Stanwyck in *Double Indemnity* comes to mind, although her language was never this colorful), and who knows how long it will be until our next opportunity?

Director John Dahl has fun with this material, filming the modern-day noir potboiler with such gusto that it's impossible not to fall under its spell, nor under the influence of its sultry, completely conscienceless leading lady. Dahl, the man behind the twisty Red Rock West, saturates this picture with atmosphere. Every time Bridget takes another pull on her cigarette, we're reminded of a time when 98% of new releases where in black-and-white.

Sap #1 is Bridget's husband, Clay (Bill Pullman). At her prompting, he gets involved in a drug deal that nets him $700,000. He thinks that he and his wife are going to use this to feather their nest egg, but Bridget

has other plans — why split what she can have all to herself? No sooner has Bill gone into the shower than she grabs the money and runs, heading for the small upstate New York town of Beston, where people always say "hello," "please," and "thank you," and no one locks their doors at night.

Sap #2 is Mike Swale (Peter Berg), a Beston native who thinks the town is too small for him — until Bridget arrives. To her, he's a means to an end, something to use up and throw away. To him, she's the love of his life, and he means to make her love him in return, regardless of the cost. *Big* mistake.

The Last Seduction's dialogue, scripted by Steve Barancik and spoken by the likes of Fiorentino, Pullman, Berg, and J.T. Walsh, is scintillating, often hilarious, and occasionally insightful. The best lines are about Bridget — "Anyone check you for a heartbeat lately?" and "I love you . . . I'm sure you feel the same way — I'm sure you love you, too" — or from her — "Spare me your brainless, countrified morality."

The Last Seduction is an entertaining motion picture to immerse oneself in — significant chunks of the plot fall apart on close examination, but it holds up well enough during the watching, and nothing can dispel the power of Fiorentino's performance. RECOMMENDED

Le Samourai [France/Italy, 1967]

Starring: Alain Delon, François Périer, Nathalie Delon Director: Jean-Pierre Melville Screenplay: Jean-Pierre Melville based on the novel *The Ronin* by Joan McLeod Running Time: 1:45 Rated: Not Rated (Violence, mature themes) Theatrical Aspect Ratio: 1.66:1 In French with subtitles

Le Samourai is close to perfection. It combines stylish direction, an intelligent script, first-rate performances, and overpowering atmosphere into one of the most tense and absorbing thrillers ever to reach the screen. In trying to identify a film with a similar impact, I'm left grasping at thin air — nothing quite like it exists in the annals of motion picture history, even when considering the work of Alfred Hitchcock.

Le Samourai is developed like a chess game between two equally-intelligent, determined opponents. One, Jeff Costello (Alain Delon), is an expert hit-man whose deeds are untraceable and whose alibis are unbreakable. The other is a police superintendent (Francois Perier) who is sure that Costello is responsible for a recent murder. He believes that, with dogged persistence, he can catch someone in a lie or uncover some discrepancy in his suspect's story. As the movie progresses and an apparent checkmate draws closer, the level of tension in *Le Samourai* reaches an almost unbearable level. One standout sequence has Costello attempting to evade an intricate trap that the superintendant has set for him in the Paris Metro.

Le Samourai opens with a quote from *The Book of Bushido* (a fictional creation of writer/director Melville): "There is no solitude greater than a samurai's, unless perhaps it is that of a tiger in the jungle." The film then proceeds to illustrate how this truth applies to the protagonist. Alain Delon's performance is subtle and mesmerizing. His expression never changes, but his eyes, his bearing, and the occasional trickle of sweat speak volumes. Delon has an undeniable screen presence — when the camera focuses on him, we cannot help but look.

If you're a fan of film noir in particular or thrillers in general, you owe it to yourself to seek out a copy of *Le Samourai*. Despite its absence on many critics' "best of" lists, this motion picture deserves a place at the pinnacle of the genre. It's difficult to imagine a much more accomplished film. **MUST SEE**

The Limey [1999]
Starring: **Terence Stamp, Peter Fonda, Lesley Ann Warren**
Director: **Steven Soderbergh** Screenplay: **Lem Dobbs** Running
Time: **1:30** Rated: **R** (Violence, profanity) Theatrical Aspect Ratio: **1.85:1**

Terence Stamp is *The Limey*, and *The Limey* is Terence Stamp. Forget about everything else in this film — the supporting cast, which features Lesley Ann Warren, Luis Guzman, and Peter Fonda, Steven Soderbergh's lively direction, and even Lem Dobbs' screenplay. Without Stamp's bravura performance, there is no movie. With it, even the thinnest premise ignites the screen with white-hot passion and energy. Stamp has done some wonderful work in a long and varied career. This is not his best film, but it may be the most forceful acting he has ever accomplished.

The movie is a visceral thriller — a stylish take on the revenge picture. Call it the art film version of *Death Wish*. There really isn't anything deeper or more meaningful going on here. However, done right, as it is here, this kind of film can be immensely entertaining and satisfying. When Stamp's Wilson finds out that his daughter, Jenny, has been killed by American drug dealers, he crosses the Atlantic and goes on a one-man killing spree, knocking off one target after another as he gets close to the bulls-eye: Jenny's lover, pop music producer Terry Valentine (Peter Fonda, playing the sleazy part with relish). *The Limey* possesses several traits that allow it to

work better than the average revenge thriller. The first in Stamp's performance, which blazes with intensity and energy. The actor's work here isn't just scene-stealing, it's movie-stealing. The second is Soderbergh's style, which includes flashbacks and flashforwards, with dialogue from one scene often bleeding into its successor. The third is the brilliant, snappy dialogue which often sounds scripted, but is delightful nevertheless. And the fourth is the sense of macabre, offbeat humor that suffuses the picture, reminding us not to take anything that transpires too seriously.

The film moves. It has color, energy, life, and pizzazz — all three in abundance. And, above all, it has Stamp. If *The Limey* had been a little less well-made, I'd call it a guilty pleasure. But, because it has been crafted with a great deal of attention and care, I'll drop the "guilty" and simply call it a "pleasure." **RECOMMENDED**

Lock, Stock and Two Smoking Barrels
[United Kingdom, 1998]
Starring: **Jason Flemyng, Dexter Fletcher, Nick Moran, Jason Statham**
Director: **Guy Ritchie** Screenplay: **Guy Ritchie** Running Time: **1:43**
Rated: **R** (Violence, profanity, drugs, brief nudity) Theatrical Aspect Ratio: **1.85:1**

Surface likenesses aside, *Lock, Stock, and Two Smoking Barrels* is actually a kinder, gentler motion picture than *Pulp Fiction*. While there's as much violence, Ritchie's method is different. All of the most vicious acts occur off screen. We see the ramifications, but we miss the genuine brutality. This effectively distances the viewer from the bloodshed, allowing us to see the proceedings in an almost cartoon-like light. It's easier to laugh when the baggage of excessive, graphic violence is taken out of the equation. *Lock, Stock, and Two Smoking Barrels* contains gore, but its presentation is neither gut-wrenching nor intense.

If the criminal ranks in London are comprised of losers like this, it's a wonder that anyone gets away with anything. Eddy (Nick Moran), Tom (Jason Flemyng), Soap (Dexter Fletcher), and Bacon (Jason Statham) are a quartet of con-artists and thieves who have scraped together enough money to enter a high-stakes poker game run by the ominously-named Hatchet Harry Lonsdale (P.H. Moriarty). Eddy is an expert poker player who, because of his ability to read people's reactions, almost never loses in an honest match. But Harry doesn't believe in playing fair. With the help of his nasty assistant, Barry the Baptist (the late Lenny McLean), Harry has fixed the game. When Eddy loses a huge round, he finds himself half a million pounds in debt, with only 7 days for him and his friends to get the money. So they turn to the only possible solution: stealing from their criminal neighbors, who are led by a tough guy named Dog (Frank Harper). Dog and his crew are about to rob a group of marijuana growers who work for a local drug baron (Vas Blackwood). Also thrown into the mix are a couple of cowardly and incompetent thieves, a deadpan hitman (soccer star Vinnie Jones) and his equally deadpan son (Peter McNicholl), Eddy's irate father (Sting), a perpetually stoned girl (Suzy Ratner), and an unfortunate cop.

Ritchie's style is direct and accomplished. *Lock, Stock, and Two Smoking Barrels* keeps moving; it's kinetic, in-your-face filmmaking. This may be the first movie to capture the reckless exuberance of *Pulp Fiction* without seeming like a blatant rip-off. With memorable witticisms sprinkled throughout, the dialogue is at least as clever as the plot structure. *Lock, Stock, and Two Smoking Barrels* has plenty of laughs and a few surprises to offer to all but the most squeamish of viewers. It's a superior thriller made with the guts and gusto that too many recycled entries into the genre fail to exhibit. HIGHLY RECOMMENDED

The Man Who Wasn't There [2001]

Starring: Bob Thornton, Frances McDormand, James Gandolfini
Director: Joel Coen Screenplay: Joel & Ethan Coen Running Time: 1:57
Rated: R (Violence, profanity, sexual situations) Theatrical Aspect Ratio: 1.85:1

For dour Ed Crane (Billy Bob Thornton), the life of a hair-cutter is a thankless one, probably because, in his own words, "I worked in a barber's shop, but I never considered myself a barber." It's a few years after the second World War, and Ed finds his existence to be a joyless exercise in monotonous repetition. He goes to work every day, puts in his hours, then returns home to his philandering, alcoholic wife, Doris (Frances McDormand). Ed knows that his wife is having an affair with her boss, Big Dave Brewster (James Gandolfini), but it doesn't bother him much. He just has another smoke and scowls some more. In fact, he figures out a way he can use it to his advantage. When a sleazy salesman (Jon Polito) offers Ed the opportunity to be a silent partner in a business arrangement, Ed gets the cash by anonymously blackmailing Big Dave. "Unless you pay $10,000," the note sent by Ed reads, "Everyone will know what you have been up to." Big Dave pays, but that's only the beginning of a cycle of deceit that leads to murder, cover-ups, and a singular example of judicial irony.

The thing I appreciated the most about *The Man*

Who Wasn't There is the unhurried, sinuous manner in which the plot moves — it twists and turns without being obvious about its surprises, and doesn't rush to get there the way so many movies do. The pace is not so much slow as it is deliberate. The movie has a lot to offer, but only to those who are patient with it. How about, for example, oddball subplots involving an alien abduction and a *Lolita*-like attraction? The main narrative offers its share of unexpected moments, so, in true Hitchcock fashion, the viewer is never exactly sure what's going to happen next. Along the way, we are provided with a running voiceover narration by Ed that, for once, doesn't seem superfluous. Then there's the ending, which I won't talk about here except to say that it's deliciously ironic and entirely appropriate.

The Coen Brothers are known for making offbeat fare, from their brilliant debut, *Blood Simple*, to the off-the-wall comedy of *Raising Arizona*, to the snow-blinded strangeness of *Fargo*. Compared to those films, *The Man Who Wasn't There* is almost conventional. Those looking for the typical Coen outlandishness may be disappointed; on the other hand, those in search of a genuine Hitchcock homage will probably be pleased. *The Man Who Wasn't There* reminds us of how entertaining a thriller can be when it concentrates on storyline rather than the overused staples of car chases and shoot-outs. RECOMMENDED

Memento [2000]

Starring: Guy Pearce, Carrie-Anne Moss, Joe Pantoliano
Director: Christopher Nolan Screenplay: Christopher Nolan, based on a story by Jonathan Nolan Running Time: 1:53 Rated: R (Violence, profanity, drugs) Theatrical Aspect Ratio: 2.35:1

Memento stars Australian actor Guy Pearce as Leonard Shelby, a former insurance investigator and crime victim who is trying to find the man who raped and murdered his wife (Jorja Fox). His goal is simple — he wants revenge through execution. Nothing less will satisfy him. But there's a small matter that complicates Leonard's investigation. He has no short term memory. During the attack that ended his wife's life, Leonard suffered brain damage. Now, although his long-term memory is fine, he can't remember any recent events. He can meet the same person a hundred times and won't know their name or who they are. To combat his condition, Leonard relies upon a series of annotated Polaroid snapshots — not exactly the ideal tool by which to seek out a killer who even the police can't locate. Along the way, Leonard is aided (or perhaps hindered) by the ubiquitous Teddy (Joe

Pantoliano), who is always on hand to offer advice, and he becomes involved with the mysterious Natalie (Carrie-Ann Moss), whose motives may not be as straightforward as they initially appear to be.

Memento doesn't stop with a great premise. In fact, what really distinguishes this film is its brilliant, innovative structure. Nolan has elected to tell the story backwards. He starts at the end and finishes near the beginning. The main narrative is presented as a series of 3-to-8-minute segments, each of which ends where the previous one began. A second thread, which starts at an unspecified time in the past and moves forward to intersect with the main storyline, is used to buffer the "reverse" segments as well as to provide background information. (It also tells the important "Sammy Jankis" story, which becomes increasingly important the deeper we get into the film.) Although this approach might at first seem confusing, it doesn't take long to get used to it, and to understand how well it works with this material.

By presenting events in *Memento* backwards, Nolan allows us to get into the mindset of the main character. Like Leonard, we don't have a clear indication of what happened before the current segment of time. We know some things from the past, but not the recent past. Like him, we are presented with numerous cryptic clues, some of which may mean something other than what they initially appear to represent. And, although it might seem that an approach which reveals the story's conclusion in the first 5 minutes would lack tension, that's far from the case. *Memento* builds to a surprising yet completely logical finale, and there's plenty of suspense along the way to keep the viewer riveted. **MUST SEE**

The Minus Man [1999]

Starring: Owen Wilson, Brian Cox, Mercedes Ruehl, Janeane Garofalo
Director: Hampton Fancher Screenplay: Hampton Fancher, based on the novel by Lew McCreary Running Time: 1:50 Rated: R (Mature themes, drug use, profanity) Theatrical Aspect Ratio: 1.85:1

In most movies, serial killers are faceless villains or foils for the protagonist. In *The Minus Man*, Fancher (the *Bladerunner* scribe, making his directorial debut) attempts something different. His intention is not only for us to see things as Vann does, but for us to sympathize with the character. Murder is made to seem neat, painless, and almost insignificant; except for this minor personality quirk, Vann is a nice guy. There's something twisted and broken deep within him, but he is not evil incarnate.

Vann does not see himself as a killer; he's a mail-

man, or the lodger in a middle-aged couple's room for rent, or the would-be boyfriend of a co-worker. Murder is something he does when the compulsion takes him, but it does not define *who* he is. He views it with a chilling matter-of-factness. "I never make a plan," he confesses, "It just happens." Owen Wilson 's portrayal is effective because it's disarming. What is it that neighbors always say about a serial killer? "He seemed like such a nice, quiet young man." That's Vann. He's hard-working, courteous, considerate, and meticulous. Yet Wilson occasionally lets us glimpse a sinister undercurrent.

The film takes place in a rural Pacific Northwest town where Vann has settled for a while. He's living in a room rented out by Doug and Jane Derwin (Brian Cox and Mercedes Ruehl). The couple's marriage is on the rocks and they're looking for someone to fill the place of their daughter, who has disappeared (we never find out exactly what happened to her). Vann fits in nicely at the Derwin household, and Doug gets him a job at the post office. There, Vann is pursued by Ferrin (Janeane Garofalo), a shy mail sorter who is attracted to him but is nervous about revealing her feelings. However, even though Vann appears to be an upstanding citizen, he hides a dark secret. A rash of mysterious deaths and disappearances starts soon after arrives.

The Minus Man is not a comfortable motion picture to sit through. The lack of overt violence and gore deepens the sense of unease. Watching Vann's tale unfold, we should be gripped by revulsion; instead, there's a strange fascination. This movie may not invite emotional participation, but it gives its audience much to ponder. **RECOMMENDED**

The Mothman Prophesies [2002]

Starring: Richard Gere, Laura Linney, Debra Messing Director: Mark Pellington Screenplay: Richard Hatem, based on the book by John A. Keel Running Time: 1:59 Rated: PG-13 (Mature themes, brief sexuality, mild profanity) Theatrical Aspect Ratio: 2.35:1

Pre-destination versus free will — it's a metaphysical debate that has obsessed religious scholars and philosophers alike through the centuries. *The Mothman Prophesies* works best if you accept the former: that the future is as immutable as the past. Admittedly, that may sound like weighty material for a movie that toes the genre line between thriller and horror movie, but director Mark Pellington is aiming for a more elevated plane.

The film opens with John and Mary Klein (Richard Gere and Debra Messing) purchasing their dream house. For John, an ace reporter at the Washington Post, happiness has finally been achieved — but it's a fleeting thing. On the way home from house-hunting, the Kleins are involved in a car accident. Mary is injured, and, at the hospital, the doctors discover that she has a rare form of brain cancer. Within weeks, she has lost her battle, but, upon her death, she leaves behind a cryptic puzzle for her husband — drawings of a strange, moth-like creature and a question: "You didn't see it, did you?"

Two years later, John has come to terms with his grief, but he is still not interested in dating. He has immersed himself in his job, which takes him away from his Georgetown home to Richmond, Virginia to interview a would-be Presidential candidate. While driving in the wee hours of the morning, he loses his way and inexplicably arrives in the small town of Point Pleasant, West Virginia, more than 400 miles distant from where he expects to be. There, from a local cop, Connie Parker (Laura Linney), he learns that a number of strange things have been happening in town — people seeing apparitions and lights in the sky, hearing strange voices, and experiencing bleeding around the eyes and ears. As John investigates, he becomes convinced that what he first believed to be hallucinations may be warnings of an impending tragedy from the same moth-like being his wife sketched — a suspicion that is re-enforced in the wake of a conversation with a reclusive author named Alexander Leek (Alan Bates).

The Mothman Prophecies is more in the nature of a supernatural thriller than a traditional horror movie. Although the film features a creature of sorts, the "Mothman" is never clearly seen, nor are its nature or intentions explained. Pellington uses a lot of clever camera trickery to give the film a stylish feel. It's an approach that not only makes *The Mothman Prophecies* look interesting, but heightens the sense of tension — all without demanding clear shots of a hideous and deranged computer fabrication. RECOMMENDED

The Negotiator [1998]

Starring: Samuel L. Jackson, Kevin Spacey, John Spencer, David Morse Director: F. Gary Gray Screenplay: James DeMonaco & Kevin Fox Running Time: 2:20 Rated: R (Violence, profanity) Theatrical Aspect Ratio: 2.35:1

The Negotiator, director F. Gary Gray's entry into the summer box office sweepstakes, is what is often referred to as a "white knuckler" — a nearly-nonstop excursion into tension. Once the initial setup has

been accomplished and the film kicks into high gear, it grabs the viewer's attention and holds it for the rest of the running time. *The Negotiator* deserves a place among the best action/thrillers of the year. This is a *Dog Day Afternoon* for the '90s.

The film starts by introducing us to Danny Roman (Jackson), hostage negotiator extraordinaire. Roman has a deserved reputation for being the best, although he isn't without his detractors, such as Beck (David Morse), who thinks Roman takes too many chances. Then, one day, when Roman learns a little too much about a police conspiracy to steal money from the pension fund, he is set up for the murder of his partner. Internal Affairs honcho Inspector Niebaum (the late J.T. Walsh) goes after the unjustly accused cop with a vengeance, leading Roman to believe that he will be given no chance to clear his sullied name. Desperate, he takes 4 people (2 cops and 2 civilians) hostage, including Niebaum and an old friend (Ron Rifkin), on the twentieth floor of the Chicago Administration Building. His goal: to intimidate them into telling the truth. Soon, when the police arrive to defuse the situation, Roman is in familiar territory, but on the other side of the law. This time, he's the hostage-taker and another expert negotiator, Chris Sabian (Spacey), is trying to talk him down. Both Roman and Sabian are masters of the rules of engagement, and each recognizes that, for the Chicago police force to take Roman's threats seriously, he may have to kill one of his captives.

Any resemblance to the original *Die Hard* is not coincidental. And, like in the 1988 thriller, the approach of keeping the action confined to a small area works to heighten the tension. As was the case in *Die Hard*, the main character is a cop. He has a potential ally on the outside. The Feds are an ominous, interfering presence. And the protagonist proves to be smarter and more resourceful than his better-equipped, highly-trained opponents. There are enough significant differences to keep *The Negotiator* from seeming like a *Die Hard* clone (it is, for example, much more talky), but the most important similarity — the adrenaline rush generated by a well-made thriller — is impossible to miss. RECOMMENDED

Ocean's 11 [2001]

Starring: George Clooney, Brad Pitt, Julia Roberts Director: Steven Soderbergh Screenplay: Ted Griffin, based on the 1960 screenplay by Harry Brown and Charles Lederer Running Time: 1:58 Rated: PG-13 (Profanity, violence) Theatrical Aspect Ratio: 2.35:1

The good news is that the 2001 version of *Ocean's Eleven* represents one of the rarest of Hollywood rarities: a re-make that is actually better than the original. That's not to say that this motion picture is an unqualified success — one tends to expect a little more from a director of Steven Soderbergh's caliber. However, 2001's *Ocean's Eleven* moves along at an enjoyable clip and relies on more than the notoriety of its stars. The film is an entertaining but unambitious endeavor that combines traditional caper rhythms with comic riffs.

George Clooney, he of the great smile and unforced charm, plays Danny Ocean, a con-artist and thief who is planning his next job the day he gets out of a New Jersey prison on parole. For Danny, this is the big one: a 3-casino robbery that will net more than $150 million. Even dividing the total take by 11 (the number of participants), the payout per person is enormous. Danny's crew consists of right-hand man Rusty Ryan (Brad Pitt), inside man Frank Catton (Bernie Mac), British bad guy Bashir Tarr (Don Cheadle), pick-pocket Linus Caldwell (Matt Damon), veteran con man Saul Bloom (Carl Reiner), moneybags Reuben Tishkoff (Elliot Gould), dueling brothers Turk and Virgil Malloy (Scott Caan and Casey Affleck), electronics expert Livingston Dell (Eddie Jemison), and contortionist/gymnast Yen (Shaobo Qin). Their goal is to liberate the financial resources of the trio of Vegas casinos run by Terry Benedict (Andy Garcia) on the night of the Lennox Lewis-Wladimir Klitschko heavyweight battle. Since the money from the Bellagio, the Mirage, and the MGM Grand is all stored in the Bellagio's vault, only a single robbery is necessary. There are some obstacles — a "security system [that] rivals that of most nuclear missile silos," countless surveillance cameras, a secure elevator with multiple safeguards against unauthorized entry, armed guards, a vault door that may be impregnable, and Danny's ex-wife, Tess (Julia Roberts), who is currently Terry's girlfriend.

The movie provides an engaging 2 hours that develops in exactly the manner one would expect from this sort of production. The storyline, while certainly not a masterpiece of plotting, offers enough to keep audiences guessing and to inject a little tension into an otherwise harmless and lightweight enterprise. There are also sufficient moments of comedy to maintain an upbeat tone. The average viewer's appreciation of *Ocean's Eleven* will be influenced by expectations, and, in the case of older attendees, memories of the original. **RECOMMENDED**

One Hour Photo [2002]

Starring: Robin Williams, Connie Nielsen, Michael Vartan
Director: **Mark Romanek** Screenplay: Mark Romanek Running
Time: **1:35** Rated: R (Profanity, sexual situations, nudity) Theatrical
Aspect Ratio: **1.85:1**

One Hour Photo is an actor's triumph — a fitting destination for Robin Williams to reach after essaying increasingly darker and more dysfunctional characters in films like *Death to Smoochy* and *Insomnia*. Any lingering doubts about Williams' ability to play a role completely straight are erased by *One Hour Photo*. The film has its share of flaws, but none of them are related to the lead actor's powerful and haunting portrayal. Williams nails it.

Sy Parrish (Williams) is the "photo guy" at the local SavMart. When he goes home, he sits alone in a spartan room and watches television. His apartment is undecorated except for one wall, which is papered with hundreds of photographs — extra copies he has made over the years of snapshots brought to him by the Yorkin family — Will (Michael Vartan), Nina (Connie Nielsen), and their son, Jakob (Dylan Smith). Sy has been living vicariously through these people for more than half a decade. His precarious mental balance begins to shift when a series of events push him past the point of instability. First, his boss (Gary Cole) shows an increasing displeasure with Sy's work. Secondly, Sy's desire to enjoy more substantive contact with the Yorkins causes him to act irrationally — buying Jakob a toy, showing up at his soccer practice, and reading the same book as Nina. Sy, whose personality is the kind for which the word "postal" was coined, decides to take matters into his own hands.

For much of its running length, *One Hour Photo* is an effective portrait of a lonely, deranged human being and the increasingly frantic rhythms of his out-of-kilter existence. As far as the audience knows, Sy has no friends, no family, no past, and no future. He crosses the line from being harmless and pathetic to being dangerous when he can no longer differentiate between fantasy and reality. There comes a time when it is no longer enough for him to watch and imagine, when the role of distant voyeur no longer satisfies him. The move from passive to active participant is not only predictable but inevitable given the psychological profile put together by filmmaker Mark Romanek. Dark and unrepentant, this excursion into the epicenter of percolating mental instability is not easily dismissed or forgotten. RECOMMENDED

Open Your Eyes [Spain, 1997]

Starring: Eduardo Noriega, Penelope Cruz, Chete Lera, Fele Martinez, Gerard Barray, Najwa Nimri Director: Alejandro Amenabar
Screenplay: Alejandro Amenabar, Mateo Gil Running Time: 1:57
Rated: R (Violence, sex, nudity, profanity) Theatrical Aspect Ratio: 1.85:1 In Spanish with subtitles

Open Your Eyes touches on and passes through so many genres that it transcends categorization. At one moment, it's a melodrama. At another, it's a romance. Then film noir. Then a cautionary tale. Then a morality play. Then science fiction. Perhaps the most amazing thing is how ably and seamlessly Alejandro Amenabar blends so many diverse elements together.

Our guide through the labyrinth of *Open Your Eyes* is Cesar (Eduardo Noriega), a wealthy, self-centered, handsome dilettante who prides himself on never sleeping with the same woman twice. When his friend, Pelayo (Fele Martinez), makes the mistake of introducing Cesar to his current girlfriend, Sofia (Penelope Cruz), trouble begins brewing. Cesar, smitten by Sofia and perhaps in love for the first time in his life, sets out to lure her away from Pelayo. For her part, Sofia appears willing to succumb to Cesar's advances — until tragedy strikes. Nuria (Najwa Nimri), a woman with whom Cesar enjoyed a brief fling, becomes mad with jealousy when Cesar rejects her. While they are in a car together, Nuria accelerates to a reckless speed, then crashes the vehicle, killing herself and seriously injuring Cesar.

He lives, but at a price: his good looks are gone, marred beyond surgical repair. To avoid frightening those around him, Cesar must hide his features behind an emotionless mask. The next time he meets Sofia, she is cold and distant. However, after spending a night in a drunken stupor on the street, Cesar finds that things are looking up. Sofia, once again gentle and loving, re-enters his life. The doctors offer hope that a new technique might allow his face to be healed. But Cesar is starting to experience moments of blinding, irrational rage, and he rightly suspects that all is not as it seems.

So what's it all about? One could easily view *Open Your Eyes* as a study of dualities. Nightmares versus reality. Memories of the past versus actions in the present. Knowledge versus ignorance. Beauty versus ugliness. Madness versus sanity. All of these elements come into play as we try to piece together what's happening to Cesar. Fundamentally, *Open Your Eyes* is concerned with one issue: the vast gulf between perception and reality. When Cesar is handsome on the outside, he is rotten within. But, when the humiliation of losing his physical beauty changes him, circumstances are reversed. (Or are they?) Yet, even at that point, we have only begun to scratch the complexity of the issue, and Amenabar forces us to go much deeper. HIGHLY RECOMMENDED

The Opportunists [1999]

Starring: Christopher Walken, John Ortiz, Cyndi Lauper, Vera Farmiga
Director: Myles Connell Screenplay: Myles Connell Running Time: 1:30
Rated: R (Brief profanity, brief violence) Theatrical Aspect Ratio: 1.85:1

The Opportunists is a character study masquerading as a heist movie. Although the plot follows a clearly-defined path with little room for side trips or detours, the element that keeps viewers interested isn't the crime, but the presence of the central character, Vic (Christopher Walken). With his flawed-yet-noble personality, Vic is the kind of guy it's hard not to pull for — a former safe cracker who spent nearly a decade in jail and is now on the straight-and-narrow. *The Opportunists* presents Vic non-judgmentally, and doesn't cloud our impressions of him with melodramatic reactions from other characters. People react to him in a natural, low-key manner.

When the film opens, Vic is seen plying his new, honest trade: fixing cars. He is surrounded by people he loves, or at least feels a responsibility for: his girlfriend, Sally (Cyndi Lauper), who understands him; his adult daughter, Miriam (Vera Farmiga), who doesn't hold it against him that he was in prison for most of her formative years; and his aunt, whose space in a Catholic nursing home he pays for. But making ends meet is tough, and Vic is beginning to realize that "the regular citizen thing is not going too good." Enter cousin Michael Kelly (Peter McDonald) from Ireland, who has hooked up with a couple of local armored car security guards, Pat (Donal Logue) and Jesus (Jose Zuniga) Presenting a united front, the three of them come to Vic with a "can't miss" proposal involving a safe and a lot of loot. And Vic finds himself sorely tempted.

Writer/director Myles Connell, making his feature debut, orchestrates a leisurely pace and modulates the film's tone to incorporate humor, drama, and a little suspense. However, those expecting a twisty, convoluted caper movie in the tradition of *The Sting* will come home disappointed. *The Opportunists* employs a straightforward storyline in order to allow the characters — Vic in particular — to breathe. This understated approach works well on its own terms, and illustrates that a heist movie (even one featuring Christopher Walken) doesn't have to be in-your-face to be effective. **RECOMMENDED**

Out of Sight [1998]

Starring: George Clooney, Jennifer Lopez, Ving Rhames, Dennis Farina Director: **Steven Soderbergh** Screenplay: Scott Frank based on the novel by Elmore Leonard Running Time: 2:03 Rated: R (Violence, profanity, sexual themes) Theatrical Aspect Ratio: 1.85:1

Even without a solid script like the one turned in by Scott Frank (*Dead Again*), it would almost be worth the price of admission to see George Clooney and Jennifer Lopez together on screen. They are two of the most attractive and charismatic actors around, and, in addition to having tremendous screen presence, they're good at their craft. True to form, both are excellent in *Out of Sight,* and the constant sexual tension between them is electric.

Clooney plays Jack Foley, one of the most successful bank robbers of our time. By applying his smile, his charm, and his mind, he managed to make illegal withdrawals more than 200 times (never using a gun) before the FBI nabbed him. Now, after being broken out of jail with the help of his best friend, Buddy (Ving Rhames), he's on his way from Florida to Detroit for a big score — $5 million in uncut diamonds hidden in the home of Wall Street financier Richard Ripley (Albert Brooks), a former prison pal. But some unfinished business is trailing Jack. During his escape, he took a female federal marshal, Karen Sisco (Jennifer Lopez), hostage. Despite the circumstances, the spark between them was instantaneous and undeniable, and now Jack finds himself thinking of her constantly. For her part, even as she tracks him down, she dreams of what it might be like to have a tryst with him.

Everything in *Out of Sight* is smart — the dialogue, the characters, and the storyline. The film boasts some great scenes. In one, Jack and Karen are crammed together in the trunk of a car. His hand strokes her thigh as the two discuss Faye Dunaway movies: *Bonnie and Clyde, Network,* and *Three Days of the Condor*. In another, the two meet face-to-face in a bar and, for the first time, openly admit the attraction that has drawn them together across the long miles separating Florida from Michigan. The opening bank robbery is also masterfully presented, with Clooney oozing charisma as he asks the frightened teller, "Is this your first time being held up?"

Out of Sight contains enough to please just about anyone who enjoys an unpredictable, character-driven thriller. Despite a somewhat nonlinear structure that uses flashbacks to fill in story holes, the plot is not difficult for a thinking viewer to follow. Better still, it's compelling from start to finish. And, for the kind of movie that this is, you couldn't ask for a more appropriate closing scene. **HIGHLY RECOMMENDED**

Panic Room [2002]

Starring: Jodie Foster, Forest Whitaker, Dwight Yoakam, Jared Leto, Kristen Stewart Director: **David Fincher** Screenplay: David Koepp Running Time: 1:48 Rated: R (Violence, profanity) Theatrical Aspect Ratio: 2.35:1

Critics writing reviews of *Panic Room* will likely delve into the cliché bag and pull out some of these familiar phrases: pulse-pounding, edge-of-the-seat, white-knuckler, thrill-a-minute, etc. However trite those sayings might be, they are appropriate for the latest tautly paced and slickly executed motion picture from populist auteur David Fincher. The film's gamesmanship is superior: a cat-and-mouse affair that sometimes features the skill, moves, and counter-maneuvers of chess and, on other occasions, plays out like a game of chicken.

The premise is simple enough, and the kind of idea Hitchcock would have enjoyed toying with. Meg Altman (Jodie Foster) is recently divorced from her millionaire ex-husband, Stephan (Patrick Bauchau). Alone with her daughter, Sarah (Kristen Stewart), she moves into a large Brownstone in the Upper West Side of Manhattan. It's an amazing place, with spacious rooms, and elevator, and, most interestingly, a "panic room." Designed to keep out intruders, the small chamber is protected by steel-plated walls, ceiling, and floor, and a door that is close to impervious. The panic room has its own ventilation system, a telephone line that isn't connected to the house's main one, and a bank of video cameras that show virtually every corner of the brownstone.

On the night that Meg and Sarah move in, they find themselves locked in the panic room in an attempt to escape a trio of threatening men who break into their house. Burnham (Forest Whitaker), Junior (Jared Leto), and Raoul (Dwight Yoakam) have come to steal something specific. Unfortunately, what they want is locked in the panic room with Meg and her daughter. Thus begin the games as the robbers seek to smoke out the victims. And things become further complicated when Burnham, Junior, and Raoul realize that there truly is no such thing as honor amongst thieves.

Panic Room does what all the best suspense-based

thrillers accomplish: it keeps us on edge. It's not hard to become enveloped in the movie's spell. Fincher's style, which involves a restless, roaming camera, lots of shadows, and tension that builds to almost unbearable levels, pulls us in. Are there logical flaws? Undoubtedly, but they don't become apparent until long after the house lights have come back on. And the script rewards us with a rarity: protagonists and antagonists who are both smart. The resolution of *Panic Room* doesn't hinge on who makes the most stupid blunders, but on who outthinks the other. And there's a nice twist at the end. Unorthodox as it may be, it *feels* right. The suspense in *Panic Room* never ebbs, and that makes for a thoroughly entertaining — if somewhat exhausting — 108 minutes. **HIGHLY RECOMMENDED**

Payback [1999]

Starring: Mel Gibson, Maria Bello, Gregg Henry, James Coburn
Director: Brian Helgeland Screenplay: Terry Hayes and Brian Helgeland based on *The Hunter* by Richard Stark Running Time: 1:42 Rated: R (Violence, torture, profanity, b&d) Theatrical Aspect Ratio: 2.35:1

Directed by Brian Helgeland in his feature debut, *Payback* is a re-make of John Boorman's 1967 edge-of-the-seat movie, *Point Blank*. Both films are based on *The Hunter*, a novel by Donald E. Westlake. Porter (Mel Gibson) is a thief and a killer, which puts him in good company with the sadistic Val Resnick (Gregg Henry). Together, the pair, along with an assist from Porter's wife (Deborah Kara Unger), pulls off a $140,000 heist. But then Resnick turns greedy, shoots Porter twice, and takes all the dough. He makes a big mistake, however: not assuring that Porter is dead. Five months later, recovered from his wounds, Porter is out for revenge. With only one ally — his girlfriend, Rosie (Maria Bello) — he decides to destroy the powerful criminal organization of which Resnick is a member.

Casting Mel Gibson as Porter is an inspired choice. *Payback*'s protagonist is an inherently dislikable fellow — a vicious killer who rips out people's nose rings, leaves behind corpses to rot, and doesn't care how many people he has to wipe out to get what he wants. However, with the appealing Gibson in this role, our natural inclination is to root for Porter, which is necessary for the film to work. If we're not on Porter's side, *Payback* becomes a litany of pointless violence. Gibson does a credible job playing a surly tough guy who's a cross between Bogart and Pacino.

Payback is surprisingly stylish for an action-oriented thriller. Its look is pure film noir, with de-saturated colors emphasizing the grayness of the city streets and gloomy interiors. The voiceover narrative (which, thankfully, isn't overused) is straight out of a potboiler, as the tough guy recounts his misfortunes with lines like "Old habits die hard — if you don't kick them, they kick you." One can almost hear Bogart uttering those words. And, while there's quite a bit more graphic bloodshed and brutality here than in any of the late screen icon's vehicles, *Payback* is a worthy '90s successor to his kind of movie. **HIGHLY RECOMMENDED**

Place Vendôme [France, 1998]

Starring: Catherine Deneuve, Jean-Pierre Bacri, Emmanuelle Seigner, Jacques Dutronc Director: Nicole Garcia Screenplay: Jacques Fieschi, Nicole Garcia Running Time: 1:55 Rated: R (Profanity, sexual situations, brief nudity) Theatrical Aspect Ratio: 2.35:1 In French with subtitles

Place Vendôme, from actress-turned-director Nicole Garcia, is a character study masquerading as a thriller. Slow-moving and simmering with low-key tension, the film takes us behind the scenes of the diamond industry as it follows one woman's struggle to re-define herself. *Place Vendôme* has its share of mysteries, but none of them are revealed or resolved with the kind of narrative twists common to movies of this sort. Instead, everything unfolds unhurriedly, allowing the needs of the characters, not those of the plot, to determine what happens next.

Vincent Malivert (Bernard Fresson), a jeweler with a internationally-known shop on Paris' Place Vendôme, has accepted stolen goods and, as a result, tarnished his reputation. Unable to face the impending scandal, he kills himself, leaving his wife, Marianne (Catherine Deneuve) with 5 perfect stones and a business that is low on inventory and teetering on the edge of bankruptcy. Marianne, an alcoholic, gradually begins to piece her life together after her husband's death, returning to work and looking for a buyer for the stolen diamonds that are now in her possession. Shady characters gather around her like vultures around carrion, including Nathalie (Emmanuelle Seigner), a young employee of her husband's who was also his mistress; Jean-Pierre (Jean-Pierre Bacri), Nathalie's financially strapped ex-boyfriend who has made a deal with persons unknown; and Battistelli (Jacques Dutronc), a scam artist with a dubious past who is currently sharing Nathalie's bed. Everyone wants Marianne's diamonds for their own purposes, and, as it becomes widely known that she has them, the proverbial noose begins to tighten.

The characters in *Place Vendôme* are a world-weary lot, beaten down by suffering the consequences of a lifetime of double-crosses and betrayals. Nathalie is the exception — all of that is ahead of her. The film never tires of contrasting her with Marianne. What Nathalie is now — ambitious, energetic, and driven — Marianne once was, until she stepped falsely and ended up imprisoned in a loveless marriage that stunted her career and destroyed her self-esteem.

Place Vendôme is a beautifully filmed motion picture, brimming with atmosphere and stylish shots. Because Garcia has elected to distance the camera from the characters, we are able to regard the way in which they evolve without forming an emotional bond with them. This is not a film where we find ourselves empathizing with the heroine; instead, we are dispassionate voyeurs, observing her actions and unraveling clues about who she was, is, and will be. As in all thrillers, there are puzzles to solve and dangers to overcome, but the difference here is that it's the interaction of the characters, rather than the contortions of the plot, that hold our attention. RECOMMENDED

The Pledge [2001]

Starring: Jack Nicholson, Robin Wright Penn, Aaron Eckhart, Benicio Del Toro Director: Sean Penn Screenplay: Jerzy Kromolowski & Mary Olson-Kromolowski Running Time: 2:04 Rated: R (Violence, profanity) Theatrical Aspect Ratio: 2.35:1

The Pledge starts out like a generic police mystery, then gradually metamorphoses into something that is part character study and part psychological thriller. Beyond the opening sequences, Sean Penn refuses to allow his movie to be pigeonholed. On the surface, it's like many things we have seen before, but the rhythm and focus are different. In the end, we come away thinking that, while *The Pledge* may not be unique, it's far from what the setup leads us to believe lies ahead. As has often been his trademark both in front of and behind the camera, Penn is not afraid to traverse the road less taken.

On the day of his retirement, Reno Detective Jerry Black (Jack Nicholson) becomes involved in a particularly sordid murder investigation. An 8-year-old girl has been sexually assaulted and brutally murdered, and, when confronting the child's mother (Patricia Clarkson) with the terrible news, Jerry vows to find the killer. Soon, the police have a man in custody, but, even after the suspect's confession and subsequent suicide, Jerry isn't convinced. He thinks there's a serial killer at work — but his colleagues, believing the case

to be closed, put him out to pasture. He ends up buying a garage in an out-of-the-way Nevada town — a place where he can go fishing every day.

While there, Jerry befriends Lori (Robin Wright Penn) and her young daughter, Chrissy (Pauline Roberts). When Lori's ex-husband beats her up, Jerry opens his home as a safe haven to the pair, and they come to live with him. For a while, Jerry settles into a routine of domestic comfort — until ugly reminders of his final case begin to crop up. Soon, he is convinced that the killer is on the prowl again and that Chrissy, a dead ringer for the previous victims, is the next target. But is there really a danger, or is Jerry deluded? And, if the serial killer is real, how far will Jerry go to effect his capture? Finally, there's the question of Jerry's murky motives: is he acting to protect his "family" or because, as an ex-cop, he cannot let go of the case?

The Pledge is clever in the way that it gradually reveals things, but never gives us too much information at one time. The red herrings don't seem as cheap as they often do in murder mysteries, and Jerry is far from the infallible, all-knowing investigator. He's a flawed human being, and, only in the end do we understand the extent of that tragic character flaw. The conclusion of *The Pledge* will cause many viewers to walk out of the theaters grumbling, since there is no traditional closure. But the way in which things turn out seems right for the material and the manner in which Penn has chosen to present it. RECOMMENDED

Pulp Fiction [1994]

Starring: John Travolta, Samuel L. Jackson, Uma Thurman, Harvey Keitel Director: Quentin Tarantino Screenplay: Quentin Tarantino based on stories by Quentin Tarantino and Roger Avary Running Time: 2:29 Rated: R (Language, violence, mature themes) Theatrical Aspect Ratio: 2.35:1

This film is one wild ride. An anthology of 3 interconnected stories that take place in a modern-day Los Angeles tinted by echoes of Dashiell Hammett and Raymond Chandler, the movie impresses in every possible way. Writer/director Quentin Tarantino has merged film noir with the gangster tale and pulled them both into the '90s. *Pulp Fiction*'s 3 tales are structured to intersect and overlap at key points, even though they are not presented in chronological order. Tarantino arranges his initial scene to dovetail with his final one in a remarkable example of closure. Those confused by the structure will see everything clearly once the final line is spoken.

"Vincent Vega and Marsellus Wallace's Wife" is the

first story. It opens with Vincent (John Travolta) and Jules (Samuel L. Jackson) out on a hit for their boss, Marsellus (Ving Rhames). Along the way, Vincent confesses that he's uneasy about an upcoming job — taking out Marsellus' young wife Mia (Uma Thurman) while the main man is out of town. The source of the nervousness lies in a story circulating that Marsellus had a man thrown out a 4th story window for giving Mia a foot massage. One wrong step and Vincent could find himself in deep trouble.

"The Gold Watch" is about a boxer, Butch (Bruce Willis), who is handsomely paid by Marsellus to throw a fight. Only at the last moment does it become more profitable to renege on the deal. So, along with his French girlfriend, Fabienne (Maria de Medeiros), Butch goes on the run, hoping to live long enough to spend some of the fortune he has suddenly gained.

"The Bonnie Situation" ties together a few loose threads. It also introduces Harvey Keitel as a suave problem-solver named Wolf and Quentin Tarantino as Jim, a man worried that his wife will come home from work to find a dead body in a blood-spattered car in his garage. Sometimes, it appears, helping out Marsellus is not without its complications.

As was the case in *Reservoir Dogs,* Tarantino's crisp dialogue sparkles. The vulgarity-laced monologues and conversations ripple with humor and are ripe with points to ponder. Who else (except perhaps David Mamet) can make profanity sound so poetic? Relentless in its pace, *Pulp Fiction* is as exhausting as it is exhilarating. In between all the shootings, Mexican standoffs, and other violent confrontations exist opportunities to explore various facets of the human experience, including rebirth and redemption. With this film, every layer that you peel away leads to something deeper and richer. Tarantino makes pictures for movie-lovers, and *Pulp Fiction* is a near-masterpiece. **MUST SEE**

Rabbit-Proof Fence [Australia, 2002]

Starring: Everlyn Sampi, Tianna Sansbury, Laura Monaghan, David Gulpilil, Ningali Lawford, Kenneth Branagh Director: Phillip Noyce Screenplay: Christine Olsen, based on *Follow the Rabbit-Proof Fence* by Doris Pilkington Running Time: 1:34 Rated: PG (Mature themes) Theatrical Aspect Ratio: 2.35:1

In 1931 Australia, it is the official policy of the government, as determined by the Chief Protector of the Aborigine Populace, Mr. Neville (Kenneth Branagh), that all "half-caste" Aborigine children (the offspring of a white parent and an Aborigine parent) are to be taken from their families and raised in orphanages

where they can be civilized with the intention of marrying them to a white person or grooming them to be a domestic servant. To Neville and those like him, this policy — separating a child from his or her family — does not seem cruel or inhuman. On the contrary, Neville states (and believes) that "in spite of himself, the native must be helped."

In the small village of Jigalong, 3 half-caste children — sisters Molly (Everlyn Sampi), who is 14 years old, and Daisy (Tianna Sansbury), who is 8, and their cousin, 10-year old Gracie (Laura Monaghan) — are taken from their mothers to live in the orphanage at Moore River, more than 1,200 miles away from their home. There, they will learn the path of "duty, service, and responsibility" that every good Christian woman should adhere to. Except that Molly, Daisy, and Gracie are not like the other girls at Moore River, and, when an opportunity presents itself, they escape. Pursued by an Aborigine tracker, Moodoo (David Gulpilil), and facing a seemingly impossible trek, they nevertheless press on, finding the rabbit-proof fence that stretches north-south across nearly all of the Australian continent and following it as a means to return to Jigalong.

Although the social injustice that led to Australia's "Stolen Generations" is very much in the forefront of *Rabbit-Proof Fence,* we are drawn into the cinematic tapestry by the real and immediate plight of the children. They are our guides through this political nightmare. *Rabbit-Proof Fence* eventually becomes a kind of road picture, with the girls making their way north and meeting all sorts of people along the way — some who help, some who hinder. There's also an element of danger, with Moodoo doggedly in pursuit and the police closing in. But Molly is smart, often outthinking or outguessing everyone, and occasionally aided by a bit of blind chance.

There is a great deal of craft evident in the way *Rabbit-Proof Fence* was put together. Under the hands of some directors, a film like this could easily turn into a travelogue; as developed by Phillip Noyce, it is an exploration of the heart and soul. And, at an economical 94 minutes, *Rabbit-Proof Fence* trims all the fat and tells its heartfelt and stirring story. **HIGHLY RECOMMENDED**

The Rainmaker [1997]

Starring: Matt Damon, Claire Danes, Danny DeVito, Jon Voight Director: Francis Ford Coppola Screenplay: Francis Ford Coppola based on the novel by John Grisham Running Time: 2:20 Rated: PG-13 (Mature themes, mild profanity, violence) Theatrical Aspect Ratio: 2.35:1

In order to make an appealing movie with a lawyer as the protagonist, it's necessary to come up with a villain who can make even an attorney look good. In this case, John Grisham has found one — a big-time, sleazy insurance company. Of course, it doesn't hurt that the main character in *The Rainmaker* has his heart in the right place. Sure, Rudy Baylor (Matt Damon) may be an ambulance-chaser, but that's only an unfortunate fact of life. He's one of the few who doesn't allow the realities of practicing law to corrupt his sense of ethics.

Rudy went to law school because he believed all the myths about helping people. But, because his family had no high-placed connections, graduation found him waiting tables to pay off his student loans, rather than going to work for a prestigious firm. Eventually, Rudy hooks up with the Memphis-based ambulance-chasing outfit of Bruiser Stone (Mickey Roarke), where he's partnered with Deck Shiffler (Danny DeVito), a "para-lawyer" who knows the ropes but has failed the bar exam 6 times. Rudy is sent to the local hospital to search for new clients. What he finds instead is a young woman, Kelly Riker (Claire Danes), who has been severely beaten by her husband. The attraction between Rudy and Kelly is immediate and obvious, but she's afraid to file for divorce for fear that her husband will kill her. Pretty soon, Rudy and Deck feel the heat as a Federal probe closes in on Bruiser, so, together with only about $10,000 between them, they open up their own office.

Meanwhile, Rudy is working on his first big case: suing an insurance company for failing to make good on a claim owed to his client, a leukemia patient, Donnie Ray Black (Johnny Whitworth). When the inevitable happens and Donnie Ray dies, it becomes a wrongful death suit, with Rudy representing Donnie Ray's mother, Dot (Mary Kay Place), against a host of high-priced suits led by Leo F. Drummond (Jon Voight). But the judge, Tyrone Kipler (Danny Glover), is a fair man, and allows Rudy some latitude in presenting his case.

The Rainmaker keeps the in-trial showmanship to a minimum. While it's virtually impossible to film a courtroom drama where there aren't at least a few tricks and unexpected legal maneuvers, *The Rainmaker* does a good job of downplaying these so that they're never too difficult to swallow. Unlike many of the other films based on a Grisham book, this one is interested in telling a story rather than ambushing the audience with cheap contrivances. **RECOMMENDED**

Ransom [1996]

Starring: Mel Gibson, Renee Russo, Gary Sinese Director: Ron Howard
Screenplay: Richard Price and Alexander Ignon Running Time: 2:01
Rated: R (Violence, profanity) Theatrical Aspect Ratio: 1.85:1

It's pretty unfair to damn *Ransom* by saying that it doesn't live up to Hitchcock's standards — how many movies do, after all? *Ransom* isn't a bad thriller, it's just not a great one. There's a little too much pointless running around, a subplot that leads nowhere, and a certain creeping predictability that argues for a shorter running length. On the other hand, strong acting, smart dialogue, and a couple of neat twists counterbalance many of *Ransom*'s weaknesses.

The script, which is based on a 1956 movie of the same name, has been re-worked by novelist Richard Price to bring it up to date. Mel Gibson is Tom Mullen, the CEO of Endeavor Airlines, the world's fourth largest carrier. He's a devoted family man, paying more than lip service to his love for his wife, Kate (Renee Russo), and son, Sean (Brawley Nolte, son of Nick). One day, at a New York City school science fair, Sean is kidnapped by a gang of 4 (Lili Taylor, Liev Schreiber, Evan Handler, and Donnie Wahlberg). Handcuffed and blindfolded, the boy is held in a small, windowless room. From this hideout, the group's ringleader, corrupt cop Jimmy Shaker (Gary Sinese), makes his $2 million ransom demand. Tom calls in the FBI. The agent in charge of the investigation, Hawkins (Delroy Lindo), advises paying the ransom. At first, Tom agrees, but, as time passes and the situation becomes more desperate, he begins to believe that Sean is already dead. Finally, no longer trusting the cops and worried that he's being played for a fool, he makes a stunning decision.

Since there's no way Sean is going to be killed (or a Disney-owned company never would have released the movie), the most compelling questions relate to how he will be recovered and whether anyone will die attempting to save him. Howard wrings a surprising amount of tension out of this cat-and-mouse material. There are times when *Ransom* is genuinely gripping, most notably during the scenes in and around Tom's fateful decision. We can also be thankful that Howard spares us a lame whodunit. We know the kidnappers' identities from the beginning, and this eliminates the necessity of peppering the plot with distracting red herrings. The ending could have been steeped in unexpected irony, but the script opts instead for a conventional resolution. **RECOMMENDED**

Read My Lips [France, 2001]

Starring: Vincent Cassel, Emmanuelle Devos Director: Jacques Audiard Screenplay: Jacques Audiard, Tonino Benacquista Running Time: 1:55 Rated: Not Rated (Violence, mature themes, sexual situations) Theatrical Aspect Ratio: 1.85:1 In French with subtitles

Read My Lips, the 4th feature from director Jacques Audiard, contains elements of a romantic thriller, but is equally powerful as a drama. The two main characters are effectively developed and fully realized. In fact, it's the protagonists — in particular, the interaction between them — that drives this motion picture forward and keeps us involved. However, unlike in many character studies, the plot is more than just a simple framework. It is complex and unpredictable, and, as a result, provides the perfect means to better get to know the characters and understand the shifting nature of their relationship.

Carla (Emmanuelle Devos) is a hearing-impaired 35-year-old woman who works as a secretary in a property development company. Her life is ruled by routine — she never goes out and is always available to babysit for her friends. She longs to move forward both in her career and in her personal life, but, encumbered by her hearing deficiency, she is unsure how to do so. One day, when her bosses decide she needs an assistant, she takes on an unskilled but charismatic 25-year-old man, Paul (Vincent Cassel). Paul is an ex-con, fresh out of jail, with no place to live. Carla is immediately attracted to Paul, and he recognizes this, and decides to manipulate the attraction for his own purposes. In return for helping her with her career goals, Paul persuades Carla to use her lip-reading abilities to aid him in casing out an apartment he intends to rob.

Audiard does a remarkable job of interweaving forceful drama with thriller elements. To bring us more into Carla's world, Audiard occasionally gives us her point-of-view, not only visually but audibly. As Carla removes her bulky hearing aid, the film's audio drops off into near-muteness, giving us a sense of what it is like to be in her position. This, like many other details employed by the director, builds strong character sympathy. HIGHLY RECOMMENDED

Reservoir Dogs [1992]

Starring: Harvey Keitel, Michael Madsen, Steve Buscemi, Tim Roth Director: Quentin Tarantino Screenplay: Quentin Tarantino Running Time: 1:36 Rated: R (Extreme violence and gore, excessive profanity) Theatrical Aspect Ratio: 2.35:1

Reservoir Dogs grabs you by the throat and digs its claws in deep. From the moment that the unwitting viewer tumbles into the realm of Lawrence Tierney's gang of 8, they are hopelessly trapped there until the final credits roll. As the first outing for actor/director/writer Quentin Tarantino, this is a triumph, displaying all the marks of a longtime virtuoso of the genre.

A jewelry store robbery has gone wrong — badly wrong — for the thieves. One member of the gang is dead, and several are missing. The survivors, including Mr. White (Harvey Keitel), Mr. Pink (Steve Buscemi), and a critically-injured Mr. Orange (Tim Roth), are holed up in a warehouse, trying to figure out how to salvage the situation. Dissention and suspicion run high, as White and Pink discuss the possibility of a traitor in their midst, and the tension escalates when Mr. Blonde (Michael Madsen) shows up with a little surprise in the trunk of his car.

The cast is first-rate, and the parts the actors have to play are fully fleshed out. Tarantino invests each member of his group with a unique and multi-faceted personality. Not content with stereotypes, the writer/director digs deeper, bringing out the humanity in even someone as viciously sadistic and reprehensible as Mr. Blonde. To go along with the characters is a surprising plot, filled with wonderful little twists and turns, and pervaded throughout by the sense of not knowing what's around the corner. The non-chronological manner in which the story is told is confusing at first, but everything eventually sorts itself out.

Tarantino's directing influences, from John Woo to Martin Scorsese, are all in evidence, and their synthesis creates a high-voltage style that's entirely his own. The writing is crisp and clean, providing line after line of snappy dialogue designed to leave the viewer alternately pondering and laughing aloud. The gallows humor and dark comedy are among many of *Reservoir Dogs'* defining elements. This is one of those rare motion pictures that's both intelligent and visceral at the same time. MUST SEE

Return to Paradise [1998]

Starring: Vince Vaughn, David Conrad, Joaquin Phoenix, Anne Heche Director: Joseph Ruben Screenplay: Wesley Strick Running Time: 1:50 Rated: R (Violence, profanity, sexual situations) Theatrical Aspect Ratio: 2.35:1

Consider this situation: what if, by surrendering yourself to foreign authorities and agreeing to spend 3 years in a prison hellhole, you could save the life of a friend? That admittedly fascinating dilemma lies at the heart of Joseph Ruben's new morality play, *Return to Paradise*, a U.S. remake of the 1989 French feature, *Force Majeure*. And, while there are times when this movie gets bogged down in melodramatic clichés, it nevertheless represents an intriguing exploration of conscience, friendship, and sacrifice.

Return to Paradise opens during the mid-'90s in Malaysia, where 3 friends, Sheriff (Vince Vaughn), Tony (David Conrad), and Lewis (Joaquin Phoenix), are spending a 5-week vacation sampling the pleasures of "God's own bathtub": rum, drugs, and girls. At the end of their stay, Sheriff and Tony head back to New York, but Lewis, a Greenpeace activist, decides to stay behind to participate in a "Rescue the Orangutan" project. As a result, Lewis is there alone when a police raid uncovers a brick of hash that sends him to jail with a death sentence hanging over his neck.

Two years in the future, a young, persistent lawyer, Beth Eastern (Anne Heche), tracks down Sheriff and Tony to apprise them of the situation. Lewis is a week away from the hangman's noose, and the only thing that will save him is if his two accomplices agree to return with her to Malaysia, turn themselves in, and spend a term in prison. If one of them goes, it's 6 years. If both of them go, it's three apiece. If they refuse, Lewis dies. The dilemma for both men, who have established lives in New York City, is clear.

Thankfully, *Return to Paradise* does not cheat the audience when it comes to examining all of the ramifications, both pro and con, of making the crucial decision. It would have been easy for director Joseph Ruben and screenwriter Wesley Strick to simply use this conundrum as a plot device. But, while there are complications, Sheriff and Tony's decision (and the agonizing process of making it) remains at the forefront. Therein lies *Return to Paradise*'s strength, and the filmmakers recognize this. The film's ending is a little unanticipated, and, although there are a few too many surprise revelations in the last 20 minutes, they all work reasonably well to enhance, rather than diminish, the central theme. Ultimately, although *Return to Paradise* can be regarded as a suspense film (will they or won't they go back?), it is as effective when viewed as a drama. **RECOMMENDED**

Road to Perdition [2002]
Starring: Tom Hanks, Tyler Hoechlin, Paul Newman, Jude Law
Director: Sam Mendes Screenplay: David Self, based on the graphic novel by Max Allan Collins and Richard Piers Rayner Running Time: 2:00 Rated: R (Violence, profanity) Theatrical Aspect Ratio: 2.35:1

Over the course of more than 4 dozen TV shows and movies, Tom Hanks has yet to challenge himself with the most difficult role for a well-liked actor — that of a bad-to-the-bone villain. He comes close in *Road to Perdition*, but doesn't quite reach that destination. For, although Michael Sullivan is a murderer for hire, he also has a conscience and a soul, loves his family, and kills not because he likes it but because it's his job. In short, Sullivan is portrayed sympathetically. The film, director Sam Mendes' eagerly anticipated follow-up to *American Beauty*, is based on the graphic novel by Max Allan Collins and Richard Piers Rayner. As with many adaptations from this medium, *Road to Perdition* stuns with its atmosphere and visuals, but arguably underachieves in some aspects of its characterization and plotting.

The setting is 1931 in Al Capone's Chicago. (Capone doesn't appear in the final cut of *Road to Perdition*, although Anthony LaPaglia apparently plays him on the cutting room floor. Capone's right-hand man, Frank Nitti — the guy who ended up in the car in *The Untouchables* — is portrayed by Stanley Tucci.) Michael Sullivan is the number one hit man of suburban boss John Rooney (Paul Newman), who has treated Sullivan as a son since he took in the orphaned boy. In fact, Sullivan's filial relationship with Rooney is so close that the gangster's natural-born son, Connor (Daniel Craig), simmers with jealousy. One night, while Sullivan is on a job, Connor kills the other man's wife (Jennifer Jason Leigh) and youngest son. Only the older boy, Michael Jr. (Tyler Hoechlin), survives. Father and son go on the road, searching for revenge, closure, and a way to start anew. But Rooney, recognizing that Sullivan will not stop until Connor is dead, ruefully hires another hit man, Maguire (Jude Law), to eliminate Sullivan (but not "the boy").

Road to Perdition allows you to feel, smell, and breathe the air of 1930s Chicago. To some extent, cinematographer Conrad L. Hall is as big a star as any of the actors, since there are occasions when the setting overwhelms the characters. At its heart, *Road to Perdition* is a little drama about fathers, sons, and the covenants they make and break. Mendes illustrates how accomplished actors will respond to an assured director. Serious movie-goers embarking upon this journey will find that *Road to Perdition* leads to a satisfying destination. **RECOMMENDED**

Ronin [1998]
Starring: Robert De Niro, Jean Reno, Natascha McElhone, Stellan Skarsgård Director: John Frankenheimer Screenplay: J.D. Zeik and Richard Weisz Running Time: 2:01 Rated: R (Violence, profanity) Theatrical Aspect Ratio: 2.35:1

Personality-wise, the mercenaries in *Ronin* fit somewhere between the Magnificent Seven and the Dirty

Dozen. There are, however, only 5 of them. The most visible, and the one with the best instincts, is Sam (Robert De Niro), an ex-CIA operative who needs the money a job like this offers. Sam is joined by a Frenchman, Vincent (Jean Reno); an ex-KGB computer expert named Gregor (Stellan Skarsgård); a nervous weapons expert, Spence (Sean Bean); and an experienced driver, Larry (Skipp Sudduth). They are being paid by Deirdre (Natascha McElhone), an icy Irishwoman who is as close-mouthed about the specifics of their job as she is about Seamus (Jonathan Pryce), the man who pulls her strings. All that Sam's team knows is that they are to steal a mysterious case from its current owners before its contents are sold to a group of high-bidding Russians. However, what appears to be a straightforward ambush-and-assault operation turns ugly when betrayal and duplicity are stirred into the mix.

Despite a complex script (or perhaps because of it), there is a formula to the way *Ronin* progresses: every plot twist is accompanied by a car chase and a shoot out. So, because the storyline develops in a serpentine fashion, not only are a lot of bullets used (and, upon occasion, the artillery is a little heavier than a handgun), but there are at least 4 lengthy car chases that employ *The French Connection*'s point-of-view approach. However, while the chases are all tautly filmed, attention grabbing, and logistically complicated (especially one that features a high-speed race through a tunnel and onto an expressway *against* 4 lanes of heavy traffic), that may be one car chase too many for any movie.

Unlike many thrillers of this sort, which devolve into a series of mindless action sequences, *Ronin* manages to remain focused on the plot and the characters, even while staging increasingly complicated pyrotechnic set pieces and offering its share of white-knuckle moments. The film is consistently exciting, if a little overlong, and never fails to keep us guessing. *Ronin* also snubs a few conventions of the genre. For example, when a character departs before the midpoint, he does not suddenly re-appear later in the movie to either (a) cause trouble, (b) take revenge, or (c) save the day. That's certainly not the only reason to see this picture, but it's one of several small pleasures that, when they're all combined, make *Ronin* a significant cut above the average thriller. HIGHLY RECOMMENDED

Rounders [1998]

Starring: Matt Damon, Edward Norton, Gretchen Mol, Martin Landau
Director: John Dahl Screenplay: David Levien & Brian Koppelman
Running Time: 1:58 Rated: R (Profanity, violence) Theatrical Aspect
Ratio: 1.85:1

The director of *Rounders* is John Dahl, who is best known for two splendidly entertaining thrillers (*Red Rock West, The Last Seduction*) that had cable TV premieres before their theatrical runs, depriving everyone involved of a shot at Oscar consideration. Although Dahl loves twisty, intricate plots that focus as much on plot convolutions as on characters, *Rounders* is something of a departure. While there are a few surprises, the storyline is basically a straightforward sports comeback scenario, with the game in question being poker and the "athlete" being a player who suffers a debilitating loss. *Rounders* is character-centered, but it does not follow the serpentine trail used by Dahl's other films.

The story opens in New York City, where our narrator, law student and poker player Mike McDermott (Matt Damon), loses his life savings in a big game with a Russian mobster known as KGB (John Malkovich). The next time we see Mike is nine months later, and he has given up cards to appease his girlfriend (Gretchen Mol). But he still has the bug, and when an old friend of his, Worm (Edward Norton), is released from prison, he is lured into the lifestyle again. Soon, he and Worm are up to their old tricks, taking money from unsuspecting marks. But Worm owes a huge debt to KGB, and, when Mike makes the mistake of vouching for him, he finds that his life is on the line as well. Now, he has 2 days to make $15,000, or he can forget about finishing law school and living happily ever after.

Although *Rounders* offers interesting characters and a compelling plot, the most fascinating aspect of the movie is its exploration of the theory of gambling. This is one of those rare instances when the voiceover doesn't seem unnecessary or intrusive, because it's through Damon's narration that we learn the ins and outs of being successful at cards. Ultimately, *Rounders* doesn't try to do anything spectacular. It's a solidly enjoyable motion picture that follows a traditional trajectory. We've seen this kind of story with boxers, baseball players, ice skaters, etc. Now it's time for the cardsharks to get their turn. However, although the storyline is predictable, the intelligent dialogue and top-drawer acting more than make up for the possible deficiency. RECOMMENDED

Run Lola Run [Germany, 1998]

Starring: Franka Potente, Moritz Bleibtreu Director: Tom Tykwer
Screenplay: Tom Tykwer Running Time: **1:21** Rated: R (Sex, violence,
profanity) Theatrical Aspect Ratio: **1.85:1** In German with subtitles

Run Lola Run is a must-see for anyone who enjoys a fast-paced, innovative motion picture that refuses to be defined by norms of the genre. Directed by Tom Tykwer, this German import is a kinetic meditation on fate and destiny. It tells the story of Lola (Franka Potente, an actress with true screen presence), a '90s girl with Raggedy Ann hair, a large tattoo, and a voice so penetrating that when she screams, she can shatter glass. She's also athletic, because, as one might expect from the title, Lola spends most of the movie running.

Her dim-witted boyfriend, Manni (Moritz Bleibtreu), has lost 100,000 marks that he owes to the mob. Lola has 20 minutes to find that money and get it to Manni or he will be killed. So she takes to the streets, straining every resource to make the score before it's too late. Instead of just showing us one of Lola's approaches, however, Twyker gives us three to choose from, throwing us into an alley of alternate realities. You can essentially pick your own ending, each of which offers its share of irreverent surprises. Sandwiched in between the alternative storylines are soft-focus scenes of Lola and Manni reflecting on life and love. These sequences serve a dual purpose: to allow us to catch our breath and to deepen our sympathy for these two intensely likable characters.

Saturated with irony, the film moves at a blazing speed to the accompaniment of a relentless techno soundtrack; blink and you'll probably miss a thrown-in visual gag. Using an innovative mix of animation, still photography, slow motion, and normal cinematography, Twyker illustrates how the smallest change in what a person does can alter the rest of their life (not to mention the lives of others, including complete strangers they pass on the street). Critic Harlan Jacobson called this a "90-minute MTV video," but, while that statement captures the film's spirit, it greatly shortchanges *Run Lola Run,* which has as much depth as it has energy and action.

HIGHLY RECOMMENDED

Runaway Train [1985]

Starring: Jon Voight, Eric Roberts, Rebecca De Mornay
Director: Andrei Konchalovsky Screenplay: Djordje Milicevic, Paul
Zindel and Edward Bunker, based on a screenplay by Akira Kurosawa
Running Time: **1:51** Rated: R (Profanity, violence) Theatrical Aspect
Ratio: **1.85:1**

Long before Keanu Reeves was stuck on board a speeding bus, Jon Voight, Eric Roberts, and Rebecca De Mornay were trapped on a runaway train. Although *Speed* is a very good movie, *Runaway Train* is a more complete experience. The script is better-written, depending more on visceral thrills than those enhanced by special effects. The characters are better-rounded, and there is a fascinating exploration of man's primal instinct. *Runaway Train* belongs to a rare genre: the intelligent thriller. It will come as no surprise to educated movie-goers to learn that the script, credited to Djordeje Milicevic, Paul Zindel, and Edward Bunker, is based on an original screenplay devised by the Japenese master, Akira Kurosawa. One can almost imagine Kurosawa regular Toshiro Mifune in the role given to Jon Voight.

Not that Voight doesn't place his own indelible stamp on the part of Manny, a hardened criminal who is serving a life sentence in a maximum security prison in Alaska. Manny has recently spent three years locked in solitary confinement. Upon his release, he is hailed as a hero by the rest of the prison population. One of his most ardent fans is Buck (Eric Roberts), a dumb, garrulous, cocky rapist whose job pushing laundry carts becomes a critical element of Manny's escape plan. With Buck tagging along, Manny makes his way through the sewers under the prison, out into the cruel Alaskan wilderness, and to a remote train station. There, the two stowaway on a 4-engine train headed south, unaware that the engineer has died of a heart attack, and the only one else on board is Sara (Rebecca De Mornay), a female maintenance worker. The train is out of control and rushing down the tracks towards a collision with destiny.

When *Runaway Train* was produced, the action genre was undergoing a change from character-driven movies to pyrotechnics-based flicks. Of the thrillers developed after this one, only a select few — *Die Hard* and perhaps one or two others — have achieved this level of tautness without compromising the intelligence of the plot. Best of all, in more than a decade since its release, *Runaway Train* has aged exceptionally well. It is just as compelling today as it was during the winter of 1985-86. **HIGHLY RECOMMENDED**

The Salton Sea [2002]

Starring: Val Kilmer, Vincent D'Onofrio, Adam Goldberg, Luis Guzman
Director: D.J. Caruso Screenplay: Tony Gayton Running Time: **1:42**
Rated: R (Drug use, violence, sexual situations) Theatrical Aspect
Ratio: **1.85:1**

The Salton Sea is a thriller with an edge — which is to say that it doesn't follow the stale, standard, connect-the-dots storyline which has become commonplace in movies that explore the seamy underbelly of the criminal world. Some of the elements found here are familiar — strung-out punks, dangerous drug dealers, corrupt cops, cynical FBI agents, flash-forwards, and red herrings — but screenwriter Tony Gayton and director D.J. Caruso find interesting ways to employ them.

The movie opens with a fascinating account of the history of speed (meth) since World War II, then takes us into the world of Danny Parker (Val Kilmer), who resides in the "land of the perpetual night party." At first, Danny appears to be just another user. He and his buddies, Jimmy (Peter Sarsgaard) and Kujo (Adam Goldberg) seem to have nothing better to do than hang out, absorb the punk/goth scene, and do drugs. But there's more to Danny than meets the eye — much more. In the first place, his real name is Tom Van Allen, or at least that used to be his real name. He is haunted by memories of a beautiful wife, who may or may not be real. And Danny is a police informant for a pair of crooked cops — Morgan (Doug Hutchison) and Garcetti (Anthony LaPaglia). He's also trying to make one last big score from a dealer named Pooh Bear (Vincent D'Onofrio), so he can vanish into obscurity. Or is he? The pieces don't all quite fit, and director Caruso is keeping the last one tantalizingly out of reach until he's ready to finish the puzzle.

While the strength of *The Salton Sea* is its serpentine plot, the movie also has a nice noir look. Caruso goes a little overboard in applying a distinctive visual varnish to the product by employing a variety of camera tricks (including time lapse photography, fades, etc.), but he stays clear of the ego masturbation that is common with filmmakers like Oliver Stone. For the most part, Caruso's unconventional moments work. *The Salton Sea* is dark, as befits its grim subject matter, but not unreasonably so. And it has a sense of humor, although only those with a penchant for warped jokes will absorb Caruso's stabs at comic relief. This thriller seems conventional until you start paying attention — and that's when the payoff occurs.

RECOMMENDED

The Second Time [Italy/France, 1996]

Starring: Nanni Moretti, Valeria Bruni Tedeschi, Valeria Milillo
Director: Mimmo Calopresti Screenplay: Heidrun Schleef, Francesco

Bruni, Mimmo Calopresti Running Time: 1:20 Rated: Not Rated (Mature themes, profanity) Theatrical Aspect Ratio: 1.85:1 In Italian with subtitles

One day, a man sees a woman. Something about her strikes him as familiar and he begins to follow her. All day, he dogs her steps — to her cafeteria at work, on the bus going home, and finally, along the street leading to the prison from which she is set free by day to participate in a work release program. The man, a university professor named Alberto Sajevo, returns home. All evening, he thinks of the woman, and the next day he sets out to meet her. Their eyes lock and they have a polite conversation, but something isn't right. Neither of them offers their real name to the other — they go by assumed identities. There's a dynamic between these two that we don't understand — perhaps they don't, either. Where are things going? Why is Alberto following her? And what are his intentions?

The Second Time is one of those stories where there's no real beginning or end. The characters' lives have been going on for a long time before we first meet them, and they'll continue after the end credits have rolled. There are no obligatory flashbacks to show us important past events and no epilogue to hint at what the future might hold. The film doesn't have much of a sense of closure, but, when it's all over, we feel that we're "up to speed" and have witnessed an important event.

Much of the credit for the film's success has to go to co-writer/director Mimmo Calopresti, who knows exactly where he wants the narrative to go, and never loses control of it. If the pacing of the second half is a little uneven, that can be attributed to the escalation in tension resulting from confrontations. The first half, however, is perfectly paced. We are brought into the situation gradually, at first mildly intrigued by the characters, then burning with curiosity. The revelation, when it occurs, is a shock, but one that makes sense when examined in retrospect. Few movies today are put together this expertly. Not only does *The Second Time* address several important issues, but it does so within a framework designed to keep viewers on the edge of their seats. **HIGHLY RECOMMENDED**

Seven [1995]

Starring: Brad Pitt, Morgan Freeman, Gwyneth Paltrow Director: David Fincher Screenplay: Andrew Kevin Walker Running Time: 2:03 Rated: R (Gory crime scenes, violence, profanity) Theatrical Aspect Ratio: 2.35:1

Frequently, mystery/thrillers present us with a cast of about 6 or 7 characters, set up a sequence of grizzly murders, then "surprise" us by revealing which of those 6 or 7 characters is the guilty party. It's a time-honored method that's repeated in at least several movies each year. At the outset, *Seven* has all the hallmarks of this kind of motion picture. Fortunately, it turns out somewhat smarter and less predictable. Though not without flaws, *Seven* isn't transparent or moronic, and it doesn't insult the average viewer's intelligence.

The good guys are a pair of detectives at opposite ends of their careers. David Mills (Brad Pitt) is new on the job, full of energy and high ideals, and ready to "make a difference" by catching the crooks. William Somerset (Morgan Freeman) is in his last week on the job. His long years studying crime scenes and following up on clues have left him weary and jaded. To him, being a detective isn't about nabbing criminals — it's about methodically collecting and cataloguing evidence in case a prosecutor ever needs it.

The serial killer pursued by Mills and Somerset is choosing each of his victims based on which of the seven deadly sins (gluttony, greed, sloth, lust, pride, envy, wrath) they have most clearly violated. The deaths form a portion of a decidedly warped sermon. In their quest to end this bloody, sadistic spree, the two cops appear well-paired, as together they make the perfect detective. Mills is all brawn and little brain. Somerset, on the other hand, spends long hours in the library researching Dante and Chaucer, looking for clues that will enable him to prevent the next killing.

Seven is unnecessarily gory and runs for a little too long, but neither of these elements detracts much from the film's enjoyability (unless you have a weak stomach). The same is true of several logical flaws — they're there, but not overly apparent while the film is on-screen. *Seven* may always be grim, dark, and rainy, but at least there's a little substance beneath the atmosphere. **RECOMMENDED**

Sexy Beast [United Kingdom, 2000]

Starring: Ray Winstone, Ben Kingsley, Ian McShane Director: Jonathan Glazer Screenplay: Louis Mellis, David Scinto Running Time: 1:28
Rated: R (Profanity, violence, sexual situations) Theatrical Aspect Ratio: 1.85:1

The oddly-titled *Sexy Beast* (oddly titled because neither of the main characters is sexy, although both are certainly beasts) focuses on a husband's determina-

tion to honor a promise he made to his wife. The movie, the debut effort from British director Jonathan Glazer, is essentially a caper flick, although the best parts take place before the crime gets underway. The first two-thirds of this film represents a test of wills between retired criminal Gary (Ray Winstone) and gangster Don (Ben Kingsley), who wants Gary to come back to work with him on one more job. Don is abusive and unrelenting; Gary is more laid back (at times almost submissive).

Both Kingsley and Winstone give forceful performances, and their often vicious, occasionally volcanic give-and-take is a delight to behold. Winstone, whose tanned, plump body is the picture of a man who has gone soft in the lap of luxury, gives yet another in a long line of effective portrayals. As good as he is, however, he is constantly eclipsed by Kingsley, who tears into this role with a gusto we rarely see from the normally stately actor. Kingsley is so magnetic that the movie suffers noticeably when he's not on screen (unfortunately, there's a span of about 20 minutes when this is true). Satellite characters, such as Gary's wife, Deedee (Amanda Redman), and crime boss Teddy Bass (Ian McShane), enrich the plot by raising the stakes. Gary can cope with Don's threats and bullying when they are directed at him, but not when his wife is their target. The tension is effectively leavened with comedy to keep the tone from becoming too harrowing.

Although the chief pleasure of watching *Sexy Beast* lies in absorbing the performances of Winstone and (especially) Kingsley, Glazer displays a lively visual style that offers moments of surprise and gratification. *Sexy Beast* runs the gamut from relentless to playful. There's a priceless scene early in the proceedings featuring a boulder and a swimming pool that has to be seen to be believed. With a style that recalls recent films like *The Limey* and *Lock, Stock and Two Smoking Barrels*, *Sexy Beast* offers a suspenseful 90 minutes. **RECOMMENDED**

Shallow Grave [United Kingdom, 1994]

Starring: Kerry Fox, Christopher Eccleston, Ewan McGregor
Director: Danny Boyle Screenplay: John Hodge Running Time: 1:33
Rated: R (Violence, gore, nudity, language, mature themes) Theatrical Aspect Ratio: 1.66:1

A couple of clichés come to mind while watching Danny Boyle's deliciously diabolical feature debut, *Shallow Grave*. The first — that money is the root of all evil — is obvious. The other — that it's always the quiet ones who bear the closest watching — is only marginally more obscure.

The film starts off a little slowly with some necessary exposition to get the story jump-started. Three flatmates — Juliette (Kerry Fox), a doctor; David (Christopher Eccleston), an accountant; and Alex (Ewan McGregor), a journalist — are looking for someone to move into the vacant 4th bedroom of their suite. After interviewing an interesting range of applicants, they settle on Hugo (Keith Allen), whose outlook on life seems a good match for their own. And his willingness to pay up front with cold cash doesn't hurt.

However, Hugo's time with the trio is destined to be short. One day, he moves in; the next, he's dead, apparently of a drug overdose. Left behind in his room are his corpse, evidence of his addiction, and a suitcase full of money. This presents a dilemma for the flatmates: call the cops or dump the body and keep the cash. Because of the nature of the film, it's not hard to guess which they choose. So, while two thugs searching for Hugo begin leaving a trail of dead bodies, Juliette, David, and Alex take Hugo's remains out to the woods where they mutilate the corpse beyond recognition and bury it in a shallow grave.

There aren't any real, three-dimensional characters in *Shallow Grave,* but the stock types are played with such ability by Fox (the aloof female), Eccleston (the reclusive nerd), and McGregor (the wisecracking party boy), that it doesn't matter. Director Danny Boyle, a veteran of British TV, imbues *Shallow Grave* with a style that at times seems a little too slick.

In fact, a weakness of this film is that it occasionally tries to be too clever (bordering on smug). Several of the apparently "shocking" plot twists aren't all that surprising, but Boyle treats each new turn of John Hodge's script as if it was the most unexpected possibility. This objection is in the nature of a minor quibble, however, since it does little to detract from the viewer's overall satisfaction. Taken as a whole, *Shallow Grave* is a reasonably enjoyable (for those captivated by this sort of thing) black comedy/noir thriller. **RECOMMENDED**

The Siege [1998]

Starring: Denzel Washington, Annette Bening, Bruce Willis, Tony Shalhoub Director: Edward Zwick Screenplay: Lawrence Wright and Menno Meyjes & Edward Zwick Running Time: 1:58 Rated: R (Violence, profanity, brief nudity) Theatrical Aspect Ratio: 2.35:1

The setting is New York City, one of the most likely (and vulnerable) American targets for terrorism.

When a special branch of the United States military, under the command of General William Devereaux (Bruce Willis), takes prisoner suspected terrorist mastermind Sheik Ahmed Bin Talal, Islamic fundamentalists across the world take notice. The only warning the FBI receives is a single, cryptic message: "Release him." Then all hell breaks loose in New York. A bus is destroyed, killing 25 civilians. A Broadway theater is bombed. Hostages are taken at a school. As the wave of terrorist activity crests, the President must consider if the only way to save the city and break the grip of fear is to declare martial law. Devereaux argues against that eventuality, but is nevertheless ready to lead 10,000 men into action on American soil.

Another person not in favor of martial law is Anthony Hubbard (Denzel Washington), the FBI agent in charge of investigating the terrorist activities. His staff is comprised of smart, energetic, intelligent men and women very much unlike the usual group of moronic Feds we're used to seeing in movies. Hubbard develops an uneasy alliance with CIA agent Elise Kraft (Annette Bening), whose department knows more about the situation than they're willing to reveal. Yet, as the twin threats of a catastrophic terrorist action and the implementation of martial law grow greater, Hubbard finds that time is against him.

One of the reasons that *The Siege* works so well is that a lot is going on simultaneously, both on the surface and just beneath it. In addition to the FBI's investigation, considerable time is spent exploring the distrustful relationships that exist between various segments of the U.S. government (namely, the army, the FBI, and the CIA). This is not an attempt at a "tell all" expose of what goes into a government cover-up, but a look at the complexities inherent when so many secrets and lies are involved. *The Siege* also examines (albeit superficially) the potential for the abuse of power when the Constitution is suspended.

The Siege is many things at once: tense, exciting, disturbing, and thought provoking. In the wake of the events of September 11, 2001, one could also argue that this film is eerily prescient. **HIGHLY RECOMMENDED**

The Silence of the Lambs [1991]

Starring: Jodie Foster, Anthony Hopkins, Scott Glenn, Ted Levine Director: Jonathan Demme Screenplay: Ted Tally, based on the novel by Thomas Harris Running Time: 1:58 Rated: R (Violence, profanity, nudity) Theatrical Aspect Ratio: 1.85:1

The Silence of the Lambs opens by introducing us to FBI trainee Clarice Starling (Jodie Foster), a brilliant student who has been selected by Jack Crawford (Scott Glenn), the head of the FBI's Behavioral Science Unit, to help in the pursuit of a serial killer called Buffalo Bill, who skins his victims after murdering them. Crawford wants Clarice to approach the infamous Dr. Hannibal Lecter, or "Hannibal the Cannibal" as he has become known, and encourage Lecter to provide a profile of Buffalo Bill. Crawford claims that Lecter might be willing to open up to a woman — and he's right. The good doctor offers Clarice a quid pro quo deal. For every piece of information he shares about Buffalo Bill, Clarice must reveal one detail about her past. So, while Lecter is helping Clarice get closer to Buffalo Bill, he is also worming his way into her psyche. Perhaps surprisingly, however, she is doing the same to him.

There is little doubt that the most memorable aspect of *The Silence of the Lambs* is Anthony Hopkins' incomparable performance as Lecter. Taking over for Brian Cox, who was effective, but not especially memorable, as the good doctor in 1986's *Manhunter*, Hopkins instantly makes the role his own, capturing and conveying the charismatic essence of pure evil. To his dying day, no matter how many roles he plays in the interim, Hopkins will forever be known for this part.

Since its 1991 release, much has been written about *The Silence of the Lambs*, Hannibal Lecter, Clarice Starling, and the relationship between them. Thomas Harris was so intrigued by the characters that he wrote the sequel, *Hannibal*, which soared into the top spot on best-seller lists countrywide as soon as it was released. *The Silence of the Lambs* may not have been the best thriller of 1991, but it was the most chilling and creepy, and there's no denying that the most celebrated aspect of the film — the Clarice/Hannibal connection — could not have been accomplished with greater skill. **HIGHLY RECOMMENDED**

A Simple Plan [1998]

Starring: Bill Paxton, Billy Bob Thornton, Bridget Fonda Director: Sam Raimi Screenplay: Scott Smith based on his novel Running Time: 2:03 Rated: R (Violence, profanity) Theatrical Aspect Ratio: 1.85:1

Beware things that are described as "simple." While this is not the central message of *A Simple Plan*, it's certainly a byproduct. From the real world, we all know that things which are supposed to be simple — a basic plumbing job, minor car repairs, etc. — frequently turn into intricate nightmares, eating up time, effort, and patience in equal quantities. In Sam Raimi's superior thriller, Hank (Bill Paxton), Jacob

(Billy Bob Thorton), Lou (Brent Briscoe), and Sarah (Bridget Fonda) discover that a seemingly uncomplicated, foolproof plan to make them all rich is not without bloody ramifications.

When *A Simple Plan* begins, Hank is a happy man living out his life in a quiet, rural Midwestern town. He has everything he could possibly want: a pregnant wife he loves, a decent job, and friends and neighbors who like and respect him. Then, one winter day, something happens that is destined to change the fabric of Hank's existence. Out in the woods, he, his mentally-slow brother, Jacob, and a friend, Lou, stumble upon the snow-covered wreckage of a small plane. Inside, they find the mummified corpse of the pilot and a stash of $4.4 million in cash — "The American dream . . . in a gym bag." Hank wants to leave the money where it is and phone the authorities. Jacob and Lou, however, argue that they should claim the loot as their own, since it probably belonged to drug dealers in the first place. At first, Hank resists, but, eventually, he gives in. Soon, however, the seeds of mistrust infiltrate the small group, pitting brother against brother, and friend against friend, and, as the circle of people who know about the money expands, the threat of discovery grows, until one incident elevates the stakes to life-and-death.

Director Sam Raimi, working from a script written by Scott Smith and using groundwork laid by John Boorman (who, at one point, was set to helm this project), does a marvelous job of depicting the growing tension between the characters. While there are moments that offer shock value, Raimi's primary goal is to gradually build the suspense. He draws us into the story by making Bill Paxton's Hank a Jimmy Stewart-type of nice guy — the sort of man it's virtually impossible not to identify with — then showing his slow, gradual spiral into the abyss of greed and self-interest that captures nearly everyone who crosses *A Simple Plan*'s screen. **HIGHLY RECOMMENDED**

Smilla's Sense of Snow [Denmark/Gemany/Sweden, 1996]

Starring: Julia Ormond, Gabriel Byrne, Richard Harris, Robert Loggia Director: Bille August Screenplay: Ann Biderman based on the novel by Peter Hoeg Running Time: 2:01 Rated: R (Profanity, violence, sex) Theatrical Aspect Ratio: 2.35:1

Julia Ormond plays Smilla Jaspersen, a half-Inuit mathematician who currently resides in Denmark. One day, upon returning to her apartment, she discovers that Isaiah (Clipper Miano), the child who lives on the floor below her, has fallen to his death.

The authorities say the fall from the roof was an accident, but, citing certain irregularities about the incident, Smilla claims it was murder. Another resident of the building (Gabriel Byrne) agrees with her. When the local police stonewall her, Smilla begins investigating on her own, and, the deeper she gets, the more dangerous the situation becomes. Her inquiries lead directly to the powerful and wealthy Dr. Tork (Richard Harris), the head of Greenland Mining, who is behind a cover-up that includes, among other things, a host of prehistoric worms (I am not making this up).

As thrillers go, *Smilla's Sense of Snow* is definitely unconventional. The locations are atypical, the protagonist is a woman who doesn't run into the arms of a man at the first sign of trouble, and there aren't any car chases. The storyline is reasonably complex (not to mention a little silly) and features enough small surprises and twists to retain the average viewer's attention. And, the fact that it's a "why-dunnit" or "how-dunnit," rather than a "who-dunnit," allows us to focus on more interesting issues than identifying possible red herrings. As crisply directed by Bille August, *Smilla's Sense of Snow* moves rapidly — almost too rapidly. The plot clicks along so briskly that numerous character details get lost in the rush.

The film's climax will probably seem preposterous for anyone expecting *Smilla's Sense of Snow* to stay grounded in reality. If nothing else, the opening sequence should prepare you to accept that boundaries not normally crossed in murder mysteries will be broken. *Smilla's Sense of Snow* is not a landmark thriller, nor is it likely to appeal to those who demand a semblance of reality. But it is involving and entertaining, and features an intriguing, independent heroine. **RECOMMENDED**

Snatch [United Kingdom/United States, 2000]

Starring: Benicio Del Toro, Dennis Farina, Vinnie Jones, Brad Pitt
Director: Guy Ritchie Screenplay: Guy Ritchie Running Time: 1:44
Rated: R (Violence, profanity, brief nudity) Theatrical Aspect
Ratio: 1.85:1

Boiled down to its essentials, *Snatch* is about a group of goons, low-level gangsters, and assorted undesirables, all of whom are after the same thing — a stolen, 84 karat diamond that's the size of a chubby baby's fist. The movie is narrated by Turkish (Jason Statham), a boxing promoter who is unwillingly pulled into the story. The diamond is initially stolen in Antwerp by Franky Four Fingers (Benicio Del Toro), who brings it to London. Once there, it is hotly pursued by the likes of an American "businessman,"

Cousin Avi (Dennis Farina), his blustering British cousin, Doug the Head (Mike Reid), and his hard-nosed sidekick, Bullet Tooth Tony (Vinnie Jones). Also in the hunt are ex-KGB agent Boris the Blade (Rade Serbedzija), sadistic crime boss Brick Top (Alan Ford), and a group of inept thieves with a pet dog. To further complicate matters, we are introduced to bare-knuckle boxer Mickey O'Neil (Brad Pitt), whose fortunes become integral to the convoluted narrative's eventual resolution. Part of the fun is watching how (and sometimes why) all of these characters interact, and seeing what happens when things don't go as planned.

Snatch is raucous and crude, but never boring or predictable. It is bold, brash, and cartoonish, and never takes itself seriously. In interviews, Ritchie has claimed not to have been influenced by Tarantino, but the video clerk-cum-filmmaker's trademarks are littered around *Snatch*'s colorful landscape. However, since Tarantino's style is the result of synthesizing the approaches of directors he admires, it's possible that Ritchie arrived at something similar by having the same influences. Whatever the case, most people who enjoyed *Pulp Fiction* will appreciate *Snatch*.

Like *Lock, Stock and Two Smoking Barrels*, *Snatch* works equally well as a violent comedy or a testosterone-fueled action film (no women have significant roles, although a few extras bare their breasts). *Snatch* finds humor in all sorts of grotesque situations — some viewers will probably be discomfited by the realization that they're laughing at such gruesome material. Some of *Snatch*'s less conventional plot elements include a dog that squeaks because it swallowed a squeeze toy, a briefcase attached to a severed arm, and a unique form of pig food. The dialogue is slick and witty, and often includes bizarre digressions (such as a lengthy discourse on a peculiar way to dispose of bodies).

For those who like this kind of movie, *Snatch* represents a diversion to be reckoned with. It's a reflection of the times, and of the kinds of films that are now considered hip and cutting edge. Ritchie came out of nowhere to make a big splash with *Lock, Stock and Two Smoking Barrels*. *Snatch* doesn't take him to the next plateau of filmmaking, but it proves that he's got some staying power. **RECOMMENDED**

The Spanish Prisoner [1997]

Starring: Campbell Scott, Rebecca Pidgeon, Steve Martin, Ben Gazzara
Director: David Mamet Screenplay: David Mamet Running Time: 1:50
Rated: PG (Violence) Theatrical Aspect Ratio: 1.85:1

Joe Ross (Campbell Scott) has just invented "The Process," a revolutionary procedure that is going to give his company control of the market (to use Hitchcock terms, this is the movie's McGuffin). But, while Joe thinks his work is worth a sizable bonus, the corporation's president, Mr. Klein (Ben Gazzara), refuses to commit to a specific figure, assuring Joe only that his effort is appreciated. While on a business trip to the Caribbean, Joe runs into Jimmy Dell (Steve Martin), a mysterious, rich stranger who offers Joe a few tips about life and business. Days later, in New York, Joe meets Jimmy again, and this begins his spiral into a strange world of deception, where nothing is what it first seems to be. Soon, like so many heroes in films like this, he finds himself in an untenable position, wrongly accused with a pile of irrefutable evidence staring him in the face. The only one he can trust is his secretary, Susan (Rebecca Pidgeon), who wants more than just a working relationship with him.

David Mamet's script supplies us with a seemingly-endless series of twists and turns, only a fraction of which are predictable. At times, the audience is a step ahead of the screenplay, but, most of the time, we're playing catch-up. Although there are plenty of holes that Mamet has no interest is sewing up (trying to solve every riddle in *The Spanish Prisoner* is an exercise in futility), this is a smart film that develops a central character we can sympathize with — a modern version of Josef K. from Kafka's *The Trial*.

The most curious thing about *The Spanish Prisoner* is the ending. At first glance, it appears to be a common wrap-up that ties together several critical loose ends. There's a deus ex machina aspect to it which may indicate that Mamet is toying with the audience by sending up the manner in which this kind of movie must end to satisfy an audience. But are things as straightforward as they seem? Is this, in fact, the end, or is it just the latest twist in an incredibly complex con game?

Although most viewers of *The Spanish Prisoner* will be personally unfamiliar with the kind of sinister plot that Joe stumbles into, the concepts of corporate greed and backstabbing will hit closer to home. The subtext of this film is the same as the one in many other Mamet offerings — how the current business climate rewards those who act ruthlessly and punishes those who hold to a code of ethics. With a plot that would make Hitchcock proud, *The Spanish Prisoner* uses this outrageously elaborate, always-entertaining approach to illustrate these more serious concerns about what it takes to survive the '90s.
RECOMMENDED

Suicide Kings [1997]

Starring: Christopher Walken, Denis Leary, Jay Mohr, Henry Thomas
Director: Peter O'Fallon Screenplay: Josh McKinney, Gina Goldman, Wayne Rice Running Time: 1:47 Rated: R (Extreme and frequent profanity, brief nudity, drug use, violence) Theatrical Aspect Ratio: 1.85:1

Once upon a time, in another life, Charlie Bennett (played by the always-delightful Christopher Walken) went by the name of Carlo Bartolucci. Under that identity, as the head of the New York City Mafia, he was one of the most feared men in America. But times change, and Charlie has gone legit. Now, he's just an average, tax-paying businessman. His wits have grown dull and he lets down his guard too easily — as he discovers when he makes the mistake of trusting a group of apparently-harmless, rich, college-age kids that he meets at his regular restaurant. They are Brett (Jay Mohr), Avery (Henry Thomas), Max (Sean Patrick Flanery), and T.K. (Jeremy Sisto) — and their goal is to kidnap Charlie and hold him hostage. But, although the former organized crime kingpin nearly foils the attempt, he is eventually subdued and drugged. When he awakens, he finds himself tied to a chair inside a New Jersey mansion, and notices that his captors have cut off one of his fingers.

Charlie is quickly informed why he has been snatched. Apparently, Avery's sister, Lisa (Laura Harris), is the victim of an unrelated kidnapping, and the men holding her are demanding a $2 million ransom. Avery and his friends have decided that Charlie is an important enough underworld figure that he can use his old connections to free Lisa. And, not willing to leave anything to chance, they decide that force is the most viable form of persuasion. However, while Charlie may be out of practice, he's no dummy, and, as the tension mounts, he plays his captors off against each other, widening fissures in their relationships. Meanwhile, his faithful henchman, Lono Vecchio (Denis Leary), is closing in on the place where his boss is being held.

If you can get past some of the film's basic setup implausibilities, *Suicide Kings* is a lot of fun. It's more of a dark comedy than anything else, and several scenes are borderline-hilarious. The film is somewhat less successful in its attempt to develop a mystery — there are a few unnecessary red herrings and at least one plot twist too many. Nevertheless, this is just one facet of a clever and involving storyline, and the real meat of the movie is the verbal chess match between Charlie and the others, who treat him with mixture of fear and awe. *Suicide Kings* is a promising beginning to director Peter O'Fallon's big-screen career. It isn't a perfect motion picture, but there's enough here to earn an enthusiastic recommendation for those who enjoy this genre. RECOMMENDED

The Sum of All Fears [2002]

Starring: Ben Affleck, Morgan Freeman, James Cromwell Director: Phil Alden Robinson Screenplay: Paul Attanasio and Daniel Pyne, based on the novel by Tom Clancy Running Time: 2:07 Rated: PG-13 (Violence, profanity) Theatrical Aspect Ratio: 2.35:1

Any Clancy fan expecting an exact adaptation of the novel is living in a dream world. Such an endeavor would require a 5-part mini-series, not a 2-hour motion picture. About the only things that remain from the novel *The Sum of All Fears* are the plot outline and some character names. But, considering the events of 9/11/01, it's eerie to note how prescient Clancy was when he penned the book. The scenario is much like ones that we have heard discussed on TV and radio talkshows. A fringe group gets hold of a nuclear warhead and plans to detonate it at a major gathering point of American citizens — in this case, the Superbowl. The goal is not only to create mass hysteria, but to implicate the Russians, and possibly precipitate a nuclear holocaust that will wipe the world's most powerful nations off the map. The movie's logic is a little muddled here, but it's just strong enough for us not to question it while we're watching the movie. Enter Jack Ryan (Ben Affleck) and his boss, CIA director Bill Cabot (Morgan Freeman). Their job: present President Fowler (James Cromwell) with facts that others may not be aware of, and keep the lines of communication open between him and his Russian counterpart (Ciarán Hinds).

When it comes to the techno-thriller, Clancy is the king. *The Sum of All Fears* may be a stripped-down condensation of his vision, with all the delicious details removed, but the author's world-view is very much in evidence. Director Phil Alden Robinson does a competent job of escalating suspense and keeping the convoluted storyline relatively coherent — at least for viewers who pay careful attention.

Because of 9/11, *The Sum of All Fears* is more demanding than the usual escapist fare. The echoes of reality in its plot points make suspension of disbelief a facile thing, but therein lies a double-edged blade. Will viewers be able to abandon themselves to the rhythms of the story and the horrors contained

therein? The movie does what all good thrillers should do — provide enough shocks and surprises to keep us guessing, and never lets up on the suspense until the end credits arrive. But now that reality and fantasy have come so close together, can audiences see one without being reminded of the other? RECOMMENDED

The Swindle [France, 1997]

Starring: Isabelle Huppert, Michel Serrault, François Cluzet Director: Claude Chabrol Screenplay: Claude Chabrol Running Time: 1:44 Rated: Not Rated (Violence, profanity) Theatrical Aspect Ratio: 1.66:1 In French with subtitles

At the beginning, things seem straightforward. Betty (Isabelle Huppert) and her partner, Victor (Michel Serrault), are pulling a job at a casino. After locating a mark, a married salesman who has been lucky at the roulette wheel, Betty drugs one of his drinks, then encourages him to invite her to his room. Once he's out cold, she lets Victor in. They relieve him of less than half of his considerable winnings (leaving enough so he'll never know he was robbed), then take off in a mobile camper, heading back to Paris for a brief respite before their next job at a dentists' convention. But Betty has been plotting her own caper for a year, and it's about to come to fruition. A lover named Maurice (François Cluzet) works as a courier for an organized crime syndicate, and he has planned to run away with 5 million francs. Betty's plan is for Victor to swap suitcases with Maurice then walk off with the cash. But things are never as simple as they initially seem, and, in *The Swindle*, circumstances become complicated fast.

By the movie's mid-point, the question everyone in the audience is asking is "Who's scamming whom?" Is Betty betraying Victor in order to run off with Maurice? Is she playing Maurice for a fool? Is she double-crossing both men? Or is it something different altogether? What's Maurice's game? Is he really as infatuated with Betty as he seems to be? Are the mobsters as gullible as he thinks? And what about the ever-resourceful Victor? Will he be meekly led into a trap, like a lamb to a slaughter? Writer/director Claude Chabrol develops the plot slowly, deferring answers to all questions until the climax, while constantly posing new ones. *The Swindle* becomes progressively more intense and involving with every passing moment.

While it's often true that films about con artists incorporate a dark, offbeat sense of humor, Chabrol's script occasionally ventures into the realm of pure comedy. Chabrol manages to mix in the lighter scenes without a hint of awkwardness, and the escalating sense of tension is never derailed by this approach. This is a wonderful achievement for a filmmaker, who, even after making movies for more than 40 years, continues to surprise and delight with each new feature. **HIGHLY RECOMMENDED**

Switchback [1997]

Starring: Danny Glover, Dennis Quaid, Jared Leto, R. Lee Ermey
Director: Jeb Stuart Screenplay: Jeb Stuart Running Time: 2:00
Rated: R (Violence, profanity, nude pinups) Theatrical Aspect
Ratio: 2.35:1

A blizzard of exceptional proportions is bearing down on Colorado, threatening to close all routes in and out of the Rockies while burying the Centennial State beneath feet of snow. Sound familiar? Of course, it's a coincidence that *Switchback,* which uses this critical plot device, is opening in the wake of a mammoth late-October snow storm that crippled the American midwest, but it's great timing. Paramount Pictures couldn't have come up with a better release date if they'd planned it.

A baby-sitter caring for a young child is murdered, then the boy is kidnapped from his affluent parents' home. A doctor-turned-drifter wanders through Texas, trying to hitch a ride to Salt Lake City. An ex-railroad worker driving around in a cadillac (with an interior decorated by nude pin-ups) offers him a ride. A serial killer strikes in Amarillo, where the current sheriff is embroiled in a pitched battle for re-election against a powerful opponent. A mysterious FBI agent arrives claiming to be on the killer's trail while he's really pursuing his own agenda. These are the diverse strands that screenwriter Jeb Stuart weaves together into the tapestry of *Switchback,* his taut, intelligent directorial debut.

Unlike most thrillers, *Switchback* doesn't move at a breakneck pace that camouflages flaws by ceaseless action and non-stop edge-of-the-seat moments. Instead, this film progresses at a more leisurely pace, allowing us time to get to know each of the 4 main characters: Danny Glover's Bob Goodall, the cadillac driver; Jared Leto's Lane Dixon, the wandering ex-doctor; Dennis Quaid's Frank La Cross, the FBI agent; and R. Lee Ermey's Sheriff Buck Olmstead. By the time the final reel unspools, we've spent time with each of these men and have come to understand a measure of what makes them tick.

Switchback features an elaborately structured contest between the hero and the villain. As the title implies, the storyline for *Switchback* features a few un-expected curves, but it doesn't try to dazzle us with narrative contortions. In the end, the film is almost more disturbing than it is exhausting. For *Switchback,* Jeb Stuart can be credited with a job well done. **RECOMMENDED**

The Tailor of Panama [2001]

Starring: Pierce Brosnan, Geoffrey Rush, Leonor Varela, Jamie Lee Curtis Director: John Boorman Screenplay: Andrew Davies & John Le Carré and John Boorman Running Time: 1:49 Rated: R (Violence, profanity, sex, nudity) Theatrical Aspect Ratio: 2.35:1

As a result of his scandalous behavior, Andy Osnard (Pierce Brosnan) is on the outs with Secret Intelligence Service MI6, and they decide to exile him to Panama, described alternatively as a "nasty web of money laundering, drug trafficking, and corruption" or as "Casablanca without heroes." Once there, Andy gets to work trying to unearth some big secret that will get London's attention. He sets his sights on uncovering the true balance of power surrounding the canal, and, as his informant, he chooses an unassuming tailor with a dark secret in his past. Harry Pendel (Geoffrey Rush) is a nice, meek man with an adoring American wife, Louisa (Jamie Lee Curtis), who minds his own business but has made an unwise investment. Now, he's $50,000 in debt and the bank is ready to call in the loan. Enter Andy, Harry's "guardian angel." If Harry will spy on his wife, who is the assistant to the Canal director, Harry will find his financial woes eliminated. Soon, Harry is spinning a fiction for Andy to keep the money flowing, and Andy is apparently eating it up, because it fuels his own agenda.

The screenplay for *The Tailor of Panama,* based on the novel by John Le Carré, is a wonderfully complex and devious affair that leaves us constantly befuddled about who's using whom and who really knows what. Some characters are a lot smarter than the initially appear to be, while others are less intelligent. And, while certain individuals aren't what they seem to be, others are. The movie sorts everything out in the end, but part of the fun is playing the game along with the characters. And, to add a sense of verisimilitude to the proceedings, much of the movie was filmed on location. (Apparently, the government deemed the consideration of having Pierce Brosnan filming in the country to be more important than the negative light in which the story portrays Panamanian politics.)

The Tailor of Panama is not an action thriller; those expecting shoot-outs and car chases will be as disappointed as those on the lookout for James Bond. Instead, this plot-centered motion picture demands that its audience thinks rather than sits passively and watches. And, although the film is primarily a serious affair, Boorman gets the opportunity to take a few shots at the American military by portraying the strategists at the Pentagon as a group of inept men who don't really know or care how accurate their information is. Over the course of a long career, Boorman has experienced his share of hits and misses. *The Tailor of Panama* belongs in the former category. **RECOMMENDED**

Thirteen Days [2000]

Starring: Kevin Costner, Bruce Greenwood, Steven Culp, Dylan Baker Director: Roger Donaldson Screenplay: David Self Running Time: 2:24 Rated: PG-13 (Profanity) Theatrical Aspect Ratio: 1.85:1

For 13 days in 1962, from October 16 through October 28, the world teetered on the brink of nuclear war as the United States and the Soviet Union stood toe-to-toe, neither bending, each waiting for the other to blink. *Thirteen Days* presents a dramatized (i.e., somewhat fictionalized) view from the top. The 3 main characters are JFK (Bruce Greenwood), RFK (Steven Culp), and Kenny O'Donnell (Kevin Costner). Kenny who? If you haven't heard of O'Donnell, you're not alone. O'Donnell went to Harvard with Bobby Kennedy, worked for JFK's Senate and Presidential campaigns, then became a special advisor to the President with an office next door to the Oval Office. He was definitely in Kennedy's inner circle. However, his role in the crisis appears to have been beefed up to give star Kevin Costner more screen time and greater importance. It is unlikely that some of the decisions and actions attributed to O'Donnell in this movie actually occurred in real life. Indeed, while O'Donnell's character was included to give some "balance" to the script, Costner's presence tips the scales in the wrong direction. At times, there's a sense that *Thirteen Days* should be devoting more attention to JFK and RFK and less to a lesser player like O'Donnell.

Thirteen Days includes a lot of fascinating elements, the most obvious of which is the struggle between Kennedy's advisors as the hawks and doves seek to sway the President to their point-of-view. Each side has valid objections to the other's position, and it becomes clear that both paths could lead to disaster. Some of the more zealous members of the military, disgusted by a perceived weakness in JFK's approach, seek to trap the President into a warlike position by manipulating the rules of engagement. Meanwhile, the top minds in the United States must

attempt to puzzle out Moscow's seemingly contradictory responses to American actions. Are they willing to capitulate and deal beneath the table, or are they setting a trap to give them time to prepare the missiles for use? Tense moments include a confrontation between a U.S. warship and a Soviet sub, attempts by a U-2 plane to avoid missiles, and the final, frenzied negotiations as the deadline looms.

Although the movie runs a little on the long side, director Donaldson never lets the momentum flag. The final half-hour features some weak spots, including a little too much non-historical melodrama and several over-the-top speeches. Some historians may be annoyed at the liberties taken by Self's screenplay with the established facts, but the writer claims that he spent countless hours poring over documents and listening to tapes in order to get most of the background correct. Certain aspects were dramatized to make them more accessible to viewers. This is not, after all, a documentary. For those with a thirst for a gripping political thriller with its roots in real-life events, *Thirteen Days* represents a satisfying refreshment. **RECOMMENDED**

A Time to Kill [1996]

Starring: Matthew McConaughey, Samuel L. Jackson, Sandra Bullock, Kevin Spacey Director: Joel Schumacher Screenplay: Akiva Goldsman based on the novel by John Grisham Running Time: 2:29 Rated: R (Profanity, violence, mature themes) Theatrical Aspect Ratio: 2.35:1

It's possible to argue all day about how much of the race issue in *A Time to Kill* is a legitimate exploration of black/white tension, and how much is sensationalism used to spice up the story. The KKK has a prominent role, but couldn't a more moderate, less universally-despised group have filled a similar function? There are times when *A Time to Kill* preaches, but isn't Joel Schumacher aiming the sermon at the converted? The movie clearly touches on some important social issues, but it's up to the viewer to dig beneath the propaganda and unearth the messages that mean something. Then again, it's worth noting that this Hollywood production is actually saying something, rather than just churning out eye-popping special effects while relying on a regurgitated plot.

The basic setup has 10-year old Tonya Hailey, the daughter of Carl Lee Hailey (Samuel L. Jackson), being raped and beaten by two rednecks. Taking the law into his own hands, Carl Lee guns down the pair in front of dozens of witnesses in the Canton, Mississippi courthouse. In the process, he also seriously injures a local deputy (Chris Cooper). Carl Lee is arrested for the double murder, and faces trial. For his attorney, he chooses a local white lawyer, up-and-coming hotshot Jake Brigance (Matthew Mc-Conaughey). With a team that includes a sleazy divorce specialist, Harry Rex Vonner (Oliver Platt), an energetic assistant, Ellen Roarke (Sandra Bullock), and his old mentor, Lucien Wilbanks (Donald Sutherland), Jake goes up against the local D.A. (Kevin Spacey). When the KKK become involved, Jake discovers that his life, and the lives of everyone close to him, including his wife (Ashley Judd) and daughter, are in danger. And the defense of Carl Lee Hailey has just begun . . .

There's not a lot of real tension about what the verdict is going to be, although the film unsuccessfully tries to lead us astray. But there are enough interesting side-issues going on that there's no fear of a viewer losing interest. Despite certain drawbacks, *A Time to Kill* is involving, energetic, and occasionally thought-provoking. All things considered, this film will make for a worthwhile trip to the cinema for all, not just those who have time to kill. **RECOMMENDED**

Traffic [2000]

Starring: Michael Douglas, Catherine Zeta-Jones, Benicio Del Toro, Erika Christensen, Don Cheadle Director: Steven Soderbergh Screenplay: Stephen Gaghan, based on the min-series "Traffik" by Simon Moore Running Time: 2:25 Rated: R (Violence, drug content, profanity, sex, brief nudity) Theatrical Aspect Ratio: 1.85:1

Unlike most ensemble movies, *Traffic* does not bring all of the characters together for a dramatic finale that ties the disparate plot threads together. In fact, for the most part, the different stories do not criss-cross, and, when an intersection occurs, it's an ephemeral one. The purpose of the movie is not to show how the characters interact or to illustrate some obscure point about fate and chance. Rather, it is to illuminate how far-reaching the drug trade is, and how trafficking in narcotics can impact on the lives of many different people in a variety of circumstances. *Traffic* looks at a wide sampling of aspects of the drug trade: the men who police it on both sides of the border, the government officials who carry out the so-called war, the people who get rich by distributing it, and the victims who debase themselves to get the money for their next fix. For some, drugs equate to greed, but, for others, they represent survival.

Although there are a large number of speaking parts, the action centers around four major characters. Benicio Del Toro turns in a nicely modulated performance as Javier Rodriguez, a Mexican police officer who is caught in a power struggle between two cartels. The biggest name in the cast is Michael Douglas, who plays Judge Robert Wakefield, the new U.S. Drug Czar whose personal life is thrown into turmoil when he learns that his daughter (Erika Christensen) is an addict. Finally, Catherine Zeta-Jones is Helena Ayala, the wife of a San Diego drug lord. Helena is ignorant of her husband's activities until he is arrested and she is forced to clean up the debris of his collapsing business, as well as cope with threats to her life and the life of her son.

The narrative palette of *Traffic* is rich, tightly woven, and consistently involving, with characters that are as well developed as their necessarily limited screen time allows. In many ways, *Traffic* is not meant to be a complete story, although it has a beginning and an end. Instead, it offers a glimpse into the world of drug trafficking, giving a sense of the vast scope of the battles that must be waged for any war against drugs to be winnable. Without ever preaching, *Traffic* shows the folly of believing that facile slogans like "Just say no" mean anything when faced with the kind of real-life situations underlying every drug deal. **HIGHLY RECOMMENDED**

Training Day [2001]

Starring: Denzel Washington, Ethan Hawke Director: Anthony Fuqua Screenplay: David Ayer Running Time: 2:00 Rated: R (Profanity, violence, drug use) Theatrical Aspect Ratio: 2.35:1

Antoine Fuqua's *Training Day* is the story of an idealistic young cop who gets a hard lesson about life in the streets from a veteran. Shining with the star power of Denzel Washington (playing the most morally ambiguous role of a fruitful career) and Ethan Hawke, *Training Day* crackles with energy. It's 2 hours long, but seems a lot shorter. However, as good as most of the movie is, it could have been better had the ending evidenced more careful scripting and less of a reliance upon contrivances.

Ethan Hawke is Jake Hoyt, an ambitious L.A. cop who wants to make detective. The fastest route to that position is to join the elite team headed by legendary undercover figure Alonzo Harris (Denzel Washington). To that end, Jake has been given one day to prove to Alonzo that he's ready for the job. At first, things don't go well — Alonzo scoffs at Jake's by-the-book attitude. "You've got to hear the street, smell it, taste it," he admonishes. Then, later, "This is street justice. It takes a wolf to catch a wolf . . . It's ugly, but it's like that." So Jake starts to learn — smoking some

LSD-laced weed after Alonzo tells him, "A good narcotics officer must have narcotics in his blood." But things soon get out of hand, with Alonzo breaking the law more often than upholding it, and Jake begins to wonder what kind of hell he has lost himself in.

The movie asks hard questions and rarely gives an easy answer. It's riveting and intense, with just enough action to satisfy those who enjoy that genre and enough substance to satiate viewers who are tired of the long litany of dumb motion pictures marching through multiplexes. Unfortunately, *Training Day* doesn't deliver the complete package. The last 15 minutes are full of clichés, contrivances, and smart characters acting dumb — all in the name of providing a "pat" conclusion. The disappointing climax is not enough to take *Training Day* off the recommendation list — the rest of the film is too strong — but it diminishes its impact. RECOMMENDED

Trainspotting [United Kingdom, 1995]

Starring: Ewan McGregor, Ewen Bremner, Jonny Lee Miller, Kevin McKidd, Robert Carlyle Director: Danny Boyle Screenplay: John Hodge based on the novel by Irvine Welsh Running Time: 1:33 Rated: R (Profanity, drug use, sex, nudity, violence) Theatrical Aspect Ratio: 1.66:1

"I chose not to choose life. I chose to choose something else," says the film's narrator and main character, a 20-something Edinburgh man named Mark Renton (Ewan McGregor), near the outset of *Trainspotting*. In rejecting the yuppie culture of a nuclear family, material possessions, a paying job, and dental insurance, Renton is rebelling, but this isn't just the usual disaffection of youth — it's a deeper, more pervasive dissatisfaction with a culture he views as sick and stifling.

Renton's escape is through drugs — primarily heroin, but really anything he can get his hands on. He's surrounded by his "buddies," a group of crooks, liars, and psychos who are even more twisted than he is. There's Spud (Ewen Bremner), a shy, inoffensive junkie; Sick Boy (Jonny Lee Miller), a vicious, duplicitous con artist who's obsessed with Sean Connery; Tommy (Kevin McKidd), a "virtuous" young man fighting the temptation of heroin; and Begbie (Robert Carlyle), a nutcase who gets his thrills from beating up people.

Trainspotting is careful not to present a one-sided view of drug use. After all, why would anyone use the stuff if all it leads to is misery and unhappiness? In Renton's words, to get an idea of what it's like using heroin, "Take the best orgasm you've ever had, multi-

ply by 1,000, and you're still nowhere near it." There are no worries about the problems and concerns of everyday life, just where the next hit is going to come from. The giddiness of heroin addiction is well-illustrated during some of the film's early scenes, but it's a euphoria that gives way to tragedy.

In the end, *Trainspotting* has an anti-drug message, but it presents its case through character studies, not preaching. There are a lot of gruesome images, some of which are presented in an oddly humorous context. For example, take Renton's head-first dive into the "worst toilet in Scotland" or Spud's reaction when he wakes up in soiled sheets. Boyle's style is distinctly his own. This is a kinetic movie, where everything, including the camera, keeps moving. This isn't an examination of the Scottish drug culture from the outside looking in, it's one from the inside looking out. HIGHLY RECOMMENDED

The Truth About Charlie [2002]

Starring: Thandie Newton, Mark Wahlberg, Tim Robbins Director: Jonathan Demme Screenplay: Jonathan Demme & Steve Schmidt and Peter Joshua & Jessica Bendinger Running Time: 1:44 Rated: PG-13 (Violence, sensuality, brief nudity) Theatrical Aspect Ratio: 2.35:1

Taken on its own terms, Jonathan Demme's *The Truth About Charlie*, a '00s re-interpretation of the 1963 thriller *Charade*, is a decent — and even engaging — motion picture. It's not a great movie, or even a very good one, but, if you try not to compare it too much to the original, it works. Given the option, it's better to see *Charade*, which easily tops Demme's version for star power, if nothing else, but *The Truth About Charlie* has its own set of charms, not the least of which is Thandie Newton.

Newton is Regina Lampert, the perplexed widow of a guy named Charlie, who has about as many last names as a cat has lives. (This being a thriller, nearly every one has at least two names.) Charlie was involved in some sort of sinister plot involving betrayal, stolen diamonds, and $6 million in cash, but now he's dead and a group of nasty-looking people think Regina is hiding the money. In addition to a trio of unsavory thugs (Joong-Hoon Park, Lisa Gay Hamilton, Ted Levine) who are dogging her every move, she has to contend with a Parisian police commandant (Christine Boisson) who is unsure of her innocence and a kindly "stars-and-bars company man" named Mr. Bartholomew (Tim Robbins). Thankfully, Regina has someone to turn to in Joshua Peters (Mark Wahlberg), about whom she gushes, "You know what's wrong with you? Absolutely nothing!" That, of course, is a powerful clue that something very definitely is wrong with Joshua, and, as the body count around Regina mounts, she realizes that.

The storyline follows the typical rhythms of this sort of movie. Even if you haven't seen *Charade*, you're unlikely to be surprised by much that happens. The chief pleasure of *The Truth About Charlie* is watching Newton re-define Regina as her own. Wahlberg makes a reasonable foil for her, and there's evidence of some playful chemistry between them, but it's easy enough to determine that this is Newton's movie, and Wahlberg is along for the ride. The twisty plot is just spice added to the sauce.

From a plot standpoint, *The Truth About Charlie* doesn't venture far from the path paved by *Charade*. Militant devotees of the original will likely despise the remake, but those who view Demme's version as an affectionate homage, or those who have never seen *Charade*, will likely be entertained. I appreciate *The Truth About Charlie* in much the same way I appreciate *Charade*, proving that it is possible to like one without being disappointed by the other. RECOMMENDED

U-Turn [1997]

Starring: Sean Penn, Jennifer Lopez, Nick Nolte Director: Oliver Stone
Screenplay: John Ridley based on his book *Stray Dogs* Running
Time: 2:07 Rated: R (Violence, profanity, sexual situations) Theatrical
Aspect Ratio: 1.85:1

U-Turn is film noir steeped in excess. Although director Oliver Stone has clearly made this motion picture with his tongue planted firmly in his cheek, he nevertheless manages to capture all of the tension and mystery necessary to hold the viewer's interest. Hence, while Stone may be poking a little good-natured fun at the genre, he has also created a highly-successful entry to it.

Film noir is always more plot-conscious than character-focused, and this is pretty much the case here. Stone and writer John Ridley have populated *U-Turn* with a variety of colorful types, only a few of whom show the beginnings of multi-dimensionality. The best-developed individual is, not surprisingly, the lead. Bobby Cooper (Sean Penn) is passing through the small town of Superior, Arizona on his way to Las Vegas to pay off a gambling debt. Bobby has already lost two fingers to the Russian mob, and he wants to avoid having to give up any more. Unfortunately, the radiator hose of his classic 1964½ Mustang chooses this moment to give out. Bobby gets the car to the only garage in the area, leaves it with the mechanic

(Billy Bob Thornton) to fix, then wanders impatiently around town.

The denizens of Superior are a strange lot. There's a blind man (Jon Voight, almost unrecognizable beneath all the makeup) who doles out nuggets of wisdom, a flirtatious tease (Claire Danes) who enjoys making her boyfriend jealous, a local bully with the nickname of TNT (Joaquin Phoenix) who's spoiling for a fight, and a sheriff (Powers Boothe) who's hardly ever without a bottle in his hand. But the most bizarre citizens of the small, backwards town are Grace McKenna (Jennifer Lopez) and her grizzled husband, Jake (Nick Nolte), who lure the unsuspecting Bobby into a web of sex, vengeance, and murder.

U-Turn is definitely not for everyone — some viewers will find the juxtaposition of offbeat comedy and noir clichés too strange and others will be offended by the film's extreme violence. Nevertheless, for those who enjoy movies on the edge, *U-Turn* offers just the trajectory you might expect. RECOMMENDED

Unbreakable [2000]

Starring: Bruce Willis, Samuel L. Jackson, Robin Wright Penn
Director: M. Night Shyamalan Screenplay: M. Night Shyamalan
Running Time: 1:47 Rated: PG-13 (Violence, mature themes) Theatrical
Aspect Ratio: 2.35:1

Bruce Willis plays David Dunne, a Franklin Field security guard on his way from New York to Philadelphia by train. A horrible accident en route leaves 131 dead and only one survivor — David, who is not only alive, but doesn't have a scratch on his body. Soon thereafter, David meets Elijah Price (Samuel L. Jackson), a comic book art dealer who thinks he has an explanation for David's miraculous survival. Elijah believes that David is a real-life superhero — his body is stronger and more resilient than that of other humans and he possesses certain, as-yet untapped special abilities. Elijah makes it his purpose to convince David to accept what he is. Meanwhile, David's son (Spencer Treat Clark) is thrilled with the possibility that his dad might be like someone out of a comic book, but his wife, Audrey (Robin Wright Penn), is just interested in patching up a threadbare marriage. However, even as David begins to accept that Elijah might be correct, he discovers that, like all superheroes, he has a fatal weakness.

Looking at the screenplay, it's obvious that Shyamalan is intimately familiar with rhythms and themes of comic books. *Unbreakable* is as much an homage to the superhero books of the writer/director's youth as it is an innovative approach to the genre. Should this film be a success, it's easy to envision a number of sequels, and such a series might appeal to actor Bruce Willis because the emphasis here is on storytelling and character development rather than on action (there is only one true action sequence in the entire film). And there are additional facets of David's personality that could be explored. His half-developed, rocky relationship with his wife, for example, is tangential to the main story in *Unbreakable*, but it is instrumental in humanizing him.

Even though this film boasts more mature direction than *The Sixth Sense,* it's unlikely that it will generate the same degree of rabid repeat viewing. The earlier picture was a phenomenon; this is just a movie. As far as the superhero film is concerned, *Unbreakable* offers a fresh perspective on a genre that is typically defined by stereotypes and clichés. So, as a follow-up to *The Sixth Sense,* this may not satisfy all of Shyamalan's adherents, but, taken on its own terms, *Unbreakable* holds together. RECOMMENDED

The Underneath [1995]

Starring: Peter Gallagher, Alison Elliot, William Fichtner, Adam Trese Director: Steven Soderbergh Screenplay: Sam Lowry (Soderbergh) and Daniel Fuchs based on the novel *Criss Cross* by Don Tracy Running Time: 1:39 Rated: R (Violence, profanity, sex) Theatrical Aspect Ratio: 2.35:1

The Underneath is told primarily in flashback and flashback-within-flashback. There are 3 time lines: the far past (late 1980s), the near past, and the present. Director Soderbergh shuttles freely between the 3, employing visual clues to orient the viewer. In the far past, the main character, Michael Chambers (Peter Gallagher) is wearing a beard. In the near past, he's cleanshaven. And in the present, green filters and a grainy film stock are used.

The bulk of the story concerns Michael's return to his Texas hometown after a several-year absence. His relations with his brother David (Adam Trese) are strained, but that's nothing compared to what they are with his ex-girlfriend, Rachel (Alison Elliot). However, even after all that has happened, there's still a spark between them — something that doesn't go unnoticed by Rachel's current lover, small-time gangster Tommy Dundee (William Fichtner). To cover up a growing re-attachment between himself and Rachel, Michael, an armored car driver, approached Tommy with scheme for a robbery. Although Tommy is intrigued by the business proposition, he's not deceived about Michael's intentions regarding Rachel.

The strengths of *The Underneath* — its atmos-

phere and character-centered basis — are also its weaknesses. This is, after all, a thriller, and sometimes the pace is allowed to lag. Also, the director doesn't appear especially concerned with plot developments, except in the service of character-building. But the gallery of people inhabiting this world is fascinating, as are the ways in which they interact.

Film noir is a hot commodity. And, while twisty plots may not be Soderbergh's strength, he uses this one more-than-adequately as a play area for a batch of interesting characters, while at the same time remaining true to the genre. In the final assessment, *The Underneath* may not be a great motion picture, but it's still a cut above. RECOMMENDED

The Usual Suspects [1995]

Starring: Gabriel Byrne, Kevin Spacey, Stephen Baldwin, Kevin Pollak Director: Bryan Singer Screenplay: Christopher McQuarrie Running Time: 1:46 Rated: R (Profanity, violence) Theatrical Aspect Ratio: 2.35:1

The "usual suspects" are 5 men: Dean Keaton (Gabriel Byrne), an ex-cop-turned-crook who's known for his steely demeanor and nerves of iron; Michael McManus (Stephen Baldwin), a psycho entry man; Todd Hockney (Kevin Pollak), a hardware specialist with an instinct for self-preservation; Fred Fenster (Benicio Del Toro), McManus' partner; and Verbal Klint (Kevin Spacey), a crippled con man. As the movie opens, these 5 are being bundled into a lineup. A truckload of stolen guns has been hijacked and the cops, led by U.S. Customs Special Agent Dave Kujan (Chazz Palminteri), are primed to get their man. But no one cracks, and as the criminals sit together in jail waiting to be charged or released, they hatch a plan for an elaborate emerald heist.

The story is told in 2 different time frames. In the present, looking back on events, Klint sits across a desk from Kujan, unfolding the tale as he remembers it. But the con man is an unreliable narrator, and viewers of *The Usual Suspects* are constantly kept guessing about what "truth" is. In fiction films, we're used to getting an impartial take on "reality"; this picture twists that principle. Not everything presented in *The Usual Suspects* actually happens, and some things occur differently than shown. The opening sequence, which details the climax of the gang's capers, teases the audience about what may or may not be the ultimate resolution.

As the narrative progresses, *The Usual Suspects* constantly raises the stakes. The audience is only slowly let into the story — at the beginning, everyone on-screen knows more than we do. Gradually, however, the skein of deceptions and plot devices is untangled by the switches back and forth between present and past. This film requires that a viewer pay careful attention to details. Those who get lost have only themselves to blame — *The Usual Suspects* doesn't take any prisoners. A trip to the bathroom or the snack bar will leave you floundering when you return.

Singer does an excellent job of blending humor into his noir thriller. There's enough to avoid a sense of ponderousness, but not so much that *The Usual Suspects* becomes campy. In the way it folds its various elements into a single resolution (which the astute viewer will be able to guess beforehand), Singer's film can be accused of toying with the audience. However, at times like this, when the person tugging the strings is adept at his craft, being toyed with can be a worthwhile experience. *The Usual Suspects* is an accomplished synthesis of noir elements and, as such, is an entertaining entry to the genre. HIGHLY RECOMMENDED

Vanilla Sky [2001]

Starring: Tom Cruise, Penelope Cruz, Kurt Russell, Cameron Diaz
Director: Cameron Crowe Screenplay: Cameron Crowe, based on *Open Your Eyes* by Alejandro Amenabar and Mateo Gil Rodríguez
Running Time: 2:10 Rated: R (Profanity, nudity, sex, violence)
Theatrical Aspect Ratio: 1.85:1

Vanilla Sky (the name refers to a painting by Monet) is the quirkily titled American remake of the 1997 Spanish language feature, *Open Your Eyes*. Like its predecessor, *Vanilla Sky* is a mind-bending excursion across genres — a warped fairy tale that dabbles in romance, mythology, horror, mystery, and science fiction. There are plenty of philosophical musings on the difference between dreams and reality, and numerous occasions in which the film dares us to tell them apart. *Vanilla Sky* gives new meaning to the familiar phrase from a children's song: "Life is but a dream."

David Aames (Tom Cruise) has the world in the palm of his hand. The majority stock owner of a big-time publishing firm, David has everything he wants — a great job with short hours, a spectacular Manhattan pad, and a gorgeous female pal named Julie (Cameron Diaz) who's willing to have sex with him whenever the urge hits (which seems to be fairly often). Then, one day, confirmed bachelor David meets Sofia (Penelope Cruz), and he suddenly discovers what love is. Unfortunately, David's blossoming relationship with Sofia fans Julie's jealousy. It seems that she doesn't share David's casual view of their sexual encounters. So, feeling hurt and be-

trayed, she invites David for a ride, then crashes her car, killing herself and badly injuring him. He survives, but is maimed and disfigured, and must wear a mask to hide the mass of scars and twisted flesh that comprises his once-handsome face. (With the mask on, he looks uncannily like Michael Myers, the psycho killer of the *Halloween* series.)

In many ways, the story is pure *Twilight Zone,* but Crowe's down-to-earth approach softens and grounds it, making the characters seem more genuine, even amidst the surreal setting. In addition, the screenplay closes with a less evasive explanation of what has transpired. However, the changes are minor; this is not a case in which Hollywood has butchered the end of a foreign feature in the hope of boosting ticket sales.

In the end, *Vanilla Sky* answers all the questions it poses and wraps up most (if not all) of the dangling plot threads. However, while the explanations come in the final 15 minutes, the most rewarding aspect of the film is the journey to that point — trying to outguess the script, enjoying the carefully constructed romance between David and Sofia (is anyone better than Crowe at telling a heartfelt love story?), and appreciating the details and nuances contributed by a director who knows what he's doing. The science fiction aspects of this movie may place Crowe in unfamiliar territory (he is clearly at his best when dealing with character interaction), but he rarely seems lost. RECOMMENDED

Where the Money Is [2000]

Starring: Paul Newman, Linda Fiorentino, Dermot Mulroney
Director: Marek Kanievska Screenplay: E. Max Frye and Topper Lilien & Carroll Cartwright Running Time: 1:29 Rated: PG-13 (Mild profanity, sexual situation) Theatrical Aspect Ratio: 1.85:1

The primary reason to see *Where the Money Is,* a comedy/caper from director Marek Kanievska, can be summed up in two words: star power. Star power, that is, as in Paul Newman's. At age 75, Newman still has more than his share of charm, although it's a more mature charisma than the kind he exuded in films like *Cool Hand Luke, Butch Cassidy and the Sundance Kid,* and *The Sting.*

Where the Money Is does not have a great storyline. In fact, if not for Newman, the film would likely be both forgettable and forgotten. The dialogue includes a few nice lines, but nothing special, and the story has more than a few holes that the 3 credited screenwriters (E. Max Frye, Topper Lilien, and Carroll Cartwright) don't really attempt to plug. The premise is simple: convicted bank robber Henry Manning (Newman) arrives at a nursing home after having suffered an apparent stroke. With the exception of occasional hand tremors, he never moves or speaks. But his nurse, Carol Ann McKay (Linda Fiorentino), thinks he's faking, and, with the aid of her husband, Wayne (Dermot Mulroney), she sets out to prove it. But Carol is interested in more than getting the upper hand on Harry. She wants to spice up a moribund marriage, and thinks that robbing a bank or an armored car might be the perfect antidote to boredom. And who better to be her partner than one of the most successful robbers in U.S. history?

Where the Money Is is a genial film with a fair amount of low-key humor and a caper that is characterized by its simplicity. Moments of tension and suspense are few (in fact, there are only 2 or 3). There are no big surprises or twists — the movie has the kind of direct trajectory that Hitchcock would have found disappointing. The interplay between Newman and Fiorentino is the undisputed high point. These two form a playful relationship that, while not overtly sexual, is characterized by an erotic undertone. *Where the Money Is* may not be deep, but it is fun. The objective is met. The filmmakers have given Newman a worthy vehicle in which to display his wares. He is not upstaged by the other actors or by a busy screenplay. Watching *Where the Money Is* is like spending 90 minutes in the company of an old friend. RECOMMENDED

With a Friend Like Harry [France, 2000]

Starring: **Laurent Lucas, Sergi Lopez, Mathilde Seigner, Sophie Guillemin** Director: **Dominik Moll** Screenplay: **Gilles Marchand, Dominik Moll** Running Time: **1:57** Rated: **R** (Violence, brief nudity, profanity) Theatrical Aspect Ratio: **2.35:1** In French with subtitles

For American audiences, who have become conditioned to certain staples and formulas defining the structure of nearly every mainstream psychological thriller, *With a Friend Like Harry* may seem like a

breath of fresh air. It isn't that director Dominik Moll wanders too far from familiar territory, but the manner in which he crafts the movie allows him to reject (or at least deviate from) many of the most common clichés. Consequently, *With a Friend Like Harry* is a more energetic and interesting entry than what one has come to expect from this overpopulated genre.

For Michel (Laurent Lucas) and Claire (Mathilde Seigner), the annual family summer vacation is starting off like a nightmare — the car is not air conditioned, the baby is screaming, and the kids are misbehaving. By the time they reach a rest stop, the long hours in the car have taken their toll. There, in the men's room, Michel meets Harry (Sergi Lopez), a guy he hasn't seen in 20 years. Michel doesn't remember Harry, but Harry definitely remembers Michel. In almost no time, Harry has invited himself and his girlfriend, Plum (Sophie Guillemin), for a drink at Michel and Claire's. At first, Harry is the perfect guest — offering to help out with chores and even buying Michel and Claire a new car. But there's a darker side to Harry — his interest in Michel runs deeper than is healthy, expanding into the realm of obsession. On the evidence of one juvenile poem written decades ago, Harry believes that Michel has the potential to be a great writer, and that his talent should be nurtured, regardless of the price.

Moll has fun toying with audience expectations. Several of the murders, which would be the centerpieces of similar American films, occur off-screen. On at least two occasions, there is enough ambiguity about what actually happens that it's possible to construct entirely different versions of the event. And, by constructing the ending the way he does, Moll is able to play with us while still presenting a conclusion that is satisfying and offers a sense of closure. This is the kind of motion picture that, if he was still alive, Alfred Hitchcock would almost certainly have given his approval to. RECOMMENDED

War

Black Hawk Down [2001]

Starring: Josh Hartnett, Ewan McGregor, Tom Sizemore, Eric Bana
Director: Ridley Scott Screenplay: Ken Nolan, based on the book by
Mark Bowden Running Time: 2:23 Rated: R (Violence, gore) Theatrical
Aspect Ratio: 2.35:1

This is not an easy film to sit through, but it does what
it sets out to do and brings the audience deep into the
heart of combat. It's noisy, messy, and repetitive.
There are probably more bullets and explosions than
in any recent picture. Yet the illusion of "being there"
is so real that, at one point, I involuntarily ducked my
head to avoid being struck by something. Amazingly,
director Ridley Scott manages to convey the chaos of
the experience without losing the narrative.

Black Hawk Down opens with a quote by Plato:
"Only the dead have seen the end of war." Then, over
a color-desaturated series of images, we are presented with a brief history of why the United States
was in Somalia in the early '90s. The story begins on
October 2, 1993. Characters are introduced — Major
General William Garrison (Sam Shepard), who is in
command of the U.S. military presence in the region;
Staff Sergeant Matt Eversmann (Josh Hartnett), recently promoted to commanding a team; Company
Clerk John Grimes (Ewan McGregor), who is about to
exchange paperwork for a gun; Lt. Colonel Danny
McKnight (Tom Sizemore), in charge of a segment of
the ground troops; and Master Sergeant Paul Howe
(William Fichtner), who will challenge orders if he
thinks they are ill-advised. Together, these men, and
many others, are about to become involved in a
seemingly routine mission that will go disastrously
wrong.

The objective is to capture several key advisors to
Mohamed Farrah Aidid, the warlord who controls
Mogadishu. The United States wants Aidid out of the
way, and this seems to be the best opportunity to advance that goal. But the troops, both on the ground
and in the air, encounter stiffer resistance than expected, and this results in the downing of 2 black
hawk helicopters. The ground troops then become
divided as the raid turns into a rescue mission, and,
in part because of poor planning and in part because
of bad luck, the fire fight turns into a debacle.

This is a singularly effective motion picture. Sure, it
could have had more character development and
there are times when the gore verges on being gratuitously extreme (in particular, during the "operation"
to clamp an artery), but those are minor quibbles. On
the whole, *Black Hawk Down* is one hell of a ride. For
better or for worse, it will leave you stunned and reel-
ing. **HIGHLY RECOMMENDED**

Das Boot [West Germany, 1981]

Starring: Jurgen Prochnow, Herbert Gronemeyer, Klaus Wennemann,
Hubertus Bengsch Director: Wolfgang Petersen Screenplay: Wolfgang
Petersen based on the novel by Lothar G. Buchheim Running
Time: 2:29 Rated: R (Profanity, mature themes) Theatrical Aspect
Ratio: 2.35:1 In German with subtitles

During World War II in Germany, submarine duty was
considered a "glamour job." It was nearly every young
man's dream to be granted the privilege of serving the
Fatherland aboard one of the sleek, glorious U-boats.
As is often the case, the grim truth proved to be radically different from the shining fiction. Submarine
service was a grueling, debilitating, dehumanizing

experience, and *Das Boot* was the first motion picture to de-mythologize it completely.

The bulk of the film takes place within the boat, and follows a group of characters as they are transformed from the clean-shaven, energetic individuals who enter to the scraggly, dispirited men who eventually emerge. We see the story through the eyes of a German war correspondent (Herbert Gronemeyer) who is on board the boat for a single tour. The men are presented as he views them — a cadre of competent sailors united by bonds stronger than family or blood. The Captain (Jurgen Prochnow), an officer of great intelligence, experience, and compassion, has earned the respect of every man under his command. However, unlike in many war movies, this leader is not a tactical genius. He can, and does, make mistakes — some of which are costly. The crew is comprised of a diverse group of individuals, including a party member, a chief engineer on the verge of a breakdown, and a young man who longs for a reunion with his French fiancée.

When it comes to action, *Das Boot* is at the top of the class, and it's no wonder that, following its initial release, Wolfgang Petersen became a sought-after director. From the moment the crew first descends into the sub and we are given a tour of its innards, the sense of claustrophobia is suffocating. This feeling builds alongside the tension until the two, in concert, are almost unbearable. In later scenes, when the air supply is running out, we can feel ourselves gasping alongside the men, as if the oxygen is being siphoned out of the theater.

The battle scenes are superbly executed, not so much from a special effects perspective, but in the way that Petersen keeps us on the edge of our seats. The two standout sequences occur when the boat attacks a British caravan and when it attempts to wend its way through the treacherous straits of Gibraltar. Both are intense, nerve-wracking pieces of film making that are apt to elevate the heart rate of even the most blasé viewer. This film takes all of the drama and suspense inherent in a submarine-based story and delivers it in a near-perfect package, establishing *Das Boot* as not just a terrific adrenaline rush, but one of the best movies ever made. **MUST SEE**

Gettysburg, Ronald F. Maxwell's re-telling of 4 hot days during the summer of 1863 (based on the Pulitzer Prize winning novel *The Killer Angels* by Michael Shaara), is a spectacle that gathers power and momentum with every scene. The film is divided into 2 parts, with an intermission in between. The first section, which begins on June 30, 1863 (the day before the start of the battle of Gettysburg) and ends during the day of July 2 with Colonel Joshua Chamberlain's legendary defense of Little Round Top, is approximately 2 hours and 20 minutes long. The second part, which takes up the remaining 1:55, concentrates primarily on July 3 and the disastrous charge of Major General George Pickett and 15,000 members of the Confederate Army against the entrenched Union position atop Cemetery Ridge.

Over 50,000 were killed or wounded during this pivotal battle of the Civil War, and *Gettysburg* takes pains to breathe life and logic into the reasons for this. Yet it does far more than that. Rather than functioning as a text book come to life, the film uses its actors to flesh out characters from history, giving not only personalities to those on both sides of the struggle, but believable causes as well. We are presented with the rare opportunity to see not only the clash of arms on the field of battle, but the clash of wills beforehand.

Historical accuracy was of great concern to the producers and director. They hired a veritable army of advisors to correct even the most minute mistakes in the script (if a general given a pale horse in the movie was known to have favored a dark horse, the mount was changed), used the actual sites in Pennsylvania as often as possible (where hiding war monuments became an art), and "recruited" more than 5,000 unpaid re-enactors to fill up the screen during the battle scenes (thus helping to keep the budget at a reasonable $20 million). The result is a movie that looks and feels real.

Epic motion pictures are a rarity these days — even more rare than films about the Civil War. *Gettysburg* should satisfy both cravings. This film is perfectly placed in the wake of Ken Burns' PBS series for any who have a re-kindled interest in this segment of American history. For those with little more than a passing interest, *Gettysburg* is still gripping enough to captivate in its own right. **MUST SEE**

Gettysburg [1993]
Starring: Martin Sheen, Tom Berenger, Jeff Daniels, Richard Jordan Director: Ronald F. Maxwell Screenplay: Ronald F. Maxwell based on the book *The Killer Angels* by Michael Shaara Running Time: 4:14 Rated: PG (Violence) Theatrical Aspect Ratio: 1.78:1

Harrison's Flowers [France, 2000]
Starring: Andie MacDowell, David Strathairn, Elias Koteas, Adrien Brody Director: Elie Chouraqui Screenplay: Elie Chouraqui Running Time: 1:58 Rated: R (Graphic violence, gore, profanity) Theatrical Aspect Ratio: 2.35:1

Harrison's Flowers personalizes the war in Yugoslavia for one New Jersey couple. The year is 1991. Harrison Lloyd (David Strathairn) is an award-winning *Newsday* photojournalist who has decided to retire in order to spend more time with his wife, Sarah (Andie MacDowell), and their two children. His editor (Alun Armstrong) convinces him to stay on in the short term until a replacement can be found. Harrison's agreement has dire consequences. His next assignment takes him to Yugoslavia, where the civil unrest is turning ugly. There, Harrison disappears and is presumed dead. But, because there is no body, Sarah will not accept that he is gone. So, alone and equipped with only a camera, she heads for the epicenter of the conflict — Vukovar — and quickly learns firsthand how war can turn human beings into rabid beasts.

At its heart, *Harrison's Flowers* is a love story, albeit a graphic and difficult one. It shows the lengths to which a woman will go when presented with the slimmest of hope that her husband might still be alive. As a character observes, "If we could all be so lucky to have a woman love us that much." Sarah's journey into Yugoslavia's heart of darkness changes many things about her, not the least of which is her view of human nature, but it never shakes the core of her being. She places Harrison above her children and herself — finding him becomes central to her existence. If he has died in Vukovar, she will meet her end there as well.

Although her journey starts out as a solo endeavor, she is eventually joined by 3 other journalists, all of whom knew Harrison: Americans Kyle (Adrien Brody) and Yeager (Elias Koteas), and Brit Stevenson (Brendan Gleeson). Hardened as these men are by things they have witnessed during previous assignments, nothing prepares them for the barbarity they experience as they gain firsthand knowledge of what is meant by the term "ethnic cleansing." Writer/director Elie Chouraqui gives us a series of memorable, harrowing visual cues, none of which is more disturbing that the sight of a dead girl, shot through the head, with dried blood caking her inner thighs — evidence of what was done to her before the coup de grace was administered. Chouraqui does not dwell on such images — merely showing them is enough.

RECOMMENDED

Hart's War [2002]

Starring: Bruce Willis, Colin Farrell, Terrence Dashon Howard, Vicellous Reon Director: **Gregory Hoblit** Screenplay: **Billy Ray** and

Terry George Running Time: 2:05 Rated: R (Violence, profanity) Theatrical Aspect Ratio: 2.35:1

It's December 1944 in Belgium and Lieutenant Tommy Hart (Colin Farrell), by virtue of his privileged upbringing (he's the son of a Senator), is far away from the fighting. When a routine chauffeur mission takes him into an unexpected German ambush, he ends up being tortured by the Nazis until he gives up the location of a fuel dump. After that, he is shipped to Stalag VIA, where the U.S. prisoners of war are led by Colonel William McNamara (Bruce Willis), under the watchful eye of SS Major Wilhelm Visser (Marcel Iures). McNamara is initially suspicious of Hart, rightfully assuming that he cracked under torture, and assigns him to bunk with the enlisted men rather than the officers. Hart isn't alone there for long, however — when two black officers, Lt. Lincoln Scott (Terrence Dashon Howard) and Lamar Archer (Vicellous Reon Shannon), arrive, they are also assigned to sleep with the grunts. The current of racism in the barracks is unmistakable, with one man in particular, Bedford (Cole Hauser), expressing his outrage and hatred in unmistakable terms. Shortly after setting up Archer for having a concealed weapon in his bunk, Bedford is found murdered with Scott standing over his body. McNamara requests that Visser allow the Americans to hold a court martial hearing. Visser, amused by the idea, agrees, and Hart is given the unenviable task of being Scott's lawyer, even though he has not finished law school.

The film is less of a traditional war story than it is one man's quest for redemption. After giving in to Nazi torture, Tommy Hart attempts to find the courage and opportunity to regain his honor. By defending Scott, a man he believes to be innocent, he is given this chance — even though Scott's fate seems sealed. As portrayed by Colin Farrell, Hart is a timid individual who is learning to stand up for himself.

Hart's War works uncommonly well because of the effective manner in which it blends together its various elements: the WWII prison camp setting, the courtroom aspects, and the issues of honor, racism, and redemption. This is one of those war movies that focuses on human interaction rather than battle and action sequences (there are a few of those, but not many), and it's all the stronger because of it.

RECOMMENDED

No Man's Land [France/Italy/Slovenia/United Kingdom, 2001]

Starring: Branko Djuric, Rene Bitorajac, Simon Callow, Katrin Cartlidge Director: **Danis Tanovic** Screenplay: **Danis Tanovic** Running Time: 1:38

Rated: R (Violence, profanity) Theatrical Aspect Ratio: 2.35:1 In Bosnian and French with subtitles

Bosnia is the province of *No Man's Land* — a place whose horrific and catastrophic civil war few Americans understood and even fewer cared about. Part of that has to do with the fact that the conflict occurred half a world away; another part has to do with the superficial nature of the media coverage. But for Eastern Europe, the situation in the Balkans was of a more immediate concern. And, whereas Hollywood has used the Bosnian conflict to give us gung-ho, old fashioned war pictures, first-time Bosnian director Danis Tanovic has countered with the dark, sober *No Man's Land,* a movie that is by turns blackly satirical and hauntingly real.

The movie opens in the midst of a dense fog — an apt metaphor for the chaos that swirled around the former Yugoslavia — with a small group of Bosnian soldiers making their way towards the front lines. They get lost, and, when the mists clear, they are massacred by the Serbs. One survivor, Chiki (Branko Djuric), ends up in a trench in no man's land, temporarily safe from attack by the enemy, but unable to return to his side. Soon after, two Serbs stealthily make their way to the trench to search for survivors. Chiki eliminates one, but ends up in a standoff with the other, Nino (Rene Bitorajac). They endure an uneasy truce until they discover a third person, Cera (Filip Sovagovic), whose precarious situation represents a danger to all 3 survivors. And, when a United Nations force with an accompanying media caravan arrives, the situation becomes less, not more, stable.

No Man's Land is essentially comprised of two elements — the 3-character sequences in the trench, which reveal less about the individuals trapped there than about the depth of their people's blind hatred for one another. This is the Serb/Bosnian conflict in a microcosm, and is as compelling as it is difficult to watch. These characters bond, but not in the way we expect them to. The other aspect of *No Man's Land* is a broad condemnation of United Nations' "aid" — how politics and egos cause well-intentioned efforts to decay into exercises in incompetence. The media plays a prime role — the military ends up manipulating what the cameras see to serve their own ends because they are fearful of a public relations nightmare.

With the United States currently involved in attacking Afghanistan and with pro-military patriotic fervor at a post-World War II high, it is unclear how well a movie like this, with a clear anti-war message,

will fare. There is no doubt, however, that, like *Platoon* and *Saving Private Ryan, No Man's Land* poses some disturbing questions about the nature of hatred and the wars it spawns. **HIGHLY RECOMMENDED**

Paradise Road [United States/United Kingdom/Australia, 1997]
Starring: Glenn Close, Cate Blanchett, Jennifer Ehle, Frances McDormand Director: Bruce Beresford Screenplay: Bruce Beresford Running Time: 1:55 Rated: R (Violence, nudity) Theatrical Aspect Ratio: 2.35:1

The film opens in February of 1942 on a night of dining and dancing at Singapore's Raffles Hotel. It's a gala ball for soldiers stationed in the Pacific and their wives (or girlfriends). The party breaks up when it's announced that the Japanese advance has pushed the Allies back and the city is about to fall. While the men return to their units, the women evacuate, cramming aboard the *Prince Albert* for the boat trip back to Australia. They are a mixed bunch of Australians, English, and Americans, and petty quarrels break out in the close quarters. But these differences are all forgotten when Japanese planes attack and sink the ship. The waterlogged and weary survivors come ashore on the Japanese-occupied island of Sumatra, where they are rounded up and thrown into a concentration camp. There, over the course of the next 3½ years, they fight to survive and not lose hope. To this end, they form a "vocal orchestra" — a chorus that astounds audiences of fellow prisoners by performing hummed renditions of the work of Mozart, Dvorak, and Holst.

The exceptionally strong cast showcases American, British, and Australian actresses, all of whom show an astonishing willingness to appear in physically unflattering circumstances (no makeup, hair and skin caked with drying mud). The conductor of the orchestra, Adrienne Pargiter, is played with grit and zeal by Glenn Close, and represents her best screen work in years. Cate Blanchett essays Susan Macarthy, a timid nurse who finds her voice (in more ways than one) while in the camp. Jennifer Ehle, with her expressive eyes, is Rosemary Leighton-Jones, a beautiful young woman who dreams of being reunited with her true love. Frances McDormand, sporting an absurdly distracting accent, is the camp doctor.

Paradise Road is less a tearjerker than an honest examination of the bonds that are formed during extreme situations. Although there are some heart-wrenching moments, and several scenes of potentially-disturbing violence, the film never descends to the level of cheap melodrama. Instead, it opts for something deeper and more meaningful by allowing us to follow a group of well-rounded characters on a journey with a strong spiritual component. *Paradise Road* not only pays tribute to the human will to live, but it is a testament to music's lasting power to heal and uplift. HIGHLY RECOMMENDED

Pretty Village, Pretty Flame [Yugoslavia, 1996]

Starring: Dragan Bjelogrlic, Nikola Kojo, Velimir-Bata Zivojinovic
Director: Srdjan Dragojevic Screenplay: Nikola Pejakovic, Srdjan Dragojevic, from war reports by Vanja Bulic Running Time: 2:15
Rated: Not Rated (Violence, profanity, mature themes, sex) Theatrical Aspect Ratio: 1.85:1 In Serbian with subtitles

Pretty Village, Pretty Flame is based on a true event. It opens in 1971 with a mock newsreel depicting the ribbon-cutting ceremony for the "Brotherhood and Unity Tunnel." Ten years later, the unfinished tunnel stands abandoned and ignored. Two boys, a Muslim named Halil and a Serb named Milan, play nearby and try to frighten each other with tales of the ogre who lives inside. By the time war breaks out in the early '90s, Halil and Milan find themselves on opposite sides. When his platoon is ambushed, Milan leads the survivors into the tunnel for refuge. Outside, Halil's band waits patiently, biding their time until the Serbs run out of water and must emerge to face their deaths.

Pretty Village, Pretty Flame is told in a non-chronological fashion that makes a film like *Pulp Fiction* seem linear. The movie jumps freely across no fewer than 4 time lines (1980, 1992, and 2 different segments of 1994). The majority of the scenes take place while the soldiers are trapped in the tunnel. There are also numerous flashbacks to the beginning of the war and a time before the conflict, as well as flash-forwards to a military hospital. At first, all of this jumping around can be very confusing, especially before you know the individuals, but, as the film progresses, it becomes clear how powerful this technique is in explaining events and developing characters.

The film is a variation of the "trapped in a foxhole" story. Sandwiched in between bursts of fighting are lengthy sequences of character interaction as the disparate members of the platoon (plus an American photojournalist who doesn't speak Serbian) come to grips with their prejudices against each other, their feelings about war, and, most importantly, their fear of death. *Pretty Village, Pretty Flame* is about 7 men and 1 women ("Snow White and the 7 dwarves," one of the soldiers quips) facing their own mortality.
HIGHLY RECOMMENDED

Regeneration [United Kingdom, 1997]

Starring: Jonathan Pryce, James Wilby, Jonny Lee Miller, Stuart Bunce
Director: Gillies MacKinnon Screenplay: Allan Scott based on the novel by Pat Barker Running Time: 1:40 Rated: R (Violence, gore, profanity, sex, nudity) Theatrical Aspect Ratio: 1.85:1

Regeneration is Gillies MacKinnon's look at the horrors of war (specifically, World War I) and the effects they have on the men who must endure them. *Regeneration* does not argue that war is wrong, but it asks us to question, without looking through a haze of patriotic pride, when a nation's political, economic, or moral position is in enough jeopardy to warrant the horrifying debt of blood that will inevitably be incurred.

The majority of *Regeneration,* which is adapted from a novel by Pat Barker, takes place within the walls of Craiglockart, a Scottish hospital for those whose war wounds are to the mind and spirit, not the body. The story centers around 4 men: established poet and war hero Siegfried Sassoon (James Wilby), neophyte writer Wilfred Owen (Stuart Bunce), shell-shocked officer Billy Prior (Jonny Lee Miller), and the doctor who treats them all, William Rivers (Jonathan Pryce). Sassoon has been sent to Craiglockart to discredit him, because his current philosophy, that the war has become one of "aggression and conquest" is a source of embarrassment to his senior officers. While there, he strikes up a friendship with Owen, and the two spend many hours talking about writing. Meanwhile, Prior, who is fighting to break through a memory blockage, is romancing a local munitions plant worker (Tanya Allen). And Rivers, who is gradually taking on the burdens of all his patients, is on the way to a breakdown. His character arc — from a strong, self-assured psychiatrist to a stammering, conscience-stricken man — is the film's most dramatic.

Rivers is the individual who provides the film with its glue, and actor Jonathan Pryce breathes life into him. Rivers represents one of the actor's finest portrayals, a once-confident doctor who slowly crumbles under the onslaught of pain he absorbs from the men under his care. There is no melodrama here, just good acting and solid writing. Rivers is allowed to retain his dignity. The other primary performances, especially that of Jonny Lee Miller, are solid.

Although *Regeneration* is not as devastating a motion picture experience as *Saving Private Ryan,* it touches upon many of the same subjects. This movie is more cerebral and reserved, but it makes at least one telling point about the dehumanizing experience of war — often, the deepest wounds endured in battle are not those done to the body, but those suffered by the mind. Doctors may be able to regenerate flesh, but mending a broken spirit requires considerably more time, energy, and skill. RECOMMENDED

Ride with the Devil [1999]

Starring: Tobey Maguire, Skeet Ulrich, Jewel, Jeffrey Wright
Director: Ang Lee   Screenplay: James Schamus, based on *Woe To Live On* by Daniel Woodrell   Running Time: 2:15   Rated: R (Violence, occasional profanity, brief nudity)   Theatrical Aspect Ratio: 2.35:1

The 4 main characters — Jake Roedel (Tobey Maguire), Jack Bull Chiles (Skeet Ulrich), George Clyde (Simon Baker-Denny), and Daniel Holt (Jeffrey Wright) — are members of the "Missouri Irregulars," a poorly organized, rag-tag group that wages guerrilla warfare against Union loyalists. Like their jayhawker enemies, these bushwhackers often attack without warning or mercy, killing men and burning whole villages with seeming impunity. Roedel and Chiles fight out of loyalty to the Confederacy and because they hate the Yankees (both have lost loved ones to Federalists). Clyde, the prototypical Southern gentleman, is at war to preserve his way of life. And, Holt, the most interesting man in the group, is an ex-slave who fights for the South out of a sense of allegiance to Clyde, who purchased then freed him. Holt does not believe in Clyde's cause, but he will fight alongside his friend for as long as they both continue to breathe.

The story develops over the course of a winter, while the four men hide out in a crudely built shelter on the property of a pro-Confederacy family, the Evanses. A young widow in the household, Sue Lee Shelly (Jewel), becomes involved with Chiles, and Clyde spends much of his time visiting a local lady friend. This gives Roedel and Holt an opportunity to get to know one another, and sets up the inevitable tragedy when combat occurs and not all of the participants escape with their lives. After the Irregulars stage a bloody raid on Lawrence, Kansas (a Union stronghold), they are hunted down by Northern troops and cut to pieces. Injured survivors seek shelter with friendly families and are forced to re-evaluate their participation in the war.

As the film progresses, Ang Lee increasingly stresses the pointlessness of the Irregulars' struggle. The only thing they are accomplishing is killing people. Nothing they do has any impact on the war. This truth occurs to everyone, beginning with Sue Lee and ending with Roedel, as disillusionment convinces each of them of the folly of continuing the fight. *Ride with the Devil* also illustrates the horrible excesses that some men go to in the name of a cause.

Ride with the Devil is a different sort of Civil War story. It takes us away from the big battles of the East and to a place where things are less cleanly defined. Although Missouri was not a battleground where the Union and Confederate armies repeatedly clashed, it was nevertheless rent by strife. As was true almost everywhere else, ideological gulfs often divided families. This is the terrain into which Lee has ventured, and the resulting motion picture offers yet another effective and affecting portrait of the United States' most important and difficult conflict. RECOMMENDED

Saving Private Ryan [1998]

Starring: Tom Hanks, Tom Sizemore, Matt Damon, Edward Burns
Director: Steven Spielberg   Screenplay: Robert Rodat   Running Time: 2:50   Rated: R (Extreme and graphic gore & violence, profanity)   Theatrical Aspect Ratio: 1.85:1

Saving Private Ryan opens with a 30-minute cinematic tour de force that is without a doubt one of the finest half-hours ever committed to film. This sequence, a soldier's-eye view of the D-Day invasion of Normandy, is brilliant not only in terms of technique but in the depth of viewer reaction it generates. It is certainly the most violent, gory, visceral depiction of war that I have ever witnessed on screen. Steven Spielberg spares the viewer nothing of the horrors of battle, using every tactic at his disposal to convey the chaos and senseless waste that lies at the core of any engagement. We are presented with unforgettable, bloody images of bodies being cut to pieces by bullets, limbs blown off, entrails spilling out, and a variety of other assorted examples of carnage.

The D-Day invasion at "Bloody Omaha" Beach forms a prologue to the main story. Following the opening half-hour sequence, we learn that 2 of the 4 Ryan brothers died in this action, while a third perished elsewhere. The mother receives all 3 telegrams on the same day. The U.S. army chief of staff, General George C. Marshall (Harve Presnell), is stirred by the grief-stricken woman's plight, and decides to send a group of men into the French countryside to find and rescue the fourth son, paratrooper Private James Ryan (Matt Damon).

Captain John Miller (Tom Hanks), a hero and survivor of the Omaha Beach battle, is chosen to lead the team of 8 men whose goal is, in Miller's words, like finding "a needle in a stack of needles." His hand-picked team includes 6 men who have served with him throughout the war and one newcomer: Upham (Jeremy Davies), a French/German/English translator who has never seen active combat. Together, they strike out across the French countryside, heading in the general direction of Cherbourg. Along the way, they learn that skirmishes in small towns can be as deadly as the attack on the beach.

In *Saving Private Ryan,* there are no human villains, and the enemy isn't so much the Germans as it is the implacable, destructive specter of war. The film's central question (When is one life more important than another?) is never really answered. For those who are willing to brave the movie's shocking and unforgettable images, *Saving Private Ryan* offers a singular motion picture experience. **MUST SEE**

Stalingrad [Germany/Sweden, 1993]

Starring: Thomas Kretschmann, Dominique Horwitz, Jochen Nickel, Sebastian Rudolph Director: Joseph Vilsmaier Screenplay: Juergen Buescher, Johannes M.M. Heide, and Joseph Vilsmaier Running Time: 2:12 Rated: Not Rated (Violence) Theatrical Aspect Ratio: 1.85:1 In German with subtitles

Stalingrad, which takes place between August 1942 and January 1943, chronicles Hitler's failed invasion of the Russian city — one of the miscalculations that lost the war for Germany. More than one million died in the bloody struggle, the fatalities caused by wounds, disease, and the same bitter cold that stopped Napolean's forces more than a century earlier. *Stalingrad* faithfully re-creates the principal historical aspects of the battle while telling a more intimate tale through the eyes of a small group of German characters.

They are Hans Witzland (Thomas Kretschmann), a clean-cut lieutenant making his first trip to the front, and Manfred "Rollo" Rohleder (Jochen Nickel) and Fritz Reiser (Dominique Horwitz), two hardened veteran enlisted men. Together, these 3 make the long, weary trek down the road of senseless violence and death, losing bits of their humanity along the way. The horrors of *Stalingrad* irrevocably destroy these men, strafing their souls and crushing their spirits. By the end, it no longer matters whether they live or die — in almost every way, they're already gone.

The psychologically destructive power of war is most clearly illustrated through the changes undergone by Hans. When *Stalingrad* opens, he is a patriot serving the Führer and Fatherland unquestioningly. Soon, however, loyalty to his country is supplanted by loathing as he sees the inhumane treatment accorded to Russian prisoners of war. Then, as the battle becomes desperate, with the German army losing scores just to capture another street, the most basic of animal drives — the need to survive — asserts itself.

Ultimately, even that runs dry, and Hans finds himself groping to save a tiny vestige of the man he once was.

There isolated moments of human triumph in *Stalingrad* — like a Russian and German exchanging bread for meat, and Hans setting a woman free instead of raping her. But these are exceptions. *Stalingrad's* disturbing power comes through its portrayal of the horrific — decapitations, amputations, grizzly deaths, and mutilations. Nothing is gratuitous; everything is effective. Director Joseph Vilsmaier pulls us into the trenches with these men, who are no different from soldiers on any side in any war. *Stalingrad* is packed with tension, and the battle sequences are startlingly realistic, but it's the inescapable message that lingers. **HIGHLY RECOMMENDED**

The Thin Red Line [1998]

Starring: Sean Penn, James Caviezel, Ben Chaplin, Elias Koteas, Nick Nolte Director: Terrence Malick Screenplay: Terrence Malick based on the novel by James Jones Running Time: 2:50 Rated: R (Violence, profanity) Theatrical Aspect Ratio: 2.35:1

The Thin Red Line is the story of the Guadalcanal conflict as seen from the American side of the front line. There are 5 main characters and a host of secondary ones. The commanding officer is Lt. Colonel Gordon Tall (Nick Nolte), who's involved in this battle for all the glory he can commandeer. To that end, he has no problem ordering scores of men to throw away their lives by attacking a seemingly-impregnable position. Captain James Staros (Elias Koteas), the commander of "C" Company who is known for his kindness to his men, refuses a direct order from Tall when he believes it's a suicide mission. Sgt. Edward Welsh (Sean Penn) has a reputation for being cold and hard, but, on the battlefield, he displays his humanity by risking his own life to get pain killers to a mortally wounded soldier. Private Witt (James Caviezel), despite nearly being courtmartialed for going AWOL, distinguishes himself in combat. And Private Bell (Ben Chaplin) performs acts of astounding bravery as his memories of his perfect marriage to a beautiful woman (Miranda Otto) fuel his desire to return home alive.

One of the things that *The Thin Red Line* does well is to illustrate the terror and chaos of war. The characters here aren't macho guys marching into a hail of bullets for the glory of the moment. They're scared men staring death in the face — a death that waits concealed in the beauty of a grassy hill. You can see the panic in their eyes when violence shatters the serenity of the countryside. There is valor in *The Thin*

Red Line, but that's not the point of the film, and the characters who perform the great deeds don't feel like heroes.

After the battle for the hill is over, Malick doesn't seem to know where to go with the movie. The final hour is a fragmentary narrative about random events that occur afterwards. It isn't compelling and there are times when it borders on being incoherent. A battle occurs towards the end of the film, but most of it apparently happens off screen. One moment, a massive force of Japanese troops is advancing; the next, it's all over and a commanding officer is addressing the survivors.

Although *The Thin Red Line* will not go down as the kind of war movie classic that *Saving Private Ryan* will, there are still many reasons to see this motion picture, especially for those who appreciate epic battle stories. See it for Malick's unparalleled visual style, for the primary character portrayals, and for the effectively chaotic, in-your-face combat sequences. The movie has the capacity to engage on both an intellectual and a visceral level. RECOMMENDED

Three Kings [1999]

Starring: George Clooney, Mark Wahlberg, Ice Cube, Spike Jonze
Director: David O. Russell Screenplay: David O. Russell based on a story by John Ridley Running Time: 1:54 Rated: R (Profanity, violence, gore) Theatrical Aspect Ratio: 2.35:1

Just as the Gulf War wasn't a traditional conflict, so *Three Kings* is not a traditional war picture — there are no big battles and only a few small-scale skirmishes. Instead, this is more of an action/adventure film, and a fairly good one at that. The characters are well developed, the situations are effectively realized, and, most importantly, there's some thought-provoking content just beneath the surface. Until the ending, *Three Kings* is a surprisingly solid effort.

Three Kings should probably be called *Four Kings,* since there are 4 main characters (although it would wreck the Biblical allusion). Archie Gates (George Clooney), Troy Barlow (Mark Wahlberg), Chief Elgin (Ice Cube), and Vig (Spike Jonze) are soldiers stuck in Iraq during March 1991, just after the ceasefire declaration. Early in the film, after Troy shoots a gun-toting Iraqi soldier, Vig sums up their experience by saying, "I didn't think I'd get to see anyone get shot in this war. Take a picture." Meanwhile, Archie, who is only weeks away from retirement, isn't being cooperative with the reporter (Nora Dunn) he has been asked to escort. He is told curtly by a superior, "This is a media war. You'd better get on board." The boredom lifts for all 4 men when they come into possession of a map that shows the possible location of a secret bunker where Saddam Hussein may have hidden millions of dollars in gold bullion stolen from Kuwait. With mercenary intentions, Archie, Troy, Vig, and the Chief set out one morning with the intention of striking it rich. Reality deals them a harsh blow, however. Once away from the army camp, they come across Saddam's troops brutally massacring those Iraqi citizens who have followed George Bush's exhortation to throw off their leader's yoke. Expecting American aid, they rebelled against Saddam, only to discover that no foreign help would be forthcoming.

As action/adventure movies go, *Three Kings* is reasonably effective. It's about mercenaries who start out with hardened, cynical hearts but who grow to feel deeply for the plight of the people around them. The action sequences are expertly directed, and David O. Russell develops tension because we're never sure who's going to survive or what's going to happen next. There are also several scenes of graphic brutality that underscore the basic inhumanity of any armed conflict. *Three Kings* is solidly structured until the end, which has a tacked-on feel. The conclusion and epilogue both seem like they were added to please Hollywood executives who might not otherwise have greenlighted the project. Overall, however, *Three Kings* makes for an interesting and occasionally exhilarating examination of modern war and human brutality. RECOMMENDED

We Were Soldiers [2002]

Starring: Mel Gibson, Madeleine Stowe, Sam Elliott, Greg Kinnear
Director: Randall Wallace Screenplay: Randall Wallace, based on *We Were Soldiers Once, and Young* by Hal Moore and Joe Galloway
Running Time: 2:18 Rated: R (War violence, profanity) Theatrical Aspect Ratio: 2.35:1

We Were Soldiers is the latest in the new breed of war movies — films that throw the viewer into the midst of the chaos and brutality of the fray, giving audiences a taste of the violent, visceral nature of an armed conflict, while still allowing moments of honor and heroism to stand out. The film tells of the November 1965 battle in the Ia Drang Valley (aka "The Valley of Death"), which was the first major engagement between American and North Vietnamese troops. Before taking the story to Vietnam, however, director Randall Wallace allows us to spend some time with the American soldiers at home. This becomes crucial to the movie's later success, as it humanizes the men, presenting them as more than faceless fodder for enemy bullets. If only briefly, we see their wives and children. Then they ship off, and, in seemingly no time, are trapped and outnumbered, fighting for their lives.

The commanding officer is Lt. Colonel Hal Moore (Mel Gibson), the leader of the 1st Battalion of the 7th Cavalry. He is a student of history and a master of tactics, and his motto is to leave no man behind. Before departing for Vietnam, he has spent sleepless nights poring over books detailing previous military engagements there, and he is determined not to repeat the mistakes of those who preceded him. In the midst of battle, Moore is at his best, inspiring confidence in his men by never expecting more of them than he is willing and able to give. He seems to be everywhere, bolstering spirits and improvising defenses for each new attack by the enemy. The men under his command include daredevil helicopter pilot Snakeshit Crandall (Greg Kinnear); the gentle and well-liked Lieutenant Jack Geoghegan (Chris Klein), whose wife has just given birth; and the crusty Sergeant Major Basil Plumley (Sam Elliott in the R. Lee Ermey role), Moore's right-hand man. Another key participant is photojournalist Joe Galloway (Barry Pepper), who is temporarily forced to exchange his camera for a gun.

Once, war movies were very much arm's length affairs, but, in an era when so many lines have been crossed and so many barriers broken, such an approach no longer works. As a result, the in-your-face style of *We Were Soldiers* results in a suspenseful, intense, and exhausting cinematic experience. There are times when the film is grueling and times when it is exhilarating. The movie has the ability to keep viewers on the edges of their seats and to wring tears from their eyes. It's an amazing experience, and a second success from the team that previously cooperated to give us an Oscar-winning motion picture (*Braveheart*). Their subject, both then and now, is about the courageous of spirit and brave of heart. **HIGHLY RECOMMENDED**

Welcome to Sarajevo [United Kingdom/United States, 1997]

Starring: Stephen Dillane, Woody Harrelson, Marisa Tomei, Emira Nusevic Director: Michael Winterbottom Screenplay: Frank Cottrell Boyce, based on the book *Natasha's Story* by Michael Nicholson Running Time: 1:40 Rated: R (Graphic violence, profanity) Theatrical Aspect Ratio: 2.35:1

Welcome to Sarajevo isn't just the story of an outsider's perspective of the conflict; it's a compelling examination of the role the media played in reporting and shaping the average person's views of the war. And, while there's nothing revolutionary or extraordinary about the dramatic narrative, the subtext gives Michael Winterbottom's movie its force. As a tale focused upon the horrors of war, *Welcome to Sarajevo* doesn't cover any new ground, but as an autopsy of what the conflict meant to a worldwide television audience, this is new and disturbing material.

The British newsman at the center of *Welcome to Sarajevo* is Michael Henderson (Stephen Dillane), whose character is based on a real-life individual (just as the movie's script was developed from the non-fictional account, *Natasha's Story*). He's a veteran war reporter stationed in Sarajevo along with his cameraman, Gregg (James Nesbitt), and his producer, Jane (Kerry Fox). Other reporters include the cynical American Jordan Flynn (Woody Harrelson) and a freelancer named Annie (Emily Lloyd), who is young and driven. For his part, Michael is growing disenchanted with his network's coverage of the news, and this leads to his involvement in an ongoing story about a front-line orphanage. What begins as a series of reports turns into a crusade, with Michael imperiling both his career and his life to get one 9-year-old girl, Emira (Emira Nusevic), out of the country at a time when the official policy is "no evacuation." *Welcome to Sarajevo* charts Michael's progress from dispassionate watcher to activist.

Throughout the film, we are given glimpses of the way the journalists on the scene report the news, and what becomes of their stories. One particularly graphic massacre is bumped from the top of the hour in favor of an item about the separation of the Duke and Duchess of York. Michael's producer, Jane, warns him that his crusade about the orphanage may be falling on deaf ears. It's all about ratings. Information is less important than entertainment, and it's difficult to make such a grotesque, twisted war, where sniper fire kills innocent bystanders, entertaining. By using a combination of real archived video, faux video filmed specifically for this movie, and normal 35mm footage, Winterbottom creates a kaleidoscope of juxtaposed images. We're never sure what's true and what isn't — whether a video of writhing, bloody bodies is genuine or a realistic recreation. This technique further illustrates how blurred the line has become between authentic, hard news and its controlled, entertainment-controlled counterpart. **HIGHLY RECOMMENDED**

Western

The Ballad of Little Jo [1993]

Starring: Suzy Amis, Bo Hopkins, Ian McKellen Director: Maggie Greenwald Screenplay: Maggie Greenwald Running Time: 2:00 Rated: R (Nudity, mature themes, violence) Theatrical Aspect Ratio: 1.85:1

Once Josephine Monaghan (Suzy Amis) lost her virginity and gave birth to a bastard, her future was ruined. With her past sins hanging over her like a hangman's noose, she has no choice but to flee the constrained, pampered socialite's world she knew in the East, and head West. There she discovers that the best life she can lead as a woman is that of a prostitute, so she makes the bold decision to grab at freedom and independence by masquerading as a man. Whiskers and muscles aren't necessary. The mere appearance of a female as a male in a time when it's "illegal to dress improper to your sex" is enough to convince just about everyone.

Loosely based on the true-life story of a woman about whom little is known, the story of *Little Jo* is a masterpiece of detail and intelligence. Maggie Greenwald has done her homework, piecing together an engrossing tale that movies quickly enough to keep the easily-distracted involved, but not so rapidly that it misses the nuances of the situation. Touches of humor are mixed nicely with drama as of *Little Jo* explores the entire spectrum of human emotions. And just because Jo has chosen to live life as a man doesn't mean that she can't yearn for her lost femininity.

The focal point of this film is Jo. As played by Suzy Amis, the character is not perfectly developed, but the actress gets better as the movie unfolds. I was particularly unimpressed with her early scenes (when she's openly female), but after the "transformation," she settled into the role. Amis is not an especially emotive actress, and her Jo is reserved — perhaps occasionally too much so. The most effective scenes are those of quiet emotion, such as when Jo sheds a tear.

If you like films about the "new Old West," *The Ballad of Little Jo* is a worthwhile choice. Even for those who aren't particularly fond of Westerns, this movie still has a lot to offer. Keeping the conventions of the genre to a minimum, it strikes out in bolder directions, reflecting personalities and lifestyles through the eyes of a woman whom everyone accepts as a man. *The Ballad of Little Jo* loses its focus on a number of occasions, but never for very long, and never in a manner that jeopardizes the viewer's overall enjoyment of Maggie Greenwald's film. **RECOMMENDED**

Dances with Wolves [1990]

Starring: Kevin Costner, Mary McDonnell, Graham Greene, Rodney A. Grant Director: Kevin Costner Screenplay: Michael Blake, based on his novel Running Time: 3:03 Rated: PG-13 (Violence, animal deaths, discreet sex & nudity) Theatrical Aspect Ratio: 2.35:1

Dances with Wolves has been called a "revisionist western" — a movie that reversed the traditional roles of Cowboys and Indians. In fact, it's nothing of the sort. While it is true that the Sioux tribe is portrayed with the kind of balance and sensitivity rarely accorded to Native Americans in any movie, the Pawnee do not fare as well (as Sioux enemies, they are presented in much the same fashion that Indians were back in the '50s and '60s). And the American soldiers are depicted as genuine, imperfect human beings, not as thoughtless, vicious brutes. *Dances with Wolves* did not subvert the entire genre; it just twisted a few of the conventions.

Dances with Wolves opens with a brief Civil War prologue in which the protagonist, Lt. John Dunbar (Costner), establishes himself as a hero by providing a diversion so that a group of Union soldiers can overcome an entrenched Rebel position. Because of his bravery, he is offered a station anywhere he wants. He chooses the frontier, so he can see it before it is gone. For over a month, Dunbar is alone at Fort Sedgewick. His only companions are a friendly wolf that he names Two Socks and his faithful mount, Cisco.

The story moves into high gear with the arrival of the Sioux, led by the thoughtful Kicking Bird (Graham Greene) and the tempestuous Wind in His Hair (Rodney A. Grant). At first, there is mutual distrust, but, as Dunbar and the Sioux interact and begin to communicate (each learning a few words of the other's language), they form a truce, then a bond. His interaction with them becomes even easier when Stands With A Fist (Mary McDonnell), a white woman who has lived with the Sioux since childhood, is able to act as an interpreter. Eventually, Dunbar leaves Fort Sedgewick and moves into the Sioux camp. He falls in love with Stands With A Fist, becomes a respected member of the tribe with his own Sioux name ("Dances With Wolves"), and is able to forget the life he left behind — until the day when Fort Sedgewick is garrisoned and the soldiers find him: an out-of-uniform officer "gone Injun."

Dances with Wolves works on many levels. It's a rousing adventure, a touching romance, and a stirring drama. Although *Dances with Wolves* contains several well-executed battle scenes, there's little doubt that the most breathtaking sequence is the buffalo hunt, where the Sioux riders race alongside thousands of rampaging buffalo and bring several of them down. It's a high adrenaline sequence that marks the moment when Dunbar finally rejects his old culture to embrace his new one. Not just during that sequence, but for three hours, *Dances with Wolves* transports us to another world, and that's the mark of a great motion picture. **MUST SEE**

The Hi-Lo Country [1998]

Starring: Woody Harrelson, Billy Crudup, Patricia Arquette, Cole Hauser Director: **Stephen Frears** Screenplay: Walon Green based on the book by Max Evans Running Time: 1:54 Rated: R (Violence, profanity, sexual situations) Theatrical Aspect Ratio: 2.35:1

The Hi-Lo Country is a curious marriage of genres. This movie illustrates the result of grafting film noir onto a western. It's what happens when a femme fatale hops into the saddle and the sack with a cowboy. Unusual as the mix may be, it is ultimately successful. While the setting and scenery are exactly what one might expect from a western, the fast-paced action has been replaced by a slowly-escalating tension and the unshakable sensation of impending doom. And the voiceover narrative, with its promise of violence, would be at home in a crime thriller.

The Hi-Lo Country takes place in New Mexico shortly after the curtain has dropped on World War II. The two main characters, Big Boy Matson (Woody Harrelson) and Pete Calder (Billy Crudup), are old school cowboys. In spite of, or perhaps because of, their vast personality difference, they're the best of friends. Together, they share dreams and a workload, and ultimately fall for the same woman: Mona Birk (Patricia Arquette), the raven-haired siren whose smell and looks mesmerize Big Boy and Pete.

Although Mona flirts with Pete, she's in love with Big Boy. Pete realizes that this makes her untouchable, but even a relationship with a pretty Mexican-American girl, Josepha (Penélope Cruz), can't banish her from his thoughts. But the complications don't stop there. Mona is married to Les Birk (John Diehl), an older man who works for the biggest landowner in the district, Jim Ed Love (Sam Elliot). Big Boy resents Love's business ways, and takes out his anger on anyone who is employed by the man, including his own brother, Little Boy (Cole Hauser). As a mark of his contempt for Les, Big Boy gradually becomes unconcerned about concealing his relationship with Mona, guaranteeing that the cuckolded husband will learn of his wife's unfaithfulness and be forced to take steps to defend his own honor.

Admittedly, *The Hi-Lo Country* is encumbered by a somewhat uneven narrative. There are long stretches when things move forward forcefully, but, in between, there are transitional sequences when the proceedings grind to a halt. Flow-related hiccups aside, Frears' picture offers numerous small pleasures. In particular, it's fascinating to observe how Frears brings together two seemingly-unrelated genres in a film that, for the most part, succeeds in paying homage to both. **RECOMMENDED**

High Noon [1952]

Starring: Gary Cooper, Thomas Mitchell, Lloyd Bridges, Katy Jurado, Grace Kelly Director: **Fred Zinnemann** Screenplay: Carl Foreman Running Time: 1:25 Rated: **Not Rated** (Violence) Theatrical Aspect Ratio: 1.33:1

High Noon contains many of the elements of the traditional Western: the gun-toting bad guys, the moral lawman, the pretty girl, and the climactic gunfight. But it's in the way these elements are blended together, with the slight spin put on them by Zinnemann and screenwriter Carl Foreman, that makes *High Noon* unlike any other Western.

Cooper plays Marshal Will Kane, and, when *High Noon* opens, it's a little after 10 o'clock in the morning, and he is being married to Amy Fowler (Grace Kelly), a woman less than half his age. At the same time, trouble has arrived in Kane's sleepy Western town. Three outlaws, the henchmen of convicted murderer Frank Miller (Ian MacDonald), are waiting at the railroad station, where Miller, recently freed from prison, is expected on the noon train. He has one goal: revenge, and the target of his hatred is Kane, the man who brought him down. Kane's friends, including the town's mayor (Thomas Mitchell), the local judge (Otto Kruger), and the former Marshal, Martin Howe (Lon Chaney), urge him to flee, but he can't. Against the wishes of his Quaker wife and with no one in the town willing to stand beside him, Kane prepares to face Miller and his gang alone.

High Noon is about loyalty and betrayal. Loyalty on Kane's part — even when everyone deserts him, he stands his ground, though it seems inevitable that the action will cost him his life. And betrayal on the town's part. Many of the locals are agreed that they owe their prosperity to Kane, but they will not help him or defend him, because they believe his cause to be hopeless. There are even those who welcome Miller's return. In the end, Kane is forced into the showdown on his own, until, at a crucial moment, Amy proves herself to be a worthy wife.

The movie transpires virtually in real time, with a minute on screen equaling one in the theater. In one of many departures from the traditional Western, there is little action until the final 10 minutes, when Kane shoots it out with Miller's gang. *High Noon*'s tension comes through Kane's desperation, aided in no small part by Elmo Williams' brilliant editing as the clock ticks down to 12. For a motion picture with so little action, the suspense builds to almost unbearable levels.

As is true of nearly every great film, all of the elements mix together in *High Noon*. The Western may be one of the few truly American art forms, and *High Noon* shows exactly how much potential it can embrace. **MUST SEE**

The Newton Boys [1998]

Starring: Matthew McConaughey, Ethan Hawke, Vincent D'Onofrio, Skeet Ulrich Director: Richard Linklater Screenplay: Claude Stanush, Clark McBay, Richard Linklater Running Time: 2:02 Rated: PG-13 (Violence, profanity) Theatrical Aspect Ratio: 2.35:1

The Newton Boys illustrates that it's possible to make a film about gangsters and gunplay without an abundance of bloodshed, violence, and death. In fact, for this account, which depicts "the true story of the most successful bank robbers in the history of the United States," director Richard Linklater has consciously kept the tone playful. That's not to say that *The Newton Boys* doesn't have its grim moments, but Linklater limits the shadows. The result is a fast-paced, entertaining motion picture that replaces gritty tension with a lightly dramatic character interaction that occasionally borders on straight comedy.

The real Newton Boys started their crime spree in 1919, and finished it 5 years later, in 1924. During that time, the 4 brothers — Joe (Skeet Ulrich), Jesse (Ethan Hawke), Willis (Matthew McConaughey), and Dock (Vincent D'Onofrio) — and explosives expert Glasscock (Dwight Yoakam) broke into more than 80 banks and committed the largest train robbery in U.S. history — the famous June 12, 1924 Rondout Robbery. Their illegal activities took them from their native Texas, through dozens of small towns and major cities all across the country, and into Canada. Linklater's film recounts the Newton gang's exploits with all of the fondness of a grandfather relating a favorite story to a child.

One thing that differentiates the Newton Boys from America's numerous, other well-known bandits is that they never killed anyone. They used guns, but rarely fired them, and almost never at a living target. All they wanted was the money, and they were often kind to the men they held at gunpoint. Moreover, they viewed themselves as champions of the undertrodden — little thieves stealing from big thieves (the companies insuring the banks). Linklater presents all four brothers as happy, good-natured fellows — the kind of guys no one would mind hanging out with. **RECOMMENDED**

The Wild Bunch [1969]

Starring: William Holden, Ernest Borgnine, Robert Ryan, Edmond O'Brien Director: Sam Peckinpah Screenplay: Sam Peckinpah and Walon Green based on a story by Walon Green and Roy N. Sickner Running Time: 2:25 Rated: R (Violence, language, mature themes, brief nudity) Theatrical Aspect Ratio: 2.35:1

The movie opens during 1913 in the small south Texas town of San Rafael. The Wild Bunch — a gang of 6 — has moved in to pull off a robbery. What they don't know is that it's a setup — the sacks of money are filled with washers and there are dozens of gun-toting bounty hunters hidden in ambush. Things turn bloody and numerous innocent citizens are caught in the crossfire. The gang escapes with the bounty hunters hot on their trail.

Leading the Wild Bunch is Pike (William Holden), an aging outlaw who enjoys planning his capers as much as carrying them out. He's beginning to feel his age, however — an old wound makes it nearly impossible for him to mount his horse and he wonders how many more jobs he'll be good for. Pike's right-hand man is Dutch (Ernest Borgnine), another grizzled veteran of the robbery circuit. The gang is rounded out by Sykes (Edmond O'Brien), Angel (Jaime Sanchez), and the Gorch Brothers (Warren Oates and Ben Johnson). One member of the Bunch is missing, however. Thornton (Robert Ryan), once Pike's closest friend, was arrested as a result of a past screw-up, and now commands the mercenaries hunting his old buddies.

It's possible to view *The Wild Bunch* as a straight action picture, albeit a highly stylized one — Peckinpah's use of multiple angles and quick cuts is amazing. All the traditional elements of the genre are present: shoot-outs, male bonding, and a high body count. The director's methods of orchestrating tension are such that the movie has its fair share of edge-of-the-seat moments. But there's a lot more here. *The Wild Bunch* has level upon level of complexity even beyond the obvious metaphor of Vietnam, and has been structured to satisfy the more discriminating movie-goer.

Not only does *The Wild Bunch* illustrate Peckinpah's mastery of his medium, but it presents a story that is effective on nearly every level: the emotional, the visual, and the visceral. There aren't many epic motion pictures of this scope these days, so it's a rare treat to look back more than 2 decades and see something that is as potent and relevant today as when it was first released. **MUST SEE**

Index of Titles

Index of Directors

Index of Foreign Films

NOTES

NOTES

NOTES

NOTES

NOTES